History of Music

History of Music

FIFTH EDITION

A BOOK FOR STUDY AND REFERENCE

by

Karl H. Wörner

Translated and Supplemented by

Willis Wager

The Free Press
A Division of Macmillan Publishing Co., Inc.
NEW YORK
Collier Macmillan Publishers
LONDON

History of Music, A Book for Study and Reference, was
originally published in German under the title *Geschichte
der Musik* (Fifth Edition [1972]), © Vandenhoeck &
Ruprecht, Göttingen, 1954. Translation from the German
with the permission of Verlag Vandenhoeck & Ruprecht,
Göttingen, Vandenhoeck and Ruprecht in Göttingen.

The Free Press
A Division of Macmillan Publishing Co., Inc.
866 Third Avenue
New York, N.Y. 10022

Collier–Macmillan Canada Ltd., Toronto, Ontario

Library of Congress Catalog Card Number: 72–90547

Printed in the United States of America

printing number
1 2 3 4 5 6 7 8 9 10

Contents

Contents

vi

List of Abbreviations

Though the titles of monographs have been extensively abbreviated, they should be recognizable when encountered in library card files or other actual reference situations. The following list is largely confined to series of publications.

Adler Hdb.	*Handbuch der Musikgeschichte,* ed. Guido Adler (Frankfurt am Main 1924; 2nd ed. in 2 vols., Berlin 1930; 3rd ed. Tutzing 1961).
AfMf	*Archiv für Musikforschung* (1936–43; continuation of the AfMw and the ZfMw).
AfMw	*Archiv für Musikwissenschaft* (1918–36, 1952 ff.; 1936–43; AfMf).
AIM	American Institute of Musicology.
AMl or Acta	*Acta musicologica* (*Zeitschrift der Internationalen Gesellschaft für Musikwissenschaft,* 1931 ff.; 1928–30: *Mitteilungen der IGMW*).
BlCh	*Das Chorwerk,* ed. F. Blume (Kallmeyer 1929–38, new ed.: Möseler 1953 ff.).
Bücken Hdb.	*Handbuch der Musikwissenschaft,* ed. Ernst Bücken, 10 vols. (Potsdam 1927–34).
Chrysanders DT	*Denkmäler der Tonkunst,* ed. F. Chrysander (1869–71).
CSMSiP	*Cantica Selecta Musices Sacrae in Polonia* (Posen 1928).
DDT	*Denkmäler deutscher Tonkunst* (1892–1931).
DJM	*Deutsches Jahrbuch der Musikwissenschaft* (Leipzig 1957–).
DMT	*Dansk Musiktidsskrift* (Copenhagen 1925 ff.).
DTB	*Denkmäler deutscher Tonkunst,* 2nd series; *Denkmäler der Tonkunst in Bayern* (1900–31).
DTÖ	*Denkmäler der Tonkunst in Österreich* (1894 ff.).
DVLG	*Deutsche Vierteljahrsschrift für Literaturwissenschaft und Geistesgeschichte* (1923 ff.).
ED	*Das Erbe deutscher Musik* (see RD and LD).
Eitner Publ. or PGfM	*Publikationen älterer praktischer und theoretischer Musikwerke vornehmlich des XV. und XVI. Jahrhunderts,* ed. for the Gesellschaft für Musikforschung by R. Eitner (1873–1905).

HDEKM	*Handbuch der Deutschen Evangelischen Kirchenmusik,* ed. K. Ameln, C. Mahrenholz, and W. Thomas (1935 ff.).
Istituzioni	*Istituzioni e Monumenti dell'Arte Musicale Italiana* (1931–41).
IMBA	*Internationales Musiker-Brief-Archiv,* Berlin.
IMM	The Institute of Medieval Music, Ltd., Brooklyn, N. Y.
In et Mon	*Instituta et Monumenta.*
JAMS	*Journal of the American Musicological Society* (1948 ff.).
JbP	*Jahrbuch der Musikbibliothek Peters Leipzig* (1894–1940).
JRB	*Journal of Renaissance and Baroque Music* (1946, continued as *Musica Disciplina*).
KmJb	*Kirchenmusikalisches Jahrbuch* (1886 ff.; previously *Cäcelienkalender,* 1876–85).
Lav. Enc.	*Encyclopédie de la Musique et Dictionnaire du Conservatoire,* ed. A. Lavignac and L. de La Laurencie (Paris 1913–31).
LD	*Das Erbe deutscher Musik,* Reihe II: *Landschaftsdenkmale* (1935–42).
MB	*Musica Britannica, A National Collection of Music,* published for The Royal Musical Association, London 1951 ff.
MD	*Musica Disciplina* (yearbook of the AIM, 1947 ff.; previously *Journal of Renaissance and Baroque Music,* 1946).
MDK	*Muzyka w dawnym Krakowic* (*Music in Old Cracow*) (Cracow 1964).
Mf	*Die Musikforschung* (journal of the Gesellschaft für Musikforschung, 1948 ff.).
MfM	*Monatshefte für Musikgeschichte,* ed. R. Eitner (1869–1905).
MGG	*Die Musik in Geschichte und Gegenwart, Allgemeine Enzyklopädie der Musik,* ed. F. Blume (1949 ff.).
M&L	*Music and Letters* (1920 ff.).
MMSiP	*Monumenta Musices Sacrae in Polonia,* ed. J. Surzyński (Posen 1885–96).
MPO	*Muzyka Polskiego Odrodzenia* (Cracow 1953).
MPR	*Music of the Polish Renaissance,* ed. J. M. Chomiński and Z. Lissa (Cracow 1955).
MQ	*The Musical Quarterly* (1915 ff.).
MW	*Das Musikwerk, Eine Beispielsammlung zur Musikgeschichte,* ed. K. G. Fellerer (1950 ff.).
NOHM	*New Oxford History of Music* (London 1954 ff.).
Olms	Georg Olms, publisher, Hildesheim.
P	Jaroslav Pohanka, *Dějiny české hudby v příkladech* (Prague 1958).
PäM	*Publikationen älterer Musik,* ed. T. Kroyer (1926–41).

PGfM	*Publikationen der Gesellschaft für Musikforschung*, see Eitner Publ.
PIMG	*Publikationen der Internationalen Musikgesellschaft* (= *Beihefte der IMG*).
PMA	*Proceedings of the Royal Musical Association*, London (1874 ff.).
RD	*Das Erbe deutscher Musik*, Reihe I: *Reichsdenkmale* (1935–42, continued in 1954).
RM	*La Revue Musicale* (1920 ff., founded by H. Prunières).
RMI	*Rivista musicale italiana* (1894 ff.).
SbIMG	*Sammelbände der Internationalen Musikgesellschaft* (1899–1914).
Sch	Arnold Schering, *Geschichte der Musik in Beispielen* (Leipzig 1931, repr. 1957).
STM	*Svensk Tidskrift för Musikforskning* (Stockholm and Uppsala 1919 ff.).
StMw	(*Studien zur Musikwissenschaft, Beihefte der DTÖ* (1913 ff.).
Torchi	*L'Arte musicale in Italia*, ed. L. Torchi (1897–1907).
VfMw	*Vierteljahrsschrift für Musikwissenschaft* (1885–94).
WDMP	*Wydawnictwo Dawnej Muzyki Polskiej* (Publication of Ancient Polish Music), bks. 1–50 (Warsaw and Cracow 1928–63).
ZfMw	*Zeitschrift für Musikwissenschaft* (1918–35, continued as AfMf).
ZHMP	*Zródła do historii muzyki polskiej* (Sources for the History of Ancient Polish Music), bks. 1–7 (Cracow 1962–3).
ZIMG	*Zeitschrift der Internationalen Musikgesellschaft* (1899–1914).

Translator's Preface

The motives and movements involved in any project of major importance are inherently interesting. They are of even greater interest when they suggest overtones of classical myth. Particularly is this true of the writing of this book by Karl H. Wörner, who, like Orpheus, was cut down by death after he had completed his song but before its echoes had died away.

I knew Karl H. Wörner as one of the sterling musicologists in my age group—first through his published works, then by direct correspondence that ensued from my translating his reports for the "Current Chronicle" section in *The Musical Quarterly*, and eventually through the hospitality of his home in Detmold, that jewel-box of a town on the edge of the Teutonberger Forest. In 1958 he became a *Dozent* at the Northwest Music Academy there, and from 1966 a full professor.

Back in the 1930's he had published articles in the *Zeitschrift für Musikwissenschaft*. These had, to some extent, derived from his Berlin doctoral dissertation (1931) on the *leitmotif*. In the 1940's he had brought out new and fresh approaches to Mendelssohn (1947) and Schumann (1949), which showed his awareness not only of the historical material but also of the state of music in the middle of the present century. In 1949 Schott in Mainz issued a book by him which suggested that he had particular talents over and above the pursuing of mere "special studies" —the gift of clearly comprehending a multiplicity of details under larger points of view. This volume was entitled *Musik der Gegenwart: Geschichte der Neuen Musik* (Music of the Present: History of the New Music).

This intimation of the possession of special gifts of what might in a metaphorical sense be called harmony and counterpoint was confirmed by two magnificent publications, one from the press of Schott in Mainz and the other from that of Vandenhoeck und Ruprecht in Göttingen, which appeared in 1954: *Neue Musik in der Entscheidung* (New Music at the Crossroads) and the first version of the present volume, *Geschichte der Musik* (History of Music). They were soon reissued, and thus he had opportunities to expand and perfect what had appeared before. His revised and increasingly enlarged editions of his history of music came out in 1956, in 1961, and in 1965. The third edition was brought out also in Japanese translation, and the fourth was translated into Spanish and Czech. All this gave him further opportunity to perfect the ambitious enterprise which he had undertaken.

His aims had been to bring the details of music together into a larger whole, to involve the reader more actively in the process of learning about it, and to preserve a sense of wonder before the elemental marvel manifested in the music of man. The history was prefaced with three quotations which enunciate these themes. One was from the concluding section of the book itself: "Meaning becomes evident if detail is related to a whole." Another is from the contemporary German philosopher Ernst Bloch's essay *Subjekt-Objekt* (1962): "Learning comes from active encounter with its material. All knowledge involves constant realization that it lives in a state of Becoming and that it breaks through the crusts." The third was from Nicolaus Steno (1673): "Beautiful is that which we see, more beautiful that which we know, but by far the most beautiful that which we do not comprehend." The themes which Karl H. Wörner thus enunciated for his history of music were its integrity, its dynamic nature, and its ultimate incomprehensibility. As he clearly stated in his preface, he wished to present his work as a great fugue in which the various nations carried the individual voices.

There had been strong motivation on his part to contribute to better understanding among the peoples of the earth, especially in that medium so dear to their hearts, music. In this field he had had unusually wide and intimate experience—writing newspaper and magazine criticism, serving as vocal and operatic coach, regularly attending the Bayreuth and Darmstadt festivals, preparing and bringing out books on Romantic and modern composers. Notable among the latter are his study of Schönberg's *Moses and Aaron* (1959, translated into English and published by Faber and Faber in 1963) and his monograph on Karlheinz Stockhausen (1963). His interests and sympathies in music were unusually wide.

He had been a prisoner of war in the United States. In conversation he told me that after having come into direct contact in the United States with his American colleagues and their work he had written an entirely different style of German. From this I saw clearly one factor in the unusual lucidity with which he handled many complicated musicological details. With great pride he showed me his personal library, in which the contributions of his American colleagues were prominently represented.

Our collaboration in preparing this English-language version was cut short by his untimely death at 59. His detailed notes toward a further revision were the basis of the fifth German edition, and it is on this current (1972) German version that the present version has ultimately been based. From the start of its preparation he had insisted that it be a matter of active collaboration between us, rather than a sheer translation. Throughout there are sections in which I have enlarged the account to deal more extensively with the various developments in the music of the Americas.

One of the unusual features of this book is the scheme according to which it is organized. The basic structure is chronological. But it does not go straight through from the beginnings to the present and mow down everything in its path. Instead, it starts out chronologically from the earliest traceable evidences of music-making and goes on through the

Renaissance. Then it takes up in separate chapters the principal types of music that have flourished in the more recent period, such as opera, symphony, keyboard music. Though the chronological sequence is here also maintained, the limitation of focus to the particular genre of music enables the reader to gain a more detailed conception of what has occurred during this period so well represented in the concert repertoire. Then, in a final section, the author returns to the general chronological conception encompassing all types of music now being made and likely to be made in the near future. Hopefully, this type of organization and presentation will serve the needs of those persons interested in the whole sweep of the development of music, as well as those interested in the genesis and growth of the special genres or areas in which they are particularly involved.

Karl H. Wörner's *History of Music* is intended to serve the needs of study and reference, to satisfy immediate interests, and to be a possession of lasting value to which the user can return again and again. In Germany, the very homeland of musicology, it has become the indispensable guide for those preparing to take their doctoral orals in this subject. The present volume will act as a guide through a complex and fascinating area in which the United States during the past quarter-century has rather unexpectedly become the heir of the European traditions of the intensive historical study of music. The fact that this book arose from the mature considerations of an active scholar of European musical life who was also a participant in it makes it unusually relevant to the needs of both the special student and the general music-lover.

Willis Wager

Author's Preface

The History of Music here presented stil bears essentially the same title and subtitle as it did in its first edition that appeared in 1954, but its scope has more than doubled. A book for study and reference, it undertakes to provide complete coverage for the history of the music of Europe.

One of its novel features is the special treatment of the Scandinavian countries and of Poland, to an extent not hitherto attempted in any German study of these areas. Another of its novel features appears in the extended paragraphs on the period around 1725 and on the 19th century. Moreover, I have undertaken to carry the discussion up to the immediate present, not only in the sense of having a chapter on the 20th century but also in that of including many details with reference to the particular genres of music, so that the presentation has at many points in the book been carried on to the present day. It goes without saying that in this edition an attempt was made to supplement the bibliographical references in order to bring the indications of new editions up to date and to incorporate into the discussion some idea of the results of very recent research in musicology throughout the world.

It may be interpreted as evidence of the proven worth of this book and of the indispensable position which it has achieved that eminent specialists have been willing to help in the preparation of the fourth edition, particularly my colleagues Jan Maegaard, M. A., of Cophenhagen, who has revised the sections on the Scandinavian countries, and Krzysztof Bieganski, M. A., of Warsaw, who has performed a similar service in connection with the Polish sections. The section on Egypt was revised by Professor Hans Hickmann of Hamburg, and the paragraphs on the music history of Bohemia, Moravia, and Slovakia by Dr. Ivan Vojtěch of Prague. For material in the paragraphs on opera in the U.S.S.R. I am indebted to Professor Schneerson of Moscow. The names of previous collaborators are mentioned in the preface to the third edition. Their contributions, for the most part further expanded, have been included in this edition. Hans Wörner has completed the index. To all, for their unselfish helpfulness, I give my hearty thanks.

Most magnanimously the publishing firm has given me its support, sparing neither effort nor cost in presenting the book in completely new form. The fact that within but a relatively few years the book could go into a fourth edition speaks in its favor, as does also the fact that the third edition is already published in Japanese and that this fourth edition is being translated into Spanish and Czech.

The ultimate point in a history of music is that it may serve the purposes of understanding and may open up new avenues of artistic achievement. No renaissance of old music without the corresponding musicological preliminaries, no awareness of non-European music without research, no Neoclassicism without historical studies. Knowledge may deepen emotion.

It was not a historian but a composer, Robert Schumann, who wrote, over a century ago, "Art will be the great fugue in which the various peoples will resolve their differences in song." May this history of music be a contribution to the understanding of peoples, and—quite over and above its literal meaning—may that be its true value.

Heiligenkirchen bei Detmold
August 15, 1965

Karl H. Wörner

Publishers' Note to the Fifth German Edition

Work on the History of Music, which Karl H. Wörner had continuously been engaged in ever since he prepared the first edition in 1954, was abruptly terminated by his sudden death on August 11, 1969.

The fifth edition, herewith presented, was completed entirely from the manuscripts and notes that Karl H. Wörner had been preparing. This edition, which is not fundamentally altered from the fourth, was seen through the press by Frau Irmhild Wörner, Ernst O. Wörner, and Dr. Ekkehard Kreft.

The Polish section was revised by Dr. Mirosław Perz of Warsaw, acting for Krzysztof Biegański, M. A., now deceased, and the Scandinavian section by Torben Schousboe, M. A., of Copenhagen, for Jan Maegaard, M. A.

In addition to the American edition being published in New York by The Free Press, there is a Dutch edition being brought out by Het Spectrum in Utrecht and a Czech edition by the Supraphon state publishing agency in Prague.

History of Music

1. Introduction

The present work is a history of the music of Europe. As late as the beginning of our present century the writer of a book such as this would not have tried to go further back into the past than ancient Greek times. But now he finds that the horizon has widened to include a global view, in which Europe takes its place. Many phenomena in European music are now seen more clearly in a view extending beyond Europe. Justifiably, then, this work begins with a glance at the origins of music and at prehistory on the one hand, and at the world of the tribal peoples and some of the ancient high civilizations of the East on the other, so that from such a vantage point we may become aware of contacts and even parallels between them and Europe.

Recently Walter Wiora has made a first attempt at a global survey—sometimes relying, of course, more on hypotheses derived from the general systematic conceptions that he has adopted than on historical data in the strict sense of the term. He divides the total picture of music history into four ages, combining "the study of surviving tradition with that of origins" and relating "regional as well as temporal divisions":

1. Aboriginal and early history with its survival among primitive and in archaic folk-music of the higher cultures;
2. Music of the ancient higher cultures from Sumerian and Egyptian to Late Roman times, as well as its widespread continuation and development through the higher cultures of the East;
3. Western music from the early Middle Ages, differing from the music of other higher cultures in many respects, such as the presence of polyphony, harmony, and large forms like the symphony;
4. Music in the age of technology and industrial culture, which embraces all countries of the earth, unites the legacy of previous cultures into a "universal museum," and carries on its intellectual concert life as well as furthering the development of various

other of its aspects such as technique, research, and composition before a "world public."

From the start, an enlarged view poses questions about history—for instance, in speaking of something as "ahistoric," "prehistoric," or "historical." The branch of study that undertakes research among tribal peoples is ethnology. These peoples—sometimes referred to as "primitives" or "people living in a state of nature"—have a tightly knit culture of their own, with definite peculiarities, antiquated traits, and an ancient tradition. But they have no history in the strict sense of the term. They live in what seems to them a harmoniously closed world, in which everything is organized statically from the beginning. Each individual is incorporated unquestioningly into it and develops within it. Hence there is no causal thinking, no logical abstraction, and no need for self-discovery, learning, or judgement.

Only after a course of events has come to be linked in a relationship of cause and effect does historical awareness make its appearance. It presupposes the will to organize, articulate, and relate. Events are then interpreted in the sense of a plan, which is perceived as they transpire.

Historians make a distinction between prehistory and history. The dividing line comes with the discovery of writing. The written word is the basis of historical study. Only those peoples have history who have written about themselves. Compared with prehistoric peoples, they have a different kind of self-awareness.

The musicologists have not as yet made as sharp a distinction between prehistory and history as have the historians. The distinction, however, has its reasons for being. The discovery of notation and the consequent introduction of notational sketches mark a mighty leap in the cultural consciousness of a people. So long as they feel no need to write out the tones and are satisfied with oral tradition, the sound passes from ear to ear, from one generation to another. Presumably they— unlike us today—did not conceive of the composition as an artistic tonal creation and a tightly interwoven form, or of the work as in any sense final. Prehistoric man, in making music, knew only the form that always renews itself in the very act of music-making. In spirit it was closer to the act of improvisation. Though the musician may have had traditional images, melodic patterns, or models to guide him as he made music, he felt that the height of his artistic achievement lay in the richness with which he transformed his model. Although even here he may have achieved clearly recognizable musical forms, he had not yet conceived of music as in our sense of the term an art form with its own laws, independent of the word—even when it had linked itself to the word. Only in the transition from prehistoric to historic time did both developments come together—that of music being conceived of as an autonomous art and that of a need being felt to hold the new and unique unmistakably firm in written notation.

The earliest evidences of notation we can find come to us from early Egyptian and Sumerian times. In terms of dated notation, the next examples come from the Hellenistic world, beginning around the 2nd century B.C. The fact that the ancient Greeks have left us only fragments of their music in notation shows clearly that their desire to write the music down was still quite secondary and perhaps arose only because the oral tradition was waning. Therefore—quite over and above the imperfections in our knowledge—we cannot write a history of *the* music of the ancient peoples. At best, we can only try to give a history of the traditions and reports *about* their music. We are somewhat similarly limited in writing of the music of the Greeks.

In order to have music in any very real sense of the word we must have intervals or distances between the tones that are definite, usable, and meaningful. For them to be definite they must be tonally fixed. To be used they must be susceptible of transposition to different pitch levels and must be able to enter into various tonal combinations that are articulated rhythmically. In other words, we must have available to us successions of tones that appear constant, firm, independent of pitch-level, transposable, and repeatable in various combinations. Sometimes these are referred to as motifs. Finally, some sense must be fulfilled; there needs to be some meaning to it all. Music is not music if it has no sense to it—though, of course, throughout history this "sense" has taken on the most diverse forms.

The words "primitive" and "civilized" as applied to peoples are nothing but familiar and sometimes useful means of indicating features of their ways of life. On the one hand, there is the music of the so-called higher cultures of the Orient and Western Europe; on the other, the music of the tribal or primitive peoples. There are some fundamental differences. The music of civilized peoples has

1. far greater melodic and tonal differentiation;
2. connection between their prevailing system of measurements and acoustical phenomena;
3. absolute pitches, established on musical instruments;
4. tonal systems that have been developed on instruments and then have also become obligatory in vocal music;
5. a theory of *ethos*, with a religious and philosophical basis;
6. certain definite melodic models or normative tonal patterns, such as the *patet*, the *raga*, or the *maqam* (in European music the *modes*);
7. a consciously cultivated historical tradition;
8. a musical profession, in which there are distinct differences in technical achievement and social position;
9. a recognized body of musical knowledge and the attendant development of "schools"; and
10. a distinction between art-music and folk-music, and thus stratification between older and newer musical elements.

Western Europe is the only part of the world that has really opened up and developed the area of harmonic polyphony in its musical practice. This characteristic feature has now penetrated all those lands that Europe colonized, such as America. A succession of further non-European countries, including Japan and more recently China, has taken over harmonic polyphony and to some extent incorporated it into their own original music.

Bibliography

K. Jaspers, *Vom Ursprung und Ziel der Geschichte* (1949); W. Wiora, *Die vier Weltalter der Musik* (Stuttgart 1961).

I Aboriginal and Primitive Music

2. The Origin of Music

Any pronouncements regarding the origin of music must be largely theoretical. Present-day anthropological and musicological research deals with the following questions:

1. During what chronological period of human history did music begin?
2. What level of development had man reached at that time?
3. What meaning did his music have for him?
4. What was his music like?
5. Does the present—the simplest forms of music among primitive peoples today—cast any light on the origins of music?

The bulk of our present information pertains to the second half of the last, or Fourth, Glacial Era in Europe, the period from the Aurignacian to the Magdalenian (50,000–10,000 B.C.). The human beings of this time, including the so-called Cro-Magnon man, looked very much like you and me. They were hunters who lived in huts or caves; and their artistic achievements, such as cave paintings and portable sculpture, as well as other archaeological finds, indicate that they performed sacrifices, held funerals for the dead, and followed a monotheistic faith centered around a Great Mother deity, the source of all fertility. Even farther back, in the Third Interglacial Epoch, between the Riss and Würm Eras (183,000–118,000 B.C.), and during the first half of the Fourth Glacial (the Neanderthal, or Mousterian, Period, up to 60,000 B.C.), there are signs that an elemental monotheism may have been observed and that the dead were interred with all the formal funeral trappings.

The earliest remains of musical instruments—pipes made from reindeer bones—have been traced to the Old Palaeolithic, or Early Old Stone Age, whose beginnings have been set at 600,000 B.C. From the Fourth Glacial Period there are three types of musical instruments that have survived: pipes made from the toe-bones of animals, flutes with three regularly spaced finger holes, and end-blown flutes of hollow cylindrical bone. Also there are bull-roarers, or flat pieces of solid material strung on thongs by which they were whirled through the air, producing a roaring sound. On the walls of the Cave of the Trois Frères in the Department of Ariège in France is depicted a magician with his animal mask and musical bow, indicating that music then had reached a stage far more advanced than is usual among primitive peoples of today such as the Vedda of Ceylon.

The latest methods of dating, particularly the use of Carbon 14, have not been applied as widely to fossil musical instruments as they have to other kinds of archaeological evidence. It appears that, as these techniques are extended and refined, we may have to revise many of our dates. Today, the beginning of the Post-Glacial Period is set at about 7000 B.C.; the Magdalenian at about 11,500 B.C.; and the oldest of the wall paintings in the Lascaux Cave in France at around 13,600 B.C. But from the best available evidence we must conclude that all the culture periods were considerably more recent than was previously assumed.

From all indications music, like art, was for man of the Fourth Glacial Era steeped in magic, just as it is for primitive peoples today. Whether sung to words or to syllables obscure in meaning, or whether created with the musical bow or bull-roarer, the link with magic was there. Similarly, in the sound-production of language itself and in the most elemental use of musical instruments, the essence of what led to music and contributed to its development originated in the supernatural and magical.

The oldest musical pipes that have been found are essentially whistles for purposes of signaling. Between them and the development of flutes with finger-holes there lies a big step in the history of the human spirit, explicable only if one proceeds from the assumption that the road to music led by way of magic. It is a step as great as that from the imprints of hands on cave walls to actual fresco paintings on those walls. The imprints or silhouettes of human hands may, if taken out of their context, seem to be the result of caprice, but actually in their place and time they were a means of performing magic and served as an early form of art.

In trying to determine when music originated, we cannot think in terms of a fixed point in time, for we are dealing here with vast expanses of time—hundreds of thousands of years—that have not as yet been measured precisely. There are still gaps in the record. Nor can we say exactly what stage of human development coincided with the beginnings of music, largely for the same reasons. If we try to draw an analogy between primitive peoples of today and early man, we are confronted with the problem that no, or few, primitive peoples today are totally untouched by our modern technological civilization.

We can assume that as man gradually acquired the understanding to carry out purposeful activities such as hunting, food-gathering, tool-making, and using fire, he became intelligently aware of the world around him, a world that for him was endowed with a soul and with magical forces. Under the circumstances it was perfectly natural that music resulted from a combination of his vocal or instrumental tone-production and his conception of magic. There is no people on earth without music.

Thus there was no "first music," no specific time we can set to mark its emergence. There were forms, however, which developed independently, the precursors of musical instruments and particularly a type of speech sound. As original language, the latter stands before the division that later occurred between speaking and singing. Its speech elements were associated with approximate pitches, which were meaningful to the people who used them.

Despite the problems just set forth, man has constantly speculated upon the origin of music. The ancients and the men of the Middle Ages undertook to explain it by myths. Through these accounts they were expressing their belief that music was of a divine and mysterious essence, thus reflecting the attitude of early man and anticipating the beliefs of modern-day primitives. Since the 19th century, some half-dozen approaches have been made toward trying to clear up the mystery of the origin of music.

Charles Darwin, approaching the question from the standpoint of his theory of evolution, stated that music arose from man's imitating the sounds of animals, especially bird calls, the imitation being a "love call" grounded in man's sexual impulse. It is difficult, however, to conceive of bird songs as being anything more than sounds of nature and only preliminary forms toward music and language. Birds lack the will to make music, and cannot transpose their calls. Their song has no "history"; it is but an immediate and compulsive reaction to the individual animal's biological condition. What is conventionally considered a "love call," moreover, would seem to have had very little to do with the songs, or indeed the lives, of primitive peoples. Among the cave paintings of the Glacial Eras, nowhere are portrayed scenes of romantic love.

Following suggestions of Jean Jacques Rousseau and Johann Gottfried Herder, Herbert Spencer thought that music had arisen from language and constituted a tonal residue of common speech. Objections to this theory, however, could be raised on the grounds that the music of many primitive peoples lacks "speech melody" and makes considerable use of nonsense syllables—that is, of syllables without verbal significance. Spencer's idea was, in general, a theory that focused almost entirely on expression. According to it, music was derived from man's emotional utterance of sound. Against this view it might be urged that the sounds arising directly from the feelings and emotions have very little to do with music or song and are merely the immediate and reflex-like outward manifestations of inner tension. Devoid of intellectual or aesthetic significance, they lack the drive toward musical creativity.

Carl Stumpf considered song as having arisen from intensified speech and outcries. But, though the latter do utilize fixed pitches, they do not exactly constitute song.

Géza Révész stressed the close connection between the beginnings of music and one of the basic needs of man for contact with his fellows. The shout or call is essentially one of these ways of making contact in which the singing voice may be used. Thus it is close to speech-song, and is often associated with it, though the two do not necessarily coincide. In individual instances among primitive peoples, the call has a definite musical structure. People call out when their feelings are aroused. Thus the call may be considered a preliminary stage of song, and in the last analysis the origin of music is again referred to that of language. The common source of music and of language is thus attributed to the wordless call.

Karl Bücher saw music as having grown from the rhythm of men at work and from their cries of mutual encouragement in their common tasks. An objection to this theory, however, is that organized labor prevails only among higher cultures and not among primitive peoples. According to another form of the rhythm theory, the beginnings of music are derived from relationships between dance and song. But no explanation is thereby given of the way music may have arisen from the movements of the dance. Among primitive peoples dance is not necessarily linked with song, as it may be accompanied merely by hand-clapping or drumming. Often, moreover, the rhythm of the melodies is so complicated as not to suggest origin in the dance.

Leaving, for a moment, the question of from what music originated, and attempting merely to describe the way it arose, some scholars have pointed out that, according to the biologists, the development or ontogeny of a human being from conception to birth goes through approximately the same stages of structural development as, according to the evolutionary hypothesis, seem to have occurred in the development or philogeny of man from previous forms of animal life. This relationship is sometimes stated as a law, that ontogeny recapitulates philogeny. Accordingly, some scholars believe that the babble of infants is related to the early stages of music within the human race. If the babble melodies and songs of children are considered "vocal music," it is possible that there may be a relationship. Right from the first sound emitted by the new-born baby there is a sort of "singing" around the tone a^1. By the age of three, children "sing" in a descending minor third, with the lower tone stressed and repeated; and by three and a half, in a descending tetrachord at a pitch level between F and C. When the matter is carried much further, however, scholars encounter the difficulty that song and melody in even the early stages of childhood do not represent entirely original creations, but are strongly conditioned by the type of singing the child encounters in his environment.

Thus, despite much speculation, the question of how and why music began remains largely open, though the attempt to answer it entails a critical examination of some popular assumptions about the nature of music.

Bibliography

K. Bücher, *Arbeit und Rhythmus* (1896); W. Danckert, *Wesen und Ursprung der Tonwelt im Mythos* (AfMw 1955); C. Darwin, *The Descent of Man* (1871); O. Koehler, *Der Vogelsang als Vorstufe von Musik und Sprache* (*Journal für Ornithologie* 1951); G. Révész, *Einführung in die*

Musikpsychologie, ch. 8 (Bern 1946); C. Sachs, *The Wellsprings of Music*, ed. J. Kunst (The Hague 1962); W. Schrammek, *Über Ursprung und Anfänge der Musik* (Lpz. 1957); E. Seemann, *Mythen vom Ursprung der Musik* (Kongressbericht Lüneburg, Kassel 1951); H. Spencer, *The Origin and Function of Music* (1857); C. Stumpf, *Die Anfänge der Musik* (Lpz. 1911) and *Musikpsychologie in England* (VfMw 1885); R. Wallaschek, *Anfänge der Tonkunst* (Lpz. 1903); H. Werner, *Die melodische Erfindung im frühen Kindesalter* (Sitzungsberichte der Akademie der Wissenschaften, Vienna 1917).

3. On the Music of Primitive Peoples

The word "primitive" is a somewhat misleading term. In the 18th century the French began to talk about the "state of nature" and about peoples who were supposed to be living in it, and the phrase was taken over into German by Herder in 1784 as *Naturvölker*. Since the end of the 19th century the word "primitive" and its related terms have become common in many languages. But the word does not at all characterize essential traits of the groups of people so designated. These terms are still used only because no better ones are current. Under no circumstances are we to assume that the primitive peoples of the earth represent, as the etymological meaning of the word suggests, the first or absolutely original state of humanity, that is, the primary or initial stage of man's becoming man. Instead, they represent a stage of human development that is comparatively quite advanced. All primitive peoples are familiar with tools, weapons, language (with well-developed grammar), fire, preparation of food, ornament, and various possibilities of artistic expression, including music.

With this caveat, we may note two essential features of the idea of "primitive" life that differentiate it from the idea of "civilized." In the first place, the individual in primitive society—though he is a thinking adult—feels himself bound to the world of his ancestors and relatives and perpetuates this world. In the second place, everyday life for primitives is quite suffused with belief in magic powers and in the effect of supernatural forces, ancestors, and spirits of nature. Even so-called "play" or dance is bound up with expression of the supernatural. All the sounds of nature itself are regarded as spirit voices.

The study of the music of primitive peoples, sometimes referred to as ethnomusicology, is not a historically oriented discipline. The ethnomusicologist does not necessarily try to view the music of the primitive or tribal peoples as an early stage of Western European music and establish a continuous historical sequence from one to the other. Instead, he deals with the music as a cultural phenomenon in its own right.

He does not make the unjustifiable claim that a simpler music is necessarily older historically or the forerunner of a more complex music.

Usually he recognizes that he has no yardstick that would enable him to reach out beyond the natural connections of peoples, races, languages, and cultures in order to construct a perfectly coherent and all-inclusive system. Some ethnomusicologists have tried to do so, on the basis of historical considerations and theories of development. For example, Sachs applied the theory of the *Kulturkreis* or "cultural circle" to music; Hornbostel based his speculations on the acoustical peculiarities of fifths as blown on pipes; and Schneider wished to establish areas in terms of tonality. But none of these attempts has been entirely successful. Instead, most ethnomusicologists have been content to arrange the multifarious phenomena they encounter according to anthropological and ethnographical categories, into peoples and nations and into racial and linguistic communities. In most cultures, and particularly the so-called higher ones, elements that are older and younger stand side by side. They form, as it were, strata of various ethnic, social, and historical derivations.

Comparative Musicology, a term corresponding to Comparative Religion, flourished particularly between 1880 and 1930 under the leadership of Carl Stumpf and Erich von Hornbostel. Comparative musicologists, or ethnomusicologists, have concerned themselves principally with the music of non-European peoples. Availing themselves of the phonograph as developed by Edison, they have extensively used recordings as documentary sources and transcribed them into written notation. What they have envisioned is an ethnology of music. Folk-song research has also come within their somewhat more broadly conceived field of concern. Their comparative studies of the characteristics of non-European music have led to reflections upon possible connections between European and non-European music that may once have been prevalent and hence may be rediscoverable.

They began their work at a time when many cultures of the earth were still untouched by influences from European music. The early scholars in the field were concerned with recording original material in order to work it over later in an objective and scientific way. The insights thus gained derive from the oldest material that was at the time in existence. In very many cultures it has been subsequently obscured or even destroyed by European influences massively exerted through records, radio, and television.

Among primitive peoples music is not thought of as "art" with a separate life of its own and with its own inner laws in our sense of the term. Originally primitives sang and played for exclusively magical purposes and ascribed supernatural powers to music. To them, music was a means of performing magic. As such, music was a force that helped the primitive person assert himself against the powers of magic, for to him all nature was endowed with a soul, and he felt that he was surrounded by magical forces. Music was magic, a fetish of supersensuous content. Only among primitives of a so-called higher level do you find songs that either no longer have, or never have had, supernatural reasons for being, such as songs of love or war, lullabies, and satirical songs. In the world of the primitives there exists no difference between sacred and secular music, for their thinking is essentially religious and mystical.

Among primitives, too, music is closely linked to the body. All members of the tribe take part in music-making as they sing, dance, clap, stamp, or otherwise participate. Thus there is no distinction between "musicians" and "non-musicians," though they recognize, of course, the medicine man, shaman, magician, or priestly musician endowed with supernatural powers. Vocal and instrumental tone-production tends to be what we might consider unnatural or inhuman, intent upon the pursuit of a supernatural or totemic purpose. As primitives do not regularly use notation, they do not "compose" in our sense of the term. They may use the same melody for psychologically different purposes, performing nasally, in falsetto, with chest voice, or in other ways. The melodies always express ideas through the music. Primitives sing only if they wish to express or communicate something. In their singing they give spontaneous expression to thoughts that are quite as important as the melodies themselves, no matter whether presented vocally or instrumentally. Melody, among primitives, consists of a continual and varied repetition of the motif, with tension established between the beginning of the motif and the final note.

Melodies employed by primitive tribesmen fall into certain recognizable and basic types. The Vedda of Ceylon, the Tierra del Fuegians of South America, and the members of many other technologically undeveloped tribes have the simplest of musical motifs, consisting of two tones that alternate in a relationship of tension and relaxation, or arsis and thesis. The former tone, or arsis, carries the accent and is the tonic,

Vedda (Ceylon)   (from Wertheimer)

Example 1

while the latter, or thesis, is not stressed. Either of the two may be the final or ending note. The relationship between the two tones corresponds to natural movements in the vocal organs. Among the melodies of the oldest primitive peoples the range seldom exceeds three notes. Children's and women's songs have preserved some examples of very simple melodies of this sort, even within high cultures of the present day.

One can find tonality and tonal functions in the music of primitive peoples. In its broadest sense, tonality means a structure consisting of steps related to some center. Tonal functions represent the gradations among the tones in this system of relationships. In discussions of primitive music the term "tonal system" applies to the sum of tones that are available and musically usable. A "practical scale" is the selection from them that is encountered in the music. Tonality is thus determined by the functions that the individual tones of the practical scale possess melodically and harmonically. Discussions of the size of tonal steps often use a system of measurement introduced by A. J. Ellis, according to which a hundred cents is equivalent to the tempered half-tone.

In formulating their melodies, primitive peoples follow three recognizable principles: first, the establishment of distances between pitches, usually by stringing together descending seconds; second, the making of the main tone consonant; and third, a progressive enlargement of the intervals as the melody descends.

Accordingly, as they add descending intervals they extend the original two-tone group into a succession, either literally repeating the motif or varying it as it descends step by step. Thus they may expand the two-tone motif to three tones, with the middle one the tonic. In accordance

Uitoto (Colombia), Song of the god Husiniamui for the "bai" festival

Example 2

with the principle of establishing tonal distance, repetition leads to a stairway-like melodic structure or *treppenmelos,* such as may be observed among the American Indians and the Papuans. Eventually the octave is established as a framework interval. The principle of establishing tonal distance is structurally predominant in the practical scales of the American Indians and Asians, and the additive principle accounts for the attachment of other intervallic steps as tones are further connected and the melodic system is extended.

When the octave has been established as the framing interval, it assumes a tonal as well as a melodic function. The extreme tones of the octave seem to stand in reciprocally consonant relationship with the tonic, which lies between them. Thus, as primitives expand their tonal space they come to apply the principle of consonance.

Ecari (Western New Guinea), "Oegva Song" (from Kunst)

Example 3

This principle operates in terms of the interval of the fifth also. It leads to a triadic type of melody with major and minor thirds, in which the octave plays a secondary role and the fourth no role at all. This type of melody, with its major and minor thirds, is found among the North American Indians, Melanesians, and Negroid peoples—particularly among the pygmies of Africa and Asia. Triadic melody, moreover, is an all-inclusive European stylistic feature that cuts across racial and geographical boundaries. As early as the Middle Ages it led an independent existence alongside features that seem more closely related to the five-note scale and the church modes.

The consonance principle is also manifested in the "fanfare" type of melody frequently encountered among the Papuans of New Guinea. They employ short motifs in thirds, which are not subdivided. As they use unvaried short motifs, they perpetuate a very primitive form of triadic melody, dispensing with the anticipatory stages. On the other hand, the Indians developed some triadic melodies by ranging motives side by side; and, as they enlarged the melodic movement, they neglected the tonal degrees that had been generated by narrowly gradated, micromotivic

Navaho (Arizona), Riding Song   (from Bose)

Example 4

melodic movement. In general, the Negroid peoples of Africa and Oceania and the early peoples of Northern Europe especially stressed the consonance principle in their scalar practice. As the interval of the third came to determine their melodies, acting as a structural and stepwise interval, the way was opened for the appearance of polyphonic forms.

Moni, Papua (New Guinea), "Cadio-Cadia"   (from Kunst)

Example 5

A third principle that primitives follow is that they take longer steps as they descend. In other words, from the midpoint in the range the descending steps tend to be longer than the ascending. This melodic feature conforms with physical and physiological laws. Just as the reduction of tension in a string lowers the tone, so does the relaxation of lip pressure. Hence, in three-tone motifs with the tonic in the middle, the second descending step tends to be the longer.

Marind-Anim (New Guinea), "aroeiam" song, gad-zi species   (from Kunst)

Example 6

The principles of establishing tonal distance and of consonance are aboriginal melodic features. From very earliest times the distance principle has manifested itself in stepwise movement, in a tendency to move about a core tone with evenly pulsing rhythm, and in the alternation of the voice as it is raised and allowed to return to rest. The consonant principle, moreover, has appeared in the presence of a horizontally established general consonance within which the voice has a tendency to hover about a state of repose.

In even the simplest situations the fifth, fourth, and octave provide the framework or the core intervallic structure. The development of a system of two, three, four, or five tones presumably goes back to the Old Stone Age. These aspects of tonal arrangement are so elemental that they have come to be regarded as "natural."

Groups of primitive people on the earth differ less in their melodic types than in their characteristic voice quality. They do so in accordance with physical peculiarities that are racially established and are apparently inherited. The particular tone-color and manner of vocal recitation accordingly seem to be innate and not readily transferable from one people to another.

Ethnologists have long drawn distinctions among food-gatherers, hunters, herders, and farmers, mainly on the basis of the form of their economic and cultural life. Marius Schneider has undertaken to make a similar classification of music. He ascribes music derived from and still dependent on the free rhythms of speech to the hunting peoples. This is frequently interrupted by calls or cries, but it makes little use of slurred tones and sequences. The feeling for form was predominantly determined by the meter, representing a strongly individual expression of the urge to make music. To the agricultural peoples, on the other hand, he has attributed a predominantly *arioso* style, with more of a tonal basis and with rounded forms, the music more group-oriented and directed toward achieving an equilibrium between meter and melody. He has assigned a position between these two extremes to the pastoral peoples. He regarded this schematic distribution as purely hypothetical, for the purpose of suggesting some kind of order in the musical material now available. Within the music of any people, of course, there are many ambiguities and transitions, as well as the residue of previous cultural stages.

Although primitive peoples have no history in the narrow sense of the term, they do undergo changes in style. Their music, moreover, is something that has arisen and is constantly undergoing change. In attempting to visualize this phenomenon, we should consider the words and the tones as an inseparable unit: the music is determined by the poetic form and the speech-rhythm. Curt Sachs refers to some melodies as being born of the words, or "logogenic," and others as being born of emotion, or "pathogenic." A third type, melodically born or "melogenic," has been developed in higher cultures, balancing the former two. Side by side with them, special types of melody, which are not confined to certain tribes or nations, prevail among certain peoples, such as the "stairway" melody of the Indians, the leaping melody of the Mongolians, the garland-like melody of the Near Easterners, and the strictly measured and square melody of the Chinese.

Primitive music is distinguished by extreme richness in its rhythmic features. The later, or so-called higher, cultures tend to schematize rhythm into metrical patterns.

In phrasal structure, primitives tend to proceed in successions of somewhat similar units, which may be referred to schematically as a a^1 a^2. Even among the early cultures, however, there are recognizable though embryonic forms that involve contrast, such as a b , a b c , and a b a . As singing is a much more spontaneous procedure among primitives than among peoples of higher cultures, their "repertoire" is much more inclusive and frequently is improvised.

Primitive man visualizes the world as filled with good and evil spirits whose voices may be heard in the sounds of nature. All living beings as well as inanimate things have been created by totemic divinities, the mythic progenitors of man, when they sojourned on earth. Thus everything was at some time divinely created. The divinities died and descended into the grave, but their bodies live on in the totems. As man must care for them, there is a totemic order in the society of the individual tribes. The individual, a human being with obligations to a definite totem, takes on its peculiar characteristics. He behaves like it, imitating its sound with his voice, as well as wearing a mask to simulate it and copying its bodily gestures. Identifying himself in this manner with his totem, the human being thinks in terms of magic and of mystical unity. The individual sound and the rhythmic sonority are thus equated with individuals and things. Since they are a mystical substance, they are indestructible. Hence music has an all-controlling significance in the lives of primitive peoples. It unifies man with the spirits and lends him their powers. In this relationship, we see the origin of musical symbolism.

Among the simplest primitive cultures there are apparently no instruments. The tribesmen make rhythmic sounds, using wooden sticks, spears, stampers, rattles, and other hollow objects. Thus they take the first step in the development of instruments of music. Initially these were tools used by the group as its members clapped their hands, pounded the bare earth with their feet, circled around the dancing pole, and heightened their actions with boards, rattles, or staves. By the time instruments appear there has already occurred considerable individualization of function and a certain degree of specialization within the culture. Thus one finds hollow bones or whistles, bamboo tubes, musical bows, shell and horn trumpets, other hollow objects, jew's-harps, pipes and flutes, drums, and xylophones. Instruments such as these imply a separation between performer and public. As the culture becomes further specialized, the musician receives professional training.

Two branches of primitive music that have attracted particular interest are the American Indian and the African. Some American Indian tribes have preserved melodies of two or three tones into the present century. Basically it is a one-voiced music, sometimes with a recorder-type instrument, against a steady percussive background. Some tribes, however, sing without drumming. There are, of course, different musical styles in different areas. The Plains Indians, for instance, sing in descending thirds instead of in the tetrachordal or pentachordal patterns usually found in the early Asian and Mediterranean civilizations.

When the ancestors of the American Indians migrated to the new continent from Northeastern Asia by way of the Bering Strait during the Middle Stone Age, they brought with them musical patterns not entirely different from those that prevailed at the time in Northern Europe and in tribal Africa. Thus a considerable body of very old tribal music has been maintained to our own day, carefully preserved in oral tradition because of its connections with a nature-centered religion in which music and dance form an essential part of the ritual.

During the last few centuries there has been a tendency on the part of American Indians to fuse tribal differences into a pan-Indian musical style. In the 18th century a musical development associated with the peyote cult came north from Mexico, and in the 19th century still another musical development was joined to the Ghost Dance movement, which envisioned an Indian resurgence.

African music has been more productive in its encounter with European music on American soil, resulting in the Negro Spirituals, blues, and jazz. The portion of Africa that has been most influential on present-day music, by way of America, is West Africa. The music there is varied and complex, often exhibiting seven-note diatonic melodies, polyphony, and extensive improvisation by the leader within a basically antiphonal or responsorial form. It is the polyrhythmic aspect of African primitive music, however, that is most impressive and has been most interesting and fruitful, particularly during the present century.

If American Indian music carries, like a fossil imprint, some of the lineaments of older tribal music, Afro-American music has been actively developing during the past few centuries and, particularly, the past few decades.

Bibliography

F. Bose, *Musikalische Völkerkunde* (Freiburg i. B. 1953); A. Häusler, *Neue Funde steinzeitlicher Musikinstrumente in Osteuropa* (Acta XXXII, 1960); E. v. Hornbostel, *Musikalische Tonsysteme* (Geiger-Scheel, Hdb. der Physik VIII, 1927); J. Kunst, *Ethno-Musicology* (Amsterdam 3rd ed. 1959); R. Lachmann, *Die Musik der aussereuropäischen Natur- und Kulturvölker* (Bücken Hdb.); B. Nettl, *Music in Primitive Culture* (Cambridge, Mass. 1956); C. Sachs, *Geist und Werden der Musikinstrumente* (Potsdam 1929), *The Rise of Music in the Ancient World* (N. Y. 1943), and *Vergleichende Musikwissenschaft* (Lpz. 1930); M. Schneider, *Die historischen Grundlagen der musikalischen Symbolik* (Mf IV, 1951) and *Primitive Music* (NOHM I); O. Seewald, *Beiträge zur Kenntnis der steinzeitlichen Musikinstrumente Europas* (Vienna 1934); C. Stumpf, *Beiträge zur Akustik und Musikwissenschaft* (1898–1901); W. Wiora, *Älter als die Pentatonik* (Studia Memoriae Bélae Bartók Sacra, 2/1957); *Jahrbuch für musikalische Volks- und Völkerkunde* (Berlin 1963–   ); *Sammelbände für Vergleichende Musikwissenschaft*, ed. C. Stumpf and E. v. Hornbostel (3 vols., 1922–3); *Zeitschrift für Vergleichende Musikwissenschaft* (4 vols., 1933); art. Blasquinte (MGG).

4. Non-European Polyphony

Although the non-European countries did not develop harmonic polyphony in our sense of the term, they show polyphonic beginnings that often utilize very primitive kinds of melodic material. Three quite self-contained regions seem to have been sources of polyphony. The first includes Polynesia, Melanesia, Indonesia, Indo-China, and the Philippines. The second extends from the Southern Caucasus to Europe. The third covers Central and South Africa. According to Marius Schneider, polyphony was created and employed widely by ancient races of mankind but was carried on further only by what he calls the white and black races, that is, by Negroid and by European peoples.

The occurrence of major and minor thirds as either structural or stepwise intervals in their melodies favors the development of polyphonic forms. Melodic movement in narrower intervals, on the other hand, inhibits this development. The high cultures of Asia accordingly have not developed polyphony as a distinct feature of their style. Melanesians, Negroes, and other short-statured Negroid peoples have comparatively rich polyphonic forms in their vocal music, using imitation, canon, ostinato, drone, and polyphony in two and three voices.

We may distinguish several types of non-European polyphony, for there are many different ways in which tones may sound together: in heterophony, in parallelism, in imitation of each other, with one voice serving as a drone or ostinato, and with all voices combining in accordance with primary forms of sonority.

Regarding the first, variant heterophony, we should note that when people sing together they are usually indulging in a kind of variation that is linked with the subjectivity of the individual singer. What is involved here is merely a matter of small variants, in which one singer differs from another. These occasional diads or simultaneous variants are limited to simple and slight melodic deviations. In general, the term "heterophony" is applied to melodic divergences from the main voice supplied as variation or paraphase by an accompanying vocal or instrumental part.

This practice has been found among the primitives of Southern Asia and South America, where the oldest form of polyphony appears among peoples to whom consonant intervals are as yet unknown. The heterophonic polyphony in Siamese and Javanese orchestral music consists of variants on a basic melody. The gongs roughly indicate the melody, and the metallophones and xylophones outline its finer details. Singing voices, flutes, and spike fiddles supply their own variations, while the big gongs mark emphases and accents (Example 7).

Literally, "heterophony" means "diversity of voices." The concept goes back to Plato, who understood by this term a certain technique that professional players used when accompanying the singing voice with

Siam, Piece for Orchestra "Kham hom" (Sweet Words)   (from Stumpf)

Example 7

an instrument. They carried and ornamented a somewhat independent melody on their instrument, producing consonant diads. Since the days of Stumpf and Adler, however, "heterophony" has come to mean the unison ornamented by a second voice, and thus a melodic variation of the main voice by the second. Sachs has glossed the term with the phrase, "that kind of simultaneous tone-production that occurs on the basis of tradition and improvisation."

Another way in which voices sometimes sound together in European music derives from their following parallel courses. This technique is known as "organum" and was especially widespread in medieval European

practice. Essentially it is a homophonic type of polyphony. The main
voice, which lies below, is accompanied by parallel octaves, fifths, and
fourths—in some instances even by seconds. The singing thus occurs simul-

Mogemoc (Western Carolines)   (from Herzog)

etc.

Example 8

taneously at different voice-levels. This practice is particularly common
among primitive peoples of East Africa and of the Caucasus and among
the folk in Iceland. Sometimes one hardly knows whether to classify an

Iceland   (from von Hornbostel)

Example 9

example of such singing as polyphonic. When the singers have noticeably
enriched the sound with parallel voices, they have probably intended
polyphony. But when they have only meant to broaden the sound toward
the end of the stanza or song for dynamic effect, they probably have not.
Certainly the practice as used in the Middle Ages can be classified as
polyphonic.

Parallelism of this type may be slightly modified, in response to
certain tonal requirements. Notably the tribesmen in the Bismarck
Archipelago, in Annam, and among the Batwa and the Zulus sometimes
replace fifths and fourth by seconds, third, and sixths to maintain a given
tonality.

Still another type of non-European polyphony occurs when voices
imitate each other in the course of antiphonal singing. The result may be
an overlapping between two choruses or between the leader and the
chorus, which produces true polyphony. The beginnings of canon are
found among even quite primitive peoples and among the Polynesians,
particularly the Samoans. The canon is one of the oldest and most primitive forms of vocal polyphony. As song and body movement are closely

Bateke (Congo), Dance song for antiphonal chorus   (from Bose)

Quickly

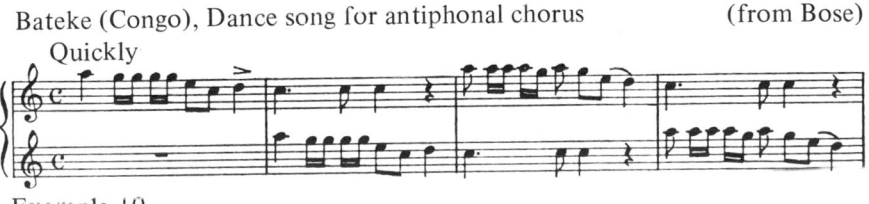

Example 10

related among primitive peoples, the canon is associated with the idea of the chase and of hunting, as in the "caccia" and "chasse" during the Middle Ages.

In its original state, antiphonal singing may take one of three forms. The chorus may repeat the entire stanza that the leader has sung (referred to as *choral repetition*), or it may repeat only the refrain of the stanza sung by the leader (called *refrain repetition*), or the leader may sing the first half-stanza, and the chorus add a second half-stanza. When the melodic line is clearly divided into such a stanza and refrain, it is known as *choral refrain*.

Although "overlapping" led to accidental canon, it later developed into a conscious two-voiced linear artistic practice. The simultaneous occurrence of the sounds, however, was intended only as enrichment of the sonority and does not constitute harmonic structure.

Semang (Malacca), Vocal Canon   (from Kolinski)

Example 11

Free imitation between voices at wide distances is also to be found, notably in the Solomon Islands, Borneo, and the Philippines.

Polyphony between two completely independent voices with a lower voice as an ostinato motif has also been recorded in the Solomon Islands, Borneo, and Annam.

Dayak (Borneo), Dance Song   (from Schneider)

Example 12

In its earliest form the ostinato is simply the rhythmically articulated clapping of hands. Further ostinato forms result when instruments of little or no melodic capability are introduced, and their role is limited largely to repetition of a rhythmically accompanying motif. Often there exists little recognizable relationship between the vocal melody and the instrumental ostinato or drone.

The drone is a deep-sounding voice, like an organ-point, which is sustained for an extensive period and is quite distinct from the independent upper voice. The principle, maintained by the bagpipe, is quite ancient and widespread. The simplest form of the drone is essentially an "overlapping" of the voices, while the leader of the half-chorus holds on to the final tone through the entry of the main chorus or while the final tone of the choral voice is sustained through the whole preliminary part of the ensuing stanza.

Finally, types of simultaneity among tones in non-European music-making may be explained simply in terms of primary forms of sonority, such as in the gong orchestras of China, Java, and Siam. In Java the ensemble is called a gamelan. The music of the Siamese and Javanese ensembles represents a well-developed example of "heterophonic polyphony." The reverberations of the variously tuned gongs, like church bells, produce the sonorous harmony of a pentachord, for example, in ascending order, c d f g a c'.

Such a form of sonority was considered by Rudolf Ficker to have been "primary" in early human music-making—the sort of sound one hears when listening to a peal of bells from a distance or to a gamelan. It is simply a fused body of sound. Polyphony, he felt, is "a compromise between two heterogeneous manifestations of energy—sonority and melody." He maintains that the former was basic, not the latter. "Certain acoustical and physical processes in nature," he wrote, "may be regarded as a starting-point for the development of music"—quite as much as can the unaccompanied melodic lines that monopolize our written records of Greek and early medieval music. He was prompted to devise this hypothesis by a number of considerations, among them the fact that we find polyphony in peoples around the world and that we have reports of concerted music-making in ancient times.

In discussing melody, he distinguished between two types, one of which he thought of as basic and the other as derivative. The first is more usual in the Near and Middle East, where no chordal-type accompaniment is appropriate or suggested by the structure of the music. This type of melody uses tonal material apparently unrelated to the principle of consonance. The modes or patterns have little to do with the natural overtones. We sometimes speak of the patterns as using third-tones or quarter-tones, but in so doing we are reading a foreign conception into their structure, as if melodies *should* be in whole steps. These so-called microtonic melodies are fundamentally means of moving in particular directions by narrow steps and of creating fanciful and decorative melismas.

The other type of melody—secondary and derived in character—suggests by its structure that it is meant to be heard within a matrix of sound that relates in some way to the natural overtone series. It calls for an awareness of sheer sonority, an experience of the fusion of sounds being produced simultaneously.

Primary sonority, accordingly, gives rise to a secondary type of melody, which is subjected to the principle of consonance in its further use for purposes of polyphony. Thus the relationship between the "primary form of sonority" and polyphony is an indirect or mediated one. Ficker's explanation, moreover, is purely speculative, but it may serve as a warning against assuming that the written record of evidence available to us from the past covers all that may have existed.

Whatever the origins of polyphony, it early and widely brought together man's needs for unity and variety, tension and release, motion and rest. Among primitive tribes this was a matter of routine and instinct.

The bane of primitive life was its large element of inertia, habit, and convention. To overcome these there had to be the impact of tribe on tribe and the conscious efforts of many individuals not only in the field of what we usually think of as the making of music, but also in that of activities that may not at first seem to be strictly musical—philosophy, mathematics, and the sciences—so that music could find a basis also in nature as man understood it. There were a relatively few areas in which this took place, all either Asian or Mediterranean, and all in a certain amount of early contact with each other.

Bibliography

G. Adler, *Über Heterophonie* (JbP 1908); W. Danckert, *Tonreich und Symbolzahl in Hochkulturen u. in der primitiven Welt* (Bonn 1966); R. v. Ficker, *Primäre Klangformen* (JbP 1929); A. Hammerich, *Studien über island. Musik* (SIMG 1899–1900); E. v. Hornbostel, *Phonographierte isländische Zwiegesänge* (Deutsche Islandforschung, Breslau 1930) and *Über Mehrstimmigkeit in der aussereuropäischen Musik* (Kongressbericht Vienna 1909); F. Hornburg, *Phonographierte Mehrstimmigkeit* (Mf III, 2); C. Sachs, *The Rise of Music in the Ancient World* (N. Y. 1943) and art. Heterophonie (MGG); M. Schneider, *Geschichte der Mehrstimmigkeit* (2 vols., Bln. 1934 and 1935) and "Ist die vokale Mehrstimmigkeit eine Schöpfung der Altrassen?" (Acta XXIII, 1951).

II The Music of Ancient Civilizations

5. The Far, Middle, and Near East

Ancient China

According to traditional legend, a basic tone—referred to as Yellow Bell (*huang chung*)—was established under the mythical Five Emperors, in the third millennium B.C. This tone was the sound of a pipe approximately a foot long according to the then-prevailing unit of measurement. The aim was to find the norm that had been determined by nature—or, in other words, the true norm. After each dynasty fell, this basic or central tone (serving on certain occasions as tonic or *kung*) was reset, on the assumption that the norm of measurement had to be brought anew into a right order with the universe, as if the old dynasty had somehow pitched the tune too high or too low. According to one tradition (which we shall follow here for purposes of simplicity), the ancient basic tone approximated that of a closed flute pipe a little over nine inches long and produced the sound of F above Middle C. Actually the length of the pipe varied considerably under different dynasties—around eight inches under the Chou dynasty and thirteen under the Ming. There are different versions of the Chinese system at different periods, but the fundamental principles remain the same.

By overblowing, the Chinese musical theorists derived from this basic tone the five, and later twelve, "norms" or *lü*'s. Arranged in a circle of fifths, these tones were interpreted as corresponding to the organization of the universe:

F	G	A	C	D
kung	shang	kio	chi	yü
middle	west	east	south	north
Saturn	Venus	Jupiter	Mars	Mercury
whole year	autumn	spring	summer	winter
whole life	age	childhood	manhood	old age
whole day	evening	morning	noon	midnight

yellow	white	blue	red	black
thoughts	care	anger	joy	fear
wind	cold	sunshine	heat	rain
prince	bureaucrat	people	work	objects
meat	bone	muscle	hair	skin
feeling	taste	smell	face	hearing
sweet	sharp	sour	bitter	salty
etc.	etc.	etc.	etc.	etc.

Ancient theorists further extended and elaborated on the system.

This all-inclusive traditional cosmology is the formula for an organic connection among music, the universe, nature, and human life. It has a certain priority in its systematic aspects. If in some form it really goes back to the time of the Mythical Emperors, it is the oldest of the cosmologies, though it was not systematized and written down until the Han dynasty (206 B.C. to 220 A.D.). The Chinese cosmological scheme may well be the starting-point for the other Asian conceptions, all based on number. The precise relationship between China and Babylon, however, has not yet been clearly established.

The scale was formed from a selection of the twelve *lü*'s. The oldest Chinese scale had five steps ordered in such a way that there were no half-steps, that is, it was pentatonic and anhematonic. It is represented more or less by F-sharp, G-sharp, A-sharp, C-sharp, and D-sharp, or the five black keys on the piano.

The ritual songs and dances of China were characterized by strict order and precision. The effort to achieve simple and symmetrical order manifested itself in rhythm that was uniform and "square," articulated in a two-by-two pattern. The ceremonial of the imperial court music was apparently well developed as early as the second millennium B.C.

According to Li Ki (*ca.* 100 A.D.), music was taken to be the "norm for heaven and earth, the principle of equilibrium and harmony." Belief in its ethical power was a consequence of its cosmic meaning. A comprehensive influence on human feelings was attributed to music. This view is often traced to Plato; but more than a century before him Confucius (551–475 B.C.) had also developed the idea that music, ethics, and education were interrelated.

Confucian hymn

Example 13

The creation of this cosmology was one of the most magnificent achievements of the human spirit. In it, for apparently the first time, world relationships involving the cosmos and man were grasped intellectually and brought into a system that was not at all rigid, but was meaningfully organized on a basis of number or abstract order. The numerical conception, which is intellectually and emotionally basic to everything that happens, was thus linked inseparably to music. Here man first triumphed over the concept of relationships based on magic.

Music gained a new meaning. Its powers were harnessed. As man adapted himself to the cosmos, music gained an ordered influence over his inner life and assumed a constructive, ethical, character-building role. A new scale of values thus came into being, emerging from the center of the system and playing a part in the inner organization of the state and of education. The significance of this newly won image was not in the least diminished by the fact that the old conception of music as a magical force occasionally reappeared.

As far as we can visualize the situation today, we find this cosmology being developed more or less simultaneously in three areas of the earth —China, Babylon, and Egypt—under similar conditions of man's relationship to his surrounding world. Great floods of the Yellow and Yangtze Rivers, the Tigris and Euphrates, and the Nile made these lands fruitful only when the power of nature was handled in an orderly way. This became possible only after the inhabitants had united into a civil community, observed nature, built dams, and so on. Along with this organized management, they developed writing, a calendar, astronomy, cities, wealth, intercontinental trade, and, eventually, successful wars of expansion. Though the three areas were in many respects similar, the Chinese gave music a more central position in their image of the world than did the Babylonians and Egyptians. In this respect they carried out a tendency which the Dutch sinologue J. J. N. de Groot has designated as "universalism."

Viewing Chinese music historically, we find that it was referred to, and its instruments were represented pictorially, as early as one of the oldest dynasties, the Shang or Yin (*ca.* 15th–11th century B.C.). From an allusion made by Ssena Ts'ien (145–*ca.* 86 B.C.) we gather that notation existed then, but the first actual written indications of the music that we have come from the T'ang dynasty (618–907). Therefore, although we know something about the earlier music, we cannot objectively reconstruct it. With perhaps more justification than in our own tradition, however, we can hypothesize certain aspects of later music as having prevailed in the earlier period, since in China there has been a notable tendency to preserve and return to older forms—in contrast to the West, where music has from the first been subjected to constant change.

Chinese musical development, according to tradition, began with the Mythical Emperors Fu-shi and Huang-ti, who are said to have discovered music and the *lü*'s and used the Yellow Bell as the basic tone of the system.

During the Chou dynasty (11th cent.–249 B.C.) music was strictly incorporated into the ceremonials of feudal society. Our most important source of information for the period is the "Book of Songs." The belief that music was a magical power controlling the forces of nature and raising the spirits of the dead changed gradually into the idea that it was significant in the formation of human character. A specifically designated Minister of Music was responsible for the precise maintenance of the court ceremonial. Music was regarded as an important factor in education, where it particularly exercised its ethical and character-building power. Along with native folk-music there was music for worship, state service, work, and family celebrations, all of which entailed a rich panoply of instruments. There was a well-developed theory of the tonal system, basically pentatonic and derived from the fundamental tone *kung*, but one that allowed for the further tonal resources of a twelve-degree chromatic scale.

Music from the states of Cheng and Wei gradually introduced a change in style. Secondary tones, deviations, and half-steps often modified the basic pentatonicism; and a distinction appeared between the historical repertoire and what writers around 300 B.C. considered "new music." When Confucius (551–479 B.C) and the Confucianists attributed high ethical qualities to music, they were referring to that of the earlier time. By the end of the Chou dynasty the theories of a system of twelve tones had been established. But in 213 B.C. there was a great burning of the books, and as a result most of the significant Chou writings have been lost.

During the Han dynasty (206 B.C. to 220 A.D.) attempts were made to reestablish the old ritual and make music more significant. There was a revival of previous practice and theory, especially at the imperial court, and from the West an incursion of foreign music and musical instruments. Influenced by Babylonian theory, the old conception of a cosmology based on music was systematized and set down in written form, at approximately the same time that Confucianism reached its height.

As the empire expanded under the Chin (265–411) and Sui (560–618) dynasties, foreign cultural features from Iran, India, and Central Asia became more evident, but the old court ceremonial of the Chou dynasty was perpetuated as the ideal. Indian influence was responsible for the beginnings of musical theater. Early in the Sui dynasty musicians came to the Chinese court from Turkestan. From Kucha there came a famous musician who propagated the idea of seven types of tonality resulting in a system of eighty-four scales, or seven scales for each of the twelve *lü*'s. Emperor Wen, who reigned from 581 to 604, was responsible for a reorganization of court musical activity and founded seven musical divisions. Each admitted the practice of one single style—one for the music of East Turkestan and Tibet (which had come by way of West Liang), another for indigenous Chinese secular music, another for Korean, another for Indian, and so on. The number of the divisions with their subsidiary orchestras was then increased to nine, indicating the cultivation of all influences in the court music of the "Middle Kingdom."

The T'ang dynasty (618–906) is considered the flowering-time of Chinese music, though today we have only the indications of pitch for the notes of a relatively few melodies. The multiple court orchestra gave rise to the fusion of some foreign influences. The art of dance flourished; and conversational or banquet music was cultivated at the court, in two departments. The imperial office of music supervised musical life and continued in formal existence until 1912. As foreign and native elements fused, a new Chinese secular music came into being. In 714 the Emperor ordered that two conservatories be founded to further the development of secular music, but liturgical music was not to be changed. The poet Li T'ai-po cultivated secular song, and a new song-form originated.

Known as the *tiu*, it was mostly epic in content. Evidence of incipient cultural petrifaction, however, began to appear as early as the Sung dynasty (961–1280). Though the 13th century developed the Chinese theater into a popular art form that is still cultivated, court music began to decline despite occasional attempts at restoration. In contrast to its earlier period of flowering, it displayed many of the typical phenomena of decadence. The present-day Chinese national opera and its distinctive style was born in the 17th and 18th centuries. Though theatrical music flourished, art music continued to decline steadily.

The Near and Middle East

For at least three millennia Mesopotamia, Arabia, and Iran formed a self-contained area of musical influence. The predominating cultural center was Mesopotamia. There was infiltration of less advanced tribes, such as the Semitic Bedouins from Arabia to the south and Indo-Europeans from Iran to the north. But they assumed the ancient cultural heritage they found on arrival and were eventually assimilated.

The Mesopotamians seem also to have influenced other lands. Egypt, Palestine, Phoenicia, Syria, Babylonia, Asia Minor, Greece, and Italy knew the harp, lyre, double oboe, and frame drum. As the instruments traveled, their names became part of the various languages. The significance of the Hittites and Phrygians in ancient Asia Minor and of the Phoenicians in Syria has been conjectured but so far not fully established. On the basis of later evidence some rather certain conclusions are possible with regard to Palestine.

Over and above details, however, two salient facts remain clear. First, it is obvious that from about 3000 B.C. on into the Christian Era, Egypt enjoyed a very high cultural development, unique in antiquity for its exclusiveness and autonomy. It had an absolute monarchy, a highly centralized governmental structure, and a strictly organized bureaucracy. The priesthood wielded significant power and was responsible for a representational and architectural art of monumental character, a hieroglyphic type of writing, great learning, and a rich literature. The Egyptians obviously influenced their neighbors in Greece and Rome. Second, it has become increasingly recognized that from about 3000 B.C. to 600 B.C. there was very high cultural achievement in Mesopotamia, led by the Sumerians, Akkadians, and Assyrians. The oldest writing and a magnificent architectural and pictorial art have been discovered there. Sumerian literature flourished around 2000 B.C., and Babylonian or Akkadian literature first flowered around 1700 B.C. and then again from 1400 to 1050 B.C. Around 650 B.C. the Assyrian king Assurbanipal built a library in Nineveh for the Babylonian and Assyrian literature then available. The Mesopotamians were notably interested in astronomy. Their culture had a deep and wide-ranging influence on that of other countries, notably Greece and the lands where Hellenism flourished.

In these high cultures music played an important role in worship. As would be expected from this emphasis, it was a part of cosmological thought, involved an extensive array of instruments, and was the concern of a professional class. In addition to the state-organized musical activity, of course, there was an extensive and independent folk-music, largely ignored in the written record. But we have our oldest accounts of an organized and systematic music from the Sumerians and the Egyptians.

Egypt

The time of Egyptian glory is usually visualized in terms of the Old Kingdom from about 2800 to 2160 B.C., the Middle Kingdom from 2160 to 1580 B.C., and the New Kingdom when Egypt was a great power from 1580 to 1085 B.C. During its final period (1085 to 332 B.C.) it was conquered by Alexander the Great, and Ptolemaic rule was established.

Primitive music prevailed throughout prehistoric, predynastic, and archaic times, which included the first two dynasties as preliminary to the music of the Old Kingdom. Means of music-making included the clapping of hands, stamping of feet, dance-ornaments, clappers, rattles, small bells, conches, cane flutes, bull-roarers, and vertical flutes.

Judging from the pictorial record, the Old Kingdom had a highly developed stage of musical culture from the start. Written documents report the activities of a musical profession and name prominent vocal and instrumental musicians. Already quite distinct from folk-music, the music of the court and temple included primitive polyphony, antiphonal songs of worship, solo songs with instrumental accompaniment, songs and dances in commemoration of the dead, and a dance in two sections accompanied by the *iba* or sistrum. Instrumental ensembles for the accompaniment of solo and group song contained one or more harps shaped somewhat like a multistringed hunting bow, one or more end-blown flutes, the double clarinet, and percussion instruments such as clappers, sistra, rattles, and (very rarely) large frame drums. The leader of the vocal and instrumental ensemble led his group by hand signals, or cheironomy, which scholars of today have succeeded in interpreting. This was a first step toward objectifying the tones, which were given names, with syllables for the steps. The trumpet also appeared for the first time in the Old Kingdom.

From the Middle Kingdom we have the first texts of hymns sung by harpers. The measurement of genuine excavated flutes permits us to assume that there were scales with large steps. There is evidence of antiphonal music-making, sung dances, hymn-like songs, and initial attempts at notation. We also find the earliest literary sources associating the stars cosmologically with music and dance. There was further development of the sistrum, the ivory rattle, the rattle-ornament made of precious metal, and the arched harp. In addition to instruments introduced earlier, there appeared also the horn with finger-holes, and, particularly, the African cylinder drum stretched with leather straps.

During the New Kingdom a revival of music occurred, but it was in terms of development in style rather than sonority. This change in style was influenced by the Near East and seems to have been related to a number of historical developments, such as the invasion of the Hyksos shortly before the beginning of the New Kingdom, closer trade relations with Asia, and notable princely marriages between the ruling houses of the Near East and Egypt. There ensued a full flowering of music and the establishment of schools for singers. Dated inscriptions on graves name many musicians, both male and female, who were vocal and instrumental virtuosi and temple singers. Measurements of wind instruments and of the fretted lute establish the fact that the intervals in the scales became smaller during the New Kingdom. Singing was antiphonal and responsorial, and there were new forms of solo singing, choral and instrumental accompaniment, strophic songs, and folk songs, with liturgical music in full flower. Instruments from Asia Minor now appeared with considerable frequency: the lyre, the lute, the angular harp, the double oboe, and both round and square frame drums. Earlier instruments were now developed further. The bow-shaped harp appeared in new types, such as the boat-shaped shoulder harp and the standing harp; and the sistrum was made in the shape of a horseshoe and of a *naos* or temple. Military music flourished under the conquering monarchs. Trumpets, for example, have been discovered in the tomb of Pharaoh Tutankhamen. Among the new instruments were metal bells, bronze cask drums, and cymbals of mussel shells.

During the late period, up to the conquest of Egypt by Alexander the Great, there were two opposing tendencies. On the one hand, there was extensive influence from Egyptian contacts with neighboring peoples outside, such as the introduction of the Cybele cult, of dance music, and of music as background for conversation. Foreign women musicians were much in evidence. On the other hand, the conservative priesthood sharply opposed foreign influences.

There is considerable similarity between the Egyptian and the Greek tonal systems. Herodotus and Plato have left us reports on Egyptian musical culture pointing out its stress on *ethos* and the close relationship between music and education.

During the late period, many new types of instruments were added to the already extensive resources. These include the nine-string lyre, giant cask or frame drums, little bells, fork cymbals, barrel drums of the Darabukka type popular in modern Egypt, smaller types of bound drum, castanets, and small metal cymbals. In addition, under the Ptolemies and in Coptic Egypt, there were small bronze bells, basket rattles, rattle drums, goblet-shaped barrel drums, bull-roarers, vessel flutes, the horn, pan-pipes, various types of aulos, new types of lyre, the hydraulis, the jew's-harp, the transverse flute, hand rattles, bone flutes, and fretted lutes. Under the Romans, the tuba and bucina were added. According to recent discoveries notation was developed further in the late period.

Babylonia, Assyria, Asia Minor, and Syria

The early musical development elsewhere in this area took place against a backdrop of more rapidly changing political forms and leadership.

The Sumerians were living in Babylonia by about 3000 B.C. Of unknown racial origin, they have left early evidences of an advanced culture and are credited with being the inventors of the oldest extant writing. They had extensive trade relations with Egypt. Their governmental system was that of a number of city-states existing side by side. In some respects they seem to have been similar to the Semitic Akkadians, who around 2700 B.C. came into the area from Arabia, with King Sargon I as founder of the Akkadian empire. About 2300 B.C. the land fell under the rule of the wild northern tribe of the Guti from Iran. When the latter were overthrown, the Sumerians and the Akkadians united in the so-called Third Dynasty of Ur, which ruled from 2050 to 1950 B.C. After numerous struggles for power, Mesopotamia was united under the famous lawgiver Hammurabi of Babylon (ca. 1700 B.C.) with Babylon as the capital and intellectual center. Around 1530 B.C. there was a brief invasion of the Hittites from the north, followed by the overthrow of Babylon by the northern mountain Kassites, who ruled the land for about six hundred years.

The Hittites had pushed into Asia Minor from Europe around 2000 B.C. Labarnas was the founder of the empire. Its older period extended up to about 1700 B.C., but it declined as the Hurrites became powerful in Northern Mesopotamia and Syria. About 1400 B.C. the Hittite realm revived, and under Suppiluliuma in about 1350 B.C. achieved very great political and cultural brilliance. North Syria was conquered, putting an end to the empire of the Mitanni, who had been responsible for the oldest cultural state in North Syria and had wielded great power during the 17th and 16th centuries B.C. in Northern Mesopotamia.

Meanwhile in 1300 B.C., the Assyrians began their rise with the foundation of their great kingdom. They were the powerful warrior people of the ancient Orient, ruling in Babylonia, Armenia, Syria, Palestine, and for a while even in Egypt. Their splendid metropolis was Nineveh, which flourished until its destruction in 612 B.C. They reached the height of their power under Ashurbanipal, who ruled from 669 to 630 B.C.; but they declined rapidly, and Babylon passed from their realm.

Nebuchadnezzar II of Babylon, who ruled from 605 to 562 B.C., conquered the western province of the Assyrian realm, Palestine, and Syria, and destroyed Jerusalem in 586 B.C. Thus he established the Neo-Babylonian or Chaldean realm and made Babylon its center, a world-city. After his death, however, Babylon fell to the Persian king Cyrus in 539 B.C., and the Babylonian empire ended. After having dominated international communication in the Near East for some two thousand years, Babylonian written culture declined, as Aramaic became the vernacular in Mesopotamia by the 8th century and cuneiform writing was replaced by the alphabetic script.

The Sumerian period of greatest development had occurred about the middle of the third millennium B.C. Early Sumerian history is usually classified into the Uruk VI-IV periods from about 3000 to 2800 B.C., the Jemdet-Nasr period from about 2800 to 2600 B.C., and the Mesilim period from about 2600 to 2500 B.C. The zenith came with the Ur I period from about 2500 to 2350 B.C. and was followed from about 2350 to 2150

B.C. by the Akkad period, from about 2130 to 2050 B.C. by that of the Guti, and from about 2050 to 1950 B.C. by Ur III.

The Sumerians of 3000 B.C. have left pictures, actual instruments, and cuneiform texts that give us an idea of their musical culture. During the Ur I period instrument-making flourished. Excavated examples display great technical perfection and artistic finish. The principal instruments were the harp, lyre, sounding staves, sistrum, and a small type of drum. Possibly they also had wind instruments. The lyre was the most important instrument used in worship.

The practice of sacred music was in the hands of professional musicians who, to some extent, enjoyed priestly status and included women in their ranks. Many of the musicians, even as early as the Mesilim period, are known by name. Music was always combined with religious texts, which were either sung or recited in a sort of speech-song. There is no evidence of a music performed solely on instruments, nor is there any extant written music in any notation that has been acceptably deciphered. There does exist an actual clay tablet of about 800 B.C. with a hymn concerning the Creation inscribed on it in Sumerian and Semitic and with some accompanying syllables that are clearly not part of the verbal text and are presumably the notation of the music. Probably each of these syllables represents not a single note but a whole little group of notes.

So far as the texts are concerned, there are two large groups: the first, songs and hymns in praise of gods and kings, and the other, laments uttered in times of sorrow over the destruction of cities and temples or over the absence of Tammuz during his sojourn in the underworld. Later the Jews and early Christians modelled their worship-service on the religious literature of the Mesopotamians. There was extensive liturgical music associated with the temples of the gods. According to pictorial representations, music played a considerable role on occasions of drinking and feasting in celebration of the highest liturgical festival, that of the New Year. In extant sources there is no indication of an entirely secular music. The Sumerians regarded music as a gift of the gods. The liturgical music that the gods had instituted, accordingly, was something in which the divine took on life and was regarded primarily as a means of fulfilling the needs of the gods themselves.

The Akkadians, Babylonians, and Assyrians took over the Sumerian cultural heritage and developed it further. According to a report in Plutarch, the Babylonians related the seasons to music, spring standing to autumn in the interval of a fourth, spring to winter in that of a fifth, and spring to summer in that of an octave. In this respect Babylonia suggests a parallel with China, though there are differences of detail in the two accounts of the relationship between tones and the seasons. These differences have been interpreted as indicating that the Chinese system was based on the over-blowing of a flute, the Babylonian on the stopping of a sounding string. Apparently, also, the orchestras in the Mesopotamian area were highly developed, as seen in the Biblical description of the Assyrian king Nebuchadnezzar's orchestra, in the book of Daniel.

Palestine (1700 B.C. to 70 A.D.)

The period of the patriarchs Abraham, Isaac, and Jacob is usually dated from around 1700 B.C. About 1500 Palestine fell under Egyptian rule. Some time after 1250 Moses freed his people from bondage. The Judges ruled from about 1200 to about 1050 B.C. Under Joshua the Jewish people conquered Palestine, and the land was divided among the twelve tribes. The judge and prophet Samuel designated Saul as king. Under David, from 1025 on, the kingdom flourished and under his son Solomon in 950 reached its highest point. After Solomon's death, it was divided into the kingdom of Israel in the north and Judah in the south, with Jerusalem as its capital. The Assyrians conquered the kingdom of Israel in 721 B.C. and exiled the Israelites. In 586 Nebuchadnezzar II destroyed the southern kingdom of Jerusalem and the First Temple. As a result, the Jews were led captive into Babylonia, returning in 539. After the middle of the 5th century B.C. the community became a priestly state, first subject to the Persians, then after 332 to the Macedonians, and later (after 301) to the Ptolemies. From 135 B.C. to 8 A.D. the Maccabees were the ruling dynasty of kings and high priests. In 63 B.C. Pompey conquered Jerusalem. In 70 A.D. Titus destroyed Jerusalem and the Second Temple and dispersed the Jews.

Paralleling somewhat the political developments, musical culture advanced during two distinct periods. The transition occurred around 1050 when the Judges were succeeded by the Kings. The music of the synagogue has wide ramifications and exhibits features of complicated growth and development, carrying on further old forms derived from Syrian, Greco-Alexandrian, Byzantine, Coptic, Abyssinian, and Roman cultures.

The first important period is that of the patriarchs and the judges. As with primitive tribes, the entire people took part in the singing, playing, and dancing. Women especially were involved in music-making. The character of the music was hymn-like and passionate.

The second important period is that of the kings. From 1025 on, the brilliant era under David marked the beginning of a more organized type of music. The first official corporate body of professional musicians was established. Temple music flourished. The Levites played a clerical or professional role in the musical service. The most important instruments had apparently been taken over from Syria: the *tof*, or frame-drum; the *kinnor*, or yoke-lute or lyre; and the *shofar*, or ram's horn without mouthpiece.

In trying to determine what the music was like, we are aided by the fact that there are still today some Jewish congregations which separated from the parent body before 600 B.C. and did not participate in the development of Jewish ritual music after the destruction of the First Temple in 586 B.C. and after the Babylonian Exile. They continue on as segregated groups in the Yemenite area of Southern Arabia, in the regions once dominated by Babylonia and Persia, and in Syria and North Africa. From their synagogue music, according to A. Z. Idelsohn, we can infer certain characteristic features of temple music during the period of the kings. There were loud, ecstatic appeals to God, such as are frequently indicated in the Bible. The manner of rendition is similar to a recitative,

Melodic punctuation (Psalm 81,2)   (from Idelsohn)

Harninu lélohim ù - senu - - - - - ,   hariù lé - lohe ja - àkov ——.

Example 14

Melodic grouping (Joshua 1,2)   (from Idelsohn)

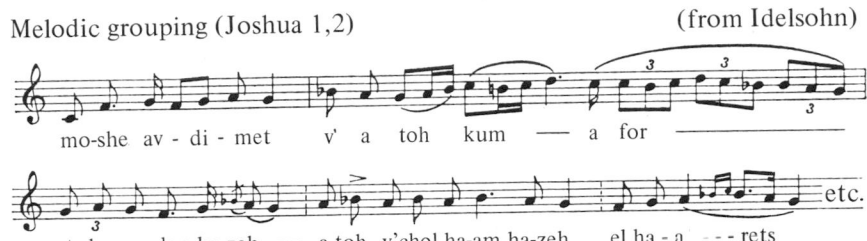

mo-she av - di - met v' a toh kum —— a for ————

et ha-yar-den ha-zeh ——, a-toh v'chol ha-am ha-zeh,   el ha - a - - - rets

Example 15

midway between monotonous recitation and free melody. The musical style is simple and archaic. Its basic steps, however, are increased by the insertion of other intervallic steps, thus exemplifying both the distancing and additive principles that appear in the music of primitive tribes. The melodies were made up entirely of individual fixed particles, with their stepwise intervals. Thus what might be called "composition" meant the free disposition and freely changing combination of this limited number of basic motifs. The freedom which the composer—or, generally, the singer himself—had available to him was that of putting the motifs together and introducing ornamental enrichments or decorations and transitions from one motif to another. Here we may recall that our word "compose" comes from the Latin *componere*, meaning "to put together."

There were special fixed motifs for the reading of the Pentateuch, the Prophets, the Psalms, prayers, and various other portions of worship. The text was accordingly combined with the basic motives, whatever they might be. In the earlier period, there was a change of motif from half-line to half-line; in the later, from word to word. The rhythm was more free than metrical.

Ancient Hebrew traditions were, of course, continued in early Christian music.

Bibliography

H. Avernary, *Formal Structure of Psalms and Canticles in Early Jewish and Christian Chant* (MD 1953); B. Bayer, *The Material Relics of Music in Ancient Palestine and its Environs* (Tel Aviv 1963); F. Behn, *Musikleben im Altertum und frühen Mittelalter* (Stuttgart 1954); H. G. Farmer, *The Music of Ancient Egypt* and *The Music of Ancient Mesopotamia* (NOHM I); F. W. Galpin, *The Music of the Sumerians and their Immediate Successors, the Babylonians and Assyrians* (N. Y. 1937); P. Gradenwitz, *The Music of Israel* (N. Y. 1949); H. Gressmann, *Musik und Musikinstr. im Alten Testament* (Religionsgeschichtl. Versuche u.

Vorarb. II, Giessen 1903); H. Hartmann, *Die Musik der sumerischen Kultur* (Diss., Frankfurt a. M. 1960); H. Hickmann, *Ägyptische Musique* (MGG), *Die ältesten Musikernamen* (Musica, Heft 3, 1951), "Instruments de Musique," in *Catalogue général des antiquités égyptiennes* (Cairo 1949), *Musicologie Pharaonique* (Kehl/Rhein 1956), *Musik im Austausch der Völker* (Musica, Heft 11, 1959), *45 siècles de musique dans l'Egypte ancienne* (Paris 1956), and *Rythme, mètre et mesure de la musique instr. et vocale des anciens Egyptiens* (Acta 1960, Fasc. I); H. Husmann, *Grundlagen der antiken u. orientalischen Musikkultur* (Bln. 1961); A. Z. Idelsohn, *Hebr.-orient. Melodienschatz*, 10 vols. (Lpz., Jerus., Vienna 1914–32); H. Kraeling and L. Mowry, *Music in the Bible* (NOHM I); J. Kunst, *Ethnomusicology* (The Hague 1959); R. Lachmann, *Musik d. Orients* (Breslau 1929); L. Picken, *The Music of Far Eastern Asia* (NOHM I); K. Reinhard, *Chin. Musik* (Eisenach and Kassel 1956); S. Rosowsky, *The Cantillation of the Bible* (N. Y. 1957); A. M. Rothmüller, *Die Musik der Juden* (Zurich 1951); C. Sachs, *The Rise of Music in the Ancient World* (N. Y. 1943), *Musik des Altertums* (Breslau 1924), *Die Musik der Antike* (Bücken Hdb.), *Geist und Werden d. Musikinstr.* (Potsdam 1929), *The Mystery of the Musical Notations in Babylonia* (Paper, AMS, N. Y. 1939), and *Die Tonkunst der alten Ägypter* (AfMw II, 1919–20); M. Schneider, *Die hist. Grundlagen der mus. Symbolik* (Mf IV, 1951); W. Stauder, *Die Harfen und Leiern der Sumerer* (Frankfurt a. M. 1957) and *Die Harfen und Leiern Vorderasiens in babyl. und assyrischer Zeit* (Frankfurt a. M. 1961); E. Werner, *The Sacred Bridge* (London and N. Y. 1959); Xia Ye, *Zur Entwicklung der chin. Opernstile* (Beiträge zur Musikwissenschaft, 1961, Heft 3); *Musikgesch. in Bildern, Bd. II, Lieferung 1: Ägypten* (Lpz. 1962); MW (Hebräische Musik); *Sammelbde. f. Musikwiss.*, ed. C. Stumpf and E. M. v. Hornbostel (Munich 1922ff); arts. Chinesische Musik, Handzeichen, Hethiter, Jüdische Musik (MGG).

6. The Music of Greece

First, in the general history of the Greek development, Indo-European tribes migrated from the north into Greece during the second millennium B.C. There they clashed with a people who were living in Asia Minor and on the islands and who ruled the east coast. This led to the Trojan War (*ca.* 1200 B.C.) and the successful completion of the Dorian migrations about 1100 B.C. During the early first millennium Sparta took the lead: Lycurgus established its constitution between 850 and 800, and during the 8th and 7th centuries B.C. it assured itself of dominance in the Peloponnesus by the two Messenian wars. The historical period began in 776 B.C., when dates were first recorded in terms of Olympiads. Around the middle of the first millennium Athens was in its glory: Solon's constitution was established in 594 B.C., and during the Golden Age of Pericles from 478 to 429 B.C. there was a flowering of the sciences and the arts. The Peloponnesian War, in which Sparta defeated Athens, raged from 431 to 404 B.C., and Thebes took over control from 379 to 362 B.C. Rule passed to the Macedonians after the Battle of Chaeronea in 338 B.C. and to the Romans in 146 B.C.

Reviewing this sequence of events in terms of cultural history, we find that the Minoans in Crete passed through the early period in the development of their civilization from 2600 to 2000 B.C. and reached maturity from 2000 to 1400 B.C., with Cnossos as their center. About 1700, under their influence, cities were established on the mainland, notably at Mycenae and Tiryns. The flowering of Cretan-Mycenaean high culture occurred from about 1500 to about 1400 B.C., and the so-called Late Mycenaean Period from approximately 1400 to about 1250 B.C.

In the Greek area, however, even more brilliant cultural heights were to be attained in the course of the ensuing millennium—an achievement so rich and varied that any way of indicating the developments during these mere five centuries is bound to seem cluttered. From 950 to about 750 B.C., "Geometric Art" prevailed in the Greek minor arts and ceramics. Homer, around 800 B.C., sang of the Trojan War. During the 8th century the Archaic style was being developed in the graphic arts. Toward the end of the century Hesiod formulated in poetry many of the myths, distinguishing among the Nine Muses. Lyric poets such as Tyrteius of Sparta, Mimnerus of Ionia, and Arion of Lesbos were active around 625. With the 6th century B.C. there came the beginnings of the Dorian architectural style, a strict and archaic sculpture, and speculation about nature on the part of the "Pre-Socratic" philosophers. Sappho of Lesbos sang of nature and love. Other outstanding figures were Pythagoras of Samos, the poet Xenophanes, and Thespis with the beginnings of tragedy in Athens. The temple of Artemis in Ephesus was built about 550 B.C. Three figures active in the early 5th century were the dramatist Aeschylus (525–456 B.C.), the poet Pindar (*ca.* 520–448 B.C.), and the sculptor Phidias (*ca.* 500- *ca.* 435 B.C.), in whose work can be observed the replacement of the Archaic by the Classical style. The high point in the Doric style of architecture occurred around 500. Other notable 5th-century figures are the historian Herodotus (*ca.* 495- *ca.* 424 B.C.), the lyric poet Anachreon (*ca.* 500 B.C.), and the dramatists Sophocles (496–406 B.C.) and Euripides (484–406 B.C.). In the 5th century also occurred the transition from Dorian to Ionic style. Socrates lived from 470 to 399 B.C., and the historian Thucydides died about 395, the comic dramatist Aristophanes about 388, the founder of Greek medicine Hippocrates about 377, and the sculptor Praxiteles in 330. Attic vase painting experienced its culmination between about 450 and 340 B.C., and the high point in the Ionic style occurred about 400 B.C. Plato (427–347 B.C.) and Aristotle (*ca.* 384–322 B.C.) summed up and transmitted the Greek heritage of philosophical thought to posterity. By 350 B.C. the period of Hellenism had begun.

The continued influence of the Greeks' idea of music on the history of Western thought is nearly as great as that of their work in other arts on subsequent architecture, sculpture, philosophy, and poetry. This may at first seem strange, for the few fragments of Greek music preserved do not even come from the Classical period. They give little idea of the nature and artistic effect of the music, for they speak to us but faintly when considered from a subjective and artistic point of view. The influence of Greek music is thus not due to its qualities as a sheer matter of sound. Instead, other aspects of the music must have been responsible for its importance. Europeans during the centuries from the beginning of the Christian era to the present have been stimulated to artistic inspiration, to imitation of the ancient models, and to research principally by four types of concern with Greek music:

1. by the music as idea, or the concept of *musiké,*
2. by Greek tragedy,
3. by the theory of *ethos* and of *katharsis,* and accordingly by the place of music in education, and
4. by musicology.

The Greeks, in their time, created an entirely new idea of music. In the early stages of mankind and among primitives, music had figured as magic. The high cultures of Asia had incorporated it in cosmological systems. These older conceptions lingered on. Perhaps an echo of the magic role is to be heard, for example, in the myth of Orpheus—though here music developed its magic power purely in the service of the beautiful and the good in accordance with the human and rather specifically Greek conception of the gods. Perhaps cosmology among the Greeks still continued to coincide with music and number as a basis in Pythagorean teachings; but it had there the character of an esoteric theory, known only to a secret society, to a small closed circle. What the human mind developed in Greece during less than five centuries, from Homer in the 9th century to Aristotle in the 4th, was the concept of *musiké.* In it the sonorous aspect of music found its entire and sole consummation in the service of the arts of poetry and the dance. Music entered and suffused both the divine and the human realms. The beautiful received its objective value through the good. Artistic experience and ethically edifying forces combined indissolubly in a single unity.

The Greeks differentiated music and language from the graphic and plastic arts. Poets and musicians were always regarded as prophets favored by the gods. The graphic and plastic artists, on the other hand, were considered workmen, at least up to Hellenistic times. Expressive value was assigned only to the audible as against the work of the plastic artist, which Plato considered but a mirror-image of worldly things.

If one speaks of ancient Greek music, he understands by the term a certain historically limited period. It begins with Homeric times about 800 B.C.—that is, after the Dorian migration—and ends in the period from about 350 to 300 B.C., with the onset of Hellenism. Although a more detailed chronicle of it will be given later, it might be well to start with an idea of some of its general characteristics.

The first is its Oriental origin. The Greeks' musical conceptions and practice had their homeland in the Orient. These were invested by the Greeks with the clarity of a carefully considered theory, which has been passed on to us. Greek music accordingly played the role of an intermediary between Oriental and Occidental cultures. We can discern many traits of Greek music in the East, such as the *ethos* theory that appeared previously in China and Egypt, the tonal system worked out in terms of the universe such as had been developed in China, Egypt, and Babylon, ways of constructing the scale used by the Babylonians and the Hebrews, and certain instruments previously found among the Hittites and the Egyptians.

Music, of highest significance for the entire culture, operated almost entirely in conjunction with the arts of poetry and dance. Independent instrumental music existed only to a limited extent and merely as solo-playing. The ancient Greeks had no harmonic polyphony as we know it, but they had achieved the highest perfection in purely monodic melody with differentiated rhythmic structure. In singing, they perhaps employed the nasal tone-production of the Orient and made very fine distinctions of pitch in ways not quite familiar to our ears.

Notation, to be sure, appears in connection with Greek music. But, though the few preserved examples are legible, they do not permit us to revive the music with thorough effectiveness as sheer sound. Greek music is a music that had its being in the very act of its production, that is, it did not rely on written notation in quite the way that Western music does. Greek notation did not arise until after the Classical period, when the integral relationship between language and music in *musiké* was disappearing. The purpose of writing it down was to delay the break-up and to preserve the tradition of musical practice. To make much actual sound from Greek notation, we would thus really first have to know Greek music. What one wishes to reconstruct, accordingly, proves to be a precondition of the reconstruction itself.

Although we can scarcely make the music ring out authentically, we can predicate the essence of it on the basis of ancient writers' reports, of poetic allusions and especially of music theory. *Musiké* originally had to do with the overt sounding of metrical speech, of verses. Since a verse could be recited in no other way than by singing, it contained within itself and from its very beginning a musical element. Thus *musiké* is not what we understand by music; rather, it was the poet's work as heard, at once music and poetry. This unity, which we today are no longer able to imagine with perfect ease, began to fall apart at the end of the 5th century, after the Classical period. Music and poetry went their ways, and only thereafter can we speak of music and of poetry, for both from then on existed independently each for its own sake. Only then could they be combined with each other, and only then was it possible to set poetry to music in our sense of the word.

On into the 5th century *musiké* was bound most closely with dance. A relic of this connection exists in our word "orchestra," which comes from the Greek *orchesis,* meaning originally the dancing place and later the circular stage area in the theater. The rhythm of the 8th-century Homeric hexameter seems to have been that of a circle dance. The choral lyric of the 7th and 6th centuries and the 5th-century choruses of Classical tragedy are also to be understood from the dance. The very word *choros* meant a circle and did not acquire its present meaning until Christian times.

The unity of *musiké* ruled out a purely contemplative or passive aesthetic enjoyment. Right on into the Classical period, song unequivocally possessed preeminence. The really sonorous aspect of music was called *melos*. According to Plato, *melos* was composed of *logos*, or word, *harmonia*, or modulation (that is, the relation in terms of tension between successive tones), and *rhythmos*, or order of movement. Tone and *rhythmos* had to subordinate themselves to the word. The tone was in a direct and natural way bound to the word, which was rich in thought and content. The musical *rhythmos* was not to be separated from the metrical aspects. In the eyes of the Greeks, according to Abert, *rhythmos* was "the real life-principle of the music"; it was a human attitude and therewith had the significance of an ethical category. Likewise, the *nomos* had legal force: it was the norm and the statute.

The music of the Classical period was never an independent art in our sense of the term, and for this reason it was hardly comparable to our music. The high significance of Greek music, which in this sense has never again been attained by any other Western people, lay in its direct relationship to life and to the gods, a union that required no intermediaries. Music was not an addition, but an essential component in worship, state festivals, celebrations, and sociability. "The music of the Greeks," according to Wegner, "permeated the whole realm in the lives of gods and men with all-inclusive validity." It was incorporated into life in a completely organic way and was at the same time an instructional means for improving the developing citizen of the state and for educating him morally.

From Greek music there have been derived two complementary principles, the Apollonian and the Dionysian. Apollo's instrument was the lyra, as well as the phorminx, which accompanied the dance and the recital of the Homeric epics. But in the 7th century B.C. the subjectively oriented lyric and in the 6th the dithyramb made their appearance and introduced a Dionysian and ecstatic element. For them, the aulos came into widespread use. A new character manifested itself in Greek music with this instrument, which was related to the shawn and the oboe, was sacred to Dionysus, and had come from Asia Minor, where it had been associated with the legendary figure of Olympus of Phrygia. The myth of the competition between Apollo with his lyre and Marsyas with his aulos reflects the clash between the two different musical attitudes. Apollo was victorious. The lyra and the aulos were distinctive of two essentially different forms of musical activity: the lyra of one based on concord and instrumentalism, the aulos on one that was embodied in line and operated through the human voice or such instruments as imitate the human voice. These two instruments were not used together until the rise of tragedy in the 5th century. Toward the end of the 5th century music began to free itself from verse in the new dithyramb. The unity of *musiké* fell apart. Purely instrumental music with its element of virtuosity predominated.

Friedrich Nietzsche in "The Birth of Tragedy" (1871) recognized in the Apollonian and the Dionysian two attitudes toward art that were separate in both origin and aim: the Apollonian as the "pictorial art of the sculptor" and the Dionysian as the "nonpictorial art of music." He assigned to the Apollonian principle the realm of dream, of the beautiful light of the inner imaginative world, of higher truth, of measure, of simple, transparent beauty, and of the individual. To the Dionysian he attributed intoxication, forgetfulness of self, magic transformation, excess, a mystic feeling of identification, titanic and barbaric lust for life, and universality. The one principle is not conceivable without the other, for they are "two interwoven artistic instincts." He felt that they were united in Attic tragedy.

It is in the realm of theory, accordingly, that Greek music has been highly important. The pentatonic scale originally formed its basis. As elements were added from the linear musical culture of Asia Minor, however, the five steps became seven through the insertion of two "irrational" tones, or slurred notes or pitches at first not precisely fixed.

Though the tonal system was not described until Hellenistic times, it was based on a decidedly linear and melodic music. Influences and intermixtures from foreign races had produced it; chromatic and enharmonic features with their quarter-tones had thoroughly infiltrated and modified the original music of the Greeks. In contrast to the "linear" music of Asia Minor, it can be taken as having been a "full-sounding" music, in which the pentatonic basis may well have had great significance.

The tonal system was founded on the interval of the fourth, on the descending series of four tones, the tetrachord. If two tetrachords are joined as suggested in Example 16, the result is the full scale, the octave species of the particular mode. The main modes or *harmoniai* are differentiated by the placement of the half-tone steps within the tetrachord:

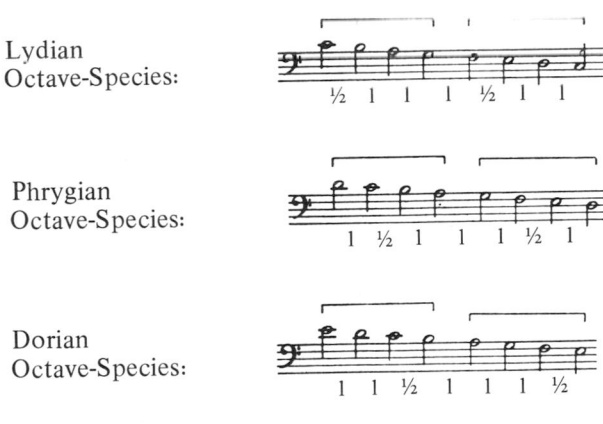

Example 16

From these scales one can construct two auxiliary scales, for example the Hypodorian (A-A) and the Hyperdorian (B-B), by appending above and below tetrachords that correspond to the basic scale and by filling out the result to the full octave:

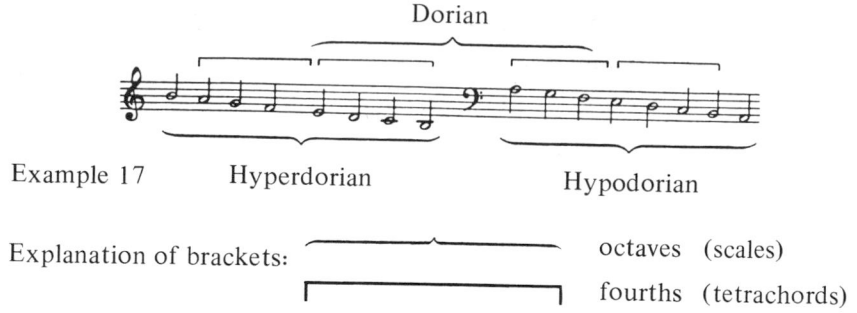

Example 17   Hyperdorian   Hypodorian

Explanation of brackets:  octaves (scales)

fourths (tetrachords)

In a corresponding manner one can obtain the Hypophrygian (G-G) and the Hyperphrygian (A-A), and the Hypolydian (F-F) and the Hyperlydian (G-G). The Hypodorian was also known as the Aeolian, and the Hyperdorian as the Mixolydian, the Hypophrygian as Ionian (or Iastic), and the Hyperphrygian as the Locrian. The Hypo- modes stood a fifth lower, the Hyper- modes a fifth higher. If the Dorian octave was filled out above and below by a tetrachord in each direction and a tone was added at the lower octave, there resulted the "perfect" system, or *systema téleion*. The two middle tetrachords were called "disjunct" or *diezeugménon;* the outer ones, "conjunct" or *syneménon.*

Example 18

The scales were transposed so that they might be applied to the normal range of the lyra or kithara, which originally—being pentatonic —had but four or five strings, but later had from seven to seventeen.

The tetrachord, as such, could be made up in various ways. These determined the three tonal species, or *genera*: diatonic, chromatic, and enharmonic. The descending diatonic tetrachord consisted of two whole steps and a half step: for example, A-G-F-E. The chromatic had an irrational step leading to its second tone: A-irrational tone-F-E. The enharmonic had such a step in the third postion: A-F-irrational tone-E.

Greek rhythm, both musical and spoken, was based not on the stress of the individual words but on the quantity of the individual syllable, that is, on whether it was short or long. A syllable, if long, could not be contracted in length, nor if short could it be extended. In other words, quantity was fixed and could not be influenced. Like a solid body, the separate syllable was removed from any lengthening stress or subjective emphasis that might draw it out—removed, as it were, from any possibility of its being influenced by whoever delivered it. As the words with their syllables—and, accordingly, their quantities—were arranged side by side and as certain combinations were repeated, there resulted rhythms or verses. These are not rhythms in the sense in which we speak of rhythms in our music, for they arose from the mere additive arrangement of quantities side by side and did not require a framework or background as in Western rhythm—in the form of marking time or giving the beat— to endow them with meaning. Greek rhythm is thus no self-sufficient musical rhythm but is at the same time a speech-rhythm. Verse-rhythm unifies *musiké*. A great deal is known about Greek rhythm, not only on the basis of the accounts of the theoreticians, but also especially on the basis of similar rhythmic attitudes maintained still today in the folk-music of Greece and the Balkans. Thus, for example, the rhythm of the circle-dance typical of modern Greek folk-music "Syrtós Kalamatianós" ♪•♪♪ can be traced back to the time of Homer.

The Greeks had two systems of notation for the tonal area they used, which may be represented as a little over three octaves descending from G above high C to E-flat. The so-called vocal script, used for purely vocal music, consisted of the letters of the Ionic alphabet, introduced into Athens in 403 B.C. The instrumental script was a combination of the old Dorian and Ionic letters and was used for the instrumental accompaniment of song, for duets, and for purely instrumental music. The origin of the instrumental script is assigned to the 6th century B.C. But in the 5th century at the latest the instrumental script had come into general use, as did also the vocal script before the beginning of the 4th century. Notation was not just a theoretical matter but from the very beginning was linked with musical practice. Compositions were written and music was made from the notation, although—according to Pöhlmann —great scope was still accorded oral tradition in performance practice and instruction. Rhythm was not indicated, as it was implied by the meter of the text. Greek melodies fit the accentuation of the text closely. For over a century ancient Greek notation has been transcribed: two scholars, Bellermann and Fortlage, working independently of each other, produced the first successful transcriptions of Greek notation at about the same time in 1847.

Although Greek musical theory gives special information about the tonal system and the ethos theory, its source value is limited by the fact that it had, since Plato, a strongly speculative and constructivistic trait, but little connection with musical life. There are no handbooks that concern themselves with practical questions about music until the second century A.D. Musical practice was carried on essentially by oral tradition. Also, the writing about music from Plato to Boethius was mainly concerned with the music of the early 5th century B.C. Musical practice did not at all correspond to the state and attitude of theory.

Plato uses a term, *heterophony*, which has come to figure prominently in discussions of primitive and Oriental music. By this term he apparently meant the continuing alternation of the melody between song and instrumental accompaniment. Heterophony occurs as a melodic variation added by way of decoration or ornamental paraphrase of the main voice by a second one, usually the accompanying instrumental voice, with no polyphony or counterpoint in our sense of the term. The passage where he uses the word occurs in the *Laws* (VII, 812 d-e): "The music teacher as well as the pupil must use the lyra on account of the fixed tuning of the strings, bringing tones in tune with other tones. Heterophony and the variety of lyra music in which some melodies come from the taut strings and others from the composer of the melody, with the addition also of tonal steps from narrow to broad, quick to slow, and high to deep as something consonant and dissonant, and moreover with the annexing of multifarious rhythmic ornaments to the tones of the lyra—all this sort of thing we are not to expect of those who are to acquire a cursory knowledge of music in three years." According to Handschin's interpretation, however, Plato describes as heterophony not the "ornamented unison" but the consonant diad to which ornaments are added. The use of diads, apart from the octave, was limited only to instrumental performance and the accompaniment of song and did not extend to purely vocal ensemble.

An important feature of Greek musical theory is *ethos*, which is related to the idea of catharsis. Music had a dominant role as the moral pillar of the political and educational structure: for according to the Greek view music, depending on its particular kind, had a positive or negative effect on the human will. Music stood in the service of religion and the state. In Sparta, Thebes, and Athens it was an educational requirement to learn how to play the aulos and to participate in the chorus. Practice of melodies took place in historical sequence: first the old hymnody of the legends of gods and heroes and only later contemporary music. In Arcadia it was a civic duty to take instruction in music up to the age of thirty. Writers on education especially stressed Doric melodies. Plato's musical ethics, as set forth in the *Republic* (II, 399 a-c), allowed only two models for the musical instruction of youth: the Dorian mode, which was considered serious and character-building, and the Phrygian, which stirred men to warlike deeds. The Lydian was rejected because of its soft character.

The Dorian, the Phrygian, and the Lydian were generally believed each to have it own characteristic. The Dorian was manly and courageous: it strengthened the will, restored one to composure, helped one stand firm in all vicissitudes, and made men stronger than fate. The Phrygian was wild, passionate, and ecstatic; hence it was the principal mode for dithyrambs. The Lydian was the mode of lament, of the tender and intimate. Corresponding to these three differences in ethos there were three stylistic types. The diastaltic inspired one to decision and action and was suitable for tragedy. The hesychastic supported equanimity and was suitable for the religious choral lyric. The systaltic was boundlessly subjective and was appropriate to the love lyric, drinking song, or complaint. For the Dorian the instrument was the kithara; for the Phrygian, the aulos. This contrast is at the basis of Nietzsche's pair of concepts, the Apollonian and the Dionysian—the former a suprapersonal, quiet, and reserved type of artistic attitude; the latter subjective, uninhibited, and orgiastic.

The three tonal genera also have ethical significance. The diatonic corresponded to the Dorian. The chromatic was excluded from tragedy. The enharmonic had special meaning in the music of Classical tragedy. The culmination of the theory of ethos is found in the third book of Plato's *Republic*.

Another important feature of Greek musical theory is the concept of *nomos*. In the beginning it designated primarily the song of worship as a distinct category. Then the term was supplanted by certain designations of types, such as the paean, dithyramb, hymn, and threnody. To the concept of *nomos*, accordingly, there adhered an occasional meaning connected with the characteristic nature of the individual culture and the god, with the particular statutes and norms. Later, *nomos* came to mean the melody with characteristic details of melodic steps, rhythm, tonal genus, and form. Usually it was linked with the name of a famous artist but was repeated and replayed, and in the latter tradition it acquired variations, yet did not lose the features that were characteristic of it. The Greek *nomos* is the counterpart of the Indian *raga*, the Persian *maquam*, the Javanese *patet*, the Tunisian *taba'*, the minnesingers' "tune," and the meistersingers' "tone." Historically, the *nomos* theory starts from the name of the kitharist Terpander of Lesbos (*ca.* 675 B.C.), though legend associates it earlier with Olympus. Terpander was said to have increased the number of *nomoi* to seven. In the Pythian games at Delphi in 586 B.C., Sakadas of Argos was victorious with the Pythian *nomos* for the aulos, in which he described the victory of Apollo over Pytho.

The music took on many individual artistic forms. The *hymnos* was a lofty art-song for the gods, usually accompanied by a stringed instrument. The general category of *hymnos* included distinct types. The paean, for example, was originally a festive song to Apollo, who was regarded as its creator, but later it came to include songs of victory or of propitiation, usually for chorus and accompanied by the kithara. Another type of *hymnos* was the dithyramb, or song praising Dionysus and dedicated to his cult, usually choral, and accompanied by auloi or the barbiton. Other types of music were for purposes of praising individuals: the threnos lauded and lamented the dead in a song of mourning, usually accompanied by the aulos; the elegy was a lamentation, originally a variety of the threnos; and the enkomion was a song in praise of the living, by way of celebration, accompanied by the phorminx, lyra, or auloi. There were still other types: the prosidion, or processional song, usually with aulos accompaniment; the hyporchema, or dance-song involving dance, strings, and song; the hymenaios, or bridal song, for weddings, with aulos accompaniment; the embateria, or marching song popular in Sparta, with aulos; work songs; and the skolion, or drinking song, either for individual or group, accompanied by the aulos or barbiton.

Plucked strings held the place of honor among the instruments. The most venerable was the phorminx, a four-stringed lyre with curved soundboard, the two vertical arms being joined by a horizontal crossbar. The phorminx is first mentioned by Homer about 800 B.C., as an instrument that accompanied song. It is also depicted in vase painting of the same period.

In the 7th century the phorminx was transformed into the kithara, which had a big box-like resonating body, was finished straight underneath, and was flat in front but swelled out substantially behind. The high arms of the kithara at first reached out in a bow but later were bent out at right angles. The strings, which have a screw-fretboard, were stretched over a bridge and attached at the end of the soundbox. The entire instrument was of wood. Normally in the Archaic and Classical periods it had seven strings. The kithara was played almost exclusively by men and mostly while standing, with the left hand pressed to the left side of the body, so that the fingers gripped the strings and—according to Sachs' interpretation—provided "the real play of melody," while the fingers of the right hand or a plectrum "prevented movement from stopping after each verse by rhythmically striking the individual string or perhaps sweeping all the strings."

While the phorminx led directly to the kithara, the lyre, or lyra, was an offshoot of this development. It was lighter than the kithara, taking two forms: the tortoise lyre or *chelys*, which had a resonance chamber made of actual or simulated tortoise shell and arms in the form of antelope or goat horns; and the barbiton, which had a somewhat similarly constructed resonance chamber and very long arms, originally straight but later curved at the end and projected so that one was on top of the other. The barbiton was lighter than the chelys. Both forms coexisted during this period but were differently used: the lyre and kithara belonged to Apollo, the barbiton to Dionysus. An offshoot of the kithara was the cradle kithara, which had a cradle-shaped soundbox, rectangular arms, and seven strings.

The harp made its appearance only after 450 B.C. In contrast to the Egyptian arched or bow-shaped harp, the resonating body and the string-holder of the Greek harp formed a wide angle. The number of strings varied. This was the instrument preferred by women.

In general contrast to these plucked strings the *aulos*—or, in the plural, *auloi*, for it was normally doubled—belonged to a later stratum of instruments. The aulos was a shawn with a double reed—a long pipe with a mouthpiece, to which were attached the reeds that were inserted in the mouth. There were four finger-holes on the upper side of the pipe and a fifth on the under side. The aulos was almost without exception used as a double aulos. Both pipes, however, were not inseparably attached, and they could be used singly. Their sound was sharp and penetrating.

The syrinx or pan-pipes consisted of five, seven, or nine pipes of different length, arranged side by side.

There were also percussion instruments: the *tympanon* or frame drum, the *krotala* or castanets, and metal cymbals in pairs.

Among the examples of extant music, a dozen are of particular interest. One is a fragment of the first *stasimon* or stationary song of the chorus from Euripides' tragedy *Orestes* (408 B.C.). The piece of music that we have, however, has been preserved for us on a piece of papyrus from the time of Augustus Caesar and was first published in 1892. As the notated manuscript is dated over four hundred years after the play was written, this can scarcely be regarded as Euripides' music.

Somewhat closer to the ancient Greek period, however, are two hymns to Apollo, from the walls of the Athenian Treasury at Delphi, where they had been chiseled in relief on the stone during the 2nd century B.C. Discovered in 1892, they are of considerable musical importance.

Perhaps the most immediately attractive of the remains is a song that was engraved on a memorial column erected by a man named Seikilos.

The time of origin of this *skolion* was about 100 B.C. Discovered in 1883, it has since become quite widely known. The eight-measure, symmetrical

Song of Seikilos

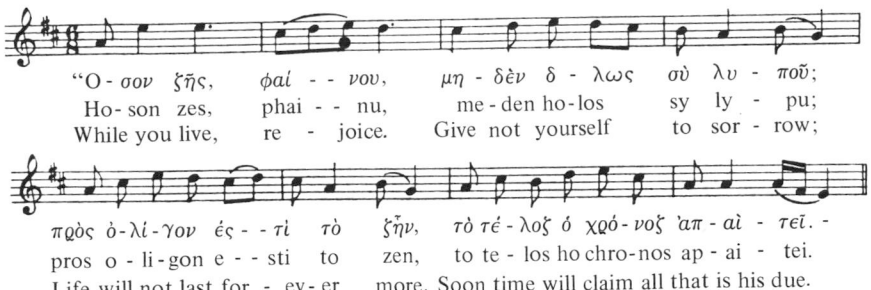

"O - σον ζῆς, φαί - - νου, μη - δὲν δ - λως σὺ λυ - ποῦ;
Ho - son zes, phai - - nu, me - den ho - los sy ly - pu;
While you live, re - joice. Give not yourself to sor - row;

πρὸς ὀ - λί - γον ἐς - - τὶ τὸ ζῆν, τὸ τέ - λος ὁ χρό - νος 'απ - αἰ - τεῖ. -
pros o - li - gon e - - sti to zen, to te - los ho chro - nos ap - ai - tei.
Life will not last for - ev - er more. Soon time will claim all that is his due.

Example 19

stanzaic song-melody consists of two four-measure sections, and its structure corresponds to the four lines of the epigram. The rhythm is even, in 6/8 measure, and the melody is purely diatonic. The structure is consonant, basically two successions of triads.

There are three fragments in the Berlin papyrus—one of a choral paean, another a passage about the suicide of Telemonian Ajax, and a third which has not as yet been successfully interpreted. These date from the 2nd century A.D. and are notable for the fact that they combine vocal and instrumental music. They were first edited in 1918.

There are also three hymns by Mesomedes, a Cretan kithara-player: one to the Muse, another to the Sun, and a third to Nemesis. These date from the 2nd century A.D. and have strictly diatonic features. They were first published in 1501 by Vincenzo Galilei, the father of the famous astronomer.

There is an early Christian hymn preserved on papyrus that was found at Oxyrhynchos in Egypt. It dates from the end of the 3rd century A.D. and was first published in 1922. This is the oldest document of Christian music and is not particularly representative of Classical Greek music, as the melody is constructed according to the Semitic principle of forming melodies from fixed particles, as explained in connection with the early music of Palestine.

There is also an instrumental example in an anonymous musical treatise, but the period and composer are unknown. It was first edited in 1841.

The music for the First Pythian Ode of Pindar, who died in 436 B.C., has been shown to be a forgery. Publication of it goes back to Athanasius Kircher (1601–1680), in the first volume of his *Musurgia Universalis* (Rome 1650).

In all, there are about thirty-three examples of Greek music of some antiquity still in existence. A complete inventory, with references to some that are still unpublished, appears in the appendix to E. Pöhlmann, *Griechische Musikfragmente* (Nuremberg 1960).

All the extant pieces have come from the Hellenistic, Roman, or Early Christian periods or were not written down until after the beginning of the Christian Era. Nothing that we have was notated anywhere near the 5th-century Classical period of Greece.

We do have, however, some idea of the way the Greeks looked at music and the course it took during their history. On this basis and by way of survey and summary, we can review the history of their music and musical theory.

They conceived of music as being of divine source. Its essence had its home in the realm of the gods. The Greeks were the only people to lay great stress on the musicianship of some of their divinities. Gods and men alike made music, finding in it a noble form of expression. Many cycles of legends report musical feats of mythical personalities. Orpheus forced his way into the underworld by singing and playing on his stringed instrument, appeased wild animals and moved them to listen, and awakened the sensibilities of the rough Thracians, but when they were thus moved to anger the frenzied Thracian women killed him. Thamyris ventured to surpass the Muses in song, and they thereupon deprived him of his sight and his artistic skill. In the course of a music lesson Linos reprimanded Hercules, who promptly killed him. Among Linos' other pupils was, reputedly, Musaios. Amphion, son of Zeus and Antiope, softened the stones with his lyre-playing when he built the walls of Thebes. Arion, playing on his lyre, plunged into the sea to escape pirates; but his music attracted a dolphin, which carried him on its back to safety. There is scarcely any way to tell precisely when ideas of magic gave way to aesthetic conceptions, or how long and to what extent they remained current side by side.

Very little is known about the music in the cultures of the Greek area before the Homeric period. Pictorial evidence from the islands of Thera and Keros, where the Cyclades culture flourished toward the end of the 3rd millennium B.C., shows the double aulos and a harp constructed like the Oriental arched harp. From the Cretan culture of the 2nd millennium, there are also only pictorial remains. They show us the aulos, a seven-stringed lyre, and the sistrum, imported from Egypt, which during the New Kingdom had cultural and political relations with Crete. From the Mycenaean culture during the latter half of the 2nd millennium the principal evidence has been supplied by archaeologists who have unearthed some lyres of presumably eight strings.

Subsequent to the 12th-century Dorian migration, evidence of the Greek attitude toward music and its cultivation during the Homeric period, around 800 B.C., appear in the *Iliad* and the *Odyssey* and in Late Geometric vase painting around 750 B.C. and later. Instrumental music and song belonged integrally together. As the divinities such as Apollo and the Muses made music, so did also the heroes themselves. Achilles, as described in the *Iliad*, on occasion sang. Also, the heroes were entertained with song at their banquets; there were *aoidoi*, whose heroic song arose directly from divine inspiration—an idea that no doubt went back to the very old human conception of the magical force of music.

The Greeks of Homer's day were familiar with various forms of song: the festive hymn presented by male chorus in honor of the divinity, the lament for the dead sung by a leader and women's chorus, and the hymeneal on the occasion of the bridal procession and marriage feast. They also had work-songs, dances, and songs of a phorminx-accompanied circle. There was, of course, the playing of plucked-string instruments and song in the course of the sociability of everyday life. The predominant instrument was the phorminx, or four-stringed lyre with somewhat rounded soundboard. During this time, aulos music was felt to be rather foreign. When the *aoidoi* presented portions of epics, they prefaced them with a "proemium," a hymn to the gods, which in its musical form gave rise during the 7th century to the kitharodic nomos. This was a strictly normalized strophic song in seven sections, which continued as an actively cultivated musical form into the beginning of the 3rd century B.C.

Perhaps partly mythical and partly historical, Olympus flourished about 750 B.C., his name symbolizing the fusion of the music of Asia Minor with that of Greece. Among the Greeks Olympus was supposed to have been the first classic master of art-music, the founder of what was known as aulody, or song accompanied by the aulos, and of the enharmonic tonal genus.

A radical change undoubtedly took place between 700 and 650 B.C., under the influence of impulses from the Orient. There ensued a stronger subjectivization and individualization both of the human being and of the music. The aulos became popular. In 676 Terpander of Antissa on Lesbos, who is said to have introduced the seven-stringed lyre and given it canonical status in place of the previous four-stringed one, won the kithara competition at the festival of Apollo Karneios in Sparta. Thaletas (about 665), born on Crete and reputedly a pupil of Olympus, was said to have introduced the aulodic music of the Cretan cult of Apollo into Sparta and to have collaborated in founding the *gymnopaidia,* or exercises performed by naked youths.

Apparently around 700 B.C. the art of the *aoidoi* split into two traditions: first, into that of rhapsodes, who declaimed their recitations, and second, into the lyrics of the Lesbian kitharody. From approximately 700 on, kitharody, or solos sung to the kithara, included two separate branches of art: the kitharodic nomos and the true lyric.

About 650 B.C. the great time of the musical lyric began, introduced by Archilochus of Paros and carried on into an era of subjective poetic expression, manifesting itself in love lyrics, political songs, satirical poems, and didactically reflective verse. Archilochus expanded the rhythmic and metrical possibilities of expression, introduced a technique combining melodic and dramatic features, and gave greater independence to the instrumental accompaniment, allowing it at times to take a course that deviated from the melody. Rhythm was refined and won an all-embracing character as a general order of life. As an instrument for accompaniment the aulos continued to increase in popularity.

About 600 B.C. the two most significant lyricists, Sappho and Alcaeus, were active—the former a poetess much celebrated and rich in subjective expression. Both came from the island of Lesbos. Anacreon of Teos, who flourished about 550 B.C., is also significant for his convivial songs.

Choral song had great significance earlier in Crete and later in Sparta, where it flowered between the 7th and 5th centuries B.C. In Sparta music served the state. The paean in honor of Apollo was distinct from the dithyramb for Dionysus, as well as from processional songs and those of lamentation, marriage, and victory. The fully developed choral lyric had its earliest exponent in Alcman, who was born at Sardis in Lydia, became active as a choral leader in Sparta during the 7th century, and composed both hymns and secular songs. The most significant exponent of the victory-song was Pindar of Thebes (d. 436 B.C.).

In terms of professional status, the poet soon became separate from the performer. Formerly, they had usually been one and the same person. But the performers of the choral lyric were professionals.

Both musical and gymnastic contests figured in competitive festivals such as the Olympic games (instituted in 776 B.C.), the Pythian games at Delphi in honor of Apollo, the Carneia and gymnopaidia in Sparta, and the Panathenea and the Dionysia in Athens.

As early as 600 B.C., aulos music achieved full artistic importance along with kithara music. At the Delphic games of 586 B.C., Sakadas of Argos is said to have won the musical competition with a famous Pythian nomos. The artist, we learn, represented on his aulos—that is, without song—the struggle of Apollo with the dragon. We can but conjecture what the musical character of this nomos may have been. In vase painting after 550 B.C., there seems to have been a preference for depicting social scenes in which the aulos plays a prominent role. About this period Pythagoras was supposed to have charged aulos-playing with being undisciplined, ignoble, and harmful. In general, he emphasized the influence of music on moral culture. This conviction then spread, particularly in Attica, with Damon, Plato, and Aristotle, among whom music was highly regarded for its contribution to moral training.

The Periclean era (478–429 B.C.), with the High Classical period in the field of the plastic arts, ushered in also a new period in the history of music, the high point of which perhaps lies in the drama. Tragedy arose from the dithyramb of the Dionysus festival. The Classical writers of Greek drama were Aeschylus (525–456 B.C.), Sophocles (496–406 B.C.), and Euripides (484–406 B.C.). The precise part that music played in the drama has not been established in detail. The most important musical forms were the choral songs of entry, of retaining position on stage, and of exit, choral songs with pantomimic dance, and lyric dialogues usually mournful in character. The chorus was made up of twelve and later fifteen singers. With Sophocles—according to Wegner—the music stood "only in a relation of content, of fact to the dramatic action," but with Euripides it was "quite different in its intrinsic value as well as in its possessing essentially a moody character throughout all of his tragedies." Euripides introduced into the artistic formulation of drama a literary and musical innovation that can be compared to the concept of the solo aria. Figures in his dramas, particularly women, have an inward, intuitive connection with the music and seek in it consolation for their sorrow.

The representations in pictures on vases at the same time show a new form in the indication of psychic participation in the music. Particularly, women seem to have become responsible for the new musicality. Also there were changes in instrumentation: the cradle kithara achieved at this time its widest diffusion, the harp began to be more frequently represented, and the aulos sharply declined.

Between Sophocles and Euripides there stood the development of a new style in the later dithyramb. The main representatives were Phrynis of Mytilene (*ca.* 450 B.C.) and his pupil Timotheus of Miletus (*ca.* 400 B.C.). Strongly subjective traits led to innovations in the way the work was formulated or modulated and to virtuoso coloratura. The tonal area was enlarged, the number of strings on the kithara was raised from eleven to twelve, and epic and dithyrambic rhythms—and with them, nomoi—were intermingled. Further representatives of this typical virtuoso music were Philoxenos of Cythera and Melanippos the Younger.

As the musicians became more subjective, they overstepped Classical limits. After 425 B.C. the Dionysian element with the aulos and other orgiastic instruments won the upper hand again. Music now freed itself from the connections which it had previously maintained with poetry, the dancing circle, mime, liturgy, or the community; and it became autonomous art or artistry in the hands of great virtuosi, who constituted a professional class.

At this point in time Plato (427–347 B.C.) raised his voice in protest. With his assumption of an ethos theory of music which his pedagogical attitudes favored, he linked up with the old Greek conceptions and tried to erect a dam to hold back innovations. His viewpoint was based on the claim of the ideal, the first great synthesis of an already historical achievement in a time when the connection with the old works had already been lost. Plato's tendency, explicitly reactionary, was hostile to any innovation.

Aristotle (about 384–322 B.C.), like Plato, gave music a place in education, but also granted it a place in life as a source of amusement. He differentiated between morally good and sensuously beautiful music and even considered instrumental music as having a right to exist by itself. Here he paved the way for the era of Hellenism. He represented a tendency to aestheticism and an orientation toward aesthetic value, toward enjoyment of form along with indifference to content.

There is no reason to doubt that alongside the highly placed professional singers there had also been from very early times many wandering singers who found their own public, perhaps particularly in the marketplace.

So far as the history of theory is concerned, we do not have any written sketches actually formulated in the earlier period. Pythagoras of Samos, in the latter half of the 6th century B.C., taught orally. Associated with his name are the divisions of the string on the monochord, the system of fifths, the system of numbers, and the conception of music as producing *katharsis*, or purification.

After 500 B.C. the Classical period of Greek music theory began with the establishment of ethical and aesthetic norms. Damon of Athens—

statesman, friend of Pericles, and musician—is taken as a pioneer in the ethos theory, which was developed by Plato (427–347 B.C.) to its full form. Plato, no professional musician, was the first Greek author to concern himself with music in his writings. Aristotle (*ca.* 384–322 B.C.) made the transition from musical ethics to aesthetics, as he considered music significant not only in building character but also in providing recreation and noble pastime. He developed theories taken over from Pythagoras about *katharsis,* maintaining that music and poetry stimulated human feelings and, in so doing, purged the individual of an excess of such emotions. By its very nature, music—like poetry—was a matter of imitation. Music imitated man and his character, arousing his emotions.

The formulation of musical theory in its more systematic aspects and the further development of musical aesthetics occurred entirely during the Hellenistic era.

Bibliography

H. Abert, *Antike* (Adler Hdb.) and *Die Lehre vom Ethos in d. griech. Musik* (Lpz. 1899); F. Bellermann, *Die Tonleitern u. Musiknoten der Griechen* (1847); K. Fortlage, *Das mus. System der Griechen* (1847); T. Georgiades, *Der griech. Rhythmus; Musik, Reigen, Vers u. Sprache* (Hamburg 1949) and *Musik u. Rhythmus bei den Griechen* (Hamburg 1958); F. A. Gevaert, *Histoire et théorie de la musique de l'antiquité* (2 vols., 1875–95); O. J. Gombosi, *Tonarten u. Stimmungen der antiken Musik* (Copenh. 1939); H. Görgemanns and A. J. Neubecker, "*Heterophonie" bei Plato* (AfMw 1966); I. Henderson, *Ancient Greek Music* (NOHM I); A. Howard, *The Aulos or Tibia* (1893); H. Husmann, *Olympos. Die Anfänge der griech. Enharmonik* (JbP 1937); E. Jammers, *Rhythm. u. tonale Studien z. Musik der Antike u. des Mittelalters* (AfMf 1941 and 1943); K. v. Jan, *Musici Scriptores Graeci* (Lpz. 1895, new ed. Hildesheim 1962); H. Koller, *Musik u. Dichtung im alten Griechenland* (Munich 1963); F. Nietzsche, *Die Geburt der Tragödie* (1871); E. Pöhlmann, *Griech. Musikfragmente* (Nuremberg 1960); T. Reinach, *La musique grecque* (Paris 1926); L. Richter, *Die Neue Musik der gr. Antike* (AfMw 1968); H. Riemann, *Hdb. der Musikges. I, 1* (2nd ed. 1919); C. Sachs, *Die griech. Instrumentalnotenschrift* (ZfMw VI, 1924), *Die Musik der Antike* (Bücken Hdb.), *Musik d. Altertums* (Breslau 1924), and *The Rise of Music in the Ancient World* (N. Y. 1943); R. Schäfke, *Geschichte der Musikästhetik in Umrissen* (Tutzing 2nd ed. 1964); M. Schneider, *Die mus. Grundlagen der Sphärenharmonie* (Acta XXXII, 1960); W. Vetter, article "Musik" (Pauly-Wissowa, Real-Encyclopädic der class. Altertumswiss., Neue Bearbeitung, vol. 16, 1, 1933); M. Vogel, *Apollinisch u. Dionysisch. Geschichte eines genialen Irrtums* (Regensburg 1967); M. Wegner, *Das Musikleben der Griechen* (Bln. 1949); R. Westphal, *Die Musik d. griech. Altertums* (1883); arts. Akzent, Alkaios, Alkman, Anakreon, Apollon, Archilochos, Arion, Aristoteles, Athena, Dionysos, Ethos, Griechenland, Hesiod, Homer, etc. (MGG).

7. Hellenism

According to the great scholar of the Hellenistic period Johann Gustav Droysen, Hellenism represented a cultural era in which the Orient and the Occident, including Rome, were suffused with the Greek cultural heritage, which in turn was influenced by the Oriental cultural heritage. This era began at approximately the time of Alexander the Great and ended with the close of the rule of Augustus Caesar (d. 14 A.D.). The levelling of national cultures gave rise to an international mixed culture, eclectic in its imitative creative achievement, museum-like in character, increasingly eager for virtuosity through emphasis on public performance and composition, and increasingly erudite in a way acquired through systematic study.

Fundamental changes in the social structure affected the consumption of artistic goods. Sociologists have established that in the 6th century B.C. the Greeks discovered the autonomy of the artist, in the 5th enjoyed the consequences of this discovery, and in the 4th found this autonomy turning into aestheticism. The Hellenistic era, according to Arnold Hauser, was marked by a "virtuoso play of wilful forms, a high degree of experimentation with abstract expressive possibilities, and a freedom that confused and devaluated classically oriented standards." In the history of Greek music the collapse of the concept of *musiké* occurred in the 4th century B.C. Although the comparatively few musical examples, preserved only from the Hellenistic period, do not enable us to reconstruct the history of the music clearly, we may assume that some of the insights gained from the history of the visual and literary arts may also apply to music. The dissolution of the classical idea of *musiké* is surely to be traced back to a change in the structure of society and a shift in the class whose taste and patronage influenced what was done.

About 300 B.C. the unity of *musiké* disappeared. But the Hellenistic era, which succeeded the Classical period, was not simply a time of decay. Of course, if one looks on *musiké* as the ideal, one is tempted to consider the emancipation of the several arts and the ensuing break-up of the unity that had prevailed among poetry, music, and dance as "decline." Consequently, then, all music since 300 B.C. to the present day would be a decadent phenomenon. But the terms "flowering" and "decay" are merely metaphors and are scarcely valid as abstract value judgements in a rational account of history. In actuality it was for the first time through this emancipation that music approached our modern conception, in that the musical element at last won preponderance over the previously emphasized element of the poetic content and finally, after 1600, in the form of instrumental music ushered in an entirely new epoch.

What did the people of the Hellenistic era achieve in music?

We must, first of all, recognize the fact that the thirty-three extant pieces of early Greek music, which happen all to come from the Hellenistic period, convey to us little idea of the actual sound of the music and, accordingly, of its artistic effect. Of the musically creative achievement of Hellenism we have no really adequate historical view.

We have, furthermore, little data on the role of music in the Greek mysteries, which include the Elusinian mysteries in Athens, the Dionysian, and the Orphic. There were also mystery cults that had been brought in from the Orient—of Cybele and of Attis, of Isis and Osiris, and of Mithra. Thus we have little knowledge of a music in which presumably Classical Greek elements had come into a new fusion with traits of Oriental music. As we know so little about this cult-music, we can only write off this aspect of the period as something that—except for pictorial and literary allusions—has been quite lost, however significant it undoubtedly was.

The literary sources that have been preserved give the impression that virtuosity or a high degree of specialization prevailed. "Virtuosity," however, should not be taken as an entirely derogatory word, in contrast to the unity of *musiké* and the personality of the poet-musician. In quite recent times the concept of virtuosity has become associated in the minds of many with the ideas of decline and fall. Viewed positively, however, the period had an exclusive professional class of singers and instrumentalists and achieved a significant increase in all aspects of the technique of composition and performance. The support of cultural and business life had become the special prerogative of the city bourgeoisie; and in this dominant stratum of society music enjoyed outstanding regard as a type of cultivation that has a strongly aesthetic emphasis—in domestic life, in the theater, in social gatherings, and at banquets. It was a part of a well-rounded cultivation. On the basis of what musical examples we have, we can feel ourselves justified in assuming that Classical music still had strong and continuing influence. Particularly significant are the two Apollo hymns and the Seikilos song, for there is in them nothing contrary to the simplicity that has been ascribed to Classical music, and for this very reason they have been characterized by Vetter as the last echoes of the musical practice of the 6th–5th centuries B.C.

The achievement of Hellenism in musical science—that is, in the theory of music—was unquestionably superior to that of the Classical period of Greek music. If Aristotle (d. 322 B.C.) already had made contact with the era of Hellenism, his pupil Aristoxenos of Tarentum (b. about 350 B.C.) was the founder of a genuine ancient musicology and the first great representative of the new era and its scientific way of thinking. He set up the nomenclature and the system of transposition scales or *tonoi* and conceived of the octave scale as also a regularly distributed chromatic structure. The highest court of appeal was for him the sense of hearing; he held to experience and thus opposed the Pythagoreans and their specifically mathematical way of thinking. The underlying controversy was one of "harmonists" versus "canonists," qualitative tonal definitions *vs.* quantitative tonal differences. Aristoxenos' reliance on the ear instead of on the mathematical purity of tone was the first step toward tempered tuning. He developed a significant theory of rhythm, with differentiation among three elementary kinds: dactyllic, iambic, and paionic. Compared with Aristotle, he can be said to have emphasized the aesthetic conception of music, though he placed the ethical beside it and still gave it considerable stress.

Under Alexander the Great, who ruled from 336 to 323 B.C., the Greek city of Alexandria, adjacent to Egypt on the Western mouth of the Nile, was founded in 332. From 300 to 230 B.C. this city was at the height of its cultural activity, with a circle of learned men at the Museum and the development there of considerable specialization. It also was a center of musical science. A whole series of Alexandrian scholars made important contributions to the theory of music. Euclid, about 300, measured tonal relations mathematically; Eratosthenes, in the 3rd century B.C., established a theory of tonal relations; and Didymos of Alexandria, about 30 B.C., established the difference between the large and small whole tone—a relationship known as the Comma of Didymus or the Syntonic Comma. Philodemos of Gandara, of the 1st century B.C., an Epicurean contemporary of Cicero, adopted a formalistic approach and entirely separated aesthetics from ethical theory. The inclusion of music in the quadrivium of arithmetic, geometry, astronomy, and music goes back to the Roman Marcus Terentius Varro, of the 1st century B.C.—a conception which was to prevail throughout the Middle Ages.

As we move on into the Christian era, we find many other writers working in the Hellenistic tradition. As the 1st century gave way to the 2nd, Plutarch served as intermediary in transmitting many facts to us—though he may have been at times not very critical of his sources. He is one of those authors who make compilations and include valuable individual observations. Claudius Ptolemy, of the 2nd century A.D., gave an exhaustive account of scalar theory, of transposition scales, and the definitive treatment of the essentials of musical calculation, thereby achieving a notable synthesis of ancient theory. Aristides Quintilianus, of the 2nd or 3rd century, who used the older sources, is indispensable in his presentation of general theory, music philosophy, ethos theory, and notation. Kleoneides, in the latter half of the 1st century, is the most significant later representative of Aristoxenos' views. Gaudentios, of the 2nd century, enlarged Aristoxenos' theory. The Neo-Pythagorean Nikomachos, in the 2nd century, wrote a book on harmonic theory; and Sextus Empiricus, in the latter half of the 2nd century, represented—as did also Philodemos— the formalistic attitude toward music and tried to achieve further abstraction of the element of soul and spirit in musical speculation. In the 4th century Bakcheios was the author of a catechism, written in dialogue form, about the main questions of musical theory; and Alypios has given us a basis on which to decipher the notation. Martianus Capella, of the 5th century, followed Aristides Quintilianus.

Boethius, who died in 524 A.D., has left us his five books "De Institutione Musicae." He was the last great theoretician of ancient music at a time when the older practice was disappearing. At this time, there was confusion and misunderstanding in the matter of the modes, the octave species, and the transposition scales of the ancients. His work provided the basis for almost all medieval theory.

Bibliography (see also that for Greece)

I. Düring, ed., *Die Harmonielehre des Ptolemaios, Ptolemaios u. Porphyrios über die Musik, Porphyrios' Kommentar z. Harmonielehre des Ptolemaios* (3 vols., 1930–4); G. Fleischhauer, *Die Musikergenossenschaften im hellenistisch-römischen Altertum* (Diss. Halle 1959); H. Schäfke, tr., *Aristeides* (1937); H. Weil and T. Reinach, ed., *Plutarch über die Musik* (1900); R. Westphal, *Aristoxenos* (2 vols., 1883–93); arts. Alypios, Aristides Quintilianus, Aristoxenos, Boethius, Didymos, Eratosthenes, etc. (MGG).

8. Rome

In time, Rome established a certain political order within the Hellenistic world. It stood in a dependent cultural relationship to Greece and made no important independent contribution to the history of music. The Romans had triumphal, wedding, funeral, and convivial songs, accompanied by the tibia, or aulos. Latin drama had no chorus. In the Roman Empire there were many sensational kithara virtuosi, among them the Emperor Nero himself. The distinctive feature of the music was the exclusive emphasis on technique and the clever development of the technical apparatus. According to Seneca's Eighty-fourth Letter, massed instruments were played at Roman theatrical productions. Though no documents of Roman musical works have been preserved, we know that in Roman musical theory the two tetrachords were filled out from below upwards, to make the octave.

In short and in view of the lack of musical works and of fruitful literary sources, it must be realized that a clear picture of the music and musical life in Rome is not today available. In general, this section of the music history of late antiquity belongs to Hellenism. But, at all events, if we are to judge from the sources, we are to assume that there was no creative development worth mentioning. The musical life of the Hellenistic-Roman epoch was extensively based on associations that concerned themselves with the ritual, military, artistic, and general cultivation of music.

In late antiquity there seems to have been some practical use of polyphony for purposes of musical display. But, in contrast to the tendency toward mass-effects and popular appeal in the music, there was also an antithetical tendency to split up into special groups directed sharply toward aesthetic aims, such as the musical rendition of bucolic poetry, mathematical speculation, and reflection upon the nature of music.

Bibliography (*see also that for Hellenism*)

J. Quasten, *Musik u. Gesang in d. Kulturen d. heidnischen Antike u. christl. Frühzeit* (Münster 1930); L. Richter, *Griechische Traditionen im Musikschrifttum der Römer* (AfMw 1964); J. E. Scott, *Roman Music* (NOHM I); G. Wille, *Die Bedeutung d. Musik im Leben d. Römer* (Diss. Tübingen 1951).

9. The North in Pre-Christian Times

In view of important later developments in Europe there is special relevance to our considering its northern portions—with reference first to their general history and then to the evidences of music there.

Wandering hunters left few traces during the Reindeer Age, from the end of the glacial era to about 6000 B.C. From 6000 to 4000 B.C.—or during what is sometimes called the Millerup Period—the climate was more that of an inland region around the landlocked Baltic. Hunters and fishermen established their first permanent settlements and left behind them bone and staghorn implements. During the Older Stone Age from 4000 to 3000 B.C., waterways connected the Baltic and the Atlantic Ocean, and a damp sea-climate prevailed. There was fashioning of tools from flint. Then, during the Newer Stone Age from 3000 to 1500 B.C., the inhabitants practiced agriculture and animal husbandry in the warmer and drier sea climate, and fashioned finer tools of polished-flint. Their economy was based on barter.

During the Older Bronze Age, from 1500 to 800 B.C., a distinctly high culture flourished, with active foreign trade, the purchase and working of bronze and gold, and the weaving of woolen cloth, which made its first appearance in Europe. In the Newer Bronze Age, from 800 to 400 B.C., there was a cult of the sun; and cliff drawings show that the people had tools and ships. Then, during the Older Iron Age, from 400 B.C. to 500 A.D., there was at first a decline in trade, with incursion of Celtic cultural influence from Central Europe and, a little later, Roman influences with increasing prosperity, the first runic inscriptions, and finally the westward migrations of the Teutonic and other peoples.

From 500 to 800 A.D., during the Newer Iron Age, Roman influences declined, and there were constant defensive conflicts. The Viking period ensued from 800 to 1000: excess of population led to maritime and military activity, settlements in France, Ireland, and England, and thrusts into the Mediterranean area, from Sweden, and into Russia, with the establishment of Novgorod and Kiev. During this period Christianity was widely disseminated in the North.

Though the evidence is scanty, it does show that music was fostered. Archaeological discoveries from the beginning of the Bronze Age include wind instruments, or rather guttural-sounding idiophones, such as animal horns and *lurer* (singular, *lur*). Two bridges perhaps belonging to an instrument like the lyre, from the 8th century A.D., have been found in Sweden. Archaeologists have in the North also found many cast-bronze *lurer*, always precisely tuned together in pairs. This doubling of the instrument, however, does not warrant our concluding that there was two-voiced playing. Most of the *lurer* have been found in what is now Denmark, a few in Norway, southern Sweden, and northern Germany, which from the time between 1100 and 500 B.C. was closely linked with the Scandinavia of the Bronze Age. With the Iron Age, however, the *lurer* entirely disappeared. Quite probably they had been used in worship.

Another source of evidence has been provided by cliff drawings, which have been found in Sweden in some abundance. Among those in Bohuslän are figures that apparently represent men blowing *lurer*. If this interpretation is correct, then it is established that *lurer* were held upright while being played, so that their form suggests that of a monstrous aurochs horn, and hence also their being produced in symmetrical pairs.

A third source of evidence is that provided by literary documents. The oldest of these that refer to music are found in Old Icelandic literature, written down in the 12th century but in part going back to the 10th. Iceland toward the end of the 9th century was first colonized from Norway, later also from Scotland, Ireland, and the islands to the north of Scotland proper. There is a reference to the harp in the epic *Völuspa*, or "Vision of the Prophetess," contained in the Older Edda. A melody for this poem, preserved in a tradition that is to be regarded with some caution, is considered the oldest piece of Nordic melodic heritage that has come down to us. Study of Icelandic folk songs gives much information about early ways of singing. In content the 10th-century heroic epics that were later incorporated into the prose Volsung Saga are related to the German *Nibelungenlied*. As for the manner of their delivery, it presumably was like that of a recitative, accompanied by the harp. The texts often ascribe magic power to harp-playing. The name *Gróttusöngur*, from one of the heroic epics, may be related to the Celtic harp *chrotta*, the Irish *crot*, and the Middle European *rotta*.

From Finland and Estonia comes the *Kalevala*, an epic poem from the immediately pre-Christian period. Neither linguistically nor culturally does it have anything in common with the Norse epics of gods and heroes, but belongs to a rather specifically Baltic-Finnish culture. Performance in melodic formulae of essentially five tones was surely connected from the beginning with the five-string plucked *kantele*, the playing of which is often described in the epics.

Bibliography

H. C. Broholm, W. P. Larsen, and G. Skjerne, *The Lures of the Bronze Age* (Copenh. 1949); A. Hammerich, *Studien über die altnordischen Luren* (VfMw 1894) and *Studien über island. Musik* (SIMG 1899–1900); J. Leifs, *Isländ. Volkslieder* (Wolfenbüttel 1929); arts. Finnland, Finnisch-ugrische Musik (MGG).

III The Music of Medieval Europe

10. Music History of the European Middle Ages

What is understood by the Middle Ages in Europe? What expanse of time do they include? And what special epoch is the European medieval period in music history?

The answer may somewhat differ according to which of three points of view one has adopted in posing the question—that of general history, that of intellectual and cultural history, and that specifically of the history of music.

The presentation of the history of music in the following chapters is concentrated exclusively on the history of music in the West. There are various reasons for this.

Our attention is directed entirely to the history of that music which we consider ours. It has always belonged to us. It surrounds us from childhood. It arose and developed within our Western area where we have our being. Right on into what is for us the present, its life-stream has flowed in an uninterrupted current.

The past in the history of music has a direct and vital place in our present—at least certain portions of it do. In concert, in opera, in church, at home, in school, music lives in the main on works of the past. Research into the history of music creates ever new and deepened relationships with the past, and contemporary composers increase our awareness of stylistic traits of historical music as they try to fuse elements of style from the past into their creative work.

Peculiar to Western music up to the present are two basic traits that link all epochs with each other and differentiate Western from non-European music: dynamism and the development of harmonic polyphony. Dynamism is peculiar to the history of the European peoples and their mentality. It leads also in the history of music to ever-renewed possibilities of form and expression, creates therewith a relatively quick change in the course of history, and favors at the same time the full versatility of creative individuals. The other trait, harmonic polyphony, involves the subordination of one or more voices to the melody, the leading voice. Polyphony thereby gives rise to the chord, and in the polyphonic development of several voices the chord plays a superior role in maintaining order and enforcing acoustical law.

The Middle Ages from the Point of View of General History

The questions initially posed may be viewed first from the historical point of view. Historians usually have distinct ideas of ancient, medieval, and modern history. In medieval history they consider three different cultural worlds: Byzantium, Islam, and the West. The historical task that devolved on the men of these three worlds resulted from three common circumstances: they linked up with the peoples of antiquity, were obliged to defend this heritage against the pressure of new and barbarian peoples, and at the same time were involved in educating these peoples.

The historical question of the chronological limits of the Western Middle Ages is not to be decided from political vantage-points alone. Events in intellectual, cultural, and religious history also help to determine the boundaries. The history of the West began when the Teutonic spirit clashed with that of Latin Christianity. In this varied and fruitful encounter the Teutons both received and contributed. The unity of Europe was maintained by churchmen and laity as its two most important sources of support. The collapse of these pillars hastened the end of the Middle Ages. The mingling of the Teutonic peoples with the Romanized Mediterranean population had especially important results.

Distinctly medieval forms of group activity arose from the fusion of Teutonism and the Christian church. The medieval state was ruled by a limited monarchy and the nobility. All rulers were Germanic in origin, genealogically as well as legally; the secular head of the West was the German emperor. More than the emperor, however, the Pope often was the powerful symbol of the unity of the West. At the end of the 12th century the power of the Empire collapsed, and a European system of states arose. The Reformation finally broke the unity of Europe under the Roman church. At the same time, the rising power of the princes put an end to the freedom of the nobility and of the bourgeoisie.

These events help establish the time-span of the Middle Ages. When the two elements of Teutonic and Roman culture interpenetrated, something new first arose among the Anglo-Saxons, the Franks, and the Alemanni, and here the way led to the Middle Ages. Politically and culturally the empire of the Franks was the first new creation, at once significant and decisive for the future. In this sense the history of the Middle Ages began around 500.

The transition to the Middle Ages came gradually, almost imperceptibly. The new society that arose involved a new aristocracy and a new socially responsible class alongside the clergy. First of all, the church of Rome in the West cultivated church song in a way that was significant for the establishment of musical culture; and then, after the 9th century, north of the Alps, it formulated polyphony, in addition to developing the trope and sequence. In these matters of refinement the church was still in a monopolistic position.

The Middle Ages from the Intellectual and Cultural Point of View

The question of what the Middle Ages were may also be seen from the point of view of intellectual and cultural history. The time-span of the Middle Ages has been considered the medial epoch in Western history between antiquity and the modern period in various and changing ways, some of which should be here mentioned. The Neo-humanists, notably Winckelmann and Goethe, considered the Middle Ages the anti-Classical period, a time of asceticism, hostile to the world, denying the senses. In the view of Heinrich von Eicken, the church was the source of this wish to fight and conquer the world.

A more positive version of the same idea was advanced by Heinrich Troeltzsch, who saw in the idea of the church a sense of something that integrated the medieval world-view. The church was the representation of the God-given order of being, in which an ethical claim was to be assimilated; and the resulting asceticism was a way for guiding the attitude of the individual life and will. St. Thomas Aquinas was regarded as the center of the medieval world-view, as the great representative of Aristotelian organismic thinking and Stoic natural law. St. Augustine, on the other hand, has been seen by Bentheim as the real instigator of the medieval world-view, with his affirmation of Neoplatonic ideas of the world.

While the German Romantics recognized the Teutonic character of the Middle Ages, the influence of antiquity on the Middle Ages stood in the foreground for Carl Schmitt and Stefan George, who stressed the "classical Middle Ages" as a fusion of the ancient heritage and the Christian idea of God. This conception, which brought the antitheses of paganism and Christianity together, may be even today regarded as still characteristic of many historians; but it has received a rather sharply scientific or objective character as individual traits of the Middle Ages have been traced back into antiquity. In this view also belongs the idea of the church as a Christian continuation of the ancient imperial force, or an *ecclesia militans*. Accordingly there has occurred a certain resolution of the great antitheses that seemed to underlie the Middle Ages. The mystical aspects went back to Orphism. Mysticism and scholasticism were closely related; they were not mutually exclusive, but stood in a certain polar relationship of tension to each other. Faith and asceticism stood side by side, for the Middle Ages was acquainted with various levels of piety. The Stoic manner had much in common with that of the Christian saints: St. Francis was an example of the road to harmony by way of asceticism.

Each of these characterizations takes the Middle Ages more or less as a unit in cultural history, while in actuality an earlier and a later medieval epoch can be clearly marked off as different from each other. The early Middles Ages was under the influence of St. Augustine and was linked with Greek patristic and Neoplatonic thought. The central intellectual figure of the later Middle Ages, on the other hand, was St. Thomas Aquinas. A deep cleft has been felt to exist in the nature of the later Middle Ages, a crude juxtaposition of what Dvorak called the "idealism and realism in the Gothic." The great turning-point was the period around 1200.

Three cultural periods are to be distinguished in the Middle Ages: first, an early medieval period based on an agriculturally oriented feudalism; then a high medieval period of courtly chivalry; and, finally, a late medieval period dominated by the urban bourgeoisie.

The Middle Ages Viewed Musicologically

The question of the nature of the Middle Ages can finally be approached in terms of the history of music. Here we must bear in mind that the basis for a history of music has to be the music itself. Of all considerations this must be the beginning and the end. All the studies that can help in the clarification of music and its history should be pursued. Primarily this means notation, performance-practice, study of instruments, and music theory as presupposition for the conception of music as an actually sounding event, as the art of tone. Secondarily—and providing that the primary works as far as possible have been covered—it means the interpretation of the sense of the music: aesthetics, knowledge of symbols, and the idea of value. Ancillary to research are several areas of knowledge which can, however, offer but secondary and supporting contributions, such as theory of society, general history, history of liturgy, and philology. The history of music can also, though to a limited extent, be clarified by the general history of art. The transferral of style concepts and epoch-divisions from art-history directly into the history of music has proved to be but a temporary expedient.

When does the time-span of the Middle Ages begin in the history of music? Authoritative views here oppose each other. Hugo Riemann, in his *Handbuch der Musikgeschichte*, says: "At the entry to the music-history of the Middle Ages there rises the powerful structure of the music of the Christian church," and he speaks then of the "liturgical chant of the ancient church." Arnold Schering, in subdividing the history of music in his *Tabellen zur Musikgeschichte*, extends antiquity on to 500 A.D. and assigns to the Middle Ages the span from 500 to about 1520.

The time-scheme adopted in the present book indicates the history of music in the Middle Ages as beginning at the point in time when the meeting of the Teutonic spirit with the music of the Roman Catholic church led to new musical and artistic results. This occurred with the new forms developed in the trope and sequence, appearing after 850 and continuing on to about 1200. To the same period is assigned the oldest tradition of organum as the first form of Western polyphony, documented around 900.

"History extends as far back as verbally documented tradition. . . . History exists only where also there is a knowledge of history, where tradition, documentation, and awareness of the origin and present state co-exist. . . . History is ever for man the clear past, the area of assimilation of what has been; it is awareness of origin." Transferred to the history of music, these ideas of Karl Jaspers, in his *Vom Ursprung und Ziel der Geschichte* (1949), imply several corollaries:

1. Documented tradition presupposes notation.
2. Notation was discovered when it was felt necessary that music be brought from its perishability, from the transitoriness of sound, to awareness or to a state of being repeatable.
3. This need arose even more when music began to free itself from its original unity with the word.
4. The autonomous powers of music accordingly became freer than they had been previously.
5. The history of music represents only secondarily the connection between music and the word, instrument, liturgy, or society. Primarily the history of music is the history of features that are essentially musical.
6. All the more, the autonomy of music demands tradition, that is, the possibility of its being carried on and systematically taught.
7. With the increasingly conscious relationship to music, a further and more intense significance attaches itself to the various ways of considering music, such as those pursued in philosophy, aesthetics, ethics, theory, and pedagogy.
8. Documented tradition, or notation, stands opposed to oral perpetuation, and also to the practice of arbitrary enrichment from the "music-making instinct" and the affective nature of the performance.
9. We have seen music developing from the complete ahistoricity of primitives through the partial or relative historicity of the Greeks—a "history" of their music being but an account of glimpses of their music passed on to us by tradition—to full historicity. This great cleft was finally bridged in the 10th century A.D. north of the Alps. It was connected with new creations, the trope and the sequence. But even earlier we have documentary evidence of the transition from Old Roman to New Roman melodies.
10. The more and more precisely developing notational systems are results of the development of polyphony.
11. Reliable notation became the document of history. For us, it is the document for the contemplation of history. For men of the time, it was the document of the particular situation that impressed itself more and more decisively on history.

On the Music of the Middle Ages

The era of the Middle Ages in music history is made up of two clearly divided portions, the dividing-point occurring around 1200. The first period brought within the framework of monastic song new creations for the ornamentation of the liturgy: sequence, trope, polyphony. The monasteries were the intellectual centers; and learning, literature, art, and music proceeded from them. The transitional point coincides in time with the effect of the Notre Dame School in Paris, beginning with the latter half of the 12th century. The sphere of activity from which new ways were shown was no longer the cloister but the metropolitan cathedral, the world-church. After, as well as before, however, the creative and performing agents were clerics. Music was a purely liturgical clerical art—beside which a freer clerical art of the conductus and one-voiced Latin songs won more and more ground. In this second period music flowered also as the chivalric art of a certain class, particularly in the French and German love-song. In the 14th century the secular art even came to dominate over the sacred, but in the 15th a balance was reached.

If we accordingly proceed from the view that the music of the Middle Ages was the fruit of the encounter of the Teutonic spirit with Christendom, we must not overlook the significant influence of antiquity upon it, which is perhaps most palpable in music theory. Distinctive of this is, for example, the position of Boethius, who was condemned to death in 524 A.D. His work brought together once again the Greco-Roman tradition and became the authority for it so far as the entire Middle Ages was concerned. The time around 1200 A.D. represented a turning-point: before 1200 the conception of music was extensively neo-Pythagorean and Platonic in tendency; after 1200, it was more practical and empirical, and somewhat Aristotelian. The idea of harmony, for example, was taken over from antiquity and strongly developed in a speculative way, being now given Christian reinterpretation as the reconciliation of opposed sonorities.

During the Middle Ages under Charlemagne the cultural heritage of Classical antiquity was received in a creative way. Thus this ancient world became, to a certain extent, a living cultural experience; and the not yet fully completed struggle for the possession of the ancient Classical spirit began—a struggle for the conscious rediscovery and regaining of something that had been lost.

Music belonged with arithmetic, geometry, and astronomy to the quadrivium of the "Seven Liberal Arts" and was a required study in instruction during the whole Middle Ages. The trivium included grammar, dialectic, and rhetoric.

The Pythagorean Archytas of Tarentum, who lived from about 400 to 365 B.C., had already placed astronomy, geometry, arithmetic, and music in one category. Music, according to him, is an art; it is, however, also a science with objects of study in which, as Aristides Quintilianus said at the turn of the 1st to the 2nd century A.D., there prevails "certain and unmistakable knowledge."

Comprehensive Bibliography on the History of Medieval Music

H. Abert, *Die Musikanschauung des Mittelalters* (Halle 1905); W. Apel, *The Notation of Polyphonic Music 900–1600* (4th ed. 1949, Cambr., Mass.); E. Apfel, *Beiträge zu einer Gesch. d. Satztechnik von der frühen Motette bis Bach* (Munich 1964) and *Studien zur Satztechnik d. mittelalterl. Musik* (2 vols., Heidelberg 1959); H. Besseler, arts. "Ars antiqua" and "Ars nova" (MGG), *Die Musik d. Mittelalters u. d. Renaissance* (Bücken Hdb.), and *Studien zur Musik d. Mittelalters I* (AfMw 1925),

II (AfMw 1927); M. F. Bukofzer, *Studies in Medieval and Renaissance Music* (N. Y. 1950); J. Chailley, *Histoire musicale du moyen âge* (Paris 1950); R. v. Ficker, *Die Musik d. Mittelalters u. ihre Beziehung z. Geistesleben* (DGLV 1925) and *Formprobleme der mittelalterl. Musik* (ZfMw VII); J. Handschin, *Der Geist des Mittelalters in der Musik* (Gedenkschrift, Bern 1957), *Musikgeschichte* (Lucerne 1948), and *Die Rolle der Nationen in d. mittelalterlichen Musikgesch.* (Schweiz. Jahrbuch f. Musikwissensch. 1931); A. Hughes, ed., *Early Medieval Music up to 1300* (NOHM II); F. Ludwig, *Die geistl. nichtliturgische, welt. einst. u. d. mehrst. Musik d. Mittelalters* (Adler Hdb.) and *Repertorium organorum recentioris et motetorum vetustissimi stili. vol. I, 1: Catalogue Raisonné der Quellen* (Halle 1910); A. v. Martin, *Das Problem der mittelalterl. Weltanschauung* (DVLG III, 1925); G. Reese, *Music in the Middle Ages* (N. Y. 1940); H. Riemann, *Gesch. d. Musiktheorie im 9.–12. Jh.* (Lpz. 2nd ed. 1921) and *Handb. d. Musikgesch.* (1, 2, Lpz. 2nd ed. 1921); O. Ursprung, *Die kath. Kirchenmusik* (Bücken Hdb.); J. Wolf, *Gesch. d. Mensuralnotation von 1250–1460* (3 vols., Lpz. 1904) and *Handb. d. Notationskunde* (I, Lpz. 1913); *The New Oxford History of Music* (II and III, London 1954 and 1960).

New Editions in Collective Volumes: W. Apel, *French Secular Music of the Late 14th Cent.* (Cambridge, Mass., 1950); P. Aubry, *Les plus anciens monuments de la musique française* (Paris 1905); H. Besseler, *Capella, Meisterwerke mittelalterl. Musik* (Kassel 1950 ff.); F. Blume, *Das Chorwerk* (Wolfenbüttel 1929–38, new ed. 1953–); C. v. d. Borren, *Polyphonia sacra. A continental miscellany of the 15th century* (Burnham 1932); E. de Coussemaker, *L'Art harmonique au 12e et 13e siècles* (Paris 1865); F. Ghisi, *Italian Ars nova music* (Rome 1946); A. Hughes, *Worcester Medieval Harmony of the 13th and 14th Centuries* (Burnham 1928); H. Husmann, *Die mittelalterl. Mehrstimmigkeit* (MW); J. Stainer, *Dufay and his Contemporaries* (London 1898); J. F. R. Stainer, C. Stainer, and E. W. B. Nicholson, *Early Bodleian Music* (2 vols., London 1901); G. de Van, *Monuments de l'Ars nova* (Paris 1938); J. Wolf, *Gesch. d. Mens. Not.* (3rd vol. of exs.); W. Wooldridge, *Early English Harmony I* (1897); *Corpus mensurabilis Musicae* (cited as AIM, Rome 1947 ff.); *Monumenta Polyphoniae Liturgicae Ecclesiae Romanae* (Rome 1947 ff.).

Collections of Sources: E. de Coussemaker, *Scriptores de musica medii aevi* (4 vols. 1864, new ed. 1908 and 1936); M. Gerbert, *Scriptores ecclesiastici de musica sacra potissimum* (3 vols. 1784, new ed. 1905 and 1931).

11. Byzantium

In 325 the Council of Nicaea was held, and Constantine the Great raised Christianity to a state religion. In 330, he transferred the imperial residence to Byzantium. Thus arose significant Byzantine art and literature, which were to be maintained there for over a thousand years. The Eastern Roman Empire, with Byzantium as its center, was founded in 395. There the Emperor Justinian I established his code of laws, the *corpus juris civilis*, between 530 and 534.

In 1054 the Eastern and Western portions of Christendom split apart, in what is known as the Great Schism. In 1204 Constantinople was conquered in the Fourth Crusade, and a Latin empire was established there from 1204 to 1261. From 1261 to 1453 Byzantium was under the rule of the Palaiologoi. In the 14th and 15th centuries Byzantine scholars brought the study of Greek to Italy. In 1453 Constantinople was conquered by the Turks under Sultan Mohammed II, and the Eastern Roman empire came to an end.

Throughout its period of flourishing, the social order of the Eastern Roman empire had remained firm on its urban and commercial basis—in contrast to the cultural collapse of Rome in the West under pressure from the extensive migrations of peoples. Constantinople was a metropolis, a center with an international population and a reservoir of trade. Its culture was that of an absolute monarchy, with stress on uniformity, convention, and stasis. Both in church and state, power was united and wielded autocratically, with tendencies to Caesaropapism. Art and music were specifically a matter of the imperial court.

"Byzantine music" refers to the music of the Byzantine cultural circle, thus not only the music of the Greek-Orthodox church but also the secular music of the imperial court in Byzantium up to the fall of the Empire in 1453.

The only pieces of Byzantine secular music we have are some songs of greeting and congratulation, usually referred to as acclamations and polychronia. We do know something about the place of music in the life of this court from ceremonial books describing its order and usages, the most famous of which is that of the Emperor Constantine VII Porphyrogenetos. Secular music, according to these books, was customarily sung antiphonally, with instrumental accompaniment, and was supplied with interludes, particularly on the organ.

Byzantine sacred music, which is related to the sacred music of the Eastern Christian churches using other languages, is—like Gregorian chant—a one-voiced and linear music without instrumental accompaniment, though for the early period it is to be assumed that the organ was used in the church. In Byzantine chant a melody is often accompanied by a sustained tone, or *ison*, which seems to be a survival of simple polyphony of the drone type. The singers were usually divided into two choirs, or *psaltai*, which sang antiphonally.

Beginning with the reign of Constantine the Great (324–337), Byzantium became the center of Byzantine sacred poetry and music. The development of sacred poetry occurred in various stages. First, there was a time of preparation, particularly in the 5th century, when the first type of Byzantine sacred music that we find is the troparion. Short passages were inserted in the psalmody between the individual Psalm verses. Later the insertions were more extensive, and the Psalm text became secondary. Troparia approximated hymns. Finally, *troparion* came to mean church song in general.

In the 5th century, Byzantine hymn poetry began to blossom forth, and during the 6th and 7th it came into full flower. The main form was the kontakion, which consisted of from twenty to thirty stanzas of similar construction, introduced and closed with from one to three differently constructed stanzas. The leading representatives of hymn-poetry were Sophronios of Jerusalem, the patriarch Sergios of Constantinople, the Syrian Romanos, and the monk Anastasios. Romanos, the most significant of them, was especially influenced by the Syrian hymnodist Ephrem (d. 373).

Finally, the period of the great kanon poetry occurred during the 7th and 8th centuries. The kanon was composed of nine odes, each of usually four stanzas. Perhaps the nine odes were originally insertions, after the manner of troparia, into the nine canticles, the Biblical odes or songs of praise. The first great kanon-poet was Andreas of Crete, who lived from about 660 to 740, and his main work is known as the "Great Kanon." Besides him, the most significant representatives are John of Damascus, who lived from about 674 to 749, and his foster-brother Kosmas of Jerusalem.

The 9th century brought with it the period of the hymnographers, or the poets who wrote only the texts for the hymns, their melodies being composed by so-called melurges. After 850 there was a separation between poet and composer, as well-known melodies were used for new texts. Religious hymns were absorbed into the liturgy of Constantinople, and the forms of the liturgy were firmly established in the 8th century.

The 13th and 14th centuries brought a new flourishing of hymn composition with enriched melody. Also during this time there was differentiation between simple and highly ornamented singing. Arabic elements intruded into vocal music. Composers of this epoch were John Kukuzeles, Josaphat Kukuzeles the Younger, Manuel Chrysaphos, John Glykys, John Laskaris, and Metrophanes Blemmydes.

Theoreticians of the 14th and 15th centuries classified Byzantine songs into three stylistic groups:

1. the hirmologic songs—that is, the melodies of the odes of the kanons, which were collected in the hirmologion,
2. the sticheraric songs, one stanza hymns, somewhat comparable to the antiphons of the Latin church and contained in the sticherarion,
3. the melismatic songs, which are preserved in the kontakarion and other liturgical song-books.

Byzantine theoreticians like Psellos of the 11th century, Pachymeris around 1300, or Bryennios of the 14th century follow ancient Greek musical theory in not dealing much with musical practice. But the treatise called "Hagiopolitis" and especially the numerous instructional treatises called "Papadikai" do tell us how the music was performed.

Byzantine notation involves a distinction between ekphonetic signs and neumes. The ekphonetic signs show the musical course of the "lection tone" in the books that contain the readings. Though the neumes are a vocal notation, they give not the individual tone but the interval between two tones. Byzantine neumes are thus an intervallic notation, which developed out of the ekphonetic signs. This development took place in three stages: early Byzantine notation between 950 and 1200, middle between 1100 and 1450, and late between 1400 and 1821. The modern

Greek notation of Chrysantos of Madytos, which has been used since 1821, is a practical simplification of Byzantine notation.

As in Gregorian chant, distinction is made in Byzantine church music among eight modes or the *oktoechos,* four of which are authentic or *kyrioi* and four plagal or *plagioi.*

The church in the East had neither a common liturgical language nor a unified liturgy. There were differences of detail in liturgy, poetry, song forms, and notation among the Syrian, Byzantine, Coptic or Egyptian Christian, Abyssinian or Ethiopian, and Armenian churches. Each of them had come to have an individual and highly wrought music. An independent development is also shown by Russian church song, which began to take shape at the end of the 10th century with the Christianization of Russia from Byzantium.

Bibliography

O. Fleischer, *Die spätgriechische Tonschrift* (Neumenstudien III, Bln. 1904); J. Handschin, *Das Zeremonienwerk Kaiser Konstantins* (Basel 1942); J. Raasted, *Intonation Formulas and Modal Signatures in Byzantine Musical Manuscripts* (Diss. Copenh. 1966. Monumenta Musicae Byzantinae, Subs. VII); G. Reese, *Music in the Middle Ages* (N. Y. 1940); L. Tardo, *L'antica melurgia bizantina Grottaferra* (1938); J. B. Thibaut, *Monuments de la Notation ekphonétique et hagiopolite de l'église grecque* (Petersburg 1913); C. Thodberg, *Der Byzantinische Alleluiarionzyklus* (Diss. Copenh. 1966. Monumenta Musicae Byzantinae, Subs. VIII); O. Tiby, *La musica bizantina* (Milan 1938); H. Tillyard, *Byzantine Music and Hymnography* (London 1923); E. Wellesz, *A History of Byzantine Music and Hymnography* (Oxford 1949), *Byzant. Kirchenmusik* (Adler Hdb.), *Byzant. Musik* (Breslau 1927), art. Byzantinische Musik (MGG), *Early Christian Music* (NOHM II), *Eastern Elements in Western Chant* (Oxford 1947), *Music of the Eastern Churches* (NOHM II), and *Trésor de musique byzantine* (I, 1934). New eds.: *Monumenta Musicae Byzantinae,* ed. Carsten Höeg, H. J. W. Tillyard, and E. Wellesz (Copenhagen, Levin and Munksgaard, 1935 ff.: Monumenta, Transcripta, Lectionaria Subsidia); MW.

12. The Music of the Early Church Through the 6th Century

The background of church history against which the musical developments are to be seen may be divided into seven periods. First, there was the Apostolic Age, beginning with the birth of Jesus Christ of Nazareth sometime between 6 B.C. and 7 A.D., and extending through his crucifixion about 33 A.D. and the subsequent leadership of his followers by St. Peter and then by St. Paul (who was converted to Christianity about 35 A.D.). Next came the Post-Apostolic Age, from the death of St. Peter and St. Paul during the Neronian persecution in 64, through the destruction of Jerusalem and the dispersal of the Jews in 70, to the rule of Hadrian around 130. The third phase was that of the Apologists (130–180), during which Christianity spread, encountering the Gnostic and Neo-Platonic movements. In the fourth period, differences over dogma occasioned many disputes, from which Christianity emerged victorious and quite sharply defined, particularly through the efforts of the Alexandrian school of Catechumens (Clemens and Origen). The fifth period spanned the 3rd century, during which Christianity became a dominant spiritual force in late antiquity. The 4th century saw the last persecution of the Christians in 303 under Diocletian. Thereafter, Christianity was practiced openly: the Edict of Milan in 313 assured Christians freedom of worship, and this period became known as the classic period of the Greek Church. There were, however, doctrinal conflicts, such as that over Arianism. During this time St. Ambrose (340–397), Bishop of Milan, was instrumental in the conversion of St. Augustine (354–430), who was to become an important bishop, church father, and author of the *Confessions* and *De Civitate Dei*. It was during this century that monasticism and convent life spread. In the final period, during the 5th and 6th centuries, Rome assumed primacy in matters of church law, and exercised strong leadership in the persons of Leo II the Great, around 450, and Gregory I, who was Pope from 590 to 604. It was a period of mass migrations of peoples, during which the church acted as a unifying bond in the West.

Church historians understand the period of the ancient Christian church as the time of the development of Christianity on the soil of the ancient world. This development began during the reign of Emperor Tiberius (14 to 37) and ended during that of Pope Gregory the Great from 590 to 604, after serious inroads on the Western Roman empire had been finally made by the invasion of the Lombards. It can be considered as the history of the spread of Christianity, or as its absorption of elements of Hellenism, which infused it with certain features of antiquity and enabled the old to continue on in a new form.

The Hellenistic aspects of Christianity may be considered, inversely, as a part of the history of Hellenism, for Christendom adopted the Greek language and concerned itself to a great extent with the Greek conceptions of mysteries and mysticism, and the speculations of the Neo-Platonists and Stoics. The period of the ancient Christian church is one of great synthesis as Antiquity lived on in altered form. It is hardly feasible to give a strictly musicological description of the epoch, since only quite isolated bits of notation exist. The presentation of the music can be based only on literary evidence, such as church poetry and particularly reports by Church fathers.

Early Christian song arose in the Eastern Roman Empire and may be regarded as an outgrowth of Jewish temple music, the music of late antiquity, and Mediterranean musical practice.

In examining the relationship of Christian to Jewish music, we should recall that the singing of the Psalms was especially emphasized not only in the Jewish but also in the Christian liturgy. One could safely take for granted that the same texts would receive similar musical treatment and that the Christian psalmist closely followed the traditions of the Jewish cantors. More conclusively, certain musical phenomena, such as melismatic punctuation and the melodic ornamentation of the last syllables of a sentence or part of a sentence, are quite widespread in the music of the southeastern Mediterranean coast, and accordingly are also a part of Jewish and Christian psalmody.

How closely Gregorian chant is linked with the music of antiquity has been a matter of differing opinion among scholars, and the discussion is by no means closed. The evidence is meager: we have but few fragments of ancient music, which are not available to us as full-bodied sound. Also, the oldest written sketches of Gregorian chant date from the 8th or 9th century at the earliest. Thus we cannot be too dogmatic about the connections. Even the comparison of individual melodies does not yield much since the Christian melodies are structurally quite different from the melodies of the ancients. The fact that, for example, the Seikilos song and the Psalm Sunday antiphon "Hosanna filio David" have tones in common may be fortuitous. In the Seikilos song there is no recognizable festal tone, while the antiphon is related to a *finalis* (G).

A significant feature of Early Christian music and of medieval musical conceptions is the ethos theory, which perpetuated ideas formulated by the ancient Greeks and earlier peoples. Through Boethius' and Cassidorous' works of musical theory, for example, this influence extends—along with Greek musical theory generally—far into the Middle Ages.

The latest research points more and more to Mediterranean musical practice as the common basis of both ancient pagan and early Christian music. This point is substantiated by the fact that they share many idioms of melodic construction and manner of delivery. Thus scholars have succeeded in tracing the melodies of the antiphons back to a limited number of melodic types or models. Hieronymus, toward the end of the 4th century, and St. Augustine (d. 430) observed some resemblance between the singing of the melismatic *alleluia* and folk-music, particularly in the melodious calls of Roman sailors and workmen in the fields or at the winepress.

The Christian service of worship, in contrast to Jewish temple music, consistently excluded instruments. The organ did not enter the church until the 9th century. The apostle St. Paul, in Ephesians 5:19 and Colossians 3:16, recommended the singing of "psalms, hymns, and spiritual songs." This passage refers probably to the two main branches of song for the divine service: psalmody, or psalm-singing, and hymnody, or the singing of newly written texts. Liturgical song, an essential component of the divine service, was further developed within the framework of the liturgy. The conservative attitude of the early Christian church led to the preservation of the musical elements assimilated from the Jewish service of worship.

Thus three different types of song are to be distinguished: (1) psalmody, or the rendition of the Psalms, or the songs of praise and doxologies derived from the Psalms; (2) hymns, or songs of praise, rendered syllabically, or with each syllable sung to its own individual tone; (3) spiritual songs, particularly alleluias, and other songs of ecstatic character with richly ornamented melodic features.

Psalmody may take the form of singing the whole Psalm, individual verses of it, or a group of selected Psalm verses combined into a new whole. The individual verses were presumably sung to the same melodic formula, in which the repetition of tones was taken for granted as a means of fitting the melody to whatever might be the number of syllables. This recitative-like and declamatory rendition of the evenly held pitches is psalmody in the narrower sense, comparable to the *accentus* in Gregorian chant. In the beginning only simple melodic types were used. The development of new elements occurred but slowly.

| Initium | Tenor | Mediatio | Tenor | Finalis |

Hymnody originally included only free-verse poems, written in a sort of stately, rhythmically articulated prose, for example, the Greek version of the "Great Doxology" or expression of praise, "Gloria in excelsis Deo." The hymn poems of St. Ambrose were the first to make use of verse. The hymns had been taken over from the Jewish liturgy and were free paraphrases of Biblical texts for the enrichment of the liturgy. Hymns in the Latin language appear for the first time in the late 4th century. The oldest extant Latin hymns, perhaps after Syrian models, are those of Hilary of Poitiers (d. 367) and St. Ambrose (d. 397). We have three fragments of hymns by Hilary and fourteen hymns by St. Ambrose, although the attribution of two of the latter are somewhat questionable. The hymns were a principal component in the service of the hours. It is not certain that the melodies traditional to the Ambrosian hymns came from St. Ambrose himself.

The melismatic style of performance has arisen from the synagogue song as well as from Mediterranean folk-song. The word "melismatic" in this connection means the singing of several tones to one syllable of text, resulting in a richly ornamented melodic line of tones predominantly arranged in stepwise succession. The alleluia is most characteristically sung in melismatic style. The word "alleluia" or "hallelujah" was originally a combination of two words, meaning "praise Jah," Jah being the shortened form of Jehovah. The melisma on the last syllable of the word "alleluia" is called a *jubilus*.

The psalms and hymns were probably sung responsorially or antiphonally. Responsorial performance consisted of alternation between leader and chorus. This may have meant that the solo parts were sung with changing text to the same melody and that the choral parts formed a textually and musically constant refrain (ab ab). Antiphonal performance consisted of alternation between two halves of the choir. Thus, theoretically, there could have been various possibilities: the simple corresponding repetition of the parts by the two halves of the choir (aa aa aa etc.); a changing repetition, in which the halves of the choir, responding to each other, carried the same melody, but the new parts were provided with new melodies (aa bb cc dd . . .); or a procedure by which the two halves of the choir responded to each other with the same melody, and an independent refrain was brought in by the whole choir (aa b). Though many alternatives are logically possible, they are only in part actually represented among the remains of the period.

The practice of antiphonal performance in singing is an ancient custom. It first spread among Christian groups in the middle of the 4th century and derived directly from the ancient Jewish temple song. The quick dissemination took place from monasteries in Syria and Palestine, which had taken over the practice from the Jewish communities, particularly in Antioch, and Milan became the principal gateway to the West.

Antiphonal singing was originally a matter of performance practice. The term *antiphon* indicated an inserted portion of song—of whatever length—that introduced the Psalm, was repeated between each line, and finally brought it to a close, thus enriching the formal make-up of antiphonal psalmody. Originally the antiphon consisted of refrain-like interjections of the congregation, often in the vernacular, but later it developed into a textually and musically independent art form and was adopted into the Mass. The main field in which it flourished, however, remained the Office.

From the 3rd century on, the bishopric of Rome won growing significance as the center of Western Christian church song. The development succeeded first in close connection with East and West Syria.

At approximately the end of the 3rd century, Greek was replaced in the Roman liturgy by Latin. The 4th century saw great liturgical and musical reforms in Italy, emanating from Rome and Milan. The Milanese rite is known as Ambrosian chant, named after the bishop there, St. Ambrose (d. 397). Ambrosian chant and the Milanese liturgy seem to have arisen under particularly strong Greek and Syrian influences. Gregorian and Ambrosian melodies may go back to a common source attributable to the church at Jerusalem. Ambrosian chant, as it has come down to us, is representative of the late 4th–early 5th centuries. The first manuscripts that we have, however, come from no earlier than the 10th or 11th. Ambrosian chant may well be regarded as a source of the Roman chant of Gregory I. It has its own style, with melodic and rhythmic formulas.

The Gallican repertoire included the music of liturgies that had been used in France for about four hundred years, from the beginning of the 5th century to the 9th. Gregorian chant is considered a substratum of the oldest religious and secular song that is of Eastern and Western provenance. The artistic development of liturgical song began in the 4th century, after the Edict of Milan in 313.

A changed social function of art corresponded to the new Christian ideal of life. In Classical Antiquity the work of art had a predominantly aesthetic meaning, but in the Christian era it came to have a meaning that was not primarily aesthetic, or a meaning that, at all events, was not confined to the purely aesthetic. It undertook to inculcate moral instruction.

13. Sacred Monody Since the Second Half of the 7th Century

Gregorian Chant

Definition of the Concept

The rise of Gregorian chant in the latter half of the 7th century is considered today a manifestation of the distinctly Roman and Latin spirit. Gregorian chant was the first great musical and artistic achievement of Christendom, and is the oldest musical art-form still in use in the West. Artistic concern with Gregorian chant developed predominantly north of the Alps after 800 A.D. and took several forms:

1. as new creation. New compositions arose through the discovery of new forms, such as the trope and the sequence;
2. by metamorphoses of the basic form, conditioned mainly by the times but also partly by the countries;
3. by the attempts to restore the historically basic form;
4. by the direct influence of Gregorian chant on musical composition, particularly of Catholic church music—for example, in the typical cantus-firmus Mass.

Gregorian chant is the liturgical music obligatory on all Catholic Christianity. Music received a completely new order of value with Gregorian chant, the basis of which lies in Christian theology.

What is usually called the "chant," or in German, *choral,* is the music of the texts of the Western Catholic liturgies in Latin. The music of the chant is monodic, without instruments, diatonic and modal in the sense of the church modes. Rather peripheral to it are some other bodies of church melody that are similar in function. The liturgies of the Eastern church, not being in Latin, are not strictly part of the chant being considered here, though they are obviously related to it. In German, the same word, *choral,* is also used for the vernacular congregational song of the Reformed churches since the 16th century.

Up to the Carolingian period there were independent liturgical traditions that strongly diverged from one another. The most important were the Milanese or Ambrosian, the Gallican (in Gaul), the Spanish or Mozarabic, and the Irish or Briton Christian, which perhaps influenced the Anglo-Saxon. Efforts at reform and unification since the 6th century were in the main directed toward the liturgy and the liturgical texts rather than toward the music. Not until Charlemagne and Pope Leo III joined forces was the unification of the liturgy and of liturgical chant carried out in all France. All regional traditions, except for the Milanese, sooner or later disappeared; and the musical repertoires linked with these liturgies suffered the same fate.

Gregorian chant in an inclusive sense—or what is referred to in German as *Gregorianik,* or Gregorianism—is the song in Latin of the Roman Catholic church of liturgical and semi-liturgical character from the middle of the 7th century to the present. The concept comprehends not only the historical repertoire but also all the new compositions, including hymns, tropes, and sequences.

The Nature of Gregorian Chant

The bases of Gregorian chant are the liturgical texts, originally in Greek and then somewhat later in Latin, as the liturgical language was also Greek in Rome until well on into the 3rd century. These texts are entirely in prose, and thus of a completely different verbal nature from the verse to which ancient music was always linked.

Gregorian chant is monodic, linear, and without instrumental support or accompaniment. It takes two basic forms: *accentus,* or liturgical recitative, and *concentus,* or free Gregorian melody.

Accentus is the *modus legendi choraliter,* the "manner of reading chorally" or the delivery of the Latin text in a declamation raised to singing, with a note for each syllable. This spoken and melodic expression served for prayers and readings and was limited to a tonal range of from about two to six notes. Further notes or figures, often called "accents," were applied to the points of articulation in the text: comma, colon, and period. Thus delivery was articulated according to the elements that gave it psalmodic and recitative-like declamation.

Concentus, on the other hand, included three styles: the syllabic, the group, and the vocalised and melismatic. The first two styles appeared in antiphonal choral singing, such as that of the Introit and Communio songs of the Mass and the antiphons of the Office. The third style appeared in responsorial solo song, such as that of the Gradual, Alleluia, Offertory of the Mass, Responsorium of the Office, and Matins. In the melismatic style, distinction is made among punctuating melismas or melismatic ornamentation toward the end of a word before a syntactic section, cesural melismas, final melismas, and interpretational melismas for stressing important words. A particularly extended form of the melisma appears in the alleluia vocalises, which are important in the origin of the sequence. On the last syllable of the alleluia, there normally occurs a melisma that is called a *jubilus.* The melismatic technique was of Oriental provenance and had been assimilated from synagogue music.

Over and above the general differentiation between *accentus* and *concentus,* there is perhaps a more useful distinction among three types of chant: lectio, psalmody, and song. In the lectio, or reading of a text such as that of the Gospel, the main concern is that the result be verbally intelligible. An individual recites on one tone, the lection tone, with purely musical and but slightly melismatic punctuation. Psalmody was presented by the choir, its two halves alternating in correspondence with the parallelism of the parts of the text. The emphasis was on clarifying by musical means the construction, not the content, of the sentence structure of the text. As for song, there is a difference between choral and solo song. In choral song—for example, in the songs of the Ordinary of the Mass, such as the *Kyrie, Gloria, Credo, Sanctus,* and *Agnus Dei*—the music realizes the language not only in its sentence-structure but also as gesture, as movement. In solo song—such as responsorial songs like the gradual, tract, and alleluia—language plays a subordinate role in contrast to all the other types. Here music alone predominates. This is explained by the position of the Gradual in the liturgy. Between the Epistles and the Gospel, between the two readings of the "service of instruction" or "lessons," a musical number is inserted, as a sort of intermezzo. In the early Christian period a singer came up on the steps of the ambo and performed a piece of music. Improvising freely, he sang a melody rich in multiple melismas. The original situation is reflected in the term for it, related to the Latin word for "steps": above, on the ambo, only the Gospel might be read.

According to Ferretti there are in Gregorian chant three types of melodic formulation to be distinguished: original melodies, melodic types, and melodic formulas. Original melodies are exclusively linked with a text and characterize the typical features of a festival or its special place in the liturgy. Melodic types, on the other hand, are prototypes that are applied as a sort of model to different texts, although the texts may have a great variety of meanings. This type predominates in the antiphons of the Office. Melodic formulas, finally, function like pieces in a mosaic. The formulas are detached from melodies that are already at hand and are added to each other logically in a new context.

The History of Gregorian Chant

By the beginning of the 7th century in Europe there were various chant repertoires—Old Spanish or Mozarabic, Gallican, Milanese, Roman, Benevontani. Sometime before the death of Pope Gregory I the Great in 604, there was a rearrangement of texts and unification of liturgy in Rome. Born about 540 of Roman ancestry, Gregory was at first a high Roman official, then a monk, later Papal adviser, and in 590 became Pope. Through his efforts the missionizing of Britain was begun in 594. The connection between Gregory and the reform of the chant was perhaps more nominal than actual: the details of the liturgical and textual reorganization that go back to him are still not entirely clear. Not until three centuries after his death was he credited with having changed the music. The Gregory legend perhaps arose from the wish to see a great event that had a significant effect on church history and music linked by name with a known historical personality.

The music belonging to the texts organized under Gregory I is the "old Roman" melodies. Nothing is known about their previous history. Some seem to have been adapted from Eastern sources, while others may have been Italian. They are contained in two manuscripts.

In the latter half of the 7th century this material was mostly reformulated in Rome and was replaced to a comparatively minor extent in what Stäblein has called a "creative act of the first order." From the

Middle Ages to our own day this "new Roman" chant is what is known as Gregorian. The reformulation involved a fundamental stylistic change in its musical history. Probably three men who were serving at St. Peter's at the time were most directly responsible—Catolenus, Maurianus, and Virbonus. The new stylistic form, according to Stäblein, lies in the "consistent and systematic flexibility, the classic equilibrium of the melodic line in its rise and fall, the sensitive apportionment of the syllabic and melodic aspects, the rational execution of the whole, and the concern with formally clear disposition," which may be regarded as a "manifestation of Roman nature."

The "new Roman" chant spread north of the Alps, coming from Rome in the south and from England in the north. Extensive missionary activity had been carried on in and from England in the wake of Gregory I's initial steps, and a flourishing chant school was established at Canterbury by 630. The Anglo-Saxon monk Boniface, from Wessex, introduced the chant into Germany. King Pippin (d. 768) was first responsible for its spread in France, and his son Charlemagne gave it exclusive authority.

The actual work of dissemination centered in the singing schools. Metz, for example, was founded from Rome, and Tours from England. A music school highly influential in Alemmania was the Benedictine monastery at St. Gall, in Switzerland, founded about 625; but by the 11th century it was eclipsed in significance by the monastery at Reichenau.

A new era began with the adoption of Gregorian chant by peoples north of the Alps—and, in a sense, the music history of the Middle Ages itself then began. The North became the leader and disseminator. As early as about 800, activity undertaken on the basis of quite different musical assumptions had begun to manifest itself, altering traditional melodies. Also, the melodies that were now created for new feasts bore new musical traits of hexachordal melody. The trope and the sequence now became especially significant. Out of the chant, which in the 8th and 9th centuries was uniform, there again developed in the course of the Middle Ages special traditions, particularly among the monastic orders.

With the 12th century came various efforts to reform the chant—in 1134 by the Cistercians, between 1245 and 1256 by the Dominicans, and at other times by the Carthusians, Franciscans, and others. These efforts continued sporadically until a definite stage, under Papal authority, was reached by the Council of Trent, between 1545 and 1563, which established the final liturgical forms still used today. This interrupted and closed the process of development in the liturgy, particularly in the Mass, which had not attained its present order until the High Middle Ages and which was still in flux on into the 16th century. From then on, liturgy and liturgical song stood codified in the uniform missal of Pope Pius V, the *Missale Romanum*, of 1570, and in the *Graduale Romanum* of 1614. Though Pope Gregory XIII commissioned Palestrina and Zoilo to undertake choral reform in 1577, after a short time the work was suspended. In connection with the *Editio Medicaea*, which goes back to the edition of 1614, the reform carried out by Anerio and Suriano was along lines laid down by the Council of Trent. Papal liturgical reform had thus come to an end, and the supervision of further use of the completed codification was assigned to the especially created Congregation of Rites.

During the 17th and 18th centuries, in accordance with the change in musical taste at the time, slightly altered versions of the melodies were introduced into the liturgical song-books.

The 19th century brought a fundamental choral reform. It proceeded from the efforts of the Benedictines to renew the chant, specifically from the researches begun in the mid-19th century by the Benedictines of Solesmes in northern France and particularly by Abbé Guéranger, who played a prominent role in its development. During the latter decades of the 19th century several publications in the field of the chant appeared. These included a notable series, the *Paléographie Musicale*, which was begun in 1889, and was edited by Dom A. Mocquereau and J. Gajard. In 1901 Pope Leo XIII assigned the task of reestablishing chant regulations on the basis of old manuscripts to the monks of Solesmes. Then in 1903 Pope Pius X issued his *Motu Proprio* and sanctioned the *Editio Vaticana*, which, along with the Gradual that appeared in 1908, was declared obligatory on the whole Roman Church. A significant recent development is the revision of the order of the Mass in 1969, permitting much more extensive use of the vernacular.

The melodies of the *Editio Vaticana* do not always go back to the oldest versions extant. Instead, versions were often taken into account that had been sung through the centuries in a long tradition and were for this reason felt to be significant.

The songs of the Mass are contained in the Gradual, those of the service of the hours in the Antiphonal. The *Liber Usualis* is a modern compilation of the songs of both the Mass and the Office. Coming thus from the Gradual and the Antiphonal they are used for Sunday and festival days.

The Notation of Gregorian Chant

Fundamentally, Gregorian chant is a music the essence of which is its sounded form. It therefore really needs no notation. With advancing Christianization, foreign peoples were called upon to adopt Christian dogma in the resounding form of the Gregorian melodies. Thus there arose a need for providing the newly converted peoples with mnemonic aids for the unfamiliar and carefully memorized melodies. Accordingly the neumes came into existence. They are signs that help one recall a melody he has already learned. They first appeared in the 8th century, but did not appear with much frequency in liturgical manuscripts until the 9th century.

The word *neume* in Greek means a "hint" or "sign." Neumes developed not only from the punctuation and accent marks, but also perhaps in conjunction with the hand movements of the precentor and choir leader during rehearsal of the melodies. Neume scripts are differentiated according to region—southern Italian, Aquitanian, French, German, and so on. All these families of scripts have in common the basic neumatic forms shown in the example with but slight deviations.

. Punctus, / or — Virga, ⌒Flexa or Clivis, ⌣Pes or Podatus,

/. Scandicus, /∴ Climacus, ○Porrectus, ∼Torculus .

The liquescent neumes are signs added to the basic neumes. They stand at the places where a sort of vowel is inserted in speaking, between the final consonant of one word and the initial consonant of the next and where, correspondingly, a tone might be also inserted in the melody.

By a quite early date neumes were arranged diastemmatically for more precise indication of the pitch. For purposes of differentiating the height of the tone they were written in a higher or lower relationship to each other, as if they were being notated on a lined staff. We have manuscript examples of this practice from the 9th century, but it had

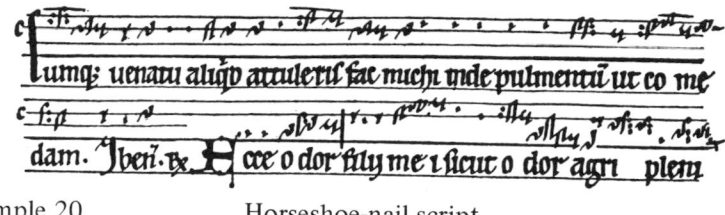

Example 20   Horseshoe-nail script

Punctum	**Virga**	**Bivirga**	**Punctum inclinatum**
Podatus vel Pes	**Clivis vel Flexa**	**Epiphonus**	**Cephalicus**
Scandicus	**Salicus**	**Climacus**	**Ancus**
Torculus	**Porrectus**	**Torculus resupinus**	**Porrectus flexus**
Pes subpunctis	**Scandicus subpunctis**	**Scandicus flexus**	**Climacus resupinus**
Strophicus	**Pes strophicus**	**Clivis strophica vel cum Orisco**	**Torculus strophicus vel cum Orisco**
Pressus	**Alii Pressi vel neumae appositae**		**Trigon**
Quilisma	**Neumae longiores seu compositae**		

Example 21   Chant notation (quadratic form)

apparently been in use earlier. This phenomenon, however, was perhaps not originally part of the idea of the neumes. Their form changed in the early period when they were placed on or near lines in order to indicate differences in pitch. They were written in quadratic notation, which is still used today for Gregorian melodies in the liturgical books. In Germany they were written in the so-called Gothic or "horseshoe-nail" script (*Hufnagelschrift*), which was still being used in liturgical books as late as the 18th century.

The present-day notation of Gregorian chant uses four lines, which are counted upwards, and a ledger line may be added above and below. The C-clef stands on the second, third, or fourth line, and the F-clef, when it appears, almost always is used on the third line. The notation of the melodies, running in the diatonic series from Do (Ut) to Si, is not bound to an absolute pitch, but is relative. The prefixed clef determines the arrangement of whole and half steps. The singer's voice level determines how high a composition should be sung. The Gregorian notes, or neumes, are either single tones or groups of more than one tone.

There are various and quite contradictory theories regarding the rhythmic significance of the neumes and thus the rhythm of the chant. Perhaps the only undisputed fact is that the virga indicates a longer durational value than the punctum.

The chant may well have had no such regulated rhythm as that which developed under the exigencies of polyphony. As Gregorian chant was not composition as we know the term, but was music that lived as it sounded, being passed on exclusively by word of mouth for centuries, it varied in rhythmic presentation according to locality and country. Today the chant is sung in such a way that all the tones have about the same duration. This is in accordance with the idea of "equalism," defended by the Benedictines of Solesmes as the rhythmic theory to be applied to the ancient chant. Some other scholars have held an alternative idea, that of "mensuralism," which involves a belief that there was differentiation among the durational values.

The Church Modes in Medieval Theory

The early 5th century "De Musica" of St. Augustine, a work on meter and rhythm, was followed in the early 6th century by the five books of the Roman Boethius *De institutione musicae*. These works provided the basic sources for the speculative theory of the Middle Ages, preserving some aspects of the Greek and Roman tradition. The Anglo-Saxon cleric Flacus Alcuin, who died in 804, was the first to write about the system of church modes and to distinguish between authentic and plagal. About 850 Aurelianus Reomensis followed him with his *Musica disciplina*. Hucbald of St. Amand, who died about 930, provided the modal series that has become classical for the liturgical music of the Middle Ages in his *Harmonica institutio*. Guido d'Arezzo in his *Micrologus de disciplina artis musicae* developed modal theory according to hexachords and solmisation syllables. The *Musica* of Hermannus Contractus, who died in 1054, contains the clearest and most uniform presentation of the Middle Ages. The octave species C and A were first admitted as main tonalities by Glareanus in his *Dodekachordon* (1547).

The Church Modes (or Tones)

The scale taken over from the Greeks provides the original tonal material and is the basis of Gregorian chant and all the music of the Middle Ages. It begins with A—later G, indicated by the Greek letter Γ, or gamma—and ends with a¹. This tonal material, though presented in a row like a scale, does not have the character of our scale as a succession of tones arranged in a musically sensible way according to an order of tensions. The most usual make-up of the tonal material occurred in the system of the church modes, variously referred to as church tones, octo-echos, modi, or tonoi. They are scalar sections, which contain the tonal material of related melodies. Not being scales that exist apart from the music, they have at their basis ideas of melodies, whose tones are brought together in the modes. The word "modus" indicates a sort of pattern, like the "nomos" that was dealt with under Greek music.

The individual modes were originally characterized by certain idioms that constantly reappeared in the melodies, for example, the idiom according to which melodies of the same tone closed ultimately on the *finalis*. The placement of the whole and half steps was not decisive—as it is in modern major and minor—for the assignment of a melody to a mode. Instead, the mode is established by the end-note or *finalis*, the main tone or *repercussa*, the range of the melody, and certain melodic turns.

Melodic conceptions also lay at the basis of the ancient modes, or *harmoniai*. But they were essentially different from those of the Gregorian chant. A tonality in Gregorian—unlike the ancient melodies—expressed itself by being directed toward a *finalis*. The church tones assumed only the names of the ancient modes and otherwise had not much in common with the earlier system.

The church tones are sections from a diatonic scale that is built upon A and spans two octaves. The tones are indicated by the letters of the alphabet; B-flat and B-natural pass for one and the same tone, but, according to the course of the melody, appear with a tendency that is directed either downwards (B-flat) or upwards (B-natural).

Authentic and plagal modes are differentiated. The individual mode is determined by the *finalis* and by the tenor, sometimes referred to as the tone of repercussion, or tuba. The authentic and the related plagal modes have the same *finalis*. The authentic is constructed above the *finalis*, but the plagal has its *finalis* in the middle of the scalar section. The authentic modes have the tenor a fifth above the *finalis*; the plagal, the tenor a third or a fourth above the *finalis*.

The eight modes were first numbered in the 8th century and were provided with designations such as Protus authentus, Protus plagalis, Deuterus authentus, and so on, as indicated in the accompanying table. The numbering I–VIII appeared in the 9th century, the application to them of the names of the ancient modes in the 10th. Glareanus in his *Dodekachordon* of 1547 was the first to increase the number of the eight church modes by adding to them the Aeolian and the Ionian, which correspond to modern major and minor. Originally there were also modes on A, B-natural, and C, but they later were lost, except for traces.

Mode	Older nomenclature	Newer nomenclature	Scalar section	Finalis	Tenor
I	Protus authentus	Dorian	D–D	D	A
II	Protus plagalis	Hypodorian	A–A	D	F
III	Deuterus anthentus	Phrygian	E–E	E	B (C)
IV	Deuterus plagalis	Hypophrygian	B–B	E	G (A)
V	Tritus authentus	Lydian	F–F	F	C
VI	Tritus plagalis	Hypolydian	C–C	F	A
VII	Tetrardus authentus	Mixolydian	G–G	G	D
VIII	Tetrardus plagalis	Hypomixolydian	D–D	G	B (C)

An asterisk has been placed above the tone of repercussion or recitation:

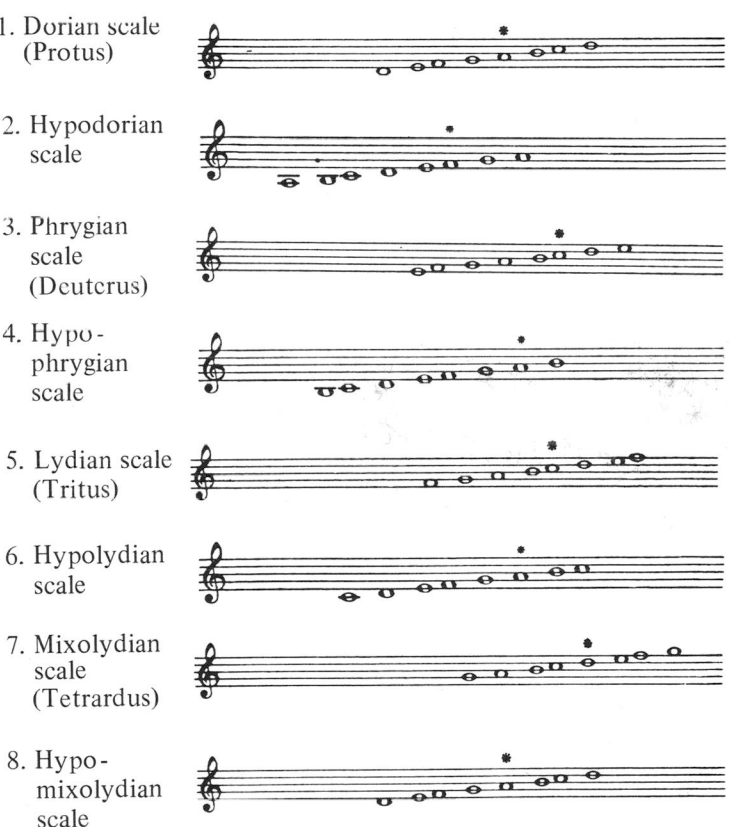

1. Dorian scale (Protus)

2. Hypodorian scale

3. Phrygian scale (Deuterus)

4. Hypo-phrygian scale

5. Lydian scale (Tritus)

6. Hypolydian scale

7. Mixolydian scale (Tetrardus)

8. Hypo-mixolydian scale

Example 22

The entire musical theory of the Middle Ages is based on the church tones.

The Hexachord System and Solmization

The hexachord, a series of six successive tones, is a section of the medieval scale, arranged in such a way that the half-step between *mi* and *fa* always occurs between each succession of two whole steps. The concept of the hexachord as a six-tone group was formulated by Guido d'Arezzo, though the designation "hexachord" does not come from him.

Born shortly before 1000 and living to about 1050, Guido, a monk and teacher at the cathedral school of Arezzo, was one of the most significant theoreticians of the Middle Ages. Among developments accredited to him are:

1. the principle of a notational system of lines a third apart, which became the basis of European notation;
2. the introduction of a yellow *do*-line and a red *fa*-line between or on the lines representing thirds, to make the placement of the half-step visually clear;
3. the development of a method of training the gift of musical perception by imprinting the tones on the memory with the help of the "didactic melody" for the hymn to St. John;
4. a guide to improvisation;
5. a basic description of the practice of organum; and
6. apparently the "Guidonian hand" and the theory of mutation, or transposition of the hexachord a fifth and a fourth higher.

The hexachord that Guido set up was the result of a methodological idea of making the individual tones of a certain melody known and of firmly impressing them on the memory. For this purpose he took the melody, probably his own, for the Sapphic poem ascribed to Paulus Diaconus of the 8th century, the hymn to St. John, patron of singers (after Luke 1:62 ff.):

Ut queant laxis *re*sonare fibris *mi*ra gestorum *fa*muli tuorum,
 *Sol*ve polluti *la*bii reatum, Sancte Johannes!

Literal sense of the words: "That thy servants may be able to sing with relaxed muscles the wonders of thy deeds, remove from polluted lips all offense, Saint John!"

Example 23

Imitation of some formal aspects of the text: "*U*tterly we pray: *R*elax our throats this day, *M*iracles to sing, *F*ar and wide praise to bring, *S*olemnly adore, *L*aying our gifts before *O*ur patron Saint John."

On the basis of this melody the pupils were to make clear to themselves the special position of the tone in the context of the neighboring tones. The six tones that occur at the beginning of the six half-lines of the first three Sapphic verses in the melody are C D E F G A; the corresponding six syllables of the verses are *ut, re, mi, fa, sol, la*.

The actual theory of the hexachord, here shown diagrammatically, was first worked out in the latter half of the 11th century, after the death of Guido, and was perhaps first fully completed around the middle of the 13th century. It is very closely related to solmization theory, which was also not developed until after Guido. The purpose of the hexachordal theory is to make clear through the solmization syllables all the tones of the diatonic scale, in the wider sense the entire tonal material of medieval music, including the twofold step involving B-flat and B-natural.

The Greek letter gamma, standing for G, is the name of the lowest note of the system. It is at the same time the *ut* of the lowest hexachord. The other tones take their names from the alphabet plus the corresponding tone syllable. From time to time a new hexachord begins with the tones G, C, and F.

The half-step always lies between *mi* and *fa*. The three hexachords are thus simply transpositions of the same series to different tonal levels.

The hexachord on C is called *hexachordum naturale*, that on F *hexachordum molle*, and that on G *hexachordum durum*. *Durum* and *molle* designate the manner in which the B-natural or B-flat is written, for the former has a symbol that is angular or hard (*durum*), the latter one that is rounded or soft (*molle*).

The transpositions of the hexachord are called mutations.

Solmization theory gives the individual tones definite names according to their place in the hexachord. The tone-names do not designate absolute pitches, but indicate the place of the individual tone within the hexachord and the tones surrounding it in the hexachordal framework. Accordingly the solmization name remains true to the tone, although it shifts onto another absolute pitch through the transposition of the hexachord. The Guidonian hand facilitated visualization of the hexachordal system and the solmization theory. It served to train the tonal imagination, assisted the memory, and helped lead the singers.

It is not correct to conceive of the hexachord as a major series, for there is no leading-tone step from the seventh to the eighth degree as the most important center of tension in the major scale. In the beginning the hexachord was a scalar section; in its further course—through systematic training—there developed a type of musical thinking in hexachords that had its place alongside the church modes. The hexachord accordingly became somewhat independent. Hence it came about that—as the article on the hexachord in *Musik in Geschichte und Gegenwart* states—"the themes of numerous compositions of the 15th to 17th centuries refer to, or directly represent, a hexachord." In the 18th century hexatonic fugal themes still appeared. But they were more like relics, having lost any genuine connection with the historic hexachordal theory.

	The Hexachords							
	1	2	3	4	5	6	7	
E							la	E la
D						la	sol	D la sol
C						sol	fa	C sol fa
B♮/B♭						B♭ fa	B♮ mi	B♭ fa B♮ mi
A					la	mi	re	A la mi re
G					sol	re	ut	G sol re ut
F					fa	ut		F fa ut
E				la	mi			E la mi
D			la	sol	re			D la sol re
C			sol	fa	ut			C sol fa ut
B♮/B♭			B♭ fa	B♮ mi				B♭ fa B♮ mi
A		la	mi	re				A la mi re
G		sol	re	ut				G sol re ut
F		fa	ut					F fa ut
E	la	mi						E la mi
D	sol	re						D sol re
C	fa	ut						C fa ut
B♮	mi							B♮ mi
A	re							A re
Γ	ut							Γ ut

Example 24

The "Guidonian Hand" is a means for aiding the memory and for helping the leader direct the singers by hand signals, or cheironomy.

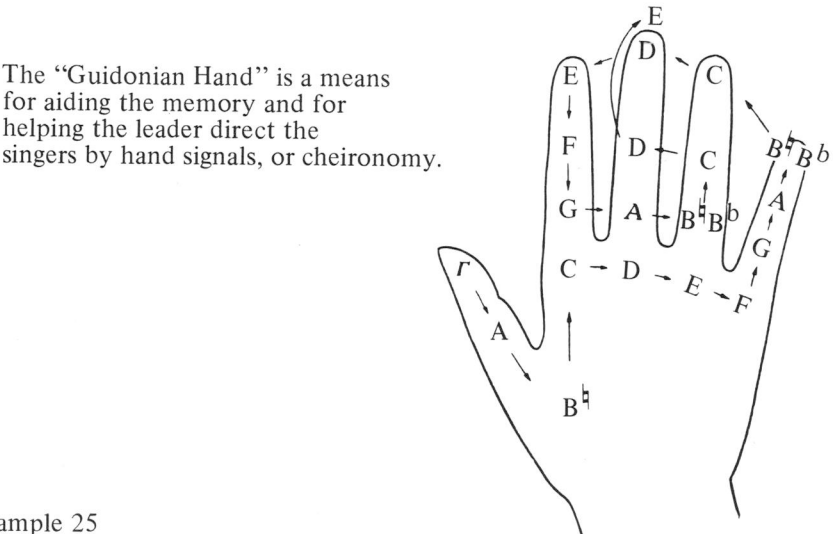

Example 25

Trope and Sequence

Hymn, trope, and sequence—as explained earlier—are also considered part of Gregorian chant. The hymn had taken shape as one of the primitive Christian forms, along with the psalms and spiritual songs. In contrast to the traditional neo-Roman repertoire, however, the hymn, trope, and sequence present new poetic works. Their text is thus not taken from the Bible. Musically they are—in preponderant number—new compositions. Particularly the trope and the sequence are accordingly the two types in which the creative activity of the peoples north of the Alps first pioneered within church music to enrich the historical Gregorian chant. The way was accordingly opened up for tendencies within the Gregorian tradition that were bound to time and place, which were imprinted in the different textual and musical forms of the trope and the sequence. The neo-Roman chant, obligatory and unified in the whole Carolingian empire, was thus the primary stratum on which they developed as a secondary stratum. With them, influences of secular music north of the Alps first penetrated the Gregorian tradition. Thus by the time of Charlemagne the cultivation of church song and the training of the singers were at their height. Church singing followed the Gregorian antiphonary or antiphonale. An outstanding personality in this field of the liturgy during the first half of the 9th century was Amalar of Metz.

The musically creative achievement of the trope and the sequence was thus no longer carried on merely by word of mouth but was fixed musically in notation and poetically by the written word. Accordingly, it is possible to consider in an objective way the music north of the Alps in its historical course. The unnotated and therefore undocumented "prehistoric" period yielded to a "historical period," with which—during the Carolingian period—the history of music in the Middle Ages north of the Alps began. The oldest musical written copy of a sequence is dated before 900. The first textual sketch of a sequence was also made in the latter half of the 9th century; it is only a little older than the first musical one. As a form the sequence flourished, but after the 13th century its significance steadily declined.

Considering first the trope, we might note that the word itself goes back to the Greek *tropos* and literally means "turn." As no uniformity prevails in the terminology, we might follow Joseph Smits van Waesberghe's suggestion and observe the distinction made by C. Blume and H. Bannister between the *sequela* and the *sequentia* and that made by H. Husmann between the *prosa* and the *prosula*. Accordingly these are:

Sequelae: exclusively the *distinctiones*, or sections, in the *melodiae longissimae* of the second alleluia-jubilus.

Sequentiae, or sequences: *sequelae* provided with texts.

Tropus: the pieces of Gregorian chant developed by the addition of introductions and insertions.

Prosulae: syllabic songs that arise from the placing of texts under the tones of a melisma.

There are two principal types of trope: (1) an insertion into the antiphonal forms of Gregorian chant, principally in the Mass (*Introit, Communio,* and *Offertorium*), where it may have an introductory function, and (2) an addition, or an appendage, to parts of the Ordinary of the Mass, principally the *Kyrie, Gloria, Sanctus, Agnus Dei,* and less often the *Credo.*

Example 26 is cited by Jacques Handschin in the *New Oxford History of Music,* Vol. II, from the Bologna University MS. 2824, fol. 3. The original text is here set in italics, the troped in Roman letters:

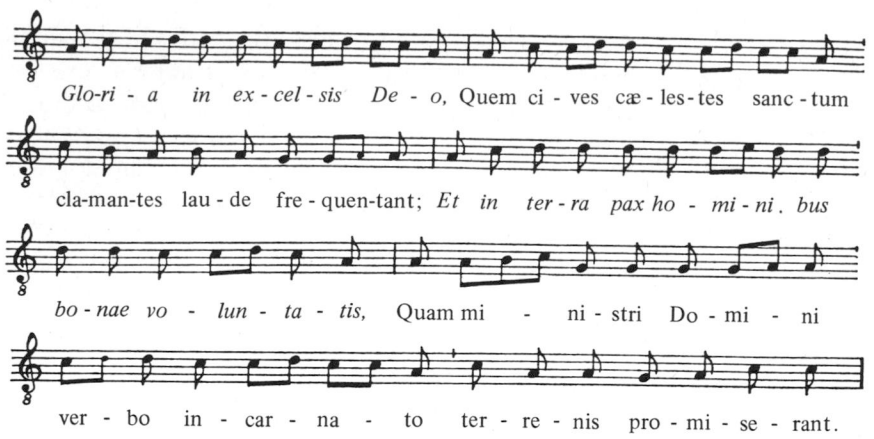

Gloria in excelsis Deo, Quem cives caelestes sanctum
clamantes laude frequentant; Et in terra pax hominibus
bonae voluntatis, Quam ministri Domini
verbo incarnato terrenis promiserant.

Example 26

The religious drama of the Middle Ages grew out of the principle of troping. This drama had its beginning in the dialogued trope that introduced the Easter and Christmas introits, led on to little dramas that were sung and performed in the church, and was finally played as "sacred drama" or "mystery" outside the church. As "trope" it involved a very extensive expansion of the liturgical text in conjunction with the dramatic action.

The first documents of polyphonic music from the Carolingian period are, in a sense, "musical tropes." Also the later motetus can be conceived of as a trope.

The first important name in the history of the trope is that of the monk Tuotilo of St. Gall (d. 915), a contemporary of Notker Balbulus. Tuotilo composed the well-known Christmas trope "Hodie cantandus."

The other new form that ushered in the 2nd millennium is the sequence. It regularly goes *x aa bb cc dd . . . y*—in other words, there are unlike stanzas of paired lines, enclosed by a free introduction and a free ending. For new texts of this type new melodies were also created. The introductory and closing parts of the sequence were sung by the whole choir, the other parts by the half-choirs in alternation.

As to its origin and history, Notker Balbulus of St. Gall (d. 912) wrote that singers found it difficult to learn by heart the melismas of the alleluia, that is, the flourishes involved in the jubilus, the elaboration of the last vowel *a* of the *alleluia*. While concerned with this problem, he had occasion to see an antiphonary that a monk who had fled from the destruction of the Jumièges monastery near Rouen (in 862 or 851) had brought with him to St. Gall. In this book, Notker said, he saw that the melismas had been underlaid with texts. He was not satisfied with the poetic quality of the texts, however, and began to compose texts himself.

Notker's influence on the sequence is disputed. He is, from one point of view, regarded as the creator of the sequence, from the other as author of its final form. Actually, it seems impossible to establish precisely what his own creative achievement was. As before Notker there were already sequence melodies with and without text (for example, those from Metz and St. Martial of Limoges), he is not the first poet of sequences; but he had the distinction, according to Handschin, of having "introduced sequence poetry into a circle that previously had known only the melismatic form of these tonal successions."

Not fully clarified, moreover, is the question of where the interpolations—partly without text, partly with—came from before finding their way into the liturgy. So far there are four explanations:

1. the singers' improvisations on the Gregorian *alleluia;*
2. the pre-Gregorian *alleluia,* shortened by Gregory I;
3. Byzantine models; and
4. Irish-Celtic forms of secular music, of which other traces have practically disappeared, in conjunction with what Handschin calls an "antistrophic or sequence-like form in the heathen cult-rhythms of Late Antiquity." In other matters, too, there were close ties between the Celtic-Irish culture and Late Antiquity.

Present-day scholars have drawn a distinction among three types of sequence, developed from the beginning to about 900:

1. The standardized church sequence, which was the most widespread. It occurred in the Mass between the alleluia and the evangelium. The succession was as follows: allcluia with jubilus —verse—repetition of the alleluia, this time with substantially expanded jubilus. This expansion of the jubilus was called in the West a *sequentia,* that is, "that which now follows," or "the succesive melodic parts"—and in Northern Italy and in the East, *longissima melodia.* This expansion of the original jubilus now bore the sequence text. The designation in the Middle Ages and still today in France is *prosa*—or, more properly, *prosa ad sequentiam*—and in Germany it is referred to as a *Sequenz,* which is a characterization of the music. The literary form is a succession of double versicles (*aa bb cc dd*); two text-lines of equal length are distinguished from the preceding and following pairs by their differing length. The musical form assigns to both lines of text the one line of melody, which is thus repeated. Textually, it follows the syllabic principle.
2. The non-parallel church sequence. Like the preceding but without parallelism of the versicles.
3. The "archaic" sequence, so called because the few examples come from a time perhaps before the "classical period" of Notker about 900. There are no connections with an alleluia or a melismatic textless jubilus. The verse portions and melodic sections are here not so regularly distributed as in the two preceding types, but partial or complete repetitions do occur.

The development of these types took place during a span of some four centuries. The first or "classic" period of sequence poetry extended from about 850 to the middle of the 11th century. Prominent writers in this period were Wipo of Burgundy (d. after 1048), who is known for his "Victimae paschali laudes"; Berno of Reichenau (d. 1048); and Hermannus Contractus, who lived from 1013 to 1054 and is best known for his "Ave praeclara maris stella." At the same time there were parallel developments in the St. Martial monastery at Limoges, in France. The

Wipo (ca. 1000 to ca. 1050), Easter Sequence "Victimae paschali laudes" (around 1040)

1. Vic - ti - mae pa - scha - li lau - des im - mo - lent Chri - sti - a - ni.
   Let all Christians of-fer praises to the Pass - o - ver victim.

2. A - gnus red - e - mit o - ves: Chri - stus in - no-cens
   Lamb, all the sheep re - deem - ing: Christ the in - no - cent

Pa - tri re - con - ci - li - a - vit pec - ca - to - res.
bring - ing re - con - ci - li - a - tion with the Fa - ther.

3. Mors et vi - ta du - el - lo con - fli - xe - re mi -
   Lo, death and life in con - flict had what won - der - ful

ran - do: dux vi - tae mor - tu - us, re - gnat vi - vus.
out - come: Lord of life made mortal, yet reigns liv - ing.

4. Dic no - bis, Ma - ri - a, quid vi - di - sti in vi - a?
   Tell us, O Ma - ri - a, what on the way thou sawest?

5. Se - pul-chrum Chri-sti vi - ven - tis, et glo - ri am vi - di re - sur-gen - tis:
   The grave of Christ the liv - ing one, the glory I saw of Him a - ris - en:

6. An - ge - li - cos te - stes, su - da - ri - um et ve - stes.
   An - gels as wit - ness - es, shroud and bu - ri - al gar - ments.

7. Sur - re - xit Chri-stus spes me - a: prae - ce - det su - os in
   My lord is ris - en, all my hope: to Ga - li - lee he has

Ga - li - lae - am. 8. Sci - mus Chri - stum sur - re - xis - se
gone be - fore you. Well know we that He has ris - en

a mor - tu - is ve - re: tu no - bis, vic-tor Rex, mi - se - re - re.
from death and cor - rup - tion. On us, vic - to-rious King, show thy mer - cy.

Example 27

second period, in the 12th century, brought with it the rhymed sequence, especially created by the Augustinian order. The main representative was Adam of St. Victor, who died in 1177 or 1192 at the St. Victor monastery near Paris. The sequence then approximated the hymn. Melodies were no longer taken from the jubilus, but were new creations. Finally, in the third period, all stanzas or verses were constructed alike, as in the song or hymn, for example in the "Dies irae" by Thomas of Celano (d. ca. 1250) and in the "Stabat mater" by Jacopone da Todi (d. 1306).

The Council of Trent at its sessions between 1545 and 1563 reduced the great number of sequences in the liturgy to four. There was the "Victimae paschali laudes" for Easter, the "Veni sancte spiritus" for Whitsuntide, the "Lauda Sion salvatorem" by St. Thomas Aquinas (d. 1274) for Corpus Christi, and the "Dies irae" by Thomas of Celano (1190–about 1250) in the Requiem. In 1727 the "Stabat mater" by Jacopone da Todi (about 1230–1306) was added for the Festival of the Seven Sorrows of Mary.

Lauda and Cantiga

The lauda, or song of praise, was a type of monodic sacred song in the vernacular that arose in Italy in the latter half of the 13th century. Interestingly enough, this was about the time that the troubadour and trouvère art, which had never flourished significantly in Italy and Spain, was waning in France. The lyricism responsible for the lauda originated in popular religious movements, such as that of St. Francis of Assisi (d. 1226) and of the Penitentes, who began to figure in central Italy about 1260. The lauda thus stood outside the liturgy of the church. It was sung at meetings of organized fraternities called *laudesi*, which sang them in public on various occasions, particularly in processions.

The first epoch of the lauda, which was monodic, lasted till 1400. The musical form corresponded to that of the French virelai. It was a refrain form, sung antiphonally by solo and chorus, in a somewhat *da capo* or *ABA* format. The solo began with the refrain, or *ripresa*, which might be more specifically designated as *a*; and this *ripresa* was then repeated by the chorus (A). There ensued a middle section consisting of two *piedi* (*b b*¹) and a *volta* (*a*¹), the latter paralleling the *ripresa*. Finally, the chorus sang the refrain (A) again. Thus the form was *a A b b*¹ *a*¹ *A*. The piedi *b* and *b*¹ were not always musically identical, nor did the volta always have the same melody as the refrain. The lauda derived from the sequences and minstrel music of the Crusades, Latin songs of the Franciscans, and Gothic minstrel music of the Ars nova. During this first epoch the most widely known poet was Jacopone da Todi (d. 1306), and the most famous work was St. Francis's song to "Brother Sun," the "Cantico de lo frate Soli."

During the course of the second epoch, from about 1400 to 1600, one also finds polyphonic laudi in plain settings. The dialogue laudi led to the sacred drama of Italy, or *sacra rappresentazione*, and further to the oratorium, or *oratorio volgare*. The lauda around 1500 was closely related to the *frottola* in musical structure.

In Spain, at about the same time as the first epoch of the lauda, there arose particular interest in songs related to the Virgin Mary. Brought together in collections, they were known as *cantigas*. The poet of the texts in the greatest of the collections, the *Cantigas de Santa Maria,* was Alfonso X, King of Castile, who reigned from 1252 to 1284. The melodies may well have come from court musicians or from traditional melodic sources. The form of the cantiga is the same as that of the virelai.

In placing these collections in their proper historical perspective, we have to go back to the *Reconquista* or retaking of Spain from the Moors. In 1212 the Christian army of the kings of Castile, Aragon, and Navarre won complete victory over the Caliph of the Almohades in the battle of Navas de Tolosa. The outstanding king of the *Reconquista* was Ferdinand III, who reigned from 1217 to 1252. His son, the compiler of the *Cantigas,* conquered Cadiz and Cartagena.

This point in history coincides with another significant cultural phenomenon, i.e., the full bloom of the early Galician-Portuguese poetry. The kings Ferdinand III and Alfonso X cultivated music at their court, attracting French troubadours, German minnesingers, and musicians conversant with the Notre Dame repertoire, as well as Moorish and Jewish minstrels.

There are two opposed theories concerning the origin and source of these songs: that the music is of Arabic origin and that it derives from Gregorian chant, folk-song, troubadour song, and motet melodies.

German Sacred Song up to the Reformation

The Middle Ages were replete with various song forms in the German language, which were related to the *cantiones,* or medieval monodic Latin songs. Though mostly sacred in content, they were not strictly part of the liturgy, as they had no definitely assigned place in the order of worship, but were in stanza form and usually had a refrain.

A very early instance of the use of German in the liturgy is to be found in the *Allerheiligenlitanei* or All Saints' Litany, in which the *Kyrie* —as early as 973—was sung by the congregation as *"Kyrie eleison, unde die heiligen alle helfant uns! Kyrie eleison."* *Rufe,* or exclamatory calls of this sort, began the Germanizing of the Latin church-language and continued throughout the entire Middle Ages. Examples of the two-line formula calls are: *"Da helfe uns der Herre Christ"* and *"Gelobt sei Gott und Maria."*

The vernacular church-song in Germany was called the *Leise.* For every church festival of the year there were non-liturgical *Leise,* or folk-like church songs. For example, the Easter *"Christ ist erstanden"* was written down in 1325; as were the Christmas *"Gelobet seist du, Jesu Christ"* in 1370, the Whitsunday *"Nu bitten wir den Heiligen Geist"* in the 13th century, and the pilgrims' *"In gotes namen varen wir"* in approximately the same period. Numerous Christmas songs have been handed down, such as *"Joseph, lieber Joseph mein,"* traceable back to

1305, and *"Es ist ein Ros entsprungen,"* probably from the 15th century. The songs written in Old High German did not undergo the linguistic change to Middle High German, with the exception of the 9th-century Frisian St. Peter song, the earliest German church song extant.

From the 12th century on, we have German versions of various Latin hymns which are still in use in the church. They include *"Komm, Heiliger Geist"* based on *Veni sancte spiritus,* the antiphon *"Mitten wir im Leben sind"* based on *Media Vita,* and *"Wir glauben all an einen Gott"* based on the Credo. The German adaptation of the sequence is called the *Leich,* consisting of pairs of strophes, each pair constructed differently and involving a different modal melody.

Among the several figures of special artistic significance as translators and adapters of hymns and sequences in the late Middle Ages there are Hermann, Monk of Salzburg (*ca.* 1370); Oswald von Wolkenstein (d. 1445); and particularly Heinrich von Laufenberg (d. 1460), a poet of original creative ability, known for his *"Ich weiss ein lieplich engelspil"* and *"Ich wölt, daz ich doheime wer."* As early as about 1500 there was widespread use of a type of song in the German Catholic Church that started with a statement affirming the collective feeling or experience of the group, which was sometimes referred to as a *Wir-Lied* ("We"-Song). In 1537 the first Catholic song-book of this new type, Michael Vehe's *Ein New Gesangbuechlin Geystlicher Lieder,* containing fifty-two songs, appeared in Leipzig.

During the Crusades of the 12th century there were many songs known as *Kreuzfahrerlieder* (crusaders' songs), such as Walther von der Vogelweide's *"Nu allerst lebe ich mir werde."* Sacred *minnelieder* appeared in the 13th century.

In Europe during the 14th century the plague years, which culminated in 1349, precipitated widespread activity among the Flagellants, or *Geissler,* who in their processions sang distinctive songs known as *Geisslerlieder.* Influences from the Italian lauda were fused with elements from the sacred art-song and folk-song. A typical *Geisslerlied* is the *"Maria muoter reinu mait"* in F major, which along with other melodies, evidences the popular feeling for the major mode.

Hybrid poetry, or *Mischpoesie,* involving the combination of Latin and German, is represented notably by *"In dulci jubilo, nu singet und seit fro."*

In the middle of the 14th century, the *aubade* or morning-song of the minnesinger (a dialogue between the lover and the watchman, warner, or death) combined itself with motifs from church thought and led to the sacred morning-song. It blossomed particularly under the cultivation of Hermann, Monk of Salzburg, and Heinrich von Laufenberg.

The 15th century gave rise to the "contrafacta" and parodies. Originally secular songs were refashioned into sacred songs, or new sacred texts were applied to well-known melodies. Though further discussion of this development is more appropriate to a consideration of the Reformation, the terms "contrafacta" and "parody"—often used in musicological writing—might appropriately be here clarified. *Parody,* with reference to music, has two meanings: (1) It can refer to a kind of transformation in which a musical work, in whole or in part, is taken up and re-illuminated in a new context, altering the real musical substance, i.e., the thematic, harmonic, or other material; (2) it can refer to change or distortion that seeks to transform one thing into something else, particularly of a comic nature. Parodies, in this second sense, did not become common till the 19th century, for example, operatic parodies. As for "*contrafacta*," there is a process in German known as *Kontrafaktur,* by which originally secular songs were transformed into sacred songs though the melody was preserved, or new sacred texts were written for already familiar secular melodies. The practice of making contrafacta can extend to whole works, as in Bach's reworking of individual secular cantatas in whole or in part into sacred cantatas. Thus the six cantatas which together form the so-called Christmas Oratorio, in their meditative parts, are all contrafacta or parodies of already existing and predominantly secular cantatas by Bach himself.

Czech Pre-Hussite, Hussite, and Post-Hussite Song

Early developments among the Czechs are to be seen against a background of the political and religious history of this Central European area. Moravia was converted to Christianity by the "apostles to the Slavs" Cyril (d. 869) and Methodius (d. 885), who were Greeks from Salonika. Their activities led to the introduction of a Slavic ecclesiastical and literary language based on the so-called Glagolitic alphabet. During the latter half of the 9th century a Czech ruling family, the Přemyslids, gained power and wielded it until 1306, winning from 1253 to 1278 a prominent European position under the Přemysl king Otakar II. After the fall of this ruling family, however, Bohemia passed in 1310 into the hands of the Luxembourg rulers, Henry VII, Count of Luxembourg, who reigned from 1308 to 1313, and his son John. From 1346 to 1378, under John of Luxembourg's son, who was born in Prague in 1316 and ruled as Charles IV, Bohemia became the heartland of the German realm. This was its "Golden Age": Prague had been an archbishopric since 1344, and in 1348 it opened the first Central European university in the area. The King from 1378 to 1419 was Wenzel IV, the eldest son of Charles IV. But in 1400 he lost the imperial crown. Jan Hus, professor at Prague and adherent of the teachings of the Englishman John Wycliffe, was imprisoned in 1412, condemned as a heretic, and in 1415 burned at the stake by the Council of Constance. In 1416 his friend Hieronymus of Prague suffered a similar fate. The Czechs then experienced a period of national and religious revolts and wars, in which the Hussites and the radical Taborites under Žižka took a strong position. Under the King of Bohemia, Georg Podiebrad, a union was created, the *Unitas fratrum Bohemorum.* Despite or because of these developments, Czechoslovakia achieved a certain distinction: Czech was the most cultivated Slavic literary language of the time. In 1620 at the Battle of White Mountain near Prague, Frederick V was killed; and there ensued a Catholic Restoration, with a reinstitution of absolutism in Bohemia and a systematically organized return of the country to Catholicism.

Returning now to our particular concern here with sacred monody, we find song within the church following two paths:

1. the Slavic liturgy, with Cyril and Methodius the chief representatives, from the late 9th century on; and
2. the Latin or Roman liturgy, which won the upper hand and consolidated its position with the founding of the bishopric of Prague in 973.

The early extant music manuscripts belong in general to the Latin liturgy and Gregorian chant: the oldest documents are the 11th-century Proprium now in the Prague National Museum and the late 12th-century missal from the monastery in Vyšší Brod.

Reform and spread of the Gregorian chant was due principally to the efforts of the dean of the St. Veit canonical choir Vít. The Prague troparium of 1235 is apparently related to this reform activity, as are the activities of Bishop Tobiáš z Bechyně toward the end of the 13th century. The height of this movement came during the reign of Charles IV from 1346 to 1378, who also, however, approved the renewal of the Greek liturgy with Old Slavic chant in the monastery of Emausy, and a fragment of the Gradual from Emausy is preserved today in the Strahov Library. At the same time, Ambrosian chant was being introduced from Milan, and further establishment of the Roman liturgy was effected by the founding of the Prague archbishopric in 1344 and the reforms of the first archbishop Arnošt of Pardubice. As early as the era of the last Přemyslids, around 1300, the first Czech hymn-writer, the Dominican priest Domaslaus, was active. There are remains of many manuscripts from the 13th and 14th centuries, including missals, graduals, antiphonaries, and collections of sequences. Probably the most significant 14th century composer was Master Záviš of Zapy (about 1350–1411), a professor at Prague University. The third Prague archibshop Jan of Jenštejn (*ca.* 1350–1400) is often named in connection with the *Leich* "*Decet huius cunctis horis,*" which is the first example we have of Czech mensural writing, and with the three-sectioned Latin song "*Mittitur archangelus fidelis.*"

The oldest Czech secular folk-songs are known to us only indirectly, through their having been officially censured. From as early as the pre-Hussite era we have four popular spiritual songs. The oldest, "*Hospodine, pomiluj ny*" (God, be gracious unto us) derives from the Czech troping of the *Kyrie.* The second song, "*Svatý Václave*" (St. Wenzel), acquired later a somewhat similar social significance. The third, "*Buoh všemohúcí*" (Almighty Lord), was introduced by Konrad Waldhauser as a popular song that came after the sermon in the liturgy. The practice became so widespread in the 14th century that the Prague synods of 1406, 1408, and 1410 had to deal with it. However, the disapproval of popular spiritual songs by the Synod of 1408 came too late. A series of new songs was heard at the Bethlehem Chapel in Prague in 1409, including "*Navštěv, nás, Kriste žádúcí*" (Visit us, dear Christ) and "*Vstalt jest Buoh z mrtvých*" (Christ is risen).

This significant trend is associated with the name of Master Jan Hus, who was born in 1370 at Husinec in Southern Bohemia and became

Professor and Rector of Prague University. He was burned at the stake by the Council of Constance in 1415. Several songs are ascribed both to him and to Master Hieronymus of Prague, who was also burned in 1416. Their contribution to that hymn repertoire has not been entirely clarified, though it has been shown that Hus wrote the final version of the text *"Jezu Kriste, štědrý kněže"* and the melody of the song *"Navštěv, nás, Kriste žádúcí"* (Visit us, beloved Christ).

As a result of the revolutionary Hussite movement following Hus's death, there was a great increase in the number of spiritual songs and liturgical reforms, which included the Bohemianization of the Mass. The Czech cantional of Jistebnice (about 1420, now in the Prague National Museum) is a very rich source. This was the official liturgical book of the group led by the Prague priest Jan Želivský (d. 1422). Presumably the revolutionary song *"Povstaň, povstaň, veliké město Pražské"* (Rise up, great city of Prague) also comes from this group. The Jistebnice Cantional mentions only two names as composers: Jan Hus and the Taborite priest Jan Čapek. In addition, polemic, military, and propaganda songs evolved from within the broader sphere of influence of the movement.

Hussite songs can be classified into those of the Taborite and those of the Prague camp. There is considerable historic significance in the fact that the Hussite movement drew popular song into the church and thereby instigated a previously unexpected development of popular musical creativity. Hussite song preceded Lutheran song. Hand in hand with this artistic development went the social cultivation of church song by the so-called literati brotherhoods. Begun in the late 14th century, they flourished during the post-Hussite period and brought together both the educated ("literati"), the outstanding members of the congregations, and the simple townsmen and workers, into a sort of fraternal organization with strictly established duties and rules. In contrast to the meistersinger, the members were all practicing artists. The brotherhoods were divided into "chorale literati" (for the practice of monodic song) and "figural literati" (for that of polyphonic song). In terms of their more strictly religious features, there were "chalice literati" (concerned with advancing the Hussite tradition) and Catholic or Evangelical (Bohemian Brothers). The cantionals include significant examples of the Czech art of manuscript illumination.

Scholars have so far estimated the total number of cantionals from the post-Hussite period at forty for the Utraquist church in eighty editions, twenty for the Lutheran church in about fifty editions, fifty for the Bohemian Brothers in fifteen editions, and seven for the Catholic. The literati cantionals contain both chorale and figured songs. Particularly significant are the *"Sborník vyšehradský"* or collective volume of Vyšehrad (about 1450), the *"Kutnihorský graduál"* or Kuttenberg Gradual (late 15th century), *"Franusův kancionál"* or Franus' Cantional (1505), and *"Královéhradecký speciálník"* or Special Collection of Königgratz (about 1550).

The heritage left by Hussite song on native soil is the contribution of the Bohemian Brothers, though in time it lost its original revolutionary aspect. *"Lukášův kancionál"* (1501) begins this series of contributions.

Michael Weisse in *"Ein Gesangbüchlein"* (1531) chose and translated texts for the German members of the movement. The most significant editorial achievement of the 16th century is represented by the Šamotuly Cantional *"Písně chval Božkých"* (Songs in Praise of God, 1561), organized by an editorial commission headed by the bishop of the Bohemian Brothers Jan Blahoslav (1523–71), who also wrote the first Czech work of music theory, *"Musica"* (1558). The Šamotuly Cantional contains 735 songs with a total of 450 melodies, of which 221 were newly composed. Another cantional is that of Kralice (1615). Notable, also, is the cantional of Jan Amos Komenský, better known as Comenius (1592–1670), which was brought out while he was in exile in Amsterdam in 1659 during the Counter Reformation. Comenius' Cantional, exemplary from the literary point of view but not quite so impressive musically, closes the series. The movement of the literati brotherhoods, which failed after the defeat of the Reformation forces in the Battle of White Mountain (1620), revived toward the end of the 17th century. In 1785, however, a governmental order finally ended their activity, which was accompanied by a serious loss of records and manuscripts.

Reports of medieval secular song from the beginning of the 15th century indicate that there was activity in the Czech area on the part of wandering scholars and minstrels as early as 1200, or perhaps even earlier. Cracow University was closed from 1370 to 1400, and some of the students went abroad, mostly to Prague. Thence came the tradition of the Bohemian singing movement in Poland around 1400. Many satirical and political songs were connected with Hussite religious conflicts. The church in 1415, however, forbade the singing of secular songs in the vernacular; and since few remains of this period are preserved, what we know of secular Polish chivalric song comes from indirect sources.

Poland

A brief general view of the initial half-millennium of Polish history will provide a framework for the medieval developments there. Though the ruling family traced its origin back to Piast, the legendary king of the Poloni or field-dwellers, it was not till the middle of the 10th century that the small ancestral holdings were united into an all-Polish state. This ruling family, incidentally, retained the Polish throne till 1370, and ruled in Masovia till 1526 and in Silesia till 1675. Poland was converted to Christianity, and the Latin liturgy was introduced. The first bishopric was founded in Poznań in 968, and in 1000 an independent church hierarchy was established under the archibishopric of Gniezno. Bolesław I. Chrobry, who reigned from 992 to 1025, established a strong Slavic state; but the gradual decline of the political significance of Poland was assured by its being split up into partial states in 1138.

In 1227 the abandonment of the principle of seniority, which accorded the princes of Cracow precedence, further weakened Polish unity. In 1320 the kingship was reestablished by Władysław Łokietek. His son, Kazimierz III, the Great, who ruled from 1333 to 1370, increased the political significance of the country and brought order in domestic

matters, establishing the University of Cracow in 1364. During the ensuing century Poland continued to gain strength: after a short regime of the
Anjous from Hungary, the Jagiellonian dynasty came to the throne,
when Jadwiga, the daughter of Louis of Hungary, married the Grand
Duke of Lithuania Władisław Jagiełło (1386–1434), and thus effected
a union between Poland and Lithuania. In 1410, the victory at Tannenberg and a thirteen-year war against the German knights strengthened
Poland's position in the northwest. The Polish-Lithuanian bloc, one of
the great powers of Europe, was a mainstay for Hussite Bohemia and for
Hungary. Kazimierz Jagiellończyk IV, who ruled from 1447 to 1492,
placed his sons on the Bohemian and Hungarian thrones.

There was Gregorian chant in Poland in connection with the first
centers of the Latin liturgy, especially the late 10th-century bishoprics
and the monasteries in the Bishopric of Poznań and, after 1000, additional
bishoprics and monasteries, such as Gniezno, Wrocław, Cracow, Trze-
meszno, and Kruszwica. As Christianization was carried on mainly by
foreign clerics, there was a development of Gregorian chant in Poland of
the early Middle Ages, first under the influence of the liturgies of Cologne
and Salzburg. The first documentary reports on liturgical music come
from 1003 and 1008. In 1003, for instance, two boys sang Psalms during
the Pre-Mass of St. Martin in the Hermitage of Międzyrzecz. In 1008 the
brothers there went through the church in procession.

The oldest liturgical manuscripts, a gift of Emperor Otto III to the
hermits of Międzyrzecz and part of the dowry of Rycheza, the wife of
Mieszkos II, were destroyed during the reversion to heathendom from 1034
to 1038. The more important documents of a later period are the Sacra-
mentarium of Tyniec from about 1060 (at the Warsaw National Library),
the Missale Plenarium from between 1070 and 1131 (at the library of
the cathedral chapter at Gniezno, MS. 149), and the Evangelarium of
Płock from about 1130 (also at the Warsaw National Library), as well
as the so-called Salzburg-Wrocław Ordinarius Pontificalis antiquus of
the 11th to 12th century (at the library of the Wrocław cathedral chapter,
MS. 149) and the 11th to 12th century Pontificale of the Cracow bishops
(Jag. Libr. MS. 2057). Among the diastematic manuscripts are the
liturgical books of the Clarissines of Cracow and Stary Sącz, which date
from 1232 or 1234. The oldest preserved examples of diocesan chant are
the Gradual of Wiślica from about 1300, the Antiphonary of Kielce from
1372, and a Płock manuscript from the 14th century.

After the brief reversion to heathendom, Cracow was the main
center for the cultivation of the chant, under Bishop Aaron of Brunvilare,
a Benedictine from Cologne, who died in 1059. Cracow exercised influence over the diocese of Wrocław. It was not till towards the end of the
11th century that the Archbishopric of Gniezno was reestablished. It is
likely that the first Polish chant, the antiphon to St. Adalbert, "*Magna
vox laude sonora*," was written in connection with the dedication of the
reconstructed cathedral in 1090, 1097 or 1127 at the latest, by the archbishop Jakub of Żnin.

With the creation, around 1080, of the first cathedral schools in
which the young people learned the chant, a precondition for the Poloni-

zation of the clergy was established. At the beginning of the 13th century there were new monastic centers, some purely Polish, under the Dominicans and the Franciscans. These were probably responsible for liturgical compositions associated with native or favorite patrons such as Adalbert, Stanisław, Jadwiga, Jacek, Kinga, Wacław, and Florian.

These compositions included rhymed stories or offices, hymns, and sequences. For St. Adalbert there is an office *"Benedic regem cunctorum"* from the first half of the 13th century, as well as some fifteen sequences, of which seven are of Polish origin, and some hymns. For St. Stanisław, there is an office *"Dies adest celebris,"* written by the Dominican monk Wincenty of Kielce in 1254–5, as well as a hymn *"Gaude mater Polonia"* and twelve sequences. For St. Jadwiga, there are three 13th-century rhymed stories from Silesia, and so on. Though some of these works are contrafacta based on songs of secular origin, there are also many original compositions among them. During this period over sixty hymns and over two hundred sequences were written.

The practice of dramatizing the Palm Sunday and Resurrection processions presumably began during the early 13th century in the cathedral at Poznań. The dialogues are in Latin, and not until a century and a half later are the first Polish Easter songs documented. Only the educated levels of society, particularly the clergy, understood liturgical song in Latin. Unlike Germany, Poland had almost no early exclamatory songs or *Rufe*, except for a single reference to one in 1249. The introduction of the Polish language into the worship service in the middle of the 13th century was a clerical move backed by the people as a reaction against the wave of German colonization that threatened to engulf them in the first half of the 13th century. At first there was just the Polish recitation of the Creed and the Ten Commandments on a very simple Psalm tone, which was the result of the activities of Bishop Pełka of the Wrocław Synod in 1248 and of Archbishop Jakub Swinka of the Łęczyca synod in 1285–7.

The oldest known Polish song is the one usually referred to as the *Bogurodzica*, or Mother of God, which is documented from as early as 1407 in MS. 1619 at the Jagiellonian Library. The initial and oldest portion of the song, addressed to the Virgin Mary (the "Deesis" motif) is not very closely related to Gregorian chant and, instead, shows close connection with nonliturgical music, particularly the music of chivalry. The beginning of the song coincides with a composition by Jehan de Braine (d. 1240) *"Par dessor l'ombre d'un bois."* The chronicler of the Jagiellonian epoch Jan Długosz (d. 1480) called the *Bogurodzica* the *carmen patrium.* We know that it was a war song of Polish knighthood, sung on the battlefield of Tannenberg in 1410. It was neither a trope nor a lay, hence Długosz's epithet for it, a "song of the fathers."

In the 14th century there appeared a succession of Easter songs: *"Wstal smartwich crol nas Synboży,"* a contrafactum of the *"Triumphat Dei filius,"* which was later absorbed into the *Bogurodzica;* the Polish translation of the *"Victimae paschali," "Presstwe swete weschrznene";* *"Chrystus z martwychwstał je,"* a Polish version of the *"Christ ist erstanden";* *"Wszegoswiata wszystek lud,"* and *"Wesoły nam dzień nastal."*

"*Jesus Chrystus Bóg człowiek*" and "*Zdrowa crolewna mathko*" (from the "*Salve Regina*") come from the end of the 14th and the beginning of the 15th century.

The first Polish Christmas songs appear about the middle of the 15th century: "*Chrystus się nam narodził*" (1435); "*Jezu Chryste nasza radiość*"; "*Stała sie rzecz wielmi dziwna*" (1442); "*Zdrów bądź królu angielski (anielski)*," a contrafactum of the "*Grates nunc omnes*"; and, somewhat later, "*Mesyasz wierny Chrystus nasz*," "*Nuż wy bielscy panowie*," "*Panna Pana porodziła*," "*Stała się nam nowina*," as well as "*Augustus kiedy królował*."

Other songs are also traceable in the 15th century, including some fifteen Marian songs, such as the "*Żale Marii*," or Mary's Sorrows, of about 1470, in free sequence form, and "*Radości wam powiedam*." We also have five eucharistic songs, three Whitsunday songs, a mourning song, and several songs about saints. In all, there are some sixty songs with Polish texts from the 14th and 15th centuries—translations or paraphrases of Latin sequences and hymns, translation from the Bohemian, or original compositions. Some, such as the "*Pieśń o bożym umęczeniu*," or Song of God's Passion, written in 1488 by Władysław of Gielniowo (d. 1505), are closely connected with Polish folk music.

Catholic Church Music in Scandinavia

Similarly, a brief general view of the initial half-millennium of Scandinavian history is indispensable for an understanding of medieval musical development there. In 826 the Benedictine monk Ansgar came as the first missionary to this region, settling in southern Jutland and also twice penetrating farther into Sweden. He left behind church structures in Hedeby and Ribe and in Birka that give evidence of his work there. Harald Blåtand, who died in 985, was the first Danish king converted to Christianity. At the beginning of the 11th century Denmark, Norway, Sweden, and Iceland were officially converted. In the 12th century Sweden brought military pressure to bear on Finland and gradually united the whole country under its rule, with Turku/Åbo as the capital. Around 1060 the first bishoprics were in Lund, then Denmark, and in Skálholt, Iceland. In 1104 Lund was the seat of the archbishop. In 1152 Trondheim was the seat of the archbishop for Norway and Iceland, and in 1164 Uppsala for Sweden and Finland.

Presumably these churchmen were concerned with music, but there are comparatively few direct sources that can be traced. The only considerable number of manuscripts and fragments that remain are from Finland. They point to influence from Cologne until 1330, when the Roman Dominican liturgy was adopted in Turku/Åbo. Remains of early music in other sections point to English and German influence, and then, after about 1200, Roman, transmitted through France. The council inaugurated by Archbishop Absalon in Lund in 1188 was certainly intended to unify church song in the North. New works included mostly sequences and offices for local saints, such as the rhymed office of St. Thorlak from the second quarter of the 14th century, from Iceland. Probably pre-existing melodic material was used in almost all instances.

The few extant service books such as graduals and missals suggest that there was faithful preservation of the Roman rite. There are no distinctively national or individual features. Several secondary sources such as choral statutes and councils indicate that there was zealous cultivation of choral song. There was, however, no separate center for the training of singers in the North. The main centers for study were Cologne and, particularly, Paris.

A collection of seventy-four clerical, non-liturgical, Latin school-songs was edited in 1582 by the Finn T. P. Ruuta under the title *"Piae cantiones"* in Griefswald, prepared for the cathedral school in Turku/Åbo and widely used throughout Scandinavia. It contains a repertoire of clerical songs of the wandering students, certainly medieval. Some few of the songs, whose sources are not traceable, suggest northern origin.

The German *Leise* and the mid-European Marian songs were often imitated and translated. Both types, much favored in the 15th century and the Reformation, paved the way for later Protestant church song.

Bibliography

Exs. Sch 2–6; *Guido*, "Micrologus" new ed. AIM; *Glareanus* "Dodeka-chordon" new ed. in Ger. tr. PGfM 1899, also Hildesheim.

Trope and Sequence: C. Blume and H. Bannister, "Liturgische Prosen erster Epoche," in: *Analecta Hymnica LIII*, Lpz. 1911; H. Husmann, "Sequenz und Prosa," in: *Annales Musicologiques II*, 1954, pp. 61–91. *Guides to Sources:* M. Gerbert, *Scriptores ecclesiastici de musica sacra potissimum* (3 vols., Paris 1784, new ed. Graz 1905 and Milan 1931); E. de Coussemaker, *Scriptores de Musica medii aevi* (4 vols., Paris 1864–7, new ed. Graz 1908 and Milan 1931); G. M. Drevens and C. Blume, *Analecta hymnica medii aevi* (55 vols., 1886–1922; contents listed in MGG, art. Analecta hymnica); A. Mocquereau and J. Gajard, *Paléographie musicale* (16 vols., Solesmes, Tournai 1889 ff., facsimiles of sources); *Monumenta Monodica Medii Aevi* (Kassel 1956–   : Bd. 1, Hymnen 1: "Die mittelalt. Hymnenmelodien des Abendlandes"); *Monumenta Musicae Sacrae*, ed. Hesbert (Solesmes, now Saint Wandrille). *Periodicals: Revue du chant grégorien* (1892 ff.); *Revue grégorienne* (1911 ff.); *Jb. für Liturgiewissenschaft* (1921 ff.), called since 1950 *Archiv für Liturgiewissenschaft. Helpful Ref. Work:* K. Marbach, *Carmina scripturarum* (Strassburg 1907): compilation of texts of liturgical chants according to their sources in the Bible. *General:* A. Baumstark, *Vom geschichtl. Werden d. Liturgie* (Freiburg i. B. 1923); T. Klauser, *Abendländ. Liturgiegesch.* (Bonn 1949); J. A. Jungmann, *Missarum sollemnia* (2 vols., Vienna 2nd ed. 1949). *Introduction:* D. Johner, *Neue Schule d. Greg. Choralgesanges* (Regensburg 1906, 7th ed. 1936 with the title: *Grosse Choralschule*). *Studies:* H. Anglès, *Gregorian Chant* and *Latin Chant before St. Gregory* (NOHM II); C. W. Brockett, *Antiphons, Responsories, and Other Chants of the Mozarabic Rite* (IMM); W. Bulst, *Hymni latini antiquissimi* (1956, with basic intro. and bibl.); K. G. Fellerer, *Der greg. Choral* (Regensburg 1936); P. Ferretti, *Esthétique grégorienne* (Paris 1938); O. Fleischer, *Neumenstudien* (3 vols., Lpz. 1895–1904); F. A. Gevaert, *La mélopée antique dans le chant de l'église latine* (Ghent 1895) and *Les origines du chant liturgique d l'église latine* (Ghent 1890); J. Handschin, *Trope, Sequence, and Conductus* (NOHM II), *Über Estampie u. Sequenz* (ZfMw XII and XIII), and *Zur Notker-Frage* (Gedenkschrift, Bern 1957); H. Hucke, *Greg. Gesang in altrömischer u. fränk. Überlieferung* (AfMw XII, 1955); H. Husmann, *Die St. Galler Sequenztradition* (Acta 1954), *Sinn u. Wesen der Tropen* (AfMw 1959), and *Tropen- u. Sequenzhandschriften* (1964); A. Z. Idelsohn, *Parallelen zwischen Greg. u. hebräisch-orient. Gesangsweisen* (ZfMw IV, 1921–2); E. Jammers, *Der Choral als Rezitativ* (AfMw 1964), *Der greg. Rhythmus: Antiphonale Studien* (Strassburg 1937), *Der mittelalterl. Choral* (Mainz 1954), *Musik in Byzanz, im päpstl. Rom u. im Frankenreich. Der Choral als Musik der Textaussprache* (Heidelberg 1962), and *Rhythmische u. tonale Studien zur Musik d. Antike u. d. Mittelalters* (AfMf 1941 and 1943); D. Johner, *Der greg. Choral* (Stgt. 1924) and *Wort u. Ton im Choral* (Lpz., 2nd ed. 1953); A. Mocquereau, *Le nombre musical grégorien* (2 vols., Tournai 1908–27); R. Molitor, *Die nachtridentinische Choralform zu Rom* (2 vols., Lpz. 1901–2); H. Oesch. *Berno u. Hermann von Reichenau als Musiktheoretiker* (Bern 1961); G. Reichert, *Strukturprobleme der älteren Sequenz* (DVLG 1949); T. Schrems, *Die Gesch. d. greg. Gesanges in d. prot. Gottesdiensten* (Freiburg, Switz. 1930); L. Smoldon, *Liturgical Drama* (NOHM II); P. Söhner, *Die Gesch. d. Begleitung des gr. Chorals in Deutschland vornehmlich im 10. Jh.* (Augsburg 1931); H. Spanke, *Aus d. Vorgesch. u. Frühgesch. d. Sequenz* (Z. f. dt. Altertum 1934); W. v. d. Steinen, *Notker der Dichter u. s. geistige Welt* (2 vols., Bern 1950); G. M. Sunyol, *Introducción a la paléografía musical gregoriana* (Montserat 1925); O. Ursprung, *Die antiken Transpositionsskalen u. d. Kirchentöne* (AfMf V, 1940); J. Smits van Waesberghe, *Guido of Arezzo* (MD 1951); H. Wagener, *Die Begleitung des Gr. Chorals im 19. Jh.* (Regensburg 1964); P. Wagner, *Einführung in d. greg. Melodien* (3 vols., Lpz. 1895–1921); E. Wellesz, *Eastern Elements in Western Chant* (N. Y. 1947); *Der Greg. Choral* (MW); *Etudes grégoriennes* (1954–   ); *Kongress-Bericht Jumièges* (Rouen 1955); *Le Graduel Romain. Edition critique par les Moines de Solesmes, vol. II: Les Sources* (Solesmes 1957); Publs. of the Greg. Akademie at Freiburg, Switz. (1903–   ); arts. Alleluja, Antiphon, Choral, Choralreform, Frühchristliche Musik, Gallikanische Liturgie, Guido von Arezzo, Hexachord, Jumièges, Sequenz (MGG).

Lauda and Cantiga: ex. Sch 51; K. Jeppesen, *Die mehrst. ital. Lauda um 1500* (Lpz. 1935); F. Liuzzi, *La Lauda e i primordi della Melodia italiana* (2 vols., Rome 1935); G. M. Monti, ed., *Bibliografia delle Laude* (Florence 1921–5); F. Stichtenoth, *Die Melodien der Laudenhandschriften Cortona und Florenz* (Diss. Göttingen 1923); O. Ursprung, *Katholische Kirchenmusik* (Bücken Hdb.); J. A. Westrup, *Medieval Song* (NOHM II); arts. Cantigas de Santa Maria, Dialog, Lauda (MGG).

Sacred Song in German to the Reformation: exs. Sch 12, 25; W. Bäumker, *Das kath. dt. Kirchenlied in seinen Singweisen v. d. frühesten Zeit bis gegen Ende d. 17. Jh.* (4 vols., Frbg. i. B. 1883 ff.); A. Hübner, *Die dt. Geisslerlieder* (Bln. 1931); J. Müller-Blattau, *Die dt. Geisslerlieder* (ZfMw 1935); P. Runge, *Die Melodien der Geissler d. Jahres 1349* (Lpz. 1900); W. Steinecke, *Die Parodie in der Musik* (Diss. Kiel 1934); P. Wackernagel, *Das dt. Kirchenlied v. d. ältesten Zeit bis zum Anfang d.*

17. Jh. (5 vols., Lpz. 1864–77); arts. Cantio, Geisslerlieder, Gemeindegesang, Kontrafaktur, Lied, Parodie (MGG); on *lai, leich,* and *leise,* see also arts. in *Reallexikon der dt. Literaturgesch.,* ed. P. Merker and W. Stammler, II (1926–8).

Czech Pre-Hussite, Hussite, and Post-Hussite Song: exs. P 1, 2, 16, 19, 27, 44; J. Bužga, *Zur mus. Problematik der alttschechischen Kantionalien* (MF 1959); Z. Nejedlý, *Das Verhältnis des hussitischen Gesangs zu der vorhussitischen Musik* (Prague 1904); C. Schoenbaum, *Zur Problematik der Musikgesch. Böhmens u. Mährens* (MF 1957).

Poland: H. Feicht, *Die polnische Monodie des Mittelalters* (MAEO) and *Mittelalterliche Choralprobleme in Polen* (Musik des Ostens II, 1963); F. Feldmann, *Darstellung u. Quellen zur schlesischen Geschichte* (Breslau 1938); B. Rajeczky, *Sur le Kyrie Ungaricum du manuscrit 1267 de la Biblioteka Jagiellońska* (Feicht-Festschrift); art. Koleda (MGG).

Catholic Church Music in Scandinavia: E. Abrahamsen, *Eléments Romans et Allemands dans le chant Grégorien et la chanson populaire en Denmark* (Diss., Copenh. 1923); T. Haapanen, *Die Neumenfragmente der Universitätsbibl. zu Helsingfors* (Kongressber. Basel 1925); A. Hammerich, *Medieval Musical Relics of Denmark* (Lpz. 1912); H. Husmann, *Studien z. geschichtl. Stellung der Liturgie Kopenhagens* (Dansk Aarbog for Musikforskning 1962); C.-A. Moberg, *Der greg. Gesang in Schweden während der Reformationszeit* (KmJb 1932), *Die liturg. Hymnen in Schweden* (Copenh. 1947), and *Über die schwedischen Sequenzen* (Diss., Uppsala 1927); T. Norlind, *Schwedische Schullieder im Mittelalter u. in der Reformationszeit* (SIMG 1900–1); R. A. Ottósson, *Sancti Thorlaci Episcopi Officia Rhytmica et Proprium Missae* (Copenh. 1959); G. R. Woodward, ed. *Piae Cantiones* (London 1910); "Piae Cantiones" (facs. new ed. in Documenta Musicae Fennicae 10, Helsingfors 1967).

14. Medieval Secular Monody

The development of medieval secular monody took place against the historical background of the Holy Roman Empire and the Romanesque. The "Holy Roman Empire of the German Nation" was founded in 962, with the crowning of Otto I as emperor. From 1024 to 1125 the Salic emperors ruled, with the widest extension of the realm under Henry III. From 1138 to 1254 the Hohenstaufens were in power, with Frederick I (Barbarossa) as emperor from 1152 to 1190. Then, from 1254 to 1273, there was an interregnum, during which the cities flourished. The Crusades occurred during the period from 1096 to 1229. From 987 to 1328 the Capetian kings ruled in France. In art, the Romanesque period was from about 1000 to about 1220; the Gothic from about 1220 to about 1550.

The flowering of secular monody was a phenomenon of what is usually referred to as chivalry. It manifested itself notably in France and Germany, but—at least so far as the music is concerned—at slightly different times, as suggested by the following chronological table:

	FRANCE	GERMANY
about 1080	Beginning of troubadour art	
1145–1195	Bernart de Ventadorn	
about 1150–1318		First flowering of the *Minnelied*
about 1170	Beginning of trouvère art	
about 1200	Culmination of troubadour art	
1207		Singing competition at the Wartburg
1230		Walther von der Vogelweide d.
1286–7	Adam de la Halle d.	
1318		Heinrich von Meissen, known as Frauenlob, d.
about 1380–1445		Second flowering of the *Minnelied*
1445		Oswald von Wolkenstein d.

This poetry and music of chivalry—usually referred to as that of the troubadours, trouvères, and minnesingers—is a notable historical artistic expression. It is amply preserved for us in notated music manuscripts and represents the first substantial musical development emanating from a secular level of society. A significant secular art, accordingly, found a place alongside the music of the church. It originated in Provence and, determined by the supranational character of chivalry, bore fruit in the art of the chivalric class in northern France, England, Germany, and other countries.

After 1200 knighthood began to develop as a self-contained social class. This was the first modern form taken by a culture organized around the court. The leading role thus passed from the clergy to chivalry. The secular poet crowded out the poetizing cleric. This new culture had in its nature some strongly feminine traits, particularly in the love songs. Increasingly it assigned a role to woman in both culture and art, as well as in society, that she had never before known. In the course of the history of chivalric poetry and music, representatives of various social classes played leading roles—kings and princes in Henry VI and William of Aquitaine, high nobility in Jaufré Rudel and Bertran de Born, lesser nobility in Walter von der Vogelweide, middle-class minstrels in Marcabru and Bernart de Ventadour, and members of the clergy. During the Late Middle Ages this culture rather suddenly and distinctly became bourgeois, but during most of the medieval period it is difficult to see any differentiation in the work of various poets in this tradition on the basis of the social levels from which they came.

One might wonder how this music came to be preserved for us in notated form. Why did the members of this social class, practicing a secular art, feel this was important? Why were both the poetry and the music often set down—in a somewhat novel notation—instead of being left to oral tradition as previously? As knighthood became conscious of being a distinct social group, it also became aware of history. It recognized its own artistic activity as something with its own right to be and its own basis alongside church music. The Crusades especially encouraged this awareness of rank and feeling of solidarity that extended beyond national boundaries.

The first independent creative activity of peoples north of the Alps for which we have clear evidence today occurred, as we have seen, in the trope and the sequence. Then, in the music of chivalry, a second great objectively verifiable act of fusion took place. It involved a union between impulses from sacred music and those from folk-music, which is otherwise not specifically documented; and it was accompanied by individual creative activity on the part of chivalric poet-composers. The poetry and music of knighthood came as an artistic outgrowth of feudal society.

Troubadours and Trouvères

Troubadour art began and reached its first height at the court of Count William IX of Aquitaine (1068–1127). From here it spread to the courts of the French and English kings. Eleanore of Aquitaine, the granddaughter of William IX, was married to King Louis VII of France from 1137 to 1152 and then to Henry Plantagenet, who, as Henry II, became King of England in 1154. One of her daughters, Maria, was married to Henry I of Champagne, who died in 1181; and the other, Aëlis, was the wife of Count Thibaut V of Blois, who died in 1191.

The first high point in this art was achieved by Bernart de Ventadorn (1145–1195), who composed only love songs. Early in troubadour art there appeared two trends that were to be richly developed: one, the *trobar clus*, a learned and later somewhat mannered and affected way of writing with recondite words and images, and the other, a simple and more folk-like style. Around 1200 the art of the troubadours attained its peak. It then quickly declined and disappeared as a result of the changed political situation in southern France, especially with the Albigensian War from 1209 to 1229.

The troubadour song of Provence was carried on further in the trouvère art of northern France, where its individual character was interwoven with something original that seemed to go back to a significantly older, popular artistic practice. The trouvère art created the heroic epic or *chanson de geste*. The best known poem of this type is the *Chanson de Roland*. Secular and sacred music intepenetrated trouvère art: sacred melodies were used for secular texts and vice versa. Poetic song-forms attained very great richness, and greater musical ability manifested itself among the northern French than among the Provençal poets. In troubadour art the preference had been for forms of the "hymn type"; but in trouvère art it seems to have leaned basically toward those of the "litany type." The first great period of trouvère art was the last third of the 12th century. About 1200 society began to be somewhat differently organized, as the commercial and cultural aspect of the cities attracted artists. Song of a class-consciously chivalric character declined. The learned townsman became the author, and members of the clerical class took part. A third period began around 1250 and extended to 1300. Though there had been associations of singers before, called *puis*, in which the townsmen also took part, these organizations now became the real supporters of the musical life, and in connection with them there arose the idea of the competition and the contest, in which individuals were "crowned" for the best achievements. The city of Arras became a center for the *puis*. Toward the end of the 13th century, however, their productive strength was exhausted, and they sank to a level of mere idle amusement.

The first historical evidence of bourgeois participation in European musical culture, however, is provided by trouvère song in its third phase, during the latter half of the 13th century, as well as by the song of the Meistersingers. The bourgeoisie took over the class-art of the chivalric aristocracy to develop it further in a very self-conscious and self-reliant way, especially in Germany. Its character was persistently conservative; it assured the continuation of the tradition even after the forms could no longer be filled with their proper artistic content. Not only the bourgeoisie in general but also the individual bourgeois trades or guilds, in particular, thus demonstrated their class-consciousness.

This music has been regarded as deriving from various sources: from popular song, widespread in the early Middle Ages; from the songs of the wandering minstrels and traveling singers, who maintained traditions going back to the mimes and *histriones* of Late Antiquity; and from Gregorian chant, particularly the sequence. The sources of the poetical texts have been attributed to impulses from antiquity such as the lyrics of Ovid and Horace, from the Persian-Arabic love-lyric, and from the Latin lyrics of the 12th century. Soon the new art received the national stamp of the individual European peoples. In a comparatively short time the troubadour art had spread widely from its place of origin in the province of Limousin, south of the Loire, centering in the Benedictine monastery of St.-Martial in Limoges.

The Art of the Troubadours and Trouvères

The troubadours, in general, lived south of the Loire. Their language was the *langue d'oc*, or Southern dialect. The trouvères, on the other hand, lived mainly north of the Loire. Their language, the *langue d'oïl*, led to modern French. Their activities coincided in point of time with the flowering of knighthood, more or less during the two hundred years from 1080 to 1280.

Troubadour song developed in three phases. The first, from about 1080 to 1150, included William IX of Aquitaine, Cercamon, and Marcabru; the second, from about 1150 to 1200, Bernart de Ventadorn, who ushered in the first golden age; and the third, from about 1200 to 1230, Peire Vidal, Folquet de Marseille, and Raimbaut de Vaqueiras, as well as—during the second half of the 13th century—Guirault Riquier.

The art of the trouvères began in the last third of the 12th century. Richard the Lion-Hearted, Blondel de Nesles, and Châtelain de Coucy belong chronologically to the first group; Gace Brulé to the second group, in the first quarter of the 13th century; and Thibault de Champagne, among others, to the third, within the second quarter. In the late period, to which Adam de la Halle also belongs, the initiative passed on over to the bourgeoisie who, as we have seen, had joined together in associations of singers called *puis*.

Troubadour art differed from trouvère more in language than in music. To some extent, there were members of the high nobility among the troubadours, such as Guilhem IX, Count of Poitiers and Duke of Aquitaine (d. ca. 1127), the first troubadour known by name; Counon de Béthume, diplomat in the Crusade of 1204; Johann de Brienne, King of Jerusalem; Pierre Mauclerc, Duke of Brittany; and Thibault, Count of Champagne, later King of Navarre (d. 1253). All these men were both poets and musicians; for, as Folquet de Marseille (d. 1231) said, "A verse without music is like a mill without water."

The connecting link between folk-music and troubadour art was provided by the jongleurs, whose name derived from that of the Latin *joculator*, and by the *menestrels*, the entertainers or traveling singers in Germany. They performed the music which the troubadours had composed, and perhaps on occasion also made up tunes of their own. The jongleurs often traveled about, as singers, jugglers, acrobats, or bear-trainers; but also among them were artists of higher station, sometimes in a definite relationship of service at the court—that is, as court poets—or traveling from court to court throughout all Europe. The minstrel or *Spielmann* represents a fusion of the traditions of the Early Medieval court singer and the mime of Antiquity. The "strolling scholar" wrote Latin; socially he was often *déclassé*, being a wandering, runaway cleric or a former and now vagabond student.

A higher level of musician, a professional class of jongleurs with school training, arose from among the minstrel folk during the 13th century. In 1288, with the founding of the Nicolai Brotherhood in Vienna, practicing musicians were brought together under the protection of the nobility and of a mock-prince, the "piper king." In 1321 a guild-like union of French instrumental musicians was established as the "Confrérie de St. Julien des ménestriers" in Paris. Along with all this there were traveling minstrels everywhere.

The type of song that flourished from about 1300 to 1530 can be spoken of as pan-European. There were many links between the various nations: traveling singers, such as Oswald von Wolkenstein; *histriones* and traveling players, who were in movement from Portugal to Poland; penitential processions; and pilgrimages, which throughout the year formed an important feature of life over wide areas of Europe. In this way individual melodies traveled from country to country.

Outstanding troubadours were Count Guilhem of Poitiers (1087–1127), Marcabru (first half of the 12th century), Gaucelm Faidit (last half of the 12th century), Raimbaut de Vaqueiras (d. 1207), Bernart de Ventadorn (d. 1195), who, according to Gennrich, brought the art of the troubadours "to a hitherto unattained height," Peire Vidal (d. 1205), and Raimon de Miraval (about 1200).

Outstanding trouvères were King Richard I (the Lion-Hearted) of England (d. 1199), Blondel de Nesle (born about 1155), Quesnes de Bethune (d. 1224), Thibault IV of Champagne, King of Navarre (d.

1253), Gace Brulé (d. about 1220), and Adam de la Halle (about 1237 to about 1286), servant of Robert II, Count of Artois, and composer of the pastoral drama *"Le Jeu de Robin et de Marion."*

The School of Arras in the 13th century was a center for the trouvères, including Jean Bretal and Adam de la Halle.

The compositions of the troubadours and trouvères are preserved in collective manuscripts, called *chansonniers*. Troubadour chansonniers preserve for us 273 melodies and some 2600 poems; trouvère, about 1700 melodies and about 2400 poems.

The music is in "square" or "quadratic" notation, written without indication of rhythm. The rhythm is assigned to the notation in accordance with the theory of the rhythmic modes. The six basic rhythmic types, which were associated by the mensural theorists with ancient rhythm, are listed in example 28. By counting back from the rhyming syllable, one

1. Modus	Trochee	— ‿
2. Modus	Iamb	‿ —
3. Modus	Dactyl	— ‿ ‿
4. Modus	Anapest	‿ ‿ —
5. Modus	Spondee	— —
6. Modus	Tribrach	‿ ‿ ‿

Example 28

can determine whether a verse has a rising (iambic or anapestic) or a falling (trochaic or dactyllic) rhythm. The second mode, or iambic with accented short and unaccented long, is characteristic of the Western Romanic area.

The Musical Forms

On the basis of the music, Gennrich classified troubadour and trouvère forms under four main headings, according to whether they derived from the litany, rondel, sequence, or hymn.

The first type, based on the same idea as the litany in the church service, includes four sub-types:

Chanson de geste, or epic chronicle of the deeds of famous heroes or the lives of saints. There is continuous repetition of melodic units *a* and *b*. Through the *chanson de geste* melodies have practically all disappeared, enough remains to give us an idea of them.

Laisse, involving a succession of two formal elements *a b* as in the *chanson de geste* but with the half-cadence being followed by a full cadence, either *a a a a . . . b* or *a b a b a b a b. . . .*

Rotrouenge, in which the same melody is repeated for several lines, with a refrain regularly forming the close.

Chanson avec des refrains, or song with several refrains, in which all stanzas end in refrains that are varied or different from each other. In the *chanson à refrain* the same refrain appears without variation.

The second basic type goes back to the rondel, or stanzaic song consisting of one unit sung first by the leader and then by the chorus, and then another unit first by the leader and then by the chorus. This appears in the following three sub-types:

Rondeau, in the simplest form of which there are six lines of text, set to two short melodic elements in alternation between leader and chorus, in which the chorus has one refrain: *a* (solo), *A* (chorus), *ab* (solo), *AB* (chorus). In a slightly more elaborate form the refrain also stands at the very beginning: *AB aA ab AB.*

Virelai, in which a refrain *A* stands at the beginning and the end of the stanza. Each stanza has a short repeated melodic unit *b* (referred to, in German, as two *Stollen*) and a concluding unit *a* (or *Abgesang*), which has the same melody as the refrain. Thus the pattern is *AbbaA.*

Ballade, in which an independent musical number is introduced, giving the basic pattern *aabC.*

The third basic type goes back to the sequence, in which the melody appears first in a section, then in a repetition of this section with different words, then a new section, then repetition of it with still different words, and so on. Sequence-type troubadour and trouvère melodies include the *lai, estampie,* and *note.* Here, as in the parent sequence-form, the same melodic group is repeated to changing texts. Among these secular counterparts to the sequence, the *lai* or *leich* is vocal, the *estampie* instrumental.

Finally, springing from the same root as the hymn, are the *vers,* in which each stanza is through-composed, and the *canzone,* consisting of two *Stollen* and an *Abgesang* that often at the end coincides musically with the end of the *Stollen* (*ab ab cdb*).

The Poetic Forms

On the basis of the words, the songs of the troubadours and trouvères fall into a number of distinct types. The *sirventes,* or "service-songs," were songs of praise, satire, or mockery, usually with moral, political, or personal content. They are so called from having been normally addressed to the feudal lord. The *Planch* or *planctus* ("lament") was a song of mourning on the death of a great personage such as a king, queen, or nobleman. As a form it goes back to the 7th century. The *aubes* was a dialogue between the lover and the watchman, warner, or death. The *tenso, partimen,* or *jeu-parti* was a discussion by several persons singing in alternation, mostly on questions of love. The designations *canson, vers,* and *chanson* refer to simple or artful stanzaic songs, usually about love. The *pastorela* was also a love-song, with suggestions of a rustic setting and usually of the relationship between a knight and a shepherdess or country girl. The *balada* or *dansa* was a dance-song, usually with choral refrain alternating with intervening soloistic portions.

The Minnesingers

German *Minnelieder* grew out of the art of the French troubadours. We know that the Minnesingers often translated from the French and were otherwise indebted to French models. The relationship between the two cultures was also fostered by the marriage of Frederick Barbarossa and Beatrix of Burgundy in 1156. The trouvère Guiot de Provins followed her to Germany, and we still have a song of his with its German imitation. The Minnesingers, moreover, borrowed from Gregorian chant, from popular song, and from the Latin poetry of the wandering students, the most important manuscript of which is perhaps the Carmina Burana, collected about 1280 in Bavaria and provided with relatively few melodies in neumes. The textual motifs of *Minnelieder* are in great part taken from the lyrics of the troubadours and the trouvères; also the forms, almost without exception, come from this source.

The Minnesinger repertoire developed in two great epochs. The first flowering occurred between 1150 and 1318, the year of the death of Heinrich von Meissen, called Frauenlob. It culminated between 1190 and 1230, in the work of the Minnesingers Walther von der Vogelweide (about 1170 to 1230), Heinrich von Morungen, Reinmar der Alte, Hartmann von Aue, and Neidhart von Reuenthal. Today it is not known for certain whether in 1205 the singing contest at the Wartburg was held under the auspices of Count Hermann of Thuringia.

This first period of its flowering permits still further subdivision. The time up to about 1250 included the "classical" epoch of song composition, when the Minnesingers were mostly of noble birth. The period after 1250—marked by the composition of *Sprüche*, or fables of political or social import—was one in which the poets were mostly of the middle class and began to call themselves "masters."

The names of the most important Minnesingers may be grouped by regions:

Austria: Reinmar der Alte, Neidhart von Reuenthal (last traceable in 1237), and for a while Walther von der Vogelweide

Bavaria and Swabia: the Counts of Regensburg and Reitenburg, Meinloh Sevelingen, Friedrich von Hausen, Tannhäuser, Ulrich von Lichtenstein, and Reinmar von Zweter

Thuringia: Heinrich von Veldeke, Heinrich von Morungen, Walther von der Vogelweide, and Wolfram von Eschenbach

Upper Saxony: Heinrich von Meissen, otherwise known as Frauenlob.

The medieval lyric is quite varied in character. The poetic content in the courtly *Minnelied* centers on the knight's courtship of the lady, conceived of as his "serving" her. The *Spruch* deals more with didactic and political themes. The melodies are modal, with sparing use of melismas. The Minnesingers preferred to compose in *Bar*-form (*aab*, or two *Stollen* and an *Abgesang*). The music observes the syllable stress, and allows a free number of intervening unstressed syllables. As a rule, the same person wrote both the words and the music. Soloistic one-voiced song was accompanied instrumentally by the fiddle or the harp, as shown in the pictorial representations in the "Great Heidelberg Song-Manuscript." As the two musical voices collaborated, there were undoubtedly some heterophonic deviations between them; and occasionally there were brief instrumental preludes, interludes, or postludes.

The most important forms were the *lied, tagelied, leich,* and *spruch.* The *lied* corresponded to the Provençal *canso* and was an idealistic love-song. The *tagelied* was the Provençal *alba* or watchman's song. The *leich,* essentially the same as the *lai,* included as sub-types the sequence *leich* and the dance *leich*. The *spruch*, literally a "saying" or "proverb," was a fable of political or social content.

The manuscript sources most extensively provided with melodies are the song codices from Jena and Colmar, containing respectively 91 and 107 melodies, which were prepared in the late 14th or 15th century. In the former, the one-voiced melodies are sketched out in square notation, and in the latter in Gothic neumes. The music is to be interpreted not according to the modal theory, but the rhythm is to be derived from the rhythm of the text. The most significant purely textual manuscript without melodies is the Great Heidelberg Song-Manuscript, written in the 14th century. The melodies of German *Minnelieder* that have been preserved come only in very small part from the written versions of direct or approximately contemporary sources, which have been transmitted for the most part by the Meistersingers in presumably altered versions. Over sixty melodies by Neidhart von Reuenthal are preserved in five different sources; and only three by Walther von der Vogelweide, in a 14th-century manuscript, including the "Palestine Song" of 1228. Other of his melodies come from Meistersinger tradition. The Jena manuscript notably contains the work of some lesser composers from the 13th century, the Colmar that of some from the 14th.

The second flowering of the *Minnelied* occurred from about 1380 to 1445. It was already under way at the time of the decline of chivalry and the rise of the Meistersingers. Thus the forms of the *Minnelied*, the *Meisterlied*, and the German *Volkslied* or folk-song overlap with the beginnings of German polyphonic forms, as will be seen later. Three individuals figure prominently in this period, linking the late form of the *Minnelied* with polyphony and providing a transition to the forms of German polyphonic song. One is Hermann, Monk of Salzburg, who lived at the court of Archbishop Pilgrim (1365–1396) and is credited with the first attempt at polyphonic song-forms in three compositions, preserved in the Mondsee Vienna song-manuscript. Another is Hugo of Montfort (1357–1423) in Bregenz, whose songs are preserved in one voiced melodies that come from the musician Bürk Mangolt. The third is Oswald von Wolkenstein, who lived from about 1377 to 1445 and is regarded as the last of the Minnesingers. In the course of his adventurous life he traveled widely. His forty songs in two and three voices are eclectic in character, with various direct borrowings from the French.

Denmark

Among the more substantial farmers and other freemen in Northern Europe there was widespread interest in harp-playing and in furthering the art of the *skalds*. Presumably these forms of music prevailed before chivalric song made its appearance. Medieval culture bloomed fully in central and western Europe before spreading to the North. The natives there often opposed this development at first and held firmly to the patterns of life that had been established from pre-Christian times. Icelandic sagas recounting the history of local families and legends of Norwegian and Danish royalty show that harp-playing and the skaldic art were highly regarded as skill and were even considered a form of magic. The same attitudes are also manifest in Saxo Grammaticus' *Gesta Danorum* (about 1200). Entertainers and minstrels traveled through Northern lands and occasionally were received at royal courts. They were, however, resented by the skalds and could not claim social equality with them.

During the 12th century medieval culture spread to the North, where a "chivalric age" attained full development between about 1250 and 1350. There was then a significant flowering of Danish "folk-tunes." This term, however, is somewhat misleading, as the songs in question belonged to a courtly art, which only later was taken up popularly and thus was rescued from oblivion. The repertoire that has been preserved to date consists entirely of dance songs. Though familiar with the art of the German minnesingers, the anonymous poet-composers of these "folk-tunes" may well have been educated in Paris. The songs are often in two lines with medial and terminal rhyme or in four lines with refrain. There is epic presentation of contemporary, historical, or supernatural incidents. They were sung by a leading singer or by singers in alternation, who also led the dance, while the rest of the group joined in on the end-rhymes and the refrain. A similar type of song was apparently also current in Sweden.

Only one melody *"Drømte mig en drøm i nat"* is preserved for us in an actual, though incomplete, manuscript version of about 1350, included in the *Codex runicus*, in square notes and runic characters. Most of the texts were collected and written out during the 16th and 17th centuries, but very few melodies from earlier periods have been handed down. It was not until about 1800 that a beginning was made toward rescuing the melodies from oblivion. An early edition was issued by H. W. F. Abrahamson, R. Nyerup, and K. L. Rahbek as the 5th volume in the *Udvalgte danske Viser fra Middelalderen* (1814). Since then there has been a succession of more inclusive and systematic collections of similar intent.

Poland

With the beginning of the 15th century, we have reports of secular song in Poland. Jan Długosz (d. 1480), the chronicler of the Jagiellonian epoch, refers to two historical songs which were popularly sung in his day, one about the death of Prince Roman at Zawichost in 1205 and the other about Ludgarda, the wife of Prince Przemysław, who was strangled by order of her husband in 1283. From many decrees of synods that forbade all usages connected with the rites of heathen cults and from Latin sermons about them we know the beginnings of folk-songs which accompanied these forbidden practices: *"Miły miłą miłuje"* or The Dearest Loves His Dearest (about 1390), *"Nie wybiraj junochu oczyma"* (about 1460), *"Dusza z ciała wyleciała"* (about 1470), and others. From about 1200 or earlier, there are documents attesting to the presence of wandering scholars and minstrels. An interesting example of a wandering scholar's song is the Gregorian antiphon with secular words "*Defectus misit nos,*" first written down in 1510.

The tradition of the Bohemian singing movement appeared in Poland at the end of the 14th and beginning of the 15th century—possibly as a result of the temporary closing of the University of Cracow from 1370 to 1400 and the transfer of some of the students to Prague. Favorite songs were "*Buoh všemohúcí,*" sung in the Polish phonetic version "*Bog fschechmogączi,*" and many satirical or political songs in connection with religious conflicts such as the Hussite movement. The danger that Hussite influences might spread to Poland led the church authorities in 1415 to forbid the singing of secular songs in the vernacular. One of the few extant remains is the somewhat frivolous scholar's song written down in 1416 about the woman who would not give the student's horse any oats. The text comes from the Polish-Bohemian linguistic border, as does the work of Jędrzej Galka of Dobczyn "*Pieśń o Wiklefie*" (1447) to the melody of the Christmas song "*Imber nunc coelitus.*"

We do not have any very direct knowledge of Polish chivalric songs on secular themes, though they are mentioned in the chronicles of Gallus (1113) and of Wincenty Kadłubek (1202). After the death of Bolesław Chrobry in 1025, the knights sang a *carmen lugubre,* and by means of a chivalric song Kazimierz the Renovator was honored for having rebuilt Poland after the period of heathen reaction (1038–9). Many songs arose in connection with military events in which Bolesław Krzywousty was engaged in Pomerania, such as the conquest of Kołobrzeg (1104) and the Battle of Nakło (1109), in which Bolesław Kędzierzawy fought with the Pruzzi (1166). It is likely that these works were structurally like the sirventes, and these indications show that it was also quite likely that the chivalric lyric flourished in Poland.

The Meistersingers

In the bourgeois world of the cities the *Meistersingers* carried on the traditions of the *Minnesingers.* A transition is provided by the work of Heinrich von Meissen, who established the *Meistersinger* school in Mainz. At first there were traveling masters, such as Hans Rosenplüt or Michel Behaim (d. 1474), but gradually schools developed. Later only the schools in the cities survived and were in close connection with the guilds. Mainz had one as early as 1370. During their heyday from 1440 to about 1600 the main centers were Mainz, Colmar, Augsburg, Nuremberg (which flourished in the second third of the 16th century), Strassburg, Freiburg, Ulm, Zwickau, Prague, Danzig, and Breslau. Despite the artistic decline in the 17th century, individual schools remained in existence. The last Meistersinger guild was dissolved in 1839 in Ulm, and the last Meistersinger died in 1876.

Musically, the unaccompanied, monodic song of the Meistersingers followed the Minnesingers' model. The Meistersingers were both poets and singers. They had high regard for the discovery of new tunes and "tones" as an artistic achievement and gave them distinctive names such as the "Blue-Knightspur Tune" or the "Departed-Gluttony Tone." These names then became traditional. Melismas were called "blossoms." The rules according to which judgment was to be rendered were set down in the *Tabulatur* and were enforced by the "marker." The local singing schools had precise regulations for admission, education, and continuation of studies. Gradations were established between pupils, school-friends, singers, poets, and masters. The schools had insignia, badges, and flags. The songs of the Meistersingers represented, for the most part, only an amateur art, somewhat overdone in terms of the rules of verse technique, stressing elements of craftsmanship in artistic creation and setting its practitioners apart from the minstrels. Along with polyphonic song as a specially oriented type of music, the work of the Meistersingers is an especially noteworthy expression of bourgeois musical culture in Germany.

Among well-known masters were Hanz Folz, Hans Rosenplüt, and particularly Hans Sachs (1494–1576) in Nuremberg. His "Silver Tune" with the words "*Salve, ich gruss dich schone*" is a Protestant paraphrase of the "*Salve Regina*" of particular artistic merit.

Bibliography

Exs. Sch 11–15, 78, 79; W. Apel, *Rondeaux, Virelais, and Ballades in French 13th Century Song* (JAMS VII, 1954); J. B. Beck, *Die Melodien der Troubadours und Trouvères* (Strassburg 1908); H. Brinkmann, *Entstehungsgesch. d. Minnegesanges* (1926); J. Chailley, *Autour de la Chanson de Geste* (AMl 1955); K. Drescher, *Nürnberger Meistersinger-Protokolle von 1575–1689* (2 vols., 1898); E. Faral, *Les Jongleurs en France au moyen âge* (Paris 1910); F. Gennrich, *Der mus. Nachlass der Troubadours* (Darmstadt 1958), *Grundriss einer Formenlehre d. mittelalterl. Liedes* (Halle 1932), *Mittelalterliche Lieder mit textloser Melodie* (AfMw 1952), and *Rondeaux, Virelais u. Balladen* (2 vols., Dres. 1921, and Göttingen 1927); K.-W. Gümpel, *Hugo Spechtshart von Reutlingen. Flores musicae (1332–4)* (Wiesbaden 1958); A. Hauser, *Sozialgesch. der Kunst u. Literatur* (Munich 1953); J. A. Huisman, *Neue Wege zur dichterischen u. mus. Technik Walthers v. d. Vogelweide* (Utrecht 1950); H. Husmann, *Die mus. Behandlg. d. Versarten im Troubadourgesang der Notre-Dame-Zeit* (AMl 1953), *Zur Grundlegung der musikalischen Rhythmik des mittellateinischen Liedes* (AfMw IX, 1952), and *Zur Rhythmik des Trouvèregesangs* (Mf 1952); E. Jammers, *Die Melodien Hugos von Montfort* (AfMw 1956) and *Untersuchungen über d. Rhythmik u. Melodik d. Melodien d. Jenaer Liederhandschrift* (ZfMw VII); K. K. Klein, ed., *Die Lieder O. v. Wolkensteins* (Tübingen 1962); A. Kühn, *Rhythmik u, Melodik Michael Behaims* (Diss. 1907); W. Lipphardt, *Unbekannte Weisen zu den Carmina burana* (AfMw 1955); E. Lommatzsch, *Leben u. Lieder der provenz. Troubadours. I. Minnelieder* (Bln. 1957); H. J. Moser, *Gesch. d. dt. Musik I;* G. Müller, *Studien z. Formproblem d. Minnesangs* (DVLG I, 1923); W. Müller-Blattau, *Trouvères u. Minnesänger* (Saarbrücken 1956); B. Nagel, ed., *Der dt. Meistersang* (Heidelberg 1952, Darmstadt 1967); W. Nagel, *Studien z. Gesch. d. Meistersänger* (Langensalza 1908); A. Pillet and H. Carstens, *Bibliographie der Troubadours* (Halle 1933); W. Salmen, *Der fahrende Sänger im europäischen Mittelalter* (Kassel 1960), *European Song 1300–1530* (NOHM

III), and *O. von Wolkenstein* (MD 1953); H. Spanke, *Bez. zwischen roman. u. mittelalt. Rhythmik* (Bln. 1936) and *Marcabrustudien* (Göttingen 1940); W. Stammler, *Die Wurzeln des Meistergesanges* (DVLG I, 1923); H. Venderwerf, *Deklamatorischer Rhythmus in den Chansons der Trouvères* (Mf 1967); J. Wendler, *Studien zur Melodiebildung bei O. v. Wolkenstein* (Tutzing 1963); J. A. Westrup, *Medieval Song* (NOHM II); R. Wustmann, *W. v. d. Vogelweide* (Strassburg 1913); H. Zingerle, *Tonalität u. Melodieführung in d. Klauseln der Troubadours- und Trouvèreslieder* (Munich 1958); R. Zitzmann, *Die Melodien d. Kolmarer Liederhandschrift* (Würzburg 1944); arts. Ballade, Jeu parti, Lai, Leich, Lied, Meistergesang, and on individuals (MGG). *Source Readings on the art of the Meistersinger:* A. Puschmann, *Grundl. Bericht d. dt. Meistergesanges samt der Tabulatur, 1571* (new ed. 1888); C. Spangenberg, *Lob, Nutzen u. Wirkung d. löblichen Gesellschaft d. Meistersinger, 1598* (new ed. 1861); C. Wagenseil, *Buch v. d. Meistersinger holdseliger Kunst, 1697* (most important source for R. Wagner). *Editions:* P. Aubry, *Le Chansonnier de l'Arsenal* (facs. and transcr., Paris 1909); C. Appel, *Die Singweisen Bernarts von Ventadorn* (Halle 1934); J. Beck, *Les Chansonniers des Troubadours et des Trouvères* (2 vols., facs. and transcr., Paris 1927 and 1938); G. Cohen, *Adam le Bossu, dit de la Halle, Le Jeu de Robin et de Marion* (Paris 1935); E. de Coussemaker, *Oeuvres complètes du trouvère A. de la Halle, poésies et musique* (Paris 1872); A. Jeanroy et al., ed., *Lais et descorts français du XIIIe siècle* (Paris 1901); A. Jeanroy, ed., *Le Chansonnier d'Arras* (facs., Paris 1925); F. A. Mayer and H. Rietsch, eds., *Mondsee-Wiener Liederhandschrift* (Bln. 1894–6); P. Meyer and G. Raynaud, eds., *Le Chansonnier de St-Germain* (facs., Paris 1892); K. K. Müller, ed., *Jenaer Liederhandschrift* (facs., Jena 1896, transcr. by G. Holz, F. Saran, and E. Bernoulli, Lpz. 1901); G. Münzer, ed., *Das Singebuch des Adam Puschmann, nebst den Originalmelodien des Michael Behaim u. Hans Sachs* (Lpz. 1907); P. Runge, ed., *Hugo von Montfort* (Lpz. 1906) and *Kolmarer Handschrift* (Lpz. 1896); R. Staiger, *Die Liederhandschrift des Benedict von Watt* (Lpz. 1914); J. Tiersot, *Sur le jeu de Robin et de Marion* (Paris 1899); *Carmina burana* (facs., IMM, Brooklyn, N. Y.); *Heinrich Frauenlob* (DTÖ 20, 2); *Adam de la Halle* (coll. ed. in prep. AIM); *Neidhardt v. Reuenthal* (DTÖ 37, 1); *Troubadours, Trouvères, Minne- u. Meistergesang* (MW); *Oswald v. Wolkenstein* (DTÖ 9, 1).

Minnesänger: Neidhart von Reuenthal new ed. DTÖ 37, 1; *Walther von der Vogelweide* ex. Sch 12; *Heinrich von Meissen* new ed. DTÖ 20, 2, and Sch 21; *Hermann, Monk of Salzburg* new ed. in Mondsee-Wiener MS; *Hugo von Montfort* new ed. 1906; *Oswald von Wolkenstein* DTÖ 9, 1, and Sch 46.

Denmark: E. Abrahamsen, *Éléments Romans et Allemands dans le chant Grégorien et la chanson populaire en Danemark* (Diss., Copenh. 1923); E. Dal, *Nordisk folkeviseforskning siden 1800* (Copenh. 1956, with Engl. summary); H. Thuren, *Das dänische Volkslied* (ZIMG 1907–8); art. Danemark in "Folklore musical" (Paris 1940).

Poland: new ed. in H. Kowalewicz, *Cantica Medii Aevi Polono-Latina* (Warsaw 1964).

Meistersinger: Sachs exs. Sch 78, 79.

15. Medieval Polyphonic Music

The cultural history of France played an especially important role in early medieval polyphony. From 987 to 1328, the Capetians were the hereditary rulers, and the authority of the crown was greatly strengthened under Philip Augustus, who reigned from 1180 to 1223; Louis IX (the Saint) from 1226 to 1270; and Philip IV (the Fair) from 1285 to 1314. Thus began French centralization. Great monastic orders were established: the Cluniacs at Cluny in 910, the Cistercians at Citeaux in 1098, and the Premonstratensians at Prémontré in 1120. Universities were founded, notably at Toulouse in 1229 and the Sorbonne in 1254. The 13th century was called the High Scholastic period, and Roger Bacon (d. 1294), Albertus Magnus (d. 1280), and St. Thomas Aquinas (d. 1274) were its leaders. The house of Valois ruled in France from 1328 to 1589 while the more than a century-long Hundred Years' War raged between France and England from 1339 to 1453.

The salient points in early polyphonic development may be listed thus:

about 850 to about 1130	Early organum
latter half of 9th cent.	"Musica enchiriadis," formerly ascribed to Hucbald of St. Amand (d. about 930)
about 1030	Treatise by Guido d'Arezzo (d. 1050)
beginning of 11th cent.	Winchester Tropar
12th cent.	St. Martial organa
2nd quarter of 12th cent.	Santiago de Compostella organa
toward 1100	Beginning of the motet
about 1150 to about 1250	Notre Dame Epoch. Leonin and Perotin. Organum and Conductus
about 1180	Beginning of modal rhythm (Northern France)
about 1180 to about 1250	Dominance of modal rhythm
about 1250	Transition to mensural notation
about 1250 to about 1320	Ars antiqua
about 1250	d. of Franco of Cologne, who represented, with Adam de la Halle, the older group of motet composers
about 1270	Report of Anonymus IV
1286–7	Adam de la Halle d.
from about 1280	Petrus de Cruce, representative of younger group of motet composers
1291–1361	Philippe de Vitry
about 1290 to after 1351	Johannes de Muris
about 1320	Beginning of Ars nova. Philippe de Vitry's *Ars nova* treatise
about 1300 to 1377	Guillaume de Machaut

There has been much speculation about the origin of Western polyphony. European music differs from non-European (or from that which has been directly stimulated by European styles), in that it is essentially harmonic and polyphonic. Musicologists have been particularly concerned with trying to establish:

1. What the historical situation was in which Western music began to go its own way, toward harmonic polyphony;
2. Why it did so; and
3. How early medieval European polyphony was related to the polyphony that presumably existed in antiquity and particularly to the various polyphonic forms of non-European music.

In trying to clarify these matters, they have hypothesized origins among the ancient Greeks, the Teutons, and various non-European peoples. All three possibilities are tantalizingly suggestive, but none seems objectively conclusive.

As to the hypothesis of the ancient Greek origin of polyphony, some musicologists have proceeded from the fact that the people of antiquity at least were aware of the basic concepts of simultaneous sounds in music and actually practiced them to some extent. This was certainly not a complete technique of polyphonic music-making in our sense of the term, but the germ of it was there. In Late Antiquity polyphony seems to have been used for musical show. It is likely that the ancient practice was carried on even in the Papal chapel, where, according to sources attributed to the 8th century, there was a group of paraphonists who performed music presumably based on fifths. Theoreticians called the first notated evidences of Western polyphony "diaphony"—or, more commonly, "organum."

The Greeks called the theory of tonal simultaneity *symphonia,* and the Latins translated the word as *consonantia.* Intervals were classified by the Greeks into two groups. The first included the octave, or *antiphon,* in which one voice sounded *against* the other; the fifth; and the fourth, or *paraphon,* in which one voice was thought of as sounding *beside* the other. The second group included the other intervals, which were called *diaphon,* or one voice sounding apart from the other (in Latin, dissonant). The diaphonic intervals usable in the melody were called *emmelic,* or "in the melody"; the opposite was *ekmelic,* or "outside the melody."

As for the hypothesis that Western polyphony came from the Teutons, some scholars have pointed out that Teutonic music was supposed to be "sonorous," whereas Gregorian was monodically "linear and melodic." It is thereby credited with the potential for developing European harmonic polyphony.

In elaboration of this Teutonic theory, musicologists recognize that the music of the Teutons was characterized by larger intervals and leaps than that of the Mediterranean cultural circle, which was typified by small intervallic steps. They attempt to support this view further by observing elements of pentatonic structure (free of half steps) in the oldest folk-songs and children's counting rhymes, such as those found in Westphalia, as well as in the Teutonic choral dialect of Gregorian chant.

But what, really, do we know about the music of the Teutons? Since there was no written notation, we can draw inferences from Roman literary and pictorial evidence and from instruments that have been found. Tacitus makes a number of allusions to music in his *Germania:* to "carmina antiqua," which celebrated incidents in mythology; to war songs in battle; to "songs of happiness"; and to the *barbitus* (meaning uncertain). From numerous bits of evidence up to the 7th century it seems that the style of Teutonic music and its manner of delivery must have been quite different from that of the Roman. Among the instruments found, the *lurer* are outstanding in instrumental quality and craftsmanship. Moreover, horns from the Bronze Age, used in religious worship, have been excavated, as well as lyres and harps.

The lurer, distinctive wind instruments from the Bronze Age, were widespread throughout Denmark, Scandinavia, and Northern Germany around 1000 B.C. Though the instruments, found in pairs, are precisely tuned together, they do not lend themselves to the assumption that they were played together polyphonically. Instruments constructed in pairs but not used harmonically are to be found in Palestine, Afghanistan, India, and Tibet. The *lurer* are not military instruments, but instruments of worship. They are between about five feet and seven and a half feet long. From the recurrence of pairs of *lurer* tuned in unison, R. v. Ficker concluded (in accordance with his speculations on "primary forms of sonority") that "the music of the *lurer* was decidedly a music of sonority, but not one of 'polyphony.'"

In support of a third possible source of Western polyphony, comparative musicologists have based a theory on their systematic research into the polyphony of non-European peoples, from primitive tribes to high cultures. Hucbald's organum seems "primitive" if one makes the mistake of viewing it as the beginning of Western polyphony. In reality, however, it is a matter of "completely developed musical phenomena" and, according to Marius Schneider, is "the end-point in a rather long succession of developments." Although it does seem likely that one should assume a direct relationship between the non-European examples and polyphony from the time of Hucbald to that of the St. Martial school, comparison of the forms in detail permits one to draw some remarkable analogies. For early European polyphony three areas are hypothesized:

1. the early French-Italian area with essentially tetrachordal structure, stressing the fourth;
2. the early English and partly northern French area with pentachordal structure, stressing the third and fifth; and
3. the St. Martial school in the 12th century, in which the first two types completely intermingle and lead to new harmonic forms.

Although the method of comparative research into melodies is somewhat indirect, it does yield some idea of the music of the early period in Europe and of the roots of Western music. The fact has been established that, as Wiora writes, "some types and formulae" of European music of the Middle Ages are pre-medieval, such as the patterns for singing epic songs or *chansons de geste,* the *Geisslerlieder,* and the Easter songs *"Christ ist erstanden"* and *"Erstanden ist der heilig Christ."* These come from types of melody that must have been substantially older. Three bodies of melody have been compared with some degree of thoroughness:

folk-traditions in outlying regions of Europe, from the Balkans to Ireland, from Spain to Finland; medieval notated versions of sacred and secular songs, old strata of Gregorian chant, and refrains of social songs from the troubadours and trouvères on; and non-European music, especially of peoples with Eurasian and Eurafrican connections, such as the Finno-ugric tribes, the Kirgiz, and the Mongols.

Early Organum (*from about 900 to about 1130*)

The first records of the oldest form of Western polyphony, organum, are handed down to us as examples in musical treatises. The most ancient of these are the treatises of Cologne and Paris, the Musica Enchiriadis, and the so-called Bamberg Scholia. The main source is the Musica Enchiriadis, a treatise on music theory widely disseminated throughout Europe from the latter half of the 9th century, formerly ascribed to Hucbald of St. Amand (d. 930). The Musica Enchiriadis explains two different types of organum: that at the fifth and that at the fourth.

In organum at the fifth the given Gregorian cantus firmus was doubled simultaneously at the fifth and octave, thus producing what is otherwise known as "paraphony" or parallel song, at different voice-levels.

Sit glo-ri-a do-mi-ni in saecula, laetabitur dominus in o-pe-ri-bus su-is

Example 29

For organum at the fourth, on the other hand, rules were given for a definite way of presenting a cantus firmus that was placed over the accompanying voice.

vox principalis:

vox organalis: Rex coe-li do - mi - ne ma - ris un - di - so - nis.

Example 30

Te hu - mi - les fa - mu - li mo - du - lis ve - ne - ran - do pi - is

Example 31

The two voices begin in unison; but the "vox organalis" performs its accompanying role on a stationary tone until the main interval of accompaniment, the fourth, is reached. Then the accompanying voice moves along with the cantus firmus in parallel fourths to end again at the unison. According to the theoreticians' description, the diads thus arising are spread out over a considerable tonal area by doubling, and they are paraphrased. Organal music-making is called *concentus concor-*

diter dissonans, or a fusion of both voices while keeping their individualities intact, and is also called *diaphonia cantilena,* or "twin song." If several singers and instrumentalists participated, and if each sound was to some extent paraphrased, the resulting succession of sounds must have been rather heavy, *cum modesta morositate,* and thus, slow. Not only does the use of instruments lend itself to this music on the basis of its sonority (the name *organum* means "instrument"), but it has been directly alluded to by the theoreticians themselves.

The best known evidence for the use of instruments in this period is the dedication of an organ of twenty-six bellows and over four hundred pipes in 980 at Winchester Cathedral in England. When two monks played this organ, one presumably had the *vox principalis* and the other the *vox organalis* of an organum.

The earliest preserved forms of organum have been explained by Heinrich Husmann as being modeled on the organ—not in the sense that polyphonic music was already being performed on that instrument, but in the sense that it arose from the characteristic sonority of the organ of the time, which had mixtures, octaves, and fifths. The organ was accordingly a "polyphonic" instrument and the model for vocal music-making. Organum at the fifth conformed strictly to this pattern. Organum at the fourth, however, already exhibited a comparatively free form and introduced dissonant intervals.

Perhaps the oldest record of organum, written by an Irish philosopher active in France, Johannes Scotus (or Johannes Erigena, *ca.* 810–885), follows the teaching of the Musica Enchiriadis in his *"De divisione naturae,"* but gives no independent description of its practice. The first treatise after the Musica Enchiriadis to concern itself again with organum comes from the 11th-century "Micrologus de disciplina artis musicae" (*ca.* 1030) of Guido d'Arezzo (d. 1050), who described and taught much the same thing, but in a somewhat different manner. He did not use the same system or the Dasia notation of the Musica Enchiriadis. He therefore had to set up the rules for organum on a somewhat different basis.

The next treatise on organum, the Milan treatise *"Ad organum faciendum,"* was written a little later than Guido's "Micrologus." The anonymous writer acknowledged Guido as a source and even borrowed examples from him. But there is an essential difference between his and the older theoretical work: the cantus firmus now does not lie above, but below the accompanying voice. As yet, there is no completely satisfactory explanation for this shift of relative positions.

The first collection of organa is the so-called Winchester Tropar, from the beginning of the 11th century (MS. Cambridge Corpus Christi College 473). It contains 164 two-voiced organa, which are, however, notated in unlined neumes and therefore cannot be reliably transcribed today. Although one can recognize that an organal voice corresponds more or less to each tone of the cantus firmus, one cannot tell whether the accompanying voice lies above or below the cantus firmus.

The process of making the individual sounds independent brought with it a further retardation of the progress from note to note, so that the Gregorian melody was no longer heard as melody. It was, however, still of central importance as "cantus firmus," or "petrified song," and the intellectual basis of the whole.

The history of organum is divided into five stages: first, each voice developed an autonomous area of sonority, or of sonorous space (*Klangraum*), in organum at the fifth (Ex. 29); then individual steps of sonority were developed in organum at the fourth (Exs. 30 and 31). Then, during the 12th century, the voice that had been added to the cantus firmus began to move in rhythmically free melismas. As a reaction to this trend the voices were subjected to a strict metrical order, as in the Notre Dame School. Finally, the voices acquired their own individual texts, leading to the development of the motet around 1100.

The unusually slow development of polyphony until about 1150 is attributed to the strongly conservative temper of the times, which held firmly to values once they had been established. This inertia corresponds to the pre-capitalistic and pre-rationalistic economy and to a pre-individualistic intellectual concept and attitude; the idea of progress was as yet unknown. Polyphonic music was to be found in the worship service of the church and in the possession of a clerical elite, and was not yet an object of aesthetic enjoyment. Its characteristic feature was that of clinging to whatever was typical and formalistic, maintaining intact the transcendental orientation.

Beginning with the 12th century we face an altered situation. Dom Anselm Hughes has described it as occurring in the following sequence:

1. The manuscripts both of Gregorian chant and of polyphony began to establish the exact pitch.
2. Rules for the organization of the lapse of time in the music must have come to be observed, for in the one voice there stand two or more notes against only one in the other voice.
3. A new situation, accordingly, arose in the relationship of the individualized voices to one another.
4. The idea of a harmonic cadence came into existence.
5. The range of voices was now greater.
6. Accordingly, there now appeared the first notated examples of three-voiced composition.

The new style was also called organum, but it was in no way a continuation of the old. Instead, it was an entirely new creation of the period around 1150 and is referred to as "classical organum."

This new stage of development appeared in some sixty-five organa of the school of the St. Martial monastery in Limoges, southeast of Poitiers. These are preserved in three manuscripts in Paris and one in London, written in diastematic neumes. They date from the end of the 11th to the beginning of the 13th century. Melismas were placed over the extended tones of the cantus firmus, and the cantus firmus thus took another step in the direction of petrifaction. The originally improvised performance of the *vox organalis* began to turn into a sort of *res facta*, or composition. In the formation of the counter-voice one can observe a process of linearization, clearly under the influence, and after the model, of Gregorian chant. Melismas that seem to be in rather free rhythms and improvised are quite like those of the Gregorian Gradual and Responsory.

We cannot establish precisely the point at which the entirely free rhythmic melismas pass over into a more mensurally oriented interpretation. When a third voice was added as a triplum to the duplum, presumably there was a rhythmic interpretation in accordance with modal theory.

The same technique as in the St. Martial organa appears in the organa of the St. John liturgy of the famous and much visited Spanish pilgrimage-place of Santiago de Compostela. It is contained in the *Codex Calixtinus*, written in the second quarter of the 12th century.

The 12th-century "Vatican Treatise" gives directions for performing the individualized sounds in an improvisatory way, with an abundance of extended examples.

These organa were usually based on tropes and sequences, that is, the cantus firmi usually came from the secondary stratum of Gregorian chant that had developed north of the Alps during the Carolingian period.

In the church service, the organa served to formulate, in a festive way, the liturgy of the Mass or the office of the feast day from which the cantus-firmus text had been taken. The position of organum within the liturgy was determined by the cantus-firmus text.

Around 1100 the English theoretician Johannes Cotto formulated for the first time the law of obligatory counter-movement thus: "If the main voice ascends, the accompanying voice descends, and vice versa."

Notre Dame School in Paris (Notre Dame Epoch) Mid-12th to Mid-13th Century

As the family seat of Hugh Capet, who was king from 987 to 996, Paris was the principal city of the growing Capetian empire and included the famous cathedral-school of Notre Dame. The clerical schools, made famous by Peter Lombard and Peter Abelard, were united around 1200 into the university, a leading institution in Europe, with some twenty thousand students. The Gothic cathedral of Notre Dame on the Ile de la Cité in the Seine was begun about 1163, and the construction continued into the 14th century.

Most scholars subdivide the period thus: the time from about 1150 to about 1250 they call the Notre Dame Epoch, and that from about 1250 to about 1320 the Ars Antiqua. About 1320 there followed the Ars Nova, which during the 14th century spread throughout France and eventually gained exclusive influence. Although this subdivisional scheme has been followed here, it might be noted that Heinrich Husmann has recently included the whole period from about 1150 to about 1320 under the heading "Old Art."

Considering it in detail, we must realize that the period from the middle of the 12th century constitutes a distinct segment in music history, in several respects:

1. While polyphony had heretofore been an art cultivated essentially in monasteries, the central church of Notre Dame in Paris now assumed the leadership. The practice of polyphonic music-making in the liturgy had become general in the cathedrals and larger

monasteries of England, France, and Spain—for example, at Winchester, Chartres, Worcester, Notre Dame in Paris, Compostela, St. Martial in Limoges, and St. Gall.

2. A basic change occurred in the incorporation of polyphony into the liturgy there. Whereas polyphony had previously been associated more with tropes and sequences, Gregorian chant was now composed polyphonically in the liturgy.

3. The names of composers were recorded for the first time in the history of polyphonic music which shows that the public was now aware of the polyphony that was emerging from the anonymity of the monastic world and that the composer was being accorded full recognition for his artistically creative efforts.

4. The conductus now made its appearance as an art of the clerical class alongside the liturgically connected polyphony in the organum.

Organum

From then on, the word *organum* became a designation for the species of polyphonic liturgical work in the narrower sense, after having previously been applied to all polyphonic music.

The musical zenith of the organa was to be found in the works of the Notre Dame School in Paris around 1200. One of the clearest sources of information about it is the report *"De mensuris et discantu,"* written about 1270, possibly by an English music student who was in Paris and who is usually referred to as Anonymus IV because he was placed by Coussemaker as the fourth anonymous author in the first volume of his *Scriptores.* According to this treatise, there was an active circle of musicians in Paris about 1200 whose main leaders were the older master Leoninus, or Leonin, and the younger master Perotinus Magnus, or Perotin the Great. The world church, rather than the monastery school, became the center of music. Music had now won significance beyond the narrower circle of its place of origin, and the period of the Notre Dame School was the first great epoch in the history of Western music. The works, objects of wonder in the whole world of that day, exercised a far-reaching influence upon music thereafter. But the Notre Dame School in Paris was only one significant center, and the art of the organum, conductus, and motet was widespread throughout France, England, and Spain.

Leoninus' contemporaries regarded him as *optimus organista,* which may refer to the fact that he was the best organum-composer of his day. He was responsible for the *"Magnus Liber Organi de Gradali et Antiphonario,"* a cycle for the entire church year, consisting of two-voiced organum compositions on responsory-melodies of the Mass and Office as cantus firmi. Rather than utilize tropes and sequence melodies for cantus firmi as before, he employed two different methods of composition:

1. In the portions of the cantus firmus that bore syllabic text, he placed extended and rhythmically free melismas over each cantus-firmus tone. These sections were called organum portions.

2. In the originally more melismatic cantus-firmus portions he utilized a predominantly note-against-note setting in which only short upper-voice melismas belonged to the moving, rhythmized tenor. These sections were called discantus parts. In them we encounter modal rhythm for the first time.

Master Perotinus Magnus (about 1200) was called by his contemporaries "*optimus discantor*," and he was even more admired than Leoninus. He was responsible for extensive revision of the *Magnus Liber Organi*. Although he changed little in the organal parts, he composed all the discantus parts anew and gave them stricter rhythm. As a result of this revision, he was called *optimus discantor*. The new compositions were called *clausulae*. To all appearances, the same procedure as had occurred in the development of the sequence was here repeated—that is, melismas were supplied with underlying text. There were folk-like influences in the melodic formation of the clausulae. The added texts are in Latin, Anglo-French, and French.

The art of Perotin, the Notre Dame School, and organum in general culminated in the three-voiced organa, or *organa tripla*, and the two extant four-voiced organa, or *organa quadrupla*. The latter are the "*Viderunt [omnes fines]*," at the beginning of the Gradual of the third Christmas Mass, and "*Sederunt principes*," at the beginning of the Gradual for St. Stephen's Day. In these, the individual cantus-firmus tones are held as long pedal points extending far beyond what would be a hundred measures in modern transcription. They establish the spaces, or *Klangräume*, in which the sonority transpires, and the three upper voices move above them in an artful fabric. Although the individual voices are formed after the model of the melody of Gregorian chant and organa of the St. Martial epoch, they depend on, and are restrained by, the modal rhythms, particularly that of the third mode. Melodic formulae, melodic paraphrasing, and the interchange of melodies between voices are characteristic features of the upper voice structure. The interchange of voices, known in German as *Stimmtausch*, means that one phrase consisting of elements that might be designated as *AB* is accompanied by another voice with the elements *BA*. This practice led to the procedure known as imitation, wherein one voice seems to be imitating what the other voice has just done.

As regards performance, Heinrich Husmann has adduced proof that the individual voice was sung by three singers at most and that the performance was purely vocal and soloistic.

During the course of the 12th century comprehensive stylistic changes took place: Leonin's style was linear and melodic, Perotin's was sonorous and vertical.

The free rhythm of the coloratura melismas of Leonin suggests the flexibility of Oriental models. The melismas consisted mostly of seconds, occasionally of thirds, and rarely of larger intervals. The soloistic upper voice frequently dropped an octave, quickly touching on all the intervening steps as in *portamento* or *glissando*. The main constructive principle in the formation of the melody was provided by the sequence.

In Perotin's music, on the other hand, we find a quite different structure: over the individual long-held cantus-firmus tones, a sonority was constructed that tended to stress the natural overtones—a "sound of nature"—consisting of the fifth, the fifth and the octave, or the fourth, or the fourth and the octave. This was ornamented, filled out melodically, and paraphrased, and short motifs were assigned to the individual voices. Thus, a unity of sonority and rhythm arose from the interchange of the various voices and the alternate intermingling of the motives. With the occasional change of the cantus-firmus tones, a new area of sonority manifests itself, and the conception of sound becomes predominantly static and free from tension.

Conductus

Along with the organa around 1200, a new type, the polyphonic conductus, came to the fore. It was significant in the development of musical composition, but, in contrast to the motet, did not continue to lead a separate existence for very long and was eventually absorbed into other *genres*. During the 12th century, various kinds of monodic songs, mostly sacred but in some instances also secular, were designated as *conductus*, which means a song of accompaniment. These accompanied the appearance of a character performing in a sacred drama or the procession of the deacon to the reading desk during the Mass. About 1200 an as yet unexplained change in the concept took place. Ever since the Notre Dame period, the term *conductus* had been the designation for a type of polyphonic music based on a non-liturgical tenor, the whole fashioned after a Latin poetic model of festive or serious character, which was sacred or secular in content. If the tenor melody was entirely or essentially syllabic, then all the voices moved in strictly rhythmized setting note-against-note. But if the tenor melody was melismatic, then the entire setting, and particularly the end of the piece, was melismatic and resembled the upper-voice complex of a three-voiced or four-voiced organum. The lower voice of the conductus was not, however, freely devised. It occasionally utilized melodic material that had been taken over from songs of the trouvères and troubadours but had been provided with new texts. From this usage it is concluded that there was no difference between secular and sacred melody. Music thus had a completely neutral relationship to the texts. One could no longer assume an individual word-tone relationship, either actual or potential. It became entirely a matter of metrical considerations.

Two types of conductus were differentiated: one with and one without melismas or ornaments (conductus *cum cauda*, and conductus *sine cauda*). In the *caudae* the main emphasis was on the melody of the lower voice rather than on the harmonic leading. According to Dom Anselm Hughes, it apparently incorporated melodies from older dances and songs of unidentified origin.

There were no fixed rules for performance. In some sections the intention must have been for an exclusively vocal performance; in others, exclusively instrumental. Often what was done must have been determined by the local situation and the available possibilities. It suits the nature of this music that different interpretations should be possible, according to the conditions under which it is given. Usually, in medieval practice, the polyphonic parts that were essentially harmonic were sung soloistically.

The conductus flourished principally from about 1175 to about 1235. Along with the organum it was the main form, and as an art was widespread among the clerics and peculiar to their particular social class. The theologian and Parisian church chancellor Philippe (d. 1236) was a notable poet of conductus texts.

Three manuscripts remain the most important sources of the music of the Notre Dame School: Wolfenbüttel 677 (or Wolfenbüttel Helmstedt 628) from the beginning of the 14th century; Florence Biblioteca Laurentiana Pluteus 29, 1, a manuscript written about 1300 in France and splendidly adorned with miniatures; and Wolfenbüttel 1206 (or Wolfenbüttel Helmstedt 1099), also of French origin.

The works are handed down in score, written in quadratic notation, as were also the songs of the troubadours, trouvères, and minnesingers. They utilized the same notation and ligatures as Gregorian chant has done in liturgical books up to the present day. The notes are to be read in accordance with the rhythmic modi. The rhythmic value of the individual note is derived not from its outward form but from the rhythmic schema of the modus on which the course of the individual voice is based. The modus was indicated by the succession of certain ligatures, or graphic notational signs which join two or more tones into one symbol. A three-toned ligature followed entirely by two-toned ones indicated the first mode; a string of two-toned ligatures ending with a three-toned one, the second mode; a single note and then purely three-toned ligatures, the third mode.

The theoreticians recognized six modi, although the fourth does not occur in the music we have, and the fifth is used almost exclusively for the rhythmicization of the lowest voice, the tenor. The sixth mode was first encountered in the tripla of 13th-century motets. These modes operated entirely in triple rhythm.

but perhaps usually to be transcribed more correctly thus:

Example 32

The Second Half of the 13th Century (Ars Antiqua)

The period from about 1250 to about 1320, is, in two respects, transitional in character. It is musically transitional in that the motet became the main form, and in it attempts were made to solve various problems, particularly those having to do with rhythm. It is transitional also in terms of musical theory, in that the mensural theory (theory of measurement) received particular attention. The epoch is often referred to as Ars antiqua. The principal theoretical work of the time, the "*Speculum musicae,*" was written about 1330 by Jacques de Liège, an author of conservative attitudes toward a period in which Ars nova had already been established.

Ars antiqua was flanked on the one side by the Notre Dame epoch and on the other by Ars nova. The designation "Ars antiqua" made its appearance about 1320 in Paris along with that of "Ars nova." Ars antiqua was marked by the rise and development of the motet and the related development of mensural notation.

The oldest motets were composed as early as the two-voiced repertoire of the St. Martial School, which originated in Aquitanian monasteries at the end of the 11th century. At the close of the Notre Dame epoch one more frequently finds *clausulae* of still mostly liturgical function being reworked into motets. The motet flourished from the middle of the 13th century through the 14th, and persisted in the 15th and 16th along with the Mass as the most important type of polyphonic music. In the Middle Ages the motet was the most important form of composition in both secular and sacred music. Many of the musical works that come to us from between 1250 and 1375 are motets, and their style began to influence the settings of sections of the Ordinary of the Mass at that time.

The motets of the St. Martial school used chant melodies in the tenor, while the freely composed upper voice troped the tenor text. The motet of the Notre Dame school, on the other hand, arose from the discant portions of the organa. The upper voices of a section of discant or even of a three- or four-voiced organum were underlaid syllabically with texts, which paraphrased the chant text presented by the tenor. The *duplum* (the voice over the tenor) was from then on called motetus, after the underlaid troping text. This designation is derived from the French *mot,* "word," and points to a contrast with the upper voice of the organum, which was sung wordlessly, as in a vocalise. The third and fourth voices over the tenor were then called, as before, triplum and quadruplum. The greater number of motets by far were three-voiced and out of the designation of the voice as *motetus,* the generic name *motet* arose.

A number of special terms have been proposed to distinguish different kinds of motets. Husmann calls motets with similar and simultaneous texts in the upper voices "conductus motets" because the upper voices are rhythmically similar within themselves, form a conductus, and together stand in contrast to the tenor.

Organum motets are those in which text has been assigned not only to the upper voices of clausulae, as in a conductus, but also to the organal portions (i.e., entire organa).

The double motet is a three-voiced piece in which the two upper voices (motetus and triplum) each has a text of its own. Since the text of the tenor is not counted, the three-voiced compositions are called double motets.

The triple motet is a four-voiced composition, in which each of the three upper voices appears with its own text, with the cantus firmus in the tenor. The highest voice is called the quadruplum.

The homophonic double motet is a later form of the conductus motet that eventually succeeded it. Its simple style of composition has been retained, but both of the upper voices have their own texts.

The tenor consists in the main of a relatively few notes performed in long note values, usually in the fifth modus. Often, only the first word of the liturgical text of the tenor was written down. Both of these features imply instrumental performance. The tenor text (although it was not heard in words) was represented by the melody of the cantus firmus, and lies at the basis of the idea of the whole piece, since the composition proceeds from the tenor as "something given."

Cantus firmi in the 13th century were usually liturgical melodies which were often taken from the cantus-firmus repertoire of the "*Magnus Liber Organi.*" In the 14th and particularly the 15th century, more and more secular tenors are to be found, though even in secular motets predominantly liturgical melodies were used as tenors.

As the upper voices gained independence and distinction through their own texts, it was appropriate that they should also be treated in a different way musically. Toward the end of the 13th century in the so-called Pierre de la Croix style, the triplum became a voice that was mobile, rhythmically rather free, and inclined to move along in short, quick note-values. In more tranquil movement, the motetus formed a middle member between the lively triplum and the tenor. In 13th-century secular motets, texts of different subject-matter and language were used in the upper voices more and more. For example, the liturgical melody of the tenor could be mated with a censorious Latin poem in the motetus and a French chanson in the triplum. The motet thus became an autonomous work of art, in which artistic fantasy had free play.

As the tenor continued to break away from the original context with greater frequency (as did the whole compositional form of the motet), it lost also the intellectual verbal significance of its origin. Accordingly the way was opened for purely instrumental presentation of the tenor, and for the three-voiced mixed vocal and instrumental form in which the tenor was presented instrumentally and the two upper voices vocally. Motets probably were performed as solos well into the 15th century.

Each individual voice of the motet may move in a different rhythm. At crucial points, however, the voices meet in perfect consonance, establishing certain rhythmic centers of gravity.

Among the Ars antiqua motets, a distinction is often made between earlier and later pieces. The older are associated with Franco of Cologne (d. *ca.* 1250), who, according to Besseler, was the same person as Franco of Paris, and with Adam de la Halle (d. *ca.* 1288). The younger Ars antiqua motets are associated with Pierre de la Croix, who was active till sometime after 1280.

The works of the Notre Dame school, particularly the conductus, were widely disseminated during the 13th century and were cultivated well into the 14th.

The *Piae Cantiones* (1582), a collection of sacred pieces assembled for the cathedral school in Turku-Abo, Finland, includes some polyphonic compositions in a style similar to that of Ars antiqua. Some of the numbers exhibit *Stimmtausch*. Also from Denmark there are scattered indications that two-voiced organa continued in practice—for example, in some Marian and Goliardic songs preserved in a monastic collection of about 1470–80.

The *hoquetus*, which appeared toward 1200 in northern France, and can be traced through to the Ars nova, is a technique of composition and fixed style of performance in which two voices that happen to lie close to each other alternate tones or groups of tones. The one voice sounds when the other pauses, so that there is a musical connection between the two voices. The etymological derivation of the word *hoquetus*, or hocket, is probably from the Arabic. It is also possible that this technique of composition spread from Oriental sources into France by way of the Arabic cultural center in Sicily.

In addition to the great Notre Dame manuscripts, the main documentary sources for Ars antiqua are the Bamberg (Ed. IV, 6), Montpellier (Ecole de méd. H. 196), and the Spanish Las Huelgas manuscripts. All three have been published in facsimile and musicological transcription. The motets are mostly notated in such a way as to cover the whole width of the page, divided into two columns, the triplum to the left, the motetus to the right, and the tenor below the two.

Since quadratic notation in accordance with the modal theory no longer sufficed for the unambiguous achievement of the greater mobility that especially made its appearance in the 13th-century motet triplum, an attempt was made to give the individual note a definite value. With the transition to mensural notation about 1250, the following note-values then developed, of which each contained, as "perfectio," three values of the next lower category:

$$\text{◗} = \text{Maxima (Duplex Longa)}, \quad \text{◗} = \text{Longa},$$
$$\text{▬} = \text{Brevis}, \quad \text{◆} = \text{Semibrevis}, \quad \text{♦} = \text{Minima}.$$

However, the two-fold subdivision of the values was not carried through until the late 13th century. Also at this time the minima was more and more frequently subdivided into its still lower category, the semiminima (♪).

The Ars antiqua manifested remarkable increase in the use of notes which did not belong to the diatonic scale. The system for the chromatic raising or lowering of tones was called *musica ficta* or *musica falsa,* and the first theoretician to deal with the question was Johannes de Garlandia (*ca.* 1195–1272), in his *De Musica mensurabili. Musica ficta* poses a large group of interrelated questions that are difficult to answer today, and the problem of the tritone stands at the center of them. The manuscripts sometimes notate the accidentals and sometimes do not.

The best known theoreticians of Ars antiqua are Hieronymus de Moravia (*ca.* 1250), Johannes de Garlandia the Elder (*ca.* 1240), Johannes de Garlandia the Younger (*ca.* 1300), Franco of Cologne (*ca.* 1250, Franco of Paris), Anonymus IV (*ca.* 1270), Pierre de la Croix, the Parisian master Johannes de Grocheo (*ca.* 1300), and Jacques de Liège (*ca.* 1330).

The 14th Century in France (Ars Nova)

The music of the 14th century is usually given the comprehensive name *Ars nova,* after the treatise of that title by Philippe de Vitry (*ca.* 1320). In de Vitry's sense, "Ars nova" not only indicates a radical change in the art, but also relates especially to innovations in mensural notation. From remarks by other writers, too, it is to be understood that music at the beginning of the 14th century was felt to be new, in contrast to that of the 13th century. A Papal bull of 1324–1325, issued by the Avignon Pope John XXII, opposed Ars nova music and urged a return to the old music—that is, to the works of the Notre Dame school and Ars antiqua —with a threat of ecclesiastical penalties if this were not carried out.

Hugo Riemann introduced the concept of the "Ars nova" as a description of an epoch in his *Handbuch der Musikgeschichte.*

The Italian music of the 14th century, in contrast to the quite different French, is perhaps better referred to as *Trecento* music.

The main characteristics of Ars nova are:

1. the new type of mensural notation;
2. the preponderance of secular over sacred music;
3. the almost exclusive prevalence of polyphonic music while monodic composition considerably declined in importance, though, significantly enough, Machaut composed a great many monodic *virelais* and *lais;*
4. the wide influence of art-music, which engaged the attention of but a limited circle of receptive listeners;
5. the autonomy of music as a work of art, independent of the previously decisive extra-musical considerations;
6. the significance of Italy, which took its place beside France in music;
7. the isorhythmic motet;
8. polyphonic song—embracing the ballade, the rondeau, and the virelai—which now attained the same significance as the motet; and
9. in the great personalities of Ars nova in France, the authority of the composer freed itself perhaps for the first time from the previous spirit of the humble workmanlike cleric.

Works of the Notre Dame school were still cultivated and written out as church music at the beginning of the century but eventually retired more and more into the background.

The music of Ars nova in France and the Trecento in Italy was mainly an art of urban and bourgeois culture, and the influence of the bourgeoisie tended toward secularization. As early as 1100 the monasteries were supplanted by the central city churches as institutions responsible for culture, and now even music tended to become worldly. The secular motet of Ars antiqua and Ars nova corresponds to the zenith of the Gothic in the plastic arts, embracing its ideals of truth to nature, depth of feeling, sensuousness, and sensibility. The motet with text in more than one language is characterized by traits of universalism, internationalism, and cosmopolitanism.

Polyphony developed notably in the Ordinary of the Mass. It found its way into the Mass quite early through a purely improvisatory technique of organum-singing. Extant written documents show two-voiced organa note-against-note. At first, only the Kyrie and Gloria were chosen for polyphonic treatment. Further polyphonic setting of sections of the Ordinary paralleled the development of the polyphonic technique of composition. And, according to the sources, the school of Notre Dame duly participated. Sections of the Ordinary in two and three voices were written during the 13th and 14th centuries; as early as the 12th there were scattered mensurated sections.

In the sacred polyphonic compositions of the 14th century, particularly during its latter half, the focus was on the setting of the five parts of the Ordinary (*Kyrie, Gloria, Credo, Sanctus,* and *Agnus Dei*) in place of the previously set Proper portions of the Mass and Office. Stylistically these sections moved in the framework of the distinctly secular forms of the conductus, motet, ballade, madrigal, and caccia. Numerous manuscripts (particularly the Ivrea, Apt, and Aosta) give a picture of polyphonic church music at Avignon during the time of the Schism (1378–1415). In these manuscripts there is little evidence that the Mass was thought of as constituting a musical whole. In other words, it was not conceived of as a cycle—a sequence of five interrelated parts, in the course of which some central musical idea unfolded.

On the other hand, a cyclic order appears in a few isolated examples, at first rather timidly. There is the three-voiced Mass of Tournai about 1300, named after the place where the manuscript is preserved. There is the fragmentary three-voiced Mass of Toulouse. And there is the Mass of Besançon or of the Sorbonne, Paris. Though somewhat cyclic, they are stylistically uneven and have about them the air of compilations. The Mass of Tournai, for instance, has three movements in the pre-14th-century style and two in 14th-century style. The *Kyrie, Sanctus,* and *Agnus Dei* must have seemed antiquated, as there is no *cantus firmus,* the rhythm is modal, and they represent the so-called "conductus-setting." The *Gloria* and *Credo,* on the other hand, show 14th-century traits with respect to sonority and rhythm: duple rhythm and mobile upper voices. Perhaps the Mass of Tournai did not originate as a cycle. But gradually the Masses of the century began to develop cyclic features. One feature that helped to encourage this was the fact that they all concluded with a motet over the "*Ite missa est*" as cantus firmus, with a Latin sacred text in the motetus and a French secular one in the triplum.

By far the outstanding work of the era is the four-voiced Mass by Guillaume de Machaut. It was quite certainly not written for the coronation of Charles V in Reims in 1364, as has been asserted by some commentators. As a composition, this Mass was rounded out by Machaut into perfect unity, though a cyclic unification was not achieved, and perhaps not even attempted. The *Kyrie, Sanctus,* and *Agnus Dei* display as cantus-firmus sections the structure and workmanship of the isorhythmic motet. The textually rich sections of the *Gloria* and *Credo,* on the other hand, are without cantus firmus, after the manner of the so-called conductus settings.

The Mass of Besançon is the oldest example of a Mass containing elements of the parody-mass.

Viewed in terms of its social function, the Ars nova motet was an art of connoisseurs belonging to a definite social class, in which the French language prevailed. It constituted a representational and festal music mainly associated with the clergy, but did not serve any liturgical purpose. This art was centered in France, primarily in Paris and later notably also in Avignon.

The double motet was the main form of the Ars nova motet, and it appeared with secular French texts, though it appeared less often with sacred texts in French and occasionally Latin, or one Latin and one French text. A liturgical cantus firmus was usually at the basis of the tenor, even in secular motets. The principal characteristic of the Ars nova motet was its isoperiodic or isorhythmic construction. The tenor was rhythmized in long note-values over a certain portion of the composition. The rhythmization of this section was then strictly repeated two or more times, although in the new period the pitches of the notes were different from those in the previous one. A rhythmically equal section or period of this type was called a *talea,* or, in French, *taille* (section).

In view of the length of the Ars nova motet, the liturgical cantus firmus was often too short to form the tenor of an entire piece. It was then reduced to repetitions of the cantus firmus. The melodic repetition of the cantus firmus was called *color.* Color and talea, repetition of the melody and repetition of rhythmic sections, often occurred together. It was not necessary, however, that they coincide.

A distinction exists between the terms "isoperiodic" and "isorhythmic." In an isoperiodic motet, only the tenor is articulated in rhythmically identical periods, or at least the layout for such a manner of articulation for the tenor is to be found only in the upper structure of the composition. An isorhythmic motet, however, may have rhythmically identical but melodically different portions in the upper voices as well as in the tenor.

The isorhythmic aspect was complicated by the shortening of the note-values in the repetition, by the retrograde repetition of periods, and by other artful devices. But isorhythm was a basic element in the construction of the composition. On into the 15th century, certain motets were laid out isorhythmically for special occasions such as festivals, enthronements, and coronations, although isorhythm was otherwise no longer used. The constructive element, to which special significance was attributed, was characteristic of the art of the 14th century. The introduction of isorhythm went back to Philippe de Vitry, and isolated examples of isorhythmic treatment occur as early as the music of the 13th century.

Three different types of poetry, all with refrain, figure in this period: the ballade, called by Machaut *ballade notée*, in contrast to a ballade that was not intended for composition; the rondeau; and the virelai, called by Machaut *chanson balladée*. Musically they form one type, which has several distinguishing features: most of the pieces are in three voices (occasionally in four); the top voice is decidedly melodic, and the two lower voices (tenor and contratenor) are instrumental. The tenor has no cantus firmus. Friedrich Ludwig called this type "French ballade form," Arnold Schering "discant song," and Jacques Handschin "cantilena." Its manner of composition has been called by Heinrich Besseler "song-setting" or "cantilena-setting." Normally a rendition of this music involved three performers: a male singer with a falsetto voice and two instrumentalists.

The chasse or chace, of which few examples are extant, is a three-voiced canon at the unison on a French text, which usually depicts scenes of hunting and pursuit in a witty way. It is not certain whether this is related to the type of canon popular in the 14th century that depends on *Stimmtausch* and is to be understood more as a means for achieving sheer sonority. The best known of these canons is the English "Sumer is icumen in." The French *chasse* may well have had no relationship to the Italian *caccia* of the Trecento.

The *hoquetus* technique was often used at the ends of motets. It rarely occurred as an independent composition, though the hoquetus "David" by Machaut is a notable exception.

There is as yet a void in the research into the connections between music and language in Ars nova.

Compositionally Ars nova is distinguished by the use of a new voice in the tenor region, the contratenor. Sometimes the contratenor moves below, sometimes above the tenor and supports it in its task as main voice of the composition, or it fills out with sonority a two-voiced discant-tenor composition into a three-voiced one. The contratenor appears for the first time in the four-voiced motet compositions of Philippe de Vitry, where, together with the tenor, it forms the basis of the composition, as one might expect in a motet. In cantilena-setting, however, the contratenor simply fills out the sound.

The tradition of Ars nova music begins with the manuscript of the *Roman de Fauvel* from the year 1316. This is a satirical poem, the action of which centers around a dun-colored horse named in the title. In the poem there are various bits of music, among which are thirty-three polyphonic pieces, including two isorhythmic motets by Philippe de Vitry. After the *Roman de Fauvel* compositions, in the Ars nova tradition, come the manuscripts of Machaut's works. These manuscripts are executed for the most part with great elegance. The order in them is as follows: one-voiced lais, motets, Mass, hocket "David" (in some manuscripts at the end), ballades, rondeaux, and virelais. The main Ars nova documentary source is the Ivrea manuscript, from the latter half of the century, reflecting the repertoire of the papal chapel at Avignon. This was an important ecclesiastical center, as it was the home of the Pope from 1309 to 1377 and of an Anti-Pope during the time of the Schism from 1377 to 1417. The Ivrea manuscript contains thirty-seven double motets, twenty-five non-cyclic settings of the Ordinary, four chasses, and eleven appended rondeaux and virelais. Likewise, close to the Papal chapel stands the later Apt manuscript, written at the beginning of the 15th century and containing thirty-four non-cyclic pieces from the Ordinary, four double motets, and three polyphonic hymns, from the period approximately between 1350 and 1420. In line with 15th-century trends, the stress here is not on motets, but on sections of the Mass.

Ars nova notation was developed from French mensural notation and systematically dealt with by Philippe de Vitry and Johannes de Muris. In the upper voices minima and semiminima prevail. Equal recognition is accorded to both two-fold and three-fold subdivision of note-values:

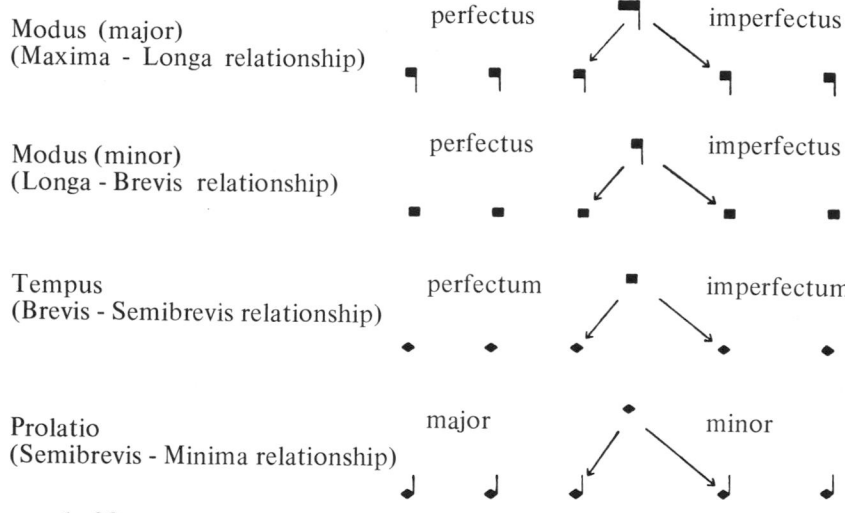

Example 33

Red notes indicate a temporary change from a triple to a duple rhythm, and vice versa.

The first duple rhythm expressly indicated in the notation appears in the Montpellier manuscript with the motet *Je ne puis/Flor de lis/Douce Dame*. In the music itself the duple rhythm is continuously maintained along with the triple. This becomes especially clear if one notices the larger aspects of the rhythmic layout of the piece: it may be triple in detail, but, when more comprehensively considered, it reveals duple and quadruple groupings.

The most significant French composers and theoreticians are Philippe de Vitry, Johannes de Muris, and Guillaume de Machaut.

Philippe de Vitry was born in 1291 at Vitry in Champagne. From 1351 on, he was Bishop in Meaux, where he died in 1361. During his career he was adviser to Charles IV of France, who reigned from 1322 to 1328, and was also a favorite of the Pope in Avignon. Famous as a personality, he corresponded with Petrarch and proved talented in many ways—in music, poetry, theory, politics, and diplomacy. Only a comparatively few of his works are preserved. He wrote the treatise *"Ars nova"* about 1320.

Johannes de Muris (b. *ca.* 1290, d. *ca.* 1351) a mathematician and astronomer in Paris, became the systematic theoretician of Ars nova, particularly with his *"Ars novae musicae"* (1319) and his *"Libellus cantus mensurabilis."*

Guillaume de Machaut (*ca.* 1300–1377) was the most significant poet, musician, and personality of the 14th century. He was outstanding in court and diplomatic circles and traveled widely in Europe. From 1323 to 1346 he was secretary to Duke John of Luxembourg, King of Bohemia, then was with Charles of Navarre, and from 1360 was constantly associated with the French court, in the service of the Duke of Berry and later of the Dauphin. At his death in 1377, he was canon of Reims.

Machaut maintained a somewhat conservative tendency in 14th-century polyphonic music, renewing, in a way, the ideas of trouvère art and reviving the spirit of chivalry in a type of song that had its roots in a stratified society. His extant musical works include forty ballades, twenty rondeaux, twenty-three motets, thirty-two virelais, eighteen lais, and a complete four-voiced Mass.

The main artistic achievement of Machaut is his work of a secular polyphonic character that, as a whole, can be described as belonging to the general category of "discant song" or "cantilena." He helped develop a new type of three-voiced setting in which the freely invented main voice lies in the upper part, the middle part is called the tenor, and the lowest part the contratenor. The top part is vocal, the two lower parts are instrumental.

More specifically he used four particular forms:

1. Ballades, in compositions which he called *ballades notées*, to distinguish them from ballades not specifically intended for musical setting. They were in two, three, or four voices. Those in two had a cantus and an instrumental tenor. In those of three voices, the leading upper part was sung, and the two lower parts—tenor and contratenor—were played on instruments. Those of four voices had their instrumental accompaniments expanded by means of a contratenor with a triplum as the topmost instrumental voice. Up to the time of Dufay, the ballade was the leading form of secular polyphony in France and was adopted as the ballata in Italy. The layout was usually tripartite (a^1 a^2 b c), being essentially the *Barform* with refrain.

2. Rondeaux, which he usually composed in three voices, had an instrumental tenor and contratenor as accompaniment. In musical construction this form is like the rondeau of the troubadours. Machaut, however, intellectualized its musical technique and provided it with musical and poetical enigmas, such as simultaneous forward and retrograde movement in two voices. The designation "rondeau" corresponds to the Latin term *rondellus*.

3. Virelais, which Machaut called *chansons balladées*, were predominantly one-voiced and, in form, followed the troubadour

pattern: refrain (A), stanza (bba), refrain (A), stanza (bba) . . . refrain (A), the concluding strain of the stanza (a) and the refrain (A) having the same melody.

4. The lais that Machaut wrote are usually one-voiced. The lai is made up of numerous two-sectioned stanzas of changing poetical and musical form, in which only the first and last stanzas are alike, the two parts of the stanza being sung each to the same melody.

Other notable composers include Thomas de Donai, Vauquier de Valenciennes, Garinus de Soissons, Guisard de Cambrai, Reginald de Bayeux, Egidius de Murino, Jean Vaillant, Pierre des Molins, and Solage.

The 14th Century in Italy (Trecento)

In understanding the cultural history of the times, we must realize that when the confederation of Lombard cities was founded in 1167, the influence of the German emperor sharply declined in Italy. Out of the confusion of the general political fragmentation of Italy between the 12th and 15th centuries, family dynasties emerged in positions of prominence in the cities of Milan (Visconti, Sforza), Florence (Medici), Mantua (Gonzaga), and Modena (Este), as did the Papal State, Venice, Naples, and Savoy-Piedmont. After 1200 an Italian literature arose: Dante Alighieri (1265–1321), Petrarch (1304–1374), and Boccaccio (1313–1375); and Italian painting flourished, notably in the work of the Florentine Giotto di Bondone (d. 1337). The universities of Padua (1222), Naples (1224), Rome (1303), and Florence (1349) were founded; and there was a brilliant flowering of intellectual life, which gave rise to Humanism, as well as significant increase in trade.

Excluding examples in musical treatises, the first polyphonic music in Italy made its appearance in the 14th century. This was, of course, at the same time as the Ars nova appeared in France. Northern Italy, particularly Florence, fostered a kind of secular music vocally conceived that reflected a love of melody and clear chord progressions. It was performed by singers and instruments. Although this music lacked the emphasis on construction so characteristic of French Ars nova, it was not entirely independent of the French in form after the second half of the 14th century. But no sooner had this Trecento art, with its joy in the life of this world, come into flower than it began to fade. By the end of the 14th century, Italian music was entirely under French influence; from the second half of the 14th century on, the music of each country influenced the other. This music was an exclusively social art of the elegant world of the courts and patricians. The musicians preferred to set the work of contemporary poets, including Boccaccio. Meanwhile, liturgical music was notably neglected.

The most important source material is the Squarcialupi Codex (MS. Florence Bibl. Laurentiana Pal. 87), usually referred to by the name of its former owner, the Florentine organist Antonio Squarcialupi (1417–1480). Written sometime after 1420, it contains in its 352 secular works two thirds of the extant known repertoire of a dozen famous Italian composers of the Trecento period. Most of these pieces are madrigal, caccia, or ballata in form.

The derivation of the name "madrigal" is by no means clear. Perhaps it comes from *mandra,* meaning "herd"; thus *mandrialis* would imply "pastoral." Perhaps it comes from *matricalis,* meaning "maternal" or "native," or perhaps it is related to *materialis,* which would stand in antithesis to *moralis,* that is, secular in contrast to sacred. The Trecento madrigal, with its exclusively secular and Italian texts, dealt with erotic, allegorical, political, and satirical matters. The poetic form consisted of two brief stanza-like strophes of two or three lines each and a concluding strain in the form of a three-line ritornello. The ritornello is melodically different from the strophes, which are usually sung to the same music. During the first half of the century the madrigal was composed in two voices, with the freely composed main melody in the upper voice. Both, or all three, of the voices were vocal in character. The Trecento madrigal, however, has no direct connection with the madrigal of the 16th century.

The *caccia* is the counterpart in Italian of the *chasse,* which dealt in French with hunting and other lively scenes, using three-part canonic form. The name of the form may refer to the text or to the musical structure. Both upper voices were treated canonically over a free instrumental supporting voice. The format consisted of a long main portion with a short ritornello. The exact historical relationship between the chasse and the caccia, however, is not yet clear.

The *ballata,* like the conductus, was originally composed in two or three voices. In the latter half of the 14th century, Francesco Landino in particular adopted the typical French discant song (cantilena, or French ballade form) as a three-voiced song with the vocal part and the two instrumental lines as lower voices. He created a mixed form when he assigned these parts to two singing voices and the contratenor to an instrument. The form of the ballata, with its A b b a A pattern, corresponds to that of the French virelai, or what Machaut called *chanson balladée.*

Trecento music was characterized by a typically Italian singing quality and a strongly tonal feeling—two features novel for polyphony. These characteristics, however, were less evident in the latter half of the century when French music became more influential, and few Italians seem to have favored the isorhythmic motet.

It was not until the latter half of the Trecento that Florence came to the fore as the second music center in Northern Italy after Padua, which retained its central position into the early years of the 15th century. Verona and Milan were also centers for a while. In Florence, the cultural development was supported particularly by the rising bourgeois aristocracy. Pisa and Lucca were included in the Florentine circle, and Perugia became prominent around 1400. Naples had no real school in the Trecento.

For political reasons, the focal point of development in Northern Italy shifted to Venice in the 15th century.

Recently a number of two-voiced pieces have come to light in Italy, from the late 13th and early 14th centuries. Apparently the art of two-voiced improvisation was widespread in the 13th century in Italy; at the same time works in the vernacular stood side by side with those in Latin and shared many features with them. The roots of Trecento art are to be sought here, in the compositions of clerics, rather than in Provençal organum or in the conductus of the Notre Dame epoch. The composition of early Trecento music is typically Italian. Only during the course of the 14th century, particularly the latter half, did the French influence become more and more significant. The work of Johannes Ciconia provides a definite link between French and Italian style.

Italian music of the 13th century was principally one-voiced, and even in the 14th century monody remained the most widespread form of music-making. Trecento music, according to von Ficker, was an exclusive art, created by the clerics of a few northern Italian courts and later by some Florentine societies interested in music and literature. It was not consciously unconventional: the writings of Marchetto da Padua, such as his *Lucidarium* (1317–8) and his *Pomerium* (1318–9), did not represent a new theory, as did the writings of de Vitry and de Muris, but simply a compendium of current practice in Italy. Also, the technique and style of composition in Italy was somewhat simplified after 1400, as less complex polyphonic forms were introduced during the transition to Italian music in the latter half of the 15th century. The construction of contrafacta and parodies in Italian Trecento works extended on into the 15th century, when we first encounter examples of the parody Mass.

Italian Trecento music spans three generations of composers. The first, with Florence as its center, cultivated the two-voiced madrigal and the three-voiced caccia. The most significant of its composers were Giovanni da Cascia (Giovanni da Firenze) and Jacopo da Bologna. Then too, there were Donato da Cascia (Donato da Firenze), Niccolò da Perugia, Vincenzo d'Armina (Vincenzo da Rimini), and Piero, as well as Ghirardello da Firenze, a somewhat younger contemporary of Giovanni da Cascia.

The principal master of the second generation and most significant composer of the whole epoch was Francesco Landino. Born about 1335 in Fiesole, he was blind from childhood. He is traditionally believed to have been awarded the laurel wreath for his organ playing by the King of Cyprus in 1364. We know that he lived in Florence from 1375 on, and by 1381 he had become one of the most famous of the Florentines, as composer, musician, poet, and theoretician. He played many instruments and was famous for his skill in improvisation. After his death in Florence on February 9, 1397, he was buried at the church of San Lorenzo, where he had long been active as organist. He left behind a total of 154 compositions, most of which are ballate. His extant compositions include nine two-voiced and two three-voiced madrigals, two cacce, ninety-one two-voiced and forty-two three-voiced ballate, and eight ballate in versions for two or three voices.

The predominance of the ballata in his and his contemporaries' work attests to the French influence that characterized also the third generation of Trecento composers. Other composers active in Landino's time were Bartolino da Padua and Lorenzo da Firenze.

We have manuscript collections from two other places outside these northern Italian centers of development. One, the Chantilly manuscript, presumably written at the court of Naples, contains motets and discant songs derived from French sources that are treated with even more rhythmic artistry. The other, the Turin manuscript, written perhaps at the beginning of the 15th century in the Lusignan court on Cyprus, contains mixed Italian and French stylistic elements.

Peculiarities of Italian mensural notation of the Trecento, such as the writing of the notes on six instead of five lines and the manner of subdividing the brevis, show its independence from the modal epoch in France. The brevis can contain not only two or three but as many as twelve semibreves. The fact that they belong together in one note value is made clear by points of subdivision. This manner of dividing the brevis opened the way to new rhythmic possibilities beyond those of French mensural notation.

Johannes Ciconia, who emigrated from Liège to Italy between 1389 and 1393, provides a link between the 14th and 15th centuries. Besseler speaks of the "Ciconian Epoch" as the time of the first fruitful encounter between North and South. Ciconia reached the height of his creative activities during the first half of the 15th century, writing mostly motets and Masses. He adopted procedures of free improvisation and created the typical "imitative motet" and the "four-voiced motet with discant duet." He used a free harmonic support in place of the cantus firmus as the lowest voice. The harmonic aspect of his work is clearly marked by the relationship between tonic and dominant. Besseler has said that the motet, which was the large form of Ars nova, adopted the really new aspect of Trecento music, "tonal harmony." Thus a synthesis was effected. He further asserts that Johannes Ciconia was the "first great Netherlander whom we see deflecting the course of music history around 1400 with astonishing versatility and all-European significance." Born in Liège presumably between 1335 and 1340, he is known to have first gone to Avignon in 1350. Between 1358 and 1367 he traveled with Cardinal Gilles d'Alboronoz in Italy, and from 1368 to 1402 or 1403 he was again in Liège. As early as 1403 he was referred to as a "master" in Padua, where he eventually died in 1411. He was the author of an extensive treatise entitled "Nova Musica."

The "Ciconian Epoch" extends from about 1370 to 1411. The principle of the imitative motet inherent in the work of the "Ciconia School" manifests itself even in the *Gloria* and *Credo* of the Mass. The technique, however, remained localized and was never carried on further. Ciconia was important for his use of models from the madrigals in the early form of the parody Mass.

He was, however, only one of many "Netherlanders" who were active in Italy around this time. Several others who came from the famous singing schools of Reims, Tournai, and Cambrai, were associated with the Papal chapel at Rome.

The Late 14th Century in France and Italy

During the late Trecento, Italy came more and more under French influence, partly because of the return of the Pope from Avignon to Rome in 1377 with his private choir that he had developed in France and partly because of the direct influence of the private chapels of high foreign prelates. Many of the names of Italian composers at the close of the 14th and the beginning of the 15th century are known, particularly those from northern Italian cities. Venice, with St. Mark's (where a choir school was founded in 1403) and Rome (after the end of the Schism in 1420) were significant centers of music that exerted a powerful influence on the North. Ciconia was one of the first composers from the Netherlands active in Italy.

In France, composers continued to write in forms and techniques that had been distinctively used by Philippe de Vitry and Guillaume de Machaut, including the motet (usually isorhythmic), the ballade, the rondeau, and the virelai. But more and more they favored the ballade, or "discant song," the rondeau, and the virelai, and began to neglect the motet, which had previously been the most actively cultivated type of composition.

The predominant style of the last two decades in France was essentially different from Vitry's and Machaut's in that the rhythmic and notational features became more carefully differentiated and far more complicated, particularly in the song-settings. Toward the end of the century, the concept of Ars nova disappeared from the remarks of the theoreticians and was supplanted by a sort of catch-phrase that crept in, referring to "subtilis" and "subtilitas," implying, as Ursula Günther has pointed out, a prevalent idea that Ars nova had been supplanted by an Ars subtilior (a more complicated art). Interestingly enough, Ars nova itself had earlier been referred to as an *ars subtilior* by Jacques de Liège. Datable works of the more subtle style are to be found only after Machaut's death in 1377. Apparently the new style had spread quickly and widely during the last two decades of the century. The extraordinary enrichment of music through the expressive possibilities of rhythm belongs among the achievements of this Ars subtilior, if we may call it that. Offshoots of it are recognizable in the early work of Dufay. In terms of cultural history, Ars subtilior belongs to the time of the Schism, the decline of ecclesiastical order, the confusion in religious and political matters, and the strife between parties in France under King Charles VI. It was a time during which *l'art pour l'art* was openly favored and during which many traditional religious and political values were shaken. Willi Apel has referred to somewhat the same phenomenon as simply "mannerism."

After Machaut's death, Paris and the French court seem to have formed the center of musical culture. The French kings Charles V (who reigned from 1364 to 1380) and Charles VI (from 1380 to 1422) maintained exceptional court chapels with the best musicians. New names appear among the composers—Jean Vaillant, Jehan de Suzay, Solage, Baude Cordier, Grimace, J. Galiot, Jacob de Senleches, Guido, J. Simonis de Haspre, and Jean Cunelier. The last representatives of this central French music school in Paris included Carmen, Cesaris, Tapissier, and Baude Cordier. Eventually it lost its separate identity and was absorbed into the Franco-Flemish musical development.

But while the Parisian school flourished, the rhythmic structure of the ballades and motets became increasingly rich and complicated. The sense of the words was often disregarded, their rhythm and declamation being often completely subordinated to the music. The subject-matter of the texts was primarily love and secondarily allegory and mythology. The ballades represented the last glitter of this highly refined court culture, which collapsed after the Battle of Agincourt in 1415. The French army was destroyed by the English, and Paris was conquered. The political and cultural predominance of France was increasingly weakened by the war that continued between England and France for more than a hundred years, from 1339 to 1453. Italian and French elements began to fuse. A new element from England was being added, that decisively influenced music at the beginning of the 15th century.

The most important source material of the transitional period is the Chantilly manuscript, containing 113 polyphonic settings, written at the beginning of the 15th century in Italy on the basis of a French manuscript no longer extant. There are other manuscripts in Continental libraries: one at Turin, written between 1413 and 1434 by French musicians on Cyprus, another at Lucca, and one at Modena, Faenza 117.

These manuscripts introduce further refinements in mensural notation, including auxiliary signs of the most various sort and significance. The minima and semiminima prevailed in the upper voices, and red notation indicated changes in rhythm. As a result, the notation became quite complicated.

The "Avignon School" was noteworthy. Obviously in conformity with the Papal bull issued by John XXII against Ars nova, Masses such as those in the Ivrea manuscript were written in which an attempt was made to achieve an ascetic style distinctly different from that of secular music. The last representatives of the Avignon School were active up to the beginning of the 15th century, and the most important manuscript is that from the Apt Cathedral.

England to the End of the 16th Century

The English influence on European music was related to her regaining political independence from France. In 1066 Duke William of Normandy, as William I (William the Conqueror), became king of England and reigned until 1087. Under him French customs and language prevailed. After his death the Anglo-Norman double kingdom was divided, but was reunited by Henry I in 1106. Henry II, who reigned from 1154 to 1189, continued to rule about a third of France. From the ensuing period, it will be recalled that Richard I (Richard the Lion-Hearted), who reigned from 1189 to 1199, was imprisoned during the Third Crusade and that as of 1215 the Magna Charta formed the basis of the English constitution. In 1339, under Edward II, a war of succession broke out with France. By the end of the 14th century, however, the English language had won precedence over French as a result of its having been used in the London Records Office and in Wyclif's translation of the Bible. In 1415 Henry V conquered the French army at Agincourt and was recognized as heir to the French crown. Toward 1453, however, all the possessions in France as far north as Calais were lost. After the conflict between the houses of York and Lancaster over the throne, usually referred to as the War of the White and Red Roses, the House of Tudor succeeded to the throne and continued to rule till 1603, with Henry VII from 1485 to 1509 and Henry VIII from 1509 to 1547. Under the latter, the Act of Supremacy, passed in 1534, established a state church and broke all ties with Rome. Edward VI was king from 1547 to 1553, followed by the Roman Catholic monarch, Mary Queen of Scots, who ruled from 1553 to 1558. Elizabeth I reigned from 1558 to 1603, a period marked by the defeat of the Spanish Armada in 1588 and by the increasing significance of England in commerce and industry. The House of Stuart came to the throne and ruled from 1603 to 1625 with James I as king of Great Britain and Ireland. From 1649 to 1660 England was a republic with Oliver Cromwell as Lord Protector. Under Charles II, who ruled from 1660 to 1685, the monarchy was restored.

It has been variously suggested that Western polyphony arose in England and spread from there, but this supposition is no longer tenable. The fact that vestiges of a quite old, native, more sonorously oriented music had been preserved in England may be related to the traditionalism characteristic of the country, but it hardly allows us to ascribe to it the origin of European polyphony.

England did, however, contribute very significantly to the development of polyphonic art. To follow the matter historically, we must consider first the particular nature of native English polyphony and then its relationships to that of the Continent.

Concerning native English polyphony, Giraldus Cambrensis, Archdeacon of St. David's in Wales, refers to a popular, improvised polyphonic manner of singing widespread in Wales and Northern England around 1200 in his *"Descriptio Cambriae."* He does not give notated examples, but says that the practice goes back to the Danish and Norwegian Vikings. A further bit of support for the assumption of a polyphony originally peculiar to England and Scandinavia is handed down to us by the Icelandic parallel songs in fifths, or *tvísöngur*, which resemble some other non-European examples of polyphony. This practice may have existed around 1300, although the first manuscript documenting it is dated 1473.

In general, very little is known specifically about the secular music of this time, though inferences may be drawn from sacred music. The obviously oldest preserved document of a perhaps popular type of polyphony is the two-voiced hymn *"Nobilis, humilis,"* in honor of St. Magnus (d. 1115), the patron saint of the then Norwegian Orkney Islands at the northern end of Scotland. This hymn is preserved in a manuscript at the Uppsala University Library dating from the end of the 13th century. The music uses successive thirds, in accordance with a practice that was called in the 15th century "gymel," or *cantus gemellus*, "twin-song." Apparently it enjoyed special favor in the earlier period in England. Various further indications of its popularity are provided by examples of a gymel-like conductus. Their peculiar sonority was later embodied in the English discant style. The theoreticians Anonymus IV and Walter Odington speak of a British preference for thirds and sixths. Doubtless this simple form of song with note against note in parallel movement sprang from origins somewhat similar to those of organum at the fifth. It is also a precursor of the later fauxbourdon, to which Bukofzer gave the name "English discant." During the course of the 14th century this technique gave rise to the "new English discant," in which more attention was paid to the independence of the vocal line.

Throughout the 13th and 14th centuries England apparently retained elements from an older stratum of musical practice in a somewhat popular type of polyphony. It involved a preference for thirds and sixths as consonances and for the tones of the major series. As French music began to make fruitful contact with English in the 15th century, these elements yielded significant results.

The "Summer Canon," with the secular text "Sumer is icumen in," preserves for us an example of English music around 1300. It is distinguished by folk-like melodic writing in major, a predilection for fullness of sonority, and its simple and improvisatory construction. In it, the upper four voices, as they have usually been interpreted, move in triple time over a two-voiced basis of sonority or *Pes* in the 5th modus, which establishes a constant change between but two sounds. The result is a perpetual "canon" at the unison which employs continuous exchange of voices (*Stimmtausch*). In a recent study of the piece, Bukofzer maintained that the upper voices were originally in duple time and that the previous dating "about 1240" should be replaced by a later one, sometime after 1300; but Schofield has rejected Bukofzer's dating, and Besseler also attributes the piece to the late 13th century. The Summer Canon also contains sacred words in Latin, an indication that the Middle Ages did not make a sharp distinction between sacred and secular composition. It is the first known self-contained canon in art-music.

E. Apfel's recent research has brought out the independence of English music from that of the Continent with special clarity. He has found that the oldest English motets contain the seeds of all the characteristics of English compositional technique that were developed during the 15th century. Early English manuscripts contain many freely composed motets and rondelli, approaching the type of the conductus. Such compositions, however, are not found in France. These and other considerations suggest that England enjoyed a high degree of musical autonomy at this time.

The English composers were the first to master composition in three and four voices on the basis of the new technique of sonority after the Notre Dame period, and they did not begin with a composition in two or three parts and simply add a supplementary voice. Instead, perhaps following some Continental model, they wrote cantus-firmus motets, conceived in three or four voices from the very start. Until well into the 15th century, it was only in England that composers cultivated the conductus, trope, and sequence polyphonically. Also the practice of developing an entire cantus firmus in a conductus-like setting has been documented almost exclusively in England. The setting of the Ordinary of the Mass in the manner of the motet was English. The new 15th-century setting of Masses and motets, which Apfel calls the "sonorously free discant setting," came from England.

To clarify the terminology, Apfel has proposed that henceforth a discant setting intended simply to increase sonority should be called "multiple two-voiced setting." In it the composer has successively added two or three spatially limited but somewhat independent voices to a lower voice (the cantus firmus) or to a succession of whatever tones happened to be lowest in the two voices (the "solus tenor"). Thus each of these voices forms a two-voiced setting of its own with the lowest voice or *solus tenor*. The result is not really a composition in two or three voices. Apfel has therefore proposed that the free discant setting be called "expanded two- and three-voiced setting." In cases where the composer has added yet another supplementary voice called a "contratenor" to a two- or three-voiced scaffolding-setting, Apfel would simply call the sonorously free discant setting a three- or four-voiced setting, according to the *total* number of the voices. In such case it is truly a matter of settings in three or four voices.

Passing on to a consideration of English polyphony, and more specifically in its relationship to that of the Continent, we may note the importance of England in the early history of organum. It was the Irish philosopher Johannes Scotus (Erigena) who, in the 9th century, left us the first verbal account we have of organum, though he did not provide any notated examples. Organs seem to have been introduced into England probably by the end of the 7th century, and organ-building reached a notable stage of development in England in the 10th century. There is a report of an organ at Winchester with more than four hundred pipes, on which polyphonic music was performed by two players. The first collection of organa is the Winchester Tropar, from the 11th century. The Norman invasion in England of 1066, of course, occasioned a most direct confrontation between the French and English cultures.

No strict separation between the compositional methods of the conductus and the motet appears in the polyphonic English music of the 13th century. We have samples of it in the so-called Worcester Fragments of the late 13th and early 14th centuries. These are mainly sequences or tropes of the Ordinary. There is little polytextuality. The setting is mostly simple, free of elaborate construction, in two or three voices, or often two-voiced, becoming three-voiced only at the end of the piece. The rhythm is characterized by Handschin as "less constrained" than in other works of the time from the Continent. The Worcester Fragments are rich in three-voiced examples with parallel chords of the sixth. The manuscript shows that there must have been an important group of composers at the Worcester Cathedral.

Be - a - ta vi - sce - ra   Ma - ri - ae vir - gi - nis

Example 34

During the 14th century English music had its own Ars nova similar to the French, though conservative and restrained in comparison with the Continental development. The scarcity of extant sources makes even isolated references to the names of composers important in establishing the fact that musical life flourished in connection with the Chapel Royal. As late as the 13th century the monasteries exercised musical leadership, until it passed on to the cathedrals and, by the end of the century, to the Chapel Royal. While secular music predominated in France and Italy during the 14th century, church music is almost all we have from England during that time. It mainly appears in musical settings of the Ordinary of the Mass, though there is frequent setting of only the *Kyrie,* which in 14th-century England was usually sung chorally.

The compositional manner was conservative. Moving out from and returning to chords composed of fifths and octaves, the sonority of the setting was determined by parallel thirds and sixths. These introduced an element that pressed ahead and at the same time bound the centers of sonority together. During the 14th and early 15th centuries this technique of composition was called *discantus,* or discant. The word *fauxbourdon* first appeared around 1430. For the most part all the voices carry the same text; but there are also instances of different voices carrying different parts of one text, especially in those portions amply supplied with words, such as the *Gloria* and the *Credo* (for example, at *"Patrem omnipotentem"* and *"Et in unum Deum"*). The cantus firmus may lie not only in the tenor but also in the middle voices and even in the top voice. The pieces are notated in score, as in the works of the Notre Dame School. In 14th-century England such works were still being copied, as is evidenced by one of the four large extant Notre Dame manuscripts written in England at the beginning of the 14th century.

Most of the manuscript sources for English music of the 14th century have disappeared, and no single manuscript is preserved complete. The Old Hall manuscript is the main source for the period from 1400 to 1430. It stems from the repertoire of the Chapel Royal, probably from the reign of Henry IV (1399–1413), and contains 138 works by Dunstable, Power, Piamor, Benet, Forest, and other composers of the English school. The next most important source is the Trent Codices. Although they contain compositions principally by the Netherlanders, there are also thirty pieces by Dunstable, ten by Power, and several others by English composers such as Sturgeon, Damett, Cooke, Byttering, Pycard, and W. Typp.

Around 1400 English music was strongly influenced by late French Ars nova, examples of which appear in the Old Hall manuscript. This influence manifests itself through isorhythm in the motet and Mass compositions, hocket, and complicated rhythms in the style of the late

French ballade and motet. The special English tradition appears in a syllabic *parlando* style, and simple conductus-like pieces. Here, Gregorian chant, like a religious symbol, was the backbone of the musical design, whereas in France it was but one of many bases for polyphonic structure. If Gregorian chant was the cantus firmus in the upper voice, it received increasing melodic enrichment, or "discant coloration." The result was a completely new melodic line, the Gregorian background of which was no longer recognizable. This development gave rise to a new melodic style. The great creative achievement of English music here lay in its having effectively restrained the rhythmic energies of Continental Gothic music by the force of its melody. Hand in hand with this went the tendency to think in chord-progressions and to favor the succession of imperfect consonances of the third and sixth. This led to the beginnings of Classical counterpoint and linear voice-leading on the basis of harmony. Thus the English development was to revolutionize Franco-Flemish music and ultimately Continental music in general.

Two musicologists, Besseler and Bukofzer, have arrived at differing interpretations of what took place. According to Besseler, English discant had been from early times an unwritten practice of improvisation over the cantus firmus. The cantus firmus lay in the lowest voice and was presented without ornament. Fauxbourdon on the Continent, on the other hand, was a complete composition in which the cantus firmus was in the upper voice and was colored, but was always accompanied only by sixth chords and combinations of the fifth and octave. This practice of composition first appeared on the Continent in pieces that were written around 1430, particularly in those of Dufay. From here it spread quickly and was soon referred to as "fauxbourdon style."

Bukofzer, on the other hand, started from the assumption that Gregorian chant could be fused into polyphonic composition in either improvised or written-out form. The first method was traditionally called "discant," and is described at length by various English theoreticians and composers of the early 15th century, notably Leonel Power, Richard Cotell, various anonymous writers, John Hothby, and by the Italian theorists Guilelmus Monachus and Burtius. This practice involved two or more singers, who followed certain understood procedures. While the Continental musicians normally limited themselves to one system in contrary motion with emphasis on perfect consonances, English composers preferred parallel motion in thirds and sixths. In the "sight system" or *discantus visibilis* they developed a method of imagining the voices to be supplied above the four lines of the staff on which the song was written. Continental discant and English discant thus differed in matters of interval and motion, and both had the cantus firmus below.

With the spread of English music to the Continent, English discant was adopted, but was changed into fauxbourdon. The cantus firmus moved into the soprano, and the Gregorian chant was colorfully ornamented. The result was essentially a melody in free discant style. Accompaniment was furnished by two deeper, supporting voices at the distance of a sixth (or octave) or a fourth. The harmonizing in parallel motion doubled the melody, hence the expression "false bass." In fauxbourdon, improvisation extended in the first place only to the middle voice, which without notation was simply improvised a fourth below the melody, and in numerous compositions was simply indicated by the word "*a faux-bourdon.*" Fauxbourdon became famous through the work of Binchois and particularly through that of Dufay, who perhaps might even be called the discoverer of this manner of composing. It enjoyed great popularity as a simple and modest sort of liturgical music. Apparently the fauxbourdon fashion reached England only after its appearance on the Continent. Later in the century the term had various meanings, and today it is still used for any string of chords of the sixth.

John Dunstable (*ca.* 1380/1390–1453) was the most significant composer of the English school as well as of the early 15th century in general and the great instigator of the new epoch in music that began about that time. The circumstances of his life are not entirely clear. He was in the service of Henry V's brother, the Duke of Bedford. The widespread fame of Dunstable during his lifetime suggests that he may have been in France for some time with the Duke. A journey to Italy also lies in the realm of possibility, and would have brought him in contact with various influences. He is buried in the church of St. Stephen's Walbrock, where his epitaph refers to him as a musician, mathematician, and astronomer.

In Dunstable's some fifty-eight extant works, elements of older musical strata which English music preserved in its particular way mingled with elements of the French and Italian music of the 14th century and brought forth something new. In the background of his music there were doubtless some hitherto unknown sources of cantabile melodic style. His entire manner of composing has a quality of improvisation and freedom about it. This quality came as a relief from the artfulness of much of the late-14th-century music, particularly that of France, and fostered new musical developments.

The special character of Dunstable's music lies, moreover, in the new treatment of dissonance that he consistently maintained. He purified French Ars nova counterpoint of its dissonances that resulted from syncopation, thus creating what Bukofzer termed the "pan-consonant" style, in which structural dissonance was prepared for and anticipated. The principle of preparing all structural dissonances was to prevail in music for the following two centuries.

The extant works of Dunstable are predominantly sacred. Of his thirty motets, twelve are isorhythmic and thus maintain the style of the French festal or representational Ars nova motet. He created a new type in the "declamation motet" by lightening the close polyphonic texture so that all voices could have an equal chance to present the text in the rhythm that resulted from the words. Together with Leonel Power and Benet, he united for the first time the individual movements of the Mass with a tenor that is liturgical but does not belong to the Mass. The result was the "tenor Mass," in each movement of which the basic melody of the cantus firmus was varied through the use of discant coloring. Although musicologists today do not credit all these innovations to Dunstable alone, they attribute them generally to a group of English composers of whom he was the head. His merit, according to Bukofzer, lies in his "having transmitted the traits of English music through the classical guise of European music." His Mass *"Rex seculorum"* and motets *"Alma redemptoris," "Veni sancte spiritus," "Salve scema sanctitas," "Crux fidelis,"* and *"Quam pulchra es,"* and his chanson *"O rosa bella"* are among his more noteworthy works.

Martin le Franc, in his *Champion des dames* (*ca.* 1440), credits Dunstable with having had a strong influence on Dufay and Binchois. The poem cites the "contenance angloise" and the "frisque concordance" as the distinguishing features of the new English style of composition. Clearly there was a contemporary awareness of the difference between Continental and English music. Composers on the Continent were stimulated by the music of Dunstable and his English contemporaries. Thus a new music (an *ars nova*) was inaugurated from England, which was hailed by the famous theoretician Johannes Tinctoris in the latter half of the 15th century as "the source and origin of the new art" (*novae artis fons et origo*), making Dunstable famous through the Continental response to his music.

After Dunstable's death, numerous English composers continued on their own firmly traditional ways without much exchange of influence with the Continent until about 1530. Not till after 1520 was there much contact with the Netherlands, nor till after 1530 did they tend to employ imitation throughout an entire composition, though many composers from the Continent went to England after 1500.

The most important manuscripts of the period from about 1460 to 1520 are the great choirbooks of Eton College, Lambeth Palace, and Gonville and Caius College at Cambridge. These are characterized by a conservative approach and by the flowering of a style of coloration. The larger forms of English choral music were constructed according to mid-15th-century cantus-firmus practice, richly ornamented in counterpoint and usually intended for five or six voices, occasionally for seven or eight. This Late Gothic style had become so typically English by the beginning of the 16th century that it could absorb Renaissance elements, such as imitation and the division of the choir, without losing the traits of the original style—a tendency culminating in the Masses and motets of John Taverner (*ca.* 1495–1545).

Other important composers were Christopher Tye (*ca.* 1500–1573), Robert White (d. 1574), John Shepherd (*ca.* 1525–*ca.* 1563), and Thomas Tallis (*ca.* 1505–1585). The most significant composer of church music in Latin during the period of Queen Elizabeth I was William Byrd (1543–1623), famous for his Masses and motets, and at the same time an important figure in music generally. In addition, there were Thomas Morley (1557–1603), Richard Deering (d. *ca.* 1630), and Peter Philips (*ca.* 1560–*ca.* 1633). These men gave special attention to anthems, which at that time meant, stylistically, motets with English text. William Byrd also wrote works in English for the Anglican worship service, as did Thomas Weelkes (d. 1623). Under Henry VIII, Edward VI, and during the era of Elizabeth I (throughout the 16th century) musical life and productivity reached unusual heights in England, especially in the secular field. Its Continental affiliations were particularly with Italian music, and the madrigal became an especially brilliant manifestation of the English musical impulse.

Polyphony in Poland to about 1500

The earliest extant examples of polyphonic music in Poland come from the late 13th century. They are two brief *"Benedicamus"* organa in the antiphonary of the Clarissines in Stary Sącz. Up to the 15th century parallel development occurred along two different lines: first, the traditional continuation of the simple practice of organum and in the 15th century that of fauxbourdon; and, second, polyphonic achievements commensurate with those elsewhere in Europe on the part of composers of both foreign and Polish origin. Although the practice of organum was mostly carried on in an improvisatory way, it left its imprint in chant manuscripts; obviously it was widespread among circles of the clergy, particularly among those on a rather lower level of authority. It is possible that the two *"Benedicamus"* organa are connected with this practice.

Further examples of manuscripts of this sort include the Christmas *lectio "Iube domne benedicere"* in the appendix to the Gradual of the Clarissines in Stary Sącz, from the latter half of the 14th century; two tropes *"Surrexit Christus hodie"* in Graduale 205 M of the Clarissines in Cracow, from the second half of the 14th century; and two portions of the Mass, the *Sanctus* and the *Agnus Dei*, in the Biblioteka Narodowa in Warsaw, MS Lat Q 201, from the beginning of the 15th century. Also from the 15th century are MS 14 RL of the Bernhardiner Monastery in Cracow; the MSS 554, 686, and 1267 of the Jagiellonian Library in Cracow; MS 2216 in the Library of the Polish Academy of Sciences in Cracow; two manuscripts in the Library of the cathedral chapter in Cracow; and MS A 52 in the Saxon Landesbibliothek in Dresden, dating from the beginning of the 16th century. Examples of improvised fauxbourdon practice appear in the MS Kras 52 in the National Library in Warsaw (*ca.* 1430). It contains interesting notes such as "Per bordunum" and "in quinta incipiendum est" for the contratenor voices, which are notated either only initially or not at all, and various marginal notes relating to counterpoint. The same technique is also present in portions of the great and artistically significant Magnificat of Nicolaus Radomski. The practice of organum that is related to fauxbourdon developed no further than a certain specific note-against-note technique, which can be observed in some pieces in MS 1361 in the Raczyński Library in Poznań from the end of the 15th century—a technique still well known in the 16th century.

The polyphonic art that was modern in the Middle Ages is but sparsely documented in Poland. Fragments of motets from the 14th century in Gradual D 2 of the Clarissines in Stary Sącz show that Ars antiqua was known in Poland. But, after these, the next manuscript comes from the early 15th century (MS 2464 of the Jagiellonian Library in Cracow). The contents of this anonymous manuscript (evidently a school exercise, containing comments by a teacher named Rambowski) go back to the 14th century and involve various texts in polyphonic settings. It is on the borderline between primitive and educated technique. More interesting are the two-voiced portions of the Mass in a parchment leaf that originated from Cracow at the end of the 14th century. It contains anonymous settings of the *Gloria*, the *Kyrie*, and the *Sanctus* preserved in only fragmentary form, and is, except for the *Gloria*, scarcely legible. It was apparently composed in ballade style and written in French mensural notation.

The strongest evidence of the high culture of Cracow and, in general, of its wide contacts with what was then the new European music, appears in MS 52 in the Krasiński Library in Warsaw and MS 378 in the National Library at Warsaw, dating from the first half of the 15th century: these contain works by Ciconia, Zacharias, Grossin de Parisiis, and Egardus. They also contain a unique record of the most eminent Polish composer of this period, Mikołaj of Radom: his nine three-voiced works, including three pairs of *Glorias* and *Credos*, a *Magnificat*, a *Historiographi aciem* in ballade style, and a piece without text. According to Ludwig, his work shows that he was "familiar with the most advanced technique." Also some anonymous compositions are to be found, of which at least three are Polish. The most interesting of them are the hymn "Cracovia civitas" and a student song "Breve regnum." Further development in the 15th century is documented by songs incorporating Polish text including "*Chawla tobie Gospodzinie*" in the Kórnik Library, MS 801 (*ca.* 1450), which is the first example of white mensural notation in Poland, and "*O nadroższy kwiatku,*" written on a late-15th-century parchment leaf that was until 1944 in the National Library in Warsaw. Quite significant too is the late-15th-century MS 1361 in the Raczyński Library in Poznań, which, in addition to the examples of simple note-against-note practice that have been mentioned (among them a Polish song in fauxbourdon "*Bądz wiesoła*"), contains compositions in which the voices imitate each other throughout. Also included are works that appear in the *Trent Codices* and the *Glogau Songbook*. Though this manuscript comes from a provincial monastery, we may assume that there was an extensive late 15th-century art in the larger Polish centers. Unfortunately the record of all this has been lost, but there is evidence that the musical culture in Cracow, where Heinrich Finck received his musical training, was quite rich.

Bibliography

Anc. Greek Origins: J. Handschin, *Musikgeschichte* (Lucerne 1948); H. Husmann, *Die mittelalterliche Mehrstimmigkeit* (MW); C. Stumpf, *Geschichte des Konsonanzbegriffes* (I: In Antiquity, 1897) and *Die pseudoaristotelischen Probleme* (1897); P. Wagner, *Über die Anfänge des mehrst. Gesanges* (ZfMw IX, 1926–7). *Teutonic Origins:* H. C. Broholm, W. P. Larsen, and G. Skjerne, *The Lures of the Bronze Age* (Copenh. 1949); R. v. Ficker, *Primäre Klangformen* (JbP 1929); art. Germanische Musik (MGG); art. Musik (Reallexikon der Vorgeschichte, Bln. 1927). *Origins suggested by Compar. Musicol.:* M. Schneider, *Gesch. d. Mehrstimmigkeit* (2 vols., Bln. 1934–5).

Early Organum: Guido "Micrologus" new ed. AIM; *Milan Treatise* new ed. in E. de Coussemaker, *Histoire de l'Harmonie au moyen-âge* (Paris 1852); *Codex Calixtinus* new ed. Santiago de Compostela 1944; W. Apel, *From St. Martial to Notre-Dame* (JAMS II); H. M. Bannister, *Un Fragment inédit de "Discantus"* (Revue grégorienne 1911); H. Besseler, *Die Musik des Mittelalters u. d. Renaissance* (Bücken Hdb.); J. Chailley, *L'école mus. de St. Martial* (Paris 1960); E. de Coussemaker, *Histoire de l'Harmonie au moyen-âge* (Paris 1852); R. v. Ficker, *Der Organumtraktat d. Vatikanischen Bibliothek* (KmJb 1932), *Die Musik des Mittelalters und ihre Beziehung zum Geistesleben* (DVLG III, 1925), and *Formprobleme der mittelalterlichen Musik* (ZfMw VII); W. H. Frere, *The Winchester Tropar* (Publ. of the H. Bradshaw Soc., vol. VIII, London 1894, texts only); T. Georgiades, *Musik u. Sprache* (Heidelberg 1954); J. Handschin, *Musikgesch.* (Lucerne 1948) and *Zur Gesch. d. Lehre vom Organum* (ZfMw VIII); A. Hughes, *The Birth of Polyphony* and *Music in the Twelfth Century* (NOHM II); W. Krüger, *Die authentische Klangform des primitiven Organums* (Kassel 1958); F. Ludwig (Adler Hdb.) and *Die mehrst. Musik d. 11. u. 12. Jh.* (Kongressbericht Vienna 1909); G. Reese, *Music in the Middle Ages* (N. Y. 1940); H. Riemann, *Gesch. d. Musiktheorie* (1898, 2nd ed. 1921); G. Schmidt, *Strukturprobleme d. Mehrstimmigkeit in St. Martial* (Mf 1962); H. Spanke, *St.-Martial-Studien* (Zeitschr. f. franz. Sprache u. Literatur 1930–2); H. Spanke and II. Anglès, *Die Londoner St.-Martial-Conductushandschrift, La música del Ms. de Londres, Brit. Museum Add. 36881* (Bulletí de la Biblioteca de Catalunya, VIII, 1928–32); L. B. Spiess, *An Introduction to the Pre-St. Martial Sources of Early Polyphony* (Speculum XXII, 1947); E. Steinhard, *Zur Frühgesch. d. Mehrstimmigkeit* (AfMw 1921); W. von den Steinen, *Karolingische Kulturfragen* (Welt als Geschichte, 1950); O. Ursprung, *Die kath. Kirchenmusik* (Bücken Hdb.); E. Waeltner, *Das Organum bis z. Mitte d. 11. Jh.* (Diss. Heidelberg; Kongressbericht Oxford 1955) and *Der Bamberger Dialog über das Organum* (AfMw 1957); P. Wagner, *Die Gesänge d. Jacobus-Liturgie zu Santiago de Compostela* (Freiburg, Switz. 1931); W. Waite, *The Rhythm of the Twelfth Century Polyphony in France* (Yale Univ. Press 1954); F. Zaminer, *Der vatikanische Organum-Traktat* (Tutzing 1959); arts. Organum, Saint-Martial (MGG).

Notre Dame School: exs. Sch 9, 10, 16. *Anonymus IV* new ed. in Coussemaker, Script. I, also Brooklyn 1959. *Other new eds.* of Notre Dame comps.: J. H. Baxter, *An Old St. Andrew's Music Book* (London 1931, facs. of Codex Wolfenbüttel Helmstedt 628); L. A. Dittmer, *Codex Wolfenbüttel Helmstedt 1099 W_2* (facs. IMM, Brooklyn, N.Y.) and *Firence, Biblioteca Mediceo-Laurenziana, Pluto 29, 1* (facs., IMM, Brooklyn); R. v. Ficker, *Musik der Gotik. Perotinus, Organum quadruplum Sederunt principes* (Vienna 1930); H. Husmann, *Die drei- u. vierstimmigen Notre-Dame-Organa* (PäM 11). *Studies:* L. A. Dittmer, *Änderung der Grundrhythmen in den Notre-Dame-Handschriften* (Mf 1958); R. v. Ficker, *Probleme d. modalen Notation* (AMl XVIII–XIX); A. Geering, *Die Organa u. mehrst. Conductus in d. Handschriften des dt. Sprachgebietes vom 13. bis 16. Jh.* (Bern 1952); F. Gennrich, *Bibliographie der ältesten franz. u. lat. Motetten* (Darmstadt 1957); E. Gröninger, *Repertoire-Untersuchungen zum mehrst. Notre-Dame-Conductus* (Regensburg 1939); J. Handschin, *Trope, Sequence and Conductus* (NOHM II), *Zur Gesch. von Notre Dame* (AMl IV) and *Zur Frage d. Conductus-Rhythmik* (AMl XXIV); H. Husmann, *Das System d. modalen Rhythmik*

(AfMw XI), *Die dreist. Organa d. Notre-Dame-Schule* (Diss. Berlin 1932), *Die Offiziumsorgana d. Notre-Dame-Zeit* (JbP 1935), *Notre-Dame u. St. Victor* (Acta 1964), and *The Origin and Destination of the Magnus Liber Organi* (MQ 1963); T. Karp, *Towards a Critical Edition of Notre Dame Organa Dupla* (MQ 1966); F. Ludwig, *Perotinus Magnus* (AfMw III), *Repertorium organorum recentioris et motetorum vetustissimi stili* (I, 1, Halle 1910, new ed. and II, IMM), and *Über den Entstehungsort d. grossen Notre-Dame-Handschriften* (Adler-Festschrift 1930); M. Machabey, *A propos des Quadruples Pérotiniens* (MD 1958); A. M. Michalitschke, *Studien z. Entstehung u. Frühentwicklung d. Mensuralnotation* (ZfMw XII) and *Theorie des Modus* (1923); F. Reckow, *Der Musiktraktat des Anonymus IV* (Wiesbaden 1967); H. Schmidt, *Die drei- u. vierst. Organa d. Notre-Dame-Schule* (1933); H. Tischler, *The Evolution of the Harmonic Style in the Notre Dame Motet* (AMl 1956); art. Conductus (MGG).

Latter Half of the 13th Century: exs. Sch 18–20; *Piae cantiones:* J. Handschin, *Das älteste Dokument für die Pflege der Mehrstimmigkeit in Dänemark* (Acta 1935); G. R. Woodward, ed., *Piae cantiones* (London 1910, facs. new ed. in *Documenta Musicae Fennicae 10*, Helsingfors 1967). *Johannes de Garlandia "De Musica mensurabili"* new ed. Coussemaker, Scriptores I. *Jacques de Liège "Speculum musicae"* new ed. vols. 1 and 2, Rome. *Other eds. of Ars Antiqua:* H. Anglès, *El Códex de las Huelgas* (3 vols., Barcelona 1931, facs. with transcr.); P. Aubry, *Cent motets du XIIIe siècle* (3 vols., Paris 1907, facs. and transcr. of Bamberg MS); J. H. Baxter, *An Old St. Andrew's Music Book* (London 1931, facs. of Wolfenbüttel Helmst. 628); E. de Coussemaker, *L'Art harmonique aux XIIIe et XIVe siècle* (Paris 1856); Y. Rokseth, *Polyphonies du XIIIe siècle* (4 vols., Paris 1935–48, facs. and transcr. of the Montpellier MS); J. Wolf, *Gesch. d. Mensuralnotation von 1250–1460* (vols. 2 and 3 are devoted to examples, with facs. and transcr. 1904). *Studies:* E. Apfel, *Beiträge zu einer Geschichte der Satztechnik von der frühen Motette bis Bach* (2 vols., Munich 1964–5) and *Der Diskant in d. Musiktheorie des 12.–15. Jh.* (Diss. Heidelberg 1953); A. Auda, *Les "Motets Wallons" du manuscrit de Turin: Vari 42* (Brussels 1953); H. Besseler, *Die Motette von Franco von Köln bis Philipp von Vitry* (AfMw VIII); F. Gennrich, *Abriss der frankonischen Mensuralnotation* (2nd ed. Darmstadt 1956) and *Bibliographie d. ältesten franz. u. lat. Motetten* (Darmstadt 1957); A. Hughes, *Music in Fixed Rhythms* and *The Motet and Allied Forms* (NOHM II); H. Husmann, art. Bamberger Handschrift (MGG) and *Die Motetten d. Madrider Handschrift* (AfMf II); F. Ludwig, *Die 50 Beispiele Coussemakers aus d. Handschrift von Montpellier* (SIMG 5, 1903–4), *Die Quellen d. Motetten ältesten Stils* (AfMw V), and *Repertorium organorum recentioris et motetorum vetustissimi stili I, 1* (1910); W. Meyer, *Der Ursprung des Motets* (Ges. Abhandl. z. mittelalt. Rhythmik, Bd. 2, 1905); A. Michalitschke, *Studien z. Entstehung u. Frühentwicklung d. Mensuralnotation* (ZfMw XII); H. Riemann, *Gesch. der Musiktheorie* (1898, 2nd ed. 1921); M. Schneider, *Der Hochetus* (ZfMw XI); F. J. Smith, *The Speculum Musicae of Johannes Leodiensis. A Commentary to Book I* (IMM, Brooklyn, N. Y.); J. Wolf, *Gesch. d. Mensuralnotation von 1250 bis 1460* (3 vols., 1904) and *Handbuch d. Notationskunde* (2 vols., 1913–9); arts. Franco von Köln, Hieronymus de Moravia, Hoquetus, Jacobus von Lüttich, Johannes de Garlandia, Johannes de Grocheo, Motette, and Notre-Dame-Epoche (MGG).

14th Century in France: Mass of Tournai new ed. by Coussemaker 1861, further AIM; *Fourteenth Century Mass Music in France* (text and music AIM); *Sumer is icumen in* Sch 17; *Philippe de Vitry* new ed. AIM, compl. ed. in *Polyphonic Music of the 14th Century* (Monaco 1956); new ed. of "Ars Nova" treatise in AIM; H. Besseler, *Die Motette von Franco v. Köln bis Philippe de Vitry* (AfMw 1927); A. Machabey, *Notice sur Philippe de Vitry* (RM 1929); art. Vitry (MGG). *Johannes de Muris:* art. (MGG). *Guillaume de Machaut:* eds.: *Mus. Werke*, 3 vols. in PäM, ed. F. Ludwig; 4 vols., ed. H. Besseler, 1954; *Oeuvres* (Poetic Works, 3 vols., ed. E. Hoepffner, Paris 1908–21); New coll. ed. 1949–   Rome, I. Mass, ed. G. de Van; V. Chichmaref, *Oeuvres lyriques de G. d. Machaut* (2 vols., Paris and St. Petersburg 1909); sels. Sch 26 a, b, 27; numerous separate eds. of the Mass; *Studies:* S. Cape, *The Machaut Mass and Its Performance* (The Score, London, June 1959 and Jan. 1960); O. Gombosi, *Machaut's Mass Notre-Dame* (MQ 1950); U. Günther, *Chronologie und Stil der Kompositionen G. d. M.* (AMl 1963); R. H. Hoppin, *Notational Licenses of G. de M.* (MD 1960); A. Machabey, *G. de M.* (RM 1930–1) and (2 vols., Paris 1955); G. Reaney, *G. de M.: Lyric Poet* (M&L, vol. 39, Jan. 1958), *The Ballads, Rondeaux, and Virelais of G. de M.* (AMl 27, 1955), *The Poetic Forms of Machaut's Musical Works* (MD 1959), and *Towards a Chronology of Machaut's Musical Works* (MD 1967); G. Reichert, *Das Verhältnis zwischen mus. u. textlicher Struktur in d. Motetten M.s* (AfMw 1956); art. Machaut (MGG). *Machaut's Contemporaries:* M. A. Baird, *Changes in the Literary Texts of the Late 15th and Early 16th Centuries* (MD 1961); U. Günther, *Datierbare Balladen des späten 14. Jh.* (MD 1961–2); R. H. Hoppin, *Notes biographiques sur quelques musiciens du XIVe siècle* (Compte-rendu du Colloque International d'Ars Nova, Liège 1959); G. Reaney, *New Sources of Ars Nova Music* (MD 1965).

14th Century in Italy: Marchetto da Padua "Pomerium" new ed. AIM; *Francesco Landino:* sel. Sch 23; coll. ed. Cambridge, Mass. 1939, new coll. ed. in prep. AIM; *Polpphonic Music of the 14th Century, vol. IV: The Music of F. L.* (Monaco 1958, suppl. vol. of Commentary Notes to vol. IV). *Johannes Ciconia:* sel. Sch 29; new ed. in prep. AIM; S. Clercx, "Un musicien liégois et son temps" (*Revue Belge de Musicologie* 1955–6, *Annales Musicologiques III*); Kongress-Bericht Utrecht 1952; *La capella musicale del duomo di Milano* (IeM); art. Ciconia (MGG). *Ars Nova and Trecento*, eds.: W. Apel, *French Secular Music of the Late Fourteenth Century* (Cambridge, Mass. 1950); P. Aubry, *Le Roman de Fauvel* (facs. Paris 1907); E. de Coussemaker, *Messe du XIIIe siècle* (Paris 1861); A. Gastoué, *Le manuscrit de musique du Trésor d'Apt* (Paris 1936); F. Gennrich, *Rondeaux, Virelais und Balladen* (2 vols., 1921–7); W. T. Marocco, *Fourteenth Century Italian Cacce* (Cambridge, Mass. 1942); N. Pirotta, *Fourteenth Century Music in Italy I* (AIM); L. Schrade, ed., *Polyphonic Music of the 14th Century* (Monaco 1956–   ); G. de Van, *Les monuments de l'Ars nova* (I, 1, Paris 1938); J. Wolf, *Der Squarcia-lupi-Codex* (Lippstadt 1955), *Gesch. d. Mensuralnotation v. 1250–1460* (3 vols., of which 2 and 3 are of exs., facs. and transcr., 1904), and *Mus. Schrifttafeln* (MS facs. 1923); *Matteo da Perugia* (IeM, nuova serie, vol. 1); *The Music of Jacopo da Bologna* (Berkeley and Los Angeles 1954); *Trienter Kodices 5 and 6, sels.* (DTÖ 61 and 76); *over-view:* cf. gen. discussion of Middle Ages, also H. Besseler art. Ars nova (MGG); *Studies:* W. Apel, *The French Secular Music of the Late 14th Century* (AMl 18–19,

1946–7); E. Apfel, *Der Diskant in d. Musiktheorie d. 12.–15. Jh.* (Diss. Heidelberg 1953); H. Besseler, *Studien z. Musik d. Mittelalters* (AfMw 7 and 8); R. Bragard, *Le Speculum Musicae* (MD 1953–4); L. Ellinwood, *F. Landino and his Music* (MQ 1936) and *The 14th Century in Italy* (NOHM III); K. v. Fischer, *Ein Versuch zur Chronologie zu Landinis Werken* (MD 1966), *Kontrafakturen u. Parodien ital. Trecentowerke* (Annales musicologiques V), *On the Technique, Origin, and Evolution of Italian Trecento Music* (MQ 1961), *Studien zur Musik des ital. Trecento u. frühen Quattrocento* (Bern 1956), *Trecentomusik—Trecentoprobleme* (AMl 1958), and *Zur Entwicklung der ital. Trecento-Notation* (AfMw 1959); F. Gennrich, *Grundriss einer Formenlehre d. mittelalterl. Liedes* (Halle 1932); F. Ghisi, *Strambotti e laude travestimento spirituale della poesia musicale del Quattrocento* (Collectanea Historiae Musicae I, 1953); O. Gombosi, *Machauts Mass Notre Dame* (MQ 1950); U. Günther, *Der mus. Stilwandel der franz. Liedkunst in d. 2. Hälfte des 14. Jh.* (Hamburg 1957) and *The 14th Century Motet and its Development* (MD 1958); V. L. Hagopian, *Italian Ars Nova Music. A Bibliographic Guide to Modern Editions and Related Literature* (Berkeley and Los Angeles 1964); H. Harder, *Die Messe von Toulouse* (MD VII); R. Jackson, *Mus. Interrelations between 14th Century Mass Movements* (AMl 1957); K. Jeppesen, *Die ital. Orgelmusik am Anfang d. Cinquecento* (Copenh. 1943); A. von Königslöw, *Die ital. Madrigalisten des Trecento* (1940); F. Ludwig, *Die mehrst. Messe des 14. Jh.* (AfMw 7) and *Die mehrst. Musik des 14. Jh.* (SIMG 4); A. Machabey, *G. de Machaut* (RM 1930–1) and *Notions scientifiques disseminées dans les textes musicologiques du moyen âge* (MD 1963); W. T. Marrocco, *The Music of Jacopo da Bologna* (Berkeley 1954); N. Pirotta and E. Li Gotti, *Paolo Tenorista "exta moenia"* (*Estudios dedicados a Menendez Pidal*, vol. III, Madrid 1952); N. Pirotta, *Il Codice di Lucca* (MD 1950–1) and *M. de Padua and the Italian Ars Nova* (MD 1955); G. Reaney, *A Chronology of the Ballades, Rondeaux, and Virelais Set to Music by G. de Machaut* (MD 1952), *Ars nova in France* (NOHM III), *Concerning the Origins of the Rondeau, Virelai, and Ballade Forms* (MD 1952), *Fourteenth Century Harmony and the Ballades, Rondeaux, and Virelais of G. de Machaut* (MD 1953), *The "Ars nova" of Philippe de Vitry* (MD 1956–7), *The Ballades, Rondeaux, and Virelais of G. de Machaut* (AMl 1955), *The Ms Paris, Bibl. Nat., Fonds Italien 568* (Pit) (MD 1960–1), and *The Poetic Forms of Machaut's Musical Works* (MD 1959); C. Sartori, *M. da Perugia e Bertrand Feragut* (AMl 1956); A. Schering, *Studien z. Musikgesch. d. Frührenaissance* (1914); L. Schrade, *A Fourteenth Century Parody Mass* (AMl 27, 1955); H. C. Slim, *Francesco da Milano* (MD 1965); F. J. Smith, *Ars nova. A Re-Definition?* (MD 1964–5); G. Vecchi, *Su la composizione del Pomerium di M. da Padova e la Brevis Compilatio* (Quadrivium I, Bologna 1956, and separately publ. Bologna 1957); J. Wolf, *Florenz in d. Musikgesch. d. 14. Jh.* (SIMG 3); *L'Ars Nova Italiana del Trecento. Convegni di studio 1961–7* (Certaldo 1968); arts. Ballata, Caccia, Chasse, Color, Florenz, Italien, Rondeau (MGG). *Notation:* W. Apel, *The Notation of Polyphonic Music 900–1600* (Cambr., Mass. 1942, 4th ed. 1949); J. Wolf, *Gesch. d. Mensuralnotation von 1250 bis 1460* (3 vols., 1904) and *Handbuch d. Notationskunde* (2 vols., 1913–9).

Late 14th Century in France and Italy: MS. *Faenza 117* facs. new ed. in MD 1959. *Avignon School:* R. v. Ficker, *The Transition on the Conti-*

nent (NOHM III); A. Gastoué, *Le Manuscrit de musique polyphonique du trésor d'Apt* (Paris 1936); U. Günther, *Das Ende der Ars nova* (Mf 1963), *Das Wort-Ton-Problem bei Motetten des späten 14. Jahrhunderts* (Festschrift Besseler, Leipzig 1961), and *Zur Biographie einiger Komponisten der Ars subtilior* (AfMw 1964); G. Reaney, *The Ms Chantilly* (MD 1954); arts. Color and Messe (MGG). *Eds.:* W. Apel, *French Secular Music of the Late Fourteenth Century* (Cambridge, Mass. 1950); *Early 15th-Century Music* (Cordier, Cesaris, Carmen, Tapissier), AIM.

England to the End of the 16th Century: Gymel ex. Sch 33. Sumer is icumen in Sch 17. Fauxbourdon Style ex. Sch. 33. John Dunstable: new ed. The Old Hall MS (Burnham 1933–8), coll. ed. MB VIII; exs. Sch 34–37; *Studies:* C. v. d. Borren, *The Genius of Dunstable* (PMA, London 1921); M. Bukofzer, *English Church Music of the 15th Century* (NOHM III), *John Dunstable and the Music of his Time* (PMA, London 1938), *The Music of the Old Hall MS* (MQ 1948–9), and *Über Leben und Werke von Dunstable* (AMl 1936); L. A. Dittmer, *Auszug aus The Worcester Music-Fragments* (Diss. Basel 1955); C. Stainer, Dunstable (SIMG II); arts. Dunstable, England (MGG). *Editions:* M. Bukofzer, coll. ed. of Dunstable, MB VIII (1954); A. Hughes, *Worcester Medieval Harmony of the 13th and 14th Centuries* (London 1928); A. Ramsbotham, H. B. Collins, and A. Hughes, *Old Hall Manuscript* (3 vols., 1933–8); J. Stainer, *Early Bodleian Music* (2 vols., London 1901); sels. from Trent Codices in DTÖ 7, 27, 31, 40; *The Worcester Fragments* (AIM). *Studies:* E. Apfel, *Der klangliche Satz u. d. freie Diskantsatz im 15. Jh.* (AfMw 12, 1955), *Die klangliche Struktur der spätmittelalt. Musik als Grundlage der Dur-Moll-Tonalität* (Mf 1962), *Studien z. Satztechnik der mittelalt. engl. Musik* (2 vols., Heidelberg 1959), and *Zur Entstehung des realen vierst. Satzes in England* (AfMw 1960); M. Bent, *Sources of the Old Hall Music* (PMA 1967–8) and *The English Chapel Royal before 1300* (PMA 1963–4); H. Besseler, *Bourdon und Fauxbourdon* (Lpz. 1950), *Das Neue in d. Musik d. 15. Jh.* (AMl 26, 1954), and *Tonalharmonik und Vollklang* (AMl 24, 1952); M. Bukofzer, *English Church Music of the 15th Century* (NOHM III), *English Medieval and Renaissance Music* (N. Y. 1950), *English Music of the Mid-Fifteenth Century* (NOHM), *Fauxbourdon Revisited* (MQ 38, 1952), *Gesch. des engl. Diskants u. des Fauxbourdons nach den theoret. Quellen* (Strassburg 1936), *Popular and Secular Music in English* (NOHM III), *Sumer is icumen in* (Univ. of Calif. Publ. in Music, 1944), *Studies in Medieval and Renaissance Music* (N. Y. 1950), *The Gymel: the Earliest Form of English Polyphony* (M&L 1935); *Popular and Secular Music in England* (NOHM III), *The Music of the Old Hall MS* (MQ 1948–9), *Über Leben u. Werke von Dunstable* (AMl 8, 1936), and art. Dunstable (MGG); L. A. Dittmer, *An English Discantuum Volumen* (MD 1954), *Auszug aus The Worcester Music-Fragments* (Diss. Basel 1952, 1955), *Beiträge zum Studium der Worcester-Fragmente* (MF 1957), *Binary Rhythm, Musical Theory and the Worcester Fragments* (MD 1953), and *Veröffentlichungen mittelalterl. Musikhandschriften Nr. 5* (Worcester Add. 68, Westminster Abbey 33327, Madrid Bibl. Nac. 192) (Brooklyn, N. Y. 1959); R. v. Ficker, *Die frühen Messenkomp. der Trienter Codices* (StMw 11), *Die Kompositionstechnik der Trienter Messen* (StMw 7), *Epilog zum Faburdon* (AMl 25, 1953), and *Zur Schöpfungsgeschichte des Fauxbourdon* (AMl 23, 1951); T. Georgiades, *Engl. Diskanttraktate aus d. 1. Hälfte d. 15. Jh.* (1937); J. Handschin, *The Summer Canon and its Background* (MD 3 and 5); F. L. Harrison,

English Church Music in the 14th Century (NOHM III), Faburden in Practice (MD 1962), and Music in Medieval Britain (London 1958); A. Hughes and M. Bent, The Old Hall Manuscript (MD 1967); S. W. Kenney, "English Diskant" and Discant in England (MQ 1959); W. Korte, Die Harmonik des frühen 15. Jh. (1929); G. Reaney, Some Little Known Sources of Medieval Polyphony in England (MD 1961); E. H. Sanders, Cantilena and Discant in 14th-Century England (MD 1965) and Tonal Aspects of 13th-Century English Polyphony (Acta 1965); J. Travis, Miscellanea Musica Celtica (IMM); B. Trowell, Faburden and Fauxbourdon (MD 1959); E. Trumble, Fauxbourdon, an Historical Survey, I (IMM); N. Wallin, Hymnus in honorem Sancti Magni comitis Orchadiae: Codex Upsaliensis C 233 (STM 1961); arts. England, Leonel (MGG). Early Tudor eds.: The Eton Choirbook (MB X–XII); Tudor Church Music (I and III, Oxford 1923–9); Music of Scotland 1500–1700 (MB XV); Studies: H. B. Collins, John Taverner's Masses (M&L 1924–5); F. L. Harrison, Music in Medieval Britain (London 1958), English Polyphony c. 1470–1540 (NOHM III), and Church Music in England (NOHM IV); A. Hughes, An Introduction to Fayrfax (MD 1952); E. B. Warren, The Life and Works of Robert Fayrfax (MD 1957).

Polyphony in Poland: new eds. MDK; H. Feicht, Quellen zur mehr-stimmigen Musik in Polen vom späten Mittelalter bis 1600 (MAEO).

IV   Renaissance Music

16. The Transition to Modern Times

The transition from the Middle Ages to the subsequent historical period involved political, sociological, intellectual, and cultural changes so fundamental that they have continued to function even down to the present.

Politically and sociologically, the end of the Middle Ages significantly weakened the Holy Roman Empire and the Papacy, to the extent that national states developed, particularly in France, Italy, and Bohemia. The collapse of the *imperium* and dissolution of the *Universitas Christiana* marked the disappearance of Western unity. In Germany new cities arose from merchant settlements and took their places beside the cities that go back to the ancient Roman centers such as Cologne, Mainz, Worms, Strassburg, Regensburg, and Passau. The so-called free cities retained their legal significance and political independence; greater weight was placed on the guilds; princely absolutism developed; and armies of mercenaries supplanted knighthood in military significance.

Intellectually and culturally, the medieval image of the world was shattered by an expanding point of view. There were important discoveries in a number of fields: Christopher Columbus discovered America (1492); Vasco da Gama followed the sea-route to India (1498); and the globe was first circumnavigated from 1519 to 1521. European culture and Christian missions began spreading over the earth; interest in geography and science increased; and there was a complete realignment of world trade. The Spaniards and Portuguese became great powers, as did the Netherlanders and the English later.

There was a new orientation toward antiquity. Humanism, or the study of ancient Greek learning and poetry, goes back to 14th-century Italy, where it had been instigated particularly by Petrarch. From the

16th century on, it was the main force in education. The movement was given great impetus by refugee Greek scholars who had fled from Constantinople after it had been conquered by the Turks (1453). The ensuing movement is usually referred to as the Renaissance, which in its original sense meant a "rebirth" of art but in an enlarged sense has come to imply a new vision of the world and man. The Renaissance was inspired by the rediscovery of antiquity, and first arose in Italy. Medieval ways of working were soon displaced as artists discovered the laws of perspective and strove to imitate nature.

The Renaissance in general is often seen as having had three phases: the Early Renaissance in Italy or Quattrocento (1420–1500), the High Renaissance (1501–1530), and the Late Renaissance or Cinquecento (1530–1600). Humanism, particularly in Germany, is divided into two phases: one early (1400–1480) and the other more mature (1480–1600), led by Rodolphus Agricola, Reuchlin, and Ulrich von Hutten.

A direct manifestation of the same spirit occurred in ecclesiastical organization during the Reformation, spearheaded by Luther in Germany, Zwingli and Calvin in Switzerland, and the Anglican Church and Puritanism in England. In the Roman Catholic Church this precipitated the Counter Reformation (Catholic Restoration), which focused on the Council of Trent (1545–1563) and the development of the Jesuit Order (from 1540).

During this time the natural sciences took initial steps toward their modern phase in the work of Nicolaus Copernicus (d. 1543), Theophrastus Paracelsus (d. 1541), Giordano Bruno (d. 1600), Galileo Galilei (d. 1615), and Johann Kepler (d. 1630). A heliocentric world-picture replaced the geocentric one. Around 1450, Johann Gutenberg of Mainz discovered printing.

Having previously drawn a distinction between the history of music in antiquity and in the Middle Ages, we shall do the same for that in the subsequent age. Specifically, we might ask whether there is really anything that unites the whole history of music from the end of the Middle Ages to the present.

The following considerations point toward an answer:

1. The period around 1400 shifted the geographical focus of the history of music. During the entire Middle Ages leadership in the development of polyphony and the songs of the troubadours and trouvères centered in France. Italy did not decisively emerge until a short period during the latter two thirds of the 14th century. After 1400, however, England through John Dunstable entered significantly into the history of music. Although England's creative participation diminished after Dunstable's death (1453), a synthesis between English style, 14th-century French tradition, and Italian Trecento music occurred in works as early as those of Guillaume Dufay, beginning the epoch of Franco-Flemish music. At this point the focus shifted from the northern part of Western Europe, which during the 15th century was not very highly unified, either nationally or politically.

The second shift in geographical focus occurred about the middle of the 16th century and had a decisive effect upon the entire history of music in modern times: Italy, renewed by its own productive intensity, took its place alongside the countries to the North. The first achievement of Italian composers made its appearance in the form of the music of the Trecento. Initially they followed the lead of the Fleming Willaert, who taught the mastery of the compositional style of the Netherlands to his many Italian pupils. But, around 1550, Venice and Rome came to the fore, the latter particularly with Palestrina. By the end of the century, during the transition to the 17th-century High Baroque, Italy had attained a leading position in Europe.

2. The political and sociological changes that introduced the new age into world history had notable consequences in the history of music. During the 15th and 16th centuries they appear in especially sharp outline: the entry of the bourgeoisie into musical practice and their increasing participation, the cultivation of secular polyphonic song, the work of the meistersingers (in a certain sense Protestant church music also), and the growth of instrumental dance music.

3. A fundamental change in the conception of music had already set in by 1300 and had overthrown the authority of Boethius. Before his death in 524 Boethius had set up the three-fold division that was retained throughout the whole medieval period: *musica mundana, musica humana,* and *musica instrumentalis. Musica mundana* was the harmony of the spheres, unavailable to the human ear. *Musica humana* was the harmony between the body and the soul. *Musica instrumentalis* was the play of instruments, and thus, though only one member of this trinity, the actual music of our human world. According to Boethius, God had ordained contemplation as the ultimate purpose of music.

Johannes de Grocheo (probably a professor at the Sorbonne about 1300) thought the only music that existed was that which made sound. He abandoned the realm of speculation and distinguished between music as a science and as an art: as a science it dealt with basic matters, but as an art it contributed to the practical understanding of the activity itself. He created a new three-fold division: folk-music, canonic music, and sacred music. Folk-music served as a buffer against the inborn misfortunes of men. Canonic music was for the educated and for those who seek out the fine points of the arts. Secular music served the common man, and preserved the welfare of the state; sacred music served to praise the almighty Creator. Though Johannes de Grocheo retained some tendency to theologize music, he pioneered in establishing the bases of modern musical aesthetics. Also new at this time was the idea that music should be given specialized social status.

Zarlino, in his *Istituzioni harmoniche* (1558), dissolved the universal connection between music and theology and strengthened the position of secular music, thereby implementing the trend toward considering music as sonic art. Music was both *scienza* and *arte*. As a *nobile scienza* it was to be based on knowledge and brought under laws and rules established by experimentation and the mathematics of acoustics. One made music to pass the time in leisure, banish earthly care, and preoccupy oneself nobly. Tones, intervals, and especially the modes had a certain affective character, which was experienced and felt through the senses. Sorrow and joy were the two ruling emotions. Music of the time of Zarlino aroused these emotions, and it was expected that the listener would react accordingly. He was to be attentive, willing, and well-disposed. Accordingly, Zarlino in presenting music entirely abandoned the attempt to theologize and placed all the more emphasis on aesthetic principles. His theories highly emphasized the subjective and were directly related to the music of the time.

4. Although the ancients have left ample evidence of their widespread cultivation of music in their literature and fine arts, the music itself of antiquity is extinct. In 1581 Vincenzo Galilei published the three hymns of Mesomedes for the first time. Examples of ancient Greek music could scarcely have been much read in the 16th century. The inspiration they exerted on Renaissance music, accordingly, came by way of literary sources, and led to the humanistic school-song, to the *chanson mesurée*, and finally to opera.

As a consequence, the impulses of Humanism and the Renaissance, though great powers in the history of the spirit, had only a limited and indirect influence upon creative work in music. On the other hand, we must not overlook the influence of antiquity on the entire Middle Ages (as exerted, for example, on Boethius in the theoretical realm) or the influence of Petrarch's humanistic poetry on the musical form of vocal music (in, for example, the 16th-century Italian madrigal).

5. Rather than begin with the antithesis between the Middle Ages and modern times, we shall begin with the special stylistic antithesis between Late Gothic and Renaissance. The differences between the two have been formulated by Hellmuth Christian Wolff thus:

Late Gothic was characterized by

1. Absolute music-making, without regard for the composed text.
2. Constructivistic, purely musical layout.
3. Flowing forms, streams of melody proceeding toward the "unending," with no sharp sections or subdivisions.
4. Linear leading of the voices without particular regard for a fused sound, parallel structure, or tonal layout.
5. Heightening of expressive feeling, of inner excitement, piling-up of voices, ornaments, and the dissonant succession of sounds.

The Renaissance, on the other hand, sought

1. Textual clarity of the music (adaptation of the music to the meter of the verse) and intelligibility of the texts that had been set to music.
2. Emotive interpretation of the texts.
3. Clarity and comprehensibility of the formulation in sharp sections with clear layout.
4. Attention to sound, to what is heard.
5. Careful expressive restraint.

When, where, and how did the transition from the Late Gothic to the Renaissance occur?

The Renaissance first manifested itself in the work of Dufay and Binchois around 1430. It can be observed in the way they delimit the musical periods, employ repetition, and introduce dance rhythms, broken chords, and parallel leading of several voices. It also appears in their use of the cyclic variation-Mass wherein the cantus firmus remains constant in all the movements.

The Renaissance in the Netherlands reached its culmination about 1500 with Obrecht and Josquin. At the same time, Late Gothic traits appeared in Agricola and Pierre de la Rue. Ockeghem was a representative of the French Late Gothic, with Renaissance elements.

In the first half of the 16th century the Late Gothic and the Renaissance coexisted. In Gombert the Gothic blossomed anew.

Around 1550, there was a heightened outburst of emotion that used sonorous and harmonic as well as declamatory means in Orlando di Lasso and Philippe de Monte. Accordingly, there was a trend away from the moderation of Renaissance style.

Though the Middle Ages and the Renaissance differed on some points, they agreed on others. One such point, only recently established by musicologists, is the development of relationships among the various parts and the whole based on numerical symbolism, as in the Masses of Dufay, Ockeghem, Obrecht, and Josquin.

Considering Renaissance music from the artistic point of view, we find that it is characterized by certain general features. There is a parallel between it and the visual arts of the Renaissance. In painting, for instance, there is close observation and study of nature and representation of the world as reported to us by our five senses; likewise in music there is a life-affirming quality in the choice of texts in the vocal music of secular society. The course of the melody and the vocal performance of the musical works are in agreement with each other. With their vocal character, the compositions represent a human quality generated by their physical aspect, the breath. The imitation of nature and the unification of the composition through the use of an *a cappella* style correspond to the recording of nature in the sciences and the scientific execution of central perspective in painting. The visible world was rationally conceived on the assumption that it was suffused by a trait that has much of the scientific method in it, is naturalistic, and avoids metaphysical symbolism. This unifying principle appears in music through the simultaneous composition of all the parts. In contrast to the additive composition of the Middle Ages, there now appeared a prevailing lightness, flow, elegance, and grace. The music is serene, melodically and rhythmically flowing; the language of the form is articulate and often rhetorical. The work of art as an indivisible unity gained perspicuity; and the power of the total effect proceeded from the principle of unity. The listener entered into a totality that he immediately grasped as he heard it. This unity of presentation and impression of totality correspond to the logical succession and relationship of the individual elements. The Renaissance motet, for example, contains a certain logic seemingly based on laws of proportion that are as yet not fully understood. There is an inner consistency in the agreement of individual elements, which depend on the text, as a new musical section begins with each new section of the text. An agreement of parts stemming from the text is the essence of the new ideal of beauty.

The musical rationalization of the Renaissance is but a part of the greater rationalization that gripped all phases of life (particularly the economic) in Italy. The full range of these new features was first reflected during the 15th century, not so much in the works of Italian composers as in the compositions of the Burgundian Dufay (though its presence there might be explained by his long residence in Italy). After Trecento music faded, Italy spawned no great creative personalities until the middle of the 16th century.

Are there common traits, accordingly, in the music that has prevailed from the end of the Middle Ages, or the beginning of the Renaissance to our present day? If so, do they justify our considering this a self-contained epoch under the heading "modern times"? The following points can be maintained in support of an affirmative answer:

1. Discovery of a new ideal of sensuous sonority in the parallel thirds and sixths of fauxbourdon, which retains a significance on into the music of Richard Strauss.
2. Development of the principle of variation as a melodic technique, at first in Dufay's Masses.
3. Architectonics through organization into periodic structures of groups of measures, through subdominant or dominant cadences, through repetition of individual sections, and through contrast of various groupings of sonority.
4. Organization of the whole according to one ultimate standard—the listener's ability to comprehend. Music was thus brought directly and forcibly to bear on achieving its effect.
5. Musical language of the emotions as the composer's spontaneous means of access to the performer and the hearer, released by the Humanist movement.

The conception of the Renaissance period in music, however, is still the subject of fundamental discussion. Heinrich Besseler in his article on the problem of the Renaissance in music (in the *Archiv für Musikwissenschaft*, 1966, as well as in an article on Vitry in *Musik in Geschichte und Gegenwart*) would begin the Renaissance as early as Philippe de Vitry (1291–1361), maintaining that this composer was the first to raise the Ars nova motet to the status of autonomous art. Previously the composer had been largely hidden within the group to which he belonged, but Vitry came forward as a personality, even working his own name into some of his compositions. In his hands the motet, previously bound to typical elements, now became an individual work of art—that is, each composition, in accordance with the particular nature of its text, was an entity unto itself, no longer entirely comparable to another piece.

Besseler also sees reasons for establishing the Renaissance in France as early as the 14th century. In England Walter Odington considered the major and minor third consonant. At that time this usage was quite unusual: it was not until a century later that Ramos de Pareja formulated it as a general rule. Also Machaut (d. 1377) gives in his *Livre du Voir Dit* an autobiographical account of his private love affair.

The later period of the Ars subtilior followed Vitry and Machaut in France, but Renaissance-like features appear in the work of Johannes

Ciconia (d. 1411), who provided his motets with something like a basis in tonal harmony, in which Besseler sees "a unification of music that rests on sympathetic human experience." This approach to tonal harmony was carried on further, by Guillaume Dufay (d. 1474). Besseler sees a move toward the full Early Renaissance by John Dunstable (d. 1453) with the development of a "pan-consonant" style in which dissonance was admitted only as a prepared suspension—a move which leads to the vocal style of Palestrina. From about 1440 to 1540 the Mass stood at the very center of musical composition. The art of polyphonic song was the Renaissance ideal. This was a humanized conception, a vocal art that increasingly became the model of instrumental music. The ideal of artistic autonomy was intrinsic, an art that was self-contained and free.

Besseler would apply the term "mannerism" to art after 1530 on the basis of its leading "away from tonality and the human" through the principle of mensuration and free distribution of word accent toward an "art of the superhuman," which ends with the epochal change about 1600. Then a new period begins with the Baroque.

Consideration of these matters is still fluid and by no means closed, as appears from the juxtaposition of the outlines of the concept of the Renaissance as given by Wolff and by Besseler. It is perhaps difficult to apply the concept of mannerism extensively to an epoch in musical style. Mannerism is not an epoch, but rather a specific type of expressive intention that appears at various stages of the Renaissance, the Baroque, the Romantic Era, and the present, but never entirely dominates any era exclusively.

As an era in the history of music, the Renaissance may be summarized thus:

1. Little is known about the type of artist that functioned in the Ars nova of 14th-century France. Apparently it was not until the Renaissance (*ca.* 1450 to 1600) that the concept of the musician as the modern artist was born. He became fully aware of himself and of the fact that the consciousness of the world was mirrored in his personality and his work and as such was understood, evaluated, respected, and honored by influential circles in his surrounding world. Thus, the modern idea of genius was born. Genius is a divine gift, and the work is determined by the quality of genius. Through the originality and power of his spirit, the genius sets himself above tradition and establishes the laws of the work. Genius is unique, inborn, and nontransferable.

2. The varied functions of music, as they had already appeared in Ars nova, now came to be sharply juxtaposed against each other: music for the church and for public festivities in contrast to music for connoisseurs; music for the learned in the socially upper circles in contrast to music for the broad mass of people. *Musica reservata* sums up the idea of a socially determined claim to a highly refined music. Separate styles gradually appeared in accordance with this classification.

3. This refinement reached its peak at the end of the 16th century in chromaticism. The conception and interpretation of the chromatic and enharmonic tonal *genera* of ancient Greek music influenced the chromaticism of this period.

4. Corresponding to the demand of the visual arts that nature be imitated, vocal composition strove to imitate nature through the characteristic feaures of the individual word—an attempt often formulated in the phrase *imitar la natura, imitar le parole.*

5. The culminating point of the Renaissance was reached in a fusion of the Netherlands compositional art and Italian musical feeling. Apparently the Italian love of vocalism, euphony, and form played a great role, as they always have in Italian folk-music.

6. At the beginning of the 16th century composers finally arrived at a basically new way of thinking: they abandoned the medieval technique of successive composition and instead simultaneously conceived and developed the individual voices. Thus, while the previous thinking had been additive, in that further voices came in by way of supplement to a given voice, composition was now conceived of as a whole complex. Musical form became an individual composition that resulted from whatever the artistic formulation might be.

7. The era of the Renaissance, especially in the 16th century, brought with it the almost absolute breakthrough of polyphonic music to a broad social audience that had not previously been reached. The process was hastened by the discovery and spread of music printing. The new universal form of musical cultivation gripped all countries of Europe. Particular national styles appeared on a secondary level, but the dominant style was derived from the combination of Franco-Flemish and Italian music.

8. The new idea of the creative artist did not alter the fact that he still worked to satisfy a demand. Music was composed for a definite purpose and thus developed a concrete relationship with practical life. The work of art was determined by the commission, not by some subjective whim of the artist, his association of ideas, or his personal life. Nevertheless music was autonomous in the sense of following its own self-contained laws.

The Beginnings of Music-Printing

Movable type was used in the earliest days of music-printing. A German printer, Hahn, utilized this method in Rome in 1476, as did also Jörg Reyser in Würzburg and Octavianus Scotus in Venice. They double-printed Gregorian chant—that is, they first printed the lines and then the notes. Petrucci in Venice applied this process to mensural music in 1498, and in 1501 he began issuing his editions—first with Netherlands chansons, then Masses, and so on—in the form of part-books, for which he first printed the text, initials, and lines, and then superimposed the notes. He brought out the first printed lute tablature in 1507. The German printer Oeglin in Augsburg also became active in 1512, and Schöffer in Mainz the following year.

Not until 1525 did Pierre Haultin in Paris discover how to do simple type-printing of music, impressing the lines and the notes simultaneously. Haultin's type was also used for organ and other keyboard music in 1530. Attaignant began issuing his editions in Paris in 1527.

Verovio in Rome first printed music from copper plates in 1586. Only in 1700 were soft metal plates stamped, in a fashion similar to the process widely used today.

The most important figures in 16th-century printing and publishing of music were: Petrucci, Antigo, Scotto, Gardano, Angelo, and Verovio in Italy; Oeglin, Schöffer, Rhau, Petreius, Johann vom Berg, Neuber, Ott, Grapheus, Gerlach, and Egenolff in Germany; Haultin, Briard, Granjon, Attaignant, Le Roy, and Ballard in France; Susato, Bellère, and Phalèse in the Netherlands; and Wynkyn de Worde, Tallis, Byrd, and Este in England.

Bibliography

H. Besseler, *Das Renaissanceproblem in der Musik* (AfMw 1966), M. v. Crevel, *J. Obrecht, Opera omnia, Editio altera, Missae VI* (Amsterdam 1960); F. Feldmann, *Numerorum mysteria* (AfMw 1957); D. Heikamp, *Zur Struktur der Messe L 'homme armé super voces musicales von Josquin Desprez* (MF 1966); M. Henze, *Studien zu den Messekompositionen von J. Ockeghem* (Bln. 1968).

17. Franco-Flemish Music of the 15th and 16th Centuries

By way of general history it should be understood that during the 15th century the power of the Duchy of Burgundy increased under Philip the Good (1419–1467) and Charles the Bold (1467–1477). In fact, Burgundy became the center of European culture; its best painting came from the brothers Hubert and Jan van Eyck, notably the Ghent altarpiece completed in 1432. The Burgundian cities reached the height of their eminence in 1477, when Marie of Burgundy married Maximilian I and Burgundy came under Hapsburg rule. At the same time (1450–1550) the Netherlands provinces were becoming increasingly important. Antwerp became the center of world trade, and the Renaissance blossomed in the Netherlands. In 1548 Charles V united all seventeen provinces of this region into the league of the "Burgundian Circle." In 1555 Philip II of Spain ascended the throne, which he occupied till 1598. But the Netherlands revolted, and in 1579 formed the Utrecht Union, as the seven northern provinces withdrew from Spain and became the Republic of the United Netherlands.

By way of introduction, it should be noted that Kiesewetter in 1829 and Fétis in 1869 concerned themselves with the "merits of the Netherlanders in music" and were awarded prizes by the Society of Dutch

Musicians. Since then, musicologists have spoken of the "Netherlands Schools."

But recently some scholars have questioned the way the period has been subdivided. First of all, the concept of the "Netherlands Schools" does not correspond to the outlines provided by the political framework of the 15th century. During that time, areas which are today French, Belgian, or Dutch belonged to the Netherlands and Burgundy. The ancestry of the composers involved has offered a further point of critical attack. Among the main composers, only Obrecht (from Bergen op Zoom) and Sweelinck (who came later) were Dutch, and none of the great composers really came from Burgundy. Dufay, Binchois, Josquin, and Lassus were born in the French-speaking province of Hainaut, which at that time belonged to Germany and today includes parts of France and Belgium. Isaac, Ockeghem, Willaert, and Gombert were Flemings. Besides, the activity of most of these composers took them far beyond their native regions.

The question of the time limits and, accordingly, the divisions into "schools" also poses some problems. Such boundary-lines overlap, as often in the history of art. Also an attempt to organize the period in terms of age-groups or generations has not proved entirely successful, for in many instances the birth-years have not been definitely established.

Recognizing these difficulties, Jacques Handschin has proposed that the entire epoch be designated "Franco-Flemish music of the 15th and 16th centuries," bringing together related phenomena in chronological episodes. H. Husmann has found the designation "Burgundian-Flemish" appropriate for the 15th century.

Hellmuth Christian Wolff regards the epoch as "a great stylistic unity characterized by strict polyphonic technique and linear equivalence of all voices," and contrasts it with the Italian music of the same and subsequent times, more homophonic and inclined to fuse sonorities. During the period we are here considering, we see Gothic and Renaissance tendencies interrelated in a way that was at once contemporaneous, coexisting, and opposing. In the previous chapter we have seen the implications of these two styles and their general course of development.

In its broadest outlines, the musical development of this era occurred in six phases:

First period (first half of the 15th century):
Guillaume Dufay (*ca.* 1400–1474)
Gilles Binchois (*ca.* 1400–1460)
Second period (latter half of the 15th century):
Johannes Ockeghem (*ca.* 1425–between 1494 and 1496)
Third period (end of the 15th century to the death of Josquin):
Jakob Obrecht (*ca.* 1450–1505)
Heinrich Isaac (*ca.* 1450–1517)
Josquin des Prez (*ca.* 1440–1521)
Fourth period (second third of the 16th century):
Nicolas Gombert (*ca.* 1500–*ca.* 1560)
Adrian Willaert (*ca.* 1490–1562)
Jacobus Clemens non Papa (*ca.* 1510–*ca.* 1557)

Fifth period (latter half of the 16th century):
  Philippe de Monte (1521–1603)
  Orlandus Lassus (1532–1594)
Holland in transition from the 16th to the 17th century:
  Jan Pieterszoon Sweelinck (1562–1621)

First Period

The First Half of the 15th Century

During the early 15th century three dominant musical traditions arrived at a stage of mutual influence: the music of France, centered in Paris; Italian music of the Trecento; and English music, headed by Dunstable. This encounter occurred in Northern France and Burgundy. The preferred musical forms were the Ordinary of the Mass, the hymn, the secular and sacred motet, and the chanson. They were cultivated by the court chapels in the administrative centers and by the great cathedrals. The Burgundian court under Philip the Good (1419–1467) and Charles the Bold (1467–1477) took the lead, bringing together many significant musicians. Among them, Guillaume Dufay created a new style. From the Northern French and Burgundian center the so-called Netherlanders, musicians of France, Burgundy, Flanders, and Holland, emigrated particularly to Italy, then to Germany and Spain. Everywhere they stimulated musical life and, especially in Italy, were themselves stimulated by it. They were active in both secular and sacred music, which enjoyed about equal favor throughout the 15th and 16th centuries.

Seen from an external point of view, the presence of English composers on the Continent is explained by the fact that the English occupied France in 1415 after their decisive victory at Agincourt. After 1416, English choirs came to be greatly admired, and it is quite possible that John Dunstable visited the Continent at this time.

Burgundian culture of the 15th century represented a fusion of the Romance and Teutonic spirits, of Low German character with French form. The last great exponent of Burgundian style was Charles V (d. 1558). Simultaneously the Late Gothic was enjoying something of an Indian summer in the work of Nicolas Gombert, from about 1530 to 1550. The epoch embodied the greatest antitheses between Gothic and Renaissance, between artificiality and naturalness, and between what was far from life and what was close to it.

Considering secular music first, we find that the chanson, or discant song, was cultivated with special love as a widespread form of art. It supplanted or perpetuated in different guise the ballade, or cantilena setting, such as Machaut had written. The Burgundian chanson was a three-voiced composition with tenor, cantus or discantus, and contratenor. The song-like solo melody of the top voice was accompanied by two instrumental lower voices; the tenor was song-like in character and supported the cantus as a counter-voice, while the contratenor was supplementary. This type of Burgundian chanson represented a milestone in the development of song. Obviously under Italian influence, it also

achieved simplicity of form and expression. The fact that verbal declamation coincided with musical rhythm was a new development. The
chansons of Binchois are the oldest evidence of the instrumentally accompanied song, displaying unity of poetry and music. The principle of
imitation manifested itself quite early in the chanson and was fully
developed in all voices by about 1450. Words or phrases of a text were
seldom repeated.

A typical feature was the cadence in which the highest voice leaps
up a third and the lowest voice an octave:

Example 35  Contratenor

The lowest voice may also make a leap of a fourth up or a fifth down, thus:

Example 36  Contratenor

When the chanson has four voices, they often form a cadence thus:

 then:

Example 37

The contratenor meanwhile was divided into a *contratenor altus,* or "high
contratenor," and a *contratenor bassus,* or "low contratenor," that led
into the region of a deeper sonority than had previously been used in
music. From the lowest to the highest, the voices were called Contratenor
bassus, Tenor, Contratenor altus, and Superius.

In the course of this development composers gradually dispensed
with the differences between vocal and instrumental parts and fashioned
all the voices melodically. The texts were secular and in verse form. The
most important form was the rondeau, perpetuating, as in Machaut, the
old form of the troubadours. It was characterized by fresh and lively
melody in triple time, clear layout with dominant-tonic or subdominant-
tonic cadences, song-like fluidity in the voices, and dance-like rhythm.
These characteristics were also common to the sacred music of the time.

In sacred music, the predominant form was the usually four-voiced
setting of the Ordinary of the Mass in a somewhat altered chanson composition with the cadences just described. Other types of sacred writing,
though secondary in importance, were the Proper of the Mass, compositions of the Office, and motets.

In the composition of the Ordinary, three types of Masses developed
from the application of the cantus-firmus principle:

1. Discant Masses. In basing their Mass-sections on liturgical melodies, composers gave these melodies figural treatment in the discant,
paraphrasing them melodically and rhythmically. In this respect they
differed from their English contemporaries. Netherlanders of the Dufay

period used paraphrase with the help of typical turns and cadence formulae, while at the same time English composers were using the cantus-firmus tones only as a framework for new melodic composition. It was not until the latter half of the century that the English method of melodic coloration became general on the Continent.

2. Tenor Masses. In the 15th century, composers began trying to give a particular musical unity to the parts of the Ordinary—that is, to unify the *Kyrie, Gloria, Credo, Sanctus,* and *Agnus* of any one Mass. Since, however, in each of the sections the appropriate liturgical cantus firmus was different, composers now began to use the same melody as the cantus-firmus basis for all parts, in order to achieve the unity they sought. The cantus firmus, which bestowed its name upon a particular Mass, was often of foreign origin and might be a sacred or Gregorian melody or a secular melody. The composer was also free to invent a cantus firmus, for example, Josquin's Masses *La sol fa re mi* and *Hercules dux Ferrariae.* The cantus firmus of the latter was derived from the vowels of the title: e u e u e a i e (re ut re ut re fa mi re). Favorite songs were taken up by numerous composers as cantus firmi of Masses, for example, "*L'homme armé*" or "*Se la face ay pâle.*" The cantus firmus might appear in the tenor after the manner of the motet practice of the 13th and 14th centuries in long note-values or organ points, or it might be rhythmically enlivened and lightly ornamented. The connection between the setting of the Ordinary and the liturgy through the liturgical cantus firmus was lost, but cyclic musical unity was achieved in its place. The Mass had now become a musical work of art, an achievement that seems first to have taken place in England, since the oldest tenor Masses are by Dunstable.

L'hom - me, l'hom - me, l'homm' ar - mé L'homm' ar -
mé doibt on don - ter. On a fait par tout cri - er
Que chas - cun se viengu' ar - mer D'un hau - bre - gon de fer.

Example 38

The presumably original form of the tune "*L'homme armé,*" probably the tenor of a chanson by Busnois, is no longer extant. "*L'homme armé*" is the cantus firmus in Masses by Dufay, Busnois, Ockeghem, Obrecht, Loyset Compère, Pierre de la Rue, Morales, Palestrina (in two instances), and Carissimi. There are, in all, some thirty known "*L'homme armé*" Masses.

In an article on Josquin's Mass "*L'homme armé super voces musicales*" in *Die Musikforschung* (1966), Dieter Heikamp makes a plausible case for the allusion here being to Christ. This interpretation is largely based on the symbolism of numbers. The weapons of the Christian struggle are the insignia of the Passion and the instruments and wounds of the Crucifixion, which were often represented in Late Medieval art.

3. Discant-Tenor Masses. In these, the chanson melody was in the tenor as cantus firmus and was at the same time colored in the discant.

The cyclic variation principle in the Mass goes back to Dunstable, with his Mass *Rex seculorum,* and to Dufay. An entirely new architectonic principle of formulation appeared. The cantus firmus remained the same in all movements of the Mass and stood in a relationship of more or less strict variation to each other, the entire course of the *Kyrie* forming the basis for the other four movements. This was a technique of melodic variation that differed from discant coloring, and involved principally the top voice, while the tenor retained the cantus firmus in long-held notes.

Characteristic of the early Netherlanders before 1430 were the clearly marked, piquant rhythms in duple time and the syllabic parlando style. These features are found also in early Dufay, and before him in the Old Hall manuscript. The stylistic change under English influence occurred between 1420 and 1430.

Sacred music that did *not* belong to the Ordinary was especially influenced by the secular three-voiced discant song. As in secular music, there was a general development in the direction of vocalization, as influences that had originated in fauxbourdon gave the individual voices an extensive rhythmic and melodic life in terms of a harmonically organized union of sonority.

The motets of the Dufay period are distinguished from those of the 14th century by their sacred content and four-voiced construction. The form of the isorhythmic motet was the first taken over in the tenor motet. The song-like treatment of the upper voice appeared in the song-motet with emphasis on the discant. Under the influence of Italian and English motets, strict architectonics were abandoned in favor of a free, effective structure, which permitted the development of independent individual portions. In place of the isorhythmic order of the upper voices there often appeared isomelody—that is, the upper voices, in correspondence with the tenor sections, were made up of similar melodic elements that seemed to be answering each other. The principle of thematic variation of the Mass also entered into the motet. On occasion the text already determined the form and expression of the music, as individual parts were set off from each other by individual musical expression.

The typical cadence is:

A typical cadence :

Example 39

Along with big motets for festive occasions, marriages, funerals, and the dedication of cathedrals such as Dufay's motet "Nuper rosarum flores" of 1436 for the dedication of the cathedral in Florence, there are song-motets that suggest a kind of sacred music for domestic use, the setting of which, however, corresponds to that of the discant song or chanson.

Around 1430 the decisive stylistic change occurred. While Gothic music was predicated on the sharp contrast between the rhythm of the declamation and that of the music, composers now tried to reconcile these two elements, in conformity with the sense of the words. A *cappella* style appeared, and instrumental influence strongly declined. Isorhythmic form was gradually replaced by free melodic variation, and polytextuality gradually disappeared.

The Trent Codices are the most inclusive manuscript sources of the music of the period. In the main they were prepared at the order of the royal secretary of Emperor Friedrich III, who reigned from 1440 to 1493. In all, they contain 1,864 sacred and secular compositions of Northern French, Flemish, English, Italian, and German composers and represent the repertoire of the imperial court chapel. From the seven books of the collection brought together between 1440 and 1465, we can distinguish between an older and a younger group of composers. Further sources are MSS Bologna, Bibl. G. B. Martini Q 15; Aosta, Seminario; Oxford, Bodleian, Canonici misc. 213; and Bologna, Bibl. Univ. 2216.

There are many aspects of the performance practice in the Dufay era that are problematical and apparently will never be entirely settled. The manuscripts give little information. It is rather certain that unaccompanied vocal renditions are justified only in motets and portions of the Mass in fauxbourdon style. Where singing voices and instruments collaborated, the clarity of the vocal line seems to have been the main consideration. Otherwise, the decisive considerations seem to have been the availability of voices and/or instruments for a particular performance. It is conceivable that this "vocal" music was, on occasion, rendered entirely by instruments. Although we are sure that instruments were used in church music, we do not know the exact details of their use.

Liège and Cambrai were the leading music centers and composition schools. Although we do not know how the composers were trained, we may assume that the training of singers and composers followed somewhat similar lines.

The two principal masters of the first period are Guillaume Dufay and Gilles Binchois. Along with them the well-known composers of the time were:

> Johannes Regis (*ca.* 1430–*ca.* 1485), Dufay's secretary at Cambrai, later active in Mons, and still later in Soignies, where he died.
>
> Jacques Barbireau (d. 1491), choirmaster at the Antwerp cathedral.
>
> Heyne von Ghizeghem (dates unknown), who was active in Cambrai and at the court of Charles the Bold of Burgundy.
>
> Antoine Busnois (d. 1492?), who served Charles the Bold and was recognized especially by Tinctoris—after Ockeghem perhaps the most famous composer of the time.

Guillaume Dufay (1400–1474), who was born probably in Hainault of Flemish-Walloon ancestry, was admitted as choirboy in Cambrai about 1409 or 1410, and appeared as a composer as early as 1420. He was in the service of the Malatestas in Rimini and Pesaro, perhaps from 1420 to 1426. He was again in Cambrai between 1426 and 1428. Between 1428 and 1433 he was in the Papal chapel at Rome, then was on leave of absence for two years, and returned to the Papal service—but at Florence and Bologna —from 1435 to 1437. In 1436 he was granted a canonry at Cambrai Cathedral; from 1437 to perhaps 1444 he was in Savoy; and from 1445 on, he was perhaps mostly in Cambrai, where he died on November 27, 1474.

Even during his lifetime Dufay was very highly esteemed. He and Dunstable, about thirty years his senior, spurred each other on to greater activity. Bukofzer draws a parallel between the artistic relationship of the two men and that of Haydn and Mozart. Dufay's fame suggests the broader possibilities of communication that had been established, enabling him to travel and to accept commissions for significant compositions intended for festivals of an impressive nature. His self-awareness left an imprint on the words of a motet that he wrote in anticipation of his own death, *"misere tui labentis Dufay"* (have mercy on Thy Dufay dying). During his career he became involved in some of the political events of his day. He was an outstanding personality and the leader of his era in music, largely through the broad scope of his work.

Dufay's style of composition—and, to some extent, early Renaissance style generally—is characterized by the song-like flow of all the voices. The harmonic principle appears in the formation of the melody, as in the structure of the melody the thirds of triads are linked with transitional notes, the voices are paralleled in thirds, and there is rich use of discant and fauxbourdon technique. In fact, Besseler would acclaim Dufay as the discoverer of fauxbourdon. In Dufay's compositions there is a strong tendency toward fused sonority, with frequent dominant and subdominant cadences. He developed the principle of the cyclic variation in the Mass. Occasionally he uses canons to intensify particular passages. He articulates the parts of the composition through sections and through the delimitation of measure groups, yet there is no periodization through groups of two or four measures. The rhythm of his work is rather sharp, at times almost dance-like. In the motets, the architectonic structure is indicated through variously grouped sonorities, but there are no repetitions of individual sections. Throughout his work four voices became the norm. The significance of the four voices in Dufay can in general be understood in this way: the bass bears the harmony; the tenor gives support and furnishes the axis of the construction; and the two upper voices, particularly the superius, carry the melody. In the layout of the movements Dufay works with effects of strong contrast, alternating duple and triple measures, as portions in two and three voices retain independent significance. Examples of imitation among the voices are rare. Each voice is extensively independent. Harmonic effects through cadences are frequent. Dufay has three degrees of relationship between the word and the tone: at the one extreme, he gives absolute precedence to the musical element; at the other, he observes close relationship between word and tone; and, at times, he joins the music and the text together rather liberally, according to syntax rather than according to the separate word. The note values of the cantus firmus are, in the repetition, occasionally augmented or diminished in exact proportion. Dufay's late Masses exercised influence for decades, leading to the extension of the Mass, the proportionately ordered relationship between individual movements, and the use of sacred and secular cantus firmi.

After Dufay, the next most important composer was Gilles Binchois. Born about 1400 in Mons in Hainault, he began as a soldier, but in 1430 became a singer in the Burgundian court chapel. Though he composed many sacred works, he was more active in the secular field of the typical Burgundian song. He died in 1460, apparently in Mons.

Second Period

The Second Half of the 15th Century

Dufay (d. 1474) exerted significant influence well on into the 15th century. But the more distinctive composers of this period tended to concentrate on church music and especially on setting the Ordinary of the Mass as a self-contained musical unit. They seem suddenly to have lost interest in the motet, favoring instead the chanson, which they preserved in elaborately prepared manuscripts known as *chansonniers*.

Everywhere they began writing in such a way that one voice imitated the other throughout a composition. This stylistic feature was rich in promise for the future. At first, according to Riemann, they introduced imitation of head-motives, of rhythmic features, and of motives that had been derived from the text. As these types of imitation extended over entire settings, the technique became known as "through-imitation"— that is, the sectional initial imitation in all voices. Through-imitation led to the equalization of the importance of the various voices and laid the groundwork for *a cappella* polyphony, which reached its zenith during the 16th century in the music of Palestrina. Four-voiced structure, which prevailed as early as the late work of Dufay, became the rule. Under the influence of the chanson, the composition seemed to open up, for example, by dividing the choral sound into portions for two and for three voices.

The course of the music was not defined by the measure as we understand it, but was based on the principle of "hovering accent" in the individual voice, in which the single beat bound the course of the whole quite loosely. The concept of "tactus" in early music is not the same as the modern idea of "time." Tactus involves the regulation of the elapse of time through a rhythmic unit without preconceptions of stressed and unstressed values. Modern "time" first came into being in the art-music of the Baroque Era.

The cantus firmus began to fill out all the voices and was treated in various ways. It could still, as in the old manner, appear in long notes in the tenor or bass; but it was also free to "wander" through all the voices. This is characteristic of the transition from the cantus-firmus Mass to the type in which the voices imitate each other throughout.

Thus arose in the Netherlands a musical art that has become almost proverbial for its complicated polyphonic construction. Ockeghem's *Deo gratias,* for example, has thirty-six voices, of which nine enter canonically at the distance of a measure followed by four different nine-voiced canons. However, only eighteen voices, at the most, are heard at the same time. In the "riddle canons" the inscriptions over the voice entries refer to such matters as inversion of intervals and crab movement, and are disguised in verbal puzzles that must be solved before performance. The culmination of this trend occurred during the period between 1475 and 1525. The deeper sense of riddle canons is still not entirely clarified, but under no circumstances were they just a matter of the composers' playing games with each other. It is possible that they may have had theological implications.

The main composer of this period was Johannes Ockeghem. Jean Pyllois, Petrus de Domarto, and Guillaume Faugues were among his contemporaries.

Johannes Ockeghem was born about 1425 in East Flanders, presumably in Dendermonde, and in 1443–4 became a singer in the choir of Notre Dame in Antwerp, perhaps also studying with Binchois. In 1448 Ockeghem served in the chapel of Duc Charles de Bourbon, and from 1452–3 to the end of his life in the chapels of the French kings Charles VII, Louis XI, and Charles VIII in Paris. In 1459 he was invested by the King with the important office of treasurer of the Abbey of St. Martin in Tours. From 1465 on, he was honored with the title *maistre de la chapelle de chant du roy.* In 1469 he was probably on a diplomatic mission to Spain, in 1484 on one to Flanders, and as early as the 1470's was regarded as the most famous musician of the period. His death between 1494 and 1496 in Tours was mourned throughout Europe; he had been highly esteemed for both his artistry and his human qualities, as evidenced by the elegies on his death. Through his own personality and his many private pupils, he exerted significant influence on the younger generation and on the period as a whole.

His music exhibits more antique traits than does Obrecht's, later in the century. The melodic aspects in Ockeghem are still less polished and flowing, triple rhythms prevail, imitations are seldom used, and through-imitation occurs only at voice entries. He adopted elements of the declining motet in the then predominant style of the discant song or chanson. In comparison with the style of Dufay and its striving toward fusion of sound, the melody in Ockeghem is much more animated, rich in syncopations, counter-movements, and voice-crossings. Most of his Masses have been worked out in accordance with the principles of cyclic variation, as in Dufay. At the same time, Ockeghem introduced something new in his development of a principle of free motivic variation, in which motifs of the model are constantly renewed through extension and variation. Also Ockeghem considerably extended Dufay's principle of choosing the first head-motif of the discant as the point of departure for ever new variations. Historically, Ockeghem was principally significant for his Masses, though he further developed the style of the period and significantly deepened the possibilities of expression.

Ockeghem's pupils presumably included Josquin des Prez, Loyset

Compère (d. 1518), Antoine Brumel, Pierre de la Rue (d. 1518), Jean Verbonnet, and Antoine Busnois.

Third Period

End of the 15th Century to the Death of Josquin

About the turn of the 15th century the third period ushered in a stylistic revolution that was ultimately to affect all features of Renaissance music. The latter half of the 16th century represents the continuation of these stylistic developments. This change in style revealed itself most clearly in the creative work of Josquin des Prez and brought to full bloom the *a cappella* style of the 16th century. It was manifest in the striving for clearer articulation of structure and in the development of a musical idiom of the emotions.

As composers made the voices imitate each other more and more closely, they arrived at a structure that at once was smoother and required clearer articulation of its parts. The melodic material of the cantus firmus was frequently spread out over the whole composition. The voices were led more and more in song-like lines. The various technical possibilities, such as cantus-firmus work, canon, and through-imitation, were fused or used side by side. By bringing individual voices together, or by dividing the choir, the composers made it sound as if more than one group were singing: there was, in other words, a multi-choral effect. Thus they clarified the layout of their pieces by articulating the sections with cadences and imitative reentry of the voices. But sometimes the attempt to perfect the formal order conflicted with the wish to make the words musically distinct. The text, accordingly, was interpreted primarily in terms of its over-all linguistic structure, was declaimed more as sentences than as words. A striking feature of the writing is the love of full choral sound, sonorous musical splendor, and euphony in the union of the vocal lines.

The emotional language, or affective idiom, that prevailed translated the expression of individual words or sentences in the music. Tendencies toward the development of an expressive art entailed a new relationship between word and tone. This manifested itself, for example, in the relationship between definite musical motives and words, such as a descending passage on the words *descendit de coelis*. Composers discovered the expressive value of the dissonance. They developed music as expression, with its own idiom in sacred and in secular music, as well as in individual genres, predominantly the Mass, motet, and chanson.

The leading composers of the period were Jakob Obrecht (*ca.* 1450–1505) and Josquin des Prez (*ca.* 1440–1521?).

The following composers were more or less of the same age:

Heinrich Isaac (before 1450–1517), who will be considered in detail among the German musicians of the time.

Loyset Compère (d. 1518).

Antoine Brumel (*ca.* 1460–*ca.* 1520), active in Chartres, Laon, and Paris, and perhaps choirmaster in Ferrara after 1505.

Pierre de la Rue (d. 1518), until 1512 at the court of Philip the Fair in Brussels.

Johannes Ghiselin, or Giovanni Verbonnet, in 1491 and 1503 in Ferrara and then in Bergen op Zoom.

Anton Divitis (*ca.* 1475–1526?), who served in the chapel of Philip the Fair and then was in the service of Louis XII in France.

Alexander Agricola (*ca.* 1446–1506), a composer of either Flemish or German ancestry, from 1474 in Milan and from 1500 in the service of Philip the Fair.

Caspar Weerbecke (*ca.* 1455–after 1506), a singer in the Papal chapel in Rome.

Antoine de Fevin (*ca.* 1470–1511 or 1512).

Jean Mouton (d. 1522 at St. Quentin), who was a pupil of Josquin and a teacher of Willaert and in 1513 became a member of the chapel of Louis XII of France.

Although our knowledge of the lives of these composers is somewhat incomplete, their position in their time is best judged by the fact that they are represented by works in the early editions printed by Petrucci.

The leading theoreticians were Johannes Tinctoris (d. 1511), Ramis de Pareja, Franchoni Gafori (Franchinus Gaffurius, d. 1522), and Giovanni Spataro. An important theoretician—though he belonged to the next generation—was Pietro Aron (*ca.* 1470–*ca.* 1545).

Tinctoris has given us a clear idea of the situation in the latter half of the 15th century, rather from a music critic's point of view. He saw England as the origin and source of the "new art," and he recognized a unique and hitherto unknown culmination of certain trends in music in the then contemporary leading generation of Dufay's pupils. *Suavitas* (sweetness) and *varietas* (variety) were for him the qualitative criteria of good music.

Johannes Tinctoris (*ca.* 1435–1511) was possibly at the Cambrai cathedral in 1460 and, according to his own report, taught the choirboys at Chartres. In 1474 he was at Liège, and about 1472 he entered the service of King Ferdinand I of Naples. We are not sure where Tinctoris was during the latter years of his life or where he died. Musician, mathematician, cleric, pedagogue, teacher of law, and one of the great Humanists, he was also the most prominent and comprehensive theoretician of his time. We have twelve of his treatises, including his *Diffinitorium musicae*, the first printed music dictionary. Perhaps the most important of the treatises is his *Liber de arte contrapuncti*.

Jacob Obrecht was born probably on November 22, 1450, in Bergen op Zoom, of Dutch ancestry. However, nothing is known of his youth and early training. His career is clearly documented, beginning around 1476 when he was choirmaster in Utrecht, from 1479 to 1484 at Bergen op Zoom, and in 1484 at the cathedral in Cambrai, where he was also consecrated as a priest. The following year he was in Bruges, in 1487 was on leave at the court in Ferrara, in 1492 went to Antwerp, and in 1496 returned to Bergen op Zoom. Two years later he was again in Bruges, probably spent from 1500 to 1504 in Antwerp, and then was in Ferrara, where he died, presumably of plague, in 1505.

Obrecht carried on further the process initiated by Ockghem that was to transform musical composition, endowing it with fundamental smoothness or polish. Most frequently the voices imitated each other to some extent, and there were the beginnings of through-imitation. Duple rhythm became more and more significant. Obrecht was the music teacher and friend of Erasmus of Rotterdam, the great Humanist. Glareanus in his *Dodekachordon* (1547) praised the "sublimity and vein of moderation" with which Obrecht wrote—in other words, he saw him as exemplifying the Humanistic attitude toward life. In this respect Glareanus contrasted him with Josquin, whose subjectivism, or "excesses of an effervescent genius," he found objectionable. This criticism of Obrecht, however, seems not to have been shared by all his contemporaries. Although he was active in his day, he exerted influence somewhat as if he were a significant outsider, in that he had no known pupils or followers.

Wolff sees Obrecht's music as fully bearing the stamp of the Netherlands Renaissance style. This is shown in the new, clearly disposed melody and the significance of the sequence, as well as the imitation and *ostinato* techniques, motivic repetitions, and strict four-measure periods. The cantus firmus is laid out in individual sections, clearly separated from one another. It appears in turn in the various sections as cantus firmus, with not only the tenor or discant voice being taken as model, but the entire composition, with many individual motives from all the voices. Accordingly, the principle of strict thematic work was developed further. Unlike Ockeghem with his principle of free motivic variation, Obrecht is bound much closer to the cantus-firmus model. Everywhere there is a recognizable effort to make the compositional work more clearly audible —that is, to convey the formal relationships and the structural order directly and impressively to the consciousness of the listener. The rhythm increases in sharpness and accentuation. The most numerous and important of Obrecht's works are his cyclic settings of the Mass. In the new complete edition brought out in Amsterdam in 1960, M. van Crevel has chosen a new way of transcribing and editing the Mass *Sub tuum praesidium.* Taking as a basis the theory of proportions outlined by Tinctoris in his *Proportionale*, he sets up a numerical table with symbolic background for the music—a table that has direct relationship to theology, as M. van Crevel has explained in his preface.

The most celebrated of the composers around 1500 was Josquin des Prez, who had been born about 1440 in the French-speaking area of Burgundy, though the exact place is not known. He was a choirboy in the collegiate church of St. Quentin, and perhaps—possibly as a result of his voice changing—became a private pupil of Ockeghem, with whom Josquin felt strong personal ties, as suggested by his elegy, *Déploration de Johan. Ockeghem.* He may also have been for a while in contact with Dufay. There is documentary evidence that Josquin was in Italy at various times after 1459, as a bass singer in the Milan Cathedral choir and perhaps in the Sforza court chapel in Milan (1472). He took holy orders as early as 1479. From 1486 to 1494 he was in the Papal Chapel in Rome, which he left presumably between 1494 and 1500. Perhaps for a short time he was at the court of René II, Duke of Lorraine.

By the end of the century Josquin was known and admired as one of the foremost musicians of the period. From 1498 to 1515 he was connected with Louis XII, King of France, who invested him with a prebend in St. Quentin. In 1503 he went to the court of Duke Hercules I of Ferrara, who at this time had at his disposal the most significant court chapel in Italy. A considerable number of Josquin's works appeared in print from the press of Petrucci in Venice, beginning in 1501. At that time Josquin was personally connected with the house of Hapsburg, particularly with Margarete of Austria (1480–1530), who became Regent of the Netherlands in 1506 and maintained a residence in Mechelen. The last place with which Josquin was associated was Condé sur l'Escaut in Hainault. Here he was active as provost of the chapter, though we do not know in what year he assumed this post. According to one not too reliable source, he died there on March 27, 1521, though according to another he lived until 1524. He was buried before the high altar of Notre Dame in Condé. Among his pupils were Nicolas Gombert, Benedictus Appenzeller, and Hieronymus Vinders.

We can reconstruct some idea of Josquin's personality from the incomplete source material of the biography and his posthumous fame. He must have enjoyed a particularly trusted position during his later years in his relationships with his patrons. Apparently he was an unusually self-aware, distinctive personality, giving creative law (in the sense of artistic autonomy) precedence over the routine requirements of his offices. The image of a religiously oriented way of life emerges from his music, which acquired depth in the late period as he dispensed with secular cantus firmi in his later Masses and motets. Numerous opinions from the period stress the absolutely sovereign mastery with which he controlled his material. Luther, for example, declared: "He is master of the notes, which he makes do what he wishes." Other opinions of the time stressed the subjective and the confessional aspects of his music.

His works include twenty complete Masses; separate settings of portions of the Ordinary; spiritual motets, hymns, and the Magnificat; secular compositions with song texts; and textless compositions such as canons, instrumental movements, and other works.

Around 1500 Josquin was celebrated for having developed a most highly individual manner of expression in his Masses, motets, and chansons. Although some traits in his compositions were still linked with the 15th century, he did pioneering work as far as the whole 16th century was concerned. As late as fifty years after his death, his works maintained a leading position, up to the time of Lasso and Palestrina. The first Masses that Petrucci printed in Venice in 1502 were Josquin's. Adrianus Petit Coclico (presumably his pupil) refers to what purports to be Josquin's manner of teaching in a treatise of 1552, in which he introduces the concept of *musica reservata*. Italian contemporaries compared Josquin with Michelangelo. Josquin initiated two main lines of development: the expressive trend that led to Lassus and the purely musical trend that led to Palestrina. Josquin created a new chanson-type in the expressively conceived and through-imitated chanson. According to Wolff, the Netherlands Renaissance style was perfected through Obrecht; and although the same might be said of the style of Josquin, his style attained its perfection more in the sense of the Italian Renaissance. Thus a simplification was achieved. Josquin was at his boldest in his motets; in his Masses he was more conservative. In Josquin's period the motet, in which the text was the source of inspiration, became a focal point of creative activity.

Josquin's style was characterized by unprecedented clarity and lucidity in the articulation of the music. It is characteristically constructed in antithetical groups and periods underlined by a principle of the repetiton of small sections. Sequence and ostinato are abundant, and through-imitation assumed in his works the predominant role that it was to maintain throughout the 16th century. His Mass *Pange lingua* is one of the first in which the voices imitate each other consistently throughout. He developed what Kroyer has referred to as "imitation in pairs," with two voices grouped as a pair and precisely imitated by a second pair. He formulated succinct, brief, and precise melodies that were determined by the rhythm of the text, thus presenting characteristic, self-contained motifs. The choir is often "split," with several voices being brought together and juxtaposed. Contrapuntal inflections are telescoped and concentrated and surrounded by voices that are deliberately designed to serve the all-inclusive architectonics and the resulting sonority.

The musical material is Gregorian cantus firmus, though usually only a short section of the chant is chosen to be reworked. Whereas Obrecht for the most part repeats ostinato themes note for note, Josquin handles them in liberal variations, as in the varied ostinato of his Mass, *La sol fa re mi*. This technique heralds the ostinato aria of the 17th century. The architectonic aspects of Josquin's work are significant, in that they were developed in a purely musical way by multiform variations of individual motives. His music was very artistic; works of great clarity of expression stand side by side with works of heightened dramatic excitement. The effect of these pieces must have been shocking to some of his contemporaries, as it was to Glareanus, who criticized him in the *Dodekachordon* (1547) for insufficient gravity and for extravagance. Though such critics of Josquin seem to have been in the minority, he was otherwise highly praised in all quarters, as demonstrated by numerous comments that we have from famous contemporaries such as Luther.

From the present viewpoint, Josquin was one of the greatest composers of all time. His rich mastery of style and his artistic power continually come as a surprise to the listener. He was the first great expressive composer in the history of Western music. The greatness of his phenomenal compositions basically eludes any attempt to classify them. His inspiration seems to have sprung principally from the depths of his religious feeling, and his clarity of form might be traced in part to the influence of Italian popular music, such as the frottola and the lauda. In connection with Josquin's work, also, we notice a tendency toward verbalization about music that weakens the autonomy of the purely musical aspect. Musical interpretation was still subservient to the theological, though in places verbal interpretation determined the formal layout and the choice of themes. Declamation was determined by the meter of the text.

Germany Between 1450 and 1550

German musicians of the 15th and 16th centuries may be grouped by generations thus:

Born *ca.* 1410:
  Conrad Paumann (d. 1473)
  Anonymous composers of settings in various manuscript song-books, such as the Lochamer, Glogauer, and Münchener.

Born *ca.* 1440–50:
  Adam von Fulda (d. 1505)
  Heinrich Finck (d. 1527)
  Arnold Schlick (d. after 1527)

Intermediate generation:
  Paul Hofhaimer (1459–1537)
  Thomas Stoltzer (*ca.* 1470–1526)

Born *ca.* 1480–90:
  Ludwig Senfl (d. 1542 or 1543)
  Sixtus Dietrich (*ca.* 1492–1548)
  Benedictus Ducis (*ca.* 1485–1544)
  Balthasar Resinarius, whose real name was Harzer (*ca.* 1480–after 1549)
  Adam Rener (*ca.* 1485–1520)
  Arnold von Bruck (*ca.* 1490–1554)
  Hans Buchner (d. 1538)
  Lorenz Lemlin (d. before 1549)
  Johann Walter (d. 1570)
  Georg Rhau (d. 1548)
  Martin Agricola (d. 1556)

Born *ca.* 1510:
  Georg Forster (d. 1568)
  Jobst von Brandt (d. 1570)
  Caspar Othmayr (d. 1553)
  Stephan Zirler (d. after 1570)

It was only after 1450 that German sacred vocal polyphony began to display characteristic individual traits. The oldest known document is a manuscript of the Benedictine St. Emmeram monastery in Regensburg, containing compositions of the period from about 1375 to about 1450 not only by English and Franco-Flemish musicians but also by Germans of local significance. Its particular quality is characterized by Dèzes as a striving for "full, satiated sound, robust heartiness of rhythm, and heart-warming melodic formulation." The pieces that are German in origin exhibit a polyphony of their own that is further documented in the Trent Codices. Toward the end of the century there was a notable tendency to stress the musical construction of the piece. The three-voiced setting of the *Missa Auleni* (*ca.* 1450), an outstanding German Mass, is notable as being in a special style. Before and after the turn of the century there is a striking tendency on the part of German composers to ally themselves with the leaders of the Franco-Flemish epoch. Isaac, a Fleming, was of special significance in Germany. In the first half of the 16th century German compositions began to play an important role even in Catholic vocal music. Many polyphonic pieces from the Catholic service were adopted by the Protestants.

During the era of Maximilian I, who reigned from 1493 to 1519, sacred vocal music was especially cultivated at the princely courts. The court chapels of Maximilian became the centers of activity in Innsbruck, Augsburg, and Vienna, seconded in rank by the chapels in Munich, Heidelberg, Torgau (at the court of Friedrich the Wise), and Ludwigs-burg (Stuttgart). Leading composers were Heinrich Isaac, Heinrich Finck, Adam von Fulda, Paul Hofhaimer, Thomas Stoltzer, and Ludwig Senfl. Among Isaac's pupils who served under him as members of Maximilian's chapel choir are Senfl, Sixtus Dietrich, Benedictus Ducis, Balthasar Resinarius, and Adam Rener.

Heinrich Isaac was born about 1450 in Flanders, and about 1480 he became organist at the court of Lorenzo the Magnificent in Florence, succeeding the organist Antonio Squarcialupi. In 1484, along with Hofhaimer, he was at the court of the Archduke Sigismund in Innsbruck. After returning to Florence, he became in 1494 court composer to Maximilian I in Augsburg. He was also active at the court of Friedrich the Wise in Torgau, in Florence, and with a chapter of the cathedral in Constance, for which he composed the *Choralis Constantinus*. After 1514, he seems to have been mostly in Florence, where he died in 1517. One of the great composers of his era, internationally active and universally significant, he was also effective as a teacher, notably of Ludwig Senfl. Master of various languages, Isaac composed with facility to French, Italian, German, and Latin texts. His German songs figure among his vocal pieces of a social nature, and at this time he was the outstanding composer in this field. He exerted a comprehensive influence on German music during the first half of the 16th century, especially on song and, later, on the chorale arrangements of the new Protestant church music. The *Choralis Constantinus* is a gigantic undertaking, in the style of the Franco-Flemish music of the period, a collection of motets as *propria* for the whole church year utilizing the prescribed Gregorian melodies. The composition was begun in 1508, completed by Senfl, and printed in 1550. Isaac also wrote secular works, song arrangements, and instrumental settings. During his lifetime he enjoyed European fame, and some of his contemporary commentators rated him alongside Josquin. As of the time Isaac was active at the court of Maximilian I, German music first began to relinquish its conservative attitude.

Heinrich Finck was born in 1444–5 in Bamberg. By 1491 he became choirmaster at the court of the Polish kings in Cracow. From 1510 to 1513 he held a similar position in Stuttgart, and from 1520 at the cathedral in Salzburg. Then from 1525 till the end of his life in 1527 he was in Vienna. Being somewhat older than Isaac, he may be considered the first great German composer. He should not be confused, however, with his grandnephew Hermann Finck (1527–1558), who wrote an extensive theoretical work, *Practica Musica* (1556).

Adam von Fulda was born about 1445 in Fulda and as of 1490 was active as choirmaster at the court of Friedrich the Wise in Torgau. He also served as an instructor at the University of Wittenberg and as court historiographer. He died in 1505 at Wittenberg. He was a composer of rather impersonal sacred vocal settings that served the needs of the court chapel and was also the author of a theoretical treatise, *De Musica* (1490).

Paul Hofhaimer was born in 1459 in Radstadt (Salzburg), and in 1479 became court organist at Innsbruck under Archduke Siegmund. In 1490 he passed into the service of Maximilian I along with the other members of the court chapel and was later given a title of nobility. But in 1500 Hofhaimer also entered the service of Friedrich the Wise in Torgau. From 1507 to 1518 he was again in Augsburg, and as of 1519 he was cathedral organist in Salzburg, where he died in 1537. As a leading organist, composer, and teacher, he was particularly significant for his song-settings.

Thomas Stoltzer was born about 1480 in Schwiednitz, became choirmaster at the court of King Ludwig II of Hungary in Ofen, and died in 1526.

Ludwig Senfl was born between 1488 and 1490 in Zurich and studied under Isaac in Constance. Up to 1519 he was in the court chapel of Maximilian I as violist and Isaac's deputy, and in 1517 he succeeded his teacher there as court composer. In 1523 he transferred his activities to the court chapel in Munich, where he died in 1542 or 1543.

Fourth Period

The Mid-16th Century

The composers who represent the fourth and fifth periods took Josquin's innovations for granted. They knew how to equalize the elements of line and harmony and to utilize expressive devices. Beyond this, they sought to give the style ever greater refinement. They took as the norm a structure of four equally balanced voices, occasionally increasing the number of voice parts to five or six. They achieved a prevailing *a cappella* type of polyphony in which all voices took equal part in the structure of the composition and always presented the same text. In practice, however, they would freely assign the vocal parts to instruments or would add instruments to the voices. Actually, they rather left the distribution of parts to the performers. In the planning of compositions, the composers introduced further refinement by the way they employed imitation throughout. In accordance with the taste of the times, they gave the chorus great sonority and arranged the voices in a way that divided the ensemble, causing short, more chordal sections to alternate with longer, more vocally independent sections.

The relationship between music and text was still closer than in the music of Josquin, though some theorists seem to have demanded even closer relationship, as though it were aesthetically indispensable. Musical motifs were derived from the tonal contours of the language. The verbal content was assimilated by the musical idiom. There are examples of musical word-painting, and theorists even developed a musical rhetoric, or "theory of figures," as in figures of speech.

A stylistic change took place between 1540 and 1550, particularly under Italian influence. It involved the relationship between word and tone; more particularly, it dealt with a clear emotional and pictorial realization of the text by musical means. Several features also paralleled this: a shift from a melismatic to a more syllabic style, from the strictly polyphonic to a more chordal division of the chorus, the use of echo-effects, and a harmonically conceived structure involving considerable use of chromaticism. This phenomenon was accompanied by a preference for scenes that were more dramatically alive than the motet texts.

Various theoreticians dealt exhaustively with ornaments, *coloraturae*, which the singer added to the written voice as decorative dressing in the form of runs and flourishes. It was assumed that the singer had the right to vary his notated text by improvising diminution or subdivision of the indicated note values.

Adrianus Petit Coclico, presumably a pupil of Josquin, used in his *Compendium musices* (Nuremberg 1552) for the first time the concept of *musica reservata*. The ten manuscript sources so far discovered from the Netherlands, Italy, France, and Germany imply that the term *musica reservata* referred to works that were intended to be heard by an educated circle of listeners. Within the sphere of the Netherlands influence there was a clear inclination toward the sacred, whereas in that of the Italian there was a preference for the secular. Music was thus "reserved" in its sociological and aesthetic character. Federhofer has concluded that, although individual sources associated different principles of formation with *musica reservata,* these principles were perhaps to be understood only as supplementary characterizations of its various chronological and geographical variations and were not necessarily applicable to its practice in general. Most scholars today have concluded that a unified way of conceiving of the term may not have existed. Generally considered, *musica reservata* is a vocal chamber music reserved for connoisseurs and amateurs.

During the fourth period composers developed the *Missa parodia,* or "parody Mass" form, in their setting of the *Ordinarium Missae* as a self-contained musical unit. They selected a motet, chanson, or madrigal and, taking it as a whole polyphonic composition, made it the basis of the Mass they were writing, alluding to it evocatively and in a more or less concealed way. In so doing they were giving artistic evidence of the wish, widespread in the 16th century, to treat secular elements spiritually. Earlier composers had exhibited the same or a similar tendency in what is sometimes referred to as the "connection Mass," the "transcription Mass," or the "Mass based on a model." The 14th-century Besançon Mass and Ciconia's Masses are the earliest we know that show such features.

According to what we so far know of the technique of the parody Mass, there were two forms. The one was a continuation of the tenor Mass. One or more melodies were taken from the model, and the melodic and linear structure prevailed over the imitative technique. But in the latter half of the 16th century the preponderant emphasis was on the second form, wherein the harmonic idea of the model determined the parody and took up the chordal successions and the characteristic alternation between chordal and polyphonic writing. Literal quotation appeared. Seen as a whole, the technique of the parody Mass paralleled the general development of vocal composition in the 16th century. The reinterpretation of secular songs, especially of dance songs and love songs, making them sacred or religious through the parody Mass, corresponds to a new style of life and experience of the period.

The motet took on a special significance. It included textually almost all liturgical movements of the Mass, as well as Biblical and newly written texts. The motet in the 16th century appeared principally in three forms:

1. The cantus-firmus motet of the older type, in which the composer transcribed the cantus firmus either in the tenor or in another voice.
2. The motet form without cantus firmus, in which the composer followed a free style of expression.
3. The motet form in which the composer gave a virtually independent musical setting to each section of the text. Thus he developed a form that has retained its validity to the present day. In each section he introduced new musical motives, beginning with the voices imitating each other and declaiming the text in a way derived from the words.

The fourth period brought with it the rise of polychorality, which had appeared during the previous century in the Venetian school, and the development of the newer Italian and French secular song-forms such as the madrigal, villanella, and chanson.

The main composers were Nicolas Gombert, Adrian Willaert, and Jacobus Clemens (non Papa).

Nicolas Gombert—born about 1500, presumably in Flanders—was a pupil of Josquin. Perhaps from 1526 to 1540 he was a singer in the court chapel of Charles V and made many trips through Spain, Italy, and Germany. He died about 1560, probably in Tournai. At one time historians considered him the founder of the strict "classical Netherlands style," which involved through-imitation, unity of the composition, equal value of the voices, and five-voiced structure. Wolff is more inclined to consider him as belonging to a "manneristically oriented Late Renaissance" that was in many respects still linked with the Late Gothic. Gombert's motets were thematically unified by the principle of free variation.

Adrian Willaert (1490–1562) will be considered later, in connection with the Venetian school which he founded.

Jacobus Clemens (non Papa) was born in Ypres about 1510, and died perhaps in 1556 in Dixmuiden. The latter part of the name by which he is usually referred to in histories of music differentiates him from the poet also living in Ypres at that time, Jacobus Papa. Clemens non Papa was a very great motet composer. He differentiated between lyrical and epic motets according to the texts and between solo and choral motets according to the assignment of the parts. In contrast to Gombert, he maintained a generally light syllabic declamation influenced by the chanson. He assigned each syllable of the text to a separate short note and often repeated tones. His themes were also influenced by Protestant chorale melodies. In this respect he followed the style of the time, in that the connection between chorale-like syllabic aspects and polyphony was a distinctive feature of secular and sacred Netherlands songs about 1550. He came quite close to establishing cadences in harmonic style, with alternation of tonic, subdominant, and dominant. One is made aware of Josquin's strong influence in his use of archtectonics, the repetition of entire sections with new text, the divisions of the chorus, echo-effects, and contrasting groups of high and low sonority.

Gombert's French and Flemish contemporaries were Thomas Crecquillon (d. 1557), court choirmaster under Charles V in Brussels; Benedikt Appenzeller (dates unknown), presumably of the Netherlands; Jacobus Vaet (d. 1567), choirmaster of the imperial chapel in Vienna; Johannes Lupi (d. 1539), in Cambrai; Pierre Manchicourt (d. 1564), who served under Philip II; Clément Jannequin (*ca.* 1485–*ca.* 1559); Jean de Richafort (*ca.* 1480–*ca.* 1547); and Claude de Sermisy (d. 1562).

Gombert's contemporaries in Italy were Philipp Verdelot; Jakob Arcadelt, who died some time before 1572; and Cipriano de Rore (1516–1565).

After the death of Josquin the hegemony of the Franco-Flemish school ceased. Frenchmen like Jannequin, Pierre Certon (d. 1572), and Sermisy broke away from the Netherlands manner to derive ways of formulating their ideas from the French spirit and particularly the French language. They were inclined more toward the use of short phrases and cogent melodies, toward the sharp separation and articulation of the sections, the declamation of the text syllable by syllable, and the emphasis on intelligibility of the text. The leading publisher of the time, Attaignant, brought out numerous editions of Masses and motets. The schools of Paris and Lyons were the leaders in the field of church music.

Fifth Period

The Late 16th Century

Though Italy increasingly assumed leadership in the second half of the 16th century through the development of distinctive schools in Venice and Rome, the musicians of Northern French and Flemish origin still figured prominently in Europe as composers and occupied the most important positions everywhere. All the European countries regarded a style that was free of strong national roots as being indispensable for the achievement of high artistic value. It was taken as a matter of course that a composer had mastered what was considered "compositional technique," and for some time this assumption was the criterion. Increasingly the composer became an expert technician and more skillful in placing musical expression at the service of the text. Thus he succeeded in developing a moving and pictorial musical language. He concentrated particularly on the madrigal, which, as Alfred Einstein observed, was "the cockpit of all innovation and experiment." The composer often achieved highly dramatic effects with polyphony. In church music he devoted his principal efforts to the motet.

The main composers were Philippe de Monte and Orlando di Lasso. In this connection it is perhaps significant that precisely these two composers reached the high point of their careers in countries other than their native land.

Philippe de Monte was born in Mechelen (1521). After some activity in Italy, he became a member of the English court chapel (1555), and as of 1568 he was choir-director at the imperial court in Prague and Vienna. He died in 1603, in Prague. Most of his compositional efforts were devoted to the motet and madrigal. Like Orlando di Lasso, he was one of the great and universal minds of the Renaissance and was highly admired even during his own lifetime. A prolific composer of madrigals, he wrote over a thousand, of which 144 are sacred. His music is related in character more closely to Palestrina's than to Lasso's. It lacks great dramatic contrasts, and the emphasis and feeling are somewhat more lyric. During the thirty-five years of his leadership the court chapel of the Emperors Maximilian II and Rudolf II was one of the foremost institutions of its kind in Europe.

Orlando di Lasso—or, in the Latinized form of his name, Orlandus Lassus—was born around 1532 in Mons, Hainault, and died on June 14, 1594, in Munich. Not too much is known of his youth, but quite possibly he was a choirboy in Mons. Early in his career he seems to have been in Italy, at Mantua and Milan; and toward 1550 he was in Naples and then at the Lateran in Rome. In 1555–6 he was again in the North, at Antwerp. During the autumn of 1556 he transferred his activities to Munich, where he was in the court chapel of Duke Albert V, first as tenor, then as choirmaster. From that place, he made numerous journeys that included Italy and Paris. Around 1570 he was at the height of his European fame. In his later years, his work evidenced increasing seriousness and strictness, as well as a kind of moodiness, under the influence of the Counter Reformation.

Lassus possessed a very great mastery of composition and enormous creative power. He wrote some two thousand compositions, including over fifty Masses and twelve hundred motets. The latter are his principal works. In 1604 under the title *Magnum opus musicum*, 516 of them were published by his sons. In the motets he displays an inexhaustible power of imagination and invention; and he was, in general, the most versatile and universal composer of his century. As a significant Renaissance man of intellect, he was distinctly the "cosmopolite" of the 16th century, master of all styles and idioms, able to compose in various languages.

Lassus absorbed the musical world of his time as any highly gifted person does, sovereignly taking up and mastering all impressions in order to let them reflect synthetically through the prism of his own personality. He quickly outgrew the tradition-bound world of his native surroundings. Early travel in Italy first widened his artistic horizons. Naples seems to have left him with especially vital secular impressions—of the commedia dell'arte, the villanesca, and Southern Italian folk-music in general. At the Lateran in Rome he succeeded Animuccia and Lupacchino and was Palestrina's predecessor. As early as his middle twenties Lassus had mastered all the possibilities that he could for his motet style. The universality, versatility, expressive potential, and meaning of his technique of composition continually impress one as being nearly unlimited. After Lassus developed his artistic powers in Italy, he appeared in Antwerp, apparently without public musical position, moving in the circles of the brilliant merchant class. His subsequent position in Munich offered him the opportunity for unique development of his potentialities as an artist and an organizer. Lassus's middle age and maturity coincided with the decades of the Council of Trent's protracted activity, from 1545 to 1563. The years after 1581 brought with them a particularly intense inward religious emphasis, with some traces of mysticism. In the years from 1581 to 1585 Lassus wrote almost a third of his tremendous life's work. The final period of his activity displays the concentration of a distinctly aged style.

His pupils included J. Reiner, Leonhard Lechner, Johann Eccard, F. Sale, Gregor Aichinger, and Giovanni Gabrieli.

Lassus's works include sacred compositions (motets, hymns, litanies, lamentations, Masses, and Passions), secular work (madrigals, villanescas, chansons, and settings of German texts), and instrumental compositions.

His style, particularly in the motets, may be characterized as a new, boldly heightened, dramatic expression of feelings, associated with tone-painting, which by its illustration of the text had already elicited distinct elements of the Baroque musical idiom. He abandoned the restraint of the Renaissance and helped to create the transition to Baroque style. In a sovereign way he mastered every compositional technique of his century, such as strict polyphony and through-imitation, free imitation, cantus-firmus work, homophony, homorhythm, rhythmic imitations, and polyrhythm. As the last representative of the old polyphonic spirit of Netherlands composition, he was at the same time quite "modern" in his creative activity. In his work, polyphony was already strongly determined by harmonic considerations. Along with his polyphonic mastery, he made use of harmonic effects, cadences, quickly changing chords, and leaping basses that were connected with cadences and changes of harmony. With this heightened emotional idiom he helped quite directly in preparing for the monodic style. He counteracted the dangers of formlessness inherent in the predominance of emotion by adopting the Netherlands principle of variation as a means of unifying his compositions.

Holland in the Transition from the 16th to the 17th Century

The particular style and tradition of the Franco-Flemish School came to an end with the close of the 16th century. The history of Dutch music in the transition from the 16th to the 17th century comes to a focus in the personality of a national composer, Jan Pieterszoon Sweelinck (1562–1621).

Sweelinck was reputed to have been one of Zarlino's pupils in Venice and from 1500 was active as organist in Amsterdam. In addition to organ music, he wrote sacred and secular vocal music, particularly psalms and chansons. In his vocal and organ compositions (usually of the ricercar type), he combined influences from Venice with those from England (the variation technique) and fused them into a distinct national Dutch style, which established the form of the organ fugue in a way that has become classic. He was a composer of great significance, and his influence as a teacher extended well on into the 17th century. A specific consideration of his organ works, however, is perhaps more appropriately reserved for a discussion of the music for that instrument.

Under the dominating influence of Calvinist politics and society—an influence which crowded out the Catholic and numerous other Protestant points of view—it was not easy to develop large musical forms such as the opera, Passion, or cantata. Music stood in the service of bourgeois society and lacked great tasks. Most significant is the importance attached to organ-playing, the cultivation of domestic music in the assembling of well-to-do citizens in *collegia musica,* and the presentation of public concerts mostly in private houses of prosperous merchants in what were called *Musikherbergen,* where the host and his guests made music together.

Poland in the 16th Century

During the 16th century Poland's position in the European power-structure was improved under the rule of the two greatest monarchs of the Jagiellon family, Sigismund I (1506–1548) and Sigismund II Augustus (1548–1572). The Polish-Lithuanian union of 1569 was strengthened, and the *Nihil novi* constitution (1505), which made the royal rule dependent on the senate and house of representatives, became the basis of the Polish parliamentary system. Through a general state reform, further limitations were placed on the influence of the higher nobility in favor of the lower nobility. Toleration of the Protestant movement prevented religious wars. Thus Renaissance culture flourished—in science (Copernicus), literature (Rej and Kochanowski), architecture, and sculpture. Influences from abroad—particularly Italy—were combined with Polish elements. After the death of the last Jagiellon ruler, the king was for the first time freely chosen; the choice fell first on Henri Valois, who ruled from 1573 to 1574, and then on Stefan Batory, from 1575 to 1586, under whom the governmental system was stabilized as a republic with a nobility.

The first of the three rulers from the house of Wasa, Sigismund III, during his reign from 1587 to 1632 succeeded in involving Poland in a succession of dynastic conflicts, which contributed to the slow decline of Polish political power. In his domestic policy he tried to establish absolutism, based to some extent on religious intolerance. Under his rule the capital was moved in 1596 to Warsaw, which now became the most important cultural center of the country.

The manuscript remains of anonymous Masses and motets discovered in Lvov show us that the great works of the Netherlands before 1530 were known in Poland. These Masses include one based on *L'homme armé* and another on *Je ne demande.*

The center of musical life in the 16th century was Cracow. There, Western music of Finck, Senfl, Willaert, Josquin, Lasso, Gombert, Sermisy, Jannequin, and others was known. It appears in the repertoire of the royal chapel, with its tradition dating back to the 14th century, and in two organ tablatures, one (1537–48) of Jan of Lublin and the other (1548) of the Holy Spirit Monastery. The founding of the Rorantists' choir (an *a cappella* men's chorus) in 1543 at the Wawel Cathedral, an entirely Polish group, played a great role in the development of Polish composition. The so-called Dissidents' movement was particularly active in spreading music among the people.

Renaissance composers in Poland produced both purely liturgical music and compositions based on nonliturgical or secular texts. The sacred music was that of the Latin liturgy and Biblical texts and included Masses and motets. The nonliturgical compositions included some on secular and Polish texts intended for general music-making, with roots mainly in the Protestant movement.

In the field of liturgical music, two leading composers and theoreticians active in the first quarter of the 16th century were Jerzy Liban (*ca.* 1464–after 1546) and Sebastian of Felsztyn (*ca.* 1485–after 1536). Their works included antiphons, sequences, and alleluias, belonging stylistically to the German school.

The two tablatures of the repertoire of the court chapel from the second quarter of the 16th century contain compositions for the Proper and parts of the Ordinary that are signed with the initials N. C., N. Ch., and N. Z. Though N. Z. has not yet been precisely identified, he seems to write in the oldest style of the three and presumably goes back to the time around 1500. N. C. (Nicolaus Cracoviensis) is the outstanding composer of the three. His highly developed style shows evidence of the influence of Josquin in Poland, as does the single motet by N. Ch. (Nicolai Chrzanoviensis). There is some doubt, however, as to whether these three composers are the sole authors of these works, as the instrumental reworking permits no certain conclusions regarding authorship or the original vocal form of the pieces.

Wacław of Szamotuły (*ca.* 1526–*ca.* 1560) is somewhat more definite. In 1547 he was accepted at the royal court in Wilno "pro componista" and, as of 1555, was at the court of Prince Radziwiłł Czarny. Though his works are incompletely preserved and include only three Latin motets and some polyphonic songs on Polish texts, the composer was fully recognized both within and outside of Poland. In tablatures and non-Polish printings his works stand alongside those of Josquin, Gombert, Lasso, and others. His motets, *"In te Domine speravi"* (1554), *"Nunc scio vere"* (extant in an organ transcription), and *"Ego sum pastor"* (1564), are replete with vocal imitation throughout.

Another prominent composer of liturgical music was Marcin Leopolita (*ca.* 1540–1589) of Lvov, who from 1560 to 1564 was *compositor cantus* at the royal court. His best known composition is the *Missa paschalis,* based on a cantus firmus taken from four early Easter-melodies, *Chrystus Pan zmartwychwastal, Chrystus zmartwychwastal jest, Wstał Pan Chrystus,* and *Wesoły nam dzień nastal.* Melodic aspects of these songs appear in all the voices. The recurrent motive of the Mass is the first section of the first song. The melodic models are freely modified and developed contrapuntally. Three motets are also preserved in organ transcriptions, an additional one in tablature (without text), and a fifth in part books from Olkusz.

Still another composer of liturgical music at mid-16th century is Krzystof Borek, of whose work two Masses are extant.

Finally, Tomasz Szadek (*ca.* 1550–after 1611) was accepted in 1569 as a singer in the royal chapel and from 1575 to 1578 was a member of the Rorantists Choir and vicar of the cathedral. Two of his Masses have been preserved, *Dies est laetitiae* (1578), with its cantus firmus from a Latin Christmas song, and *Pisneme* (1580), with its cantus firmus from Crecquillon's chanson *Puis ne me peult venir.*

Composers of motets include Marcin Wartecki (mid-16th century), Marcin Paligonus (16th–17th century), Walenty Gawara (16th–17th century), and Mikołaj Zieleński (*ca.* mid-16th century to some time after 1650), representative of the Venetian school in Poland.

The Americas Through the 16th Century

By way of orientation to general history, one should realize that the main concentration of Indians in ancient America was in Mexico, Central America, and Peru and was dominated by Aztecs, Mayans, and Incas respectively. Distinctive civilizations flourished there at approximately the same time as in Eurasia, the Mayans being the first to achieve a highly developed urban civilization at about the same time as the Han dynasty in China and the Romans in Europe. In 1521 the Mexican capital was taken by the Spaniards, and by the end of the century the culture of the Iberian peninsula dominated the Latin American area.

Early Spanish chroniclers make it clear that Indian music in these centers of high culture was integrated into a religious cult, organized on a 260-day cycle, and was entrusted to a carefully trained and highly esteemed caste; errors in performance were punishable by death. The music, fundamentally monodic, was a matter of group performance involving instruments as well as voices. Existing syrinxes or *antaras* from very early times in Peru suggest highly developed and precise tonal awareness. Indians throughout the Spanish-American area took quickly to Gregorian chant and to the polyphonic Spanish music that was then at its height, and instruction in church music was actively used by the missionaries as a means of proselytizing.

Long experience on the part of the Indians with dramatic ritual and historical drama offered fertile field for European-type musico-dramatic presentations. As early as 1539 the Indians at Tlaxcala celebrated Easter, in Aztec, with a religious play or *auto sacramental* about the fall of Adam and Eve. Another *auto, Los Pastores,* has been recorded in recent times from the oral tradition into which it passed as it became religious folk-drama. Also, rather simple religious songs known as *alabados* were introduced by the Spanish missionaries and have been studied from modern recordings of the music as it has been orally preserved.

Twelve liturgical books containing music were printed in 16th-century Mexico, of which the first was an *Ordinarium* (1556). Begun while the Council of Trent was still in session, this version is close to the one arrived at by that body. The first music composed and printed in America is attributable to Juan Navarro, a Franciscan originally of Cadiz. Essentially like Gregorian chant, it supplemented the Passion music contained in a volume that the Bishop of Michoacan ordered printed in 1572 that came off the press in 1601 as the *Quatuor Passiones*.

Hernando Franco, who came to Guatemala from Spain around 1554, was serving as choirmaster in Mexico City soon after 1570. He composed seven Magnificats and other religious works, including two lively hymns with Aztec texts in honor of the Virgin. Another 16th-century composer, Juan de Lienas, wrote three Masses and other religious works.

In the field of secular music, the dances later known as the sarabande and the chaconne are considered to have come from 16th-century Mexico. Initially they seem to have aroused official disapproval in Europe, but they soon caught on; today most listeners know them from their later and quite elaborate treatment by Baroque composers. Sachs suggested that these dances may have originated among the Negroes in New Spain, who by 1580 outnumbered the Spaniards there. If these dances are Afro-American, this is a strikingly early precedent for the more recent Afro-American jazz influence on European music.

General Bibliograpy

H. Besseler, *Die Musik des Mittelalters u. d. Renaissance* (Bücken Hdb.); C. van den Borren, *Etude sur le XVe siècle musical* (Antwerp 1941); J. Handschin, *Musikgesch.* (Lucerne 1948); H. Leichtentritt, *Gesch. d. Motette* (Lpz. 1908); R. B. Lenaerts, *Die Kunst der Niederländer* (MW); J. Marix, *Historie de la musique et des musiciens de la cour de Bourgogne sous le règne de Philippe le Bon* (Strasbourg 1939); A. Orel, *Die mehrst. geistl. (kath.) Musik von 1430–1600* (Adler Hdb.); A. Pirro, *Hist. de la musique de la fin du XIVe siècle à la fin du XVIe siècle* (Paris 1940); G. Reese, *Music in the Renaissance* (N. Y. 1959); H. Riemann, *Hdb. d. Musikgesch. II, 1* (Lpz. 1907); A. Schering, *Studien zur Musikgesch. d. Frührenaissance* (Lpz. 1914); O. Ursprung, *Die kath. Kirchenmusik* (Bücken Hdb.); P. Wagner, *Gesch. d. Messe I* (Lpz. 1913); H. C. Wolff, *Die Musik der alten Niederländer* (Lpz. 1956); arts. Cantus firmus, Niederländische Musik, and Motette (MGG); *new eds. in coll. vols.: Altklassische Polyphonie* (MW); *Collectio operum musicorum Batavorum*, ed. Commer (12 vols., Bln., 1844–58); *Das Chorwerk*, ed. Blume (Wolfenbüttel 1929–38, new ed. 1953–); *Maîtres musiciens de la renaissance française*, ed. Expert (23 vols., Paris 1894–1908); *Monumenta Polyphoniae Liturgicae Sanctae Ecclesiae Romanae* (1947– , Rome); *Musica divina*, 1853–69, ed. Proske and Schrems (8 vols., Regensburg); *Musica sacra*, 1839–87, ed. Commer (Regensburg, Bln.); *Trésor musical*, ed. Maldeghem (29 vols., Brussels 1865–93); *Van Ockeghem tot Sweelinck*, ed. A. Smijers (1939–).

First Half of the 15th Century: Motets Sch 30; new ed. Altniederl.

Motetten (Kassel); sel. of Trent Codices in DTÖ 7, 11, 19, 27, 31, 40. *Studies:* E. Apfel, *Der Diskant in d. Musiktheorie des 12.–15. Jh.* (Diss. Heidelberg 1953) and *Der klangliche Satz und der freie Diskantsatz im 15. Jh.* (AfMw 12, 1955); H. Besseler, *The Ms Bologna Biblioteca Universitaria 2216* (MD 1952); C. van den Borren, *Dufay and his School* (NOHM III); E. Dannemann, *Die spätgot. Musiktradition in Frankreich u. Burgund vor dem Auftreten Dufays* (Heidelberg Diss. 1930, Strasbourg 1936); F. Feldmann, *Untersuchungen zum Wort-Ton-Verhältnis in den Gloria-Credo-Sätzen von Dufay bis Josquin* (MD 1954); R. v. Ficker, *Die Kolorierungstechnik der Trienter Messen* (StMw 7), *Die frühen Messenkomp. d. Trienter Codices* (StMw 11), and *The Transition on the Continent* (NOHM III); T. Georgiades, *Musik u. Sprache. Das Werden der abendländischen Music dargestellt an der Vertonung der Messe* (Heidelberg 1954); B. Meier, *Die Harmonik im cantus-firmus-haltigen Satz des 15. Jh.* (AfMw 1952); A. Orel, *Einige Grundformen der Motettenkomp. in 15. Jh.* (StMw 7); Burgund (MGG). *Johannes Regis* coll. ed. (2 vols., AIM). *Jacques Barbireau* coll. ed. 1954–7 (2 vols., AIM). *Heyne von Ghizeghem* coll. ed. in prep. (AIM). *Antoine Busnois* coll. ed. in prep. (AIM). *Guillaume Dufay:* coll. ed. in 6 vols. (1947– , AIM, Rome), sep. ed. J. Stainer, *Dufay and his Contemporaries* (London 1898); BlCh; Sch 38–40; H. Besseler, *Neue Dokumente zum Leben u. Schaffen D.s* (AfMw 1952); R. Bockholdt, *Die frühen Messekompositionen von G. D.* (2 vols., Tutzing 1960); C. van den Borren, *D.* (Brussels 1925), *D. and his School* (NOHM III), and *Etudes sur le XVe siècle musical* (Antwerp 1941); C. Hamm, *A Chronology of the Works of D., Based on a Study of Mensural Practice* (Princeton 1964); art. Dufay (MGG). *Gilles Binchois:* new eds. DTÖ Trienter Codices, BlCh, Stainer (*Dufay and his Contemps.*); chansons of Binchois (Mus. Denkmäler II, Mainz 1957); *Codex Escorial* (facs., Kassel); C. van den Borren, *Pièces polyphoniques profanes de provenance Liègoise* (Brussels 1950); E. Droz, Y. Rockseth, and G. Thibault, *Trois Chansonniers français du XVe siècle* (Paris 1927); Sch 42–43; *Studies:* J. Marix, *Hist. de la musique et des musiciens de la cour de Bourgogne sous le règne de Philippe le Bon* (Strasbg. 1939) and *Les musiciens de la cour de Bourgogne au XVe siècle* (Paris 1937); art. Binchois (MGG); *new eds. in colls.: Der Kopenhagener Chansonnier* (ed. Jeppesen, Lpz. and Copenh. 1927); *Poètes et mus. du XVe siècle* (ed. Droz and Thibault, Paris 1924); *Trois Chansonniers fr. du XVe siècle* (ed. Droz, Thibault, and Rokseth, Paris 1927).

Latter Half of the 15th Century: E. Apfel, *Der Diskant in der Musiktheorie des 12. bis 15. Jh.* (Diss. Heidelberg 1953); L. K. J. Feininger, *Die Frühgeschichte des Kanons bis Josquin des Prez* (Diss. Heidelberg 1937); art. Kanon (MGG). *Johannes Ockeghem* coll. ed. vol. I Lpz., PäM I, 2; vol. II, N. Y. 1947; BlCh; Sch 52; M. Brenet, *J. de O.* (2nd ed. 1911 in *Musique et Musiciens de la vielle France*); M. Henze, *Studien zu den Messekompositionen J. O.* (Bln. 1968); E. Krenek, *A Discussion of the treatment of dissonances in Ockeghem's Masses compared with the contrapuntal theory of J. Tinctoris* (St. Paul 1947) and *J. O.* (N. Y. 1953); D. Plamenac, *Autour d'Ockeghem* (RM 1928); W. Stephan, *Die burg.-niederl. Motette z. Z. O.s* (Würzb. 1937); R. Zimmermann, *Stilkritische Anmerkungen zum Werk O.s* (AfMw 1964); art. Ockeghem (MGG).

End of 15th Century to Death of Josquin: N. Bridgman, *The Age of Ockeghem and Josquin* (NOHM III); W. Fischer, *Zur Kennzeichnung d. mehrst. Setzweise um 1500* (StMw 5); art. A cappella (MGG). *Hein-*

rich Isaac: new ed. *Choralis Constantinus* DTÖ 5, 1, and 16, 1; *Book III,* Ann Arbor 1950; Secular works, song transcripts., and instr. pieces DTÖ 14, 1; Sch 55 and 56; W. Senn, *Musik u. Theater am Hof zu Innsbruck* (Innsbr. 1954); P. Blaschke, *Der Choralis Constantinus* (KmJb 1931); W. Lipphardt, *Die Geschichte des mehrst. Proprium Missae* (Heidelberg 1950). *Loyset Compère:* coll. ed. in 6 vols. 1958–   (AIM); L. Finscher, *L. C. and His Works* (MD 1958–62); *Antoine Brumel:* coll. ed. 1951– (AIM); A. Pirro, *Dokumente über A. B.* (ZfMw XI, 1929); *Pierre de la Rue:* new ed. *Liber Missarum,* Milan and Kassel 1941; BlCh, Sch 65; H. C. Wolff, *Die Musik der alten Niederländer* (Lpz. 1956); art. P. de la R. (MGG); *Johannes Ghiselin:* C. Gottwald, *J. G., J. Verbonnet* (Wiesbaden 1962); *Alexander Agricola:* coll. ed. in prep. (AIM); *Gaspar Weerbecke:* coll. ed. in prep. (AIM); G. Croll, *G. v. W.* (MD 1951); *Antoine de Fevin:* B. Kahmann, *A. de F.* (MD 1950–1); *Jean Mouton:* Sch 66; P. Kast, *Studien zu den Messen des J. M.* (Frankfurt a. M. 1955); *Franchinus Gaffurius:* coll. ed. of mus. works, 1955–   (AIM); *Johannes Tinctoris:* coll. ed. of mus. works (AIM); "Proportionale" in Coussemaker, *Scriptores IV; Jacob Obrecht:* coll. ed. 1908–21 (Lpz. and Amsterdam), new coll. ed. 1951–   (Amsterdam); Sch 54; O. Gombosi, *J. O.* (Lpz. 1925); E. H. Juten, *J. O.* (Annales de l'Academie Royale d'Archéologie de Belgique 67, 1930); B. Meier, *Zyklische Gesamtstruktur u. Tonalität in den Messen J. O.s* (AfMw 1953); art. Obrecht (MGG); *Josquin des Prez:* coll. ed. (Amsterdam 1921–   ); sel. comps. in PGfM VI and BlCh; Sch 59–62; F. Blume in Kallmeyer's "Drachentöter" (1929); M. E. Brockhoff, *Die Kadenz bei Josquin* (Kongress-Bericht Utrecht 1952); C. Dahlhaus, *Studien zu den Messen J. de P.* (Diss. Göttingen 1952); J. H. Lovell, *The Masses of J. de P.* (Diss. Ann Arbor 1960); H. Osthoff, *Besetzung und Klangstruktur in J.s Werken* (AfMw 1952) and *J. D.* (2 vols., Tutzing 1962 and 1965); A. Smijers in PMA, London 1927; O. Ursprung in Bulletin de la Société "Union Musicologique" (1926); W. Wiora, *Der religiöse Grundzug im neuen Stil u. Werk J. des P.* (Mf 1953); art. Josquin (MGG); *Adrianus Petit Coclico* treatise (1552) facs. new ed. 1954.

Germany between 1450 und 1550: K. Dèzes, *Der Mensuralkodex des Benediktiner-Klosters Sancti Emmerami* (ZfMw X); H. J. Moser, *Gesch. der deutschen Musik I* (Stuttgart 2nd ed. 1921) and *Kleine deutsche Musikgeschichte* (enl. ed. Stuttgart 1949); H. F. Redlich, *Central Europe* (NOHM IV); M. Ruhnke, *Beiträge zu einer Geschichte der deutschen Hofmusikkollegien im 16. Jh.* (Bln. 1963); J. Sittard, *Gesch. der Musik u. des Theaters am württembergischen Hofe I* (Stuttgart 1890); F. Stein, *Gesch. des Musikwesens in Heidelberg* (Heidelberg 1921); O. Ursprung, *Münchens mus. Vergangenheit* (Munich 1927); F. Walter, *Gesch. des Theaters u. der Musik am kurpfälzischen Hofe* (Lpz. 1898); H. Zenck, *Die Musik in Deutschland von 1450–1550* (in: Numerus und Affectus, Kassel 1959) and *Sixtus Dietrich* (Lpz. 1928). *Missa Auleni:* BlCh; new ed. *Der Mensuralkodex des Nikolaus Apel* (ED 32); art. Aulen (MGG). *Heinrich Isaac:* see above. *Heinrich Finck:* new ed. *Liedsätze und Motetten* (PGfM 8), hymns and a Mass (BlCh), songsettings (DTÖ 37, 2); Sch 87; art. Finck (MGG). *Adam von Fulda:* "De Musica" repr. in Gerbert, *Script. III;* W. Ehmann, *A. v. F.* (Bln. 1936); art. Fulda (MGG). *Paul Hofhaimer:* nos. incl. in Moser, *P. H.* (Stuttgart 1929); song-settings (DTÖ 37, 2). *Thomas Stolzer:* repr. of Lat. hymns and psalms (DDT 65, RD 21 and 25; sel. works I, Lat.

Sacred Music and Instr. Pieces (RD 22); song-settings (RD 20); secular pieces (DTÖ 37, 2); L. Hoffmann-Erbrecht, *T. S.* (Kassel 1964). *Ludwig Senfl:* coll. ed. intro. in RD, song-settings (PGfM; RD 10, 15; DDT 34); Masses, motets, Magnificat (RD 5, 13; DTB 3, 2); Sch 76, 84–86; E. Löhrer, *Die Messen v. L. S.* (Lichtensteig 1938); W. Schuh, *L. S.* (in *Grosse Schweizer*, Zurich 1938); B. A. Wallner (in *Münchner Charakterköpfe der Gotik*, Munich 1938).

The Mid-16th Century: W. Applebaum, *Accidentien und Tonalität in den Musikdenkmälern des 15. und 16. Jahrhundert* (Diss. Berlin 1936); H. Brandes, *Studien z. mus. Figurenlehre im 16. Jh.* (Bln. Diss. 1935); M. van Crevel, *Adrianus Petit Coclico* (The Hague 1940); R. Dammann, *Spätformen der isorhythmischen Motette im 16. Jh.* (AfMw X, 1953); H. Federhofer, *Eine neue Quelle der Musica reservata* (AMl Vol. XXIV, Fasc. I–II, 1952) and *Monodie u. Musica reservata* (DJM 1960); E. Ferand, *Die Improvisation in der Musik* (Zurich 1938); K. Huber, *Ivo de Vento* (Munich Diss. 1917); R. B. Lenaerts, *16th Century Parody Mass in the Netherlands* (MQ July 1950); E. Lowinsky, *Secret chromatic art in the Netherlands motet* (N. Y. 1946); discuss. of Lowinsky's book by M. v. Crevel in *Tijdschrift d. Vereeniging v. Nederlandsche Muziekgeschiedenis XVI*, 1946; E. Lowinsky, *Tonality and Atonality in 16th Century Music* (Berkeley and Los Angeles 1961); B. Meier, *Reservata-Probleme* (AMl 1958) and *The Musica Reservata* (MD 1956); H. H. Ungerer, *Die Beziehungen zwischen Musik u. Rhetorik im 16.–18. Jh.* (Würzburg 1941); Adrian Petit Coclico, *Compendium musices* (facs. repr. 1954, Kassel); *Die Improvisation* (MW); arts. Diminution, Musica reservata, and Musikalisch-rhetorische Figuren (MGG). *Nicolas Gombert:* H. Eppstein, *G. als Motettenkomp.* (Diss. Bern 1934); J. Schmidt-Görg, *N. G.* (Bonn 1938). *Jacobus Clemens (non Papa):* coll. ed. 1951– (AIM, Rome) in 21 vols.; K. P. Bernet Kempers, *Bibliog. of the Sac. Works of C. n. P.* (MD 1964), *C. n. P. u. s. Motetten* (Augsburg 1929), and *Zur Biogr. C. n. P.* (ZfMw IX); J. Schmidt, *Die Messen des C. n. P.* (ZfMw IX). *Benedikt Appenzeller:* new ed. Werke I, Lpz. 1923. *Others:* N. Bridgman, *The Franco-Flemings in the North* (NOHM IV); F. Lesure, *France in the 16th Century* (NOHM IV).

The Late 16th Century: *Philippe de Monte,* collected edition (Bruges and Düsseldorf 1927–1939); G. van Dorslaer, *La vie et les œuvres de P. de Monte* (Brussels 1921). *Orlando di Lasso:* coll. ed. Lpz. 1894–1927, carried on further in Kassel 1956; coll. ed. of letters in facs. in prep. (IMBA); sels. Sch 125–127; C. v. d. Borren, *O. de L.* (3rd ed. Paris 1930) and *Roland de Lassus* (Brussels 1943); L. Balmer, *O. de L.s Motetten* (Bern and Lpz. 1938); W. Boetticher, *Aus O. d. L.s Wirkungskreis* (Kassel 1963), *Neue Forschungsergebnisse im Gebiet der mus. Renaissance* (Göttingen 1964), *Neue Lasso-Funde* (Mf 1955), and *O. de L. u. s. Zeit,* vol. 1 (Kassel 1958, vol. 2 containing a catalogue of the works, in prep.); J. Huschke, *O. d. L.s Messen* (AfMf V); H. Leuchtmann, *Die mus. Wortausdeutungen in den Motetten des Magnum opus musicum von O. de L.* (Strasbourg, Baden-Baden 1959); E. Lowinsky, *Das Antwerpener Motettenbuch O. d. L.s* (The Hague 1937); A. Sandberger, *Ausg. Aufsätze zur Musikgesch.* (Munich 1921), *Beitr. z. Gesch. d. bay. Hofkapelle unter O. d. L.* (I and III Lpz. 1894–5), and *O. de L. u. die geist. Strömungen seiner Zeit* (Munich 1926); E. Schmitz, *O. L.* (Lpz. 1915); art. Lasso (MGG). *Other Neth. Comps. of this Era:* DTÖ 90, *Niederl. u. ital. Musiker der Grazer Hofkapelle Karls II* (1564–90).

Holland in Transition from 16th to 17th Century: Sweelinck: coll.
ed. in 10 vols. (Lpz. 1894–1901).

Poland in the 16th Century: J. Chomiński, *Die Beziehungen der
polnischen Musik zu Westeuropa vom XV. bis zum XVII. Jh.* (MAEO); M.
Perz, *Der niederländische Stil in Polen zwischen 1500 u. 1530* (Kongress-
Bericht Lublana 1967). *Jerzy Liban* new ed. MDK; art. Liban (MGG).
Sebastian of Felsztyn: new eds. MMSiP 2, MDK, MSt; art. Felsztyn
(MGG). *Wacław of Szamotuły:* new eds. MMSiP 2, MDMP 9, MPO,
MPR, MSt. *Krzystof Borek:* new eds. MDK, MSt. *Tomasz Szadek:* new
eds. MMSiP 1, WDMP 33, MDK. *Marcin Paligonus:* new ed. MSt. *Walenty
Gawara:* new ed. MDK.

18. The Venetian School

Founded in the 5th century A.D., the city of Venice under the rule
of its *Doge* began to show activity by 697 and in the 10th century began
extending its power along the eastern coast of the Adriatic. It absorbed
some Greek islands in the process and established itself as the queen
first of the Adriatic and then of the Mediterranean and as leader in the
rich Levantine trade until well into the 17th century. During the 15th
and 16th centuries, the city became a center of Italian Renaissance art
and the birthplace of the famous Venetian School of Painting, whose most
illustrious members were Bellini, Giorgione, Titian, Palma Vecchio, and
Tintoretto.

The fame of Venice as a center of music began with the founding of a
schola cantorum at St. Mark's Cathedral in 1403. This cathedral had been
long in existence: its foundations, laid in the 9th century, had been
enlarged in 1063 and achieved their present completed form early in the
15th century. There were two organs on facing balconies. The placement
of the organs, presumably, inspired Adrian Willaert to develop instrumental and vocal polychorality by setting off the tone of the organs
against each other and against the vocal and instrumental choirs assigned
to them.

Characteristics of the Venetian polychoral music-making as it
reached its climax were:

1. Collaboration between two, three, or four corporate sources of
   sound, placed separately and at some distance from each other
   within the enclosed area.
2. Choirs of various makeup, either of the same or different components. A choir might consist, for example, of Soprano, Alto,
   Tenor, and Bass or represent one of various pitch levels, such as
   high, middle, or low.
3. The involvement of instruments, first in rather free selection and
   then, as more definite ideas of tone color were worked out, the
   selection of specific instruments.

4. The collaboration of choirs, sometimes as if in dialogue, sometimes as if solo, according to a definite compositional conception.
5. The employment of all available musical means to heighten the
intended effect on the listener.

The Prehistory of Venetian Polychorality

The use of choruses in alternation was, of course, a very old and
widespread practice. In one way or another it is quite familiar to
primitive peoples and among the ancient civilizations.

Around 1500 cathedrals and other important churches usually had
at least two and regularly three organs: the "postif," or organ without
pedals in the choir area among the singers, the "portatif," or small portable
organ to be used anywhere in the church as support for the choir, and
the big built-in organ with various registers that was juxtaposed with the
monophonic or polyphonic choir in what was known as alternatim-
practice, according to which the choir and the organ took turns in
rendering the musical material.

Something resembling polychorality was perhaps first used as a compositional technique by Ockeghem, who introduced sonorously different
pairs of voices in alternation, as did Josquin and many others after him.
This style, however, was always marked by horizontal or linear imitation,
not by vertical antiphony.

The actual individual who is said to have first used the sound of the
organs at San Marco together was Annibale Padovana (*ca.* 1527–1575).
He developed to some extent the concertizing or alternate collaboration
between them, and it became part of the permanent scheme of the worship service there.

Even earlier, during the latter half of the 15th century, there is
evidence of alternating polyphonic psalmody using double choirs in Italy.
Obviously Fra Ruffino Bartolucci d'Assisi, who was cathedral choirmaster in Padua from 1510 to 1520, followed this practice when he wrote
eight-voiced double-choired Psalms *a coro spezzato* (with separated
choir), in which the Psalm verse is distributed in separate words or short
groups of words alternately between the two choirs. From the stylistic
point of view, this suggests incipient Venetian polychorality, though
Ruffini's choral treatment is syllabic and homophonic.

Characteristics of the Venetian School

Although we can detect earlier tendencies in the direction of polychorality in Italy, we must attribute special historical influence to Adrian
Willaert's eight-voiced Psalms for Vespers, printed in 1550. Though a
Fleming, he founded the Venetian School that was soon to be represented
almost exclusively by Italian composers. One of its outstanding characteristics was its use of polychorality. Treating choirs antithetically and joining
them to achieve a special effect on the listener became an art of spatial
sonority. A new dimension of space was discovered in the listeners'

musical consciousness. Perhaps one may wish to draw a parallel here to the opening-out of space in world discovery and the recognition of a heliocentric cosmology that had taken place in Europe shortly before. From the strictly musical point of view, however, we may note that in the Venetian School the organ was released from its previous dependence on vocal music.

The conductor deployed the various groups of singers or instrumentalists in *coro spezzato* or *coro battente*. He often set them off against each other in dialogue form, and frequently introduced echo effects. By the end of the 16th century his desire to heighten the color and show had led to his use of five choirs of vocal and instrumental tone-colors. The antiphonal grouping fostered *concertante* practice. He tended to neglect finely differentiated details of polyphony and concentrate on great, broad sound-effects, often achieved mainly with chordal writing. He took musical motifs from the turns of phrase in the natural declamation of the text. Increasingly he used chromaticism to heighten effects. Thus he developed a melodic idiom filled with images and emotions and with some details of realistic tone-painting.

In laying out a composition he devised a plan that would use the possibilities of the available musical means in a variously echeloned way, section by section, so that the voice-entries could always seem new and all come together at the end for a great final effect. The alternation between soli and tutti, accordingly, had a strongly form-producing, organizing significance.

Giovanni Gabrieli brought this development to its peak. His polychoral music—and that of the Venetian School generally—was quite demonstrative, in the sense of exerting its effect directly on the hearers. This aspect of it is understandably based on social and historical features. It proclaimed the powers of the day in church and state, and was akin to their festivals, balls, weddings, and birthday celebrations. Also it evidenced the power and might of the Counter Reformation.

The epochal significance of the Venetian School, moreover, lies in the development of instrumental music and of early monody in its Renaissance and Baroque phases. On the basis of the *canzona francese,* polychoral and motet principles were carried over into instrumental music. Thus polychoral instrumental canzone and sonatas were written as independent instrumental pieces. Giovanni Gabrieli, for instance, composed his *Sacrae Symphoniae* in 1597, and had as many as five choirs with twenty-two voices in his *Canzoni e Sonate* (1615). Such pieces had both secular and sacred uses—in the latter, for instance, as instrumental interludes in place of the organ in the worship service. His *Sonata pian e forte* is the first printed instrumental work with the dynamics indicated. Also his *Sonata con tre violini e basso se piace* is the first monodic instrumental composition of this period.

Venetian style continued to be influential during the 17th century, especially in Rome and Germany. In fact, the principle of polychorality belongs to one of the characteristic stylistic features of music in the

Early and High Baroque. Thus some scholars tend to see the Baroque era in music as beginning in Venice about the middle of the 16th century.

As to the way the music of the Venetian School was actually performed, the main choir—regularly consisting of four singers for each voice part—stood beside the main organ. The second choir was the *cappella,* which had a similar complement of singers to each part. The third choir was a "high choir," the fourth a "low choir." The director stood with the first choir, as indicated in Ludovico Viadana's *Salmi à 4 Chori per cantare e concertare* (Venice 1612). The total number of singers at San Marco around 1550 must have been nearly forty. Instruments were also employed and either played independent parts or duplicated voice parts, serving to substitute for them or to strengthen them. The choirs were arranged in a way that was spatially divided (*per choros*), either on balconies or on supports specially set up for them. The director's role involved a responsibility for not only rhythmic and metrical exactness but also the balance in sonority between the choirs and the instrumentalists. On occasion supplementary choirs were added to strengthen the full choirs (*ripieni*).

Details in the varying practices of actual performance have been explained also by Michael Praetorius. The indication *cappella* meant, in the first instance, a purely vocal rendition and, in an expanded sense, referred to the choir that, at the most, consisted of voices alone. The choral voices might be designated *cantar sodo* or *alla Romana*—that is, without ornament and without emphasis or expression—or *cantar d'affetto* or *alla Neapolitana,* that is, with expression. The freely improvised ornamentation by diminution, anticipation, accents, and other decorations were known as *cantar passegiato, alla Lombarda, gorgia,* or *coloratura.* Freely improvised addition of more voices was *contrappunto alla mente.*

Representatives of the Venetian School

The founder and head of the Venetian School was, as we have seen, Adrian Willaert, who was born around 1490, probably in Bruges, studied music under Jean Mouton, and arrived in Rome possibly in 1516. Thereafter he resided briefly in Ferrara and then in 1524 became master of the choir at St. Mark's Cathedral in Venice, where he died in 1562. Willaert's influence on the latter half of the 16th century was extraordinary, especially in regard to the imitation of the word in music, in accordance with ideas often referred to as *imitar la natura* or *imitar le parole.* His pupils included Andrea Gabrieli, Cipriano de Rore, and Giuseppe Zarlino, who referred to Willaert (perhaps in slightly exaggerated admiration) as the father of modern music. His main works are motets, and he led in the development of the Italian madrigal and the ricercar.

Cipriano de Rore, countryman of Willaert and his pupil, was born in 1516, probably in Antwerp. In 1563, de Rore succeeded Willaert as director of the choir at St. Mark's, a post he held until his death two years later. Like Willaert, de Rore is noted particularly for his contributions to the madrigal.

Claudio Merulo, who was born in 1533, was assigned to the second organ at St. Mark's in 1557 and succeeded to the first organ in 1566. From 1586 until his death in 1604 he was court organist at Parma. As might be inferred from this brief sketch of his career, Merulo is known chiefly for his organ works.

Girolamo Diruta, born in 1561, studied under Zarlino, Merulo, and Andrea Gabrieli and for a time was cathedral organist in Venice and from 1603 choirmaster at St. Mark's Cathedral. Diruta was the author of a basic theoretical work on organ playing, *Il Transilvano*, published in two parts in 1593 and 1609.

Giovanni Croce was born in 1557, became Baldissera Donato's successor as master of the cathederal choir in 1603, and died in 1609.

Giuseppe Zarlino was born in 1517 and died in 1590. He was a pupil of Willaert, reputedly a teacher of Sweelinck, and in 1565 successor to de Rore as master of the choir. Zarlino was one of the most significant theorists of the first half of the 16th century. His fame rests mainly on his *Istitutioni harmoniche*, published in 1558; his discovery of the dual nature of harmony; his work with form and style that transcended church modes; and his establishment of the third in the relationship of 4:5, which Ramis de Pareja had projected earlier in 1480. The fourth book of the *Istitutioni* contains, in ten rules, the basis for the handling of text in polyphonic music. Zarlino's book *Dimostrationi harmoniche* appeared in 1571, and a collected edition of his theoretical writings appeared in 1589.

Andrea Gabrieli, who was born sometime between 1510 and 1520 in Venice and died there in 1586, was a pupil of Willaert. From 1536 he was a singer at St. Mark's, and he became Merulo's successor at the second organ in 1564. Among his pupils were his nephew Giovanni Gabrieli, Hans Leo Hassler, and Gregor Aichinger. He traveled extensively, visiting the Bavarian court chapel as early as 1562, and was in touch with Orlandus Lassus. Through his compositions he enhanced the Venetian style with works that were highly articulate and rich in contrasts. His versatility extended to motets, Masses, madrigals, and orchestral and organ works. By introducing the *stile concertato* and timbre as elements in polychoral construction, he moved beyond the mere juxtaposition of two or more essentially similar choirs to the achievement of the greatest possible contrasts in color between various combinations of voices and instruments.

Giovanni Gabrieli, who was born about 1555 in Venice and died there in 1612, was, as has been mentioned, the nephew and pupil of Andrea Gabrieli. He perhaps also studied with Lassus, and from 1575 to 1579 served under his direction in the Munich court chapel. In 1584 Giovanni Gabrieli succeeded his uncle as second organist at St. Mark's, and in 1586 he became first organist. By 1600 he had become widely known and highly regarded, attracting from all countries numerous pupils, most significantly Heinrich Schütz. In the motets of Giovanni Gabrieli the Venetian School reached its climax. In originality, imagination, and creative versatility he was unsurpassed. He endowed polychorality with a new dimension by employing as many as twenty-two voices. He introduced specially notated orchestral choirs, used chromaticism to heighten the realism of his emotional idiom, and pioneered in monody, the orchestral sonata, the polyphonic sonata in simple setting, and the madrigal. His main works are the *Sacrae symphoniae* I and II (1597 and 1615) and the *Canzoni e sonate a 3–22*, which appeared posthumously in 1615. A well-known extract from the first book of *Sacrae Symphoniae* is the *Sonata pian e forte*. Giovanni Gabrieli trained many pupils. We have the names principally of those who came from countries north of the Alps to study under him. The most significant composer of this group is Heinrich Schütz; the most significant theoretician, Michael Praetorius.

Continued Influence of the Venetian School

By the middle of the 16th century the polychoral style had come into widespread use throughout northern Italy. In 1613 Gabrieli's mantle and the rich heritage of the Venetian School fell to Claudio Monteverdi, who maintained the tradition brilliantly. After 1637 Venice became the center of Italian opera. Another significant development was the fusion of the Venetian polychorality and the style of the Roman School into a colossal Baroque style in Rome.

Other Italian composers also carried on the Venetian style, in Venice and elsewhere: Giuseppe Guami (d. 1611) in Venice and Lucca; Tiburtio Massaino; Adriano Banchieri (d. 1634) in Bologna; and Paolo Agostino (d. 1629).

In other countries, also, composers were influenced by Venetian polychorality and chromaticism: in Spain, Juan Bautista Comes of Valencia (d. 1643); in Holland, Jan Pieterszoon Sweelinck (1562–1621); and in Germany and Bohemia, Jacob Handl, Hans Leo Hassler, and Hieronymus Praetorius—and somewhat later, Michael Praetorius and Heinrich Schütz.

Hans Leo Hassler was born in Nuremberg in 1564 and presumably first learned to play the organ from his father. In 1584 he was in Venice studying with Andrea Gabrieli and became closely associated with Giovanni Gabrieli. Returning to Germany, he became in 1585 chamber organist to the Fugger family in Augsburg and in 1601 organist of the Frauenkirche and leading musician in Nuremberg. From 1604 to 1608 he was in Ulm, but was active mainly as a merchant. In 1608 he became chamber organist to the Elector of Dresden. He died in Frankfurt am Main while on a journey in 1612. He had become famous as a composer during the 1580's, and was given a title of nobility by Emperor Rudolf in 1595. Having mastered the Italian forms of early Venetian polychorality and the madrigal, he imbued them with a certain German depth and warmth of feeling. He continued to influence German music, particularly through his social songs, the *Lustgarten,* and through his Protestant church music, *Kirchengesänge simpliciter* and *Psalmen fugweis.*

Hieronymus Praetorius, brother of Michael Praetorius, was born in Hamburg in 1560, succeeded his father as organist of St. James' there in 1586, and died in 1629. Within his own lifetime his works were issued in a collected edition.

Bohemia

In Bohemia groups of *literati* were responsible for cultivating Czech polyphony during the 15th and 16th centuries, as well as for introducing the European repertoire into even small communities. Works by such composers as Lasso and Isaac were performed, as well as those by composers active in the imperial chapel founded at Prague in 1526. During the reign of Rudolf II from 1576 to 1612, Prague became one of the most important centers of European music, graced by Philippe de Monte, Charles Luyton, Jakob Regnart, and Jacobus Gallus.

Jacobus Gallus was the greatest composer active in Bohemia at the time: his name is a Latinized form of the German Jakob Handl (*Handl* meaning, literally, "little rooster"); originally, in Slavic, his name was Jokap Petelin. Born in 1550 in Reifnitz, Lower Krain, he perhaps spent part of his youth in Italy, became a singer in the Viennese court choir in 1574, and transferred his activities first to Olomouc in 1579 and then to Prague in 1585, where he died in 1591. His main work was the *Opus musicum* I–IV (1586–90), and he is particularly known for his *Ecco quomodo moritur*.

Following the lead of Prague, significant choirs were established in various Bohemian castles such as the Rožmberk choir in Krumlov in 1552 and Kryštof Harant's choir in the Pecka castle about 1600. Some of the prominent Bohemian composers were Jan Trajan Turnovský, active in the second half of the 16th century, composer of a cantus-firmus Mass, *Dunaj, voda hluboká;* Jiří Rychnovský (d. 1616); Jan Campanus Vodanský (1572–1622); and, most important, Kryštof Harant z Polžic a Bezdružic (1564–1621), who wrote a five-voiced Mass, *Dolorosi martyr*, and a motet, *Maria Kron*. There are also many notable anonymous compositions.

Poland

Although Waclaw of Szamotuły had written an eight-voiced Mass (no longer extant) even before 1560, the first exact information we have of a Polish polychoral work, a twelve-voiced Office, comes to us from 1590. The collection *Melodiae Sacrae* was printed in Cracow in 1604 and contains the double-choired eight-voiced motet *Beata es virgo Maria* of Andrzej Staniczewski (16th–17th century). The music, however, is only partly extant. The rest of this printed collection includes several polychoral works by Italian composers who were active in Poland.

The polychoral technique is fully evidenced in the two collections, *Offertoria totius anni* and *Communiones totius anni* (printed at Venice in 1611) by Mikołaj Zieleński, organist and choir director to the Primate Baranowski. They contain 121 pieces for voices or for voices and instruments of from one to twelve parts. Three purely instrumental compositions are transcriptions of *a cappella* pieces. The Baroque style is represented in the polychorality (for example, a twelve-voiced Magnificat), in the tone color (such as contrasts in manner of setting, dynamics, and rhythm), and in the stress placed on the emotional and illustrative facets of the text and the naturalistic handling of individual words. Some of these "communions" for solo voice with organ accompaniment may well be considered the first Polish solo concerti. The works of Zieleński hold their own beside those of Giovanni Gabrieli. Zieleński is one of the most important of the Polish composers before Chopin.

The principal source of the general repertoire and polychoral music known in Poland before 1630 is the Peplin Tablature, consisting of scores with appended organ tablature, containing 899 pieces in six books, notably some polychoral motets by various composers, including Andrzej Rohaczewski and several members of the Polish royal choir in Warsaw, as well as Luca Marenzio, Giulio Osculati, Asprilio Pacelli, Andres Hakenberger, and Annibale Stabile.

General Bibliography

G. d'Alessi, *La Capella Musicale del Duomo di Treviso* (Treviso 1954) and *Precursors of A. Willaert in the Practice of "Coro Spezzato"* (JAMS 1952); H. Besseler, *Die Musik des Mittelalters u. d. Renaissance* (Bücken Hdb.); P. Winter, *Der mehrchörige Stil* (Frankfurt a. M. 1964); C. v. Winterfeld, *Giov. Gabrieli u. s. Zeitalter* (3 vols., Bln. 1834); *New Printings in Coll. Eds.: Classici musicali italiani* (Milan 1941–3); *Istituzioni e Monumenti dell'Arte Musicale Italiana* (I and II, Milan 1931 and 1932); *L'Arte Musicale in Italia* (Torchi I, II, III, Milan 1897– , vol. of exs. to Winterfeld's Gabrieli); J. W. v. Wasielewski, *Instr. Sätze vom Ende des XVI. bis Ende des XVII. Jh.* (Bln.). *Sonata pian e forte* Sch 148. *Adrian Willaert:* coll. ed. (Rome 1950–); vol. I of coll. ed. in PäM 9; sels. Sch 104, 105; H. Beck, *A. W.s Messen* (AfMw 1960); A. Carapetyan, *The "Musika Nova" of A. W.* (JRB 1946); E. Hertzmann, *A. W. in der weltlichen Vokalmusik seiner Zeit* (Diss. Bln. 1929); R. Lenaerts, *Notes sur A. W.* (Brussels 1935); H. Zenck, *A. W.s "Salmi spezzati"* (1550) (Mf 1949); and *Studien zu A. W.* (Lpz. 1929); Pref. to IeM. *Cipriano de Rore:* coll. ed. 1959– (AIM); A. Johnson, *The Masses of C. de R.* (JAMS 1953); J. Musiol, *C. de R.* (Halle 1932). *Girolamo Diruta:* art. Diruta (MGG). *Giuseppe Zarlino:* new eds. of "Istituzione" N. Y. 1965, Ridgewood 1966; of "Dimostrationi" N. Y. 1965; R. Flury, *Z. als Komponist* (Winterthur 1962); H. Zenck, *Z.s Istitutione harmoniche als Quelle zur Musikanschauung der ital. Renaissance* (ZfMw XII). *Andrea Gabrieli:* new ed. IeM; Torchi II, III; *Classici mus. ital.* V; sep. eds.; Sch 130; D. Arnold, *A. G. u. d. Entwicklung der "cori-spezzati"-Technik* (MF 1959). *Giovanni Gabrieli:* coll. ed. 1956– (AIM); IeM I and II; Torchi II and III; many sep. eds.; S. Kunze, *Die Instrumentalmusik G. G.s* (2 vols., Tutzing 1963). *Hans Leo Hassler:* new eds. organ works (DTB 4, 2), canzonette and Ger. songs (DTB 5, 2), madrigals (DTB 11, 1), cantiones sacrae (DDT 2), Masses (DDT 7), sacri concentus (DDT 24–25), Lustgarten (PGfM), Psalmen fugweis (PGfM), Kirchengesänge simpliciter (Kassel); coll. ed. 1961– (ed. C. Russell Crosby, Jr.); A. Sandberger, *Bemerk. z. Biogr. H. L. H.s* (DTB 5, 1); E. F. Schmid, *H. L. H. u. s. Brüder* (Ztschr. d. hist. Vereins f. Schwaben, Bd. 45, Augsburg 1941); R. Schwartz, *H. L. H. unter d. Einfluss d. ital. Madrigalisten* (VfMw IX); art. Hassler (MGG). *Hieronymus Praetorius:* new ed. sel. works DDT 23; B. Friedrich, *Der Vokalstil des H. P.* (Diss. Hamburg 1932).

Bohemia: exs. in P 74–76, 94. *Jakob Handl:* "Opus musicum" new ed. DTÖ 6, 1; 12, 1; 15, 1; 20, 1; 24; 26; sel. Sch 131; P. Pisk, *Das Parodieverfahren in den Messen von Gallus* (StMw V).

Poland: new eds. in AMiP 1–7; MMSiP 1, 2; MPO; MPR; WDMP 12, 31, 36, 41, 45, 53; MMiP Ser. 1, vol. 1; MSt.

19. The Roman School

Ushered in by the Council of Trent (1545–1563), the Counter Reformation strengthened the Roman Catholic Church and gave impetus to the ecclesiastical arts, particularly architecture, painting, and music. The Jesuit order, founded in 1540 by St. Ignatius Loyola, played a prominent part in this development. Many rulers and noblemen also supported the Counter Reformation, notably Philip II, King of Spain from 1556 to 1598, Ferdinand I, King of Germany from 1556 to 1564, and the various Dukes of Bavaria. In Italian art, the first half of the 16th century is usually considered High Renaissance and Early Baroque; and the late 16th and the 17th centuries, High Baroque.

Italian church music during the first half of the 16th century has not yet been exhaustively investigated. The three-volume collection *Italia Sacra Musica,* edited by Knud Jeppesen (Copenhagen 1963), first shed some light on it, revealing how Italian composers like Costanzo Festa (*ca.* 1480–1545) had mastered the style of the Franco-Flemish school and also developed an independent quality of their own. Next to Festa, Gasparo Alberti (*ca.* 1480–1560) is perhaps the most significant composer among those here first published. The fact that Rome did not recover its musical productivity before the 16th century is no doubt due to the slow economic and cultural recovery after the return of the Papacy from Avignon. Rome became a European center only after 1500—and, from the musical point of view, a quite special sort of center.

Although the history of the *capella pontifica* in Rome extends back to the early days of the Papacy, it distinguished itself in the middle of the 16th century by a musical style very much its own and by a group of composers known as the Roman School. These men exercised a continuing influence and have maintained a constant significance in the history of music on to the present day. They wrote in a strictly church style and were comparatively more conservative in attitude than the Venetian School. Thus the Netherlands compositional techniques of the Josquin period fused with these composers' native Italian sense of melody and euphony.

Palestrina was the outstanding composer of the Roman School. His predecessor was Costanzo Festa, a singer in the Papal choir, who died in 1545 at Rome. Festa was one of the first Italians to adopt an *a cappella* style in which the parts imitated each other throughout. An older Italian contemporary of Palestrina's was Giovanni Animuccia (*ca.* 1500–1571), who was choirmaster at St. Peter's. He wrote outstanding madrigals and laudi, and his Masses prepared the way for Palestrina's.

Although the record of Giovanni Pierluigi da Palestrina's birth is not exact, he was born apparently about 1525 in Palestrina, near Rome. He was a choirboy at Santa Maria Maggiore in Rome, and he probably studied with Firmin le Bel. From 1544 to about 1551 he was organist in his native city, in 1551 became choirmaster at the Cappella Giulia, and in 1555 singer in the Papal choir. In 1554 he published his first book of Masses, dedicated to his patron, Pope Julius III. By this time Palestrina had married, and in 1555 he was dismissed by Pope Paul IV, who wished to reestablish the clerical character of the Schola. A month later Palestrina was appointed choirmaster in the Lateran church, a position he held until 1560. In 1555 his first book of four-voiced madrigals appeared. From 1561 to about 1566 he was choirmaster at Santa Maria Maggiore, then became a music teacher in the Seminario Romana. From 1567 to 1571 he was in the service of Cardinal d'Este. Then Palestrina, from 1571 to his death on February 2, 1594, was choirmaster at St. Peter's, where he lies buried. During his lifetime and after his death he had great influence. His works consist of 105 Masses, over five hundred motets, and over a hundred madrigals.

The so-called Palestrina style, or *stile alla Palestrina,* represents the very perfection of vocal polyphony in the second half of the 16th century. It is characterized by complete balance of harmony and melodic line, by symmetrical flow of melody and rhythm throughout, by equable distribution of melismatic and syllabic treatment of the text, and by balance between the chordal and contrapuntal portions of the composition. The melodic movement is mostly stepwise, and the rhythm is constantly flowing and often complementary. The voices imitate each other, and there is perfection and great equanimity in the treatment of dissonance for that time, with exact control of the way the voices approach and leave the dissonant relationship. The structure is usually for five or six voices, with individual motets having as many as twelve, which are grouped, splitting the resulting body of sound and creating apparent polychorality. One might call it an orchestration of the choral sonority.

In general, we may characterize Palestrina's music as being in a lyric and epic tonal idiom. Considered from a modern point of view, it was quite reactionary and decidedly conservative, though appropriate to its period in its treatment of *a cappella* style. It is more or less related to the music of Josquin's late period, though it does not exactly undertake to revive it. Palestrina's music does not have the imaginative power and emotional content of Lasso's. The individuality of Palestrina's work rests in his unique concentration and equability of the artistic idiom, and (at least as compared with Lassus) in the elimination of dramatic differences and sharp accents of a striking nature. The Palestrina style gained particular historical significance as the polyphonic ideal in instruction books such as Fux's *Gradus ad Parnassum* (1725) and through the Palestrina Renaissance of the 19th century that was connected with the Romantic Movement. In 1868 this phenomenon gave rise to the tendency in music known as Caecilianism and the founding of the Caecilian Society. Palestrina's music reflects High Renaissance society and Papal Rome, in its aristocratic and conservative aspects, claiming to exercise authority for "eternity" and maintaining an equanimity in which there is little place for the display of uncontrolled emotion.

Toward the end of the 16th century the art of counterpoint (particularly canonic writing) enjoyed a distinct revival, spreading out from Italy and particularly from Rome. Throughout the 17th century many works of contrapuntal theory appeared, beginning with Giovanni Maria Artusi's *Arte del Contrapunto* (1586–9). In conjunction with this revival, many composers wrote strongly polyphonic vocal compositions, particularly Masses and canons.

Palestrina has been credited with "saving church music," though his efforts were not as single-handed as has been popularly represented. There had been growing complaint about the condition of church music from the very beginning of the 16th century. Clergymen and others, including Erasmus of Rotterdam, protested that the text had grown unintelligible, that instruments were being over-used, that a secular spirit prevailed, and that the chant itself needed reform. Pope Pius IV requested that the Council of Trent deal with questions of church music. Several cardinals officially prepared the material for the deliberations. They were assisted in this task by various specialists in music, including the Flemish composer Jacobus de Kerle (*ca.* 1531–1591). In 1561 de Kerle composed his *Preces speciales* in a mixed polyphonic-homophonic expressive style that was at that time somewhat modern, and the work found favor with the Council. Otto Ursprung has even suggested that de Kerle should be regarded as the "savior of church music." The Council decided in 1563 that the then contemporary polyphonic church style should be recognized, that there should be greater emphasis on intelligibility of the text and on ecclesiastical dignity (*pia gravitas*), that there should be avoidance of any elements that were "lascivious and impure" (i.e., secular), and that the Roman breviary and missal should be reformed. In 1564 the Pope authorized a commission of cardinals to carry out the Council's decision in Rome. In this connection Palestrina, who published his second book of Masses in 1567, was named as a model and was mentioned in the preface. His *Missa Papae Marcelli*, presumably composed in 1562–3, stands at the end of this volume. Because of its date and its unusually close integration of music and text, Jeppesen plausibly connects it with the Council of Trent, but adds that many aspects of this epochal event "have not yet been sufficiently clarified." One should not overlook the fact that authoritative power and force characterized the principle of the Council of Trent's restoration. To a great extent that meant an end to liberalism, even in church music.

The focal point of Palestrina's creative activity is to be found in the now authenticated 105 Masses and the motets. Among them all types of Mass usual at the time are represented: some on free themes, or themes invented by the composer; some on Gregorian chant; some on popular melodies; and some on previously composed polyphonic works, thus being so-called parody Masses. He based only eleven of his Masses on nonliturgical themes. Fifty-one are parody Masses, of which twenty-eight are based on polyphonic works by other composers and the rest on works by Palestrina himself.

There were notable contemporaries of Palestrina in Spain, similarly adept in the *a cappella* style. In fact, they constitute a distinct school. Cristóbal de Morales (*ca.* 1500–1553) and Bartolomeo Escobedo (*ca.* 1500–1563) were singers in the Papal choir in Rome and later were active in their own native land. Among their pupils were Francisco Guerrero (1528–1599), who became choirmaster in the Seville cathedral, and Tomás Luis da Victoria (*ca.* 1540–1611), who was first in Rome and later in Madrid.

In Rome itself Ruggiero Giovanelli (d. 1625) succeeded Palestrina in his office and maintained the Palestrina style, as did Palestrina's pupils Giovanni Maria Nanino (d. 1607), Annibale Stabile (d. 1604), and Antonio Dragoni (d. 1598). Felice Anerio (d. 1614) and Francesco Suriano (d. 1621) also received their start in the Roman School and carried on the Palestrina style as a tradition. By the middle of the 16th century Rome and Venice had become the two main centers of sacred music. There was also notable cultivation of sacred music elsewhere, especially in Naples, Mantua, and Milan.

The colossal style of the Roman Baroque developed in the 17th century, assimilating some elements of Venetian polychorality. Orazio Benevoli (d. 1672), Paolo Agostino (d. 1629), Antonio Maria Abbatini (d. 1677), and Virgilio Mazzocchi (d. 1646) figured in this development. Benevoli's festival Mass for the dedication of the Salzburg cathedral in 1628 represents the epitome of this style. It is written for fifty-three voices, including sixteen vocal, thirty-four instrumental, two organs, and basso continuo. Contemporaries, reflecting Counter Reformation and Jesuit influences, likened this style to what was presumably heard in the heavenly realms.

After 1560 the Counter Reformation exercised an increasing influence on music. The era was one of spiritual anguish and renunciation, of asceticism and dogmatic torment. Many composers were caught up in it, and Palestrina retracted his early secular madrigals. In the last two decades of his life Lasso dealt with material of increasingly deep spirituality such as his *Penitential Psalms* (1565), which Osthoff has characterized as having been written with "heightened symbolism and passionate fervor." After 1560 there was a tendency to write sacred madrigals, and after 1570 the motet reflected the increased veneration of the Virgin Mary and the saints. Composition of " penitential Psalms" became more and more significant. The reform of Gregorian chant was completed in the Editio Medicea (1614).

After the Council of Trent, many Catholic song-books appeared, particularly in Germany, after 1567 as counterparts to the Protestant hymnals. These largely Jesuit-instigated efforts elicited a reaction among the Protestants, who went one step further by joining the German language, the chorale, and the word of the Bible. This development led to the chorale motet and the sentence motet.

Catholic song-books that appeared in Germany during the 16th and

17th centuries include a *Hymnarium durch das gantze Jar verteutscht* (1524), Georg Witzel's *Deutsch Betbush* (1537), Michael Vehe's *Ein New Gesangbüchlein Geystlicher Lieder* (1537), *Dillinger Gesangbuch für die Bamberger Diözese* (1561), Johann Leisentritt's *Geistliche Lieder und Psalmen* (1567), *Gross Catholisch Gesangbuch* (1625), *Kölner Jesuitengesangbuch* (1623), Friedrich Spee's *Trutznachtigall* (1629), and Angelus Silesius's *Heilige Seelenlust* (1657).

General Bibliography

H. Besseler, *Die Musik d. Mittelalters u. d. Renaissance* (Bücken Hdb.); H. Coates and G. Abraham, *The Perfection of the a cappella Style* (NOHM IV); H. Osthoff, *Einwirkungen der Gegenreform auf die Musik des 16. Jh.* (JbP 1934); H. Leichtentritt, *Gesch. d. Motette* (Lpz. 1908); O. Ursprung, *Die kath. Kirchenmusik* (Bücken Hdb.); P. Wagner, *Gesch. d. Messe I* (Lpz. 1913); *New Printings in Coll. Eds.: Classici musicali italiani* (1941–); *Hispaniae Schola musica sacra* (8 vols., Lpz. and Barcelona); *I Classici della musica italiana* (1919– , 36 vols.); *Monumenta Polyphoniae Liturg. Sanctae Eccl. Romanae* (1948– , Rome); *Musica divina* (ed. Proske, 1853–); *Musica sacra* (ed. Commer, 1839–).

Early 16th Century: Italia Sacra Musica (3 vols., ed. K. Jeppesen, Copenhagen 1963). *Costanzo Festa:* coll. ed. AIM; *Hymni per totum annum* (*Monumenta polyphoniae italicae* III); Torchi I and II; Sch 120–122. *G. P. da Palestrina:* two coll. eds.: 33 vols. (Lpz. 1862–1907); 1939– , ed. Casimiri, Rome. Monographs by Baini (Rome 1828), Baini-Kandler (Lpz. 1834); M. Brenet (Paris 1905); E. Schmitz (Lpz. 1914); R. Casimiri (Rome 1918); A. Cametti (Milan 1925); etc. E. Apfel, *Zur Entstehungsgesch. des Palestrinasatzes* (AfMw 1957); A. Feil, *Zum Gradus ad Parnassum von J. J. Fux* (AfMw 1957); K. G. Fellerer, *G. P. da P.* (Regensburg 1930, 2nd ed. Düsseldorf 1960; cf. Jeppesen's discuss. in Acta III, 74), *Der Palestrina-Stil u. s. Bedeutung in d. vokalen Kirchenmusik d. 18. Jh.* (Augsburg 1929), and *Church Music and the Council of Trent* (MQ 1953); S. Hermelink, *Dispositiones modorum. Die Tonarten in d. Musik Palestrinas u. s. Zeitgenossen* (Tutzing 1960); K. Jeppesen, *Der Palestrina-Stil u. d. Dissonanz* (Lpz. 1925, Engl. 1927), *Marcellus-Probleme* (Acta XVI), and *Kontrapunkt, Lehrbuch der klass. A-cappella-Polyphonie* (Danish 1930, Amer. ed. 1939); C. A. Miller, *Erasmus on Music* (MQ 1966); R. Schlötterer, *Struktur u. Komp.-verfahren in d. Musik P.s* (AfMw 1960); O. Ursprung, *Die kath. Kirchenmusik* (Bücken Hdb.) and *Restauration u. Palestrina-Renaissance in d. kath. Kirchenmusik d. letzten zwei Jh.* (Augsburg 1924); K. Weinmann, *Das Konzil von Trient und die Kirchenmusik* (Lpz. 1919). *Contemporaries of Palestrina:* H. Anglès, *Spain and Portugal* (NOHM IV); *Francesco Guerrero, Opera omnia* (Barcelona 1955–); *Hispaniae Schola musica sacra* (8 vols., Lpz. and Barcelona); *La música en la corte de los Reyes Católicos* (Barcelona 2nd ed. 1960); Cristóbal de Morales, *Opera Omnia* (ed. H. Anglès, Barcelona, 1952–); coll. ed. of works of Victoria (8 vols., Lpz.); C. Winter, *Ruggiero Giovanelli* (Munich 1935); art. Gemeindegesang (MGG). *Orazio Benevoli, Mass* DTÖ 10, 1.

20. The Spanish School

In the background of the development of a distinctive Spanish school in music lies the political union involved in the marriage in 1469 of Isabella I of Castille (who reigned from 1474 to 1504) and Ferdinand II of Aragon (who reigned from 1479 to 1516). The daughter of this marriage and heir to the throne, Joanna the Mad, married the Hapsburg Philip the Fair. Their eldest son, Carlos I, came to the throne of Castille and Aragon in 1516 and to the German throne as Karl V in 1519. He abdicated in 1556 and was succeeded by his son Philip II, who ruled from 1556 to 1598. In 1581 the northern provinces of the Netherlands broke away; in 1588 the Spanish Armada was destroyed. On the other hand, in 1571 the Turkish fleet was destroyed at Lepanto, and in 1581 Spain gained control of Portugal. After Philip's death, however, Spanish power declined sharply. As a matter of cultural history, Spain was eminent in painting during the Baroque, producing such artists as El Greco, Jusepe de Ribera, Francisco de Zurbarán, and Bartolomé Esteban Murillo, and such authors as Miguel de Cervantes, Lope de Vega, and Pedro Calderon.

As early as the last decade of the 15th century one can distinguish works of sacred music by Spanish composers from those written in the prevailing Franco-Flemish period style. Masses by Juan de Anchieta (1462–1523), Pedro Escobar (d. 1514), and Alonso de Alba distinguish themselves by their simplicity of technique and a somewhat archaic manner, which is to a high degree combined with powerful spirituality. The simplicity of the forms corresponds to an ideal of subordination of the compositional technique to the expressive power in both the music and the text.

Religious music bore a distinctly national trait during the Golden Age of Spanish music, the 16th century. There was further development of the particular features that had already manifested themselves by the end of the previous century: simplicity of technique, power of feeling, mysticism, and dramatic tension. In these respects the music of the Spanish school made contact with the expressive power of the painting that flourished at the same time. The development and establishment of these national peculiarities are all the more remarkable in view of the fact that the best of the Spanish composers were quite familiar with the music of the Franco-Flemish, Venetian, and Roman schools. This is related to the love of music shared by Karl V, his wife the Empress Isabella (d. 1534), and Philip II, who on their trips through Europe took their personal musicians with them. Philip II was regarded as a veritable Maecenas of Spanish music. During the 16th century two court choirs were active, one Flemish and the other Spanish, each practicing its own kind of music. Spanish composers often used Flemish models in their parody Masses and on many occasions transcribed Flemish vocal compositions for the organ or the vihuela.

Creative activity focused on three schools, the Andalusian, the Castilian, and the Catalan.

The main composer of the Andalusian school was Cristóbal de Morales (*ca.* 1500–1553), who was a member of the Papal choir in Rome from 1535 to 1545. He was singled out for special honor by the Pope, and later served in Toledo, Marchena near Seville, and Malaga. Morales was the first Spanish composer who attained international recognition for his work, which includes twenty-two extant Masses and over eighty motets. He anticipates the ideas of the Council of Trent and the particular manner of Palestrina in the purity of his idiom.

Francisco Guerrero (1527 or 1528–1599), a pupil of Morales, served as choirmaster at the cathedral of Seville and wrote eighteen Masses and over a hundred motets. His concern, like his teacher's, was primarily with sacred music.

Juan Navarro (1528–1580), a pupil of Morales, was active in Avila, Salamanca, and Palucca.

The Castilian school is quite the peer of the Andalusian. The work of Tomás Luis da Victoria (*ca.* 1548–1611) represents its high point. Victoria studied at the Collegium Germanicum in Rome, where he was a pupil of Palestrina, and in 1571 became Palestrina's successor at the Collegium Romanum. From 1578 to 1585 he was chaplain for the Congregazione dei Preti dell' Oratorio under Neri, and was then in Madrid from about 1587 to his death. Together with the compositions of Morales, those of Victoria form the very center of Spanish creative activity in church music. We have twenty Masses and forty-four motets by Victoria. His style recalls Palestrina's in the agreement of line and harmony, and is by no means its inferior in religious depth.

The Castilian school also included Juan Escribano (*ca.* 1480–1557), of Rome and Salamanca; Bartolomé Escobedo (*ca.* 1500–1563), of Salamanca, Rome, and Segovia; and Diego Ortiz, who lived during the first two thirds of the 16th century in Spain and Italy and was both a composer and a theoretician.

The main representative of the Catalan school was Juan Pablo Pujol (1573–1626), of Tarragona, Zaragoza, and Barcelona. He was the most significant Spanish composer in the first third of the 17th century.

Along with the three schools that have been mentioned, there were also the Valencian school, represented mainly by Juan Bautista Comes (1568–1643), and the Aragonian school.

Bibliography

Hispaniae Schola musica sacra (8 vols., Lpz. and Barcelona); *La música en la corte de los Reyes Católicos* (Barcelona 2nd ed. 1960); sel. works, J. B. Comes (2 vols., Madrid 1888); coll. works, Guerrero (Barcelona 1955–   ); coll. works, Morales (Barcelona 1952–   ); coll.

works, Juan Pujol (Barcelona 1926–   ); coll. works, Victoria (8 vols., Lpz.); *studies:* H. Anglès, *Spain and Port.* (NOHM IV); R. Casimiri, *Il Vittoria: nuovi documenti* (Rome 1934); H. Collet, *Victoria* (Paris 1914); H. v. May, *Die Kompositionstechnik T. L. de Victorias* (Bern 1943); R. Mitjana, *C. de Morales* (Madrid 1920) and *F. Guerrero* (Madrid 1922); M. Palau, *La obra del Músico J. B. Comes* (Madrid 1944); F. Pedrell, *Victoria* (Valencia 1919); G. Reese, *Music in the Renaissance* (rev. ed., N. Y. 1959); R. Stevenson, *C. de Morales* (JAMS VI, 1953); G. A. Trumpff, *C. de Morales* (Diss. Göttingen 1938).

21. The Vocal Art of 16th-Century Society

The leading European countries—Italy, France, Germany, and England—suddenly came forth with a socially oriented music around 1500. The reason can be understood only in the light of the social circumstances that prevailed during the transition from medieval to modern times. Musicians and publishers brought out many printed editions, beginning with anthologies and later turning to collections of works by individual composers. The titles make it clear that the numbers contained in them could be sung or played on instruments, inviting every possibility: all parts sung, all played on instruments, and an alternation or mixture of these media. The medium used was contingent upon current availability. By the beginning of the second third of the 16th century, collections increased in number and included some compositions intended for instruments alone. In the main the pieces fall into two groups: dances and free compositions.

Italy

Many folk-song elements appear in Italian secular music of the 16th century. A quite extensive polyphonic music of folk-like song existed side by side with the courtly social madrigal. It can be traced from the latter half of the 15th century to its fusion with the monodic forms at the beginning of the 17th century. Italian composers seem rather to have monopolized it. By virtue of its very nature it was independent of the madrigal and included all forms of the stanzaic song with refrain or repeated sections. Its origin presumably goes back to an Italian improvisatory practice connected with Italian dance-music and took its point of departure from the *bassa danza*. Accordingly, the bass part of the dance retained the elements that moulded the form. Often there were ostinati or melodies in the bass that established the dance rhythm. They led to a four-voiced note-against-note setting, with stress on the two outer voices. Even in highly developed musical forms the ostinato bass is often still recognizable.

Frottola

The word "frottola" is probably derived from the medieval "frocta" and originally meant an "assortment or a bouquet of pleasant things"— in this instance, of verses. In the collective volumes of the Venetian printer Petrucci, "frottola" designates many different poetic forms set to music. Frottole are of two types, the Florentine carnival song and the Mantuan frottola.

The Florentine carnival song, or *canto carnascialesco*, was a song in three or four voices for the masked procession. It is predominantly homophonic, note-against-note, and stanzaic with refrain. The simple melodies are usually assigned to the topmost voice or the tenor. In content, the emphasis is on the lively texts. It was the first significant musical evidence of a new Italian national style, which from then on established itself as equal in rank to the music of the Franco-Flemish school and was in many ways related to the Franco-Flemish chanson. This rebirth of Italian music dates from about 1480. It quickly reached its height toward the end of the 15th century under Lorenzo de' Medici (d. 1492), when the carnival celebrations developed hitherto unknown brilliance.

The Mantuan frottola, on the other hand, was a smaller imitation of the Trecento ballata, rather than a parody of the Franco-Flemish chanson, and it exemplifies the native Italian art of song. The form was that of the ballata: *ripresa* (refrain), *mutazioni* (piedi), and *volta*. Usually only the ripresa was set to music. A succession of similarly constructed stanzas with final rhymes ended in a refrain. The refined art of the Mantuan frottola included mostly love-poems of somewhat superficial feeling, slightly ironical and supercilious, often containing a touch of improvisation. They were built on the musical foundation of the Italian dance bass, or *bassa danza*. The setting was regularly four-voiced note-against-note, homophonic, and intended for solo with instrumental accompaniment, with the melody in the soprano. Arrangements for song and lute have been occasionally preserved. Also *a cappella* performance was possible. The character of the music is light and flowing.

The Mantuan frottola was rather a generic term, which included the frottola in the narrower sense, oda, strambotto, sonetto, and canzona. The frottola was principally cultivated for and by the nobility. The first efflorescence of the form occurred during the years after 1490 at the Mantuan court under Isabella d'Este, the wife of Francesco Gonzaga. Moving out from Mantua, the interest in frottole quickly spread to the cities of Ferrara, Florence, and Venice.

Mantuan frottole for the most part were printed, in contrast to Florentine carnival songs. Numerous works, which to some extent go back to the latter half of the 15th century, were published after 1501 in Italy. Between 1504 and 1514 Petrucci brought out eleven books of frottole, in which he seems to have notably improved the texts. The most productive among the many composers were the Italians Marchetto Cara (d. after 1525), who was at the Mantuan court of the Gonzagas during most of his career, and Bartolommeo Tromboncino (d. *ca.* 1535), who also lived in Mantua and moved to Ferrara in 1513. The frottola was most popular during the first three decades of the 16th century, and the last printed publication appeared in 1533. The frottola was replaced in popularity by the villanesca and the madrigal.

A variation of the frottola is the *villota* (*alla Padovana, alla Mantovana, alla Bergamasca*), which became popular about 1540 and was usually homophonic and four-voiced.

Villanella

The word "villanella," which derives from *villano*, means "rustic ditty." The first publications devoted to this type of song appeared in 1537 in Naples, the homeland of the villanella. The first printed edition contained *Canzone villanesche alla Napoletana.* After 1560, the designations *villanesche, villanelle alla Napoletana,* and *canzoni Napolitane* were widely and indiscriminately used. As early as 1541, publications also appeared in Venice. During the latter half of the 16th century the name "villanella" prevailed.

In terms of its text, the villanella is a *strambotto* augmented by a refrain. A strambotto has an eight-line stanza, each line consisting of eleven syllables. The lines rhyme alternately. A refrain is added to the strombotto stanza, resulting in a villanella.

In terms of its music, the villanella consisted originally of a song-like soprano melody which was accompanied by thirds and fifths. According to Ludovico Zacconi in his *Prattica di musica* I (1592) and II (1622), the Southern Italians sang in parallel triads, and this practice was imitated here. Under the influence of the madrigal and the French chanson, however, the villanella quickly freed itself from this atavistic simplicity. The bass turned into a counter-voice, and the melody was artfully treated.

The structural idea involved in the three voices of the villanella (two soprano and one bass) is the basic concept behind the Baroque trio sonata. It formed the sharpest contrast to the artful settings of the Franco-Flemish school. Through its unaffected nature and fresh folk-like qualities it contributed substantially in the latter half of the 16th century to the creation of new forms and new compositional techniques, and influenced the madrigal in the direction of naturalness.

Thus mixed forms approximating both the madrigal and the villanesca appeared. For example, a villanesque melody was arranged in the artful style of the madrigal, or the primitive villanesque technique was adopted to parody the art-form of the madrigal. The villanella was finally expanded to four or five voices. A derived form was the *balletto*, or dance song. The villanella type was particularly imitated in Germany, England, and France and was fused with forms peculiar to these countries.

At the end of the 16th century, the Italian madrigal and the villanella were brought together in madrigal comedies by such composers as Orazio Vecchi and Adriano Banchieri. The dialogue of the personages who appeared were choral rather than soloistic and were always set polyphonically in the style of the madrigal and its related vocal genres.

Madrigal

The madrigal originated as a conscious reaction away from the frottola style. It emanated from a circle headed by the cardinal and poet Pietro Bembo. The writing of verse for madrigals as a kind of utilitarian poetry suddenly became the vogue. The structure was free. It consisted mostly of lines of eleven and seven irregularly mixed syllables, revealing no stanzaic structure but ending with an epigram. Many of the madrigal poems expressed an attitude of dedication or homage. Following the model of Willaert's work issued in 1559, composers especially preferred to set poems by Petrarch, Ariosto, Sannazaro, and Tasso. The madrigal was an art of a select fashionable group, and was cultivated socially for festive occasions; but it also shared some of the original aims of chamber music, to satisfy the participants' own joy in making music. The cities of Venice, Ferrara, Milan, Bologna, Florence, Rome, and Naples were especially involved in the development of the madrigal. Madrigal compositions belonged in the realm of *a cappella* art—that is, the setting was designed to make the individual voices equally significant. Though polyphonic structure prevailed, the compositional technique often betrayed the transition from polyphony to homophony. Musically, the madrigal arose from a fusion of the *canto carnascialesco*, the *lauda*, the *frottola*, the French *chanson,* and the *motet.*

The designation *accademia* was adopted by many associations of professional and amateur musicians for the cultivation of the madrigal. They were to be found in many places throughout Italy. The members sang mainly for their own pleasure, with or without listeners; but they also sang at various festivities and on family occasions. One of the first of these academies was the *Accademia Filarmonica* in Verona, founded in 1543.

The madrigal developed in three periods:

First Period: The initial collection of printed madrigals extant, *Madrigali novi di diversi eccellenti musici,* appeared in 1533 in Rome—presumably preceded by a first edition (1530), of which no copy has been preserved. Jacques Arcadelt's first book of four-voiced madrigals was printed in 1539 in a second edition, and by 1654 it had gone through thirty-six printings.

Leading composers of this period were Jacques Arcadelt, of Florence, Rome, and Paris (d. before 1572); Philippe Verdelot (*ca.* 1490 to some time before 1552), of Venice and Florence; Adrian Willaert (d. 1562 in Venice); Cipriano de Rore (d. 1565); Ihan Gero (dates and circumstances of life unknown); Costanzo Festa, master of the Papal choir in Rome (d. 1545); and Alfonso della Viola, choirmaster in Ferrara.

Musicians of the Franco-Flemish school and of France (Arcadelt, Verdelot, and Willaert) played a striking role during this period, and the responsibility for founding the Italian madrigal must be ascribed principally to them. They were felt somewhat to be "foreigners" in Italy, though two members of the group, Festa and Alfonso della Viola, were Italian.

At first the madrigal followed the frottola stylistically and was characterized by note-against-note writing. The pieces were predominantly four-voiced. There was close relation between the muisc and the verse structure. The melody was in the upper voice, though each individual part had inherent melodic aspects by virtue of the voice-leading.

Adrian Willaert and Cipriano de Rore held the key positions. In his day Willaert's creative work was considered *musica nova* because of its stress on emotion and its chromaticism, which incidentally may have been stimulated by studies of antiquity. Rore's madrigals, which began appearing in 1542, represented the first flowering of this type of art. They pointed the way to Monteverdi in their setting of Petrarch and their imitation of the pictorial language of the poems in the music while preserving unity of composition.

Second Period (the classical full bloom of the madrigal): The setting now expanded to five voices, sometimes grouped antithetically in such a way as to constitute subdivisions of the choral ensemble. Homophonic and imitative portions alternated, creating declamatory effects. The harmony was often enriched by occasional alterations to suggest musically pictorial and emblematic details.

Leading composers of this period were Orlandus Lassus (d. 1594); Philippe de Monte (d. 1603); Palestrina (d. 1594); Andrea Gabrieli (d. 1586); Giovanni Gastoldi, of Mantua (d. 1622); and Baldassare Donati, of Venice (d. 1603).

Whereas the composers of the first period had been largely "foreign," those of the second were predominantly Italian. In dealing with their native language, they brought a new treatment of the text into the music.

The transition to the third period brought with it further heightening of the tone-painting as musical symbolization of the expression of the text. The theorists of the time, particularly Zarlino, called for *imitazione della natura.* The artistic result was not naturalistic, but involved a highly exaggerated individualism of expression and experience. All possibilities were expressively "significant," including the voice-leading, voice range, differences between homophonic and polyphonic treatment, rhythm, syncopation, movement of the voices, change of time, and pictorial aspects of the notation.

Third Period: Very bold chromaticism developed in the interests of expression that often had dramatic features; and virtuoso tone-painting, very trenchant delineation, passionate feeling, and a dramatic representational quality evolved. Characteristic motives were developed, and sometimes there was *concertante* development of individual motives. Bits of declamation significantly pointed toward incipient melody. The development of chromaticism was a joint result of the tendency to work in a spirit of the humanism of antiquity and to imitate the chromatic and enharmonic aspects of ancient Greek music. By the last third of the 16th century, leadership had finally passed into the hands of the Italian composers. During this third period, obviously they represented only a rather thin, educated, and exclusive social stratum.

Leading composers of this third period were Luca Marenzio (1553 or 1554–1599) of Warsaw and Rome; Carlo Gesualdo, Prince of Venosa (*ca.* 1560–1613); Claudio Monteverdi (1567–1643); Heinrich Schütz, whose op. 1 appeared in 1612; Giaches de Wert (1535–1596); and Luzzasco Luzzaschi (d. 1607).

Burgundy and France

In the 15th century the French word *chanson* ("song") became a collective term for works of French and Burgundian polyphonic vocal art. The texts were exclusively French, but during the 16th century the composers of the Franco-Flemish period began to set also Dutch, Italian, and German texts. The chanson texts in the 15th century were predominantly merry, life-affirming, and amorous. The art was an exclusively courtly and aristocratic one. In this form the vocal art of the 15th century made contact with the polyphonic songs of the 14th century. The time between the death of Guillaume de Machaut and the beginning of Dufay's work has been divided into two sections:

1. From about 1380 to the beginning of 1400, including works by Solage, Trebor, Senleches, Gailot, Suzoy, and the Italians Philipoctus de Caserta and Matheus de Perusio.
2. From the beginning of 1400 to about 1430, represented by the composers Petrus Fontaine, Johannes Ciconia, Lebertoul, Nicolas Grenon, Loqueville, Hugo and Arnold de Lantins, Tapissier, Carmen, and Cesaris.

Among the composers of this first section, Matheus de Perusio, active in Milan (d. *ca.* 1418), is considered the main exponent of an altered style that involved a quite new and simplified melodic form containing the seeds of imitative counterpoint, a predominance of the upper voice, tonic-dominant cadences as closes, and consonant effect.

The Chanson in the 15th Century (Burgundo-Flemish Period)

The *chanson*, or discant song, was the main artistic form of secular music in the 15th century. The outstanding composer of it was Guillaume Dufay (*ca.* 1400–1474), and his most significant contemporary was Gilles Binchois (*ca.* 1400–1460). A French national style developed, which, though not bound to any school, was copied in Italy. It manifested a light and soaring quality, elegance, flowing declamation, and the agreement of musical with verse rhythm. Fifteenth-century composers in this form equalized the voices and made them more singable, and more artfully developed from the melody of the song itself.

According to Wolff, Dufay's chansons were intended for four types of performance:

1. Upper voice sung, two lower voices instrumental (after the model of Machaut's ballade and virelai).
2. Outer voices sung (after the model of the Italian ballata).
3. Tenor sung, with two accompanying instrumental voices.
4. Played entirely on instruments.

How these types fitted chronologically into the composer's work has not been established. Presumably they ran concurrently. Thus there were various ways the chanson might be performed in the 15th century: the discant or tenor might be sung, while the contratenor was played on the lute, viol, little organ, or harp; or all the voice parts might be played by instruments.

Dufay's contemporaries between 1460 and 1480 were Mouton, Hayne, Busnois, Jéhan, Fedé, Boubert, Barbingnant, Ockeghem, and Caron.

In the second half of the 15th century, composers refined the contrapuntal work in the chanson, adopting the techniques of imitation and canon. Thus they emphasized even more the meaning and expression of the words. The chanson accordingly lost its earlier identity as an artful musical construction and became a composition more inspired by the text.

Josquin des Prez (*ca.* 1450–1521?) was active at the midpoint of this transformation, which also involved a sociological change. The Burgundian courtly and aristocratic art of song in the 15th century gave way to a bourgeois art of small proportions that made innovation and experiment possible. Such middle-class tendencies in the art of song were typical of the late Middle Ages and the transition to the Renaissance. The bourgeoisie thus became more and more responsible for its own culture, as it was in its own way responsible for the new economic form of capitalistic and productive enterprise.

Josquin's chansons mark the culminating point in the Netherlands art of song. He sythesized the most highly artful polyphony and the expressive elements of the Renaissance. As a result, he wrote chansons that were formally lucid and meaningfully declaimed in accordance with the syllables, metre, and content of the verses. He employed the principle of repetition, introduced homophonic and homorhythmic portions, and achieved a fusion of sound. Often he augmented his writing for three or four voices to that for five or six, and he used French texts almost exclusively.

Among his contemporaries were Alexander Agricola, Loyset Compère, Pierre de la Rue, Stockhem, Ghiselin, Obrecht, Isaac, Benedictus Ducis, and Appenzeller.

The Chanson in the 16th Century

The rise of the chanson from the 15th to the 16th century was determined especially by the growth of a prosperous bourgeoisie. This social development was paralleled by the increasingly apparent transition on the part of the more folk-like art to a more cultivated one and by the stylistic change from the Burgundian to the 16th-century chanson. Also influential on it was the development of the lyric. The spread of the chanson occurred particularly as a result of the initiative of several music printers and publishers in France and in the Netherlands, such as Pierre Haultin, Pierre Attaignant, Robert Ballard, Adrian Le Roy, Etienne Briard, Tielman Susato, and Pierre Phalèse de Louvain. The high point in the development of the French national chanson occurred mainly during the reign of Francis I from 1515 to 1547.

The period that began about Josquin's time developed the chanson, which, as a rule, was four-voiced and in which the voices imitated each other and were freely articulated. Its architectonic plan was organized more and more in accordance with the verses, in which the composers emphasized the sections of text by musical episodes. The idea of the setting involved a constant alternation between homophony and polyphony, with numerous subtleties in the grouping of voices, imitation of the declamatory intonation, tone painting, background and interpretation of individual words (such as those for joy or pain), repetitions of tone and word, syllabic declamation of the text, and novel expression of feeling. This style inaugurated the first period of the Italian madrigal.

The instrumental form of the *canzone francese* is a transcription of the typical French chanson.

The period following Josquin brought with it the great epoch of the national French chanson. Beginning about 1530, it resulted in numerous printed editions issued by the main publishers Attaignant in Paris, Jacques Moderne in Lyons, and Tilman Susato in Amsterdam. After 1550 the lead was taken by the publishing firm of Adrian Le Roy and Robert Ballard in Paris. The spread of the chanson during the 16th century was closely related to music printing. Between 1528 and 1552 Attaignant published over fifty collections containing more than fifteen hundred chansons.

Two types developed: the melodiously presented sentimental chanson and the merry chanson with lively parlando movement in the voices. The leading poet was Clément Marot. The texts included all aspects of life, particularly the erotic.

Among the composers were Nicolas Gombert (*ca.* 1500–*ca.* 1560), Adrian Willaert (*ca.* 1490–1562), Pierre Certon (d. 1572 in Paris), Jacobus Clemens non Papa (*ca.* 1510–1555 or 1556), and also one of the first madrigalists, Jacques Arcadelt (d. before 1572 in Paris).

In the second half of the 16th century the chanson form was fundamentally altered as a result of the influence of French poets and humanists and of Italian music, particularly the madrigal. The new chanson was stanzaic, syllabic, and homophonic, with the main melody in the upper voice. Declamation closely followed the text of the poem. The new type was first called *vaudeville* or *voix de ville*, and later *air* or *air de cour*. Toward the end of the century, beginning about 1570, it was the main form of secular music in Paris. A group of poets known as the Pléiade was especially influential. Pierre Ronsard was their head, and the movement resulted in the Académie de Poésie et de Musique, founded in 1570–1 under the leadership of Jean-Antoine de Baïf. The most important composers to favor this type of composition (*chanson mesurée*) were Guillaume Costeley, Claude Le Jeune, and Jacques Mauduit (d. 1627). The main concern of the Académie was with a *musique mesurée*, in which *vers mesurée* with its long and short syllables was fitted to a music of correspondingly long and short note values, with due regard for all other aspects of the verse.

Meanwhile, the polyphonic chanson continued, and the madrigal was particularly influential upon its form. The forms of the villanella and the *canzone alla napoletana* also became popular. The leading masters of the polyphonic chanson were Jacques Arcadelt and Orlando di Lasso.

The main composers, accordingly, were Guillaume Costeley (d.

1606), Claude Le Jeune (*ca.* 1530–1602), Orlando di Lasso (d. 1594), and Jan Pieterszoon Sweelinck (d. 1621, in Amsterdam).

In about the middle of the 16th century Netherlands printers, notably Susato, began to issue collections of chansons in Flemish.

Among the works of this era, the program chanson achieved special significance as a form of vocal program-music in which the music closely depends on the word-painting of the text. There was widespread imitation, especially in Italy, of pieces depicting battles (such as Jannequin's "Battle of Marignano"), street scenes, the hunt, and bird concerts.

Though following the exigencies of programmatic characterization, the composers did not lose sight of the over-all formal layout. Their work notably influenced the Italian madrigal.

The main composers were Clément Jannequin, with 395 chansons (d. *ca.* 1559), Claudin de Sermisy (d. 1562, in Paris), and Crequillon (d. presumably in 1557).

Germany

Older Folk-Song

The idea of the folk-song can be characterized in somewhat the following way:

1. The word and the tune are united. The tune belongs integrally to the text.
2. The folk-song may well include all aspects of life in its subject matter.
3. The folk-song has not been composed literally by the folk as a whole. There are always individuals at work, though their names may remain mostly unknown. There can also be tunes—of art songs, for example, by known composers—which may become folk-songs by gaining popular currency, such as Schubert's *Am Brunnen vor dem Tore.*
4. The tune of the folk-song is fluid—that is, in the course of being "sung over and over again," it is transformed or changed.
5. In contrast to popular songs and hits, the folk-song has a longer life span.
6. The folk-song has no great "artistic value," but it is valuable in terms of *its own* intrinsic nature.
7. The tune of the folk-song, as a one-voiced melody, has its own individuality.

The oldest song literature is known only from reports that it existed or from its written texts. Occasionally scribes tried to indicate the notes in neumes, but today these are illegible. By comparing various recorded melodies, musicologists have established that particular types and formulae are premedieval. But the actual notes of the music remain inferential.

Many popular tunes evolved into medieval church songs. The Penitential Songs (*Geisslerlieder*) of 1349, for example, are preserved for us in chant notation and come from melodic types that must be substantially older. A few folk-tunes of the Middle Ages are noted in 15th-century manuscripts. The best sources we have for recovering the notes of some of the folk-songs come to us from the end of the Middle Ages, when the practice arose of using a folk-song as the cantus firmus for a polyphonic composition.

Polyphonic Arrangements in the 15th Century

The earliest polyphonic arrangements of German songs are found in the work of the Monk of Salzburg and Oswald von Wolkenstein. But these constitute the end of minnesong and contain no real folk heritage. There are, however, four German song-manuscripts of the 15th century: the *Lochamer Song-Book,* originating around 1460, probably in Nuremberg, and presumably owned by Wolflein von Lochamer of that city; the *Schedel or Munich Song-Book,* written between 1460 and 1467 in Nuremberg and Leipzig by Hartmann Schedel; the *Glogau or Berlin Song-Book,* from around 1477 to 1488 in Glogau, Silesia; and the *Rostock Song-Book,* which originated around 1470–80.

These collections contain mainly one-voiced sketches, along with some settings for two and three voices; the *Glogau Song-Book* even has a song for four voices. The tune normally lies in the tenor or descant and occasionally in the bass. Usually only one voice is provided with text, and some of the texts have been left out entirely. The model for these contrapuntal arrangements was provided by the Franco-Flemish chansons, especially those of Dufay and Ockeghem. The collections were primarily intended for music-making in the home. Well-known tunes from the *Glogau Song-Book* are "Elslein" and "Es liegt ein Schloss in Österreich," and from the *Lochamer,* "Ich spring' in diesem Ringe" and "Ich fahr dahin." Moser has professed to find differences between folk-tunes and court tunes. The court tunes predominate in German polyphonic song between 1450 and 1550. Their texts represent a belated flowering of Middle High German epigrammatic poetry. The tunes are perhaps often part of the folk heritage, but they were surely retouched by composers of the time. Also, vice versa, many original tunes of known composers have been absorbed into the folk heritage. The character of the songs corresponds to the needs of people in various occupations and situations; thus there are agricultural, minstrel, military, amorous, and political songs. Occasionally the names of composers are given, but Konrad Paumann is the only one of outstanding significance. The pieces are quite uneven in the technical quality of composition. The difference between court and folk tune lies in the court tune's greater melodic range and in the fact that the melodic formulation is influenced by one of the modes (Ionian on F is the most widely used). The *AAB* form predominates.

Polyphonic Social Song in the 16th Century

There were three stages in the development of the polyphonic social song:

1. *At the beginning of the 16th century:* This was the era of Maximilian I. The first printed collections were issued by Erhard Oeglin

(Augsburg 1512), Arnt von Aich (Cologne ca. 1512), and Peter Schöffer (Mainz 1513). Four-voiced setting predominated. As the cantus firmus lies in the tenor, this type is often called the "tenor song." Introductions and interludes are marked by initial imitative treatment. The entire structure is articulated according to the melody line of the song. The cantus firmus was mostly sung, and the other voices were performed instrumentally. The independent instrumental transcriptions for clavier, organ, or lute were an important branch of social song and of domestic musical culture.

During the first two decades of the 16th century the court tune predominated. The three printed works, according to Moser, mainly contained the repertoire of individual court choirs. The composers represented in the collections were active in princely courts. They can be divided into two generations: one born around 1440, including Adam of Fulda, active at Torgau (ca. 1445–1505); Heinrich Finck, of Cracow, Stuttgart, Salzburg, and Vienna (1444 or 1445–1527); and Heinrich Isaac, of Innsbruck and Augsburg (ca. 1450–1517); and another generation born around and after 1460, including Paul Hofhaimer, of Innsbruck, Augsburg, and Salzburg (1459–1537), and Thomas Stolzer, of Ofen (ca. 1480–1526).

2. *In the late 16th century:* This was the era of Karl V. Presumably as a result of the troubled times, a break of twenty years occurred in the publication of song collections. When they reappeared the major new publications were the collections of Ott, *Gute und neue Liedlein* (Nuremberg 1534 and 1544); Egenolf *Gassenhawerlin und Reutterliedlin* (Frankfurt a. M. 1535); Schöffer and Apiarius, *Fünff und sechzig teutscher Lieder* (Strassburg 1536); and Forster, *Ein Auszug guter und neuer teutscher Liedlein* in five books (Nuremberg 1539–56). The physician Georg Forster (ca. 1510–1568) came to Nuremberg in 1547 and was the collector, editor, and arranger of this significant publication. He united in one person the functions of composer and poet with those of song collector, arranger, and publisher.

The printed publications of songs in the second third of the 16th century represent the German bourgeois world, the middle-class music that was at home among the upper and lower levels within this social stratum. The possibilities of printing in collective editions or in single sheets met a demand that the work of art be brought into daily life in a generally available form. This had a certain commercial character. All human levels were included in the texts. The song repertory had its roots in bourgeois awareness and also included the tunes of the court.

As of *ca.* 1530, all four voices were vocally conceived. The composition, which centered about its often well known and traditional melody, was handled in various ways. The setting was always polyphonic and the structure—in accordance with the layout of the cantus firmus—was clear and perspicuous. At least five approaches were adopted on various occasions:

1. The cantus firmus might be placed in the tenor and free contrapuntal voices might be set against it, as in the older type of motet.

2. Sections of the cantus firmus might be imitated in the counter voices, utilizing in many instances a cantus-firmus structure.

3. The voices might imitate each other throughout, as in the through-imitative motet.

4. The melody might be given a canonic layout.

5. The cantus firmus might be in the cantus or top voice part, and the setting might be note-against-note in a rather homophonic manner.

One particular type of song that sometimes appears in this repertoire, the *quodlibet,* had a significance of its own. A union of different melodies into a whole, it usually had a burlesque effect. It is represented in a collection assembled by Wolfgang Schmeltzl in 1544.

The most important song composers in the age of Karl V have been divided into an older and a younger group. The older (born around 1490) includes Ludwig Senfl (*ca.* 1486–1542 or 1543), a pupil of Isaac's in Constance, active in Innsbruck and Munich, the most fruitful and significant song composer of the group, who did his outstanding work in the polyphonic cantus-firmus type of song; Arnold von Bruck, court choirmaster in Vienna (d. after 1554); Sixt Dietrich (*ca.* 1490–1548); Benedikt Ducis (*ca.* 1480–1544); Laurenz Lemlin, of Heidelberg (b. *ca.* 1495?); and Thomas Sporer (*ca.* 1485–1534). The younger group, born around 1510, included Caspar Othmayr (d. 1553), Stephan Zirler, and Jobst von Brant; all three were members of a Heidelberg group led by Laurenz Lemlin.

The humanistic school-song forms a type of its own. Petrus Tritonius in 1507, Martin Agricola, Paul Hofhaimer, Ludwig Senfl, and Benedikt Ducis composed Horatian odes in four-voiced setting, note-against-note, in the meter of Classical verse.

3. *In transition to the 17th century:* Most of the German song composers of the eras of Maximilian I and Karl V had died by the middle of the 16th century. The following period, which closed around 1620 with the beginnings of the thoroughbass song, was dominated by the increasing influence of the Italian social song, which the younger generation of composers particularly favored. They introduced the older cantus-firmus technique into the villanella and the madrigal, bringing various individual varieties of song to maturity on German soil. Thus German song melodies were often transcribed *alla madrigalesca* or *alla villanesca.* Now too, the freely invented choral song, or song-motet, occupied a special place.

The composers, some of whom were originally Italian and Franco-Flemish, included Matthäus Le Maistre, of Dresden (d. 1577); Antonio Scandello, of Dresden (d. 1580); Jakob Regnart, of Innsbruck and Prague (d. 1599); Leonhard Lechner, of Nuremberg and Stuttgart (d. 1606); Orlandus Lassus (1532–1594); and Johannes Eccard, of Königsberg and Berlin (d. 1611).

The most significant German song composer around 1600 was Hans Leo Hassler (d. 1612). He wrote Italian madrigals and combined the Italian compositional technique with German forms and German melodic feeling in his collections of German songs. Blume regards the "Lustgarten" as the "prototype of the social and student song of the 17th century." Hassler's German song collections are the *Neue teutsche Gesang nach Art* der welschen Madrigalien und Canzonetten (1596) and *Lustgarten neuer teutscher Gesäng, Balletti, Gaillarden und Intraden* (1601).

Significant musicians of the first third of the 17th century were Christoph Demantius, of Zittau and Freiburg i. S. (d. 1643); Melchior Franck (d. 1639); Valentin Haussmann; and particularly Johann Hermann Schein, choirmaster at St. Thomas' in Leipzig (d. 1630). Schein's song collections are the *Venuskränzlein* (1609), *Musica boscareccia oder Waldliederlein* in three books (1621–8), *Diletti pastorali* (1624), and *Studentenschmaus* (1626). In the second and third of these collections he had already made the transition to the 17th-century choral and solo song with thorough-bass accompaniment.

England

England had a secular polyphonic song tradition of its own before it flowered during the Elizabethan period around 1580. Extant examples show that it was related to European 15th-century song literature in general.

The stimulus to native creativity, however, came from Italy. Italian madrigals were known in England perhaps before 1550. But by the last decade of the 16th century English composers themselves showed a great. increase in activity. English poets had first become interested in Italian literary models, had proceeded to imitate them, and finally had developed further their own native art of verse.

The history of the English madrigal was begun during the reigns of Elizabeth I (1558–1603) and James I (1603–6125), and was concluded at the beginning of the Puritan era. In 1588 the collection *Musica Transalpina* appeared, made up almost entirely of significant Italian madrigals in English translation. It released a flood of further publications that were either translated from Italian or composed by native English musicians. Luca Marenzio and Giovanni Giacomo Gastoldi particularly served as models, and there was extensive imitation of the Italian musical forms. The madrigals have an English character by virtue of their native musical feeling, the way in which the voices are led melodically and are made to produce a full sound, their feeling for nature, the original conception and re-experiencing of the text, and the traits seemingly derivative of folk music. This was the "Golden Age" of English music. In contrast to the Italian madrigal, the English was more popular, expressed the rising English bourgeoisie, and did not share the Italian penchant for chromaticism, over-refinement, and subtle differences. It had stronger roots in a positive feeling for life and was perhaps more strongly bound to tonality. The madrigalists in England were not able to achieve as high a literary standard in their texts as the Italians.

After 1600 the madrigal had reached the height of its popularity, and the "ayre" became the more popular form. Here the main voice part was on top and was sung, while the other voice parts were either sung or played on instruments. At this time there were many arrangements for solo voice and lute.

A distinctive English development of the 17th century was the "catch." Catches are canons of three and more voices on light-hearted texts. The first collection appeared in 1609.

The main composers of the "Golden Age" of English music were William Byrd, Thomas Morley, John Dowland, John Wilbye, Thomas Tomkins, Thomas Weelkes, and Orlando Gibbons.

William Byrd was born in 1542 or 1543, probably in London or Lincolnshire. Not much is known of his youth and early training, but in 1563 he became organist of Lincoln Cathedral, and in 1574—together with Tallis—organist in the Chapel Royal of Queen Elizabeth I. Later he was in Harlington, Middlesex, and Stondon, Essex, and died in 1623, probably in Stondon. He was one of the most significant and versatile composers of his time, writing Masses, motets, anthems, madrigals, compositions for the virginal, and chamber music—including dances, chorale transcriptions, and fancies.

Thomas Morley was born in 1557, studied under Byrd, and became organist of St. Paul's Cathedral in London. In 1592 he became a Gentleman of the Chapel Royal. Beginning in 1593, he issued five collections of madrigals and, in 1597, brought out a treatise, *A Plaine and Easie Introduction*. He died in 1603. Founder of the English madrigal school, he was the first to assimilate the Italian madrigal style completely and to adapt it popularly to English conditions.

John Dowland was born in 1562. Renowned as lutenist, he was for a considerable period in France, Germany, Italy, and Denmark. In 1616 he entered the service of the English court. In 1625 or 1626 he died in London. He is significant for his lute songs, or ayres, his compositions for lute solo, and his madrigals.

John Wilbye was born in 1574, was active at Hengrave Hall in the service of Sir Thomas Kytson, and later was at Colchester. He died in 1638. By many he is considered the outstanding member of the English madrigal school.

Thomas Tomkins, the most famous member of a well-known family of English musicians, was born about 1573, studied under Byrd, became organist of the Chapel Royal, and later held a similar position at Worcester Cathedral. He died in 1656, in Martin Hussingtree, Worcester. He was a composer of madrigals, church music, virginal pieces, and chamber works.

Thomas Weelkes was born presumably between 1570 and 1580, became organist of Winchester College and later of Chichester Cathedral, and died in 1623 in London. He was a significant madrigalist and church composer, the most bold and uncompromising of the English madrigalists. Between 1597 and 1608 he issued five collections.

Orlando Gibbons, born in 1583 in Oxford, was a member of an outstanding family of musicians. As a youth he was a choirboy at King's College in Cambridge, and later, in 1605, he became organist of the Chapel Royal and then of Westminster Abbey. He died in 1625 in Canterbury. His sacred compositions, madrigals, and virginal and chamber works are quite significant.

Denmark

Music flourished under King Christian IV (1588–1648), who enlarged the choir by giving regular appointment to thirty-one singers, thirty instrumentalists, and sixteen trumpeters. He attracted significant musicians to his service, including John Dowland and Heinrich Schütz, and provided Danish musicians with the possibility of studying abroad. Among them were:

Melchior Borchgrevinck, of Dutch family background, who by 1587 had been given a court appointment and was sent to study with Giovanni Gabrieli. In 1600 Borchgrevinck was court organist and in 1618 master of the court choir. In 1605–6 he brought out fifty-two madrigals by Italian and Danish composers in two books at Copenhagen under the title *Giardino novo bellissimo*. He died in 1632.

Mogens Pedersøn, born about 1585, became a pupil of Borchgrevinck and of Giovanni Gabrieli between 1599 and 1600 and from 1605 to 1609. He was in England from 1611 to 1614. Returning to Denmark, he became assistant choirmaster in 1618 and died in 1623. Book I of his *Madrigali a cinque voci* appeared in Venice in 1608, and ten madrigals of a lost second collection (1611) have been found in a manuscript copy made by Francis Tregian (B. Mus. Egerton 3665). Two madrigals of his appeared in Brachrogge's collection of 1619. He also issued a volume *Pratum spirituale* in Copenhagen in 1620.

Hans Nielsøn (Giovanni Fonteio), born about 1585, pupil of Borchgrevinck, studied with Giovanni Gabrieli between 1599 and 1600 and from 1602 to 1604 and with the English lutenist Gregorius Howett in Wolfenbüttel from 1606 to 1608 and in Heidelberg in 1611. Returning to Denmark he was active as a chapel singer and court lutenist, became assistant choirmaster 1623–4, and died sometime after 1626. His *Il primo libro di madrigali a cinque voci* (Venice 1606) contains twenty-one pieces, of which No. 7 is in the second book of Borchgrevinck's collection.

Hans Brachrogge, born about 1585, pupil of Borchgrevinck, studied with Giovanni Gabrieli from 1602 to 1604 and was in England from 1611 to 1614 and in Italy in 1619. In his homeland he sang in the court choir in 1611 and died some time after 1638. His collection *Madrigaletti a III voci* (Book I, Copenhagen 1619) contains twenty-one pieces, of which Nos. 8 and 17 are by Pedersøn.

Truid Aagesen (1593–1613), organist at the Vor Frue Kirke in Copenhagen, issued *Cantiones trium vocum* (Hamburg 1608) under the name Theodoricus Sistinus.

Poland

In the 16th century a distinctively Polish type of song existed, mostly in small stanzas, usually not through-composed, simple, often note-against-note. In themes these pieces were predominantly religious, often being versions of Psalms and moralizing songs, though among them there were some secular numbers on historic and political themes. The sources for these are Jan of Lublin's organ tablature (1537–48); the Holy Spirit Cloister organ tablature (1548); the song books of Puławy (1545–56) and Zamość (1558–61); and the Cracow lute tablature of the late 16th century. Also there are the melodies in Makołaj Gomółka's Polish Psalter (1580) and various individual printed sources. Among the transcriptions of Polish songs contained in organ tablatures there are some artful settings, e.g. Nicolaus Cracoviensis' *"Aleċnade mną Wenus,"* but there are also some simple folk-dances and historical songs.

The so-called Dissident movement around 1550 focused greater attention on Polish Renaissance song. Folk-like cantus firmi and compositions rhythmically related to folk-music appear among many compositions in Protestant song books.

Among the historical songs there are pieces with "royal" themes (including the *"Pienie o electii krala polskiego Sigmunta wtórego,"* the first song printed in Poland, in 1531). There are also texts which represent important political events.

Wacław of Szamotuły (*ca.* 1526–*ca.* 1560) and Cyprian Bazylik (*ca.* 1535–*ca.* 1591) were active in the Reformation and especially significant. Their Psalms, hymns, and confessional songs are of great artistic value and show technically complicated polyphonic work. The existence of many contrafacta indicate the popularity of these composers.

Mikołaj Gomółka (*ca.* 1535–after 1591) had been trained in the royal choir at Cracow and Wilno, and was a member there until 1563. His major work is a *Psalter of David,* printed in Cracow in 1580, to a text by Jan Kochanowski, the greatest Polish poet of the 16th century. Kochanowski's talent had no narrowly sectarian aims, but was generally oriented toward aesthetic and poetic expression. Likewise, Gomółka set this text to music not for the church service but for purposes that transcended the limits of a specific group. Hence this psalter is not like other comparable European examples, nor does it resemble 16th-century Polish church songs. It can be considered a Polish equivalent to the apolitical secular forms of music such as the madrigal or chanson. Gomółka's Psalms generally have no cantus firmi, but in some cases only initial citations with symbolical or programmatic function. The unity of the text and music is indicated only for the first stanza or, if non-stanzaic, for the very opening. This represents the first significant attempt to give Polish a strict and consistent musical formulation as a language of poetic art. It greatly influenced Polish work in the chanson and madrigal, as well as the Polish folk-song. It is a composition of quite mature harmonic achievement, juxtaposing major and minor and utilizing augmented chords and chromaticism. Many of its madrigalian features show close relationship to the construction and symbolism of Netherlands composition. In general, it represents a combination of Italian *maniera* with Netherlands compositional technique and Polish spirit. It is the most inclusive and outstanding work that preserves for us some aspects of Polish music during the closing years of the Renaissance.

Bibliography

A. Einstein, *Die mehrstimmige weltliche Musik von 1450–1600* (Adler Hdb.); N. Fortune, *Solo Song and Cantata* (NOHM IV).

Italy: Frottola: F. Ghisi, *I Canti Carnascialeschi* (Florence 1937) and *Strambotti e Laudi* (Florence 1953); K. Jeppesen, *La Frottola. I: Bemerkungen zur Bibliographie der ältesten weltlichen Notendrucke in Italien. II: Zur Bibliographie der handschriftlichen musikalischen Überlieferung des weltlichen italienischen Lieds um 1500* (Acta Jutlandica XL:2–XLI:1, Aarhus 1968–9; vol. III in prep.); R. Schwarz, *Die Frottola im 15. Jh.* (VfMw 1886); art. Frottola (MGG). *Villanella:* B. M. Galanti, *Le Villanelle alla Napolitana* (Florence 1954); G. M. Monti, *Le villanelle alla napoletana* (Città di Castello 1925); W. Scheer, *Die Frühgesch. der ital. Villanella* (Nördlingen 1936); M. Vajro, *La canzone napolitana* (Naples 1957). *Madrigal: Willaert,* ed. BlCh; *Rore,* coll. ed. 1959– ; *Gero,* Torchi I; *Marenzio,* PäM 4, 1; 6; *Gesualdo,* coll. ed., 10 vols., Hamburg; Torchi IV; IeM V; *Monteverdi,* coll. ed.; *Schütz,* coll. ed.; *Studies:* Academia di Scienze, Lettere ed Arti di Modena, ed., *Horazio Vecchi* (Modena 1950); D. Arnold, *Marenzio* (London 1965); A. Carapetyan, *The Concept of Imitazione della Natura* (JRB 1, 1947); E. J. Dent, *The 16th Century Madrigal* (NOHM IV); A. Einstein, *Die mehrst. weltl. Musik von 1450–1600* (Adler Hdb.) and *The Italian Madrigal* (3 vols., Princeton 1949); H. Engel, *Luca Marenzio* (Florence 1956); J. Haar, ed., *Chanson and Madrigal 1480–1530* (Cambridge, Mass. 1964); E. Helm, *Secular Vocal Music in Italy* (NOHM III); E. Hertzmann, *A. Willaert in d. weltl. Vokalmusik s. Zeit* (Lpz. 1931); J. Hol, *Horazio Vecchi als weltl. Komponist* (Basel 1917); F. Keiner, *Die Madrigale des Gesualdo di Venosa* (Lpz. 1914); E. Kiwi, *Studien z. Gesch. d. ital. Liedmadrigals im 16. Jh.* (Würzbg. 1937); D. T. Mace, *Pietro Bembo and the Literary Origin of the Italian Madrigal* (MQ 1969); H. F. Redlich, *Das Problem des Stilwandels in Monteverdis Madrigalwerk* (Bln. 1931); A. Sandberger, *Aufsätze zu Lassos Komp. in ital., franz. u. dt. Sprache* (Ausg. Aufsätze z. Musikgeschichte, Munich 1921); H. Schultz, *Das Madrigal als Formideal* (Lpz. 1939); W. Weismann, *Die Madrigale des Carlo Gesualdo* (DJM 1960); art. Madrigal (MGG). *New eds.: Canti carnascialeschi* (of the Lorenzo Magnifico period, ed. Masson, Paris 1913); *Chansons italiennes de la fin du XVIe siècle* (ed. Wotquenne, Lpz., Brussels, London); *Das mehrstimmige Lied des 16. Jh.* (MW); Gesualdo, coll. ed. (Hamburg 1957–62), *Madrigals* (Rome 1942–58); *Le Frottole nell'edizione principe di Ottaviano Petrucci* (In et Mon I); *Petruccis Frottole,* Books I and IV, 1504–5 (PäM 8); Torchi, *Arte mus. in Italia* I, II, IV; BlCh; Sch 69–72, 98–101, 106, 140, 164–167.

Burgundy and France: D. v. Bartha, *Benedictus Ducis und Appenzeller* (Wolfenbüttel 1930) and *Probleme d. Chansongesch. im 16. Jh.* (ZfMw XIII); H. Besseler, *Hat M. de Perusio Epoche gemacht?* (Mf 1955); C. v. d. Borren, *The French Chanson* (NOHM IV); M. Brenet, *Musique et musiciens de l'ancienne France* (Paris 1911); A. Einstein, *Die mehrst. weltl. Musik von 1450–1600* (Adler Hdb.); H. Expert, *A propos de la musique fr. à l'époque de la renaissance* (Lav. Enc.); W. Gurlitt, *Burgundische Chanson und dt. Liedkunst* (Kongressber. Basel 1924); J. Haar, ed., *Chanson and Madrigal 1480–1530* (Cambridge, Mass. 1964); K. P. Bernet Kempers, *J. Clemens non Papa's Chansons* (MD 1961); F. Lesure, *C. Jannequin* (MD V, 1951); J. Levron, *C. Jannequin* (Paris

1948); W. Marggraf, *Tonalität und Harmonik in der franz. Chanson zwischen Machaut und Dufay* (AfMw 1966); P.-M. Masson, *Le mouvement humaniste* (Lav. Enc.); H. Prunières, *Nouv. Hist. de la Musique* (Paris 1934); T. W. Werner, *Musik in Frankreich* (Breslau 1927); H. C. Wolff, *Die Musik der alten Niederländer* (Lpz. 1956); H. Zingerle, *Zur Entwicklung der Rhythmik u. Textbehandlung in den Chansons von 1470 bis 1530* (Innsbruck 1954); arts. Chanson, Madrigal (MGG). *New eds.*: C. v. d. Borren, *Pièces polyphoniques profane de provenance Liègoise* (Brussels 1950); E. Droz, Y. Rockseth, and G. Thibault, *Trois Chansonniers français du XVe siècle* (Paris 1927); H. Expert, *Les maîtres musiciens de la Renaissance française* (23 vols., Paris 1894–1908); R. J. v. Maldeghem, *Trésor musical* (Collection authentique de musique sacrée et profane des anciens maîtres belges), 29 vols., 1865–93; *60 chansons aus der ersten Hälfte des 16. Jh., franz. u. niederl. Komponisten* (PGfM 23); *Chansons von Binchois* (Mainz); coll. eds. of J. Cesaris, J. Ciconia, B. Cordier, T. Crequillon in prep. (AIM), coll. ed. of Dufay (1947–   , AIM); coll. ed. of chansons, Jannequin (Paris 1965–   ); Codex Escorial (facs., Kassel); Sch 24, 35, 40–42, 53, 68, 116–118, 133, 144.

The Chanson in the 16th Century: Costeley and Claude le Jeune (Expert, Maîtres), Lassus and Sweelinck (coll. eds.), Jannequin's Battle of Marignano (new ed., Expert), Jannequin (coll. ed., Paris 1965–   ; Expert, Maîtres; Cauchie, Heft 2), Sermisy (Expert, Renaissance), Crequillon (Commer, Maldeghem). *Studies:* F. Lesure, *C. Goudimel* (MD 1948) and *C. Jannequin* (MD 1951); D. P. Walker, *The influence of Musique mesurée à l'antique* (MD 1948) and *The Rhythm and Notation of Musique mesurée* (MD 1950); D. P. Walker and F. Lesure, *Claude le Jeune and Musique mesurée* (MD 1949).

Germany: H. Albrecht, *C. Othmayr* (Kassel 1950); O. Baumann, *Das deutsche Lied in den Orgeltabulaturen* (Bln. Diss. 1934); H. Besseler, *Das Lochamer Liederbuch aus Nürnberg* (Mf I); K. Gudewill, *German Secular Song* (NOHM IV) and *Zur Frage der Formstrukturen der deutschen Liedtenores* (Mf I); W. Gurlitt, *Burgundische Chanson- u. dt. Liedkunst d. 15. Jh.* (Baseler Kongressber. 1924); R. v. Liliencron, ed., *Deutsches Leben im Volkslied um 1530* (Stuttgart, n. d.); H. J. Moser, *Gesch. d. dt. Musik* (Stuttgart 2nd ed. 1921) and *Kleine dt. Musikgesch.* (Stuttgart 1949); H. Osthoff, *Das Niederländer u. d. dt. Lied (1400–1640)* (Bln. 1938); C. Petzsch, *Das Lochamer Liederbuch* (Munich 1967); C. P. Reinhardt, *Die Heidelberger Liedmeister des 16. Jh.* (Diss. Heidelberg 1938); H. Rosenberg, *Untersuch. über d. dt. Liedweise im 15. Jh.* (Bln. Diss. 1931); W. Salmen, *Das Lochamer Liederbuch* (Lpz. 1951); O. Wessely, *A. v. Bruck* (Cologne 1968); arts. Glogauer Liederbuch, Humanismus, Lied, and Hartmann Schedel (MGG).

Older Folk-Song: colls.: F. M. Böhme, *Altdeutsches Liederbuch* (Lpz. 1877) and *Volkstümliche Lieder d. Deutschen im 18. u. 19. Jh.* (Lpz. 1895); L. Erk and F. M. Böhme, *Deutscher Liederhort* (3 vols., Lpz. 1893–4); R. v. Liliencron, *Die hist. Volkslieder d. Deutschen vom 13. bis 16. Jh.* (4 vols., Lpz. 1865–9, texts only); J. Meier, *Deutsche Volkslieder, Balladen* (Bln. 1935–9); H. J. Moser, *Tönende Volksaltertümer* (Bln. 1935); *Landschaftl. Volkslieder* (37 booklets), ed. Verband dt. Vereine f. Volkskunde (1924–   ); Sch 44–47, 85–88, 111, 124, 125, 132, 139, 141, 152, 154, 187; *studies:* W. Danckert, *Das europ. Volkslied* (Bln. 1939) and *Grundriss d. Volksliedkunde* (Bln. 1939); H. Mersmann, *Grundlagen einer mus. Volksliedforschung* (AfMw 1922–

4); H. Naumann, *Grundzüge d. dt. Volkskunde* (Lpz. 1922); J. v. Pulikowski, *Gesch. d. Begriffs Volkslied im mus. Schrifttum* (Heidelberg 1933); W. Salmen, *European Song 1300–1530* (NOHM III); A. Sydow, *Das Lied* (Göttingen 1962); W. Wiora, *Älter als die Pentatonik* (Studia Bélae Bartók Sacra, 2/1957 Budapest), *Das echte Volkslied* (Heidelberg 1950), *Europ. Volksgesang* (Cologne 1952, MW), and *Europ. Volksmusik u. abendländische Tonkunst* (Kassel 1957); art. Lied (MGG).

Polyphonic Arrs. in the 15th C.: Lochamer Liederbuch facs. Kassel, new ed. in *Chrysanders Jhb.*, Bd. II; *Glogauer Liederbuch* new ed. in RD 4 and 8; *Rostocker Liederbuch* new ed. Halle 1927.

Polyphonic Soc. Song in the 16th C.: colls. printed by Oeglin PGfM 9. *Arnt von Aich*, new ed. Kassel 1930. *Peter Schöffer*, facs. 1913, sels. BlCh. *Heinrich Finck*, PGfM, 8; DTÖ 37, 2; Sch 87. *Isaac*, DTÖ 14, 1. *Hofhaimer*, DTÖ 37, 2, and in Moser, *Hofhaimer. Stoltzer*, DTÖ 37, 2; RD 20 and 22. *Ott coll.*, PGfM I-III. *Egenolf coll.*, facs. 1927, new ed. Hildesheim. *Forster coll.*, PGfM 29 and RD 20. *Senfl*, RD 10, 15. *Arnold von Bruck*, DTÖ 37, 2. *Dietrich*, RD 23. *Sporer*, coll. ed. 1929–   . *Othmayr*, sel. works ED 26. *Humanistic schoolsong*, Sch 73, 74. *Scandello*, Sch 132. *Regnart*, PGfM 19, Sch 139. *Lechner*, PGfM 19. *Lassus*, coll. ed. *Eccard*, PGfM 21. *Hassler*, DTB 5, 2, PGfM 15, Sch 152. *Schein*, coll. ed., Sch 187.

England: compl. works of English madrigalists in *The English Madrigal School*, 36 vols., ed. E. H. Fellowes (London 1913–24); G. Bontoux, *La Chanson en Angleterre au temps d'Elisabeth* (Oxford 1936); E. J. Dent, *The 16th Century Madrigal* (NOHM IV); E. H. Fellowes, *The English Madrigal* (London 1925), *The English Madrigal Composers* (London 2nd ed. 1949), and *The English Madrigal Verse 1588–1632* (London 1920); J. Kerman, *The Elizabethan Madrigal* (New York 1962); P. Warlock, *The English Ayre* (Oxford 1926); art. Madrigal (MGG). *William Byrd:* coll. ed. 20 vols. (1937–50), ed. E. H. Fellowes, London; Sch 145; O. Becker, *Die engl. Madrigalisten Byrd, Morley u. Dowland* (Lpz. 1901); E. H. Fellowes, *W. B.* (London 2nd ed. 1948); W. Gray, *Some Aspects of Word Treatment of W. B.* (MQ 1969). *Thomas Morley:* "Plaine and Easie Intro." facs. new ed. 1937, also London 1952. *John Dowland:* new ed. in *The English School of Lutenist Songwriters;* Sch 146; art. Dowland (MGG). *John Wilbye:* H. Heurich, *J. W. in seinen Madrigalen* (Augsburg 1931). *Thomas Tomkins:* D. Stevens, *T. T.* (London 1957); S. de B. Taylor, *T. T.* (London 1933). *Thomas Weelkes:* D. Brown, *T. W.* (London 1969). *Orlando Gibbons:* E. H. Fellowes, *O. G.* (London 1925).

Denmark: new eds. in *Dania Sonans;* BlCh; *Folke- og Skolemusik I,* 5 and XVI, 2 (Copenh. 1934–5 and 1965); A. Hammerich, *Musikken ved Christian den Fjerdes Hof* (Copenh. 1892). *Studies:* T. Dart, *Tregian's Anthology* (ML 1951); R. Gerbert, *Vorwort zu BlCh* 35; K. Jeppesen, *Vorwort zu "Dania sonans I"* (Copenh. 1933); art. Dänemark (MGG).

Poland: new eds. in MPO, MPR, CSMSiP 28, 34, 47–49, and MDK.

V Music of the Seventeenth to Nineteenth Centuries

22. The Baroque and Classical Periods

In presenting the history of music, one has to set up divisions into sections and chapters that seem meaningful and that are distributed according to epochs, types, and countries. This is required by the very nature of the material and for didactic reasons. A distinction has to be made, for instance, between prehistory and history, and similarly between antiquity and the Middle Ages.

Once one has begun to draw such lines, however, and has allowed his sense of order to come into play, he cannot very well stop there, but must strive to articulate larger units. He finds, for instance, that he cannot very well compare the "modern period" with the concept of the "Middle Ages" as a self-contained unit. The comparison of Medieval and Modern, he finds, cannot be fruitfully applied to the history of music, as can the comparison of the Late Gothic and the Renaissance. By the same token the Baroque, Classical, and Romantic eras are to be understood as higher entities.

The Baroque Era

The question regarding the relative value of music in the scheme of things was answered in two ways during the Baroque Era: the heavenly and the earthly, or the cosmological and the terrestrial.

Cosmologically, it must be realized that research in the field of the natural sciences in general, and astronomy in particular, made decisive advances during the Renaissance and was being carried on further during the Baroque Era. Baroque thinkers thus achieved a historically unique synthesis of intuition and knowledge, of vision and of the observation of nature. The German astronomer Johannes Kepler (1571–1630) represented one culminating point in this development as he pioneered in his mathematical computation of planetary orbits. He united the factual research of his time with the age-old intuitive Oriental view of the connection between the cosmos, number, and music. In his main work, *Harmonia mundi*, or Harmony of the World (1619), he sketches an inclusive world-view, pervaded by observation of nature, aesthetic awareness, and philosophical conception.

The book of nature, according to Kepler, is written in numbers and mathematical figures. Simple numerical relationships and geometrical regularities prevail. This order is one of the basic assumptions in his view of the beauty of nature and the inherent harmony in all its relations. In fact, his conviction that the universe is mathematically ordered is a motive for his research. Aesthetic wonder at the beauty and order of the universe is his starting-point. In a way, he was carrying the Pythagoreans' speculations about numbers into the empirical realm. He saw all parts of the universe as homogeneous. The sublunar world was no longer the realm of imperfection, in contrast to the spiritual realm of the starry heavens. Matter and motion were the same in both; the universe was undivided throughout. No longer did there exist differences of nature and value between heaven and earth.

The order of the macrocosm, as in the microcosm, corresponded to the basic tones of music. Kepler found the steps of the scale expressed in the relationships between the visible movements of the planets. In the *Harmonia mundi*, Book V, Chapter 6, he showed that musical modes were distributed among the planets. Saturn was associated with the Mixolydian mode, Jupiter with the Dorian, Mars with the Lydian, and the earth with the Phrygian. He calculated that in heaven no more than six voices sound together, and concluded that

> The movements of heaven are nothing else but a constant polyphonic music . . . comprehensible to the understanding, not the ear . . . a music which by dissonant tensions, as by syncopes and cadences throughout (as men apply them in imitation of those natural dissonances), heads straight for certain provided resolutions each with its six members (as it were, its six voices) and thus in the immeasurable flow of time sets up distinguishing marks. It is therefore no longer strange that man, the imitator of his Creator, has finally discovered the art of polyphonic song, which was unknown to the ancients. He wished to play the continuous duration of world time in the short part of an hour with an artful symphony of several voices and so far as possible get a taste of the divine Creator's pleasure in his works, in the lovely feeling of bliss that this music, in imitation of God, gives him.

Thus Kepler took a total view and considered the over-all relationship of the cosmos and man. He was able to do so by using number. In this way, he found a philosophical explanation, primarily for the interrelationships within the whole and secondarily for the influence of music on man's inner life.

Over against this synoptic view, however, there was also a terrestrial, or earthly, way of looking at music. It renounced the cosmological superstructure and arrived at an autonomous theory of the affections, or emotional states. During the Renaissance, Zarlino (1517–1590) had made this the leading philosophy of music. Now, in the Baroque, it was systematized. The cornerstone was laid by René Descartes (1596–1650), founder of Rationalism, in his *Passiones animae* (1649). He also wrote in 1650 a *Compendium musicae* that was published posthumously. "The purpose of tone," he wrote, "is to give us pleasure and to call up in us various emotions." Thus the influence of music on man's inner life became posited as a fact, which led to further investigation into what properties of tone—such as pitch, duration, strength, and tempo of succession—released particular responses. Present-day psychologists take the term that was used, "affect," to mean any heightened experience of feeling. The affects, the "passions of the soul," Descartes defined as "notions or feelings or excitements of the soul which one quite particularly relates to himself and causes by any stirring of the animal spirits to be entertained and strengthened." These "animal spirits" are the "most mobile and fine particles of the blood thinned by the heart's warmth, which continually in great number press toward the caverns of the brain and have the property of being very small and of moving very quickly, like the elements in the flame of a torch. Hence they never loiter, but in every possible way put the body in motion."

The theory of the affections, or the affects, was also significantly set forth by Athanasius Kircher (1601–1680), professor at the University of Würzburg and a naturalist, in his *Musurgia universalis* (1650) and his *Phonurgia* (1673); Marin Mersenne (1588–1648) in his *Harmonie universelle* (1636); and Johann Mattheson (1681–1764) in *Der vollkommene Capellmeister* (1739).

The terrestrial point of view, by which music was immediately dominated, led to a revolution in secular music, which has given a particular cast to music from 1600 to the present. If one thinks of the time scheme from this point of view, one can begin the "modern period in the history of music" around 1600.

New developments that occurred around 1600 include:

Opera

Oratorio

Independent orchestral music

Soloistic instrumental music with continuo

Song accompanied by thorough-bass, with either solo voice or soloistic voice parts

Separate and more individualized music for organ and other keyboard instruments

Recognition of a whole series of instruments now quite familiar to us as having individual character and hence deserving a soloistic literature and special handling according to their particular nature in orchestral compositions

Highly brilliant music for vocal solo

Very strong emphasis on professionalized musicianship, which was soon carried even further to virtuosity

Although the most striking break came around 1600, individual traits characteristic of Baroque music had already made their appearance earlier or were very soon to appear. The predominantly sonorous and chordal impulse in Venetian music had begun around 1550, the new affective idiom a few decades later, thorough-bass technique developed around 1600 and then spread very quickly, and the individualization of instrumental sonority was quite marked around 1620–1630. Accordingly, it is not possible to specify a single year for the transition from Renaissance to Baroque, but the following roughly chronological division attempts to be true to the general picture:

ca. 1560–ca. 1620: Early Baroque

ca. 1620–ca. 1680: Main or High Baroque

ca. 1680–ca. 1740: Late Baroque

From the point of view of art-history and sociology Arnold Hauser, in his *Social History of Art* (1953), sees in the Baroque the final dissolution of the cultural tradition of the Middle Ages. He views mannerism as a last and futile attempt to restore medieval unities. During the Baroque the feudal aristocracy lost any political significance it may have had as a warrior caste. The political ties of feudalism turned into national states that were absolute and essentially modern. Christian unity disintegrated into churches and sects. Philosophy broke away from religiously oriented metaphysics and was refashioned into the "natural system of the sciences." Art overcame medieval objectivity and stressed the expression of subjective experience. In music, the decisive change about 1600 corresponds to this new view of things.

The artistic tendencies of mannerism form a particular movement in the history of music during the epoch of the Early Baroque. The urge to push characteristic types of individual expression beyond all bounds and become unlimitedly subjective, the over-stressing of specific elements in the signification of individual words, the extreme emphasis on separate impulses, the constant unrest, and the high degree of individuality that consciously isolates itself by addressing itself to only a quite small section of society—all are features of mannerism. Renaissance unity and proportion of form were dissolved, logic was brushed aside, and the voices became extremely individualized. The chromatic aspects of form supplanted the diatonic. This egocentricity increased most strongly in the late madrigal and early monody and pressed on from here into early opera (Monteverdi's *Orfeo*, 1607) and the cantata. Ostensibly, mannerism in music addresses itself to an intellectual aristocracy, while the music of the Early Baroque strives for a broader, more popular effect. This intellectual stratum in the 16th century, however, was by no means small; it was international; and mannerism was its special way of expressing itself and of making itself understood, knit together as it was precisely through a common taste for that aspect of things that was difficult, highly complicated, and "dark." "Manneristic arts of deception" are examples of an artistic style of expression that broods over final period styles. This applies as much to the 14th century with Ars nova and Ars subtilior as it does to the time around 1600, as much to the Romantic period around 1830 as to the music of the Schönberg circle around 1910–50 (Schönberg died in 1951, Webern in 1945, Berg in 1935) or to the era of serial music between 1949 and 1960. But mannerism became a musically expressive style particularly during the decades roughly between 1580 and 1630. It marked with artistic expression a crisis that terrified the close of the 16th century.

In the three-fold division of the Baroque, individual personalities take their places thus:

Early Baroque (*ca.* 1560–*ca.* 1620):
    Italy: Adrian Willaert (*ca.* 1490–1562)
              Orlando di Lasso (1532–1594)
              Luca Marenzio (*ca.* 1550–1599)
              Giovanni Gabrieli (*ca.* 1555–1612)
              Carlo Gesualdo, Prince of Venosa (*ca.* 1560–1613?)
              Claudio Monteverdi (1567–1643)
  Germany: Jakob Handl (Jacobus Gallus) (1550–1591)
              Leonhard Lechner (*ca.* 1550–1606)
              Hans Leo Hassler (1564–1612)
              Michael Praetorius (1571–1621)
              Johann Hermann Schein (1586–1630)
  Holland: Jan Pieterszoon Sweelinck (1562–1621)

High Baroque (*ca.* 1620–*ca.* 1680)
    Italy: Claudio Monteverdi (1567–1643)
              Girolamo Frescobaldi (1583–1643)
              Francesco Cavalli (1602–1676)
              Giacomo Carissimi (1605–1674)
              Orazio Benevoli (1605–1672)
              Marc' Antonio Cesti (*ca.* 1623–1669)
  Germany: Heinrich Schütz (1585–1672)
              Samuel Scheidt (1587–1654)
              Johann Jakob Froberger (1616–1667)
              Adam Krieger (1634–1666)
    France: Champion de Chambonnières (*ca.* 1602–*ca.* 1671)
              Jean-Baptiste Lully (1632–1687)

Late Baroque (*ca.* 1680–*ca.* 1740):
    Italy: Arcangelo Corelli (1653–1713)
              Alessandro Scarlatti (1659–1725)
              Antonio Vivaldi (*ca.* 1680–1743)
              Domenico Scarlatti (1685–1757)
  Germany: Dietrich Buxtehude (1637–1707)
              Johann Joseph Fux (1660–1741)
              Reinhard Keiser (1674–1739)
              Georg Philipp Telemann (1681–1767)
              Johann Sebastian Bach (1685–1750)
              George Frederick Handel (1685–1759)
    France: François Couperin le Grand (1668–1733)
              Jean-Philippe Rameau (1683–1764)
  England: Henry Purcell (1659–1695)

The individual epochs brought forth particular traits and developments. The Early Baroque, for example, included the rise of the Venetian School and Florentine opera. Composers at St. Mark's in Venice developed polychorality and a strongly chordal style with great sonorous color and splendor. For the first time they specified their definite intentions with regard to instrumental sonority. They discovered the architectural aspects of the composition as a formal principle of construction and the way it brought about a heightening of the expression of feeling in the music. In their hands instrumental music gradually made itself independent of vocal models, particularly in Venetian music for organ and for orchestra. Giovanni Gabrieli wrote the first Baroque monodic instrumental composition. In Florence, moreover, there was further development of the monodic style with the rise of opera. Monody infiltrated all new and all traditional types, including instrumental music, which experienced special favor. This led to the development of the concertante principle.

The High Baroque represented the culmination of the 17th-century history of opera in the Venetian opera school and the beginning of the French national opera. Oratorio also reached a climax with Carissimi in Rome. Stylistic possibilities discovered in the Early Baroque had now suffused the traditional forms and created new ones. The era of the High Baroque was sharply distinguished by boundless freedom in meeting new situations with new formal combinations. Instrumental music, particularly for organ and clavier, became more individually distinct. Chamber music forms originated, including French dances and the orchestral suite as developed by Lully, as well as the French overture. The concertante principle became one of the most important possibilities in compositional technique. Although the instrumental families of the Renaissance and Early Baroque were further developed, there was a simplification in the instrumental resources for the performance of the thorough-bass, which was now simply played by the organ or cembalo.

During the Late Baroque, forms became more definite and were schematized into types. There was a sort of absolutism about quite definite, individual musical forms that occurred principally in three areas: the opera, the concerto, and the overture. The musically oriented opera of the Neapolitan School was developed, with its succession of self-contained musical numbers and recitatives. The *da capo* aria was established. Paralleling the "number" opera, there were also "number" oratorios and "number" cantatas. Instrumental forms included the concerto grosso and the solo concerto. The sonata took on the forms of the *sonata da chiesa* and the *sonata da camera*. Fugues became monothematic, with the theme being answered at the fifth. The overture became, on the one hand, the French or Lully overture and, on the other, the Italian operatic *sinfonia,* or Scarlatti overture. These gave rise to overture suites and suites for orchestra, keyboard, and lute, employing an Allemande-Courante or a Sarabande-Gigue combination as the core movements.

To characterize the Baroque period as a whole, we may observe that it stands in a different relationship to its predecessor than did the Renaissance. While Late Gothic and Renaissance stood diametrically opposed to each other, the Baroque was a gradual outgrowth of the Renaissance. During the almost two hundred years of the Baroque, music undertook to comply with nearly all the demands that are made of it still today, with respect to forms and tasks, ideal aims and sociological duties, and subjective and abstract aspects. Consequently it is scarcely possible to ascribe to it characteristics that will fit all the works that came into being during this great period in Europe. The road from the works of the Early Baroque (Giovanni Gabrieli and Monteverdi) to the major achievements of the Late Baroque (Bach, Handel, Scarlatti, and Rameau) is so very long, devious, and varied that the attempt to give a generally inclusive characterization must seem foredoomed to failure.

If some traits are here emphasized, it is with the implied reservation that they are properly applicable to individual works and accordingly cannot be transferred generally to all. Among these are, for example, the Baroque drive toward the large, the monumental; the sense of the direct; the theatrical orientation of effect; the heightening of the emotional to the impassioned; the linking of the subjective with musical symbols, figures, and flourishes; the assignment of abstract character to subjectivism; the combination of other-worldly yearnings with this-worldly and mundane desires and wishes; and the combination of spirituality with sensuousness. Such abstractions from the works, on the one hand, and from the living flow of musical change, on the other, make a very limited contribution to understanding.

The attempt must accordingly be made to see the matter from musical viewpoints that were developed in the Baroque era. The following are here suggested:

1. Development of thorough-bass, sometimes referred to as figured bass, *Generalbass*, and *basso continuo*—that is, the practice of indicating the chordal structure of the accompaniment by placing numbers or figures under the bass line. The phrase "thorough-bass era" was first used in music history by Hugo Riemann in 1911 as a designation for the period approximately identical with the Baroque. Thorough-bass was the form taken by a certain way of conceiving of composition that almost exclusively dominated the whole era. It especially emphasized the outer voices by giving them the melody and the bass, and accordingly de-emphasized the middle voices, which then served as harmonic supports between them. Chords were reduced to type, and notes foreign to the harmony were eliminated from the standard chords. The *Cento Concerti Ecclesiastici* (1602) of Ludovico (Grossi) Viadana (*ca.* 1560–*ca.* 1627), sometime choirmaster of the Mantua Cathedral, is of special historical significance, as he was the first to introduce figured bass into sacred music.

2. Individual treatment of the bass in the bass variation (or "ground," as was common in keyboard music), the *basso ostinato* (chaconne, passacaglia, and ostinato aria), and in quasi-*ostinato* forms such as the slow movements of solo concerti.

3. Rise of major-minor tonality. By the 16th century the modes, or sections of the scale, incorporated in the system of church tones, had been much influenced by a feeling of major and minor. The modal and the major-minor principles then existed more or less independently or interdependently side by side until in the Late Baroque, when major and minor finally carried the day. Thus the concept of major-minor tonality was created and definitely fixed; it prevailed in art music for over two centuries. Along with it came the concepts of tonal tension and harmonic center, involving the tonic, dominant, and subdominant.

The development of equal temperament roughly paralleled that of major-minor tonality. There were a number of stations along the way toward the final acceptance of equal temperament, notably the acoustical work of Andreas Werckmeister in 1691 and Johann Sebastian Bach's *Well-Tempered Clavier*, Part I, in 1722, which used all the major and minor keys, as well as all the diatonic, chromatic, and enharmonic possibilities of modulation. Since Bach's day the diatonic and the chromatic have become polar phenomena in the idea of music bound to major and minor. From Bach to Reger and Richard Strauss composers have time and again made forays into the extreme possibilities offered by diatonicism and chromaticism.

4. The first breakthrough on the part of chromaticism occurred in the transition from Early to High Baroque. In the individual works of Giovanni Gabrieli, Gesualdo da Venosa, Claudio Monteverdi, Heinrich Schütz, and others shortly before and after 1600, one finds chromatic passages of extreme boldness in the leading of the musical lines as well as in the confrontation of one chord with another. Chromaticism broke all the rules that had been established earlier with regard to the introduction and resolution of dissonance. Its use was exclusively determined by expression. Don Nicola Vicentino (1511–1576) led the way with his madrigal compositions and his book *L'antica musica ridotto alla moderna prattica* (1555), in which he tried to apply Greek tonal genera, as he understood them, to the polyphonic music of his own day.

5. Distinct character of the modern measure. Composers of art music in the Gothic and the Renaissance did not think in terms of the modern measure, but instead let the temporal course of the music be regulated solely by the "tactus" or counted unit. Simultaneously, however, folk-music and some closely related art-music such as the frottola, lauda, villanella, and chanson were already being made up of something like measures in our sense. Around 1600, then, composers generally began to think of their work as organized in measures in the sense of a regular succession of heavy and light beats. This conception, which prevailed up to about 1950 as a rule for compositional layout, notation, and performance, had finally come to be widely held during the period of the Late Baroque.

6. The *old* and the *new*. In the Middle Ages as the composers of Ars antiqua were challenged by those of Ars nova, individuals operating from different artistic bases confronted each other. The result was an overt opposition between the old and the new, with the development of a distinct dualism. Essentially this same situation recurred at decisive moments in history—for example, during the middle of the 15th century and around 1600. Giulio Caccini called his collection of solo songs that first appeared in Florence in 1602 "Le Nuove Musiche." Monteverdi distinguished in 1607 between the *Seconda Prattica* and the *Prima Prattica*. The latter was the compositional style that had prevailed since Ockeghem. In it "the music was not the maidservant but the mistress of the word." But in the *Seconda Prattica,* poetic speech was the mistress of the music. In terms of subsequent developments, however, this situation worked out somewhat differently from previous situations of a similar nature, in

that henceforth the old was no longer discarded and consigned to oblivion, but retained an independent and constituent share in subsequent musical practice. This applied particularly to the continuance of the Palestrina style as *stile antico* or *stylus gravis,* which maintained its stubborn adherents for centuries. It remained with its own right to exist, though, during the Baroque era and later, styles often changed quickly and decisively. Every composer to the present has mastered the Palestrina style, and every composer until Mozart wrote in contemporary idiom, though he occasionally would write in the old style of which he was also a master. The old style had a life of its own and a quite sharply defined place in church music, socially, alongside the new music. There was no longer any rivalry between the two styles.

7. *Affect* and *rhetoric.* The Romantics, who rediscovered Bach, heard his music with the ears of their time and interpreted it in the spirit of their own music. It has been reserved for students in our century to open up the way to a more historically correct manner of performance and, at the same time, to find insight into the special assumptions under which the composers of the Baroque wrote. Their creative processes were not consummated under identical or even related intellectual, psychological, and sociological conditions as in the Romantic Era. The composer of the Baroque Era thought and composed in a strictly articulated system of rules and signals, which were inserted according to circumstances but had subjective effect. These signs, replete with meaning, were to some extent linked with rhetoric. Music thus became a sign language. Today these signs are more often classified as symbols and are more strictly interpreted than they were in the last century.

In Bach's vocal works Schweitzer pointed out "twenty to twenty-five basic themes" in which "are rooted almost all characteristic expressions, which attract one's attention by their regular reappearance in the cantatas and Passions." Schering followed up this observation by introducing the concept of the "sonorous emblem," or symbol. He succeeded in distinguishing four levels of symbolism in Bach: one expressive of the affect or state of feeling; a second concerned with acoustical, optical, and dynamic matters; a third that was rather technological; and a fourth that was ideological. In doing so, Schering was the first to recognize how closely these elemental themes and symbols were connected with rhetorical figures of speech.

Huber distinguished six "primal motifs" in the music of Schütz: (1) the organ point, which implies the basis, rest, perseverance, restraint, and firmness; (2) undulatory and pendulating motifs, or a pulsating glide back and forth or up and down, expressive of peaceful release, redemption, or such feelings as doubt or weeping; (3) rising motifs, suggesting awakening or regaining strength; (4) sinking motifs, associated with falling asleep or becoming weaker; (5) motifs that first rise and then sink, the rise symbolizing ascent to a height and the sinking something like fate; and (6) motifs that first float down and then rise, which are used with such ideas as the announcement of something or the idea of being saved.

Musico-rhetorical figures are those musical figures that are applied in a way corresponding and analogous to the use of rhetorical figures. Although they have existed in polyphonic music at least since Dufay, they became a matter of conscious instructional theory in composition only with the 16th century. These instruction books dealt with what they referred to as the "themes," according to a body of theory known as *musica poetica,* which undertook to teach the making of compositions in a way analogous to that of making a work of verbal art. In *musica poetica* the figure is, of course, a musical form. All *figurae musicae* have a musical sense and in the treatises are always defined in terms of music and the technique of composition.

In the Late Baroque, the major-minor epoch and bourgeois musical culture began. Between 1722 and 1725 the foundations were laid for a development that continued during the major-minor epoch (*ca.* 1725–*ca.* 1910). This development represents the last completed period in the relationship between music and history. To some extent it still continues today in the character of bourgeois musical culture. Its establishment is documented by five events of the early 1720's:

1. 1722: Part I of the *Well-Tempered Clavier,* which Johann Sebastian Bach brought together in Cöthen. This revealed the development of equal temperament and the use of all its consequences for metrics, harmony, and the establishment of musical periods.

Bach's *Well-Tempered Clavier* was based on two fundamental developments of his day. First, major and minor came into practically exclusive use around 1700 and crowded the church modes almost completely into the background. Second, the way for the development of evenly tempered tuning had been theoretically prepared by physical acoustics.

In his preface Bach says his work is intended "for the service and use of musical youth eager for instruction as well as for those who in this study are already proficient" and that the music has been "set down and completed for special pastime." Without specially stressing the fact, the Preludes and Fugues go through all the keys, according to Bach's previous allusion in the title. Earlier, in 1711, Johann David Heinichen was the first to set forth the circle of fifths in his *Anweisung für den Generalbass,* and Mattheson referred to its practical value in his *Neuer-öffneten Orchester* (1713). As early as 1702 Johann Caspar Ferdinand Fischer (d. 1746), choirmaster at the court in Baden, wrote preludes and fugues in twenty keys in his *Ariadne musica.* This series assumes the availability of equal temperament, as provided by Werckmeister. Johann Pachelbel (1653–1706) also wrote keyboard suites that went through seventeen keys.

2. 1722: Rameau's *Traité de l'harmonie.* Here the functional relationships between the chords in major and minor were recognized.

The complete title of the treatise by Jean-Philippe Rameau reads, *Traité de l'harmonie réduite à ses principes naturels.* It is based on the work of Giuseppe Zarlino of Venice (1517–1590), who recognized the dual nature of harmony in his *Istituzioni harmoniche* (1558). But the way for Rameau's specific contribution was prepared by the physical and acoustical research of his time. In 1700 Joseph Sauveur in Paris proved the natural composition of sounds from the series of the harmonic overtones, and in 1714 combination tones were discovered by Giuseppe Tartini. Rameau established the concept of the *centre harmonique,* thus introducing functional thinking as a logic of chord successions in composition. He also established the concept of the tonic, or *son principal,* the dominant, and the subdominant and recognized the nature of the deceptive cadence. Approaching chords in terms of their structural foundation in thirds, he saw the difference between *harmonie parfaite* in major and minor and derived chords. He was the first to formulate the double form of the minor scale, differentiating the ascending minor scale from the major scale only by the minor third, while the descending minor scale renounces the leading tone, or *note sensible,* and also lowers the sixth step, for example: D-minor ascending D, E, F, G, A, B, C-sharp, D; descending, D, C, B-flat, A, G, F, E, D.

3. 1725: The theoretical work of composition *Gradus ad Parnassum* by Johann Joseph Fux of Vienna (1660–1741) evinced a historical and retrospective viewpoint.

With this work, written in Latin and in the form of a dialogue between teacher and pupil, Fux set the precedent for an intensive preoccupation with a historically oriented period-style and for the fusion of this style with whatever style currently prevailed, regardless of whether the intention was to bring the two together or keep them separate. As one of the most representative composers of the Late Baroque, Fux stood at the very peak of the Neapolitan style, but consciously tried to return to the style of Palestrina. Thus, in a way, he was a traditionalist who attempted to comprehend the Palestrina style pedagogically and to articulate it from his own point of view stressing the organization of the measures, the harmonic connection, and the subjective effect on the feelings. His textbook, which enjoyed immediate and widespread popularity (1725 in Latin, 1742 in German, 1761 in Italian, 1773 in French, 1791 in English), has structurally influenced almost all counterpoint textbooks up to the present. Here a "double vision" begins: the effort on the part of the composer to communicate with his peers and, at the same time, to digest academically the historical heritage.

4. 1725: Founding of the *Concerts spirituels* in Paris that gave birth to modern concert life and the bourgeois concert public.

This was the first entry of the concert into the Renaissance-type culture, with adaptation to the prevailing forms of society. Distinctive features of concert life accordingly developed: organization; individuality; social esteem of the artist, with corresponding rewards; and, eventually, an emphasis on virtuosity. In Germany and Switzerland about 1600 the Collegium musicum arose, at first privately and later publicly. It gave concerts and was supported by bourgeois society of the urban culture. The founding of the *Concerts spirituels* in Paris in 1725 was a milestone along the way to public concert life. The first concert was at once a great social event. In 1724 a "Musical Society" was founded in London. In Hamburg, at about the same time, Telemann organized public concerts with paid admission and printed programs.

5. 1722: Mattheson's *Critica musica* in Hamburg. This first example

of regular musical reportage marks the beginning of periodical music criticism and musical journalism.

The full title of this pioneer work was, translated: *Critica Musica, i.e. thoroughly correct investigation and judgment of many partly preconceived and partly ingenuous opinions, arguments, and objections, thus to be found in old and new printed and unprinted writings on music. So far as possible, for the uprooting of all gross errors and for the furthering of a better crop of pure harmonic knowledge, composed in various parts and brought out piece by piece by Mattheson. First issue. Hamburg, in May 1722.*

Johann Mattheson was born in 1681 in Hamburg and died there in 1764. He had broad musical training and in 1690 became a singer in the Hamburg opera, at the same time serving as choral coach, composer, and director. In 1706 he became secretary of the English society in Hamburg and later was councilor to the legation. He made numerous diplomatic journeys and had wide acquaintance with the musical life of the time. His activity as a composer was extensive. From 1718 to 1729 he was director of church music at the cathedral in Hamburg. From about 1735 on, he was afflicted with total deafness. His principal significance lies in the encyclopedic, aesthetic, literary, and journalistic realm. He was a pioneer in music journalism, which subsequently—partly in the sense of criticism, partly of publicity—has become a product of our musical life. As a child of the Enlightenment, he consistently strove to place his insights into music on rational and empirical bases. Along with this, he combined a body of thought that had been developed through his contact with the English and French Enlightenment. *Critica Musica,* published from 1722 to 1725 in twenty-four issues, was the first musical periodical in Germany and marked the beginning of music criticism in the narrower sense as a periodically published report and criticism. Further important writings of Mattheson's were *Das neu-eröffnete Orchester* (The Recently Inaugurated Orchestra), *Grundlage einer Ehren-Pforte* (Foundation of a Triumphal Arch, a biographical dictionary of musicians), *Der vollkommene Capellmeister* (The Perfect Conductor), and *Grosse General-Bass-Schule* (Complete School of Thorough-Bass).

The Classical Era

By the term "Classical Era" music historians understand, in the narrower sense, the period of Viennese Classicism, with Haydn, Mozart, and Beethoven as the three principal Classical composers. The concept of Viennese Classicism can be sharply defined from the point of view of musical style. But from another point of view it is perhaps less definite, sharing the general characteristics of the Classical, as it applies not only to the arts but also to the general conduct of human life. In this more general sense the Classical displays traits of aspiration consistent with ability and the will-to-form with the ability to carry it out; feeling balanced with understanding, and emotion with logic; opposites overcome in a higher unity, as the artistic, individual, and solitary fate is represented within the range of the generally valid and the generally human;

and harmony of all the parts regarded as the ideal of beauty. There is a tendency to stress that which is typical and generally valid, lasting and timeless, in accordance with laws and norms.

Musical and stylistic distinctions may be made between
1. The Pre-Classical transitional period (*ca.* 1720–*ca.* 1760),
2. the Early Classical period (*ca.* 1760–*ca.* 1780), and
3. the High Classical period (1781–*ca.* 1810).

The Pre-Classical Transitional Period (ca. 1720–ca. 1760)

Instrumental music was the center of the musical development of the new style, and it was here that the great changes of form took place. The sonata as a cyclic form stood at the very heart of the matter, as did an individual new movement-form within it, the sonata allegro. Also the Classical rondo and the song forms, particularly in the slow movements, participated in this change. A difference of expression went hand in hand with the differences in form. Sociologically, this whole period was led by the aristocracy and the upper bourgeoisie. Referring to the fundamental aspect of this development, Arnold Hauser has written: "In the latter half of the 18th century a revolutionary change took place, the advent of the modern bourgeoisie with its individualism and its will to be original. This removed the idea of style as that of conscious and willed community in matters of the spirit and gave the idea of intellectual property its present-day sense."

From the point of view of music history, the 18th century was a distinctly transitional period. Although the Baroque Era had reached its fulfillment around the middle of the century with Bach and Handel, a stylistic change had set in long before and by about 1780 had already led to a new zenith in Viennese Classicism. Confronting the period of the Late Baroque there appeared a general simplification of the stylistic means. Melody began to reign supreme over compositional structure, invention, and expression. Simplicity, directness, and inwardness became the standards. Preparations for a break with the past had been gradually taking shape, and then at last occurred. The connection with folk-song, which enjoyed universal favor, was in its way new. A fusion of folk-like elements and art music occurred in the Classical Era. As a synthesis, this represented a perhaps unique and unrepeatable artistic and creative achievement.

Three new basic concepts of expression came into being: first, the *galant* or courteous; second, the *empfindsam* or sentimental as style-concepts of the Rococo in music; and, finally, the *Sturm und Drang*, or "Storm and Stress," as the first onslaught of musical Romanticism. The development of the *galant* style began around 1700, that of the *empfindsam* about 1730, and the *Sturm und Drang* set in somewhere about 1760. Elements of the new styles constantly overlapped and continued to mix, both with themselves and with the style of the Baroque Era. During these decades, change and transition were so fluid that the complete works of an 18th-century composer seldom embody just one style, although a particular style may be individually developed in particular works or movements.

Taking each of these three stages in more detail, we find that the *galant* style appeared in French lute music of the 17th century, had spread over into French *claveçin* music, and was taken up also in Germany in the second third of the 18th century, where it tended to reduce the Baroque stress on compositional layout, rhythm, and ornaments. Music in the *galant* style was ·written predominantly in a transparent, thin setting for two or three voices. The layout was homophonic and simple. Playful and graceful turns were especially favored, as were also other rococo-like ornaments. The composer often played with small and almost microscopic motifs, or he strung tonal thoughts together without much logical connection.

The *empfindsam* style, on the other hand, led to a type of expression that was rich in contrasts and predominantly cantabile. Composers in this style loved an abundance of expressive dynamic opposites and also heaped up certain formulated turns, such as the sigh motif. The sigh (*Seufzer*) is a particular succession of notes known as an anticipation, in which the anticipatory note is shorter than the note of resolution, and both notes are slurred in *portamento* fashion.

When the *Sturm und Drang* finally appeared, it was an avowal of uninhibited subjectivism. It manifested itself in sudden opposites of dynamics, melody, and instrumentation, in heightened display of orchestral effects such as the *crescendo* and the *forte-piano,* or abrupt succession of loud and soft. Thus the new movement expanded the gamut of expression beyond that of the *empfindsam* style in the direction of more expressiveness. The *Strum und Drang* was the musical counterpart of the predominance of nature over reason which was for the first time proclaimed by Rousseau in 1751. The slogan "back to nature" dominated the period. The first clear phase of the *Sturm und Drang* began around 1760 in the music of Schobert, Beck, and C. P. E. Bach. It was carried on further by Haydn, Mozart, and others, and paralleled the literary movement of the same name. It placed genius at the pinnacle of human values and thereby gave a central position in the work to artistic creation as an act that was secret, unfathomable, and dependent on higher inspiration.

A change in the sociological structure was inseparably linked with the change in expression. The stylistic revolution of the 18th century was related to sociological changes and was entirely dependent on the rise of the new class, the bourgeoisie.

The new period was dominated by *ratio,* or reason. The concept arose out of the economic activity in the Netherlands. It was given a philosophical basis in England and had its first social effects in France. Accordingly, the bourgeois concert made its appearance. The composer wrote for a "public" whose anonymity he surmounted by his individuality.

Thus the virtuoso performer and performance secured a new meaning. Virtuosity became a profession, and the child prodigy was one of its species. The spirit of the Enlightenment, with its ideas of the natural and the rational, was the soil from which the new art sprang.

Thus began the period of bourgeois musical culture. The bourgeois music-lover became the real patron and art-critic. He replaced the aristocracy and the church in their previous functions as the giver of orders and bread. At the same time, through public financing and private musical life, the bourgeois music-lover assumed the authority for forming his own musical judgment, which gave rise to the concept of a musical public involving the layman, the concert, the opera, the music publisher, and the press.

The free market came into being. The middle-class subjectivism that replaced courtly art has been essentially the prevalent aesthetic concept to the present day. At the end of the 18th century the bourgeois attitude toward art was decisive in all matters. It had a character that was in part more progressive, in part more conservative. At the very end of the 18th century the musical taste of the aristocracy was the same as that of the upper bourgeoisie. The neo-Baroque traits, for example, of Mozart's late work, with its French overture and its fugues, represent the progressive bourgeoisie which became classically oriented in feeling and which to some extent redirected the function of these forms. The modern bourgeoisie first appeared in England, with such writers as Thomson, Young, Macpherson, Richardson, Fielding, and Sterne. The rise of the bourgeoisie brought the criteria of refinement that are still basically valid today. These changes also brought with them the development of modern scientific thinking.

The Early Classical Period (ca. 1760–1780)

About 1760 Joseph Haydn and about 1770 the young Wolfgang Amadeus Mozart entered into this development. Haydn and Mozart moved to the fore and decisively aided in leading the Classical Period to greater heights. These are the two decades during which both Haydn and Mozart passed through the separate phases of the *galant,* the *empfindsam,* and the *Sturm und Drang* styles. The influence of Carl Philipp Emanuel Bach on them and on others of their day was especially great. The styles were manifested in single works, often even in individual movements, and were brought—not always, but occasionally—to surprisingly new artistic results. At the same time, Mozart was making his foray into the separate European musical styles. With Haydn, refinement of the creative process occurred more slowly and more narrowly than with Mozart, yet no less persistently. Haydn was perhaps the first to attempt to build the Baroque form of the fugue into the string quartet (for example, the final movements of his Quartet Op. 20, Nos. 2, 5, and 6). But an abrupt pause of almost ten years intervened in his writing of quartets. As seen from the point of view of Haydn and Mozart, the Early Classical Period was a time of preparation, of collecting, of bringing together, of taking up first one thing and then another and exhausting it.

The High Classical Period (1781–ca. 1810)

The rise of the Classical Period was concurrent with a complete change in the aesthetics of music and the ascription of sense and value to it. In the middle of the 18th century the theory of affects was given a special nuance in the theory of imitation. The founder was Charles Batteux (1713–1780). In his *Traité des beaux arts, reduits à un même principe* (1743), he developed the theory by reducing all the arts, including music, to the imitation of "beautiful nature." The "most elegant object of dance and music should be the imitation of feelings or passions. . . . Hence it follows that everything which is mere action, idea, or picture is not too well adapted to music. Hence there also arises the fact that long tales, lectures, transitions, metaphors, wit—in a word, everything that has been written from memory or reflection—stubbornly resists the tonal art. Everything, on the other hand, that is the expression of the feelings seems to yield to it almost of itself." During the 18th century the previous scope of music was significantly widened, as was the area of aesthetics, although the aesthetic theory of imitation was finally discarded. In this connection, the following quotations (taken from Hermann Pfrogner, *Musik. Geschichte ihrer Deutung*, Freiburg i. Br., Munich 1954) suggest various views expressed during the second half of the 18th century:

> Music, which in its beginnings was perhaps only intended to represent noises, has gradually become a mode of reciting, or simply a language, by means of which the different feelings of the soul—or, better, their passions—in different ways are brought to expression. (Jean le Rond d'Alembert, 1751)

> The stronger and truer the declamation, which is the model of melody, and the closer the one conforms to the other, the truer and fairer the melody will be. (Denis Diderot, *ca.* 1761–1762)

> The melody, imitating the inflections of the human voice, expresses complaints, cries of sorrow and joy, threats, and sighs. All voiced signs of the passions are its realm. It imitates the accents of speech and turns of feeling in every dialect in certain inner stirrings: it not only imitates, it speaks itself, and its inarticulate but lively, fiery, passionate diction has a hundred times more power than the mere word. Thence arises the strength of musical imitation, the power of song over tender hearts. (Jean Jacques Rousseau, 1753)

> What, then, is true musical expression? I answer: it is such a concordance of melody and harmony as moves us in the strongest way and arouses in us those passions or emotions which the poet seeks to arouse in us. (Charles Avison, 1752)

> The entire power of music can be determined according to three different effects—as it takes effect on the hearing, on the passions, and on the imagination. In other words, it can be considered in so far as it simply flatters the senses, elicits emotions, or inspires ideas. Of these effects the last two determine what is called the moral or expressive power of music, and only in them can one consider something that could be called imitation. Music can be said to imitate something only in so far as it expresses something. (Thomas Twinning, 1789)

> Music, on the other hand, moves directly, and, in this respect, immeasurably excels painting. . . . Ask composers what passages they like

best in their works, prefer to all others, and think of most often with secret
affection—whether it is not those in which their music is speaking and has
a certain delivery. (Christian Gottfried Krause, 1752)

Thus the tones are signs that copy feeling and passion with gradually
understandable truth and arouse the hearts of men with irresistible effect.
No other sign may in this respect be placed beside them, and music is thus
a unique art that can copy feelings and passions in the full sense of the
word. (Karl Heinrich Heydenreichs, 1790)

During the High Classical Period—that is, up to about 1810—Haydn,
Mozart, and Beethoven clarified their styles. Especially Haydn did so.
In his late work he makes a general, universal, and humanitarian communication to his fellow man through his music—most purely and comprehensively in his London Symphonies, *The Creation*, and *The Seasons*.

The artistic principle of Classical music, as has been generally recognized, consists in contrast. The liveliness of Classical music arises from
continually successive contrasts of tone-color, harmony, rhythm, and
above all motive or theme. The motif takes a central position in composition. The principle develops most fruitfully in so-called thematic work,
which has continued in operation right on to the present. The principle
was quite noticeable in Vivaldi, was further developed by J. S. Bach, and
was rediscovered—presumably by Haydn. It appeared in the composition of the symphonies, but not until the string quartets Op. 33, Nos. 1–6
—the "Russian" quartets and the "Scherzi" or "Maiden" quartets—was it
raised to a formative principle. "They are," declared Haydn himself, "of
an entirely new special sort."

In the compositional proceedings perhaps the primary feature was
the discovery of the large melodic period. Thus "thematic work" set in
with motivic sectors being cut out of the thematic melodic arch and being
treated independently. They then took their place at the heart of the
compositional proceedings. Their linkage, combination, repetition, alteration, expansion, and contraction, according to their rhythmic, harmonic,
modulatory, polyphonic, and dynamic possibilities, were somewhat like
ever-changing lighting, new flashes of thought, and transformations. As
the principle was carried through, the element of surprise also played a
great role. At every moment the "connoisseur" among the listeners was
intellectually and emotionally presented with new musical situations that
he had to assimilate. The continuing artistic appeal rested on the unity
of intellectual and emotional forces and on the continuous linkage of
spiritual and intellectual processes with inner emotional experiences.

The music was written for the connoisseur as well as for the amateur.
To both it offered equal satisfaction and ever new stimulation. The antithesis between the connoisseur and the amateur was indicated in 1789
by Johann Wolfgang von Goethe in his *Wahrheit und Wahrscheinlichkeit
des Kunstwerkes* (*Truth and Plausibility in the Work of Art*):

A perfect work of art is a work of the human spirit. It wishes to be apprehended by a spirit of harmonious origin and education, and this latter also
finds excellence and perfection according to his nature. Thereof the com-

mon amateur has no idea; he treats a work of art like an object that he encounters in the marketplace; but the true connoisseur sees not only the truth of that which is imitated but also the merits of what has been selected, the cleverness of the combination, the spiritual aspect of the tiny art-world; he feels that he must raise himself to the art-work in order to enjoy it; he feels that he must compose himself from his scattered life, live with the art-work, look at it repeatedly, and thereby give himself a higher existence.

The notated example is the first theme of the *Symphony No. 104* (*London Symphony*) in D major by Joseph Haydn. The third and fourth measures individualize themselves in the Development section into several new combinations.

The principle of thematic work is a principle of selection. Its development is inconceivable without the variation principle, which was placed in an entirely new light through the intellectual work with motives during the Classical Era. Both principles were constantly bracketed together. The transformational possibilities were especially rich in what seemed to be outwardly "insignificant looking" material. This is shown in the following examples of some of the metamorphoses which Beethoven carried out in the first movement of the *Eroica* (op. 55) with the fanfare-like first theme, originally derived entirely from the "tones of nature," though the variations in dynamics and phrasing which he derived still further from the theme are not presented in the quotations.

In visualizing the forces that resulted from the developments of musical form during the Baroque and Classical Eras, we need to bear in mind the distinction between those forces that "seek the center" of the work of art (or are "centripetal") and those that "flee from the center" (or are "centrifugal"). These tendencies coexist in any given period, and act and react upon each other. In some ways, the historical precedent during the period of the Late Baroque, when certain forms developed and became schematized as types, was repeated around 1780 and characterized the Viennese Classical and subsequent periods. These latter periods brought with them the sonata allegro form, the simple song form, the rondo form, and the cyclic variation in the upper voices.

Every formal development, as has been observed, is a reciprocal action of centripetal and centrifugal forces, which in the individual epochs alternately prevail. Thus the course of musical form is constantly diverted from one to another. Centrifugal formal tendencies are those that reject every move to focus on one point. The result is either an inherent flow in their course, recognizing little or no paragraph-like organization, or a stringing-together of individual formal parts that have life independently within themselves. Schematically considered, this stringing-together produces an endless succession in a purely additive way. Thus the parts either can grow playfully out of improvisation, from sheer "playing," or they can be put side by side in the utmost musical concentration as extremely individual units. In each instance we have to do with expressed "moments," with "music of the instant" in the literal sense of the term as an outcome of the unrepeatable.

Momentary form, as a manifestation of centrifugal tendencies, may appear in any one of three ways. First, the whole movement may be monothematically an uninterrupted flow, and may be organized only harmonically, as in Bach's *Well-Tempered Clavier* I, *Preludes in C major and in D minor;* Chopin's *Piano Sonata in B-flat minor* (4th movt.) or his *Preludes in E-flat major and minor;* or in Prokofieff's *Piano Sonata No. 7* (3rd movt.) A second possibility is that the whole movement may be predominantly monothematic, interrupted by little episodes or incorporated into a higher formal order, as in Bach's *Well-Tempered Clavier* I, *Preludes in C-minor and in D-major;* Beethoven's *Piano Sonata Op. 31,*

No. 2 (last movt.); Schumann's *Toccata in C-major;* or in Schönberg's *String Quartet No. 3* (1st movt.) where the rhythm is homogeneous. A third possibility is that the movement may consist of a stringing-together of independent, self-contained parts. This may be done in a playful manner, derived from improvisation, as in Bach's *Well-Tempered Clavier* I, *Preludes in B-flat major* or Mozart's *Fantasy for Piano, K. V. 394.* Or it may be marked by extreme individualism in expression, as in Beethoven's *Piano Sonata Op. 106* (introduction to the fugue) or his *Cello Sonata Op. 102, No. 1* (Adagio, introduction to the last movement), or in Schönberg's *Erwartung.* Or, finally, there may be a combination of these two possibilities, side by side, as in Bach's *Chromatic Fantasy.*

In instrumental music centrifugal tendencies crowded in as the French chanson and the Renaissance motet were imitated instrumentally. These centrifugal tendencies were then operative around 1600 to a heightened degree in the madrigal, in monody, and later in the impassioned recitative. They were determined by the layout of the text as prose and by the felt values as subjective moments of expression. The expression-laden *recitativo accompagnato* around 1700 was for the first time transferred to instrumental music by Francesco Antonio Bonporti (1672–1749), a pupil of Corelli. Apparently Johann Sebastian Bach wrote the recitative of his *Chromatic Fantasy* with this idea in mind.

There are many examples of such instrumental recitatives in musical literature, sometimes explicitly so designated and sometimes not. For example, there are such passages in Johann Sebastian Bach's *Chromatic Fantasy* (around 1720); C. P. E. Bach's *Prussian Sonata No. 1* (1742), *Fantasia* in the *6th Sonata,* among the eighteen examples in his *Versuch,* and *Fantasia* in his *Musikalisches Vielerley* (Hamburg 1770); Joseph Haydn's *Symphony No. 7* (*Le Midi,* 1761, 2nd movt.); Louis Spohr's *Violin Concerto No. 8 in the Form of a Vocal Scene* (1816); L. v. Beethoven's *Piano Sonatas Op. 31, No. 2,* and *Op. 110, String Quartets Op. 131, 132, and 135, Symphony No. 9* (Finale), and *Piano Concerto No. 4* (2nd movt.); Frederic Chopin's *Piano Concerto No. 2* (2nd movt.); and Hector Berlioz's *Romeo and Juliet* (Love Scene).

During the Romantic Era prose passages of this kind in instrumental music increased in importance; their "speaking" character was heightened more and more in Berlioz, Liszt, and Wagner. Passages of this sort were then no longer indicated expressly as recitative; they were to be performed strictly in tempo, as had already appeared in the Finale of Beethoven's *Symphony No. 9.*

A second centrifugal form pushing into the contrast-filled multitude of separate parts was provided by improvisation, based on free fancy, the impulse of the moment at the instrument. Here the player was not led by a form that had been previously thought out but by the favorable aspects of the moment, not by the composition but by impulse, not by considered laws of art but by inspiration vouchsafed to him in the sudden flash, not from the calculation involved in the written record on the music paper but from the mood. So he put part beside part in a row, image beside image, from moment to moment. Composers have tried to capture this music of the instant in a whole succession of written "compositions."

Such bits of form in fantasies, preludes, and toccatas, especially for the organ and other keyboard instruments, have taken their places since the 16th century as equally privileged alongside the closed, centripetal forms. Special heights in this tendency were achieved in the Baroque Era, in the *Sturm und Drang* by Carl Philipp Emanuel Bach, the Mannheim School, and Schobert, in Mozart, Beethoven, and in the Romantic Era. As "fantasy-like development sections" the centrifugal momentary form found favor even in the sonata allegro form. Currently, Stockhausen has raised momentary form directly to the status of a formal quality.

Bibliography

The Baroque Era: M. Bukofzer, *Music in the Baroque Era* (N. Y. 1947); S. Clercx, *Le Baroque et la Musique* (Brussels 1948); R. Dammann, *Der Musikbegriff im dt. Barock* (Cologne 1967); R. Haas, *Musik des Barocks* (Bücken Hdb., Potsdam 1928); P. H. Lang, *Music in Western Civilization* (N. Y. 1941); J. Müller-Blattau, *Geschichte der Fuge* (Kassel 3rd ed. 1963); C. Sachs, *The Commonwealth of Arts* (N. Y. 1946); *Die Fuge* (MW); art. Barock (MGG). *Renaissance to Baroque:* H. Brandes, *Studien zur mus. Figurenlehre im 16. Jh.* (Bln. 1935); H. H. Eggebrecht, *H. Schütz. Musicus poeticus* (Göttingen 1959); W. S. Huber, *Motivsymbolik bei Schütz* (Basel 1961); M. Ruhnke, *Joachim Burmeister. Ein Beitrag zur Musiklehre um 1600* (Kassel 1955); A. Schering, *Das Symbol in der Musik* (Lpz. 1941); A. Schmitz, *Die Bildlichkeit der wortgebundenen Musik Bachs* (Mainz 1950); G. Schünemann, *Geschichte des Dirigierens* (Lpz. 1913); A. Schweitzer, *J. S. Bach* (Lpz. 1908); H. H. Ungerer, *Die Beziehungen zwischen Musik u. Rhetorik im 16. bis. 18. Jh.* (Würzburg 1941); art. Figuren, Musica theorica, practica, poetica (MGG). *Rise of Bourgeoisie in Music:* L. Balet, *Die Verbürgerlichung d. dt. Kunst, Lit. und Musik im 18. Jh.* (Strassburg 1935); E. Preussner, *Die bürgerliche Musikkultur* (Hamburg 1935, 2nd ed. Kassel 1951); E. Rebling, *Die soziol. Grundlagen der Stilwandlung d. Musik in Deutschland um d. Mitte des 18. Jh.* (Saalfeld 1935). *Sturm und Drang:* E. Bücken, *Der galante Stil* (ZfMw VI); H. H. Eggebrecht, *Das Ausdrucksprinzip im mus. Sturm und Drang* (DVLG 1955); F. Ritzel, *Die Entwicklung der "Sonatenform" im musiktheoretischen Schrifttum des 18. und 19. Jh.s* (Wiesbaden 1968). *High Classical Period:* St. A. Markus, *Musikästhetik, 1. Teil, ein Beitrag zur Geschichte der Nachahmungsästhetik und Affektenlehre sowie der idealistischen Musikästhetik in Deutschland* (Lpz. 1967).

23. The 19th Century

The Relative Position of the Various Nations

During the 19th century, the leading musical nations belonged to the German-speaking portion of Central Europe, namely, Austria and Germany. As various other nation states became more powerful, special developments spread among them. Even though France and Italy played significant roles in the music history of this century, they were somewhat apart from the major developments of the century as a whole.

Italy's predominance in the mid-16th century, which to a great extent determined the music of the 17th and 18th centuries, was replaced by the Viennese Classical development. Vienna became a center distinguished by the great tradition.

At the same time, other cities such as Berlin, Leipzig, Dresden, Munich, and Weimar (through Liszt's efforts) achieved independent significance. As a result of Beethoven's 19th-century musical significance, instrumental music remained the real center of creative activity. Nothing equalled the rank of instrumental music in German-speaking countries until the operas of Richard Wagner appeared during the second half of the century. The musical life there was determined by an unbroken chain of significant composers, an abundance of notable practicing musicians with composers again at their head, and by the eminent educational centers, especially in Vienna, Leipzig, Berlin, and Munich. Composers and composition students came from all over the world to study in Austria and Germany. Numerous composers and practicing artists toured abroad. The musical life of England and the United States was fructified by German-speaking artists. The European nation states that carried on their old traditions under altered circumstances or for the first time gained real significance in modern music history are, in alphabetical order, Bohemia, Denmark, England, Finland, Norway, Poland, Russia, Spain, and Switzerland.

During this century France was somewhat outside the main stream of development. The 1789 revolution was an expression of new ideas that gave music a new social basis. There were mass assemblies. In the 19th century, French music was most stimulated by Beethoven, Weber, Schubert, and Rossini; later by Meyerbeer, Liszt, and Chopin; and finally by Wagner, Offenbach, and the great Russians. Despite some strong national factors and a firm native tradition, it was thus influenced from abroad and came to some extraordinarily wide contrasts in Berlioz, Franck, Bizet, and Debussy. Berlioz and Franck formed opposite polarities, as did Wagner and Brahms. The greatest French musical achievements lay in the fields of opera, symphony, oratorio, and operetta.

Italian opera assumed a special place in history during this century. A particular stratification of public taste, resulting from the Revolution of 1789, played a part in the creation of a public for this kind of opera. Whereas 18th-century opera had stressed music, 19th-century opera stressed action. Though Italian opera lost its previous European preeminence, it prospered in Italy in the works of Rossini, Donizetti, Bellini, Verdi, Mascagni, Leoncavallo, and Puccini.

Music and Society

The relationship between the musician and his public was different in the 19th century from what it had been in the previous one. Many distinctive features of 19th-century history were established in 1789.

The French Revolution, with its emphasis on freedom, equality, and popular sovereignty, had determined the character of the subsequent period. It caused the demolition of monarchistic absolutism, increased self-participation and self-determination on the part of the bourgeoisie, the beginnings of revolutionary nationalism, and a radical secularization. The century was characterized by the Industrial Revolution, the enlightenment of the masses, and a rising growth in population. Life took on new dimensions through the technology of the steam engine and electricity. The natural sciences emerged, while philosophy retired to the background, though socialistic theories were formulated upon philosophical bases. Imperialism became the characteristic political feature of both the older powers and the new nation states.

The many altered conditions for the musician—for that matter, for the creative personality in general—posed problems that concerned his very existence. The 19th century created the "free composer." No longer did he work as he was obliged to do as a servant of the aristocracy or as a member of the church. Instead, he worked for an unknown public, for an undetermined number of anonymous hearers whose favor he was obliged to court without being acquainted with them. Thus a cleft developed in the composer's side of the relationship. At one extreme was his individualistic exhibitionism of his personal world of ideas and inspiration that totally disregarded either the hearer or player; and at the other, his "tossing off" of what people perhaps might like to play and hear and his adjustment to the market situation. The one extreme led to his almost superhuman efforts to create a public for himself through the world of ideas, to influence that public with intentions that projected far beyond the musical into the pseudo-religious, philosophical, and cosmological realms (for example, on the part of Wagner and Liszt). The other extreme led to music as an entertainment industry, the history of which began in the 19th century. Criteria of courtly taste still prevailed well into the 18th century. In so far as the bourgeoisie departed from them, the experience of art became irrational. Likewise, creative activity, marked by highly exaggerated individualism, became irrational and anomalous to the extent that aesthetics took on the character of metaphysics in the Romantic Era.

The claim of the composer to be an exceptional human being with the status of priest and prophet may be illustrated by numerous quotations: Beethoven, "Only divine art, only in it are the means that give me power to sacrifice the best part of my life to the heavenly muses" (1824); C. M. von Weber, "All the power and the purity of steadfast will—these alone consecrate man to be the true priest of his art" (1816); Schumann, "Artists are prophets"; Liszt, "The word of God is revealed in the creations of genius" (1852); Mahler, "Man is, as it were, himself only an instrument on which the universe plays" (1896); Scriabin, "If I have recognized that everything is my creation, my free wish, and that outside me nothing exists—I thereby become an absolute being" (1905); Berlioz, "I belong to the religion of Beethoven, Weber, Gluck, and Spontini" (1854); Wagner, "Individual loneliness is boundless" (1872); Hugo Wolf, "The comet's course of genius cannot be directed along traditional lines. It creates the order and raises its will to law" (1885); Schönberg, "The natural laws of the gifted man are the laws of future mankind" (1921).

The insecurity of the composer's existence usually drove the musician in two directions, to become either a practicing artist or a teacher. This combination of the composer and the practicing musician led to the phenomena of the conductor-composer and the virtuoso-composer. A temporary accord was reached in ideal individual instances—in, for example, Beethoven as a pianist, Weber as a conductor, Chopin as a pianist, Mendelssohn as a conductor and pianist, Liszt as a pianist and conductor, Wagner as a conductor and stage director, Mahler as a conductor, and Richard Strauss as a conductor. A third distinct outcome was the combination of composer and music aesthetician, writer, or in individual cases even publicist, as exemplified by Weber, Berlioz, Schumann, Wagner, Liszt, and Hugo Wolf.

The music that resulted from these changed conditions for the musician is to be understood, first, in the light of the process of secularization that made it independent of its religious, theological, and ecclesiastical supports. On the one hand, it experienced a growing trend toward the worldly—or, specifically, toward the mundane—and, on the other, toward a subjectivization by way of the composer's introduction of his private world, making a sort of individual confession that sometimes alluded to even most highly personal matters. The "Romantic" as an element of expression had its deepest basis here and opened entirely new areas to music.

Another distinctive feature of 19th-century music history is the pluralism of the public—its ability to undergo rapid changes, like Proteus in the ancient myth. From 1800 to 1900 the population of Europe grew from 187 to 447 million. In perhaps like proportion there was an increase in the demand for and consumption of music. A more detailed view of this phenomenon can be gained from various points of view.

Music such as Beethoven's last quartets, that at first seemed unapproachable, won its own public. Music such as Wagner's "Tristan," that was at first considered unperformable, constantly raised the technical and artistic achievement. Liszt's extraordinary pianistic virtuosity became the technical standard for concert pianists. The same was true of Paganini's violin technique. Music first written for a definite social circle, such as Chopin's works for piano, now belonged to the world.

The bourgeoisie bore the torch of culture, fulfilling this role by attending concerts and operas, participating in amateur choruses and orchestras, and making music at home. Groups of amateurs assembled in men's choruses or singing societies, sometimes referred to as *Liedertafel*, and in mixed choruses or choral and oratorio societies. Such men as Pestalozzi and Nägeli in Switzerland and Zelter in Berlin were involved in this development. A new piano literature, known as salon music, was sometimes a feeble imitation of virtuoso music, in a smaller, shallower, and depreciated version. Its advent coincided with the first great flowering of piano virtuosity. Between 1830 and 1848, or between Thalberg's first epoch-making season and Liszt's last year of concertizing, virtuosity reached its height. Typical representatives of salon music were Louis

Barthélémy Pradher and his pupils Franz Hünten, Henri Rosellen, and Heinrich Herz. Paris was its center. With the increase in population, music rose prodigiously as an entertainment factor and as an adjunct to life. Passive consumption of music became typical. Whether danced to or merely listened to, waltz-music reached its height in Vienna. A new literature proceeding from dance music was consumed. Open parks where military concerts were given, excursion resorts near the city, dance halls, and amusement parks such as the Prater in Vienna became the centers of entertainment. Music first made its way in to cafés in Paris after 1850. The institutions of 19th-century musical life were organized in a thoroughly capitalistic manner. It was not until the 20th century that the schism between "serious" and "light" music manifested itself in its full sharpness.

Music in the 19th century also found a distinctive type of expression in the growing political activity of the working class, in workers' songs and workers' choruses.

A third influential feature of 19th-century musical life was the improvement of communication. It was the age of the steamship, with the first of such vessels going from New York to Liverpool in 1818. Steam navigation was established on the Rhine by 1825. It was also the age of the railway that saw passenger traffic between Liverpool and Manchester by 1830 and between Nuremberg and Fürth by 1835. And it was the era of the electric telegraph, with the first telegraph lines between Baltimore and Washington in 1844, the era of the telephone, which was discovered in 1861, and the era of wireless telegraphy, which began in 1897. Proximity and speed of contact in musical life such as had never before existed appeared hand in hand with the construction of regular concert halls. Modern communication brought the touring artist or virtuoso and his international audience together. Music festivals flourished. Although the first music festival in the modern sense dates from 1698 in England and there were Handel festivals there as early as the second half of the 18th century, the first German music festival was held in 1810 at Frankenhausen in Thuringia. The Lower Rhenish Music Festivals, first held in 1817, achieved special significance. Bayreuth Festival performances of the *Ring des Nibelungen* in 1867 achieved an international character that would not have been possible in Europe before the railways.

In undertaking to divide the 19th century into epochs, one finds that the course of music parallels the course of political events and the intellectual and cultural history. The clearest break occurred about the middle of the century. Today the concept of Romanticism is generally limited to the first half of the 19th century.

The Make-up of Music History

The First Half of the 19th Century

During the first half of the century the central impulse proceeded from a notable group of Romantic composers up to 1830. Thereafter the French and Italian Romantic Movements presented quite notable developments of their own.

The first group represented what is usually referred to as the "historical Romantic era." Wackenroder, Tieck, and Schelling had prepared the way for it by 1800 with their writings on aesthetics. The first important work appeared about 1816, and the era ended more or less with Schubert's death in 1828.

Outstanding members of this first group were as follows:

Ernst Theodor Amadeus Hoffmann (1776–1822) wrote "Undine" in 1813–4, an opera involving magic and the first artistically significant Romantic opera. As early as 1809 he produced literary works, including criticism of Beethoven and other composers, and sketches that were significant for their combination of musical and literary aesthetics and for their basic formulation of the Romantic conception of music. Three of his tales are the basis of a well known opera by Offenbach.

Louis Spohr (1784–1859) wrote his *Violin Concerto No. 1* in 1802 and in 1816 an opera *Faust*, which took its place alongside E. T. A. Hoffmann's *Undine*. He wrote his *Violin Concerto No. 8* in 1816 "in the form of a vocal scene." Among his other operas, *Jessonda* (1823) is the most significant and *Der Berggeist* (1825) is the historically most important one, with its division into scenes.

Carl Maria von Weber (1786–1826) wrote music for *Rübezahl* (1804), his first opera *Silvana* (Frankfurt a. M. 1810), and patriotic songs for Körner's *Leyer und Schwert* (1814). Weber achieved the first artistic climax of the Romantic Era in German opera with *Der Freischütz* (Berlin 1821), which was followed by *Euryanthe* (Vienna 1823) and *Oberon* (London 1826).

Heinrich Marschner (1795–1861) continued the tradition of German opera significantly between 1828 and 1833 with his *Vampyr, Templer und Jüdin*, and *Hans Heiling*, featuring the supernatural and abnormal and including descriptions of nature.

Franz Schubert (1797–1828) applied strong Romantic emphases to his vocal and instrumental compositions, such as "*Der Erlkönig*" (1816), *Symphony in B-minor* (1822), *Müllerlieder* (1823), *Wandererfantasie* (1823), *Winterreise* (1826), string quartets in D-minor, and G-major (1826), and the last three piano sonatas and the *Great C-major Symphony* (1828).

Of this first group, E. T. A. Hoffmann, Weber, and Schubert died before 1830, a year of crisis, with the July Revolution in Paris, the disturbances in Germany, and the Polish uprisings. By the beginning of the 1830's Spohr and Marschner had passed the height of their creative activity.

A second group of composers appeared with significant artistic works as early as 1830. Through them, the Romantic Era became a European event. Recognition extended beyond linguistic boundaries, partly in response to political considerations. Chopin and Liszt, as interpreters and composers, created the first European musical internationalism. Music became the Romantic art par excellence.

Outstanding members of the second group were:

Hector Berlioz (1803–1869), whose *Symphonie fantastique* (1830) was of epoch-making significance for all orchestral program music and opera. All of Berlioz's major orchestral works, however, were composed before 1840.

Felix Mendelssohn-Bartholdy (1809–1847), with his Overture for Shakespeare's "Midsummer Night's Dream" (1826), his first version of the overture *The Hebrides* (Fingal's Cave), called "The Lonely Island" (1829); and *Six Songs without Words, Book 1* (1830).

Frédéric Chopin (1810–1849), whose early piano works were written before 1830, the *Twelve Etudes, op. 10,* between 1828 and 1832 and the *Piano Concerto in E-minor* in 1830.

Robert Schumann (1810–1856) wrote the *Abegg-Variations* and the *Toccata, op. 7,* in 1830 and from 1829 to 1831 worked on *Papillons,* from 1834 to 1835 on *Carnaval,* and in 1834 on the *Symphonic Etudes.*

Franz Liszt (1811–1886) was strongly influenced by a cluster of ideas that emerged in Paris around 1830—the July Revolution, Count Saint-Simon's ideas of Christian Socialism, F. de Lamenais's Christian Democracy, and French Romanticism. His *Années de Pèlerinage* and *Album d'un voyageur,* written in 1835–6, reflected a new individual relationship to nature through a Romantic style of expression.

Berlioz, Liszt, Richard Wagner (1813–1883), and Giuseppe Verdi (1813–1901) were the only members of this group who continued to work significantly beyond the middle of the century and to develop much that was new. Berlioz had written his Requiem in 1837, and among his subsequent works were *The Damnation of Faust* in 1846 and the opera *The Trojans* after 1850. After 1850 Verdi succeeded in focusing his stylistic intentions during his middle creative period, and Wagner undertook his reform of opera in accordance with philosophically oriented conceptions. Liszt also addressed himself to orchestral composition and then to his major sacred works.

The Historical Romantic Era

The Romantic Era began in literature shortly after 1750 in connection with the revival of Shakespeare. It coincided with a movement stressing the return to nature. The epoch of the *Sturm und Drang,* which was centered in the German theater, also involved music during the 1760's, beginning with Schobert, Beck, and C. P. E. Bach. This movement led to a hitherto unknown heightening of expression. Many people affected by it liked to interpret compositions extramusically. For example, texts by the poet Gerstenberg as well as Hamlet's "To be or not to be" soliloquy were assigned to a keyboard fantasy of C. P. E. Bach's in 1783 (as described by Chrysander in the *Vierteljahrsschrift für Musikwissenschaft* VIII). The spirit of C. P. E. Bach continued to influence the works of Haydn, Mozart, and Beethoven. Romanticism in music reached significant heights of artistry as early as Mozart's keyboard *Fantasies in C-minor* (K. V. 396 and 475).

Romantic music can be characterized roughly by five traits. In keeping with the nature of the movement, they involve opposing tendencies, but as a whole form a self-contained period style.

1. Representation of unusual states of the soul and life, and accordingly a predominance of extramusical impulses over musical form. This

tendency was connected with the discovery and characteristic treatment of quite new harmonic, rhythmic, melodic, coloristic, and formal means. For example, the individualism of the artist became autobiographical in some pieces, such as Berlioz's *Symphonie fantastique: Scenes from the* suggested the secret and the irrational, as in Chopin's *Nocturnes;* Schumann's *Traumeswirren, op. 12.* The "Faust" idea appeared in many works, such as Schumann's *Faust-Szenen* and Liszt's *Faust-Sinfonie.* Also related to the "Faustian," Manfred appeared in Schumann's *Manfred-Overtüre.* The night was presented as the opposite to life, to the day; and thus it suggested the secret and the irrational, as in Chopin's *Nocturnes,* Schumann's *Nachtstücke, op. 23;* his *In der Nacht,* from op. 12; and Wagner's *Tristan und Isolde.* Sometimes the stress was on loneliness, hopelessness, the idea of there being no way out, a sense of the deepest depression and despair of life, as in Schubert's *Winterreise. Vice versa,* sometimes there was a sense of exaltation over the commonplace by a sort of magically induced fanciful soaring, as in Schumann's *C-major Fantasy, op. 17,* 2nd movt.; his "Soaring," from the *Phantasiestücken, op. 12;* and his "Spring Night" from the *Eichendorff Song Cycle, op. 39.*

2. The discovery of a new relationship between man and nature and its representation in music. Nature was variously seen. It was at times an element that threatened man, that was hostile to him, as evidenced by its catastrophic aspects, as in the "Wolves' glen scene" in the *Freischütz,* or in Liszt's "Storm" in the first book of his *Années de Pèlerinage.* At other times it was indifferent to man—inaccessible, inhospitable, and uninhabitable, as in Mendelssohn's *Hebrides Overture.* The ocean is represented accordingly in Weber's *Oberon* and Wagner's *Flying Dutchman.* Mountain peaks are also so suggested in Liszt's *Berg* Symphony and Wagner's *Ring.* At still other times, nature was conceived of as an elemental force bound up with the fate of man, as in the *Frieschütz, Walküre,* and *Siegfried.*

3. Assimilation of older elements, especially the revival of polyphony and Baroque forms under the influence of J. S. Bach. A somewhat subordinate tendency toward Historical Classicism ran concurrently with Historical Romanticism and will be considered in an ensuing section.

4. Study of the folk-heritage in music and imitation of folk-like melodic simplicity.

The folk-song movement inevitably involved assimilation and imitation of the musical folk-heritage. The roots of this movement go far back —in England to the amateur work of Young, Macpherson, and Bishop Percy and in France to the ideas of Jean Jacques Rousseau. In Germany, the philosopher Johann Georg Hamann paved the way, but it was Johann Gottfried Herder (1744–1803) who really introduced the folk-song movement into Germany. He helped form the scholarly concept of "folk-song" (*Volkslied*) and started the collection of it in a systematic way. In his sense of the term, Johann Wolfgang von Goethe carried the work on further in his great original poetic achievements, which particularly inspired the Berlin song-school in the 18th century and the composers of *lieder* in the 19th.

The Romantic concept of the folk-song had been established by the end of the 18th century. August Wilhelm Schlegel (1767–1845) played a decisive role in formulating this concept as he limited the idea of "folk-poetry" to songs that "were composed expressly for and among the lower classes." Achim von Arnim and Clemens Brentano edited a collection of texts, *Des Knaben Wunderhorn* (1806), which became basic for the 19th century, encouraging further collecting activity. The research of Ludwig Uhland (1787–1862) and August Heinrich Hoffmann von Fallersleben (1798–1874) gave new stimulus to scholarly research. Friedrich Silcher (1789–1860) and Wilhelm Zuccalmaglio (1803–1869) were outstanding collectors as well as poets in their own right. During the second half of the 19th century, Rochus Freiherr von Liliencron (1820–1912), Ludwig Erk (1807–1883), and Franz Magnus Boehme (1827–1898) produced fundamental works of research.

5. Predilection for exotic effects through employment of foreign national coloring or the folkloristic heritage. Many individual composers, such as Chopin, bore the distinct stamp of definite national elements and traits.

As early as about 1810 the Romantic trend toward dominance of content over form had sharply set in with Beethoven and led to the extension of the cyclic form to seven movements, as in the *Quartet in C-sharp minor*. It also led to the small forms of the *Bagatelles* and to the division of the musical composition into separate movements. Only occasionally did Beethoven introduce programmatic titles to elucidate his intention.

Judged from a broader historical perspective, the music of the Romantic and the Classical eras must be seen as a unity. The following features are common to both epochs:

1. The idea of the human, of the irradiation of music individually on man through the moral impulse
2. The claim of autonomy for music, of the right of the work of art to follow its own laws, and to be free in pursuing its aims

It is in many instances very difficult to separate in music the Classical from the Romantic music, particularly during the numerous transitions. As Blume has said:

> The distinction depends perhaps essentially on the symbolic power of the form and on the independent consummation on the part of the listener: if the content of a piece of music rests more in a self-contained symbolic form and invites the listener to consummate the experience on his own, it will be felt to be more Classic; if the formal power of the music is weaker but it it yet compels the listener by the demonic qualities of its power to fascinate, it will be felt as Romantic.

The boundary-line between Classic and Romantic in aesthetics, however, is not so ambiguous. At this point a sometimes lofty and remarkably poetical trait invades aesthetics and usually casts systematization to the winds, substituting the values of the essayist or the pure poet. The emphasis, the exuberance of the language, the passionately confessional tone has for us today an often significantly higher power of suggestion than does the music itself. In the music itself we do not often find the boundlessness of which the aestheticians of the Romantic Era spoke so much—except possibly in the mature works of Beethoven and in a relatively few other compositions. Romantic musical aestheticians saw music as having its roots in the suprasensible. The Neo-Pythagorean and medieval heritage of ideas, which now began to reappear, was never systematized, but was only dressed in a somewhat new form, as can be seen in these passages cited from Pfrogner's study:

> Were our limited sensibility to allow us to look into the realm of the spirits, we would be astonished to see how definitely they follow harmonic laws; we would see that our earthly music is but a picture, a hull, an emblem of the eternally spiritual. In all relationships of man to the universe, to God, to society, to himself, or to his inner nature, he acts according to the laws of the tonal art. Too, the inner character and the guidance of the soul is true music and is based on harmonic laws. (Friedrich H. Dalberg, 1787)

> Music is the only art which reduces the most manifold and contradictory promptings of our heart to the same beautiful harmonies, the only art which plays in like harmonious tones with joy and sorrow, with despair and veneration. Hence music infuses in us the true serenity of soul, which is the most beautiful jewel that man can acquire;—that serenity, I say, when everything in the world seems to us natural, true, and good, when we in the wildest agitations of men find a beautiful unity, when we with pure heart feel all beings related to us and near to us, and, like children, behold the world as through the faint light of a lovely dream. (Wilhelm Heinrich Wackenroder and Johann Ludwig Tieck, 1799)

> The forms of music are forms of eternal things, in so far as they are considered from the real point of view. For the real point of view of eternal things is that from which the infinite is begotten of the finite. But this same development of the infinite into the finite is also the form of music; and as the forms of art on the whole are the forms of things-in-themselves, thus the forms of music are necessarily considered forms of things-in-themselves or ideas entirely from their real point of view. (Friedrich Wilhelm Joseph Schelling, 1803)

> When music is spoken of as an independent art, should not the meaning always be only instrumental music, which, scorning every help, every admixture of another art (poetry), clearly articulates the peculiar nature of this art, recognizable only in it? It is the most Romantic of all arts—almost, one might say, the only truly Romantic art; for the infinite alone is the subject with which it deals. Orpheus' lyre opened the gates of Hades. Music opens a realm hitherto unknown to man, a world which has nothing in common with the world of the external senses, which surrounds him and in which he leaves behind all definite feelings in order to devote himself to an unspeakable yearning. (E. T. A. Hoffman, 1813)

Historical Classicism

Monteverdi's insistence that the kind of composition with which he had identified himself constituted a *Seconda Prattica overo Perfettione della Moderna Musica* (1605) came from a new historical awareness. The *stile antico* and the *stile moderno* were opposites, but both were historical reality and artistic necessity. From his time on, styles were seen as historical actuality. Thus a historical situation was created that has had importance in terms of the principle involved right up to the present— though, to be sure, the circumstances have differed from time to time. Since his day, a dualism has existed in the history of music. In the 18th century it led to the differentiation between the *stile antico* and the style that happened to be in vogue, as well as to the compromise solution of the *stilus mixtus,* which brought together what Quantz in 1752 called "pieces both in the so-called laborious and in the stirring and capitivating manner of writing."

Mozart created a new and different situation when—in 1782 in Vienna—the Baron van Swieten showed him a selection of the works of J. S. Bach and Handel, including both parts of the *Well-Tempered Clavier* and the *Art of the Fugue.* Mozart's assimilation of these impressions led immediately to a series of sketches for fugues and completed fugal compositions on subjects which derived mainly from Bach and Handel. If Classicism means the voluntary seeking-out of a style that has been viewed in historical perspective and the attempt to fuse it with the individual's own period-bound and personality-bound idiom, then Mozart was the first Classicist in the history of music. He did not succeed in synthesizing this idiom with his own until he came to the *C-minor Mass* and the *Requiem,* which he did not live to complete. Meanwhile, however, he fashioned a new formal type that succeeded in fusing the sonata allegro form with contrapuntal forms by incorporating strongly fugal sections, notably in the Finale of the *Quartet in G-major* (K. V. 387), the Finale of the *Jupiter Symphony,* and the Overture to *The Magic Flute.*

The rediscovery of Bach and Handel in the 19th century resulted in their works being subjected to a kind of analysis that became a matter of course for every aspiring composer. Beethoven's late works were quite individual new polyphonic creations. Schumann maintained that the "deeply combinatory, poetic, and humoristic elements in most of the new music" of his day were related to Bach. When Schumann wrote these words in 1840, he was thinking of "all the so-called Romantics" in Germany, and he specifically mentioned Mendelssohn, Bennett, Chopin, and Hiller. Schumann considered the preludes and fugues of the *Well-Tempered Clavier* "characteristic pieces" and "tone-pictures," and he interpreted them in this way. For "practice in the *capriccio* style" he recommended such models as the fugues in C-minor, D-major, E-minor, F-major, and G-major from the first part of the *Well-Tempered Clavier.* This attitude of Schumann throws a new light on his own piano works. Many pieces, for example in the *Kreisleriana,* consist of the repetition of a single figure and thus point to the preludes in C-major, D-major, or D-minor of the *Well-Tempered Clavier,* Book I. The finale of Chopin's *B-flat minor Sonata* derives from the same impulse. Mendelssohn's E-major *Capriccio for Piano,* Op. 14, shows the influence of Bach in the characteristic gigue-theme with its imitations at the beginning of its Allegro section. Bach's polyphony was revived in the texture of the inner voices in Schumann and Chopin as Romantic expressive art. In 1840 Schumann's involvement with polyphony entered into a new phase. He and his wife were studying fugue, and he methodically repeated this type of study in 1842, 1845, and again in 1853, using the *Well-Tempered Clavier* and Cherubini's theory-book. The direct artistic results were Schumann's fugal works, op. 56, 58, 60, and 72.

Mendelssohn's personality and work were related to the world of Bach and Handel even more closely than Schumann's. If Mozart was the first Classicist, Mendelssohn was the first composer of rank who attained a decidedly Classicistic attitude. He had been trained by Zelter, and from early youth he was closely associated with Bach and Handel's works. In 1829, at the age of twenty, Mendelssohn appeared as the director of the first revival of the *St. Matthew Passion*. Thus he revived and continued the formal heritage of the then historical Baroque and Classical Eras and raised the idea of doing so to a stylistic principle that continued remarkably operative for the rest of the century. As man and artist he was thoroughly conservative. In 1833 he wrote: "Men must come, continue along the way—they will lead the rest further on or will turn back to the old and correct masters, in a direction that really ought to be called 'forward.'" When he made the personal acquaintance of Chopin and Berlioz, he felt that he "did not agree with them." Mendelssohn's first biographer, Wilhelm Adolf Lampadius, wrote in 1848 that "in the midst of the collapse of art, among so many weeds growing rankly over its debris," Mendelssohn with his "intellectual energy has guarded his noble-mannered, thoroughly excellent Classical orientation and has maintained it victoriously in his own creations." The tendency to deal with art in Lampadius' very critical way reechoes in the writing of the whole century. The lines of opposition between the conservative and the progressive parties were sharply drawn, and the cleft extends deeply into the present. Historical retrospect, at all events, reveals that the party of progress was also bound to tradition even more closely than observers at the time were able to recognize.

The Second Half of the 19th Century

In the latter half of the century the problems were extensively changed. In politics the leading issues were imperialism and nationalism; in economics, the Industrial Revolution, investment capitalism, social problems, and the class struggle; in science, the reorganization of the world picture through Darwin's evolutionary theory; in philosophy, the pessimistic pantheism of Schopenhauer and Nietzsche's psychological criticism of society. Meanwhile Christianity was seeking again to win ground theologically. It was an extremely restless time, involved in constant ferment and precipitate events. The problems were recognized to but a limited extent, with consequent increase in the continuing subconscious tension and uneasiness.

Music became the sounding board for ideas that were philosophically oriented, involving a world-view that was often quasi-religious. The intellectual tensions were most strongly apprehended in Wagner's *Ring des Nibelungen*. It was a time of Romantic realism. Likewise Liszt's symphonic poems reflect the world-view in the poetic realm of music.

The intellectual forces of the period were also in part oriented toward the theologically Christian and ecclesiastical aspects of religion. Protestantism found its voice in Brahms, and Roman Catholicism in Liszt, Bruckner, and the leaders of the Caecilian movement to revive Catholic church music. The musical means being employed were significantly increased—in the instrumentation of Wagner's *Ring* and the full-evening length of the late symphonies of Bruckner. Other works, however, exhibited quietness, intensification, and cultivation of the intimate—the songs of Brahms and Hugo Wolf, chamber composition, and piano miniatures. There was strong emphasis on intellectual profundity and continuing or so-called eternal values in life. This inwardness was compensation and equivalence for the externalizing of various aspects of life, with the beginnings of "mass culture." Realism and the psychological criticism of society that appeared in literature left its imprint in music only outside the German-speaking areas—for example, in Mussorgsky's *Boris Godunov* and Bizet's *Carmen,* in individual operas of Verdi, and in the *verismo* movement in Italy around 1890.

In German-speaking areas two trends whose opposite natures were considered insurmountable at the time made their appearance. From the present point of view they seem rather to have been complementary traits with a common basis. The one trend was the "Neo-German School" under Liszt; the other was Romantic Classicism, led in music by Brahms.

The leader of the "Neo-German School," of the "party of progress" in music, was Liszt, from the time when he became music director of the court in Weimar in 1848. The group that flocked around him included Joachim Raff (1822–1882), Hans von Bülow (1830–1894), Peter Cornelius (1824–1874), Hans von Bransart (1830–1913), Karl Tausig (1841–1871), and Felix Draeseke (1835–1913). The character of the music of the "Neo-German School" was Romantic-Realistic. The word *Zukunftsmusik* ("music of the future"), first used in a derogatory sense and later adopted as a slogan, was perhaps coined around 1855 by the critic Bischoff after Wagner's essay, *The Art-Work of the Future (Das Kunstwerk der Zunkft).* In 1860 a manifesto, signed by Brahms, Joachim, Grimm, and Scholz, indiscreetly and prematurely reached the press, stating "that they could only deplore and condemn the products of the leaders and pupils of the so-called Neo-German School as something that was contrary to the innermost nature of music." Opposition was driven to the very extremes, even though individual composers such as Peter Cornelius and Hans von Bülow had already effected a reconciliation. The art of Wagner and Liszt, however, did not finally carry the day until the generation born after 1860. Thus the majority of the composers at the time of Wagner and Liszt continued along the roads indicated by Mendelssohn and the late Schumann, in the sense of 'a Classicistically oriented music that did not entirely exclude programmatic impulses. According to its own inner nature it was Romantic-Classicistic.

The resulting antitheses also left in aesthetics a precipitate; and the opposed positions seemed at that time irreconcilable.

Friedrich von Hausegger, in his *Die Musik als Ausdruck (Music as Expression),* 2nd ed., 1887, wrote:

What is the nature of music? Whence does it come? What tasks does it have to fulfill? These questions have no merely theoretical significance. Their answer will give us the yardstick for measuring the value of music and the plumb-line for judging it. The nature of music is expression—or, more clearly, expression raised to the noblest effect. Herein lies the high, often misconstrued value of this art. True art is true religion. Since the means of expression active in the instrumental work are drawn from the expressive ability of the human organism and under its influence are transformed into a state of effectiveness, they are able to communicate with the listener directly as expression and as such and in such a manner as to set up a reaction. It is therefore an error to think that instrumental music is merely tonal play.

Eduard Hanslick, on the other hand, in his *Vom Musikalisch-Schönen* (*On the Musically Beautiful*), had clearly taken the opposite position in 1854. In the preface to a later edition, Hanslick states what he considered music to be:

When I wrote this essay, the spokesmen for the "Music of the Future" were in loudest voice and perhaps had to incite people of my persuasion to respond. When I prepared the second printing, Liszt's program symphonies had just appeared, which—more completely than anyone had previously managed to do—dispense with the independent meaning of the music and only hint at what the listener is to consider the form intended. Since then we also now have Richard Wagner's *Tristan, Nibelungenring*, and his theory of the "infinite melody," that is, of formlessness raised to principle, the sung and spiritual opium dream, which now has a temple of its own for the cult in Bayreuth.

Tonally animated forms are one and all the content and subject-matter of music. The elemental aspect of music is euphony, its nature rhythm. By the specifically "musical" we understand something that is beautiful, that—independently, and not requiring a content derived from without—consists solely of tones and their artistic combination. The meaningful relations in sounds attractive in themselves, their concord and discord, their flight and self-attainment, their soaring and expiring—all this makes up that which in free forms comes before our inward view and pleases us as beautiful.

This antithesis continues to be sharply drawn still today. Stravinsky in his *Autobiography* (1937) wrote:

"Expression" has never been an inherent property of music, and in no respect is the right of music to exist dependent on "expression." If, as almost always happens, music seems to express something, that is an illusion and not reality. It is nothing but an external trimming, a property that we supply to the music in accordance with old tacitly accepted convention and with which we invest it as with a label, a formula—in short, it is a cloak which we from habit or insufficient insight confuse with the thing itself and which we have drawn over it.

Anton Webern, on the other hand, in 1932 expressed himself thus:

Man cannot exist otherwise than as he expresses himself. Music does it in musical thoughts.

The problematic aspect of this matter was not resolved until it was viewed from the vantage-point of a holistic psychology. Expressive music may well be a concept that is opposed to music that is play, ornament, or formality; but the opposition is a question of accentuation. The radical confrontation is a pseudo-problem. The difference between music as expression and music as play does not rule out the possibility that perhaps expressive characteristics are proper to playful music and, vice versa, that strongly expressive music can also have strict form.

Music always means something and always is linked with some kind of sense. That is its primary aspect as a phenomenon. There is no music without meaning. The meaning is that which clings to the music, which it conveys, what it says and thereby communicates. The concept of expressionism concentrates on a single aspect of this meaning. In the word "expression" there is always a quite subjectively colored connotation. Thus there clings to it the sense of the individual, the personal, the subjectivistic, the distinctly feeling-laden, the emotional. The concept of meaning placed on a more comprehensive level than the specialized idea of expression overcomes the contrast that the second half of the 19th century pushed to the point of irreconcilable opposition. Every piece of music has the characteristic of meaning.

In the countries outside Austria and Germany the aesthetic and artistic assertions of these two parties did not occupy such a central position. They were but a side issue. Between about 1860 and 1890, Russia and Bohemia gained very great significance as musical countries. During the years after 1890 France moved into the center with Impressionism and replaced the German predominance, while Austria with the Viennese atonal school around 1910 pursued a course that was quite isolated. The development of every composer in the 19th century, of no matter what nation, revolved primarily around Beethoven in instrumental music and secondarily in either the Mendelssohn-Schumann-Brahms or the Berlioz-Liszt-Wagner orbit. An original genius like Mussorgsky was an almost completely exceptional phenomenon.

A whole generation of musicians was profoundly moved by the experience of *Tristan.* Wagner completed the score in 1859; it appeared in print in 1860; and the first performance was given in Munich in 1865. His work had many meanings for the new generation. To some, it was music as expression and poetic idea, world-view and philosophy. To others, it was interpretation of a metaphysics of love and erotic transcendence. To still others, it was the high-point in certain developments in harmony. It marked the culminating point in the formal progress of the symphony in so far as its structure was concerned. Its parts were linked by the "infinite melody," and the themes, or leitmotifs, were the symbolic vehicles of the unutterable. In it, the instrumentation became the individual medium of dramatic psychology. Stimulated by Liszt and Wagner, the generation then in its youth was, in part, strongly swayed by a fanatical belief in progress.

Representatives of the *Tristan* generation were Gustav Mahler (1860–1911), Hugo Wolf (1860–1903), Richard Strauss (1864–1949), Hans Pfitzner (1869–1949), Max Reger (1873–1916), Arnold Schönberg (1874–1951), Franz Schreker (1878–1934), Anton Webern (1883–1945), Alban Berg (1885–1935), and Rudi Stephan (1887–1915). Of the non-German musicians, Claude Debussy (1862–1918), Alexander Scriabin (1872–1915), and Zdeněk Fibich (1850–1900) reflected the influence of Wagner in an especially productive and independent way.

Many members of the *Tristan* generation have expressed what this work meant to them:

"When I came out of the Festspielhaus speechless, I then knew that the greatest, most painful thing had occurred to me and that I would bear it undesecrated with me through my life" (Gustav Mahler, 1883, after his first visit to Bayreuth).

"The Romantic Movement was not to be surpassed after Wagner. After Wagner the Romantic and the erotic were completely exhausted" (Richard Strauss to Emil Tschirch, about 1901).

"With one chord music succeeded in expressing feeling: the feeling of love, longing, penitence, or readiness for death—the final two measures of the Prelude to *Tristan* say more to the hearer than the most beautiful poem in words" (Richard Strauss to Josef Gregor, 1935).

"Yes, the 'old wizard' has bewitched us young men, so that we may wander along such paths" (Hugo Wolf to Rosa Mayreder. 1895).

"In the heyday of my artistic awakening, then, when we young people discovered for ourselves Schopenhauer, Richard Wagner, and Ibsen, *Tristan* was one of the works that entirely captivated me for a long time" (Hans Pfitzner, *Impressions and Pictures of My Life*, 1947).

"I was really ready to disregard the Classical composers for Richard Wagner, however highly I otherwise esteemed Beethoven" (Max Reger, 1888).

"Through acquaintance with Zemlinsky, Schönberg came into the society of young artists. An ardent enthusiasm for Wagner prevailed in this circle, especially for *Tristan*, of which no performance was missed and of which the style, instrumentation, and middle-voice leading was made the subject of searching discussions" (E. Wellesz, *Arnold Schönberg*).

The incidents to which Wellesz refers occurred presumably around 1896. Schönberg himself, in his *Progressive Brahms* (1933), wrote about the situation at the end of the century:

That was the attitude of the time; those who did not love Wagner clung to Brahms, and *vice versa*. . . . What seemed unbridgeable in 1883 was no longer a problem in 1897. The greatest musicians of this period—Mahler, Strauss, Reger, and many others—had grown up under the influence of both masters. They all reflected the intellectual, emotional, stylistic, and technical achievements of the preceding period. What once had been the subject of discussion was now referred to as the difference between the two personalities, between their styles of expression—which, after all, were not so opposed to each other as to rule out the union of the particular features of both in one work.

Bibliography

G. Knepler, *Musikgeschichte des 19. Jh.* (2nd vol., Bln. 1961); for further refs., see bibl. of *Symphony during 19th century*; E. Bloch, *Das Prinzip Hoffnung, Teil I–V*, esp. ch. 51 (Frankfurt a. M. 1959); I. Stravinsky, *Chroniques de ma vie* (1936); A. Webern, *Der Weg zur Neuen Musik* (ed. W. Reich, Vienna 1960); A. Wellek, *Musikpsychologie und Musikästhetik* (Frankfurt a. M. 1963); K. H. Wörner, *Das Zeitalter der thematischen Prozesse in der Geschichte der Musik* (Regensburg 1969), *Der Expressionismus in der Musik u. sein Verhältnis zur Vergangenheit* (Convegno Internazionale di Studi sull'Espressionismo, Florence 1964), and *Neue Musik in der Entscheidung* (Mainz 2nd ed. 1956).

24. Catholic Church Music from the Seventeenth Century to the Present

Music in the Catholic Service

Since the 14th century there have been many Papal pronouncements that relate in one way or another to music. The Mass in accordance with the Tridentine Rite was promulgated by Pope Pius V in 1570; and since it provides the framework within which Catholic church music has been written since that time it is more or less the basis of the ensuing discussion of music in the Catholic service. The first inclusive definition and regulation of church music was Pope Pius X's *Motu proprio* "*Inter pastoralis officii*" of 1903. It has also been confirmed and supplemented by his successors several times. In it the Church has defined *musica sacra* as an "essential component of the solemn liturgy" and assigned it the task of "giving greater power to the liturgical text" and thereby "stirring the faithful to piety and rendering their spirit more receptive" to the grace communicated by the divine mysteries.

Thus the Church has demanded that Church music possess the qualities proper to the liturgy (*proprias liturgiae qualitates*), or, more specifically:

1. "Holiness" (*sanctitatem, sancta esse debeat*)—that is, it ought to be sacred, to express "transcendence" as opposed to "worldliness"
2. "Excellence of form" (*bonitatem formae*) and, accordingly, "the character of true art" (*verae artis specimen*)
3. "Universality" (*universitas*)—it should have qualities that are supranationally valid and beyond merely local and national limits.

Liturgical and Musical Forms of the Mass

Central to the Catholic liturgy is the Mass, which has two basic forms, one sung and the other read.

In the sung Mass, the *Missa in cantu* or *Missa cantata*, the priest who is celebrating it sings the portions assigned to him, following certain prescribed melodies from the Gregorian repertoire. He uses a smooth recitative style, or *accentus,* as do also the people when they give their responses, or acclamations. In the early days of the Church, the priest improvised, but he no longer does so today. Except in the *tractus,* the choir and the congregation—or the leader or leaders and the choir (*schola*)—sing the other songs antiphonally. For these the Church recommends the Gregorian melodies available in Papally approved books. The songs of the Proper have only one melody each, those of the Ordinary more than one—the Credo six, the rest of the Ordinary eighteen. The choir and the congregation may use other monodic or polyphonic pieces from the past or the present that conform to the requirements outlined. If the people cannot sing the Gregorian or other settings that have been chosen, the choir may act for them, singing portions that really belong to the congregation.

In very recent times a development that has been in a process of preparation for centuries and that has been strong in German-speaking areas has been confirmed by the granting of permission (*benignissime tolleretur*) that, where the bishops consider it advisable, the congregational and choral songs of the Latin liturgy may be replaced by those in the vernacular if there are not the necessary resources for the execution of the songs in Latin. The songs are to conform as closely as possible to the content of the official liturgy, but they should not be literal translations of the liturgical texts. The result is the German rite, or *Deutsches Amt.* According to a recent extension of this policy the vernacular is now generally used by the Roman Catholic Church.

In the *Missa lecta,* or read Mass, however, the priest who is celebrating it speaks the official liturgical texts. Sometimes he says them antiphonally with those who are assisting at the altar. At all events, the congregation simply responds with the acclamations in a speaking voice.

In smaller congregations, on rare occasions, the people also participate with still further texts, and the result is sometimes referred to as a recited Mass, or *Missa recitata.* Such possibilities open the way for considerable variety: prayer-leaders, or precentors, may sing or speak vernacular texts with or for the congregation. These do not belong to the real liturgy of the Mass, but are more in the nature of "pious exercises" or "private worship" (*pia exercitia* or *cultus privatus*). Here too the reminder is to be observed "that they be clearly in agreement with the separate parts of the Mass" (*ut singulis Missae partibus plane congruant*). Again, among some congregations it has been granted that even a translation of the liturgical texts themselves may be used. Thus, proceeding out from the Mass, a broad field has opened up for the development of the vernacular church-song and other forms of monodic and polyphonic sacred music in the vernacular.

The tendency toward variety in this respect has been strong in German areas, and through the "liturgical movement" of recent decades the following three types have been formulated. In 1942, they received a final stamp of recognition in the "Outlines of the Fulda Bishop's Conference on the Formulation of the Pastoral Worship Service." In all three, the acclamations are rendered in turn by the priest and the congregation in Latin, but the other parts of the Mass differ, thus:

1. Community Mass (*Gemeinschaftsmesse*): A vernacular translation is used, modelled after the *Missa cantata* as set forth in the precepts for the "High Mass" or *Hochamtsregel*. This is spoken partly by the prayer-leader, or *Commentator*, and partly by the people.

2. Devotional and Sung Mass (*Bet-Sing-Messe*): In place of a part of the sung liturgical portions, there are vernacular songs adapted to them, the other texts being spoken partly by the prayer-leader, partly by the people.

3. Sung Mass (*Singmesse*): Songs are adapted to portions of the Mass, and the Lessons are given by the *lector* in the vernacular.

Although an older form of the sung Mass that blanketed even the acclamations and Lessons with an uninterrupted succession of songs and organ interludes is still in widespread use, it is no longer recommended by the Church.

The Mass has two parts, the Ordinary and the Proper. The Ordinary includes all portions that retain the same text unchanged every time the Mass is celebrated. Five of them are sung antiphonally between the choir and the congregation: *Kyrie, Gloria, Credo, Sanctus,* and *Agnus Dei.* Only by exception and surrogate are they to be presented by the choir alone. Since the 14th century, polyphonic cycle-settings have been to an increasing extent written with this possibility in mind and, in an essentially inadmissible part-for-the-whole narrowing of the idea, have come to be called "Masses." The Proper of the Mass, on the other hand, includes those portions which are "proper" to whatever liturgical day is being celebrated or are "common" to a similar group of festival days and hence are called "*Commune.*" The songs of the Proper, of the *Commune,* are the *Introitus, Graduale, Alleluia, Tractus, Sequence, Offertorium,* and *Communio.*

Liturgical days are distinguished in kind and importance. The most important ones constitute a cycle of festivals for the church year (*Proprium de tempore*). They are of five types: 1. Feasts; 2. Octaves, or celebrations of high festivals extending through eight days; 3. Sundays; 4. Week-days; and 5. Vigils, or days of preparation, formerly night-watches before high festivals. Of lesser importance is the cycle of festivals for saints (*Proprium* or *Commune de sanctis*). These are the saints' feast-days, arranged in five orders of rank according to the degree of the festivity. Finally, on days of lower liturgical rank, in place of the Mass that is proper to the day, there can be the celebration of a votive Mass, in response to a particular wish that such a Mass be celebrated.

There is a definite structure to the celebration of the Mass. It consists of a service of words and a service of sacrifice. The first part, or service of words, includes the pre-Mass and the Mass of the Catechumens, to which in early times the converts receiving training in preparation for baptism and baptized penitents were admitted. The second part is the divine service of the meal. The food in it is the bread and wine that have been consecrated or substantially transformed and have become Christ, who sacrificed himself through death on the cross. Thus the unique redeeming crucifixion of Christ is transferred from past to present. For this reason this second main part of the Mass is also referred to as the sacrificial Mass or festal sacrifice or divine service of sacrifice, with the faithful partaking of the sacrificial food. This second or sacrificial service consists of the "preparation of the gifts," or *Offertorium*, the "eucharistic high prayer" when the priest repeats the words of Jesus at the Last Supper ("This is my body, which is given for you . . . , this is my blood, which is shed for you. . . . Do this in remembrance of me"), and the "Communion," when the priest and the faithful partake of the holy sacramental food.

The separate parts of the Mass fall within these main outlines. The accompanying table indicates their relationship, as well as those who, in a *Missa cantata*, sing them. The following abbreviations are used: Ch Choir, Co Congregation, L Lector, M Ministri or those serving at the altar other than the Priest, P Priest, Pr Precentor or choir-leader, S Schola or rest of the choir. A transverse line means "and/or."

	ORDINARIUM	PROPRIUM
LITURGY OF THE WORD	Entry (P & M)	*Introitus* (S)
	Prayer at steps (P/M)	
	Kyrie (Ch/Co)	
	Gloria (intonation by P, continuation by Co)	
		Oratio (P/Co)
		Reading (P or L)
		Vocal interludes (Pr/S)
		Evangelium (P or L)
		Sermon, optional (P)
	Credo (intonation by P, continuation by Ch/Co)	
LITURGY OF THE EUCHARIST	1. Preparation of sacrificial gifts with prayers of presentation (P/M)	*Offertorium* (Pr/S)
		Secreta, Oratio (P/Co)
	2. Eucharistic prayer	
	Preface (P/Co)	
	Sanctus (Ch/Co)	
	Canon (P/Co)	
	3. Communion section	
	Pater noster (P/Co)	
	Breaking of the Bread (P)	
	Agnus Dei (Ch/Co)	
	Prayer of Peace/Kiss of Peace (P/M)	
	Prayers preparatory to Communion	
	Receiving of Communion (P/M/Co)	*Communio* (Pr/S)
		Postcommunio, Oratio (P/Co)
	4. Dismissal and Blessing	
	Ite, missa est (P/Co)	
	Blessing (P)	

Although the foregoing outline of the Tridentine Rite indicates the basis of most of the music that has been written so far for the Catholic service, it should be realized that a new Ordo Missae was promulgated by Pope Paul VI on April 3, 1969, as a result of the Second Vatican Council.

The new rite carries further tendencies that have been previously noted and gives them a kind of general official recognition that they had not had before.

Of note in the new rite is the absence of the distinction between High Mass and Low Mass (i.e., sung Mass and read Mass). In the outline given on the next page, there are many options. With the further permission of vernacular texts the development of liturgical music is likely to vary still more from country to country. The Latin texts are, nevertheless, normative and music is being prepared for the new texts. As with the Tridentine Rite it is customary to have a recessional hymn, which is not considered part of the Rite itself.

Returning, however, to the outline of the Tridentine Rite, which officially prevailed during the period of music that we are here primarily considering, we are to understand musically the sung portions of the Mass only on the basis of the prayers they contain, their literary form, and their history in the development of the liturgy. These aspects are touched on in the following notes on individual types of song in the Mass, beginning with those performed primarily by the priest and moving on to those rendered antiphonally between the choir and the congregation or by the choir entirely.

With the acclamation "*Dominus vobiscum*" (The Lord be with you), the priest introduces all the prayer texts of the *Oratio* and *Prefatio*, which are given in solemn liturgical recitative, or *accentus*. The congregation responds to him with the cry, "*et cum spiritu tuo*" (and with thy spirit). He concludes the prayer-texts with the formula "*per omnia saecula saeculorum*" (for ever and ever), and the congregation answers "*Amen.*" The latter formula, when it continues directly from a silent prayer, shows that this prayer also was originally sung by the priest—for example, at the Canon, which continues the *Paternoster*. Further on, the proclamation of the Gospel, the breaking of the bread, and the kiss of peace, as well as the dismissal blessing, are introduced by the same or similar acclamations, and likewise with the answering cry of the congregation. Musically the richest acclamation is the dismissal call, "*Ite, missa est*" (Go, you are dismissed). *Missa* is the Latin past participle of *mittere* (to send), and means dismissal in the sense of being charged with a mission, hence "Mass" or *Missa* as the name for the whole celebration through which its primarily missionary and social character is stressed. The cry, "*Ite, missa est,*" was taken over from the formulae used in the Roman popular assembly. If another liturgical celebration such as a procession is joined to the celebration of the Mass, instead of the cry of dismissal, a call of blessing is used: "*Benedicamus Domino*" (Let us praise the Lord).

Prominent in the priest's part are the *Oratio*, the *Lectio*, and the *Evangelium. The Oratio*, or prayer, is taken from the precisely formulated official compilation of the *Orationes* of the faithful, introduced by "*Oremus*" (let us pray). The *Lectio* is from the letters of the Apostles— hence sometimes referred to as the Epistles—or it is from the Book of Revelation or from the Old Testament. The *Evangelium* is a selection or *Sequentia* from one of the four Gospels.

The priest (or *Lector*) sings—or, in earlier times, improvised—these

	ORDER OF THE MASS	PRIEST/ MINISTER	CHOIR/SCHOLA/ CONGREGATION
INTRODUCTORY RITES	Entrance Greeting		May sing the introitus or a seasonal alternate or approved hymn
	Penitential Rite and Kyrie	May be sung	May be sung
	Gloria (on occasion)	May be sung	May be sung
	Opening Prayer	May be sung	Response, "Amen," may be sung
LITURGY OF THE WORD	First Reading		
	Response		May be sung
	Second Reading		
	Gospel Acclamation		May be sung
	Gospel	May be sung	
	Homily		
	Profession of Faith		May be sung
	General Intercessions	May be sung	May be sung
LITURGY OF THE EUCHARIST	Preparation of the gifts		May sing the psalm or a seasonal alternate or approved hymn
	Orate fratres		
	Prayer over the gifts	May be sung	Response, "Amen," may be sung
	Preface Dialogue	May be sung	Responses sung
	Preface	May be sung	
	Preface acclamation	May be sung	May be sung
	Eucharistic Prayer	May be sung	
	Memorial acclamations	May be sung	May be sung
	Concluding acclamation	May be sung	May be sung
	Lord's Prayer/ Doxology	May be sung	May be sung
	Prayer for Peace		
	Sign of Peace		
	Fractio		Lamb of God may be sung
	Communion		May sing same option as at the entrance
	Meditative Period of thanks		May employ song
	Prayer after communion	May be sung	Response, "Amen," may be sung
	Dismissal	May be sung	Responses sung

texts on an even pitch, interspersing little turns of melody or punctuational flourishes only at pauses in the sentences. These flourishes are more richly developed and follow each other more closely in the *Paternoster* and in the *Preface,* so that the even pitch of the recitation scarcely appears. Originally the priest maintained the same vocal melody in the continuation of the last *Paternoster* prayer (*embolismus* or insertion) and in the Canon. Of this, however, there remains only the resumption of the melody in the closing words *"per omnia saecula saeculorum,"* so that the congregation can answer *"Amen."*

The Eucharistic Prayer occupies a central position in the Sacrificial Service. The word *eucharista* means "expressing thanks," in accordance with the prototypes of the Last Supper and the Israelitish paschal meal in which the Bible reports that first "he said thanks. . . ." Originally it was intended as a unit, the congregation coming in on the *"Sanctus,"* with the words of transubstantiation being inserted. Thus the first portion, which is still sung, received the name *Prefatio,* or laudation. The oldest *Sanctus*-melody, which appears in the Vatican edition under *Ordinarium-cyclus XVIII,* consists of the same melodic formulae as that of the *Prefatio.* Not until the Middle Ages did richer and richer settings appear. The continuation of the eucharistic prayer, which is today rendered silently, has at the present time—as a result of the insertion of prayers of petition and offering—largely lost its original character of thanks and praise and now is known as the "canon," which means the plumb line or guiding principle, because it is the core of the entire celebration of the Mass.

Passing on to songs in the Mass that are sung antiphonally between the choir and the congregation, we have the five major portions of the Ordinary.

The *Kyrie* is so called from the litany-cry *"Kyrie eleison,"* which is Greek for "Lord, have mercy." The *Kyrios* addressed here is the Lord in the sense of absolute dominion, *Christus* as the "ruler of all," or *Pantokrator,* enthroned on the right hand of the Father. Hence, in alternation with *"Kyrie,"* Christ is addressed in the phrase *"Christe eleison."* Originally the people sang these calls on coming into the celebration of the Mass, in a succession not fixed in number, as the antiphonal response to a precentor's call to prayer. After the introduction of a psalm specifically for the entry, in the *Introitus,* and the omission of the calls to prayer, they were stylized into a three-fold repetition of each sentence in the *Kyrie-Christe-Kyrie* succession as a quasi-litany, thus two-fold alternation between choir and people. This litany arrangement has largely been lost in the later polyphonic settings.

The *Gloria* presumably goes back to the 2nd century A.D., when it was originally a private prayer. At first it was reserved for only the bishops, but gradually it was incorporated as a festive entry-hymn into the celebration of the Mass. This feature of its use is preserved to the present time in that it is used as an entry-hymn on festive days. In form it is a free succession of Psalmodic verses and litany-like cries, suggesting alternation from verse to verse between groups of singers.

The *Credo* is a version of the "Apostles' Creed," expanded by the Council of Nicaea in 325 A.D. and the Council of Constantinople in 381 A.D.

At first it was related particularly to the baptismal confession, and only later was it assimilated into the celebration of the Mass—as far as the Roman liturgy is concerned, in about the year 1000. The individual articles of the faith follow a succession that resembles verse and that is structurally somewhat like the *Gloria.*

The *Sanctus,* together with the *Benedictus,* is one of the oldest elements in all the liturgies. The first part is the cry of adoration uttered by the angels before the throne of God, from the prophet Isaiah's vision of heaven. The second part is the cry of allegiance uttered by the Jews from the Gospel account of Jesus' entry into Jerusalem, antiphonally constructed (a-b-a) with the *Hosanna* as the framing verse for the "*Benedictus. . . .*" Only, contrary to the liturgical structure of the song, the expansion of later polyphonic settings led to the separation of the *Benedictus,* which was not usually sung until after the transubstantiation. The separation of the *Benedictus* also destroyed the a-b-a form of *Hosanna-Benedictus-Hosanna.*

Like the *Kyrie,* the *Angus Dei* is an extremely old litany cry, but it was not incorporated into the Roman Mass until the 8th century—after the Greek model—and was soon stylized to the three-fold repetition. Not until the 10th to 12th centuries did the custom gradually arise of inserting at the last cry, in place of the "*miserere nobis,*" the prayer for peace, "*dona nobis pacem.*" This change came about because of the kiss of peace that was given at the same time in the clerical choir, though it was later understood in the sense of a prayer for political peace.

Considering now the choral portions of the Proper, we should note that they begin with the *Introitus,* which is essentially a psalmodic song with refrain, or antiphon. From the beginning of the 5th century the Introitus was added to the older litany of entry. As the antiphon became more and more richly formulated, however, the psalm was correspondingly shortened; and as early as about 600 there remained only one verse of the psalm and the closing and related "*Gloria Patri . . . ,*" or Doxology. The musical form was, accordingly, a-b-b-a (Antiphon-Psalm verse-*Gloria Patri*-Antiphon).

Between the Reading and the Gospel the choir may sing songs of various structures on different occassions. In the foregoing table these have been indicated simply as "vocal interludes," in which four different types of song are often used.

The first type of interlude-song is known as the *Graduale* or, as it was originally called, *Responsorium graduale. Responsorium* means "reply," and *graduale* refers to the *gradus* or steps leading up to the *ambo,* or chancel, from which the Lector reads. In this type of song the *Psalmista* sang on the steps of the *ambo,* and the people or the choir responded with a sort of refrain. As with the *Introitus,* however, the psalm was shortened to one verse (*versus*). Thus, after a long development that went back to the synagogue worship-service, the Gradual as it can be traced from the time of Gregory I consisted of a very richly ornamented song laid out in essentially a-b-a form: *Responsorium-Versus-Responsorium.*

Another type of song which may be used as an interlude is the *tractus,* or psalm without refrain. *Tractim* in Latin means "in one motion, without a break." It was performed by one or more precentors. Originally it had been coordinated with a second Reading, which was later dropped. Like the *Graduale,* it developed into a richly melismatic form and was accordingly abbreviated to but a few verses.

A third type of interlude-song is the *Alleluia,* which involves richly melismatic jubilation on the final vowel of the word "Alleluia," expressing the inarticulate joy over the Resurrection at Easter. After the precentor has sung this onomatopoetic word without its final flourish, the choir repeats it with the concluding melisma or *jubilus* and develops it into great curves of melody. Then the precentor sings the *versus,* which continues the jubilus melodically, using a text that is Biblical or in the nature of a free prayer. The repetition of the alleluia with jubilus rounds off the song to an a-b-a form. On feast-days and Sundays related to Easter this song has replaced the older *Tractus,* and even in Eastertide itself has replaced the Gradual (except during the octave of Easter, when an older stage in the development is preserved), so that at the present time two alleluias are sung after the *Lectio.* Though these are to be understood as one song with two verses (a-b-a-c-a—the so-called Great Alleluia-song), their unity from the musical point of view is not entirely admissible, as the second *versus* with its alleluia has an entirely different melody, usually in even another mode or ecclesiastical key. At all events, in this instance after the first singing of the alleluia, the repetition after the *versus* is omitted.

Finally, in the *sequence,* which arose in the 10th century, the initial and final sections were sung by the whole choir and the intervening paired lines were sung each by half-choir antiphonally. The Council of Trent reduced the number of sequences to four. A fuller discussion of the *sequence,* however, is more appropriate in connection with the time of its flourishing in the Middle Ages.

Proceeding with the choral songs of the Mass, we come to the opening of the sacrificial part of the service of worship. Here, the *Offertorium* was originally choral psalmody with refrain, or antiphon, for the sacrificial procession of the faithful and for the preparation of the offerings. Soon after its introduction in the 5th century, it developed as a result of the improvisatory technique of ornamentation into richly melismatic solo psalmody with a choral antiphon, which was also richly ornamented. In the course of the Middle Ages, however, as a result of the omission of the sacrificial procession of the faithful, there was increasing neglect of the solo verses. By 1570 only the choral antiphon was left—like a body without a head. The new liturgical regulation recommends its being again supplemented by Psalm verses.

The *Communio,* likewise, was originally choral psalmody with antiphon for the communion procession of the faithful, introduced in the 5th century. Though the simpler choral melodic aspects have been preserved, the Psalm likewise was dropped, with the neglect of frequent communion by the faithful in the Middle Ages. After the communion decretals of Pius X, a development in the direction of restoration ensued, reestablishing the original form: Antiphon-Psalm-Antiphon.

The explanations that have been given for the musical form of the songs in the *Proprium* apply primarily to their settings in Gregorian chant. Since, however, this form is based jointly on the textual content and the liturgical function of the songs of the Proper, a polyphonic setting must also take extensive account of this given form. Polyphonic settings of the Proper—though not so widely known as those of the Ordinary—are quite as numerous, at least until well into the 18th century. Only the practice in church music during the past century or so has neglected the Proper of the Mass. As a result of an increasing tendency, fostered by Pope Pius X, to encourage the people to take a more active part (*actuosa participatio*), the legitimate form of which is the sharing in the Ordinary of the Mass, the way is again prepared for recognition of the fact that the real field for polyphonic church music is the *Proprium Missae*.

A special form in which the Mass is often composed polyphonically is represented by the "Requiem," or Mass for the Dead. It takes its name from the first word of its *Introitus: "Requiem aeternam dona eis, Domine"* (Give them eternal rest, O Lord). The texts peculiar to the Mass for the Dead belong to the group of votive Masses. Here a practice that was sometimes followed in the 16th century has come to prevail generally for other liturgical occasions as well, namely the so-called Plenary Mass. The phrase comes from the Latin *plenarius,* meaning "all-inclusive." In a Plenary Mass the Proper and Ordinary are composed in a cyclic form, arranged according to the succession in the celebration of the Mass.

Still another large segment of the Catholic worship-service is included in the *Officium,* or Prayer of the Hours. Although the Mass, which is celebrated at least once a day in every church, is the core of the Catholic service of worship, the Prayer of the Hours is a cycle of reading and prayer that cannot be omitted in an account of this subject. At the present time it is carried out daily by a deputy for the whole church—corporately in monasteries and individually by priests in silent recitation with their breviaries. It also called the *Officium,* or Office, because it represents an official duty. It consists of the following hours of prayer:

Matins, meaning "dawn." It is also sometimes referred to as the *Mette* or, if earlier, as *Vigilia,* meaning "night-watch." According to the strictness of the order, this is celebrated at night or in the early morning.

Lauds, or morning praise, at sunrise.

Prime, about seven A.M. or—according to the old reckoning—"at the first hour" of the day.

Terce, at the third hour, thus about nine o'clock.

Sext, at the sixth hour, thus about twelve o'clock.

Nones, at the ninth hour, thus about three in the afternoon.

Vespers, or *laudes vespertinae* or *vesperae,* meaning "evening praise," at sundown, about 6 P.M. This is the evening counterpart to the morning celebration of the Mass, the most festive hour of prayer in the *Officium.*

Compline, or *completorium,* meaning "completion of the day's work," before going to sleep, about 8 P.M.

The silent individual recitation is not confined to fixed hours.

Texts from the Office have also been set to music of high quality, both in Gregorian chant and in many other works during the further history of music.

Particularly during the past few centuries certain general musical designations for several types of Masses have been widely used.

The *Missa Solemnis* figures prominently in music of the 18th and 19th centuries. This is a solemn, festive Mass, with strong emphasis on expression through the use of instruments, often involving a symphony orchestra with trumpets and tympani.

The *Missa Brevis,* or "concise" version of the Mass, has figured prominently since the 16th century. The designation *Missa Brevis* carries no implications as to the instrumentation or disposition of the voices.

The *Alternatim-Mass,* approved in 1600, has some portions that are played on the organ, with simultaneous recitation of text, and other portions that are sung by the choir. In the course of the Mass, these portions alternate, the *Credo* being entirely sung.

The *Organ Mass* is a solo organ Mass, widespread in France until well into the 19th century.

The *Missa Concertata,* which came in with Viadana in 1607, marks a stage in the gradual introduction of *concertante* episodes into the traditional form of Classical polyphony. By the middle of the 17th century these elements began to assume greater importance than the more traditional portions in this type of Mass.

The *Cantata Mass,* or *Number Mass,* introduced by the Neapolitan School, is a type in which the music determines the form. The text is organized into thematically self-contained sections like choruses, arias, duets, and trios.

The *Pastoral Mass,* or *Missa Pastorale,* appeared before 1600 but became much more widespread in the 18th century. It is a Mass for Christmastide, utilizing Christmas songs and pastoral melodies.

The *German Catholic Sung Mass* appeared in 1726 as a Mass in one or more voices accompanied by the orchestra. It might be characterized as a free song-cycle.

The *Protestant Mass,* or Partial Mass, includes only the *Kyrie* and *Gloria.*

The *Protestant Song-Mass,* which made its appearance with Michael Praetorius in 1619, is a polyphonic setting of the German version of the Ordinary, also involving congregational songs.

The 17th Century

There were four styles of 17-century Catholic church music:

1. Concert style, or *stile concertato,* which made its appearance in the Venetian School and reached a culminating point with Giovani Gabrieli, who died in 1612. This led to the concertante Mass and motet, ranging in the variety of its resources from the solo to the many-voiced choir, from the simple *basso continuo* accompaniment to the orchestral setting. There is a connection between concert style and expressive style.

2. Operatic style involving arias and recitatives, or *stilo concitato.*

This came into church music from the theater and involved dramatic word-interpretation in the declamation and in the musical structure itself.

3. Roman colossal style.

4. Strictly contrapuntal style, in which the *stile antico* persisted. *Stile antico* and *stile moderno* were united in *stile misto,* or *stylus mixtus,* the "mixed" church style. In it, passages of counterpoint and fugue stand alongside *arioso* portions.

While monody was developing in secular music, there was a parallel development in sacred. Thus the solo motet with *basso continuo* (*Geistliche Konzert*) came into being.

The term *concerto* was first used in 1587 by Andrea Gabrieli. Then it appeared again in Adriano Banchieri's *Concerti ecclesiastici* for eight-voiced double choir (1595). As published, this work is the first modern score with bar lines and an organ part as *basso continuo* for the first choir. The numbers in Lodovico Viadana's *Cento Concerti Ecclesiastici* (Venice 1602) are the first sacred concerti for one, two, three, and four solo voices with figured bass. Viadana's new work inspired quite a following, in somewhat the same way as did Giulio Caccini's *Nuove Musiche* (Florence 1601).

During the first half of the 17th century, Italian and German composers were trying to combine the concertante style with the new expressive style. In Italy, as we have seen, there was Adriano Banchieri (1567–1634), who applied the *concertante* principle to the motet in his double-choired *Concerti Ecclesiastici* (1595). Also there were Alessandro Grandi in Venice (d. 1630); Tarquinio Merula (d. after 1652); Francesco Turini (d. 1656); Giovanni Rovetta, Monteverdi's successor at San Marco in Venice (d. 1668); and Marco da Gagliano in Florence (*ca.* 1575–1642). In Austria there were Johann Stadlmayr (1560–1648), choirmaster in the court of Archduke Maximilian in Innsbruck; Christoph Straus, who was choirmaster of the Viennese court chapel from 1616 to 1620; and Giovanni Valentini, who was court organist in Vienna from 1619 and the teacher of Johann Kaspar Kerll.

Then, during the latter half of the 17th century, Italian composers in particular tried to develop the solo style in the cantata and to achieve expressive *coloratura* and declamatory *parlando.* For purposes of choral declamation they simply used series of chords.

In this development Italian composers took the lead: Bonifazio Graziani (1605–1664), choirmaster in Rome; Francesco Cavalli (1602–1676), leading composer of the Venetian opera school and choirmaster at San Marco in Venice; Maurizio Cazzati (*ca.* 1620–1667), choirmaster in Mantua; Antonio Draghi (1635–1700), who after 1658 held various court positions in Vienna and ultimately was court choirmaster; Agostino Steffano (1654–1728), a leading composer of chamber duets and cantatas; and Claudio Monteverdi.

German composers also participated in this movement, with the following taking a prominent part in the latter half of the 17th century: Johann Heinrich Schmeltzer (*ca.* 1623–1680), who from 1649 held various court positions in Vienna and in 1679 was court choirmaster; Heinrich

Ignaz Franz Biber (1644–1704), who from 1673 was at the court in Salzburg; and Johann Kaspar Kerll (1627–1693), who was a pupil of Giovanni Valentini, Carissimi, and Frescobaldi, later became choirmaster of the Munich court, served from 1677 as court organist in Vienna, and later in his career returned to Munich.

The fact that church music flourished in Vienna during the 17th and 18th centuries was essentially due to the interest of the emperors Ferdinand III, Leopold I, Joseph I, and Karl VI, whose reigns spanned the period from 1637 to 1704. They were themselves notably active as composers.

Italian and South German influences met in Austria. According to Orel, a stylistic transition is provided by the work of a composer who became court choirmaster in Vienna in 1649, Antonio Bertali (1605–1669). He subordinated the role of the concertante instruments, emphasized that of the voices, developed melodic phrases in a song-like manner, and prepared the way for the fugue on the *Amen*.

Guido Adler spoke of a typically Austrian-Baroque stylistic trend and of a Viennese School, to which are also to be reckoned Antonio Draghi (1635–1700) and the choirmaster of the Viennese court along with Fux, Marc Antonio Ziani (1653–1715). Instead of juxtaposing several choirs, these composers used soli and tutti within a single choir, setting off the passages for soli in bold dynamic and contrapuntal contrast with those for tutti. As the solo passages became more and more song-like, elements of coloratura were introduced. These composers, moreover, liked to conclude solos with choruses and to insert solos between choruses by way of contrast. They also used tone-painting. Modulation was effected by typical relationships, such as those of tonic, subdominant or dominant, parallel key, or borrowed dominant.

In composing the movements they developed a certain architectonic uniformity. The *Kyrie* was in three sections: a (*Kyrie*)-b (*Christe*)-a (*Kyrie*). The *Gloria* and *Credo* were subdivided into the separate verses or articles of faith. The *Sanctus* had the form a (*Sanctus*)-b (*Osanna*)-c (*Benedictus*)-b (*Osanna*). The *Agnus Dei* was in three sections, corresponding to the three implorations.

Among these composers in Vienna, a special position was occupied by Johann Joseph Fux, the greatest native composer of the Austrian Baroque. He was born in 1660 in Steiermark. As early as 1696 he was an organist in Vienna, in 1698 he became court composer, in 1711 assistant choirmaster, and in 1715 choirmaster. He died in Vienna in 1741. His works include numerous church compositions, among which the *Missa canonica* (1715) is his major contrapuntal work. He also wrote organ and other keyboard pieces, church sonatas, suites, operas, and a theoretical work on counterpoint, *Gradus ad Parnassum* (1725).

In his church compositions Fux mixed the *a cappella* style with the orchestrally accompanied expressive style. To some extent his works show Neapolitan influences and also to a large extent are decidedly contrapuntal in attitude. The contrapuntal textbook *Gradus ad Parnassum* is a presentation of the Palestrina style from a personal point of view with emphasis on the regulation of time, the establishment of harmonic connections, and the effect on the listener. For some two hundred years it was the basis of instruction in counterpoint and has served as a starting-point for almost all subsequent textbooks on the subject.

In France church music was dominated by declamatory stylization, which tended to establish a balance between aria and recitative. The outstanding composers were Jean-Baptists Lully (1632–1687); Henri Du Mont (1610–1684), of Paris and Maastricht; Pierre Robert (1618–1699); and Michel-Richard Delalande (1657–1726).

In Bohemia, Catholic church music flourished after the restoration of Catholicism in 1621. Four notable composers were the organist Adam Michna z Otradovic (*ca.* 1600–1676) from Jindřichův Hradec, composer of the well-known collections of songs, *Česká mariánská muzika* (Czech Marian Music), *Svatoroční muzika* (Music of the Holy Year), and *Loutna česká* (The Czech Lute); Antonín Planický (1692–1735); the famous composer of organ works Bohuslav Matěj Černohorský (1684–1742), head of an active school of composers that included several remarkable contrapuntalists; and, in Prague and later in Dresden, Jan Dismas Zelenka (1679–1745), who wrote numerous church and instrumental compositions, particularly oratorios. Černohorsky was presumably the teacher of Gluck.

The musical situation in Poland cannot be understood without some awareness of the 17th-century historical background. The country was ruined economically by wars and the growing power of the magnates. Disruption of the Imperial Diet, conspiracies of the old nobility, natural catastrophes, and egoistic interests of foreign kings during what is sometimes referred to as the Saxon period, along with other causes, led to the partition of Poland.

There were, however, many centers of musical culture, and during the 17th century they increased in number. There was the royal chapel, at which the artistic level was high—witness the visits of Luca Marenzio, Annibale Stabile, and Tarquinio Merula. There also were numerous centers of the higher nobility where musical works for the stage were cultivated. Ecclesiastical dignitaries had their chapels, and there were church ensembles and city chapels as well. We now know of some one hundred fifty musical groups active around 1750. With the cosmopolitan orientation of the nobility the Polish repertoire disappeared almost entirely, and what native art there was had to look to church ensembles for any support. Gradually bourgeois culture exerted greater influence on church music, making it more secular and, at the same time, more Polish.

Two trends appeared in church music, one more modern, stressing vocal and instrumental concerts and the Concert Mass, and the other more traditional, emphasizing the *a cappella* style.

Preliminary forms of the vocal and instrumental concert appeared in 1611, in the work of Mikołaj Zieleński, a Polish representative of the Venetian School. Another composer, one of the most notable figures in the Polish Baroque, is Bartłomiej Pękiel, who became choirmaster of the royal chapel in Warsaw in 1649, was later director of the cathedral choir in Cracow, and died in 1670. His works are mainly *a cappella*, including some Masses of great stylistic richness; but he also composed a highly significant work, the only Polish Baroque oratorio we have, *Audite mortales*. Other composers were Marcin Mielczewski (*ca.* 1600–1651), choirmaster of Prince Ferdinand's chapel and Bishop of Płock; Jack Różycki (*ca.* 1640–1707), director of the royal chapel in Warsaw and Dresden; Damian Stachowicz (*ca.* 1658–1699) of the Piarist Order in Łowicz; Stanisław Sylwester Szarzyński (active at the turn of the century) of the Cistercian Order; and Grzegorz Gerwazy Gorczycki (1665–1734), choirmaster at the Cracow cathedral-school.

Among compositions of more traditional trend, settings of the Ordinary of the Mass figure prominently in the work of Mielczewski, Franciszek Gigli-Lilius (*ca.* 1600–1657), Gorczycki, Jan Fabrycy (*ca.* 1615–1655), Andrzej Paszkiewicz (second half of the 17th century), Aleksander Leszczyński (1616–1680), Jan Radomski, in the second half of the 17th century, and I. A. Langrocki, at the turn of the century. There were also some Italian composers influential in Poland, such as Pacelli, Anerio, and Scacchi, as well as some anonymous composers. As has been mentioned, Bartlomiej Pękiel wrote some significant works in rather a traditional style, notably the *Missa pulcherrima*.

Among the more conservative works of the time, there are motets, usually having to do with the Blessed Virgin or the Passion. Hymns appeared in the cycle of Jacek Różycki. Notable among the Psalms is the *Benedictio mensae* (1611) by Wojciech Dębolęcki (1585–6 to 1645–7), the first Polish composer to use the *basso continuo* in his *Completorium* (Venice 1618). In the canon collection *Da pacem Domine* (1634) by Andrzej Chyliński there is great contrapuntal art, based on one theme, as in the *Art of the Fugue*.

In the Americas during the 17th century there was sharp juxtaposition of Roman Catholic church music and long-established American Indian ritual music in South America. At Cuzco in 1610, for example, thirty thousand Indians held a twenty-five-day festival celebrating the beatification of St. Ignatius Loyola in ceremonies including mock battles, acclamations, and hymns. Also at Cuzco, in 1613, a 720 page *Ritual* was printed, including a four-voiced *a cappella* composition with text in the Indians' language, "composed to be sung in processions as they enter their churches on Lady-Days." The music has periods of uneven length, and there are occasional syncopations. At Lima Cathedral a succession of Spaniards served as choirmaster, and some of their religious compositions have survived, notably those of Tomás de Torrejón (1644–after 1719) and Juan de Araujo (*ca.* 1646–1714).

In Mexico a number of religious *villancicos* were composed, the texts of some being by a famous Mexican poet of the period, Sister Juana Iñes de la Cruz. These songs were issued in fifteen collections between 1677 and 1691. Other composers were born in Europe but early came to Mexico and are represented by extant works in Mexico archives. These composers include Pedro Bermúdez (fl. 1605), Francisco López y Capilla (fl. 1645), Juan de Padilla (fl. 1650), and Antonio de Salazar (fl. 1690). The practice of Roman Catholic service music was extended to New Mexico by the San Felipe Mission and was spread by the French along the St. Lawrence and Great Lakes. Notably, Fr. Louis André employed music as a means of proselytizing, by way of the children, at Green Bay, Wisconsin, in the 1670's. By the end of the century Fr. Sebastian Hale had a vested choir of forty young Indians in Maine.

The 18th Century

The style of the Neapolitan School widely influenced Catholic church music in the 18th century. Composers of this group further introduced self-contained formal parts into the composition of the Mass. As a result, the Mass took on the character of a *Cantata Mass*, with independent numbers such as choruses, recitatives, arias, and duets, and with emotionally toned contrasts in the music.

Then, especially in the latter half of the 18th century, composers began to unify the movements and link them together according to the basic principles of musical form and architectonics. They stressed the metrical aspects of the music and often repeated words of the text. Thus they produced the typical "Number Mass," in which they developed individual sections of text symphonically as self-contained musical numbers. W. A. Mozart, for example, treated individual movements in free rondo form.

This increase in subjectivity, expressed in the personal attitude towards prayer in contrast to its being conceived of liturgically, is traceable to the influence of opera. The liturgical texts were set with an eye to the emotional effect. The melodic aspects were the same as in secular works. Harmonically, the major-minor orientation came to the fore. Also, the operatic or symphonic orchestra of the time with the strings arranged in choirs and the soloistic wind instruments entered into church music.

The composers most influential in the new development were the Italians Alessandro Scarlatti (1660–1725), Leonardo Vinci (1690–1730), Leonardo Leo (1694–1744), Francesco Durante (1684–1755), Geminiano Giacomelli (1686–1743), and Giovanni Battista Pergolesi (1710–1736).

At the same time as the Neapolitans were developing a more subjective church style, other composers were maintaining the *stile antico,* or strict *a cappella* style. Also the Neapolitan composers themselves wrote some Masses in strict style, though they often showed some traces of influence peculiar to the time. But the *stile antico* remained alive in the 18th century consciousness as the official church style, particularly for *a cappella* Masses performed in Advent and Lent.

Special significance is to be attached to the conservative trend in Northern Italy. It was represented here by a number of composers, one of whom was Padre Martini (1706–1784) in Bologna. As music historian and theoretician he was perhaps the most learned scholar of the time. He wrote a book of contrapuntal theory, *Saggio di Contrapunto* (1774), and tried in his compositions to unite the strictness of the older type of writing with the new expressiveness. Bologna was the meeting-place of the *Accademia Filarmonica,* founded in 1666, to which members were admitted only after having passed examinations in strict counterpoint. In 1770 Mozart, at the age of fourteen, was admitted to the Academy.

In Rome the colossal style was further cultivated during the 18th century. Attempts were made to combine *a cappella* style, polychorality, and *stile moderno.*

Along with Vienna, Dresden was the main center of Catholic church music of the Neapolitan trend in Germany. The direct influence of Naples was exerted by the activities of the Italian Antonio Lotti (1667–1740) and Giovanni Alberto Ristori (1692–1753). The main connection with Italy, however, was established by Johann Adolf Hasse (1699–1783), who wrote an extensive body of church music in the Neapolitan style. Composers attached to the Dresden court chapel included Johann Christoph Schmidt (d. 1728), Johann David Heinichen (1683–1729), Johann Zelenka (1679–1745), Johann Georg Schürer (*ca.* 1720–1786), Johann Gottlieb Naumann (1741–1801), and Franz Seydelmann (1748–1805).

Mannheim was also a source of influence on church music. The orchestral idiom developed there passed into the symphonic treatment of sacred composition. Of the Mannheim composers, particularly Franz Xaver Richter (1709–1789) and Ignaz Holzbauer (1711–1783) wrote church music. Also connected with the Mannheim circle was Abt Vogler (1749–1814), a personality who exerted considerable influence through his compositions, theoretical writings, and pedagogical activity. Among his pupils were Carl Maria von Weber and Giacomo Meyerbeer.

In Vienna a fusion of the Venetian with the Neapolitan style was achieved by Antonio Caldara (*ca.* 1670–1736), who in 1716 became assistant choirmaster in the Viennese chapel. He juxtaposed choral and soloistic sections in a typical Cantata Mass with self-contained Neapolitan arias, in which he often also used an instrument along with the voice in concertante fashion. In the choral portions, he still kept the soli formally subordinated to the choruses and alternated homophonic and more or less strict polyphonic sections. At the end of the *Gloria* at the words *"Cum sancto Spiritu"* and in the *Credo* at *"Et vitam venturi"* he normally introduced a fugue.

The Viennese tradition of the 17th century was further maintained in the 18th century by two Austrians who were choirmasters at St. Stephan's in Vienna, Georg Reutter (1656–1738) and his son, a pupil of Caldara, Johann Georg Reutter (1708–1772) as well as by a pupil of Fux, Georg Christoph Wagenseil (1715–1777), who became court composer in 1739. Thus the ground was laid for the composers of the Viennese Classical period.

In Vienna at this time a distinction was sharply made between the *Missa Solemnis,* or festive Mass, and the *Missa Brevis,* or short Mass, consisting of only the *Kyrie, Gloria,* and *Credo.* The *Missa Solemnis* was for special occasions; the *Missa Brevis,* for ordinary Sundays. In the *Missa Solemnis* the five sections of the Ordinary were divided into more or less numerous and independent choral movements and arioso solo songs as in a cantata, which were given quite a broad treatment with rich instrumentation. Although in 1784 Joseph II issued decrees that the worship service should be simplified and instrumental music should be banned, these provisions were removed after his death.

Joseph Haydn's and Wolfgang Amadeus Mozart's works of church music also belong in the circle of the Viennese tradition. Although a fuller consideration of their and some of their successors' careers will be given in connection with the secular forms of music in which they excelled, some details specifically relating to their church music will be included here.

Joseph Haydn, born in 1732 in Rohrau in Lower Austria, early sang as solo soprano at St. Stephan's Cathedral under Johann Georg Reutter the Younger, but after change of voice in 1749 was without regular employment. Eventually, however, he became private conductor to Prince Esterházy in Eisenstadt in the 1760's, and from then until he was pensioned in 1790 he wrote the majority of the works that made him famous throughout Europe. He became a close friend of Mozart in 1781. On two occasions during the 1790's he made trips to London, but the latter years of his life were spent primarily in Vienna, where he died in 1809.

Haydn's works of church music include twelve Masses, which diverge sharply from each other in character and type. His first Mass came into existence around 1753. The only Cantata Mass that he wrote was the *Cecilia Mass* (1782), which is remarkable for its length, use of coloratura, and introduction of recitative with ensuing aria. There occurred a fourteen-year hiatus between 1782 and 1796 in his composing of Masses, no doubt attributable to the Josephian era. After 1796 he wrote six big festive Masses: the *"Holy"* Mass (1796), the *"Kettledrum"* Mass, *Lord Nelson Mass* (1798), *Theresa Mass* (1799), *Creation Mass* (1801), and *Harmony Mass* (1802). All six utilize the Classical symphony orchestra, employ significant contrapuntal work, and involve effective juxtaposition of soli and chorus. These are compositions of a life-affirming character and manifest the influence of Austrian folk-music. In addition to the Masses he also wrote some other church music, including two *Te Deums*, Offertories, a *Stabat Mater* (1773), and a Requiem.

Wolfgang Amadeus Mozart was born in 1756 in Salzburg, son of the assistant conductor and court composer Leopold Mozart. After appearances and tours as a child prodigy and artist during the 1760's and 1770's, he entered the service of the Archibishop of Salzburg and of Joseph II, spending the last decade of his life mostly in Vienna, where he died in 1791.

In all, he wrote fifteen Masses, a Requiem (which he left unfinished), Offertories, and numerous individual compositions of sacred choral music. During his Viennese period after 1782, he composed the unfinished *Mass in C-minor,* the *Ave Verum,* and the *Requiem.* His principal activity in the field of church music occurred during his services at Salzburg. He thus experienced, at various times, influences from the Viennese and Salzburg traditions, from Hasse and the Neapolitans, and occasionally from the *stile antico* through his contacts with Padre Martini. Mozart's first complete Mass (K. V. 139) was written in 1768. The Mass K. V. 167 introduced a free rondo form in the *Credo,* which had accordingly been composed from a purely musical point of view. The historical significance of Mozart's Masses from this period is thus largely due to the novelty of this formal approach. The works of the Viennese years after 1782, however, represented an independent fusion of influences from Bach and Handel, particularly in the *torso* of the *C-minor Mass,* K. V. 417a,

1782–3, and in the *Requiem*. They were a stylistic synthesis of Classicism and Baroque. The *Requiem*, written by Mozart up to the *"Lacrimosa,"* was completed by his pupil Franz Xaver Süssmayer; many details in this matter are still not entirely clear.

Composers in Austria at the Time of Haydn and Mozart

Church musicians in Salzburg included Johann Ernst Eberlin (1702–1762), Anton Cajetan Adlgasser (1728–1777), and Leopold Mozart (1719–1787). Particular significance within the framework of practical Church music can be ascribed to Michael Haydn (1737–1805). Going back to Gregorian chant, he harmonized it contrapuntally in chordal setting.

Church musicians in Vienna included Florian Gassmann (1729–1774), successor to J. G. Reutter as conductor at the court, and Johann Georg Albrechtsberger (1736–1809), court organist, from 1793 choirmaster at St. Stephan's cathedral, significant as a theoretician and author of the *Gründliche Anweisung zur Komposition* (1790) and as teacher of Beethoven.

In Poland, up to the middle of the 18th century, the Neapolitan style predominated. Then gradually there was a "secularization" of religious composition. National elements—emphasizing the Polish aspects of music, particularly in the so-called Polish Masses—were introduced. This tendency had appeared as early as the end of the 17th century in the dioceses of Chymno and Silesia, for example in the Lenten Mass *Stworzycielu wszechmogący*, in Christmas songs, and in the *Planctus*, or fragments of the Passion. Among the liturgical forms, the disappearing vocal concert was replaced particularly by Marian-oriented litanies, Psalms, and *Magnificats*. The Mass enjoyed a flowering-period in the latter half of the 18th century.

In America during the 18th century, opera began to compete with the church service for the focal point of the composer's attention in the older centers of Latin American development. The influential church composer Tomás de Torrejón in Lima wrote a musical score (performed and printed in 1710) for Calderón's *La púrpura de la rosa*. The first native choirmaster at the Mexico City cathedral, Manuel Zumaya (fl. 1720), also wrote music for a libretto translated from a Neopolitan opera. An Italian, Ignacio Jerusalem, became choirmaster in Mexico City in 1764, having begun his career there as an opera conductor.

As the older centers in New Spain were taking the path of Western European music, some of the newer centers were less advanced along it. Cuba (with Esteban Salas) and Venezuela (with José Lamas and Cayetano Carreño) were at the height of their development of religious composition. Other areas were just beginning: in 1769 the California Franciscan missions were started, with much attention to plainsong, *alabados*, and native orchestras. In 1813 Fr. Narciso Durán (1776–1846) at the San José Mission brought out a book of chants harmonized in parts.

Roman Catholic music was in use at St. Mary's Church in Philadelphia, where on July 4, 1779, a festival *Te Deum* for choir with organ and other instrumental accompaniment was sung at a service attended by the President and members of Congress in commemoration of the

Declaration of Independence. A volume of *Litanies, Vespers, Hymns, and Anthems as they are sung in the Catholic Church* was published at Philadelphia in 1787, consisting of two-part music, some of it adapted from secular works.

The 19th Century

The church music of Beethoven and Schubert, like that of Haydn and Mozart, is also linked with the Viennese tradition.

Ludwig van Beethoven was born in 1770 in Bonn, son of a tenor in the Electoral Chapel. At first he was a pupil of his father, who wished to make a child prodigy of him. In 1787 Beethoven went to Vienna, hoping to become Mozart's pupil; in 1792 he finally moved to Vienna, where, except for brief trips, he spent the rest of his life. He was Haydn's pupil in 1793, also studying with other musicians there. At first he appeared in Vienna mainly as a pianist, but, partly as a result of increasing deafness, turned more to composing. In 1809 a group of noblemen established an income for him. Highly individualistic, he was the first musician of modern history to free himself from any relationship of servility toward prince or church. He died in Vienna, in 1827.

His works of church music include his *Mass in C, op. 86* (1807) and his *Missa Solemnis in D, op. 123* (1823). Both of these Masses were composed in accordance with a definite liturgical practice. But they transgressed liturgical bounds in their handling of the music and in their subjective confessional character. Beethoven himself, in a letter to the publisher, Breitkopf and Härtel, viewed the possibility of concert performance and translation into German. Stylistically, his *C-major Mass* related to Hayden's Masses. Distinctive stylistic features of the *Missa Solemnis,* written during his third creative period, include the extension of the fugues, the predominance of the choral sections, the unification of the sonorous ensemble (chorus, soli, and orchestra) in a way unlike the contrasting of timbres characteristic of an earlier era, the lengthening and enlargement of the periods, the emotional effect of the idiom, and the highly subjective and confession-like interpretation of the text.

Franz Schubert was born in 1797 in Lichtenthal, near Vienna, the son of a teacher. Trained as a boy soprano at the Vienna court chapel, he eventually became a free-lance composer in Vienna. In 1825 and 1827 he applied unsuccessfully for the position of vice-choirmaster, and in the latter year a concert of his works was arranged—the only public concert of his works during his lifetime. He died in Vienna in 1828.

His works of church music include six Masses, a German Mass, and smaller church works. These Masses, as Orel observed, "grew out of the general, popular feeling of the Viennese soil" and were in significant ways quite opposite to Beethoven's Masses. They are distinguished throughout by characteristically Schubertian melodic feeling. His *Mass in A* (1819–22) and *Mass in E* (1828) are outstanding. They are in the nature of festive Masses. In its particular melodic and harmonic qualities Schubert's church music especially points toward the future.

Considering the situation in church music in Vienna as a whole, we might observe that Beethoven and Schubert were in some ways isolated from their surroundings. Church music of a practical nature was being written by many of their contemporaries, including Antonio Salieri (1750–1825), Abt Maximilian Stadler (1748–1833), Abt Vogler (1749–1814), and Simon Sechter (1788–1867). Abt Vogler expressed the Christmas mood in his "Pastoral Masses." Sechter is better known as a theoretician, famous for his three-volume *Grundsätze der musikalischen Komposition* (1853–4) and for his having been Bruckner's teacher.

Munich during the 19th century was a notable center of Catholic church music, in which a conservative tradition led from Peter Winter (1754–1825) and Kaspar Ett (1788–1847), by way of Franz Lachner (1803–1890), to Josef Rheinberger (1839–1901).

In France, the most significant composer during the era of Beethoven was the Italian Luigi Cherubini (1760–1842). His numerous works of church music include Masses and two Requiems and are distinguished by high regard for the liturgy, mastery of *a cappella* style and full-sounding handling of the singing voices and the orchestra. Of native Frenchmen, the outstanding composer was Hector Berlioz (1803–1869). He went far beyond the scope of the liturgy in his *Requiem*, performed in 1837 at the cathedral of the Invalides in Paris in celebration of the capture of Constantine and in memory of the French soldiers who had fallen in battle. In the *"Tuba mirum"* he used five orchestras and eight pairs of kettledrums.

The Neo-French School tended to move in a Classicist direction. Its soft melodic aspects, according to Fellerer, "often seriously transgressed the limits of sentimental expression." Composers of this group concentrated on rather small artistic forms for practical use. Among representatives of this trend were Charles Gounod (1818–1893), Ambroise Thomas (1811–1896), and César Franck (1822–1890). Franck's compositions specifically for the church service are much less significant than his oratorios and organ music. In 1894 the *Schola Cantorum* was founded in Paris and became the center of the French church-music movement that had developed from this tradition.

In Italy, the emotionally effective dramatic features in the character of the music and the treatment of the orchestra in the work of Simon Mayr (1763–1845) exerted significant influence on church music. Compositions by Gaetano Donizetti (1797–1848) and Giocchino Rossini (1792–1868) contain dramatic and expressive soli and work with large choral and orchestral effects. Rossini's *Stabat Mater* is particularly significant. Far superior in artistic format is the *Requiem* of Giuseppe Verdi (1813–1901), written in memory of the poet Alessandro Manzoni, who died in 1873. This composition of Verdi's reaches out far beyond the liturgy and today is almost exclusively heard only in the concert hall. In all of its parts it is of remarkable beauty, of great expressive power in its melodic aspects, and harmoniously balanced in form but primarily dramatic in conception.

During the 19th century Italy experienced a reform movement comparable to Caecilianism in Germany, with emphasis on *a cappella* art. Giuseppe Baini (1775–1884) laid the foundations for Palestrina research.

Alongside Beethoven and Schubert, only two further 19th-century composers of more than passing significance contributed to Catholic church music, Franz Liszt and Anton Bruckner.

Franz Liszt was born in 1811 in Raidig, Hungary, of German ancestry. Trained as a child prodigy in Vienna, he later moved to Paris, where he came under the influence of the Romantic Movement in literature and was associated with Chopin and Berlioz. In 1848 he became master of the court chapel in Weimar and, as a leader in the Neo-German School, wrote his first orchestral works and took a stand for the new music of his day. In 1865 he took minor holy orders in Rome, was much of the time on tour, and moved between Rome, Weimar, and Budapest. He died in 1886, in Bayreuth.

His works of church music include the *Gran Festival Mass* (1858), for the dedication of the basilica at Gran; the *Coronation Mass* (1867), for the crowning of Emperor Franz Joseph I as King of Hungary; the *Mass* for men's choir (1848, rev. 1869); the *Missa Choralis* (1865); the *Requiem* (1867–8); and numerous smaller church choruses.

Both festival Masses were written in the neo-Romantic spirit and are characterized by programmatic elements, brilliant effects, and dramatic and theatrical enhancement of the text by the music. In the *Gran Festival Mass* he used not only Gregorian elements but also leitmotifs to unify the movements thematically and symbolically. Inspired by the *Gran Festival Mass*, the Swedish composer August Södermann (1832–1876) wrote the only important contribution from Scandinavian countries to 19th-century Catholic church music in his *Katolsk Messa* (1875). In the *Mass* for men's choir, the *Missa Choralis*, and the *Requiem*, Liszt held more closely to the liturgy than he had done in his previous Masses, and he strove for simplicity by using and imitating melodies from the Chant. Thus his efforts here tended in the direction of the reforms advocated by Proske, Witt, and other members of the Caecilian movement.

Anton Bruckner was born in 1824 in Ansfelden, in Upper Austria, and early served as a choirboy in St. Florian's Seminary, becoming eventually a teacher and cathedral organist there. In 1865 he became cathedral organist in Linz, in 1868 teacher at the Vienna Conservatory, and in 1875 lecturer on music theory at the University of Vienna. He died in Vienna, in 1896. Recognition of his work, however, did not become very widespread until a quarter-century after his death.

His works of church music include the *Mass in D Minor* (1864, revised in 1876), *Mass in E Minor* (1st version 1866, 2nd version 1882), *Mass in F Minor* (1867–8, revised in 1876 and 1890); and the *Te Deum* (1881, revised 1882–4). The Masses which Bruckner composed for liturgical purposes are Orchestral Masses, involving a full symphony orchestra. The only exception is the *Mass in E Minor,* which he wrote for eight-voiced choir with wind accompaniment. The style is quite symphonic; according to Orel, Bruckner was the creator of the "Mass in modern symphonic style." He succeeded in achieving a liturgical type of expression, distinctive of church music, on the basis of the symphonic development of the 19th century. The music, distinguished by a lofty ecclesiastical spirit, possesses the same stylistic elements as the Bruckner symphonies:

broad melodic lines, motivic development and use of sequence, double thematicism with individualized treatment of the accompaniment, and expansion of the tonality, particularly through harmonic relationships involving the interval of the third. Fugues appear in traditional places and are contrapuntally significant.

The most important Polish composer to write Masses was Józef Elsner (1766–1854). He composed twenty-two Latin Masses and nine Polish Masses as a cycle of songs on a Polish text, as well as numerous other works of church music. Thus he perpetuated the traditions that had been begun by composers in Mannheim and Vienna, stimulated by influences from Naples. Similar characteristics are shown by the church works of Karol Kurpiński (1785–1857) and of Stanisław Moniuszko (1819–1872), whose compositions include seven Latin and Polish Masses, of individual style, that carry on traditions of late Viennese Classicism.

The major representatives of Caecilianism were Józef Surzyński (1851–1919) and Mieczysław Surzyński (1866–1924). Affiliated with the Regensburg School, the former did research in the history of Polish music, founded the publication *Monumenta Musicae Sacrae in Polonia,* and was highly regarded both as teacher and composer.

There was also, however, some 19th-century work in Poland that was unaffected by the Caecilian movement, notably compositions by Gustaw Roguski (1839–1921), Władysław Zeleński (1837–1921), Mieczysław Sołtys (1863–1929), and Piotr Maszyński (1855–1934).

In Latin America the theater and the piano dominated the musical scene during the 19th century, and instead of a fruitful union of Spanish and Indian sacred music there ensued a denaturing of the sacred by the secular, principally Italian opera. Toward the end of the century, however, this trend was counteracted by Caecilian influences in the work of the Ratisbon-trained Mexican José J. Vlázques, organist at the Shrine of the Virgin of Guadalupe and director of the Querétaro School of Sacred Music.

In the United States, Catholic service-music continued to be written, but as a comparatively minor part of the composition during the period. Bishop John Cheverus published a collection of hymns and anthems (1800) and a manual (1830) that represented the musical usage among Roman Catholics in Boston. Benjamin Carr (1768–1831), who came from England in 1793, published the volume *Masses, Vespers, and Litanies* (Philadelphia 1805), including a Mass and a *Te Deum* of his own composition; but his religious compositions were only a part of his extensive musical activity, which included journalism, opera, concertizing as pianist and singer, and choral conducting. Also, as but part of extensive and varied activity, John Knowles Paine (1839–1906) wrote a Mass, which he conducted at the Singakademie in Berlin (1868); and the earliest important work of Mrs. H. H. A. Beach (1867–1944) was a Mass for soli, chorus, orchestra, and organ, first performed by the Handel and Haydn Society in Boston in 1892.

Toward the end of the century the Caecilian movement exerted an especially strong influence in the United States through Catholic church musicians from the German-speaking area who came to the New World, particularly the Swiss John B. Singenberger (1848–1934), composer of fourteen Masses and other religious works. Msgr. Henry Tappert (1855–1929), Ludwig Bonvin (1850–1939), and Hubert Gruender (1870–1940) were active. American-born Sr. Mary Cherubim, head of the Alverno College of Music in Milwaukee, composed and published two Masses and sixteen motets.

The Movement to Reform Catholic Church Music in Germany

The Catholic church music reform movement in Germany was carried on by the clergy. It became influential around the middle of the 19th century, focusing on the revival of 16th-century sacred *a cappella* music, Caecilianism, and musicological research into choral literature.

The Heidelberg lawyer F. J. Thibaut (1774–1840) prepared the way for the revival of 16th-century *a capella* music with his essay *Über Reinheit der Tonkunst* (*On Purity in Music*), which appeared anonymously in 1825 and was reprinted eight times by 1907. For many years he had privately assembled a group of amateurs in Heidelberg to sing Handel oratorios and Palestrina works. In his essay he made some quite practical and perceptive recommendations, which continued to have their effect for almost a century.

More methodical moves toward reform appeared by mid-century, as Regensburg became the center of a movement introduced by Karl Proske (1794–1861) with his edition of *Musica Divina*, a collection of sacred works of the Palestrina period. The instigator of these ideas was Franz X. Witt (1834–1888), who in 1868 founded the *Allgemeiner deutsche Caecilienverein* for the improvement of Catholic church music in Germany. The musicological leader of the movement, Franz X. Haberl (1840–1910), was the editor of the collected edition of Palestrina. In the Caecilia Society there developed two extreme tendencies, one of which followed strictly the 16th-century ideal while the other showed itself open to current influences, such as chromaticism and the use of leitmotifs. The latter movement, New Caecilianism, promptly made contact with 19th-century music. Many works of church music written during the 19th and 20th centuries were influenced by Caecilianism, but their significance did not extend much further than carrying out the specific aims of the movement itself.

The 20th Century

During the 20th century various Papal pronouncements have established the position taken by Rome on questions of church music. Pope Pius X's *Motu propio* of 1903 established it along definitive lines. Further aspects were dealt with in Pope Pius XI's *Constitutio Apostolica* of 1928 and Pope Pius XII's *Liturgical Encyclical* of 1947 and circular letter *Musicae Sacrae Disciplina* (On Church Music) of 1955.

In Germany Catholic church music of the present day is characterized by:

1. the choral movement, which is particularly promoted in the abbeys of Maria Laach and Beuron;

2. the popular choral movement, which strives to encourage the active participation of the people in the liturgical worship-service and is particularly supported by the Gerleve and Grüssau abbeys and by the Youth Movement; and
3. newly created works in the spirit of contemporary music, with the main emphasis on the art of vocal composition through expressive line.

Among the leaders have been Joseph Haas (1879–1960) and Heinrich Lemacher (b. 1891), both of whom—the former in Munich, the latter in Cologne—have trained a great many pupils. Haas, a pupil of Reger's, wrote *"Eine deutsche Singmesse"* after Angelus Silesius *a cappella*, *"Deutsche Vesper,"* several Masses, including the *Speyer Cathedral Festival Mass*, the Christmas-song play *"Christnacht,"* a folk-oratorio on St. Elisabeth, and a *Te Deum* (op. 100).

Further contemporary Catholic church-composers include:

Germany: Joseph Ahrens (b. 1904), Kurt Doebler (b. 1896), Otto Jochum (b. 1898), Joseph Lechthaler (b. 1891), Franz Philipp (b. 1890), Gottfried Rüdinger (1886–1946), Kaspar Rosseling (1894–1960), Herman Schroeder (b. 1904), Otto Siegl (b. 1896), Gerhard Strecke (b. 1890), and Heinrich Weber (b. 1901).

Austria: Joseph Messner (b. 1893), Karl Koch (b. 1887), Karl Walter (b. 1892), Ferdinand Andergassen (b. 1892), Ernst Tittel (b. 1910), Anton Heiller (b. 1923), Hermann Kronsteiner (b. 1914), Joseph Kronsteiner (b. 1910), and Hans Bärenfeind (b. 1908).

Switzerland: Paul Hübner (b. 1918), Oswald Jaeggi (b. 1913), and Albert Jenny (b. 1912).

Holland: Marinus de Jong (b. 1891), Jan Mul (b. 1911), Jan Strategier (b. 1911), and Jaap Vranken (b. 1923).

Belgium: Floor Peeters (b. 1903).

Denmark: Bernhard Lewkovitch (b. 1927).

Poland: Karol Szymanowski (1882–1937), with his *Stabat Mater* (1929), *Veni Creator* (1929), Fragment of a "Litany to the Blessed Virgin" (1933), and numerous solo songs; also Witold Maliszewski (1873–1939), Henryk Opieński (1870–1942), Wacław Gieburowski (1877–1945), Bolesław Wallek-Walewski (1885–1944), Feliks Nowowiejski (1877–1946), Jan Adam Maklakiewicz (1899–1945), and Krzysztof Penderecki (b. 1933), *"Passio et mors Domini nostri Jesu Christi Secundum Lucam."*

United States: Nicola A. Montani (1880–1948), J. Alfred Schehl (1882–1959), Pietro Yon (1886–1943), R. K. Biggs (b. 1886), Joseph J. McGrath (b. 1899), Carlo Rossini (b. 1890), and J. Vincent Higginson (b. 1896).

Several significant composers of the 20th century have shown themselves receptive to religious motifs and liturgical tasks, sometimes treating themes of a spiritual character, whether from denominational commitment or their general approach to life. Arnold Schönberg (1874–1951), Paul Hindemith (1895–1963), and Willy Burkhard (1900–1955) have appeared from the German-speaking area with this particular emphasis at various times. Darius Milhaud (b. 1892), Arthur Honegger (1892–

1955), Igor Stravinsky (1882–1971)—whose works include a Mass (1948) —and Oliver Messiaen (b. 1908) have appeared from the French-speaking area. Similarly, there have been Ildebrando Pizzetti (b. 1880), Giorgio Federico Ghedini (b. 1892), Ettore Desderi (b. 1892), and Luigi Dallapiccola (b. 1904) in Italy, and Benjamin Britten (b. 1913) in England. Among composers in the United States who have written Masses are Roger Sessions (b. 1896), Virgil Thomson (b. 1896), Paul Creston (b. 1906), Vincent Persichetti (b. 1915), Lou Harrison (b. 1917), Leonard Bernstein (b. 1918), Louis Mennini (b. 1920), and Daniel Pinkham (b. 1923).

Monophonic and Polyphonic Catholic Passions

Music relating to the Passion—that is, the suffering of Jesus as presented in the four Gospels—belongs, in a way, to the history of the oratorio. Although the oratorio requires separate consideration, the Passion will be dealt with here because of the distinctness of the material and its special relationship to the music of worship.

The monophonic Latin Passion is the reading of the account of the Passion during Holy Week in the Gregorian lesson-tones. It is sung on four days of this week: Palm Sunday (St. Matthew 26 and 27), Tuesday (St. Mark 14 and 15), Wednesday (St. Luke 22 and 23), and Good Friday (St. John 18 and 19). In Gospel manuscripts as early as the 9th century there are indications of various pitches and manners of delivery for the individual roles of the Evangelist, the main personages, and the *turba*, or response of the crowd. At first these details were presented in the manuscripts by letters, such as *c*, meaning *celeriter*, "fast," added to the Evangelist's part. From the very beginning, different pitch levels were assigned to the three main roles of the Evangelist, Christ, and the *turba*, as well as to the parts of other individual personages. This arrangement was confirmed later as the contours of the melodies were suggested by neumes. The first evidence of the allotment of parts to several singers is contained in an English manuscript of the 13th century.

Not until the middle of the 15th century do polyphonically indicated *turbae*-choruses appear, but it seems natural to assume that they were improvised earlier. Initial stages of further development are shown in a number of manuscripts. In a document from the parish church at Füssen around 1450 there are simultaneous *turbae*-recitatives on three steps of the Passion tone at a distance of a fifth and a fourth. This type of procedure was further developed by Johann Walter and by composers who used the *falsobordone* style of the Italian Passions. In the British Museum MS. Egerton 3307 of around 1450, moreover, the *turbae* and the soliloquists are given in three-voiced English descant style. This procedure was to be further devleoped by R. Davey and in the Modena Passions. In the Modena MS. Est. M. 1. 12, around 1480, there are polyphonic *turbae* in Continental *fauxbourdon* style, with the cantus firmus in the upper voice. Finally, in the Passion-harmony or setting of the accounts of the same incidents in all the Gospels that was earlier ascribed to

Obrecht but that is now regarded as being by Longaval, written shortly after 1500, we find the through-composed, liturgical Passion-tone always in one of the four voices and the technique in general that of Italian *falsobordone* with motet-like liberties. This method of setting the Passion was to be further developed in the German Protestant Passions.

In the 16th and early 17th centuries in Upper Italy there were many Responsorial Passions, in which polyphony might be used for only the *turbae,* or for the *turbae* and the soliloquists, or for fundamentally all passages of direct discourse, even those of Christ. The last type came to be cultivated with particular frequency. The earliest known works, written before 1541, were by Giovanni de Albertis, whose three Passions perhaps Antonio Scandello brought to Germany. The through-composed type of Passion seldom appeared in Italy, but it did appear there in works by Vincentino Ruffo, Jan Nasco, and Cipriano de Rore.

On German soil, settings of the Passion extensively related to the Italian style did not appear until after 1550, in works including four Responsorial Passions by Orlandus Lassus. Under Lassus' influence, J. Reiner wrote three Passions. For the court chapel in Prague, in accordance with Antoine Longaval's Passion-harmony, Jacobus Gallus wrote three Passions and Jakob Regnart one. In England around 1490 R. Davey wrote a responsorial *St. Matthew Passion.*

Connected with the execution of the Council of Trent's reforms, there was a decline in the artistic value of polyphonic liturgical responsorial settings of the Passion. In the Catholic worship-service the place of the Oratorio-like Passion was quite subordinate. On the other hand, there have been many Catholic oratorios of the Passion from the beginning of the 17th century to the present, among others the Sepulchre Oratorios in Vienna, numerous settings of the Passion poem *La Passione di Jesu Christo* by Metastasio, and works by Ernst Eberlin, *Der blutschwitzende Jesu* (The Bloody Sweat of Jesus), Joseph Haydn's *Die sieben Worte des Erlösers am Kreuz* (The Seven Words of the Redeemer on the Cross), Ludwig van Beethoven's *Christus am Oelberg* (Christ on the Mount of Olives), Franz Liszt's *Christus,* Charles Gounod's *La Rédemption,* and Lorenzo Perosi's *La Passione di Christo secondo* S. Marco.

By way of summary of this extensive development, it might be noted that Passions have been variously classified. According to one somewhat older system there are three main types—the choral and dramatic, the motet or figural, and the oratorio Passion. According to a more recent and thorough classification, however, there are five principal types:

1. The Responsorial Passion History, in which only the *turbae* are polyphonic and in which the Passion tone is used as the cantus firmus. Composers from Johann Walter to Orlando di Lasso—in his *St. Mark* and *St. Luke Passions*—have composed works of this type. Also of this same type is the Responsorial Passion. Here, in addition to the *turbae,* some of the soliloquies, and occasionally also those of Jesus, are polyphonic. The Passion tone, however, is not so strictly maintained. Meiland, Scandello, and Gesius—in his *St. John Passion*—have written such works.

2. The Through-Composed Passion History, in which the Evangelist's report is also polyphonic and the Passion tone is used as cantus firmus.

Longaval, Resinarius, and Galliculus have written Through-Composed Passion Histories. As with the Responsorial Passion, moreover, there is a secondary type, the Through-Composed Passion, that also belongs in this category. In it the adherence to the Passion tone is somewhat relaxed and the composition is much more declamatory. Cipriano de Rore, Jan Nasco, and Daser wrote Through-Composed Responsorial Passions. In the Through-Composed Passion the composer may use as his text the complete version of a particular Evangelist or the shortened version of a Gospel account of the Passion. Still a third possibility is that he may take his text from the Passion-harmony, or *Summa Passionis*, as a résumé of the Biblical passages in all four Gospels. Though Protestant composers resorted more to the Passion harmony, particularly in the Seven Last Words of Christ on the Cross, three Catholic composers—Longaval, Gallus, and Regnart—used it in their Passions.

3. The Motet-like Passion, which is polyphonic throughout and is a free transcription, with elements in the setting such as are found in the motet. This type is exemplified by works of Gallus, Lechner, and Demantius.

4. The Oratorio-like Passion, in which monodic choral parts are replaced by monodic recitatives and, on rare occasions, by free chorale-like recitations, as in Schütz. Chorales, arias, and choral sections are often inserted into the liturgical texts.

5. The Passion Oratorio, in which the text of the Passion from the Gospels is replaced by a free compilation of Biblical and non-Biblical texts from the subject-matter of the account of the Passion.

General Bibliography

G. Adler, *Zur Gesch. d. Wiener Messkomp. in d. zweiten Hälfte d. 17. Jh.* (StMw 4); K. G. Fellerer, *Der Palestrinastil u. s. Bedeutung in d. vokalen Kirchenmusik d. 18. Jh.* (Augsburg 1929) and *Gesch. d. kath. Kirchenmusik* (Düsseldorf 2nd ed. 1949); A. Gottron, *Kirchenmusik u. Liturgie. Die kirchlichen Vorschriften für Gesang u. Musik beim Gottesdienst* (Regensburg 1937); H. Lemacher and K. G. Fellerer, *Hdb. d. kath. Kirchenmusik* (Essen 1949); A. Orel, *Die kath. Kirchenmusik von 1600–1750*, and *Die Kath. Kirchenmusik seit 1750* (Adler Hdb.); O. Ursprung, *Die kath. Kirchenmusik* (Bücken Hdb.) and *Restauration u. Palestrina-Renaissance in d. kath. Kirchenmusik d. letzten zwei Jh.* (Augsburg 1924); P. Wagner, *Einführung in die kath. Kirchenmusik* (Düsseldorf 1919); *Die Messe* (MW); arts. Caecilianismus, Messe (MGG).

17th Century: Viadana, Cento Concerti Ecclesiastici, new ed. Kassel 1964. *Stadlmayr,* new ed. Hymns in DTÖ 3, 1. *Straus,* DTÖ 30, 1. *Draghi,* Masses in DTÖ 23, 1. *Steffani,* DTB 6, 2. *Schmeltzer, Biber,* and *Kerll,* DTÖ 25, 1, and 30, 1. *Ferdinand III et al.,* new ed. *Österreichische Kaiserwerke.* J. J. *Fux:* coll. ed. 1959–ᅠ, Kassel; DTÖ 1, 1 and 2, 1 (Masses, motets), DTÖ 23, 2 (Partitas), DTÖ 85 (keyboard mus.), DTÖ 17 (opera), DTÖ 9, 2 (ch. sonatas and suites); Sch 271, 272; L. Köchel, *J. J. F.* (1872, incl. thematic index); A. Liess, *Die Triosonaten von J. J. F.* (Bln. 1940), *Fuxiana* (Vienna 1958), and *J. J. F.* (Vienna 1948); J. H. v. d. Meer, *J. J. F. als Opernkomp.* (3 vols., Bilthoven 1961); art. Fux (MGG). *Du Mont:* art. (MGG). *Michel-Richard Delalande:* N. Dufourcq, ed.,

Notes et références à une histoire de M.-R. D. (Paris 1957). *Bohemia:* new eds. in P 106, 107, 112, 115. *Poland:* new eds. in MDK, MMSiP, WDMP, CSMSiP, ZHMP 7, MSt; Z. M. Szweykowski, *Some Problems of Baroque Music in Poland* (MAEO); arts. on individuals (MGG). *America:* O. F. DaSilva, *Mission Music in California* (Los Angeles 1941); G. T. Edwards, *Music and Musicians of Maine* (Portland 1928).

18th Century: Pergolesi: Sch 275. *Padre Martini:* W. Reich, *P. M. als Theoretiker* (Diss. Vienna 1934). *Lotti:* DDT 60. *Hasse:* Sch 310; W. Müller, *H. als Kirchenkomp.* (Lpz. 1911, PIMG, Beihefte 2. Folge, Heft IX). *Caldara:* Sch 273; DTÖ 13, 1. *Reutter:* DTÖ 88. *J. Haydn:* coll. ed. Ser. 23, Bd. 1, Masses (1951); C. M. Brand, *Die Messen J. H.s* (Würzburg 1941). *W. A. Mozart:* coll ed. Ser. I, II, III, Supplement. *Austrian Contemps. of Haydn and Mozart:* new eds. church comps. of M. Haydn in DTÖ 22 and 31, 1, with thematic catalogue, notes, and additions in Jancik) and L. Mozart (DTB 9, 2); H. Jancik, *Michael Haydn* (Vienna 1952); A. M. Klafsky, *M. Haydn als Kirchenkomp.* (StMw 3); F. Kosch, *Gassmann als Kirchenkomp.* (StMw 14); A. Weissenbäck, *Albrechtsberger als Kirchenkomp.* (St.Mw 14). *Poland:* new eds. in WDMP 55, 64; ZHMP 8, 10, 12, 14, 15. *America:* G. Chase, *America's Music* (N.Y. 2nd ed. 1966).

19th Century: Beethoven: coll. ed. Ser. XIX; L. Dikenmann-Balmer, *B.s Missa solemnis* (Zurich 1952). *Schubert:* coll. ed. Ser. XIII; O. Wissig, *S.s Messen* (Lpz. 1909). *Salieri:* K. Nützlader, *S. als Kirchenkomp.* (StMw 14). *Bruckner:* M. Auer, *B. als Kirchenmusiker* (Regensburg 1927); H.-G. Scholz, *Die Form der reifen Messen A. B.s* (Bln. 1961). *America:* L. Ellinwood, *The Hist. of Am. Church Music* (N. Y. 1953); K. G. Fellerer, *Hist. of Cath. Ch. Mus.*, tr. F. A. Brunner (Baltimore 1961); R. Stevenson, "Church Music" in *100 Yrs. of Music in Am.*, ed. P. H. Lang (N. Y. 1961).

20th Century: Jos. Haas: K. Laux, *J. H.* (Düsseldorf 1954).

The Passion: K. v. Fischer, *Zur Gesch. der Passionskomp. des 16. Jh. in Italien* (AfMw 1954); G. Schmidt, *Grundsätzliche Bemerkungen zur Gesch. der Passionshistorie* (AfMw 1960); A. Schmitz, *Oberital. Figuralpassionen des 16. Jh.* (Mainz 1955); art. on Passion (MGG), incl. B. Stäblein on *Die einst. lat. Passion.*

25. Protestant Church Music from Luther to the Present

Some understanding of German church history during the 16th and 17th centuries is indispensable to a conception of the music for the Protestant—or, as it is usually referred to in Germany, the Evangelical— service of worship. The early incidents focus around the personality of Martin Luther (1483–1546).

In 1517 he posted his ninety-five theses, precipitating an order from the Diet of Augsburg the next year that he retract them. He refused, and in 1520 he burned the bull excommunicating him. In 1521 the Diet of

Worms was held and issued its Edict. Luther accordingly began translating the Bible. The Second Diet of Speyer was held in 1529, the Diet of Augsburg in 1530. The Nuremberg religious peace was established in 1532.

After Luther's death religious conflict continued. The Schmalkaldener War occurred from 1546 to 1547. The Augsburg religious peace was established in 1555. Around 1560 the Evangelical movement was at its height, and Germany was nine-tenths Protestant. In 1608 the Protestant Union was formed, and in 1609 the Catholic Liga. The Thirty Years' War raged from 1618 to 1648.

In the latter part of the century there was a trend toward Pietism, with its emphasis on Bible study and personal religious experience. Philipp Jakob Spener published his *Pia Desideria* in 1675, and A. H. Francke took the lead in various Pietistic developments at Halle.

Luther and the Evangelical Worship-Service

Martin Luther wrote three essays on the order of worship. The first, "*Von Ordnung Gottesdiensts in der Gemeinde*" (1523), established the three basic types of the Evangelical service: Mass, matins, and vespers. Luther's second essay, "*Formula Missae*" (1523), distinguished between worship-services for "religious foundations and cathedrals" and those for village and rural congregations. In the larger cities there were school and cantorial choirs, which performed the main parts of the Mass, matins, and vespers in Latin. The smaller congregations, however, had a simplified service of worship, entirely in German. Luther's third essay, "*Deudsche Messe und ordnung Gottesdiensts*" (1526), created the basis of a German Mass. In place of separate parts of the Mass there appeared congregational songs in German. For example, instead of the Credo there was "*Wir glauben all an einen Gott.*"

Technically trained in music, Luther composed thirty-six songs. In at least twenty of these the melodies are certainly his own. His songs derive largely from pre-Reformation German songs, liturgical songs of the Catholic church, folk-songs and other popular components, religious and poetic elements from the Bible and the Psalms in particular, and the Hussite chorale. From these models Luther brought together various traits and fused them into congregation song—or, as it is sometimes referred to in German, "we"-song (*wir-lied*)—of general ecclesiastical and popular effect.

Up to the middle of the 17th century church song, which served as a sort of creed in the service, was the center of Protestant church music. In chorale arrangements, chorale preludes, and song motets it extensively determined the musical forms of the Evangelical worship service.

Protestant Song-Books

The first Protestant song-books were brought out in 1524. One was the Wittenberg *Achtliederbuch*, consisting of eight "songs" or texts for singing and four melodies; another, the Erfurt *Enchiridien*, of fifteen melodies and twenty-five songs; and still a third, the Strassburg *Kirchenampt*. All three of these have been newly brought out in facsimile editions.

Also in 1524 there appeared the *Geystliche gesangk Buchleyn. Wittenberg*, edited by the Torgau choirmaster and one of the musical advisers to Luther, Johann Walter (d. 1570). It contains thirty-two songs, some rather old and some new, in settings of from two to six voices. They are contrapuntal arrangements, with the chorale usually in the tenor, though there are also some with it in the upper voice. The last of many constantly enlarged editions appeared in 1551.

These publications of 1524 were followed by a great succession of song-books with one-voiced melodies. Though we do not today have a copy of the first edition of Klug's song-book that appeared at Wittenberg in 1529, we know that it contained the first printing of the melody for "*Ein feste Burg.*" Two other important early Reformation song-books, both published at Leipzig in 1530, are those of Blume and Schumann. Another is the Bapst song-book (Leipzig 1545). A little later in the Reformation era, two especially extensive collections are those of Spangenberg (1568) and Keuchenthal (1573).

Polyphonic church-song arrangements were also published in profusion after Walter's song-book of 1524. The most important collection was that edited by the publisher Georg Rhau and brought out at Wittenberg in 1544, *Newe deudsche Geistliche Gesenge . . . Für die gemeinen Schulen* (New German Spiritual Songs for the Common Schools). It contained 123 polyphonic chorale arrangements by Senfl, Stoltzer, Dietrich, and others. The types of setting are like those in the secular songs of that day. There are linear and polyphonic settings with the cantus firmus in the tenor, and there are settings involving largely coordinate voices that imitate each other. Some of these settings point ahead towards the chorale motet. The songs in this volume are presented in the order of the church year.

In the worship service the chorale was performed in any of three ways—by the congregation in unison and without any accompaniment or instrumental support, by the choir school in the figured version with the tenor as cantus firmus, and by the organ as a solo. The chorale was always sung in its entirety (*per omnes versus*). In practice, the congregation, choir, and organ took turns in presenting the individual stanzas. This method of presentation was referred to as *alternatim*. The way in which the organ took its turn led to the so-called organ chorale.

The sharp difference between the one-voiced, unaccompanied congregational song and the figured version of the chorale melody was somewhat softened by the fact that in the latter the melody appeared in the descant in its simpler and more chordal form. Thus the congregation could follow and sing along with the chorale in the soprano, and even take it over. This procedure was normal until the 17th century, when the organ began to accompany congregational singing.

The model of these four-voiced settings, note against note, was Claude Goudimel's psalm-settings, which were completed in 1565. Goudimel's settings utilized the French translation of Marot and Beza, and as a result of their unusual popularity in Germany they were soon imitated. In 1565 Ambrosius Lobwasser translated the Goudimel psalter into German and retained the Goudimel melodies. Lobwasser's influence extended to the Leipzig preacher Cornelius Becker, whose versification of the Psalms was set to music by Calvisius, Schein, and Schütz in 1628. Under Goudimel's influence in 1586 Lucas Osiander issued *Fünfzig Lieder und Psalmen* in simple four-voiced cantional setting, or setting with the chorale in the discant. Numerous song-books of this type appeared, including the *Dresden Gesangbuch* of Rogier Michael (1593), Bartholomäus Gesius (Frankfurt a. O. 1954), Seth Calvisius (1597), the *Eislebener Gesangbuch* (1598), Melchior Franck (Coburg 1602), and the *Kirchengesänge simpliciter* of Hans Leo Hassler (1608).

In the 17th century the practice of thorough-bass prevailed, and in the song books the figured bass appeared along with the chorale melody. Performance tended to be more and more in terms of a simple harmonic setting. In the latter half of the 17th century there occurred the transition to the exclusively isometrical notation of the chorale melodies, in contrast to the old polymetrical melodic formulae—in other words, they were written out in predominantly equal notes and equal measures, instead of in the often unequal units in which they had earlier been notated.

Among the influential song-books of the 17th century were J. H. Schein's *Kantional* (1627), Johann Crüger's *Brandenburgisches Gesangbuch* (1640), and the *Gothaische Kantional* in three parts (1648). Particular influence was exerted by Johann Crüger, who until his death in 1663 was the choir-director of the Nicolaikirche in Berlin. Crüger's *Praxis pietatis melica* contained songs by Paul Gerhardt (d. 1676) and went through over forty editions in the course of a century.

In 1704 there appeared the first part of the song-book of the Piestistic movement, Freylinghausen's *Geistreiches Gesangbuch*. It dominated the 18th century and influenced further song-books of the period, such as Witt's in 1715, Bronner's, Detzel's in 1731, Schemelli's in 1736, König's, and Reimann's. With the increasing influence of secular music in the latter half of the 18th and in the 19th centuries, the chorale became more and more a song of feeling. We find this in the chorale books of Kühnau, Hiller, Kittel, and Schicht. Then, some time before 1850, there began a reform movement, the later phases of which are still with us today.

In the Scandinavian countries, Hans Thomissøn's *Den danske Psalmebog* (1569), with its 219 melodies, set a standard for congregational song. Similarly significant for the principal church service was Niels Jesperssøn's *Gradual* (1573), which gave Danish congregational songs as alternatives beside portions of the Latin Mass. Both books were introduced into Norway. Their counterparts in Iceland, issued in 1589 and 1594, became the basis for the monodic chorale that was sung up to the end of the 19th century. In Sweden, during the early years after the Reformation, the brothers Olaus and Laurentius Petri fostered the development of a conservative attitude toward the liturgy. Eleven small collections of church songs were issued in the 16th century, and in 1611 there appeared an order of the Mass according to German and Danish models. In Finland many German church songs were translated into Finnish, and the melodies were taken over with little change.

The influence of the basso continuo song became noticeable toward the end of the 17th century. In Sweden this appeared in H. Vallerius' edition of *Den svenska psalmboken* (1697), which gave the melody and the figured bass, showing also the influence of Crüger's *Praxis pietatis melica*. A one-voiced edition of Vallerius' Psalmbook appeared in 1702 in Finnish. In Denmark the basso continuo influence appeared in the one-voiced melodies in the *Gradual* (1699) assembled by Thomas Kingo and still more directly in the devotional books for private use such as Kingo's *Aandelige Siunge-Koor* (Spiritual Chorus, 1674–1681). The numbers became more isometric and the melody more ornamented, and in Denmark even arias and dance-songs were added. This tendency was carried on further in a pietistic direction by Erik Pontoppidan's *Nye Psalme Bog* (1740) and by the first printed chorale book with basso continuo in Denmark, F. C. Breitendich's publication of 1764.

Chorale Motet and Sentence Motet

Except for congregational song the Protestant church did not as yet have any music that was distinctively its own in style during the first fifty years of the Reformation. In its worship-service it used the traditional and contemporary Catholic motet literature. Protestant composers wrote original works, such as the polyphonic chorale arrangements of Johann Walter that appeared in 1524 or the settings in Rhau's collection *Newe deudsche Geitsliche Gesenge* (1544). But they represented stylistically the traditional types of the polyphonic German song arrangements. In one type, the cantus firmus stood over against the other voices, note-against-note. In another type it was paraphrased or accompanied by freely devised voices. In still a third type, the cantus firmus was imitated by the other voices. Under the influence of Franco-Flemish song settings, this third type led to the style in which the voices imitated each other throughout.

Rhau in Wittenberg issued several collections of Latin Masses, hymns, motets, and other works written by various European composers. In the middle of the century Nuremberg was the center of Evangelical music publishing. Here Hans Ott issued in 1537–1538 the motet collection *Novum et insigne opus musicum,* and Montan and Neuber in 1558 the *Evangelia.* The works of these collections, which were used in the churches of both denominations, do not, however, represent anything specifically Protestant even in content.

While a decline in musical invention of new chorale melodies was noticeable in the latter half of the 16th century, there was nevertheless an increase in the Evangelical polyphonic arrangements of songs or chorales. Orlando di Lasso's song settings provided the model. At the end of his creative activity, these represented the type of the song-motet. Polyphonic arrangement, with and without the chorale in the tenor or in the discant, reached a first culminating point under Lasso's influence in the song settings of Leonhard Lechner, of Nuremberg and Stuttgart (about 1553–

1606). Also Johannes Eccard, of Königsberg and Berlin (1553–1611), was responsible for some polyphonic arrangements in the *Preussische Festlieder,* edited by Strobäus and brought out in 1642–1644. Lechner and Eccard were Lassus's private pupils and represented most clearly the school of Lassus in Germany. Many composers cultivated the song-motet during the years from 1570 to 1630. Their grand master was Michael Praetorius, of Wolfenbüttel (1571–1621), who in his *Musae Sioniae* (1605–11) wrote 1244 compositions on 537 chorale melodies.

Along with the song-motet the sentence-motet or *Spruchmotette* acquired increasing significance. Its texts were particularly taken from the Psalms and Gospels. During the 17th century they gradually displaced song in the position of predominance. Also here Lasso's influence was felt, as was shown in various expressive features and in the realistic interpretation of the text. After 1600 German won priority over Latin in the Evangelical worship service. Among the many representatives of the song-motet and sentence-motet were Meiland, Gesius, Eccard, Hassler, Demantius, and Lechner.

The complete repertoire of Evangelical musical practice in the worship service around 1600 was contained in the four-volume compilation *Florilegium Portense* (1603–21) of Erhard Bodenschatz, choir director at Schulpforta (d. 1636). It included works by fifty-eight composers, among whom were Gallus, Lasso, Hassler, and many of their Italian contemporaries, and was still in use during J. S. Bach's time.

In the 17th century, wedding and funeral motets came to be written for double chorus. They were originally conceived of as *a cappella,* but as sung with the resources of the choir-school they were usually supported by instruments. These compositions established a tradition in which Bach wrote his motets: the eight-voiced "*Singet dem Herrn,*" the Funeral Motet, the eight-voiced "*Der Geist hilft unsrer Schwachheit auf,*" the eight-voiced "*Fürchte dich nicht,*" the eight-voiced "*Komm, Jesu, komm,*" the five-voiced "*Jesu, meine Freude,*" and the four-voiced "*Lobet den Herren, alle Heiden.*"

The generation after Bach included Doles, Hiller, Rolle, Homilius, Schicht, and Türk. They tended to neglect the cantata and turn to the motet, in the sentimental style of the period, and made more and more modest technical demands on the performers.

The repertoire of the art of the motet cultivated at the Danish court in the mid-16th century is represented by two groups of part-books, one that appeared in 1541 and another in 1556. These contain more than three hundred settings of European and predominantly Netherlands repertoire, partly by composers who for varying periods of time were active in this area, including Jørgen Preston, Johan Paston (who was later called to Sweden), and Adrian Petit Coclicus. The first significant Danish composer was a pupil of Gabrieli, Mogens Pedersøn (about 1580–1623), in whose collection *Pratum spirituale* (1620) there are twenty-nine five-voiced chorale motets. The motet "*Cor mundum crea in me Deus*" by Caspar Ecchienus (about 1600) is the first known Norwegian composition of this type.

Among the composers active in Sweden were Vincenzo Albrici

(1631–1696), who wrote the first motet in Swedish, *"Fader vor"* or Paternoster, in 1654, and Christian Ritter (*ca.* 1650–after 1725), who wrote fifteen church concerti as well as other works in Stockholm between 1678 and about 1700.

Sacred Concert

New Italian stylistic traits were quickly adopted beyond the Alps after 1610. Though at first they did not much alter the way Evangelical church music focused spiritually on the chorale melody and the proclamation of the Scripture, they soon brought in:

1. Giovanni Gabrieli's sonorous display of instrumental and vocal choirs and the alternation between instrumental ritornelli and vocal sections;
2. concertizing music-making as if various voices, instruments, or bodies of sound were vying with each other;
3. virtuoso vocal soli;
4. a style of monody that Michael Praetorious referred to as "madrigalesque"; and
5. thorough-bass.

All forms of religious music were subjected to the concertizing idea as a principle of composition. They might bear the most various designations or titles suggested by poetic or religious imagination, such as symphoniae, concerti, sacred concerts, motetti concertanti, or harmoniae. But essentially in all of them the composer faced, first of all, the special stylistic problem of this period—how to connect the chorale melody with the concertizing principle. Eventually he solved this problem at the expense of the chorale. He subordinated the chorale, perhaps most notably in the work of Heinrich Schütz.

The sacred concert can be considered the "cantata" of the 17th century, although the designation *cantata* in this connection was not usual at this time. The types of instrumentation were quite various: monochoral works with continuo, monochoral and polychoral works with instruments, soloistic compositions for one or more voices with instruments. The composer decidedly made the word predominate over the music. He was strongly stimulated by the text in devising the free and varied layout of the musical form. Often he developed dialogue-like alternating speeches and whole scenes. He placed side by side different methods of composition—homophonic and polyphonic, declamatory and concertizing. The text, which was mainly taken from the Bible, he integrated symbolically by musical means. By using the declamatory principle of a musical rhetoric, he raised the word to the heights of a penetrating musical idiom, enriching it from the text by tone-painting in a realistic and subjectively emotional way.

In actual performance the singer or instrumentalist customarily enriched the written-out vocal and instrumental text as notated, or the *res facta*, by freely improvising ornaments such as diminutions, coloraturas, passages, runs, and trills. In this he was guided by diminution exercises such as those contained in Lodovico Zacconi's *Prattica di musica* (Venice

1592), in which Zacconi distinguishes between "essential ornaments" and free, impulsive ones. The "essential" ones are invariable figures, like trills, mordents, or turns. The free ones are figures and runs that were always inserted in an impromptu way. When vocalists and instrumentalists collaborated, the leader determined the best way for them to make use of the available means. In so doing he was not violating the composer's intention with regard to sonority. If the leader found it suitable, the composer intended him to augment the sound and achieve a powerful effect, particularly at the end of the piece.

The sacred concert was the real focal point in the encounter between Evangelical church music and the stylistic innovations from Italy. Of decisive significance in the outcome was the creative work of three composers called at the time the "three great S's": Heinrich Schütz (1585–1672), Johann Hermann Schein (1586–1630), and Samuel Scheidt (1587–1654). Schein's *Opella nova* came first chronologically, Part I appearing in 1618 and consisting of chorale arrangements in concertizing style for one or two singing voices, one or two instruments, and basso continuo. Scheidt's sacred concert works came next, dating from 1621, Part I of his *Symphoniae sacrae* appearing in 1629. Finally, Heinrich Schütz issued his *Kleine geistliche Konzerte* in 1636 and 1639. Church music of the sacred concert type was then written by all the choir leaders of the 17th century, including Johann Staden, Gregor Aichinger, and Andreas Hammerschmidt.

Cantata

By the middle of the 17th century a transition began which was to lead from the sacred concert to the 18th-century type of Protestant composition we usually call generically a *cantata*. The change arose from the widespread emphasis on a contemplative approach to the word of the Bible and a tendency to add meditative lyrics to it. They were given an arioso formulation, so far as the music was concerned. Thus they became song-like arias, developed in stanzas; and after 1710 they took the typical form of the *da capo* aria. Their model was Italian opera.

A great many choir directors—or, as they were called at the time, "cantors" (and are still so called, their functions including not only directing but also composing)—participated in this transition from the sacred concert to the cantata. They form three groups, in roughly the eastern, northern, and southern parts of Germany. The list of Saxon and Thuringian cantors includes Andreas Hammerschmidt, Johann Rudolf and Johann Georg Ahle, Friedrich Wilhelm Zachow, and the cantors at St. Thomas's in Leipzig, Schelle, Knüpfer, and Kuhnau. The North-German group includes Georg Böhm, Matthias Weckmann, Christoph Bernhard, Thomas Selle, Franz Tunder, and Dietrich Buxtehude. And the South-German circle, particularly at Nuremberg, is represented by a group including Erasmus Kindermann, Johann Philipp Krieger, and Johann Krieger.

The clergy raised many objections to the operatic elements, but these were eventually overcome by the free lyrical poems of the orthodox

Lutheran pastor in Hamburg, Erdmann Neumeister (1671–1756), with his *Geistliche Cantaten statt einer Kirchenmusik* (1st ed. 1700, 2nd ed. 1704). In general he alternated recitatives and arias, but he made the texts for the recitatives as free of stanzaic regularity and sometimes of rhyme as the texts that may be found in some madrigals. Hence his recitatives have been referred to as "madrigalesque." The form of the setting of the recitative was syllabic with a strongly declamatory character, the model of which was the delivery of the great pulpit orators of the time. Neumeister's cantata texts were imitated by other writers, including Salomo Franck (1659–1725) and Christian Frederich Henrici, who wrote under the pseudonym of Picander (1700–1764). Cantata texts appeared to some extent in print and served as devotional tracts.

Musically the cantata of the 18th century went back to the chorale or sentence motet, the sacred concert in its choral and soloistic forms, and the model of opera with the development of the scene articulated into recitative and aria or arioso.

Thus two typical forms of cantata—with many intermediate forms— arose during the Bach period: the chorale cantata and the free lyrico-poetic cantata.

The chorale cantata focused on the song of the church and, to a certain extent, renounced free lyric poetry, as only the individual stanzas of the chorale were being set to music. The chorale melody was the musical heart of the work. Individual stanzas were developed in the manner of a chorale fantasy, in which the chorus and soli alternated in presenting portions of the chorale. If any newly composed verses were incorporated, they often merely paraphrased the thoughts expressed in the chorale. Johann Sebastian Bach turned particularly to the chorale cantata after 1740, as in such works as *"Lobe den Herrn"* (No. 137), *"Wachet auf, ruft uns die Stimme"* (No. 140), and *"Wie schön leuchtet der Morgenstern"* (No. 1). Although a musical starting-point for the chorale cantata was provided by the chorale variation in the work of Samuel Scheidt, Bach developed a form of his own. He set to music the first and last stanzas of the chorale in the original poetic version, but he paraphrased the middle stanzas in recitatives and arias in the style of the textually freer or madrigalesque cantata. Thus the chorale melody could permeate the freely composed poetry as musical material, while it entirely dominated the original chorale stanzas.

The free lyrico-poetic cantata carried the rhymed poetical text, inspired by thoughts from the Bible, in the form of recitatives and *da capo* arias. Biblical quotations and chorale stanzas were added. The poet often preferred to develop a scene after the operatic model. In detail, the form was fixed by Erdmann Neumeister's poetic models. He at first versified free elaborations on Biblical texts in recitatives and arias, and thus he developed what Blume has called a cantata aiming at edification (*Erbauungskantate*). Then, after 1711, he combined the Biblical text and the chorale with reflective verses of a contemplative nature and thereby developed a kind of cantata that undertakes to fulfill some of the functions of a sermon (*Predigtkantate*). A third type takes selections or *perikopai* from the Bible and juxtaposes them against a series of reflections on them, resulting in a cantata contemplative of Biblical passages (*kontemplative Perikopenkantate*). Usually the congregational chorale formed the conclusion. There were manifold possibilities of musical performance for all types of cantata, as there were cantatas for one or more solo voices with or without choir, and an orchestra of varying make-up always collaborated. The organ, and to some extent the cembalo, presented the thorough-bass. The performers were obliged to read the music from manuscript, as printed versions were very rarely available.

The cantata was a regular part of the Sunday service, which took its place in the order of worship shortly before the sermon. Relating in its text directly to the worship-service of the particular occasion, the cantata was thus something like a Sunday sermon or festival set to music. Cantatas in two sections were presented one before and the other after the sermon. An annual cycle embraced about sixty to seventy cantatas for the entire church year, beginning with the first Sunday in Advent.

Passion

As we have seen, the Passion originated under Catholic auspices and took several forms. As a part of Evangelical church music it continued its development in a number of directions.

German Responsorial Passion

As for the most fundamental and conservative type, no doubt the medieval tradition of monodic singing of the Passion in Latin was uninterruptedly continued during the Lutheran Reformation. The beginning of the Responsorial Passion in German goes back to Johann Walter (d. 1570), with his *St. Matthew Passion* and his *St. John Passion*. Luther's special instructions on which lesson-tones were to be chosen for the Gospel and the Epistle exerted considerable influence on the early Protestant Passion. But after 1550 the medieval Passion tone came back into exclusive use. In accordance with the special treatment of the *turbae* and the Passion tone, the numerous German Responsorial Passions have been classified by Ameln and Gerhardt as falling into one or another of six different groups.

The German Responsorial Passion remained to some extent a component of the liturgy of the Evangelical divine service until well on into the 19th century; it had the principal share in the Passion observance up to the 17th century. There are many compositions in this form, including works by Meiland, Besler, Mancinus, Vulpius, and Christoph Schultze. Originally the *turbae* were in *falsobordone* setting, with use of the cantus firmus. Jakob Meiland was the first to relax these connections in 1567 and thereby to heighten the dramatic possibilities. For the text of the *conclusio* (*Gratiarum actio*), Meiland was the first to use a song-stanza, and in this he was widely imitated. Heinrich Schütz's three Passions are German Responsorial Passions. They are the *St. Matthew*, the *St. Luke*, and the *St. John*—the *St. Mark* not having been authenticated. The oldest is the *St. Luke*, which was written after 1653; the other two were written about 1665-6.

Through-Composed Passion

A less restricted type, moreover, extended the polyphonic aspects throughout the composition. There were essentially three varieties in Protestant music. One, in Latin, was of only limited significance in the hands of Protestant composers. Longaval's Passion here furnished the model. Within the Protestant area it was followed in such Latin Passions as those of Galliculus (1538), Resinarius (1543), Daser (1578), Bucenus (1578), and Gesius (1613).

A second variety, in the vernacular, included works by Burck (1568), Lechner (1594), and Demantius (1631). To some extent these composers relaxed the connection with the traditional Passion tone. For texts they mainly used the Passion-harmony compiled from the accounts in all four Gospels. Lechner's *St. John Passion* is the most significant work of this type.

In a third variety the composer simply assigned the monodic voice of the Evangelist to the choir and treated all the other speeches polyphonically. Giovanni de Albertis had provided a model for this type of Passion, and Antonio Scandellus in 1568 had imitated it. Further works along this same line were those of Gesius in 1588, Beber in 1610 at the latest, and Rogier Michael, though the music of his Passion is no longer extant.

Oratorio-Like Passion

Toward the middle of the 17th century, the Passion story was at first expanded with further Biblical texts and stanzas from the song books and later also with contemporary sacred reflective lyrics composed for the occasion. The starting-point for this type of Passion was provided around 1640 in Hamburg by the work of Thomas Selle, who in 1643 wrote a *St. John Passion* in which there were contemplative choruses on Biblical texts as intermezzi. We have only the text of a *St. Matthew Passion* (1664) of Thomas Struthius, in Danzig, but we know that it contained lyric poetry and chorales. Solo arias and orchestra appeared in Christian Flor's *St. Matthew Passion* (1667). Further early works included Johann Sebastiani's *St. Matthew Passion*, composed at the latest by 1663 and printed at Königsberg in 1672 and Thiele's *St. Matthew Passion* (1673). In Thiele, a pupil of Schütz, the emphasis lay on the arias over free madrigalesque poetry of meditative character with instrumental movements, or *ritornelli*. The Passion verse of Brockes (1712) was set to music by Händel (1716), Telemann, Keiser, Mattheson, and others.

Bach's *St. John Passion* combined the Gospel text with chorales and separate portions of Brockes's text. The religious aspects were somewhat humanized. The subjective element was embodied in the sympathetic Christian as observer. The organic link between the Scriptural text and the freely written poetry, including the chorale, was characteristic of Bach. The text of this *St. Matthew Passion* was by Picander.

The number of oratorio-like Passions written throughout the 17th and 18th centuries was extraordinarily great. Their musical basis had been provided by the incursion of monody, thorough-bass, and concertante instrumental voices.

Passion-Cantata and Passion-Oratorio

To conclude our survey of the basic types of the Passion in Protestant music, we might observe that the Passion Cantata and Passion Oratorio were not always entirely distinct as types. Often the Passion Cantata was somewhat shorter. Both were inclined to omit the actual Biblical text of the Passion. The text consisted of freely composed verse together with stanzas of songs. The direct liturgical relationship in the Passion Cantata was the connection with the sermon; hence in the foreground stood unambiguously the reflective characterization of the account of Jesus' suffering. Occasionally several Passion cantatas were combined into a new whole. The widely known Passion "*Seliges Erwägen*" (1728) of Telemann, for example, consisted of nine parts.

The final steps toward the complete poetic formulation of the Passion material were taken after 1700 in Hamburg, the main center for Passion compositions of an oratorio-like nature, paralleling Neumeister's cantata-libretti. Poets of the Passion in Hamburg were Postel (1704), Hunold (Menantes), and Brockes. Hunold's verse for the "*Blutiger und sterbender Jesus*" (Jesus Bleeding and Dying, 1704) excludes the Biblical text entirely. But the Evangelist was again introduced in the celebrated Passion poem of Brockes, "*Der für die Sünde der Welt gemarterte und sterbende Jesus*" (Jesus Martyred for the Sins of the World and Dying, Hamburg 1712), which was set to music by some dozen composers.

The poem "*Der Tod Jesu*" (The Death of Jesus) by K. W. Ramler, with its strongly lyrical and sentimental character, enjoyed special popularity in the latter half of the century in Karl Heinrich Graun's musical setting (1755), the first performance of which took place no longer in the church but in the theater. Thus the Passion Oratorio finally moved out of the framework of church worship. The spread of the Protestant Passion Oratorio then reached out also beyond the regions of Germany associated with the Evangelical church on into Catholic areas and became an ecumenical and somewhat social affair.

In more recent years the worship aspect has been restressed, giving rise to works connected with the Passion that have been composed by Hugo Diestler, Hans Friedrich Micheelsen, Kurt Thomas, Ernst Pepping, Siegfried Reda, and Frank Martin.

Cantorial Schools and Cantors from the 16th Century to the 18th Century

Evangelical church music was supported by the cantorial schools (*Kantoreien*) that had already been urged by Luther as city unions of voluntary members. Until well into the 18th century the church choir consisted of boys' and men's voices. Instruction in music was given in Latin schools to the boys, who were educated there as boarding pupils. The "cantor" was the music teacher. In official rank he came after the *rektor* and also taught Latin. Each class usually had five hours of singing lessons a week. The pupils were trained to perform church music. Low voices were provided by older pupils or students from outside (*ad-*

juvanten). In procession—that is, as *kurrende*—the cantorial school sang Christmas songs during the evenings of Advent in the streets and before the houses of the city, from which additional income resulted for the choirmaster and for the pupils, often otherwise penniless. Singing at weddings and funerals also contributed to their support.

In general, *kantorei* means the choir of singers who were in the service of a church or a princely court and who carried on their activity professionally. Perfecting the divine service and participating in secular events were among their duties. A corresponding institution had played an outstanding role during the Middle Ages, in Rome, in the episcopal sees, and in the great princely residences. The singing-school at Metz, for instance, had figured prominently in the early history of Gregorian chant. Thus the *kantoreien* were simply maintaining an old tradition. Only after the Reformation were these groups of practicing singers no longer active in a professional capacity.

A long-standing tradition was also being maintained by the numerous choirmasters, cantors, and organists in Evangelical church music from the middle of the 16th to the 18th century. The following list suggests some of the most important of them, arranged in order of their year of birth:

Johann Walter (1495–1570), court choirmaster in Torgau under Friedrich the Wise, became in 1526 head of the cantorial school there. Friend and musical adviser of Luther, in 1548 he became choirmaster to the Elector Moritz and founded the choir in the Dresden court chapel. His principal works include the "*Wittenberger Geystliche gesangk Buchleyn*," "*Gothaer Cantional*," and a *St. Matthew Passion*. He also wrote some songs, one of the best known of which is "*Wach auf, wach auf, du deutsches Land*" (1561).

Sixt Dietrich (*ca.* 1490–1548), originally a choirboy in Constance, became in 1517 choir-prefect there. In 1527 he turned Protestant, and by 1540 he had a friendly relationship with the Luther circle in Wittenberg. He is largely known for his chorale arrangements.

Leonhard Lechner (about 1553–1606), a pupil of Lasso, was active in Nuremberg and became court choirmaster in Stuttgart. Between 1570 and 1575 he was probably in Italy, as he was the first in Germany to display accomplished mastery of polychorality. He wrote a *St. John Passion*, "*Deutsche Sprüche von Leben und Tod*," motets on the Canticles, and "*Neue teutsche Lieder*."

Hieronymus Praetorius (1560–1629), son of Jakob Praetorius the Elder (d. 1586), became, like his father, organist at St. James's in Hamburg.

Michael Praetorius (1571–1621), brother of Hieronymus Praetorius, was choirmaster in Wolfenbüttel.

Bartholomäus Gesius (d. 1613) was cantor in Frankfurt a. O.

Philipp Dulichius (1562–1631) was cantor in Stettin.

Christoph Demantius (1567–1643) was cantor in Zittau and Freiberg i. S.

Johann Staden (1581–1634) was organist in Bayreuth and Nuremberg.

Johann Hermann Schein (1586–1630) was cantor of St. Thomas's in Leipzig.

Samuel Scheidt (1587–1654) was a pupil of Sweelinck and became court organist and later choirmaster in Halle.

Thomas Selle (1599–1663) was music director of the five main churches in Hamburg.

Andreas Hammerschmidt (1612–1675) was cantor in Zittau.

Franz Tunder (1614–1667) was organist at St. Mary's in Lübeck.

Johann Erasmus Kindermann (1616–1655) was organist in Nuremberg.

Johann Rosenmüller (*ca.* 1619–1684) was active in Leipzig, then in Italy, and later court choirmaster in Wolfenbüttel.

Matthias Weckmann (about 1619–1674), who studied under Schütz, J. Praetorius, and Scheidemann, became organist at St. James's in Hamburg in 1655.

Joh. Rudolf Ahle (1625–1673) was organist in Mühlhausen i. Thür.

Christoph Bernhard (1627–1692), pupil of Schütz and Carissimi, became assistant choirmaster in Dresden, later cantor of St. James's in Hamburg, and subsequently returned to Dresden. As leader of the Collegium Musicum that Weckmann had founded in 1660, he helped make it important in the early history of the German oratorio.

Dietrich Buxtehude (1637–1707), having grown up in Helsingborg and Helsingør, was organist there. Then, in 1668, he succeeded Tunder as organist in St. Mary's in Lübeck, where he maintained the "*Abendmusiken*" that Tunder had founded. He influenced Bach and was particularly significant for his organ works and cantatas.

Johann Philipp Krieger (1649–1725) was court choirmaster in Bayreuth and later in Halle and Wiessenfels.

Johann Krieger (1652–1735), brother of Johann Philipp Krieger, was cantor in Zittau.

Georg Böhm (1661–1733) was organist at St. John's in Lüneburg.

Friedrich Wilhelm Zachow (1663–1712) was organist of the Marktkirche in Halle and teacher of Handel.

George Philipp Telemann (1681–1767) became organist of St. Thomas's in Leipzig in 1702 and, two years later, choirmaster to Count Promnitz in Sorau. In 1708 he was concert-master in Eisenach, and in 1712 church choirmaster in Frankfurt a. M. In 1721 he became music director of the five main churches in Hamburg. His activities were extensive in all fields of music—church music, oratorio, cantata, opera, instrumental music, and song.

Christoph Graupner (1683–1760) was court choirmaster in Darmstadt, and composer of church works, operas, symphonies, and keyboard works.

Johann Friedrich Fasch (1688–1758) became court choirmaster in Zerbst in 1722.

Gottfried Heinrich Stölzel (1690–1749) was court choirmaster in Gotha.

These and other *cantors* of the 16th to 18th centuries form the background against which Heinrich Schütz and J. S. Bach are to be visualized.

The position of cantor at St. Thomas's in Leipzig was a distinguished one, often referred to in German as simply the *Thomaskantor*. Among the musicians who held this office, with the years of their service or of their completion of it, are Josef Scharnagel (*ca.* 1505), Georg Rhau (1519–20), Johann Hermann (1531–6), Wolfgang Jünger (1540), Johann Brückner (*ca.* 1541); Ulrich Lange (1594), Wolfgang Figulus (1551), Melchior Heyer (1564), Valentin Otto (1594), Sethus Calvisius (1615), Johann Hermann Schein (1630), Tobias Michael, assisted by Johann Rosenmüller (1657), Sebastian Knüpfer (1676), Johann Schelle (1701), Johann Kuhnau (1722), and Johann Sebastian Bach (1750).

A list of notable Protestant musicians of this period should also include some of the outstanding individuals in the Scandinavian countries:

Johan Lorentz the Younger (1610–1689), son of the organ builder of the same name, organist of the Vor Frue Kirke, Copenhagen, in 1629 and of the Nikolajkirke and Holmens Kirke about 1635. An outstanding organist, he gave concerts three times a week in the Nikolajkirke.

Johannes Schröder (d. 1677), organist at St. Peter's Church in Copenhagen and teacher of Johann Philipp Krieger.

Christian Geist (*ca.* 1640–1711) of Mecklenburg, a member of the Swedish court chapel from 1670 to 1679 and then active in Copenhagen at the Helliggeistkirke. In 1689 he succeeded Johan Lorentz at the Holmens Kirke. He composed sacred concerts, numerous separate compositions, arias, and dialogues in concertante style.

Thomas Schattenberg (*ca.* 1580–after 1622), organist at St. Nicholas' Church, Copenhagen, beginning in 1604. Among his compositions are some four-voiced motets, *Cantiones sacrae* (1620), and some three-voiced madrigals, *Flores amoris* (1622).

Andreas Düben the Elder (*ca.* 1590–1662), pupil of Sweelinck, the first of a family of highly significant musicians in Sweden. About 1620 he came to Stockholm as court organist, was later the organist of the German church, and in 1640 became court choirmaster.

Gustav Düben the Elder (1624–1690), son of Andreas Düben, organist of the German church in Stockholm and court choirmaster. His compositions include a setting of the Paternoster *Fader vor* (1663), *Surrexit pastor bonus* (1664), and some songs with thorough-bass, *Odae Sveticae* (1674). He was responsible for the so-called Düben Collection, containing numerous compositions by Tunder, Buxtehude, Bernhard, Albrici, Geist, Ritter, Carissimi, Abbatini, Durante, and others.

The account of the notable publications of books of Protestant church songs should also include some that appeared in Poland. The Reformation spread widely in the middle of the 16th century. The Protestants, usually referred to there as the Dissidents, had established many printing presses, which were issuing songs for one or more voices. Their artistic level was not homogeneous, and there was great variety in the technique of the polyphonic arrangements. The melodies mostly followed the old Latin and Polish church music, as well as Bohemian and German themes that were common to the Lutheran chorale. The polyphonic arrangements, however, were mostly Polish.

The first Polish song-book was *Piésni duchowne a nabozne* . . . , by

Jan Seklucjan (Königsberg 1547). At brief intervals thereafter, further collections appeared, among them Walenty of Brzozów's (1554), translated from the Czech; Dawid Jakub Lubelczyk's psalter (1558); the Cracow Cathechism (1558); Jan Zaręba's *Pieśni chwał boskich* (1558); Groiki's *Pieśni duchowne* (1559); Nieśwież's song-book (1563); Kraiński's song-book (1599); and Piotr Artomius Krzesichleb's *Cantional to iest pieśni krześciańskie Toruń* (1587, further editions to 1728).

As the individual church congregations in Poland became more firmly established, they tended to bring their usages more closely into conformity with those of other centers of Protestant church music in Europe. Rybiński's psalter of 1603, for example, was provided with tunes "after the melodies of the French psalms."

Early Protestant activity in America was influenced by Calvin's particular form of the movement, as it had taken shape in Geneva, according to which only unaccompanied psalms should be sung in the church service. Thus the whole congregation could overtly participate, and verbal meaning could dominate sheer sound. For this purpose, metrical versions —that is, translations into the native language using ballad meter, with tunes—were published on the Continent and in England by 1562. The French or Genevan psalter was used by 16th-century Huguenots coming to the New World and was the basis of the Ainsworth Psalter (Amsterdam 1612) brought by the Pilgrims to Plymouth in 1620. The official English Sternhold and Hopkins Psalter was the one used by the non-Separatist Puritans, who settled at Boston in 1630 as a spearhead of reform within the Church of England. By 1640 they had printed there the Bay Psalm Book, which by the end of the century had been reissued more than forty times within Great Britain itself, some of these later editions including notation for a music so plain as to suggest that it may have served simply as an outline for what was in practice sung. As in primitive music, a line was normally sung or spoken first by a leader and then sung by the group, according to a practice known as "lining out." From the musical point of view, Massachusetts Bay psalmody contracted: in the 1640 edition, forty-eight tunes are indicated; in the 1698, only thirteen.

Writers in both England and America during the early 18th century tried to improve the situation by insisting that the congregation should learn to sing from notes and took steps to make it possible for them to do so—for example, Thomas Symmes in his "The Reasonableness of Regular Singing" (Boston 1720). Soon the "singing school" became a popular institution throughout the Colonies. This gave rise shortly after mid-century to the writing of significant anthems by New England composers, such as William Billings (1746–1800), well known for his "fuguing tunes," and Oliver Holden (1765–1844). Unlike 17th-century psalmody, the compositions had a through-composed plan and varied treatment, needing to be rehearsed and not exactly manageable by just everyone who felt he had the Spirit. Like other temporarily unfashionable music, older traditions of psalmody retreated to the backwoods, soon to be joined there by hymn-singing traditions as they passed out of fashion.

In Pennsylvania, however, a more direct manifestation of newer

Central European Protestant music appeared. Aside from somewhat eccentric individuals like Conrad Beissel (1690–1768) with a system for composing music very much his own, there was a real group of serious Moravian composers centered at Bethlehem, Pennsylvania, notably John Antes (1741–1811) and Johann Friedrich Peter (1746–1813)—the former a native of the region. A *collegium musicum* flourished at Bethelehem as early as 1744. The music cultivated there often involved both voices and instruments, and included string trios, quartets, and quintets—of a musical quality that identifies itself immediately as belonging to the same type of composition as that from which the great 18th-century German masters like Haydn and Mozart developed and as being related to the great Czech musical migration of the 18th century.

Within the specifically American tradition, the Moravians had direct influence on John Wesley, the founder of Methodism, who published at Charleston, South Carolina, in 1737 a "Collection of Psalms and Hymns" —the first hymnal designed specifically for use by a Church of England congregation. This religious institution had heretofore confined the singing in church to Psalms. The tunes for these new hymns were of quite various origin and, as this particular type of song gained favor, occasioned some original tune-composition. This development then proceeded from America to England—and ultimately, through missionaries, was to influence musical practice in some quite remote countries, not only Christian, as can be observed in the English section of "Standard Buddhist Gathas and Services" (Kyoto 1939). Among the quite active American compilers and composers of hymn-tunes were Thomas Hastings (1784–1872), Lowell Mason (1792–1872), and William B. Bradbury (1816–1868).

Schütz and Bach

Heinrich Schütz—or, in the Latinized form of his name, Henricus Sagittarius—was born on October 14, 1585, at Köstritz in Reuss and died in Dresden on November 6, 1672. A choirboy at the court of the Landgrave Moritz the Learned of Hesse in Kassel, he was at first a law student, but in 1609 received a stipend from the Landgrave that permitted him to study under Giovanni Gabrieli in Venice. After his return in 1613 he was court organist in Kassel, and from 1617 to the end of his life court choirmaster in Dresden. During this war-torn period, however, he was for several years court choirmaster in Cophenhagen. In 1628–9 he made a second trip to Italy and was in personal contact with Monteverdi in Venice. After 1644 he was again mostly in Dresden, working indefatigably in helping to restore German court chapels and church-choirs. Schütz had many private pupils, including Heinrich Albert, Weckmann, Bernhard, Adam Krieger, Johann Jakob Loewe, Theile, and Dedekind.

At Schütz's funeral he was eulogized as the "iron-gray father of German men of music" (*eisgrauer Vater der deutschen musici*). Mattheson in his *Ehrenpforte* (1740) referred to him as the "general apprentice-master of the makers of German music" (*allgemeiner Lehrmeister der deutschen Musikanten*). W. C. Printz in his *Historische Beschreibung der Sing- und Klingkunst* (1690) was responsible for the practice of referring to Schütz, Schein, and Scheidt as the "three famous S's" (*drey berühmten S*) of the 17th century.

As to his style, Schütz in his early youth was influenced by the art of Lasso and Hassler. While he was studying with Giovanni Gabrieli he adopted several picturesque Venetian features. These included polychorality, which left a brilliant imprint on his "Psalms of David" (1619), affective chromaticism of the third period of the Italian madrigal, and Monteverdi's operatic monody. It was during his first creative period of quite highly stressed subjectivity, which lasted up to 1628, that Schütz wrote his *Cantiones sacrae,* his *Auferstehungshistorie,* and his opera "Daphne."

After going to Italy a second time and renewing contact with Monteverdi, Schütz reduced the number of performers that he required for his works—perhaps partly as a result of wartime conditions—but retained always his quite personally experienced type of expression, notably in Part I of the *Symphoniae sacrae* and in the *Kleine geistliche Konzerte.*

Toward the end of the 1640's, he first showed a lessening of the subjective in favor of a more dogmatic type of utterance in his *Symphoniae sacrae* II and III and his *Geistliche Chormusik.* Musically, thus, he achieved close union of the parts and transcended the antitheses and contrasts that had been presented by the style he had adopted. In this third phase Schütz created mature works that are most highly balanced and unified. His towering significance in the 17th century lies almost exclusively in his Evangelical church music, and here it is a matter of his own fusion of styles into a most vital and powerful communication of a Protestant profession of faith.

He was the most significant personality and composer to appear in German music of the 17th century. For Evangelical church music he notably fulfilled three tasks: artistic, political, and theological. Artistically, he had mastered several Italian stylistic features that were regarded as innovations during the first three decades of the 17th century: such stylistic innovations as polychorality, the monodic principle, the concertante style, and the use of emotionally toned chromaticism. He transferred these Italian stylistic developments to German Protestant church music. Twice he had been to Italy: once from 1609 to 1612 as a pupil of Giovanni Gabrieli in Venice and again from 1628 to 1629. He brought these stylistic features together artistically into a many-sided achievement of unique significance. Politically, also, he played an important role in his persistent efforts to establish German court chapels and cantorial schools, particularly after the Thirty Years' War. He trained numerous pupils and, through his personality, provided a model for his time. Theologically, his significance lay in his music as a confession of Protestant faith of inflexible firmness and outstanding artistic ability to express powerful religious impulses.

His major works of Evangelical church music are his *Psalmen Davids* (1619); *Auferstehungshistorie* (1623); *Cantiones sacrae* (1625); Becker's Psalms (1628); *Symphoniae sacrae* I (1629); *Musikalische Exequien* (1636); *Kleine geistliche Konzerte* I and II (1636 and 1639);

Symphoniae sacrae II (1647); *Geistliche Chormusik* (1648); *Symphoniae sacrae* III (1650); *Zwölf geistliche Gesänge,* including the *Deutsche Messe* (1657); *Matthäus-, Lukas-,* and *Johannespassion* (1665–6); Christmas Oratorio (1664); *Die sieben Worte* (1645); and 119th Psalm and German Magnificat (1671), of which only the German Magnificat is extant in its entirety.

Johann Sebastian Bach was born on March 21, 1685, in Eisenach and died on July 28, 1750, in Leipzig. He was the youngest son of the musician appointed by the court and the town Ambrosius Bach (1645–1695) and a member of a widespread Thuringian family of musicians, going back to Hans Bach, who was born about 1520. In the family there were town pipers as well as cantors and organists. By the age of ten Bach had lost both parents and was brought up by his oldest brother, Johann Christoph, organist in Ohrdruf. There young Johann Sebastian became acquainted with the organ works of Pachelbel. In 1700 Bach entered grammar school and soon became choir prefect at St. Michael's School in Lüneburg. There he received musical impressions from a number of sources. He heard the organists Georg Böhm and Johann Jakob Loewe, formerly a pupil of Schütz; in Hamburg he heard Johann Reinken and Vinzenz Lübeck, and in Celle he became acquainted with French court music of the Lully tradition. Early in 1703 Bach was appointed violinist to Prince Johann Ernst II in Weimar. In the autumn of that year he became organist in Arnstadt. During the months between October 1705 and February 1706 he went to Lübeck to study under Buxtehude. In 1707 J. S. Bach married his cousin Maria Barbara Bach, and among the children to be born of this first marriage were Wilhelm Friedemann and Carl Philipp Emanuel. Also in 1707 Bach became organist of St. Blasius's at Mühlhausen; and in 1708 he became court organist and in 1714 court concert-master under Duke Wilhelm Ernst in Weimar. During the Weimar years, which were intellectually stimulating for Bach, he wrote his major organ works, notably the *Orgelbüchlein,* which originated presumably in 1717; he composed numerous church cantatas; and he became concerned with the Italian concerto form, beginning with keyboard transcriptions of Vivaldi and other concerti. From 1717 to 1723 Bach was in charge of music at the court of Prince Leopold von Anhalt in Cöthen. Although the Prince was a great lover of music, he was an adherent of Reformed Protestantism, which favored very modest musical accompaniment to worship. Bach, accordingly, wrote very little there specifically for the church, and instead composed his major works of keyboard and chamber music, such as Part I of the "Well-Tempered Clavier," the inventions, suites, instrumental sonatas, violin concerti, and six "Brandenburg Concerti" (1721).

In 1720 Bach applied unsuccessfully for the position of organist at St. James's in Hamburg. After the death of his first wife, he married Anna Magdalena Wülcken in 1722; and Johann Christoph Friedrich and Johann Christian were to be born of this second marriage. From 1723 to the end of his life he was cantor of St. Thomas's and music director in Leipzig, though he experienced increasing difficulties in working with those in authority over him. From 1729 to 1739 Bach was also leader of the student Collegium Musicum that had been founded by Telemann. In 1736 Bach was named "court composer" by Elector August III of Saxony after having applied three years before by submitting the *Kyrie* and *Credo* of his B-minor Mass. In 1747 Bach became a member of Mizler's "Society of Musical Sciences," and in the same year he played before Frederick the Great in Potsdam. During the Leipzig years he composed the St. John and St. Matthew Passions, the Christmas Oratorio, the B-minor Mass, numerous cantatas, major organ works, and other instrumental music, including Part II of the "Well-Tempered Clavier," the "Musical Offering," and the "Art of the Fugue."

To summarize Bach's life specifically in relation to church music, the places where he lived and came in contact with various kinds of Protestant church music establish the framework of his career:

Eisenach and Ohrdruf (to 1700): encounter with Thuringian church music, organ works of Pachelbel.

Lüneburg (1700–1703): contact with the organ composers Georg Böhm and Johann Jakob Loewe, the latter a pupil of Schütz; in Hamburg with Johann Reinken and Vincent Lübeck.

Arnstadt (autumn 1703–1707): first position as organist in Arnstadt; 1705–6, visit with Buxtehude in Lübeck for purposes of study.

Mühlhausen (1707–1708): organist.

Weimar (1708–1717): court organist. Church cantatas, organ works (*Orgelbüchlein*).

Leipzig (1723–1750): cantor at St. Thomas's. *St. John* and *St. Matthew Passions*, Christmas Oratorio, church cantatas, organ works.

Bach's historical mission of summing up the centuries-old development of Western music characterizes also his church music. It is the direct expression of his distinctively orthodox Lutheran religious faith. To him music was "for the honor of God and the recreation of the spirit." The works came into being purposefully in fulfillment of the church office assigned to him and were closely linked with the liturgy. They uniquely brought together a powerful musical impulse, an encompassing spiritual expressiveness, and a strong sense of pervading inspiration. He embodied his religious ideas in musical symbols, some of which have been fully elucidated only recently.

His vocal church music had two important bases. One was the Evangelical chorale. Notably he made 371 chorale settings and also numerous cantus firmus variations. The other basis was the then new fusion and penetration of Scripture with free lyric poetry. This appears notably in the extant Passions (*St. Matthew*, 1729, and *St. John*, 1723), in most of the cantatas (of which we have some two hundred, organized in five annual cycles), and in the six cantatas linked in a cycle known as the Christmas Oratorio. Also in the organ works, which will be considered in detail under the heading of keyboard literature, he summed up all the traditional forms: preludes and fugues, toccatas, fantasies, and chorale preludes.

His *B-minor Mass* is a work of special importance. The title "High Mass" was not applied to it until 1845. It is no "Mass" in the sense of the composition of the five parts of the Ordinary, but it consists of four independent compositions: the *Missa* (the setting of the *Kyrie* and *Gloria*, composed in 1733), the *Symbolum Nicenum* (the setting of the Nicene Creed, composed in 1732), the *Sanctus* (composed in 1736), and the sections from *Osanna in excelsis* to *Dona nobis pacem* (composed 1738–9). Bach wrote the movements for separate use in the Leipzig worship service. In 1733 he presented the *Missa* to the Elector of Saxony and asked to be considered for the "composing of church as well as orchestral music," and, accordingly, in 1736, he was named "royal Polish and electorial Saxon court composer."

Bach stands beside Handel as the most sublime phenomenon at the end of the Baroque Era. He combines and universalizes the centuries-old Western musical development. His musical greatness consists not in the creation of new forms, but in a unique exploitation of traditional ones. His idiom often reaches out far beyond his period, and particularly on into the Romantic Era. His music is filled with very strong personal individuality, containing moving content and utilizing forms linked with the times. Very often in his music, Bach imitates or "paints" in tone certain procedures that are quite pictorial. He also used a system of musical symbolism and seems to have carried out in his work many esoteric number relationships. Blume has attempted to describe Bach's style in somewhat the following terms: there is a profound penetration into the various forms, as, for example, in Bach's multiplication of polyphonic elements in the concerto form. Bach has a great deal of long-lined ornamental work in the melodic voices. Often he uses an intensifying technique of chromatic alteration, and his motives and linear formations seem laden with energy. He preferred the rhythm to progress uniformly and often handled the bass in ostinato fashion. His polyphony on occasion becomes dense, his melody reaches out widely, and his metrical construction is quite precise.

After Bach's death, his work was almost completely forgotten by the general public. The memory of it, however, lived on among his pupils— his sons, Krebs, Homilius, Nichelmann, Doles, Müthel, Agricola, and Kirnberger—and among individual connoisseurs. After 1800 the rediscovery of his work began, coinciding to a great extent with a period of renewed interest in history. Bach's work and personality have since then shone with incomparable radiance. A milestone in the Bach Renaissance was the revival of the *St. Matthew Passion* in 1829 by the Berlin Singakademie under the leadership of Mendelssohn.

Protestant Church Music Since Bach

In the middle of the 18th century the Evangelical church lost its dominating influence in spiritual and practical life. Church music accordingly declined in significance. Theology suffered from the influence of the Enlightenment, and the new religion of reason gave little place to church music.

The cantata declined in significance and became a sort of brief dramatic oratorio with simplified forms and cantabile melodic and chordal structure.

The oratorio flourished in the concert hall. Its particular nature was determined by the predominance of feeling, of lyricism. The three oratorio poems by K. W. Ramler, *Tod Jesu* (Death of Jesus), *Auferstehung und Himmelfahrt* (Resurrection and Ascension), and *Die Hirten bei der Krippe* (Shepherds at the Manger), which were set to music by numerous composers, are idyllically bourgeois and represent a high-point in the achievement of touching sentimentality.

Also the new church-song led away from the church. Christian Fürchtegott Gellert (1715–1769) produced a new type in his *Geistliche Oden und Lieder* (Spiritual Odes and Songs, 1757), determined by a combination of Pietistic, Rationalistic, and Sentimental tendencies. Many composers set Gellert's verses to music. Also Friedrich Gottlieb Klopstock (1724–1803) came to the fore as a poet of new songs and paraphraser of old ones. Matthias Claudius (1740–1815) was responsible for *Der Mond ist aufgegangen* (The Moon Has Risen). A type of "sacred song," represented by C. P. E. Bach and J. A. Hiller, made its appearance. The new "chorale book," intended for organ as accompaniment to congregational singing, was written in four-voiced setting. The most important chorale books in the latter half of the 18th century were those of J. Christoph Kühnau, Johann Adam Hiller, and Johann Christian Kittel. The compositions, according to Blume, are to be regarded as utilitarian music without much real artistic significance.

After Evangelical church music reached an artistic nadir around 1800, several developments helped to renew interest in it:

1. The collection of sacred folk-songs in such publications as "Des Knaben Wunderhorn" (1806) by Arnim and Brentano
2. Newly written poetry by Novalis
3. Nationalism aroused by the War of Liberation and expressed in verse by Arndt, Körner, and Schenkendorf
4. Historical research
5. A revival of interest in the music of Johann Sebastian Bach

In 1829 the so-called Berlin Song-Book made its appearance, and in 1833 Josias von Bunsen's attempt to set up an Evangelical book of common song and prayer, *Versuch eines allgemeinen evangelischen Gesang- und Gebetbuches*. These first Reform song-books ushered in a movement that was to continue to the present day. The preliminary work was done through research by such scholars as Karl von Winterfeld, Philipp Wackernagel, Johann Zahn, and Albert Fischer. Their efforts made many older works of Evangelical church music available in reprints, such as editions of Denkmäler as well as other collective and selective volumes. The achievement of the 19th century extended practically to a reform of the liturgy and of the song-books. As these efforts increased, however, the production of new music for the Protestant worship-service declined.

A first approach to a new church music in the Protestant spirit was made by Johannes Brahms in his motets Op. 29, 74, and 110, in his *Fest- und Gedenksprüchen* (Festive and Memorial Sentences), Op. 109, and in his "Eleven Chorale Preludes" posthumously published in 1902.

An important connecting link between Brahms and the new church music was provided by Arnold Mendelssohn (1855–1933), a secondary-school music teacher and composer of church music in Darmstadt, who in 1919 became a member of the Berlin Academy. He was mainly significant for his chorale cantatas and motets. Mendelssohn was the teacher of Paul Hindemith, Kurt Thomas, and Heinrich Spitta.

The significant advance that Evangelical church music has made since 1920 consists of certain tendencies that look to the past and certain other tendencies that look to the immediate present. As to the historically oriented movement envisioning a renaissance of earlier aims, we should realize that the Psalmists, the church fathers, and Luther shared the fundamental attitude that music meant divine worship. The renaissance movement in Evangelical music during the past half-century has reinstated this assumption in the thinking of many composers. A new relationship to the work of Johann Sebastian Bach has been achieved. The "Art of the Fugue" in Wolfgang Graeser's version, for example, was first performed in 1924 by Karl Straube. In 1925 organists and organ-builders began setting for themselves the special aim of recreating in the present the Baroque idea of organ sonority. The organ had become the principal instrument in the service. In connection with the singing movement started by the collection *Zupfgeigenhansl* (1908), Renaissance and Baroque vocal music was rediscovered by many who were in charge of church music. In particular, the works of Heinrich Schütz and Michael Praetorius were again performed. Song-books of the 16th century, such as those of Bapst and Goudimel, appeared in reprints. A new liturgical movement gave new meaning to the Mass, and particularly to the idea of sacrifice in it. This served to restore some equilibrium in the worship service, as over against the rationalistic focus on the sermon.

The movement in which organists and organ-builders were involved began to take shape in the early years of the 20th century as three pupils of Charles Marie Widor in Paris—Matthias, Rupp, and Albert Schweizer—consciously rejected the then prevailing type of organ, which imitated the Late Romantic expressive and nuanced orchestral sonority. At the beginning of the 1920's, the Alsatian musicians' aims were adopted in Germany. Wilibald Gurlitt in Freiburg im Breisgau had the organ of the German Early Baroque reconstructed according to the specifications of Michael Praetorius in his "Syntagma musicum," and Christhard Mahrenholz restored a High Baroque organ. The restoration of the Schnitger organ of St. James's church in Hamburg filled out the historical picture. Thus the original sounds were again available for the historical notation. The efforts released a new ideal of sonority, which found fruit in contemporary organ composition. Three organ conventions in Germany—one at Hamburg in 1925 and two at Freiburg im Breisgau in 1926 and 1927—resulted in productive discussions.

Passing on to new works of church music, we might note that they to some extent stand on the same level of significance as contemporary secular music. The separation between secular and sacred music, which prevailed in the 19th century, no longer prevails. Of these composers none writes exclusively for the church. The works involve a rejection of the Romantic idea of sonority and an awareness of the vocal world of the

Renaissance, the instrumental world of the Baroque, and Gregorian chant.

The wide area in which a number of tendencies have confronted each other includes organ music (organ chorales, partitas, preludes), Mass compositions (in Latin or German), the chorale (chorale settings for choirs, chorale motets), the sentence motet, and the Passion. Composers who have been concerned with this movement and some of their relevant works are the following:

Ernst Pepping (b. 1901), *Passionsbericht des Matthäus, Spandauer Chorbuch,* motets, German chorale Mass, *Missa "Dona nobis pacem,"* organ works, Paul-Gerhardt song-book, and "Christmas Story according to St. Luke."

Hugo Distler (1908–1942), organ works, Mass, "Year Cycle" (choral compositions), chorale motets, *Geistliche Chormusik,* German chorale Mass, chorale Passion, and "Christmas Story."

Johann Nepomuk David (b. 1895), organ works (chorales), motets.

Heinrich Kaminski (1886–1946), organ works (chorale sonata), motets, *Magnificat,* "Passion," and "Mass in German."

Hans Friedrich Micheelsen (b. 1902), organ works, chorale motets, *Tod und Leben* (Requiem), "Sacred Concerti," solo cantatas, and Passions.

Siegfried Reda (1916–1968), chorale prelude for organ, sentence motets, sacred concerti, and Requiem.

Kurt Thomas (b. 1904), *Kleine geistliche Chormusik,* Mass in A-minor, and "Passion according to St. Mark."

Willy Burkhard (1900–1955), organ works, cantatas, Mass, and oratorio *Das Gesicht Jesajas.*

Walter Kraft (b. 1905), choral works, "Canonic chorale motets," and oratorio *Christus.*

Helmut Bornefeld (b. 1906), chorale work for organ, motets, and *Kantoreisätze.*

Adolf Brunner (b. 1901), Missa, motets, and sacred concerts.

Johannes Driessler (b. 1921), motet, *Sinfonia Sacra,* oratorio *Dein Reich komme, Denn Dein Licht kommt* (cantata), and *Der grosse Lobgesang.*

Günther Raphael (1903–1960), motets and organ works.

Heinz Werner Zimmermann (b. 1930), motets, psalms, and organ works. Church music with jazz elements.

Church Music in the Scandinavian Countries Since 1750

The isometric chorale—that is, the kind that maintains equal measures and more or less equal notes throughout—had become the norm in German publications beginning with the late 17th century, but in Scandinavian countries this development appeared about a century later. In Denmark and Norway it was established with the chorale books of Niels Schiørring in 1781 and 1783, of H. O. C. Zinck in 1801, and of C. F. E. Weyse in 1839. The same trend appeared in Sweden with J. C. F.

Haeffner's chorale book, first published in 1820. In 1838 Norway obtained its own chorale book, compiled by O. A. Lindeman.

The active writing of new church-song texts, especially those of N. F. S. Grundtvig, resulted during the second third of the 19th century in many new melodies composed in Denmark in the style of the Romantic song. In certain circles these created a new, lively type of congregational song. This specific situation was made possible by the fact that, from the 19th century on, the Danish chorale books were no longer authorized, and the choice of melodies accordingly remained free. New melodies were printed along with the traditional chorales in the chorale books of A P. Berggreen (1853) and V. Bielefeldt (1900) and in the Norwegian chorale book of L. M. Lindeman (1877), but the leading collections of melodies for the Grundtvig congregations were those of Henrik Rung (1857, rev. 1868) and the chorale book of Christian Barnekow (1878). In Norway folk-melodies were introduced into the *Koralbok for den norske Kirke* (1926).

The reform movement became quite strongly pronounced in Denmark with Thomas Laub (1852–1927). In 1887 his book *Om Kirkesangen* opposed the stiff, slow chorale and the poor quality of the Romantic church song and advocated instead the restoration of the modally harmonized, rhythmically lively, early Protestant chorale. His collection "Dansk Kirkesang" (1918) contained about 130 old melodies and about 70 new ones composed by him in the style that had prevailed around 1600. This tendency was carried further in *130 Melodies* (1936), edited by J. P. Larsen, F. Viderø, and M. Wöldike. The same principles were followed by P. Steenberg's Norwegian collection (1949) and an inter-Scandinavian committee's *Nordisk Koralbog* (1961). *Den Danske Koralbog* (1954) by J. P. Larsen and M. Wöldike undertook to do justice to both the Romantic tradition and the reform movement. In Sweden in 1963 the chorale book of 1939 was supplied with an appendix, in which the melodic forms and accompaniments were influenced by the German Evangelical book of church songs and by German practice.

As for Finland, in 1903 for the first time since the song book of 1702 a new official chorale book was issued under the supervision of editors headed by R. Lagi, O. I. Colliander, and R. Faltin. This book included Finnish folk-melodies. There was a further tendency toward a stronger national character in the new chorale book of A. Maasalo, T. Kuusisto, and A. Lehtonen (1944). The *Sálmasöngsbók* used in Iceland was edited by Sigfús Einarsson and Páll Isólfsson in 1936.

The movement toward liturgical reform, prompted by the study of Gregorian chant, also manifested itself in the revival of the prose portions of the Mass and the principal Offices. Mass books were authorized in Sweden, Norway, and Finland, while in Denmark J. P. Larsen's *Messetoner* (1935), as well as the antiphonaries, remained a matter of possible private use in the prayers of the Hours.

In the field of religious art-music, the most significant Swedish composer of the 18th century was J. H. Roman (1694–1758), who set many Psalms to music, some scored for many voices and instruments including solo and continuo, among which is a *Svenska messan* or *Missa brevis* in Swedish. Church music was also written by Ferdinand Zellbell the Younger (1719–1780).

Romantic church music was represented in Denmark primarily by C. E. F. Weyse (1774–1842) and J. P. E. Hartmann (1805–1900). Weyse's *Den ambrosianske Lovsang* (1826) and especially the cantatas for the main church festivals—such as a Christmas cantata (1818), a Whitsunday hymn (1820), and an Easter cantata (1821)—were an early and successful attempt to revive Protestant church music. Additional cantatas were written by Hans Matthison-Hansen (1807–1890). The Swedish composer G. Wennerberg (1817–1901) composed settings for Psalms. In the course of the 19th century there was great interest in smooth choral hymns for liturgical purposes, to some extent influenced by Caecilianism and particularly represented in Sweden by J. A. Josephson (1818–1880), Otto Olsson (1879–1964), and John Morén (1854–1932).

Though important impulses have manifested themselves in Denmark during the 20th century in the field of church music, Sweden and Norway have shown even more fruitful activity both in performance and composition. In Denmark, the following have composed motets in the spirit of the reform movement: Carl Nielsen (1865–1931), Knud Jeppesen (b. 1892), Vagn Holmboe (b. 1909), and Bjørn Hjelmborg (b. 1911). In Sweden, there have been Gunnar Thyrestam (b. 1900), Torsten Sörensen (b. 1908), and Torsten Nilsson (b. 1920). And in Norway there have been Per Steenberg (1870–1947) and Rolf Karlsen (b. 1911). Motets influenced by more recent trends in secular music include those by Leif Thybo (b. 1922) in Denmark, Sven-Erik Bäck (b. 1919) and Sven-Eric Johanson (b. 1919) in Sweden, and Knut Nystedt (b. 1915) and Egil Hovland (b. 1924) in Norway, where Fartein Valen (1887–1952) was unique in writing intensively expressive motets in free atonal style.

The organ movement appeared in Denmark with works by Carl Nielsen, Knud Jeppesen, Svend-Ove Møller (1903–1949), Finn Viderø (b. 1906), Leif Kayser (b. 1919), and Leif Thybo, and in Sweden with works by Valdemar Söderholm (b. 1909) and Stig Gustav Schönberg (b. 1933). New developments since 1950 have contributed much to the work of the Swede Bengt Hambræus (b. 1928), with his almost hypnotic organ works.

Church Music in the United States During the 19th and 20th Centuries

In the United States during the 19th and 20th centuries the impulse behind the creation of hymn-tunes in the early 19th century was perpetuated among Southern white and Negro groups and gave rise to "Negro spirituals," which were later to find their way again into general Protestant use and to be utilized in instrumental works by recognized composers. It also continued operative among wide segments of the Protestant world, as indicated by the popularity of the "gospel hymns" —which reinstated a certain amount of the "general participation" idea from earlier psalmody—as they figured in revivalistic tours in the United

States and abroad, conducted by D. L. Moody and I. D. Sankey around 1875 and Billy Graham at mid-20th century.

Among more educated levels in leading urban centers, however, two trends in Protestant musical worship manifested themselves during the 19th century: a dominant tendency to favor a stationary and somewhat professionalized quartet, with organ or choir accompaniment, and an at first subordinate tendency (but stronger as the century proceeded) to have a vested choir enter in procession, singing and usually preceded by the crucifer, and take its place in the chancel. This latter tendency was a conscious revival of Gothic practice and was associated with the Oxford Movement, which was not unrelated to Caecilianism. The outstanding composer in the "sacred quartet" tradition was Dudley Buck (1839–1909), who studied in Leipzig and Paris, composed many anthems, pioneered in giving organ recitals, and taught numerous pupils who were to be active church-music composers. His larger choral works, notably "The Light of Asia" and "The Voyage of Columbus," were performed in both Europe and America. The outstanding composer sympathetic to the medievalistic tendency was Horatio W. Parker (1863–1919), who studied under Rheinberger in Munich. Parker's outstanding religious composition was *Hora Novissima* (1893), to a Latin text by Bernard of Cluny—an oratorio for choir, chorus, orchestra, and organ. Originally performed in church—as many of the well-known oratorios by 18th- and 19th-century European composers were not—this highly wrought and unified work reestablished an important relationship that had been interrupted in Protestant church music. Later it was performed at the Three Choirs Festival in Worcester, England; and Parker's "Wanderer's Psalm" was commissioned for the Hereford Festival of 1900 and his "Star Song" for the Norwich Festival of 1902. Also in the latter year he received an honorary Doctor of Music degree from Cambridge University. From 1904 to 1920 he was Dean of the Yale University School of Music. Both Buck's and Parker's works embody some aspects of the approach to music that is usually referred to on the Continent as neo-German.

An outstanding American composer also active within the Episcopal church and writing both secular and sacred music is Leo Sowerby (b. 1895), in the latter field notably a Passion, "Forsaken of Man" (1940), and an oratorio on a Franciscan text, "The Canticle of the Sun" (1946). William Grant Still (b. 1893) wrote a cantata "And They Lynched Him on a Tree" (1940), Virgil Thomson (b. 1896) an Anglican Mass for unison chorus and organ (1958), and Normand Lockwood (b. 1906), "Land of Promise" (1960) for a General Conference of the Methodist Church, as a "dramatic portrait of Rocky Mountain Methodism."

There has been renewed interest in various aspects of the early Protestant music of America within the past few decades. Charles Ives (1874–1954) brings many of the hymns into his Third and Fourth Symphonies (1904, 1910–11). Ross Lee Finney (b. 1906) has a choral and orchestral work based on tunes from the Ainsworth Psalter. Henry Cowell (1897–1965) wrote a series of compositions for various instrumental resources, "Hymns and Fuguing Tunes" (1942–57), and William Schuman (b. 1910) wrote an orchestral "New England Triptych" (1956) on the basis of the 18th-century American composer William Billings' "fuguing tunes."

General Bibliography

F. Blume, *Die ev. Kirchenmusik* (Bücken Hdb., Kassel 2nd ed. 1965); J. D. v. d. Heydt, *Gesch. d. ev. Kirchenmusik* (Bln. 1926); H. J. Moser, *Gesch. d. dt. Musik* I and II, and *Die ev. Kirchenmusik in Deutschland* (Bln. and Darmstadt 1953); K. F. Müller and W. Blankenburg, eds., *Leiturgia, Hdb. des ev. Gottesdienstes* (Kassel); A. Schering, *Ev. Kirchenmusik* (Adler Hdb.); O. Söhngen, *Theol. Grundlagen der Kirchenmusik* (in: Leiturgia, Kassel 1957); W. Stahl, *Geschichtl. Entwicklung d. ev. Kirchenmusik* (Bln. 2nd ed. 1920); new eds. in coll. vols.: BlCh; *Hdb. d. dt. ev. Kirchenmusik* (Göttingen, 1941–   , ed. Ameln, Mahrenholz, and Thomas): *I. Der Altargesang, II. Das gesungene Bibelwort, III. Das Gemeindelied, IV. Das gottesdienstliche Orgelspiel* (abbreviated here as HDEKM); *Musik um Luther. Die in den Jahren 1538 und 1534 von d. Verleger u. Drucker Georg Rhau hrsg. Musikdrucke* (Kassel 1954–   ). Luther "Deudsche Messe" facs. Kassel, "Wir glauben . . ." Sch 77, melodies new ed. in *Weimarer Lutherausgabe*, Bd. 35; H. Abert, *Luther u. d. Musik* (Ges. Schriften u. Vorträge, 1929); W. Gurlitt, *Joh. Walter* (Lutherjb. 1933); H. J. Moser, *Die Melodien d. Lutherlieder* (1935); J. Rautenstrauch, *Luther u. d. Pflege der kirchl. Musik in Sachsen* (Lpz. 1907); W. Stapel, *Luthers Lieder u. Gedichte* (Stuttgart 1950). *Achtliederbuch, Erfurter Enchiridien*, and *Strassburger Kirchenampt*, facs, new eds. *Geystliche gesangk Buchleyn* PGfM 7 and Walter, coll. ed. vol. I; Sch 80. *Blume* and *Babst* song-books, facs. new eds. Kassel. *Rhau song-book*, DDT 34. *Goudimel's psalm-settings*, facs. new ed. Kassel; Sch 142, 143, 189. *Song-book studies:* A. Fischer and W. Tümpel, *Das dt. Kirchenlied des 17. Jh.* (6 vols., 1904–16); E. E. Koch, *Gesch. d. Kirchenliedes u. Kirchengesangs der christl., insbes. d. dt. ev. Kirche* (8 vols., Stuttgart 1866–76); J. Kulp, *Die Lieder unserer Kirche* (Göttingen 1959); C. Mahrenholz and O. Söhngen, eds., *Hdb. zum Ev. Kirchengesangbuch* (Göttingen); W. Nelle, *Gesch. d. dt. ev. Kirchenliedes* (Hamburg 2nd ed. 1909); P. Pidoux, *Le Psautier huguenot du XVIe siècle* (2 vols., Basel 1962); A. Schering, *Die metrisch-rhythm. Grundgestalt unserer Choralmelodien* (Lpz. 2nd ed. 1927); L. Schöberlein and F. Riegel, *Schatz d. liturg. Chor- u. Gemeindegesanges* (3 vols., 1865–72); P. Wackernagel, *Das dt. Kirchenlied von d. ältesten Zeit bis Anfang d. 17. Jh.* (5 vols., 1864–77); J. Westphal, *Das ev. Kirchenlied* (5th ed. 1918); C. v. Winterfeld, *Der ev. Kirchengesang u. sein Verhältnis zur Kunst d. Tonsatzes* (3 vols., Lpz. 1843–7); J. Zahn, *Die Melodien d. ev. Kirchenlieder* (6 vols., Gütersloh 1889–93); coll. ed. of Goudimel in 15 vols., in prep. (IMM, Brooklyn, N. Y.); arts. Gemeindegesang, Gesangbuch, Kantional (MGG). *Thomissøn* "Psalmebog," *Jesperssøn* "Gradual," *Vallerius* "Psalmboken," *Kingo* "Gradual," and *Breitendich* chorale book: facs. new eds.

Chorale Motet and Sentence Motet: exs. Sch 107–110, 123. *Eccard* "Preussische Festlieder," new ed. 1858. *M. Praetorius:* coll. ed.; Sch 159–162. *E. Bodenschatz:* O. Riemer, *E. B. u. s. Florilegium Portense* (Diss. Lpz. 1928). *Pedersøn* "Pratum spirituale": ed. K. Jeppesen (Dania sonans I, Copenh. 1933). *Christian Ritter:* T. Norlind, *Zur Biographie C. R.s* (SIMG 1910–1).

Sacred Concert: Schein "Opella nova," Sch 188. *Schütz* "Kleine geistliche Konzerte," Sch 190. Adrio, *Die Anfänge des geistl. Konzerts* (Bln. 1935); F. Blume, *Das monodische Prinzip in d. prot. Kirchenmusik* (Lpz. 1925); H.-O. Hudemann, *Die protest. Dialogkomp. im 17. Jh.* (Kieler Diss. 1941); arts. Dialog, Kantate (MGG). *Performance Practice in the 17th Century:* E. T. Ferrand, *Die Improvisation* (MW); R. Haas, *Aufführungspraxis der Musik* (Bücken Hdb.); M. Kuhn, *Die Verzierungskunst in der Gesangsmusik des 16.–17. Jh.s* (Lpz. 1902); M. Praetorius, *Syntagma musicum, III. Bd., Wolfenbüttel 1619* (new ed. Lpz. 1916, also Documenta musicologica, Kassel); A. Schering, *Aufführungspraxis alter Musik* (Lpz. 1931); art. Aufführungspraxis (MGG).

Cantata: A. Dürr, *Zur Chronologie der Leipziger Vokalwerke J. S. Bachs* (Bach-Jahrbuch 1957) and *Studien über die frühen Kantaten J. S. Bachs* (Lpz. 1951); H. J. Moser, *Gesch. d. dt. Musik II;* W. Neumann, *Bach. Sämtliche Kantatentexte* (Lpz. 1956) and *Hdb. der Kantaten J. S. Bachs* (Lpz. 1947); K. F. Rieber, *Die Entwicklung d. dt. geistl. Solokantate im 17. Jh.* (Freiburg Diss. 1926); A. Schering, *Über d. Kirchenkantaten vorbachischer Thomaskantoren* (Bach-Jb. 1912); E. Schmitz, *Gesch. d. Kantate u. d. geistl. Konzerts I* (Lpz. 1914); F. Smend, *J. S. Bachs Kirchenkantaten* (6 bks., Bln. 1947–9, 2nd ed. 1950); L. F. Tagliavini, *Studi sui Testi delle Cantate sacre di J. S. Bach* (Milan 1956); C. S. Terry, *Bach's Cantata Texts* (London 1926); F. Treiber, *Die thür.-sächs. Kirchenkantate z. Z. d. jungen Bach* (AfMf 1937); H. Werthemann, *Die Bedeutung der alttestamentlichen Historien in J. S. Bachs Kantaten* (Tübingen 1960); R. Wustmann, *Bachs Kantatenwerk* (Lpz. 1913); F. Zander, *Die Dichter der Kantatentexte J. S. Bachs* (Diss. Cologne 1967); Kantate (MGG).

Passion: Walter "St. Matthew Passion" new ed. in Kade, HDEKM, also "St. John Passion." *Resinarius:* BlCh. *Burck:* PGfM 22. *Lechner* "St. John Passion" new ed. Kassel 1926; HDEKM. *Demantius:* BlCh. *Selle* "St. John Passion": BlCh. *Johann Sebastiani* "St. Matthew Passion" DDT 17. *Theile* "St. Matthew Passion" DDT 17. *Basic repr. of Prot. Passion:* HDEKM; studies: K. Ameln and C. Gerhardt, *J. Walter u. d. ältesten dt. Passionskomp.* (Monatsschrift f. Gottesdienst u. kirchl. Kunst 1939) and *J. Walter u. d. ältesten dt. Passionshistorien* (Göttingen 1947); W. Braun, *Die mitteldeutsche Choralpassion im 18. Jh.* (Bln. 1960); P. Epstein, *Zur Gesch. d. dt. Choralpassion* (JbP 1931); K. v. Fischer, *Zur Gesch. d. Passionskomp. des 16. Jh. in Italien* (AfMw 1954); O. Kade, *Die ältere Passionskomp. bis 1631* (Gütersloh 1893); W. Lott, *Zur Gesch. d. Passionskomp.* (AfMw III, VII); H. J. Moser, *Die mehrst. Vertonung d. Evangeliums I* (Lpz. n.d.) and *Zur Frühgesch. d. dt. Generalbasspassion* (JbP 1920); A. Schering, *Gesch. d. Oratoriums* (Lpz. 1911); G. Schmidt (HDEKM); arts. Historia, Passion (MGG).

Cantorial Schools . . . 16–18th Century: D. Krickeberg, *Das prot. Kantorat im 17. Jh.* (Diss. Bln.-West 1963); F. Sannemann, *Die Musik als Unterrichtsgegenstand in den Lateinschulen des 16. Jh.* (Bln. 1904); G. Schünemann, *Gesch. d. dt. Schulmusik* (Lpz. 1928); A. Werner, *Gesch. d. Kantoreigesellsch. in Sachsen* (Publ. d. IMG Beiheft 9, Lpz. 1902) and *Vier Jahrhunderte im Dienst d. Kirchenmusik* (Lpz. 1933); art. Kantorei (MGG). *Johann Walter:* new ed. Kade (Passion comp.); coll. ed. in 3 vols. (Kassel); HDEKM; W. Ehmann, *J. W.* (Musik u. Kirche, Jg. 1934); C. Gerhardt, *Die Torgauer Walter-Handschriften* (Kassel 1949); W. Gurlitt, *J. W.* (Lutherjb. 1933). *Sixt Dietrich:* new eds. DDT 34; HDEKM;

H. Zenck, *S.D.* (Lpz. 1928, PäM 3, 2; also new ed. of 13 hymns). *Leonhard Lechner:* coll. ed. 1954–   , ed. K. Ameln (Kassel); HDEKM; K. Ameln, *L. L.* (in Schwäbische Lebensbilder, Bd. 7, Stuttgart); M. Schreiber, *L.L.* (Diss. Munich 1932); art. Lechner (MGG). *Hieronymus Praetorius:* sel. works DDT 23; B. Friederich, *Der Vokalstil des H. P.* (Hamburg 1932). *Michael Praetorius:* coll. ed. 20 vols. Wolfenbüttel, Berlin; new ed. of the "Syntagma musicum" I (Kassel 1959), II (PGfM 13, also Kassel 1958); III (Lpz. 1916, Kassel 1959); HDEKM; F. Blume, *Das Werk des M. P.* (ZfMw XVII); A. Forchert, *Das Spätwerk des M. P. Ital. u. dt. Stilbegegnung* (Bln. 1959); W. Gurlitt, *M. P.* (Lpz. Diss. 1915); R. Unger, *Die mehrchörige Aufführungspraxis bei P.* (Wolfenbüttel 1941). *Bartholomäus Gesius:* HDEKM; art. Gesius (MGG). *Philipp Dulichius:* motets in DDT 31 and 41; art. *Dulichius* (MGG). *Christoph Demantius:* motets in BlCh; German songs in LD Sudetenland, Bohemia, and Moravia I; "St. John Passion" in BlCh; HDEKM. *Johann Staden:* sel. works DTB 7, 1, and 8, 1. *J. H. Schein:* coll. ed. Lpz. 1901–23; HDEKM; new Schein ed. 1964 (Kassel); W. Reckziegel, *Das Cantional von J. H. Schein* (Bln. 1963); A. Prüfer, *J. H. S.* (1895) and *S.s Stellung in d. Gesch. d. dt. Liedes* (Beiheft d. IMG 1908). *Samuel Scheidt:* organ works DDT 1; coll. ed. Hamburg 1923–   ; HDEKM; E. Gessner, *S., geistl. Konzerte* (Bln. 1961); C. Mahrenholz, *S. S.* (Lpz. 1924); *Thomas Selle:* S. Günther, *Die geistl. Konzertmusik T. S.s* (Diss. Giessen 1935). *Andreas Hammerschmidt:* sel. works DDT 40; sacred concerti DTÖ 8, 1. *Franz Tunder:* cantatas in DDT 3; Sch 211; W. Stahl, *F. T. u. D. Buxtehude* (AfMw 1926). *J. E. Kindermann:* works in DTB 13, 21–24. *Johann Rosenmüller:* instr. works in DDT 18; F. Hamel, *Die Psalmkomp. J. R.s* (Strasbourg 1933); A. Horneffer, *J. R.* (Bln. Diss. 1898). *Matthias Weckmann:* motets in DDT 6; coll. wks. LD Schleswig-Holstein 4; Sch 212, 213; G. Ilgner, *M. W.* (Wolfenbüttel 1939). *J. R. Ahle:* vocal works in DDT 5; HDEKM. *Christoph Bernhard:* cantatas DDT 6; *Heinrich Schütz's Theory of Comp. as understood by his pupil Christoph Bernhard* (new ed. Lpz. 1926); Sch 213. *Dietrich Buxtehude:* coll. ed. Hamburg 1925–   ; cantatas (DDT 14); chamber music (DDT 11); organ works I–II (Lpz. 1938–9); new organ works (Stockholm 1950); vocal works (8 vols. Hamburg 1925–   ); keyboard works (Copenh. 1942); organ works I–IV (Copenh. 1952); *Studies:* F. Blume, *Das Kantatenwerk D. B.s* (JbP 1941); M. Geck, *Die Vokalmusik D. B.s und der frühe Pietismus* (Kassel 1965); S. A. E. Hagen, *D. B.* (Copenh. 1920); J. Hedar, *D. B.s Orgelwerke* (Stockholm 1951); K. Jeppesen, *D. B.* (DTM 1937); C.-A. Moberg, *D. B.* (Helsingborg 1946); H.-J. Pauly, *Die Fuge in den Orgelwerken D. B.s* (Regensburg 1964); A. Pirro, *D. B.* (Paris 1913); O. Söhngen, *Die Lübecker Abendmusiken* (Musik u. Kirche 1957); W. Stahl, *Franz Tunder und D. B.* (AfMw 1925); C. Stiehl, *Die Familie Düben u. die Buxtehudeschen Mss.* (MfM 1890); arts. Abendmusik, Buxtehude (MGG). *Johann Philipp Krieger:* cantatas DDT 53–4; organ works DTB 18. *Johann Krieger:* keyb. works DTB 18. *Georg Böhm:* coll. ed. Lpz. 1927–   ; J. Wolgast, *G. B.* (Bln. Diss. 1924). *F. W. Zachow:* sel. works in DDT 21–22. *G. P. Telemann:* new ed. of intermezzo "Pimpinone" RD I 6, of oratorios and cantatas DDT 28, of instr. mus. DDT 61–62, DDT 29, and of songs DDT 57; many indiv. new eds.; sel. ed. 1950–   (Kassel); ed. of letters in prep. (IMBA); W. Menke, *Das Vokalwerk T.s* (Kassel 1942); M. Schneider in DTD 28; E. Valentin, *G. P. T.* (Burg 1931) and *T. in s. Zeit* (Hamburg 1960). *Christoph Graupner:* cantatas DDT 51–52; sel.

(Kassel); F. Noack, *G.s Kirchenmusiken* (Darmstadt 1916). *Johann Friedrich Fasch:* B. Engelke, *J. F. F.* (Diss. Lpz. 1908). *Cantors of 16th–18th Centuries: new eds. in coll. works:* RD 1 and 2 (Altbachisches Archiv); RD 9 (Orgelchoräle um J. S. Bach); DDT 49–50 (Thüring. Motetten der ersten Hälfte des 18. Jh.); DTB 6, 1 (Nürnberger Meister in der zweiten Hälfte des 17. Jh.); *Musikgesch. Leipzigs* (1st vol. by R. Wustmann, Lpz. 1909, 2nd and 3rd vols. by A. Schering, Lpz. 1926 and 1941); *St. Thomas zu Leipzig. Bilder u. Dokumente,* ed. B. Knick (Wiesbaden 1962); art. Leipzig (MGG).

Scand. Countries: Johan Lorentz: B. Lundgren, *J. L. in Kopenhagen* (Kongressbericht Cologne 1958). *Christian Geist:* sel. works in ED; art. in MGG. *Düben family:* A. Düben, "Pugna triumphalis" ed. N. Fransén, Stockholm 1932; *G. Düben* works in *Monumenta Musicae Svecicae,* vol. 5; B. Grusnick, *Die Dübensammlung. Ein Versuch ihrer chronologischen Ordnung* (STM 1964 and 1966); T. Norlind, *Die Musikgesch. Schwedens in den Jahren 1630–1730* (SIMG 1899–1900).

Poland: G. Kratzel, *Die altpolnischen protestantischen Kantionalfrühdrucke* (Mf 1965); art. Kraiński (MGG).

America: coll. ed.: W. T. Marrocco and H. Gleason, *Music in Am.* (N. Y. 1964); *studies:* A. P. Britton, *Theoretical Introductions in Am. Tunebooks to 1800* (U. of Mich. Diss. 1950, Ann Arbor, Univ. Microfilms 1505); R. T. Daniel, *The Anthem in New Eng. before 1800* (Evanston 1966); L. Ellinwood, *The Hist. of Am. Church Music* (N. Y. 1953); H. Engelke, *A Study of Ornaments in Am. Tune Books 1790–1800* (USC Diss. 1960, Ann Arbor, Univ. Microfilms, L. C. No. Mic. 60-558); I. Lowens, *The Origins of the Am. Fuguing Tune* (JAMS, 1953); D. M. McCorkle, *John Antes . . .* (MQ 1956); W. S. Pratt, *The Music of the Pilgrim* (Boston 1921); A. G. Rhau, *John Frederick Peter* (MQ 1937); R. Stevenson, *Prot. Ch. Mus. in Am.* (N. Y. 1966).

Heinrich Schütz: coll. ed., 18 vols., begun in 1885 by Philipp and Friedrich Spitta; new col. ed. (Kassel) begun in 1955; Stuttgart coll. ed. in 36 vols. begun in 1966. Numerous indiv. eds., HDEKM, Sch 189–192. A. A. Abert, *Die stilistischen Voraussetzungen der Cantiones sacrae von H. S.* (Wolfenbüttel and Bln. 1935); W. Bittinger, *Verz. der Werke* (Kassel 1960); H. H. Eggebrecht, *H. S. Musicus poeticus* (Göttingen 1959); M. Geier, *Kurtze Beschreibung des H. H. S.' mühseligen Lebenslaufs* (1672, facs. new ed. Kassel 1935); R. Gerber, *Das Passionsrezitativ bei H. S. u. seine stilgesch. Grundlagen* (Gütersloh 1929); W. S. H. v. Hasleberg, *Motivsymbolik bei H. S.* (Basel 1958); G. Kirchner, *Der Generalbass bei H. S.* (Kassel 1960); W. Kreidler, *Der Stile concitato bei S. u. Monteverdi* (Kassel 1934); H. J. Moser, *H. S. Sein Leben u. Werk* (Kassel 2nd ed. 1954); E. H. Müller, ed., *S.'s coll. letters and other writings* (Regensburg 1931); J. Piersig, *Das Weltbild des H. S.* (Kassel 1949); A. Pirro, *S.* (Paris 2nd ed. 1924); W. Schuh, *Formprobleme bei H. S.* (Lpz. 1928); P. Spitta, *Die Passionen nach den vier Evangelien von H. S.* (Lpz. 1886); *Die Komp.lehre H. S.' in d. Fassung s. Schülers Christoph Bernhard* (new ed. Lpz. 1926); *S.' Memorial an den Kurfürsten von Sachsen von 1651* (Kassel 1936).

J. S. Bach: compl. ed., 50 vols. of the *Bachgesellschaft* begun in 1851, continued by the *Neue Bachgesellschaft;* "Die Neue Bach-Ausgabe," ed. by the Joh.-Seb.-Bach Institut at Göttingen and by the Bach-Archiv at Leipzig, beginning in 1954; *Them.-system. Verzeichnis der mus. Werke* ed. by W. Schmieder (Lpz. 4th ed. 1966). Mizler's *Nekrolog* (1754);

Hiller (1784); Forkel (1802, mod. repr. 1925); P. Spitta (2 vols., Lpz. 1873 and 1880, 5th ed. 1962, repr. 1964); A. Pirro (*L'esthétique de Bach*, Paris 1907); A. Pirro (*Bach*, Paris 1906); A. Schweitzer (*Bach le musicien poète*, 1905); C. S. Terry (London 1928); H. J. Moser (Bln. 1934); R. Steglich (Potsdam 1935); F. Hamel (Göttingen 1951); F. Smend, *Bach in Köthen* (Bln. n. d.); W. Vetter, *Der Kapellmeister Bach* (Potsdam 1950); series of arts. on Bach (MGG). Extensive special research. *Bach-Jahrbücher* since 1904. Compl. ed. of letters (Regensburg 2nd ed. 1950); documents (Kassel 1950); *Bach-Gedenkschrift* (Zurich 1950); *Bach-Probleme, Festschrift* (Lpz. 1950); K. Geiringer, *The Bach Family* (London 1958); *Bach-Dokumente* (3 vols., Kassel 1964–   ); H. Keller, *Die Orgelwerke B.s* (Lpz. 1948); W. Neumann, *Hdb. der Kantaten J. S. B.s* (Lpz. 1947); A. Schering, *B.s Leipziger Kirchenmusik* (Lpz. 1936); R. Wustmann, *B.s Kantatenwerk* (Lpz., 1913).

Protestant Church-Music since Bach: H. Hoffmann, *Vom Wesen d. zeitgen. Kirchenmusik* (Kassel 1949); A. Niebergall, *Ev. Gottesdienst heute* (Kassel 1953); E. Schlink, *Zum theol. Problem der Musik* (Tübingen 1947); O. Söhngen, *Die Wiedergeburt der Kirchenmusik* (Kassel 1953) and *Kämpfende Kirchenmusik* (Kassel n. d.); R. H. Wallau, *Die Musik in ihrer Gottesbeziehung* (Gütersloh 1948); Zeitschrift "Musik und Kirche." Scandinavia: S. Sorensen, *Allgemeines über den dänischen protestantischen Kirchengesang* (Kieler Schriften zur Musikwissenschaft Bd. 16, Kassel 1965). America: G. Chase, *America's Music* (N. Y. 2nd ed. 1966); L. Ellinwood, *The Hist. of Amer. Church Music* (N. Y. 1953); J. T. Howard, *Our Am. Music* (N. Y. 4th ed. 1965); R. Stevenson, *Protestant Church Music in Am.* (N. Y. 1966).

26. Opera

Prehistory of Opera

Music in Dramatic Art Before 1600

Before the advent of actual opera, several dramatic forms with music had appeared:

1. Medieval liturgical festival plays. These arose particularly in Southern Germany and the German part of Switzerland. They came from the St. Gall movement that had fostered tropes and sequences—a development with which the names of Tuotilo and Notker are associated. Spoken Passion and mystery plays with incidental music developed from the originally sacred *singspiel*, which spread to Northern France and England. Proving quite popular, they grew into folk-plays. The *sacre rappresentazioni*, which were usually presented in church, were of particular significance in Italy during the Trecento.

2. School comedies and moralities, from the 14th to the end of the 17th century, containing choral songs as incidental music. Later, directly influenced by opera, they were expanded and provided with instrumentally accompanied solos. The 16th-century drama of the Humanists and of the schools contained choruses set carefully after Classical metri-

cal patterns. We have examples by Tritonius, Hofhaimer, and Senfl. At Jesuit secondary institutions school-opera was still significant during the 18th century. The drama of the Humanists introduced three important new features: (1) the transformation of the pageant-type medieval play into a work of verbal art; (2) the separation of the stage and the audience for purposes of heightening the illusion; and (3) concentration of time and place in the action, thus overcoming what Hauser has called the epic limitlessness of the Middle Ages.

3. Song-plays. The oldest preserved example of this richly cultivated type of art is Adam de la Halle's "Le Jeu de Robin et de Marion" (Naples 1283), which has fourteen incidental songs in it. Scholars are still not sure exactly how it was presented—whether, for instance, it was really given dramatically, with dialogue.

4. Incidental music in Renaissance drama, of which one of the earliest examples is Politian's "Orfeo" (1471). In Rome, from 1480 on, when important personages appeared on the stage, they were accompanied by music. The number of plays with music increased about the middle of the 16th century. In 1585 Sophocles' "Oedipus" was presented in Vincenza with music by Andrea Gabrieli.

5. Intermezzi. Originally, dramatic scenes that were merry or comic developed plots of their own and grew in significance. But still they remained entr'actes and were provided musically with canzone, choruses, and dances. With the collaboration of Cavalieri, Malvezzi, Marenzio, and Caccini they became more prominent in the latter half of the 16th century. Of similar importance as preparation for actual opera were occasional poems written in homage and presented on festive occasions, involving allegory and semi-dramatic elements and often including such forms as the *canti carnasciuleschi, mascherate, canzonette, cantate, veglie,* and *balletti.* They were known in Venice as *rappresentazione.*

6. Pastoral dramas, beginning with Boccaccio's "Ninfale Fiorentino." The culminating points were Tasso's "Aminta" (1577) and Guarini's "Pastor fido" (1581). Imitations of Theocritus' and Vergil's late Classical idylls and eclogues, known as *favole pastorale,* widened the range of material in the Florentine, Roman, and early Venetian operas. The *commedia dell 'arte,* which had developed from the *mimi* and the *atellane* of Antiquity, gained in significance, especially in the later Venetian and Neapolitan opera.

7. Madrigal comedies. In these the group sang the whole composition, which had been written as a madrigal, but the text purported to be a conversation between two or more people. Thus a quasi-dramatic action was presented, though probably without costumes or scenery. Among the madrigal comedies were Alessandro Striggio's "The Gossip of the Women on Wash-Day" (1567), Orazio Vecchi's "Amfiparnasso" (1597), and Adriano Banchieri's "La pazzia senile" (1598). This type continued until the beginning of the 17th century.

Preliminary Developments in Monody

In addition to these dramatic forms involving music, there were developments in music itself that prepared the way for operatic monody

—that is, for solo song accompanied by chords in harmony, which made its appearance about 1600 as a style of performance revolutionary in its effect. It entailed a degree of unification that had not been present before, subordinating all details to a single principle. It is comparable to the composition of a painting in which everything can be related to a central point on a single diagonal. Several forms paved the way for monody:

1. The Spanish villancico, the Italian frottola, and the German and French Humanists' songs, which to some extent had almost developed homophonically accompanied declamation.

2. Arrangements for song and lute of Cara's and Tromboncino's frottole, Verdelot's madrigals as reworked by Willaert, and the proverbios of the Spanish lutenists Luis Milan, Luis de Narvaez, Alonso de Mudarra, Auriquez de Valderrábano, Diego Pisador, Miguel de Fuenllana, and Esteban Daza. These lute pieces, along with many original songs, were printed between 1536 and 1576. In this general category, also, belong Spanish solo songs accompanied by the vihuela de mano.

3. Other solo versions of polyphonic pieces. Toward the end of the 16th century there appeared printed music that contained the tablature for voice with cembalo and lute right along with the polyphonic version of sacred and secular canzonette, as in Cosimo Bottegari's "Libro de Canto e Liuto."

4. "Pseudo-madrigals" are madrigals set up as if they were monodies, with the melody in the upper voice and the other voices accompanying it harmonically. Examples of this form are to be found in Luzzasco Luzzaschi's duets and trios with cembalo accompaniment, which were printed in 1601.

5. Vincenzo Galilei's setting in recitative style, around 1590, of parts of the lamentations of Jeremiah and the lament of Ugolino from Dante's "Inferno." The music of his recitative settings, however, is no longer extant. Father of the noted astronomer, he studied under Zarlino and discovered the ancient hymns of Mesomedes.

6. Instrumental solo-playing on the viola with cembalo accompaniment, traceable as early as 1553 in the "Tratado de Glosas sobre Clausulas" by Diego Ortiz, at Rome. Here there is explanation with practical examples of how the solo instrument is to be brought together with the cembalo, as well as how vocal compositions such as madrigals and motets are to be arranged for the cembalo. There are also further instrumental books of this sort by Ganassi dal Fontego (1542 and 1543), Juan Bermudo (1555), and Tomás de Sancta Maria (1565).

7. The development of a kind of cipher-writing above the lowest voice, known as thorough-bass, among Italian organists. The earliest example of this practice dates from 1587. After 1600 figured bass quickly spread and became fairly general. This practice became known by various names—basso continuo, basso seguente, basso fondamentale, General-bass, bezifferter Bass, basse chiffré, and basso figurato. It is a sort of musical shorthand in which the structure of the chords is expressed by numbers over the bass voice. The top voice and the bass had thus

become the two centers of the musical conception and stood in a polar relationship to each other while the middle voices simply fulfilled a supplementary role.

Italy

Seen from a longer-range view of general history, the 17th century was to bring with it for Italy a period of literary, artistic, and political decline. From 1628 to 1849 it was strongly influenced from abroad and from 1750 to 1800 was actually under foreign rule, with the Bourbons in Parma, Naples, and Sicily, the Hapsburg-Lorraine family in Tuscany, and the Austrians in Milan. After the victory of Bonaparte at Marengo in 1800, the Italian political structure was reorganized; but in 1813–1814 Napoleon's power was overthrown, and Austria conquered Upper Italy. In 1815, through the Congress of Vienna, Austria dominated Italy. From 1820 to 1831 there were uprisings in Naples, Sicily, and Sardinia, with King Carlo Alberto of Sardinia appearing as the champion of Italian independence. The union of Italy was achieved during the period from 1849 to 1871: from 1852 to 1861 Cavour was at the head of the Italian ministry, and from 1861 to 1878 King Victor Emmanuel II ruled.

17th Century

Back in the late 16th and early 17th centuries, Italy was still in a period of Baroque splendor, the developments being focused around various centers such as Florence, Mantua, Rome, and Venice. It was at Florence that the beginnings of opera appeared, within a group known as the Florentine Camerata. During the years from around 1580 till the end of the century, discussions of art occurred at the house of Count Bardi and, after 1592, at that of Jacopo Corsi between patrons, scholars, poets, and musicians. A third group, led by Emilio de' Cavalieri, included the musicians Vincenzo Galilei, Piero Strozzi, Giulio Caccini, Jacopo Peri, and the poets Ottavio Rinuccini and Gabriello Chiabrera. In 1581 Galilei published a treatise in dialogue form, "Della Musica antica e della moderna," which adopted a position frontally opposed to contrapuntal music. Galilei himself made some attempts to compose in the monodic style, perhaps stimulated to do so by the discovery of the hymns of Mesomedes. In 1592 Jacopo Corsi took over the leadership of the circle. The artistic result of the period was the development of the monodic style with the collaboration of Emilio de' Cavalieri, Giulio Caccini, Jacopo Peri, and Marco da Gagliano, with strong influence from the madrigal vocal style as it was represented by the composers of the third period of the madrigal. In his preface Caccini called for "Nuove Musiche" (1601) in which the music would have to subordinate itself to the text.

"Dafne," the first opera, was presented at the house of Jacopo Corsi in Florence in 1597—a date that has sometimes been given incorrectly as 1594. The text was by Ottavio Rinuccini, the music by Jacopo Peri (d. 1633). The music, however, is not extant.

In 1600, for the marriage of Henry IV of France to Maria de' Medici, the "Euridice" of Rinuccini and Peri was given its first performance in the Pitti Palace in Florence. The work made a very great impression on the people of the time. The same text was also set to music by Giulio Caccini (d. 1610), and the work was performed in 1602.

According to Peri's preface to "Euridice," *stile rappresentativo* or *recitativo* was a kind of composition midway between speech and song. It changed the harmony of the accompaniment only if logical or grammatical reasons demanded it. The voice of the singer remained on the same chord. Giovanni Battista Doni asked that the composer take the delivery of a good actor as his model. The text must be clearly understood; the music was to conform to the word.

There were also other operas performed shortly after 1600 in Florence, including Marco da Gagliano's "Dafne," which used Rinuccini's text (Mantua 1608) and one by Francesca Caccini, the daughter of Giulio Caccini. In these operas, however, there were no further new elements.

Like Florence, Mantua was an early center of interest in opera, and it was there that the first important composer in this form, Claudio Monteverdi, brought out his work. Born in 1567 in Cremona, he was a pupil of Ingegneri and early evidenced talent—in fact, he was already a published madrigalist at sixteen. From 1590 to 1612 he served the court at Mantua, first as singer and violinist and later as choirmaster. In 1613 he succeeded Giulio Cesare Martinengo as choirmaster at St. Mark's in Venice and served there till his death on November 29, 1643.

Monteverdi was one of the boldest and most inventive of the musically creative personalities of history, being responsible for a whole group of innovations that have been enumerated by H. F. Redlich somewhat as follows. First of all, Monteverdi showed harmonic and chromatic daring in his madrigals, especially in Books II and V (1590–1605). He combined, for the first time, singing voices with an obligatory instrumental ensemble in accordance with precise formal law in his Mantuan operas and his "Scherzi Musicali" (1607). In his "Orfeo" (1607) he included symphonic ritornelli structurally and individualized the accompanying instrumental resources in a fully composed score. From opera he carried over the dramatic recitative style into sacred music, first in his solo motet "Nigra sum" (1610). He refashioned the *stile concitato*. In the "Combattimento" (1624) he introduced the four-voiced string movement into the completely composed score and first used the tremolo and pizzicato. He used typical characterizing motives in his operas and took conscious steps toward a number of operatic forms, including the da capo aria, the bipartite and tripartite aria, the coloratura variation aria, the concertante chamber duet, and the passacaglia variation—particularly in his late Venetian operas. Basic to his achievements is his declaration, in 1607, that he represented the *Seconda Prattica*, in opposition to the linear art developed by Ockeghem, or *Prima Prattica*, in which "the music is not the servant but the mistress of the word."

In 1607 Monteverdi's "Orfeo" was first given in Mantua. The poetic text was by Striggio. It was a gifted composer's combination of the new style with available forms into a musico-dramatic unity. Declamatory expression was heightened, with characterizing dramatic motifs in the recitatives; and there were strophic songs with refrains, choruses, dances, and independent orchestral sections, which recurred in the manner of a *leitmotif*. Tone-color was significantly used in the orchestra.

Monteverdi wrote some further stage works for Mantua, including "Arianna" (1608), the *mascherata* in Ottavio Rinuccini's "Il Ballo dell' Ingrati," and the "Combattimento di Tancredi e Clorinda" (1624). Of the "Arianna" all that we have is the highly expressive "Lamento d'Arianna." The "Combattimento" is from Tasso's "Jerusalem Delivered" and utilizes the *stile concitato*, a style of sacred music, dramatic in character, in which the instrumental portion serves autonomously in the dramatic action to express anger and scorn. The "Scherzi musicali" of 1632 already point ahead to the late works, which were composed in Venice. During the years between 1616 and 1630 he wrote ten operas and ballets, of which but few are extant.

A third center that was affected by the opera movement was Rome, where developments occurred in the direction of allegory and comedy. In 1600 there was a performance of the sacred opera "Rappresentazione di Anima e di Corpo" by Emilio del Cavaliere (d. 1602), an allegorical play; in 1606, the pastoral drama "Eumelio" by Agostino Agazzari; in 1610, "La Morte d'Orfeo" by Stefano Landi, with a libretto by the composer; in 1626, "La Catena d'Adone" by Domenico Mazzocchi; in 1632, "S. Alessio" by Stefano Landi, his most significant work; in 1633, "Erminina sul Giordano" by Michelangelo Rossi; in 1639, "La Galatea" by Loreto Vittorio; and in 1656, "La vita humana" by Marco Marazzoli.

The style of the Roman opera involved the gradual assimilation of polyphonic elements into the choruses, dramatic enlivenment of the recitative, and development of self-contained forms in the solos. In the texts there was a preference for the allegorical, with the introduction of personified concepts. Thus the moralizing sacred opera containing edifying reflections developed—a type of opera that later fused with the oratorio. In Stefano Landi's opera "Il San Alessio" there were for the first time merry dance songs to characterize the ferryman Charon. Thus comic elements found initial entry into opera.

Rome was the homeland of the full-length *buffo* opera. Its founder was Cardinal Giulio Ruspigliosi, who was later Pope Clement IX. He wrote two comic opera libretti, "Che soffre speri," set to music in 1639 by Domenico Mazzocchi and Marco Marazzoli, and "Dal male il bene," set by Antonio Maria Abbatini and Marco Marazzoli and performed in 1653. Further development of the *buffo* opera was taken over by Venice and then in the 18th century especially by Naples.

Mazzocchi was no doubt reflecting the taste of the time when in his preface to "Catena d'Adone" (1626) he complained of the *tedio del recitativo*. Soon the recitative was further developed, and Giovanni Battista in his "Trattato della musica scenica" (1640) could draw a distinction between the *stile recitativo* as the naturally declamatory flow of speech, the *stile espressivo* as the cantabile expression of feeling, and the *stile rappresentativo* as the dramatically enlivened, passionate accent.

The institutionalizing of opera, however, occurred in a fourth Italian city, Venice. After the opening of the first regular opera house, the Teatro S. Cassiano in Venice, in 1637 with Francesco Manelli's opera "L'Andromeda," opera became a component of Venetian public cultural life. By 1700 sixteen opera houses had been founded in Venice. The theater was supported by the Venetian public itself. This underlying sociological shift created a completely new basis for the development of opera. Venetian opera had three public social levels: the lower bourgeoisie of Venice, the foreign princes as box-holders, and the great Venetian merchants. Cavalli represented the aristocratic culture, Cesti the bourgeois. Opera in Venice was one of the antecedent forms of the later bourgeois musical theater.

Monteverdi wrote a number of operas for Venice: two that are no longer extant, "L'Adone" (1639) and "Le Nozze de Enea con Lavinia" (1641), and two that we have, "Il Ritorno d'Ulisse in patria" (1640) and "L'Incoronatione di Poppea" (1642). Here he had transcended 16th-century stylistic traits, expanding the recitative to reveal beginnings of the arioso, developing the varied strophic song, and deepening the melodic expression. He placed less emphasis on polyphony, reducing the extent of the choruses and instrumental sections and simplifying the make-up of the orchestra. Thus he fused the instrumental and vocal portions into a dramatic whole, inventing instrumental motives in connection with the dramatic action and developing ostinato forms in accordance with dramatic intention. The final duet of the "Incoronatione" is one of the first examples that we have of the *da capo* form.

The two main composers of Venetian opera were Caletti-Bruni, or Cavalli, and Cesti.

Pier-Francesco Caletti-Bruni, known as Cavalli, was born in 1602 in Crema, rose from singer in St. Mark's chapel in 1668 to choirmaster there, and died in 1676 in Venice. Of his forty-two operas, the most successful was "Giasone" (1649). He also wrote "Le Nozze di Teti e di Peleo" (1639), "L'Egisto" (1643), and—for the marriage of Louis XIV—"Ercole amante" (Paris 1662).

In his style of composition, he was at first connected with Roman opera, but later created the Venetian style. He favored a more terse, more dramatically striking type of expression, instead of dwelling on the musical characterization of the personages in the opera. Also he displayed great richness of invention. He transformed the recitative into arioso song by using coloratura elements both decoratively and thematically. With individualized song-like sections he established a transition to bipartite and later tripartite arias. Often he constructed his arias and duets over a basso ostinato. At the climactic points in the action he introduced duets. He frequently presented solemn death scenes, which became a definite musical type in opera.

Marc'Antonio Cesti, born in 1623 in Arezzo, was presumably a pupil of Carissimi's. In 1645 he became *magister musicae* at the theological seminary in Volterra. He entered the service of the Archduke in Innsbruck, in 1652. From 1659 to 1662, he was a member of the papal choir. After being again in Innsbruck for a while, he was from 1666 to

1669 assistant choirmaster in Leopold I's chapel in Vienna. He died in 1669 in Florence. His principal works are "Il Pomo d'oro" (1666 or 1667), a festival opera performed in Vienna on the occasion of Leopold I's marriage; "La Dori" (Florence 1661); "Il Tito" (1666); "L 'Argia" (Innsbruck 1655); and "Le Disgrazie d'Amore" (Vienna 1667).

Cesti's style is marked by the development of great, self-contained musical scenes, culminating in lyrical moments. In general, he preferred elegiac, dreamy moods, with love-duets of extreme tenderness, and often with dramatic melodic lines of great softness. Occasionally, however, he assimilated farcical elements and folk-like songs into his work.

There were three phases in the development of Venetian opera. In the first, from 1637 to about 1660, expression in the recitatives was heightened and the arioso parts were gradually developed, the sinfonias remaining still largely chordal. In the second, from about 1660 to about 1680, bipartite and tripartite arias were developed in organic connection with the recitatives that preceded them, and fugue began to appear in the sinfonias. In the third, from about 1680 to the end of the century, the fugal style was intensified, entering even the ritornelli of the arias. During this time there was a transition to the Neapolitan type of opera, in which there was less emphasis on the dramatic effect and more on the formal order of the music.

Cavalli and Cesti belonged to the first and second phases, as did Francesco Sacrati and Pietro Andrea Ziani. Sacrati's "La finta pazza" was given in Venice in 1641 and in Paris in 1645. Giovanni Antonio Boretti, Carlo Grossi, and Carlo Pallavicino belonged to the second and third phases. Giovanni Legrenzi, Giovanni Maria Pagliardi, Domenico Freschi, and Carlo Francesco Pollarolo belonged to the third phase.

The style of Venetian opera was characterized by two somewhat complementary tendencies. On the one hand, composers and public seemed to prefer historical, mythical, and allegorical materials, viewing them according to their own current taste. On the other hand, they were inclined to project their immediate experiences into the forms of the past. There was considerable emphasis on theatrical architecture, machinery, and other equipment. The theater-architect Giacomo Torelli played a significant role in this development. To accommodate the frequently changing scenes, the theaters developed twelve principal types of sets, including ones in which the gods might manifest themselves and in which the characters might visit the underworld. Also the composers established individual fixed musical types, such as the *lamento,* often constructed over an ostinato bass. The stylistic peculiarities often ascribed to the Neopolitan school alone, such as the *da capo* aria, the coloratura aria, the aria with concertante solo instruments, and also the infiltration of folklike melody, had already manifested themselves in Venice.

Alongside heroic opera, in the latter half of the 17th century, comic opera developed as a means of satirizing the heroic opera style and led to the full flowering of a decidedly parodistic and comic opera. This development may be considered as a quasi-folk influence, on the part of the public. The main representative of this trend was Pietro Andrea Ziani. Particularly, also, Legrenzi mixed heroic and comic styles.

18th Century

The Neapolitan Opera School (1690–1800)

Opera Seria

The 18th century has been termed by Blume the "century of opera par excellence." Certainly the Neapolitan school, from 1690 to 1800, can claim a prominent place in such an estimate, and opera seria a prominent place in the work of this school.

Although some of the individual stylistic peculiarities of Neapolitan opera had been previously developed in Venetian opera, the influence of two men established the type of Neapolitan opera seria. They were the text-poets Apostolo Zeno (1668–1750) and Pietro Metastasio (1698–1782). Zeno, successor to Silvio Stampiglias as court poet in Vienna, wrote the texts for forty-seven operas and twelve oratorios. There were also fifty-seven published opera texts by Metastasio, the celebrated court poet in Vienna under Maria Theresa.

Both Zeno and Metastasio were connected with Classical French tragedy. They placed heroic and courtly figures on stage and completely satisfied the taste of the refined world with elegant images of fashionable and aristocratic society. The characters in these libretti had no particular inner development, but remained typical. Psychologically, the action was based mainly on intrigue. Its structure was schematic. The polished, melodically flowing and flowery verses were basic to the stereotyped musical forms of the *da capo* aria and to the typical affective and coloristic features of the music. Because Neapolitan opera stressed music at the expense of the text and developed solo singing to such an extreme that it gradually foundered on the excesses of its virtuosity, it sometimes figures in histories of music as opera *per se*.

The action was articulated into recitativo secco, recitativo accompagnato (obbligato), and arias. Recitativio secco, a very flowing form of recitative with cembalo accompaniment, advanced the external action. The arias were points of rest, or of affective expression, to characterize states of the soul. Metastasio did not write any arias that advanced the action, but only arias that commented on it and drew similitudes. The recitativo accompagnato—orchestrally accompanied, declamatory, with emphasis on expression—often stood before the aria and also, at the time of Gluck, advanced the action.

The construction of the *da capo* aria was tripartite, ABA. When the first part was repeated as the third, it was then provided by the singer with freely improvised ornaments. A lyric quatrain lay at the basis of both parts A and B. Part B was often the contrast to A in key, meter, and tempo. Part A was itself again bipartite. Its parts were separated from each other by a cadence on the dominant or parallel key and an ensuing ritornello. The second part, usually provided with coloraturas, had some of the character of a development and led back to the usually shortened first section. At the end of it came the singer's free cadenza. The aria was the basis of the orchestral ritornelli—four in all, which stood at the beginning, at the end of the two sections of the first part, and at the close of the second part.

Alongside the aria there occasionally appeared also the song-like cavatina. In ensemble sections only duets were significant.

The tripartite Neapolitan overture or sinfonia (Allegro, Andante, Allegro) was a sort of rushing upbeat without being linked in content with the opera. The tripartite aspect was later the model of the Classical symphony.

Very great importance was attached to the scenery of the performance and to its being brilliantly cast with vocal virtuosi—with the *prima donna* and the *primo uomo,* a castrato. Castrati, who had begun to play a significant part in opera during the late 16th century, became well established by about 1650 and dominated Neapolitan opera completely. Famous castrati of the time were Senesino, Cafarelli, Farinelli, and Crescentini. Famous women opera singers were Tesi, Bordoni-Hasse, Cuzzoni, Mingotti, Agujari, and Gabrielli. The artistic standard was *bel canto,* the ideal of beautifully sonorous music-making, which also influenced instrumental music strongly.

The *stagione* was the well-established opera season during carnival time, from the second day of the Easter holidays to June 15 and from September 1 to November 30. The composer wrote only on commission for a certain production and entirely in view of the vocal peculiarities of the singers that had been secured for the performance. Practically all composers wrote both serious and *buffo* operas. Except in France, Neapolitan opera had a position of almost unlimited world domination.

A *pasticcio* was a mixed opera, which different composers participated in composing, usually act by act.

Representatives of the Neapolitan School of Opera

Alessandro Scarlatti and the Older Neapolitans (to 1730)

Alessandro Scarlatti was regarded as head of the school. Its founder had been Francesco Provenzale, whose music parted company with the finer psychological musical style of the Venetians and approached the character of absolute music.

Francesco Provenzale (1627–1704), a Neapolitan, was a teacher in the S. Maria di Loreto Conservatory and later became its director. From 1686 to 1699 he was conductor at the S. Gennaro Theater. As early as 1653 he began to write operas, among which are "Il schiavo di sua moglie" (? 1671) and "Stellidaura vendicante" (Naples 1678). Among his pupils were Alessandro Scarlatti, Domenico Sarri, and N. Fago.

Alessandro Stradella (about 1645–1682) was involved in some circumstances that are not very clear today and was murdered in Genoa. We have several operas and oratorios, cantatas, trio sonatas, and concerti grossi of his, pointing in some ways ahead to features of Neapolitan style.

Alessandro Scarlatti, born in 1660 in Palermo, had his first opera produced in 1679 in Rome. From 1680 to 1684 he was master of the court choir for the Swedish queen, who was living there. Also he was in

Naples as leader of the conservatory, court conductor (1684–1702, 1708–1718, and 1722–1725), and for a while also choirmaster. He died in 1725. Among his pupils were Logroscino, Durante, and Hasse.

Sixty-four of his 114 operas are extant, the best known being "La Rosaura" (Rome 1690), "Teodora" (Rome 1693), "Tigrane" (Naples 1715), and his last opera, "Griselda" (Rome 1721). He also wrote the comic opera "Il trionfo dell'onore" (Naples 1718).

As to the style of his work, he started from the point reached by the Venetians Stradella, Legrenzi, and Pallavicino. Surpassingly gifted and enormously prolific, he wrote significant music that was individually felt and that was original, serious, and careful, with a feeling for greatness, many-sided in the control of expression, and ranging from the charming to the vehement. It was a music of dramatic power and melodic richness, containing occasional Neapolitan provincialisms. In it, the *da capo* aria predominated, but Scarlatti also employed strophic songs, brief duet passages, and occasional ensembles. He developed an aria style of considerable pathos. In his later works the instrumentation became richer and richer. Scarlatti, Handel, and Steffani were the most significant representatives of the early Neapolitan music-centered opera. Scarlatti's points of contact with the later Neapolitans, however, were limited. Instead, his creative work presents a summation of the stylistic development of the whole Baroque era.

Leonardo Vinci (1690–1730), court conductor in Naples, was a brilliant melodist, with fiery expressive qualities. He showed a preference for Neapolitan provincialisms, was particularly masterful in individual accompanied scenes, and conveyed a strong general effect of virtuosity.

Leonardo Leo (1694–1744), a pupil of Provenzale, succeeded Scarlatti at S. Onofrio Conservatory in Naples. Teacher of Jommelli and Piccinni in Naples, he was outstanding as a composer of comic opera and church music.

Niccolò Porpora (1686–1768) exerted extensive influence as composer, conductor, and singing teacher in Venice, Vienna, Dresden, London, and then again in Venice, Vienna (where he taught Haydn), Dresden, and Naples. Versatile in musical expression and calculating in effect, he represented a culminating point of virtuosity in the Aria.

Giovanni Battista Pergolesi (1710–1736), pupil of Durante and Feo, displayed great melodic ability, with a somewhat effusive tendency to display gentle feeling. He wrote five serious operas, but was most significant in the *buffo* opera.

George Frederick Handel (1685–1759) also belongs, historically, to the school of Scarlatti. His career was many-sided, including also oratorios and orchestral and keyboard works. Born and trained in Halle, he received early impressions of native opera in that general area of Germany, hearing works by Johann Philipp Krieger at Weissenfels and by Telemann at Leipzig. In 1703 he became a violinist in the Hamburg opera and soon was active as harpsichordist, conductor, and composer. He wrote four operas in German there, the first of which, "Almira" (1705), is extant. In 1706 he went to Italy, where he came in contact with the Neapolitan operas and solo cantatas of Alessandro Scarlatti, as well as with the opera in Venice. Handel's first Italian opera was presumably "Rodrigo." His "Agrippina" was written for Venice in 1709. Influences of Scarlatti and Corelli seem to have contributed to a strongly transitional period in his work, but his style again became clearer in his first opera written for London, "Rinaldo" (1711). In further operas he maintained the clarity of the Italian formal structure.

His connection with London came from the fact that between 1711 and 1716 he was court conductor for the Elector of Hanover, who in 1713 became King George I of England. At the King's order Handel opened his "first academy" (in a sense, the Royal Academy of Music) at the Haymarket Theater in London in 1720 with "Radamisto." In this and subsequent operas Handel tended to place the ethical above the purely affective aspects of his music. Under Bononcini's influence he was able to gain popularity through lighter, more song-like treatment of the material in "Ottone" (1723). But he did not bring the orchestral and vocal elements together into really big scenes until his "Giulio Cesare in Egitto" (1724), which was followed by a whole series of outstanding operas such as "Tamerlano" (1724) and "Rodelinda" (1725). At the same time, however, one can also detect influences of Leonardo Vinci. In 1728 Handel also set some of Metastasio's texts to music. The principle of strict schematization in the *da capo* arias and recitatives now advanced side by side with the principle of tension in scenic construction. Handel's operas in London were originally intended for a small but dominant social stratum, which included outstanding individual connoisseurs of music.

As a composer of operas in London, Handel encountered cross-currents within the British aristocracy, intense competition with Bononcini, and difficulties with temperamental vocal stars. In 1728 he faced bankruptcy—hastened, perhaps, by the success of Gay and Pepusch's "Beggar's Opera." In 1729 Handel tried to make a recovery, and again in 1734; but these efforts ended in 1737 with a physical and financial breakdown. Although he did eventually come back, his work as a composer after 1740 was largely in the field of oratorio.

His operas belonged principally to the Neapolitan style, although there were unmistakable Venetian influences in the polyphonic recitatives, the scenes of pathos, and the slumber scenes. He united German feeling and Italian formalism, excelling all his Italian contemporaries in suggesting human characters by means of melody. In his operas he submitted to prevailing conventions, and his efforts at musical reform were largely reserved for his later oratorios.

Among his works there are over forty operas. His principal works for the London "academies," with the dates of first performance, include "Radamisto" (1720), "Muzio Scevola" (1721), "Floridante" (1721), "Ottone" (1723), "Flavio" (1723), "Giulio Cesare" (1724), "Tamerlano" (1724), "Rodelinda" (1725), "Scipione" (1726), "Alessandro" (1726), "Admeto" (1727), "Riccardo I" (1727), "Siroe" (1728), "Tolomeo" (1728), "Lotario" (1729), "Partenope" (1730), "Poro" (1731), "Ezio" (1732), "Sosarme" (1732), "Orlando" (1733), "Ariadne in Crete" (1734), "Il Pastor Fido" (1734), "Terpsichore" (1734), "Ariodante" (1735), "Alcina" (1735), "Atalanta" (1736), "Giustino" (1737), "Arminio" (1737),

"Berenice" (1737), "Faramando" (1738), "Serse" (1738), "Giove in Argo" (1739), "Imeneo" (1740), and his last opera, "Deidamia" (1741).

Second Neapolitan School (*Hasse and His Followers*)

Another German, Johann Adolph Hasse (1699–1783), was the leader of the Neapolitan School in its second phase. His Italian colleagues called him *Caro Sassone,* or "dear Saxon." Born at Bergedorf near Hamburg, he was a pupil of Alessandro Scarlatti and Niccolò Porpora in Naples. He married the famous opera singer Faustina Bordoni. Having won his first Italian operatic success in 1723 in Naples, he soon extended his activities to Venice, and from 1731 on he was largely in Dresden, making various trips from there to Italy, London, and Paris. He died in Venice. Along with Scarlatti and Handel he was one of the most significant dramatic composers of the period. Having achieved international fame during his lifetime, he exerted great influence on the younger Neapolitans, as well as on Gluck, Haydn, and Mozart. He wrote some sixty-five operas, fourteen intermezzi, and numerous pasticcios. His works include the operas "Artaserse" (Venice 1730), "Cleofide" (Dresden 1731), "Didone abbandonata" (Hubertusberg, near Dresden, 1742), "Arminio" (Dresden 1745), and "Solimano" (Dresden 1753).

Hasse's significance arises from the fact that he had a high conception of the operatic and dramatic layout in both its larger and its smaller aspects. Also, in the *secco* recitatives he achieved vivid dramatic expression, with a strong sense of wide-spanned forms, a great talent for melody, and a distinct ability to characterize his personages. As with Handel's work, his also showed outstanding mastery of the Italian forms combined with a German power of feeling. His art took its point of departure from such works as Keiser's German operas, but did not attain greatness until it was enriched in Italy by French elements. In his later career Hasse seems to have worked for a reform of opera. He had extensive correspondence with Metastasio about the development of accompagnato scenes, renovation of the chorus, and instrumental sections and dances. Thus the narrow and stereotyped aspects of poetry and music in Neapolitan opera elicited reform efforts long before Gluck.

Hasse's efforts toward renovation of opera were carried on further by Jommelli, Traëtta, di Majo, Terradella, and Perez. Gluck with his opera reform was simply maintaining a tradition.

Niccolò Jommelli (1714–1774), a pupil of Prota and Feo, first appeared as a composer in Naples with a comic opera in 1737, but as he turned to opera seria he sided stylistically with Hasse. A friend of Metastasio at Vienna in 1749, Jommelli was court conductor in Stuttgart from 1753 to 1769. There he came into contact with Rameau's operas, and learned much from them; and after 1769 he was again in Naples, though not so popular with his countrymen as he had been before. He wrote eighty-two operas, of which fifty-three are extant.

A pioneer in the new style and one of the most important forerunners of Gluck, Jommelli has scenes that are amply laid out with ensembles and choruses. He reworked Metastasio's texts to render the *accompagnati* more significant and to displace the *secco* recitative. His work was also marked by the strong dramatic power of his operatic idiom, by the beginning of the incursion of *buffo*-like stylistic elements, and by his detailed characterization in the ensembles.

Tommaso Traëtta (1727–1779), a pupil of Durante, was in Parma as early 1758–63, where he came under the influence of Rameau's operas. In Vienna he was one of the circle around Count Durazzo, whose version of Quinault's "Armida" he set to music in 1761. In 1763 he composed "Ifigenia in Tauride," to a text by Coltellini. Traëtta made an approach to Gluck's reform in the "Sofonisba" (Mannheim 1762), with its recitatives after the model of Rameau and with the *da capo* aria transformed into the *dal segno* aria. In the "Antigona" (Petersburg 1772) there are evidences of the influence of Gluck, among whose forerunners Traëtta was the most versatile and imaginative of the composers.

Josef Mysliveček (1737–1781), a Czech born near Prague, was highly celebrated in Italy as "Il divino Boemo" or "Venatorini." He wrote some thirty operas, as well as oratorios, symphonies, and chamber music. A friend of Mozart, he was gifted as a melodist and shows folk influences in his work.

Francesco di Majo (1732–1770) at fifteen was court conductor in Naples, and during his career wrote nineteen successful operas. In feeling he was allied with a new generation. His work shows individual expression in touching, tender melodies with chromatic and other features that strongly influenced Mozart. His orchestral idiom was enriched by the influence of *buffo* opera, and his arias with concertante instruments were inspired by the new dramatic spirit. Two new forms of the *da capo* aria were developed: one—the *dal segno* aria—in which the *da capo* portion was shortened by half and the second section of the first part was immediately repeated, and the other in which the middle section B was foreshadowed in the main section A.

Domenico Terradellas (1713–1751), a Spaniard born in Barcelona and one of Durante's pupils, was predominantly active in Italy and achieved his main success with "Artaserse" (Venice 1744).

Davide Pérez (1711–1778), born in Naples, began his career as a composer in Lisbon in 1752. Previously he had been in Naples, Vienna, and Rome. He was significant as a dramatist. During his lifetime his operas "Demetrio" (Palermo 1741) and "Solimano" (Lisbon 1757) were regarded most highly.

Christoph Willibald Gluck, with his Italian operas, also belongs to the school of Hasse. Born on July 4, 1714, at Erasbach in Weidenwang Parish, Upper Palatinate, Gluck died on November 15, 1787, in Vienna. From 1731 he studied logic and mathematics at the Karlsuniversität in Prague and was there a church singer and perhaps for a while a pupil of the Bohemian composer and organist Černohorsky. In 1736 he was briefly in Vienna, and then in Milan, where he became a pupil of Sammartini. In 1741 he wrote his first opera "Artaserse" for Milan. By 1745 he had written eight successful operas in Neapolitan style and two pasticcios. In connection with these activities he made a trip to London; on the way, in Paris, he probably came in contact with Rameau's operas. In 1746 he wrote his first opera for London, "La caduta dei Giganti"

(The Fall of the Giants). He was personally acquainted with Handel. As conductor of the Mingotti traveling opera troupe Gluck was in Dresden, Hamburg, and Copenhagen; then probably for a longer period he was in Prague. By 1752 an opera composer of European renown, he was imperial court composer in Vienna. There he wrote his French comic operas, in which he showed considerable terseness of musical characterization.

Between 1741 and 1762 Gluck wrote twenty-two Italian operas and pasticcios. Although we have only the libretto of his first opera "Artaserse" (Milan 1741), we have both the words and music of his "Cleonice" (Venice 1742) and "Demofoonte" (Milan 1742)—all three with Metastasio texts. In 1743 Gluck wrote "Tigrane" for Crema, and Act I of the pasticcio "Arsace"; in 1744 "Sofonisba" and the pasticcio "La finta schiava" for Milan, but more notably "Ipermestra" for Venice, "Poro" for Turin (1744) and "Ippolito" for Milan (1745); in 1746 "La caduta dei Giganti," his first opera for London, and the pasticcio "Artamene." Also he wrote some works for the Mingotti traveling operatic troupe: "Le nozze d'Ercole e d'Ebe" (1747) for Pillnitz, "Semiramide riconosciuta" (1748) for Vienna, "La Contesa de' Numi" (1749) for Copenhagen, "Ezio" (1750) for Prague, and "Issipile" and "La Clemenza di Tito" (1752) for Naples. Before "Orfeo" Gluck wrote—among his serious operas—"L'Innocenza giustificata" (1755) for Vienna, "Antigone" (1756) for Rome, "Il re pastore" (1756) for Vienna, and "Tetide" (1760).

Gluck's Italian operas, which anticipate many significant traits of his later masterpieces, are in form and content Neapolitan operatic works in the style of Hasse and, as such, maintain the Metastasio type. Musically they are particularly under Jommelli's influence and, so far as instruments are concerned, have adopted Sammartini's change of style.

In 1762 Gluck began his reform of opera, which will be discussed later. Collaboration with the librettist Calzabigi in that year, in Vienna, led to his first opera intended to exemplify his program of reform, "Orfeo ed Euridice." This was followed, for Vienna, by "Alceste" (1767) and "Paride e Elena" (1770). The emigration of Gluck to Paris in 1772 occasioned the continuation of the reform with "Iphigénie en Aulide" (1774), "Armide" (1777), and "Iphigénie en Tauride" (1779). Gluck and Alxinger together translated the "Iphigenia in Tauris" into German (Vienna 1781).

The Neo-Neapolitans

The Neo-Neapolitan School fostered a social type of opera that Gluck failed to reform. The musical pattern in it quite dominated the dramatic structure. With the growing influence of the sentimental and elegant styles, there came a preponderance of the melodic element and a preference for the graceful and trifling. Heroic pathos gave place to rhetorical gesture. There was further development of virtuoso coloratura and of the orchestral idiom. The chorus declined. *Secco* recitative was more and more carelessly handled. The *da capo* aria became more and more multiform, being handled as a *dal segno* aria, a shortened *da capo* aria, or as an aria with concertante solo instruments. There was even a carry-over from the sonata-allegro and the rondo forms, as contrasting themes appeared. Also there were small song-like cavatinas. Opera buffa began to influence opera seria in certain melodic aspects such as the use of diminutively articulated themes and characterizing motives, in the form of ensembles and the finale, and in the handling of the orchestra. Opera seria, however, still remained long an affair of courtly spectacle and festivity and persisted in Mozart's "La Clemenza di Tito" (Prague 1791).

Johann Christian Bach (1735–1782), the youngest son of J. S. Bach by his second marriage and sometimes referred to as the "Milan" or "London" Bach, was born in 1735 in Leipzig. After his father's death he became a pupil of his brother Carl Philipp Emanuel Bach in Potsdam and perhaps about 1757 a pupil of Padre Martini in Bologna. In 1760 he was converted to Roman Catholicism and became the cathedral organist in Milan, writing successful Italian operas. In 1762 he became master of music to the Queen in London and, with Karl Friedrich Abel, founded the Bach-Abel Concerts there. He wrote successful operas for London and in the 1770's also for Mannheim. In London, in 1764, he met eight-year-old Mozart, whom he had strongly influenced. Johann Christian Bach died in 1782 in London.

During his lifetime he was highly celebrated. He possessed unusual talent for the new style and at the same time for the modish features that went with it. He combined his remarkable training as a composer with a great gift for melodic invention. His strength and his influence on the period were tied up with the courteous (*galant*), tender (*empfindsam*) and virtuoso, gentlemanly phases. He gave his public a decidedly society-centered art. His light touch and his versatility in conjunction with his distinguished craftsmanship made him prolific in all fields—opera, the symphony, the overture, chamber music, keyboard pieces, and church compositions.

In his operas he was a typical representative of the *galant* or polished style, with euphonious, fervent Italian melodic aspects, rich in contrasts. He showed diversity of form in his arias, under varying influences; and in his later works there was a sentimental, dreamy trait. He preferred pieces with virtuoso obbligato parts for wind instruments. In melody he exerted significant influence on Mozart. His operas included "Catone in Utica" (1761) for Italy, "Orione" (1763), "Zanaida" (1763), "Adriano in Siria" (1765), and "Caratacco" (1767) for London, and "Temistocle" (1772) and "Lucio Silla" (1776) for Mannheim.

Giuseppe Sarti (1729–1802), a pupil of Padre Martini in Bologna, was active with the Mingotti traveling opera troupe. Later he was a conductor in Copenhagen, Venice, and Petersburg, and served as choirmaster at the cathedral in Milan. He was the teacher of Cherubini. A significant representative of the Neo-Neapolitan group, he had definite dramatic talents and a taste for amplitude and versatile melodic expression. His most famous opera was "Giulio Sabino" (Venice 1781). His work also shows great richness of form, particularly in "Alessandro e Timoteo" (Parma 1782).

Niccolò Piccinni (1728–1800), who studied in Naples, was a successful composer of the Neo-Neapolitan School. In 1776 he was called to

Paris to play a role as opponent to Gluck, but later sided with him—most significantly, however, in *buffo* opera. Piccinni wrote 127 operas, influenced by elements from opera buffa and in turn reinfluencing it. In them there was a further relaxation and enrichment of form, with poetic, sensitive, and often Romantic expression. The rondo finale, for instance, was developed. For Paris he wrote operas under Gluck's influence: "Roland" (1778), "Atys" (1780), "Iphigénie en Tauride" (1781), and "Didon" (1783). His most important opera was "La Cecchina ossia la buona figliuola" (Rome 1760).

Pietro Guglielmi (1727–1804), pupil of Durante in Naples, wrote over a hundred operas and was especially eminent in *buffo* opera. He introduced folk-like elements and often maintained a light, teasing tone, even with serious texts. His rhythm was lively and unrestrained, with a predominance of coloratura in concertante arias.

W. A. Mozart imitated the Neo-Neapolitans in his early operas, but lagged behind his models because of his youth and inexperience. In all, he wrote seven Italian *opere serie:*

"Mitridate, Re di Ponto" (Milan, December 1770), text by Vittorio Amadeo Cigna-Santi, in the style of Metastasio.

"Ascanio in Alba" (Milan, October 1771), *azione teatrale* by Giuseppe Parini, an allegorical shepherds' play, with effective choruses and dances.

"Il sogno di Scipione" (Salzburg, May 1772), *azione teatrale* by Metastasio, a congratulatory festival play in dramatic form in homage to Archbishop Hieronymus Count of Colloredo.

"Lucio Silla" (Milan, December 1772), text by Giovanni de Gamerra, revised by Metastasio, a work that shows a substantial increase in the composer's power of musical expression.

"Il re pastore" (Salzburg 1775), *serenata drammatica* by Metastasio, a dramatic pastoral like "Ascanio in Alba."

"Idomeneo, Re di Creta" (Munich 1781), text by Giovanni Batista Varesco after a French model in Metastasio's style, but enriched by choruses and ballets of the Parisian type. This is Mozart's most mature opera seria, under the influence of exponents of the Late Neapolitan style like Giuseppe Sarti and Johann Christian Bach and of C. W. Gluck, particularly in the choruses.

"La Clemenza di Tito" (Prague 1791), text by Metastasio, reworked by Caterino Mazzolà. This was composed as an opera seria in eighteen days under difficult circumstances, being intended for the coronation of Emperor Leopold II as King of Bohemia. It is most significant for the great first finale.

Opera Buffa

The beginnings of opera buffa as full-length opera, to occupy a whole evening, go back to the comic libretti "Che soffre speri" (1639) and "Dal male il bene" (1654) of Cardinal Ruspigliosi, later Pope Clement IX, in Rome. Composers in Venice, particularly Pietro Andrea Ziani, developed parodistic and comic opera as satire on the heroic opera style by inserting comic scenes into the serious action. In so doing, they were carrying on the tradition of the old improvised comedy usually referred to as commedia dell'arte, which had itself grown from folk-operatic roots.

With the beginning of the 18th century operatic composers in Naples took the lead in developing two types of comedy, the intermezzo and the full-length *buffo* opera. The former had developed out of the comic episodes they had begun to insert into the material of their operas. In plot, these insertions were independent of the main action. Soon the composers turned these episodes into little independent presentations that were given between the acts of the opera seria. At the same time, they were developing the full-length *buffo* opera.

The texts were from popular life and were often in Neapolitan dialect. The old commedia dell'arte types were adapted, such as the character masks of Arlecchino, Brighella, and Pulcinella. The action was short, lively, and filled with fun. Influence from the Italian folk-spirit was always evident. The musical forms were closely allied with South Italian folk-music; for example, they included the Siciliano, with its dotted rhythm in quiet 6/8 or 12/8 measure. There were characteristic melodic types, short hopping motifs, and song-like forms. *Da capo* aria appeared. In contrast to opera *seria*, opera *buffa* became more and more formally free, mobile, and natural. Its action was distributed among self-contained musical numbers and *secco* recitatives.

The first example of a complete comic Neapolitan opera was "Patrò Callieno della Costa," the text of which was by Agasippo Mercotelli (perhaps a pseudonym) and the music by Antonio Orefici (Naples 1709). From this period of the beginnings, we have only the texts. The first period of Neapolitan opera *buffa* extended from 1709 to 1730 and included as composers Leonardo Vinci (1690–1730) and Leonardo Leo (1694–1744), who along with their serious operas also wrote opera *buffa* in both its intermezzo and its full-length forms—for example, Vinci's "Li Zite'n galera" (1722). The most significant intermezzo was "La Serva padrona" (1733) by Giovanni Battista Pergolesi (1710–1736), an inspired musical comedy of striking characteristic features and high melodic charm, which attained world success through being presented by touring troupes. The performance of 1752 in Paris gave rise to the founding of the French *opéra comique*. Pergolesi wrote four full-length operas and several intermezzi. The authenticity of many of Pergolesi's works, however, has been questioned.

The further rise of opera *buffa* was favored by satirical attacks on opera *seria*, particularly in Benedetto Marcello's essay "Il teatro alla moda" (Venice 1721), as well as by further attacks launched by aestheticians and other writers like Frederick the Great's chamberlain in Berlin, Count Francesco Algarotti (d. 1764), with his "Saggio sopra l'opera in musica" (1755). On the stage, also, opera *seria* was satirized in John Gay's "Beggar's Opera" (London 1728), the music for which was assembled by Johann Christoph Pepusch.

In the second period of opera *buffa*, at the beginning of the 1730's, works exhibited new traits. After 1750 *buffa* surpassed *seria* everywhere in significance and popularity. The development soon led to finer musical comedy, with its serious and sentimental scenes, as there was less emphasis on comic character-masks. There was usually a sentimental pair of lovers. Opera *buffa* became bourgeois melodrama. With Piccini's "Buona figliuola" (1760), after Goldoni, the development was completed. Coarser comic scenes, involving disguises, mistaken identity, scenes of drunkenness and slapstick, and parodies, declined in favor of pieces displaying bourgeois virtue. With 1735 the success of Carlo Goldoni (1707–1793) in comedy marked a turning-point. Along with him the most important poets of opera *buffa* were Trinchera, Cerlone, Casti, and Lorenzi. Trinchera was more a satirist, while Francesco Cerlone tended to bring in the Romantic, fabulous, and wonderful. Casti and Lorenzi carried on their activities past the beginning of the 19th century, Giovanni Battista Casti to 1803 and Giovanni Battista Lorenzi to 1805. But by mid-18th century opera buffa had begun to include three principal kinds of material —that of the original comic forms, a second deriving from folk-opera but tending toward magic and the improbable, and the third represented by the village idyll.

Hand in hand with this development went that of a musical *buffo* style, which among the Neo-Neapolitans was often taken over into the opera *seria*. Among its characteristics was the subordination of the text to the music, even in formal details such as the frequent repetition of small textual phrases. A naturalistic *buffo* idiom was established, with considerable use of *parlando*. Instrumental features included little hopping motifs, short grace-notes freely applied, and liberal use of thirds and sixths in accompaniment of the touching melodies. Many typical melodic and rhythmic features served purposes of characterization. The orchestra, particularly the wind instruments, played a dramatic role, and the ensemble became increasingly significant. Three types of ending developed—the aria finale, the chain-like finale, and the rondo finale.

Representatives of Buffo Opera Between 1730 and About 1800

Rinaldo da Capua (d. after 1771) was a celebrated composer, writing principally for Rome; but comparatively little of his work is extant.

Niccolò Logroscino (d. 1765 ?) went far beyond Pergolesi and became one of the main exponents of the new *buffo* style, with numerous sudden flashes of burlesque in his "Governatore" (Naples 1747).

Giuseppe Maria Buini (d. 1739) was the head of an independent center of *buffo* opera that had began to develop in Venice, but today we have only libretti of his works.

The composers of the second Neapolitan School, mainly concerned with opera *seria,* only occasionally turned their attention to opera *buffa.* Its great upsurge and enormously increased production did not occur until a little later, with the Neo-Neapolitans. The works were, however, no longer confined to Naples alone, as Venice had become an independent center, and opera *buffa* henceforth possessed a generally Italian character. All the opera theaters of Europe competed for the presentation of Italian *buffo* operas.

Baldassare Galuppi (1706–1785) was the leader in the Venetian *buffo* opera. A pupil of Lotti, he began in 1728 writing for the stage at Venice, soon had achieved European fame, and was from 1741 to 1743 in London. In 1748 he was assistant choirmaster at St. Mark's cathedral in Venice, soon becoming head choirmaster. From 1765 to 1768 he was in St. Petersburg. In the course of his career he wrote over a hundred operas.

Niccolò Piccinni (1728–1800), as *buffo* composer, was the most significant of the Neo-Neapolitans. His work brought with it several new features—a tender and inward tone, witty stylization of folk-tunes, an increase in the extent to which the orchestra collaborated in the dramatic action, and a great richness of form full of dramatic life, as in the chain-like finale in independent individual sections. As early as "Zenobia" (1756) we find in his work numerous stylistic elements of the Mannheim School, which apparently had been stimulated by the Italian opera *buffa*. The bourgeois melodrama "Buona figliuola" (Rome 1760), based on Goldoni, was most successful during the second half of the 18th century.

Giovanni Paisiello (1740–1816), pupil of Durante, was significant as a *buffo* composer and active in Naples, St. Petersburg, and Paris. He wrote over a hundred operas, including "Il Barbiere di Siviglia" (St. Petersburg 1782), "La Moniara" (1798), and "Nina pazza per amore" (1789). Stylistically related to Piccinni, he displayed realistic *buffo* elements and achieved significance in his invention of realistic character-izing motives, exaggeration of comic expression, strong folk-like accent, moving and compelling rhythm, and brilliant orchestral coloring, to some extent with Italian folk-instruments. He had a very strong influence on Mozart.

Pietro Guglielmi (1727–1804) was active as composer of both serious and comic operas, with over a hundred to his credit.

Pasquale Anfossi (1727–1797), born near Naples, pupil of Piccinni, became known throughout Europe for his operas, more than seventy in number, written for performance in Naples, Paris, London, Dresden, and other cities. In 1791 he became choirmaster at the Lateran in Rome. In delicacy of expression he was especially influential on Mozart through the operas "L'incognita perseguitata" (Rome 1773), "La finta giardiniera" (Rome 1774), and "La pescatrice fedele" (1776).

Domenico Cimarosa (1749–1801), a Neapolitan, pupil of Sacchini and Piccinni, was active in Italy, Petersburg, and Vienna. Of his numerous operas, "Il matrimonio segreto" (Vienna 1792) is his masterpiece, marked by significant heightening of the ensemble technique.

Ferdinando Paër (1771–1839), active in Italy, Vienna, Dresden, Warsaw, and Paris, wrote forty-three operas, to some extent influenced by Mozart and, later, by Beethoven and Cherubini.

A special style of Viennese opera buffa developed in the work of Florian Gassmann (1729–1774).

In the *opere buffe* of W. A. Mozart this type of opera reached its artistic perfection. During his earlier years he wrote two:

"La finta semplice" (composed for Vienna 1768 but not performed), with text by Marco Coltellini. Using Gassmann's music as a point of departure, the composer seems more to have been writing a sort of school-exercise.

"La finta giardiniera" (Munich 1775), with text by Raniero de' Calza-bigi, translated by Mozart around 1780 into German as "Das verstellte

Gärtner-Mädchen" (The Disguised Gardener-Maiden). The music was influenced by the Italian *buffo* composers, including Anfossi, who had set the same material; but Mozart's work here represents a great advance over the "Finta semplice."

During his mature period Mozart wrote three Italian *opere buffe:*

"Le nozze di Figaro" (Vienna 1786), *commedia per musica* after Beaumarchais (1784) by Lorenzo da Ponte. Perhaps this is the most significant comic opera of all, unique in the combination of characterization of the personages through music, the comedy of the situation, and the plumbing of psychological depths. Musically it is of unique richness.

"Don Giovanni" (Prague 1787), *dramma giocoso per musica* by da Ponte, a unique combination of the tragic with the comic, in which the demoniacal element breaks through. Quite individual characters are developed, and all the artistic means of opera *buffa* and *seria* are united. Mozart has here combined some very fine psychological detail-work with realistic means.

"Così fan tutte" (Vienna 1790), text by da Ponte entirely in the spirit of the Italian *buffo* operas with their types, mistaken identities, disguising, and parody of opera seria. It is Mozart's richest ensemble opera, of ironical humor and constantly lifelike delineation, but also full of melodious sound, enthusiasm, tender feeling, and elegance. In accordance with the material, it is of a style thoroughly its own.

19th Century

The traditions of Italian opera were notably maintained and furthered during the 19th century by Rossini, Donizetti, Bellini, and Verdi.

The Gluck reform operas of the late 18th century had little organized following in Italy. Neapolitan opera died out, with several dozen names of opera composers who did not manage to carry on further the brilliance of the school.

The first musician on Italian soil to change the general appearance of opera and give it renewed vitality by adopting new instrumental and vocal means was Simon Mayr (1763–1845), who was born in the Bavarian town of Mendorf, of German ancestry. He was a pupil of Bertoni in Venice, in 1802 became a church musician in Bergamo, and died there. He began writing operas in 1794, and is credited with a total of sixty-one stage works. Between 1796 and 1815 he was especially successful, adopting all the then modern means, and thus effecting a fundamental stylistic change in relation to Neapolitan opera. There are evidences of Gluck's influence in the larger choral and ensemble scenes and the autonomous instrumental music. The orchestra was given a significantly greater role. Musical effects were heightened by altered harmony, and there was a special feeling for dramatic effects. Mayr exerted extensive influence, particularly on Berlioz, Meyerbeer, Spontini, and Saverio Mercadante (1795–1870).

A composer who helped Italian opera seria regain world domination was Gioacchino Rossini (1792–1868). Called the "Swan of Pesaro" after the city of his birth, he wrote thirty-nine operas, between 1810 and 1829, with the height of his creative work during the decade from 1815 to 1825.

He died on November 13, 1868, in Ruelle, near Paris. Among his operas the following are outstanding: his first great successes in Venice in 1813, "Tancredi" and "L'Italiana in Algeri"; "Il barbieri di Siviglia" (Rome 1816), with text by Cesare Sterbini, along with Mozart's operas and Verdi's "Falstaff" a culminating-point in Italian opera buffa; "Otello" (Naples 1818), with text by Marquis F. Berio di Salsa after Shakespeare and with music without secco recitative; "Mosè in Egitto" (Naples 1818); "Semiramide" (Venice 1823); and his last stage work "Guillaume Tell" (Paris 1829), with text after Schiller by V. J. Etienne de Jouy and H. L. F. Bis, a work that tended more towards "grand opera." After 1829 Rossini wrote no more operas, and only occasionally church music, including his *Stabat mater*. In opera buffa, however, he is of towering significance for his rich melodic invention, his outstanding formal gifts, his light hand in poetical, moody flashes of thought, and his brilliant mastery of the singing voices, for which, beginning in 1815, he wrote in the score each individual ornament.

Along with Rossini, the most significant *buffo* composers were Donizetti and Bellini.

Gaetano Donizetti (1797–1848), a pupil of Mayr, wrote over seventy operas. From about 1830 to 1844 he was particularly successful in Italy, Vienna, and Paris. The Late Neapolitan *buffo* opera was renewed in "L'Elisir d'Amore" (Milan 1832) and in "Don Pasquale" (Paris 1843). "La fille du régiment" (1840) was an *opéra comique* for Paris. A significant example of his work in serious opera was "Lucia di Lammermoor" (Naples 1835).

Vincenzo Bellini (1801–1835), a pupil of Zingarelli in Naples, showed a preference for Romantic material, thus paralleling the early German Romantic Movement. Winning success all over Europe, he did significant work in serious opera, especially "La sonnambula" (Milan 1831) and "Norma" (Milan 1831).

With the 19th century there appeared in Italy dozens of opera composers whose individual traits can hardly be seen with complete distinctness. But the unique greatness of one composer, Giuseppe Verdi, eclipses all others. He was born probably on October 10 and was christened on October 11, 1813, in Le Roncole near Busseto in the Parma region, then under Napoleonic rule, and died on January 27, 1901, in Milan. His family background is that of farmers and small merchants who had lived in Le Roncole for some two hundred years, his father being the owner of a modest retail store. Early evidencing musical talent, he was a pupil of Ferdinando Provesi in Busseto, and at sixteen was already a well-trained musican. In Milan from 1832 to 1834 he was further encouraged by the conductor Vincenzo Lavigna to pursue contrapuntal and literary studies of Classical and Late Baroque works. In 1836 he was *maestro di musica* in Busseto. During that same year he completed his first opera, "Oberto" (Milan 1839), and married Margherita Barezzi, who died in 1840 after the death of their two children in the course of the two previous years.

According to an autobiographical sketch dictated in 1879, Verdi himself regarded his artistic career as "actually beginning" with "Nabucodonsor" or "Nabucco" (Milan 1842), his first distinctly popular success, particularly as the Italians spontaneously took the chorus of captive Hebrews, *Va pensiero,* as also expressing their own feelings under political oppression. With this work Verdi assumed a prominent position in Italy, alongside Donizetti. The success was repeated with "I Lombardi alle prima crociata" (Milan 1843). The artistic traits of the later Verdi were already formed in "Ernani" (Venice 1844). New musical and dramatic elements appeared in "I due Foscari" (Rome 1844), such as characterizing themes returning from time to time, greater interpenetration of recitative and self-contained musical numbers, and sharp delineation of character and mood. Verdi now undertook numerous commissions for operas, so that he later spoke of the ensuing period as his "gallery years." Nevertheless the operas that followed, though of uneven value in detail, reveal in many traits a consecutive artistic development. If it is not always consistent, at least it is discernible—beginning with "Oberto" and ending with "Falstaff."

Around 1845 he enjoyed European fame. In carrying out his artistic conceptions, he became more and more rigorous: for example, he insisted that the duet "Fatal, mia donna, un murmure" from "Macbeth" (Florence 1847) be rehearsed a hundred fifty times. Increasingly Verdi undertook to reform the Italian operatic stage. The libretti now being worked out according to his intentions, he sought for bold material, great characters, and strong situations, rather than for the presentation of a particular philosophy of life.

With "Macbeth" there began a new chapter in the history of Italian opera. The first performance of "I Masnadieri" was given in London, of "Les Vêpres Siciliennes" and "Don Carlos" in Paris, and of "La Forza del Destino" in Petersburg. "La Battaglia di Legnano" (Rome 1849) was his last political opera; it became tinder for the Italian revolution of 1849. "Rigoletto" (Venice 1851) and the operas written after it are still in the international repertoire.

Verdi acquired in the valley of the Po a farm, Sant' Agatà, which he later cultivated himself and made his homestead. In very great inner creative repose he wrote the last three operas and the Requiem.

Not until the past four decades has there been adequate general evaluation of Verdi. His work has a development, shows an independent conception of music drama, and focuses strongly on the music. The idiom was novel, and the melodic invention and the characterizing motives serving the demands of human portrayal and of a musico-dramatic total work of art were quite his own. The over-all conception grew out of the history of Italian opera. In terms of his personal character, he was unusually humane, generous, and magnanimous, truly royal in his impulse to be independent, averse to everything superficial, and temperamentally disposed to passionate patriotism.

His twenty-six operas seem to fall into three major groups:

1. From "Oberto" to about 1850. His beginnings are to be found in Donizetti and Bellini, though these initial feaures are joined with Verdi's own musical invention, with its distinct rhythm and melody. Early he was swayed by the Italian political movement, his name V.E.R.D.I.

being used as a symbol for Vittore Emmanuele Re di Italia. Works of the first group include "Un Giorno di Regno," Verdi's first comic opera (Milan 1840); "Nabucodonosor" (Milan 1842); "Ernani" (Venice 1844); "I due Foscari" (Rome 1844); "Attila" (Venice 1846); "Macbeth," text by Francesco Maria Piave (Florence 1847); "I Masnadieri," text by Andrea Maffei, after Schiller's "Robbers" (London 1847); "La Battaglia di Legnano," text by Salvatore Cammarano (Rome 1849); and "Luisa Miller," text by Salvatore Cammarano, after Schiller (Naples 1849).

2. Beginning of the great international successes. Here there was significant psychological refinement of the musical workmanship with great dramatic effect, in works including "Rigoletto," text by Francesco Maria Piave after Victor Hugo's "Le Roi s'amuse"(Venice 1851); "Il Trovatore," text by Salvatore Cammarano after a Spanish drama by A. García Guitiérrez (Rome 1853); "La Traviata," text by Francesco Maria Piave after the novel "La Dame aux Camélias" by Alexandre Dumas (Venice 1853); "Les Vêpres Siciliennes," text by Augustin Eugène Scribe and Charles Duveyrier, the first of the two operas composed by Verdi in French (Paris 1855); "Un ballo in Maschera," text by Antonio Somma after "Gustave II" by Scribe (Rome 1859); "La Forza del Destino," text by Francesco Maria Piave after a Spanish drama (St. Petersburg 1862); and "Don Carlos," Verdi's second opera in French, text by François Joseph Méry and Camille De Locle (Paris 1867).

3. Late works. These include "Aida," text by Antonio Ghislanzoni (Cairo 1871); "Otello," text by Arrigo Boito, after Shakespeare (Milan 1887); and "Falstaff," Verdi's second comic opera, text by Arrigo Boito, after Shakespeare's "Merry Wives of Windsor" (Milan 1893).

For Italy—and for the world—Verdi is as significant as Wagner is for Germany. Without being influenced by Wagner, he led Italian opera to a new culmination. His dramatic characterization was carried to the ultimate in psychological refinement, through melody and through characterizing motive, though not accomplished symphonically as in Wagner. The focal center in Verdi's opera was man and the human in all its phases from the tragic to the comic. Verdi's human beings were never, as in Wagner, vehicles for clusters of cosmic or philosophical ideas. In the late works Verdi succeeded in attaining an organic alternation between formal sections complete in themselves and connecting arioso or declamatory portions. Thus he attained unification of the work in the service of the dramatic whole. The richness and originality of his always distinguished melodic invention are inexhaustible; the rhythm is most compelling. "Falstaff" represents a completely new Italian *buffo* style.

A trend that appeared in Italian opera during the late 19th century is known as *Verismo*, from the Italian *vero* or "true." Still within Verdi's lifetime Italian opera took new paths that were related to those of naturalistic drama. The way for Veristic opera had already been prepared by works like "Boris Godunoff" (1874) and "Carmen" (1875). Its aims were set forth as the program for the ensuing dramatic representation in the prologue to "Pagliacci." There the title character says, in effect: "The poet describes the world as he really sees it." The first Veristic operas were "Cavalleria rusticana" (1890) by Pietro Mascagni (1863–1945) and

"Pagliacci" (1892) by Ruggiero Leoncavallo (1858–1919). The world success of these operas was never again achieved by the two composers with their numerous other works. Influences from Verdi and Wagner, with predominance of compelling melodies, were linked in an effective dramatic style with broadly successful result. In this manner Eugen d'Albert (1864–1932), among others, wrote numerous operas; particularly well known is his "Tiefland" (Prague 1903). An artistically quite remarkable representative of Verismo in Italy was Umberto Giordano (1867–1948), particularly with his early operas "Andrea Chénier" (Milan 1896), "Fedora" (Milan 1898), and "Siberia" (Milan 1903).

20th Century

The last outstanding culmination of distinctive artistry and international success on the part of Italian opera occurred in the work of Giacomo Puccini (1858–1924), a composer of great ability, careful and finely detailed workmanship, and consistently brilliant total effect. He was born on December 22, 1858, in Lucca, of an old family of composers and conductors, was trained as a church musician in Lucca, and then from 1880 to 1883 was a pupil of Amilcare Ponchielli and Antonio Bazzini at the Milan Conservatory. His first opera, "Le Villi," was composed in 1883 in a competition held by the Sonzogno publishing firm. Though not awarded the prize, it was performed in Milan the following year. The music showed the influence of Verdi and had a strong sense of theatrical effect. In his second opera, "Edgar" (Milan 1889), Puccini began to develop his own idiom, marked by dramatic construction of separate scenes, individual melodic characterization and invention, harmonic tension, artful handling of voices and orchestra, richness of moods, musical poetry, exoticism, and compelling stage-effects.

Now established as a composer, he retired to his villa Torre del Lago and calmly wrote his works. He rejected an invitation to teach composition at the Milan Conservatory. His first masterpiece was "Manon Lescaut" (Turin 1893), with libretto by Marco Praga, Domenico Oliva, and Luigi Illica, based on Abbé Prevost's novel. He was considered the greatest Italian composer after Verdi, his world fame beginning with "La Bohème" (Turin 1896), on a libretto by Guiseppe Giacosa and Luigi Illica, after Henri Murger's novel (Turin 1896). He maintained his success with "Tosca," on a text by Guiseppe Giacosa and Luigi Illica, after Victorien Sardou's drama (Rome 1900); "Madame Butterfly" (Milan 1904), with libretto by Guiseppe Giacosa and Luigi Illica, after D. Belasco's dramatization of a story by J. L. Long; "La fanciulla del West" ("The Girl of the Golden West," New York 1910); and "La Rondine" ("The Swallow," originally planned as an operetta for Vienna, Monte Carlo 1917).

His later style, marked by highly clarified external effects and significantly refined musical delineation, appeared in a group of three one-acts under the collective title of "Trittico" ("Triptych"), consisting of "The Cloak," "Sister Angelica," and the distinguished comic opera "Gianni Schicchi," with text by Giovanni Forzani (New York 1918). "Turandot," which the composer did not live to finish but which was completed by Franco Alfano (Milan 1926), has a text by Guiseppe Adami and Renato Simoni, after Gozzi. It represents the composer's most mature work. Decidedly big in form, it is flat-surfaced in scenic construction and well balanced between motivic work and melodic layout. The action is deepened by the music and carried on into the tragic realm. In it there are exotic elements of the utmost refinement, entirely new and buffoonish humor in the ministerial portions, and supreme mastery in the management of musical means. Puccini died on November 29, 1924, in Brussels.

Several composers born around 1880 considerably changed the physiognomy of Italian music. They consistently rejected Late Romanticism, Impressionism, and Verismo, becoming again aware of Italian music of the late 16th, 17th, and 18th centuries, particularly "old Italian" instrumental music. They rediscovered Monteverdi, the two Scarlattis, and Vivaldi. This generation succeeded in regaining a leading position in European music for Italian instrumental composition.

In opera the relationship to the libretto was changed. The poet Gabriele d'Annunzio (1863–1938) exerted decisive influence by reestablishing the perspective of the Italian and Latin literary tradition. Members of this generation of the 1880's who especially assumed leadership were Ildebrando Pizzetti (b. 1880), Gian Francesco Malipiero (b. 1882), and Alfredo Casella (1883–1947). Malipiero was particularly active in the operatic field, with works based on material from Shakespeare, Euripides, Calderon, Pirandello, and E. T. A. Hoffman.

New music has been written by Luigi Dallapiccola (b. 1904), with his operas "Il Prigionero" (Florence 1950), "Job" (*sacra rappresentazione,* Rome 1950), and "Ulysse" (Berlin 1968). Another Italian composer who has written music of significant novelty is Luigi Nono (b. 1924), with his ballet "Der rote Mantel" (Berlin 1954) and his opera "Intolleranza 1960" (Venice 1961). The material indicates a high sense of human responsibility toward the problematic aspects of present-day life, and tends to be comprehended in complex self-contained units, with application of the twelve-tone technique.

Outside this group with its intense will-to-style and rejection of society-centered and conventional opera, there is a composer who was born in Italy in 1911 and lives in the United States, Gian Carlo Menotti, who has written Veristic and realistic operas with eclectic music.

France

By way of general historical background to the developments in France, it will be recalled that the country was ruled by the house of Bourbon for two centuries, from 1589 to 1789, notably by Louis XIV from 1643 to 1715. In 1789 the French Revolution broke out, continuing to 1795. Napoleon I became hereditary monarch of the French from 1804 to 1815, but he was banned to St. Helena in 1815 after the Second Peace of Paris. King Louis XVIII reigned from 1814 to 1824, and Charles X from 1824 to 1830, until his abdication was precipitated by the July Revolution in Paris. At first Count Louis Philippe of Orléans was vice-regent of the empire, and he was followed by King Louis Philippe I. The

February Revolution occurred in Paris in 1848, and from 1848 to 1852 France was a republic with Prince Louis Napoleon as president. From 1852 to 1870, however, Napoleon III headed the Second Empire, which was brought to a close by the Franco-Prussian War of 1870–1 and the Peace of Frankfurt am Main; in 1870 France was declared a republic.

Lyric Tragedy (Tragédie Lyrique)

There were several preliminary forms of dramatic and musical activity in France that are regarded as forerunners of the opera:

1. Folk-comedies, carnival festivals, and moralities
2. Secular comedies of the troubadours and trouvères, such as Adam de la Halle's "Le jeu de Robin et de Marion" (Naples 1283)
3. *Entremets*, or masks and processions, at the 14th-century courts of France and Burgundy
4. Sung masquerades, for which the most important poets of the nation wrote texts, beginning about 1550

In 1570 the poet Jean-Antoine de Baïf and the musician Thibault de Courville founded the Académie de Poésie et de Musique in Paris. Its purpose was to renew the theater, after the ancient model, by bringing all the arts together, including stage dancing. The artistic idea of the *ballet de cour* was first projected in the "Ballet comique de la Royne" (1581), a joint work of various authors, led by Balthasar de Beaujoyeux. The *ballet de cour* remained the favorite form of the court. It was especially cultivated from around 1610 to 1620. As an autonomous art-form independent of the Italian discovery of opera, it consisted of a succession of dances held together by a dramatic idea and accompanied partly by song, partly by instruments.

Opera as developed in Italy had but limited influence on the art of the French stage. There were three futile attempts to find a place for Italian opera in France:

1. In 1645 there was a production of Sacrati's "Finta pazza," in 1646 of Cavalli's "Egisto," and in 1647 of Luigi Rossi's "Orfeo," with ballet insertions, written for Paris.
2. In 1654 there was a performance of Caprioli's "Le nozze di Peleo e di Teti," with numerous ballets.
3. In 1662, for the marriage of Louis XIV, Cavalli wrote "Ercole amante" for Paris as a combination of Italian opera and French *ballet de cour*, to a text by Buti.

The result of these attempts seems to have been largely a sharpening of peculiarly French traits, though Lully shows some influence from them in his music and Quinault in his texts; and a party favorable to Italian opera formed in Paris.

In 1651 the *ballet de cour* began to receive new impetus. The poet Isaac de Benserade gave it increased literary significance. Meanwhile Molière and Lully were collaborating on spoken comedy in the *comédie-ballets,* which contained dance and *buffo* scenes. The court was interested in art. Louis XIV himself danced solo roles. After 1670, however, musical tragedy under Lully took the lead.

Jean-Baptiste Lully was born November 28, 1632, in Florence and died March 22, 1687, in Paris. A native Italian, he came to Paris in 1646, first as "garçon de la chambre"—not, as sometimes erroneously stated, as a scullion—of the Princesse de Montpensier. He had striking gifts as a violinist and was active in the domestic musical ensemble. In 1653 he became composer for the Parisian court and was named by the king "Compositeur de la musique instrumentale." He played the violin in the king's string orchestra, "Les vingt-quatre violons," was charged with setting up an orchestra of his own, "Les petits violons," consisting of sixteen violinists, and at the same time composed numerous divertissements and ballets. In 1661 he was named "Surintendant de la musique," meanwhile becoming naturalized, and in 1662 he became "Maître de la musique de la famille royale." On more than one occasion Molière and he worked in direct personal contact in producing comédie-ballets and pastorales. In 1672 the king granted him the privilege of founding an Académie royale de musique, which was the beginning of the French national opera. The climax of his career occurred in 1680 when he became Secrétaire du roi. He died as a result of a foot injury incurred through a misplaced blow from the staff with which he was conducting.

Lully was a commanding personality of despotic will, the first great theater director in the history of opera and a dictatorial leader of the orchestra. He became the creator of French national opera and of a French national operatic style; for he recognized with sure artistic instinct the possibilities that presented themselves and, favored by Gluck, knew how to carry through his artistic aims with great tenacity. His creative work stands in very close conjunction with French absolutism, with the culture of French Classicism, particularly as formulated in drama, and with the great art of the ballet at the court. In a sense, what he was striving to create was a "total work of art," or the sort of thing that Wagner was later to call the *Gesamtkunstwerk*, artistically convincing and epoch-making for France. Lully increasingly freed French music from Italian influence. He created, moreover, a French *buffo* style of his own, in collaboration with Molière. As composer of dance pieces and organizer of them into suites, Lully influenced Europe in orchestral music, particularly in the matter of general style and in the specific form of the French Overture. Bach and Handel adopted the Lullian orchestral suite. German pupils of Lully were Johann Sigismund Kusser, George Muffat, and Johann Caspar Ferdinand Fischer.

His works include operas, comédie-ballets, ballets, sacred music, instrumental works, and songs.

Taking as points of departure the *ballet de cour* and the *comédie-ballet*, French imitation of Italian opera led to the establishment of the pastorale. An example of this—though the music is not extant—is the "Pastorale d'Issy" (1659), with libretto by Pierre Perrin and music by Robert Cambert. In 1669 Perrin received from the King the privilege of presenting operas. In 1671 Cambert opened the first operatic enterprise with the pastorale "Ponome," of which the music is in part preserved. This was followed in 1672 by the pastorale "Les peines et les plaisirs de l'amour." Perrin ran into debt and was imprisoned. Lully secured from him the privilege of giving performances and in 1672, with the favor of Louis XIV, opened the Académie Royale de Musique with a pastorale "Les fêtes de l'amour et de Bachus." From 1673 to 1687 Lully wrote ballets and an annual musical tragedy for Paris, including "Alceste" (1674), "Thésée" (1675), "Persée" (1682), "Roland" (1685), and "Armide," with text after Tasso (1686). The texts of all six of these are by Philippe Quinault. They were followed by "Acis and Galatée," with text by Jean Galbert de Campistron (1686). All these works were printed by Ballard during Lully's lifetime.

Lully's creative work is representative of the state and society as Louis XIV conceived of them, with the court and Paris as the scene of action. Paris was not only the center of the world but also was decisive in all questions of taste and cultivation. Art had general validity in the sense of a community of the elite. It was anti-individualistic and represented an authoritarian court culture.

The lyrical tragedy of Lully was generally related to the Classical French theater of Corneille and Racine and imitated its heroic and impassioned declamation in the recitative, with many changes in measure. The music followed the word of the poet closely. Drama prevailed. Quinault, the poet of most of Lully's texts, chose his material from Greek and Roman mythology and legend and from medieval heroic story. He adopted the Classical five-act layout, the verse structure in Alexandrines varied with iambic pentameter, and the rationalistically developed plot. His envisaged ideal was a renaissance of ancient Greek tragedy. The result was a distinctly French work of art bound firmly to the culture of Louis XIV's court and society, magnificent in its showmanship and stage effectiveness. The air, usually bipartite or tripartite in simple song-form, was strictly syllabic in its melodic aspects and was basically not very different from recitative. On occasion there were little duet passages. The chorus and the ballet were of great significance. An independent prologue in honor of the king formed the beginning of each opera. There were definite heroic and idyllic types of scene, such as funerals, sacrificial and priestly episodes, and tempests involving the sea and thunderstorms. The orchestra played a significant role, with precisely worked out instrumentation, independent instrumental pieces of picturesque character, pure program music, and big forms—often chaconnes—in the ballets. As early as 1658, in the ballet "Alcidiane," Lully's overtures assume a tripartite form: first there is an introductory slow portion in solemn dotted rhythm, then a fugal Allegro, and finally a repetition of the introductory section. The string ensemble was five-voiced.

The model of Quinault and Lully dominated French opera style for the next fifty years. André Campra (1660–1744) and his pupil André Destouches (1672–1749) particularly came to the fore. Italian influence was responsible for the development of vocal style. But with Campra the harmony and instrumental colors continued to play a dramatically significant role.

The old *ballet de cour* continued, though without the collaboration of court society in the dance, in the form of the big opera ballet, called the *comédie-ballet* or the *opéra-ballet*. As a reaction to the monotony of *tragédie lyrique,* quite large ballet scenes, consisting of prologue and entrées, were assembled, with the addition of bravura and recitative. In 1684 women began to participate on the stage as dancers.

The interim period between Lully and Rameau permitted the pro-Italian operatic party in Paris to regain strength. A literary dispute began in 1702 with the essay "Parallèle des Italiens et des François" by the Abbé Raguenet. It was aligned with the later controversy that began in 1752 between the Buffonists and the Anti-buffonists and was resumed in 1772 between the Gluckists and the Piccinnists.

The French operatic party was significantly supported by Jean-Philippe Rameau. Born in 1683 (christened on September 25) in Dijon, Rameau was the son of an organist and presumably early studied with his father. Many details in his life, especially during his first forty years, are not as yet clarified; but we know that at eighteen he decided to become a musician and for this purpose spent a few months in Italy, principally in Milan. In 1702 he became an organist in Clermont, and in 1706 went to Paris, where he heard Louis Marchand, the most famous French organist of the period. In the same year Rameau's first "Livre de pièces de clavecin" was published in Paris. In 1709 he succeeded his father as organist at Notre Dame in Dijon, in 1713 was in Lyons, and then again was organist of the cathedral in Clermont, though details of these years are not very clear. In 1722 or 1723 he settled permanently in Paris. The "Traité de l'Harmonie" appeared in 1722, the "Pièces de Clavecin" in 1724. In 1726 he married Marie-Louise Mangot. In 1732 he obtained the position of organist at Ste. Croix de la Bretonnerie, which is his first recorded regular position after that in Clermont. His "Nouveau système de musique théorique" appeared in 1726. As early as 1723 he seems to have become interested in opera, and in 1733 he made his first and decisive contact with the stage by composing "Hippolyte et Aricie." This work initiated the series of Rameau's great operas. In 1745 he received the title of Royal Composer of Chamber Music. His theoretical work "Démonstration du principe de l'harmonie" appeared in 1750. He died September 12, 1764, in Paris.

Rameau's historical significance lies principally in his operas, his keyboard music, and his theoretical writings. As theoretician he developed insight into triadic chord-construction and the reduction of inversions to basic chords, as well as the interpretation of tones foreign to the harmony. He introduced the concept of the *centre harmonique* and accordingly developed functional thinking as a logic of the succession of chords in their significance for composition. Also he advanced the concepts of *son principal*, or tonic, *dominante*, and *sousdominante*, or subdominant, with the seventh chord in its first inversion, and recognized the nature of the deceptive cadence. Rameau was one of the great epochal phenomena in the age of the Late Baroque.

Rameau's work in opera falls into two periods, the first from 1733 to 1739 and the second beginning in 1745, the year he was called to the court. His main operas, written for Paris, were "Hippolyte et Aricie," with text by Simon Joseph de Pellegrin (1733); "Castor et Pollux," with text by Pierre Joseph Justin Bernard (1737); "Dardanus," with text by Charles Antoine Leclerc de la Bruère (1739); "Zoroastre," with text by

Louis de Cahusac (1749); and the opera-ballet "Les Indes galantes," with text by Louis Fuzelier (1735).

As for Rameau's operatic style, his first opera—brought out when he was fifty—further developed the Lullian *tragédie lyrique* in the light of the ballet tradition. The large operatic scenes and solo scenes with chorus made a lasting impression on Gluck. Also noteworthy are Rameau's significant expansion of the orchestral idiom in program pieces, the strong enlivenment of the orchestra in recitative, the rich fashioning of the material in solo scenes and ensembles, and the great harmonic and contrapuntal opulence. The music maintains magnificent linear aspects in both the heroic and the tender passages. The influence of Italian opera is especially evident in the handling of solo song, with occasional coloratura passages and *da capo* arias.

While Rameau was still alive *tragédie lyrique* was outstripped in success and public significance by *opéra comique*. Not until 1774, with the appearance of Gluck, did the great heroic opera receive renewed impetus, which led the way to the great operatic controversy.

The incidents that led to Gluck's reform of opera began in Vienna and arose from the interest of the stage-manager Count Durazzo (1717–1794) and the participation of Raniero de' Calzabigi (1715–1795). The dramatic ballet "Don Juan" (1716) was their first collaborative work. Calzabigi wrote three reform texts in Italian for Gluck, all of them presented in Vienna: "Orfeo ed Euridice" (1762), "Alceste" (1767), and "Paride ed Elena" (1770).

Gluck began with a reform of the text, insisting that a dramatically and psychologically based action with large ideas and simple structure should stand at the center of the work and that the music should follow the poetry. He believed that the poetic foundation should determine the musical expression, and that the music should seek simple, genuine expression and sharp delineation of the characters. The *da capo* aria was replaced by various other forms—from the simple song to the freely through-composed number. The orchestrally accompanied recitative had special significance in the service of the drama and of the chorus, which had a dramatically participative role. Thus impulses of Italian and Viennese origin as well as those stemming from Rameau and Handel combined in a personal style of compelling power and very high significance, upheld from a quite responsible artistic point of view.

The French attaché in Vienna, du Gand Lebland du Roullet, served as intermediary in the continuation of the reform in Paris. Gluck's reform operas for Paris in French were "Iphigénie en Aulide" (1774), with text after Racine by du Roullet; "Orphée" (1774), the French version of which was by Pierre Louis Moline; "Alceste" (1776), the French version of which was by du Roullet; "Armide" (1777), with text by Philippe Quinault; and "Iphigénie en Tauride" (1779), with text by Nicolas François Guillard. Gluck's last work was "Echo et Narcisse," with text by Louis Théodore de Tschudy (1779). With his French operas Gluck reformed *tragédie lyrique*. He strengthened his own declamatory and arioso styles in connection with the French language and found common ground with Lully and Rameau in the airs, ensembles, and orchestral ritornelli.

The conflict between the Gluckists and Piccinnists began in 1774. It renewed the old dispute over the relative merits of Italian and French opera and occasioned a number of publications. The Dauphine Marie Antoinette was on Gluck's side, as was Rousseau. At the end of 1777 the Italian party called Piccinni to Paris, but his "Roland" was written under Gluck's influence.

With many adherents in Paris, Gluck exerted continuing influence in France. Paradoxically enough, a Gluck tradition was formed in Paris and maintained largely by Italian composers. It adhered to heroic and impassioned material from ancient sources and to consistent dramatic structure. The music served the purposes of the drama.

The main representatives of this tradition were:

Jean Baptiste Lemoyne (1751–1796), with "Electre" (1782) and "Phèdre" (1786).

François Joseph Gossec (1734–1829), with "Thésée" (1782), after Quinault's libretto.

Antonio Sacchini (1730–1786), a Neopolitan, pupil of Durante, successful in Italy and London. He came to Paris in 1781, where he wrote "Oedipe à Colone," first performed in 1786 at Versailles, his most significant work for grand opera.

Antonio Salieri (1750–1825), who was born near Verona, became a pupil of Gassmann, and made the acquaintance of Gluck's work in Vienna. In 1771 he wrote "Armide" for Vienna, more or less in accordance with Gluck's conception of opera. Later he went to Paris, where he wrote his main operas, "Les Danaides" (1784), "Les Horaces" (1786), and "Tarare" (1787). In 1788 he became court conductor in Vienna and later leader of the court choir. He taught Beethoven, Schubert, and Liszt. In all, he wrote about forty operas and numerous church works.

Luigi Cherubini (1760–1824), born in Florence. Arriving in Paris in 1787 just before the outbreak of the French Revolution, he wrote many works, some of which come under the heading of "Revolutionary" or "Terror" opera, to be discussed later. Eventually he became head of the Paris Conservatoire.

Johann Christoph Vogel (1756–1788), a German, born in Nuremberg, best known for "La toison d'or" (Paris 1786) and "Démophon" (posthumously performed, Paris 1789).

E. N. Méhul (1763–1817) and J. F. Lesueur (1760–1837). Méhul had brilliant dramatic talent and was rich in ideas. His writing tends toward the melodramatic and the increased use of the *leitmotif* technique. Lesueur wrote one of the most extreme of the terror operas and was active as a teacher.

Charles Simon Catel (1773–1830), pupil of Gossec and Henri-Montan Berton (1767–1844).

Gasparo Spontini (1774–1851), born in the Papal State, pupil of Piccinni. Spontini's early operas are in Neo-Neapolitan style. But in 1803 he went to Paris, where he effected a fusion of the qualities of the

Gluckist school with Italian softness, thus becoming, as Kretschmar has called him, a "modernized Gluck." Melodically, rhythmically, and orchestrally his music is unusual in its dramatic power. It helped prepare the way for the sensational effect of French *grand opéra*. His greatest successes were in Paris. From 1820 to 1841 he was court conductor in Berlin. His main works were "La Vestale" (Paris 1807), "Fernand Cortez" (Paris 1809), "Olimpie" (Paris 1819), "Alcidor" (Berlin 1825), and "Agnes von Hohenstaufen" (Berlin 1829).

A distinct type, known as French grand opera, developed during the second quarter of the 19th century. It had been prepared for by Auber's "Muette de Portici" (Paris 1828) and Rossini's "Guillaume Tell" (Paris 1829). But the first actual example of the type was Meyerbeer's "Robert le Diable" (Paris 1831).

The style of this type of opera implied a wish for material with showy historical background, for pompous mass scenes with large ensembles and ballets, and for a plot that could exert an immediate effect on a public strongly influenced by French Romanticism. Composers in this style developed brilliant vocal scenes, involving recitatives, arias, and ensembles, of a rather Italian style for big voices, with strikingly dramatic orchestral force and sensational operatic effect. Berlioz, Verdi, and Wagner were influenced by the instrumentation developed by composers in this style.

The leading grand opera composer was Giacomo Meyerbeer (Jakob Liebmann Beer), who was born in 1791 in Berlin and died in 1864 in Paris. From 1805 to 1807 he studied composition under Zelter in Berlin, and in 1810—along with Weber and Gänsbacher—he began his studies under Abt Vogler. At first Meyerbeer wrote German operas that were on the order of *singspiele*. In 1816, on Salieri's advice, he went to Italy, and was successful with his Italian operas, which show the influence of Gioachino Rossini and Simon Mayr. During a break in his creative activity from 1824 to 1830, Meyerbeer went to Paris in 1826 where, with Augustin Eugène Scribe as his librettist, he conformed to the French style and secured world success with his grand operas. In 1842, in Berlin he became General Music Director of Prussia. Considerable portions of his operas were of significant originality, and up to the turn of the century his works held a dominant place in the operatic schedules of Europe. His main operas were "Robert le Diable" (Paris 1831), "Les Huguenots" (Paris 1836), "Le Prophète" (Paris 1849), "L'Africaine" (Paris 1864), "Das Feldlager in Schlesien" (Berlin 1844, given in Paris in 1854 as "L'Étoile du Nord"), and "Le Pardon de Ploermel" (Paris 1859).

Jacques Fromental Halévy was born in Paris, son of a German father and French mother, and died in 1862. After studying with Cherubini, he wrote numerous operas, most successfully the grand opera "La Juive" (Paris 1835) and the comic opera "L'Éclair" (Paris 1835).

Hector Berlioz (1803–1869) wrote three operas characterized by an increase in theatrical means, particularly on the part of the orchestra, with great dramatic release and full richness of Romantic harmony. His operas constitute a distinctly French national version of Gluck's artistic point of view. Although fuller discussion of his work is more appropriately given under the heading of the symphony, it should be noted here that his operas were "Benvenuto Cellini" (Paris 1838), "Béatrice et Bénédict" (Baden-Baden 1862), and "Les Troyens" (the first part given its first performance in Karlsruhe 1890, the second part in Paris 1863).

The three operas of Félicien César David (1810–1876) also figure in this development. Of these the most successful was "Lallah Roukh" (Paris 1862). David had traveled through the Near East, and exotic aspects of his style included repetitions of motives, ostinato basses, minor dominants, and avoidance of the traditional cadence. His works achieved unusual orchestral sonorities.

A fusion of the elements of *tragédie lyrique* and of *grand opéra* with *opéra comique* led to *drame lyrique*. Composers who worked in this style preferred legendary and historical material that often possessed a fabulous or Romantic character and was expressed in a dramatically effective way. After laying on exciting ground-colors, they dwelt lyrically on a free alternation between number and recitative. The melody was of predominantly lyrical expression, and the drama was heightened by choruses and lavish ballets.

Among the most significant composers of *drame lyrique* were Gounod and Massenet.

Charles François Gounod (1818–1893), a pupil of Halévy, Paër, and Lesueur, studied Italian *a cappella* music as a Prix de Rome holder and later came into personal contact with related German music in Vienna, Leipzig (where Mendelssohn headed the Conservatory), and Berlin. He wrote some dozen operas, including "Faust," with text by Jules Barbier and Michel Carré, after Goethe (Paris 1859) and "Roméo et Juliette," with text by the same librettists, after Shakespeare (Paris 1867).

Camille Saint-Saëns (1835–1921) wrote some twenty operas and ballets, including the opera "Samson et Dalila" (Weimar 1877, French text by Ferdinand Lemaire, German version by Richard Pohl) and "Henri VIII" (Paris 1883).

Alexis Emanuel Chabrier (1841–1894), Edouard Lalo (1823–1892), Gabriel Fauré (1854–1927), and Charles Marie Widor (1844–1937) also composed examples of *drame lyrique.*

The greatest success in the theater was gained by Jules Massenet (1842–1912), particularly with his soft, often sentimental melodic lyricism. He wrote operas, some still holding strongly to the *grand opéra* style and some tending more to the manner of *opéra comique*. Among his more than a score of operas were "Le Cid" (Paris 1885), "Thaïs" (Paris 1894), "Manon" (Vienna 1884), "Werther" (Paris 1892), and "Don Quichote" (Monte Carlo 1910).

Léo Delibes (1836–1891) took up a position rather between *opéra comique* and *drame lyrique* with his opera "Lakmé" (Paris 1883), but was most effective in his dramatically enlivened ballets "Coppélia" (1870) and "Sylvia" (1876).

Gustave Charpentier (1860–1956), at the turn of the century, showed influences of Verismo in his "Louise" (Paris 1900), but also used Impressionistic stylistic means.

After about 1870, French opera often found itself set off in antithetical opposition to Wagner.

César Auguste Franck (1822–1890), the head of the French Classicistic School, wrote five operas: "Le valet de ferme" (unpubl. comic opera); "Ernelinde" and "Tom Jones" (both operas completed around 1880); "Hulda" (composed between 1882 and 1885 and performed at Monte Carlo 1894); and "Ghiselle" (1888–1890, unfinished at the composer's death but performed at Monte Carlo 1896). None of Franck's notable pupils, such as Vincent d'Indy (1851–1931) and Ernest Chausson (1855–1899), was primarily an opera composer.

The artistically most significant opera after 1900 in France was Debussy's "Pelléas et Mélisande" (Paris 1902), on a poetical text by Maeterlinck. This work formed the culminating point in Impressionism in music. In it Debussy seems to have envisaged a return to *drame lyrique*. The singing voice declaimed, almost syllabically and without much passion, while the orchestra painted a sonorously atmospheric background that was moody but at the same time restrained, with unique refinement of feeling, sonority, painting, and musical poetry.

Claude Debussy was born on August 22, 1862, in St. Germain en Laye and died on March 25, 1918, in Paris. He completed his studies in 1880 at the Paris Conservatoire. In 1881 and 1882 he served as pianist for a while in the household of Madame von Meck in Russia, where he became acquainted with works of Tchaikovsky, Borodin, and Musorgski. In Paris he pursued further study in composition with Ernest Guiraud (1837–1892, composer of the recitatives in Bizet's "Carmen"). In 1884 Debussy was awarded the Prix de Rome for his cantata "L'Enfant prodigue." In Rome, and later also in Solesmes, he studied Gregorian chant. He visited London in 1887 and the Bayreuth festivals in 1888 and 1889, being for a while influenced by Wagner, particularly by "Parsifal." At the same time he made contact with Impressionistic painters and Symbolist poets such as Mallarmé. At the Paris World's Fair of 1889 he encountered music of the Far East. The crucial year was 1892, with the Prelude to the Afternoon of a Faun, after Mallarmé, and the beginning of the opera "Pelléas and Mélisande." Thereafter, particularly from 1900 on, he exhibited an increasingly close relationship to the history of French music, especially that of the Renaissance, of Rameau, of Couperin, and of the 19th century. His permanent residence was Paris, with occasional concert tours as conductor to Vienna, Budapest, Italy, Russia, and Holland.

Debussy's point of departure was French music, and especially that of his circle—Massenet, Lalo, Chabrier, Gounod, Bizet, and Fauré. But he found the road to freedom in his creative work by way of Wagner, Musorgski, Gregorian chant, the music of the Far East, and later more and more by way of French music. He also made contact with the other arts in their Impressionistic and Symbolistic phases and with philosophical and religious tendencies as expressed by the Rosicrucians and by d'Annunzio. To appreciate fully the phenomenon of Debussy one must always bear in mind that he aspired to be a "musicien français." Not only did he successfully lead the history of French music to a new brilliant climax unique in its individuality, but also he fused the French past with the present into a new, uncommonly protean image, which is not to be reduced to any formula and is resistant to every classification. Debussy is a Classicist and also—in terms of his significance—a classic. He was revolutionary not only in his attitude toward music but also through his high regard for the church modes, the occasional abandonment of functional harmony, the use of pentatonicism, the whole-tone scale, and parallel voice-leading in chords. He founded Impressionism in music and led it to its peak. Nevertheless his art is not to be thought of as merely "impressionistic" in the superficial sense of the term, as an art of the casual first impression. His artistic scope is much more inclusive. The development and the transformation of his creative gifts are rich and highly significant. His late works, in their way, prepare for the coming Classicism. With him France took over the leading role in the history of European music and replaced Germany in the position of preeminence.

Opéra Comique

Opéra comique goes back to 1640, when comedies with incidental music were played outside the city walls. These presentations were called vaudevilles, apparently from *voix de ville,* meaning street ballads or popular songs. The name *opéra comique* implies a less exalted idea than opera itself and suggests a parody of opera style.

The transition from comedy with incidental music to *opéra comique* as a conscious art work was achieved by the playwright and poet Charles Simon Favart (1710–1792). Originally dependent on the Italians whose *buffo* operas were translated into French, *opéra comique* soon became differentiated from *opera buffa:* the materials were taken from the timely and immediate, from the everyday life of the bourgeois world, with its descriptions of the customs of the classes and the bourgeois festivals and usages and its tendency toward moralizing characterization. In it there was a preference for the reproduction of external situations, including nature descriptions—for example, of thunderstorms.

Rousseauistic ideas gradually appeared: there were contrasts between city and country. Melodrama spread. The transition to Romantic material occurred especially in Marmontel and Grétry. The most significant poets of *opéra comique* in the 18th century were Charles Favart, Jean Michel Sedaine, and Jean François Marmontel. They surpassed the Italians in wealth of ideas, realism of character depiction, and liveliness of language. The action was divided up into spoken dialogue and musical numbers. All the musical forms were represented, from simple strophic song to *da capo* aria and numerous ensembles. The rhythmic aspects were especially lively. The vocal style had its roots in the French dance song and the social song. The orchestral part possessed great dramatic liveliness. After Grétry, leitmotivic principles appeared in the action and the music.

Symphonic principles of development were gradually taken over into opera, for example, in Cherubini. *Opéra comique* was the typical expression of the bourgeois tendencies in French opera that set in about the middle of the 18th century. During the 18th century, as the novel became the really progressive work of art, a deepening and refining of psychology penetrated opera. Viewed in general, this prepared the way for one of the strongest influences in the further unfolding of opera, that is, the development of the action on the basis of psychological verisimilitude. Further ahead lay the back-to-nature movement instigated by Rousseau.

Opéra comique gained its independence as a work of art after 1750 in connection with the Buffonist controversy. This arose from the fact that in 1752 Italians began playing *buffo* operas, including Pergolesi's "Serva padrona." The performances occasioned a quarrel between rival parties, opposed on ostensibly aesthetic grounds. The Antibuffonists were the nationalistically minded French, the partisans of Rameau, called *coin de roi* because they assembled in the theater under the king's box. The Buffonists were the adherents of the Italian operatic art, who assembled in the *coin de la reine*. Most of the Philosophes, including Rousseau, Diderot, and Grimm, belonged to this latter group. In 1754 the Italians had to leave the city. Some composers tried to imitate *opera buffa*, for example Jean Jacques Rousseau in the *singspiel* for which he composed the words and music, "Le Devin du Village" (Fountainebleau 1752). This work was parodied by Favart in his "Bastien et Bastienne," which became the basis of an early *singspiel* by Mozart.

Jean Jacques Rousseau (1712–1778), a gifted musical amateur and poet who was much concerned with the philosophy of culture, exerted great stimulus on 18th-century musical life. He wrote numerous essays on music, including in 1767 the "Dictionnaire de musique." His "Le Devin du Village" was influential in France and Germany, as was also his poetical monologue with accompanying music, "Pygmalion" (Lyons 1770).

During these years twelve comic operas that Gluck composed in Vienna were performed. They belong not so much to the tradition of the German *singspiel* as to that of the French *opéra comique* as represented by Philidor and Monsigny. Some are designated as *comédies mélées d'ariettes*, or comic operas interspersed with little arias, with which Gluck had replaced some of the elements of vaudeville. Others are simply vaudeville compositions for which the text has been supplied by Favart and the "airs nouveaux" by Gluck. The first piece was apparently "Tircis et Doristée" (1756). The most important were the one-act "Le cadi dupé" (The Cadi Duped, 1761) and the three-act *opéra bouffon* "La rencontre imprévue" (The Unforeseen Encounter, or "The Pilgrims of Mecca," 1764) with the same material as Mozart's "Entführung." For Gluck, preoccupation with *opéra comique* led to his sharpening his abilities in musical characterization, turning to the comic and folk-like, and practicing in smaller forms.

Thus in the course of more than a century *opéra comique* had eliminated much of its vaudeville and by 1763 had achieved some maturity. There were two groups of *opéra comique* composers, one consisting of Duni, Philidor, and Monsigny, and the other headed by Grétry.

Egidio Ronualdo Duni (1709–1775), born near Naples, a pupil of Durante, won his first great operatic successes in Italy and in 1757 went to Paris. He was the founder of *opéra comique* as a dramatic and musical work of art, in which music served entirely the demands of the drama.

His Italian melodic traits were linked with French declamation, sharp musical characterization, and formal richness. In some twenty-three operas he wrote for Paris he composed bourgeois genre pieces and comedies of magic on Favart's texts, developing individual types of opera that retained their vitality in the 19th century. His works include "La fée Urgèle" (Fontainebleau 1765), "Le peintre amoureux" (Paris 1757), "Les moissoneurs" (Paris 1768), and "L'isle des foux" (Paris 1760).

François André Philidor (1726–1795), born in Dreux, pupil of Campra, began writing operas for Paris in 1759. He had a strong feeling for realism and even caricature. In his operas he introduced sensational effects in presenting situation and character. He increased the ensemble, often used orchestral tone-painting, and for the first time introduced an *a cappella* quartet in opera. His operas include "Blaise le savetier" (Paris 1759), "La maréchal ferrant" (Paris 1761), "Le bûcheron" (1763), "Le sorcier" (Paris 1764), and "Ernelinde, Princesse de Norvège" (Paris 1767).

Pierre Alexandre Monsigny (1729–1816), born in Fauqembergue, wrote his first opera "Les aveux indiscrets" (1759) as a unique attempt to introduce into *opéra comique* the style of the *tragédie lyrique* with its through-composed recitatives and absence of dialogue. With his outstanding melodic talent and formal richness, the material was deepened and the orchestral part differentiated. His operas include "Le Roi et le fermier" (Paris 1762), "Le Déserteur" (Paris 1769), "Le Faucon" (1772), and "Félix ou l'enfant trouvé" (Fontainebleau 1777).

André Ernest Grétry (1742–1813), by nationality a Belgian, was born near Paris, studied in Rome, and began in 1768 to write operas for Paris. Participating also in the French Revolution, he successfully expanded the range of material in his operas, introducing romantic subject-matter and themes of revolution, terror, and freedom. He also exhibited magnificent richness in the mastery of forms, unusual dramatic imagination, and consistently folk-like and natural expression. The ensembles followed the Italian model of *buffo* opera. The reminiscent motif was taken up as the dramatic leading idea in "Richard the Lion-Hearted." Grétry's operas were very popular in all Europe. His principal works are "Le tableau parlant" (1769), "Les deux avares" (1770), "Zémire et Azor" (1771), "Richard Coeur de Lion" (1784), "La caravane du Caïre" (1783), "Panurge dans l'Isle des Lanternes" (1785), "Raoul Barbebleu" (1789), and "Guillaume Tell" (1791). He published his reminiscences in *Mémoires out Essais sur la musique*, 3 vols. (Paris 1789).

Toward the end of 18th century *opéra comique* became the mirror of political and bourgeois life more strongly than before. The type of the revolutionary and terror opera with immediate, realistic content was a product of the events of the time. Threatened by political rulers, man lived in anxiety and oppression. The counterpart to this was the depiction of scenes from happy bourgeois family life. Compensating divine justice appeared. Tone-painting in the music as expression of atmosphere won an entirely new significance. The main period of the terror opera included roughly the years 1790 to 1810. The type continued on, especially in Germany, and influenced many composers such as

Beethoven, Weber, Simon Mayr, and Meyerbeer. Comic material was often entirely dropped, as were also even the inserted comic pieces.

The opera of revolution and terror pioneered in several aspects of musical expression and characterization, right on through the work of Beethoven and Berlioz. These aspects included the use in opera of symphonic developmental techniques of splitting up and transforming the sound-producing body, the beginnings of a move to go on beyond the separate musical numbers towards an opera of through-composed scenes, the layout of the harmony and rhythm in breathless crescendi, and the use of extreme contrasts of dynamics and orchestral effects.

From now on, *opéra comique* as the designation of a type meant opera with spoken dialogue.

Composers of terror or rescue operas included most notably Cherubini, but also a number of others:

Nicolas d'Alayrac (1753–1809) was successful not only in lyric comedies and vaudeville presentations but also in lyric drama, particularly "Les deux Savoyards" (comedy, 1789), "Raoul, Sire de Créqui" (comedy, 1789), and "Léhéman ou la tour de Neustadt" (1801), all first performed in Paris.

Ferdinando Paër, who was born in 1771 in Parma and died in 1839, was a conductor in Dresden, Warsaw, and Paris. In his opera "Leonora ossia l'amore coniugale" (Dresden 1804) he used the libretto that Beethoven was to use in "Fidelio."

Jean François Lesueur (1760–1837), teacher of Berlioz, Ambroise Thomas, and Gounod, wrote "La caverne" (Paris 1793), the most extreme of all the terror operas; "Paul et Virginie" (1794); "Télémaque" (1796); and "Ossian ou les Bardes" (Paris 1804).

Étienne Nicolas Méhul (1763–1817) began about 1800 to combine *opéra comique* and the opera of the Gluck school, particularly in "Joseph in Egypt" (Paris 1807).

Luigi Cherubini (1760–1842) was born a Florentine but, like Lully, became entirely French, though not naturalized. He was a pupil of Sarti and won his first operatic successes in Italy and London. In 1787 he appeared in Paris and soon became a significant representative of the Gluck school. He achieved great European success, also with Masses, two Requiems, and chamber music. He was, moreover, widely recognized as a teacher of theory and became director of the Paris Conservatoire, influencing strongly the French and German Romantic Movement. During the period around 1800 he was by far the outstanding composer in France. He wrote many operas of great dramatic breadth: "Lodoiska" (1791), a terror opera; "Eliza, ou le voyage aux glaciers du Mont Saint-Bernard" (1794), which included elements of Romantic nature; "Médée" (1797), a tragic opera; "Les deux journées" ("Der Wasserträger," 1800), a predecessor of "Fidelio"; "Anacréon" (1803); and "Les Abencérages" (1813), a Romantic opera. All these operas were first performed in Paris.

About 1810 *opéra comique* revived through the infusion of folk-like elements in the sense in which Grétry had used them, but after 1830 it declined, particularly as a consequence of the undistinguished nature of the texts. Composers of *opéra comique* included the following:

Niccolò Isouard (1775–1818), born an Italian, settled in Paris by 1799. He was successful in "Michel-Ange" (1802), "Cendrillon" (1810), "Le billet de loterie" (1811), and "Joconde" (1814), all first performed there. His was a light, lively tone, with charming vocal music, and his music was also widely popular in Germany.

François Adrien Boieldieu (1775–1834), who came to Paris in 1796, was in St. Petersburg from 1805 to 1810 but returned to Paris. In 1817 he succeeded Méhul in his position as teacher of composition. Boieldieu's music was very gracefully contrived, with charming harmony, transparent writing, and a light, fluid, comic manner. He was especially successful with "Zoraîme et Zulnar" (1798), "Le Calife de Bagdad" (1800), "Jean de Paris" (1812), "Le petit chaperon rouge" (1818), and "La Dame blanche" (1825), all first performed in Paris.

Daniel François Esprit Auber (1782–1871), a pupil of Cherubini's and court conductor to Napoleon III. Auber wrote some fifty operas, which may be seen as falling into three groups. Up to 1820 he took Grétry, d'Alayrac, and Boieldieu as points of departure. Between 1820 and 1848 he composed his most important works. After 1848 there was a distinct decline. His talent lay in easy invention of melodies, their fluent development, and rich ensemble sections. He was especially successful in "Le maçon" ("Maurer und Schlosser," 1825), "La fiancée" (1829), "Fra Diavolo" (1830), and "La Part du Diable" (1843). With "La muette de Portici" (1828) Auber produced an effective first contribution to grand opera. All these works were first performed in Paris. A performance of "La muette de Portici" in 1830 set off the revolution that led to the separation of Belgium from Holland.

Louis Joseph Ferdinand Hérold (1791–1833), pupil of Adam, Catel, and Méhul in Paris. Hérold wrote some thirty operas, including "Zampa" (1831) and "Le pré aux clercs" (1832), both first performed in Paris.

Adolphe Charles Adam (1803–1856), pupil of Boieldieu, composer of fifty-three stage works, of which "Le postillon de Lonjumeau" (1836) and "Si j'étais roi" (1852) were especially successful.

After 1848 there occurred a basic change of style. The direction that *opéra comique* had taken led further and further into shallowness, and approached the operetta, for example in "Les dragons de Villars" (Paris 1856), known in Germany as "Glöckchen des Eremiten," by Louis Maillart (1817–1871). A new trend utilized the means of grand opera and turned to romantic material with realistic coloring. Spoken dialogue was sometimes dispensed with entirely, being absorbed in the speech recited to music or in the recitative, but the old division according to numbers was retained. Among the most successful musicians who wrote works of the new type were Jacques Offenbach and Charles Louis Ambroise Thomas (1811–1896), composer of thirteen operas, including "Mignon" (1866).

Jacques Offenbach was born in 1819 in Cologne and died in 1880 in Paris. The son of a Jewish cantor, he came to Paris early and studied 'cello at the Conservatory. His musical career began with his serving as 'cellist in the orchestra of the Opéra Comique. He became conductor of the Théâtre Français, and soon thereafter composer of stage works. In 1855 he became director of his own theater. He wrote over a hundred operettas, including "Orphée aux enfers" (1858) and "La belle Hélène" (1864), rich in melodic and rhythmic ideas, with unsurpassed mastery as a type of the parodistic operetta. His greatest success came in his operettas mirroring Parisian life during the Second Empire, quite closely linked with the life of the times. "Les contes d'Hoffmann" (1881, first performed in Paris) is an *opéra comique* of surpassing significance. With its musical characterization of the demonic and buffoonish and with its melodic richness, it has a place of its own among the works of Offenbach and of his period.

Offenbach regularly called his one-act pieces "operettas" and his compositions in several acts "opéra bouffe"—a designation referring to the satirical and critical tone of the pieces. His works that we have come to know as "classical operettas" are opéra bouffe. Operetta flourished between 1855 and 1867, the years of the two Parisian world expositions. Hauser has referred to it as the "most original and in many respects the most expressive artistic product of the Second Empire."

A trend toward realistic opera occurred in the work of Georges Bizet (1838–1875), a pupil of Halévy, winner of the Prix de Rome in 1857. As his main work he composed "Carmen" (Paris 1875), after a story by Mérimée. Previously Bizet had written several operas, including "Les pêcheurs de perles" (Paris 1863), "La jolie fille de Perth" (Paris 1867), "Djamileh" (Paris 1872), and "Ivan le terrible" (composed probably in 1865, first performed at Bordeaux in 1951). "Carmen" is a number-opera with spoken dialogue, the recitatives being composed later by another hand. There is sporadic use of the leitmotif. The melodic invention is rich and especially lyrical, the formal talent strong, the writing transparent, and the instrumentation clear. It has very great theatrical effect with strongly realistic means.

About this time the artistic means of *opéra comique* so fused with *drame lyrique* that it becomes no longer feasible to classify the operas according to types.

20th Century

France has been influential in establishing three recent trends in the music of the world: first, through the Impressionism of such composers as Debussy and Ravel; second, through the Neo-Classicism of the late Debussy and the group that called itself "The Six," with which Stravinsky also became associated in 1920; and, third, through serial music, introduced in 1949 by Messaien.

Most significant new impulses for the musical stage have come from Darius Milhaud (b. 1892). Between 1913 and 1923 he set to music Paul Claudel's translation and reworking of the Aeschylean trilogy in the "Orestie," which was given its first complete stage performance in Berlin in 1963. This work is characterized by the strictly self-contained nature of the individual musical numbers, polytonality, rhythmic declamation of the speaking voice against a purely percussive background, statuesque or oratorical basic character, and a narrowing of the gap between liturgy and theater. Within the framework of the heroic material, there was for the first time an absolute triumph over Wagnerian music-drama. In

"Christophe Colomb" (Berlin 1930), perhaps the most significant stage work of Milhaud's, to a poetic text by Paul Claudel, the idea of the "epic theater" was interpreted from the point of view of Catholic theology. His opera "David" (Milan 1956) is indebted to Jewish history. The one-act "Le pauvre matelot" (Paris 1927), with text by Jean Cocteau, is Veristic; the three "Opéras minutes" (composed in 1927) deal with classical material, which has been more or less compressed to brief ten-minute length.

Stylistically Igor Stravinsky (1882–1971), as he was connected with Neo-Classicism, belonged in the French-speaking area. One of his most widely known works is "Oedipus Rex," a scenic oratorio after Sophocles by Stravinsky and Jean Cocteau in Latin, given in concert form in Paris in 1927, staged in Berlin in 1928. Also his "Histoire du soldat," based on an idea of Charles Ferdinand Ramuz, a story "to read, to play, and to dance," was first performed at Lausanne in 1918. Arthur Honegger, though from Switzerland, also belongs to the French-speaking area and has written significant stage works, but they will be discussed under the work emanating from that country.

German-Speaking Countries

By way of general history, it will be recalled that Germany was a loose confederation after the Peace of Westphalia in 1648 and that the empire was but an empty form. In 1785, at the instigation of Frederick the Great of Prussia, the League of German Princes was formed. From 1813 to 1815 Germany fought its war of liberation against France, eventuating in the Congress of Vienna, which established the system of European states. There was the German Confederation and the Holy Alliance. In 1830 the July Revolution in France had its reverberations across the Rhine. Constitutional government was established in Saxony, the Hesse electorate, Brunswick, and Hanover. In 1848 there were the March riots in Berlin and Vienna. A National Assembly was called in Frankfurt am Main, and in 1871 at Versailles the Reich was established. King Wilhelm I of Prussia was crowned German Kaiser.

From the Beginnings to About 1750

Since Germany acquired its impetus to develop opera largely from Italy and France, an adequate account of the history of opera in Germany must err, if at all, on the side of inclusiveness. Thus the ensuing account includes works in German that served as beginnings toward a national form in text and music under the influence of Italian and French opera. It also includes the works of Italian composers that were introduced directly into Germany or were written particularly for performance there. Finally, it includes also French operas that were adapted for German performance. The somewhat foreign nature of the early phases of opera in Germany will be realized from the fact that between 1720 and 1740 German national opera was completely submerged beneath the Italian.

The earliest evidences of opera in Germany appear in two early-17th-

century productions, which seem to be rather derivative in their antecedents. In 1627 "Dafne" was presented in Torgau near Dresden, on the
occasion of the marriage of Georg, Landgrave of Hesse, to Sophia
Eleanora, Princess of Saxony. The music, which is no longer in existence,
was composed by Heinrich Schütz; and the text was the "Dafne" of
Rinuccini, translated by Martin Opitz, the leader of the Silesian school
of poets. In 1644 "Seelewig," or Soul Eternal, a so-called "Freudenspiel"
or "joyous play" in the manner of the school drama and the moralities,
was presented in Nuremberg. The basis of it is a sacred poem by Philipp
Harsdörffer, which was set to music by Sigismund Theophil Staden.

After these beginnings there were developments in the various cities.
Except for Hamburg, however, these were not very notable artistically—
partly because of economic and political consequences of the Thirty Years'
War.

In Hamburg, the first permanent opera house "am Gänsemarkt,"
or At the Goose Market, was opened in 1678 with the sacred opera
"Adam und Eva," the text of which was by Richter and the music by
Johann Theile, a pupil of Schütz. It was the first of several Biblical and
allegorical operas. Despite the opposition of the clergy, opera made its
influence felt in Hamburg.

The leading composers of the first ten years of opera in Hamburg
were N. A. Strungk and J. W. Franck. Nikolaus Adam Strungk (1640–
1700) had previously been in Dresden and then in Leipzig. Johann
Wolfgang Franck (b. 1644) wrote an opera "Die drei Töchter Cecrops"
that was given at Ansbach in 1679. To some extent the German works
were arrangements of Italian and French models or the result of stimulation exerted by the Italian and French operas, particularly Lully's, often
in translation.

The Hamburg opera led in the movement toward a national opera in
Germany. It achieved its first artistic culmination in 1695 under J. S.
Kusser and its second after 1697 under Reinhard Keiser. The decline in
artistic development began in 1710. In 1738 German operatic performances were discontinued. In 1750 the Theater am Gänsemarkt was demolished, but during the seventy-two years of its existence over 280
operas had been presented there.

The texts originally dealt with religious subjects. Then, under French
and Italian influence, they came to include mythological material, leading
to an aesthetic controversy in which even the preacher Elmenhorst, among
others, intervened with his "Dramatologia" (1688). There was a strongly
folk-like touch, especially in the work of Christian Postel and Barthold
Feind. After 1700 farcical opera was established, with folk-scenes and
dialect. In relation to the French opera the low level of German poetry
is especially striking. The stage setting in the Hamburg performances,
however, was noteworthy.

Composers responsible for the development of opera in Hamburg
were:

Johann Sigismund Kusser (1660–1727), pupil of Lully in Paris,
connected with the opera in Brunswick, and in 1695 leader of the opera
in Hamburg. In operatic works for Brunswick, Hamburg, and Stuttgart,

his music was particularly influenced by the French and also stimulated by Steffani.

Reinhard Keiser (1674–1739), born near Weissenfels, pupil at St. Thomas's in Leipzig and associated with Kusser in the opera at Brunswick. In 1697 and thereafter, with some interruptions, he wrote operas for Hamburg, and his works accompanied the fate of the Hamburg opera from its period of splendor to its decline. Of his 116 operas, only thirty-five are extant. Their style reveals Italian and French influences that had been exerted on Keiser's significant and independent personality. In the judgement of many of his German contemporaries, he was the greatest opera composer in the world. His music was independently developed, and his compositions were artful, with a feeling not only for great tragic scenes but also for elegant ones. His declamatory recitatives were in the manner of Johann Sebastian Bach. In the instrumentation there was great richness of invention.

George Frederick Handel, of whose four German operas for Hamburg we have the brilliant early work "Almira" (1705).

Johann Mattheson (1681–1764), who composed numerous works, including operas, oratorios, cantatas, a Passion after Brockes, chamber music, and keyboard works. He was also significant for numerous theoretical essays, including "Das neueröffnete Orchester" (3 parts, 1713–21), "Grosse Generalbass-schule" (1731), "Critica musica" (2 vols., 1722), "Der vollkommene Capellmeister" (1739), and "Grundlagen einer Ehrenpforte" (1740).

Georg Philipp Telemann (1681–1767), who began in 1721 to work with Keiser in the writing of several dozen operas for Hamburg. Telemann had special talent for comic scenes, notably in "Pimpinone" (Hamburg 1725).

In Brunswick, beginning in 1639, festival presentations with numerous German sacred *singspiele* took place at the court. The words for them were written by Duke Ulrich, the music by Johann Jakob Löwe. In the 1680's French and Italian works were presented. In 1690 a public opera house was erected, which was arranged and managed after the Venetian model. The main period of its flourishing occurred under Johann Sigismund Kusser and after 1707 under Georg Kaspar Schürmann (1672–1751), whose "Ludovicus Pius" or "Ludewig der Fromme" was given at Brunswick in 1726. Schürmann (1672–1751), a pupil of Kusser, also set to music German historical material, including "Heinrich der Vogler" (Brunswick 1718), in works that particularly show French and Italian influence. Hasse and Karl Heinrich Graun got their start in Brunswick under Schürmann's leadership. After 1735 the opera came entirely under Italian influence.

At Hanover, Italian and French operas were at first favored at the court. In 1689 the new opera house was opened with Steffani's "Enrico Leone." By 1688, Hanover had become an important center for the cultivation of opera through the activity of the court conductor Steffani and through that of his friend Handel, who in 1711 became his successor. In 1714 the opera was disbanded when the court was transferred to London.

Agostino Steffani was born in 1654 in the Venetian town of Castelfranco and died in 1728 in Frankfurt am Main. A pupil of J. K. Kerll in Munich and of Bernabei in Rome, he became in 1675 court organist in Munich and then was briefly in Paris, where he was influenced by Lully. In 1682 Steffani was named titular abbot and later bishop, fulfilling also a significant role as diplomat. In 1681 he became director of chamber music for the Elector in Munich, in 1688 conductor for the Hanover court, and in 1703 for the Wittelsbach court in Düsseldorf. Later he was in Padua and was frequently on tour. Steffani's significance for the history of music lies in his combination of Italian, French, and German elements, for example, in his very early adoption of the *da capo* aria and of the Lully-type overture. He also exerted influence on Handel in the development of the cantabile aspects of his compositions. Steffani was famous for his chamber duets. In all, he wrote eighteen operas for Munich, Hanover, and Düsseldorf.

At Weissenfels, operatic performances were given from 1680 to 1736. The mythological dramas and ballets in German are among the earliest impressions that Handel had of opera. The court composers were Johann Krieger (1649–1725) and his son Johann Gotthelf Krieger.

At Altenburg, German opera was fostered in connection with school comedies. The principal composers were Grosser and Stölzel.

The first opera in Dresden was Schütz's "Dafne" (1627). Ballets were performed as early as 1622. From 1662 on, Italian opera reigned supreme in Dresden, especially through the significant activity of the Italian composers Giovanni Andrea Bontempi (1624–1705) and Carlo Pallavicino (about 1630–1688). In 1686 a permanent Italian opera was established, with the collaboration of German composers, among whom was Nikolaus Adam Strungk, court conductor in Dresden. During the 18th century, with Antonio Lotti (1667–1740), and beginning in 1731, with Johann Adolph Hasse (1699–1783), Dresden became the German center of Neapolitan opera.

The first opera in Leipzig was "Das bezwungene Ofen" (1685). A permanent opera house opened in 1693 with Nikolaus Adam Strungk's "Alceste," and operated under Strungk's leadership until 1720. Of his operas only arias are preserved. The Leipzig operatic performances, especially supported by the students, were mostly translations of Italian works, with predominantly mythological material.

In Nuremberg notable cultivation of a sacred and moralizing opera began in 1643. From the early period we have "Seelewig" (1644) by Sigismund Theophil Staden. From about 1670, Renaissance material was presented in the Nuremberg opera.

In 1712 at Durlach German operas were first presented at the court of the Margrave of Baden. Of these "Die romanische Lucretia" (1715) by Casimir Schweitzelsperg is extant, but almost all the other scores of the composers to the house of Durlach have been lost.

The first operatic performance in Munich was "L'arpa festante" (1653), by Maccioni. Johann Kaspar Kerll (1627–1693) wrote Italian operas, but the music has almost entirely disappeared. In the ensuing period opera at Munich was entirely under Italian influence, and the leading composers were Ercole Bernabei (about 1620–1687), Agostino Steffani (1654–1728), and Pietro Torri (about 1665–1737).

Vienna, which from the operatic point of view was a branch of Italy, yet had its own particular features. There were great operatic presentations after the Venetian model. There were also direct artistic relations with Venice that began under Ferdinand III from 1637 to 1657 and continued under Leopold I from 1658 to 1705, Joseph I from 1705 to 1711, and Karl VI from 1711 to 1740. Apparently Monteverdi's "Ritorno d'Ulisse" was performed in Vienna in a revised version, and in 1642 "L'Egisto" by Cavalli was also given there. Cesti was assistant conductor in the imperial court at Vienna from 1666 to 1669. In 1666–7 "Il Pomo d'oro" was presented as a festival opera.

From 1669 to 1700 Antonio Draghi (1635–1700) composed over a hundred stage works for Vienna. Giovanni Bononcini (b. 1670) was also active there.

From 1700 to 1731 Johann Joseph Fux (1660–1741) exercised increasing influence in Vienna, composing eighteen pompous but strictly conservative tragic operas, thus foreshadowing the later reform. The Italians Antonio Caldara (about 1670–1736) and Francesco Conti (1682–1732) were also there as Fux's colleagues. Apostolo Zeno, court poet in Vienna, established the pattern of the Neapolitan opera in his texts, and this pattern was taken over by Metastasio.

From 1680 to about 1720 the German national style of music drama gradually developed. One may perhaps infer that in the lost music of Schütz's "Dafne" (1627) there was German operatic imitation of the Italian monodic style. In Staden's "Seelewig" (1644) the recitatives are outweighed by the strophic solo songs and the duets in dialogue on popular and sacred melodies.

In German opera of the decades before and after 1700, there were characteristic song-like elements in form and expression, for example, in extant arias by Johann Philipp Krieger and Nikolaus Adam Strungk. The song-like layout appears even in the big arias of Keiser, who likewise was acquainted with popular strophic songs with farcical coloring. In the works of the principal German composers, especially Kusser and Keiser, there are striking influences both Venetian and French. The Italian influences appear in the aria formations, *da capo* movements, and duets; the French in dance and chorus sections and the description of situations. The declamation in recitative and arioso was modelled after the Protestant church cantata and French opera and represented in many ways the dramatic culmination of the composition. In the principal works, according to Schiedermair, the German character was shown in the sense for dramatic truth and the sensitivity of expression.

The Movement To Establish German Music Drama

In the middle of the 18th century there was a literary movement that called for a national opera of heroic mold in German. It was supported by Scheibe, Klopstock, Lessing, Herder, and also the painter Friedrich

Müller. Wieland took the decisive step by drawing up aesthetic demands and carrying them out in practice. His libretto "Alceste" in five acts was set to music by Anton Schweitzer (1735–1787), and it became the first through-composed German full-length opera of the 18th century, with strongly declamatory recitatives, arias, choruses, and significant orchestral participation (Weimar 1773). A second opera by Wieland and Schweitzer was "Rosamund" (Mannheim 1780).

A further attempt was "Günther von Schwarzburg" (Mannheim 1777) with text by Anton Klein and music by Ignaz Holzbauer (1711–1783). The music was strong in feeling, versatile in its use of forms, and quite expressive in the accompanying recitatives. It exerted a lasting influence on Mozart and Beethoven.

The German reform movement was also represented by Johann Gottlieb Naumann (1741–1801), who was born near Dresden and was active in Stockholm and Dresden. He began in the operatic style of Hasse but, influenced by Gluck, attained significant independent works, among which were "Cora och Alonzo" (Stockholm 1782) and "Gustaf Wasa" (Stockholm 1786). They belong to the French operatic type, with German and Italian traits such as the use of extended forms, choruses, recitatives, and reminiscent motifs.

A follower of Naumann was Friedrich Ludwig Aemilius Kunzen (1761–1817) in Copenhagen, whose principal work was "Holger Danske" after Wieland's "Oberon" (1789).

A French form that was imitated in Germany and eventually took on qualities of its own there was the musically accompanied monologue, usually referred to in German as a *melodram* or *monodram*. The original form was invented by Jean Jacques Rousseau (1712–1778), who wrote the monologue "Pygmalion" (Lyons 1770), with music by Horace Coignet. In order not to have the French language sung, it was spoken and instrumental interludes were interspersed between the declamation to support the pantomime. Rousseau's "Pygmalion" was set to music by numerous composers, including Franz Aspelmayr and Anton Schweitzer (Weimar 1772).

The model of Rousseau was imitated in numerous German "melodramas," for which Georg Benda (1722–1795) created a new style in his "Ariadne" (Gotha 1775) and "Medea" (Leipzig 1775). Henceforth the spoken word and the music were heard together. Benda's melodramas, which were highly prized by Mozart and others, brought on a whole series of similar works by other composers. The new genre was regularly called "monodram" because the monologue of a heroine usually formed the center of the scenically represented action. If a second character was added, writers of the time called the result a "duodram." The musical style of the German *melodram* goes back to the highly exaggerated manner of expression of Hasse's *recitativo accompagnato* and to the mime-oriented music of dance dramas of the French ballet-master Jean Georges Noverre, which were set to music by Florian Deller (d. 1773), Johann Joseph Rudolph, Josef Starzer, Franz Aspelmayr, and others. The *melodram* was adopted as a means of achieving special dramatic expressive power in the *singspiel* and the *opéra comique*.

The German Singspiel *in the 18th Century*

A musico-dramatic form that contributed greatly to the formation of a German national opera was the *singspiel*, which derived from the English ballad-opera. It gave rise in the German-speaking area to two significant branches, one in the North and the other in the South. While the efforts of Wieland, Schweitzer, and Holzbauer remained isolated phenomena, the *singspiel* represented a new and concerted advance toward a German national opera. The initial beginnings toward a *singspiel* in conscious contrast to *opera seria* was "The Beggar's Opera" by Gay and Pepusch (1728). It was imitated by an Irishman named Coffey in "The Devil to Pay" (London 1731) and by others. In 1743 a German translation was presented in Berlin under the title "Der Teufel ist los" or "Die verwandelten Weiber," presumably with the original English melodies. In 1752 the same work appeared in Leipzig, reworked by Christian Felix Weisse with melodies by Johann Georg Standfuss. He established the German *singspiel* as dialogue interspersed with songs, presented by actors. In 1766 there followed a third adaptation with the music of Johann Adam Hiller under the influence of the *opéra comique* and the Berlin song-school.

In the beginning the *singspiel*, which enjoyed widespread favor as an art of the bourgeoisie, consisted of song-like pieces inserted in the spoken dialogue. Italian forms, such as coloratura arias, appeared only occasionally. Further development paralleled that of *opéra comique*, works of which were often translated and recomposed. What were in the beginning rustic and workingmen's pieces yielded to the Romantic magic play. The comic declined in favor of the sentimental. During the years between 1773 and 1785, the poetic level was raised significantly by Goethe's *singspiel* contributions, which were frequently set to music: "Claudine von Villa Bella," "Erwin und Elmire," "Jery und Bätely," "Lila," "Die Fischerin," and "Scherz, List und Rache." Gradually the musical forms were enriched by further adoption of Italian and French elements such as the Neapolitan overture, recitative, and ensemble and choral numbers. These features, however, detracted somewhat from the original folk-like aspects.

Notable composers of *singspiele* in Northern and Central Germany were Hiller, Benda, André, and Neefe.

Johann Adam Hiller (1728–1804), choir director at St. Thomas's in Leipzig, wrote "Die verwandelten Weiber" (Leipzig 1766), "Lisuart und Dariolette" (Leipzig 1766), "Lottchen am Hofe" (Leipzig 1767), "Die Jagd" (Weimar 1770), and "Der Erntekranz" (Leipzig 1771). His *singspiele* became increasingly stylized and operatic. The texts were mostly by Felix Weisse, using Favart's libretti as models.

Georg Benda (1722–1795) wrote "Der Dorfjahrmarkt" (1775), "Walder" (1776), "Julie und Romeo" (1776), and "Der Holzhauer" (1778), all first performed in Gotha. They have rather large scenes with a corresponding freedom in the formal treatment, accompanied recitative, and ensembles.

Johann André (1741–1799), founder of the music-publishing firm in Offenbach that bears his name. Among his *singspiele,* "Das wütende

Heer" (1780) was a forerunner of the text of the "Freischütz," and "Die Entführung aus dem Serail" (1781) was on the same text as Mozart's work. His compositions were characterized by folk-like melodic invention.

Christian Gottlob Neefe (1748–1798), court organist in Bonn and teacher of Beethoven, wrote numerous *singspiele,* including "Die Apotheke" (Berlin 1771) and "Amors Guckkasten." In certain of his works there were rather strong beginnings toward musical characterization and the adoption of romantic and exotic elements, for example, in "Zemire und Azor" (1776), "Die Zigeuner," and "Adelheid von Veltheim" (Frankfurt am Main 1780).

The South German *singspiel* had three centers, the Swabian, Bavarian, and Austrian. The first two had but limited significance.

As early as the 18th century Vienna had *singspiel*-like theatrical burlesques of strongly local character. For performance of this sort young Haydn wrote the *singspiel* "Der neue krumme Teufel" (Vienna 1752). In contrast to this native local and folk art, the Northern and Central German *singspiel* never took root.

The artistic rise of the *singspiel* in Vienna did not begin until 1778 when by command of Joseph II, who ruled from 1765 to 1790, the Viennese "National *Singspiel*" was opened with Ignaz Umlauf's "Bergknappen." In contrast to the circumstances in Middle and Northern Germany, it involved exclusively singers of rank. In the individual style that developed there were noticeable traces of Italian opera, both *seria* and *buffa,* and of French *opéra comique,* as well as a trace of the Viennese *opera buffa* of Florian Gassmann (1729–1774) and of the Viennese popular manner in the text and music.

From the textual point of view, several types appeared at about the same time:

1. The Viennese magic *singspiel* under Paul Wranitzky (1756–1808) and Wenzel Müller (1767–1835)
2. The bourgeois melodrama with incidental farcical numbers. Two composers of this type of opera were Johann Schenk (1753–1836), Beethoven's teacher, who in 1796 wrote the "Dorfbarbier," and Josef Weigl (1766–1846), who in 1809 wrote "Die Schweizerfamilie"
3. A remarkable transition to the comic opera that occurred in the work of Karl Ditters von Dittersdorf (1739–1799), with large ensembles in the manner of Viennese opera buffa. His masterpieces were "Doktor und Apotheker" (1786) and "Hieronymus Knicker" (1789).

The Viennese *singspiel* was the historical soil from which Mozart's German operas sprang. They provided German opera for the first time with world significance. Mozart wrote six theatrical works in German:

"Bastien und Bastienne," a *singspiel* (Vienna 1768). The text was Friedrich Wilhelm Weiskern's translation of "Les Amours de Bastien et Bastienne," which Charles Favart in 1753 had written as a parody on Rousseau's "Le devin du village." The South German *singspiel* character and influences of Hiller predominated in Mozart's music.

Incidental music to Gebler's "Thamos, König in Ägypten" (composed in 1773 and 1779), which included choruses, entr'acte music, and *melodram.*

"Zaide," a *singspiel,* about 1779, text by Johann Andreas Schachtner. This work was not performed, the music not having been completed, and it was published only after Mozart's death. The material is related to the "Entführung."

"Die Entführung aus dem Serail," a *singspeiel* (Vienna 1782), text after Christoph Friedrich Bretzner, reworked by Gottlieb Stephanie the Younger. This was the first work in the history of the German *singspiel* that far surpassed the rest—as Goethe said, "laid all the rest low." It had vigorous formulation and musical characterization, particularly of Osmin. Also it introduced Turkish local color, and in the finale various characters take turns in singing as in vaudeville. The Mozartian relationship between word and tone is here firmly established, carrying out the composer's idea that "in an opera, poetry must by all means be the obedient daughter of the music."

"Der Schauspieldirektor," comedy with music (Vienna 1786), text by Gottlieb Stephanie the Younger. This work was written for performance on a particular occasion.

"Die Zauberflöte," a *singspiel* (Vienna 1791), text by Emanuel Schikaneder. This is one of the most significant German operas, of very great musical maturity. In it the most various musical forms of opera— including aria and folk-song, coloratura, ensemble, accompanied recitative, fugato with a Protestant chorale, and solemn choruses—are united into a dramatic and musical whole. The music characterizes the classical ideal of humanism and develops a new type of musical symbolism, in such features as the three solemn chords or the sixth as an interval. Portions of the music develop a distinctively German musical style; other portions, such as the Queen of the Night's aria, are in the Italian manner. It has classic unity in its handling of the exigencies of drama and musical form.

Out of the Viennese *singspiel* grew Beethoven's "Fidelio," strongly influenced by the French Revolution opera. The material, which went back to an event in the Reign of Terror, was written by Jean Nicolas Bouilly as "Leonore ou l'amour conjugal." This topical drama was immediately set to music by Pierre Gaveaux in 1798 in Paris; moreover, it was also set in Italian by Ferdinando Paër (Dresden 1804) and by Simon Mayr (Padua 1805). Beethoven's work was in three versions: that of 1805 with libretto by Joseph Sonnleithner in three acts with "Leonore Overture" No. 2, that of 1806 in two acts with "Leonore Overture" No. 3, and that of 1814 with a libretto revised by Georg Friedrich Treitschke in two acts with the "Fidelio Overture" in E major. The work combined Viennese *singspiel* influences with peculiarities of the Italian opera and the French terror opera, such as that of Gaveaux, Paër, and Cherubini. Its uniqueness in all musical literature was due to the ethical aspects of the music, its deeply passionate nature, the volcanic dramatic power, and the moving depth of its psychological penetration.

19th Century

Franz Schubert (1797–1828) provided a transition from Viennese *singspiel* to Romantic opera. Though his stage works are not very significant in the history of opera, he wrote some fifteen of them, including *singspiele*, magic operas, a song-play, and the grand operas "Alfonso und Estrella" (composed in 1821–2) and "Fierrabras" (composed in 1823). In these works there is a lack of sharp dramatic characterization and purely theatrical force. Instead, the lyrical predominates; but there are some individual traits, such as those deriving from the use of *melodram* and the reminiscent motif.

Ernst Theodor Amadeus Hoffmann (1776–1822) also provided a transition to the Romantic Era. He was a pupil of Reichardt, and in his capacity as lawyer he was government counsel. In 1808 he became a conductor in Bamberg and in 1814 counsel in the highest court of appeals in Berlin. With great gifts as a writer of Romantic fiction and a draftsman, he gained significant influence as a result of his music criticism and writings on the arts in, for example, "Der Dichter und der Komponist" (1813). His twelve stage works were predominantly *singspiele*, with the exception of "Undine," after Friedrich de la Motte Fouqué (Berlin 1816). In only individual traits, however, did their music represent an advance into the realm of Romantic expression. Fully developed Romanticism was not to make its appearance until the work of Carl Maria von Weber.

Romantic Opera

The texts of German Romantic operas were often based on folk-legend, as well as on historical and heroic material. They stressed a new connection between man and nature, between natural and supernatural powers that manifested themselves in human life through such figures as Samiel and Kühleborn, to lead to a dangerous interplay between the two realms. The imaginative effect was heightened by the idea of salvation. Popular descriptions of surroundings were favored. Though the music showed acquaintance with Italian forms, it adopted new elements through the use of material related to folk-song. Musical expression was heightened by an entirely new symbolic use of sound in the instrumentation and a quite novel harmony. The leitmotif won heightened significance. Recitative and aria were gradually transformed into the dramatic scene.

German Romantic opera soon developed two main types, in the Romantic national opera and the grand historical opera. As early as the 1830's German opera had been declining in originality and significance and was being overshadowed by French opera. But in 1843 Richard Wagner intervened for the first time decisively in the history of German national opera with the "Flying Dutchman" (1843), "Tannhäuser" (1845), and "Lohengrin" (1850), to lead the type of the Romantic national opera to its ultimate culmination.

Carl Maria von Weber and German Romantic Opera

With "Der Freischütz" Romantic national opera stood alongside the Italian and French as meriting equal recognition for its artistic significance. In this work of Weber's it was validly formulated as implying an accord between nature and human feeling, a Romantic attitude toward nature, the idea of salvation, musical chiaroscuro, and folk-scenes. The music contained heterogeneous elements, from the *singspiel*, Italian opera, and *opéra comique*. But they were synthesized in an ingenious way and, to some extent, constituted a form that was most highly original and forward-looking in its ideas. By means of sound, it symbolized life in the forest and among hunters and suggested the demonic element in nature. Similarly it was original in its instrumental coloring and in its use of the leitmotif. In "Euryanthe" Weber tried to create the type of a through-composed German Romantic grand opera and to unify the form.

The operas that Weber early completed were "Das Waldmädchen" (1800), "Peter Schmoll" (1803), "Silvana" (1810), and "Abu Hassan" (1811). His masterpieces were "Der Freischütz" (Berlin 1821), "Euryanthe" (Vienna 1823), and "Oberon" (London 1826).

Another active composer of German Romantic opera was Ludwig (Louis) Spohr (1784–1859). A significant violin virtuoso, he was the founder of modern German violin playing, with his "Violinschule" (1831). He made extensive concert tours and in 1822 became court conductor in Kassel. Between Schubert and Schumann, he and Weber were the leading Romantic composers. He wrote nine symphonies, twelve violin concerti, chamber music, and ten operas, including "Faust," on a text by Joseph Karl Bernhard after the old folk-play (composed in 1813, first performed by Weber in 1816 in Prague), "Zemire und Azor" (Frankfurt 1819), "Jessonda" (Kassel 1823), "Der Berggeist" (1825), "Pietro von Albano" (Kassel 1827), "Der Alchimist" (Kassel 1830), and "Die Kreuzfahrer" (Kassel 1845). As to the style of Spohr's operas, there were many features of his work that pointed toward the future. In conjunction with Mozart there occurred in him a development of chromaticism that anticipated, for example, the *Tristan* chord. Also in Spohr's work there was development of the declamatory recitative and of the leitmotif. In places, also, Spohr possessed expressively melodic and cantabile traits that were very much his own.

Still another important composer of German Romantic opera, influential on Wagner, was Heinrich Marschner (1795–1861). After having conducted opera in Dresden, he went to Hanover in 1831. He was successful, and his work has been historically significant, especially in the operas *Der Vampyr* (Leipzig 1828), *Templer und Jüdin* (Leipzig 1829), and *Hans Heiling* (Berlin 1833), through the Romantic use of instrumental color, the characterization, and the folk-like elements.

German Comic Opera

Side by side with Romantic opera, German comic opera led an existence of its own. Up to about 1850 it fused old elements of the *singspiel* with influences of the *opéra comique*. Its most successful composer was Albert Lortzing (1801–1851), actor, *buffo* tenor, conductor, and poet-composer, who led a restless, rather troubled life, wandering from city to city in Germany. Between passages of dialogue in his operas, for which he wrote the text himself and in which he tried especially to create "roles," there are arias, strophic songs, and ensembles incorporated as self-contained musical forms. The *singspiel* tone predominated in the amiable, always folk-like melodies of these merry, down-to-earth compositions. His most successful works were *Die beiden Schützen* (Leipzig 1837), *Zar und Zimmermann* (Leipzig 1837), *Der Wildschütz* (Leipzig 1842), and *Der Waffenschmied* (Vienna 1846). In *Undine*, after Friedrich de la Motte Fouqué (Magdeburg 1845), the same style was transferred to a Romantic type of material.

Other composers of German comic opera were Otto Nicolai and Friedrich von Flotow. Otto Nicolai (1810–1849) had been a pupil of Zelter and in 1841 became court conductor in Vienna and founder of the Vienna Philharmonic concerts. Moving to Berlin in 1847, he wrote four Italian operas and a notable opera with German text *Die lustigen Weiber von Windsor,* after Shakespeare's *Merry Wives of Windsor* (Berlin 1849), which in its Italian lightness and art of handling the ensemble is one of the best German comic operas.

The work of Friedrich von Flotow (1812–1883), particularly *Alessandro Stradella* (Hamburg 1844) and *Martha* (Vienna 1847), displays the predominant influence of Auber and Adam.

During the latter half of the 19th century the composers of German comic opera tried to keep themselves largely free of Richard Wagner's influence, which was increasing at this time. Despite some contact with it, however, two composers, Peter Cornelius and Hermann Goetz, wrote comic operas that represent high points of artistic achievement.

Peter Cornelius (1824–1874), a pupil of Dehn in Berlin, became a champion of the Liszt-Wagner circle in Weimar. Beginning in 1860, he taught at the Imperial Music School in Vienna; later, in 1865, he served under Wagner in Munich. He died in 1874 in Mainz. In the *Barbier von Bagadad* (Weimar 1858) he wrote a comic opera of distinctive character, the peculiar charm of which consisted in its tender lyrics and burgeoning melodic aspects, while Berlioz was particularly influential on the musical characterization of the comic scenes. Cornelius' second opera, *Der Cid* (Weimar 1865), is also noteworthy.

Hermann Goetz was born in 1840 in Königsberg and died in 1876 in Hottingen near Zurich. Having been a pupil of Hans von Bülow in Berlin, he became organist in Winterthur and wrote *Der Widerspenstigen Zähmung,* after Shakespeare's *The Taming of the Shrew* (Mannheim 1874).

German opera entered a new phase and its most brilliant period with Richard Wagner, who was born on May 22, 1813, in Leipzig and died on February 13, 1883, in Venice. After the early death of his father, he was taken in 1814 to Dresden, where he spent his childhood, his stepfather being the actor Ludwig Geyer. Wagner attended the Kreuzschule and early received theatrical impressions of Weber's operas and decisive influence from the Beethoven symphonies. In 1827 he returned to Leipzig, and in 1831 began to study philosophy at the University and counterpoint with the choir director of St. Thomas's, Weinlig. In 1833 Wagner became conductor in theaters in Würzburg, Magdeburg, Königsberg, and Riga. In

Königsberg he married Minna Planer; and in 1839 they fled from Riga to escape creditors, going by way of London to Paris. There, though he found great difficulty in making a living, he wrote the *Flying Dutchman*. In 1842 he returned to Germany and was named Royal Conductor in Dresden after the successful first performance of *Rienzi*. During the Dresden period he composed *Tannhäuser* and *Lohengrin*.

In 1849 he participated in the Dresden May Uprising and was forced to flee—with a warrant out against him—by way of Weimar to Zurich. Not until 1860 was he pardoned. He wrote there the reform essays and the *Nibelung* libretto. Also there he composed the *Rheingold*, *Walküre*, *Siegfried* (up to the middle of Act II), and *Tristan und Isolde*. In 1861 *Tannhäuser* was performed in Paris, and he conducted concerts in Vienna, Russia, and elsewhere. In 1864 there occurred a decisive turn in his fortunes, thanks to the support of Ludwig II of Bavaria; and in 1865 came the first performance of *Tristan* and in 1868 of the *Meistersinger* in Munich. In 1870 he was again married, to Cosima von Bülow, daughter of Liszt and of the Countess d'Agoult. In 1872 the cornerstone was laid for the festival theater in Bayreuth. He moved to Wahnfried in 1874, and in 1876 the festival performances opened, with the first private presentation of the *Ring des Nibelungen*. In 1882 *Parsifal* was first performed in Bayreuth.

In surveying Wagner's career as a whole, Westernhagen has seen the first half of it, from 1813 to 1849, as consisting of four periods:

1. 1813–1833: residence in his native area, including his early and student years in Leipzig and Dresden.
2. 1833–1839: travel, as interpreter of the works of others in Würzburg, Lauchstädt, Rudolstadt, Magdeburg, Königsberg, and Riga.
3. 1839–1842: enforced recall to his creative role, in Paris.
4. 1842–1849: appointment as Court Conductor in Dresden.

The turning-point in his career came in 1849 and is associated with the revolution that ensued upon the Dresden May Uprising. The second half of his life has again four principal episodes:

1. 1849: exile from his native land, and experiences in Zurich, London, Venice, Lucerne, and Paris.
2. 1861–1865: travel, as interpreter of his own works in France, Belgium, Austria-Hungary, Russia, and Germany—from the performance of *Tannhäuser* in Paris to that of *Tristan* in Munich.
3. 1866–1872: voluntary retirement for creative work at Triebschen.
4. 1872–1883: final period as the "Master of Bayreuth."

His works were composed in the following order: *Symphony in C* (first performance 1833 in the Gewandhaus); 1832, first opera, *Die Hochzeit* (The Wedding, fragment); 1833, libretto and music of the *Feen* (Fairies), after a fairy-tale by Gozzi; 1836, *Das Liebesverbot* (The Love-Ban) after Shakespeare's *Measure for Measure* (first performance in Magdeburg); 1838–1840, composition of *Rienzi*, after a novel by Bulwer (first performance, Dresden 1842); winter 1839–1840, *Faust-Ouvertüre;* July-Aug. 1841, composition of the *Fliegende Holländer* (Flying Dutchman, first performance, Dresden 1843); 1843, *Das Liebesmahl der Apostel* (The Agape of the Apostles); 1844–5, *Tannhäuser* (first performance,

Dresden 1845); 1846–8, *Lohengrin* (first performance, Weimar 1850, under Liszt); 1851–2, writing of the *Nibelung* text; 1853, beginning of work on composition; 1857, interruption in Act II of *Siegfried;* 1859, completion of *Tristan;* 1867, completion of *Meistersinger;* and 1874, completion of *Götterdämmerung*. Though the first sketch of *Parsifal* is dated as early as 1865, the libretto was written in 1877, and the music was completed in 1882.

Westernhagen accordingly groups the compositions thus:
First creative period (to 1848):
    1. *Feen, Liebesverbot, Rienzi* (early works)
    2. *Holländer, Tannhäuser, Lohengrin*
Turning-point in his work (1848–53):
    Major writings on the theory of the arts.
Second creative period (1853–82):
    1. *Rheingold, Walküre, Siegfried* (Acts I and II).
    2. *Tristan, Tannhäuser* (Paris version), *Meistersinger*
    3. *Siegfried* (Act III), *Götterdämmerung, Parsifal*

Wagner's reform of opera was undertaken not only through his compositions but also through his theoretical writings. They may be classified thus:

Stories and essays: including *Ein deutscher Musiker in Paris* (Winter 1840–1).

Reform writings (1849–51): *Die Kunst und die Revolution, Das Kunstwerk der Zukunft, Das Judentum in der Musik, Oper und Drama* (3 parts).

Autobiography: *Mein Leben* (written 1865–80).

On performance practice and music history: including *Über das Dirigieren* (1869), *Über Schauspieler und Sänger, Beethoven* (1870).

The late writings on philosophy, particularly that of religion: *Deutsche Kunst und deutsche Politik* (1868), *Was ist deutsch?* (1878), *Religion und Kunst* (1880), *Heldentum und Christentum* (1881).

Nietzsche's essays on Wagner are *Richard Wagner in Bayreuth,* which is the fourth number in his *Unzeitgemässe Betrachtung* (1876), *Der Fall Wagner* (1888), and *Nietzsche contra Wagner* (1889). Westernhagen has established that Nietzsche found the main terms that he used in his criticism of Wagner—such as "Romantic," "mystique," "pessimism," "nihilism," and "decadence"—in Paul Bourget's *Essais de psychologie contemporaine,* 2 vols. (Paris 1883 and 1885). Bourget himself in these essays never referred to Wagner, but the main points in his criticism of the times were simply applied by Nietzsche to Wagner. Thus Nietzsche's characterization of Wagner is derived from what Bourget wrote in analyzing the influence of the German spirit on France and French literature of the 19th century.

Wagner had written operas in more than one of the conventional styles before he undertook to reform opera. He had started out with the Romantic style, in the *Feen*. In the *Liebesverbot* he tried the style of the French *opéra comique* and of Italian opera. In *Rienzi* he imitated French grand opera. But for the first time in the *Flying Dutchman* he found a body of material that had enough poetic power to make the music effective. With *Lohengrin* he abandoned the division into numbers. From the *Ring* on, Wagner combined legend with tendencies from Schopenhauer's philosophy. Beginning with the *Rheingold,* and most completely in *Tristan,* he fulfilled the demands of his reform essays.

In Wagner's *Gesamtkunstwerk,* or "total work of art," all the arts were united under the leadership of drama. "Music is female," he maintained. "The creative power lies outside her, and unless she is made fruitful by this power—that is, the power of poetry—she cannot bear." He replaced the traditional operatic forms with the symphonic flow of the orchestral idiom, the "unending melody," the instrumental seeds of which were musical tone-symbols or leitmotifs. As in a Beethoven symphony, they were "developed," or subjected to musical changes, yet always in very close dependence on the dramatic development. He replaced the sung melody and the recitative with *Sprachgesang,* a kind of utterance between speech and song, an emotionally heightened stage diction transcribed as music. In a unique way he intensified the orchestral language, the instrumentation, the differentiation of the harmonic aspects through chromaticism, and the seemingly inexhaustible richness of musical moods. The insight into the world of the time presented in Wagner's stage works follows from his experience of life and analysis of human relationships.

Dozens of German opera composers were contemporaries and successors of Wagner. They composed works of various types: (1) monumental operas, (2) fairy-tale operas, (3) light operas, (4) Veristic operas, affiliated with the Italian development, and (5) folk-operas.

1. Monumental opera has a dependent and imitative relationship to Wagner. This appears, for instance, in the work of August Bungert (1845–1915), who wrote a tetralogy, *Homerische Welt* (*Kirke,* Dresden 1898; *Nausikaa,* Dresden 1901; *Odysseus' Heimkehr,* Dresden 1896; and *Odysseus' Tod,* Dresden 1903). This epigonic relationship is also represented by Felix von Weingartner (1863–1942) in his trilogy *Orestes* (Leipzig 1902), as well as in his *Shakuntala* (Weimar 1884) and in his *Genesius* (Berlin 1892); by Felix Draeseke (1835–1913) in *Herrat* (Dresden 1892); by Max von Schillings (1868–1933) in *Ingwelde* (Karlsruhe 1894); by Cyrill Kistler (1848–1907) in *Baldurs Tod* and *Kunihild* (Sondershausen 1884); and by Richard Strauss in *Guntram* (Weimar 1894).

2. As a composer of fairy-tale operas Engelbert Humperdinck (1854–1921) was the most successful with *Hänsel und Gretel* (Weimar 1893). He also set to music the fairy-tale material of *Die Königskinder* (New York 1910), *Die sieben Geisslein,* and *Dornröschen.* Alexander Ritter (1833–1896) wrote the operas *Der faule Hans* (Munich 1885) and *Wem die Krone?* (Weimar 1890); and Siegfried Wagner (1869–1930) the *Bärenhäuter* (Munich 1899), *Herzog Wildfang,* and *Kobold* (Hamburg 1904).

3. The yearning for a light or serene opera with partly *singspiel*-like forms appeared as one escape from the Wagnerian influence. A number of composers wrote operas of this type, usually referred to as *heitere Opern:*

Hugo Wolf (1860–1903) in *Der Corregidor* (Mannheim 1896), Max von Schillings in *Der Pfeifertag* (Schwerin 1899), Ludwig Thuille (1861–1907) in *Theuerdank, Lobetanz* (Karlsruhe 1898), and *Gugeline* (Bremen 1901), Hans Sommer (1837–1922) in *Saint Foix*, Anton Urspruch (1850–1904) in *Das Unmöglichste von allem* (Karlsruhe 1897), Eugen d'Albert (1864–1932) in *Abreise* (Frankfurt 1898), Emil Nikolaus von Reznicek (1860–1945) in *Donna Diana* (Prague 1894), and Ermanno Wolf-Ferrari (1876–1948) in the operas *Die neugierigen Frauen* (Munich 1903), *Die vier Grobiane* (Munich 1906), and *Susannes Geheimnis* (Munich 1909).

4. Veristic opera had developed in Italy, but among the Verists of German origin Eugen d'Albert was the most successful with *Tiefland* (Prague 1903).

5. The typical folk-opera achieved a broader basis, as represented, for example, by Wilhelm Kienzl (1857–1941) with *Evangelimann* (Berlin 1895). In this connection also belong Cyrill Kistler with *Röslein im Haag* and *Der Vogt auf Mühlstein;* Hans Sommer with *Loreley, Meermann,* and *Münchhausen;* and Julius Bittner (1874–1939) with *Die rote Gret* (Frankfurt 1907), *Der Musikant* (Vienna 1910), and *Der Bergsee* (Vienna 1911).

20th Century

During the post-Wagnerian and Late Romantic epoch Richard Strauss and Hans Pfitzner have had special artistic significance as the outstanding opera composers active in Germany itself.

Richard Strauss was born on June 11, 1864, in Munich and died on September 9, 1949, in Garmisch. During his lifetime he had a most brilliant career as conductor in opera and concert. In 1885 he became assistant and soon thereafter successor to Hans von Bülow as leader of the Meiningen court orchestra. In 1886 he was third conductor of the Munich court opera, in 1889 first conductor in Weimar, in 1894 conductor of *Tannhäuser* in Bayreuth, in the same year court conductor in Munich jointly with Hermann Levi, and in 1894–5 successor to Bülow as leader of the Berlin Philharmonic. During this time he also fulfilled engagements as guest-conductor in many countries of Europe and America. From 1898 to 1918 he was first conductor of the Royal Opera in Berlin, being also named in 1908 General Music Director. From 1919 to 1924 he, together with Franz Schalk, was director of the Vienna State Opera. In 1924 Strauss withdrew from all offices, but from 1933 to 1935 he became President of the Office of Music for the Reich in Nazi Germany.

The historical significance of Richard Strauss lies in the area of symphonic program music and opera. He was educated first under the supervision of his father, who played first horn in the Munich court orchestra, and then under the court conductor F. W. Meyer. Strauss's early training was quite Classical. But in 1886 in Meiningen Alexander Ritter (1833–1896) revealed to him the world of Liszt and Wagner. His intuition led him—as he wrote later, about 1940—to think of "music as expression" and of the composer "as the subconscious mouthpiece of the world spirit." From Berlioz and Liszt, Strauss led the way to the summits of international success and the achievement of certain effects in this direction, so far unsurpassed, particularly with *Till Eulenspiegel.* The opera of Strauss's that has had the greatest success is *Der Rosenkavalier.* In his operatic work he searched widely for what seemed to him a good, interesting, and absorbing libretto. He shows influences of Expressionistic colorism and of Naturalism, particularly in *Salome* and *Elektra,* where also he occasionally abandons tonality. In the second version of *Ariadne auf Naxos* he brilliantly combines 18th-century opera with post-Wagnerian style. In *Frau ohne Schatten* he wrote a symbolistic fairy-tale opera. His power of musical invention, however, declined significantly in the operas written after *Intermezzo.* But in the Wagner-Liszt succession Strauss was the representative German composer of the period before World War I.

Strauss's operas began in the Wagner tradition, the first one being *Gutram,* for which the composer wrote the text (Weimar 1894). Next he wrote the one-act *Feuersnot,* on a text by Ernst von Wolzogen (Dresden 1901). But he began to achieve world operatic renown with his musical settings of the spoken dramas *Salome* by Oscar Wilde (Dresden 1905) and *Elektra* by Hugo von Hofmannsthal (1909). Like Wagner he subordinated the music to the drama, concerning himself in many ways with the problem of making it possible for the hearer to follow the text, through a new *parlando* and through various aspects of musical form, especially in his lighter operas such as *Der Rosenkavalier* (Dresden 1911) and *Ariadne auf Naxos* (first version, Stuttgart 1912; second version, Vienna 1916). The text of both these operas was by Hugo von Hofmannsthal, the first version of the latter being a one-act after Molière's *Le Bourgeois Gentilhomme* and the second version having also a prelude. A distinct decline in Strauss's inventive power appeared after 1920, however, with *Intermezzo,* to a text by the composer (Dresden 1924); *Arabella,* to a text by von Hofmannsthal (Dresden 1933); *Die schweigsame Frau,* to a text by Stefan Zweig (Dresden 1935); and *Capriccio,* to a text by Clemens Krauss (Munich 1942). Strauss's operas do not have the ethical-instructive and philosophical bent of Wagner's. Strauss's individuality consists in the great abundance of musical characterization, the harmonic colorfulness, the palette of sonorities, the sense of tone-painting, the melodic richness, the song-like elements, and the masterful handling of the voices. Special historical significance is to be ascribed to *Ariadne auf Naxos,* which in its stylistic connections with the 18th century adopts elements of opera buffa and opera seria and transforms and reformulates them in a masterful way.

Hans Pfitzner was born in 1869 in Moscow and died in 1949 in Salzburg. Having studied at Hoch Conservatory, he became a conductor in 1894 at Mainz, at Berlin in the Theater des Westens, and in 1911 at Strassburg, where he was also especially active as a teacher. In 1920 he began giving the master class in composition at the Prussian Akademie der Künste in Berlin, and in 1929 at the Akademie der Tonkunst in Munich. But after 1939 he had to relinquish his regular professional position.

His operas were *Der arme Heinrich* (Mainz 1895), *Die Rose vom Liebesgarten* (Elberfeld 1901), *Das Christelflein* (composed in 1906, revised in 1917, first performed in Dresden 1917), *Palestrina* (Munich

1917), and *Das Herz* (Berlin 1931). These have symphonically through-composed scenes with *leitmotive* and wide-spanned song-like formal aspects. *Palestrina* is a significant drama of ideas in a distinctly post-Wagnerian sense, representing the artist as an instrumentality of higher powers.

The final turning-away from Romanticism in the libretto and from the symphonically executed leitmotif technique first occurred in the German-speaking area in the work of two composers of German-Italian origin: Busoni and Wolf-Ferrari.

Ferruccio Busoni (1866–1924) wrote his own libretti, including *Arlecchino* (Zurich 1917) and *Doktor Faust* (Dresden 1925, completed by Philipp Jarnach). Rejecting programmatic music, he returned to Bach and Mozart, calling for a "young Classicism" (*junge Klassizität*). He adopted figures of the commedia dell'arte in *Arlecchino* and of the old puppet play in *Doktor Faust,* and developed the acts of the opera in self-contained musical scenes, using to some extent old forms.

Ermanno Wolf-Ferrari (1876–1948) wrote many operas, in which he anticipated Strauss, Busoni, and Stravinsky in returning to 18th-century Italian *buffa* and utilizing *parlando*-singing, a transparent orchestra, self-contained forms, and melodious and gracefully serene homophonic music.

In the 1920's the general image of the period was determined by the attempt to combine the 18th-century musically oriented opera—sometimes referred to as the "music opera"—with the new Neo-Classical tonal idiom that was distinctive of the era. The musician who took the lead, in terms of an impressive quantity of composition, was Paul Hindemith (1895–1963). His most influential operas were *Cardillac* (Dresden 1926), which has individual musical numbers throughout, and *Mathis der Maler,* for which he wrote the text (Zurich 1938).

A noteworthy composer, quite active between 1925 and 1932, was Kurt Weill (1900–1950), a Busoni pupil, who emigrated in 1933 to Paris, London, and then the U.S.A. In collaboration with Bert Brecht, a new form of the musical theater was developed, focusing on the instructive piece and on so-called epic opera. Weill's work includes *Die Dreigroschen-oper* (Berlin 1928), *Mahagonny* (Baden-Baden 1927), and *Aufstieg und Fall der Stadt Mahagonny* (Leipzig 1929). In the U.S.A. Weill carried on further these possibilities in various directions.

An attempt to achieve a new dramaturgic total conception involving music, speech, visual aspects, and dance was made by Carl Orff (b. 1895) in *Carmina Burana* (Frankfurt a. M. 1937) and in other works, including *Trionfo di Afrodite* (Milan 1953); *Antigonae,* on a text by Hölderlin (Salzburg 1949); *Ödipus der Tyrann,* on a text by Hölderlin (Stuttgart 1959); and *Prometheus* (Stuttgart 1968).

Further German opera composers include Werner Egk (b. 1901), Boris Blacher (b. 1903), Giselher Klebe (b. 1925), and Hans Werner Henze (b. 1926). In East Germany Ottmar Gerster (b. 1897), Paul Dessau (b. 1894), and Rudolf Wagner-Régeny (b. 1903) have composed operas.

In the Austrian portion of the German-speaking area, a typically

Late Romantic composer was Franz Schreker (1878–1934), who wrote numerous operas, including *Der ferne Klang* (Frankfurt a. M. 1912), *Die Gezeichneten* (Frankfurt 1918), *Der Schatzgräber* (Frankfurt 1920), and *Irrelohe* (Cologne 1924). He wrote his own libretti, dealing with human beings in quite alienated psychological states. The music maintained high orchestral coloring throughout and often bordered on atonality.

About 1900 there were folk-operas of a certain popularity, particularly those of Wilhelm Kienzl and Julius Bittner. Higher artistic claims may be made for the work of Emil Nikolaus von Reznicek; Franz Schmidt (1874–1939), with his *Notre Dame* (Vienna 1914); Alexander von Zemlinsky (1872–1942), who was a significant conductor and composed numerous operas; and Egon Wellesz (b. 1885), a musicologist and composer of various operas between 1920 and 1930.

Unique figures of the 20th century were Arnold Schönberg (1874–1951) and Alban Berg (1885–1935).

Schönberg's operas were *Erwartung,* a monodrama, with poem by Marie von Pappenheim, written in 1909 (Prague 1924); *Die glückliche Hand,* a drama with music, to a libretto written by the composer, 1908–13 (Vienna 1924); *Von heute auf morgen,* to a text by Max Blonda, 1928–9 (Frankfurt a. M. 1930); *Moses und Aron,* on a text by the composer, for the third act of which we have only sketches, 1930–2 (first concert performance Hamburg 1954, first stage performance Zurich 1957). *Erwartung* and *Die glückliche Hand* are in free atonality and athematic style, the music being at every moment individual in terms of the psychology of the text, the action, or the natural atmosphere. Twelve-tone technique appears in *Von heute auf morgen* and *Moses und Aron.* The latter was perhaps the culminating point in Schönberg's creative activity. There is in it considerable theological involvement in the question of the idea and image of mankind. The music unites Bach's tonal symbolism with Wagner's motivic technique, and the symphonic development evidences supreme mastery of all potentialities.

Berg's operas were *Wozzeck,* to a text by the composer, after Büchner, 1917–21 (Berlin 1925) and *Lulu,* to a text by the composer, after Wedekind, 1929–35, the third act remaining only in a sketch of the score (Zurich 1937). *Wozzeck* is an expressionistic music drama, in free atonality. The material is treated in an earthy and human way. There are fifteen scenes, at times in self-contained forms. The formal layout is modelled on Schönberg's *Pierrot Lunaire,* and the element of alienated psychology and the depiction of nature is somewhat like that in Schönberg's *Erwartung.* In *Lulu,* where twelve-tone technique is used, there is a further highly increased psychological representation of complicated human characters and situations, which have been brought together and formulated in closed musical forms.

Further Austrian composers of operas include Krenek and von Einem. Ernst Krenek (b. 1900), composer of numerous operas, including *Zwingburg,* the first "scenic cantata" (Berlin 1924); *Karl V,* an opera undertaking to present a historical world-view (Prague 1938); *Leben des Orest,* a mythological grand opera (Leipzig 1930); and *Johnny spielt auf,* a so-called jazz opera (Leipzig 1927). Gottfried von Einem (b. 1918) has also composed operas, including *Dantons Tod,* after Büchner (Salzburg 1947).

In Switzerland as well as Germany and Austria the post-Wagnerian situation in opera around 1900 was clearly revealed in the work of Friedrich Klose (1862–1942), with his *Ilsebill* (Karlsruhe 1903); Hans Huber (1852–1921); Walter Courvoisier (1875–1931), with his *Lanzelot und Elaine;* Volkmar Andreae (1879–1962); and Karl Heinrich David (1884–1951). The strongest personality of this generation, so far as his work for the stage is concerned, was Othmar Schoeck (1886–1957), significant as lyricist, in *Penthesilea* (Dresden 1927), *Massimilla Doni* (Dresden 1937), and *Schloss Dürande* (Berlin 1943).

The outstanding Swiss composer among the members of the generation born after 1890 was Arthur Honegger (1892–1955). His principal stage works, originally in French, were *Judith* (Lausanne 1925), *Antigone,* with text by Jean Cocteau, after Sophocles (Brussels 1927), and *Jeanne d'Arc au bûcher,* with text by Paul Claudel (Paris 1950). In them there was a fusion of Romance and Germanic elements, with his own union of numerous suggestions from Gregorian chant and the Protestant chorale, from Bach to Strauss and Stravinsky. The style was lapidary, with the presentation in large planes, vital and simple and yet linked with a high understanding of art and a strict sense of architectonics. *Jeanne d'Arc* is one of the most important contributions to the epic, polydimensional theater, and at the same time an expression of a profound theological world-view.

To Honegger's generation belongs Frank Martin (b. 1890), from the French-speaking part of Switzerland. His operas include *Der Sturm,* after Shakespeare (Vienna 1956).

To the younger generation belong Heinrich Sutermeister (b. 1910), with works including *Romeo und Julia* (Dresden 1939), and Rolf Liebermann (b. 1910), who has composed operas of current significance, *Leonore 40/45* (Basel 1952) and *Penelope* (Salzburg 1954).

England

In relating operatic development in England to that on the Continent, we should recall that the Stuart line of kings had close ties with the Bourbons in France, but that with the 18th century the alignment shifted to one with Germany. Of the Stuart line, which ruled from 1603 to 1689, James I was King of Great Britain and Ireland from 1603 to 1625. Charles I reigned from 1625 to 1649, when he was beheaded and England became a republic between 1649 and 1660 with Oliver Cromwell (d. 1658) as Protector. Then, from the Restoration of the Stuarts in 1660 to 1685 Charles II reigned, and from 1685 to 1688 James II. From 1689 to 1702 William III was king, and war was waged with Louis XIV of France between 1688 and 1697. From 1702 to 1714 rule was in the hands of Queen Anne. The War of the Spanish Succession was fought from 1701 to 1714, with the Peace of Utrecht in 1713. In 1714 Great Britain began to be ruled by the House of Hanover: George I, previously elector of Hanover, ascended the English throne; and from 1727 to 1760 King George II reigned, and England began to achieve great-power status and maritime supremacy.

Opera in England was preceded by the masques, which by the first third of the 17th century—through the work of Ben Jonson, John Milton, and others—had taken the form of a distinctive literary type with incidental vocal and instrumental music. These were secular, mostly mythological dramas, which either were presented on stage with scenery but with little acting by the performers, or else were given entirely in concert style. Monody appeared in the airs and dialogues of the masques. At the beginning of the 17th century there occurred further extension of the music, the orchestra, the choruses, and the dances. The Italian recitative style was adopted. The masques were also further developed during the Commonwealth under Cromwell.

English opera began at the instigation of the poet Sir William Davenant, as a result of the impression made on him by Italian operas in Paris and by the French dramatic art. Taking its start from loosely connected scenes, Davenant's *The Siege of Rhodes* (London 1656) was the first opera that was sung throughout, the music having been written by four different composers. Opera during the Restoration period eventuated in the much favored heroic play. It supplanted the masque, which remained as the operatic intermezzo. As spoken theatrical work with incidental music, opera became in England a distinctive and much favored form. Numerous theatrical pieces were arranged for this type of presentation. Composers included Matthew Locke, Henry Purcell, Giovanni Battista Draghi (brother of Antonio Draghi), and John Banister. At the court of Charles II there was special interest in French opera; but, in general, Italian influences prevailed.

The unique culmination of English national operatic art was provided by Henry Purcell, who was born in London, probably in 1658 or 1659, and died in the same city November 21, 1695, being buried in Westminster Abbey. Son of a member of the court chapel, he became in 1669 choirboy in the Chapel Royal, where he gained familiarity with English church music, such as the anthems of Tallis, Byrd, Child, Blow, and Humfrey. He was a pupil of John Blow, Captain Cooke, and Pelham Humfrey. After his voice changed, he continued to serve in the court chapel, and in 1679 became Blow's successor as organist of Westminster Abbey, in 1682 organist of the Chapel Royal, and in 1683 conductor at the court of Charles II, James II, and William III. Purcell's first printed composition appeared in 1675, and his first collection of trio sonatas in 1683. Most of his anthems he composed rather early, and most of his stage works during the last six years of his life.

Purcell was England's greatest composer, already recognized and celebrated during his lifetime. He was a genius in synthesizing High Baroque and English Restoration elements, combining French influences from Lully and particularly Italian influences into a style very much his own, which is felt to be thoroughly English. Purcell had at his disposal formal mastery and richness, individual melodic power of expression, sense of magnitude, and fluent and highly euphonious melody. His stage works reveal him as a born dramatist. Most of his work has so far exhibited undiminished vitality. In addition to his opera *Dido and Aeneas* (London 1689) and numerous other compositions for the stage, he composed church music, congratulatory and other secular songs and odes, and instrumental works for chamber ensemble and for harpsichord.

The peak in Purcell's creative work for the stage was his opera somewhat after the French model, *Dido and Aeneas*, which consists of a prologue and three acts. The dramatic style is lively, with choruses influenced by Lully, but also with recitatives and arias showing strong Venetian influences, a French overture, great tragic scenes, preference for ostinato variations in arias, and music of quite significant originality of expression and invention. The other scenic musical works of Purcell were only incidental music to spoken drama.

After 1700 the national English opera came almost exclusively under Italian influence, which culminated in the work of George Frederick Handel. Individual counter-currents led in 1728 to works that included notably *The Beggar's Opera* by John Gay, for which Christoph Pepusch had assembled the music from old folk-songs, popular tunes, and operatic airs of various composers and for which he wrote an overture of his own.

National English operatic efforts continued in the numerous ballad operas, or *singspiele,* made up of folk-songs in the 18th century in England and America.

19th and 20th Centuries

Among English musicians the real rise in their own creative achievements did not begin until the last third of the 19th century. During the period before the "Renaissance of English Music" Bennett and Field were especially notable.

William Sterndale Bennett (1816–1875) was educated at the Royal Academy of Music in London, was active as a director and teacher in London, in 1856 became Professor of Music at Cambridge, in 1866 Director of the Royal Academy of Music, and in 1871 was knighted. A friend of Mendelssohn and of Schumann, he represented an English Romantic tendency connected with the Leipzig circle. His works include an oratorio, *The Woman of Samaria,* cantatas, a symphony, overtures, and piano compositions.

John Field (1782–1837), born in Dublin, received his piano training from Clementi, with whom he was in Paris and Vienna, and in 1802 went to Petersburg, where he was highly celebrated as a concert pianist and piano teacher. Beginning in 1821 he was in Moscow; and, taken ill during a concert tour through Western Europe in 1833, he died in Moscow. Field pioneered especially in the lyrical piano piece of the Romantic period and of the 19th century, particularly in his Nocturnes.

Other notable British musicians included George Onslow (1784–1853), Henry Bishop (1786–1855), and Michael William Balfe (1808–1870), who wrote 19 operas in English as well as other operas in Italian and French.

The years from 1880 to 1900 are often referred to as the "Renaissance of English Music." During these two decades England began to return to a creative musical role. Performance facilities, the cultivation of music in the churches, the great choruses that sang oratorios, and the readiness to welcome foreign artists on concert tour had been quite evident since the days of Handel and continued to prevail. Concert life had greatly increased since the 18th century. Revival of native tradition and gradual severance from the predominance of German music are tied up with the movement around 1880 and the names of Hubert Parry (1848–1914), Charles Villiers Stanford (1852–1924), and Alexander Campbell Mackenzie (1847–1935). The development of English musical style that began around 1900 was linked up with the discovery of English folk-song. Then, after World War I, there occurred the break with the 19th-century tradition.

Opera had never been incorporated into English musical life as an organic component, but had been a part of the social scene, the presentation being in the hands of foreign troupes. An exception, however, was the ballad opera. Beginnings were made from this form, with its stress on self-contained musical numbers bound together by dialogue, as Arthur Sullivan (1842–1900) in collaboration with his librettist William Schwenck Gilbert between 1871 and 1896 wrote 14 operettas and comic operas for the stage. Many of these, such as *H.M.S. Pinafore* (London 1878), were world successes. Sullivan attempted also to take the step to the serious opera, with *Ivanhoe* (London 1891).

Most of the composers since the Renaissance of English music also wrote operas; Hubert Parry wrote one, Charles Villiers Stanford seven, Alexander Campbell Mackenzie six. Frederick Delius (1862–1934) wrote six, his main work being *Romeo und Julia auf dem Dorfe*, text by Jelka Delius after Gottfried Keller (Berlin 1907; first English performance, London 1910); and Ralph Vaughan Williams (1872–1958) also wrote six. Despite this extensive composition of operas, however, a real English repertory has hardly resulted. It was not until quite recently that a beginning in this direction was made by Benjamin Britten (b. 1913), the most significant composer for the stage since Purcell. He possesses an unusual sense of the theater and of the idiomatic aspects of the English language in connection with music. Stylistically he is often quite eclectic and conservative. Perhaps his most important opera is *Peter Grimes* (London 1945), a world success. The musically strongest one is *The Turn of the Screw* (Venice 1954).

Within the English-speaking area, moreover, there have been many operatic works composed by Americans, either native or naturalized. Though this development requires separate discussion, it should be noted that Igor Stravinsky's opera *The Rake's Progress*, with text by W. H. Auden and Chester Kallmann, after a series of pictures by Hogarth (Venice 1951), is stylistically in the tradition of the 18th-century number opera. Also George Gershwin (1898–1937) found a distinctive way towards an American opera in *Porgy and Bess* (Boston 1935), in which there are influences from the Veristic opera in the dramatic touches and the high degree of integration with the world of the American Negro in the use of spirituals and other songs and the exploitation of tone-color.

Czechoslovakia

By way of general historical background for the Czech operatic development during the 19th and 20th centuries, it should be observed that during the 19th century the economic and cultural individuality of the Czech bourgeoisie grew in intensity, as over against the Viennese administration's adherence to centralization. In 1871 the Czechs demanded an agreement that would correspond to the "Austrian-Hungarian Agreement" of 1867, but the demand was rejected. During the ensuing years verbal and physical struggles continued between Czechs and Germans in Bohemia and in the Viennese imperial council. A new party of the Young Czechs had formed against the unsuccessful party of the so-called Old Czechs. The aim was to federalize the empire in favor of Czech domination in Bohemia and Moravia and union with Hungarian Slovakia. In 1918 Austria-Hungary fell, and the Czechoslovakian Republic was proclaimed in Prague, with Masaryk as president until 1935. His successor, Eduard Beneš, continued in office until 1938. In that year, the conference in Munich was prelude to an invasion by German troops into the Sudeten-German area. In 1939, after the German invasion, Bohemia and Moravia became a protectorate of the Reich, until their liberation in 1945.

Though the Czech national opera was not established until the 19th century, opera existed in this area earlier. In Bohemian countries, from the beginning of the 18th century, it was fostered primarily in cities such as Prague and Brno and in the castles. The permanent court theater was supported by such noble families as those of Sporck, Lobkowitz, Questenberg, Rottal, and Schrattenbach. From the Sporck theater in Prague came the Ständetheater in 1798. Operatic life in the 18th century was under the influence of the German and Italian schools of opera. The first attempt to present a Czech opera in Italian style was made in 1730, with the opera, *O původu Jaroměřic*, by Franktišek Václav Míča (1694–1744), performed in Czech, German, and French.

At the beginning of the 19th century, however, more effective efforts were made to establisha a Czech national opera. As early apparently as about 1800 Mozart's *Zauberflöte* was produced in Czech; in 1823, Weigl's *Schweizerfamilie;* in 1824, Cherubini's *Wasserträger;* also soon thereafter, Weber's *Freischütz.* The individual most responsible for Czech operatic life of the 1820's was František Škroup (1801–1862), author of the first Czech *singspiel Dráteník* (Wire-Binder), on a text by J. K. Chmelenský (Prague 1826), and of the folklike *singspiel Fidlovačka,* on the text by J. K. Tyl (Prague 1834), containing a song *Kde domov můj*, the source of the Czech national anthem. For various political and sociological reasons it was not until the 1860's that there was an upsurge in Czech cultural life and thus also in Czech opera, particularly through the appearance of the creator of what is today regarded as Czech national music, Smetana.

Bedřich Smetana was born on March 2, 1824, in Litomyšl, East Bohemia, and died on May 12, 1884, in Prague. As early as 1843 he was active in Prague as a music teacher. Having studied the piano, he was encouraged by Johann Friedrich Kittl (1806–1868), the Director of the Prague Conservatory of Music, and was trained in composition by Joseph Proksch (1794–1864). These two, with the music historian August Wilhelm Ambros (1816–1876), formed a group that adhered to Neo-Romantic ideas such as were exemplified by Berlioz, Liszt, and Wagner. In 1848, sympathizing with the revolutionary conflicts, Smetana opened a music school of his own in Prague. Under the pressure of political affairs he left his native land in 1856, to take over the leadership of the Philharmonic Society in Göteborg. After the fall of the Bach absolutism, Smetana returned in 1861 to Prague and indefatigably devoted his talents to serving the cultural life of his nation.

The revival then beginning led in 1861 to the founding of the *Hlahol* singing society, as well as to that of numerous other groups and the development of the patriotic singing movement. In 1862 it also led to the opening of the Czech provisional theater, and in 1863 to the organization of the artists' society, *Umělecká Beseda*. It is particularly to Smetana's credit that he helped raise the national musical culture to an international level. From 1863 to 1865 he was director of the *Hlahol* singing society, in 1864 and in 1869 conductor of the Czech Philharmonic Concerts, from 1864 to 1865 music critic on *Národní Listy*, from 1863 to 1870 chairman of the music division of the *Umělecká Beseda*, and from 1866 to 1874 first conductor of the provisional theater. In 1874 he suffered from deafness, withdrew from public offices, and concentrated entirely on composition; in the last years of his life he underwent clinical psychiatric treatment.

Smetana's life was a continued struggle for the advancement of his artistic position and against the reproach that he wished to force the Neo-German trend on Bohemia. The music scholar Otakar Hostinský (1847–1910), among others, stood tirelessly at his side and aided him in his efforts. Basic Smetana research was begun by Hostinský's pupil Zdeněk Nejedlý, a pioneer in Czech musicology.

The actual history of Czech national music begins with Smetana, who founded it. In only a qualified sense can his music be said to have been influenced by Franz Liszt. Instead, it is an inspired stylization and monumentalization of the essential element in the intonation of Czech folk-song. Without actually quoting, it takes national melody as a point of departure and incorporates in it features of both dance and song. Smetana transcended the pre-Revolutionary conception of the 1830's and '40's that a national music was to be created only by quotations and imitations of folk-songs.

Over and above the historical national contribution, Smetana was a personality of unique historical significance. He approached national materials in his operas personally and at the same time in a historically Romantic way, and in his musical comedies he developed the figures individually from real life. In the symphonic poem Smetana and Liszt created a new type, based on the laws of musical dramaturgy. According to Helfert, Smetana's music is a synthesis of Romantic inspiration and of strict Classical architectonics.

In addition to symphonic poems, chamber music, piano pieces, songs, and choruses, he wrote eight operas: *Braniboři v Čechách* (The Branden-burgers in Bohemia, text by Karel Sabina, 1862–3, Prague 1866), *Prodaná nevěsta* (The Bartered Bride, text by Karel Sabina, Prague 1866), *Dalibor* (text by Joseph Wenzig, Prague 1868), *Libuše* (text by Joseph Wenzig, 1871–2, Prague 1881), *Dvě vdovy* (Two Widows, text by Emanuel Züngel after French material by Mallefille, Prague 1874), *Hubička* (The Kiss, text by Eliška Krásnohorská, Prague 1876), *Tajemství* (The Secret, text by Eliška Krásnohorská, Prague 1878), and *Čertova stěna* (The Devil's Wall, text by Eliška Krásnohorská, Prague 1882).

Three of Smetana's operas are based entirely on Czech history. *The Brandenburgers in Bohemia* deals with the revolt of the people against the Brandenburg occupation, from 1278 to 1283. *Dalibor*, like *Fidelio*, is a song of freedom recounting the tradition of the legendary Czech knight Dalibor, of the 15th century, who was a symbol of Czech musi-cality. *Libuše* recounts the myth of the origin of the state ruled by the Czech kings, the Přemyslides. It is today the national Czech festival opera. A second main area in the operatic works of Smetana is comedy. *The Devil's Wall*, which has its comic features, deals with Czech his-torical material from the 13th century. His comic operas are quite indi-vidual types of musical comedy. *The Bartered Bride* is a folk-comedy of much common sense and truth to life. *The Kiss* is a lyrical work, full of the poetry of simple feeling, naive and folk-like. *Two Widows* is a comedy full of sparkling humor and life. *The Secret* was the culmination of Smetana's entire style in the comic opera. His work in opera has, along-side its basically optimistic feeling, a distinctive historical Romanticism that is to be understood from the political situation, as he was demon-strating the historical national consciousness and its reaction to political constraint. In *The Bartered Bride* Smetana starts from Mozart's *Marriage of Figaro* and raises the figures above parody and farce to create a new type of realistic comedy from the milieu of Czech country life.

The most important figure in Czech opera after Smetana is Antonín Dvořák (1841–1904). Since his most significant work is in the symphony and chamber music, details of his career are more appropriately con-sidered under those headings. But he did write music of all types, including ten operas: *Alfred* (text by Karl Theodor Körner, 1870); *Král a uhlíř* (The King and the Charcoal-Burner, text by Bernhard Guldener, pseudonym of J. B. Lobeský, Prague 1874), *Tvrdé palice* (The Block-head, one-act, text by Josef Štolba, 1874, Prague 1881), *Vanda* (text by Beneš-Šumavský, Prague 1876), *Šelma sedlák* (The Farmer a Rogue, text by Josef Otakar Veselý, Prague 1878), *Dimitry* (text by Marie Červinková-Riegrová, Prague 1882), *Jakobín* (The Jacobin, text by Marie Červinkova-Riegrová, Prague 1889), *Čert a Káča* (The Devil's Cat, text by Adolf Wenig, Prague 1899), *Rusalka* (text by Jaroslav Kvapil, Prague 1901), and *Armida* (text by Jaroslav Vrchlický, 1902–3, Prague 1904).

In subject-matter the world of the folk-like rustic milieu predom-inated (*The Blockhead* and *The Farmer a Rogue*) and of the Czech folk-tale (*Rusalka, The Devil's Cat,* and *The King and the Charcoal-*

Burner). Precisely here, though the main emphasis in Dvořák's work as a composer did not lie in the field of opera, he created his most significant stage work, *Rusalka*. It enriched the Czech repertoire with a new type of fairy-tale opera, full of poetic magic, touching lyricism, and simple wisdom, and attained world renown.

Zdeněk Fibich (1850–1900), called the "third classic master of Czech national music," was born in Všebořice in Central Bohemia, and received extensive musical training, culminating in study abroad at Leipzig, Paris, and Mannheim. From about 1871 to the end of his life he was in Prague, where he taught music privately, though briefly from 1873–4 he was a music teacher in Vilnius. From 1875 to 1878 he was in Prague, second conductor of the Interim Theater, from 1878 to 1881 choir leader of the Orthodox Church and from 1899 to 1901 stage-critic of the National Theater.

He wrote seven operas: *Bukovín* (The Bukovinian, text by K. Sabina, 1870–1, Prague 1874), *Blaník* (text by Eliška Krásnohorská, 1877), *Nevěsta Messinská* (The Bride of Messina, text by Otakar Hostinský after Schiller, 1882–3, Prague 1884), *Bouře* (The Tempest, text by Jaroslav Vrchlický after Shakespeare, Prague 1895), *Hedy* (text by Anežka Schulzová after Byron's *Don Juan*, Prague 1896), *Šárka* (text by Anežka Schulzová, Prague 1897), and *Pád Arkuna* (The Fall of Arcona, text by Anežka Schulzová, 1898, Prague 1900).

Smetana's immediate successor in the dramatic realm, Fibich made it quite his own, though he was still deeply influenced by Smetana in subject and in general musical expression in the early opera *Blaník*. *The Bride of Messina* is the most significant musical tragedy of Czech operatic literature. *The Tempest* is treated rather as a Romantic fairy-tale opera. The last three operas have an individual view of the world of Wagnerian Romantic tragedy. *Hedy*, which is not without reason called the Czech *Tristan*, particularly enters the sphere of the development of erotic myth. Especially notable is *Šárka*, an opera created from myth and at the same time a Czech national heroic epic in somewhat the manner of Smetana's *Libuše*.

In addition to opera, Fibich composed works in the form of the *melodram*. His contribution to this genre was to show the way from the concert *melodram* to the dramatic *melodram*, from the chamber-music form with piano accompaniment to the orchestral form, from illustrative description to the synthesis of music and poetry, so that his sixth and final concert *melodram* is *Hakon* (1888), a self-contained melodramatic-symphonic poem. In the form begun by Georg Benda, the word was here linked with an unbroken stream of music in such a way that anything which might turn aside the declamation or the music was removed. In this style a work unique in world literature was composed, Fibich's melodramatic scenic trilogy *Hippodamia*, to a text by J. Vrchlický, with the following parts: *Námluvy Pelopovy* (Pelops' Courtship), *Smír Tantalův* (Tantalus' Atonement), and *Smrt Hippodamie* (Hippodamia's Death). In these, the drama is underlined by use of the leitmotif.

Josef Bohuslav Foerster (1859–1951) was an immediate successor to Fibich in the Smetana tradition. He was active mainly in Prague, except during the years from 1893 to 1918 when he and his wife, the opera singer B. Lauterer-Förster, moved to Hamburg and later Vienna. In 1918 he returned to Prague and became Professor at the Conservatory and in 1922 at the Master-School. He was artistically related to Fibich in the sense of being highly intellectual, active also in literature and painting, and maintaining a relationship to the *melodram*. But he was yet more inward, naive, and subjective in expression than Fibich. Foerster had rich lyrical gifts, composing many song cycles. He had a decided sense of the dramatic and was the creator of the psychologically deepened music drama of Czech operatic literature.

Of the six operas that he wrote, the first three have found a permanent place in the Czech repertoire: *Debora,* on a text by Jaroslav Kvapil (Prague 1893); *Eva,* on his own text, after *Gazdina roba* by Gabriela Preissová (Prague 1899); and *Jessika,* on a text by Jaroslav Vrchlický, after Shakespeare's *Merchant of Venice* (Prague 1905). The opera *Eva* is the most significant one, presenting a psychologically deepened description of the tragedy of a simple Czech woman from the country—a work influenced by the Russian literary realism especially strong in the 1890's.

Continuing the Dvořák tradition, Vítězslav Novák (1870–1949) wrote principally symphonic and chamber music. He also composed two pantomimes, *Signorina Gioventù* and *Nikotina* (1929); four operas, including particularly *Lucerna* (The Lantern, Prague 1923), based on a much favored classic Czech play by Alois Jirásek.

Proceeding along lines begun by his teacher Fibich, Otakar Ostrčil (1879–1935), son of a well-known family of Prague doctors, at first taught at the Prague school of commerce. From 1908 to 1922, however, he directed an amateur orchestral association with notable results. From 1914 to 1918 he was leader of the municipal Weinberg Theater (*Vinohradské divadlo*). In 1919 he served as theater critic. Then, as successor to Fibich's pupil Karel Kovařovic (1862–1920), he conducted the opera at the Prague National Theater. In this position, which he held for the rest of his life, he was largely responsible for a brilliant era in the history of this foremost Czech theater.

He wrote five operas: *Vlasty skon,* or Vlasti's Death, to a text by Karel Pippich (Prague 1904); *Kunálovy oči,* or Kunal's Eyes, to a text by K. Mašek, after a story by Julius Zeyer (Prague 1908); *Poupě,* or The Bud, to a text by František Xaver Svoboda (Prague 1911); *Legenda z Erinu,* or the Legend of Erin, on his own text, after Julius Zeyer (1920); and *Honzovo království,* or Hansen's Kingdom, to a text by Jiří Mařánek, after a story by Tolstoi, 1932 (Prague 1935).

The first opera, *Vlasta's Death,* which grew out of the national mythic soil, reveals Ostrčil's close study of Fibich. The second and fourth of the operas are also based on myth—East Indian and Irish, respectively—which has been deepened and dramatized psychologically. *The Bud* is in the tradition of Czech musical comedy, which developed further the psychological aspect opened up in Foerster's *Eva*. Ostrčil's last opera was an artistic appeal against the danger of Fascism and imperialistic war in the 1930's. Ostrčil was one of the immediate heirs to the dramatic art of Smetana. He conceived of Wagner's idea of music drama in a way of his own and adapted it to Czech cultural and moral traditions. Developed from Fibich's Romanticism, Ostrčil's music achieved distinctive expressive style. Basically it is one in which characteristic polymelodic and individual melodic details are consistently subordinated to a monumental tectonic construction.

Otakar Zich (1879–1934) was also manifestly pursuing aims similar to Smetana's in the comic one-act opera *Malířský nápad,* or The Painter's Idea (Prague 1910), the tragic opera *Vina,* or The Debt, 1915 (Prague 1922), and the comic opera *Preciézky,* or *Les Précieuses,* 1924. Aims similar to Smetana's also appear in the work of Otakar Jeremiáš (1892–1962), who wrote a music drama *Bratři Karamazovi,* or The Brothers Karamazov, on a text by Jaroslav Maria, after Dostoievsky's novel, 1924–7 (Prague 1928), and in the work of Iša Krejčí (b. 1904) who wrote an *Antigone,* after Sophocles, composed 1933–64, and a *buffo* opera *Pozdvinžení v Efezu,* or Confusion in Ephesus, to a text by J. Bachtík, after Shakespeare's *Comedy of Errors,* 1944.

Rudolf Karel (1880–1943), on the other hand, was more related to the world of Dvořák's musical lyricism, with his opera *Smrt kmotřička,* or Godmother Death (Brno 1933). Also the Dvořák tradition appears in the work of Boleslav Vomáčka (b. 1887), who wrote the opera *Vodník,* or The Water-Carrier, 1933–6; and in that of the Brno composer Jaroslav Kvapil (1892–1958), who wrote *Pohádka máje,* or A Fairy-Tale of May, 1940–2.

An important figure in the development of Czech national music and particularly in that of opera was Leoš Janáček, who was born June 3, 1854, in Hukvaldy, Moravia, member of a family long active as teachers and musicians. In 1865 choirboy and instrumentalist in Brno, he was a pupil of Pavel Křížkovský (1820–1885), founder of the Czech choral style connected with the folk-music heritage. At the Prague organ school, moreover, he was a pupil of Zdeněk Skuherský (1839–1892) and František Blažek. After passing the examination to teach in the regular school system, Janáček taught music at the teachers' training institution in Brno and was conductor of the Brno Beseda society, with which he affiliated a women's chorus and an orchestra. A close friend of Dvořák's from these years on, he devoted himself in 1879 to further study for a year at the conservatories in Leipzig and Vienna. In 1881 he founded and directed the Brno organ school. For the first time in 1896 he visited Russia, which he regarded as the "mother of all Slavism" and which left a strong imprint on many of his works. After the first performance of his opera *Jenufa* in Prague in 1916 he became internationally known, and the new political situation after 1918 brought him new honors in his native land as well. He was appointed Professor of the Master Class in Composition at the Prague Conservatory, with Brno as the center of his activities. During the 1920's he received various honors at home and abroad, and on August 12, 1928, he died in Ostrava.

After he returned from Vienna in 1880 he vacillated between Romanticism and folk-music. During the ensuing eight years he decided to concentrate on the latter. The decision was strongly encouraged by his acquaintance with František Bartoš, who had done research in dialects. Together they began studying folk-song systematically in 1888—thus before Vaughan Williams, Bartók, and Kodály. After sporadic earlier choral settings, Janáček composed his *Dances from the Lach* and the *Suite for Orchestra* in a way distinctively his own. In 1897 he wrote the cantata *Amarus*, the first major work of Slavic character. From about 1894 to 1903 he was working on his opera *Jenufa*, which—like all of his major works—contains three elements: the national and the social worlds and the intimate sphere of experience. Musically it is the result of his involvement with Moravian–Slovakian folk-music, his collecting and harmonizing folk-songs and folk-dances, and his transcriptions of speech-melodies. Janáček was one of the great original geniuses in the history of music. Although traces of influence from schools such as Impressionism and Verism and from individual composers are perceptible, still in his style he was fundamentally independent, self-creative, and without exact prototype. A dramatist in all that he wrote and of an enormous vitality, as a realist he was at the same time a musician of feeling. His sources of inspiration are the nature of his homeland, its folk-song, and speech-melody as he had come to observe it by carefully listening to people as they talked. This is also the basis of his thematic work as well as the actual instrumental motives that he elaborated in a way all his own and—while observing the monothematic principle—with an apparently unbounded creative richness. The music is tonally conceived, favoring church modes and occasionally also the whole-tone scale. Meters that are either incomplete or expanded to quintuple and sextuple units are characteristic of his work.

He wrote orchestral and choral works, a Mass, chamber music, piano compositions, and songs; but he also wrote nine operas: *Šárka*, after a poem by Julius Zeyer (1887, 2nd version 1888); *Počátek románu*, or Beginning of a Novel, on a text by Jaroslav Tichý, after Gabriela Preissová, 1891 (Brno 1894); *Její pastorkyňa*, or Jenufa, after a play by Gabriela Preissová, 1894–1903 (Brno 1904); *Osud*, or Fate, on a text by Fedora Bartošová, 1903–4 (Brno 1958); *Výlet pana Broučka na měsíc*, or Excursion of Mr. Brouček to the Moon, 1908–17, and *Výlet pana Broučka do XV. století*, or Excursion of Mr. Brouček into the 15th Century, 1917, a two-part opera, with text by František Serafín Procházka, after the satire of Svatopluk Čech (Prague 1920); *Káťa Kabanová*, with libretto by the composer, after the drama *The Storm* by Alexander N. Ostrovski, 1919–21 (Brno 1921); *Liška Bystrouška*, or The Sly Little Fox, with text by Rudolf Těsnohlídek, 1919–23 (Brno 1924); *Věc Makropulos*, or The Makropulos Secret, with libretto by the composer, after Karel Čapek, 1923–5 (Brno 1926); and *Z mrtvého domu*, or From the House of the Dead, with libretto by the composer, after Dostoievsky, 1927–8 (Brno 1930).

In Bohemia the idea of the Romantic Era had led gradually from the idealization of folk-art to the activity of patriotic singing societies and then to the art of Smetana, which intensified its national materials and gave them international appeal. In Moravia, on the other hand, it remained attached to the ideal of folk-art and expressed itself most significantly in the compositions of Pavel Křížkovský and in the folklore movement. Even Janáček, Moravian through and through, devoted himself passionately to folklore research. But he saw the limits of a style of composition that limited itself to this manner. Especially in his ballet *Rákocz Rákoczy* (1891) and in his opera *Beginning of a Novel* he creatively recognized the problem here involved. The extreme possibilities can be found in his imitatively Romantic opera *Šárka,* on the one hand, and in his folkloristic miniatures, on the other. While searching between these two extremes and after much struggle and temporary reversion to folklorism and—as in his opera *Fate*—to Romanticism, he at last succeeded in discovering his own artistic world in the opera *Jenufa.*

Janáček's operas are prose set to music. Musically, they are permeated with the "speech melody," or the musical imitation of the realistically spoken word in all individual circumstances of life, and by the very original handling of the thematic work. The thematic invention in the instrumental work is mostly traceable to a germinal motive. In its modification, transformation, and reformulation his imagination was inexhaustible. Variants ensue from the psychological development of the realism, in close connection with the drama. Thus he made a new contribution to the principle of the leitmotif and attained astonishing psychological unity. In the subjects of his operas he was mainly a realist, though symbolism and allegory also played a role. Through his music he embraced absolutely all life situations within the dramatic power of his expression. His works represented a new chapter in the history of Czech opera, and individual compositions have won acceptance throughout the world.

Janáček's powerful achievement influenced some of his younger contemporaries. Vít Nejedlý (1912–1945) composed works related to his artistic realm of expression, notably in 1938 an opera *The Weavers,* after G. Hauptmann. Also Emil František Burian (1904–1959) was strongly influenced by Janáček's operatic style in the opera *Maryša,* on a text after the play of that name by the Mrštík brothers, 1938.

One of the most recent composers from this area to achieve international fame was Bohuslav Martinů (1890–1959), who was born in Polička and studied composition in Prague with Joseph Suk and in Paris with Albert Roussel. From 1923 to 1940 he was in Paris, from 1940 to 1953 in the U. S. A., and from 1953 to 1959 in Switzerland and Italy. He composed sixteen operas, most notably *Hry o Marii* (1933–4), *The Theater behind the Gate* (1936), *Comedy on the Bridge* (1935), *Julietta* (1936–7), *Mirandolina* (1954), and *Greek Passion* (1955–8). Also he wrote twelve ballets. The music in the stage works is Neo-Classicistic, linked in *Julietta* with Surrealistic influences.

The movement to establish a Czech national opera was followed by a comparable movement among the Slovakians. The first significant Slovak composer of the 19th century was Ján Levoslav Bella (1843–1936), born in Liptovský Mikuláš, and early in his career a Catholic priest and writer of church music. Coming under the influence of Neo-Romantic ideas in the 1870's, however, he left Catholicism and, through Ludevít

Procházka, was in close touch with the artistic world of Smetana. In 1881 he went to Transylvania, but in 1923 he was again on Slovakian soil. He completed only one opera, *Kováč Wieland,* or Wieland the Smith, with text by O. Schlemm, after Richard Wagner's sketch, 1880–9 (Bratislava 1926).

After the liberation of Slovakia from German Fascism in 1944, the national Slovakian opera flourished in the folk-democratic state in connection with the rise of a national culture. The first opera of this period was *Krútňava,* or Katrena, with text by Š. Roza (Bratislava 1949), composed by Eugen Suchoň (b. 1908), on a subject from Slovakian village life. Suchoň, a pupil of Vítězslav Novák, carried Janáček's realism further. The musical idiom in his opera derived from Slovakian folk-like melody with its frequent alterations, which the composer considered harmonic interpretation of its peculiarly Slovakian melodic aspects. Another opera of Suchoň's, *Svätopluk* (Bratislava 1960), was based on national history.

Ján Cikker (b. 1911), pupil of Vítězslav Novák, wrote two Slovakian national operas, *Jánošík,* to a text by Š. Hoza (1954), and *Beg Bajazid,* to a text by J. Smrek (1957). While the first opera was composed predominantly as a great symphonic and dramatic picture, the second centered more on the vocal aspect. A climactic point in the Slovakian opera was reached in Cikker's two stage works, *Mr. Scrooge,* after Dickens (1958), and *Vzkriesenie,* after Tolstoi's story *Resurrection* (1960).

Russia

The general historical background of the development of Russian opera covers approximately the past two centuries. The first university in Moscow was founded in 1755 and the academy of arts in Petersburg in 1758, during the reign of the Empress Elisabeth from 1741 to 1761. She was followed by Catherine II of Anhalt-Zerbst from 1762 to 1796, Paul I from 1796 to 1801, and Alexander I from 1801 to 1825. During this period two writers came to the fore, the poet Alexander S. Pushkin (1799–1837), with *Eugene Onegin* and *Boris Godunoff,* and Nikolai Gogol (1809–1852), with various novels and comic stories. In 1812 Napoleon invaded Russia, and after his defeat Nicholas I ruled from 1825 to 1855 and Alexander II from 1855 to 1881. During this time painting enjoyed a high position among the arts, and three outstanding writers of fiction made their appearance, Ivan Turgeniev (1818–1883), Fyodor Dostoievsky (1821–1881), and Count Leo N. Tolstoi (1828–1910). Under Alexander II there were extensive reforms, such as the abolition of serfdom in 1861 and the revision of the legal system in 1864, as well as a broadly democratic tendency and a significant rise of journalism. The Russo-Turkish War occurred in 1877–8. Under Alexander III from 1881 to 1894 and Nicholas II from 1894 to 1917, three further important writers appeared, Anton Chekov (1860–1904), Maxim Gorki (1869–1935), and Alexander Blok (1880–1917). Also during this time Vladimir Ilitch Ulyanov, or Nikolai Lenin (1870–1924), began his activities: the first convention of the social-democratic workers' party was held at Minsk in 1898 and the second in 1903, with Lenin as leader of the majority or

Bolshevik party. After the Russo-Japanese War in 1904–5, an attempt at revolution proceeded from a strike in Petersburg. But in 1917, with the arrival of Lenin in Petrograd, the Revolution itself occurred.

Like England and Germany, 18th-century Russia was an outpost of Neapolitan opera. Francesco Araja, Baldassare Galuppi, Giovanni Paisiello, Tommaso Traëtta, Domenico Cimarosa, Catterino Cavos, and Guiseppe Sarti were active there. The first Italian opera presented in the court theater in Petersburg, in 1736, was Francesco Araja's *La forza dell'amore e dell'odio*. The period of greatest brilliance was the reign of Catherine II from 1762 to 1796. The first public opera house in Russia was opened at Moscow in 1776, being in 1780 moved to a new building on the site of the present Bolshoi Theater. The first public court theater in Moscow was founded in 1806. The work of the Italians, however, did not contribute very directly to the actual development of Russian opera. Possibly the only exception was the work of Catterino Cavos (1776– 1840), who was in Petersburg from 1789 to his death and who set Russian material to music and used Russian folk-melodies in his operas, thus helping to clear the ground for the Russian national opera.

Russia had a remarkable type of *singspiel* of its own during the latter half of the 18th century, written by various pioneers and fore-runners of Russian opera, such as Solovski, Michail Martinski (1750– 1820), Vassili Alexeivich Pashkevich (1742–1800), Dimitri Stephanovich Bortniansky (1751–1825), Yevstignei Ipatovich Fomin (1761–1800), Stephan Ivanovich Davidov (1777–1825), and Alexei Nikolaievich Vertov-sky (1799–1862).

The first operas of lasting historical significance in Russia were written by Michael Glinka, who was born on June 1, 1804, in a land-owning family at Novospaskoie, near Smolensk. At first he was taught piano at home and then further in boarding school at Petersburg, where he received instruction in violin and also briefly in piano with John Field. From 1822 to 1828 Glinka was in the civil service. For reasons of health he was for a time in the Caucasus, where he came to know the folk-music of the Georgians. From 1830 to 1833 he was in Europe, visiting Milan, Rome, and Naples and meeting Mendelssohn and Berlioz; and in 1833–4 he studied theory with Siegfried Dehn in Berlin. Having returned to Petersburg, he wrote the opera *Ivan Sussanin,* or The Life for the Czar (Petersburg 1836), the first Russian national opera, followed by *Ruslan and Liudmila* (Petersburg 1842). From 1844 to 1847 he was abroad again, renewing acquaintance with Berlioz in Paris and study-ing folk-music in Madrid and Seville. In 1852, also, he was in Paris. But from 1854 to 1856 he was living near Petersburg, and there he came into friendly contact with the composers Dargomishski, Balakirev, and Serov and the reviewer Vladimir Vassilievich Stassov (1824–1906). Returning to Berlin to study counterpoint and church modes with Dehn in 1856, Glinka died there on February 15, 1857.

Glinka is considered the "father of Russian music." In national Rus-sian art-music he was the pioneer. The première of his *Ivan Sussanin* at

Petersburg in 1836 marked the birth of Russian national opera and, at the same time, inaugurated the period of nationalism in the history of Russian music. During his sojourn in Italy from 1830–1833 he derived lasting impressions of Italian music as exemplified in the operas of Bellini and Donizetti and in church music. His composition studies in theory, harmony, and counterpoint were professionally directed in Berlin by Siegfried Dehn, who encouraged him in his intention of composing "in a Russian way." Glinka's patriotic opera *Ivan Sussanin* is a happy fusion of formal elements of Western opera with the spirit of Russian folk-song. The opera was a national creation, strong in dramatic expression, and a guide for the following period. He is of significance in his orchestral work *Karmarinskaya* and in some of his songs. The best, however, is in the two operas. In his opera *Ruslan and Liudmila* Glinka introduces numerous Oriental elements, utilizing here perhaps for the first time in music the whole-tone scale. Over and above his historical merits, Glinka has elicited intensely patriotic admiration from all Russian musicians of all possible persuasions.

In addition to his orchestral works, chamber music, piano compositions, and songs, he composed two operas: *Ivan Sussanin,* or The Life for the Czar, to a text by Baron Georgy Fedorovich Rosen (Petersburg 1836) and *Ruslan and Liudmila,* to a text by five collaborators, after Pushkin (Petersburg 1842). As for the style and particular features of these operas, they were consciously national creations, effecting a highly significant synthesis of formal elements from the operas of Mozart, Weber, Cherubini, and the Italians, with the spirit of Russian folk-song. They have a strong sense of the dramatic and are basically of patriotic character.

Glinka's successor was his friend Alexander Sergeievich Dargomishski (1813–1869), who was strongly influenced by him. At first Dargomishski was a public official, but in 1835 he returned to private life. There he carried on extensive music study, pursuing it during visits to Paris, Brussels, and Vienna. In 1867 he was Anton Rubinstein's successor as Director of the Imperial Russian Music Society. Dargomishski's principal works were *Russalka,* or The Nymph, on a text by the composer after Pushkin (Petersburg 1856) and *The Stone Guest,* to a poetical text by Pushkin, a work for which he did not complete the music—but it was supplemented by César Cui and instrumented by Rimski-Korsakov (Petersburg 1872). The significance of this music arises from its national character, replete with folksong-like melodies. It was a pioneering effort in the realistic declamation of recitative. Dargomishski said, "I want the sound to express the word directly. I seek truth."

In Russia the beginning of the 1860's brought great national creative development also in music, with Petersburg and Moscow as centers. Leaders in organizing it were the brothers Anton Grigorievich Rubinstein (1829–1894) and Nikolai Grigorievich Rubinstein (1835–1881), each with his own attitude toward Central European music.

Anton G. Rubinstein was internationally famous as a pianist. He was a versatile composer, with numerous operas to his credit, including *The*

Demon, after Lermontov (Petersburg 1875). He also wrote symphonic poems, an Ocean Symphony, an oratorio, *Christus,* and piano works. A writer on music and an organizer, he was the founder of the Imperial Russian Music Society in Petersburg in 1859 and of the Conservatory in Petersburg in 1862, serving as the initial director of the latter institution. He was the first Russian musician to enjoy equally high recognition as composer and interpreter. In addition to bringing the artistic standards of central and western Europe into Russian musical life, he gave Russia European methods of education in music.

Nikolai G. Rubinstein, on the other hand, was not prominent as a composer. He was, however, significant as a director and teacher and was an eminent pianist. Founder and first director of the Conservatory in Moscow in 1866, he directed the concerts of the Moscow branch of the Imperial Russian Music Society from the year of its founding in 1860 to his death. This society not only contributed a great deal to introducing the music of the West into Russia but also strongly supported and encouraged Russian creative work. The conservatories in Petersburg and Moscow were organs of the Music Society. Music schools and classes were also organized elsewhere in Russia. Nikolai Rubinstein was essentially closer to the national sources of Russian art than was his brother.

During this period the outstanding critic was Alexander Nicolaievich Serov (1820–1871), himself also a composer of operas.

The Western European accounts of Russian music history have long been accustomed to distinguish between the "Westerners" and the "Mighty Group" and to see in the attitude of these musicians a dualism, a taking of front-line positions in opposition to each other, to be transcended only by Tchaikovsky and Rimski-Korsakov. According to the results of specialized Soviet musicological research, however, this conception is too schematic and superficial and hence is no longer tenable. In reality the historical events were essentially more complicated. It is also incorrect to label the "Five" musical dilettantes. Although they were not all primarily professional musicians, they were technically trained in music.

Under the designation "Mighty Group," "Innovators," "Band of Five," "Balakirev Party," "Russian National School," or "Young Russian School," the five composers Musorgski, Borodin, Cui, Balakirev, and Rimski-Korsakov are usually grouped together.

The designation "Mighty Group" seems to have been taken from a review written by Stassov. In 1867 a concert was given in connection with an ethnographic exhibition under the leadership of Balakirev. Stassov ended his account of the concert with the words: "God grant that our Slavic guests may never forget this concert. God grant that they forever retain the memory of how much poetry, feeling, talent, and ability have been displayed by the little but mighty group of Russian composers."

Modest Petrovich Musorgski was born on March 21, 1839, in Karevo, not far from Pskov. Son of a landowner, he received his first piano instruction from his mother and then from a German governess, and early became acquainted with folk-music. In 1849 he entered the Peter-Paul School in Petersburg and in 1852 the Ensign Guards' School, where he received piano instruction from Anton Herke. From 1856 to 1859 he served as an officer in the Infantry Guard regiment. By 1856 he was in contact with Borodin, Dargomishski, Cui, and Balakirev, and thus he became one of the "Mighty Group," whose intellectual and musical leader was Mili Balakirev and whose spokesman was the critic Vladimir Stassov. Here Musorgsky developed into an individual composer, turning unreservedly to the national aspects of his music. After he had fulfilled his military service in 1859, he lived till 1863 without professional occupation; but he was then obliged to take a civil-service position in the Engineering Department of the Ministry of Transportation, which he held until a year before his death. During the years from 1865 to 1872 he wrote his first songs, which included the cycle *The Nursery*. Also during this period he wrote the operas *Boris Godunov, The Marriage,* and the orchestral work *A Night on Bald Mountain.* Then, during the years from 1872 to 1880, he composed the operas *Chovanshtchina* and *The Fair at Sorotchinzi,* the song-cycles *Sunless* and *Songs and Dances of Death,* and the piano work *Pictures at an Exhibition.*

Musorgski was entirely conscious of the novelty of the road he was taking. In a letter to Stassov, he said: "The artistic representation of beauty alone, in its purely material significance, is crude childishness— the babyhood of art. We should cultivate steadily and conquer the comparatively unexplored area of human nature and the behavior of the masses. There lies the true mission of the artist. Let's push on to new shores." But Musorgski's significance was not realized in his own day. He died on March 28, 1881, in Petersburg.

Musorgski was perhaps the greatest and certainly the most original talent in music that Russia has so far produced. His achievement, in a certain sense unique, lay in the creative directness with which he understood how to characterize. He was unlimited in his possibilities of expression, embracing all human life. This ability gained its special stress through his aesthetic insistence on realistic representation in his way of imitating the spoken word and of appropriating his heritage of folk-music. Although in this respect he had been somewhat anticipated by Glinka and Dargomishski, he excelled them in spontaneity, tension, and breadth. In his *Boris Godunov* Musorgski wrote not only the first naturalistic and realistic or Veristic opera in Russia, but also the first social drama in music. "Musical folk-drama" is the subtitle of *Chovanshtchina.* This work is entirely uninfluenced by the conventions of Italian opera or of Wagner's reform ideas. Likewise Musorgski in his program music deviates entirely from the direction taken by Berlioz and Liszt, giving a realistic and not an idealizing interpretation to the program. The same character of representation distinguishes Musorgski's songs, which in this respect stand unique in the history of the 19th-century *lied.* In the evaluation of many of Musorgski's works a distinction must be made between the original versions and the revisions, mostly by Rimski-Korsakov.

His works include four operas, orchestral works, piano works, and numerous songs.

Aleksandr Porfirevich Borodin was born in 1833 in Petersburg and became professionally a physician and professor of chemistry at the Academy there. He was strongly inspired by Balakirev. In 1877 Borodin went to Germany, where he enjoyed the friendship of Franz Liszt. Later, in 1881, he spent a summer vacation in Germany, and from 1885 to 1886 he was in Belgium. He died in 1887 in Petersburg. His works include the opera *Prince Igor*, two symphonies, chamber music, and songs.

César Antonovich Cui (1835–1918) was born in Vilnius, his father being French and his mother Lithuanian. From early childhood he received instruction from Stanislaw Moniuszkow. Cui attended the engineering school in Petersburg and by profession became Professor of Fortifications at the Military Engineering Academy. In 1856 he became acquainted with Balakirev and in the following year with Dargomishski. With particular love for the works of Schumann, he carried on his own very fruitful creative work as composer and his extensive activity as music critic. As composer he did not show very strongly marked individuality. In him the distinctly Russian traits are weak and are at their best in his musical miniatures.

Mili Alexeivich Balakirev was born in 1837 near Nishni-Novgorod. At first he followed scientific pursuits and studied music only incidentally. As early as 1855 he appeared in public as a brilliant pianist in Petersburg. He received strong encouragement from Glinka, after whose death in 1857, particularly from 1861 on, he became the intellectual and professional leader of the "Five." In his role as spokesman he was explicitly compared by Stassov with Robert Schumann. In 1862 Balakirev founded in Petersburg the "Free Music School," a school standing over against the Conservatory, and conducted its concerts of new Russian music. From 1867 to 1869 he was also Director of the Concerts of the Imperial Russian Musical Society and from 1883 to 1895 Director of the court choir. He died in 1910 in Petersburg. His works include orchestral and piano compositions and songs.

Nikolai Andreevich Rimski-Korsakov was born on March 18, 1844, in Tichvin, in Novgorod province, the son of a nobleman, and early received musical instruction. In 1856 he entered the naval school in Petersburg, where he took further instruction in music and received lasting impressions from Petersburg operatic and concert life. In 1861 he first made contact with Balakirev. After returning from a world tour during 1862–5 on the training ship "Almas," Rimski-Korsakov remained in the naval service. In close contact with the other members of the "Five," however, he wrote his first two symphonies, the symphonic poems *Sadko* and *Antar*, and his first opera, *The Girl from Pskov*. In 1871 he accepted a professorship of composition and instrumentation at the Petersburg Conservatory. Although he left the naval service in 1873, he remained until 1884 inspector of all the ships' bands. From 1879 to 1882 he conducted the concerts of the "Free School of Music" founded by Balakirev, and from 1886 to 1890 he was leader of the "Russian Symphony Concerts" in Petersburg. He also on many occasions conducted abroad. He was, moreover, from 1883 to 1893 teacher and acting director of the court vocal chapel led by Balakirev. As in 1905 during revolutionary activities Rimsky-Korsakov took the side of the students, he was discharged from his position, but he returned to the faculty eight months later. He died on June 21, 1908, in Liubensk.

Rimsky-Korsakov was one of the great national phenomena in the history of Russian music. Proceeding from the ideas of the "Five" with regard to folklore and realism, he created a life-work important in scope and significance, the main part of which lies in opera and symphonic program music. In the history of music he is the past master of combined orchestral colorism and fairy-tale fantasy. He also led the Russian fondness for Oriental idioms to a climax, yet in his hands an artistic unity arises from the combination of these Orientalisms and Russian folklore. Foreign influences of Wagner and Liszt are relatively limited. Rimski-Korsakov was not only a magnificent artist in instrumentation but also a creative musician who worked entirely in the spirit of the individual instruments and proceeded from their technique. Special credit is due him for his service in behalf of the works of other composers, particularly his friends Musorgski and Borodin, though many aspects of his "arrangements" are today much disputed. Rimsky-Korsakov was a highly significant teacher; among his pupils were Alexander Glasunov, Anatol Liadov, Anton Arenski, Mikhail Ippolitov-Ivanov, Alexander Gretchaninov, Nikolas Tcherepnin, Maximilian Steinberg, Igor Stravinsky, and Ottorino Respighi. He was also the composer of a substantial list of works, including fifteen operas, three symphonies, symphonic poems, symphonic suites, overtures, chamber music, choral pieces with orchestra, and piano compositions.

Borodin and Musorgski had come to know each other in 1856. In Dargomishski's house they met Cui and Balakirev. Though Rimski-Korsakov had already joined them in 1861, he did not definitely do so until after his return from his trip around the world. The high point of their activities thus occurred during the 1860's. About 1870 contact ceased. The members of the group acquainted each other with their own compositions, and Balakirev was their most important critic. They also studied works by foreign composers, particularly Beethoven and Schumann. The attitude of the "Five" was progressive and at the same time national. Their aim was to gain entry for Russian song into art music. As Musorgski said, "I am touched by everything Russian." They also wished to raise the battle-cry on behalf of the international efforts in the current musical life of Russia and to elevate musical realism to the status of true art.

Musorgski attained the most significant results of the "Five," so far as Russian opera is concerned. He carried on further what Glinka and Dargomishski had been doing, and obtained world recognition for his *Boris Godunov* (based on Pushkin's drama and first performed at Petersburg in 1874). There are three versions of it: the first, 1868–70, is the "original *Boris*"; the second version was completed in 1872; and the third version was Rimski-Korsakov's arrangement. The work involves a completely new, most highly original and pioneering handling of the material, carrying on the realistic treatment of the word in the recitative and the melody after Dargomishski's model. It also contains harmonic innovations and a previously unexampled power of suggestion in the stage realism. Musorgski, moreover, possessed a strong sense of the comic in music.

Musorgski worked on *The Marriage* in 1868 but left it a fragment, which Rimski-Korsakov published; later Alexander Tcherepnin and Michail M. Ippolitov-Ivanov supplemented and instrumented it. It is a comic opera after Gogol, and in it Borodin adopted prose dialogue in a lifelike and realistic musical setting. *Chovanshtchina,* with text by the composer, took shape between 1873 and 1880; but Rimski-Korsakov arranged it, and it was given in Petersburg in 1886. *The Fair of Sorotshinzy* was composed between 1875 and 1880, but it remained a torso, available in arrangements by César Cui and Nikolas Tcherepnin.

Borodin worked on his only opera, *Prince Igor,* between 1869 and 1875, writing his own text; but his music was supplemented by Rimsky-Korsakov and Alexander Glazunov, and the opera was presented at Petersburg in 1890. In it, Borodin carried on from Glinka. "I am attracted," he wrote, "to the song, to the cantilena, not to the recitative . . . and moreover to well-rounded, broadly disposed musical form." He derived the dramatic characterization from the melody, conceiving of the work in amply proportioned scenes arising from the musical form, as he said, "painted distinctly and clearly in large areas with big, strong strokes." Though he reproduced national coloring, he did not use overtly folkloristic themes.

In opera, alongside Musorgski, Rimski-Korsakov is the most important of the "Five." His fifteen operas are *The Maiden of Pskov,* to a text by the composer, 1868–72, new version 1891 (Petersburg 1873, 1895); *May Night,* to a text by the composer, after Gogol, 1878 (Petersburg 1880); *Snow Flakes,* to a text by the composer, after Ostrovski, 1880–1 (Petersburg 1882); *Mlada,* to a text by the composer, 1889–90 (Petersburg 1892); *A Night Before Christmas,* to a text by the composer, after Gogol, 1894 (Petersburg 1895); *Sadko,* to a text by the composer and V. I. Byelski, 1896 (Moscow 1898); *Mozart and Salieri,* a drama by Pushkin, 1897 (Moscow 1898); *Vera Sheloga,* 1898 (Moscow 1898); *Czar's Bride,* to a text by Lev A. Mei, 1898 (Moscow 1899); *The Tale of Czar Saltan,* to a text by V. I. Byelski, after Pushkin, 1899 (Moscow 1900); *Servilia,* to a text by the composer (Petersburg 1902); *Katschei the Deathless,* to a text by the composer (Moscow 1902); *Pan Voievoda,* to a text by I. F. Tyuvenev (Petersburg 1904); *Legend of the City of Kitesh and the Maiden Fevronia,* to a text by V. I. Byelski, 1904 (Petersburg 1907); and *Coq d'Or, or* The Golden Cockerel, to a text by V. I. Byelski, after Pushkin (Moscow 1909).

In terms of subject-matter, these operas are almost entirely Russian. In their more purely musical aspects, Rimsky-Korsakov displayed great versatility and stressed musical realism. Basically, he maintained, "an opera is, above all, a work of musical art. . . An opera text may be considered and judged only in connection with the music, both so far as *mise en scène* and literary form or verse structure are concerned." In terms of style, he showed superlative mastery in the orchestral coloring.

Sometimes he quoted, borrowed, and freely imitated Russian folk-song for purposes of dramatic characterization, yet also he used Oriental features. He composed in self-contained musical numbers, though he also used a leitmotivic technique. The harmony is rich, and sometimes he uses church modes. In *Mozart and Salieri* he has recitatives that follow Dargomishski's model in the matter of melodic declamation. Rimsky-Korsakov also had a feeling for the comic in music.

Although Peter Ilich Tchaikovsky's life and works will also be discussed under the heading of the symphony, it should be noted here that he was born in 1840 in Votkinsk, studied law, and entered the civil service in Petersburg; but he also studied at the Petersburg Conservatory from 1861 to 1865. While teaching music at the Moscow Conservatory and writing as a music critic, he composed his first four operas. In the latter part of his career he traveled much abroad, but he died in Petersburg in 1893.

In all, he composed ten operas: *The Voyevode,* to his own text, after a comedy by Ostrovsky, 1867–8 (Moscow 1869); *Undine* (1869–70, not performed); *Opritshnik,* or The Bodyguard, to a text by the composer, after a drama by Lashetshnikov, 1870–2 (Petersburg 1874); *Vakula the Smith,* to a text by Y. P. Polonski, after Gogol, 1874 (Petersburg 1876; revised 1884 as *The Little Slippers,* Moscow 1887); *Eugen Onegin,* to a text by the composer and K. S. Shilovsky, after Pushkin, 1877–8 (Moscow 1879); *The Maid of Orleans,* to a text by the composer, after Schiller, 1878–9 (Petersburg 1881); *Mazeppa,* to a text by the composer and V. P. Burenin, 1881–3 (Moscow 1884); *The Sorceress,* to a text by I. V. Shpazinski, 1885–7 (Petersburg 1887); *Pique Dame,* to a text by Modest Tchaikovsky, after Pushkin, 1890 (Petersburg 1890); and *Iolanthe,* to a text by Modest Tchaikovsky, after a drama of Henrik Herz, 1891 (Petersburg 1892).

In contrast to Rimski-Korsakov, who preferred the legend and myth of the Russian world, Tchaikovsky sought for himself opera material in life as he had subjectively experienced it and with which he could identify himself. Throughout his whole career he was attracted to opera, and twice he found material that quite particularly inspired him: in Pushkin's *Eugen Onegin* and *Pique Dame.* In these, he wrote in 1891, he was enthralled by "the humanity, the simplicity of the action. . . . Feelings, moods, and pictures (perhaps experiences), to which the text led me along, to bring them truly, honestly, and simply to expression through the music—in this sense I am a realist and grass-roots Russian." Influences, more from French and Italian than from German opera, were raised to a new, higher unity in a world of psychology and feeling, the character of which is Russian. *Eugen Onegin* established the world fame of Tchaikovsky. Still today it is the best loved and most often performed opera in Russia. Tchaikovsky's operatic style was thoroughly individual and unmistakably his own. He particularly excelled in the melodic art of characterization with its strongly realistic sense of the dramatic and the theatrically effective, in the lightly sketched and dramatically self-reliant form that was usually conceived in terms of numbers, in the mastery of voice-leading, and in symphonic and musical development.

Soviet Union

The operas that have been written in the USSR run into the hundreds, and—as usual—but few have really found a place in the repertoire. At the head there stand works of Prokofieff, Shostakovich, Chrennikov, and Kabalevsky. Also from the Asiatic republics there are many operatic works by composers who had never written operas previously. The folkloristic material of the individual republics has also been used by Russian composers, including Reinhold Glièr (1875–1956), Sergei Vassilenko (1872–1956), Vladimir Vlassov (b. 1903), Vladimir Fere (b. 1902), and Evgeni Brusilovsky (b. 1905).

Sergei Prokofieff (1891–1953) achieved great international success with many works, including *The Gambler* (Brussels 1929), *The Love of the Three Oranges* (Chicago 1921), *The Fiery Angel* (radio performance, Paris 1954), *War and Peace,* after Tolstoi (two versions 1946 and 1955), *Semion Kotko* (Moscow 1940), *Betrothal in the Cloister* or *The Duenna,* after Sheridan (Leningrad 1946), and *The Story of the True Man* (Leningrad 1948).

The first Soviet operas were written in the early 1920's. They included *For a Red Petrograd* by Arseny Gladkovsky (1894–1945), on a libretto by V. Lebedev; *The Revolt of the Eagles* by Andrei Paschenko (b. 1885); and *Decembrists* by Vassili Solotariov (1873–1964). The aim was to represent or suggest incidents in the Revolution.

The late 1920's brought forth operas such as *Ice and Steel* by Vladimir Deshevov (1889–1955) and *The North Wind* by Lev Knipper (b. 1898). Dmitri Shostakovich (b. 1906) revealed a characteristic fusion of Western European influences in *The Nose,* after Gogol, and in an opera that for a while occasioned much controversy, *Lady Macbeth of the District of Minsk* (Leningrad 1934). Further operas from the '30's were *And Quiet Flows the Don,* after Sholokov, by Ivan Dserchinsky (b. 1909), *The Farmer from the Village of Kamarinsk* by Valeri Shelobinski (1913–1946), *Warship Potemkin* by Oles Tchishko (b. 1895), and *In the Storm* by Tichon Chrennikov (b. 1913).

A special role in the formation of the repertory was played by Dmitri Kabalevsky (b. 1904). His operas include *Colas Breugnon* (*The Master of Clameci,* after Romain Rolland, 1937), *In the Fire* (*Before Moscow,* 1943), *The Family of Taras* (1947–50), and *Nikina Varshina* (1955).

Yuri Shaporin (b. 1887) wrote the opera *The Decembrists* (1957), after Alexei Tolstoi's drama.

Further opera composers include Konstantin Dankevich (b. 1905) with *Bogdan Chmelnitzky* (1951); Yuli Meitus (b. 1903) with *The Young Watch* (1947); Vissarion Shebalin (b. 1902) with *The Taming of the Shrew,* after Shakespeare (1955); Tichon Chrennikov with *The Mother,* after Gorki (1957); Kirill Moltshanov (b. 1922) with *Twilight* and *Corno Street;* Antonio Spadavecchia (b. 1907) with *The Brake* and *Soldier Schweik;* Grigori Shantir (b. 1923) with *The City of Youth;* Rodion Shtshedrin (b. 1932) with *Not Love Alone;* Nazib Shiganov (b. 1911) with *Jalil,* after the Tatar poet; the Esthonian composer Eugen

Kapp (b. 1908) with *Flames of Revenge;* Gustav Ernesaks (b. 1908) with *Storm Coast;* Marger Zarin (b. 1910) with *To New Shores;* the Georgian composer Otar Taktakishvili (b. 1924) with *Mindia;* the Ukrainian composer Georgi Maiboroda (b. 1920) with *Arsenal;* and Vano Muradeli (b. 1907) with *October.*

From the 19th century on, the ballet has played a very important role in creative work for the stage.

Poland

The general history of Poland, against which the development of opera there is to be understood, focuses on a series of partitionings and a subsequent struggle for political freedom and union. Economic life in this area had been active as early as the mid-18th century, leading to the development of cities, of popular education, and of the system of instruction. From 1764 to 1795 the arts were under the protection of King Stanisław August Poniatowski. Despite the first partitioning of Poland in 1772, the economic and cultural situation continued to improve: the Commission for National Education was the first ministry for adult education in the world, there was an extensive literature of the Enlightenment written by such figures as Krasicki and Naruszewicz, and research in the sciences was carried on by the Śniadecki brothers. A constitution was proclaimed on May 3, 1791. The second partitioning of Poland occurred in 1793, leading in the year following to the uprising under Kościuszko. The third partitioning came in 1795, with complete loss of independence. From 1807 to 1815 there was a duchy of Warsaw, founded with Napoleon's help. The Congress of Vienna was responsible for the final partitioning of Poland, and in 1830–1 occurred the November Uprising. The so-called Great Emigration, notably to Paris and including Mickiewicz, Słowacki, Krasiński, and Chopin, had an effect on the homeland. Further liberation movements—those of Cracow in 1846, of Poznań in 1848–9, and of the whole kingdom in 1863–4—led to still more oppressive measures. As a result of relative national freedom in the Austrian sector, cultural life concentrated in Cracow and Lvov. In 1905 there was the Workers' Revolution in the Kingdom of Poland. In 1918 the country was declared a republic.

The history of opera in Poland can be traced back to the 17th century. In 1628 there was an Italian opera performance in Warsaw, presumably of Sande Orlandini's *Galathea.* In 1633 the first permanent "opera stage" was inaugurated at the royal castle with Piotr Elert's *La fama reale.* Up to 1646 the royal court had witnessed eleven operas presented there, stylistically belonging to the Florentine and Roman circle.

During the latter half of the 17th century operas were performed only sporadically. Beginning in 1699, when an opera was given in connection with the coronation of August the Strong, the Dresden opera regularly gave guest performances in Warsaw. In 1725 at Warsaw, Poland had its first public opera theater, the repertoire consisting exclusively of works by Neapolitan composers.

From about 1725 on, Italian operas became more and more frequent at the courts of the nobility, and by mid-century had become quite usual there. A special role was taken by the Radziwiłł court in Nieśwież, where around 1749 *singspiele* with Polish text were performed, such as *Przejrzane nie mija* and *Opera pasterska,* thus marking the first step toward the creation of Polish opera.

The opening of a professional Polish theater in Warsaw on the initiative of King Stanisław August in 1765 established the basis for the origin of the first genuine Polish operas. In 1778 Maciej Kamieński (1734–1821) presented there *Nędza uszczęśliwiona.* It had an extensive overture in the Italian style and almost twenty numbers, including arias, duets, mass scenes, national elements, and the rhythms of Polish folk-dances.

Further representatives of early Polish opera were Jan Dawid Holland (1746–1815), Michał Kazimierz Ogiński (1731–1803), Antoni Wejnert (1751–1850), and Gioacchino Albertini (1751–1812). During the years from 1778 to 1794 at least twenty-seven Polish operas were presented.

Jan Stefani (1746–1829) wrote what was perhaps the greatest work of early Polish opera, *Cud mniemany czyli Krakowiacy i Górale,* with text by W. Bogusławski (Warsaw 1794)—a great success, with strongly patriotic emphasis, realistic treatment of folk customs, and stylization of Polish folk-music.

Early in the 19th century there was intensive cultivation of opera, stressing patriotism in many ways—principally historical works, represented most significantly by Józef Elsner and Karol Kurpiński.

Józef Elsner (1766–1854) was Director of the Warsaw National Theater and the Music Academy, and he was also the teacher of Chopin. In his own right he was a productive and versatile composer but without much truly creative individuality. In all, he wrote nineteen operas, of which the only successful ones were *Leszek Biały* (Warsaw 1809) and *Król Łokietek* (Warsaw 1818).

Karol Kurpiński (1785–1857) was Elsner's successor at the National Theater and director of the principal theater from 1833 to 1840. A composer, teacher, and author, he wrote thirty stage works, of remarkable significance for the Polish historical and comic opera. He was the most significant opera composer before Moniuszko.

The earliest musical version of Goethe's *Faust* was by the Governor of the grand duchy of Poznań Prince Antoni Radziwiłł (1775–1833). The score, written between 1806 and 1830 in close collaboration with Goethe, was presented piecemeal in 1810, 1816, 1820, and 1830; and the first performance of the entire work occurred in 1835 at the Berlin Singakademie. There are twenty-five numbers, only part of which are in traditional opera form, the rest being in free or rhythmized declamation with orchestral accompaniment—peculiarities that bring the work close to the Wagnerian conception of music drama. The musical ideas are versatile, original, and deeply expressive, with poetic melodic aspects that parallel those of Schubert and of Wagner in his earlier works.

The efforts to create a big national opera, however, were realized by Stanisław Moniuszko, who was born on May 5, 1819, in Ubiel near Mińsk. After studying in Warsaw from 1827 to 1830 with August Freyer and in Berlin from 1837 to 1839 with the director of the Singakademie Karl F. Rungenhagen, he went to Vilnius, and in 1841 he became organist at St. John's church, director of the Vilnius theater orchestra, and teacher of music, numbering among his pupils César Cui. In 1839 he wrote his first stage work in Vilnius, the operetta *Night's Lodging in the Apennines.* His next works were in Early Romantic style, as he tried to achieve a new manner of stylizing Polish folk-music. In 1842 in Petersburg he made an unsuccessful attempt to gain a place in the Czar's chapel. The first or Vilnius version of the opera *Halka* he completed in 1848. A second trip to Russia in 1849 was crowned by the success of his cantata *Milda* and of the concert overture *Fairy Tale,* dedicated to Dargomishski. A turning-point occurred in Moniuszko's life and work in 1858, with the presentation of a new four-act version of *Halka* at the Warsaw Theater, of which he became director. He visited Liszt in Weimar, and in 1862 made the acquaintance of Rossini, Auber, and Gounod in Paris. His next operas, *Flis, The Countess,* and *Verbum nobile,* established his fame as a composer. The performance of his *Haunted Castle* in Warsaw in 1865 occasioned a patriotic demonstration. Moniuszko's works were performed abroad, *Halka* being given in Prague, Moscow, and Petersburg. In 1864 he became a teacher of theory, instrumentation, and composition at the Warsaw Musical Institute, and in 1871 he issued a harmony textbook. He died on June 4, 1872, in Warsaw.

He and Chopin are the most important representatives of the Polish national style. Unlike Chopin, however, he adhered closely to native traditional art and did not especially stress the idea of revolution. There is a national emphasis in the themes of his libretti and song-texts, in the creative use of sources from Polish, Lithuanian, and Belorussian folklore, and in his various patriotic touches. Moniuszko learned the technique of composition from models like Loewe, Schubert, Mendelssohn, Lortzing, Bellini, Donizetti, Auber, Glinka, and Dargomishski. Particular values appear in the richness of melodic invention, the fluid and natural harmony, and the freshness of rhythmic ideas, mostly originating from folklore. Chopin's work has unfortunately eclipsed the artistic values of Moniuszko's, but he took the lead in creating the Polish national opera and in serving as musical mentor to very broad levels of the Polish people.

His more important stage works include the following: *Halka,* with text after W. Wolski (two-act version Vilnius 1848, four-act version Warsaw 1858); *Bettly* (Vilnius 1852); *Flis* (Warsaw 1858); *Hrabina,* or The Countess (Warsaw 1859); *Verbum Nobile* (Warsaw 1861); *Straszny Dwór,* or The Haunted Castle (Warsaw 1865); and *Paria,* after Delavigne (Warsaw 1869). He also wrote numerous operettas or *singspiele.* The libretti are mostly on Polish themes. They show Polish society with its specific stratifications, failings, merits, and conflicts: in *Halka,* for example, there is social conflict between the nobility and the farmers. The form and musical characterization of individual social circles and their personages are traditional, but certain aspects of the melody and rhythm are unconventional, as is also the creative transformation of Polish motives and of the traditional aristocratic song and dance. The lyrics of the arias are Slavic; and there is clever construction in the ensemble, especially in its comic touches, with a sure feeling for stage effect. Moniuszko holds first place in the history of Polish opera..

The political and economic situation in the latter half of the 19th century did not encourage the composition of Polish operas. Practically the only theaters were at Warsaw and Lvov, and they were beset with financial difficulties, strict political censorship, repertoire-politics, and a conscious preference for foreign works. Between 1864 and 1914, at the most, there were works in the Moniuszko operatic tradition.

Some composers, however, continued stubbornly on their own way: Antoni Minchejmer (1830–1904), Ludwik Grossman (1835–1915), Stanisław Duniecki (1839–1870), Władysław Żeleński (1837–1921) with *Goplana* (Cracow 1896) and *Janek* (Lvov 1900), Zygmunt Noskowski (1846–1909), Henryk Jarecki (1846–1918) with *Mindowe* (1880), and Roman Statkowski (1859–1925) with *Filenis* (London 1903) and *Maria* (Warsaw 1904).

One of the best known of the Polish composers is Ignacy Jan Paderewski (1860–1941), famous also as a pianist and statesman. He was trained at the Warsaw Conservatory under Strobel, Janotha, Schloezer, and Roguski, in Berlin under Kiel and Urban, and in Vienna under Leschetizky. In 1885 he taught at Strassburg. As pianist he attained world fame, giving concerts in Vienna in 1887, in Paris and London in 1891, in New York, in Austrialia in 1904, and in Africa in 1912. In 1885 he made his debut as a composer and enjoyed fame after the Dresden premiere of his opera *Manru* (1901). In 1919 he was Prime Minister and Minister of Foreign Affairs for the Polish government. In 1935 he undertook to supervise the first Polish edition of the collected works of Chopin. *Manru*, Paderewski's only opera, is in the tradition of the Wagnerian music-drama. It is effective on stage, and the maturity of the composition and its deeply expressive character place it qualitatively beside Moniuszko's *Halka*. The style is Late Romantic, enriched with strong Slavic and gypsy elements. Still today it is regularly included in the Polish repertoire.

Other Polish composers at the turn of the century were Mieczysław Sołtys (1863–1929); Felicjan Szopski (1865–1939); Henryk Melcer-Szczawiński (1869–1928); Henryk Opieński (1870–1942); Tadeusz Joteyko (1872–1932); Feliks Nowowiejski (1877–1946) with *Legenda Bałtyku* (Poznán 1924); Adam Wieniawski (1879–1950); Bolesław Wallek-Walewski (1885–1944); Ludomir Michał Rogowski (1881–1954); and Ludomir Różycki (1884–1953) with *Eros and Psyche* (Breslau 1917), *Casanova* (Warsaw 1923), and *Beatrix Cenci* (Warsaw 1927).

An outstanding Polish composer of the 20th century with significant work both in opera and in orchestral and ensemble music is Karol Szymanowski (1882–1937). Though his life and works will also be considered under the heading of these other forms, it should be noted here that he was born in the Ukraine, studied in Warsaw, and in 1927 became director of the Warsaw Conservatory. His opera *Hagith*, with text by F. Dörmann, 1912–3 (Warsaw 1922), is related in structure and idiom to Strauss's *Elektra*. It belongs to an early creative period in his career, when he still felt strong connections with traditions of Polish Romantic music and used Neo-Romantic means. At the same time, *Hagith* is somewhat transitional, as it shows tendencies on the composer's part to modernize the idiom through the coloristic sonority and harmony of Impressionism and to give it some of the dynamic features that one associates with Bartók and Stravinsky. Szymanowski's second opera, *King Roger*, with text by the composer and J. Iwaszkiewicz (Warsaw 1926) became an international event. The action is set in 12th-century Sicily and shows the conflict between the heathen and the Christian world. Characterization occurs through stylization, using such means as modal elements, Orthodox church music, and Orientalisms; and a great unity of idiom is achieved. It clearly belongs to a later period in the composer's style and—like all his work—is deeply subjective, ecstatic, dramatic, full of pathos, and contemplatively mystical.

More recent work is by Apolinary Szeluto (1884–1966), Raul Koczalski (1885–1948), Tadeusz Szeligowski (1896–1963), Aleksander Tansman (b. 1897), and Witold Rudziński (b. 1913).

Scandinavia

Denmark and Sweden to 1750

By way of general history during the period when opera spread to the north of Europe, it should be noted that from 1611 to 1721 Sweden was a major power, conquering what is now southern Sweden in 1658. But after the Norse war of 1700 to 1721 it lost its predominance. Absolutism, established in 1680, was replaced by a free constitution under Gustav III but was restored in 1772. Absolutism, however, prevailed in Denmark from 1660 to 1848. There was considerable scientific and humanistic advance during this time: in Denmark, by Niels Steensen (Steno) (1638–1686) in physiology and geology and by Ole Rømer (1644–1710) in establishing the speed of light and, in Sweden, by Emanuel Swedenborg (1688–1772), Andreas Celsius (1701–1744), and Carolus Linnaeus (1707–1778).

Up to about 1750 cultivation of opera in Copenhagen and Stockholm was almost exclusively in the hands of Italians, French, and Germans, either connected with theatrical troupes or acting as individuals. G. F. Hoyoul (d. 1652) wrote court ballets for Copenhagen. Heinrich Schütz was in Copenhagen in 1633–5, 1637, and 1642–4 and may well have collaborated in dramatic presentations. Caspar Förster the Younger (1616–1673) wrote *Il Cadmo* (1663) and opera ballets. Music for the first Danish opera, P. Schindler's *The United Contention of the Gods* (1689), is no longer extant, though the libretto is preserved. At the second performance the opera house, which had been built specially for it, burned. In 1702 Bartolomeo Bernardi (d. 1732) was given a court appointment. In the 1720's Reinhard Keiser was active in Copenhagen.

In Sweden during the latter half of the 17th century, Pierre Verdier composed French ballets. French operas of the Lully school were introduced perhaps as early as 1699 by Claude de Residor's opera troupe. French taste was manifested by H. P. Johnsen's *The Bartered Bride*

(1742). From 1752 to 1754 the Roman Vincenzo Albrici was the leader of an Italian opera company in Stockholm.

The Gustavian Opera in Sweden

After 1750 Italian opera was more intensively fostered, at first by A. N. von Höpken (1710–1778) and then by F. Zellbell the Younger (1719–1780), who was influenced by Handel. The main representative of the Neapolitans at the court of Gustav III from 1771 to 1792 was a former pupil of Padre Martini's, Francesco Uttini (1723–1795), who in 1767 became court conductor. J. G. Naumann (1741–1801) was very successful in Stockholm from 1777 to 1778 and from 1782 to 1786 as composer and reorganizer of the court chapel. His reform style culminated in the Swedish operas *Amphion* (1778), *Cora och Alonso* (1782), and *Gustav Wasa* (1786). The main representative of Gluckian opera was the German Joseph Martin Kraus (1756–1792), who came to Sweden in 1778 and remained there the rest of his life, bringing out notably *Proserpina* in 1781 and *Aeneas i Carthago* in 1790. The ultimate effect of the Gluck influence appeared in J. C. F. Haeffner (1759–1833). Toward the end of the century Abt Vogler (1749–1814) was in Sweden for a rather long time. The operas *Gustaf Adolph och Ebba Brahe* (1788) and *Dido och Aeneas* (1799) marked the appearance of Mannheim sentimentality and Romantic elements.

Rationalism and Romanticism in Denmark

Resuming as part of the background the subsequent general history of Denmark, we note that during the Napoleonic wars Denmark fought against England and that Copenhagen was bombed in 1807, leading to governmental bankruptcy in 1813. In 1849 a new legal system was adopted, with legislative parliament and constitutional monarchy. There were wars with Prussia. In 1920 Northern Schleswig was united with Denmark. Throughout the 19th century a number of Danes figured prominently in science and literature: H. C. Ørsted, who described electromagnetism in 1820; N. F. S. Grundtvig (1783–1872), who fathered the Danish folk high school; and Hans Christian Andersen (1805–1875); Søren Kierkegaard (1813–1855); and the poet J. P. Jacobsen (1847–1885).

More specifically regarding opera, the theaters were completely closed from 1730 to 1746 under the pietistic king Christian VI, but after his reign opera was actively fostered. Mingotti's troupe was in Copenhagen from 1747 to 1756. Conductors included Christoph W. Gluck, Francesco Uttini, Paolo Scalabrini (1713–1803), and Giuseppe Sarti (1729–1802). The last two were royal directors of music and actively helped to create a Danish opera. Though the writer of comedies Ludvig Holberg (1684–1754) came out in favor of opera and wrote a libretto *Artaxerxes*, after Metastasio, it was never set to music. The Norwegian writer N. K. Bredal pioneered in writing the unsuccessful pasticcio *Gram og Signe* (1756), which Sarti set to music. The first attempts to create a Danish *singspiel* met with similar fate; only Scalabrini's music for the satirical tragedy *Kærlighed uden Strømper* (Love without Stockings, 1773), by the Norwegian poet J. H. Wessel, is performed still today.

Johan Ernst Hartmann, the German-born father of a significant Danish family of musicians, established the basis for something new with his Gluck-influenced *Balders Død* (1779) and *Fiskerne* (1780), to libretti by Johannes Ewald, and with *Gorm den Gamle* (Gorm the Old, 1785), with text by B. C. Boye.

Johann Abraham Peter Schulz (1747–1800) was royal conductor of music from 1787 to 1795. His Danish *singspiele,* whose smooth cadences were regarded as mysterious, aided in developing a national school in the 19th century. His works include *Høstgildet* (The Harvest Feast, 1790), *Peters Bryllup* (Peter's Wedding), and *Indtoget* (The Entrance, both in 1793).

Friedrich Ludwig Aemilius Kunzen (1761–1817) was first in Denmark from 1784 to 1789 and was later royal conductor of music from 1795 to 1817, exhibiting the influence of Schulz and Naumann, and later of Mozart. He wrote sixteen operas and *singspiele* for Copenhagen, notably *Holger Danske* (1789), to a text by Jens Baggesen, after Wieland's *Oberon.* Further stage works include *Hemmeligheden* (The Secret, 1796), *Erik Ejegod* (1798), and *Gyrithe* (1807).

Edouard Dupuy (1770–1882), who was in Copenhagen from 1800 to 1809, wrote *Ungdom og Galskab* (Youth and Madness, 1806).

Christoph Ernst Friedrich Weyse (1744–1842), born in Altona, came to Copenhagen in 1789 to study with Schulz, and then remained in Zealand. With Weyse the Schulz-type of *singspiel,* which had already begun to be considered Danish, underwent a further development of lasting significance. More strongly gifted lyrically than dramatically, Weyse introduced many of his best songs and ballads into his stage works. His *singspiele* include *Sovedrikken* (The Sleeping Potion, 1809), *Ludlams Hule* (Ludlam's Cave, 1814), *Floribella* (1824), and *Festen paa Kennilworth* (1836). His works, which exhibit simplicity of expression and occasionally approach the Romantic expressive manner, are connected closely with the literary flowering of the young Romantic movement in the writings of Adam Oehlenschläger and B. S. Ingemann. As their contemporary and as the teacher of J. P. E. Hartmann, Niels W. Gade, and A. P. Berggreen, Weyse is considered a classic of Danish music.

Friedrich Kuhlau (1786–1832), born in Uelzen, pupil of C. F. G. Schwencke in Hamburg, came to Denmark in 1810. Somewhat along the *singspiel* lines of the *Magic Flute* and the *Freischütz,* he wrote half-a-dozen notable theatrical works: *Røverborgen* (The Robbers' Castle, 1814), a dramatic scene *Euridice in Tartarus* (1816), *Trylleharpen* (The Magic Harp, 1817), *Elisa* (1820), *Lulu* (1824), and *Hugo og Adelheid* (1827). He also wrote incidental music for several plays, including the National Festival Play *Elverhøj* (Elves' Hill, 1828). In it the Danish royal hymn, *Kong Kristian stod ved højen Mast,* appears, the melody going back to J. E. Hartmann and beyond. Also the music for this play includes some of the earliest arrangements of northern folk-tunes. His work has taken suggestions from Mozart's *Magic Flute* and from Cherubini, Beethoven, Weber, and Rossini. The form is clear, the counterpoint and instrumentation are well considered, and the harmony is daring. He is most convincing in the characterization of situations and of types, which are often worked out contrapuntally. In Denmark he pioneered in the creation of understanding for Beethoven and the young Romantics. In constant awareness of developments abroad, he encountered much opposition from the conservative party led by Kunzen and Weyse. Though his work was successfully presented, it did not form a school.

Pantomime ballet was introduced in Copenhagen by Vincenzo Galeotti (1775–1816). For him the Dane Claus Schall (1757–1835) wrote numerous ballet scores. After Galeotti, the Noverre pupil Antoine Bournonville was called from Sweden, his son August Bournonville (1805–1879) becoming the classic master of the Danish ballet tradition from 1829 to 1877. Through him ballet received the position of the central art at the royal theater. As author of thirty-six ballets he encouraged numerous Danish composers.

After Kuhlau and Weyse, the opera developed more in the lyrical than the dramatic direction, turning to legendary material and medieval history.

Johan Peter Emilius Hartmann (1805–1900), like Weyse, was indebted to the literary Romantic Movement, developing a "Nordic" style quite his own. His work maintains a simple and determined manner of expression, shows a preference for melancholy or tragic minor moods, and often introduces abrupt modulations. He came into prominence with an opera built up of folk-song material, *Liden Kirsten* (1846), on a text by Hans Christian Andersen, in which he introduced lyrics of love and nature that have become almost folk-songs. The Norse cadence appeared particularly in his late ballet work, in connection with the Edda material.

Further composers include Peter Heise (1830–1879), with *Drot og Marsk* (1878); C. F. E. Hornemann (1840–1906); P. E. Lange-Müller (1850–1926); and August Enna (1859–1939).

Romantic Opera in Sweden

Resuming the general historical background, we might note that in 1866 a legislative parliament was established in Sweden. Outstanding personalities in Swedish cultural development were August Strindberg (1849–1912) and Hjalmar Söderberg (1869–1941).

The only significant opera composer at the beginning of the 19th century in Sweden was Edouard Dupuy (1770–1822), trained in Paris and Berlin. He came to Sweden in 1793, went to Copenhagen six years later, and then returned to Sweden in 1810 as royal conductor of music. His work was related to *opéra comique* and to Mozart, in the charming *singspiele Föreningen* (The Union, 1815), *Balder* (1819), and *Felice* (1821). A pupil of Dupuy's, Franz Berwald (1796–1868), wrote *Estrella de Soria* (1841) and *Drottningen av Golconda* (The Queen of Golconda, 1864).

Swedish national opera was largely a creation of the last third of the 19th century. Ivar Hallström (1826–1901) was the first to interpret the old Norse material in the Romantic sense. His main work was *Den bergtagna* (The Enchanted, 1874). He also wrote the fairy-tale play *Den förtrollade katten* (The Bewitched Cat, 1869). August Söderman (1832–

1876) did not finish any operas but, inspired by Romantic realism, prepared the way through his declamatory vocal style, his mastery of the orchestra, and his creation of a lyric cadence that has come to be thought of as specifically Swedish.

Andreas Hallén (1846–1925), a pioneer as composer, director, and writer, was trained in Leipzig, Munich, and Dresden. From 1879 to 1883 he taught singing in Berlin, then resided in Sweden. In addition to certain affiliations with folk-song, he showed Wagnerian traits in *Harald der Wiking* (1881), *Häxfällen* (1896), and *Waldemarsskatten* (1899).

Wilhelm Stenhammar (1871–1927), a pupil of E. Sjögren and Hallén, wrote two operas.

Wilhelm Peterson-Berger (1867–1942), after training in Stockholm and Dresden, became from 1896 to 1930 an influential music critic for *Dagens Nyheter* in Stockholm. In his entire work he strove to adapt the idiom of Beethoven and Wagner to the Northern manner of expression inaugurated by Grieg and Söderman. His work, always to his own texts, has strongly personal features and occasionally uses impressionistic means. His main composition was *Arnljot* (1910), and the legendary drama that had perhaps the greatest success was *Adils och Elisiv* (1927).

During the next generation, there was a reaction against the Wagnerian influence. Ture Rangström (1884–1947) wrote two notable operas, *Kronbruden* (Stuttgart 1919, Stockholm 1922), after Strindberg, and *Medeltidig* (Medieval, 1921)—works that are very much his own, interwoven with a lyrical tone much like that of folk-music and with modal suggestions. Inspired by Richard Strauss, Nathanael Berg (1879–1957) wrote operas that include *Leila* (1912), *Engelbrecht* (1929), and *Genoveva* (1947). Kurt Atterberg (b. 1887) also wrote five operas that bear a strong imprint of Swedish folk-song.

Norway

It should be realized that Norway belonged to Denmark until 1814, when it was united with Sweden under one ruler. In 1905, however, it became an independent kingdom. Its major dramatist was Henrik Ibsen (1828–1906).

It lacked a court theater in the sense that most other European countries had one; hence opera was fostered at various theaters in a desultory way until in 1958 *Den norske Opera,* supported by the national government and the city of Oslo, was founded. Any development of a specifically Norwegian art of opera, accordingly, had to take a different course from that of other countries and perhaps can scarcely be said to have occurred. Waldemar Thrane (1790–1828) wrote in 1825 *Fjeldeventyret* in the manner of a Schulz *singspiel,* and also composed some songs in the Norwegian folk manner. The first national-romantic opera, *Fredkulla* (1858), was written by M. A. Udbye (1820–1889). Around 1900 several composers wrote works produced on foreign stages before appearing in Norway, such as S. Aspestrand's *Die Seemannsbraut* (Gotha 1894), G. Schjelderup's *Norwegische Hochzeit* (Prague 1900), and Christian Sinding's *Der heilige Berg* (Dessau 1914). Catharinus Elling's

Kosakkerne (1897) and the operas of Johannes Haarklou (1847–1925), *Fra gamle Dage* (In Olden Times, 1894), *Væringerne i Miklagaard* (1901), *The Emigrants* (1903), and *Mari-Sagnet* (1909), were first performed in Oslo or in Trondheim. Arne Eggen (b. 1881) wrote the opera *Olav Liljekrans* after Ibsen (Oslo 1940). Geirr Treitt (b. 1908) composed an opera *Jeppe* (1966), and Arne Nordheim (b. 1931) a twelve-tone ballet, *Katharsis* (1961).

Finland

Historically, Finland belonged to Sweden up to 1809. It was thereafter ruled by the Russian Czar until in 1918 it achieved national independence.

The first national opera, *Kung Karls jakt* (1852), was written by the German-born "Father of Finnish Music," Fredrik Pacius (1809–1891). Oskar Merikanto (1868–1924) wrote in Finnish *Pohjan neiti* (Girl of the North, 1908); and Erkki Melartin (1875–1937), *Aino* (1909). Selim Palmgren (1878–1951) composed *Daniel Hjort* (1910) in Swedish.

Since World War I, a Finnish opera repertoire has developed. Two works by Leevi Madetoja (1887–1947) are considered national operas: *Pohjalaisia* (The People from Österbotten, 1924), exhibiting passionate love of freedom and utilizing folk-melodies from Österbotten, and *Juha* (1935). Ilmari Krohn (1867–1960), Armas Launis (1884–1959), Väinö Raitio (1891–1945), Tauno Pylkkänen (b. 1918), and Tauno Marttinen (b. 1912) have written in the national and Romantic spirit, to some extent influenced by newer tendencies.

Post-Romantic Opera in Denmark and Sweden

Romantic realism, strongly represented in Sweden, faded away almost entirely in Denmark. Carl Nielsen (1865–1931) wrote two operas, *Saul og David* (1902) and *Maskerade* (1906). The former is like an oratorio, far removed from all realism, with polyphonic choral movements, extended arias and duets, and modal elements. The latter, based on a comedy by Holberg, is classicistic *buffo*. Both works have become models for later composition.

Further composers include Hakon Børrensen (1876–1954), Poul Schierbeck (1888–1949), Knud Jeppesen (b. 1892), Paul von Klenau (1883–1946), Jørgen Bentzon (1897–1951), Knudåge Riisager (b. 1897), Ebbe Hamerik (1898–1951), Finn Høffding (b. 1899), S. S. Schultz (b. 1913), Herman D. Koppel (b. 1908), Poul Rovsing Olsen (b. 1922), Ib Nørholm (b. 1931), and Per Nørgaard (b. 1932). Riisager composed *Etude* (1948), *Månerenen* (The Moon Reindeer, 1961), and other ballets.

Other Swedish composers include Hilding Rosenberg (b. 1892) and Gunnar de Frumerie (b. 1908). Rosenberg composed *Resan til Amerika* (1932), *Lycksalighetens ö* (Island of Happiness, 1945), and an opera-oratorio tetralogy, *Joseph och hans bröder* (1945–8), after Thomas Mann.

Modern operas, to some extent inspired by Schönberg, have been composed by Sven-Erik Bäck (b. 1919), with *Tranfjädrarna* (1956), *Gästabudet* (1958), and *Fågeln* (1961); by Karl-Birger Blomdahl (1916–

1968), with a chamber opera *Aniara* (1959) and *Herr von Hancken* (1962–4); and by Lars Johan Werle (b. 1926), with *Drömmen om Thérèse* (1964).

The Americas

Peru and Mexico

In Lima a Noah play with musical recitative, *El Arca de Noé,* was given nine times in 1672. The first dramatic work sung throughout and still surviving in score is a Venus and Adonis *presentacion* (1701) by Tomás de Torrejón (1644–1728), *La púrpura de la rosa,* to a text by Calderón. Thus in Spanish, as in English, there was a vernacular tradition of musical drama before the great international flood of Italian opera inundated the opera houses.

The rising tide of Italian opera is suggested by the fact that a Mexican-born composer Manuel Zumaya, master of the chapel at the Mexico City cathedral, in 1711 translated and set to music for his opera *Partenope* a libretto that had been used previously by the Neapolitan Luigi Manzo in 1699. The resulting opera was presented at the Mexican viceregal palace in 1711, the year in which Handel produced in London the first of his Italian operas, which were ultimately to include his own setting of this same Italian text. Soon the works of Cimarosa, Paisiello, and Rossini—in Italian—monopolized the Peruvian and Mexican stages; and when the Spanish singer, impresario, and composer Manuel García proceeded from his successes in Europe and North America to Mexico, all his presentations were given in Italian—even his own slight theatrical compositions. Some dozen Mexican composers in the course of the 19th century obtained performances for their operas in Mexico City, notably Cenobio Paniagua (1821–1882) with *Catalina di Guisa* (1859, in Italian), Melesio Morales (1838–1908) with *Ildegonda* (1866, Florence 1869), and Aniceto Ortega with *Guatimotzín* (1871)—the last-mentioned utilizing Azetc subject-matter.

A notable opera by the Brazilian composer Carlos Gomes (1846–1896) received its first performance at La Scala in 1870, *O Guaraní,* based to some extent on Brazilian Indian material.

With the 20th century the Italian monopoly weakened. Gustavo E. Campa followed French precedent in his opera, which also utilized Aztec subject-matter, *Le Roi Poète* (1901). Ricardo Castro wrote *La Légende de Rudel* (1906) to a French libretto, though when it was produced in Mexico City it still had to be sung in Italian. Since the political changes during the second decade of the present century, opera has retired from the center of Mexican composers' concern, though significant ballets have been written, as well as one-act operas by Pablo Moncayo (b. 1912), with *La Mulata de Córdoba* (1948), and Luis Sandi (b. 1905), with *Carlota* (1948). A large historical pageant-opera, Miguel Bernal's *Tata Vasco* (1941), about the first Bishop of Michoacán, encountered difficulties in getting a performance in Mexico City and was presented in oratorio form in Spain in 1948.

The United States

The situation farther north was somewhat like that in Spanish America, with so-called "ballad opera" productions in the vernacular of song and spoken dialogue. An early ballad-opera writer was James Ralph (about 1700–1762), who went along with Benjamin Franklin on his first trip to London when both were in their early twenties: the libretto of Ralph's *The Fashionable Lady* (London 1730) still exists. In 1735 at Charleston, South Carolina, an "opera" of *Flora, or Hob in the Well* was presented. By 1750 *The Beggar's Opera* had also begun to make its appearance in America, as had other works of the same type.

In the last decade of the century, shortly after the conclusion of the American Revolution, there appeared a more serious or sentimental note in the work of Europeans who had migrated to the New World: James Hewitt (1770–1827) in his *Tammany* (1794), one surviving number of which is based on an "old American Indian song"; Benjamin Carr (1768–1831) in *The Archers* (1796), on the William Tell theme; and Victor Pelissier (*ca.* 1760–*ca.* 1820) in his *Edwin and Angelina* (1796), after Goldsmith. Also active as arrangers and composers of music for the theater were Peter A. van Hagen (1750–1803) and Alexander Reinagle (1756–1809), a friend of C. P. E. Bach.

With the 19th century, Italians dominated opera and Germans orchestral, chamber, and choral music. There were some odd results. The Metropolitan Opera House in New York, for example, was opened in 1883 with Gounod's *Faust* sung in Italian; then for seven seasons it—and even *Aida, Carmen,* and *Il Trovatore*—were sung in German. Heroic efforts to break this Continental monopoly were made by William Henry Fry (b. Philadelphia, 1815–1864), whose first opera, *Leonora,* after a novel by Bulwer-Lytton, was produced in Philadelphia (1845) and later—in Italian—in New York. European correspondent for the New York Tribune from 1846 to 1852, he was in close touch with Berlioz, whom he may have influenced to undertake, after he had done so, musical composition based on Byron's *Childe Harold.* A later opera by Fry is *Notre Dame de Paris* (Philadelphia 1864). Perhaps in response to a contest announced by Ole Bull for an opera by an American composer on an American subject, George F. Bristow (1825–1898) wrote *Rip Van Winkle* (New York 1855), after Irving.

Meanwhile, of course, there were unproduced operas being written by American composers, such as James Hewitt's son John Hill Hewitt (1801–1890). The impulse behind the earlier ballad opera also continued in various theatrical forms, such as the "Negro minstrel show" or "Ethiopian opera," in which leading figures were T. D. Rice (1808–1860), D. D. Emmett (1815–1904), and E. P. Christy (1815–1862). In the middle of the 19th century such groups were very popular and even toured Europe. They developed a certain standard instrumentation and form, and bits from their repertoire, such as *Turkey in the Straw, Old Dan Tucker,* and *Dixie,* have passed into quasi-folksong currency; some of their procedures have been perpetuated in jazz. Perhaps the most substantial contribution to American music from this area was the work of Stephen Collins Foster (1826–1864), who wrote *Old Folks at Home* for E. P. Christy.

The ballad-opera tradition was also carried on in other types of musical theater, such as *The Black Crook* (1866), which was one of the first productions to include chorus girls; the Edward Harrigan and Tony Hart full evening's entertainment from *The Mulligan Guards Ball* (1879) on, and the so-called "light operas" by such composers as Reginald de Koven (1859–1920), notably *Robin Hood* (1890); Victor Herbert (1859–1924), who also wrote two grand operas, *Natoma* (New York 1911), based on an Indian theme, and *Madeleine* (New York 1914); Rudolf Friml (b. 1881); and Sigmund Romberg (1887–1951).

The vitality of the American musical theater is shown by the popularity of many works which are often simply referred to as "musicals" and are usually presented in regular theaters instead of specifically in opera houses. Their literary, choreographic, and musical aspects have shown increasing sophistication and finesse. High points in this field during the past few decades have been *Show Boat* (1927) by Jerome Kern (1885–1945), after Edna Ferber's novel; *Porgy and Bess* (1935) by George Gershwin (1898–1937), after Du Bose Heyward's novel; *Oklahoma!* (1943) by Richard Rodgers (1902–1960), after Lynn Riggs's play, and *South Pacific* (1949), after James Michener's short stories; *The Music Man* (1957) by Meredith Wilson (b. 1902); *The Most Happy Fella* (1956) by Frank Loesser (b. 1910), after Sidney Howard's play; and *My Fair Lady* (1956) by Frederick Loewe (b. 1904), after a play by G. B. Shaw.

Only during the present century has the Metropolitan Opera House in New York produced any operas by American composers, beginning with a one-act by Frederick S. Converse (1871–1940), *The Pipe of Desire* (1910), and a full-length opera by Horatio W. Parker, *Mona* (1912). Among other Americans who have written operas performed at the Met are Deems Taylor (b. 1885) with *The King's Henchman* (1927) to a libretto by Edna St. Vincent Millay and *Peter Ibbetson* (1931), after Du Maurier; Howard Hanson (b. 1896) with *Merry Mount* (1924), after Hawthorne; Louis Gruenberg (1884–1964) with *Emperor Jones* (1933), after O'Neill; Gian-Carlo Menotti (b. 1911) with the *opera buffa Amelia Goes to the Ball* (1938) and the one-act *The Island God* (1942), both to his own libretti; and Samuel Barber (b. 1910) with *Vanessa* (1958), to a libretto by Menotti.

Gian-Carlo Menotti, born in Cadigliano, Italy, in 1911, came to the United States in 1928 and completed his musical studies at Curtis Institute in Philadelphia. Most of his operas bear a considerable inheritance from *Verismo*. *The Medium* (1946) was first presented at Columbia University, then at a regular theater on Broadway and subsequently elsewhere in the United States and abroad, and it was also filmed. *The Consul* (1950), *The Saint of Bleecker Street* (1954), and *Maria Golovin* (1958) were performed on Broadway and elsewhere; *Labyrinth* (1963) was written for the National Broadcasting Company; and *The Last Savage* (1963) was first performed at the Paris Opera and then at the Met.

Among native American composers who have written operas first performed in European opera houses are Henry K. Hadley, *Safie* (Mainz 1909); Arthur Nevin (1871–1943), *Poia* (Berlin 1909); Paul Hastings Allen (1882–1952), *O Munasterio* (Florence 1911), *Il Filtro* (Genoa 1912), *Milda* (Venice 1913), and *L'ultimo dei Moicane* (Florence 1916); George Antheil (1900–1959), *Transatlantic* (Frankfurt 1930); Vittorio Giannini (b. 1903), *Lucedia* (Munich 1936) and *The Scarlet Letter* (Hamburg 1938); Samuel Barlow (b. 1892), *Mon ami Pierrot* (Paris 1935); Roger Sessions (b. 1896), *Montezuma* (Berlin 1964); and Louise Talma (b. 1906), *The Alcestiad* (Frankfurt 1962), to a libretto by Thornton Wilder.

Radio and television networks have commissioned operas, notably Charles S. Skilton (1868–1941), *The Sun Bride* (NBC 1930); Henry K. Hadley, *A Night in Old Paris* (NBC 1933); Randall Thompson (b. 1899), *Solomon and Balkis* (CBS 1942); Vittorio Giannini, *Beauty and the Beast* (CBS 1938) and *Blennerhasset* (CBS 1939); Gian-Carlo Menotti, *The Old Maid and the Thief* (NBC 1939) and *Amahl and the Night Visitors* (NBC 1951).

The movies, also—both in their institutionalized form and quite individually and experimentally—have offered a field in which 20th-century composers have been active and in which very many listeners have been brought into contact—consciously or unconsciously—with contemporary technical developments in music and been made more receptive to them (or, vice versa, have been made less tolerant of procedures once regarded as acceptable). George Antheil (1900–1959) wrote *Ballet Mécanique* (1924) to accompany an abstract film. Virgil Thomson (b. 1896) provided music for the documentary films *The Plow that Broke the Plains* (1936), *The River* (1937), and *Louisiana Story* (1948). Aaron Copland (b. 1900) wrote the score for *Of Mice and Men* (1939), *Our Town* (1940), *North Star* (1943), *The Cummington Story* (1945), *The Red Pony* (1947), and *The Heiress* (1948). A vast number of other composers have been and are active in this field. They often extract suites from their scores, once these have served their purpose, or re-use portions of them in other and more abstract musical forms. The existence of a number of channels by which a composer who has inclinations towards the theater can reach his public—such as radio, television, movies, and recordings—perhaps renders some aspects of the gesture of autonomy that Wagner made in establishing a physical opera house at Bayreuth unnecessary today; and just as technical developments in transportation made Bayreuth feasible in the late 19th century, some technical developments in the matter of communications have made it possible for particular composers to reach their particular publics in other ways.

As in any active and changing field, there is always—sometimes on the periphery—consciously experimental activity. An early excursion in the unconventionally operatic was the setting of Gertrude Stein's *Four Saints in Three Acts* (*Hartford* 1934) by Virgil Thomson (b. 1896). More recently Meyer Kupferman (b. 1926) has set Gertrude Stein's *In a Garden* and *Dr. Faustus Lights the Lights*. Harry Partch (b. 1901) has set in most unconventional-sounding idiom William Butler Yeats's version of *King Oedipus* (1952) and also composed *The Bewitched* (1957) and

Revelation in the Courthouse Square (1961), after Euripides' *Bacchae*. Lester Trimble (b. 1923) has set portions of Chaucer in impeccable Middle English (1959) and has also written the opera *Boccaccio's Nightingale*. A musical composition comparable to "pop art" in painting is *in memoriam Kit Carson* (1964) by Robert Ashley, presented at the ONCE Festival in Ann Arbor and involving group and gestural activity as well as purely auditory experience. Many aspects of so-called *avant-garde* composition—such as that presented at the ONCE Festival—is intended to bring various media together and give an extreme sense of immediacy. Pursuit of these aims leads almost inevitably towards—in some sense—the theater, though not necessarily the sedate, established opera house. Particularly in the United States—where a system of state-supported theaters and opera houses does not prevail, and a great deal of activity takes place under university and local auspices—there has been a relatively rapid degree of innovation, and evidences of it are not absent from post-World-War-II composition.

Bibliography

H. Abert, *Grundprobleme d. Operngesch.* (Lpz. 1926); W. Altmann, *Katalog d. theatr. Musik seit 1861* (Wolfenbüttel 1936); F. Clément and P. Larousse, *Dictionnaire des Opéras* (Paris 1869, 3rd ed. 1905); J. Gregor, *Kulturgesch. d. Oper* (Vienna 1941); D. J. Grout, *A Short History of Opera* (N. Y. 2nd ed. 1965); H. Kretzschmar, *Gesch. d. Oper* (Lpz. 1919); A. Loewenberg, *Annals of Opera* (Cambr. 1943); H. Riemann, *Opernhdb.* (Lpz. 1887, suppl. 1893); R. Rolland, *Hist. de l'opéra en Europe avant Lully et Scarlatti* (new ed. Paris 1931); L. Schiedermair, *Die dt. Oper* (Bonn 2nd ed. 1940); *Die Oper* (articles by various authors in Adler Hdb.); art. Oper (MGG).

Prehistory (to 1600): 1. Med. Liturg. Dr.: E. K. Chambers, *The Medieval Stage* (2 vols. Oxford 1933); R. de Coussemaker, *Drames liturgiques du moyen-âge* (Rennes 1860); E. Krieg, *Das lat. Osterspiel von Tours* (Würzburg 1956); W. Lipphardt, *Die Weisen der lat. Osterspiele des 12. u. 13. Jh.* (Kassel 1948); A. Schubiger, *Das lat. Drama d. Mittelalters u. s. Musik* (Bln. 1876); E. A. Schuler, *Die Musik der Osterfeiern, Osterspiele u. Passionen des Mittelalters* (Kassel 1951); L. Smolden, *Liturgical Drama* (NOHM II); K. Young, *The Drama of the Medieval Church* (2 vols. Oxford 1933); art. Liturg. Dramen (MGG); ex. Sch. 8. *2. School Comedies:* R. v. Liliencron, *Die Chorgesänge d. lat. dt. Schuldramen im 16. Jh.* (VfM VI). *3. Song-Plays:* G. Cohen, *Adam le Bossu, dit de la Halle* (Paris 1935). *4. Incidental Music:* L. Schrade, *La Représentation d'Edipio Tiranno au Teatro Olimpico* (Paris 1960). *7. Madrigal Comedies:* exs. Torchi IV, PGfM 26.

Prelim. Developts. in Monody: 2. Arrs. for Song and Lute: exs. PäM II, Sch 96, 114. *5. Vincenzo Galilei:* F. Fano, V. G. (IeM IV). *6. Instrumental Solo-Playing:* Ortiz "Tratado" new ed. Bln. 1913, also Kassel. *7. Thorough-bass:* H. H. Eggebrecht, *Arten des Generalbasses im frühen u. mittleren 17. Jh.* (AfMw 1957); M. Schneider, *Die Anfänge d. Basso Continuo* (Leipzig 1918); article on Generalbass (MGG); *Die Monodie* (MW).

Italy: F. Abbiati, *Storia della musica II–IV* (Milan 1941–5). *17th Century: Florence:* A. Loewenberg, *Annals of Opera* (Geneva 2nd ed.

1955); O. G. Sonneck, *Dafne the first opera* (SbIMG 1913–4); *La Camerata Fiorentina* (IeM 4); exs. Sch. 171–5; V. *Galilei "Della Musica antica e della moderna"* facs. repr. Rome 1934 and Milan 1946; *Rinuccini's and Peri's "Euridice"* facs. Milan 1934, Torchi VI; *Caccini's "Euridice,"* PGfM 10. *Mantua: Monteverdi:* compl. ed. in 16 vols. ed. Malipiero (Asolo 1926–42), biogr. monographs by M. LeRoux (Paris 1951), G. F. Malipiero (Milan 1930), D. de Paoli (Milan 1945), H. Prunières (Paris 1924, London 1926), H. F. Redlich (Olten 1949, London 1952), L. Schneider (Paris 1921), and L. Schrade (N. Y. 1950); compl. ed. of letters in Ger. tr. in prep. (IMBA); A. A. Abert, *Monteverdi u. d. mus. Drama* (Lippstadt 1954); W. Osthoff, *Monteverdi-Funde* (AfMw 1957) and *Monteverdi-Studien I: Das dramatische Spätwerk* (Tutzing 1960); *La musica in Cremona* (IeM 6); *Monteverdi's "Orfeo"* facs. Augsburg 1928, ed. Sch 176, partial new ed. PGfM, numerous new versions and arrangements; *Monteverdi's "Lamento d'Arianna"* Sch 177, *"Ballo"* and *"Combattimento"* Torchi VI. *Rome: Cavaliere's "Rappresentazione"* facs. in Mantica, *Collezione*, Rome 1912, piano version 1915, exs. Sch 169–70; *Buffo opera* ex. Sch 204; W. Witzenmann, *Domenico Mazzocchi* (Diss. Tübingen 1965); art. Doni (MGG). *Venice: Monteverdi's "Il Ritorno d'Ulisse"* DTÖ 29, *"L'Incoronatione di Poppea"* facs. new ed. 1938, ex. Sch 178. *Cavalli's "Giasone,"* partial new ed. PGfM 12, exs. Sch 200–1. *Cesti's "Il pomo d'oro,"* DTÖ 3, 2, and 4, 2; *"La Dori,"* partial new ed. PGfM, exs. Sch 202–3. A. A. Abert, arts. on Cavalli and Cesti (MGG); H. Goldschmidt, *Studien z. Gesch. d. ital. Opera im 17. Jh.* (2 vols. Lpz. 1901 and 1904); R. Haas, *Die Musik d. Barock* (Bücken Hdb.); H. Kretzschmar, *Beitr. z. Gesch. d. venez. Oper* (JbP 1907, 1910, 1911) and *Die venez. Oper u. d. Werke Cavallis u. Cestis* (VfM 1892); H. Prunières, *F. Cavalli e l'opéra vénétien au 17e siècle* (Paris 1931); H. Riemann, *Hdb. d. Musikgesch. II, 2*; L. Walther, *Die Ostinato-Technik in den Chaconne- u. Arien-Formen des 17. u. 18. Jh.* (Würzburg 1940); E. Wellesz, *Cavalli u. d. Technik d. venez. Oper* (StMw I) and *Die Oper in Italien im 17. Jh.* (Adler Hdb.); H. C. Wolff, *Die venez. Oper in d. zweiten Hälfte d. 17. Jh.* (Bln. Diss. 1932 and ZfMw XVI); exs. Sch 223, 224, 226, 227, 231, and 270.

18th Century: Neapolitan Opera Seria: H. Abert, *W. A. Mozart I* (Lpz. 1919); A. della Corte, *L'estetica di P. Metastasio* (Turin 1922); F. Florimo, *La scuola mus. di Napoli e i suoi Conservatorii* (4 vols. Naples 1880–2); M. Fehr, *A. Zeno u. s. Reform d. Operntextes* (Zurich 1912); A. de Gubernatis, *P. Metastasio* (Florence 1910); R. Haas, *Die Oper im 18. Jh.* (Adler Hdb.); A. Heriot, *The Castrati in Opera* (London 1956); F.-H. Neumann, *Die Ästhetik des Rezitativs* (Strasbourg 1962). *F. Provenzale:* H. Goldschmidt, *F. P. als Dramatiker* (SIMG VII); G. Pannain, *F. P. e la lirica del suo tempo* (RMI 1925). *A. Stradella:* H. Hess, *Die Opern A. S.s* (Beiheft II 3 of the IMG 1906); new ed. of *"La Forza dell'amor paterno,"* Ricordi, Milan 1932. *A. Scarlatti: "La Rosaura"* PGfM 14; C. v. d. Borren, *A. S. et l'ésthetique de l'opéra napol.* (Brussels 1921); E. Dent, *A. S.* (London 1905, repr. 1959); A. Lorenz, *Die Jugendopern A. S.s* (2 vols. Augsburg 1927); O. Tiby, *La Famiglia Scarlatti* (JRB I 1947); art. A. S. (MGG). *L. Vinci:* S. G. Silvestri, *L. V.* (Geneva 1935). *L. Leo:* G. Leo, *L. L.* (Naples 1905). *G. B. Pergolesi:* coll. ed. 26 vols. (Rome 1939–42); A. della Corte, *G. B. P.* (Turin 1936); G. Radiciotti, *G. B. P.* (Rome 1910, 2nd ed. Milan 1935, enl. Ger. ed. 1954); art. Pergolesi (MGG). *G. F. Händel:* H. Abert, *H.* (Ges. Schriften, Halle 1929); F. Chrysander, *G. F. H.,* 2 vols.; J. Eisenschmidt, *Die szenische*

Darstellung der Opern H.s auf der Londoner Bühne seiner Zeit (Wolfen-büttel 1941); R. Steglich, *H.s Opern* (Adler Hdb.) J. A. Hasse: *"Arminio,"* new ed. ED 27 and 28; R. Gerber, *Der Operntypus H.s u. s. textl. Grund-lagen* (Lpz. 1925); C. Mennicke, *J. A. H.* (SIMG V); B. Zeller, *Das Rez. accomp. in d. Opern J. A. H.s* (Halle 1911); art. Hasse (MGG). *N. Jommelli: "Fetonte,"* new ed. DDT 32–33; H. Abert, *N. J. als Opernkom-ponist* (Halle 1908); art. Jommelli (MGG). *Traëtta:* sel. nos. DTB 14, 1, and 17; A. Nuovo, *T.* (Bitonto 1938). *Mysliveček:* ex. P 144. *Terradellas:* ex. Sch 298. *Gluck:* partial new ed. of "Demofoonte" for Gluck Soc. 1914; new ed. "Ipermestra," *Gluckjahrbuch* 1914; "Le nozze d'Ecole e d'Ebe" DTB XIV, 2; "L'Innocenza giustificata" DTÖ 41; compl. ed. by R. Gerber 1951–   Kassel; ed. of French reform operas by Pelletan (Paris 1873–96); monographs by M. Arend (Bln. 1921), M. Cooper (London 1936), A. Einstein (London 1937), R. Gerber (Potsdam 2nd ed. 1950), P. Lan-dormy (Paris 1941), H. J. Moser (Stuttgart 1940), and J. Tiersot (Paris 1910); extensive individual studies: H. Abert, *G.s ital. Opern b. z. Orfeo* (Gluck-Jhb. 1915); E. Kurth, *Die Jugendopern G.s bis Orfeo* (StMw I); W. Vetter, *G. u. s. ital. Zeitgenossen* (ZfMw VII); *Gluck-Jahrbücher;* sel. letters (Zurich 1951); compl. ed. of letters in prep. (IMBA); them. cat. (Lpz. 1904, suppl. and appendix Lpz. 1911); C. Hopkinson, *A Bibliog. of the Works of G.* (London 1959). *J. C. Bach:* H. Abert, *B.s Opern u. Mozart* (ZfMw I); M. Schwarz, *J. C. B.* (SIMG II); C. S. Terry, *J. C. B.* (London 2nd ed. 1967); A. Wenck, *Beiträge zur Kenntnis des Opern-schaffens von J. C. B.* (Frankfurt Diss. 1932). *G. Sarti:* C. Rivalta, *G. S.* (Faenza 1928). *N. Piccinni: "Roland"* new ed. in *Chefs d'oeuvre* series. *P. Guglielmi:* G. Bustico, *P. G.* (1899); F. Piovano, *Elenco cronologico delle opere di P. G.* (RMI 1905). *Mozart's Ital. Operas:* L. Conrad, *M.'s Dramaturgie der Oper* (Würzburg 1943); E. J. Dent, *M.'s Operas* (rev. ed. London 1947). *Opera buffa:* H. Abert, *Mozart I* (Lpz. 1919); N. d'Arienzo, *Origini dell'opera comica* (RMI II, IV, VI); A. della Corte, *L'opera comica italiana* (Bari 1923); N. Pirrotta, *Commedia dell'Arte and Opera* (MQ 1955); M. Scherillo, *L'opera buffa napoletana* (1916). *Pergolesi's "La Serva Padrona"* new ed. Eulenburg, Lpz.; piano arr. 1911; P 1925; *"Maestro di Musica,"* new ed. 1928; *"La finta polacca,"* new ed. 1914; Pergolesi coll. ed. 1939–   ; *Marcello's "Il teatro alla moda,"* new ed. in Ger. Munich 1917. *Satire of Opera Seria:* F. Algarotti, *Saggio sopra l'opera in musica* (1755); E. Wellesz, *Algarotti u. s. Stellung zur Musik* (SIMG 15). *Buffo Musical Style:* M. Fuchs, *Zur Entwicklung d. Finales in d. ital. Opera buffa vor Mozart* (Diss. Vienna 1932). *R. da Capua:* P. Spitta, *R. d. C.* (VfMw 1887). *N. Logroscino:* H. Kretzschmar, *Zwei Opern N. L.s* (JbP 1908). *G. M. Buini:* E. J. Dent, *G. M. B.* (SIMG 13). *B. Galuppi:* W. Bollert, *Die Buffoopern B. G.s* (Berl. Diss. 1935) and art. Galuppi (MGG); A. della Corte, *B. G.* (Siena 1949). *N. Piccinni:* H. Abert, *P. als Buffokomponist* (JbP 1913); A. Camerti, *Saggio cronologico delle opere teatrali di N. P.* (RMI VIII); A. della Corte, *P.* (Bari 1928). *Paisiello:* H. Abert, *P.s Buffokunst und ihre Beziehungen zu Mozart* (AfMw I); A. della Corte, *P.* (Turin 1922); G. C. Speziale, *P.* (Naples 1931). *Cimarosa:* M. Tibaldi Chiesa, *C. e il suo tempo* (Milan 1939). *Gassmann: "Contessina"* new ed. DTÖ 21; G. Donath, *G. als dram. Komponist* (StMw).

19th Century: T. Werner, *Die Oper im 19. Jh.: Italien* (Adler Hdb.). *S. Mayr:* H. Kretzschmar, *Die musikgesch. Bedeutung von S. M.* (JbP 1904); L. Schiedermair, *S. M., Beitr. z. Gesch. d. Oper.* (2 vols., Lpz. 1907,

1910). *Rossini:* H. Gerigk, *Das alte u. neue Bild R.s* (ZfMw XVI); G. Radiciotti,.*R.* (3 vols., Tivoli 1927–9); G. Roncaglia, *R. l'olimpico* (1946, Fratelli Bocca, ed.); H. Weinstock, *R. A Biog.* (London 1968); sel. letters (Bln., Vienna, Lpz. 1947); art. Rossini (MGG). *G. Donizetti:* W. Ashbrook, *D.* (1965); G. Barblan, *L'opera di D. nell'età romantica* (Bergamo 1948); G. Gavazzeni, *Votae musica di G. D.* (Milan 1937); A. Geddo, *D.* (Bergamo 1936); G. Monaldi, *G. D.* (Milan 1935); art. Donizetti (MGG). *Bellini:* Ital. monographs include those by de Angelis (Brescia 1935), della Corte and G. Pannain (Turin 1936), G. Monaldi (Milan 1935), and G. Policastro (Catania 1935); art. Bellini (MGG). *G. Verdi:* publs. of the Instituto di Studi Verdiani, incl. studies of "Un Ballo in Maschera" and "La Forza del Destino" (Parma-Busseto 1960–   ); studies by F. Abbiati (4 vols. Milan 1960), A. Baresel (Lpz. 1938), A. Capri (Milan 1939), C. Gatti (Verona 1951), H. Gerigk (Potsdam 1932), C. Graziani (Milan 1941), K. Holl (Bln. 2nd ed. 1943), and M. Mila (Milan 1958); J. Loschelder, *Das Todesproblem in V.s Opernschaffen* (Cologne 1938); F. Walker, *The Man V.* (London 1963); *I Copialettere di G. V.* (Milan 1913), *Briefe* (Vienna 1926), sel. letters ed. O. Büthe and A. Lück-Bochat (Frankfurt 1963); *Carteggi Verdiani*, ed. A. Luzio (4 vols. Rome 1935–47); C. Gatti, *V. nelle imagini* (Milan 1941); G. Monaldi, *Iconografia Verdiani* (Bergamo 1913).

20th Century: Puccini: studies of P. have been written in Ital. by A. Fraccaroli (1925), in German by K. G. Fellerer (Potsdam 1937) and J. Weissmann (1922), and in English by M. Carner (London 1958); P.'s letters ed. by G. Adam (Lindau i. B.)

France: H. M. Brown, *Music in the French Secular Theater, 1400–1550* (Cambr. 1963); R. Haas, *Die franz. Oper bis 1750* (Adler Hdb.); *L'opéra en France,* arts. by R. Rolland, L. de la Laurencie, H. Radiguer, V. Debay, and P. Locard, in *Lav. Enc.* (Paris 1914); R. Rolland, *Hist. de l'opéra en Europe avant Lully et Scarlatti* (Paris 1895, 3rd ed. 1931); art. Frankreich (MGG). *J.-B. Lully:* monographs by E. Borrel (Paris 1949), J. Chancel (Paris 1938), L. de la Laurencie (Paris 2nd ed. 1919), and H. Prunières (Paris 1910); *La vie illustre et libertine de J. B. L.* (Paris 1929); F. Böttger, *Die comédie-ballets von Molière u. L.* (Diss. Bln. 1930); J. Eppelsheim, *Das Orch. in den Werken L.s* (Tutzing 1962); M. P. Lacroix, *Ballets et Mascarades de Cour de Henri III à Louis XIV* (6 vols., Geneva 1868–70); F. Lindemann, *Die Operntexte Quinaults* (Diss. Lpz. 1904); H. Prunières, *Le ballet de cour en France avant L.* (Paris 1914), *L'opéra italien en France avant L.* (Paris 1913), and *Notes sur les origines de l'ouverture fr.* (SIMG XII); D. P. Walker, art. Ballet de cour (MGG), art. Lully (MGG); exs. in *Chefs d'oeuvre*, Sch 222, 232–4; coll. ed. Paris 1930–   . *A. Campra:* ex. Sch 261; new ed. of Campra and Destouches in *Chefs d'oeuvre;* M. Barthélemy, *A. C.* (Paris 1957); K. Dulle, *Destouches* (Diss. Lpz. 1909); J. Ecorcheville, *De Lully à Rameau* (Paris 1906); L. de la Laurencie, *Notes sur la jeunesse d'A. C.* (SIMG X). *J.-P. Rameau:* compl. ed. Paris 1895–1914, 18 vols.; indiv. works in *Chefs d'oeuvre*, Sch 297; compl. ed. of theoretical works in prep. (AIM); G. Girdlestone, *J. P. R.: His Life and Work* (London 1957); L. Laloy, *R.* (Paris 1908); L. de la Laurencie, *R.* (Paris 1926); P. M. Masson, *L'opéra de R.* (Paris 1936); H. Pischner, *Die Harmonielehre R.s* (Lpz. 1963). *Gluck:* "Orfeo" DTÖ 21, "Armide" Sch 313; W. Boetticher, *Über Entwicklung u. gegenwärtigen Stand der G.-Edition* (AMl 1958); F. Grimm, *Correspondance G. littéraire . . . depuis 1753–1790* (Paris

1878, 16 vols.); L. Holzer, *Die frz. Opern G.s* (StMw 13); J. G. Sieg-meyer, *Über den Ritter G . . . Briefe von ihm u. anderen berühmten Männern s. Zeit* (Bln. 2nd ed. 1837); W. Vetter, *G.s Entwicklung zum Opernreformator* (AfMw VI). *Gluck's Successors in Paris:* E. Bücken, *Der heroische Stil in d. Oper* (Lpz. 1924); M. Dietz, *Gesch. d. mus. Dramas in Frankreich 1787–1796* (Vienna 2nd ed. 1893). *Gossec:* L. Dufrane, *G.* (Paris 1927). *Sacchini:* new eds. of *"Chimène"* and *"Renaud"* in *Chefs d'oeuvre.* A. *Salieri:* new eds. of *"Les Danaides"* and *"Tarare"* in *Chefs d'oeuvre;* A. della Corte, *A. S.* (Turin 1939); G. Magnani, *A. S.* (Turin 1934). *J. C. Vogel:* A. Vogler, *J. C. V.* (Diss. Halle 1914). *Catel:* in *Chefs d'oeuvre.* G. *Spontini:* C. Bouvet, *S.* (Paris 1930); L. Ronga, *G. S.* (La Rassegna Musicale, Jan. 1951); K. Schubert, *S.s ital. Schule* (Strasbourg 1932); *Documenti Spontiniani inediti,* ed. A. Belardinelli (2 vols. Florence 1955); *S.'s correspondence with Goethe,* in prep. (IMBA). *Meyerbeer:* H. Becker, *Der Fall Heine-M.* (Bln. 1958); H. de Courzon, *M.* (Paris 1910); W. C. Crosten, *French Grand Opera, an Art and a Business* (N. Y. 1948); L. Dauriac, *M.* (Paris 2nd ed. 1930); J. Kapp, *M.* (Stuttgart 1924); *Briefwechsel u. Tagebücher,* ed. H. Becker (vol. I, to 1824, Bln. 1959). *Saint-Saëns:* J. Harding, *S.-S. and his Circle* (London 1965). *Debussy:* in English: E. Lockspeiser, *D.* (London 1936, rev. 1944 and 1951) and *D., his life and mind* (2 vols., London 1962 and 1965); O. Thompson, *D., man and artist* (N. Y. 1937); in French: M. Boucher, *D.* (Paris 1933); A. Coeuroy, *D.* (Paris 1930); A. Goléa, *Pelléas et Mélisande* (Paris 1951); C. Koechlin, *D.* (Paris 1927); A. Saurès, *D.* (Paris 1936); L. Vallas, *D. et son temps* (Paris 1932 and 1958); in German: W. Danckert, *D.* (Bln. 1950); E. Decsey, *D.s Werke* (Graz and Vienna n.d.); A. Liess, *D., Das Werk im Zeitbild* (2 vols., Strasbourg 1936); H. Strobel, *D.* (Zurich, 3rd ed. 1960); in Italian: R. Paoli, *D.* (Florence 1951). *Opéra comique:* N. M. Bernardin, *La comédie italienne en France et les théâtres de la foire* (Paris 1902); G. Cucuel, *Les créateurs de l'opéra comique fr.* (Paris 1914); A. Font, *Favart, le comédie vaudeville et l'opéra comique du 17me et 18me siècle* (Paris 1894); E. Hirschberg, *Die Enzyklopädisten u. die frz. Oper im 18. Jh.* (Lpz. 1903); R. A. Mooser, *L'Opéra comique français en Russie au 18e siècle* (Geneva 1954). *J. J. Rousseau:* "Le Devin du Village" new ed. SIMG IV, also Leipzig; new ed. of Rousseau's writings on music (Paris 1929–   ); A. Arnheim, *"Le devin du village" von J. J. R. u. die Parodie "Les amours de Bastien et Bastienne"* (SIMG V); R. Gérin, *J. J. R.* (Paris 1930); A. Jansen, *J. J. R. als Musiker* (Bln. 1884); A. Pochon, *J. J. R. et la critique* (Paris 1940); A. Pougin, *J. J. R. musicien* (Paris 1905); J. Tiersot, *J. J. R.* (Paris 1912, 2nd ed. 1920). *Gluck's Comic Operas:* R. Haas, *Durazzo und Gluck im Burgtheater* (Vienna 1924). *Duni:* art. MGG. *Philidor:* G. E. Bonnet, *P. et l'évolution de la musique fr. au 18e siècle* (1921). *Monsigny:* A. Pougin, *M. et son temps* (Paris 1908). *Grétry:* coll. ed. of the operas Lpz., 49 vols.; J. E. Bruyr, *G.* (Paris 1931); E. Closson, *G.* (Paris 1920); H. Wichmann, *G. u. d. mus. Theater in Frankreich* (Bln. Diss. 1927). *Opera of Revolution and Terror:* M. Dietz, *Gesch. d. mus. Theaters in Frankreich von 1787–1796* (Vienna 2nd ed. 1893); G. Knepler, *Musikgeschichte des 19. Jh.* (Bd. 1, Bln. 1961); R. M. Longyear, *Notes on the Rescue Opera* (MQ 1959); *E. N. Méhul:* A. Pougin, *M.* (Paris 1889); H. Strobel, *Die Opern von E. N. M.* (ZfMw VI); *L. Cherubini:* monographs by R. Hohenemser (Lpz. 1913) and L. Schemann (Lpz. 1925); *L. C. nel II centenario della nascita* (Florence 1962). *Opéra comique after*

1810: N. Isouard: E. Wahl, *N. I.* (Diss. Munich 1911); *Boieldieu:* H. de Curzon, *Les opéras comiques de B.* (RM 1933); G. Favre, *B.* (2 vols., Paris 1944–5); A. Pougin, *B.* (1875); G. de Saint-Foix (RM 1926); *Auber:* C. Malherbe, *A.* (Paris 1911); *Hérold:* R. Duhamel, *H.* (RM 1933); A. Pougin, *H.* (Paris 1906); A. Adam: *A. A., Souveniers d'un musicien* (2 vols., Paris 1857 and 1859); A. Pougin, *A. A.* (Paris 1877); *J. Offenbach:* A. Henseler, *J. O.* (Bln. 1930); S. *Kracauer, J. O. u. das Paris seiner Zeit* (Amsterdam 1937). *Bizet:* in French: Delmas (2nd ed. 1938); H. Gauthier-Villars (Paris 1911); P. Landormy (Paris 1924); in German: A. Weissmann (Bln. 1907), also H. Daffner, ed. *Nietzsches Randglossen zu "Carmen"* (Regensburg 1912); E. Istel, *B. u. Carmen* (Stuttgart 1927); *B.s Briefe aus Rom 1857–60* (1949); art. Bizet (MGG); in English: M. Curtiss, *B. and His World* (N. Y. 1958).

German-Speaking Countries: H. Kretzschmar, *Gesch. d. Oper* (Lpz. 1919); many studies of the hist. of opera in local histories of music, cf. the bibl. in R. Schaal, *Das Schrifttum z. mus. Lokalgeschichtsforschung* (Kassel 1947); R. Schaal, *Stand u. Aufgaben der mus. Lokalforschung in Deutschland* (MF 1957); L. Schiedermair, *Die dt. Oper* (Bonn 2nd ed. 1940).

Bibl. from Begininngs to c. 1750: R. Brockpähler, *Hdb. zur Gesch. der Barockoper in Deutschland* (Emsdetten 1964); R. Haas, *Die Oper in Deutschland bis 1750* (Adler Hdb.); H. Huber, *Das Textbuch d. frühdt. Oper* (Diss. Munich 1958); H. Kretzschmar, *Das erste Jh. d. dt. Oper* (SIMG III); L. Schiedermair, *Zur Gesch. d. frühdt. Oper* (JbP 1910); G. F. Schmidt, *Zur Gesch., Dramaturgie u. Statistik d. frühdt. Oper, 1627–1750* (ZfMw V–VI); H. C. Wolff, *Die Barockoper in Hamburg, 1678 bis 1738* (2 vols., Wolfenbüttel 1957). *Staden's "Seelewig"* partial new ed. MfM XIII, Sch 195. *Hamburg:* W. Schulze, *Die Quellen d. Hamburger Oper, 1678–1738* (Hamburg 1938); R. Stephenson, *Hamburgische Oper zwischen Barock und Romantik* (Hamburg 1948). *N. A. Strungk:* F. Berend, *N. A. S.* (Diss. Munich 1915). *J. W. Franck:* R. Klages, *J. W. F.* (Diss. Hamburg 1936); *Franck's "Die drei Töchter Cecrops"* new ed. LD Bayern. *J. S. Kusser:* ex. Sch 250; H. Scholz, *J. S. K.* (Diss. Lpz. 1901). *R. Keiser:* new eds. *"Krösus"* and *"L'inganno fedeli"* DDT 37–38, *"Der lächerliche Prinz Jodelet"* PGfM 18, *"Octavia"* Suppl. 6 to Handel's compl. ed.; Sch 268, 269; H. Leichtentritt, *R. K. in seinen Opern* (Diss. Bln. 1901). *J. Mattheson:* *"Der vollkommene Capellmeister"* facs new ed. 1954 Kassel; *"Grundlagen einer Ehrenpforte"* new ed. 1910; F. X. Haberl, *J. M.* (KJb 1885); H. Schmidt, *J. M.* (1897); art. Mattheson (MGG). *Telemann:* *"Pimpinone,"* RD 6; Sch 266; W. Menke, *T.s Vokalschaffen* (Kassel 1940); K. Otzenn, *T. als Opernkomponist* (Bln. 1902). *Brunswick:* G. K. Schürmann *"Ludovicus Pius,"* PGfM 17, Sch 293; F. Chrysander, *Gesch. d. Braunschweig-Wolfenbüttelschen Kapelle und Oper von 16. bis 18. Jh.* (Chrysanders Jahrbücher I 1863); G. F. Schmidt, *Die frühdt. Oper u. d. musikdram. Kunst G. K. S.s* (Regensburg 1933) and *G. K. S.* (Diss. Munich 1913). *Hanover: Steffani:* *"Alarico il Baltha"* DTB XI, 2, XII, 1; *"Tassilone,"* Denkm. rhein. Musik, Bd. 8; *J. Krieger,* exs. Sch 236a and b. *Dresden:* art. MGG. *Leipzig:* art. MGG. *Nuremberg:* S. T. Staden, *"Seelewig"* (1644), partial new ed. MfM XIII; H. Druener, *S. T. S.* (Bonn Diss. 1938); J. Haar, *Astral Music in 17th-century Nuremberg* (MD 1962). *Durlach:* L. Schiedermair, *Die Oper an d. badischen Höfen des 17. u. 18. Jh.* (SIMG XIV). *Munich:* L. Schiedermair, *Die Anfänge d. Münchener Oper* (SIMG V); M. Zenger, *Gesch. d. Münchener*

Oper (ed. T. Kroyer, Munich 1923). *Vienna:* F. Farga, *Die Wiener Oper von ihren Anfängen bis 1938* (Vienna 1947); R. Haas, *Die Wiener Oper* (Vienna 1926); E. Wellesz, *Die Opern und Oratorien in Wien 1660–1708* (StMw VI); *Monteverdi "Ritorno d'Ulisse"* DTÖ 29; *Cesti "Il Pomo d'oro"* DTÖ 2 and 4; A. Draghi: M. Neuhaus, *A. D.* (StMw I); art. Draghi (MGG); *Fux "Costanza e Fortezza,"* Sch 272, DTÖ 17.

18th-Century Movement to Establish German Music Drama: A. Schweizer: J. Maurer, *A. S. als dram. Komp.* (Beih. IMG, 1912); *Holzbauer "Günther von Schwarzburg"* DDT 8–9; J. G. Naumann: R. Engländer, *G. N.* (Lpz. 1922). *Melodram:* H. Abert, *J. B. Noverre u. s. Einfluss auf d. dram. Ballettkomp.* (JbP 1908); E. Istel, *Die Entstehung des dt. Melodramas* (Bln. 1906), *J. J. Rousseau als Komponist seiner lyr. Szene "Pygmalion"* (Beih. I of the SIMG), and *Stud. d. Gesch. des Melodramas* (Lpz. 1901); M. Steinitzer, *Zur Entwicklungsgesch. d. Melodrams u. Mimodrams* (Lpz. 1918); J. van der Veen, *Le Melodrame musical de Rousseau au romantisme* (The Hague 1955).

The German Singspiel in the 18th Century: H. Abert, *W. A. Mozart I;* G. Calmus, *Die ersten dt. Singspiele v. Standfuss u. Hiller* (Lpz. 1908); H. J. Moser, *Gesch. d. dt. Musik II;* R. Pröpper, *Die Bühnenwerke J. F. Reichardts* (Bd. I, Bonn 1965). *North and Middle German exs.* Sch 309 a and b; *Benda "Der Dorfjahrmarkt"* DDT 64; F. Brückner, *B. u. d. dt. Singspiel* (SIMG V); J. André: W. Stauder, *J. A. u. d. dt. Singspiel* (AfMf 1936); C. G. Neefe: J. Leux, *C. G. N.* (Lpz. 1925), Neefe autobiog. (1789, new ed. Cologne 1957). *Viennese Singspiel:* R. Haas, *Zum Wiener Singspiel* (DTÖ 18); V. Helfert, *Zur Gesch. d. Wiener Singspiels* (ZfMw V); W. Krone, *Wenzel Müller* (Bln. Diss. 1906); *Umlauf "Bergknappen"* DTÖ 18; *Schenk "Dorfbarbier"* DTÖ 34; *Dittersdorf* autobiog. 1801, new ed. Regensburg 1940; L. Riedinger, *D. als Opernkomp.* (StMw 1914). *W. A. Mozart's Operas in German:* H. Abert, *Mozart* I and II; E. Dent, *Mozart's Operas* (London 2nd ed. 1947). *Beethoven "Leonore Overture No. 2"* new ed. piano version by Prieger; *"Leonore Overture No. 3"* new ed. piano version by Jahn; W. Hess, *B.s Bühnenwerke* (Göttingen 1962) and *B.s Oper "Fidelio" u. ihre drei Fassungen* (Zurich 1953); L. Schiedermair, *Über Beethovens Leonore* (ZIMG VII).

19th Century: E. T. A. Hoffmann *"Undine"* new ed. piano version 1906, ed. Hans Pfitzner; sel. mus. works ed. Becking, vols. 1–4, Lpz., inc.; *Letters* (3 vols., Bln. 1960); H. Ehinger, *E. T. A. H.* (Olten 1954); G. Ellinger, ed., *Schriften und Kritiken E. T. A. H.s* (5 vols., 1912); P. Greeff, *E. T. A. H. als Musiker und Musikschriftsteller* (Cologne 1948); E. Kroll, *E. T. A. H.* (Lpz. 1923); F. Schnapp, ed., *Schriften zur Musik* (Munich 1963). *Romantic Opera:* M. Ehrenhaus, *Die Operndichtung d. dt. Romantik* (Breslauer Beitr. z. Lit.gesch. 1912); S. Goslich, *Beitr. zur Gesch. d. dt. rom. Oper zwischen Spohrs "Faust" u. Wagners "Lohengrin"* (Lpz. 1937); T. Kroyer, *Die zirkumpolare Oper. Zur Wagnergesch.* (JbP 1919); L. Spohr *"Violinschule"* new ed., sel. works new ed. F. O. Leinert (Kassel), autobiog. (2 vols., 1860–1, unabridged new ed. Tutzing 1968); R. Wassermann, *L. S. als Opernkomp.* (Diss. Rostock 1910); H. Marschner: A. Bickel, *Die Opern H. M.s* (Diss. Erlangen 1929); H. Gaartz, *Die Opern H. M.s* (Lpz. 1912); V. Köhler, *M.s Bühnenwerke* (Diss. Göttingen 1955); G. Münzer, *H. M.* (Bln. 1901). *German Comic Opera:* A. Lortzing: coll. letters, ed. R. Kruse (Regensburg 1913); E. Killer, *A. L.* (Potsdam 1938); G. R. Kruse, *A. L.* (Bln. 1899); H. Laue, *Die Operndichtung L.s*

(Diss. Bonn 1932). *O. Nicolai:* G. R. Kruse, *O. N.* (Bln. 1910) and *N.s ital. Opern* (SIMG 12); coll. essays (ed. Kruse, Regensburg); journal (ed. W. Altmann); letters to his father (ed. W. Altmann, 1924). *P. Cornelius:* compl. works (5 vols., Lpz.); autobiog. (1874); literary works (4 vols., Lpz. 1904–5); monographs by C. M. Cornelius (2 vols., Regensburg 1925) and M. Hasse (2 vols., Lpz. 1923). *Wagner:* "*Parsifal*" compl. ed. 1912–22, Lpz., new ed. in prep.; essays and poems, compl. ed. (10 vols., E. W. Fritzsch, Lpz.; 12 vols., Breitkopf u. Härtel, Lpz.; 10 vols., Bong u. Co., Bln.); various eds. of letters, including W. Altmann, *Briefe nach Zeitfolge u. Inhalt* (Lpz. 1905) and coll. letters, ed. G. Strobel and W. Wolf (Lpz. 1967–   ); autobiog. *Mein Leben* (privately printed 1870, then Munich 1911 and Lpz. 1933; unabr. ed. Munich 1963, also 1969); basic monographs: G. Adler (Munich 2nd ed. 1923); P. Bekker (Lpz. 1924), R. Bory, *Wagner. Leben u. Werk in Bildern* (Frauenfeld 1938), C. Glasenapp (6 vols., Lpz. 1876–1911), M. Koch (3 vols., Bln. 1907–18), E. Kurth *Romantische Harmonik* (Bern 1920), A. Lorenz, *Das Geheimnis der Form* (4 vols., Bln. 1924–33), E. Newman (4 vols., London 1933–47), C. v. Westernhagen (Zurich 1956 and 1968).

20th Century: Richard Strauss: monographs by J. Gregor (Munich 1939), F. Gysi (Potsdam 1934), W. Mann, *R. S.—Das Opernwerk* (Munich 1967), N. R. del Mar, *R. S. A Critical Commentary* (1st vol., London 1962), R. Specht (2 vols., Vienna 1920), M. Steinitzer (rev., Bln. 1927), and W. Thomas, *R. S. u. seine Zeitgenossen* (Munich and Vienna 1964); R. S., correspondence with H. v. Hofmannsthal (Zurich 3rd ed. 1964); R. S., *Betrachtungen u. Erinnerungen* (Zurich and Freiburg i. B. 2nd ed. 1957); *Them. Verzeichnis,* ed. E. H. Müller von Asow (Vienna 1955–   ); *R.-S.-Jahrbuch* 1954 and 1959–60; many eds. of letters; index to comps. (ed. Schuh and E. Roth, London 1964); O. Ortner, *R. S.-Bibliographie I, 1882–1944* (Vienna 1964). *Pfitzner:* coll. writings (3 vols., Regensburg 1927–9); speeches, essays, and letters, ed. by W. Abendroth (Bln. 1955); basic monograph by W. Abendroth (Munich 1935). *Schönberg:* K. H. Wörner, *Gotteswort und Magie. Schönberg's Oper "Moses und Aron"* (Heidelberg 1959, enl. version in Engl., London 1963) and *Schoenberg and the Theater* (MQ 1962).

England: C. E. Baehrens, *The Origin of the Masque* (Groningen 1929); C. Cecil, *The History of Opera in England* (Taunton 1930); J. Dent, *Foundations of English Opera* (Cambridge 1928); R. Haas, *Die Oper in England bis 1740* (Adler Hdb.); G. Knepler, *Musikgeschichte des 19. Jahrhunderts* (1st vol., Bln. 1961). *H. Purcell:* ex. Sch 247; compl. ed. of works, ed. by the Purcell Soc. (26 vols., London 1878–1928); new compl. ed., The New Purcell Society Ed., 1959–   , 5 suppl. vols. planned; D. Arundell, *P.* (London 1911); W. H. Cummings, *P.* (London 1911); J. Holst, ed., *P.* (Toronto 1959); F. de Quervain, *Der Chorstil H. P.s* (Bern and Lpz. 1935); R. Sietz, *P.* (Lpz. 1955); W. Barclay Squire, *P.'s Dramatic Music* (SIMG V); St. Favre-Lingorow, *Der Instr.stil von P.* (Bern 1950); J. A. Westrup, *P.* (London 1937, N. Y. 1962); F. B. Zimmerman, *P. An Anal. Cat. of his Music* (London 1963) and *H. P.* (London 1968). "*The Beggar's Opera*" ex. Sch 281, new ed. E. J. Dent, Oxford Univ. Press, London; A. V. Berger, *The Beggar's Opera, the Burlesque and It. Opera* (M&L XVII); G. Calmus, *Die Beggar's Opera* (SIMG VIII) and *Zwei Opernburlesken aus der Rokokozeit* (Bln. 1912); *John Gay and the Ballad Opera* (Ninth Music Book, ed. Max Hinrichsen,

London 1956). *Ballad Operas:* E. M. Gagey, *Ballad Opera* (N. Y. 1937); G. Knepler, *Musikgeschichte des 19. Jh.s* (1st vol., Bln. 1961).

Czechoslovakia: Smetana: F. Bartoš, *S. in Briefen u. Erinnerungen* (Prague 1954); V. Helfert, *Die schöpferische Entwicklung S.s* (Lpz. 1956); J. Jiránek, *Liszt u. S.* (Studia musicologica V, 1963, Budapest); E. Rychnovský, *S.* (tr. Ger., Stuttgart 1924). *L. Janáček:* H. Hollander, *L. J.* (London 1963); J. Vogel, *L. J. Leben u. Werk* (Ger. tr., Prague 1958).

Russia: B. W. Asafiev, *Russian Music from the Beginning of the 19th Century* (tr., Ann Arbor 1953); M. D. Calvocoressi and G. Abraham, *Masters of Russian Music* (N. Y. 1936); K. Laux, *Die Musik in Russland und in der Sowjetunion* (Bln. 1958); D. Lehmann, *Russland, Oper u. Singspiel in der 2. Hälfte des 18. Jh.* (Lpz. 1958); O. v. Riesemann, *Monographien zur russ. Musik I* (Munich 1923) and *Russen* (Adler Hdb.) *Glinka:* memoirs, tr. Ger. as *Aus meinem Leben* (Ostberlin 1961, Wilhelmshaven 1969); monographs by M. D. Calvocoressi (Paris 1913); W. Vetter, *Beethoven u. G.* (Beethoven-Festschrift, Bln. 1952); art. Glinka (MGG). *Musorgsky:* compl. ed. Moscow 1931–   ; M. D. Calvocoressi, *M.* (London 1956); J. Leyda and S. Bertensson, eds. and trs., *The Musorgsky Reader. A Life in Letters and Documents* (N. Y. 1947). *Rimsky-Korsakov:* compl. ed. Moscow 1944–   ; autobiog. (1908, Ger. tr. Lpz. 1928, other trs.); N. van der Pals, *R.-K.s Opernschaffen* (Paris and Lpz. 1929); G. Troeger, *Mussorgskij u. R.-K.* (Breslau 1941).

Poland: A. Nowak-Romanowiczowa, *Musik in den Theaterformen des ehemaligen Polens* (MAEO); W. Trocki, *Die Entwicklung der Oper in Polen* (Dresden 1867); O. Tschirch, *Fürst A. H. Radziwill u. seine Faust-Musik* (1907); arts. Elsner, Kurpiński, Paderewski (MGG).

Scandinavia: Norddeutsche und nordeuropäische Musik. Referate der Kieler Tagung 1963 (Kieler Schriften zur Musikwissenschaft Bd. 16, Kassel 1965); S. Walin, *Beiträge zur Gesch. der schwed. Sinfonik* (Diss. Uppsala 1941); K. Lange and A. Østvedt, *Norwegian Music* (London 1958); G. Hilleström, *Das Schlosstheater von Drottningholm* (Stockholm 1958); *The Royal Opera, Stockholm* (Stockholm 1960). *Denmark and Sweden to 1750:* C.-A. Moberg, *Essais d'opéras en Suède sous Charles XII* (Publ. de la Société franç. de musicol. II, 1933). *The Gustavian Opera in Sweden:* R. Engländer, *J. M. Kraus u. die gustavianische Oper* (Uppsala 1943), *Die gustavianische Oper* (AfMw 1959), and *Zur Psychologie des Gustavianische Opernrepertoires* (Natalicia K. Jeppesen, Copenh. 1962); H. Nyblom, *Gustav III's Opera* (Stockholm 1923); E. Sundström, *F. Zellbell d. J.* (STM 1919). *Rationalism and Romanticism in Denmark:* T. Krogh, *Zur Gesch. des dän. Singspiels im 18. Jh.* (Diss. Copenh. 1924); H. Müller, *Die mingottischen Opernunternehmungen 1732–56* (Lpz. 1915); V. C. Ravn, *Vorwort zu "Balders Død" von J. E. Hartmann* (Copenh. 1876); C. Thrane, *G. Sarti in Kopenhagen* (SIMG 1901–2). *J. A. P. Schulz:* O. K. Riess, *J. A. P. S.s Leben* (SIMG 1913–4); M. Seiffert, *S.' "dänische" Oper* (AfMw 1918–9). *Kunzen:* C. A. Martienssen, *"Holger Danske"* (SIMG 1911–2). *C. E. F. Weyse:* W. Behrend, *W. u. Kuhlau* (Die Musik 1903–4); A. P. Berggreen, *C. E. F. W.s Biographie* (Copenh. 1876). *F. Kuhlau:* K. Graupner, *F. K.* (Munich 1930); C. Thrane, *F. K.* (Lpz. 1886). *Ballet:* D. Fog, *The Royal Danish Ballet 1760–1958,* and A. Bournonville, *A Chronol. Catalogue* (Copenh. 1961). *Hartmann:* biogs. by A. Hammerich, W. Behrend, and R. Hove (Copenh. 1916, 1918, and 1934). *P. Heise:* W. Behrend, *P. H.* (Riemann-Festschrift 1909). *Romantic Opera in Sweden: W. Stenhammar:* H. Küpper, *W. S.* (Die Musik 1937–8).

America: G. Chase, *America's Music* (N. Y. 2nd ed. 1966); H. Graf, *Opera and its Future in Am.* (N. Y. 1941); E. E. Hipsher, *Am. Opera and its Composers* (Phila. 1927); J. T. Howard, *Our Am. Music* (N. Y. 4th ed. 1965); H. E. Johnson, *Operas on Am. Subjects* (N. Y. 1964); I. Kolodin, *The Story of the Met. Opera 1883–1950* (N. Y. 1953); C. McCarthy, *Film Composers in Am.* (Glendale, Cal. 1953).

27.   Oratorio

The oratorio is a work which may be described by the following traits:

1. The material represented is predominantly religious, being from the Bible, saints' lives, legend, or allegory.
2. There is no attempt to present the content scenically.
3. The artistic form derives either from dramatically developed scenes in which individual characters and choruses participate, from general impersonal reflections, or from both elements combined.
4. The intention is that the content have a lastingly edifying effect on the hearer.

17th Century

Italy

During the first half of the 17th century two different types of oratorio existed side by side, each with its own separate previous history, *oratorio latino* and *oratorio volgare*. The name *oratorio*, which probably comes from the word for a prayer-chapel, appears for the first time around 1640 in connection with the Italian dialogue oratorio.

Oratorio latino—Latin or liturgical *oratorium*—was composed in Latin prose and was connected with the official liturgy of the church. It was derived from the liturgical dramas of the Middle Ages, and after 1600, from sacred and Latin dialogues that in text followed the Scriptures and were incorporated into the liturgy. These dialogue oratorios were successors to the liturgical dramas, but they dispensed with scenic representation and introduced a solo narrator, often referred to as the *Testo, Textus, Historicus, Storico,* or *Racconto.* They were particularly prevalent first in Upper Italy and then in Rome. The part of the *Testo* was often written for chorus, as in the old Passion motets, and the voices of the soloists were often written in recitative. The choral portions were mostly homophonic. Among the composers of these dialogue oratorios or motet oratorios were Donati, Bonini, Tomasi, and—in the latter half of the 17th century—Carissimi, Gratiani, Foggia, and Marcorelli.

From 1640 to 1700 Latin dialogue oratorios were often given at

Rome, particularly in the S. Marcello prayer-chapel. A select public of lay and clerical aristocrats attended, and emphasis was placed on the exclusive nature of the occasion. Significant artists collaborated. The culminating point of the performances occurred during Lent. The works were divided into three parts, with the sermon presented between the second and third parts. The texts were predominantly taken from the Old Testament.

The most significant composer of Latin oratorios was Giacomo Carissimi (1605–1674), who had been a cathedral organist in Tivoli and then from 1628 to the end of his life director of music at S. Apollinaire in Rome and choirmaster at the Collegium Germanicum. As composer and as teacher he was highly influential, having taught such well-known pupils as Alessandro Scarlatti, J. Kerll, Christoph Bernhard, and Marc-Antoine Charpentier (1636?–1704), choirmaster at Ste. Chapelle and composer of an oratorio for Paris.

Of Carissimi's thirteen extant Latin oratorios, the principal ones are *Jonas, Jephta, Ezechias, Balthazar, Abraham et Isaac, David et Jonathas, Historia Divitis, Diluvium universale,* and *Extremum judicium Salomonis.* In them, the anonymous writer of the text has vivified the Biblical passages by adding verses of his own. He has introduced a *Historicus,* whose connecting narrative has been set to music for chorus, solo, or duet. The focal point of the music lies in the choruses, which have been written in a style that is harmonically simple, chordal, and declamatory, following the spoken accent. The chorus takes a dramatically reportorial and contemplative part in the action and exerts a powerful effect. The soloistic recitative has been adapted to the solemnity of the Latin language and has combined declamation with melodic penetration. Carissimi had a striking preference for triadic motifs in the declamation. In the music he imitated many poetic figures borrowed from rhetoric, such as rhetorical questions, repetitions, inversions, and metonymy. Also he incorporated effects of tone painting in the solo passages. Only sporadically, however, does he use structures that suggest the aria.

After the classical culminating point under Carissimi, Latin oratorio declined quite rapidly, particularly through the weakening of the texts in the direction of lyrical softness, or so-called *oratorio erotico,* though they were still predominantly taken from the Bible. The dramatic choruses diminished in significance. Gradually there occurred an approximation to the *oratorio volgare.* The recitatives were neglected in favor of the arias. After 1700 the history of Latin oratorio coincided essentially with that of Italian.

Oratorio volgare—Italian or popular oratorio—was in the vernacular, had no connection with the liturgy, and belonged to the prayer-chapels of religious confraternities. It derived from a number of sources—the *lauda,* the older dialogue oratorio, sacred monody, and sacred opera.

To consider its sources in the *lauda,* or popular Italian sacred song, we must realize that by this time there were at least three forms of the *lauda,* lyric, narrative, and dialogue, normally sung stanzaically. The dialogue *lauda* led, on the one hand, to sacred drama, the *devozione,* and later to the *rappresentazione sacra,* and, on the other, to the singing of *laude* in the devotional exercises of Filippo Neri (1515–1595). The narrative and the dialogue *lauda* combined to produce the historical *lauda,* which introduced speech and reply through narrative portions and was likewise sung stanzaically. The *lauda* was but loosely connected with the divine service. It belonged to the oratory or prayer-chapel of the clerical brotherhoods and enjoyed significant emphasis in the great popular religious movement led by Filippo Neri, who founded in 1575 a Congregazione dei Preti dell'Oratorio, an order of lay brothers, without vows, the Philippini. In Neri's day the strongly folk-like, usually three-voiced dialogue *lauda* had stanzaic form and, in general, corresponded to the secular canzone.

The lyrical *lauda,* on the other hand, was especially refashioned by Giovanni Animuccia (d. 1571) around 1570 into the motet *lauda* of from four to eight voices. In this manner also are Palestrina's two books of five-voiced sacred madrigals of 1581 and 1594. Imitations of Neri's prayer groups in numerous Italian cities on into the middle of the 17th century gave rise to an inclusive literature, in which there were already intimations of the Italian dialogue oratorio.

Another source of *oratorio volgare* was the older dialogue oratorio, which grew out of texts first written by Agostino Manni (d. 1618). The dialogue oratorio injected new life into the stanzaic dialogue *lauda,* which after 1600 had come to seem antiquated. It introduced recitative and the *Testo,* enlivened the content through rhymed independent poetic work with Bible material in changing meters, and particularly stressed the edifying tendency in texts conducive to religious contemplation.

The most important work of this nature is the *Teatro armonico spirituale di Madrigali* by Giovanni Francesco Anerio (Rome 1619). It contains through-composed music, contemplative lyrical final choruses as extended lyrical *laude,* and frequently still the choric composition of *Testo* parts on the analogy of the motet Passion. But it also has features that were then new: soloistic and recitative settings, as well as fine stylistic differences in the recitative compositions between the *stile recitativo* or narrative delivery, the *stile espressivo* or expression of emotion, and the *stile rappresentativo* or dramatic expression. Anerio's work was distinguished by the development of a cantabile manner of expression on the part of the soli and the occasional dramatic choruses.

From about 1640 on, Italian dialogue oratorios were also called simply oratorios. The music had gained predominance over the ceremonial of the prayer-chapel.

A third source of *oratorio volgare* was 17th-century sacred monody, as the principle of secular monodic literature had been carried over into sacred stories or meditations, which found favor in the prayer-chapel exercises. Among the numerous composers, particularly in Rome, were Ottavio Durante, Vittoria Loreto, Domenico and Virgilio Mazzocchi, Domenico Massentio, and Marco Marazzoli. Large operatic scenes, such as scenes of lamentation, became increasingly influential, giving rise to complex solo cantatas, such as the *Musiche sacre e morali* (Rome 1640) of Domenico Mazzocchi.

Finally, a fourth source of *oratio volgare* was sacred opera in Rome, for example the dramatic presentation of the *Rappresentazione di anima e di corpo* of Emilio del Cavaliere in 1600 in the prayer-chapel of the *Congregazione dell' Oratorio*. The adoption of the recitative as a new art form also for the expression of religious feelings had a stimulating effect on the oratorio. Further sacred operas in Rome included Agazzari's *Eumelio* (1606), Landi's *San Alessio* (1634), Rossi's *Erminia sul Giordano* (1637), and Marazzoli's *La vita umana* (1656).

In conjunction with the significant cultivation of music in Rome through the prayer-exercises of the *Congregazione dell' Oratorio*, about 1640 the oratorio had developed its own particular characteristics, and during the latter half of the century there was separate development of choral and of solo oratorio.

The growing upsurge of interest in the oratorio from 1660 on was due especially to the Philippini. *Oratorio volgare* was quite widespread throughout Italy as a component of church festivals. The areas of subject matter were widened to include saints' legends, beginning with Spagna's *Pellegrino nella patria* and including *San Alessio* (1663). Clarity was increased by the adoption of features from opera and the inclusion of operatic scenes.

A movement to reform the oratorio texts was introduced by Arcangelo Spagna (d. 1721), who in his essay *Discorso dogmatico* (1706) visualized Senecan tragedy as an ideal for oratorio poetry. He called for the abolition of the *Testo* and for unity of time and place in the structure of the action, as suggested by Aristotle. Between 1656 and 1716 Spagna wrote poetical texts for no less than thirty oratorios, and his ideas inspired Zeno and Metastasio in their later reforms. The chorus gradually retired, and in its place solo song came to the fore with expressive recitatives and arias. Toward the end of the century virtuosity gained ground, and with it emphasis on the aria at the expense of the recitative. Thus the transition began towards Neapolitan oratorio.

In the history of the Italian oratorio during the latter half of the 17th century, three strongly independent local centers arose, one in Rome, another in Northern Italy, and a third in Vienna.

In Rome, avid cultivation of Italian oratorio began about 1640, increased particularly after 1700, and lasted until well on into the 19th century. Every year as many as twelve new oratorios were performed. Of these we today have the libretti, but only a few of the scores have survived. Among dozens of composers there, Alessandro Scarlatti stands out as the most famous. In 1708 Handel's first two oratorios, *Ressurezione* and *Trionfo del Tempo,* were presented in Rome.

Soon there was corresponding activity in Northern Italy. In Florence a significant upsurge occurred about 1690, occasioned by the activities of the brotherhoods. Here again, the libretti are extant but the musical scores have almost entirely disappeared. Among the Florentine composers were Ottavio Pitoni, Francesco Maria and Antonio Veracini, Giuseppe Maria Orlandini, and A.F. Piombi. Works of the Roman school, moreover, were performed, and there was also interest in pasticcio oratorios, the music for which was written by different composers. A "scenic oratorio" developed, with divisions into scenes and distinctly changing settings, which are precisely indicated in the libretto; but this type of oratorio was seldom given actual dramatic performance.

Bologna was a long-standing center of the oratorio cult in northern Italy, with regular presentations as early as 1661. Their particular quality was a preference for outwardly showy effect and brilliant facade. Among the composers were Giulio Cesare Arresti, Maurizio Cazzati, Donati Cossoni, Giovanni Battista Vitali, Giovanni Legrenzi, and Petronio Franceschini.

Also at Modena there was a school founded by Giovanni Colonna and including Giovanni Bononcini, Alessandro Stradella, and Giovanni Battista Bassani. Bononcini wrote three oratorios that are musically characteristic of the transition to the Neapolitan School. Stradella wrote six oratorios, including *S. Giovanni Battista*, with brilliantly artistic characterization, expressive recitatives and duets. These works had direct influence on Handel.

After the appearance of Giuseppe Torelli in 1685, concert instrumental music infiltrated the Modenese oratorio more strongly. With the development of independent instrumental pieces and the illustration of situations and psychological states and with the expansion of the stanzaic aria to the *da capo* aria, the transition to the Neapolitan oratorio was made toward the end of the century. The change in style is traceable in the works of numerous composers, such as Clemente Monari, F. Antonio Pistocchi, Carlo Pollarolo, Giacomo Perti, and Attilio Ariosti.

In Vienna, the first performance of an Italian oratorio occurred in 1649. Beginning in 1660 oratorio was regularly fostered there through performances in the chapels of the imperial family during Lent for the *Santo sepolcro* celebration. These works were presented as tableaux from the Passion story before a perspectived background and might take either of two forms: one the *azione sacra* or *rappresentazione sacra* with scenery, costumes, and pantomime, and the other the *oratorio per il santo sepolcro* without stage scenery and simply as an oratorio around the sepulchre. Toward 1700 purely musical oratorio performances were introduced. Among the composers of the sepulchral oratorios before 1700 were Leopold I (d. 1705) with eight oratorios; Antonio Draghi, who from 1674 was composer in residence at Vienna; and Antonio Bertali, who became master of the court chapel in 1649.

Presumably oratorio on the Italian model was fostered also in Munich, but it has not been investigated in detail.

The German Oratorio in the 17th Century

The beginnings of a German oratorio were provided in the middle of the 17th century by the "Plays of Joy and Sorrow" in Nuremberg, usually referred to as the *Nürnberger Akte,* a combination of recitation and incidental music intended for the spiritual edification of the congregation after the divine service. An example is the *Leidende Christus,* Suffering Christ (1645), to a text by Johannes Klaj in four acts, set to music—which, however, is no longer extant—by Johann Staden.

Beginnings toward an organized cultivation of the oratorio were perhaps first made in Hamburg in connection with the Collegium Musicum there. It had been founded in 1660 by Matthias Weckmann, who was a pupil of Schütz and was organist at St. James's church. From that time until 1674 this group regularly gave concert-like performances every Thursday in the refectory of the cathedral. Of similar significance were the evening musical performances in Lübeck, or *Lübecker Abendmusiken,* begun in 1673 by Franz Tunder and carried on particularly by his successor Dietrich Buxtehude, with presentation of cantatas and oratorios on the last five Sundays before Christmas.

Numerous dialogues in the 17th-century worship service took the place of the motets in the Protestant liturgy, composed in a combination of monodic recitatives and various forms of concert music. Works of this sort were written by Andreas Hammerschmidt (d. 1675), with his *Dialoge oder Gespräche zwischen Gott und einer Gläubigen Seele,* or Dialogues or Conversations between God and a Faithful Soul, and by Johann Rudolf Ahle, Thomas Selle, Sebastian Knüpfer, Matthias Weckmann, Christoph Bernhard, and Heinrich Schütz. On occasion these dialogues were expanded to quite extensive oratorio-like works with inset chorales, as in the *Actus musicus* entitled *De Divite et Lazaro* (1649) by Andreas Fromm in Stettin.

As early as the middle of the 16th century, moreover, there had been oratorio-like Resurrection histories, such as the *Resurrectio domini Jesu Christi* (ca. 1570) by Antonio Scandellus, in two, four, and five voices throughout, the words of Jesus being set in four-part composition. This was followed by the Resurrection history of Nicolaus Rosthius (1598) and the *Historia von der fröhlichen und siegreichen Auferstehung,* or History of the Joyful and Victorious Resurrection (1623), by Heinrich Schütz. Schütz derived from Scandellus and set the speeches of the individual characters not strictly in monody but as duets. Further discussion of Passion compositions, however, belongs under the heading of Catholic and Evangelical church music.

The first German oratorio, according to Schering, was the *Historia von der freuden- und gnadenreichen Geburt Jesu Christi,* or Story of the Joyful and Gracious Birth of Jesus Christ (1664), by Heinrich Schütz. Though the style of delivery follows Italian dramatic monody, Schütz succeeded in fusing it completely with the German language. He incorporated into the action self-contained forms, which he called *Intermedien* or intermezzi (choruses, arias, trios, and a quartet), each with characteristic instrumentation and depiction of characters and scenes in a conception that is constantly intensified poetically.

An isolated experiment in oratorio was the *Historia von dem christlichen Lauff und seligen Ende Johannes des Täufers,* or History of the Christ-like Career and Blessed End of John the Baptist (1612), by Elias Gerlach.

The oratorio in Germany continued long as a peripheral form, on the outskirts of other forms such as the dialogue, the history, and the school-play. The concept of the oratorio as a specific type seems not to have gained currency until after 1704 through the texts written by Hunold Menantes, which will be considered in connection with the developments of the 18th century. In tracing the use of the word "oratorio," however, one must realize that in such phrases as *Actus oratorius* and *Stylus oratorius* the adjective is derived from *oratio* (speech) and not from *oratorio* (prayer-chapel).

18th Century

The Oratorio of the Neapolitan School

The oratorio poems of Zeno (1668–1750) and Metastasio (1698–1782) significantly influenced the literary, aesthetic, and ethical renewal of the oratorio through their greater moral profundity and preference for Biblical material as over against that from saints' legend and also through their verbal and poetical loftiness and strongly edifying emphasis. Three different areas of subject matter characterize historical, Romantic, and idyllic oratorios. The same text was often set to music by numerous composers. Zeno's first oratorio was *Sisara* (1719). He enunciated its aesthetic principles in the preface to his seventeen *Poesie sacre drammatiche* (1744). Metastasio also concerned himself seriously with his oratorio texts, which he called *componimenti sacri*. Other poets followed in his oratorio tradition, particularly Carlo Pasquini and Steffano Pallavicini.

Like Neapolitan opera, there was also Neapolitan oratorio. The line between the style of opera and that of oratorio was to a great extent erased. Typical features appeared at the same time in both, such as the *da capo* aria, accompanied recitative, and a refined development of the orchestral idiom. The chorus was neglected, and the solo oratorio prevailed. The accompanied recitative became the main element in dramatic expression, and recitative even often supplanted arioso. Rhetorical turns were imitated in the singing to heighten the declamation. In the arias the feelings or affects were indicated by typical melodic and rhythmic formulas. As over against the 17th-century oratorio the ensemble and instrumental means were considerably heightened. The work was more artful.

The musical style of Neapolitan oratorio underwent change somewhat as did that of Neapolitan opera with its three epochs of the older Neapolitans, Hasse and his school, and the Neo-Neapolitans. The Neapolitan school influenced Europe throughout the whole 18th century. In only individual cities, particularly Vienna, was there mutual influence between the local and the Neapolitan styles. Practically all the opera composers of the time also wrote oratorios. Most works in the unusually extensive output have been handed down only in manuscript and so far have not been made the subject of exhaustive musicological research.

According to Schering, the Neapolitan oratorio had three stages in its 18th-century development: one during the first half of the century, another from 1750 to 1780, and a third from 1780 to 1800. Taking up first the development from 1700 to 1750 in Italy itself, we find some of the same composers as in opera. Alessandro Scarlatti (1660–1725) wrote fifteen oratorios. In his early works around 1685 he began in the style of the Venetian composers, but after 1700 he differentiated the orchestra significantly and in the late works achieved heightened expression in the accompanied recitative. Leonardo Vinci (1690–1730) wrote three oratorios, with soaring themes of passion ranging from heroic expression to tender, ardent melody. Giovanni Battista Pergolesi (1710–1736) wrote two oratorios as significant as the *Stabat Mater,* of intensified lyric expression and of tender and pleasing tone-painting. Leonardo Leo (1694–1744) wrote five oratorios, of which the most significant is *Sa. Elena al Calvario* (1732), which influenced Hasse. Niccolò Porpora (1686–1786) composed a number of virtuoso oratorios which were widely known also outside of Italy. Among them was *David e Bersabea* (London 1734), written in competition with Handel. Niccolò Jommelli (1714–1774) wrote his first oratorio in 1743, *La Betulia liberata* for Venice, exhibiting strongly Hasse's influence and achieving greater depth than Porpora had done. Other composers include Domingo Terradellas, Rinaldo da Capua, Giovanni Battista Martini, and Giovanni Battista Casali.

The early-18th-century oratorio in Vienna differed from that of the Neapolitans in the greater depth of its musical content and the significance of its dramatic aspects. The composers strove for truth of dramatic structure, preferred strict composition, and exhibited a more lofty conception and more inclusive utilization of possible instrumental resources. The Venetian operatic tradition was carried further in the oratorio, as there was strong reserve toward Neapolitan influences. The artistic taste was determined by the emperors Joseph I, who reigned from 1705 to 1711, and Karl VI, from 1711 to 1740. After the death of Karl VI the fostering of oratorios in Vienna at the court significantly declined as a result of military preoccupations. With the founding of the musical society or *Tonkünstlersozietät* in 1771 a renewal of activity was undertaken by the bourgeoisie.

Marc Antonio Ziani (1653–1715), the court conductor who succeeded Antonio Draghi, began about 1700 writing oratorios for Vienna with strongly Venetian influences. Antonio Caldara (*ca.* 1670–1736) became assistant conductor at Vienna in 1716 and with Fux was the main exponent of the Viennese oratorio. Antonio Lotti (1667–1740) was for a while active in Vienna. Johann Joseph Fux (1660–1741) in his ten oratorios combined the art of strict counterpoint with sublime and emotional effects. Marc' Antonio Bononcini (*ca.* 1677–1726) wrote three significant oratorios between 1707 and 1711 and placed the Venetian operatic forms at the service of new expression. Giovanni Battista Bononcini (1670-*ca.* 1750), brother of M. A. Bononcini, wrote in the Neapolitan idiom a number of oratorios for Vienna and London. Giuseppe Porsile (1672–1750), with thirteen oratorios, was a highly regarded composer in Vienna. Georg Reutter the Elder (1656–1738), who in 1697 joined the court chapel, was more closely linked with Fux than with the Italians active in Vienna.

In Dresden Italian oratorios were presented from about 1730 on, notably works by Johann Dismas Zelenka (1679–1745), Johann David Heinichen (1683–1729), and Giovanni Alberto Ristori (1692–1753). From the middle of the 1730's, Johann Adolf Hasse (1699–1783) led the development in Dresden, composing between 1734 and 1750 eight works of the Neapolitan solo oratorio type. They stressed the musical delineation of emotion, whereas Handel in his arias stressed characterization. Hasse's compositions are distinguished by flourishing melody, mastery of form, and clarity of conception. The most widely known of Hasse's oratorios were *Pellegrini al sepolcro* (1742) and *Sa. Elena al Calvario* (1746, 2nd version 1772).

Passing on to the second stage in the development of Neapolitan oratorio—that from 1750 to 1780—we find that in its homeland it was strongly dependent on the stylistic and expressive means of not only *opera seria* but also *buffa*. It was entering into an artistic decline, adopting virtuoso vocal elements and suffering from melodic superficiality. Niccolò Piccinni (1728–1800) wrote several oratorios of outstanding significance in the style of the Neo-Neapolitan School, including *Gionata* (1792). Francesco di Majo (1732–1770) composed a few oratorios, including *Gesù sotto il peso della croce* (1764). Other composers included Davide Perez (1711–1778), Antonio Gasparo Sacchini (1730–1786), Domenico Cimarosa (1749–1801), and Baldassare Galuppi (1706–1785).

In Vienna the concerts of the Tonkünstlersozietät were opened in 1772 with the *Betulia Liberata* of Florian Gassmann (1729–1774). On commission from the society, W. A. Mozart in 1785 wrote the cantata *Davide Penitente*. His first Neapolitan oratorio, still dependent on Hasse, is *Betulia* (Padua 1771). Most of the Italian oratorios written by German composers belonged stylistically to the Neapolitan School, which thus included Ignaz Holzbauer (1711–1783), Leopold Anton (christened Johann Anton) Kozeluch (Koželuch) (1747–1818), Georg Christoph Wagenseil (1715–1777), and Joseph Haydn, with his *Ritorno di Tobia,* written for Vienna in 1775, revised in 1784.

The third stage in the 18th-century oratorio of the Neapolitan school, from 1780–1800, was marked in Italy itself by the influence of Gluck, which can be seen in the way the scenes were laid out, the high seriousness with which they were conceived, and the various means adopted for giving them greater profundity. These qualities appear in the oratorios of Giovanni Paisiello (1740–1816), Antonio Salieri (1750–1825), Ferdinando Paër (1771–1839), and Simon Mayr (1763–1845). Toward the end of the century the output of Italian oratorios increased. Elements from *opera buffa* crowded in more noticeably. Evaluated from the standpoint of actual oratorio practice, the artistic curve was falling. From 1786 on, at Lent in Rome and Naples, oratorios were presented as *opere sacre* on the stage. They were differentiated from other operas only by the Biblical material and the omission of the ballet. Along with Naples and Rome, the cities of Bologna, Florence, Padua, and Venice led in the fostering of oratorio.

In Germany during this period Italian oratorio was represented by a number of composers, including Johann Friedrich Reichardt (1752–1814) and Karl Ditters von Dittersdorf (1739–1799). Following Hasse in Dresden there was a younger generation in Joseph Schuster (1748–1812), Franz Seydelmann (1748–1806), and Johann Gottlieb Naumann (1741–1801). The new style was distinguished by differentiation of feeling, softer melodic expression, many gentle anticipatory ornaments, and preference for melodic sequences of thirds and sixths. At the beginning of the 19th century the influence of the Italian oratorio in Germany largely came to an end, though it lingered on in Dresden until 1826.

Handel's Oratorios

The towering figure in the 18th-century oratorio was George Frederick Handel (1685–1759), whose career figures prominently in the discussion of opera as well as in that of other musical forms. He was born on February 23, 1685, in Halle on the Saale, son of a barber and court surgeon, and died on April 14, 1759, in London. Handel's teacher was Friedrich Wilhelm Zachow, the organist at the Marktkirche in Halle, where Handel received his early impressions of Protestant church music. He came into contact with German opera as written by Telemann in Leipzig and Johann Philipp Krieger in Wiessenfels. He also early heard the concerts at the court of Sophie Charlotte in Berlin. Originally a law student, he was at the same time organist in the Reformed church in the castle at Halle and made his appearance as composer with church cantatas. In 1706 he journeyed to Italy, where he heard the concerti grossi of Arcangelo Corelli and the oratorios of Carissimi, the Neapolitan opera and the solo cantatas of Alessandro Scarlatti in Naples, and the opera in Venice. In Italy he wrote some of his early operas and oratorios.

From 1711 to 1716 Handel was the successor to his older friend Steffani as music-director to the court in Hanover. From here, he traveled on leave to England and wrote his first opera for England, *Rinaldo* (1711), and the Utrecht *Te Deum* (1713), which showed the influence of Purcell and English choral music. In 1714 the Elector of Hanover became King George I of England. Handel was conductor in the Hanoverian court chapel, and at the same time conducted in the private chapel of the Duke of Chandos in Cannons, for whom he composed, among other works, two *Te Deums* and twelve anthems. At the King's order Handel opened his "first academy" at the Haymarket Theater in London with *Radamisto* (1720). For various reasons Handel faced bankruptcy in 1728, and although he made a second attempt in 1729 and a third in 1734, these ended in failure in 1737. He suffered a stroke and was cured in Aachen. After 1740 he turned decidedly to oratorio and thereafter wrote one or two oratorios regularly almost every year. In 1751 he went blind while working on the oratorio *Jephta*. An English citizen, Handel was buried in Westminster Abbey.

His personality united his own creative genius with openness to foreign artistic impressions that he received in Germany, Italy, and England and fused them with his own nature. This power of synthesis attained its last and greatest height in the oratorios written after he was fifty-five. His work is the great culminating and concluding formulation of the expressive means of his era, the Late Baroque. His creativity is combined with a gigantic, untiring energy in carrying out his purposes. Handel was a German who found his fulfillment in England as an Englishman.

His models in the oratorio and the sources of his impulse to write in this form were Carissimi with his way of making the chorus carry the idea, the Neapolitan opera school with its dramatic solo song and *da capo* aria, Purcell and the English literature of the odes and anthems with their great choir effects, the Protestant church-music of Halle, Hamburg, and Lübeck with its varied choral treatment, and Rameau and French opera with its colorful and descriptive instrumentation.

The English public also had an influence on Handel's oratorios. Particularly in England the educated middle class, with its strong national self-awareness, felt that it was in a sense "God's chosen people." In the figures and stories of the Old Testament it felt an analogy to its own historical calling. With Handel's oratorios, written in English, an art-form in the national language gradually came to predominate over Italian opera. Until after 1870 Handel's oratorios completely dominated the concert hall and the English resources of production, enjoying unlimited popularity. His oratorios had an effect that transcends limits of time and nation; and this effect is attributable to the power and the ideas which link, include, and indeed embrace peoples. Still today *The Messiah* is the most often performed concert piece in England. Handel was the founder of the English oratorio.

The basis that sustained Handel's success in England even during his lifetime was a quite unusual efflorescence of musical life, especially among very broad social levels, as well as the fact that publishers were quite active, organizations had musical evenings, and choral singing was most widespread. Choir festivals had already been begun in the late 17th century, but particularly in the latter half of the 18th century they enjoyed enormous increase in popularity. Sociologically, Handel's oratorio concerts were supported from 1739 on by broad levels of the music-loving bourgeoisie. These concerts contributed substantially to the development of musical life in England.

His English librettists were Thomas Morell, Samuel Humphreys, Pope, Arbuthnot, Newburg, and Hamilton.

Handel's oratorios may be considered as falling into three groups. The initial ones are in Italian, *Resurrezione* and *Trionfo del Tempo*. They were first performed in Rome in 1708, and the *Trionfo* was also revised by Handel in 1735 and 1757. His *Acis and Galatea* (1720, 1732) is an oratorio-like composition with English words; but his first English oratorio was *Esther,* written for the Duke of Chandos, originally performed in 1720 and expanded in a version presented in 1732. Handel showed increasing predilection for the oratorio as a form after 1730. *Deborah* and *Athalia* were both first performed in 1733. After a five-year pause, interrupted only in 1736 by *Alexander's Feast,* there ensued *Saul* and *Israel in Egypt,* both in 1739. In fact, in 1739 Handel rented the Haymarket Theater to present in concert style an oratorio each year at Lent. Between the separate acts he himself improvised at the organ. Works of the late period include *The Messiah* (Dublin 1742), a work bearing some relationship to the North German cantata-oratorio; *Samson* (1743); *Semele* (1743); *Joseph* (1743); *Belsazar* (1744); *Heracles* (1744); *Judas Maccabaeus* (1746); *Occasional Oratorio* (1746), *Alexander Balus* (1747), *Josua* (1747), *Susanna* (1748), *Salomo* (1748), and

Theodora (1749). His last oratorio was *Jephta* (1751), followed by the revision of *Trionfo del Tempo* (1757).

As for their style and particular nature, they did not develop directly from the church service, but stand rather in very close relationship to his operas. His later creative activity in the oratorio was, in a way, an operatic reform, but it also was an achievement in oratorio that in idea approached the musical drama. In the 1730's Handel was writing significant oratorios alongside his outstanding operas, and only after his last opera, *Deidamia* (1741), did he turn exclusively to oratorio. His Biblical oratorios—except for *The Messiah* and *Israel in Egypt*, which go back entirely to the Scriptural text—contain the words of the Bible in dramatized form with lyrical and reflective additions. The works are each made up of three acts.

Handel's music always has a drive toward the great and monumental, but at the same time it has a tendency toward the folk-like and inclusive. It utilizes magnificent characterization of the personages involved, pictorial and often tone-painterly effects, impressive moods of nature, and inclusive effects in the heroic mode as well as in the tenderly lyrical, the humorous, and the satirical. It has a sureness, unique of its kind, in uniting dramatic with epic elements and radiates a strong ethical power. Alongside works like *Israel in Egypt*, which are true choral oratorios with the chorus as bearer of the idea, there are some in which the chorus is used more as Baroque decoration. In addition to great Biblical works Handel composed allegorical and mythological oratorios, such as *Alexander's Feast, or the Power of Music* (1736), *L'Allegro, il Pensieroso ed il Moderato* (1740), *Semele* (1743), and *Heracles* (1744).

The German Oratorio

In the German-speaking area during the late 17th and early 18th centuries there had been local development of the oratorio that may perhaps best be considered in terms of the regions—northern, central, and southern.

In northern Germany, the German oratorio and Passion gradually produced, from about 1670 on, a new artistic form that took shape out of the introduction of lyric poetry as supplementation, expansion, and meditation evoked by the Scripture. This development was tied up with the Passion, which also figures in the discussion of early Catholic and Evangelical music. After the model of Erdmann Neumeister's sacred cantatas, Hunold Menantes in 1704 versified in his *Blutiger und sterbender Jesus*, or Jesus Bleeding and Dying, the Passion material in lines that freely rhymed. Hamburg and Lübeck were the centers of this cultivation of oratorios and Passions in the service of the liturgy of the Protestant worship service. The peculiarity of German oratorios lay in the connection between Scripture, lyrical poetry, dramatic recitative, *secco* recitative, aria, chorale, and chorus, with distinct folk-like touches in the conception and language. After 1700 an attempt was made to free the oratorio from its liturgical connections. Johann Sebastian Bach's *Christmas Oratorio* is a succession of six cantatas, presented separately at the worship services on the six feast days from Christmas to Epiphany.

Composers in Hamburg included Johann Mattheson (1681–1764), who introduced the oratorio to Hamburg in 1715 and wrote in all about 29 oratorios. From 1718 on, Georg Philipp Telemann (1681–1767) composed oratorios, of which the most significant of the later ones is *Der Tag des Gerichts*, or Day of Judgment (1761). Reinhard Keiser (1674–1739) wrote *Der siegende David*, or Victorious David (1728); C. P. E. Bach (1714–1788), *Die Israeliten in der Wüste*, or The Israelites in the Desert (1775).

Among the composers in Lübeck were Johann Christian Schieferdecker (d. 1732), successor and son-in-law of Buxtehude, who maintained the tradition; Johann Paul Kunzen (d. 1757), successor of Schieferdecker; and his son and successor Adolf Karl Kunzen (d. 1772).

In central Germany, numerous cities had local cultivation of the oratorio, though it was of less significance there than in northern Germany. Magdeburg excelled, under Johann Heinrich Rolle (d. 1785), who wrote seventeen oratorios and various Passions and won high regard in this region.

In southern Germany and Austria, Salzburg was a center for the active cultivation of the oratorio in the 18th century. Johann Ernst Eberlin (d. 1762) wrote several oratorios, including *Der blutschwitzende Jesus*, in which there is a mingling of Neapolitan and German stylistic elements. Eberlin's influence can be seen in ten-year-old W. A. Mozart's first German oratorio, *Die Schuldigkeit des ersten Gebotes*, or Guilt of the First Commandment (1767).

An offshoot of the local cultivation of oratorio in Germany was that in Denmark. Johann Adolph Scheibe (1706–1776), born in Leipzig, became master of the royal chapel in Denmark from 1740 to 1748 but was then supplanted by the Italians Scalabrini and Sarti. An aesthetician and composer, he—along with Schulz, Kunzen, and Weyse—was a pioneer in the efforts to establish an independent Danish musical culture and a guide in the musical treatment of the Danish language. He wrote the oratorio *Der wundervolle Tod des Welterlösers*, The Wondrous Death of the Redeemer (1754); the Passion *Der døende Jesus* (1762), on his own text; and several extensive funeral cantatas, particularly one for Frederick V (1766).

The Change in Style and Content after 1750

After Handel's death there was criticism of his oratorios. It had originated in England: at first a Dr. Brown enunciated it in 1763 and then it was taken up in Germany. The objections were directed against the operatic layout, the recitative, and the action. A new theory demanded that lyric description with impressions of nature outweigh the dramatic and that the composer avoid narrative sections and specifically operatic features. This new attitude was influenced by Gluck's opera reform and by the new poetry and literature of the time. The poets of the new period —Klopstock, F. W. Zachariae (*Die Pilgrime auf Golgatha*), K. W. Ramler (*Tod Jesu, Auferstehung und Himmelfahrt*, and *Die Hirten bei der Krippe*), and Herder (*Die Kindheit Jesu* and *Die Auferweckung des Lazarus*)—to some extent took direct part in the new oratorio poetry.

They emphasized the development of a new feeling for nature that recognized its combination of sublime and idyllic aspects. They favored the sentimental and folk-like. New types of oratorio accordingly appeared. One kind resembled *The Messiah* in stressing death and resurrection. Another was concerned with the end of the world. Still others dealt with the story of the Creation or depicted the idyllic aspects of a state of nature. Oratorio performances were increasingly addressed to the secular concert-going public.

The Passion oratorios and Passion cantatas bore with particular distinctness the imprint of the new sensibility of the time, for example Georg Philipp Telemann's *Seliges Erwägen* (1729), Karl Heinrich Graun's *Tod Jesu* (1755), and Johann Adolph Scheibe's *Wundervoller Tod des Welterlösers*. Ramler's oratorio poem *Auferstehung und Himmelfahrt* was set to music by various composers, including Telemann, Agricola, Scheibe, Krebs, Zelter, and—most significantly—C. P. E. Bach.

Turning to the more northern portions of Europe to trace the late-18th-century oratorio there, we may note that J. A. P. Schulz, who was in Copenhagen from 1787 to 1795, wrote a Passion oratorio *Maria og Johannes* (1788), and also *Christi Død* (1792), *Lovsang* (1793), and *Frelserens sidste Stund* (1794), works that are midway between oratorio and cantata. F. L. A. Kunzen (1761–1817), a successor of Schulz, wrote *Opstandelsen* (1796) and *Skabningens Halleluja* (1797). J. M. Kraus (1756–1792), who was in Sweden from 1778 on, composed *The Death of Jesus* (1776), a Neopolitan oratorio with Mannheim elements. Also, in 1792, he wrote a mourning cantata for King Gustav III that displays notable invention, expression, and contrapuntal finesse.

Joseph Haydn

The turn of the century is marked by two great oratorios by Joseph Haydn (1732–1809). *The Creation* (1798) and *The Seasons* (1801) are works of his old age. In both we can see evidences of the new and somewhat Romantic attitude toward the oratorio that had arisen among writers during the latter half of the century. Haydn wrote these works after having been impressed by the performances of Handel's works in 1791 in London. *The Creation* is Milton's *Paradise Lost* as reworked by Lindley and van Swieten. The text for *The Seasons* was prepared by van Swieten directly from Thomson's poem of the same name.

Although particularly in *The Creation* Haydn follows the model of Handel in the freedom of the over-all layout and in the individual hymn-like choruses, he employs throughout a musical expressiveness that is very much his own. He has assigned the role of the *Testo* in *The Creation* to the three archangels. With constantly vivid interchange between soli and chorus, he handles the aria form with great individual freedom and richly enlivens the recitative by his treatment of the orchestral accompaniment. He also has numerous bits of humorous and felicitous tone-painting, though they are always subordintated to the over-all architecture of the musical whole. The instrumental movements are highly significant, as for example when he introduces *The Creation* with an idea of the antecedent state of chaos. Elsewhere, also, he suggests various aspects and moods of nature in a highly imaginative way. His two great oratorios are rare examples of almost ideal unity and self-containedness in their combination of very high artistic achievement with general folk-like quality. Comparing the two, however, one perhaps feels that *The Seasons* lacks coherent action and that the four parts of the work are *singspiel*-like *genre* pictures, although Haydn introduced three concretely conceived characters in Simon, Luke, and Hanna.

Haydn's oratorios have exerted significant historical effect. Right to the present there have been many imitations of the material of *The Seasons,* and during the 19th century the two Haydn oratorios were unusual favorites in the cultivation of the oratorio by the bourgeoisie in all countries of the world except Italy.

19th Century

The awakening of a new type of sensibility around the middle of the 18th century, especially in conjunction with Rousseau's ideas, shifted the personal musical statement to instrumental music. The further this tendency went in its artistic achievement, the more the day of the oratorio was over, losing its validity as a uniting art form that had comprehensively brought together the expression of the time. At the turn of the century Haydn's oratorios stood entirely isolated in their artistic greatness. As a type the oratorio acquired more and more a museum-like significance, serving as the culminating-point in concert performances and great music festivals. As early as shortly after 1750 there was an awareness, particularly in southern Germany, of a distinctly historical relationship to the art of Handel. But in England Handel was imitated despite all the criticism, and the relationship of individual composers to him at their historical distance was thoroughly classicistic. On the Continent, however, Handel left significant and fruitful results in the history of the oratorio in the work of Haydn and Mendelssohn.

Germany

The Oratorio Between Haydn and Mendelssohn

Between 1800 and 1810 the sterility in the writing of German oratorios was most striking. But after 1810 increased interest turned to religious material. The preference was for apocalyptic, suprasensual themes as counterparts to the Romantic demon opera. The music utilized Romantic, highly superficial means in conjunction with commonplace, somewhat wayward melodic aspects.

After the Paris Revolution of 1830 the interest in the choice of text, however, changed. There was use of realistic and lifelike material taken from the Old Testament, or there was interest in the secular oratorio. The numerous successful oratorios of Karl Loewe were typical of this change, as were also the men's chorus oratorios, including Richard Wagner's *Das Liebesmahl der Apostel* (1843). At the artistic head of the movement to write secular oratorio stood Robert Schumann.

Oratorio composers between Haydn and Mendelssohn include Joseph

Eybler (1765–1846) with *Die letzten Dinge* (1811); Maximilian Stadler (1748–1833) with *Das befreite Jerusalem* (1813); Friedrich Schneider (1786–1853) with sixteen oratorios, of which *Das Weltgericht* (1819) was especially successful; Bernhard Klein (1793–1832) with *Hiob* (1820), *Jephta,* and *David;* Louis Spohr (1784–1859) with many oratorios, including *Das Jüngste Gericht* (1812), *Die Letzten Dinge* (1826), and *Der Fall Babylons* (1842); and Karl Loewe (1796–1869) with *Die Zerstörung Jerusalems* (1829), *Die Fastzeiten* (1825–1836), *Johann Hus* (1842), a legendary oratorio, *Die Siebenschläfer* (1833), and a men's chorus oratorio, *Die eherne Schlange* (1834).

Mendelssohn and His Followers

The three oratorios of Felix Mendelssohn-Bartholdy (1809–1847) were conceived as a triptych in the succession *Elijah* (Birmingham 1846), *Paulus* (Düsseldorf 1836), and *Christus* (incomplete). Their significant popular success is explainable from their highly idealistic qualities and from the connection, which was new for the time, between softly expressive melody and rounded-out and balanced song-like Classical and Romantic forms with elements of the Late Baroque such as fugue and chorale transcription. Together with the oratorios of Liszt, the works of Mendelssohn form the culminating point in the sacred oratorio of the 19th century. Mendelssohn's oratorios gave rise to many imitations, though they are quite eclectic. For example, he was the model of Karl Loewe's late works, of the *Zerstörung Jerusalems* (1840) by Ferdinand Hiller (1811–1885), of the *Mose* (1841) by Adolf Bernhard Marx (1795–1866), and also of many works by composers of the Berlin Academy and the Leipzig School. In 1870 sacred oratorios began to exhibit technical features derived from the Wagnerian music drama such as the use of the leitmotif, symphonic formal development, and declamation fusing speech and song. Further development of the oratorio accordingly divided into an academic-conservative trend and a progressive trend, each with numerous representatives and party adherents.

Oratorio composers of conservative attitude in the last half of the 19th century were Martin Blumner (1827–1901) with *Columbus* (1853), *Abraham* (1859), and *Der Fall Jerusalems* (1875); Friedrich Kiel (1821–1885) with *Christus* (1874); Ludwig Meinardus (1827–1896) with *Luther in Worms* (1872); Anton Rubinstein (1829–1894) with numerous sacred oratorios; and Max Bruch (1838–1920) with *Moses* (1894).

The tradition was carried on from the 19th century by many composers, including Felix Draeseke (1835–1913) with the oratorio tetralogy *Christus* (published in 1905) and by Georg Schumann (1866–1952) with *Ruth* (1907). Their works reveal dominant influences of Mendelssohn in the solo songs, of Bach, and of Handel in the choral construction. Only on occasion was the use of the leitmotif borrowed from Wagner.

Ein deutsches Requiem by Johannes Brahms (1833–1897) occupies a place of its own. The text, which Brahms himself compiled from the Bible, describes in seven parts the mystery of mortality and resurrection, without special liturgical connections. Leading ideas are consolation and promise in the Protestant sense. The music, which was written between 1861 and 1868 and received its first complete performance in Leipzig in 1869, is for soprano and baritone solo, chorus, and orchestra. It resembles in some respects a cantata. Song-like parts and choral sections, which have been conceived as *a cappella* in character, stand in contrast to free dramatic portions and the two choral fugues.

Franz Liszt and the Oratorio of the Neo-German School

The first oratorio of the Neo-German School was written by Franz Liszt, *The Legend of St. Elizabeth* (completed in 1862 and first performed in 1865). It is the most significant saint's-legend oratorio in existence. Liszt followed it up with the oratorio *Christus,* which he composed in 1866 and which was first performed in 1873. Both works are religiously Catholic in feeling and strive in the concert hall for a liturgical effect, which they do not quite achieve because the broad folk-basis is lacking. Liszt attempted to bring the religious spirit of the church into a synthesis with the tonal means and material of the program symphony. He renounced dramatic effect and exclusiveness and favored the delineation of individual episodes. To achieve a somewhat archaic manner he adopted early ecclesiastical thematic material but harmonized it in a modern way. Separate characteristic leitmotifs appear. A remarkable feature is the symphonic participation and characterization on the part of the orchestra, which is often used for purposes of tone painting. The individual main thoughts are often developed sequentially, for example, in the prelude to *St. Elizabeth.* Liszt conceived of the *Christus,* which is based on fourteen early ecclesiastical songs, as possibly being used within the liturgy.

The Secular Oratorio

The artistically most significant secular oratorio in the earlier half of the century was *Das Paradies und die Peri* (1843) by Robert Schumann (1810–1856), on material that came from Thomas Moore's *Lalla Rookh.* The role of the Testo was sometimes handled in recitative, sometimes in arioso, and sometimes assigned to the chorus. The basic tendency was narrative, undramatic, and lyrical, with an abundance of very beautiful details. The thematic aspects were unified by main ideas that were variously modified. Schumann's *Der Rose Pilgerfahrt* (1851) is an idyllic tale entirely laid out in a lyric manner. Schumann could not work out to completion ideas he had for a great, ecumenical Luther oratorio.

The secular oratorio, increasingly cultivated in the last third of the 19th century, was further represented by Max Bruch (1838–1920) with *Odysseus* (1873), Friedrich Gernsheim (1839–1916), Georg Vierling (1820–1910), Joseph Brambach (1833–1902), and Adalbert von Goldschmidt (1848–1906).

France

It was not until the end of the 18th century that the oratorio in France, after having been introduced by Carissimi's pupil Charpentier, was revived on the initiative of François Joseph Gossec (1734–1829).

His efforts were curtailed by the Revolution, but they were resumed by Jean François Lesueur. Since then, the oratorio—often called *Mystère*—has been in France a persistently cultivated art form, which has availed itself of theatrical means more often than has the oratorio in Germany. The composer who continued the oratorio tradition after the Revolution, Jean François Lesueur (1760–1837), tried to synthesize Gregorian, Baroque, and Classic-Romantic stylistic elements under a significant outward garb of sonority, thus reviving the old *drame liturgique* as a link between drama and the worship-service, for example in his *Oratorio de Noël* (1826). His pupil Hector Berlioz (1803–1869) has written oratorios in his *trilogie sacrée L'Enfance du Christ* (1854) and his secular oratorio *La damnation de Faust* (1846), one of his most significant works. Other widely known French composers who have written oratorios are Charles Gounod (1818–1893), with *La Rédemption* (1882) and *Mors et Vita* (1885), embodying mystic and imaginative elements in a musical idiom at once Romantic and quite archaistic, thus resembling Liszt; Jules Massenet (1842–1912), with his quite effective *Marie Madeleine* (1873) and *La Vierge* (1880); Camille Saint-Saëns (1835–1921), with *Le déluge* (1876) in three parts, gentle in character; César Franck (1822–1890), with *Ruth* (1846), *La Rédemption* (1872), *Les Béatitudes* (1880), and *Rebecca* (1881), showing invention of his own and a lyrical power of creating mood; and Gabriel Pierné (1863–1937), with his *Croisade des enfants* (1904), which creates strong pictorial effects.

In Belgium Peter Benoit (1834–1901) came to the fore with rather large works, including *The Scheldt* (1867) and *The Rhine* (1889).

Czechoslovakia

The patriotic singing movement that began in the 1860's set the stage for the development of choral song and oratorio. The first classic work of this sort came from Bedřich Smetana (1824–1884), *Česká píseň*, or Czech Song (1868), to a text by Jan z Hvězdy (a pseudonym for J. J. Marek).

Antonín Dvořák (1841–1904) wrote the oratorio *Svatá Ludmila*, or St. Ludmilla, to a text by Jaroslav Vrchlický (1885–6) and the cantata *Svatební košile*, or The Spirits' Bride, to a text by K. J. Erben (1884), in addition to works of church music such as the *Stabat Mater* (1876), *Mass in D major* (1887), and *Requiem* (1890).

Josef Bohuslav Foerster (1859–1951) composed sacred works, including a *Stabat mater* (1891–2) and *Svatý Václav*, or St. Wenceslaus (1928).

Vítězslav Novák (1870–1949) wrote secular works, including the cantata *Svatební košile*, or The Spirits' Bride (1913), and a monumental symphonic cantata *Bouře*, or The Tempest, to a text by S. Čech (1910).

Novák's pupil Ladislav Vycpálek (b. 1882) wrote predominantly philosophical and religious monumental works in cantatas, with close approach to the polyphony of Bach: *Kantáta o posledních věcech člověka*, or Cantata of the Last Things of Man (1921), *Blahoslavený ten člověk*, or Praised Be Man (1933), and *České requiem*, or Czech Requiem (1940).

Jaroslav Jeremiáš (1889–1919) composed an oratorio, *Jan Hus*.

Significant vocal and symphonic works by Leoš Janáček (1854–1928) include his first cantata *Amarus* (1898) and his cantata *Věčné evangelium*, or The Eternal Gospel (1914), which was the forerunner of his great *Glagolská mše*, or Glagolitic Mass, on the Old Slavic text (1926), with strongly monothematic layout and unique in the spiritual relation of the music to the text.

Bohuslav Martinů (1890–1959) composed some small folk-cantatas between 1955 and 1959, but he also wrote some notable large works along these lines, such as the cantata *Kytice* (1937) and particularly the *Mass in the Field* (1939), the oratorio *Gilgameš* (1954–5), and *Isaiah's Prophecy* (1959).

Since the 1920's there have been many national, social, and sociopolitical cantatas, such as those of Vilém Petrželka (b. 1889); Boleslav Vomáčka (b. 1887); Emil Axmann (1887–1949); Eugen Suchon (b. 1908); Miloslav Kabeláč (b. 1908) with *Neustupujte* (1939); Václav Dobiáš (b. 1909); Otmar Mácha (b. 1922) with *Odkas J. A. Komenského* (1952–5); and Vladimír Sommer (b. 1921) with *Vokální symfonie*, to texts by Kafka, Dostoievsky, and Pavese (1958).

Italy

In Italy in the middle of the 19th century there arose new interest in oratorio of classicistic and retrospective tendency. Pietro Raimondi (1786–1853), who was choirmaster at St. Peter's, figured prominently in this development, with his oratorio trilogy *Giuseppe*. Other composers of the movement were Jacopo Tomadini (1820–1883) and Lorenzo Perosi (1872–1956).

England

From the times of Handel to the present day, England has shown remarkable interest in the oratorio through largely amateur choral organizations in metropolitan and provincial centers. As the native oratorios by English composers were entirely under Handel's influence up to about 1880 and later under Mendelssohn's, these compositions do not have great individual significance.

The beginning of what Edward Dent called the "Renaissance of English music" occurred in 1880. Since then a change has taken place. Three composers played particularly decisive roles: from Scotland, Alexander Mackenzie (1847–1935), with *The Rose of Sharon* (1884), which exhibited new Romantic traits; from England, Charles Hubert Parry (1848–1918), with *Judith* (1888), *Job* (1892), and *King Saul* (1894), which was conceived in great, powerful choral sections; and, from Ireland, Charles Villiers Stanford (1852–1924), with *The Three Holy Children* (1885) and *Eden* (1891), which reveal what Arnold Schering has referred to as an ability to unite "stylistic elements of Liszt, Wagner, and Gounod."

The culminating point in this artistic movement was achieved by Edward Elgar (1857–1934), particularly in his second oratorio, *The*

Dream of Gerontius (1900), a work reflecting a considerable breadth of Catholic sentiment. He made use of Wagner's devices of the leitmotif, colorful participation of the orchestra, and novel choral treatment. Elgar wrote, moreover, the oratorios *The Light of Life* (1896), *The Apostles* (1903), and *The Kingdom* (1906).

Scandinavia

J. C. F. Haeffner (1759–1833) was indebted to the spirit of Classicism in his oratorio *Försonarem på Golgatha* (1809).

In Denmark there had already appeared, from Scheibe on, a tendency to bring the oratorio and the cantata form together. A pupil of Schulz, C. E. F. Weyse wrote choral works, of which the most significant are cantatas. Throughout the whole Scandinavian area during the 19th century there were sacred and secular vocal works, in part oratorios and in part cantatas or extended ballads. The numerous occasional cantatas are here left out of account.

J. P. E. Hartmann (1805–1900) wrote both secular and sacred choral works, notably *Dryadens Bryllup* (1858), *Davids 115. Psalme* (1871), *Völvens Spaadom* (Vala's Prophecy, 1872), *Luther paa Warthurg* (1884), and *Hellig tre Kongers Kvad* (1894).

Along with Schumann the main representative of what Mies called the "ballad oratorio," a form which goes back to Loewe, was Niels W. Gade (1817–1890), who composed fifteen works, mostly with soli, chorus, and orchestra. His principal oratorio was *Elverskud,* or The Erl-King's Daughter (1853), which represented the high point of Romantic music in Denmark. Other of his works included *Comala* (1846) with text after Ossian, *Korsfarerne,* or The Crusader (1866), *Kalanus* (1869), *Zion* (1874), *Psyche* (1882), and *The Stream* (1889), after Goethe's *Mahomet,* stylistically related to Mendelssohn and Schumann. In Gade's ballads there is a minor cadence, linked on occasion with a lyrical and idyllic tonal idiom of his own, as in Oluf's Ballad in *Elverskud.*

Peter Heise (1830–1879) wrote the well-known choral work *Tornerose* (1873) in addition to many songs.

Carl Nielsen (1865–1931) displayed many 20th-century linear features in his *Hymnus amoris* (1896), on Latin texts, and also composed a lyric humoresque, *Fynsk Foraar* (1921).

Other Danish composers who wrote significant choral works are Knud Jeppesen (b. 1892), *Te Deum Danicum* (1942); Svend Erik Tarp (b. 1908), *Te Deum* (1933); Herman D. Koppel (b. 1908), *Tre Davidspsalmer* (1949) and the oratorio *Moses* (1965); Lief Thybo (b. 1922), *Markus Passion* (1964); and Per Nørgaad (b. 1932), an oratorio *Dommen* (1961).

In Sweden, August Södermann (1832–1876) was the creator of the national Romantic musical idiom. Among his most significant works are some extensive and dramatically conceived ballads with orchestra, two of which have chorus, *The Pilgrimage to Kevlaar* (1866), after Heine, and *Signelils färd* (1869). Solo ballads include *Tannhäuser* (1856) and *The Abandoned Mill* (1866) for baritone, *Hafsfrun,* or The Mermaid (1861), for tenor, and *The Black Knight* (1874) for bass. These show excellent characterization in the lyric and dramatic aspects, mature Romantic harmony, and superior management of the full orchestra. The melodic aspects range from simple song-like features to the Wagnerian declamatory style.

Along lines opened up by Gade, ballad oratorios were written in Sweden by Ivar Hallström (1826–1901), *Des Sängers Fluch* (1871) and Ludvig Normann (1835–1885), *Humleplockningen* (1884).

Gunner Wennerberg (1817–1901) composed the oratorios *Jesu födelse* (1860), *Jesu dom* (1901), *Jesu död* (posth.), and *Stabat mater* (1893) in addition to songs.

Influenced by Stenhammar, Sibelius, and Schönberg, Hilding Rosenberg (b. 1892) became a significant 20th-century Swedish composer, conductor, and teacher. In the 1940's he worked mainly in monumental forms such as the oratorios *Huvudskalleplatsen* (The Place of the Skull, 1938, rev. 1965), the opera-oratorio *Josef och hans bröder* (1945–8), and the symphonies with solo and chorus No. 4 *Johannes uppenbarelse* (1940) and No. 5 *Örtagårdsmästaren* (1944).

Other significant Swedish composers include Valdemar Söderholm (b. 1909), with *Saligprisningarna* (1963) and *Te Deum* (1964); Sven-Eric Johanson (b. 1919), with the chamber oratorio *Aff Sancte Christoffero* (1948); and Maurice Karkoff (b. 1927), with the oratorio-cantata *Das ist sein Erlauten* (1965).

In Norway, Edvard Grieg (1843–1907) wrote ballad-like cantatas *Foran Sydens Kolster* (1870–1) and *Landkjenning* (1872–81).

Connected more with national folk-music are, moreover, Sigurd Islandsmoen (1881–1964), influenced by his teacher Max Reger, in *Israel i fangenskap* (1930), *Heimat frå Babel* (1934), and *Requiem* (1943); David Monrad Johansen (b. 1888), writing in the national Scandinavian manner, *Voluspå* (1923–6); Ludvig Irgens Jensen (b. 1894), with *Heimferd* (1930) and *Canto d'omaggio* (1950); and Sparre Olsen (b. 1903), with *Draumkvedet* (1937) and *Ver Sanctum* (1941).

In Finland Jean Sibelius (1865–1957) composed several extensive vocal works with orchestra, such as the choral symphony *Kullervo* (1892), *Vapautettu kuningatar*, or The Rescued Queen (1906), *Oma maa*, or Native Land (1918), and *Väinön virsi*, or Väino's Song (1926). Ilmari Krohn (1867–1960) wrote *Ikiaartehet*, or Eternal Treasures (1912); and Armas Maasalo (1885–1960), a Christmas oratorio (1945).

In Iceland a monumental oratorio style was achieved by Björgvin Guðmundsson (1891–1962) in *Friður á jörðu*, or Peace on Earth, and by Jón Leifs (b. 1899), the most original of Iceland's talents, in his two *Edda* oratorios.

Poland

The first Polish Latin solo oratorio, *Audite mortales*, by Bartłomiej Pękiel (d. 1670) was performed at the royal court. During the 18th century, Italian cantatas and oratorios were performed by church ensembles, particularly by that of the Cracow Center under Pastor X. Sierakowski. The first composers were Antoni Milwid (1760) and Teodor Zygmuntowski (1786), the Jesuit father Zgierski (about 1770), Jan Dawid

Holland (1780), Feliks Michal Lang, and Jakub Gołąbek. In addition to works of churchly character, there were also secular cantatas, mostly composed for definite occasions and often presented as patriotic demonstrations.

The first great Polish oratorio was *Passio Domini* by Józef Elsner (1766–1854), written in 1835–7. The text was from hymns, psalms, and the Gospel. Solo portions included the words of Jesus (sung by soprano and bass), of Pilate, and of Judas, the main voices in turn taking over the role of the *Testo*. This was Elsner's best religious work, though it is basically Neapolitan with Classical elements.

Stanisław Moniuszko (1819–1872) wrote the cycle *Litanie Ostrobramskie* (I, 1843; II, 1849; IV 1855). Rich in compositional and sonorous contrasts between soli and chorus, the work is very expressive, being related to Beethoven's symphonies. Moniuszko created the Polish dramatic cantata. His first attempts were a cycle on texts by J. I. Kraszewski, *Milda* (1848), *Nijoła* (1852), and *Kruminé*, stories of heroes and gods of old Lithuania. Then, on a much higher level, he composed *Widma* (Warsaw 1865), based on the scene in the Cemetery Chapel from the second part of A. Mickiewicz's *Obsequies,* and *Sonnet from Crimea* (Warsaw 1868), to a text by A. Mickiewicz. Here Moniuszko displayed masterful use of the chorus, realism in depiction through sound, lyric and inspired accents, and illustrative sections, the idiom being the same as in the operas.

In the last years of the 19th century almost all the outstanding Polish composers wrote cantatas. Zygmunt Noskowski (1846–1909) composed seven solo and choral cantatas. Among his best works are *Świtezianka* (1888), *Chivalric Cantata* (about 1890), *He Who Places Himself under God's Protection* (1891), and *To the Utrata,* on the occasion of the Chopin festivities in Żelazowa Wola (1899). Other Polish cantata and oratorio composers are Antoni Minchejmer (1830–1904), Władysław Żeleński (1837–1921), and Mieczysław Sołtys (1863–1929). Feliks Nowowiejski (1877–1946) was the most eminent representative of the Polish oratorio, with his internationally successful *Quo vadis* (1903) and his *The Discovery of the Blessed Cross* (1906), which maintain the tradition of Liszt and Wagner.

Karol Szymanowski (1882–1937) composed a *Stabat mater* (1929) and a cantata *Veni creator* (1929), on the occasion of the opening of the Academy of Music in Warsaw, the most significant of the works of Polish sacred music of the 20th century, with strict simplicity of setting, frequent use of modal elements, rich instrumental color, contemplative and intense character, and strongly expressive power.

Numerous cantatas and oratorios were written between 1920 and 1939. Among the composers were Henryk Opieński (1870–1942), Ilza Sternicka-Niekraszowa (1898–1932), Stanisław Kazuro (1881–1961), Władysław Raczkowski (1895–1959), Bolesław Poradowski (1902–1967), Stanisław Wiechowicz (1893–1963), Kazimierz Sikorski (b. 1895), Roman Palester (b. 1907), and Roman Maciejewski (b. 1910).

After World War II there was a great revival of the cantata with political accents in the texts, by Stanisław Wiechowicz (1893–1963), Bolesław Woytowicz (b. 1899), Kazimierz Wiłkomirski (b. 1900),

Grażyna Bacewicz (1913–1968), Kazimierz Serocki (b. 1922), Tadeusz Baird (b. 1928), Stanisław Skrowaczewski (b. 1923), Jan Krenz (b. 1926), and Krzysztof Penderecki (b. 1933).

The United States

Various tendencies manifested themselves in American composition of cantatas and oratorios during the late 18th and early 19th centuries. Working in a Central European tradition, John Antes (b. 1740 in Fredericktop, Pa.) wrote contemplative numbers for solo and ensuing chorus, with instrumental accompaniment, in a modest form of the same general style as that used by Bach in his cantatas, and in his later career was in personal contact with Haydn. Under the leadership of William Tuckey (1708–1781), Handel's *Messiah* was performed in New York in 1770—two years before it was presented in Germany. The American and French Revolutions injected a secular and political note: an "oratorial entertainment" entitled *The Temple of Minerva* (1781), of which the libretto survives, was written by the amateur composer and signer of the Declaration of Independence Francis Hopkinson (1737–1791), and refugees from the European political disturbances of the 1790's included Victor Pelissier, who provided music for an exhibition of the *Temple of Independence* (1799), and the son of the opera composer Tommasso Traëtta, Philipp Traëtta (1777–1854), who commemorated the end of the War of 1812 with an oratorio, *Peace*.

By mid-19th century, however, German dominance had been established as firmly in cantata and oratorio as had Italian in opera. Americans normally pursued higher musical studies in Germany, and what they wrote was often Mendelssohnian or neo-Germanic. Ashael Abbot's *The Waldenses* (1852) was the first of a projected series "in honor of the different races that have struggled for liberty in the last 1600 years." The refugee of the 1790's James Hewitt's son, John Hill Hewitt (1801–1890), composer of Civil War songs for the South, wrote an oratorio *Jephtha* and several cantatas. Other composers and their works include George F. Bristow (1825–1898), *Praise to God* (1861) and *Daniel* (1867); John Knowles Paine (1839–1906), *St. Peter;* and J. C. D. Parker (1828–1916), *Redemption Hymn* (1877), *The Blind King* (1886), and *The Life of Man* (1895).

Toward the end of the century American composers of dramatic cantatas and oratorio-like choral works began to receive performances in both Europe and America: Dudley Buck (1837–1909), with *The Light of Asia* (1885) and *The Voyages of Columbus;* and Horatio Parker (1863–1919), with *Hora Novissima* (1893), *Wanderer's Psalm, Star Song,* and *The Legend of St. Christopher* (1902).

20th Century

The most remarkable phenomenon in the many-faceted picture of the 20th century is perhaps the fact that oratorio has come closer to opera, and vice versa. Concepts and names of types have appeared in discussions of 20th-century music such as opera-oratorio, scenic cantata, instructive piece, and epic theater. This development seems to have originated from a generally reflective tendency and from Neo-Classical stylistic contacts with the 18th century. Opera and oratorio have begun again to encroach on each other sharply, and works have been written in which both scenic and concert presentation have been originally intended. The contemplative intention can be either philosophical and religious, as in Paul Claudel, or political, as in Bert Brecht. The concept of "epic theater" has been also theoretically formulated by Brecht in his *Schriften zum Theater* (Frankfurt a. M. 1957). Claudel, for his part, spoke of a new poetic art of the universe, a new logic (*"nouvel art poétique de l'Univers, une nouvelle logique"*) in his *Art Poétique* (1903–4).

Works include Claude Debussy, *Le Martyre de St. Sébastien* (Paris 1911), a mystery play with text by Gabriele d'Annunzio; Arthur Honegger, *King David*, a dramatic psalm to text by René Morax (Mézières 1921, concert performance at Winterthur 1923); Arthur Honegger, *Jeanne d'Arc au bûcher*, a dramatic oratorio with text by Paul Claudel (given in concert performance at Basel in 1938 and in stage performance at Paris in 1950); Ernst Krenek, *Die Zwingburg*, a scenic cantata, op. 14, 1922 (Berlin 1924); Igor Stravinsky, *Oedipus Rex*, an opera-oratorio given concert performance in Paris in 1927 and scenic performance in Berlin in 1928; Paul Hindemith, *Lehrstück*, with text by Brecht (Baden-Baden 1929); Carl Orff, *Carmina burana*, given scenic first performance at Frankfurt a. M. in 1937; and Luigi Dallapiccola, *Job, rappresentazione sacra* (Rome 1950).

The conclusion seems appropriate to the general picture of the 20th century that oratorio and cantata are being cultivated now as ever with all possibilities of an overlapping of the two types. Also their approach in material may be referred to as universal. Insights are sought not only in the philosophical, the religious, and the political but also in the generally aesthetic realm.

Works include Ralph Vaughan Williams (1872–1958), *Sancta Civitas* (Oxford 1926); Arnold Schönberg (1874–1951), *Die Jakobsleiter*, or Jacob's Ladder, 1917, not compl. (Vienna 1961); Franz Schmidt (1874–1939), *Das Buch mit sieben Siegeln*, or The Book of the Seven Seals (1938); Joseph Haas (1879–1960), *Die heilige Elisabeth*, or St. Elizabeth (1931); Igor Stravinsky (1882–1971), *Canticum sacrum* (Venice 1956) and *Threni* (Venice 1958); Frank Martin (b. 1890), *Le Vin herbé* (1941), *In terra pax* (1944), *Golgotha* (1948), and *Der Cornet*, to a text by Rilke (1943); Paul Hindemith (1895–1963), *Das Unaufhörliche*, to a text by Gottfried Benn (Berlin 1931), *When Lilacs Last in the Dooryard Bloom'd*, to text by Walt Whitman (New York 1946), *Ite, angeli veloces*, to text by Paul Claudel (three parts, first and second Wuppertal 1955, third Brussels 1953); Willy Burkhard (1900–1955), *Das Gesicht Jesajas* (Basel 1936), *Das Jahr* (Basel 1942); Conrad Beck (b. 1901), *Der Tod zu Basel* (Basel 1953); William Walton (b. 1902), *Belshazzar's Feast* (Leeds 1931); Michael Tippett (b. 1905), *A Child of Our Time* (London 1944); Benjamin Britten (b. 1913), *War Requiem* (1962); Johannes Driessler (b. 1921), *Dein Reich komme* (Essen 1950) and *De profundis* (1952); Luigi Nono (b. 1924), *Il canto sospeso* (Cologne 1956); Hans

Werner Henze (b. 1926), *Novae de infinito laudes,* to a text by Giordano Bruno (Venice 1963) and *Das Floss der Medusa,* to a text by Ernst Schnabel (Hamburg 1968).

The fusion between oratorio and cantata in the present century has been especially evident in American works, many of which have been performed on both sides of the Atlantic—for example, Edgar Stillman Kelley (1857–1944), *The Pilgrim's Progess* (1918); Charles S. Skilton (1868–1941), *The Guardian Angel;* Henry K. Hadley (1871–1937), *Resurgam* (1923) and *Belshazzar* (1932); Randall Thompson (b. 1899), *The Peaceable Kingdom* (1936); Bernard Rogers (b. 1893), *The Raising of Lazarus* (1931), *The Exodus* (1932), and *The Passion* (1944); Louise Talma (b. 1906), *The Divine Flame;* William Schuman (b. 1910), *This Is Our Time* (1940) and *A Free Song* (1943), subtitled *Secular Cantata Nos. 1 and 2;* Alan Hovhaness (b. 1911), *Shepherd of Israel* (1953); and Lukas Foss (b. 1922), *Song of Anguish* (1945).

There are, of course, many composers in the United States concerned with the possible utilization of electronic devices and of jazz techniques. *Philomel* by Milton Babbitt (b. 1916), for example, is for soprano, recorded soprano, and synthesized accompaniment. *Homecoming* (1959) by Larry Austin (b. 1930) is for soprano and jazz quintet. A *Computer Cantata* (1963) has come from the University of Illinois machine, in the hands of L. A. Hiller and Robert Baker. Experimental work of this type has found a convenient field in the cantata and oratorio.

General Bibliography

D. Alaleona, *Storia dell'oratorio musicale in Italia* (Milan 1945) and *Studii sulla storia dell'oratorio musicale in Italia* (Turin 1908); H. Kretzschmar, *Führer d. d. Konzertsaal* (Lpz. 5th ed. 1939, rev. H. Schnoor); G. Pannain, *L'oratorio dei Philippini e la Scuola Musicale di Napoli* (Milan 1934); G. Pasquetti, *L'oratorio musicale in Italia* (Florence 1906); A. Schering, *Gesch. d. Oratoriums* (Lpz. 1911); H. Schnoor, *Das Oratorium* (Adler Hdb.); F. Vatielli, *L'oratorio a Bologna* (Rome 1938); H. Vogel, *Zur Gesch. d. Oratoriums in Wien v. 1725–1740* (StMw 14); art. Oratorium (MGG).

17th Century: G. Carissimi: coll. ed. of the oratorios (I, Rome 1951); new eds. in Chrysanders DT III: "Jephta," "Judicium Salomonis," "Balthasar," and "Jonas"; also "Jephta" (Verlag Rieter-Biedermann and Universal-Ed.), "Judicium Salomonis" (Vieweg); Sch 198; G. Massenkeil, *Die oratorische Kunst in den lat. Historien und Oratorien G. C.* (Diss. Mainz 1952) and *Die Wiederholungsfiguren in den Oratorien G. C.* (AfMw 1956); W. Müller-Blattau, *Untersuchungen zur Kompositionstechnik in den Oratorien G. C.* (Mf 1963); E. Vogel, *Die Oratorientechnik G. C.s* (Diss. Prague 1928); *M.-A. Charpentier:* C. Crussard, *Un musicien inconnu, M.-A. C.* (Paris 1945); B. E. Nielsen, *Les grands oratorios bibliques de M.-A. C.* (Dansk Aarbog for Musikforskning 1966–7). *Congregazione dell'Oratorio: L'Oratorio dei Filippini e la scuola musicale de Napoli* (IeM 5). *Dialogue Oratorios:* art. Dialog (MGG). *Cavaliere "Rappresentazione"* Sch 169, 170. *G. B. Bassani:* R. Haselbach, *G. B. B. Werkkatalog, Biographie u. künstl. Würdigung* (Diss. Zurich 1954, Basel 1955). *Leopold I:* Sch 225. *Lübecker Abendmusiken:* art. Abendmusik (MGG).

A. Hammerschmidt "Dialoge" DTÖ 8, 1. A. Fromm "De Divite e Lazaro," new ed. Denkmäler der Musik in Pommern. *Oratio* and *oratorio:* arts. Dialog, Oratorium in Deutschland (MGG).

18th Century: A. Caldara: U. Kirkendale, A. C. Sein Leben u. seine venez.-röm. Oratorien (Cologne and Graz 1966). J. J. Fux: coll. ed. J. A. Hasse "La conversione di S. Agostino" DDT 20; L. Kamienski, Die Oratorien v. H. (Diss. Bln 1912). G. F. Handel: compl. ed., 100 vols., begun in 1859 by F. Chrysander and 5 suppl. vols., and Halle ed. begun in 1955; Sch 246, 280; letters and other writings, ed. M. v. Asow (Lindau 1949). H.-Jahrbücher 1928–33, cont'd. 1955, Lpz., 1966–   . H.-Bibliog. up to 1961 compiled by K. Sasse (Lpz. 1963). G. Abraham, ed., H. A Symposium (London 1954). Monographs by F. Chrysander (2½ vols., Lpz. 1858–67); O. E. Deutsch (A Documentary Biog., London 1955); N. Flower (London 1922, new ed. London 1947); P. H. Lang (H., N. Y. 1966); J. P. Larsen (H.'s Messiah, N. Y. 1957); H. Leichtentritt (Stuttgart 1924); J. Mainwaring (London 1760); H. J. Moser (Kassel 1942); J. Müller-Blattau (Potsdam 1933); R. Rolland (Paris 1924); W. Serauky (vol. III 1738–43, Kassel 1956, vol. IV 1743–6, Kassel 1958, vol. V. 1747–59, Kassel 1959); W. C. Smith (London 1949); P. Young (H.'s Oratorios, London 1946). J. Mattheson Sch 267. G. P. Telemann: DDT 28; H. Hörner, T.s Passionsmusiken (Lpz. 1933); W. Menke, Das Vokalwerk T.s (Kassel 1942). J. E. Eberlin "Der blutschwitzende Jesus" DTÖ 55; R. Haas, E.s Schuldramen u. Oratorien (StMw VIII). J. A. Scheibe: J. Mattheson, Grundlage einer Ehrenpforte (1740, new ed. 1910); E. Rosenkaimer, J. A. S. als Verfasser des krit. Musikus (Diss. 1923).

19th Century: F. Draeseke: E. Roeder, F. D. (I, Dresden 1930; II, Bln. 1935); art. Draeseke (MGG). England: E. Elgar: M. Hurd, E. (London 1969); M. Kennedy, Portrait of E. (London 1968). America: G. W. Chadwick, H. Parker (New Haven 1921); G. E. Hastings, Life and Works of F. Hopkinson (Chi. 1926); M. D. Howe, J. K. Paine (MQ 1939); D. M. McCorkle, John Antes (MQ 1956); I. P. Semler, H. Parker (N. Y. 1942); D. S. Smith, A Study of H. Parker (MQ 1930).

28.   Music for Orchestra

Dance Music and the Orchestral Suite

Although we do not have much early music specifically for instruments alone, we do know from manuscript illustrations and other evidence that players and singers made music together as early as the Middle Ages. Instrumentalists customarily played parts in vocal pieces. Also there are some instrumental pieces for dances such as the *estampie, estampida,* or *stantipes,* in triple time.

The most important early writer to give us an account of instrumental music is Johannes de Grocheo, who lived in Paris around 1280. He distinguished between the *ductia* and the *stantipes* in instrumental music and specified the *rubebe* and particularly the *vielle* as the principal instruments for accompanying these dances. Other medieval dances were the *saltarello* and the *trotto*. One of the earliest *estampie* melodies that has been preserved for us exists as the basis of a poem written by the troubadour Rimbaut de Vaqueiras (d. 1207), *Kalenda maya*.

Many instrumental dance pieces for one or two voices are preserved in French, Italian, and English manuscripts of the 13th and 14th centuries. Predominantly major, they fall into definite periods marked by half and full cadences and use short motives in a somewhat sequential way.

During the 15th and 16th centuries instrumental pieces were occasionally interspersed also in German polyphonic song literature. Among the extant examples are works by Heinrich Isaac. Pieces without text are also included in the Berlin and Munich song books.

Since much early instrumental music was especially linked with dance, some conception of dance forms gives an idea of the formal framework within which this type of early instrumental composition occurred. During the late Middle Ages social and folk dances of the European nations of all levels were made up of an introductory and a main portion, or "fore-dance" (*Vortanz*) and "after-dance" (*Nachtanz*). The two-fold division is to be traced back psychologically to the increase in excitement as the dance proceeds. The fore-dance is the striding or treading dance in binary measure that accompanies the movements of the dancers in a ring (*Riegen*). The after-dance is the turning dance in quick triple measure that accompanies their more lively motions as they leap or whirl (*Springtanz*). This two-fold division sets up the starting point for the forms developed in European dance music, the dance suite, and instrumental music of more than one movement.

In Germany the fore-dance was usually called the *dantz*, the after-dance the *springdantz, hupfer, hupfauf*, or *proportz*. In Italy the first part was the *passamezzo, padovana* (*pavana, paduana*), or *calata;* the second part, the *saltarello, gagliarda* (*gaillarde, galliarde*), *piva*, or *romanesca*. In 15th-century France, the *basse danse* and the *tourdion,* and in the 16th the *bransle* and *amener* followed the same basic distinction. Though the *passamezzo* and the *paduan,* for instance, differed in details of movement, they were basically the same in principle and represented a contrast to the ensuing movement.

Dances of the 15th and 16th Centuries

Several dances that became widespread during the Renaissance were:

Basse danse: evidently known around 1400, perhaps derived from the *estampie,* a slow, festive dance in duple but also in triple rhythm. In 1529 Pierre Attaingnant in Paris printed a collection of eighteen examples of the *basse danse* for the lute. After 1550, however, this type of dance gradually went out of fashion.

Saltarello: evidently in use as early as the 14th century. The saltarello is an up-beat dance in triple measure. It became the after-dance of the *basse danse* and was often musically taken from the fore-dance melody, with a change of rhythm. The characteristic rhythm of the saltarello was

Quarternaria: in Germany usual as an after-dance.

Piva: full-measured and four-beat, twice as fast as the *basse danse.*

Calata: lively measure in 4/4 or 12/8 time.

Bransle (also *branle*): of French origin, from the beginning of the 16th century to the time of Louis XIV usual as a social and a folk dance. The *bransle simple* was in duple time, the *bransle double* in triple time.

Pavane, or "peacock dance": a festive fore-dance in 4/4 measure, which replaced the *basse danse.*

Passamezzo: a somewhat quick pavane of Italian antecedents.

Galliarde (*gagliarda, gaillarde*): known from the end of the 15th century, the after-dance of the pavane, and normally in triple measure.

These dances have certain common traits throughout Europe. They show the influence of folk music. The predominant melody is usually in the upper voice. Block chords support the harmony. Accents fall mostly on the main beat of the measure. Syncopations are comparatively few. The basic trait is folk-like simplicity. The music can be comprehended as consisting of mutually corresponding groups of two, four, or eight measures.

Dances of the Baroque Era

Dances that came more into use or that figured prominently in the Baroque were:

Allemande: originally a German folk-dance, re-imported by way of France and England to Germany, but not much actually danced after about 1630. Around 1600 it was simply folk-like, in binary measure, with flowing movement and homophonic voice-leading. Its after-dance was the "Tripla" (Courante). A characteristic of the allemande was the up-beat:

Courante: the after-dance of the allemande. The courante, in triple measure, reached its culmination as a dance during the latter half of the 17th century in France. There was a difference between the more solemn French courante and the more flowing, lively Italian corrente, with this rhythm and up-beat:

Sarabande: possibly originally Spanish or Latin American, about 1600 spreading from Spain to France and gradually in its expression taking on a ceremonious and pompous character. The setting was homophonic, with melodically ornamented upper voice. Among its characteristics were the slow 3/2 measure and the ending on the second beat, which in dancing involved drawing one foot along after the final step. The typical rhythm of the sarabande was:

Gigue: in duple and in triple time. In Shakespeare's day in England, it was the "jig," an incidental dance-song in plays, and from there it found its way into the English suite literature. From about 1635 it was introduced by Gautier and his school as a stylized "gigue" into French lute music and then into French clavecin and orchestral music. From about 1660 it appeared in the Italian trio sonata and at about the same time in German suite literature. There was differentiation among different individual types of gigue.

The Orchestral Suite

The suite came into being originally as a succession of dance movements. There were three ways in which they might be related to each other—by reduction, by continuation, and by variation. That is, the afterdance might have the same melody as the fore-dance, altered only rhythmically; thus the suite would be formed by reduction, as the afterdance would be in reduced time-values. Or the after-dance might use the beginning of the fore-dance and carry it on further by spinning out or copying various features of the fore-dance structure with new motives, and the suite would be formed by continuation. Finally, the fore-dance might be carried on by variations, and these might then be concluded with the after-dance. The first example that we have of this third type is a passamezzo with four variations and a saltarello in the Phalèse collection of 1583. By this time the other two possibilities of suite formation were in use.

The orchestral suite arose, according to Blume, during the first half of the 16th century. From 1530 on, Attaingnant began printing dance movements for orchestra in Paris. In 1555 there appeared in Breslau dances published by the brothers Paul and Bartholomäus Hesse. In 1571 Palèse in Antwerp printed collections. As early as the last decade of the 16th century there appeared also in Germany several printed collections of dances: in 1593 Nikolaus Rosthius, *XXX Newer lieblicher Galliardt, 4 St., I. Teil, mit schönen lustigen Texten,* or 30 New Favorite Galliards, 4-voiced, Part I, with Comic Texts; in 1594 Christoph Demantius, another collection under the same title; in 1597 Paul Lütkemann, *Der I. Teil newer lateinischer und deutscher Gesenge auff die vornembsten Feste und etliche Sonntag im Jahr nebenst nachfolgend schönen Fantasien, Paduanen, und Galliarden lustig zu singen und gar lieblich auff allerley art instrumenten zu gebrauchen. 6 St.,* or Part I, New Latin and German Songs for the Principal Festivals and Various Sundays in the Year, along with Related Fantasies, Paduans, and Galliards, Good for Singing or Playing on All Types of instruments. 6 voices; in 1598 Valentin Haussmann, *Neue artige und liebliche Tänze zum Teil mit Texten,* or New Refined and Favorite Dances, Many with Texts; Mattäus, Reimann, *Noctes Musicae,* for the lute; August Nörmiger, *Tabulaturbuch,* for the organ; and in 1600 Johann Rudenius, *Flores Musicae,* for the lute.

English orchestral dance music, introduced around 1600 by English groups of comedians with their musicians traveling in Germany, significantly influenced the German orchestral suite. English orchestral dance movements also emerged from the practice of the masked festivities, called in England simply "masques." When this association disappeared, the dance pieces began to be linked by purely musical connections, such as the contrapuntal treatment of the dance melody, unification of the movements by the same key, and retention of individual motifs in all the movements of the dance. English dances by William Brade appeared in print for the first time in 1609 at Hamburg and by Thomas Simpson in 1610 at Frankfurt am Main.

The first flowering of the German orchestral suite occurred between 1601 and about 1623. Hans Leo Hassler's *Lustgarten newer teutscher Gesäng, Balleti, Galliarden und Intraden, mit 4, 5, 6, und 8 Stimmen*, or Pleasure-Garden of New German Songs, Ballets, Galliards, and Intradas, for 4–8 voices, was published in 1601. From 1600 to 1630 new dance collections regularly appeared; but from 1630 to 1650 there were only scattered works, with interruptions of several years between them. No doubt this was related to the Thirty Years' War (1618–48).

As to the characteristic features of these early suites, the original four-movement succession of dances was called—for example, in Peuerl —Paduana, Intrada, Dantz, and Galliarde. It was extended in Schein to five movements, and in Johann Neubauer to six. The dances were arranged in pairs, for example in Schein: Paduana (in 4/4 time), Galliarda (in 3/4 time), Courante (in 3/4), Allemande (in 4/4), and Tripla (in 3/4). The orchestral setting in from four to six voices was conceived of in optionally simple or orchestral instrumentation for strings and winds without continuo. The individual voices were polyphonically independent. Coherence within a suite came from the fact that the same key prevailed throughout.

The usual order of movements in the 16th-century suite is encountered during the early 17th century only in Peuerl in 1611 and Schein in 1617. Therefore the generally used term "suite" is not entirely appropriate for the dance works of the first half of the 17th century. Instead, some dances seem to have been loosely strung together in these early-17th-century works. At the opening of this succession of dances there was usually, up to 1650, a paduan or a paduan-galliard pair of dances. As over against this, the formation of other pairs of dances appeared but seldom, as in Peuerl dantz-intrada, in Schein allemande-courante, or in Hammerschmidt mascharada-saraband, ballett-saraband, or aria-saraband —which, however, in Hammerschmidt were not connected with each other by the same motivic material, as was otherwise usual.

The formal culmination was provided by the variation suite. All the thematic material of the suite could be developed by variation from one main idea. The entire dance composition could be a variation carried through with change of the type of rhythm; motifs and rhythms could be freely interpolated, motifs regrouped, or other devices could be used. The German orchestral suite at the end of the Thirty Years' War was closely related to folk-music and yet possessed its own individual artistic nature. Thus, the term that has become usual in referring to it, "variation suite," is misleading, as the connection of various dances by variation usually applies only to the introductory pair of dances, a paduan and a galliard.

The relationship of two dances by variation was adopted from popular and practical procedures in music-making and made its appearance as early as the first extant dance-publications of Petrucci in 1508 and of Attaingnant in 1530.

The juxtaposition of several motivically related dance movements appeared in the Italian lute music of the first half of the 16th century, for example in Melchiore de Barberii's three-movement lute suites (1549).

Composers before 1630 included Hans Leo Hassler, J. Christoph Demantius, Valentin Haussmann, Melchior Franck, Johann Staden, Paul Peuerl, Johann Hermann Schein, and Samuel Scheidt.

The second flowering of the German orchestral suite began as the writing of suites revived around 1635 and increased after 1650, continuing on to 1680. Dance movements were now normally arranged in the manner of suites. The beginning was formed by a sinfonia in the style of the Venetian operatic prelude, consisting of multipartite sections of contrasting character separated by pauses filled with tension. A free opening movement appeared first in Johann Jakob Löwe's *Synfonien, Intraden, Gagliarden, Arien, Ballette* (1658). The introductory movement assumed the earlier place of the paduana and was of special musical value to Rosenmüller, who in 1667 brought out a publication in which the order of movements was Sinfonia, Allemanda, Correnta, Ballo, and Sarabanda.

The instrumentation, which in the middle of the 17th century had often been left unspecified, was gradually made definite and the continuo was adopted.

Toward the end of the century there appeared works in which free instrumental movements, not necessarily dances, followed one another. They resembled the sinfonia type. These collections were called sonatas—in, for example, Rosenmüller's *Sonate a 2, 3, 4 et 5 Stromenti* (1682). This cyclic instrumental type was displaced at the beginning of the 18th century.

Composers active in this mid-17th-century development included Johann Schop (d. 1667), Andreas Hammerschmidt, Johann Rosenmüller, Diedrich Becker, Johann Pezel, and Johann Caspar Horn.

The German orchestral suite experienced a third season of flowering, bringing with it the overture suite between 1670 and about 1740. From 1670 on, French dances, French instrumentation, and rhythm after the model of Lully were imitated in Germany. Composers now placed a French overture at the beginning of the suite. As a result, they sometimes called the whole suite an overture, after the designation of the introductory movement. They developed a brilliant orchestral style, heightened the tone color, and juxtaposed *tutti* and the solo *trio* in the manner of the Italian *concerto grosso*. Individual movements occasionally bore programmatic titles, after the manner of their French model. The whole idea of the composition was often lightened, made more lively, more transparent, active, and flowing. The fixed sequence of movements in the French suite was Allemande, Courante, Sarabande, and Gigue.

Among the composers who contributed to this development was Georg Bleyer with his *Lustmusik nach jetztiger Frantzösischer Manier* (1670), but without overture. Sigismund Kusser, of Brunswick and Hamburg, who had studied under Lully in Paris and later taught Keiser, introduced the French overture suite into Germany in 1682. Other composers were Philipp Heinrich Erlebach, George Muffat with his *Florilegium* (1695 and 1698), Johann Caspar Ferdinand Fischer, Johann Philipp Krieger, Johann Joseph Fux, and Georg Philipp Telemann. Johann Sebastian Bach wrote four overture-suites—one in C, another in B minor, and a third and fourth in D—probably in Cöthen and Leipzig, where from 1727 to 1736 he led the student Collegium, which had been founded by Telemann. George Frederick Handel wrote two extensive, free cycles of dance and concert movements with rich variety in instrumentation in his *Water Music* (1717) and *Fireworks Music* (1749).

In 16th-century Poland, as elsewhere, there was practical music intended for people of all social levels and stylized music intended for educated listeners. As for the former, every ball at the royal court began with a ceremonious procession. Probably the early form of the polonaise was used at the coronation of Henri Valois in 1574. Among the nobility there were numerous Polish dance forms, including the Springing Dance, the Candle Dance, Mill Dance, Major Dance, Minor Dance, as well as Polonized dances like the "Zeuner-Dance" and "Hayduk Dance." Among the bourgeoisie, alongside the aristocratic dances there were also the Blacksmith Dance and the Clucking Dance. Reports on the rustic dances are quite scanty, practically the only source being the tablature of Jan of Lublin. There thirty-six dances show the social differentiation and the influence of Western European models along with national traits. In the latter half of the 16th century the nobility and the bourgeoisie adopted Italian and, somewhat later, French dances.

As for the more stylized music, which was perhaps not really intended to be danced to, Polish dance was widely disseminated throughout Europe and was sometimes referred to as Chorea Polonica or Balletto Polacco. We have over three hundred examples of it in forty-one German, Swedish, Hungarian, Bohemian, English, and Dutch works. These are usually bipartite, with a contrast in meter and movement between the two parts. A few examples of the monopartite form in the 16th century are based on duple meter, while in the 17th century there are also some based on odd-numbered metrical units, reflecting French influence. The composers of most of these Polish dances were probably not Poles—except for Diomedes Cato with his Chorea Polonica in Besard's tablature of 1603 and Wojciech Długoraj with his Polish dances in the Leipzig tablature of 1619. Polish elements included the complete citation of folk melodies (in Nörmiger's publication of 1598 and in the Vietoris MS. of about 1680), the use of fragments of these melodies, and the rhythmic outlines of Polish dances. In especially artful arrangements, such as those in the collections of Haussmann and Demantius, the original peculiarities of the Chorea Polonica as a dance were lost, being linked instead more with urban types of music like the amorous or ballad lyric.

Instrumental Ensemble Music and Orchestral Music of the Renaissance and Baroque

The real development of independent instrumental music began in the 16th century. In cultural history it corresponds to the general tendency towards pronounced secularization. The type of music-making that takes place in instrumental groups amounts predominantly to a movement in secular music, the end of which is amusement or conversation. Stylistically, however, there is very little difference between the sacred and the secular in this music for instrumental groups.

The titles of many printed song-collections that appeared in various places of Europe point to the fact that the compositions could also be played by instruments alone. More and more, with the beginning of the second third of the 16th century, there were collections intended only for instrumental performance. Two main forms can be distinguished: dances and "free" compositions.

Except for dance music, instrumental music for ensemble and orchestra in the 16th century included two different types: social music of the upper classes and music that represented the church.

Renaissance training in Italy required of the perfect nobleman, the *cortigiano,* the ability to play with confidence on stringed instruments and to sing well enough to participate in social music. An idea of this is conveyed by the leading etiquette book of the time, written by Baldassare Castiglione (Florence 1528). The ensemble literature of this highly cultivated social level primarily consisted of the vocal compositions of the frottola, villanelle, madrigal, and French chanson, which could be presented by a combination of voices and instruments or entirely by instruments. They were played from either the vocal part-books or from instrumental transcriptions. The greatest part of the playing material was freely improvised and as a result is not documented by written-out versions. The collections appearing frequently in print at the end of the 16th century indicate by the designation *per cantare e sonare* that performance might be optionally vocal or instrumental. Most of the settings were *a quattro.* Viol-playing predominated.

In England, an instrumental ensemble group was referred to as a "consort." The same word also designated music that was played. The "whole consort" was composed of a group of instruments of the same family but of different size; the "broken consort," of instruments of different families. In the very inclusive polyphonic literature for instruments, the "fancy" or "fantasia" particularly plays a major role. The outstanding composers in this form were William Byrd, Thomas Morley, and Orlando Gibbons. Formally, this "fantasia" was related to the type of the Renaissance motet. A motive was first presented monodically by an instrument, then taken up and imitated by the other instruments in succession, and finally brought to a concluding cadence. Thus section followed section; in between, occasionally, there were also homophonic sections. Preceding the fantasia as an instrumental composition in England there were the

In Nomine compositions, in which an individual instrumental style, independent of dance music, was developed even before the *ricercare* compositions of composers like Willaert. The climax of English instrumental writing was reached in the two decades of the 17th century.

The form known as the *carmina* was cultivated principally in the Netherlands and Germany. This was an instrumental composition analogous to the song-setting, usually with a well-known tune as cantus firmus, and less frequently with a freely invented theme. Examples are preserved in 16th-century manuscript collections.

In the musical literature of the period the *carmina* was soon replaced by the *ricercar* and the *fantasia*. Originally these forms perhaps belonged in the realm of the keyboard instruments and the lute, though initially there was no distinction between the music and the forms for the individual instruments. Also the model was the motet. Up to the end of the 16th century, the ricercar and the fantasia maintained the basic type of the motet: sectional structure with cadences at the end, imitative thematic entries, vocal character of the thematic treatment, and no strong contrasts. Thematically the ricercar was often based on secular or sacred material, while the fantasia had traits of freer invention.

The instrumental ensemble pieces up to the end of the 16th century were often for from two to seven voices, and regularly for four or five. In Italy and Germany there was considerable development of two-voiced pieces, or *bicinia,* and three-voiced, or *tricinia.*

During the mid-16th century, Spanish instrumental music apparently played a leading role. Statements by Tomás de Sancta Maria (d. 1570) and Antonio de Cabezón (d. 1566) indicate this, as does also the important tract *Tratado de glosas* (Rome 1553) by Diego Ortiz. In Spain various possibilities that were later to be developed made their first appearance, including the form of the variation, particularly also with an ostinato bass.

The decisive turn in the development of self-contained instrumental music occurred in the *canzon* (or *canzone*). The artistic model was particularly the French chanson with its rather song-like periodic structure and the typically somewhat integrated layout in contrast to the comparatively freely-composed Italian madrigal. The designation *canzone* is found from the beginning of the 16th century on. At the beginning of the second third of this century Attaingnant published instrumental arrangements of French chansons, first for keyboard instruments, and then in versions for both vocal parts and for instruments. The principle soon was imitated in Italy. In the last third of the 16th century the *canzon francese* or the *canzon da sonar* was a purely instrumental piece. The *canzone* still retained for a long time in its principal theme the rhythm ♩ ♩ ♩ characteristic of the French chanson. The instrumental *canzone* adopted traits characteristic both of the ricercar (with its sectional make-up) and of the dance suites (such as its metrical and rhythmic features and its short motives).

The *canzone* was raised to a new artistic height by Giovanni Gabrieli in his *Sacrae Symphoniae* (1597). The decisive factor was now the orchestral sonority with its fullness and individual colorfulness and the intention of achieving by its large layout a festive effect on the hearer, both in the church and on secular occasions. The previous instrumental ensemble music, as chamber music, was now filled out by orchestral music in an entirely new way.

The independent ensemble suite with an orchestral instrumentation developed during the 1580's in the Venetian School. This development came from the instrumental transcription of vocal models. Two types arose, one that was an independent instrumental composition such as the sonata and the canzon da sonar and the other that was organically linked with an ensuing vocal piece, such as the intrada, symphonia, or ritornello. While the sonata and canzon da sonar often opened with the ♩ ♩ ♩ rhythm of the French chanson, the intrada took over the form of the pavane with the attendant galliard and thus the contrast of tempo and rhythm. Michael Praetorius, in his *Syntagma musicum*, Book III (1619), makes a distinction between the introductions to choral church compositions if they are sinfonias in the manner of the pavane or if they are ritornelli in the manner of the galliard. The word *sonata*, which literally means simply a "sounding piece," implied a purely instrumental work in general, in contrast to the *cantata*, or piece for singing voices.

Among the oldest datable compositions that may have been presented orchestrally are the ensemble pieces of the *Canzoni a sonare* of Fiorenzo Maschera published in 1584. Perhaps they may have been presented sometimes by a group and sometimes by a solo performer. The works of Andrea Gabrieli that were written before 1580 did not appear until 1615 posthumously in the collection *Canzoni e sonate*, together with works by Giovanni Gabrieli. They included compositions for from three to twenty-two voices, grouped in instrumental choirs of from three to five voices according to the principle of Venetian polychorality. The handling of the individual choirs, whether strings, woodwinds, or brasses, was often precisely established. The orchestral canzona and orchestral sonata in Giovanni Gabrieli often consisted of two short sections strictly contrasting in tempo, beat, and manner of setting, which constantly alternated and in so doing could be varied and ended with a coda. Gabrieli's contemporaries and successors multiplied the independent sections to ten or more. Their model was imitated in Germany by many composers, including Schein, Hammerschmidt, and Rosenmüller.

The typical sonata developed later than the typical canzona. The earliest sonatas so far known occur in collections that began to appear about 1580. In Giovanni Gabrieli and his followers the sonata exhibits the characteristic features of strong contrast between block-like, compact individual portions, with less emphasis on counterpoint and more on the deliberately festive and majestic character, as exemplified in Giovanni Gabrieli's *Sonata pian e forte*.

After the death of Giovanni Gabrieli in 1612 the much heightened instrumental polychorality in Venice was reduced to the use of but four to six voice parts, but the opposition of the tone colors was retained. Formally the canzona type that had been derived from the chanson was linked with the type of the Gabrieli sonata into a rich store of individual types of performance. Fugal compositions were developed out of the canzona with the imitative opening section. In the latter half of the 17th century the sonata in Venice notably declined. From then on, the trio sonata took its place alongside the church sonata.

Three interrelated types of instrumental music that developed in the Renaissance and Baroque were the church sonata, chamber sonata, and trio sonata.

Church Sonata

Traditionally, in the service of worship in Italy, the prelude, interlude, and postlude had taken the musical form of the orchestral canzona and orchestral sonata. The canzona was a series of many sections, musically rather independent of each other. Gradually these sections became more distinct, their number declined, and they grew into independent movements within a composition. Thus arose the church sonata, or *sonata da chiesa*. The term was first used in 1637 for works by Tarquinio Merula (*ca.* 1600–after 1652).

The development of the type particularly occurred in Bologna, which toward the end of the 17th century became a center of Italian instrumental music. The succession of significant instrumental composers there began in 1657 with the appointment of Maurizio Cazzati conductor in the main church of San Petronio. Soon a pupil of his, Giovanni Battista Vitali (about 1644–1692), assisted in the development, as did also Giuseppe Torelli (1658–1709), who came to Bologna in 1686, and Giovanni Battista Bononcini (b. 1670).

If in Bologna the sonata was linked with the church, the court music of the Este family—on which the church music was dependent—dominated in Modena, the second center of instrumental music. The significant musicians of Modena in the latter half of the 17th century were Giuseppe Colombi and Marco Uccellini, who became in 1654 conductor of the court chapel and was famous as a violin virtuoso. Giovanni Bononcini also figured in the Modenese development, as did Giovanni Battista Vitali, who went there in 1674. Distinctive features of Modenese instrumental music were its virtuoso character, its neglect of polyphony, and the development of a flowing chamber music style and of typical miniature sonata forms.

But it was Arcangelo Corelli (1653–1713), of Bologna, who gave the church sonata its classic form. It had four movements with the stereotyped succession of *Grave, Allegro, Andante,* and *Allegro* or *Presto.* Each of these four had its customary treatment: the opening *Grave* was homophonic or imitative, the *Allegro* was fugal, the *Andante* homophonic and in triple measure, and the finale either fugal or homophonic. For the most part the key was the same in all the movements. Likewise all the movements were organized according to the modulatory scheme of moving from Tonic to Dominant, then from Dominant to Parallel Key, and then from Parallel Key back to Tonic. The opening *Grave* had moving basses in eighth-note and quarter-note movement. The finale was usually a dance-like movement, such as a Gigue, Minuet, or Gavotte. The slow movement stood now and then in the parallel key. The fugal portions were, after the exposition, usually not developed further. The general character of the church sonata was brilliant and festive. The instruments were at least doubled in performance.

When Corelli was seventeen he was accepted in the *Accademia Filarmonica* in Bologna, and became an outstanding violinist. From 1675 on, he was in Rome. In 1687 he was the maestro di musica of Cardinal Benedetto Panfili and then became leader of the musical performances of Pietro Ottoboni, the nephew of Pope Alexander VIII. In 1700 he was leader of the instrumentalists of the *Accademia de Santa Cecilia*. In 1706 he became a member of the *Accademia degli Arcadi*, was recognized as the foremost instrumental composer of Italy, and enjoyed princely honors.

There are twelve numbers in each of his first six sets of compositions: *Sonata da chiesa a tre, op. 1* (1683), *op. 3* (1689); *Sonata da camera a tre, op. 2* (1685), *op. 4* (1694); *Sonata a Violino e Violone o Cembalo, op. 5,* the 12th number of which is the famous *La Follia* (1700); and *Concerti grossi, op. 6* (publ. 1714).

Corelli was exclusively an instrumental composer. His works have been characterized by Paumgartner as the "quintessence of the imposing evolution in Italian instrumental music that began around 1600"; they are filled with a "Baroque classicistic drive," the "striving for noble containment of rich imagination and abundance of thought and for general intelligibility in expressive presentation in concise form, and are full of aristocratic dignity." With Corelli Italian instrumental music reached its second culminating point after Giovanni Gabrieli, and Corelli's style-creating influence spread to all Europe.

Chamber Sonata

The chamber sonata, or *sonata da camera,* usually had its movements in a sequence of fast-slow-fast, and they were of a predominantly dance character. The instrumentation was soloistic.

The separation between church sonata and chamber sonata was often not carried through strictly, as indicated by the designation of pieces as usable in either context, *per chiese e camera.* On occasion, also, the chamber sonata was referred to as a *partita,* which seems to have been a term used on occasion interchangeably with "suite."

The type of *sonata da chiesa* represented by Corelli's op. 1 was soon adopted all over Europe: in Italy by Antonio Caldara (*ca.* 1670–1736), Antonio Vivaldi (*ca.* 1680–1743), Francesco Maria Veracini (1685–1750), Evaristo Felice dall'Abaco (1675–1742), Francesco Geminiani (1674–1762), Pietro Locatelli (1695–1764), and Giuseppe Tartini (1692–1770); in England by Henry Purcell (1658 or 1659–1695); and in Germany by Johann Adam Reinken (1623–1722), Dietrich Buxtehude (1637–1707), Nikolaus Adam Strungk (1640–1700), Heinrich Ignaz Franz Biber (1644–1704), Johann Gottfried Walther (1684–1748), Georg Philipp Telemann (1681–1767), and Johann Kuhnau (1660–1722), who transferred the form of the church sonata to the solo clavier in the second part of his *Klavierübung* (1692).

Johann Sebastian Bach (1685–1750) wrote three sonatas for flute, six for violin, and three for gamba. In these compositions he wrote out the keyboard part, which is therefore designated as *obligato*, or "obligatory." The other solo voice, in each composition, was played by the continuo.

One of the outstanding Czech Baroque composers was Pavel Josef Vejvanovský (about 1640–1693), music director at the Kremsier court. Among his works are some instrumental sonatas, dependent on the Venetian school. Other Czech composers were Jan Dismas Zelenka (1679–1745) and František Václav Míča (1694–1744), composer and master of the choir in the castle at Jaroměřice on the Rokytná.

In Poland the first group of instrumental ensemble-pieces is a set of three fantasies by Mikołaj Zieleński, in the collection *Communiones totius anni* (Venice 1611), in Venetian style, with echo effects and sections in the manner of the ricercar and the canzona. The Peplin tablature has canzone by Tarquinio Merula, as well as by A. Jarzębski and A. Rohaczewski.

Adam Jarzębski (before 1590–1648), violinist, architect and poet, was exclusively an instrumental composer, writing *Canzoni e concerti* (1627). Some of the twenty-seven pieces there contained are transcriptions of Christmas songs and of motets by Merula, Lasso, and other composers; others are original compositions, all canzone, artistically comparable with those of Frescobaldi, Marini, or Monteverdi. In 1612 Jarzębski served in the chapel of the Elector Johann Sigismund in Berlin and in 1621 in the royal chapel in Warsaw.

Marcin Mielczewski (*ca.* 1600–1651) introduced in his *Canzona a 3* some dance-like elements that suggest the Polonaise and the Cracovienne.

Stanisław Sylwester Szarzyński, around 1700, composed significant "sonatas," which—despite the designation—are symmetrically constructed canzone in seven sections.

In Norway, Georg von Bertouch (1688–1743), born in Germany, imitated Italian forms. Johan Helmich Roman (1694–1758), who had been trained in England, introduced the concerto grosso into Sweden.

Trio Sonata

The trio sonata is a composition of more than one movement, for two thematically active and quite equally favored soprano instruments with basso continuo. Just what the soprano instruments may be is somewhat optional: for example, they may be two violins, two oboes, or a violin and a flute. The thorough-bass, which was realized on the organ, cembalo, or lute, was always supported by an accompanying instrumental bass, which was played on the violoncello, gamba, double bass, or bassoon. The trio sonata was one of the most intensively cultivated forms of instrumental ensemble in the Baroque era.

The characteristic feature of the trio sonata—two equal high voices and one low voice—developed from vocal music. Vocal examples appear in Claudio Monteverdi's 5th book of madrigals (1605) and in his *Scherzi Musicali a 3 voci* (1607), in Ludovico Grossi Viadana's *Cento concerti ecclesiastici* (1602), in Giovanni Giacomo Gastoldi's *Balletti a 3* (1594) and *Canzonette a 3* (1592), and also in the literature of the canzonette and villanelles up to the beginning of the 16th century. The transition to the instrumental trio sonata appears in Monteverdi's *Scherzi Musicali,* where the ritornelli were written out and accordingly were no longer improvised. The oldest independent trio collections for two violins or cornet and non-figured bass come from Salomone Rossi (*ca.* 1570–*ca.* 1630) in his *Primo libro delle Sinfonie e Gagliarde* (1607, 2nd book 1608). Ludovico Grossi Viadana published in his *Cento concerti ecclesiastici* (1602) the first thorough-bass trio that can be considered in the full sense of the term a trio sonata.

Up to the middle of the 17th century the trio canzona and the trio sonata existed side by side. Gian Paolo Cima's *Concerti ecclesiastici* (1610) has a trio canzona designated *Sonata a tre.* As in a canzona, several sections follow one another. In the literature of the Early Baroque the designations *sonata* and *canzona* often have more or less the same meaning, as do also the designations *sonata* and *sinfonia.*

An offshoot of the trio sonata is the variation sonata with the two possibilities of the soprano (discant) and the basso ostinato variation. In 1613 Salomone Rossi was the first to write a *Sonata sopra l'Aria Romanesca.* A bass that might be thus designated as *romanesca* was a fixed-bass formula, which pointed back to its vocal background and could be easily altered as a bass in instrumental composition. Other designations of a similar nature were *ruggiero, ciaccona,* and *gazella.* Many composers of the day made these and other favorite discant melodies the basis for variations.

During the High Baroque, the cities of Modena, Bologna, and Ferrara assumed leadership. The form of the sonata da chiesa developed from the reduction of the number of movements to four or five. The nucleus in the crystallization patterns of all the formal structures, according to Schenk, was a pair of movements, consisting of a fugal *Allegro* in duple time (A) and a dance-like and homophonic *Vivace* or *Presto* in triple (B), which was extended by shortened or varied repetition of the first part (A') and insertion or anticipation of slow movements (X).

As has been pointed out previously, Arcangelo Corelli gave the church sonata its classic form. The church sonata and the chamber sonata differed in that the chamber sonata had dance movements while the church sonata usually did not.

The "Concerto" Concept

A type of composition for instruments that was extremely important during the Renaissance and Baroque was commonly referred to as a "concerto." In tracing its rise, we should perhaps get some idea of the first appearance of the designation and the conception that lay behind it.

In 1519 the word "concerto" was first used with musical implications. Here it meant "concertizing" in the sense of "coming to an understanding about something"—that is, in music, more or less "collaborating in instrumental ensemble-playing." At the end of the 16th century, however, a new meaning was added, that of the "contest" between sounding bodies rivalling each other, or as the alternate emergence of one or more voices from an ensemble. The word "concerto" is derived from the Latin *concertare* (with its past participle *concertatus*); the attempt to derive it from *conserere* (with the past participle *consertus*) is open to philological objections. The two different meanings of the word "concerto"—on the one hand, agreement or collaboration and, on the other, competition— are equally valid up to the middle of the 18th century. On this basis, the quite different ways in which the word is applied can be understood.

The word "concerto" (Ger. *Konzert*, Fr. *concert*, Engl. *consort*) also has the meaning of a concert event, which takes place openly and usually before a paying public.

The *concertante* element began, according to Schering, with the *discantus*. This voice, usually improvised, moved in counterpoint over a cantus firmus. Around 1550 there was reference in music theory to a "concertizing counterpoint." In Andrea and Giovanni Gabrieli the word "concerto" was the collective term for bichoral vocal pieces with instrumental accompaniment, as it was also in Michael Praetorius.

In the *Cento concerti ecclesiastici* (1602) by Viadana (1556–1645), "concerto" meant the collaboration of one or more solo voices with thorough-bass accompaniment. Johann Sebastian Bach still, on occasion, called his cantatas "concerti." The Baroque period thus knew no strict division of the genus "concerto" into species. In practice the terminology was always flexible and ambiguous. If "concerto" in the 16th century referred to playing in instrumental ensemble, by the end of the century it was also conceived of as "competition," and this change in context was connected with the contrast between Renaissance and Baroque music. Baroque music was filled with contrasts. The juxtaposition of tutti and soli is explained also from the practical needs of music-making as contrast between the mass of amateur players and the outstanding soloists.

In the history of the instrumental concerto from about 1660 on, Schering distinguished three types: concerti without prominent solo parts (concert symphonies), concerti with more than one solo part (concerti grossi), and concerti for one solo instrument (solo concerti). All these forms made their way into the church and were played in the service of worship.

Concert Symphony

The first of these three types, the concert symphony, or concerto without prominent solo parts, was a forerunner of the concerto grosso. Normally the concert symphony had three movements: *Allegro, Andante,* and *Allegro*. In contrast to the later Neapolitan opera symphony, it was often in minor and of solemn character. It was used in the church and combined certain elements of the church sonata with those of the chamber sonata. Composers who wrote concert symphonies include Giuseppe Torelli (1658–1709), Giulio Taglietti, Henrico Albicastro, and Felice dall'Abaco (1675–1742).

Concerto Grosso

As for the second of the three types, one must realize that the term "concerto grosso" refers not only to the art-form as such but also to the full instrumental choir, which is also known as "ripieni" or "tutti," the "ripienist" being the orchestral violinist. The "concertino," or small orchestra, "concertizes," in the sense of entering into competition with this full choir. In Corelli, Handel, or Geminiani the concertino has the instrumental strength of the trio sonata (two violins and basso continuo with violoncello), but at the same time it may avail itself also of wind instruments. This special form of instrumental concertizing developed after 1650. It derived from older polychoral church music and from the three-voiced wind concertino for two flutes or oboes and bassoon, which appeared in the French opera for the aria ritornelli and the ballet portions in contrast to the full instrumental choir.

The designation "concerto grosso" itself was used perhaps for the first time in 1698 as a title by Lorenzo Gregori.

Georg Muffat reported that as early as 1682 Arcangelo Corelli (1653–1713) had developed in practice at Rome the principle of the concerto grosso, bringing together as many as 150 stringed instruments. Corelli's twelve "concerti grossi" op. 6 were, however, not published until 1714 and mark the first high point in this type of musical literature. In terms of form, eight of these concerti grossi are church sonatas and four are suites.

In character this music-making is a competition, a matter of each one's making his way with alternation of choirs, a sort of dialogue, providing sonorous variety and richness of contrast. Corelli made this procedure the occasion for a systematic musical architecture. The number of collaborating players was not specified and in practice depended on the occasion, the opportunity, and the space. Alessandro Stradella (*ca.* 1645–1682) anticipated Corelli with quite similar works, presumably during the 1670's.

Corelli's principle was taken up quickly. The string trio as concertino made its way even into the suite. In the following period, particularly by 1710, the principles of the concerto grosso and the solo concerto often interpenetrated, while solo voices emerged from the ensemble of the concertino.

Concerti grossi around Corelli's time and shortly thereafter were written by a number of composers, including Giuseppe Torelli, whose works appeared about 1690–1707; Georg Muffat (1653–1704), who in his concerti grossi of 1701 was the first to bring out Corelli's principle in Germany; Giuseppe Valentini (1710); Lorenzo Gregori (1698); Francesco Geminiani (d. 1762), Corelli's pupil, the first to bring the concerto grosso to England; Pietro Locatelli (1695–1764), another pupil of Corelli's, who published concerti grossi for the first time in Holland; Francesco Manfredini (perhaps 1688–toward 1748), who issued concerti grossi in 1718; Tommaso Albinoni, with his *Sinfonie e Concerti, op. 2* (1700); Alessandro Scarlatti, with six concerti before 1710 and six concerti around 1740; and Evaristo Felice dall'Abaco, with his *Concerti a quattro da chiesa, op. 2*.

Antonio Vivaldi (*ca.* 1680–1743) was the most productive and imaginative Italian composer in the concerto form during the Baroque era. Around 1725 he wrote significant program music in his *Cimento dell'Armonia, op. 8*. Vivaldi was active during most of his life as violin teacher and orchestra leader at the Pietà music school and orphans' home in Venice. From indications in his manuscripts we can infer the manner in which his works were presented by the orchestra: he was acquainted with an extremely rich differentiation among characterizing tempi, very fine gradations in dynamics involving thirteen levels from *pianissimo* to *fortissimo*, and, it may be assumed, transitional passages of *crescendo* and *diminuendo*.

To obtain further oppositions in sonority, he used wind instruments. The sound of the trumpet, for instance, served to increase the air of solemnity in church.

Johann Sebastian Bach composed six *Brandenburg Concerti* in 1721 for the chapel of the Margrave Christian Ludwig of Brandenburg, with changing instrumentation of the concertino in the individual concerti. The instrumentation is as follows:

First Concerto, F major: *Due Corni di Caccia, tre Hautbois e Bassono, Violino Piccolo concertato, due Violini, una Viola e Violoncello, col Basso Continuo.*

Second Concerto, F major: *Una Tromba, un Flauto* (recorder), *un Hautbois, un Violino concertato, e due Violini, una Viola e Violone in Ripieno col Violoncello e Basso per il Cembalo.*

Third Concerto, G major: *Tre Violini, tre Viole, e tre Violoncelli col Basso per il Cembalo.*

Fourth Concerto, G major: *Violino principale, due Fiauti d'Eco* (recorders), *due Violini, una Viola e Violone in Ripieno, Violoncello e Continuo.*

Fifth Concerto, D major: *Une Traversière, un Violino principale, un Violino e una Viola in Ripieno, Violoncello, Violone e Cembalo concertato.*

Sixth Concerto, B-flat major: *Due Viole du Braccio, due Viole da Gamba, Violoncello, Violone e Cembalo.*

George Frederick Handel wrote twelve concerti grossi, *op. 6*, 1739, as well as oboe concerti, *op. 3*.

Significant concerti grossi were also written by other composers, including Gottfried Heinrich Stölzel (1690–1749), Georg Philipp Telemann (1681–1767), and Johann Friedrich Fasch (1688–1758).

Solo Concerto

The third type of concerto, the solo concerto, grew from the concerto grosso. Solo concerti were first published by Giuseppe Torelli in 1698, under the title *Concerti for one violin with orchestral accompaniment*. These were followed by Tommaso Albinoni in 1700 and by Giuseppe Jacchini with 'cello concerti in 1701.

The form was established by Antonio Vivaldi (*ca.* 1680–1743) and developed into the great solo concerto. He published his *Concerti, op 3, 4, and 6–12*. Many of them are extant in manuscript. The first came out probably about 1710. J. S. Bach immediately took up the form and during his Weimar period from 1708 to 1717 transcribed some of them.

The Vivaldi concerto is in three movements with the tempi *Allegro-Andante-Allegro*. The first movement consists of a succession of tutti and soli. Their number ranges from four tutti and three soli to six tutti and five soli. The succession begins according to the key-plan: Tonic-

Dominant-Parallel key. The tutti passages always have the same thematic aspects: the solo groups are either thematically independent or taken from the tutti. The tutti usually begin with broken triads. The soli favor technical effects, such as runs, arpeggiated chords, and double stops. The second and third movements formally resemble the first, but are simpler.

Vivaldi's form was taken up by Benedetto Marcello (1686–1739), Francesco Geminiani (d. 1762), Giuseppe Tartini (1692–1770), Pietro Locatelli (1695–1764), George Frederick Handel, Johann Sebastian Bach, Georg Philipp Telemann (1681–1767), Christoph Graupner (1683–1760), Johann Georg Pisendel (1687–1755), and other composers in England, France, and Sweden. Handel's solo concerti are notably for organ and for oboe; Bach's for violin and for keyboard instruments—he being the creator of the keyboard concerto.

First and foremost perhaps in Johann Sebastian Bach, the ritornello and intermezzo portions increasingly converged and fused as a result of the way the themes were handled. The first and last movements more and more assumed a developmental character, with thematic work in the sense of the Viennese Classical Era. Motives were split off from the ritornello and reworked. Particular motives were treated contrapuntally and were connected by strong modulatory passages. There were cyclic relationships, thematic connections between the first and the last movements, a contrast to the middle movement with its strongly expressive content, unification of the whole as a self-contained cycle, and remarkable anticipation of the principles rediscovered presumably in the Pre-Classical and the Viennese Classical periods. This was especially true of Bach's *Brandenburg Concerti* and of his various solo concerti.

Baroque solo concerto composition began about 1700 and flourished till about 1760. It was supplanted by classical sonata composition, which made its way into the solo concerto. Vivaldi's solo concerto form, according to Kolneder, was the first attempt in the history of music to create musical means for instrumental expression that was at once individualistic and group-oriented or concertante. Vivaldi would take a theme, split it up into parts, and elaborate on each part. This procedure was further developed by Bach, particularly during his Cöthen period.

Symphony

The Pre-Classical Transition (from about 1720 to 1760)

The changes of style that took place from about 1720 to 1760 might be grouped together under two headings, a change in formal layout and a change in sonority. The change in layout is primarily a matter of the establishment of the sonata as a cyclic form and the role which the sonata-allegro came to play in it. The change in sonority was tied up with the replacement of the keyboard by orchestral instrumentation.

The sonata as a form was quite distinctly cyclic by about 1770 in symphonic and chamber music, with the four movements *Allegro, Andante, Minuet with Trio,* and *Allegro.* Yet there were also still many varieties in the number and character of the movements. As a cyclic form the symphony had its starting-point in the Neapolitan opera sinfonia with its three movements *Allegro, Andante,* and *Allegro.* The first movement was in sonata-allegro form. The middle movement of the symphony was developed into a self-contained slow composition. Also the form of the first movement spread to the last movement, which had normally before been a dance movement.

The minuet, a dance form of the Baroque period, underwent a change. Measure and meter were not altered, but the influence of the folk-like dance character now became more striking. The form was tripartite A-B-A. Part B was called Trio, the name coming from France in accordance with the custom of assigning individual passages in the overture and ballet to two oboes and a bassoon. Particularly through Haydn the character of the minuet again changed and became a characteristic piece, and later on was called a scherzo.

The four-movement form of the symphony came into vogue in Mannheim through the compositions of Stamitz and in Vienna through those of Wagenseil, Monn, Schlöger, and Starzer. In Italy and in the North German school, on the other hand, the three-movement layout was long retained.

Practically all types of instrumental works were occasionally called symphonies in the middle of the 18th century, from about 1720 to about 1760, or from Alessandro and Domenico Scarlatti to the initial symphonies of Haydn. These early symphonic composers were developing and deepening the form. No unnecessary distinctions in this respect need be drawn between the symphony in opera, in concert, or in the chamber (such as the trio sonata and the quartet) or between that for keyboard instrument and that for instrumental ensemble (for example, in divertimenti). When the clarification of the form came, it occurred simultaneously in all the European centers of music, particularly in Naples, Rome, Venice, Vienna, Mannheim, Dresden, Berlin, Hamburg, Paris, and London, though with some fundamental differences.

The focal point of the change occurred in the opening movement, which was in sonata-allegro form. This form has three parts: Exposition, Development, and Reprise or Recapitulation. The Exposition usually presents two themes or thematic groups. They are often of a contrasting nature and, with relationship to each other, stand usually in the key-scheme of the main key to the dominant or, in minor, of the main key to the parallel key. The exposition ends with a final group in the auxiliary key. The second part of the sonata-allegro form develops the given material or its individual parts through modulatory, motivic, polyphonic, or rhythmic elaboration and then appends a bridge passage back to the main key. The final part of the sonata-allegro form, the reprise or recapitulation, repeats in the principal key the thematic material set forth in the exposition and appends a coda.

Foreshadowings of the sonata-allegro form had already been present or prepared for in previous forms. For example, the opening movement of the Neapolitan sinfonia had modulated according to the same basic scheme. Also dance forms had followed the plan of the repetitions. The

Vivaldi concerto had used its rhythmic and dynamic contrasts. And the aria had the varied and yet integrated subsections of the sonata-allegro.

Around 1720 the sonata-allegro form was firmly established as a pattern in the first movement of the Neapolitan operatic sinfonia. Many Neapolitan composers participated in the initial development, including Alessandro Scarlatti, Francesco Feo, Niccolò Porpora, Leonardo Vinci, and Leonardo Leo.

Along with the changes in formal layout there was also an important change in sonority. The keyboard as a thorough-bass instrument gradually disappeared from the orchestra. It became superfluous because the accompaniment was more and more assigned to the middle voices and gradually was developed as motives. The bass itself was on occasion treated melodically. Extended and fully written-out composition—or as Beethoven in a letter that he wrote to Hofmeister on December 15, 1800 called it, "obligato accompaniment"—took the place of free accompaniment, even in chamber music. The classical orchestra came finally to have the following instrumentation: a five-voiced choir of stringed instruments, two flutes, two oboes, two clarinets (at first only in the Mannheim and Paris orchestras), two bassoons, two horns, two trumpets, and tympani.

The new style resulting from the changes in form and sound focused at first on certain places and then spread from there.

The roots of the new style presumably lay in Italy. The various influences that came together and fused in the development of the new style and the new forms proceeded, so far as the music was concerned, primarily from the Neapolitan opera buffa, from Pergolesi's chamber music, from the sinfonia of the Neapolitan opera, and from clavier music. Also the folk-music from southern Italy helped instigate the new style, and the Italian feeling for mellifluous singing contributed to it.

Composers who influenced the development of the new style were:

Giovanni Battista Pergolesi (1710–1736), in his twelve trio sonatas (1731). These were three-movement compositions of the sinfonia type, with beginning and ending movements in major and the epilogue somewhat independently formed. They still bore traces of popular *buffo* melody and occasionally also *cantabile* first themes. The melodies were graceful, tender, and euphonious; and they were soon imitated throughout Europe. Pergolesi tended to formulate the motives in a somewhat rococo way, out of small articulated parts. There is today, incidentally, a question about the authorship of many works once ascribed to him; some of them are now attributed to Chiarini.

Niccolò Porpora (1686–1768), in his six orchestral trios (1736).

Giovanni Battista Sammartini (1700 or 1701–1775), choirmaster in Milan, teacher of Gluck. Along with Pergolesi, Sammartini pioneered in the new expressive style as it manifested itself in the dynamic and dualistic aspects of contrast, raising the melodic expression to a lofty *espressivo*. In contrast to Pergolesi, however, Sammartini made beginnings and experiments toward a symphonic synthesis.

Gaetano Pugnani (1731–1798), in the symphonies that he began composing about 1765. In 1770 he became court conductor in Turin.

Rinaldo da Capua (d. after 1771), the forerunner of the German symphonic development (according to Sondheimer) by virtue of the clarity of formal organization of the parts in his first symphonic writing and the comprehension of these parts into a larger whole.

Niccolò Jommelli (1714–1774), significant for heightening the expressive possibilities of instrumental music by transferring the vocal style of opera into the orchestral idiom in his operas and thus stimulating the instrumental music of the period. His operas—more appropriate for discussion under Italian opera—were performed in 1751 and thereafter in Mannheim. He himself was active from 1753 to 1769 as master of the court chapel in Stuttgart. It has been assumed that the *crescendo* style of orchestral presentation came by way of Jommelli's operas to the Mannheim composers. At all events, he was one of the great pioneers in establishing a connection between Italian and German music during this period.

In this development, moreover, Italian clavier music was involved in the work of the composers Domenico Scarlatti, Francesco Durante, Benedetto Marcello, and Domenico Alberti. As early as 1732 Durante wrote two-movement sonatas independently of C. P. E. Bach. Domenico Scarlatti's *Essercizi*, or sonatas, contain elements of the later sonata-allegro form. Occasionally he introduced several themes and placed them one after the other freely in a sort of development with added partial repeat, and at times he also clearly juxtaposed a first and a second theme.

After the sonata-allegro form had been established, there occurred the gradual abandonment of the three-movement layout of the cyclic *sinfonia* form. The juxtaposition of two movements, usually contrasting in tempo—slow-fast or fast-slow—was characteristic of Italian music. Since the influence of the suite led to the adoption of the minuet, one of the two movements could be a minuet. Vice versa, principles of the *sinfonia* were taken over into the suite. The contrast and accordingly the dualism between the first and second themes in the first movement of a symphony were established. In the first theme, rhythm usually was stressed. Its particular nature consisted in its triadic structure, in chordal repetition, and in the analysis and breaking of the chord. The second theme was presented melodically and found support in the aria, folk-song, and dance. If the allegro theme was constructed in a song-like way, it was spoken of as the "singing allegro." This appeared first among the Italians, in Pergolesi and others, and then among Stamitz, Schobert, and Johann Christian Bach. Mozart adopted it perhaps principally from Johann Christian Bach after first having become acquainted with Bach's works in London during 1764.

Next in importance after Italy as the seedbed of the new style was Austria. The Austrian school, with Vienna as its center, occupied an intermediary position between Italy and North Germany. From about 1740 it undertook changes on its own in the Italian symphonic type, which with the adoption of a dance movement became the typical divertimento. Two types were developed: the usually four-movement symphony with minuet and the suite with sonata-allegro form in the first and last movements. The suite had up to eight and more movements. Four-movement symphonies with minuet were written sporadically as early as 1740 by Monn and others and later again by Joseph Haydn. In the musical technique of composition the ground for the Viennese Classical era was created primarily by Wagenseil. Austrian folk-music had considerable influence on the melodic aspects of the symphony.

The first composer to perfect the German symphony in Austria was, according to Sondheimer, Georg Christoph Wagenseil (1715–1777). A pupil of Fux, Wagenseil was music teacher at the court of the Empress Maria Theresa. From Italy he took over the main outlines with the dualistic form, but he developed the details independently through his own great creative power. The reprise was constructed as a complete repetition of the exposition. Thus the proportions of the tripartite form were balanced. Wagenseil's major symphonies were written about 1760. He helped establish the technique of the later Classical era by conceiving his works thematically and motivically in terms of periods—as, at the same time, Stamitz was also doing—and by assigning motivic work to one or more principal voices.

Other composers in Vienna important at this stage of development were the organist at the Karlskirche, Mathias Georg Monn (1717–1750), and the court conductor, Johann Georg Reutter the Younger (1708–1772).

A third focal point for the stylistic change was in Bohemia. Czech instrumental music of the 17th and 18th centuries was based on the significant tradition that had developed among the castle chapels. In the latter half of the 17th century it was especially introduced into the chapel of the Archbishop of Lichtenstein-Kastelkorn in Kroměříž, at first by Henirich Biber, then later by P. J. Vejvanovský (1640–1693). The chapel at the Kuks castle in Bohemia was particularly notable, as were also those in Moravia at the Holešov, Tovačov, Náměšt, and Jaroměřice castles. Together with the intensive cultivation of church music in the cities and monasteries, there was widespread development of a multitude of instrumentalists and composers, who also sought out new possibilities abroad.

Individual aspects of Johann Stamitz's music, such as popularity of the minuet and a pre-Classical form of the sonata, appeared in the music of František Václav Míča (1694–1744), master of the chapel and tenor at the court chapel of Jan Adam Questenberg in Jaroměřice on the Rokytná.

Czech musical emigration occurred mainly in four directions: westward to Germany, France, and England, southward by way of Ljubljana to Italy, eastward to Poland and Russia, and—in greatest numbers—to Vienna. In Germany there arose two centers of Czech musical emigration, Mannheim and Berlin. In the ensuing listing of Czech musicians who gravitated toward these various centers, the Czech spelling of the names is here retained:

The Mannheim School included Jan Václav Stamic (1717–1757),

František Xaver Richter (1709–1789), Antonín Fils (1730–1760), Jiří Čárt (1708–1788), and the two sons of the founder, Karel (1745–1801) and Jan Antonín Stamic (1754–1809).

The members of one of the greatest Czech musical families resided in Berlin: František Benda (1709–1786) and his two brothers, Jan Jiří Benda, Jr. (1715–1752) and Jiří Antonín Benda (1722–1795), who later were active for many years in Gotha.

In Paris there was the pianist and composer Jan Ladislav Dusík (1760–1812) and Antonín Rejcha (1770–1836), Professor at the Conservatoire.

Two Czechs were active in Italy: Václav Pichl (1741–1805) at Milan and Joseph Mysliveček (1737–1781), who composed extensive instrumental work and was especially active in opera.

There were many Czech musicians in Vienna: František Ignác Tůma (1704–1774), Florian Leopold Gassmann (1729–1774), Jan Adam Míča (1746–1811), nephew of František Václav Mica from Jaroměřice, Leopold Koželuh (1747–1818), Jan Křtitel Vaňhal (1739–1813), František Kramář (Krommer, 1759–1831), Vojtěch Jírovec (1763–1850), the brothers Pavel (1756–1808) and Antonín Vranický (1761–1820), and Jan Václav (Hugo) Voříšek (1791–1825).

In eastern Europe there were Ivan Práč (d. 1798), the author of one of the first collections of Russian and Ukrainian folk-songs (Petersburg 1770); Jan Antonín Mareš (1719–1794), the founder of the celebrated Russian horn school; Eduard Nápravník (1839–1916); and Váša Suk (1861–1933).

Czech composers also formed an especially strong group in Vienna during the latter half of the 18th century.

They formed the nucleus of the "Mannheim School," a term introduced by Hugo Riemann referring to the circle of composers and musicians who—beginning with Johann Stamitz—were assembled in the court orchestra at Mannheim during the time of the Elector Karl Theodor from about 1741 until the transfer of the court to Munich in 1778. According to Sondheimer, the Mannheim School in a narrow sense comprised Johann Stamitz's violin and composition pupils and in a wider sense the composers active there and distinguished by what Leopold Mozart called the *Mannheimer goût* or Mannheim taste. They are credited with having brought about two important developments, the introduction of a new style of composition in the symphony and chamber music and the establishment of a new manner of orchestral playing.

As for the new compositional style, it suddenly appeared at about the same time as similar features in the work of the Italian composers Pergolesi, Sammartini, and Jommelli, and also in that of the Viennese Monn and Wagenseil. The nature of the Bohemian practical musician that characterized Johann Stamitz and his successors involved an independent subjectivism and very great musical energy in the spirit of a new era. The manner of musical expression was in many respects inspired directly by the innate Czech musicality.

The continuing significance of the Mannheim composers arose from the introduction of the minuet into the symphony, as a new movement that stood third among the now four movements; the individual development of the second theme in the first movement; the contrapuntal thematic combinations in the subjective expression of the individual voice; and the preference for particular favorite idioms, such as *Seufzer* (literally, "sighs"), *Bebungen* (tremoli, involving a principal note and three other notes playing around it), *Vögelchen* ("little birds," or mordents in which there was a preliminary upper second), *fp* ("fortepiano," or sudden change of dynamics from loud to soft), and *Orchesterwalze* ("orchestral roll," or crescendo in connection with the steady repetition of a figure from the lower to the upper register). These graces originated in part from the Neapolitan *buffo* opera.

No less important was the new development in style of playing. Under Johann Stamitz and his successor Christian Cannabich, the Mannheim court orchestra became preeminent in Europe. Of revolutionary significance was its cultivation of sonority, or—as a Berlin musical periodical of 1793 referred to it—"the same, precise delivery, the fiery, soulful execution, and the evenness in bowing," the orchestral crescendo, and expressive dynamics in all their nuances. Mannheim orchestral dynamics were stimulated and influenced by Neapolitan opera buffa in general and particularly by Jommelli, who had been specifying the crescendo in his scores even before the Mannheim composers had begun to exploit it. Also Rameau had influenced Mannheim playing, around the middle of the century. The make-up of the Mannheim court orchestra was twenty-two violins, four violas, four violoncelli, two double basses, two flutes, two oboes, two clarinets, two bassoons, two horns, two trumpets, and tympani.

Johann Stamitz was born in 1717 in Havlíčkův Brod in Bohemia, the son of German-Austrian parents, and died in 1757 in Mannheim. As early as 1742 he had appeared in Frankfurt am Main as a celebrated violin virtuoso, probably as early as 1741 in Mannheim as violinist, and become in 1745 concertmaster in the court orchestra of the Elector Karl Theodor (1742–1799). From 1748 on, he also appeared as a guest artist in Paris. As founder of the Mannheim School and as concertmaster and violinist, Stamitz won European fame and significant influence.

The composers connected with Johann Stamitz belonged to two age-groups. Among the older were the following:

Franz Xaver Richter (1709–1789) was born in 1709 in Holešov in Moravia and in 1747 came to Mannheim. Later he was conductor at the cathedral in Strassbourg and became one of the most important representatives of the Mannheim group in the symphony and in chamber music.

Anton Filtz (about 1730–1760) was born probably in Bohemia, though the precise place is not known, and in 1754 came to Mannheim, where he was at first a pupil of Stamitz. His musical idiom is especially rich in Bohemian traits.

Jiří Tschart (1708–1788) was born in Hochtanov near Havlíčkův Brod in Bohemia and became a notable violinist in Warsaw, Dresden, Rheinberg, and Berlin. For twenty years he was active in Mannheim.

Ignaz Holzbauer (1711–1783), born in Vienna, was active as a musician in his native city, in Italy, and in Stuttgart, coming to Mannheim in 1753. Among his compositions was the German opera "Günther von Schwarzburg" (Mannheim 1777).

Carlos Giuseppe Toëschi (1724–1788) was born in Italy and came to Mannheim in 1752.

The creative work of the younger generation, whose music made Johann Stamitz appear somewhat antiquated in the eyes of his contemporaries, brought the widely ranging influence of the Mannheim composers to bear on the music of Europe after about 1760, particularly on such composers as Haydn, Mozart, Beethoven, Johann Christian Bach, Dittersdorf, Boccherini, and Gossec. Under Cannabich the orchestra attained its greatest renown.

Those who belonged to the younger generation included the two sons of Johann Stamitz, Karl (1745–1801) and Anton (1754–1809). Karl Stamitz, born in Mannheim, pupil of Cannabich and Holzbauer, became violinist in the Mannheim court orchestra in 1762. Later he was in Paris, Kassel, and Jena, and was twice in Russia. He represented the *galant* style of the Mannheim School. His brother Anton Stamitz was born in Havlíčkův Brod, his father's native town, and was for many years in Paris.

Also a younger member of the group, Christian Cannabich (1731–1798), a pupil of Johann Stamitz and of Jommelli, studied in Italy and succeeded Stamitz as concertmaster at Mannheim in 1758. Repeatedly in Paris, he became famous as the greatest orchestral leader of the time and brought significant formal refinements into the first movement of the symphony.

The younger contingent included also Franz Beck (about 1730–1809), pupil of Johann Stamitz in Mannheim and of Galuppi in Venice, later active in France. At the beginning of the 1760's he enlarged the symphony significantly on the basis of development in terms of dualistic themes. In Beck the Mannheim emphasis on the great line that Stamitz had introduced was summed up and perfected, with the detail work of Wagenseil and the fusion of form and the desire for content. The culmination was reached by Beck's *op. 3* (1762) as the result of new influences that had come from the "Storm and Stress" movement. For the first time, as Sondheimer has written, the movement was "apprehended and treated in its entirety as a problem in development."

In symphonic style, the North German School with its center in Berlin at the chapel of Frederick the Great adhered in principle strictly to the typical Neapolitan *sinfonia*. The introduction of the minuet was forbidden. The contrapuntal style was characteristic and was never entirely given up, appearing in imitations, canons, fugues, and in the development sections. The "quartet symphonies" cultivated by C. P. E. Bach were symphonies for strings with continuo.

The leading composers of this North German group included the Graun and the Bach brothers:

Karl Heinrich Graun (1703 or 1704–1759), master of Frederick the Great's court chapel in Berlin, composed numerous operas (in Neapolitan style) and the cantata *Der Tod Jesu* (1755). In 1742 the Berlin opera house was opened with Graun's *Cesare e Cleopatra*. His brother, Johann Gottlieb Graun (1702 or 1703–1771), was Frederick the Great's concertmaster. The Bach brothers were Wilhelm Friedemann, C.P.E., and Johann Christoph.

The oldest son of Johann Sebastian Bach by his first marriage was Wilhelm Friedemann Bach (1710–1784), the "Halle Bach." Born in Weimar, he was a pupil and the favorite of his father, who prepared for him the *Little Clavier Book, begun in Cöthen January 22, 1720*. From 1726 to 1727 he was a violin pupil of Johann Gottlieb Graun in Merseburg, from 1733 to 1746 organist of St. Sophia's in Dresden, and from 1746 to 1764 organist in Halle. But then he resigned and, without a regular job, lived a life of poverty and misery in Halle, Brunswick, and Berlin, where he died. A novel by Brachvogel based on incidents in his career is not very reliable. Wilhelm Friedemann Bach was one of the best organists in his time. As composer he was especially significant in his keyboard and chamber works. Racing far ahead of his brother Carl Philipp Emanuel, he pioneered in the new style, particularly that of *Empfindsamkeit,* or tenderness. He was regarded as endowed with great genius, but the sociological groundwork was lacking for its individual fulfillment and public recognition during the epoch of his activity. His compositions include church cantatas and instrumental works.

Carl Philipp Emanuel Bach (1714–1788), the "Berlin" or "Hamburg" Bach, was the second of the sons by Johann Sebastian Bach's first marriage to survive his father. Born in Weimar and at first a pupil of his father, he was later a student of law at the universities in Leipzig and Frankfurt an der Oder. In 1738 he became chamber harpsichordist to the Crown Prince Frederick of Prussia in Ruppin. After Frederick the Great's accession to the throne in 1740, C.P.E. Bach became chamber harpsichordist and piano teacher in Berlin and Potsdam. In 1768 he succeeded his godfather Georg Philipp Telemann in the very distinguished position of city music director at the five principal churches in Hamburg.

Admired by his contemporaries as an "original genius," C.P.E. Bach extensively influenced the entire development of music in the latter half of the 18th century through his instrumental and particularly his keyboard compositions. He had particular effect on Haydn, Mozart, and Beethoven. His music found an individual way of expressing the dominating period-styles of the *Galant* (courteous), *Empfindsam* (tender), and *Sturm und Drang* (storm and stress). His musical subjectivism included a passionately agitated manner of expression, sharp dynamic contrasts, thematic antitheses of tension within very small space, surprising and quite bold harmonic idioms, tension-filled general pauses, instrumental recitative style, and thematic rhetoric or so-called "speaking" thematicism. In his own day many remarked on the *Gespräche* or conversations in his music—that is, the "speaking" passages particularly in his trio sonatas. His significance in the development of musical form derives from his development of the second theme and from his bringing the three-movement sonata to full maturity, but he is still more significant for having deepened its content.

His compositions include many pieces of church music, oratorios, symphonies, chamber music, keyboard works, songs, and theoretical works, notably his *Versuch über die wahre Art das Clavier zu spielen* or Essay on the True Manner of Playing the Clavier (Berlin 1753, 2nd part Berlin 1762).

Johann Christoph Friedrich Bach (1732–1795), the "Bückeburg Bach," first famous son of Johann Sebastian Bach by his second marriage, was born in Leipzig. In 1750 he became conductor to the count of Lippe in Bückeburg, making the orchestra there one of the best in Germany and spending the rest of his life at this court. In his work there are various influences of individual styles, yet he did not transmit great creative impulses of his own in the way his three famous brothers were successful in doing. His works include oratorios, cantatas, sacred songs, symphonies, and chamber music.

In addition to centers of stylistic change in Italy and German-speaking countries, there was also a focal point of late-18th-century development of the symphony in Paris, as has been shown by some hitherto unassembled material that has been published by B. S. Brook in *La Symphonie française dans la seconde moitié du 18 siècle*, 3 vols. (Paris 1962). Certainly Mannheim influences were significant. Johann Stamitz obtained his first performance in 1751 in Paris and was in 1754–5 himself active with great success there. But the ground had been prepared by French composers, and Paris was at this time the first city of Europe in musical culture. French composers in the latter half of the 18th century had added an element that was their own and quite significant. From about 1730 to 1749 there was a time of preparation, during which one of the most original and progressive French composers was Louis-Gabriel Guillemain (1705–1770). French symphonic style originated in 1750, and reached its culmination during the 1770's and 1780's. Its productive strength was extraordinarily rich.

The most significant of the French composers in the field of the symphony was François Joseph Gossec (1734–1829), who in 1773 reorganized in Paris the *Concerts Spirituels* founded by Philidor, and in 1784 the *École Royale de Chant*. His symphonies, composed from 1752 to 1809 under the influence of Stamitz and Haydn, were independent in musical invention.

London was also a focal point in the development of the new symphonic style, through the activities there of Johann Christian Bach (1735–1782). He was the youngest son of J. S. Bach by his second marriage, and is sometimes referred to as the "Milan" or "London" Bach. His symphonies, which number more than sixty, unite the Italian cantabile style with Mannheim influences. As he was a successful writer of Italian operas in Milan before coming to London, he figures also among opera composers. In London he was master of music to the Queen.

Associated with him was Karl Friedrich Abel (1723–1787), long considered to have been a private pupil of J. S. Bach. Abel came to London in 1759 and conducted the Bach-Abel concerts from 1765 to 1781.

His symphonies are related to those of his colleague and of the Mannheim School.

In Scandinavia there was peripheral development of symphonic style. Johan Helmich Roman (1694–1758)—sometimes referred to as the "Father of Swedish Music," was born in Stockholm, received his musical training from his father, and resided from 1716 to 1720 in England. Having become a member of the Swedish royal orchestra in 1711, he became its first conductor in 1727. From 1735 to 1737 he was in England again, and in Italy; and in 1745 he retired. As composer and organizer of far-reaching significance for the development of Swedish musical life, he improved the status of musicians and organized public concerts, introducing Handel's music into Sweden. His music was stylistically uneven during the transition from Baroque to Rococo, but it had traits of its own. Inspired by Handel and Geminiani, he wrote sacred choral works, somewhat like cantatas, and secular and sacred songs distinctive in layout. Numerous instrumental works figure among his compositions, including overture suites, concerti grossi, and some twenty Neapolitan-type symphonies, eight of which are in four movements. They are among the most modern of Roman's compositions and were perhaps written late, possibly influenced by Graun. He also composed for the solo violin.

Two symphonies by H. P. Johnsen (1717–1779) mark the transition to the *galant* style.

At the same time in Trondheim, Norway, Johan Daniel (1714–1787) and Johan Heinrich Berlin (1741–1804) were actively writing symphonies, concerti, and cantatas; and, in Copenhagen, Johan Ernst Hartmann (1726–1793) wrote symphonies. J. A. Scheibe's instrumental works, which were undoubtedly extensive, are no longer extant.

The Early Classical Period (about 1760–1780)

From about 1760 Joseph Haydn took part in the development of the symphony, and from about 1770 so did young Mozart. Out of the pre-Classical transition period came the early Classical period, focusing on Haydn and Mozart and including works up to about 1780.

Joseph Haydn was born on March 31, 1732, in Rohrau on the Leitha, Lower Austria, and died on May 31, 1809, in Vienna. When eight years old, he was solo soprano at St. Stephen's Cathedral under Johann Georg Reutter the Younger but had no instruction in theory. After his change of voice in 1749, he was without regular employment. During the immediately ensuing years Haydn found occasional employment as a musician and composer and accompanied Porpora, who instructed him in thorough-bass. On commission from Karl Joseph von Fürnberg in Weinzirl, Haydn wrote his first string quartet about 1755. In 1759 he became conductor to Count Morzin in Lukawetz, and there wrote his first symphony in 1759. In 1761 he became assistant conductor of Prince Esterházy's private orchestra in Eisenstadt. Becoming conductor in 1766, he continued to discharge these duties until 1790, composing there the majority of his works, which gradually made his name known throughout Europe. Frequent visits brought him also to Vienna. Here in

1781 he became a close friend of Mozart. After being pensioned in 1790, Haydn settled in Vienna. From 1790 to 1792 and in 1794–5 he was in London, directing his symphonies in the subscription concerts organized by Salomon. Influenced by his stay in England, he wrote two oratorios, *The Creation* (1798) and *The Seasons* (1801); but after 1803 he wrote no further compositions.

Haydn's lasting significance lies particularly in the fact that his work represent "moral characters" in his symphonies. In the seriousness of his embodied in his symphonies and string quartets and in the two oratorios. Geiringer finds five distinct periods in Haydn's work: 1750–60, the youthful and apprentice years; 1761–70, the time of preparation; 1771–80, the middle period, a time characterized in German cultural history as the "Storm and Stress" era, beginning with the Piano Sonata in C-Minor No. 20; 1781–90, a time of maturity, beginning with the publication of the quartets *Op.* 33 and his close friendship with Mozart; and 1791–1803, final mastery, in which there are anticipations of the Romantic Movement.

Haydn's music possesses almost inexhaustible possibilities of artistic expression, with a predominantly optimistic attitude and with significant influences from Austrian folk-music. He always stressed the moral attitude of his activity as a composer and musician, saying that he had tried to represent "moral characters" in his symphonies. In the seriousness of his conception of art and his courage in trying the unconventional, Haydn regarded C. P. E. Bach as a model, of whom Mozart said, "Bach is the father; we are the children. Whoever of us does anything right has learned it from him. . . ."

Haydn's compositions include 104 symphonies that have been shown to be reliably genuine. He also wrote over 60 divertimenti, over 50 solo concerti with orchestra, 77 string quartets (1755–1801), 38 piano trios, 30 string trios, 12 violin sonatas, 6 string duets, 175 baryton numbers, 52 sonatas and divertimenti for piano, and other instrumental works, in addition to oratorios, Masses, operas, and songs.

He wrote his symphonies between 1759 and 1795, all of them commissioned works. The first was composed in 1759 in the service of Count Morzin. From the 31st Symphony (1765) on, four-movement layout was almost always the rule. Haydn began in the style of the Viennese pre-Classical composers. The first movement was in sonata-allegro, the last often in rondo or sonata-allegro form, the two possibilities being not entirely separable. Haydn had adopted the principle of thematic work in individual numbers quite early in his career, and that principle became a focal point in the *Maiden Quartets,* or *Russian Quartets* (op. 33, 1781), which Haydn said were written "in a new and special manner," centering on compositional work as individual motifs were separated out of the theme for thematic and contrapuntal treatment. The principle was then transferred from the string quartet into the symphony.

In the 1780's Mozart's influence is perceptible in Haydn's formulation of his melodies. Using as his point of departure the late music of Mozart, Haydn brought his symphonic work to its very peak of refinement in the London Symphonies. They are particularly marked by the fact that they have slow, thoughtful introductions to the first movement, reminiscent of the French overture. After 1770 the symphonies display heightened subjective expression.

Many of them have programmatic names, such as *Le Midi* (Noon, No. 7, C, 1761), *Der Philosoph* (The Philosopher, No. 22, E-flat, 1764), *Der Schulmeister* (The Schoolmaster, No. 55, E-flat, 1774), *La Poule* (The Hen, No. 83, G minor, 1786), and *Die Uhr* (The Clock, No. 101, D, 1794). Other names refer to characteristic impulses behind the work, such as *Lamentatione—Weihnachtssinfonie* (Lamentation—Christmas Symphony, No. 26, D minor, about 1765), *Allelujah* (No. 30, C, 1765), *Trauersinfonie* (Mourning Symphony, No. 44, E minor, before 1772), *Abschiedssinfonie* (Farewell Symphony, No. 45, F-sharp minor, 1772, with the instruments leaving off one after another), *La Chasse* (The Chase, No. 73, D, 1781), *Mit dem Paukenschlag* (With the Drum-Beat, No. 94, G, 1791), *Militär* (Military, No. 100, G, 1794), and *Mit dem Paukenwirbel* (With the Drum-Roll, No. 103, E-flat, 1795).

In 1784 Haydn received from the directors of the Concerts Spirituels in Paris an order to compose six symphonies, now usually referred to as the "Paris Symphonies," which appeared in 1786 (Nos. 82–87). The twelve London Symphonies for the Salomon Concerts in London (Nos. 93–104) were written from 1791 to 1795.

The 104 symphonies of Haydn are inexhaustible in their abundant inspiration, imaginative formal construction, and experimentation with instrumental and formal possibilities, as Haydn worked toward final accord between form and content.

Wolfgang Amadeus Mozart was born on January 27, 1756, in Salzburg, son of the assistant conductor and court composer Leopold Mozart (author of *Versuch einer gründlichen Violinschule*, 1756). A child prodigy, Wolfgang was credited with his first keyboard playing at the age of three and his first composition in 1761. He made his first tour as artist in 1762, to Munich and Vienna; his second, by way of Munich, Frankfurt, and Brussels to Paris and London, in 1763–6; and his third to Vienna, Olomouc, and Brno in 1767. At this time he wrote his early operas *Finta semplice* and *Bastien und Bastienne*. From 1769 to 1771 he made his first journey to Italy, to Milan, Bologna, Florence, Rome, and Naples. For Milan he composed *Mitridate*. From 1771 to 1773 he made his second and third journeys to Italy, and composed *Ascanio in Alba* and *Lucio Silla* for Milan. In 1777–8 he made a trip to Paris by way of Mannheim. The death of his mother occurred while he was in Paris. Mozart was in the service of the Salzburg archbishop until 1781, and then— except for short trips to Prague, Berlin, and Frankfurt—continuously in Vienna, but only from 1787 in a regular position as chamber musician to Joseph II. Mozart died on December 5, 1791, in Vienna, in dire poverty.

To Goethe, Mozart was "sheer genius," endowed with an inconceivable ability to assimilate impulses from without into his own being. Hermann Abert said that Mozart "was of all great musicans the most receptive and the one with the greatest ability and need to adapt artistic impressions to his own uses. This gift of fresh feeling he retained to the end of his life." Mozart first came in contact with the circle of musicians associated with Salzburg and Vienna, including Leopold Mozart, Haydn, and Wagenseil. Also he knew the keyboard music of C. P. E. Bach. He studied the keyboard style of Johann Schobert in Paris and the symphonies of Karl Friedrich Abel and Johann Christian Bach in London. Having already encountered the operatic art of Italy, in 1777 for the second time he came in contact with the Mannheim style, the attempts of Holzbauer to write German opera, and Gluck's operas in Paris. In 1781 he encountered Haydn's new quartets, and then the art of Handel and Johann Sebastian Bach. An openness to new impressions is so clearly reflected in Mozart's creative work that Wyzewa and St.-Foix have seen in his career up to 1777 a total of twenty-four periods, each oriented toward one or more artistic models, and they have established ten further periods for the later years. In his historical influence, Mozart was most significant in the opera, the symphony, and chamber music—in opera for his handling of the German singspiel and the opera buffa, in the symphony for his last three symphonies of 1788, and in chamber music for his string quartets and quintets and chamber music with piano.

His works include 40 symphonies, 31 divertimenti and similar compositions, 25 concerti, 15 further solo concerti with orchestra, 5 concerti for two or three solo instruments, 9 quintets, 26 string quartets, 8 piano trios, 42 violin sonatas, 17 two-hand and 5 four-hand piano sonatas, 4 fantasies for piano, and other piano works, operas, Masses, vocal works with orchestra, and songs.

Of the 40 symphonies, the first is K. V. 16, in E-flat, performed in 1764 in London; the last is the "Jupiter," K. V. 551, performed in 1788 in Vienna. In the beginning Mozart was strongly influenced by the Italian opera sinfonia and by Johann Christian Bach; then he alternated among Viennese, Italian, and Mannheim influences. In the 1770's, there was a distinct heightening of feeling during the "Storm and Stress" period—in, for example, the *G minor symphony* (K. V. 183) and the *E♭ major symphony* (K. V. 184), both about 1773. The *Symphony in D* (K. V. 297) was written in 1778 in Paris. The "Haffner Symphony" was derived from the "Haffner Serenade" (D major, K. V. 385, 1782 in Vienna). Like the *Symphony in C major* (K. V. 425, 1783), it shows strong influences of Joseph Haydn. The *Prague Symphony*, without minuet, in D major (K. V. 504), was written in 1786 in Vienna.

But the culminating point of his symphonic writing was reached in the last three symphonies—in E-flat major (K. V. 543), G minor (K. V. 550), and C major (K. V. 551), the "Jupiter"—completed on June 26, July 25, and August 10, 1788, in Vienna. Each of the three symphonies has its own individuality. K. V. 550, predominantly written in minor, is the first dramatically symphonic cyclic presentation of the tragic as fate and of apparently ineluctable depression. The finale of K. V. 551, as a sonata-allegro form with strongly fugal portions, is a supreme elaboration of influences from Bach. The cantus firmus C–D–F–E, which is of Gregorian origin, appears in each repetition in altered contrapuntal reworking. Thus for the first time the principle of irreversibility, or permanent change, is here suggested. The slow introduction to K. V. 543 is connected with *Don Giovanni* and points ahead to the *Magic Flute,* and the character of lofty solemnity is here joined with a sense of the greatest mystery. In the symphony K. V. 543 there are still numerous traits borrowed from Haydn, which Mozart has now interpreted in a way entirely his own. In these three works Mozart led the symphony to its first culminating point, and accordingly in this field itself he reached his most significant achievement. They bring together everything that went before and point ahead far into the future.

For the first time, in these three symphonies, what might be called the "idea of the symphony" is clearly projected. Here the symphony has withdrawn from every influence imposed on it by society, and is thus a completely autonomous work of art. From this height it reflects back on the listeners and thereby has an inexhaustible general human effect. As it is a cyclic unity, the movements—in relation to the whole—are to be neither detached nor replaced. In content this unity represents a unique, unmistakable, and uninterchangeable idea, decidedly realizable in music, the character of which can be paraphrased in words only with difficulty. Thus, from the standpoint of the music, the composer has faced the most various technical tasks, involving cyclic unity, corresponding relationships of individual movements to each other, layout of the movements, development of the themes, and linkage of various types of form with each other. As occasion presents itself, there may be the influence of ideas from outside the realm of music, strictly considered. There may be stimuli of a quite personal nature tied up with experience, and reflection of literary or pictorial prototypes. There may also be the introduction of the human voice, use of literary texts. as direct program, and transformation of the instrumental symphony into the vocal symphony. All these possibilities are implicit in the stage in the development of the symphony that Mozart had reached in his "Jupiter."

Among the Austrian contemporaries of Mozart were Franz Asplmayer (1728–1786) and Joseph Starzer (1726–1787). Also many other composers associated with Haydn and Mozart reveal the general continuation of the great models. Some of them were quite dependent on Haydn, particularly Karl Ditters von Dittersdorf (1739–1799), who wrote over a hundred symphonies, including program symphonies on Ovid's *Metamorphoses*.

Czech composers who stylistically belong to the Early and High Classical periods include František Ignác Tůma (1704–1774), Florian Leopold Gassmann (1729–1774), Jan Adam Míča (1746–1811), Leopold Koželuh (1747–1818), Jan Křtitel Vanhal (1739–1813), Antonín Rössler (Rosetti, 1750–1792), Vojtěch Jírovec (Gyrowetz, 1763–1850), Pavel Vranický (1756–1808), Antonín Vranický (1761–1820), and Jan Václav Hugo Voříšek (1791–1825). F. X. Dušek (1731–1799) was active in Prague.

The list of Haydn's pupils includes Ignaz Pleyel (1757–1831), who in 1795 became a prominent composer and music dealer in Paris; Sigismund Neukomm (1778–1858); and Ludwig van Beethoven.

Other composers of the Early Classical Period include Luigi Boccherini (1743–1805), who went from his native Italy to Spain, where he conducted the court orchestra in Madrid. All in all, he wrote some thirty symphonies. His very numerous works of chamber music were especially popular, being rhythmically and melodically lively, playful, and bright. He was the creator of the string quintet (usually with two celli), for which he wrote about 125 compositions.

In Denmark, C. F. E. Weyse (1774–1842) composed seven symphonies between 1795 and 1799.

Historically associated with Mozart were Muzio Clementi (probably 1752–1832) and Johann Franz Xaver Sterkel (1750–1817). Clementi was particularly active in London as pianist, publisher, and piano-maker.

A composer of the transition to the High Classical period was the German-born Swede J. M. Kraus (1756–1792) with six symphonies, No. 3 in C minor (1783) dedicated to Haydn and No. 6, *Symphonie funèbre* (1792) with Beethovenian traits.

The High Classical Period (from 1781 to about 1810)

The year 1781 was important in the careers of both Haydn and Mozart, marking the appearance of Haydn's string quartets op. 33, in which the principle of thematic work was carried through. Also in the same year Mozart transferred his activities to Vienna, and there he came into contact with Haydn. The ensuing decade of mutual artistic exchange between the two composers formed the heart of the High Classical period. As early as the 1770's instrumental music was influenced by the "Storm and Stress." In Mozart's last three symphonies and in Haydn's London Symphonies expression was thus quite significantly deepened and was brought into an ideal balance with the form. When Beethoven in 1792 arrived in Vienna, the symphony already stood at a culminating point in its history.

Ludwig van Beethoven was born in Bonn and was christened on December 17, 1770; he died in Vienna on March 26, 1827. Son of a tenor in the Electoral chapel, he was at first a pupil of his father, who wanted to make a child prodigy of him. Also he received important early musical impressions from Bach's *Well-Tempered Clavier,* to which the court organist Christian Gottlob Neefe had introduced him. In Bonn he heard music performed at the residence of the Elector of Cologne. Beethoven's introduction to literature and philosophy (Goethe, Schiller, Klopstock, Kant, and Herder) came from members of the Breuning and Wegeler families with whom he was acquainted, and he developed a lifelong interest in Shakespeare and Homer. In 1789 he enrolled at the university that had just been opened in Bonn. In 1787 he was in Vienna for the first time, hoping to become Mozart's pupil. After a brief stay he was called home by the severe illness of his mother. In 1792 he finally moved to Vienna and—except for short trips—spent the rest of his life there. Here he was to receive—according to the phrase used by his patron, the great Count Waldstein—"Mozart's spirit from Haydn's hands." Beethoven was Haydn's pupil in 1793, but at that time he also studied counterpoint with Johann Schenk, fugue with Georg Albrechtsberger, and Italian vocal composition with Antonio Salieri. At first Beethoven appeared in Vienna mainly as a pianist. Through Count Waldstein he was brought to the attention of a group of aristocrats, among whom were

Archduke Rudolf and the princes and counts Lichnówsky, Lobkowitz, Esterházy, and Kinsky. Of these, in 1809, Rudolf, Lobkowitz, and Kinsky provided for Beethoven's material needs by establishing an income for him. Even before 1800 suffering from hearing disability, he wrote in 1802 the *Heiligenstadt Testament.* The malady increased and toward 1820 led to almost complete deafness. He appeared publicly as a pianist for the last time in 1814 and as a conductor in 1822. His last years were deeply troubled by concern over his adopted nephew Karl.

Goethe said of Beethoven that he had never seen an artist "more integrated, more energetic, more inward." These words indicate Beethoven's personality as an individualist of the Post-Revolutionary period, as a person with a temperament that sets stricts rules for itself, and as the intensified man of feeling. He was the first individualist among musicians of modern times to free himself from every relationship of servility toward prince or traditional and conventional church. He found the ethical keynote for his conduct of life especially in his favorite poets, Homer and Goethe. Beethoven's own thoughts are extant in numerous aphorisms jotted down in his diaries. His inner life is reflected in many of his letters, among which the one to the anonymous "Immortal Beloved" and the *Heiligenstadt Testament* (1802) are especially moving documents, as they show him to have been a man of strong feelings.

The style of his works was to some extent derived from C. P. E. Bach, Haydn, and Mozart, stimulated by the style of the Mannheim School and of the French composers Grétry and Cherubini, and influenced also by G. F. Handel. Though thus indebted to previous composers, Beethoven wrote music of unprecedentedly individualistic expression and of heartfelt human power of feeling. In the concentration of form from the musical material, he is comparable only to J. S. Bach. Dynamic contrasts, rhythmic force, melodic expansion, striking character of the motives, and thematic development are distinctly Beethovenian traits. His whole output has given rise to individual interpretations, some stressing form, some content. In general, one can distinguish three stylistic phases. In the first, up to about 1802, he was dependent on Haydn and Mozart. In the second, on to about 1812, he fashioned his forms and artistic means more individualistically. And from 1812 on, he rose more and more boldly to worlds of subjective expression which were new and yet which fused in a novel way with the forms of the variation and fugue.

His works include nine symphonies; eleven overtures, including three *Leonore Overtures, Egmont, Coriolanus, Prometheus,* and *Consecration of the House;* a violin concerto in D; five piano concerti; a triple concerto for piano, violin, and cello; a choral fantasy; two romances for violin and orchestra; thirty-two (actually, now, thirty-eight) piano sonatas; ten violin sonatas; five cello sonatas; nine piano trios; four piano quartets (three in 1785); a piano quintet with winds; two wind octets; a wind sextet; a septet and a sextet for strings and winds; two string quintets and sixteen string quartets with a fugue for each quartet and quintet; five string trios; a trio for flute, violin, and viola; an oratorio "Christ on the Mount of Olives"; several cantatas; choral songs and sixty-six songs with piano; concert arias; and two Masses, one in C and one in D.

The nine symphonies provide a focal point in this body of composition:

First Symphony, C, op. 21, composed at the latest in 1799, first performed in 1800, published in 1801.

Second Symphony, D, op. 36, completed probably in 1802, first performed in 1803, published in 1804.

Third Symphony ("Eroica"), E-flat, op. 55, composed in 1803, first performed in 1805, published in 1806.

Fourth Symphony, B-flat, op. 60, composed probably in 1806, first performed in 1807, published in 1808.

Fifth Symphony ("Fate Symphony"), in C minor, op. 67, completed in 1807, first performed in 1808, published in 1809.

Sixth Symphony ("Pastorale"), F, op. 68, composed in 1807–8, first performed in 1808, published in 1809.

Seventh Symphony, A, op. 92, composed in 1811–2, first performed in 1813, published in 1816.

Eighth Symphony, F, op. 93, composed in 1811–2, first performed in 1814, published in 1817.

Ninth Symphony with concluding chorus on Schiller's "Ode to Joy," D minor, op. 125, completed in 1823, first performed in 1824, published in 1826.

There are sketches for a Tenth Symphony (1826).

The First and Second Symphonies were written in Beethoven's first stylistic period, the Third to Eighth in his second, and the Ninth in his third. Four-movement structure is the rule, with the exception of the "Pastorale," which is in five movements. Slow introductions to the first movement, with far greater significance than in Haydn, appear in the First, Second, Fourth, and Seventh. The symphonies can be divided into the following groups: the First, Second, Fourth, Seventh, and Eighth emphasize form, while the Third, Fifth, and Ninth emphasize content, and the Sixth ("Pastorale") is a program symphony. So far as significance is concerned, the first movements at times have the predominance; and, particularly from the "Eroica" on, the center of gravity lies in the development section. The most significant adagio movements appear in the Fourth and Ninth Symphonies. Th Fifth Symphony with its striking C major finale after the C minor of the first and third movements has become the prototype for numerous later contrasts of mood in symphonies which make full use of the dialectical tension between major and minor to characterize the keys. The close linkage of the last two movements, as in Beethoven's Fifth, had already appeared in Dittersdorf's *C major Symphony*. Although the "Pastorale" as a program symphony is not entirely new in its idea, Beethoven's music is—in his words—"more expression of feeling than painting." The joyous trait of the Seventh Symphony is especially based on elemental rhythmic effects, and the Eighth is supremely serene. In the Ninth the quite new problem of introducing the singing voice in the finale was solved by the use of recitatives for the celli and double basses and by allusions to the first three movements. The first movement is uniquely monumental, richer in the abundance of themes than before, and with strictly contrapuntal elaboration. The conventional orchestra of the Haydn period was enlarged in the Third Symphony by a third horn, in the Fifth by piccolo, contrabassoon, and tympani, and in the Ninth by piccolo, contrabassoon, third and fourth horns, and tympani and other percussion.

One of Beethoven's pupils was Carl Czerny (1791–1857), who was later to be the teacher of Liszt. As a composer Czerny was prolific, with over a thousand compositions to his credit. But he is regarded today more as a significant piano teacher and author of pedagogical works for the instrument. Another of Beethoven's pupils was Ferdinand Ries (1784–1838), a piano virtuoso, composer, and conductor.

Symphonic composers contemporary with Beethoven include J. Wölfl (1772–1812) and A. Eberl (1765–1807).

The Early Romantic Period (from about 1810 to 1828)

The music history of the 19th century and of the Romantic movement in particular is characterized by seemingly contradictory tendencies and great individual differences among the various composers. Franz Schubert, however, stands out as the greatest among many symphony composers active at this time.

Ludwig Spohr (1784–1859) wrote nine symphonies between 1811 and 1850. The most significant of them as absolute instrumental works are the Third (with a slow movement as its finale) and the Fifth—both in C minor. The Fourth, or *Weihe der Töne* (Consecration of Tones, after a poem, 1832) is a program symphony, as are also the Sixth or *Historische Symphonie im Styl und Geschmack vier verschiedener Zeitabschnitte* (Historical Symphony in the Style and Taste of Four Different Epochs, 1839), the Seventh or *Irdisches und Göttliches im Menschenleben* (Earthly and Heavenly in the Life of Man, for double orchestra, 1842), and the Ninth or *Jahreszeiten* (Seasons). In style Spohr consciously imitates Mozart. The expression in his symphonies is predominantly elegiac and sentimental. Harmonically, the music is soft and highly chromatic, with mobile, gliding middle voices and with a lack of contrasts in rhythm and dynamics.

Carl Maria von Weber (1786–1826) composed two symphonies, both in C major, in 1807 at Carlsruhe in Silesia, intended for the orchestra of Duke Friedrich Eugen of Württemberg. The First Symphony, influenced by Beethoven's First, is of historical significance.

Franz Schubert (1797–1828) wrote eight extant symphonies, the first six strongly influenced by the Viennese Classical composers: the First, in D major (1813); the Second, in Bb major (1814–5); the Third, in D major (1815); the Fourth, in C minor (1816), which Schubert called the "Tragic Symphony"; the Fifth, in Bb major (1816); the Sixth, in C major (1817–8); the Seventh, in C major (1828), discovered by Schumann in 1838 in the hands of Schubert's brother Ferdinand; and the Eighth, in B minor (1822), discovered in 1865 and world-famous as the "Unfinished" in two movements, sketches for the Scherzo being also extant. There may also have been a "Gaststein Symphony."

Schubert's symphonies are characterized by song-like themes, novel continuation in the development, exploitation of the power of harmony to create mood, vacillation between major and minor, use of the horn as melodic solo instrument, and individual instrumental colors. In the Seventh Symphony, there is a fusion of the slow introduction with the allegro portion of the first movement. In his last two symphonies he linked up with Beethoven to make the transition to the High Romantic period in the symphony with strong emphasis on the composer's lyric individuality.

Richard Wagner (1813–1883) composed a symphony in C major in 1832 while he was studying music with Weinlig, the choir-director at St. Thomas's in Leipzig. Though influenced by Beethoven, it also has individual traits that characterize the later Wagnerian style.

Johann Wenzeslaus Kalliwoda (1801–1866), who was best known for his men's choruses, wrote seven symphonies between 1826 and 1843.

The High Romantic Period (from 1828 to about 1850)

Soon after Beethoven, Weber, and Schubert had died, composers manifested highly individual tendencies. These increased in distinctness and diversity throughout the 19th century. Particularly after 1850 they attracted many quite irreconcilable partisans.

Beethoven's music, greatly admired throughout the century, received highly individual interpretations in terms of form and in terms of content. Berlioz was one of the first to associate himself with Beethoven as a "program musician." The works of Berlioz became the stimulus and model for the "Neo-German School" under Liszt and Wagner, and have exerted influence by way of Richard Strauss and Arthur Honegger that has continued on to the present time. On the other hand, a more classically oriented group of composers have followed Beethoven as the master who perfected the classic symphonic form. Beginning with Mendelssohn and Schumann in his later period, this conception of Beethoven was carried on further by Brahms. But even as the "Classicists" did not rule out programmatic suggestions, whether these were explicitly presented as "programs" or not, so also in many program symphonies and symphonic poems there are indications of an effort to retain the sonata-allegro form and the cyclic succession of movements.

Felix Mendelssohn-Bartholdy, son of a banker, was born in Hamburg on February 3, 1809, and died in Leipzig on November 4, 1847. Grandson of the philosopher Moses Mendelssohn, he grew up in Berlin and was a pupil of Zelter in theory and of Ludwig Berger in piano. Manifesting precocious musical talent, young Mendelssohn was admired by Goethe as early as 1821. In 1826 Mendelssohn wrote the Overture to Shakespeare's *Midsummer Night's Dream,* and in 1829 he directed the Berlin Singakademie's revival performance of Bach's *St. Matthew Passion.* After several years on tour through Germany, Italy, France, and England, he became municipal director of music in Düsseldorf from 1833 to 1835. In 1835 he became leader of the Gewandhaus orchestra in Leipzig, which he made a music center of Europe. In 1843 he organized the Leipzig Conservatory. From 1841 to 1844 he was primarily active in Berlin, and then again in Leipzig.

Mendelssohn was the first composer to evidence a particularly historical awareness in his responsible and critical attitude toward creative work in the oratorio. Among the Romantics this attitude contributed to a somewhat retrospective trait, which has continued to manifest itself right up to the middle of the present century almost without interruption.

Gifted in many ways, Mendelssohn was a cultivated, happy, and artistic person. He had a highly stimulating effect on his period in Germany and England as an organizer, conductor, and pianist. In their day his compositions quite suited the taste of the solid citizens of what was called in Germany the "Biedermeier generation"—or, in England, the Victorians. He exerted also a great influence on the entire century through his music, especially by virtue of its melodic and formal richness. Giving new impetus to the oratorio, he sought to fuse Late Baroque forms with Biedermeier feeling. During his century he was widely acclaimed for his songs, chamber music, and piano works—particularly his *Songs without Words*. Quite melodically conceived, his music is of great formal richness.

His works include five symphonies, three stage and five concert overtures, a violin concerto, two piano concerti, numerous works for piano solo and for piano with orchestra, an octet for strings, two string quintets, seven string quartets, a piano sextet, three piano quartets, two piano trios, a violin sonata, two cello sonatas, organ works, two oratorios, church music, and songs.

His symphonies are the Symphony in C minor, op. 11, an early work, of 1824; the *Reformation Symphony*, op. 107, written in 1829–30 but rejected by the composer and published posthumously; the Symphony in A ("Italian"), op. 90, composed in 1833 and also published posthumously; the symphony-cantata *Lobgesang* or Song of Praise, op. 52, composed in 1840 for the Gutenberg commemoration in Leipzig; and the Symphony in A minor, op. 56 ("Scottish"), 1842. This last of his symphonies, inspired by impressions of nature received in the northern part of the British Isles, proved to be of continuing historical influence because of its adoption of national color and its use of predominantly song-like melodies. Though Mendelssohn in his symphonies and overtures followed many impulses that were of not strictly musical origin, he preserved the traditional form. The song-like aspects of his orchestral compositions, however, predominate over the strictly symphonic work.

Robert Schumann was born on June 6, 1810, at Zwickau, in Saxony, and died on July 29, 1856, in Endenich near Bonn. While at school he was predominantly concerned with literature, being especially impressed by Jean Paul's works; and not until 1830 while he was enrolled as a student of law did he finally resolve to devote himself to music, studying the piano under Wieck in Leipzig. After paralysis of his hand in 1831, he devoted himself entirely to his own creative work as a composer. In 1834 the *Neue Zeitschrift für Musik* began publication, with Schumann as editor-in-chief—a position which he continued to fill until 1842. In 1840 he married Clara Wieck. They moved to Dresden in 1844, and for many years he received little recognition as a composer. In 1850 he became municipal director of music in Düsseldorf. In 1854, after attempting suicide, he was confined to a sanatorium at his own request.

Schumann arrived at composition after many detours into legal study, authorship, writing, music criticism, and performance at the piano; and, as a result of his double talent for music and literature, he long engaged in composition and music criticism side by side. After he had written for about ten years almost exclusively for the piano, he mastered for himself in 1840 the *lied*, a year later the symphony, and then chamber music and oratorio. Finally, he attempted opera. He began in the style of the Romantic musical aphorism, confining himself largely to the small forms of piano music, which often took their initial impulses from not specifically musical impressions. But about 1841 he began to approach closer and closer the Classical and later also the Baroque forms, in preparation for which he pursued extensive fugal studies. His significance for his time and his continued historical importance are based on his rich and direct melodic and harmonic Romantic idiom, which he felicitously placed at the service of non-musical suggestions and which he knew how to relate to the formal world of the Classical Era.

His works include four symphonies; various overtures and orchestral works, most significantly the Overture to Byron's *Manfred;* a concerto for piano, one for violin, and one for 'cello; three string quartets; a piano quintet; a piano quartet; three piano trios; two violin sonatas; numerous smaller pieces for one solo instrument with piano; works for piano, two and four hands; two oratorios; scenes from *Faust;* and songs and choruses.

His four symphonies are today usually numbered as follows: the First, in B♭ major, usually referred to as the "Spring Symphony" (1841); the Second, in C major, completed in 1846, and actually the third in order of composition; the Third, in E♭ major, or the "Rhenish" (1850), actually the fourth in order of composition; and the Fourth, in D minor, second in order of composition (1841), but reorchestrated in 1851.

Schumann was hard pressed to fill out the form with thematic work as Beethoven had done. His work is formally best in the Second Symphony, freshest in invention in the First, and most significant in inner content in the Fourth, in which the four movements are bound together thematically in a closer way than ever before. The First and Third Symphonies are programmatically inspired. The First, related to Adolph Böttger's poem, was originally provided with descriptive titles for the four movements: *Beginning of Spring, Evening, Merry Games,* and *Full Flood-Tide of Spring.* The Third—particularly in the final movement—evokes the throbbing, colorful, but also serious world of the Rhineland.

Romantic Classicism (from 1850 to about 1900)

The greatest Romantic Classicist, Johannes Brahms, carried out in music the purposes implicit in the late work of Schumann. In the decades between 1840 and 1870 and later, many composers in Germany worked in such a spirit, which might be designated as that of Romantic Classicism. Among them, for example, were Franz Lachner (1803–1890), Ferdinand Hiller (1811–1885), Stephen Heller (1813–1888), Max Bruch (1838–1920), Joseph Rheinberger (1839–1910), and Hermann Goetz (1840–1876). Also deserving of mention are symphonies by Robert

Volkmann (1815–1883), Woldemar Bargiel (1825–1897), Carl Reinecke (1824–1910), and Albert Dietrich (1829–1908). Many composers of this time followed the lead of Mendelssohn.

Johannes Brahms was born in Hamburg on May 7, 1833, and died in Vienna on April 3, 1897. His father was a musician, being a double-bass player. Having studied with him and with Eduard Marx, he was introduced to the musical world by Schumann in his article, "New Paths," in the *Neue Zeitschrift für Musik* (1853). At first he came before the public as a concert pianist, but particularly after 1860 he became known as a composer. Except for a sojourn in Düsseldorf and temporary service as piano teacher to the Prince of Lippe and as choirmaster in Detmold, Brahms lived mainly in Hamburg. In 1862 he moved to Vienna and remained there for the rest of his life, except for trips, particularly in summer, to Switzerland, Italy, and elsewhere. In Vienna he was director of the Singakademie from 1863 to 1864 and choral director of the Gesellschaft der Musikfreunde from 1872 to 1875. Otherwise he did not hold any other public positions. Recognition of him as a composer grew appreciably after the quite significant Bremen performance of the *German Requiem* in 1868. In 1889 he was made an honorary citizen of the city of Hamburg, and in 1896 became a member of the Paris Academy.

Geiringer differentiates four creative periods in Brahms's life, a first or early period up to 1855, a second to 1867–8, a third to 1890, and a fourth to 1896. Some commentators on Brahms have suggested that his Classicism was connected with an innate stubbornness or with his peasant, laboring, or Low German ancestry; others have seen it as coming from his creative ability to link himself with the art of the past. His development as a composer occurred slowly, perseveringly, without leaps, by organic growth. His art is lyrical throughout. Hence even the sporadic dramatic passages in his music are never theatrical, never superficial. He had a particularly important relationship to folk-song, with which he liked to identify his work melodically and with which he had strong sympathies. His music is simple, plain, and lapidary, for all its often heightened technical demands. Its value lies in intensification, depth of feeling, and quietly striving power.

His works include four symphonies, two orchestral serenades, orchestral variations on a theme by Haydn, two concert overtures, two piano concerti, a violin concerto, a double concerto for violin and 'cello, two string sextets, two string quintets, a clarinet quintet, three string quartets, a piano quintet, three piano quartets, four piano trios, a piano trio with clarinet, three violin sonatas, two 'cello sonatas, piano and organ works, *Ein deutsches Requiem, Rinaldo* (after Goethe, for tenor solo, men's chorus, and orchestra), *Nänie* (by Schiller, for chorus and orchestra), *Triumphlied,* and choruses and songs.

Specifically, the symphonies are the First, in C minor, op. 68, composed between 1862 and 1876; the Second, in D major, op. 73 (1877); the Third, in F major, op. 90 (1883); and the Fourth, in E minor, op. 98 (1884–5). Along with the symphonies of Schumann, those of Brahms are highly significant as absolute music in the Beethoven spirit, with their amply projected form being developed organically from the thematic material. If the First Symphony is in thought an imitation of Beethoven's Fifth, Brahms has grown to his own full stature in the treatment of the tragic motif in the Fourth. Its fourth movement is a chaconne, the eight-measure theme of which is varied thirty-two times. The Second Symphony, basically lyrical and amiable, is often called the "Pastoral." Marked by elegiac tendencies characteristic of Brahms's late period, the Third is dominated by a motif involving the minor third and the sixth (F-Ab-F), which opens the symphony as a "motto." Where Beethoven had presented a scherzo as the third movement in his symphonies, Brahms placed a more reflective *allegretto* movement in this position in his first three symphonies and, in the Fourth, a fast movement.

Anton Bruckner, born on September 4, 1824, in Ansfelden in Upper Austria, died on October 11, 1896, in Vienna and was buried in the collegiate church of St. Florian. The son of a teacher, he became after his father's death a choirboy in St. Florian Seminary. Later he attended the teachers' college in Linz and became first an assistant teacher in Windhag and then, after having passed the examination for school principals, a teacher at St. Florian in 1845. In 1848 he became the organist at St. Florian and in 1856 the cathedral organist in Linz. After initial studies undertaken on his own, he took counterpoint lessons for years from Simon Sechter in Vienna. At Bruckner's own request he was given an examination by a committee of the Gesellschaft der Musikfreunde and received a diploma to attest to his qualifications as a conservatory teacher. From 1861 to 1863 he studied composition with Otto Kitzler, conductor of the theater orchestra at Linz, where he became acquainted with the works of Liszt and Wagner. In 1868 he succeeded Sechter at the Vienna Conservatory and at the same time served as organist for the court. In 1875 he also lectured on music theory at the University of Vienna. In 1891 he received an honorary doctorate from the University of Vienna and was made an honorary citizen of Linz in 1894. Although honored as a person during his lifetime, he achieved recognition for his creative work only very slowly. As early as 1864 he had made a final breakthrough toward free expression of his own creative potentialities. But the first performance of his Seventh Symphony under Arthur Nikisch in Leipzig in 1884 remained the only significant hearing he gained for his work as a composer of symphonies while he was alive. Subsequently, around 1920, there was a growing awareness of his work and of his creative individuality, but up to very recent years it has been largely confined to Central Europe.

His works include eleven symphonies, one string quintet, four Masses, a *Te Deum*, five German psalms, and smaller sacred and secular choral works.

As viewed from the present, his historical significance lies in his synthesis of the musical means of the two great tendencies, Romantic Realism and Romantic Classicism. These he consummated in a more intuitive than conscious way, without being widely understood by his contemporaries. His efforts, however, were not dependent on public approval or rejection.

The particular nature of the symphonic music of Bruckner consisted in its uniting a number of traits into a symphonic style of his own, some apparently coming from Wagner and some from the fact that he was originally an organist and Austrian. Wagnerian influence may be seen in his use of "nature motifs"; in the chromatic and enharmonic aspects of his compositions; and in his instrumentation, which expanded the symphony orchestra through the inclusion of eight horns, four of which alternate with four Wagner tubas. Bruckner's conception of sonority, however, seems to have come from the organ, which has left its traces in the voice-leading and the instrumentation. Also he has derived suggestions from organ improvisation in the service of the Catholic liturgy, showing his familiarity with Palestrina style and with the melodic formations of congregational song. A quite sensuous sonority is here combined with religious fervor. There are influences from Austrian folk-music, in the manner often of Mozart and particularly of Schubert. Bruckner expands the formal subdivisions in his works by adding intensification, as on the organ, without thematic development. Thus he has given the pieces a decidedly confessional character, augmenting the musical means at the finale.

A feature peculiar to Bruckner is his usually tripartite layout of the main movements, with subdivision of the separate groups into three sections. His music, deeply inspired by Catholic religiosity, is always colorful and reflects joy in the senses. A distinctly novel feature of it in the history of the symphony is the monumental style characterized by impressive themes and by the piling-up of sonorous means, with distinctive passages for the brass section. In studying the symphonies, however, one must be sure to consider them in their original form, the so-called "*Urfassung*," as written by the composer.

According to the usual way of listing Bruckner's symphonies there are nine with numbers, preceded by the Symphony in F minor (1863) and the Symphony No. 0 (1864) from the Linz period. The numbered symphonies are: the First, in C minor, first version 1865–6, first performed in Linz, 1868; the Second, in C minor, first version 1871–2, first performed in Vienna, 1873; the Third, in D minor, dedicated to Richard Wagner, first version 1873, second version 1876–7, first performed in Vienna, 1877; the Fourth, in E♭ major, sometimes referred to as the "Romantic," first version 1874, second and third versions 1878–80, first performed in Vienna 1881; the Fifth, in B♭ major, sometimes referred to as the "Catholic," first version 1875–7, first performed in Graz 1894; the Sixth, in A major (1879–81), first performed 1899; the Seventh, in E major (1881–3), first performed in Leipzig 1884; the Eighth, in C minor, first version 1884–7, second version 1889–90, first performed in Vienna 1892; and the Ninth, in D minor, only the first three movements completed and the finale sketched out (1887–96), first performed in Vienna 1903.

Turn of the Century

Gustav Mahler was the last composer in the German-speaking area who placed the focal point of his creative activity in the symphony and belonged to the great historical tradition of Austrian-German and Czech music. Born at Kalischt, in Bohemia, on July 7, 1860, he died in Vienna on May 18, 1911. He studied in Vienna at the Conservatory and the University, where he was a pupil of Bruckner. After a brilliant career as opera conductor at theaters in Olomouc, Prague, Leipzig, Budapest (in 1888), and Hamburg, he was leader of the Viennese Hofoper from 1897 to 1907, and then guest conductor at the Metropolitan Opera in New York and leader of the Philharmonic Society in New York. As a conductor he was a highly significant interpreter, through his selfless and even fanatical devotion to the work of music.

His compositions include nine symphonies and an unfinished Tenth, a symphony *Das Lied von der Erde*, a choral work *Das klagende Lied*, songs with orchestra, and songs with piano. The symphonies are: the First, in D major, after Jean Paul's *Titan*, composed 1885–8, first performed 1889; the Second, in C minor, completed in 1894, in five movements with alto solo *Urlicht* or Original Light and Klopstock's *Auferstehen* or Resurrection as chorus, first performed in 1895; the Third, in D minor, completed in 1896, first performed in 1902, the *Lied vom grossen Pan* or Song of the Great God Pan, with alto solo and children's choir; the Fourth, in G major, 1899–1900, first performed in 1901, with soprano solo; the Fifth, in C♯ minor, 1901–2, first performed in 1904; the Sixth, in A minor, 1903–4, first performed in 1906; the Seventh, in B minor, 1904–5, first performed in 1908; the Eighth, in E♭ major, 1906–7, for double choir, soli, and orchestra, the so-called *Symphony of the Thousand*, first performed in 1910. It contains in the first part a setting of the Whitsun hymn *Veni creator spiritus* and in the second part the final scene of Goethe's *Faust* II; the Ninth, in D major (1908–9), first performed in 1912; and the Tenth, unfinished, of which two movements were first performed in 1924. Mahler himself was responsible for the programmatic titles, but cancelled them before publication. The song cycle *Das Lied von der Erde*, Song of Earth, is also basically symphonic. Composed in 1908, it was first performed in 1911.

In individual movements of his symphonies Mahler approaches program music but does not depict particular incidents in a musically realistic manner. Instead, he grasps the general expression of the mood. For him, as for Wagner, the word was the vehicle of the musical idea. In many instances, however, he did not explicitly name his literary or pictorial originals. He enlarged the performance mechanism—in the Eighth Symphony, for instance, by bringing in such unusual resources as a children's choir, two mixed choirs, and eight solo voices, each with eight-fold woodwinds. In so doing, he was also willfully enlarging the cyclic form of the symphony in terms of its content, under the influence of metaphysical ideas. He maintained, however, a type of musical expression that was predominantly lyrical. In his later works, such as the *Lied von der Erde* and the Ninth Symphony, he sometimes resolved the vocal lines into very sharply differentiated instrumentation almost like that of chamber music.

Unquestionably, of all symphonists after Beethoven, Mahler entered into the Beethovenian heritage with the greatest sense of authority, administered it most fruitfully, and developed it most extensively. Not only did he excel all others in the panoramic nature of his artistic visions, but also he won from the form of the symphony the most manifold and rich nuances. Beethoven had already paved the way for the principle of steady development in his *Eroica* and his Ninth Symphony, and this principle became more and more logically definite in Mahler, as greater and greater tension was created in the separate parts of the form without any lapses into incoherence. His late works prepared the way for the "Viennese atonal school" of Schönberg, Berg, and Webern. Like them, he had roots deep in the Austrian musical tradition. As an experienced conductor, he had at his disposal a remarkable sense of instrumentation, which he never used as an end in itself but always introduced to realize his artistic intentions and make his intellectual and emotional aims clear.

Program Symphony and Symphonic Poem

On the History of Program Music

"Program music" means music that expresses something objective—usually processes in nature or human life—and establishes this intention in its title. The existence of program music goes back, in a sense, to our very earliest indications of conscious music-making; but its importance in the 19th century is based on an assumption that had been widely made as early as the century before, that the value of music resided alone in its ability to fulfill tasks of painting, description, and representation. Every composition, accordingly, was always to be based on a program—on what Schering has called a "quite definite, objectively present segment of reality." While Schering considered the discovery of an "esoteric program" indispensable to the interpretation of music, Kretschmar in his explanations was satisfied with "establishing the emotional effect." Here we observe two different points of view, either of which can be easily pushed to an extreme. The results of such extremism necessarily appear in any general consideration of the 19th century as a whole. An extremist of one camp, such as Hanslick, is willing to grant validity only to an "absolute" music, an art of "tonally actuated forms," with "no other aim than the music itself." Extremists on the other side make similar claims for "expression." These opposites outline the sharp confrontation that can take place between emphasis on content and emphasis on form.

Many well-known instrumental pieces of the 16th, 17th, and early 18th centuries expressly indicate programmatic subjects. This is particularly true in the keyboard music of the English virginalists, Froberger, Couperin, Rameau, and Kuhnau, as well as in the violin music of Biber and Tartini, and in the instrumental concerti of Vivaldi, such as his *Cimento dell'Armonia*, op. 8.

During the latter half of the 18th century, programmatic ideas made their way into symphonic literature. Examples of such program symphonies are the *Musikalische Instrumental-Kalender,* or Calendar of Musical Instruments (1748), of Haydn's predecessor in office at Eisenstadt, Gregor Joseph Werner (d. 1766); the *Sinfonia burlesca* and the *Military Symphony* of Leopold Mozart (d. 1787); the symphony *Le Portrait musical de la Nature* (1784) of Heinrich Knecht; the *Telemachus*

Symphony of Anton Rosetti (though the music of it is not extant); and the twelve symphonies on Ovid's *Metamorphoses* that Dittersdorf composed in 1783–5. Some composers (including Stamitz, Haydn, Leopold Mozart, Gossec, and Wranitzky) wrote hunting symphonies; others (including Knecht, Cannabich, Toëschi, and Beethoven), pastoral symphonies, celebrating nature. In addition to his Sixth or *Pastoral* Symphony, Beethoven composed *Wellington's Victory or the Battle of Vittoria* (op. 91), first performed in 1813. Many composers around the turn of the century also wrote battle symphonies.

Program Symphony and Symphonic Poem in the 19th Century

The history of the program symphony after Beethoven was introduced by Hector Berlioz. Berlioz was born in Côte-Saint-André (Isère) on December 11, 1803, and died in Paris on March 8, 1869. At first he was a student of medicine; then he became a pupil of Lesueur and Reicha and was strongly influenced by Gluck, Beethoven, and the French Romantic movement in literature. In 1828 and 1830 he was selected for the Prix de Rome, but otherwise did not receive in France the appreciation that was his due. Lively interest in him, however, was shown on his concert tours in Germany, Austria, and Russia from 1843 to 1847. In 1852, and again in 1855, Liszt arranged a Berlioz Week in Weimar. In Paris he was a library attendant at the Conservatory and in 1852 became the librarian. Along with his work as a composer he was responsible for extensive literary activity. In this he took an indefatigable stand for new art, which at that time meant largely program music.

Berlioz was the main point of departure for the history of French music in the 19th century. His significance is three-fold: as the "great liberator" of 19th-century French music from foreign domination both Italian and German, as founder of a distinctly French Romantic movement, and as the first to wean France away from Wagner. Berlioz was one of the most stimulating personalities in the history of 19th-century European music, with long-range influence on the Neo-German School. His music, by its nature energetic, is thoroughly conceived in orchestral colors and communicates ideas, states of mind, and suggestions that go beyond strictly musical limits. Thus, in a way, his works are theatrical, descriptive, extreme, bold, and typical of a certain aspect of French music. It is, moreover, thoroughly autobiographical, and reaches far beyond its period in the means, form, and expression that underlie it. Using the orchestra as his medium, Berlioz created a completely new idiom, the particular nature of which is still today operative. In connection with the modernity of his artistic intentions, Berlioz experienced many vicissitudes of recognition and affirmation and of rejection, irony, and scorn in the course of his life, which in this respect was filled with a deep sense of the tragic. In his character—and, correspondingly, in his music—we find for the first time an essentially modern dissociation of sensibility, along with its artistic representation.

His works include five symphonies, eight overtures to operas and plays, a Requiem (1837), two oratorios (*The Infancy of Christ* and *The Damnation of Faust*), a *Te Deum*, and three operas. The symphonies, in detail, are *Symphonie fantastique* (1830), first called *Episode from the Life of an Artist*, in five movements: Dreams-Passions, A Ball, In the Country, Procession to the Gallows, and Witches' Sabbath, with the *idée fixe* as the intellectual and musical leitmotif of the work; *Lélio, or The Return to Life* (1831), a melodramatic continuation of the *Symphonie fantastique; Harold en Italie* (1834), inspired by Byron's *Childe Harold's Pilgrimage* and originally intended as a concert piece with viola for Paganini; *Roméo et Juliette*, a dramatic symphony with soli and choruses in seven movements (1839); and *Symphonie funèbre et triomphale* (1840).

As for the particular qualities and significance of his compositions, they are connected with the art of characterization and illustration of the classical French ballet, of Lully's and Rameau's operas, and of clavecin music. They are also connected with Beethoven's *Pastoral Symphony*, with the French Romantic Movement as it found expression in the writings of Chateaubriand and Victor Hugo, and with Shakespeare and Lord Byron. Highly gifted with a significant sense for musical description and painting and the courage to dare something new, Berlioz wrote program music that has continued to exert considerable influence. Through his new instrumental effects, through the complete individualization of the various instruments, and through realistic tone-painting and the expansion of symphonic form, Berlioz exercised first an extensive influence on Liszt and Wagner, and in the latter half of the 19th century also on the younger French composers and the Neo-Romantic German school, including Strauss and Hausegger—and, more recently, on Arthur Honegger and Olivier Messiaen.

Perhaps more than any other one person, Franz Liszt was responsible for encouraging Berlioz and bringing the Neo-German School to concentrate on program music. Liszt's original compositions also exerted a powerful influence in the same direction. Franz Liszt was born of German ancestry in Raiding, Hungary, on October 22, 1811, and died in Bayreuth on July 31, 1886.

Having studied piano under Czerny and composition under Salieri, he was presented as a child prodigy in Vienna, and on his first public appearance in 1822 he aroused Beethoven's admiration. After moving to Paris, Liszt was a composition pupil of Paër and Reicha. The young artist was formed in Paris by the Romantic movement in literature. A close artistic friendship linked him with Berlioz and Chopin. This first great epoch in Liszt's life had its high point in the virtuoso period and the triumphal tours from 1839 to 1847. During these years he was highly successful in his concerts, brought his virtuosity to unprecedented heights, wrote piano works of increasing significance, and championed the music of Beethoven in an exemplary way.

The second great epoch in Liszt's life began in 1848 with his activity as master of the court chapel in Weimar, where he became the center of the Neo-German School. During this period he wrote his great orchestral works. Indefatigably and selflessly taking a stand for new composition—giving, for example, the first performance of *Lohengrin* in 1850 —Liszt founded in 1861 the Allgemeine deutsche Musikverein.

In 1861 the third phase of his life began. Liszt, who took minor holy orders in 1865 in Rome, was much of the time on tour and regularly moved between Rome, Weimar, and Budapest. During this period he composed his sacred works and oratorios.

In his day Liszt was a unique personality with a deeply fascinating power, captivating those with whom he came in contact not only by his dazzling artistry but also by his human qualities of kindness and readiness to help others, notably as exemplified by his friendship with Richard Wagner. Liszt greatly stimulated and encouraged the music of his century and beyond, through many features of his activity. He conveyed striking ideas that combined music and poetry in his symphonic poems and his keyboard rhapsodies. His harmony, with its chromatic and enharmonic aspects, was of bold and surprising innovation, as was also his instrumentation. His activity as a piano virtuoso was unique, and as a teacher he had a very far-reaching effect. He had numerous pupils and still today lives on in the pupils of his pupils as well as in his piano compositions.

He specifically designated two of his works as symphonies, the *Faust* and the *Dante*. The *Faust Symphony* (1854) is in three characteristic pictures: Faust, Gretchen, and Mephisto, and as conclusion the Chorus Mysticus for men's chorus and tenor solo. The *Dante Symphony* in two movements—*Inferno* and *Purgatorio* with choral ending—was completed in 1856.

Liszt also composed the following thirteen "symphonic poems": *Was man auf den Bergen hört* (completed in 1849 but extant in three versions), after a poem by Victor Hugo; *Tasso, Lamento e Trionfo* (1849, with a final version in 1854); *Les Préludes* (written in 1848, later revised), with a foreword from Lamartine's *Méditations; Orpheus* (1854); *Prometheus* (1850, revised in 1855), conceived as an overture for Herder's *Der entfesselte Prometheus; Mazeppa* (1851), after Victor Hugo; *Festklänge*, intended as festival music in 1853 for his anticipated marriage with Countess Wittgenstein; *Heldenklage*, going back to an idea of a Revolution Symphony, of 1830; *Hungaria* (1854); *Hunnenschlacht* (1857), inspired by Kaulbach's painting; *Die Ideale* (1857), after Schiller; *Von der Wiege bis zum Grabe* (1811–2); and *Hamlet* (1858). Priest of art, he ranged widely over the works of man.

The particular features and significance of Liszt's symphonic compositions focus on his creation of the "symphonic poem" as a new type. In this he was stimulated by Berlioz's program music. A Liszt symphonic poem is in a single movement. As artistic plan he chose four different ideological areas: material that had to do with philosophy and worldview, material of a literary character, pictorial ideas, and the world of his own experience. The programs often undertook only to direct the listener to the general character of a picture. The music was less a realistic representation of a dramatic course of action than an exploitation of the mood-content. Many aspects of these works were quite new, at least as musical means placed in the service of poetic expression: the great heroic and often theatrical nature of the themes, the lyrical impetus, the bold tone-painting, the pioneering harmonic aspects, and the orchestral effects that influenced the whole century. As an example of tone-painting, Liszt's first symphonic poem, *Was man auf den Bergen hört*, represents the impression made on him by the Alps. Formally, symphonic poems developed from the Romantic piano fantasy and the opera overture of the Classic and Romantic periods. The sonata-allegro form remained often recognizable in clear outlines.

The *Dante Symphony* corresponded formally to two symphonic poems. Following the model of Beethoven and Berlioz, Liszt introduced a chorus in the second movement. The *Faust Symphony* was, in its overall layout, a symphony with the Allegro, Adagio, and Scherzo sequence of movements. The coda was laid out as in a cantata.

During the latter half of the 19th century music was the characteristic expression of Romantic realism, culminating in the symphonic poems of Liszt and Strauss. Composers usually chose to work with materials that suggested images and symbols of the lofty aspects of a world-view or of the history of mankind. The presentation, however, lacked the innocence and spontaneity that had been characteristic of the historical Romantic era. The means through which the composer wished to work were—particularly with Strauss—more and more strongly calculated for the effect that they would make upon a broad circle of listeners.

There were also many other composers at this time actively writing program music. Joachim Raff (1822–1882)—a pupil of Liszt, and later active as teacher in Wiesbaden and Frankfurt am Main—composed eleven symphonies, including *Im Walde, Leonore,* and *In den Alpen.* Alexander Ritter (1833–1896), of great influence on Richard Strauss in his youth, wrote numerous symphonic poems.

The most significant representative of program music in Germany after Liszt was Richard Strauss (1864–1949), who was also a significant opera composer. He was particularly successful in fusing form and content, structure and subject matter. *Till Eulenspiegel* is in rondo form; *Don Quichote* is a set of ten variations; *Tod und Verklärung* is in sonata allegro form. Strauss had a musical idiom entirely his own, a remarkable feeling for the illustrative, and a highly sensitive awareness of sonority, as well as a masterful ability to deal with large forms, linked with a rich gift of musical invention.

His symphonic poems are *Aus Italien* (1886), a symphonic fantasy in four movements; *Macbeth* (reworked in 1891); *Don Juan* (1889), after Lenau; *Tod und Verklärung,* or Death and Transfiguration (1890); *Till Eulenspiegels lustige Streiche,* or Till Eulenspiegel's Merry Pranks (1895); *Also sprach Zarathustra,* or Thus Spake Zoroaster (1896), after Nietzsche; *Don Quichote* (1898); and *Ein Heldenleben* (1899). His symphonies are a Symphony in F minor, op. 16 (1884); *Sinfonia Domestica* (1904), consisting of four parts in one movement; and *Alpensinfonie* (1915).

Around the turn of the century the program symphony in Germany predominated over the absolute symphonic form. Among numerous representatives are Siegmund von Hausegger (1872–1949), Hans Huber (1852–1921), August Klughardt (1847–1902), Philipp Scharwenka (1847–1917), and Friedrich Klose (1862–1942).

France after Berlioz

As early as the middle of the 19th century many French composers were following Berlioz's example in fusing symphonic form with the cantata. Félicien David (1810–1876), for example, wrote *Le Désert* (1844) and *Colomb* (1847). *Le Désert* is a symphony-ode with particularly strange musical effects, which were responsible for his assuming the leadership in an exotic trend. L. T. Lacombe (1818–1884), with his *Manfrède* (1847) and *Les Hongrois* (1850) also followed Berlioz, as did Ernest Reyer (1823–1909) with the symphony-ode *Le Sélam* (1850).

France made contact with the absolute symphonic form of the Germans most successfully in the work of Camille Saint-Saëns and César Franck.

Camille Saint-Saëns (1835–1921), who was originally an organist and later a free-lance composer in Paris, wrote five symphonies and four symphonic poems. His main work was his Symphony in C minor (1886), in four movements, of which the first two and the last two were to be continuous in performance. The melodic aspects of his work are under Gregorian influence, orchestrally enriched with organ and piano. In all four movements there is variation on the unifying thematic basis.

César Franck, who was born in Liège in 1822 and died in Paris in 1890, was of German ancestry. After studying under Reicha at the Paris Conservatoire, he became in 1844 an organ teacher there and was also active in Paris as a church musician. His significant symphonic masterpiece is his Symphony in D minor in three movements, composed in 1886–8, containing strong motivic work with contrasting and basically song-like themes.

During the latter half of the 19th century in France, there were both types of symphony—program and abstract—giving evidence of the combined influence of Berlioz, Liszt, and Wagner, as well as Franck's classicistic tendency. Edouard Lalo (1823–1892) in his Symphony in G minor (1885–6) showed particularly refined art in harmony and sonority. Charles-Marie Widor (1844–1937), in addition to organ works, wrote five symphonies. Vincent d'Indy (1851–1931), a French composer of Spanish ancestry and a pupil of Franck's, helped found the *Société Nationale de Musique* in 1871 and the *Schola Cantorum* (projected in 1894 and opened in 1896) and was of significant influence as a teacher, also composing three symphonies and symphonic poems. Ernest Chausson (1855–1899) composed a Symphony in B♭ major (1890). Gabriel Pierné (1863–1937) wrote various symphonic works. Paul Dukas (1865–1935) wrote a Symphony in C major (1896) as well as *The Sorcerer's Apprentice* (1897), a symphonic scherzo, based on a ballad by Goethe and notable for its significant instrumental color. Albert Roussel (1869–1937) proceeded from program to absolute music in his four symphonies, the First composed as *Poème de la Forêt* in 1908 and the Fourth, in A major, completed in 1935.

The symphonic idea received a character of its own through the musical Impressionism of Claude Debussy (1862–1918), whose activities figure also prominently under the heading of opera. Debussy's main composition of the symphonic type is *La Mer* (1905), but his compositions *Ibéria, Rondes de Printemps, Nuages, Prélude à l'après-midi d'un faune,* and *Jeux* are also well known. The subtitle of *La Mer* is "symphonic sketches." By the indication "sketches" the graphic element is suggested, and the subjects are wind, sea, atmosphere, light, and colors. They are treated, however, in a quite symphonic way, with exposition and development of themes; and the forms are centripetal. Impressionism utilizes primary forms of sonority and also self-moved columns of chords, frequently pentatonic in nature. *Jeux,* composed in 1912 and presented as a ballet in Paris in 1913, became a pioneering work for music at mid-century, through such features as its art of lines, which pointed toward serial composition.

Eastern Europe

Russia

The first symphonic works in Russia were written long before the activities of the "Five." One of these earlier Russian composers was Alexander Nikolaievich Aliabiev (1787–1851), who wrote songs and one symphony (1830). Michael Glinka (1804–1857), whose career figures in the development of Russian opera, also wrote an orchestral fantasy *Kamarinskaia* on two Russian folk-songs. Tchaikovsky said that this work contained the whole future of Russian symphonic music as the acorn contains the oak. Glinka also wrote his Spanish Overture No. 1 with the title *Jota Aragonesa* and No. 2 with the title *Night in Madrid,* as well as a *Waltz Fantasy.* Anton Rubinstein (1829–1894) composed six symphonies, of which the first three were written before 1850.

Of the members of the "Group of Five," Rimski-Korsakov, Musorgski, and Borodin brought out symphonic works:

Nikolai Rimski-Korsakov (1844–1908) wrote his first symphony in the last year of his world cruise in 1865. He composed, in all, three symphonies, the Second with the title *Antar.* He also wrote some symphonic poems, notably *Sadko,* and some symphonic suites, of which the best known is *Scheherazade.* From the point of view of orchestral color his work is especially significant.

Modest Musorgski (1839–1881) composed a symphonic poem, *A Night on Bald Mountain.*

Alexander Borodin (1833–1887) wrote three symphonies, the First in E♭ major (1862–7), the Second in B minor (1870–7), and the Third, left incomplete but finished by Glasunov. These are significant works, particularly on account of the national coloring, typical of the Russian symphonic art, which Laux has characterized as the "assertion of a certain content of emotional or objective nature, namely a content of specifically national and Russian cast." They display heroically stressed basic character, strongly emotional power, and distinguished formal workmanship.

Peter Ilich Tchaikovsky successfully brought together Russian national music and the Beethovenian symphony of ideas. He was born in

Votkinsk on May 7, 1840, in the *gouvernement* of Viatka, where his father was the director of the government mines. A sensitive child susceptible to musical impressions, he showed unusual musical abilities, which received further opportunities of development when in 1848 the family moved to Petersburg. After attending the law school in Petersburg until 1859, he entered the civil service in the Ministry of Justice, where he continued until 1863. In 1861, however, he had begun studying music at the Petersburg Conservatory, recently founded by Anton Rubinstein, where he was a pupil of Nikolai Zaremba and later also of Anton Rubinstein and where he completed his studies in 1865. From 1861 to 1877 while Tchaikovsky was in Moscow, his creative powers reached their full development and he began to win recognition. Here especially he was encouraged by Nikolai Rubinstein and the publisher Peter Jürgenson. The works he wrote during the Moscow period include the first four symphonies, the first four operas (of which the fourth is *Eugen Onegin*), the ballet *Swan Lake,* and the three string quartets. In Moscow Tchaikovsky was a teacher at the Conservatory and for a while music critic on the *Moscow News.* An unhappy and catastrophic marriage in 1877 brought on a severe inner crisis, from which with some difficulty he recovered. During this period he became acquainted with Nadia Filaretovna Meck (1831–1894), whose assistance made him financially independent and whose deep understanding—achieved entirely by correspondence—he was to enjoy until 1890. He gave up entirely his teaching activities in Moscow and lived only temporarily in Russia, otherwise traveling abroad. After seven years of wandering, he took up residence near Moscow. In 1892 he moved to the house which is today the Tchaikovsky Museum, in Klin near Moscow; but his world fame contributed greatly to the restlessness of his life, involving him in many tours and conducting obligations. On November 6, 1893, Tchaikovsky died of cholera in Petersburg.

Though in the breadth of his work Tchaikovsky is one of the almost universal composers, his main significance lies in instrumental music, particularly the symphony, and in opera. His music is everywhere felt to be thoroughly Russian. He had complete mastery of all aspects of form, particularly of the German, French, and Italian music of his time. He seems to have been more influenced by the world of Beethoven, Schumann, and Mendelssohn than by that of Liszt or Wagner. Impulses from Schumann were very important to him, leading him to write many genre pictures and miniatures. His last three symphonies are concerned with ideas, somewhat as is Beethoven's Fifth. As a result of his choice of material the operas have a quite special national character, intensified significantly by the sensitive nature of the music. The national peculiarity of the music arises stylistically from the way he has used folk-song, not only in the sense of quoting it as thematic material but also in the way he has worked it up symphonically. The music also has in it suggestions of urban songs, Russian gypsy melodies, and national dance tunes—as well as of the cultivated society dance, particularly the waltz. It also has great emotional breadth and contrast, and emphasizes the emotional element in general—features which have come to be felt as particularly Russian.

In addition to symphonic poems and overtures, he composed six symphonies: the First, in G minor, op. 13 (*Winter Dreams*, 1866), first performed in Moscow in 1868; the Second, in C minor, op. 17 (1872), first performed in Moscow in 1873; the Third, in D major, op. 29 (1875), first performed in Moscow in 1875; the Fourth, in F minor, op. 36 (1877), first performed in Moscow in 1878; the Fifth, in E minor, op. 64 (1888), first performed in Petersburg in 1888; the Sixth, in B minor, *Pathétique*, op. 74 (1893), first performed in Petersburg in 1893; and the *Manfred*, op. 58 (1885), first performed in Moscow in 1886.

The title of the First Symphony, *Winter Dreams*, is not a program but an intentional bit of guidance to the listener's imagination and receptivity, somewhat as Robert Schumann likewise anticipated in the title of his *Spring Symphony*. The Second was written in Kamenka, in the Ukraine, using suggestions of local motifs which are here worked up artfully into a symphonic whole. The Third has, on the other hand, a "Western" appearance, with its invented themes. It shows the influence of Schumann, for example, in its having five movements as does Schumann's *Rhenish Symphony;* at the same time, it points ahead to the later symphonies. The last three are symphonies of ideas, like those of Beethoven. Tchaikovsky wrote of his Fourth: "My symphony is programmatic, but the program is such that it cannot be formulated in words. . . . Basically my symphony is an imitation of the Fifth Symphony of Beethoven . . . so far as the idea is concerned." Something similar applies also to his Fifth and Sixth Symphonies. The last three are masterpieces, universally significant among Tchaikovsky's compositions. Beethoven conveyed a peculiar power and sense of fate, but Tchaikovsky reformulated these aspects imposingly and overwhelmingly. The thought of the ideal, which is basic to the work, is suggested even in the slow introduction, and thematically permeates the whole symphony.

Tchaikovsky's works include ten operas, three ballets, six symphonies, orchestral suites, overtures and symphonic poems, three piano concerti, other piano works, many pieces of chamber music, notably three string quartets, a violin concerto, cantatas, choruses, songs, and duets.

Right to the present, much Russian musical creative activity has focused on the symphony. Outstanding works have been written by Alexander Scriabin (1872–1915), with three symphonies (the First in E major, op. 26, 1900–1; the Second in C major, op. 29, 1902; and the Third, op. 43, *Le Poème Divin*, 1903–4) and the one-movement symphonic poems *Le Poème de l'Extase*, op. 54 (1905–7) and *Prometheus*, op. 60 (1909–10); Alexander Konstantinovich Glasunov (1865–1936), with eight symphonies; Sergei Wassilievitch Rachmaninoff (1873–1943), with three symphonies; Nikolai Yakovlevich Miaskovski (1881–1950), with twenty-seven symphonies; Sergei Sergeevich Prokofiev (1891–1953), with seven symphonies; and Dmitri Dmitrievich Shostakovich (b. 1906), with thirteen symphonies.

Czechoslovakia

In the history of the symphony and the symphonic poem, Czechoslovakia has a remarkable place of its own. The Czech musical emigration of the 18th century had already made a significant contribution. The real history of Czech national music, both in opera and in the symphony, however, began with Bedřich Smetana (1824–1884). The center of his symphonic work was the cycle of symphonic poems *Má vlast,* or My Native Land, consisting of *Vyšehrad* (1874); *Vltava,* or The Moldau (1874); *Šárka* (1875); *Z českých luhů a hájů,* or From Bohemia's Woods and Fields (1875); *Tábor* (1878); and *Blaník* (1879). During his stay in Sweden, Smetana wrote three symphonic poems somewhat along the lines of the Lisztian school: *Richard III* (1858); *Valdštýnův tábor,* or Wallenstein's Camp (1859); and *Hakon Jarl* (1861). In the cycle *Má vlast* he created a type of symphonic poem of his own. Musically and dramatically he was independent of any literary model and instead proceeded from a musical and poetic basis, relying entirely on the poetic content. He also wrote program chamber music, including an autobiographical string quartet in E minor entitled *From My Life* (1876) and another string quartet in D minor (1882–3).

The other great figure from early Czech national music was Antonín Dvořák, who was born in Nelahozeves on September 8, 1841. From 1857 to 1859 he studied at the Prague school for organists. Then he became violist in the orchestra at Komzák, which in 1862 was developed into the orchestra of the provisional theater in Prague. Dvořák continued in that capacity until 1873. Then, on Hanslick's and Brahms's recommendation, he received an Austrian state stipend from 1874 to 1878. During these years his individuality as a composer became more and more marked, and the issuing of his *Klänge aus Mähren* and his *Slavische Tänze* in 1878 by the Berlin publisher Fritz Simrock and the efforts of the conductors Hans von Bülow and Hans Richter on behalf of his works began to pave the way for his world success. After Dvořák, rich in practical experience, had given up the orchestra in 1873, he assumed the position of organist at St. Adalbert's Church in Prague. The constantly growing international recognition of his work gradually gave him financial independence and prompted his making extensive concert tours abroad. In 1890 he received an honorary doctorate from Cambridge University and in 1891 from the Czech University in Prague. In the same year he accepted a professorship at the Prague Conservatory. This teaching responsibility he carried on to the end of his life, interrupted only from 1892 to 1895 when he was director of the privately organized National Conservatory in New York. In 1892 he was named the artistic director of the Prague Conservatory, and in 1901 its head. He died in Prague on May 1, 1904. The success won by many of his works yielded countless evidences of the high regard in which he was held by his native land and by the entire world.

As a composer Dvořák was first trained in the Classic and then in the Romantic manner. Eventually he discovered the Neo-German world of Liszt and Wagner. In 1874, however, he departed from it in order to find his own particular nature in the Slavic world. In contrast to Smetana, who drew his inspiration from Czech folk-song, Dvořák reveled in the rhythmic and harmonic riches of Czech and Moravian folk-song and eventually went farther into the folk heritage of the Eastern and

Southeastern parts of Europe until he arrived at the melodic sources of Slovakia, Ukraine, and Yugoslavia. In some compositions that he wrote in America he undertook to absorb American folk-song and the Negro Spiritual. Dvořák's complete work now and then reflects influences and suggestions that have come from the Neo-German School, but it also reflects still more certain influences that have come from the school that Brahms represented. Thus Dvořák almost always adopted a naive and pure relationship to folk-music and to spontaneous experience, reminding one in this respect of Schubert. Dvořák was Czech and accordingly quite national in his ties with the joy of singing and dancing; this was the source of the rhythmic power of his music, his joy in the sound of the instruments, and his basically optimistic attitude toward life. Gifted with extraordinary productiveness, he wrote music of all types, to achieve his most significant work in the pure musical forms of the symphony and chamber music.

His works included ten operas, nine symphonies, symphonic poems, overtures, concerti (one for piano, one for violin, and two for 'cello), chamber music, piano compositions, songs, choruses, and church music.

His nine symphonies are the First, in C minor (*The Bells of Zlonitz*), written in 1865, first performed in 1936, in Brno; the Second, in B♭ major, op. 4, written in 1865, revised and first performed in 1888, in Prague; the Third, in E♭ major, op. 10, written in 1873, first performed in 1874, in Prague; the Fourth, in D minor, op. 13, written in 1874, first performed in 1892, in Prague; the Fifth, in F major, op. 76, written in 1875, first performed in 1879, in Prague; the Sixth, in D major, written in 1880, first performed in 1881, in Prague; the Seventh, in D minor, op. 70, written in 1885, first performed in 1885, in London; the Eighth, in G major, op. 88, written in 1889, first performed in 1890, in Prague; and the Ninth, in E minor, *From the New World,* op. 95, written and first performed in 1893, in New York.

Dvořák in his youth had been concerned with the music of Liszt and Wagner. But in his period of maturity he encountered that of Brahms and thus became involved in Classical music, the form and character of which had a decisive effect on him. At the same time, this formal heritage was linked with the musical idiom of his people. He united original musicianship, great melodic richness, and rhythmic flow with a certain trained formal power. Quite apart from his place in Czech musical history, his nine symphonies, as instances parallel to those of Brahms and Bruckner, produced evidence that the history of the symphony after Beethoven could be carried on further with significance and independence also in the nonprogrammatic area. In the history of Czech music Dvořák is considered the real founder of the modern Czech symphony. As a composer of symphonies he is of world importance. His First and Second Symphonies were written in the period of his artistic beginnings. His Third Symphony, written eight years later, shows the influence of Wagner and Liszt, but already possesses a character of its own, which in the Fourth and Fifth Symphonies is more distinctly marked. After an interruption of five years, he wrote his Sixth Symphony, in which he attained mastery of technique and the full national idiom. Composed in New

York and numbered Ninth in order of composition, *From the New World* has enjoyed special favor.

Zdeněk Fibich (1850–1900) completed three symphonies (in F major, op. 17, 1883; in E♭ major, op. 38, 1893; and in E minor, op. 53, 1898) and the symphonic poem *V podvečer,* or Evening Twilight (1893). In Fibich's artistic career there were approximately three stages, during the last of which there is a predominance of the Late Romantic inclination toward nature and related tendencies characteristic of the turn of the century.

Josef Bohuslav Foerster (1859–1951) composed five symphonies, of which the third is entitled *Life* (1896), and the fourth *Magnificent Night* (1905). He also wrote the symphonic poem *My Youth* (1900) and the orchestral suite *Cyrano de Bergerac* (1903).

Vítězslav Novák (1870–1949), a pupil of Dvořák, became professor at the Prague Conservatory in 1909 and professor of the master class in 1920. At this time he founded the Modern Music Society, which later was transformed into the Czech section of the International Society for Contemporary Music. As a teacher he exerted significant and lasting influence, particularly on leading Slovak composers of today. He composed abundantly in all fields: *Slovácká suita* (1903); symphonic poems *V Tatrách* (1902); *O věčné touze,* or Of Eternal Longing (1904); *Toman a lesní panna,* or Toman and the Forest Sprite (1907); *Podzimní symfonie,* or Autumn Symphony (1931–4); *Jihočeská suita,* or South Bohemian Suite (1937); and *Májová symfonie,* or May Symphony (1943). He has often been referred to—not with complete accuracy—as a Czech representative of Impressionism. He was more than that—one of the foremost Czech masters of polyphony, and at the same time a composer whose work was inspired by Moravian and Slovakian folk-songs.

Josef Suk (1874–1935), also a pupil of Dvořák and second violinist in the Bohemian String Quartet, became professor of composition at the Prague Conservatory in 1923. An inheritor of Dvořák's lyricism, he wrote inclusive symphonic works, marked by deep and fateful personal crises: *Asrael,* or Symphony of the Angel of Death; *Anděl smrti* (1906); *Pohádka léta,* or A Summer Fairy-Tale (1908); *Zrání,* or Maturity (1917); and *Epilog* (1929). He was the principal representative of new trends in Czech symphonic composition that took the purely subjective as its point of departure.

Otakar Ostrčil (1879–1935), a pupil of Fibich, has been often called a Czech representative of Expressionism. His first work in the new style was his *Impromptu* (1911). Among his mature works are his Suite in C minor (1912); *Sinfonietta* (1921); the symphonic poem *Léto,* or Summer (1925–6);·and *Křížová cesta,* or The Crossroad (1928). Though close to the world of Mahler, he was independent of the tradition, being a Czech champion of so-called New Objectivity in modern polyphonic style.

Leoš Janáček (1854–1928), important in both operatic and orchestral composition, was the creator of a completely different and original world. His works include *Lašské tance,* or Lachish Dances (1889–90), an early composition. The culminating compositions of his mature period are the three-movement rhapsody *Taras Bulba* (1918) and the five-movement *Sinfonietta* (1926). Janáček's Expressionism was a matter of his favoring expression over form. Like Smetana, he was a consistent representative of Realism, of the direct comprehension of actual life—that is, in the unrepeatable musical uniqueness of the given moment. Hence the basic and peculiar monothematicism characteristic of his style, growing out of the unified mood of the living moment which Janáček wished to capture. Hence also his typical technique of repetition. He preferred to let the same chord sound through several metrical units, or he altered it against the background of the psychologically presupposed situation and awareness. Moreover, he established ostinati of basic rhythms, which were combined with uninterrupted changes of the rhythmic details. In this respect he showed a relationship to the *cifrování*, or ciphering principle, and to the technique of folk-like variation in general. Typical of Janáček's over-all style was a preference for static variation form and special fragmentation and suite-like succession. The characteristic figurations, moreover, gave structure to the form and expression.

Bohuslav Martinů (1890–1959) wrote six symphonies between 1942 and 1953, in the fullness of his mature creative work, carrying on from Dvořák and strongly influenced by Roussel and Stravinsky. These compositions have a new monumental and dramatic quality, representative of the modern Czech symphony. In the last period of his creative work he composed several symphonic poems.

National Slovakian music began with the collecting and harmonizing of Slovakian folk-songs. The first significant Slovakian composer, Ján Levoslav Bella (1843–1936), shared in this activity and also composed a symphonic poem, *Osud a ideál,* or Fate and the Ideal (1874, revised in 1880). There was an active group of Slovakian composers, including Mikuláš Moyzes, Mikuláš Schneider-Trnavský, Viliam Figuš-Bystrý, and Frico Kafenda. Carrying on further in directions indicated by Novák and this older group of composers, a younger generation has come to expression, including Alexander Moyzes (b. 1906), Eugen Suchoň (b. 1908), Jan Cikker (b. 1911), and Dezider Kardoš (b. 1914).

Poland

In the chapels of the Polish churches, monasteries, and cities during the latter half of the 18th century there was intensive cultivation of the sinfonia. Many works of Viennese, Mannheim, Bohemian, Italian, and French antecedents were performed in the churches of Warsaw, Poznan, Cracow, Grodzisk, Gnesen, Borek, and Mogiła. Often the players had before them the first copies of Haydn's works of the 1760's. The first symphonies written by many Polish composers were within the sphere of influence of the Neapolitan school and the early Viennese style. Gradually the making of music in church progressed to higher artistic forms for the trained listener, incorporating strong folk influence such as the rhythms of the mazurka, polonaise, and cracovienne, as well as the melodies of folk-songs.

During the first third of the 19th century, however, the chapels in the churches declined, and the cultivation of symphonic music became the task of the theater ensemble and of amateurs who were still functioning within the domestic circle. Symphonies were written principally by composers who were connected with the theater, such as Elsner, Kurpiński, and Nidecki. The program symphony representing historical events was particularly popular, such as Elsner's symphony on the Battle of Iskahar (1797) and Kurpiński's symphony *The Battle of Moshajsk* (1812). Józef Elsner (1766–1854), Franciszek Mirecki (1791–1862), and Józef Nowakowski (1800–1865) composed symphonies in accordance with the models of the Viennese Classical era. Early Romantic elements appeared in a symphonic fragment of Franciszek Lessel (about 1780–1835). The Second Symphony (1834) of Elsner's pupil Ignacy Feliks Dobrzyński (1807–1867) is notable: in 1836 awarded a prize in a competition held by the Gesellschaft der Musikfreunde in Vienna, it has the subtitle "Characteristic of the Spirit of Polish Music" and contains folk material in all movements—one of the first symphonies in musical literature to be constructed entirely of folk themes.

Since there were few regular symphony orchestras, smaller forms —such as the overture, fantasy, and suite—were much more in evidence. This was a reason for the tendency to stress a program in compositions of the "Romantic" period. The first attempt was the concert overture *Fairy Tale* by Stanisław Moniuszko (1819–1872) in rhapsodic form as a series of pictures. The generation after Moniuszko made an even more substantial contribution. In addition to Stanisław Duniecki (1839–1870) and Aleksander Zarzycki (1834–1895) there were also Władysław Żeleński and Zygmunt Noskowski.

Władysław Żeleński (1837–1921) wrote two symphonies in the Romantic tradition and two significant concert overtures, *In the Tatra* (1871) and *Forest Echo* (1888), connected with folk-song and folk-dance and containing elements that stressed tone color.

Zygmunt Noskowski (1846–1909) composed a classicistic First Symphony (1873–1875); an overture, *Eye of the Sea* (1875), his first symphonic poem, containing elements of Tatra folklore; a Second or Elegiac Symphony (1875–9); a symphonic poem *The Steppe* (1896–7), Noskowski's best orchestral composition with Slavic melody and chromatic harmony; and a Third Symphony, *From Spring to Spring* (1904), on life in a Polish village.

The symphonic poem had its greatest Polish representative in Mieczysław Karłowicz (1876–1909). After studying in Warsaw and Berlin, he became a noted violinist and director, serving in 1904 as director of the Warsaw Musical Association. In 1906 he joined the "Young Poland" group, which had been founded in 1905 by Ludomir Różycki and Grzegorz Fitelberg and included among its later members Apolinary Szeluto and Szymanowski. This group tried to draw away from the epigones of Moniuszko and to follow Neo-Romantic tendencies such as those in Strauss. Karłowicz wrote the symphonic poems *Returning Waves* (1903), *Three Eternal Songs* (1906), *Lithuanian Rhapsody* (1906), *Stanisław and Anna Oświecim* (1906–1907), *Sad Story* (1908), and *Episodes from the Masked Ball* (sketched in 1908, completed in 1911 by

G. Fitelberg). These works are related to those of Strauss in that they suggest psychological and philosophical problems and tend to stress a program. Harmonically they derive from Wagner's *Tristan*, with its dark colors. Melodically they show both German and Slavic influences—or, more specifically, the influence of Strauss and Tchaikovsky—yet these influences are enriched with special lyrical qualities. Along with Szymanowski, Karłowicz was the most renowned of the Neo-Romantic Polish writers of symphonies.

A number of composers belong to the same generation as Karłowicz: Ignacy Jan Paderewski (1860–1941), Emil Młynarski (1870–1935), Zygmunt Stojowski (1869–1946), Henryk Opieński (1870–1942), Feliks Nowowiejski (1877–1946), Grzegorz Fitelberg (1879–1953), and Ludomir Różycki (1884–1953).

Karol Szymanowski was born in Tymoshovka in the Ukraine on October 6, 1882. In 1902 he began to study theory in Warsaw with Marek Zawirski and then composition with Zygmunt Noskowski. In 1914 he traveled to Italy and Sicily, Tunis, Paris, and London, coming in contact with the newest tendencies as represented by Debussy, Ravel, and Stravinsky. In 1919 he returned to Warsaw, becoming in 1927 director of the Warsaw Conservatory and, after its reorganization, rector of the Music Academy. In 1929 he won the first prize awarded by the state for music, and in 1930 he received an honorary doctorate from the Jagiellon University in Cracow. Also about this time he began to win increasing recognition abroad. For reasons of health, as he was suffering from tuberculosis, he was often in Switzerland and France and in Zakopane, where he came into contact with Tatra folk-music, which strongly influenced the third period of his work. His writings also include a series of valuable works on the aesthetics of music. He died in Lausanne on March 29, 1937.

There were three periods in his creative activity. Before beginning to study with Noskowski, he had strong connections with the tradition of Polish Romantic music, and at the same time used Neo-Romantic means such as those of Wagner, Scriabin, and Strauss, as well as of Brahms and Reger. The greatest successes of this period were his Second Symphony (1909) and Second Piano Sonata (1910). The opera *Hagith* (1912) is a transitional work, showing influences of Strauss and a tendency to modernize the idiom through the chromatic sonority and harmony of Impressionism. Szymanowski's Impressionism, however, has a dynamic character. Among the outstanding works of this period are the piano cycles *Metopes* (1915) and *Masks* (1917), the violin cycle *Myths* (1915), and the First Violin Concerto (1917). Next there was a very brief period consisting of compositions in "pure form": the Third Sonata (1917) and the First String Quartet (1917). Then, early in 1920, Szymanowski achieved a style very much his own, for which analogies—rather than models—are to be discovered in the work of Stravinsky or Bartók. He simplified the composition and clarified the harmony, avoiding complicated polyphony and insisting on strict rhythm. In *King Roger* and in his *Stabat mater* there is a tendency to archaism, and in his Mazurkas, *Harnasie*, and Second Violin Concerto there is infusion of folk-lore, particularly from Kurpie and the Tatra Highlands. The character of

Szymanowski's music is always deeply subjective, ecstatic, and somewhat dramatic, pathetic, and contemplatively mystical.

His Overture op. 12 (1905), First Symphony (1907), and Second Symphony (1909) come from the first creative period, being of a Romantic and Neo-Romantic character. The Second Symphony is the last and most mature work of this period, combining the sonata, variation and fugue, and polyphony. The Third Symphony (1916), which is really a cantata for soprano, chorus, and orchestra, with a text after the Persian poet Mevlan Jelaleddin Rumi, contains Orientalisms, with Debussy's coloristic sonority but of a strongly dynamic character of Szymanowski's own, in its power closely connected with Expressionism. The Fourth Symphony, *Concertante*, for piano and orchestra (1932) was written within his third period of composition, in which there is notable simplification and use of folklore. In his ballet with chorus *Harnasie* (Paris 1936) he revealed mastery of orchestral treatment, traces of Impressionistic chromaticism, strict stylization of the music of the Tatragoral peoples, and bold rhythmic motifs, with occasional tectonic significance.

Further composers of symphonies include Witold Maliszewski (1873–1939), Eugeniusz Morawski (1876–1948), Piotr Rytel (b. 1884), Bolesław Wallek-Walewski (1885–1944), Łucjan Kamieński (1885–1964), Czesław Marek (b. 1891), Tadeusz Szeligowski (1896–1963), Kazimierz Sikorski (b. 1896), Bolesław Szabelski (b. 1896), Aleksander Tansman (b. 1897), Józef Koffler (1897–1943?), Jan Adam Maklakiewicz (1899–1954), Piotr Perkowski (b. 1901), Michał Kondracki (b. 1902), Jerzy Fitelberg (1903–1951), Roman Palester (b. 1907), Antoni Szałowski (b. 1907), Arthur Malawski (1904–1957), Grażyna Bacewicz (b. 1913), Witold Lutosławski (b. 1913), Andrzej Panufnik (b. 1914), Michał Spisak (1914–1965), Kazimierz Serocki (b. 1922), Stanisław Skrowaczewski (b. 1923), and Tadeusz Baird (b. 1928).

Scandinavian Countries

From the very first, symphonic writing in the North was closely linked with foreign models. But with the 19th-century spread of Romantic nationalism, the symphony in the North underwent a development which cannot be quite characterized in terms of Romantic realism and Classicism. Though the symphony held its own, it also fused with the overture, the concerto, and the symphonic poem into a form in which there scarcely seems to be any point in trying to keep the old genres sharply separated. Romantic realism with its stylistic peculiarities remained basically Central European, affecting the North only later, and then almost exclusively in Sweden. The national Romantic idiom showed an affinity for interpretations of native material in the manner of the tone poem, without departing too far from the Classicistic-Romantic style.

Franz Berwald (1796–1868), of a well-known family of Swedish musicians, pupil of his father Christian Berwald and of Edouard Dupuy, began composing in the style of the later works of Beethoven, Marschner, Spohr, and French opera. In the course of his career he developed a quite distinctive idiom of his own, with short motifs leading to unexpected melodic turns, sharp rhythmic features, abrupt modulations, and solid counterpoint. In all of his work he revealed an interest in experiment and anticipated many later deviations from the Classical norm, such as symmetrical disposition of the movement, uninterrupted transition between movements, and contraction of the scherzo and adagio, in his Septet (1828). Because of these peculiarities he was not recognized until later, and then but slowly. During the years from 1829 to 1842 and from 1846 to 1849 he was abroad; then in 1867 he taught composition at the Academy. He composed six symphonies, including *Sinfonie sérieuse* in G minor (1842) and *Sinfonie singulière* in C major (1845).

J. P. E. Hartmann (1805–1900) composed two symphonies, one in G minor (1835) and the other in E major (1848), inspired by Spohr and Marschner, an overture "Hakon Jarl" (1844), and a concert overture in C major (1852).

J. F. Frøhlich (1806–1860) wrote a symphony in E♭ major (1830).

Niels Wilhelm Gade was born in Copenhagen on February 22, 1817, and died there on December 21, 1890. Early he studied violin and was playing concerts at sixteen. He studied composition under A. P. Berggreen, a former pupil of Weyse, and later became substitute organist for Weyse. Gade contributed some songs to a collection of Berggreen's in 1838, including *Paa Sjølunds fagre Sletter*, or On Zealand's Lovely Plains, later the principal theme of his First Symphony. In 1841 he achieved striking success with the concert overture *Efterklang af Ossian*, or Echoes of Ossian, composed for a competition arranged in 1839 by the *Musikforeningen*. The next work, his First Symphony, encountered opposition, and Gade sent it to Mendelssohn, who successfully conducted its first performance. Thereafter Gade himself moved to Leipzig; in 1844 he taught at the Leipzig Conservatory and was second conductor of the Gewandhaus concerts, which he carried on after Mendelssohn's death. In 1848 he returned to Copenhagen, where he became the uncontested leader of official Danish musical life. In 1850 he reorganized the orchestra of the *Musikforeningen* and often combined it with the chorus of the St. Cecilia Society in an extensive repertoire of Classical and Romantic music presented in the course of some forty years. In 1867 he, together with Hartmann and H. S. Paulli, assumed leadership of the newly founded Conservatory. In 1851 he became organist at the Garnisons Kirke and in 1858 also undertook the honored position of organist at the Holmens Kirke. He received his professorship in 1856 and an honorary doctorate in 1879.

Gade's attitude was fundamentally conservative. He composed most of his best works before 1855. Refining his style, he was not able to renew it. Though in the late works dry academism on occasion outweighed inspiration, all his life he was accorded boundless European prestige and received many first performances outside of Denmark, in Leipzig, Bonn, Düsseldorf, and Birmingham.

In all, he wrote eight symphonies. Mendelssohn's first performance of Gade's First Symphony in C minor (1842) led to the Danish composer's European fame. Alongside it, the Fourth in B♭ major (1850), Fifth in D minor with piano (1852), and Sixth in G minor (1857) are the most significant. He also wrote seven concert overtures, of which *Efterklang af Ossian* (1840) was a charming initial work.

Gade's style is somewhat suggested by the fact that he prefaced his Ossian overture with the quotation from Uhland as a motto: "We are not bound to formula; our art is poetry." From the very beginning, his Romanticism was linked with astonishing formal and instrumental skill, even in his less inspired work. This particular quality brought him to the Leipzig High Romantic movement, of which he is known as the principal representative in the North.

Ludvig Norman (1831–1885), a Swedish composer of the Leipzig High Romantic era who was indebted to Gade, wrote four symphonies, including No. 3 in D minor (1881), as well as a concert overture in Eb major (1856).

Emil Hartmann (1836–1898), son of J. P. E. Hartmann, wrote seven symphonies, including No. 2, *Fra Riddertiden,* or From the Days of Chivalry (1884); a symphonic poem, *Hakon Jarl;* and an overture (1878), *Hærmændene paa Helgeland,* after Ibsen.

Asger Hammerich (1843–1923, from 1864 his last name was spelled Hamerik) was a significant Danish composer of symphonies. He was trained under N. W. Gade and J. P. E. Hartmann in Copenhagen, Hans von Bülow in Berlin, and Hector Berlioz in Paris. In 1869 he went to Italy, and from 1871–98 he was director of the Peabody Institute in Baltimore. After 1898 he was again in Copenhagen. He displayed notable ability in manipulating large forms, often with contrapuntal and linear writing. Of his seven symphonies (1881–98), No. 6 *Symphonie spirituelle,* in G major, op. 38, is for strings. He also wrote five Nordic Suites.

Together with Grieg, Johan Svendsen (1840–1911) brought the flowering of Norwegian music to its culmination at the end of the 19th century. Trained in Leipzig under Richter and Hauptmann, he wrote joyous, clearly disposed, well instrumented orchestral works that may be considered examples of Classically oriented Romanticism: two symphonies, in D major (1867) and Bb major (1876), the latter being Svendsen's major work; an orchestral legend, *Zorahayda* (1873); three symphonic poems, including *Carnaval i Paris* (1872); and four Norwegian rhapsodies.

The compositions of Edvard Grieg (1843–1907) tended more to the smaller forms; hence he is discussed in more detail under vocal and piano music. He did write, however, the overture *I Høst,* or In Autumn (1866), and four symphonic dances (1898).

Finnish musical life was entirely dependent on Swedish up to the beginning of the 19th century. In 1790 the *Musikaliska Sällskapet* was founded in Turku-Åbo, then the capital. After Finland's separation from Sweden in 1809, Helsinki-Helsingfors became the capital in 1812, and thereafter German influence increased. When the German musician Fredrik (originally Fritz) Pacius (1809–1891) emigrated to Finland in 1835, he helped develop a particularly Finnish music, notably composing a one-movement symphony (1850). Four years before, A. G. Ingelius (1822–1868) had composed the first Finnish symphony, with a Scherzo finnico in quintuple meter. Filip von Schantz (1835–1865) was the first to write a symphonic poem on the *Kalevala* cycle of material, in his *Kullervo*. Another composer active in Turku-Åbo at the same time was Conrad Greve (1820–1851), who had been born in Germany and had studied under Mendelssohn and David, and whose works included three overtures and some incidental music for the theater.

The Late Romantic style formulated by Wagner was followed by influential composers in all the Scandinavian countries: in Sweden, by Andreas Hallén (1846–1925) with a concert overture, four symphonic poems, two rhapsodies, and four orchestral suites and by W. Peterson-Berger (1867–1942) with five symphonies and five orchestral suites; in Norway, by Christian Sinding (1856–1941) with four symphonies; and in Denmark, by P. E. Lange-Müller (1850–1926) with two symphonies and by Rued Langgaard (1893–1952) with sixteen symphonies and many symphonic poems.

Johan Svendsen's tendencies toward Classicism were carried on further in Norway by Johan Halvorsen (1864–1935) with three symphonies and two Norwegian rhapsodies, and in Finland by Robert Kajanus (1856–1933) and by Ernst Mielck (1877–1899), a pupil of Max Bruch. Between 1895 and 1899 Mielck wrote one symphony, two overtures, an orchestral suite, two piano concerti, a violin concerto, and chamber music. Kajanus energetically promoted musical culture in the Finnish capital, founding in 1882 the *Helsingfors orkesterförening*, which in 1914 became the *Helsingfors stadsorkester*, conducted by him until 1932. His orchestral works, among the most significant Finnish compositions before Sibelius, included the symphonic poems *Kullervos död*, or Kullervo's Death (1880), and *Aino*, with its concluding chorus (1885), as well as two Finnish rhapsodies, a sinfonietta, and an *Ouvertura sinfonica*. Helsingfors' Musical Institute was founded in 1882 with Martin Wegelius (1846–1906) as its first leader.

Jean Sibelius was born in Tavastehus on December 8, 1865, and died in Järvenpää on October 20, 1957. After studying theory and composition with Martin Wegelius from 1885 to 1889 in Helsinki-Helsingfors at the Musical Institute (which was later to be renamed the Sibelius Academy) and then in Berlin with A. Becker and in Vienna with R. Fuchs and K. Goldmark, he settled in the Finnish capital in 1891 and participated actively in the cultural resistance to Russian oppression. In 1904 he moved to the village of Järvenpää, where he lived for the rest of his life. In 1900 he received an annual state stipend which enabled him to devote himself entirely to composition. In 1913 he received an honorary doctorate from Helsinki and from Yale, in 1916 the title of professor, and in 1947 an honorary doctorate from Oxford.

The early works of Sibelius were given their first hearty encouragement by Busoni and quickly gained world success. Although they are often considered "specifically Finnish" because of their national and Romantic cast and their particularly dark tone, the assured way in which this "Finnish" label is applied may perhaps be questioned. Since he drew his inspiration not from Finnish folk-music but directly from nature and mythology, the "Finnish" tone may well be his own quite personal manner of expression which has taken on certain national and Romantic connotations. It is unambiguously characteristic of only the work of his youth, such as his symphonic poems on Kalevala material and his first two symphonies. In his later symphonies he developed a more universal idiom, no longer to be measured only with the national and Romantic yardstick. At the end of the 1920's he apparently ceased composing.

In the course of his career he wrote seven symphonies, No. 1 in E minor (1899), No. 2 in D major (1902), No. 3 in C major (1907), No. 4 in A minor (1911), No. 5 in E♭ major (1915, rev. 1919), No. 6 in D minor (1923), and No. 7 in C major (1924). His eleven symphonic poems include *En Saga* (1892), a set of four legends entitled *Lemminkainen* (1895), *Finlandia* (1899), *Dryaden* (1910), and *Tapiola* (1925). He also wrote eleven symphonic poems, four suites, and a concert overture, *Karelia* (1893).

As for the style and particular features of his work, the first two symphonies and the early symphonic poems are of Romantic-Realistic, darkly colored sonorous splendor, often with ostinati. The style is emotional, to some extent influenced by Bruckner and the Russian symphonists. The works have many aspects of national and Romantic program music, such as the use of Kalevala material. But the manner of expression is Sibelius's own, without attempts to copy or adapt details of actual folk-music practice. After 1905 there occurred a change of style: the passionate and extreme effects disappeared, and there was increased simplification and concentration on aspects of the work that had to do with absolute music, culminating in the thematic asceticism of the Fourth Symphony. The sonority became lighter, more Impressionistically colored, particularly in the symphonic poems around 1910. In his late style after 1915 there was a synthesis, his thematic and dynamic aspects again more expansive, yet without the emotionalism of the youthful works, as he displayed in the last three symphonies a unique art of variation, based on thematic metamorphosis. An Eighth Symphony, if it ever existed, seems to have been suppressed by the composer.

In addition to his symphonic compositions, he wrote a violin concerto, two serenades for violin and orchestra, pieces for violin and piano, two string quartets, about a hundred one-movement piano pieces, about a hundred songs, sixteen vocal works with orchestra, choral songs, and incidental music for plays.

Carl Nielsen was born in Nørre Lyndelse, Fyn, on June 9, 1865, and died in Copenhagen on October 3, 1931. Son of a family of village musicians, at fourteen he entered upon the career of regimental bandsman. Never trained abroad, he studied theory and violin at the Copenhagen Conservatory from 1884 to 1887. Prior to 1903 he made three trips to Germany, France, Austria, and Greece. From 1889 to 1905 he was violinist in the royal orchestra, from 1908 to 1914 director of the royal theater, and then from 1915 to 1927 director of *Musikforeningen*, being mainly active in Gothenburg between 1918 and 1922. In his later years he mostly conducted his own works. Having taught at the Conservatory since 1915, he became in 1931 its director.

From an early age familiar with folk-song and classical music, Nielsen tended to reject many Romantic features that he encountered in cosmopolitan music. Thus he worked more or less with folk-song in his use of the small forms and tried to renew the symphony along classical lines in his longer works. His melodic gifts enabled him to revive 20th-century folk-related song effectively. Encouraged by J. P. E. Hartmann to treat the national and Romantic tonal idiom unsentimentally, he also had learned much about harmonic and compositional technique from J. Svendsen, C. F. E. Hornemann, and J. Brahms. Nielsen introduced elements from the church modes and equalized within any one key the treatment of major and minor thirds and of sixths and sevenths. Thus, quite early, he achieved a form of "expanded tonality." With more and more independent handling of rhythm and polyphony, he developed his own impressive symphonic style, influential on his contemporaries and successors. The most important impulse in his development was his suggestive use of melody, which became more and more distinctive and free, occasionally being carried to the very limits of tonality. There was a strong tendency toward chamber music in his later works, where the rather classical ideals were displaced under the influence of the music then current. Occasionally he wrote in a way that was almost Expressionistic, in the Sixth Symphony (1925), the flute concerto (1926), and the clarinet concerto (1928). The turning-point, in 1922, came with the Fifth Symphony and the Wind Quintet.

He wrote six symphonies: No. 1 in G minor (1892); No. 2, *De fire Temperamenter* (1902); No. 3, *Sinfonia espansiva* (1911); No. 4, *Det Uudslukkelige,* or The Unquenchable (1916); No. 5 (1922); and No. 6, *Sinfonia semplice* (1925). He also wrote a concert overture *Helios* (1903) and two symphonic poems *Saga-Drøm,* or Legendary Dream (1908), and *Pan og Syrinx* (1918).

In addition to his symphonic works, Nielsen wrote two operas, oratorios and cantatas, three concerti (one for violin, one for flute, and one for clarinet), a suite for strings, four string quartets, two violin sonatas, further chamber music, piano and organ works, songs and other vocal works, and incidental music for plays.

About the time of Sibelius and Nielsen, the following composers were among those who wrote symphonic works:

In Sweden: Wilhelm Stenhammar (1871–1927), Hugo Alfén (1872–1960), Ture Rangström (1884–1947), Kurt Atterberg (b. 1887), Gustav Nystroem (b. 1890), Hilding Rosenberg (b. 1892), Dag Wirén (b. 1905), Allan Pettersson (b. 1911), K.-B. Blomdahl (b. 1916), and Gunnar Bucht (b. 1927).

In Denmark: Jørgen Bentzon (1897–1951), Ebbe Hamerik (1898–1951), Finn Høffding (b. 1899), Svend Erik Tarp (b. 1908), Herman D. Koppel (b. 1908), Vagn Holmboe (b. 1909), Svend S. Schultz (b. 1913), N. V. Bentzon (b. 1919), P. Rovsing Olsen (b. 1922), Ib Nørholm (b. 1931), and Per Nørgaard (b. 1932).

In Finland: Erkki Melartin (1875–1937), Uuno Klami (1900–1961), N.-E. Ringbom (b. 1909), K. Tuukkanen (b. 1909), Erik Bergman (b. 1911), E. Englund (b. 1916), and Joonas Kokkonen (b. 1921).

In Norway: Fartein Valen (1887–1952) with four symphonies and several one-movement orchestral pieces, L. I. Jensen (b. 1894), H. Sæverud (b. 1897), and Klaus Egge (b. 1906).

In Iceland: Jón Leifs (b. 1899), Karl O. Runólfsson (b. 1900), and Jón Nordal (b. 1926).

The Americas

Latin America

For various historical reasons Latin America has had a predominant orientation in orchestral music toward Paris while the United States, up to the 20th century, has tended to look more to various centers in the German-speaking area. In Latin America until well on into the 18th century the church was still the artistic center; also Latin America has always had a higher degree of direct governmental patronage of music than has North America. Antonio Raffelín (1798–1882) of Cuba wrote orchestral music that was performed in Paris, and groups of composers were active in Brazil and Venezuela by the beginning of the 19th century.

As a figure whose activities spanned the three continents of the Americas and Europe, Louis Moreau Gottschalk (1829–1869), born in New Orleans, was educated in Paris where he gained the high regard of Berlioz and was considered by Chopin and Liszt one of their peers as he exploited American material in his virtuoso piano pieces somewhat as they were doing material from the folk-music of Poland and Hungary. *La Noce de los Trópicos* represents Gottschalk's orchestral work. Shortly before his death he had presented three festivals involving some thousand performers in Brazil—somewhat as others had done on a larger scale in Boston about the same time and as Berlioz had earlier done in Paris on a smaller scale with his *Requiem.*

As the various Latin American countries achieved independence during the 19th century, they fostered strong trends toward nationalism, which appeared in the programs of various orchestral works. Although within the present century Latin American orchestral composers are quite as international as any, there remains a certain carryover of this orientation toward the Latin countries of Europe. Two composers of orchestral music who have figured prominently in the 20th century are Heitor Villa-Lobos (1887–1959) of Brazil and Carlos Chavez (b. 1899) of Mexico. Both received their higher musical education in Paris and, on returning to their native countries, undertook important governmental positions in the field of music education.

Villa-Lobos composed over a dozen symphonic poems and twelve symphonies, mostly containing program elements. He also wrote for various performing combinations fourteen *chorôs,* which combine Brazilian Indian and popular features. His aim was a fusion of native and foreign aspects in his music, and a great deal of his enormous body of composition had a relationship to his activities as Director of Music Education of Rio de Janeiro. His *Bachianas Brasileiras* are what he imagined J. S. Bach would have written if he had been a Brazilian.

In a way, this may be related to the "back to Bach" movement which at one stage was so prominent a part of the neo-classical trend in Stravinsky's career. In the work of Villa-Lobos, however, it yielded a rather massive, colorful, thick sonority, with compelling rhythm often intensified by use of dissonance and native percussion instruments. Syncretism is perhaps distinctively American, as the cultures of Europe have developed by extruding dissident elements and periodically striving for what is regarded there as stylistic purity, often with somewhat thin, ascetic, and anemic results. The New World has often taken the road in the opposite direction. The style of Villa-Lobos is tonal—often polytonal—and basically harmonic.

In five symphonies and other works Chávez, American Indian in his ancestry, has amalgamated various aspects of American Indian music with those of European music as it had developed along the Franco-Russian axis. He has served as director of the National Conservatory in Mexico City and as chief of the department of fine arts in the Secretariat of Public Education. In the United States he has appeared as guest conductor and as lecturer. The style of his music is energetic, austere, controlled, rhythmically complex, and often dissonant. There are few sentimental or introspective aspects in his writing, few nuances involving light and shade. Everything is hard, precise, bright, severe, definite, and uncompromising.

Chávez has taught and otherwise encouraged many younger Mexican composers, for example a "Group of Four" including Salvador Contreras (b. 1912), Blas Galindo (b. 1910), Daniel Ayala (b. 1908), and Pablo Moncayo (1912–1958). Other active Latin American composers are Alberto Ginastera (b. 1916) of Argentina, Juan Orrego Salas of Chile, Héctor Tosar of Uruguay, and Roque Cordero (b. 1917) of Panama.

The United States

Within a general German orientation there was considerable variety in early North American orchestral music. The Moravians, who could be considered as part of the Czech emigration, were by mid-18th century fostering a Central European type of instrumental music at their collegium musicum in Bethlehem, Pennsylvania. The first orchestral score published in the United States seems to have been *The Death of an Indian Chief* (1791) by a Dane in Boston, Hans Gram. As a result of late-18th-century political unheavals in Europe—as at various times later—a number of composers emigrated to the United States and were active in orchestral composition. One of them was Alexander Reinagle (1756–1809), whose portrait C. P. E. Bach requested for his "hall of fame." Among compositions of these refugee composers were orchestral descriptions of such matters as their trip over, storms at sea, and battles, with tendencies toward the Storm and Stress style. A late phase of the Czech musical emigration brought one of the more personally colorful of the composers, the Bohemian Anton Philip Heinrich (1781–1861), to America in 1818. There he wrote hundreds of vigorous, highly individual, program-laden works, quite bizarre for his or any day, including symphonies such as *The Combat of the Condor, The Tower of Babel,*

The Indian Carnival, and musical tributes to Beethoven and Mendelssohn.

Native American composers began to play a role in the development of orchestral music by mid-19th century. George F. Bristow (1825–1895) composed six symphonies, four of which were performed by the New York Philharmonic, in which he played the violin. William Henry Fry (1815–1864), of Philadelphia, for six years foreign correspondent of the New York *Tribune* and well acquainted with Berlioz, wrote four symphonies which were performed in New York in 1853: *Childe Harold, A Day in the Country, The Breaking Heart,* and *Santa Claus.*

Two late-19th-century native composers who wrote symphonies and symphonic poems had received their higher musical education in Germany. One of them, John Knowles Paine (1839–1906), became the head of the music department at Harvard; and the other, George W. Chadwick (1854–1931), the head of the New England Conservatory. Mendelssohn was no doubt their ideal, and the problem seemed to them one of gaining recognition in the older centers of musical culture beyond the Rhine. Some native American composers, such as G. T. Strong (1856–1948) and Arthur Bird (1856–1923), even emigrated to Germany. Edward Mac-Dowell (1861–1908), the best composer of his generation, taught for a while at the Darmstadt Conservatory and on Liszt's recommendation received performance and publication in Germany before returning to the United States in 1888. MacDowell's orchestral compositions include two Indian Suites and some symphonic poems with Shakespearean and Arthurian programs.

This fundamentally German orientation among composers in the United States continued even when they did not study abroad, often being perpetuated through the traditions of the town band as well as through teachers who had been German-trained or German-inspired. One of the most original and autochthonous of the American composers was Charles E. Ives, who was born in Danbury, Conn., on October 20, 1874, and died in New York City on May 19, 1954. His father, a band-master, provided him with his early musical education. Later he studied under such German-trained American composers as Dudley Buck and Horatio Parker, at Yale, graduating from there in 1894. All through his youth he had had extensive experience of music, as organist, bandsman, and participant in various kinds of ensembles. In order to continue his activity as a composer without having to compromise his aims or become subservient to some prevailing fashion, he went into the insurance business in 1898 while continuing to compose music. Many of the technical features that were to be exploited a decade or so later in Europe appear as a regular part of his procedures during the 1890's. Polytonality appears in his *Song for Harvest Season* (1894) for voice, cornet, trombone, and organ pedal, each in a different key. His eight-voiced *64th Psalm* (1898) is bitonal. Also the placement of different music-producing groups differently in space was a regular part of his procedures, being quite effectively used in his *The Unanswered Question* (1908). His compositions include four symphonies (1898, 1902, 1904, and 1916), two piano sonatas, 114 songs, and numerous works for chorus and for various instrumental combinations. Many of his compositions are rich in allusions to well-known musical material, such as familiar hymns, popular songs, and classical works—his approach to composition being a very inclusive one. Normally the work is conceived of as if it consisted of independent strata of sound, thus reinstating features earlier characteristic of polyphony. The philosophical basis of his music retains a great deal of the Emersonian or Transcendental point of view, and Ives expressed himself quite fully on the subject of his musical aims in his *Essays before a Sonata,* published in connection with his Second Piano Sonata in 1919—the essays, he said, being for those who couldn't stand the music and the music for those who couldn't stand the essays. In his work he consciously stressed what he called "substance" rather than "manner." His innovations came no doubt from his independent observation of musical and sonorous actualities, so that his priority in point of time is a matter not of where he stood in a single evolutionary sequence but rather of the separate occurrence of similar developments at approximately the same time in different countries. Although widespread public recognition of his work did not come until mid-20th century, he influenced many prominent members of the next generation of American composers, and some of his exact contemporaries, such as Schönberg, admired his work greatly.

At the turn of the century the pattern of orientation toward Germany began to be replaced by one toward France. Charles Martin Loeffler (1861–1935), born in Alsace and educated in Paris, emigrated to America in 1881. He is well known for his orchestral composition *Pagan Poem* (1901), after Virgil. E. B. Hill (1872–1960), after studying with Widor in Paris, returned to head the Harvard music department and to write symphonic compositions based on poems by Poe (1920) and Amy Lowell (1927), as well as two symphonies, one in 1928 and the other in 1931. Charles T. Griffes (1884–1920), though having studied in Germany, carried out Impressionistic aims in his tone poem *The Pleasure Dome of Kubla Khan* (1919), after Coleridge.

Often the shift in international orientation toward Franco-Russian procedures was interpreted as an advance toward "true Americanism" in music, as was also the use of material of American Indian or Negro origin as well as suggestions of immediate experiences and details in the everyday world. A group of composers associated with the Wa-Wan Press (1901 to 1912), notably Arthur Farwell (1872–1952), wrote many pieces based on American Indian material. Henry F. Gilbert (1868–1928) with his *Comedy Overture on Negro Themes* (1905) and *Dance in Place Congo* (1906) and Louis Gruenberg (1884–1964) with his *Jazz Suite* (1926) were making use of Negro motifs on a symphonic level, while from another direction the same aim was being approached by Paul Whiteman and his "symphonic jazz" efforts, for which George Gershwin (1898–1937) wrote his *Rhapsody in Blue* (1924). Immediate bits of everyday experience were also suggested in witty orchestral scores, as in *Adventures in a Perambulator* (1915) by John Alden Carpenter (1876–1951) and *Flivver Ten Million* (1927) by Frederick S. Converse (1871–1940).

Among 20th-century American writers of symphonies a strong impact of the anti-*espressivo,* neo-classical aesthetic associated with Stravinsky was conveyed through a teacher of composition in Paris, Nadia Boulanger. Among her pupils shortly after World War I were Douglas Moore (b. 1893), Walter Piston (b. 1894), Virgil Thomson (b. 1896), Quincy Porter (b. 1897), Roy Harris (b. 1898), and Aaron Copland (b. 1900). To these more or less French-influenced composers might be added Elliott Carter (b. 1908), Ned Rorem (b. 1923), and no doubt many others. Although all have written symphonic compositions, two have addressed themselves to the problems posed by the symphony with special persistence, Walter Piston with seven symphonies written between 1936 and 1961 and Roy Harris with eight between 1934 and 1962. Piston's are quite self-contained, with not much explicit reference beyond the sheer music itself. Harris's, on the other hand, are more emotional and expansive, sometimes bringing in folk-melodies, hymns, or allusion to patriotic documents and generally suggesting epic aspects of American life and character. Both composers write tonally, often modally, and with considerable contrapuntal skill, to some extent deriving from their post-World War I training in Paris.

Other extremely active American composers have been oriented toward Italian and German tradition, taking 19th-century precedent as their point of departure. Study at the American Academy in Rome has been a factor in the work of Howard Hanson (b. 1896) with five rather subjectively emotional symphonies, Roger Sessions (b. 1896) with four that have taken him farther along a road analogous to Schönberg's, Randall Thompson (b. 1899) with three that are somewhat abstract, objective, and eclectic, and Samuel Barber (b. 1910) with two rather lyrical symphonies as well as other orchestral works. Vincent Persichetti (b. 1915) with seven symphonies written between 1942 and 1957, David Diamond (b. 1915) with eight between 1941 and 1961, and Peter Mennin (b. 1923) with seven between 1942 and 1964 may perhaps appropriately be included with these composers. The emigration of Schönberg to the United States in 1933 helped establish direct continuity with the Viennese tradition, and among his American pupils were such unlike and distinctive pupils as John Cage (b. 1912) and Leon Kirchner (b. 1919). As can be observed in the work of Ives also, Germanic precedents were so thoroughly ingrained in American musical feeling, particularly through town bands and other choral and instrumental groups, that they have formed a substantial part of the assumptions with which many Americans have approached orchestral music, for example in William Schumann (b. 1910) with eight symphonies written between 1936 and 1962. Lukas Foss (b. 1922) was born in Berlin and at fifteen came to the United States, where he has composed symphonic and other works. Among his recent efforts have been various educational activities and the fostering of corporate improvisation among chamber and symphonic groups.

Some composers of orchestral music in the United States have directly attempted to work creatively in musics other than merely those of the Western European tradition. Among composers with this special concern, Henry Cowell (1897–1965) wrote fifteen symphonies and Alan Hovhaness (b. 1911) thirteen. One development related to this trend is a considerable increase in music for percussion groups. Attempts have been made also to bridge national and stylistic antitheses and apparent impasses and contradictions by work with "electronic music," in which Milton Babbitt (b. 1916) has been quite active. He serializes everything— dynamics, note-values, and so on—the way the immediate followers of Schönberg serialized only the twelve pitches of the chromatic scale. Whether composition for a "Synthesizer" is to be considered orchestral, ensemble, or solo music, the fact remains that in at least certain branches of contemporary American composition a basis has been reinstated that is highly mathematical, abstract, and not specifically sensuous. This is at the other extreme from the tendency to explore improvisation and to allow the sound produced on the instruments to have rather free play. In one way or another technical aspects from both these extreme and antithetical tendencies may be expected to work back into the main-stream of American symphonic composition, which in the 20th century has been abundantly maintained, not only along both its Franco-Russian and Italo-German axes but also in terms of some of its non-European possibilities.

Overture

Among orchestral pieces designated as "overtures" there is consider-able variety. Some are simply pieces meant as general introductions or openings without relationship in subject-matter or theme to the ensuing action of the opera or play. For example, Rossini's overture to *The Barber of Seville* had previously served as introduction to two other of his works, including the tragic opera *Elizabeth of England*. Other overtures, how-ever, lead into the action and have closer relationship to it. There are at least four types, involving:

1. Unrelated juxtaposition of individual musical ideas of the operas, as in a potpourri-overture, like that of Johann Strauss's *Fledermaus* or as in a folk-song or student-song overture like Brahms's *Academic Festival Overture*.
2. General preparation of mood, as in Gluck's *Iphigenia in Tauris*.
3. Summary of the main dramatic impulses in the work, as in the *Leonore* Overtures II and III and in *The Flying Dutchman*.
4. Preparation of the listener for the beginning of the piece, as in *Tristan and Isolde*.

One of the first traceable instrumental introductions is the sinfonia for the *dialogo musicale Giudizio d'amore* (1599), ascribed to Baldassare Donati but probably by Emperor Leopold I. A stylistic principle impor-tant to the later overture distinctly appears here in the juxtaposition of slow and fast tempi.

Monteverdi's *Orfeo* (1607) opened with a "toccata" of three trumpet fanfares followed by a ritornello, which was repeatedly introduced during the opera with symbolical implications. Significant independent orches-tral pieces or canzone also serve as introductions to the Prologue, Act II, and Act III of Stefano Landi's opera *Il San Alessio* (Rome 1632).

The Venetian operatic sinfonia was influenced by the sonatas and canzone of Gabrieli. Up to 1660 chordal writing predominated, with alternating slow and fast sections. After 1660, however, the sinfonia either came to resemble outwardly the French overture with its contrasts in tempo of slow-fast-slow, yet usually without the fugal portion, or else made the transition to the Neapolitan form. As early as *Il pomo d'oro* (1666–7) Cesti brought into the instrumental introduction some aspects of the ensuing chorus, to bring the listener into rapport with it. The Venetian opera had many further examples of such preludes in which a program has been intended.

The Neapolitan sinfonia, moreover, prepared the way for the spread of the concert idea. The so-called Scarlatti overture was an independent, concertante tripartite instrumental piece with the succession of movements fast-slow-fast, which received its decisive first development from Alessandro Scarlatti (1660–1725) and had been already prepared for by such composers as Alessandro Stradella (about 1645–1682) and G. Perti. The first movement (Allegro) was developed in three sections into the sonata-allegro form. The second movement (Largo) was usually in the parallel key or in the similarly designated minor. Originally this second movement was only a transition to the third movement, which was lively in tempo, a Presto or Vivace with suggestions of the dance.

The French, or Lully, overture grew out of four-sectioned sinfonias which served as introduction to the *ballets de cour*. The *ballet des rues de Paris* (1647) contained, in contrast to the dances, an introductory piece designated as the overture, in a two-sectioned, or slow-fast, form. The *rhythme saccadé* (jerky rhythm) typical of the French overture first appeared in *Les fêtes de Bacchus* (1651). Around 1660 imitative passages crowded into the second or quick portion of the movement. In 1658 for the first time, Lully (1632–1687) wrote in the ballet *Alcidiane* an overture in the typical form: first the slow portion, in duple time, quite pompous, in dotted rhythm with a half-cadence on the dominant; second, a fugal portion in lively rhythm; and the third portion an optional coda that served as a reprise of the first part. The orchestration was five-voiced. Archaically strict, impersonally typical, and tenacious of convention, the French overture essentially expresses an aristocratic attitude toward life and a rationalistic trait basic to Baroque music.

The Neapolitan sinfonia mingled with the French overture in the operas of Jean-Philippe Rameau (1683–1764). He gave the overture an entirely new meaning as a programmatic introduction by reproducing musically the antecedent action in the drama. Also he enlarged the French form by adopting from Italian models certain thematic elements and the formal layout of the allegro portion. From the second third of the 18th century, the connection in content between the overture and the ensuing drama was urged by many theoreticians such as Mattheson, Quantz, Algarotti, and Rousseau.

Christoph Willibald von Gluck (1714–1787) completed the process of fusion by establishing the classical form of the overture under the influence of the concert symphony, which was in sonata-allegro form. In his preface to *Alceste* (1769), moreover, he gave public expression to his fundamental attitude toward the overture and wrote his first program overture for this opera. In his *Iphigénie en Aulide* (1774), the overture was also joined thematically with the opera. The work is in one movement with slow introduction and sonata-allegro form, except that the exposition was not repeated before the development. The overture led directly into the first scene.

Gluck's influence on the overture in W. A. Mozart (1756–1791) was first noticeable in *Idomeneo* (1781). The overture was in one movement and in the form that had been established by Gluck, as was also the overture to *Don Giovanni* (1787). The overture to the *Magic Flute* represented the height of formal perfection in the French or Lullian overture. A thematic relationship to the opera was established by the three trumpet chords. The overture to *Così fan tutte* also contained a quotation from the opera.

The Italians and the French took the most significant creative part in the further development of the overture between Gluck and Beethoven by extending the form and heightening its expressive possibilities.

Simon Mayr (1763–1845) created the prototype of the newer overtures of his day, which were characterized by very great heightening of effect through building up the coda. These overtures had great crescendi, expanded resources particularly in the wind and percussion sections, and instrumentation very much the composer's own but always calculated to achieve a powerful effect. Unexpected intervals and modulations were used, and dramatic effects were stressed, often without much inner relationship to the ensuing opera. Mayr's work had lasting influence on Spontini, Meyerbeer, Weber, Wagner, and Verdi.

Luigi Cherubini (1760–1842) wrote overtures that normally began with a slow introduction and moved on into an allegro in sonata-allegro form. In comparison with Mayr, he refined various features of the form and instrumentation in, for example, the overtures to *Anakreon, Die Abenceragen, Medea, Der Wasserträger, Elisa,* and *Lodoiska.*

In comparison with Cherubini, Étienne Henri Méhul (1763–1817) had an individual way of handling the form and of achieving forceful instrumental effects. The overture to his rescue opera *Helena* (1803) directly influenced the *Leonore* overtures of Beethoven.

Beethoven's involvement with the form and content of the overture is reflected most clearly in the three *Leonore* overtures. He wrote them in the following order: No. 1, composed in 1804 or 1807 and published posthumously; No. 2, composed in 1805 and played at the first performance of the opera; and No. 3, composed in 1806. The overture *Fidelio* in E major was performed in 1814 with the third version of the work. Overture No. 1 consists of a slow introduction, allegro, an inserted adagio (Florestan's aria), and the resumption of the allegro. Overture No. 2 is an outline of the drama. It has a slow introduction based on the Prison Scene and an allegro as in a sonata-allegro with a first theme (Leonore) and a second theme (Florestan). At the culminating point of the development the trumpet signal symbolizes the dramatic resolution. The reprise is then omitted and a transition is made straight to the coda. Overture No. 3 introduces the reprise in basically the same poetic layout.

With particular impressiveness Beethoven succeeded in fusing form and content with symphonic and dramatic force in the overture to *Egmont* (1810) and *Coriolanus* (1807). In both, there was extension of the coda.

In his overtures Beethoven followed not only Gluck and Mozart but also the German-Italian Mayr and the Frenchmen Cherubini and Méhul. The overture for the *Weihe des Hauses* (1822) is simply a copy of the Lullian overture.

Carl Maria von Weber (1786–1826) began the transition from the program overture to the potpourri overture. Weber took his thematic material entirely from the opera and, in bringing it together in the overture, gave a survey of the dramatic tensions in the action. His music had a unique plasticity of expression and a compelling verve, especially in the overtures to *Freischütz, Euryanthe,* and *Oberon.* The allegro in the sonata-allegro form was the center of the overture. It was extended to include a slow introduction and a coda.

Felix Mendelssohn-Bartholdy (1809–1847) developed the typical Romantic concert overture. He did his first work of this kind, the overture to Shakespeare's *Midsummer Night's Dream*, in 1826 as an independent piece for concert presentation. The incidental music was not composed until 1843 for a stage performance of the play in the New Palace in Potsdam. The *Midsummer Night's Dream* Overture is a significant piece of Romantic musical poetry of great formal perfection, as is also the *Hebrides* Overture (1829), composed after impressions he had received of the landscape on a trip to Scotland. Mendelssohn's other overtures, e.g. *Fairy Tale of the Beautiful Melusina* and *Calm Sea and Happy Journey,* are either concert overtures and as such favorite Romantic genre pieces or overtures to plays, for example to Victor Hugo's *Ruy Blas* and to Racine's *Athalia.*

Robert Schumann (1810–1856) wrote a significant overture to Byron's *Manfred,* strongly Romantic in mood and organic in its thematic development.

Richard Wagner (1813–1883) wrote the early overtures *King Enzio, Columbus, Polonia,* and *Rule Britannia* between 1832 and 1837. He also wrote a significant concert overture in *Faust* (in 1840 and revised in 1855), in the classical overture form. The overtures to his operas represent two types: either self-contained compositions in their content and musical aspects or compositions that lead over into the first scenes of operas. The self-contained overtures—to *Rienzi, The Flying Dutchman, Tannhäuser, Lohengrin,* and *The Meistersinger*—are program overtures of individual formal independence. The introductory preludes to *Tristan* and *Parsifal* are significant introductions into the characteristic world of the particular opera. Beginning with *Lohengrin,* Wagner called the overture a *Vorspiel,* or prelude.

During the latter half of the 19th century the formal principles of the classical overture—with its introduction and ensuing allegro in sonata-allegro form—fused more and more with the idea of the symphonic poem, so that the boundary line between the two types was almost erased. While opera gradually dropped the prelude as a sizable independent orchestral piece, the overture as a concert piece of its own gained in importance. It turned in content more and more to historical material or ideas of world literature. On occasion the poetic title was not given explicitly.

At the same time the overture annexed a broad folk-like basis in such compositions as folk-song and patriotic-song overtures. Brahms's *Academic Festival Overture* (1880) follows this trend. Almost every composer of any importance in the late 19th and early 20th centuries wrote one or another type of overture. A compilation of the material arranged according to countries appears in Botstiber's history of the genre.

At mid-20th century the use of the designation "overture" and the composition of various types continued unabated, at least among composers in the United States. Examples are *Overture to the "School for Scandal"* (1933) by Samuel Barber (b. 1910), *American Festival Overture* (1939) by William Schuman (b. 1910), *Folk Overture* (1945) by Peter Mennin (b. 1923), *A Short Overture* (1946) by Ulysses Kay (b. 1917), and *Dramatic Overture* (1951) by Gunther Schuller (b. 1925). The basis on which the designation is used seems to be that the composition introduces some other work, alludes to familiar material, or conveys briefly a somewhat high-spirited mood.

Bibliography

Dance Music and Orchestral Suite: O. Bie, *Tanzmusik* (Bln. n. d.); F. Böhme, *Gesch. d. Tanzes in Deutschland* (Lpz. 1886); F. Blume, *Studien z. Vorgesch. d. Orch.suite* (Lpz. 1925); R. Lach, *Zur Gesch. d. Gesellschaftstanzes im 18. Jh.* (Vienna 1920); A. Magriel, *Bibliography of Dancing* (N. Y. 1936); K. Nef, *Gesch. d. Sinfonie u. Suite* (Lpz. 1921); P. Nettl, *Die Wiener Tanzkomposition in der 2. Hälfte d. 17. Jh.* (StMw 8) and *Tanz u. Tanzmusik* (Adler Hdb.); G. Oberst, *Engl. Orch.suiten um 1600* (Wolfenbüttel 1929); C. Sachs, *Eine Weltgesch. d. Tanzes* (Bln. 1933); R. Sonner, *Musik u. Tanz, Vom Kulturtanz zum Jazz* (Lpz. 1930); J. Wolf, *Die Tänze d. Mittelalt.* (AfMw I); *Die Suite* (MW). *Beginnings of Instr. Music:* P. Aubry, *Estampies et danses royales* (Paris 1907); J. Dieckmann, *Die in deutscher Lautentabulatur überlieferten Tänze des 16. Jh.* (Kassel 1931); R. Eitner, *Tänze des 15.-17. Jh.* (MfM 7. Jhg. Beilage); Y. Rokseth, *The Instrumental Music of the Middle Ages and Early 16th Century* (NOHM III); J. Wolf, *Die Tänze des Mittelalters* (AfMw I); H. E. Wooldridge, *Early English Harmony from the 10th to the 15th Century* (1897); Sch 28; art. Estampie (MGG). *J. de Grocheo* new ed. SIMG I. *R. de Vaqueiras* "Kalenda maya" new ed. Aubry, *Trouvères et Troubadours* (Paris 1909). *H. Isaac* DTÖ 14, 1. *Dances of the 15th and 16th Centuries:* F. Crane, *Materials for the Study of the 15th Century Basse Danse* (IMM); M. Reimann, *Materialien zu einer Definition der Intrada* (MF 1957); arts. Basse danse, Branle, Galliarde (MGG); Sch 91, 112, 119, 134–137. *Dances of the Baroque Era:* W. Danckert, *Gesch. d. Gigue* (Lpz. 1924); E. Mohr, *Die Allemande* (2 vols., Zurich 1932). *The Orchestral Suite in the 17th Century:* W. *Brade* Sch 156. H. L. *Hassler* PGfM 15; Sch 153. V. *Haussmann* DDT 16; Sch 655. M. *Frank* DDT 16. J. *Staden* DTB VII 1, VIII 1. P. *Peuerl* DTÖ 36; Sch 157. J. H. *Schein* and S. *Scheidt* coll. eds. J. *Rosenmüller* DDT 18; Sch 220. J. *Pezel* DDT 63; Sch 221. G. *Muffat* DTÖ 1,

2 and 2, 2; Sch 251. *J. C. F. Fischer* DDT 10. *J. J. Fux* DTÖ 9. *G. P. Telemann* DDT 61–62. *Polish Dances in 16th Century:* new eds. in MPO; MPR; ZHMP 1, 2, 6, 16; WDPM 20, 22, 24; MDK; MSt; K. Hławiczka, *Grundriss einer Gesch. der Polonaise biz zum Anfang des 19. Jh.s* (STM 1968); T. Norlind, *Zur Gesch. der poln. Tänze* (SIMG 1910–1); F. Starczewski, *Die poln. Tänze* (SIMG 1900–1).

Instr. Ensemble and Orchestral Music of Ren. and Baroque: H. Botstiber, *Gesch. der Ouvertüre u. der freien Orch.formen* (Lpz. 1913); W. Fischer, *Instrumentalmusik von 1450–1750* (Adler Hdb.); E. H. Meyer, *Concerted Instrumental Music* (NOHM IV); C. Sartorio, *Bibliografia della musica instrumentale italiana stampata in Italia fino al 1700* (Florence 1952); L. Torchi, *La musica instr. in Italia nei secoli XVI, XVII e XVIII* (Turin 1901); J. v. Wasielewski, *Instrumentalsätze vom Ende des 16. bis zum Ende des 17. Jh.* (1905). *In Nomine compositions:* art. MGG. *Ortiz* "Tratado" new ed. Bln. 1913, also Kassel. *A. and G. Gabrieli:* new ed. of instr. works in IeM I and II. *Merula* Sch 184. *G. B. Vitali,* Torchi VII; Sch 241. *A. Corelli:* coll. ed. (5 vols., London 1888–91); Sch 240; B. Paumgartner, art. Corelli (MGG); M. Pincherle, *C.* (Paris 1933). *J. S. Bach:* W. S. Newman, *The Sonata in the Baroque Era* (Chapel Hill 1959). *Poland:* new eds. in WDMP. *Trio Sonata:* E. Schenk, *Triosonate* (MW). *Concerto:* art. Konzertwesen (MGG). *Viadana* "Cento concerti ecclesiastici," Sch 168; new ed., Mantova 1964. *Concert Symphony:* new ed., *Schweizerische Musikdenkmäler, Bd. 1. Concerto Grosso:* H. Engel, *Das Concerto grosso* (MW) and *Das Instrumentalkonzert* (Lpz. 1932); W. Krüger, *Das Concerto grosso in Deutschland* (Wolfenbüttel 1932); A. Schering, *Gesch. d. Instrumentalkonzertes* (Lpz. 2nd ed. 1927); *Gruppenkonzerte der Bachzeit* (ED 51). *G. Muffat:* DTÖ 11, 2, and 89. *A. Vivaldi:* coll. ed. 1947–   , Milan. *G. H. Stölzel:* DDT 29–30; W. Schmidt-Weiss, *S. als Instr.komponist* (Diss. Munich 1938). *A. Vivaldi:* Sch 276; *Accademia musicale Chigiana in Siena,* Publs. 1939–49 on Vivaldi; M. Dounias, *Die Violinkonzerte G. Tartinis* (Wolfenbüttel 1935); F. Giegling, *G. Torelli. Ein Beitrag zur Entwicklungsgesch. d. ital. Konzertes* (Kassel 1949); D. J. Iselin, *B. Marini* (Basel Diss. 1930); W. Kolneder, *Auff.-Praxis bei Vivaldi* (Lpz. 1957), *Antonio Vivaldi* (Wiesbaden 1965), and *Die Solokonzertform bei Vivaldi* (Strasbourg, Baden-Baden 1961); M. Pincherle, *Vivaldi et la musique instr.* (Paris 1948; Engl., N. Y. 1957); M. Rinaldi, *Catalogo numerico tematico delle composizioni di A. Vivaldi* (Rome n. d.) and *Vivaldi* (Milan 1943); G. Tartini, *Traktat über die Musik,* tr. A. Rubeli (Düsseldorf 1966); *Das Solokonzert* (MW).

Symphony: Gen. Bibl.: E. Bücken, *Musik d. Rokoko u. d. Klassik* (Bücken Hdb.); W. Fischer, *Instr.musik von 1750 bis 1880* (Adler Hdb.) and *Zur Entwicklungsgesch. d. Wiener klass. Stils* (StMw III); V. Helfert, *Zur Entwicklungsgesch. der Sonatenform* (AfMw VII, 1925); K. Nef, *Gesch. d. Sinfonie u. Suite* (Lpz. 1921); F. Noack, *Sinfonie u. Suite* (2 vols. in *Kretzschmars Führer durch d. Konzertsaal* (Lpz. 1932); R. Sondheimer, *Die formale Entwicklung d. vorkl. Sinfonie* (AfMw IV) and *Die Theorie d. Sinfonie i. 18. Jh.* (Lpz. 1925); R. v. Tobel, *Die Formenwelt d. klass. Instr.musik* (Bern 1935); F. Torrefranca, *Le Origini della Sinfonia* (RMI 1913–5); *Die Sinfonie* (MW); art. Klassik (MGG). *Changes in Sonority:* A. Feil, *Satztechn. Fragen in d. Komp.lehren von Niedt, Riepel u. Koch* (Diss. Heidelberg 1955); O. Schreiber, *Orchester u. Orchesterpraxis in Deutschland zwischen 1780 u. 1850* (Bln. 1938). *G. B. Pergolesi:*

C. L. Cudworth, *Notes on the Instrumental Works attributed to P.* (M&L 1949); F. Walker, *Two Centuries of P. Forgeries and Misattributions* (M&L 1949); see also under Opera. *G. B. Sammartini:* G. de St-Foix, chronol. of works in SIMG 15; R. Sondheimer, *G. B. S.* (ZfMw 1920–1). *G. Pugnani:* A. Mury, *Die Instr.werke G. P.s* (1941); E. M. v. Zschinsky-Troxler, *P.* (Bln. 1939). *G. C. Wagenseil:* G. Hausswald, *Der Divertimento-Begriff bei W.* (AfMw 1952); H. Horowitz, *W. als Sinfoniker* (Diss. Vienna); arts. Cassation, Divertimento, Serenade (MGG). *J. G. Reutter:* new ed. of Reutter's, Wagenseil's, Monn's, and Starzer's instr. works DTÖ 15, 2, and 19, 2; L. Stollbrock, *Leben u. Wirken d. J. G. R. jun.* (VfMw 1892).

Mannheim: new eds. DTB 3, 1; 7, 2; 8, 2; 15; 16: index and works: J. Stamitz, Richter, Filtz, Holzbauer, Cannabich, Toëschi, K. Stamitz, Eichner, Fränzl, Beck, Erskin, and Danzi. H. Riemann, prefaces to the new eds. in DTB, particularly 3, 1, and 7, 2; F. Waldkirch, *Die konzertanten Sinfonien d. Mannheimer im 18. Jh.* (Diss. Heidelberg 1931); *Klarinettenkonzerte des 18. Jh.* (ED 41); *Flötenkonzerte der Mannheimer Schule* (ED 51). *J. Stamitz:* P 135; P. Gradenwitz, *J. S.' Leben* (Brno 1936). *F. X. Richter:* P 136; W. Gässler, *Die Sinf. v. F. X. R.* (Diss. Munich 1940). *A. Filtz:* P 137; art. Filtz (MGG). *I. Holzbauer:* new ed. *Instr. chamber music* ED 24; art. MGG. *C. G. Toëschi:* R. Münter, *Die Sinfonien T.s* (Diss. Munich 1956). *C. Cannabich:* H. Hofer, *C. C.* (Diss. Munich 1921). *F. Beck:* R. Sondheimer, *Die Sinfonien v. F. B.* (ZfMw IV).

North German School: M. Flueler, *Die norddt. Sinf. z. Z. Friedrich d. Gr.* (Bln. Diss. 1908). *Graun brothers:* K. Mennicke, *Hasse u. d. Brüder Graun als Sinfoniker* (Lpz. 1906); art. Karl Heinrich und Johann Gottlieb Graun (MGG). *W. F. Bach:* M. Falck, *W. F. B.* (Lpz. 2nd ed. 1919); art. W. F. B. (MGG). *C. P. E. Bach:* "Versuch . . ." new ed. Lpz. 1906, tr. Engl. N. Y. 1948, facs. Lpz. 1957; themat. index, ed. A. Wotquenne (Lpz. 1905); ed. of letters in prep. (IMBA); A. E. Cherbuliez, *C. P. E. B.* (Zurich 1940); H. Jalowetz, *C. P. E. B. u. d. Wiener Klassiker* (SIMG VI); H. Mersmann, *Ein Programmtrio C. P. E. B.s* (JbP 1917); H. Miesner, *C. P. E. B. in Hamburg* (Lpz. 1929); A. Schering, *C. P. E. B. u. das "redende Prinzip" in der Musik* (JbP 1938); E. F. Schmid, *C. P. E. B. u. s. Kammermusik* (Kassel 1931); O. Vrieslander, *C. P. E. B.* (Munich 1923). *J. C. F. Bach:* G. Schünemann, *J. C. F. B.* (Bach-Jb. 1914).

Paris: B. S. Brook, *La Symphonie française dans la second moitié du 18e siècle* (3 vols., Paris 1962). *F. J. Gossec:* L. Dufrane, *G.* (Paris 1927); F. Hellouin, *G.* (Paris 1903); J. G. Prod'homme, *G.* (Paris 1949).

London: J. C. Bach: H. P. Schökel, *J. C. B. u. die Instr.musik s. Zeit* (with them. catalogue of the instr. works, Wolfenbüttel 1926); C. S. Terry, *J. C. B.* (London 1929); F. Tutenberg, *Die Sinfonie J. C. B.s* (with them. catalogue of the symphonies, Wolfenbüttel 1928).

The Early Classical Period: A. Feil, *Satztechnische Fragen in d. Komp.lehren von Niedt, Riepel u. Koch* (Diss. Heidelberg 1955); W. Fischer, *Zur Entwicklungsgesch. des Wiener klass. Stils* (StMw III); K. Westphal, *Der Begriff der mus. Form in der Wiener Klassik* (Lpz. 1935); MW; art. Klassik (MGG). *J. Haydn:* coll. ed. (Lpz. 1908–   , 10 vols. publ.); coll. ed. of the Haydn Soc., Boston, Vienna, Lpz., Wiesbaden, discontd. after 4 vols.; coll. ed. of Jos.-Hadyn-Institut e. V. Cologne (1958–   , Munich and Duisburg). E. Mandyczewsky, Themat. Index in coll.

ed.; A. v. Hoboken, *Themat. Index* (1st vol., Mainz 1957). D. Bartha, ed., *Ges. Briefe u. Aufzeichnungen* (Kassel 1965); coll. ed. of letters in prep. (IMBA). R. Forster, *H.-Ikonographie* (Eisenstadt 1932). Monographs by K. Geiringer (Potsdam 1932, Mainz 1959, also in Engl.); H. Kretzschmar, *H.s Jugendsinfonien* (JbP 1908); H. C. R. Landon, *The Symphonies of J. H.* (London 1955, and suppl. London 1961); J. P. Larsen, *Die Haydn-Überlieferung* (Copenh. 1939); L. Nowak, *H.* (Zurich, Lpz., Vienna, 2nd ed. 1959); C. F. Pohl (2 vols., Lpz. 1878, 3rd vol. by H. Botstiber, Lpz. 1927); A. Schering, *Bemerkungen zu H.s Programmsinfonien* (JbP 1939); E. F. Schmid, *J. H. Ein Buch von Vorfahren u. Heimat des Meisters* (Kassel 1934); L. Schmidt (Bln. 2nd ed. 1906); A. Schnerich (Zurich 2nd ed. 1926); L. Somfai, ed., *J. H., sein Leben in zeitgen. Bildern* (Kassel 1966); and H. J. Therstappen, *H.s sinfonisches Vermächtnis* (Wolfenbüttel 1941). *W. A. Mozart:* coll. ed., Lpz.; new coll. ed., Kassel 1955–   ; coll. ed. of letters and sketches (4 vols., Kassel 1962–   ); coll. ed. of letters of the Mozart family (Lpz. 1914), new ed. IMBA (Lindau i. B., 1949–   ); *Mozart-Jahrbücher*, 1923– ; *Chron. them. Verzeichnis d. Werke* (L. v. Köchel, 6th ed. by F. Giegling, A. Weinmann, and G. Sievers, Wiesbaden 1963); *M.-Handbuch*, ed. O. Schneider and A. Algatzy (Vienna 1963); O. E. Deutsch, ed., *M. Die Dokumente seines Lebens* (Kassel 1961); *M. u. seine Welt in zeitgen. Bildern* (Kassel 1961); H. Abert, 2 vols. Lpz. 1919–21, as 3rd ed. of work by O. Jahn (1856); A. Einstein (London 1945); R. Haas (Potsdam 1933); B. Paumgartner (Zurich 6th ed. 1967); E. Schenk (Zurich, Lpz., Vienna 1955); L. Schiedermair (Bonn 2nd ed. 1948); D. Schulz, *M.s Jugendsinfonien* (Lpz. 1900); G. de St-Foix, *Les Symphonies de M.* (Paris 1932); T. de Wyzewa and G. de St-Foix, *W.A.M.*, 5 vols., Paris 1912–46. *K. D. von Dittersdorf:* 3 symphs. in DTÖ 43, 2; C. Krebs, *Dittersdorfiana* (with Them. Cat., Bln. 1900); addenda to the Cat. in ZIMG IV. *L. Boccherini:* L. Picquot, *Notice sur la vie et les ouvrages de L. B.* (Paris 1851, new ed. with commentary Paris 1930); R. Sondheimer, *B. e la Sinfonia in "do magg.", op. 16 n. 3* (RMI 1920). *M. Clementi:* A. Casella, *M. C. et ses symphonies* (RM 1936); M. Unger, *C.s Leben* (Langensalza 1914). *J. F. X. Sterkel:* A. Scharnagel, *J. F. X. S.* (Würzburg 1943). *J. M. Kraus:* new ed. Sinf. in C min. (1783) in *Monumenta Musicae Svecicae*, Bd. 2, 1960; K. F. Schreiber, *Biog. über d. Odenwälder Komp. J. M. K.* (Buchen 1928); S. Walin, *Beitr. z. Gesch. d. schwed. Sinfonik* (Diss. Stockholm 1941).

The High Classical Period: L. v. Beethoven: coll. ed. Lpz., new coll. ed. in prep.; them. cat. ed. Nottebohm, new ed. Kastner (1913); *Catalogo storico-critico di tutte le opere*, ed. A. Bruers (Rome 1944); *Them.-bibliogr. Verzeichnis aller vollendeten Werke*, ed. G. Kinsky and G. Halm (Munich-Duisburg 1955); W. Hess, *Verz. der nicht in der Ges. Ausg. veröffentlichten Werke* (Wiesbaden 1957). Historically important studies by Wegeler and Ries (1838), Schindler (1840), Marx (1859), and Nohl (1864). Letters (ed. Kalischer, 5 vols., Bln. 1906–8). *B.s Persönlichkeit. Urteile d. Zeitgenossen* (ed. A. Leitzmann, 2 vols. Lpz. 1914); *B. in Berichten d. Zeitgenossen* (ed. A. Leitzmann, Lpz. 1921). *B.-Jahrbücher* (1908–   ). *Nbks.*, ed. Nottebohm ("Beethoveniana" 1872, 1887); ed. of conversation nbks. begun by Nohl (1924) and G. Schünemann (1941), and by K.-H. Köbler (4 vols., Lpz. 1967). Monographs by A. W. Thayer (reworked in Ger. by Dieters and Riemann, 5 vols. 1866–1908; orig. Engl. publ. N. Y. 1921); P. Bekker (Bln. 1911); G. Ernest (Bln. 1920); A.

Halm (Lpz. 1927); L. Schiedermair (Bonn 3rd ed. 1951); R. Riezler (Zurich 8th ed. 1962); R. Rolland (7 vols., Paris 1928–45); R. Bory, *B. Leben u. Werk in Bildern* (Zurich 1960); J. Schmidt-Görg, *B. Die Gesch. seiner Familie* (Munich and Duisburg 1964); A. Schmitz (Bonn 1927). Specifically on the symphonies: Grove (London 1896); Colombani (Turin 1897); Prod'homme (new ed. Paris 1949); Weingartner (Lpz. 1906); Kretzschmar (Führer durch den Konzertsaal); K. Nef (Lpz. 1928); Hutschenruyter (The Hague 1928); Chantavoine (Paris 1932); Magni-Dufflocq (Milan 1935); Oboussier (Bln. 1937). *C. Czerny:* H. Steger, *Beitr. z. C.s Leben u. Schaffen* (Diss. Munich 1924). *F. Ries:* L. Überfeld, *R.' Jugendentwicklung* (Diss. Bonn 1915). *J. Wölfl:* R. Baum, *J. W.* (Kassel 1928). *A. Eberl:* F. J. Ewens, *A.E.* (Dresden 1927).

Early Romantic Period: 19th-Century Music in Gen.: E. Bücken, *Musik d. 19. Jh. bis zur Moderne* (Bücken Hdb) and *Romantik u. Realismus* (A. Schering-Festschrift, Bln. 1937); C. Dahlhaus, ed., *Studien zur Trivialmusik im 19. Jh.* (Regensburg 1967); G. Knepler, *Musikgesch. des 19. Jh.* (2 vols., Bln. 1961); P. H. Lang, *Music in Western Civilization* (N. Y. 1941); H. J. Moser, *Gesch. d. dt. Musik III;* W. Oehlmann, *Die Musik des 19. Jh.* (Bln. 1953); H. Riemann, *Gesch. d. Musik seit Beethoven* (Stuttg. 1900). *Romantic Movt. in Music:* G. Becking, *Zur mus. Romantik* (DVLG 1924); E. Bücken, *Romantik u. Realismus* (A. Schering-Festschrift, Bln. 1937); H. Eckardt, *Die Musikauff. d. franz. Romantik* (Diss. Heidelbg. 1932); A. Einstein, *The Romantic Era in Music* (N. Y. 1946); E. Glöckner, *Stud. z. rom. Psychol. d. Musik* (Diss Bonn 1909); E. Istell, *Die Blütezeit d. mus. Romantik in Deutschland* (Lpz. 1909); H. J. Moser, *Gesch. d. dt. Musik III;* K. Roeseling, *Die Grundhaltung rom. Melodik* (Diss. Köln 1928); MW (*Romantik in der Tonkunst*). *F. Schubert:* E. Laaff, *S.s Sinfonien* (Diss. Frankfurt a. M. 1933); H. J. Therstappen, *Die Entwicklung d. Form b. S., dargestellt an d. ersten Sätzen s. Sinf.* (Lpz. 1931).

High Romantic Period: R. Schumann: Thematic catalogue (Lpz., N. Y.); monographs by H. Abert (Bln. 4th ed. 1920), W. Boetticher (Bln. 1941), E. Bücken (Cologne 1940), W. Dahms (Bln. 1916), G. Eismann (*R. S. Eine Biographie in Wort und Bild*, Lpz. 1964), J. W. v. Wasielewski (Lpz. 5th ed. 1926), and K. H. Wörner (Zurich and Freiburg i. B. 1949); S.'s coll. writings on music and musicians (Lpz. 1854, 5th ed. 1914, ed. by M. Kreisig); S.'s letters (2 vols., Lpz. 2nd ed. 1904); sel. letters and writings (ed. W. Boetticher, Bln. 1942, also with numerous previously unpubl. items supplied by G. Eismann, 2 vols., Lpz. 1956); early letters (Lpz. 3rd ed. 1891). *F. Hiller:* R. Sietz, *Aus F. H.s Briefwechsel. Beitr. zu einer Biographie* (Cologne 1958). *J. Brahms:* basic monograph by M. Kalbeck (4 vols., Bln. 2nd ed. 1908–15); biographies by A. v. Ehrmann (Lpz. 1933), E. Evans (4 vols., London 1912–38), K. Geiringer (N. Y. 2nd ed. 1947), R. Gerber (Potsdam 1938), F. May (Lpz. 1911), C. Rostand (2 vols., Paris 1954), and R. H. Schauffler (N. Y. 1933); art. Brahms (MGG); *Ein B.-Bilderbuch*, ed. by V. von Miller zu Aichholz (Vienna 1905); individual scholarly studies: W. F. Korte, *Bruckner u. B.* (Tutzing 1963); V. Luithlen, *Studie zu B.' Werken in Variationenform* (StMw 14); A. Sturke, *Der Stil in B.' Werken* (Würzburg 1932); V. Urbantschitsch, *Die Entwicklung der Sonatenform bei B.* (StMw 14). Correspondence in 16 vols., ed. (1907–   ) by the *Deutsche B.-Gesellschaft,* suppl. with the corr. with Clara Schumann, Billroth and others. *Them. Verz.nis sämtl. im Druck erschienener Werke* (Bln. 1907, enl. ed. N. Y. 1956). *A. Bruckner:* compl. ed. 1930–   in 22 vols., Musikwissenschaftlicher Verlag, Vienna; basic biog. (4 vols., Regensburg 1922–36) by A. Göllerich (1st and 2nd vols.) and M. Auer (3rd and 4th vols.); sep. studies esp. by M. Auer (Vienna 6th ed. 1949), H. A. Grunsky (Stuttgart 1922), R. Haas (Potsdam 1934), A. Halm (Munich 1914), W. F. Korte (*B. u. Brahms,* Tutzing 1963), E. Kurth (2 vols., Bln. 1926), A. Orel (Vienna 1925), F. Wohlfahrt (Lpz. 1943), and W. Wolff (Zurich 1948); letters (2 vols., Regensburg); letters, documents, reports (ed. by A. Orel, Vienna 1953); art. Bruckner (MGG).

Turn of the Century: G. Mahler: compl. ed. in process; cat. of works (Vienna 1959); monographs by P. Bekker (*M.s Sinfonien,* Bln. 1921), D. Mitchell (*G. M., the Early Years,* London 1958), A. Roller (*Die Bildnisse von G. M.,* Lpz. 1922), P. Stefan (Munich 1910), R. Specht (Bln. 1913), and B. Walter (Frankfurt a. M. 1957); letters, ed. A. M. Mahler (Vienna 1924); Anna Maria Mahler, *Reminiscences and letters* (Amsterdam 1940; Engl., Lond. and N. Y. 1946); 10th Symph. (Facs. of the sketch sheets and score, Bln. 1924); art. Mahler (MGG).

Program Symphony and Symphonic Poem: J. Bergfeld, *Die formale Struktur der sinf. Dichtungen* (Eisenach 1931); E. Bienenfeld, *Darstellung von Schlachten i. d. Programmusik* (ZIMG VIII); O. Klauwell, *Gesch. d. Programmusik* (Lpz. 1910); A. Schering, *Beethoven u. d. Dichtung* (Bln. 1936); W. Wiora, *Absolute Musik* (art. in MGG); art. Programmusik (MGG). *H. Berlioz:* compl. ed. Lpz., new compl. ed. in prep.; monographs by J. Barzun (2 vols., Boston 1950), A. Boschot (3 vols., Paris 1906–13), L. Constantin (Paris 1934), A. Jullien (1888), R. Louis (Lpz. 1904), and G. Prod'homme (2nd ed. 1913); B.'s lit. works in a Ger. compl. ed. in 10 vols. (Lpz.); B.'s *Traité d'instrumentation* (1844, available in several revisions, incl. one by R. Strauss, 1905); C. Hopkinson, *A Bibliog. of the Mus. and Lit. Works of H. B.* (Edinburgh 1951); art. Berlioz (MGG); numerous eds. of the letters. *F. Liszt:* coll. ed. 1907–   ; coll. writings (4 vols. Lpz. 1910); basic studies by L. Ramann (Lpz. 1880–94) and by P. Raabe (2 vols., Stuttgart 1931); special studies by H. Engel (Potsdam 1936), E. Haraszti (Paris 1967), Z. László and B. Mátéka (Kassel 1967), and P. Rehberg and G. Nestler (Zurich and Stuttgart 1961); letters 1835–86, ed. M. Prahács (Kassel 1967); illustrated volumes on Liszt assembled by R. Bory (Geneva 1936) and by W. Füssmann with B. Matika (Langensalza 1936), as well as by H. Weilgung and W. Handrick (Weimar 1958); letters from Hungarian collections 1835–86, ed. M. Prahács (Kassel 1966); Liszt's letters publ. by La Mara (8 vols., Lpz. 1893–1904); corr. betw. Wagner and Liszt (2 vols., Lpz. 2nd ed. 1900). *A. Ritter:* S. v. Hausegger, *A. R.* (Bln. 1907).

France after Berlioz: V. Debay and P. Locard, *Ecole rom.fr.* (Lav. Enc.); C. Le Senne, *Période contemporaine* (Lav. Enc.); G. Servières, *La symphonie en France au 19e siècle* (Ménestrel 1923). *C. Franck:* monographs incl. those by V. d'Indy (Paris 1906), W. Mohr (Stuttgart 1942), and K. Demuth (London 1949). *P. Dukas:* G. Favre, *P.D.* (Paris 1948); art. Dukas (MGG).

Eastern Europe: P. Tchaikovsky: coll. ed. Moscow 1940–   ; basic study by Modeste Tchaikovsky (Moscow 1900–2, tr. Engl.); extensive bibl. in many languages includes monographs by A.-E. Cherbuliez (*T. u. die russ. Musik,* Rüschlikon-Zurich 1948), N. van der Pals (Potsdam 1940), R. H. Stein (Bln. 1927), K. v. Wolfurt (Zurich 1952), and F. Zagiba (Zurich, Lpz., Vienna 1953); Diaries (N. Y. 1945). *A. Dvořák:*

compl. crit. ed. 1954–   Prague; J. G. Burghauser, themat. cat. (in Czech, Ger., and Engl.); J. Clapham, *D. Musician and Craftsman* (London 1966); A. Hořejš, *A.D. Sein Leben in Bildern* (Prague 1955); A. Robertson, *D.;* H. Sirp, *A.D.* (Potsdam 1939); O. Šourek, *Chron., them. u. system. Verzeichnis* (Bln. 1917), *D. in Briefen u. Erinnerungen* (Prague 1954), and *D. Werkanalysen I, Orch.werke* (Prague n.d.). *Poland:* J. Węcowski, *La musique symphonique polonaise du XVIIIe siècle* (MAEO).

Scandinavian Countries: F. Berwald: coll. ed. (Kassel 1968–   ); R. Layton, *F. B.* (London 1959). *N. W. Gade:* W. Behrend, *N. W. G.* (Copenh. 1918, also tr. Ger.); A. Nielsen, cat. of works in Aarbog for Musik 1924, suppl. K. Atlung in DMT 1939. *J. Sibelius:* H. E. Johnson, *J. S.* (N. Y. 1959); N.-E. Ringbom, *S.* (Helsinki 1948, tr. Ger. Olten 1950); E. Tanzberger, *Die sinf. Dichtungen von J. S.* (Würzburg 1943), *J. S.* (Wiesbaden 1962), and *J. S. als Sinfoniker* (Congress Report, Lüneburg 1950); B. v. Törne, *S., a Close-up* (London 1937). *C. Nielsen:* C. N., *Levende Musik* (essays, Copenh. 1925, tr. Engl. London 1953), *Min fynske Barndom* (autobiog., Copenh. 1927, tr. Engl. London 1953). Monographs by L. Dolleris (Odense 1949), K. Jeppesen (Music Rev. 1946), T. Meyer and F. S. Petersen (2 vols., with cat. of works, Copenh. 1947–8), and R. Simpson (*C. N. Symphonist,* London 1952). J. Balzer, ed., *C. N.* (Copenh. 1965, tr. Engl.).

The Americas: L. M. Gottschalk: P. Arpin, *Life of L. M. G.* (N. Y. 1852); L. M. G., *Notes of a Pianist* (Phila. 1881, new ed. N. Y. 1964); O. Hensel, *Life and Letters of L. M. G.* (Boston 1870); J. T. Howard, *L. M. G.* (MQ 1932); C. E. Lindstrom, *The Am. Quality in . . . L. M. G.* (MQ 1932); V. Loggins, *Where the World Ends* (Baton Rouge 1958). *C. Ives:* H. Bellamann, *C. I.* (MQ 1933); E. Carter, *I. Today* (Mod. Music 1944); H. and S. R. Cowell, *C. I.* (N. Y. 1955); F. Grunfeld, *C. I.* (Am. Composers Alliance Bull. 1955).

Overture: H. Botstiber, *Gesch. d. Overtüre u. d. freien Orch.formen* (Lpz. 1913). *B. Donati,* Sinfonia for "Giudizio d'amore": new ed. in Botstiber.

29. Keyboard and Lute Music

Instruments

First developed in the Orient, the organ was brought to a high state of refinement at quite an early date. In Alexandria about 250 B.C. Ctesibios built an organ for which the air supply was regulated by water pressure. In 757 A.D. the organ reached Europe from Byzantium. From the 9th century on, it made its way into the Western church. By the end of the 15th century it already had bellows, channels, cases, and shutters for the wind supply, keyboards in several manuals and pedal, stops, and many ranks of pipes with contrasting timbres. The usual forms it took were three: the *portativ,* or small portable organ; the *positiv,* or stationary organ of limited scope for smaller churches or the home; and the *regal*, a small domestic reed organ.

The clavichord derived from the monochord, as instrument traditionally associated with the Pythagoreans, who used it in subdividing a length of string and generating the various tones. In the fully developed clavichord, when the key or *clavis* was pressed down, a metal bridge or tangent at the rear of each key came up and touched the string, or *chorda*. The instrument was built in two forms, one bound or fretted (*gebunden*), the other not (*ungebunden, bundfrei*). When provided with frets, or "fretted," several keys used one string; when not, there was a key for each string. Like the finger in playing a stringed instrument, the tangent shortened the string and at the same time set it in motion. Since the tangent remained in touch with the string in this type of tone production, not only could one play louder or softer but also, by moving the finger back and forth in a "quiver," or *Bebung*, one could elicit a vibrato. During the 18th century, particularly in Germany, the clavichord was accordingly the instrument preferred for sensitive or so-called singing performance.

The harpsichord—also known as the virginals, spinet, clavecin, Keilflügel, or cembalo—was constructed in an essentially different way. When the player pressed a key down, it moved a jack that had been resting on the rear end of the key. A tongue of quill or leather, projecting from the side of the jack, then plucked the string. This produced a sharp, metallic sound, which could not be modulated. It could only be strengthened by simultaneously sounding other ranks of strings and thus duplicating the tone at the higher and lower octaves if certain stops had been pulled, as on an organ. Alongside the organ, the harpsichord was the authoritative instrument for general purposes during the Baroque.

The piano—also called the Hammerklavier, Tafelklavier, Fortepiano, and Hammerflügel—goes back to a discovery made in 1709 by the Paduan Bartolommeo Cristofori in Florence. In this instrument the key when pressed down propels the hammer against the string. Two types of action were soon developed: in the "pushing-pin" mechanism, or *Stosszungenmechanik* (later developed into the "English action" and the basis of piano construction today), the hammer sits on its own support; in the "tossing mechanism," or *Prallmechanik* (the later "German" or "Viennese action"), the hammer is directly attached to the rear of the key. In 1783 Broadwood invented and patented the pedal. Erard in 1823 worked out a double escapement mechanism to permit faster repetition of a note, according to which the hammer, after striking, did not fall completely back into its original position but was checked halfway between. Iron frames and cross-stringing were first developed in America.

Keyboard Music to 1600

14th Century

The oldest extant organ tablature, containing six two-voiced and three-voiced organ pieces, is dated about 1325 and comes from England. Three of the pieces are entirely of instrumental origin; the others are *intavolature,* or polyphonic motets paraphrased, transcribed, and to some extent reduced to organ-fingering notation. Two of these vocal originals are traceable in the early-14th-century *Roman de Fauvel* in Paris. In the British manuscript, the untitled instrumental transcriptions are dances, of a type known as the *estampie.* The English tablature has mensural notation for the upper voice and letters for the lower. This manuscript, British Museum Add. 28550, is usually referred to as the Robertsbridge MS. The keyboard pieces it contains were for their own day quite chromatic, employing all the twelve half-steps of the scale.

About 1299 in Florence, the oldest organ that we know of there was built. Also in Italy several organ-builders, known to us and forming a succession, were active during the 14th and 15th centuries. The most important document of the late 14th century is the Codex Faenza 117, earlier known as the Codex Bonadies, containing over a hundred pieces for organ or other keyboard instrument, principally transcriptions of Italian and French songs by such composers as Jacopo, Landini, and Machaut, with free transformation of the vocal upper voice and with altered adoption of the tenor. Further organ transcriptions of sections from the Ordinary (*Kyrie* and *Gloria*) on the same chant melodies may be taken as evidence for the early development of the Organ Mass. No doubt we are justified in assuming that Italian organ playing particularly flourished in the 14th century. In Florence, for example, Francesco Landino (d. 1397) was quite famous as an organist—though we have no example of his specifically organ compositions today.

15th Century

The Squarcialupi Codex of about 1460 contains 354 compositions with underlaid text. Many passages in which the principal voice has been instrumentally paraphrased suggest that the compositions were played also on the organ. This manuscript belonged to the highly regarded Florentine organist Antonio Squarcialupi (1416–1480).

Remnants of 15th-century music that we can be sure was specifically for the organ are preserved only from Germany. The oldest extant document comes from Breslau around 1425. Stylistically, however, early German organ-music seems to have derived from Italy.

A manuscript of 1448 belonging to Adam Ileborgh, rector in Stendal, is more significant musically than the earlier fragments in manuscripts from Breslau, Berlin, and Munich. The style that prevailed in the Ileborgh organ book was carried on further by Konrad Paumann, a famous blind organist at the Sebalduskirche in Nuremberg and court organist in Munich from 1450 until his death there in 1473. Paumann's *Fundamentum organisandi* (1452) is an instruction book for organ playing and composition with cantus-firmus transcriptions that include some German folksongs and three *Präambeln* or Preludes as original compositions, of which the first has the form and general proportions of a toccata. The indications are in mensural notation on the upper staff and in letters on the lower.

The *Buxheimer Orgelbuch* of about 1470 is in the manner of Paumann. Containing over 250 pieces, it is the most inclusive and important source we have for the period, including ornamented transcriptions of polyphonic compositions, reworking of borrowed tenor melodies, and sixteen preludes with freely improvised passages and, by way of variety, sections in chordal style which clearly utilize the principle of contrast. It is a collective manuscript, including contributions from various composers. The transcriptions are of works by famous composers of the period—including Dunstable, Dufay, and Binchois. Often there are different variations on one song or one ballade, with changes in the ornamentation, rhythm, and harmony. By this time the compositions had become predominantly three-voiced.

16th Century

No tablatures have been preserved from the period between about 1470 and 1512 in Germany. In the immediately subsequent period, however, German organists of the 16th century constitute a group known as the "Colorists' School." Their style involved decoration, paraphrase, and variation of the original model (songs, dances, or vocal compositions) with a flood of ornaments and passages. The vocal pieces were "reduced" to compositions for the instrument. No fundamental difference existed between organ and other keyboard music. Pieces from the sacred and the secular repertoires stand side by side in all the manuscripts, which were presumably intended for use in both the church and the home. The keyboard had a range of three octaves (F to g^2 or A to b^2).

The first printed tablature appeared in Arnold Schlick's *Tabulaturen etlicher Lobgesänge und Liedlein* (1512). It contains three-voiced and four-voiced transcriptions of secular and sacred songs, entire vocal compositions and dances, and some purely instrumental pieces as fantasies and preludes.

Further tablatures are those of the organists Leonhard Kleber in Göppingen; Hans Kotter in Freiburg, Switzerland; Hans Buchner in Constance; Elias Nikolaus Ammerbach at St. Thomas's in Leipzig; Fridolin Sicher in St. Gall; and Jakob Paix in Lauingen and Neuburg on the Danube. Kotter's are notable as containing the first known dances for a keyboard instrument.

The organ composer who far surpassed all others and attracted a wide following was Paul Hofhaimer (1459–1537), chamber organist of the Archduke Sigmund of the Tirol. Later he was organist at the Emperor Maximilian's court and at the Elector Friedrich the Wise's court, first in Torgau, then in Augsburg, and finally in Salzburg.

From this period there are three basic theoretical works that deal with organ playing in Germany: *Spiegel der Orgelmacher und Organisten* (Speyer 1511) by Arnold Schlick (d. 1517), a blind organist at the Palatine court in Heidelberg; *Musica getutscht* (Basel 1511) by Sebastian Virdung; and a work that explains much about playing and the technique of making tablatures, *Fundamentum* (before 1540) by Hans Buchner.

In Italy, what was apparently the first published tablature for keyboard instruments appeared in 1518 in Rome. *Frottole intabulate da sonar organi*. In these pieces, the homophonic style of the original frottole had been transformed through ornaments and neighboring notes as well as through leaps filled in diatonically, so that it had become a kind of polyphony. The publisher and probably also the arranger of the collection was Andrea Antico. In 1523 there appeared the first volume, *Recerchari, Motetti, Canzoni,* of a collection by Marco Antonio Cavajono or Cavazono (before 1490–after 1559), the father of Girolamo Cavazzoni. These ricercari are especially distinguished and excel in a structure that is obviously disposed in sections, exhibiting development of motifs, an orderly plan of tonalities, and richness in modulation. To some extent they are written in six voice parts.

The first culmination of Italian organ and other keyboard music coincided with the Venetian school. The many works of Girolamo Cavazzoni, Annibale Padovano, Jacobus Buus, Adrian Willaert, and Francesco Bendusi are still transcriptions of vocal originals. With the great virtuosi at the organs of St. Mark's cathedral, Claudio Merulo (d. 1604), Andrea Gabrieli (about 1510–1586), and Giovanni Gabrieli (about 1555–1612), organ music assumed independent instrumental character, developing forms of its own, though the particular nature of these forms only gradually appeared.

Among them is the *ricercar,* an instrumental composition in several sections, making it possible for several themes to be treated one after the other, as in a motet. The *fantasy* is closely related to the ricercar. The *toccata* is predominantly a virtuoso composition of prelude-like character with passages, chords, and contrapuntal entries. The *canzona* is a vocal piece in tablature. Organ Masses are liturgical organ compositions, which appear at traditional places in the Gregorian chant and transcribe it. These designations, however, did not yet indicate the formal schemes that became usual in the Baroque Era only during its late phase.

In the Italian organ or keyboard tablature the notation is given on from five to eight lines for each hand. The Venetian composers attracted an extensive school.

The theoretician of the Merulo organ-style is Girolamo Diruta, with his book of exercises in organ playing, *Il Transilvano* (1593).

In Spain, the development of organ and other keyboard playing followed the same course as in the other European countries. Theoretical works were written by Juan Bermudo in 1549 and by Tomás de Sancta Maria in 1565. The most famous composer was Philip II's court organist, Antonio de Cabezón (d. 1566), whose works were published posthumously in 1578 as a pedagogical collection, *Obras de música para tecla, arpa y vihuela.* Of these the most significant were the four-voiced *tientos,* or fantasies, a form related to the Italian *ricercar.* In the art of the variation Cabezón excelled the English virginalists, being responsible for the first extant keyboard variations, called *differencias,* on dance-like and folksong-like themes in highly developed variation technique.

The leading composer at the beginning of the 17th century was Francisco Correa de Arauxo. Correa was born about 1575, became in 1598 organist at the San Salvador collegiate church in Seville, and published in 1626 his principal work, *Facultad Orgánica,* a collection of *tientos* and *discursos.* He died presumably in 1663.

In France, the Parisian printer Pierre Attaignant brought out in 1531 seven books of tablatures with chansons, dances, compositions based on the Ordinary, and motets. The composers of the transcriptions for key-board instrument are anonymous. The high technical level permits one to assume that this first printed edition had been already preceded by manu-script collections that are no longer extant. As in all the other European countries there was an abundance of forms—transcriptions of motets, song compositions, and dances, preludes, and versettes for songs at Mass and Vespers. But the French keyboard work was particularly related to the Italian. In transcribing polyphonic pieces, French composers took account of the character and possibilities of the keyboard instrument. The orna-ments were not just applied superficially but fused into the compositions themselves, as the composers exploited the peculiar nature and scope of their instrument.

In England, during the first third of the 16th century when Henry VIII was king (1509–1547), keyboard music was being composed, but it was not printed in tablature. The works were preserved only in manu-script, notably in British Museum Add. 29996 and Add. 30513. The total of about two hundred extant liturgical organ works is greater than that in all the other European countries. Among numerous composers, the leading ones were the organist at St. Paul's in London John Redford (d. 1547), Thomas Preston, and Philip ap Ryce. MS. 29996 contains only religious works. The Gregorian cantus firmus is treated in the most various manner, especially in a sort of coloration that since Dunstable had been traditional in England. The instruments had a range of four and a quarter octaves (C to g^3). Particularly notable are the successions of variations that point the way directly to Byrd and Bull.

During the reign of Elizabeth I (1558–1603), there occurred a real flowering of a music explicitly for keyboard. This was for the virginals, a small portable instrument of the cembalo type with a single set of strings. It was considered part of a proper upbringing within a certain social class to be able to play this instrument.

The two main collections are the *Fitzwilliam Virginal Book*, which is preserved in a manuscript of about 1570–1625, and *Parthenia or the Maidenhead*, which was the first printed source, issued in 1611. The great madrigalists are here represented among the composers—William Byrd, John Bull, Orlando Gibbons, John Munday, and Thomas Morley. Further collections are *My Ladye Nevell's Booke, Will Forster's Virginal Book, Benjamin Cosyn's Virginal Book,* and *The Mulliner Book* (presumably compiled around the mid-16th century).

This body of musical literature for the virginals has a number of dis-tinctive features, one of which is the fact that it is normally written on two six-line staves, one for the right hand and the other for the left. But more important is its distinctive musical material and treatment. In addition to numerous vocal transcriptions there are preludes, fantasias, dances such as the pavane, galliard, allemande, courante, and gigue, and variations on songs and dances. The fact that English composers developed a technique of their own for this instrument influenced their colleagues on the Con-tinent to introduce moving passages, broken chords, chordal attacks, and rich ornamentation, and to develop grounds, variations often explicitly carrying out some program idea as characteristic pieces over a basso ostinato (for example, in Byrd's variations on the peal of bells), and figurated upper-voice variations.

In Poland, the first mention of an organ occurs toward the end of the 12th century, at the court (1177–1194) of Duke Kazimierz the Just. In the middle of the 13th century there is a record of the death of the first Polish organist known by name, the Dominican monk Tomasz. By the end of the 14th century the organ had become quite widespread.

The earliest Polish organ compositions come from the first half of the 16th century and include arrangements of Polish and foreign vocal works. They either adhere closely to the originals or extensively rework them for instrumental performance by omitting or transferring voices and by providing them with distinctive ornamentation. Some of the original pieces bear titles such as *preambulum* or *chorea*.

There are two notable tablatures—one of Jan of Lublin, organist at the monastery in Kraśnik, and the other of the Holy Spirit Monastery in Cracow. Jan of Lublin's tablature, written between 1537 and 1548, contains some 300 pieces, of which a number bear what are usually referred to as "monograms" of their composers: 39 are signed N. C. (Mikołaj of Cracow), one N. Ch. (Mikołaj of Chrzanów), and six N. Z. The tablature of the Holy Spirit Monastery, written in 1548, contains 101 pieces, five signed N. C. and eleven N. Z., as well as works by well-known composers such as Finck, Senfl, Stoltzer, Wüst, Hofhaimer, Cavazzoni, Verdelot, and Josquin. In addition, there are some miscellaneous and fragmentary early-16th-century remains—those of an organ tablature in the Warsaw Municipal Library and an organist's wooden desk in the Biblioteka Narodowa w Warszawie, where there are also some tablatures of Preambula, transcriptions of portions of the Ordinary, and a motet by H. Finck.

Though the late-16th-century tablatures of the Warsaw Music Society are no longer extant, they contained 77 works by Polish "Monogrammists": Jakób Sowa, Christophorus Clabon, Martinus Leopolita, and Martinus Wartecki. Largely these are transcriptions of vocal works, written down about 1590. Among them was also the *Little Warsaw Tablature*, apparently part of a larger Tablature of Warsaw Music, and transcriptions of motets by Marcin Leopolita, Wacław of Szamotuły, and Marcin Wartecki. Johann Fischer Morungensis's tablature (1595) contains some pieces by Diomedes Cato.

During the 17th and 18th centuries there was notable development of organ building on the part of native and foreign masters in, for example, Leżajsk (by Jan Głowiński) and in Jędrzejów, Kazimierz, and Olkusz (by Hans Hummel of Nuremberg). These organs were played by celebrated musicians such as Tarquinio Merula and by a pupil of Frescobaldi, Andrzej Niżankowski (d. 1655). But actual manuscript sources are few. There is only one organ tablature, of about 1660, and some other scattered remains, and the only known composers are Johann Podbielski and Piotr Żelechowski.

The 17th and 18th Centuries (Baroque)

At the beginning of the 17th century in Italy, the previous epoch was magnificently summed up and concluded by Girolamo Frescobaldi (1583–1643), organist at St. Peter's in Rome, a player of European renown. Many of his works were printed as collective volumes of toccatas, ricercari, and capricci. He continued to develop the typical Gabrieli forms, such as the monothematic ricecar. In his hands the canzone, as "variation canzone," became purely instrumental compositions and freed themselves entirely from their vocal models. The capricci were often programmatic. In the preface to his first book of toccatas (1614), he urged that the emotional effect alone should determine the performance. Thus he formulated the principle of his famous *rubato* playing. His music always exhibits long line and significant imagination. After his death, however, Italian organ music declined in importance. His most famous pupil was Johann Jakob Froberger. Despite the important achievement of Frescobaldi, the organ and the harpsichord in Italy did not develop independent status until well along toward the end of the 17th century. Frescobaldi's style was further developed by Bernardo Pasquini (1637–1710).

A formally and technically revolutionary new trend in keyboard music was inaugurated by Domenico Scarlatti (1685–1757), son of Alessandro Scarlatti and choirmaster of the Cappella Giulia in Rome. In 1720 he became court harpsichordist in Lisbon and in 1729 in Madrid. In the main he wrote one-movement sonatas, sometimes entitled *essercizi* or studies, principally after 1729. There are 555 of them, mostly transmitted to us in manuscript and in many instances forming pairs. Individual sonatas of his are important contributions to the development of the sonata-allegro form. They reveal a new style of keyboard technique, involving wide leaps, crossing of hands, quick repetition of notes, trills, and passages in thirds, sixths, and octaves. In general, they are marked by playful, virtuoso ease and witty elegance. Scarlatti was the ancestor of quite modern keyboard playing.

Particular features of Domenico Scarlatti's work were taken up by others, including Francesco Durante (1684–1755), Benedetto Marcello (1686–1739), Domenico Alberti (about 1717–1740), Giovanni Battista Martini (1706–1784), Baldassare Galuppi (1706–1785), Pietro Domenico Paradisi (about 1710–1791), and Giovanni Platti (about 1700–1763).

Though the Netherlands had an old tradition of building and playing the organ, its first great creative achievement in composition for that instrument came only with Jan Pieterszoon Sweelinck (1562–1621), who was a pupil of Zarlino in Venice and later was organist in Amsterdam. He was the outstanding composer who brought together Italian, English, and Netherlands influences in organ and other keyboard works, in the form of fantasies and toccatas, and carried on the German and Netherlands traditions in transcriptions of chorales and other songs. In his fantasies the development of themes was unified and thus he essentially approached the later principle of the fugue. He showed a preference for variations, strict contrapuntalism, virtuoso playing, and sonorous echo-effects. Highly influential on the 17th-century North German generation of organists through his teaching, he was referred to in his day as the "builder of German organists" (*Deutscher Organistenmacher*). His German pupils included Scheidt in Halle, Seifert in Danzig, Schildt in Wolfenbüttel, Scheidemann in Hamburg, and Jakob Praetorius the Younger in Hamburg. In keyboard music Sweelinck attained special importance through his variations on secular songs.

The first leading master of French clavecin music was Louis XIV's court clavecinist Jacques Champion de Chambonnières (*ca.* 1602–*ca.* 1671). By transferring the principle of the suite to keyboard music he was the creator of the French keyboard suite. His *Pièces de clavecin* (1670) are suite-like collections of numerous dances and other movements without any necessary order in their succession. The variety in the series remained characteristic of French keyboard music. Occasional super-scriptions on the movements do not indicate programs, but are rather to be understood simply as identifying labels. He developed a technique of harpsichord playing with rich ornaments, broken chords, melodic middle voices, light playing figures, and a delicate compositional technique influenced by the French lutenists and the English virginalists. Particularly through his many pupils, the entire school of clavecinists in the 17th and 18th centuries can be traced back to him.

Among those who studied with him was Louis Couperin (1626–1661). His nephew François Couperin le Grand (1668–1733), organist of the royal chapel and teacher of the royal family, led the French harpsichord art to its climax. He was the author of an instructional book *L'art de toucher le clavecin* (1716, 2nd ed. 1717). Between 1713 and 1730 he published a total of four volumes, containing twenty-seven suites, which he called *Ordres*. He lightened their sequence with numerous insertions, sometimes having as many as twenty movements. He wrote a kind of music unusually full of fantasy and wit, in moods all the way from serious gravity and mourning to the development of a Rococo-like art of the musical miniature, so far as both expression and playing technique were concerned, involving hand-crossings, repeated notes, and a most highly differentiated art of ornament. Many of the pieces have a program, such as the characterization of female types, tender moods, and scenes of great festivity. Couperin's historical significance lies in his clever synthesis of the French clavecin tradition with the style of the Italian Baroque sonata. According to Pirro, he "summed up French music" and particularly influenced Johann Sebastian Bach.

Couperin's art was carried on further by Jean-Philippe Rameau (1683–1764), but was scarcely raised to a higher degree. Rameau's keyboard works are the *Premier livre de Pièces de clavecin* (1706); *Pièces de clavecin avec une méthode pour le méchanique des doigts* (about 1724), reissued in 1731 with a "table pour les agréments"; *Nouvelles suites de pièces de clavecin* (between 1727 and 1731); and *Pièces de clavecin en concert avec un violon ou une flûte et une viole ou un deuxième violon* (1741).

Two very significant composers were active during the time between the two Couperins: Nicolas Le Bègûe (1630–1702) and Jean-Henri d'Anglebert (1628–1691).

In France organists used mainly forms that were linked with the liturgy, such as portions of the Mass, interludes, and verses of the Magnificat. Composers known for their keyboard music include Jean Titelouze (1563–1633) of Rouen; André Raison of Paris; Nicolas Gigault (1625–1702) of Paris, who brought out his *Livre de Musique pour l'orgue* (1685); Nicolas de Grigny (1671–1703), at Notre Dame in Reims, whose *Livre d'orgue* (*ca.* 1700) Bach copied out for his own use; Louis-Nicolas Clérambault (1676–1749); Louis Claude d'Aquin or Daquin (1694–1772), organist of the royal chapel and well known as clavecinist; Jean François Dandrieu (1682–1738), court organist in Paris; and Louis Marchand (1669–1732), of Paris, a serious composer, significant virtuoso and improviser, unfortunately known mainly from a somewhat fancifully embroidered account of his encounter with Bach in Dresden.

Clear separation between organ and other keyboard music occurred in France as early as the beginning of the 17th century.

Germany

In Germany during the Baroque, interest in keyboard music was so intense and the forms that developed were so various that distinctions are often made between the South German, Central German, and North German traditions.

South German keyboard music, predominantly influenced by Frescobaldi and other Italian composers and by the composers of France, showed an inclination for clearly organized, perspicuous forms, for clear sound, and for imitation among the voices on a harmonic basis. The principal emphasis was on clavichord and harpsichord music, as Catholic worship in South Germany gave comparatively little scope for individual freedom in organ playing.

One of the leading composers was Johann Jakob Froberger (1616–1667), born in Stuttgart, pupil of Frescobaldi in Rome, court organist in Vienna and later on tour through Europe as organist. In addition to writing toccatas and capriccios for organ in the style of Frescobaldi, he founded the German keyboard suite after the French model. His suites follow the sequence: Allemande, Courante, Sarabande, and Gigue. As a result, this particular succession of movements became the norm around 1650. He also unified the suite by maintaining one key throughout and by establishing inner motivic connections within it. Some of his pieces have suggestions of a program, such as a *Lamento;* others are variations in suite form, such as *Auf die Mayerin.* He was the most significant German keyboard composer before Bach. With his work German music for clavier became quite distinct from that for organ.

In connection with Froberger there arose a Viennese keyboard school, represented by Alessandro Poglietti (d. 1683), Ferdinand Tobias Richter (1649–1711), and Georg Reutter the Elder (1656–1738).

Johann Kaspar Kerll (1627–1693) was influenced by Carissimi and Frescobaldi in Rome, and later became music-director of the court chapel in Munich and court organist in Vienna. He was also of lasting influence as an organ teacher. In his compositions he fused Italian influences with German feeling and gained widespread popularity with his characteristic capriccios such as the *Cuckoo Call, Battle,* and *Styrian Shepherd.*

Georg Muffat (1653–1704), who studied in Paris and Italy, was an organist in Alsace, Salzburg, and Passau. He united German, Italian, and French styles in his *Apparatus Musico-Organisticus* (1690).

His son, Gottlieb Theophil Muffat (1690–1770), a pupil of Fux, became court organist in Vienna. Adopting the typically French overture as introduction for his keyboard suites, he has a *ciacona* with thirty-eight variations over an ostinato voice in his *Componimenti musicali per il Cembalo* (1739). He also shows strong Couperin influence in his program pieces and in the performance technique of his works. His are the next-most-important keyboard suites after Bach's and link the Baroque and the Pre-Classical Viennese eras.

Franz Xaver Murschhauser (1663–1738), born in Alsace, was active at the Munich Frauenkirche. Having been a pupil of Kerll, he exhibits many features derived from him.

The keyboard music of Johann Caspar Ferdinand Fischer (d. 1746), court conductor in Baden, shows French influence in the suites for cembalo, *Musikalisches Blumen-Büschlein* (1696) and *Musikalischer Parnass* (1738). In his *Ariadne musica* (1702) there are preludes and fugues in twenty keys, presupposing the equal temperament established by Werckmeister. They were influential on other composers, including Johann Sebastian Bach, particularly in the preludes.

Johann Pachelbel (1653–1706), born in Nuremberg, was influenced by various of Kerll's pupils. He served as organist in Eisenach, Gotha, Erfurt, Stuttgart, and Nuremberg. In his compositions he fused Southern, Middle, and Northern German styles, giving particular place to predominantly South German features. He wrote keyboard suites that proceed through seventeen keys, chorale variations in conjunction with the South and Central German schools, variations in his *Musikalische Sterbensgedanken* and in his *Hexachordum Apollinis* (1699), fugues, fantasias, and ciacone for organ. A particular type of chorale fantasy was so characteristic of him that it is often referred to as the Pachelbel type, in which the chorale melody is placed in the upper voice in extended form while the other voices imitate it.

Johann Erasmus Kindermann (1616–1655), organist in Nuremberg, wrote strongly contrapuntal organ fugues and keyboard suites. Consisting of movements arranged according to keys, they maintain certain thematic interconnections.

Central German organ music played an intermediate role between Northern and Southern. Several members of the Bach family were among the many organists particularly connected with the Protestant church. The most significant Central German composers were:

Samuel Scheidt (1587–1654), a pupil of Sweelinck and organist at the St. Maurice Church in Halle. Along with Schütz and Schein he was one of the three "great S's." His main works were the *Tabulatura nova*

(1624) and the *Görlitzer Tabulaturbuch* (1650). The former is an inclusive German work, containing the whole stock-in-trade for organ and other keyboard playing of the period. Influences from Sweelinck and from the South German organists appear in Scheidt's monothematic fantasies, echo pieces, tripartite fugues after the model of Sweelinck, variations on folk-songs, and various technical effects such as passages and the repetition of tones. His polyphonic chorale preludes point toward the future, particularly in their treatment of the cantus firmus.

The most significant of Scheidt's many pupils was the song-composer Adam Krieger (1634–1666).

Johann Krieger (1652–1735), who was born in Nuremberg, served as organist in Zittau. In his *Sechs musikalische Partien* (1697) he wrote keyboard suites, and in his *Anmuthigen Clavier-Übung* (1698) toccata-like preludes and ricercare with regular development sections.

Johann Kuhnau (1660–1722), cantor at St. Thomas's in Leipzig before Bach, was a musician of cultivation, versatility, and literary talent. In the second book of his *Klavierübung* (1692) he wrote a *Sonate aus dem B*. Then, in his *Frische Clavier Früchte oder die sieben Sonaten* (1696) he planned out the numbers rather freely but mostly in four contrasting sections: Vivace, Adagio, Allegro, and Andante. Although it is true that Kuhnau played an important role in the early development of the sonata, he did not invent the form—as he was long assumed to have done. He had at hand models in the works of G. Strozzi, Legrenzi, and Cazzati, who had transcribed trio sonatas for the keyboard. Kuhnau also was the composer of program sonatas, notably six *Biblische Historien* in 1700, which depicted such episodes as the "Combat between David and Goliath" and the "Wedding of Jacob." Kuhnau's works helped to focus the musical amateur's attention on keyboard playing.

Friedrich Wilhelm Zachow (1663–1712), organist at the Marktkirche in Halle and teacher of Handel, based his art on traditions of the chorale prelude and variation as practiced by Scheidt and Pachelbel.

The keyboard works of Georg Philipp Telemann (1681–1767) represented predominantly the *galant* or polite style. The flowing, elegant keyboard writing in suites and figures of distinctly light character was determined by Italian and French influences.

A prominent member of Johann Sebastian Bach's circle was Johann Gottfried Walther (1684–1748), city organist and court musician in Weimar. He was a relative and friend of Bach, a composer, theoretician, historiographer, and collector of contemporary organ music. He edited the *Musikalisches Lexicon* (1732), the first encyclopedia of music. For the organ he composed chorale preludes in all current styles and with significant contrapuntal art.

North German organ music occupied a leading position during the 17th and 18th centuries. It tended toward the monumental and fantastic, with ornamental flourishes, and was often laid out in contrasting sections that might be virtuoso-homophonic or fugal. The melody was often interrupted by pauses, broken chords, chromatically colored transitional chords, pedal passages and trills, and double pedaling. Mainly the organist played preludes and postludes in conformity with the liturgy. He also played fantasias, fugues, and chorale preludes.

Sweelinck was the founder of the North German organ school. His German pupils were Heinrich Scheidemann (*ca.* 1595–1663), organist at St. Catherine's in Hamburg; Melchior Schildt (1592 or 1593–1667), organist in Wolfenbüttel, Copenhagen, and Hanover; and Paul Siefert (1586–1666), organist at St. Mary's in Danzig, previously in Königsberg and Warsaw.

The Sweelinck school was carried on further in North Germany by a succession of organists, many of whom were pupils of Sweelinck's pupils. They include Matthias Weckmann (about 1619–1674), who studied with Schütz, J. Praetorius, and Scheidemann, and later became court organist in Dresden and organist at St. James's in Hamburg. There he founded the Collegium Musicum and was a close friend of Froberger. Johann Adam Reinken (1623–1722) was a pupil of Scheidemann at St. Catherine's in Hamburg and succeeded him in that position. Franz Tunder (1614–1667) was organist at St. Mary's in Lübeck. Dietrich Buxtehude (1637–1707) was the son-in-law and successor of Tunder in Lübeck. Reinken and Buxtehude particularly influenced Bach. Buxtehude continued the renowned *Abendmusiken* or evening musical programs with soloists, chorus, and orchestra during the pre-Christmas season. His music was quite imaginative, particularly in the free compositions for organ such as the preludes and toccatas. His works are of three kinds: free compositions, chorale variations, and chorale preludes. In all, there are nineteen suites and six keyboard variations. Nicolaus Bruhns (1665–1697), pupil of Buxtehude, became the organist in Husum. Vincent Lübeck (1654 or 1656–1740) was organist at St. Nicholas's in Hamburg. Georg Böhm (1661–1733), born and trained in Thuringia, was the organist at St. John's in Lüneburg. Also influential on Bach, he was midway between Central and North German organists. New subjectivity and sensitivity appeared in the old forms, contributing to the Bohemian type of chorale transcription. He was responsible for developing his own particular type of chorale adaptation, which involved brief treatment with artful decoration of the melody under the influence of French clavecin ornaments.

In Bohemia, the greatest organ composer and leader of the entire Czech school of composers was Bohuslav Matěj Černohorský (1684–1742), whose organ compositions and vocal music grew out of the spirit of Czech melody. Some of his fugues for organ are extant, as are also six of his vocal works. His pupils include Jan Zach (1699–1773), František Ignác Tůma (1704–1774), Josef Ferdinand Norbert Seger (1716–1782), and František Xaver Brixi (1732–1771).

Summary

Thus, during the transition from the 17th to the 18th century, or as the High Baroque turned into the Late Baroque, musical forms were unified and reduced to type. Organ music was clearly separated from harpsichord music. In the performance of pieces there were differences in character between the compositions for harpsichord and those for clavichord. Ricercare and canzone disappeared almost completely. The place once occupied by the ricercar was taken by the fugue with themes answering at the fifth and with the introduction of regular episodes between the development sections. There was not much elaboration of folk-song for organ; instead, transcriptions of the chorale became more and more significant. The toccata became the virtuoso performance piece, with bold and playful passages, arpeggios, chord work, and pedal soli. In clavier music, from Froberger on, the suite won increasing favor. Variation form was further developed. The artistic summary of the Baroque era occurred in the organ and clavier music of Johann Sebastian Bach.

Perhaps we should note two technical details in the presentation of some of the material on J. S. Bach's and subsequent composers' works for keyboard instruments. One is the use of a bit of German musicological shorthand for the indication of the keys in which pieces are written: capital letters for major keys and small letters for minor. Thus, for example, "Fugues in c, G, a" means "Fugues in C minor, G major, and A minor." Another is the use of the designation "clavier," which simply means "keyboard." Bach's *Wohltemperiertes Klavier* is the "Well-Tempered Clavier" because the instrument for which it was intended is not really specified. It could be the clavichord, harpsichord, or piano—or, for that matter, if one really wished, the organ. This latitude—but with primary focus on the harpsichord—is suggested here by the use of the word "clavier."

Johann Sebastian Bach

The great master of organ composition was Johann Sebastian Bach (1685–1750). His work for organ brings together the traditions of Central, South, and North Germany. He encountered the Central German traditions in Ohrdruf, Arnstadt, Mühlhausen, and Weimar—during stages of his career that have been reviewed in this book under the heading of Protestant church music. He also came in contact with the South German School during his stay at Ohrdruf, his study of Pachelbel's work, and his transcription of the Italian concerti at Weimar. The North German School he encountered in the persons of Böhm at Lüneburg, Reinken at Hamburg, and Buxtehude at Lübeck. Writing in all forms, Bach brought them to the peak of their perfection. Having mastered all the traditional types, he developed them further and heightened their content. He also achieved entirely new heights of virtuosity. Many of these virtuoso works he wrote immediately before or during the time he was in Weimar. After 1735 he returned to the organ with renewed intensity and wrote his final masterpieces.

His works include chorale transcriptions, or chorale harmonizations, and fantasies, preludes, and fugues, as well as a number of further works. The chorale arrangements include forty-six chorales in the *Orgel-Büchlein* (Weimar 1717); six chorales printed between 1747 and 1750 and known as the *Schübler* chorales; eighteen chorales, often referred to as the "great chorales," during the revision of which Bach died; the *Clavierübung*, Part III (*Vorspiele über Catechismus- und andere Gesänge*), printed in 1739; twenty-four chorale preludes in Kirnberger's collection; another group of twenty-eight chorale preludes; and four chorale variations (including the canonic variations on *Vom Himmel hoch*, printed about 1745 at the press of Balthasar Schmidt in Nuremberg). The fantasias, preludes, and fugues include eighteen Preludes and Fugues; Preludes and Fugues in c, G, a; Fantasie and Fugue in a; *Fantasia con imitazione* in b; Fantasies in C, c, G, G; Preludes in C, G, a; Fugues in c, c, G, G, g, b; Eight Little Preludes and Fugues, the authenticity of which has been questioned; and Toccatas in F, C, d, and E (*Concertata*). The further works include six Sonatas (also for pedal cembalo); a Passacaglia (c); four Duets contained in the *Clavierübung* III; a *Canzona* (d); an *Alla Breve* (D); a *Pastorale* (F); a *Trio* (d); and four *Concerti* after Vivaldi.

Turning from Bach's music for organ to that for the clavier, we find that some aspects of it derive from French suites and ornaments. Among the composers who influenced him were Domenico Scarlatti, Froberger, Fischer, and Kuhnau. But Bach soon outgrew his models in that he set entirely new intellectual tasks for keyboard players, for whom he wrote his works to serve as study material and "special pastime" (*zum besonderen Zeit Vertreib*).

Bach wrote his clavier pieces in somewhat the following order:

At Arnstadt (1703–7): one *Sonata* (D, with imitation of hens' cackling) and two *Capricci* ("in honorem J. Chr. Bachii" in E and "on the departure of a dear brother" in B♭, particularly influenced by Johann Kuhnau).

At Weimar (1708-17): study works, including his transcription of sixteen violin concerti by Vivaldi, Marcello, Telemann, and others, for the clavier and organ, and the *Toccatas* in d, g, e, f♯, and c.

At Cöthen (1717–22): *Clavierbüchlein* for *Wilhelm Friedemann Bach* (1720), a book of keyboard exercises with an exposition of elementary music theory, preludes, chorales, dances, and fugues; *Erstes Clavier-Büchlein vor Anna Magdalena Bachin Anno 1722*, containing French suites, an organ fantasy, an aria with variations, a minuet, and a chorale; fifteen *Inventions* (two-voiced) and fifteen *Sinfonias* (three-voiced inventions); *The Well-Tempered Clavier* I (1722); six *French Suites* (which appear in the books of music intended for Anna Magdalena Bach) in d, c, b, E♭, G, and E, in which the four basic movements are augmented with French dance forms to become six to eight movements.

At Leipzig (1723–1750); six *English Suites* (A, a, g, F, e, and d); six *Partitas* (or German suites), in B♭, c, a, D, G, e (printed as Part I of the *Clavierübung* in 1731), the *Italian Concerto* (transcription of the Italian concerto-form on the two-manual harpsichord), and the Partita in b (printed as Part II of the *Clavierübung* in 1735); four *Duets* (two-voiced fugues, related to the inventions) in Part III of the *Clavierübung* (printed in 1739); the *Goldberg Variations* (Part IV of the *Clavierübung*, printed in 1742), an aria with thirty variations over its bass, for two-manual harpsichord; *The Well-Tempered Clavier* II (assembled about 1744); the second *Notenbüchlein for Anna Magdalena Bach* (1725) with Partitas, French Suites, Preludes, Marches, Polonaises, Chorales, Spiritual Songs, and the Song about Tobacco; the *Chromatic Fantasy and Fugue*.

Seven *Concerti for Clavier with Orchestra* (Bach was the first to write keyboard concerti), mostly reworkings of violin concerti; three *Concerti for two Claviers and Orchestra;* two *Concerti for three Claviers;* a *Concerto for four Claviers.*

George Frederick Handel (1685–1759), organ pupil of Zachow in Halle, was to the very end of his life famed as an organ virtuoso, and as early as 1702 he was organist of the Reformed castle and cathedral church in Halle. In Hamburg and Lübeck he came into contact with Reinken, Lübeck, and Buxtehude.

His organ works consist of six organ concerti, op. 4 (1738). The further six organ concerti in each of the years 1740 and 1760 (op. 7) are concerti grossi in instrumentation (for organ or cembalo, strings, oboes, and bassoon) and in form, in which the four-movement layout of the Italian church sonata was predominant. The organ assumed the role of the concertino. He wrote these principally as entr'acte music for his oratorios.

His clavier music consists of comparatively few works—when compared with his operas and oratorios, in which he played his major role in the history of music. But his clavier music is important. The following were published by Händel himself: six fugues and the first part of the *Suites de Pièces pour le Clavecin* (1720). A second and third part were brought out in London and Amsterdam in 1733 without Handel's having seen them through the press. The Chaconne in G major, with twenty variations, and the Capriccio in G minor, belong among the works thus pirated. The eight suites of 1720 represent the German type or are successions of movements after the Italian sonata.

In 1928 seventy-six previously unknown *Pieces for the Clavicembalo* by Handel appeared in print for the first time, in two volumes.

Organ Music after Bach

After the death of Bach, significant musicians only occasionally wrote church music. Organ music lost profundity, in connection with the subjectivism of the new style and the new conception of religion as a matter of the feelings. Organ literature was held either to traditional forms in a retrospective spirit or to transcription of characteristic or mood pieces for the organ. There were well-trained and talented musicians of the Bach school, including Wilhelm Friedemann Bach and Johann Ludwig Krebs, as well as the cantors at St. Thomas's after Bach; but they proved to be particularly receptive to *galant* music. Among the levelers of organ playing was Georg Joseph Abt Vogler (1749–1814), who became popular with showy improvisations on programs that were proposed to him. Vogler introduced the virtuoso and concert-like trend.

In the 19th century great individual composers on occasion were interested in the organ as part of musical classicism or the neo-Baroque. Felix Mendelssohn-Bartholdy (1809–1847) wrote six sonatas, op. 65, and three Preludes and Fugues, op. 37, in which the melodic element predominates. Robert Schumann (1810–1856) wrote six fugues on B-A-C-H (1845) and individual pieces for the pedal-piano. With Franz Liszt (1811–1886) the organ took the final turn away from the church instrument to the concert instrument with the adoption of the sonority that had developed in the symphony orchestra. Liszt's organ works were a Fantasy and Fugue on

Ad nos ad salutarem undam, a Prelude and Fugue on B-A-C-H, Variations on Bach's *Weinen, Klagen,* a *Missa pro organo,* and a Requiem.

A consciously conservative attitude, on the other hand, was adopted in Germany by Johannes Brahms (1833–1897) and in France—or, more properly, Belgium—by César Franck (1822–1890). Brahms succeeded in effecting a synthesis of harmonic and polyphonic aspects. His works include eleven posthumous chorale preludes, op. 122; also, without opus-numbers, two preludes and fugues, a fugue in A♭ minor, and a chorale prelude and fugue on *O Traurigkeit, o Herzeleid.*

Joseph Rheinberger (1839–1901), professor of organ and composition in Munich, was a significant representative of the conservative and classically-oriented trend in Germany. In his twenty organ sonatas he attempted to fuse late-Baroque polyphonic and formal traits with the lyricism of the time. Between 1870 and 1900 Rheinberger was one of the most sought-after teachers in Germany, numbering among his pupils Humperdinck, Wolf-Ferrari, Thuille, and the Americans Chadwick and Parker.

César Franck, originally from Belgium but becoming in 1844 a church musician in Paris, wrote various organ pieces between 1859 and 1890, culminating during the latter year in three organ compositions on chorales of his own devising. Franck became the leader of a specifically French school of organists. Charles Marie Widor (1844–1937) fused the aims of the organ and of the symphony orchestra.

The attempt to connect the conception of sonority prevalent in the post-Wagnerian period with late-Baroque forms was undertaken by Max Reger (1873–1916), born in Brand (Upper Palatinate) on March 19, 1873. A pupil of Adalbert Lindner in Weiden and then of Hugo Riemann in Sondershausen (later in Wiesbaden), Reger remained in Weiden as a composer from 1898 to 1901, then moved to Munich and in 1907 to Leipzig, where he was the university music director and teacher of composition at the Conservatory. From 1911 to 1914 he was court conductor in Meiningen. He died in Leipzig on May 11, 1916. His organ works include chorale fantasies written between 1898 and 1901, two organ sonatas, fantasies on Bach (op. 46) and the Symphonic Fantasie (op. 57), preludes and fugues, variations (op. 73), and chorale preludes (op. 67). In style, his organ works show a Late Romantic expressive idiom full of bold imagination, involving very great contrasts of dynamics and content. He had certain inclinations toward a rather restless harmony, and he tended to use Late Baroque forms (fugues and chorale variations) and Protestant chorale melodies.

Danish composers for the organ in the 19th century included J. P. E. Hartmann (1805–1900), who wrote a Fantasy and a Sonata, *Langfredag-Paaskemorgen,* and Hans Matthison-Hansen (1807–1890) who wrote six symphonies and six fantasies. Swedish composers who wrote in late-Romantic style include Emil Sjögren (1853–1918) with *Legende* (1907) and Otto Olsson (1879–1964) with a fantasy and fugue on *Vi lofve dig, o store Gud* (1909) and a *Credo symphoniacum* (1925). Also, the Danes Gottfried Matthison-Hansen (1832–1909), Otto Malling (1848–1915), N. O. Raasted (b. 1888), and Rued Langgaard (1893–1952) and the Icelanders Páll Isólfsson (b. 1893) and Jón Leifs (b. 1899) wrote concertante organ music.

Since 1920 organ music has revived, particularly in Germany. Composers have rejected the idea of Romantic sonority. Some have tried to objectify the creative idea. Others—notably Olivier Messiaen and a group who continue the tradition of French organ music—have expanded the possibilities of subjective expression by emphasizing sonority, dynamics, and rhythm, combined with technically meaningful construction. Still others have operated from a somewhat Late Romantic basis and tried to expand tonal possibilities within a harmonically related polyphony—for example, pupils of Reger such as Joseph Haas, Karl Hasse, and Hermann Grabner.

In view of the place and task of the instrument, the composer has normally had one or another of three possible attitudes toward what he was undertaking to do. He might try to convey a sense of his world-view, presented as if in concert. He might follow a more religious and meditative aim—as the French school surrounding Messiaen has done. Or he might proceed in a more liturgical and confessional way, as composers in Protestant church music have been inclined to do.

The most significant composer for the organ at present, in view of his influence on the general character of new music, is Olivier Messiaen, who was born in 1908 in Avignon. From 1919 to 1930 he studied at the Paris Conservatoire under such teachers as Paul Dukas and Marcel Dupré and in 1931 became organist at St. Trinité in Paris. In 1936 he founded the Jeune France and in 1942 became professor at the Conservatoire, teaching analysis, aesthetics, and rhythmics. He has played an authoritative role as teacher of the new generation, his pupils including Pierre Boulez and Karlheinz Stockhausen. Messiaen's compositions for organ include *L'Ascension* (1934), *La Nat'vité du Seigneur* (1935), *Les Corps glorieux* (1939), *Messe de la Pentecôte* (1950), and *Livre d'Orgue* (1951). The style of his works involves a profession of faith, proceeding from a liturgically bound Catholic piety. In the unity of the religious and artistic there no longer exists opposition between the sacred and secular in music. Messiaen found his own style in the study of special rhythmic problems of East Indian, Gregorian, and medieval music. There is a strong stimulus, also, that has come from nature, particularly the song of birds. Melodically this style is often channeled within the system of six modes of limited transposability that he proposed. The pictorial quality and the splendor of the sonority are eminently French, embodying impulses from Berlioz and Debussy, as well as from Liszt. The organ compositions involve a quite individual religious idiom, linked with the composer's ideas and conceptions. Messiaen's writings include his *Technique de mon langage musical* (Paris 1944), in two volumes, and the prefaces to individual works.

Somewhat less extreme and tendentious work for organ has been maintained in the United States since 1920, usually in fulfillment of the particular church office that the composer has undertaken. Leo Sowerby (b. 1895) has written a great deal of quite vigorous organ music, fundamentally tonal. He was educated at the American Academy in Rome from 1921-4 and subsequently served for thirty-five years as organist and choirmaster at St. James's Episcopal Cathedral in Chicago, becoming in 1962 director of the College of Church Musicians at the Washington (D.C.) Cathedral. His organ works include a Symphony in G (1930), *Pageant of Autumn* (1937), and a concerto for organ and orchestra (1938). Everett Titcomb (b. 1884), also a church organist and choirmaster for forty years at the Church of St. John the Evangelist in Boston, particularly used Gregorian motifs. Although many American composers have written for the organ, such as Virgil Thomson (b. 1896), Paul Creston (b. 1906), Gardner Read (b. 1913), Gail Kubik (b. 1915), and Vincent Persichetti (b. 1915), one can hardly credit them with the kind of impact on music specifically of the mid-20th century that Messiaen had, nor has it played the central role in their careers that it did in that of the great master of keyboard literature—J. S. Bach.

Piano Music after Bach

Rococo, "Storm and Stress," Classic Era

In conjunction with the change in style that occurred before and after 1750, keyboard music gradually took on an entirely new character in its forms, its musical expression, and in the technique with which it was played. The older formal types disappeared: gone were the suites and the preludes and fugues. Composition became predominantly homophonic. The sonata and the solo concerto with orchestral accompaniment became the prevailing new forms. The development of the sonata and of the sonata-allegro form occurred in the course of the decades in different countries of Europe. Various local centers were established in Germany itself.

In the second half of the 18th century the piano supplanted both the harpsichord and the clavichord. The literature of the organ and that of the other keyboard instruments became completely separated, and from then on they remained distinct. To a hitherto unknown extent the piano became a universal instrument, and for it were written not only original compositions but also a flood of transcriptions that are hard to bring together under a single heading—piano scores of operas, piano versions of orchestral works, of chamber music, transcriptions of works for other instruments or for voice, and all sorts of arrangements. The piano is the instrument of the bourgeois era, in the good sense as it served to cultivate domestic music, in the bad sense as it fostered salon music.

The two older sons of Bach were particularly involved in the development of a North German style. The compositions of Wilhelm Friedemann Bach (1710–1784) include sonatas and piano concerti, notable in their intermediate position between the sentimental cantabile and strict style of the Late Baroque.

Carl Philipp Emanuel Bach (1714–1788) was of very great influence in his time, up to the turn of the century, both in terms of form and content. Up to about 1780 he wrote exclusively for the harpsichord and clavichord, composing over four hundred pieces in all, including more than one hundred fifty sonatas. Not all his clavier works are available today in reprints. His most important clavier collections are the six "Prussian" sonatas, dedicated to Frederick the Great (1742); six "Württemberg" sonatas, dedicated to Duke Karl Eugen of Württemberg (*Sei Sonate per Cembalo,* 1744); six sonatas as supplement to the *Versuch über die wahre Art* (1753); six sonatas (the "Amalia Sonatas" 1760 for clavier with varied reprise, i.e., with written-out ornaments); the collections *Für Kenner und Liebhaber* including sonatas, fantasias, and rondos (1779–87); and about fifty clavier concerti.

C. P. E. Bach developed the type of the German rondo, which exhibits several digressions while the French rondo has only one digression into minor. A particular feature of his work is the free, subjective, and imaginative formulation of the main thought on its return, which is neither formally nor harmonically bound to one norm. There were predominantly three movements in his sonatas, with the three sections of the sonata-allegro form in the first movement. The North German type of sonata avoided any approach to the suite, and excluded dance movements of any sort. C. P. E. Bach's *Versuch über die wahre Art, das Clavier zu spielen,* 2 parts (1753 and 1762), is basic for keyboard playing and for understanding the aesthetic conceptions of the 18th century. In expressive passages Bach introduced the "speaking principle" into keyboard music.

The two youngest sons of Bach were strongly influenced by Italy and became typical representatives of the "galant style": Johann Christoph Friedrich Bach (1732–1795), of Bückeburg, with sonatas and concerti; and especially Johann Christian Bach (1735–1782), of Milan and London, with sonatas (1765 and 1780) and concerti. They developed a cantabile, melodic style with a second theme that always contrasted, in what was often referred to as the "singing allegro." The character of their music is tender, elegiacally expressive, but always elegant. It is pleasant music, with virtuoso brilliance and further development of the sonata-allegro form by complete and shortened reprise, partly under Stamitz's influence. Johann Christian Bach wrote pieces specifically for the piano.

Johann Schobert (about 1740–1767) was perhaps of Silesian origin, presumably Wagenseil's pupil, and as Prince Conti's chamber harpsichordist one of the most celebrated keyboard artists in Paris. Schobert wrote sonatas and concerti for the harpsichord. Influenced by Stamitz's Mannheim style and still more by Wagenseil's Viennese style, he was a notable representative of the "Storm and Stress," of considerable individuality. His music displays unnaturally emotional developments of fantasy, heavy feeling, bold harmonic movement, broad song-like themes, and orchestral keyboard style achieved by the transfer of Mannheim effects to the harpsichord. Other German composers at this time in Paris were Eckard, Honauer, and Raupach. Schobert was the first to write violin sonatas, trios, and quartets with obligatory keyboard part and thus one of the first to write chamber music, after the *Pièces de Clavecin avec un violon* (about 1734) by Jean Joseph Cassanea de Mondonville (1711–1772) and after the *Pièces de Clavecin en concerts* (1741) with violin or flute and viola by Jean-Philippe Rameau. Schobert was of significant influence on young Mozart.

The leading representative of the South German or Viennese style in keyboard music was Georg Christoph Wagenseil (1715–1777). He linked up the sonata type with the suite by placing the minuet in the middle or at the end of the sonata. Surprisingly he introduced trios in minor, articulated the exposition of the first movement in three parts of the theme, and in his melody clearly revealed influence of Viennese folk-music. He wrote in a flowing, virtuoso piano style with passages in thirds and brilliant figure-work.

There were several important 18th-century keyboard instruction books. Notable among them are Carl Philipp Emanuel Bach, *Versuch über die wahre Art, das Clavier zu spielen,* or Essay on the True Manner of Playing the Clavier (1753 and 1762); Georg Simon Löhlein (1725–1781), *Clavierschule oder kurtze und gründliche Anweisung zur Melodie und Harmonie* (1765 and 1781); Daniel Gottlob Türk (1756–1813), *Clavierschule oder Anweisung zum Clavierspielen für Lehrer und Lernende* (1789) and *Kleines Lehrbuch für Anfänger im Clavierspielen* (1792); August Eberhard Müller (1767–1817), *Clavier- und Fortepianoschule oder Anweisung zur richtigen und geschmackvollen Spielart beider Instrumente* (1804), 5th ed. revised by Carl Czerny.

The technical and sonorous possibilities of the piano, which by 1800 had crowded out the harpsichord and clavichord and become generally standard, led to the development of a new keyboard style. Pianists exploited several new possibilities of modulating the tone: dynamic contrasts, *crescendi* or *diminuendi,* and *sforzati* attacks. Also they cultivated song-like playing, in imitation of the singing voice. They developed virtuosity in the handling of quickly flowing diatonic or chromatic passages, as well as passages in thirds, sixths, and octaves. They shifted hands in runs, and used broken chords. The emphasis was on neat performance. Chords were broken up into accompanying figures in the left hand (the Alberti bass), into tonal repetitions at the interval of an octave (Murky or drum bass), and into tonal repetitions on the same note.

The fifty-two sonatas of Joseph Haydn (1732–1809) span some four decades and clearly reflect the general development in the latter half of the 18th century, as Haydn assumed a more and more prominent role. His first keyboard sonata, which shows Viennese influence, is called a partita. It is of suite-like character, with unified basic tonality and, as in Wagenseil, with the minuet in the middle or final position. As early as the Largo of the Second Sonata the influence of C. P. E. Bach had begun to manifest itself, most strongly in Sonatas No. 19 and 20 (1771), with their bold freedom of form. After 1780 in Sonatas No. 37, 41, and 49 the stimulus of Mozartian melody is detectable. After that time Haydn wrote his keyboard sonatas only for the piano. Sonata No. 49 (1790) represents the culmination in his sonata-writing. Sonatas No. 50–52 belong to his late period and point forward to Beethoven and Schubert.

Of Haydn's keyboard concerti only the last two, in G and D, are musically and technically significant.

The keyboard works of Wolfgang Amadeus Mozart (1756–1791) are eighteen sonatas for two hands; five fantasies; numerous variations and smaller pieces; five sonatas for four hands; a sonata for two keyboard instruments; and twenty-five keyboard concerti, one calling for two and one for three keyboard instruments.

Mozart's keyboard work began under the influence of Scarlatti, Wagenseil, Haydn, Schobert, and Johann Christian Bach (Sonatas K. V. 279–284, composed about 1774). A stylistic change occurred in 1777 with Sonatas K. V. 309 and 311 under the influence of the Mannheim School. Sonata K. V. 331, in A major, was written probably under the inspiration of Parisian keyboard music. At the same time, in 1778, he wrote the tragic A minor sonata (K. V. 310), the character of which was significantly increased in the C minor Sonata K. V. 457 of 1784. Mozart's later affection for polyphony was particularly shown in the B♭ Sonata of 1789 (K. V. 570), in the first movement of K. V. 533, and the last sonata, in D major (K. V. 576).

Of keyboard concerti Mozart wrote only fifteen between 1782 and 1786 in Vienna for his own performance. They combine technical brilliance with significant musical content. The best-known ones are the concerti in D minor (K. V. 466), in D major (Coronation Concerto, K. V. 537), in B♭ major (K. V. 595), and in A major (K. V. 488).

Mozart's keyboard works are culminating points in his rich creative activity. His sonatas far exceed in significance those of Haydn. Their artistic richness consists in the *cantabile* quality of their invention and the originality of their content and form. The concerti are to some extent linked closely with 18th-century society-music, yet in them music never loses itself in external brilliance.

Many other composers contemporary with Mozart and Beethoven were active in writing keyboard music. In Vienna there were Leopold Anton Kozeluch (originally Johann Anton Koželuch, 1747–1818); Anton Hoffmeister (1754–1812), also a music publisher; and Johann Baptist Wanhall (1739–1813). Active over a wider geographical area were Johann Wilhelm Hässler (1747–1822), a virtuoso who toured Europe; a pupil of Haydn, Ignaz Joseph Pleyel (1757–1831), who later was active as composer, music dealer, and piano maker in Paris; and Johann Ladislaus Dussek (Jan Ladislav Dusík, 1760–1812), an international virtuoso responsible for an extensive body of keyboard work. Originally Bohemian and classically oriented, he became more Romantic in his later works.

A number of musicians, known today mainly for exercises they wrote for the piano, were generally active in their day as composers and performers: Clementi, Cramer, Czerny, and Hummel. Muzio Clementi (presumably 1752–1832) was highly regarded by Beethoven and was celebrated as a pianist. Engel has called him the "perfecter of the Classical keyboard sonata." Clementi's works included 106 piano sonatas and a collection of studies entitled *Gradus ad Parnassum*. His pupils included Cramer, Field, Moscheles, A. A. Klengel, L. Berger, and Kalkbrenner; and his influence extended to Haydn, Mozart, and Beethoven. Johann Baptist Cramer (1771–1858) wrote 84 studies that are still in use today. Carl Czerny (1791–1857), a pupil of Beethoven, wrote more than a thousand works and, along with his well-known etudes, a great deal of solo music. Johann Nepomuk Hummel (1778–1837) began as a pupil of Mozart and developed into the early Romantic era, the beginning of which he helped to precipitate with, for example, his sonata op. 81. His style is distinguished by special brilliance.

Two Swedish composers of the Mozart-Beethoven period were Johan Wikmanson (1753–1800), a pupil of J. M. Kraus and Abt Vogler, and Olaf Ahlström (1756–1835), composer of sixteen sonatas. The Dane C. E. F. Weyse (1774–1842) wrote twelve concert etudes and other works. The Irishman John Field (b. 1782 in Dublin, d. 1837 in Moscow) was the first to write nocturnes (1814), and with his elegiac, dreamy, singing expression exerted an influence on Chopin. Other composers related to Beethoven were his pupil, Ferdinand Ries (1784–1838), and Friedrich Kuhlau (1786–1832), who wrote numerous keyboard works, including a piano concerto in C major (1813).

Typical representatives of salon music were Heinrich Herz (1803–1888) and Franz Hünten (1793–1878) in Paris, who wrote variations, caprices, and potpourris that were often called fantasies.

19th Century

With the final victory of the pianoforte around 1800, the playing of that instrument took two distinct directions: virtuoso concert performance and domestic music-making. Both ways soon were carried to an extreme. There arose a virtuosity which spread all over Europe and soon declined into more or less superficial brilliance. Domestic piano-playing, fashionable as the factory-made instruments became a symbol of respectability in the home, contented itself with the literature of cheap entertainment or what was often referred to as salon music. Through the whole 19th century there runs the struggle on the part of significant composers to pull these extremes back to the middle, either through exemplary concert performance or through new works that could again serve their purposes in both the concert hall and in the home.

Ludwig van Beethoven (1770–1827), whose career as a whole is dealt with in connection with the symphony, has a similar place of importance in the literature of the piano. His works may be thus assigned to various periods in his career:

Keyboard compositions of his youth: nine variations on a march by Dressler, the three "Electoral Sonatas" (Eb, f, D), piano sonata in Eb, and variations on themes by Righini and Dittersdorf. Also at this time he wrote three easy sonatas, in G, G, and F.

The piano music with opus numbers forms three *chronological* groups: 1. op. 2–22 (1795–1800); 2. op. 26–90 (1801–1814); and 3. op. 101, 106, 109, 110, 111, 120, 126 (1816–1822).

The 32 sonatas may be classified thus in content:

Sonatas in *minor*: op. 2, 1 (f), 10, 1 (c), op. 13 (c, "Pathétique"), op. 57 (f, "Appassionata"), op. 111 (c);

Sonatas in *major*: op. 2, 2 (A), op. 10, 2 (F), op. 10, 3 (D), op. 14, 2 (G), op. 28 (D, "Pastoral"), op. 78 (F♯), op. 79 (G), op. 90 (e);

Virtuoso sonatas: op. 2, 3 (C), op. 7 (Eb), op. 22 (Bb), op. 31, 1 (G), op. 31, 3 (Eb), op. 53 (C, "Waldstein"), op. 54 (F).

Fantasia sonatas: op. 27, 1 (Eb), op. 27, 2 (c♯, "Moonlight Sonata"), op. 31, 2 (d, "Tempest Sonata"), op. 81 (E♭, "Sonate caractéristique: Les adieux, l'absence et le retour").

Late sonatas: op. 101 (A, 1816), op. 106 (B♭, 1818), op. 109 (E, 1820), op. 110 (A♭, 1821), op. 111 (c, 1821–2).

Variations: the most significant, which are comparable only to Bach's, are op. 34 (F, on a theme of Beethoven's own, 1802), op. 35 (E♭, "Eroica" Variations, 1802), 32 Variations (c, 1806, without opus number), op. 120 (33 Diabelli Variations, 1820–3).

Individual pieces: three rondos (particularly op. 51, 2, G), Rondo capriccioso ("Rage over the Lost Penny"), Fantasia op. 77, Andante in F (originally the middle movement of the "Waldstein Sonata"), Bagatelles op. 33, 119, 126.

Piano concerti: No. 1, op. 15 (C, 1796–7); No. 2, op. 19 (B♭, 1792–5); No. 3, op. 37 (c, 1800–1); No. 4, op. 58 (G, 1806); No. 5, op. 73 (E♭, 1809–10); Choral Fantasy (1808).

Far beyond what had before been thought possible, Beethoven raised expression and form to new heights and established very strong expressive contrasts. At the same time, he achieved strict architectonic organization in accordance with compelling, musically logical development and very great formal individualism. He exhibited sovereign mastery of all forms from the sonata allegro to the variation and fugue, from the miniature to the gigantic. He developed the scherzo from the minuet and made it a highly distinctive and characteristic movement. Within the sonata allegro he made the development portion the very focus of the movement and gave it substantial content. He brought the individual movements together into a cyclic whole, placing them together with sovereign freedom, with the greatest range of invention, from sheer instrumentally sketched-out four-tone motifs to the most broadly conceived melodies, with powerfully pulsing rhythm throughout, sharply opposed dynamics, and the use of all sonorous and tonal levels of the keyboard. In the piano concerti he created an entirely novel relationship between the orchestra and the solo instrument.

Romantic Piano Music

During the Romantic period, piano music developed in several directions:

1. With the widespread increase of imaginative and improvisatory elements, the big forms—those of the sonata-allegro and the rondo—lost the formal strictness and logic so characteristic of Beethoven.
2. The Romantics discovered themes that were more song-like than symphonic and that were less suitable for development.
3. Suggestions that are not strictly musical—coming from pictorial and poetic models and ideas—influenced the composition more and more.
4. A rich world was opened up in the area of musical miniatures in *genre* pictures, such as "songs without words," waltzes, national dances, scherzi, intermezzi, nocturnes, impromptus, and the like.
5. Harmony gained significance as the refined expression of mood,

at the expense of the more elemental and rhythmic aspects of the composition.

Weber and Schubert were early members in a succession of Romantic and highly individual composers who wrote for the piano.

Carl Maria von Weber (1786–1826) composed two piano concerti (C, E♭); a concert piece for piano and orchestra (f, 1821); four piano sonatas (C, op. 24; A♭, op. 39; d, op. 49; e, op. 70, composed between 1812 and 1822); numerous small forms, including the *Invitation to the Dance* (1819), variations, rondo, polonaise, and pieces for four hands.

In Weber's main works, the rhythm is lively and the idiom unusually pictorial and emotional, constantly maintaining interest by rich contrasts of invention. Technically, a brilliance is achieved far beyond that of Mozart, Hummel, or Beethoven, through the use of broken chords, effective passage work, chordal fullness, leaps, and widely separated levels in accompaniment. Weber developed his piano style particularly from that of Dussek.

Franz Schubert (1797–1828) wrote twenty-one piano sonatas, the *Wanderer Fantasy* (1822), eight impromptus (op. 90 and 142, 1827), six Moments musicaux (op. 94, about 1828), scherzi, numerous dances (waltzes and ländler), and several pieces for piano duet, including the sonatas op. 30 and 140 (*Grand Duo*), Fantasy (f), Allegro (a), marches, polonaises, variations, and other works.

Schubert's piano style is an instrumental style that has grown out of song. It says the most beautiful thing it can say in great quasi-vocal melodic curves of *cantilena,* generally renouncing the dramatic assemblage of material and the establishment of sharp thematic contrasts and never letting the technical become an end in itself. Schubert's piano compositions, with few exceptions, lack brilliance. He was no concert pianist. In compensation, they are all the richer in inward values and contrasts of feeling. Often the most beautiful mood-pictures are sketched in short pieces. Especially his miniatures were very influential on the further development of piano music. His *Impromptus* have their immediate model in the collection of the same name published in 1820 by the Czech composer Jan Václav Voříšek (1791–1825), a pupil of Jan Tomášek. During the years between 1819 and 1824, Schubert composed no sonatas. The posthumous sonatas in c, A, and B♭, however, show a new synthesis of his individuality and Classical form. The *Wanderer Fantasy* anticipates the fantasia-sonata that is in a single movement but has several sections.

After Schubert there appeared a whole succession of composers whose piano works show one or another of the general traits of Romanticism. Felix Mendelssohn-Bartholdy (1809–1847) wrote two piano concerti (op. 25 in g and op. 40 in d); three sonatas (in E, g, and B♭); forty-eight "songs without words"; fantasias; capriccios; preludes and fugues; and variations, including the *Variations sérieuses* (op. 54).

Mendelssohn's works develop an elegant and virtuoso yet sensitive and expressive type of keyboard playing and a flowing technique in the service of poetic conceptions—"elfin whispers," as they sometimes appear in scherzi and capriccios. The "songs without words," quasi-vocal instrumental music of sensitive character, became a favorite small form in piano literature. The preludes and fugues, which were influenced by the Bach renaissance, were devised in chordal and homophonic counterpoint.

Robert Schumann (1810–1856) wrote a piano concerto (in a, op. 54, the first movement having been composed as a "fantasy" in 1841, and the second and third movements in 1845), and many works for piano solo: three sonatas (f♯, op. 11, 1833–5; f, op. 14, 1835–6; g, op. 22, 1835–8); *Fantasy* (C, op. 17, 1836); and *Fantasiestücke* (op. 12, 1837). His cyclic tone-poems for piano solo include *Papillons* (op. 2, 1829–31); *Davids-bündlertänze* (op. 6, 1837); *Carnaval* (op. 9, 1834–5); *Kinderszenen* (op. 15, 1838); *Kreisleriana* (op. 16, 1838); *Novelletten* (op. 21, 1838); *Nachtstücke* (op. 23, 1839); and *Faschingsschwank aus Wien* (op. 26, 1839). His variations for piano two-hands include the *Abegg Variations* (op. 1, 1830) and the *Symphonic Studies* (op. 13, 1834). He also wrote works for piano four-hands, including *Bilder aus Osten* (op. 66, 1848).

Except for the piano concerto, the significant works of Schumann for the piano were written between 1830 and 1839, a period during which he published only piano compositions in his op. 1–23. They are almost without exception tone-poems inspired by literature even though the source of the inspiration is not always recognizable. They are to a considerable extent small imaginative musical pictures, which are often linked together with magnificent élan into self-contained scenes (or cycles) in rondo form. Even the sonatas are to be understood as fantasias. The pianistic style, which is often orchestral, was completely new in its development of a minutely articulated, melodically enlivened contra-puntalism in the inner voices (influenced by Bach), its rich use of orna-ment, and its depiction of mood by means of sonorous harmony. In the later works—not included in the foregoing list—there is after 1840 a pre-dominance of classically architectonic simplicity and preference for strictness and contrapuntal forms, particularly the fugue.

Following Schumann in piano music there were many composers who either expanded the *genre* piece toward the virtuoso or reduced it to the idyllic, particularly Franz Wüllner (d. 1902), Robert Volkmann (d. 1883), Woldemar Bargiel (d. 1897), Adolf Jensen (d. 1897), and Theodor Kirchner (d. 1903).

In Poland, before and after Chopin, one form of piano music was cultivated with especial fondness, the polonaise. Its main representative was Michał Kleofas Ogiński (1765–1833), a pupil of Józef Kołowski, Viotti, Campanelli, Lafont, and Baillot, and also a political figure, com-poser of the opera *Bonaparte au Caire*. His some twenty polonaises en-joyed great popularity. Many have titles that suggest programs and are in tripartite song form and simple keyboard style. Along with the salon music there also were compositions with higher formal order and vir-tuoso elements. The fourteen sonatas by Józef Elsner (1766–1854) were the first echo of the Classical sonatas of Haydn and Mozart. The greatest Polish piano composer before Chopin was Franciszek Lessel (about 1780–1835), who was influenced by Haydn, with Romantic elements particu-larly in the Second Piano Concerto, one of the first works to represent the national style. Virtuosity was increased in the compositions of the famous pianist Maria Szymanowska (1790–1831), a pupil of Lessel and Field. Many composers of the generation before Chopin created an almost imperceptible stylistic change to the Romantic, but their works form but a pale background to the revolutionary phenomenon of Chopin.

Frédéric Chopin was born in Żelazowa Wola near Warsaw on March 1, 1810, and died in Paris on October 17, 1849. His father was French, from Lorraine, and his mother was of Polish ancestry. After studying piano with Adalbert Zwyny and composition with Józef Elsner in Warsaw, he enjoyed early successes as a virtuoso. In 1828 he made his first trip abroad, which included a visit to Berlin. In 1829 he went on his first major concert tour, to Vienna, Prague, and Dresden; and in 1830 he made concert trips through Germany. In 1831 he went to Paris, the center of the intellectual and artistic life of the French Romantic movement. There he was celebrated as a pianist and in demand as a piano teacher; but as early as 1835 he suffered from poor health, which took the form of a respiratory disorder. From 1836 to 1847 he was a close friend of the writer George Sand, and in 1838–9 he went with her to Majorca. Otherwise, except for concert tours—such as one in 1848 to England and Scotland—he remained in or near Paris.

Chopin, an ardent patriot, felt himself always linked most closely with the national and political fate of his Polish homeland. To the present day he has been Poland's greatest composer. Though the nature of his music has very deep roots in that of the Polish nation, the connection does not consist solely in the adoption of material related to folk-song or in the stylization of national dances such as the polonaise and mazurka. For many features of his piano works Chopin was indebted to his contemporaries, including even quite minor ones such as Field, Hummel, and Dussek. He was also indebted to Carl Maria von Weber and to Beethoven. Of special significance is the influence of Johann Sebastian Bach, for whose keyboard music Chopin had extraordinary admiration. Bach's music found in Chopin's a most highly personal transformation, characterization, and individualization, extending also to a highly personal way of imitating the polyphony. The real artistic medium of Chopin's world was the piano, and he most abundantly enriched the literature for this instrument—and thereby music in general. His artistic individuality at the piano was almost unlimited. Taking his stand in the world of Classic and Romantic forms, he deepened the latter in an unanticipated way.

Over and above the national features, the unique charm of Chopin's music consists in his unparalleled mastery of piano sonority, the formulation of melody quite his own (with *cantabile* features), the inexhaustible ornamentation, the unusually rich harmonization with chromatic alterations, the bold imagination, and the unique poetry, rhythm, and compelling passion.

His piano works with orchestra include two piano concerti (e, op. 11, 1830, and f, op. 21, 1829); fantasies; and polonaises. For piano solo he wrote three sonatas (in c, op. 4, 1828; in b♭, op. 35, around 1839; and in b, op. 58, 1845); twenty-seven etudes (op. 10, 1833, and op. 25, 1837; also three smaller etudes without opus numbers); twenty-four preludes (proceeding through all the keys in the circle of fifths), op. 28, 1839; nineteen nocturnes; four scherzi (in b, b♭, c♯, E); four ballades (in g, F, A♭, f); *Fantasie* in f (op. 49, 1842); *Berceuse* in D♭ (op. 57); numerous mazurkas, waltzes, polonaises, and the like; also the *Barcarolle* in F♯ (op. 60).

Chopin's genius weighed heavily on Polish piano music of the 19th century. There were numerous imitators. A greatly gifted young composer was Antoni Stolpe (1851–1872), whose tonal idiom was mature, neo-Romantic, showing excellent feeling for the big form, with elements of a style of his own.

Among the followers—not imitators—of the artistic ideals of Chopin, a leader was Juliusz Zarębski (1854–1885), who had been a pupil of Dachs in Vienna and of Liszt in Rome. A famous virtuoso and professor at the Brussels Conservatory, he took from Chopin almost all the forms of piano music and handled them with richness of modulation, charming color in the harmonic sequences, and effects which were to become characteristic of Debussy. His most notable composition is *Serenade burlesque* (1884).

At the turn of the century the outstanding figure in Polish music was Ignacy Jan Paderewski (1860–1941). In his work, music from the Goralian region has been transcribed in the *Album of Dances and Songs from the Tatra;* and the piano concerto op. 17 and the Polish fantasy op. 19 combine the virtuosity of the Romantic concerto with stylization of folk motifs. The sonata op. 21 and the variations and fugue op. 23 were the first monumental piano compositions since Chopin, of neo-Romantic, heroic-tragic moods.

Karol Szymanowski (1882–1937), active as a composer for orchestra, wrote his earliest works under the influence of Liszt and Scriabin. In the variations op. 10, for the first time, he showed the influence of the folk-music of the Tatra headlands. The climax of the first creative period was reached in the Second Sonata (1910), a synthesis of the sonata form and the variation and fugue. The *Metopes* (1915) exhibit purest examples of Szymanowski's Impressionistic traits. In the Third Sonata (1917) he displays anti-Romantic tendencies. In his final creative period he wrote the mazurka cycles op. 50 and 62, continuing the Chopinesque idea, stylizing Polish folklore with the use of polytonality, strong dissonances, and powerful rhythmic elements. The mazurka, a folk-dance from Central Poland, was linked with the folklore of the Tatragorian area. The same style appeared in his Fourth Symphony (*Concertante*) for piano and orchestra.

Franz Liszt (1811–1886), whose career as a whole also figures in the discussion of music for orchestra, made a contribution to piano literature that can be compared only with that of his friend Chopin. Liszt's works for piano and orchestra include two piano concerti (E♭, 1848; A, composed in 1839, revised 1866–7) and the *Dance of Death* (1850, final version 1882). For piano solo he wrote some one hundred fifty original compositions, including a sonata (in b, 1852–53), *Fantasia quasi Sonata* after reading Dante (1837 and 1849), and two ballades. (D♭, b).

Most of the etudes have been reworked by Liszt more than once and clearly reveal the heightening of technique that in the course of the decades he made his own, for example the *Etudes d'exécution transcendante* and the *Paganini Etudes;* also the concert etudes, which include *Waldesrauschen* and *Gnomenreigen* (1863).

Also for piano solo he composed a number of tone pictures: *Années de Pélerinage* in three parts (published in 1855–83); *Harmonies poétiques et religieuses* (1853), inspired by poems of Lamartine; *Consolations* (1849), inspired by poems of Sainte Beuve; *Legenden* (1886); and *Der Tanz in der Dorfschenke* or *Mephisto Walzer* (1860).

In addition to these original compositions for piano he made some four hunderd transcriptions, involving transfer and reworking of material: piano scores, such as those of symphonies by Beethoven and Berlioz, and parts of Wagner operas; transcriptions of Bach's organ works; transcriptions of songs, particularly those of Schubert; fantasias on familiar operatic melodies; and nineteen rhapsodies (the twentieth remaining unpublished), brought out in two groups about 1883 and between 1882 and 1885, their melodies for the most part going back to Hungarian folk material.

Liszt's piano compositions were written in approximately three periods: first, one in which he appeared as a virtuoso—that is, up to 1848; then a second period in Weimar, during which he worked mainly in the large forms, up to about 1855; and the third period of his later life, after 1880, with harmonic and sonorous ideas that pointed toward the future. Liszt based his technique on Hummel, Czerny, and other contemporaries. Several other influences made themselves felt in the development of his own style: the literary aspects of French Romanticism, Berlioz with his bold programmatic ideas, Paganini with the novelty of his technique and delivery, and Chopin with the lyricism and rubato of his playing. Thus Liszt developed a completely new piano technique, emulating orchestral sonority. He discovered new possibilities of playing with unanticipated heightening of virtuosity, such as the playing of octaves and chords, broken chords, passages, chromatics, intervallic runs, and leaps; and he exploited dynamic effects of every sort. In individual late works he anticipated in his harmony characteristic traits of the musical Impressionism that was to come.

Liszt was the leader of a very extensive school, the last representatives of which continued into the present century. Among them, as composers for the piano, are Felix Draeseke (1835–1913), Hermann Goetz (1840–1876) with his piano concerto in B♭, Hans von Bülow (1830–1894), Eugen d'Albert (1864–1932), and Ferruccio Busoni (1866–1924). Busoni in his compositions after 1900, however, went his own way, with closer relation to Bach and Mozart, leading into a new "Classistic" development. This is seen in his piano concerto with final chorus, *Fantasia contrapunctistica*, sonatinas, and *Indian Diary*.

Johannes Brahms (1833–1897) composed two piano concerti, one in d, op. 15, completed in 1858, and the other in B♭, op. 83, 1878–81. For piano solo he composed three sonatinas (C, op. 1; f♯, op. 2; f, op. 5); variations, op. 9 (on a Schumann theme); op. 21 (No. 1, on an original theme; No. 2, on a Hungarian theme); op. 23 (four-hands, on a Schumann theme); op. 24 (on Handel); op. 35 (on Paganini); op. 56b (on Haydn); also, among other works, four ballads (op. 10); two rhapsodies (op. 79); fantasies (op. 116); three intermezzi (op. 117); scherzo (op. 4); eight piano pieces: four capricci and four intermezzi (op. 76); and the four last groups of piano pieces, op. 116–119 (published in 1892 and 1893).

Allied with the late work of Schumann but reaching back particularly to Beethoven and Bach, Brahms wrote in a piano style that he had developed entirely from absolute form. He brought the inventive and formal aspects of his work into adequate relationship with each other, not only in the sonatas or variations which bear their names in the Classical meaning of the terms, but also in the shorter pieces. Thus he expressed himself in a way that was often Romantically tinged in harmony and melody, yet was Classically formal in external appearance. He never made piano technique an end in itself, but always linked it with content. In his piano style he favored widely extended chords, broken or otherwise. Often he doubled notes at the octave, third, or sixth. Some of the compositional structures he used are polyrhythmic. All, on occasion, develop tremendous power. This tendency to pile up overwhelmingly powerful effects reached a climax in the variations on themes from Handel and Paganini.

In conjunction with Brahms there was a group that opposed the Neo-German school. The group included Albert Dietrich (d. 1908), Julius Otto Grimm (d. 1903), Bernhard Scholz (d. 1916), and Heinrich von Herzogenberg (d. 1900).

In the latter half of the 19th century there were quite significant developments in some of the countries around Germany, notably in Russia, with Tchaikovsky and Musorgski.

Peter Tchaikovsky (1840–1893) wrote three piano concerti, No. 1 in b♭, No. 2 in G, and No. 3 in E♭; a fantasy for piano and orchestra (op. 56), and two piano sonatas (op. 37, 1878, and the apprentice work op. 80). He also wrote many small pieces that bear some relationship to those of Schumann.

The main piano composition of Modeste Musorgski (1839–1881) is his *Pictures at an Exhibition*, a cycle of piano pieces elicited by an art show. These pieces describe individual drawings and paintings, and are linked together by the *Promenade*. The work contains movements unusually bold in expression. He also wrote various piano miniatures.

The French composer Charles Camille Saint-Saëns (1835–1921) wrote five piano concerti and numerous works for piano two-hands and four-hands and for two pianos.

César Franck (1822–1890) is also significantly represented with his *Prelude, Chorale, and Fugue* (1884) and *Prelude, Aria, and Finale* (1886–7), as well as his *Variations symphoniques* for piano and orchestra.

In Spain Isaac Albeniz (1860–1909) was the first virtuoso piano composer along Lisztian lines. Enrique Granados Campina (1867–1916) incorporated national elements into his piano work *Goyescas* (1912). Along with Impressionistic traits, folklore characterized the work of Manuel de Falla (1876–1946) and Joaquim Turina (1882–1949).

Among more modern Italian composers, Francesco Malipiero (b. 1882) and Alfredo Casella (1883–1947) wrote notable piano music.

In Bohemia, one of the most important piano composers was Johann Ladislaus Dussek (Jan Ladislav Dusík, 1760–1812), not to be confused with Mozart's Prague friend František Xaver Dušek (1731–1799). Dusík spent the major part of his life as an outstanding piano virtuoso and prolific composer in Paris, writing sonatas in which the style points ahead to the Romantic art of Chopin and Smetana. Another forerunner of the Early Romantic style was Jan Václav Voříšek (1791–1825), who in his rhapsodies (1818) and impromptus (1820) prepared the way for Schubert and approached in his own compositions the brilliance of Liszt. Václav Jan Tomášek (1774–1850) influenced with his *Eclogues* (1807), *Rhapsodies* (1810), and *Three Dithyrambs* (1818) not only Schubert and Voříšek but also Smetana's first compositions, the *Bagatelles et Impromptus* (1844).

In the compositions of Bedřich Smetana (1824–1884), the founder of Czech national music, the piano played an outstanding role. In this respect he was almost exclusively a composer of *genre* and program pieces. He transformed suggestions from the life of the Czech people and various characteristics of their popular melody into a musical and poetic type of pianistic expression. In the polka he wished to idealize the psyche of his nation. Toward this artistic aim he utilized Lisztian technique. Smetana's works include the cycles *Sny*, or Dreams (1874–5), and *České tance*, or Czech Dances (1877–9), six characteristic compositions op. 1 (1848), two concert etudes, *Macbeth and the Witches* (1859), and many genre pieces.

Antonín Dvořák (1841–1904) wrote predominantly *genre*-like compositions; and Zdeněk Fibich (1850–1900), intimate and lyrical piano music. His cycle of over five hundred small compositions *Moods, Impressions, and Memories* (1892–8) are directly related to Smetana.

More recent piano composers are Vítězslav Novák (1870–1949), with his *Sonata Eroica* (1900) and cycle *Pan*; Josef Suk (1874–1935), with his cycles *Of the Little Mother* (1907) and *Through Life and Dream* (1913); Leoš Janáček (1854–1928), with his cycle *On the Overgrown Path* (1902–8), sonata fragment *1. X. 1905*, cycle *In the Fog* (1912), Concertino for piano and chamber orchestra (1925), and Capriccio for piano, left hand, with winds (1926); and Bohuslav Martinů (1890–1959), with four piano concerti and a Sinfonietta gioccosa for piano and orchestra (1940).

In the Scandinavian countries, the Swede Franz Berwald (1796–1868) wrote a piano concerto in D (1855). The Dane J. P. E. Hartmann (1805–1900), in his three sonatas and genre pieces, developed his own emotional style on the basis of Spohr's and Chopin's, in conjunction with the "Northern" Romanticism of his late ballets (Sonata in a, 1885). Niels W. Gade, inspired by Mendelssohn, wrote *Aquarelle* (1850) and other works. In Norway there was considerable activity on the part of Chopin's pupil Thomas Tellefsen (1823–1874).

Edvard Grieg (1843–1907) wrote mainly for the piano. From his pen we have a concerto in a (1868), a ballade in g (1875) as a set of free variations on a Norwegian folk-song, a sonata in e (1865), and ten particularly well-liked volumes containing sixty-six *Lyrical Pieces.* He found his inspiration in melodic turns and dance-like rhythms of Norwegian folk-music. In the art of the miniature he was a master, anticipating Impressionism in his harmony.

Romantic piano music was also written by Ludvig Norman (1831–1885), with his *Concert-Piece with Orchestra;* Emil Sjögren (1853–1918), with his *Erotikon* and two sonatas; W. Peterson-Berger (1867–1942), with some hundred lyrical pieces; W. Stenhammar (1871–1927), with two concerti and two sonatas; Christian Sinding (1856–1941), with his Concerto in D♭, a sonata, and many *genre* pieces; and Jean Sibelius (1865–1957).

Transition to the More Recent Period and the Present

After Liszt, Claude Debussy (1862–1918) developed a new independent pianistic style associated with French Impressionism. A new piano technique was established for musical impression, especially in rather small tone-pictures of programmatic character exploiting all resources of the "Debussy style." These included expansion of the harmony through use of the whole-tone scale, pentatonicism, and chords in parallel motion, tone-painting with chord combinations, exploitation of all levels of the instrument for the effect of the sonorities, very delicate use of tone, very rich dynamics, organ-like full sounds, interpenetration of different lines, and occasional use of organ-points. Debussy's piano works include two *Arabesques* (1888), *Suite bergamasque* (1890), *Prelude, Sarabande, and Toccata* (1901), *Estampes* (1903), twenty-four *Préludes* in two volumes (1910), and twelve Etudes (1915).

A famous younger contemporary of Debussy was Maurice Ravel (1875–1937), who anticipated to some extent the Impressionistic piano style in his *Jeux d'eau* (1901), *Miroirs* (1905), and *Gaspard de la Nuit* (1908). Ultimately he combined it with traditional forms and traits in his *Sonatina* (1905), *Le Tombeau de Couperin* and *Piano Suite* (both in 1917), and his Piano Concerto in G and *Concerto for the Left Hand* (both in 1931).

Debussy's style also found many imitators outside of France.

Of the German composers who wrote for the piano after the time of Brahms, Max Reger (1873–1916) stood in the forefront. His piano works were closely related to his organ style. In them there is great richness of fantasy, strongly polyphonic penetration of traditional forms, and a generally restless harmony. Reger composed some of his best works in his great variations for piano on themes from Bach (op. 81), Telemann (op. 134), and Beethoven (op. 86, for two pianos), and in his only piano concerto (in f, op. 114). Together with these longer works he also wrote many short characteristic pieces of lyric and Romantic expression in collective volumes (Improvisations, Humoresques, Aquarelles, Silhouettes, and *From My Diary*).

Carl Nielsen (1865–1931) wrote a *Symfonisk Suite* (op. 8), a Chaconne, a Theme and Variations (op. 40), and a Suite (op. 45).

In the 20th century, the piano is the instrument whose literature has felt the first impact of new stylistic developments. Characteristic traits of the music may thus serve as a starting point from which to survey it.

One of the first of these developments to make its appearance was a general dissolution of tonality, as reflected in the work of Alexander Scriabin (1872–1915), who wrote ten piano sonatas, seventy-nine preludes, twenty-four etudes, and many smaller pieces. Beginning with the harmony and expression of Chopin, Liszt, and Wagner, he magnified more and more the expressionistic traits, developing new possibilities in harmony, the "mystical chord" (with the seven tones C, F♯, B♭, e, a, and d, resulting from five superimposed fourths or from the 2nd, 11th, 7th, 5th, 13th, and 9th overtones), quartal harmony, polytonal and polyrhythmic traits, ambiguous chromatics, and unusual piling up of pianistic sonority.

Charles Ives (1874–1954) wrote two piano sonatas between 1902 and 1915, the Second Sonata bearing the title "Concord, Mass., 1840–60." Independently of Europe and largely on his own, he first developed extremely radical harmony, conglomerate chords or "tone clusters," polytonality, atonality, polyrhythms, and complicated dissonant counterpoint.

Free atonality appeared in three piano pieces (op. 11) written by Arnold Schönberg (1874–1951) in 1909 and in six short piano pieces (op. 19) written in 1911. Major-minor tonality was dissolved and transformed into free atonality in an extremely concentrated idiom. His message was heightened expressionistically. He developed cellular contrapuntal structures and condensed the musical miniature to an extreme degree of concentration.

The transition from free atonality to what Schönberg spoke of as "composition with twelve tones related only to each other" occurred in his works from op. 23 to 25, on which he had been working from 1920 to 1924. Op. 23 is the *Five Piano Pieces;* op. 25 the *Suite for Piano.*

Schönberg's strictly twelve-tone piano works are the piano pieces op. 33a (1928) and op. 33b (1931), as well as the piano concerto op. 42 (1942), in which the four interrelated movements (Andante, Molto Allegro, Adagio, and Giocoso) and the collaboration between piano and orchestra carry on the tradition of Beethoven and Brahms.

Schönberg and his two pupils Alban Berg (1885–1935) and Anton Webern (1883–1945) are the classic representatives of twelve-tone composition. It is the basis of Berg's Chamber Concerto for piano, violin. and thirteen woodwinds (composed in 1925) and Webern's Variations op. 27 (composed in 1936). It also appears in the compositions of many others, including Luigi Dallapiccola (b. 1904), Wolfgang Fortner (b. 1907), and Hans Werner Henze (b. 1926). Hanns Jelinek (1901–1969) wrote a pedagogical work for piano in his *Zwölftonfibel* and *Zwölftonwerk*, as an introduction to the use of the system.

Serial composition made its first European appearance in the work of Olivier Messiaen (b. 1908), who in 1949 organized his etude *Modes de valeurs et d'intensités* in all parameters by modes. Piano works that after 1949 also exercised stylistic influence were written by Stockhausen, Boulez, Stravinsky, Cage, and Cowell. Karlheinz Stockhausen (b. 1928) composed works in which for the first time the parts of the form are exchangeable: Piano Pieces I–IV (1952–3), V–VIII (1954), IX and X (1954–61), and Piano Piece XI (1956). Pierre Boulez (b. 1925) in his First Piano Sonata (1946) adopted Webern's technique, in his Second Piano Sonata (1949) carried through the idea of rhythmic cells, and in his Third Piano Sonata (first performed in 1957) exhibited exchangeability of the parts of the form. His Structures I for two pianos (first performed in 1952) and Structures II for two pianos (first performed in 1961) are also significant. Igor Stravinsky (1882–1971) composed his Movements for piano and orchestra in 1958–9. During the post-Webern period after 1949 tones have been set like points that are precisely determined as to pitch, dynamics, rhythm, and attack. They are organized in concentrated and nonrepeating clusters and successive tonal combinations. There is also an alternation between passages of time that are precisely determined and those in which there is great mobility of tempo. Often the formal parts are exchangeable in accordance with the aleatory or chance principle, with individual possibilities of interpretation varying according to the particular situation and with various shadings in the alternation of all these possibilities. Several composers prepared the way for the so-called post-Webern epoch—Webern himself in his late works, Messiaen in his modal compositions, and John Cage (b. 1912) in his use of the "prepared piano." The development of a new technique of piano playing was also a matter of concern to Henry Cowell (1897–1965) quite early in his career. In 1912 in San Francisco he for the first time utilized so-called tone clusters by playing the piano with the forearm, elbow, and fist as well as the fingers and also by connecting his keyboard technique and harmony closely with chords built on seconds. Cowell was also responsible for the idea of sounding the strings of the grand piano directly with sticks or pieces of metal.

Tonality has generally been expanded through the piano compositions of Igor Stravinsky (1882–1971). Except for the work entitled *Movements,* they come from his neo-Classicistic period: Concerto for piano and wind orchestra (1923–4), Sonata for piano (1924), Serenade in A (1925), Capriccio for piano and orchestra (1929), Concerto for two pianos (1935), and Sonata for two pianos (1943–4).

The principal works for piano by Béla Bertók (1881–1945) were his fourteen Bagatelles op. 6 (1908), Allegro barbaro (1911), three Etudes op. 18 (1918), Improvisations on Hungarian Songs op. 20 (1920), Sonata (1926), five piano pieces entitled *Out of Doors* (1926), First Piano Concerto (1945), Sonata for two pianos and percussion (1937), and numerous works brought out for study and instruction, *For Children* (85 pieces) and *Mikrokosmos* (156 pieces). Bartók's piano music reflects the stylistic phases he went through, from the Late Romantic by way of the reworking of Impressionistic elements and the use of folkloristic material to the exploitation of motor and rhythmic impulses and finally to Classicistic clarification. His instructional works are of unique significance in 20th-century music.

Serge Prokofieff (1891–1953) wrote nine piano sonatas, five piano concerti, and numerous other piano pieces, including a Toccata (op. 11),

Sarcasmes (op. 17), and *Visions Fugitives* (op. 22), as well as *Music for Children*. His piano works form a conspicuous part of his entire creative activity. All the traits that distinguish his other works are quite clearly present in them, such as melodic richness, harmonic refinement, imagination, rhythmic power, formal skill, and brilliant pianism. As these features suggest, the composer himself was a concert pianist.

Paul Hindemith (1895–1963) wrote three piano sonatas (1936), *Ludus Tonalis* (1942), a piano concerto (1945), a suite (1922), *Kammermusik No. 2* (Piano Concerto, 1924), Piano Concerto in Two Parts op. 37, Sonata for two pianos, Concert music for piano, brasses, and two harps (1930), Sonata for piano four-hands (1938), and a Theme with Four Variations (*The Four Temperaments*) for string orchestra and piano solo (1940). Hindemith's writing for the piano was essentially determined by polyphonic thinking and by the concert situation. Neo-baroque and Classicistic traits in form and melody predominate, except for the presence of contemporary trends in the Suite (1922). *Ludus Tonalis* is a series of eleven interludes and twelve fugues, framed by a prelude, which returns as postlude in the inversion and in the crab form. The succession of the fugues corresponds to Series 1 in the succession set up by Hindemith in his *Unterweisung im Tonsatz,* or Instruction in Composition.

Olivier Messiaen (b. 1908) wrote for piano *Vingt regards sur l'Enfant Jésus* (1944); four Etudes, including *Modes de valeurs et d'intensités* (1949); *Catalogue d'Oiseaux* (1956–8); *Visions de l'Amen* for two pianos (1943); *Le Réveil des Oiseaux* for piano and orchestra (1952); and *Oiseaux exotiques* for piano and orchestra (1954). Mainly, here, the same features appear as in his organ compositions. The keyboard works represent a supreme further development of the piano technique of Liszt, Debussy, and Ravel—except for the study *Modes de valeurs et d'intensités,* in which he wrote in modes he had set up himself.

Between 1925 and about 1950 many composers in all countries wrote piano music in expanded tonality.

An important figure at the turn of the century was Erik Satie (1866–1925), who wrote many piano pieces that opened up new areas. The *Three Sarabandes* (1887) and the *Three Gymnopédies* (1888) were influenced by Debussy and Impressionism, especially in harmony. The *Pièces froides* (1897) anticipate transparent post-1920 French composition; the *Véritable Préludes flasques* (1912) were already written in the Neo-classicistic style; and the *Heures Séculaires et Instantanées* (1914) point ahead to Surrealism.

Lute Music

According to the classification of instruments set up by Sachs and von Hornbostel, lutes are complex chordophones consisting of a support for the strings and a resonance box. The two parts are in organic relationship and cannot be separated without disturbing the resonating body.

The lute has a bulging body or sound-box, over the top of which the strings extend parallel with each other. According to the instrumental classification system, most of the usual stringed instruments, whether bowed or plucked, belong to the lute family—even the European violin.

The lute in the narrower sense consists of a sound-box, which can be round, oval, pear-shaped, or of a full-length almond shape, pointed at either end. The sound-box is provided with a level top of wood or skin and may have in it one or more sound openings or holes.

The lute of European art-music, fully developed as early as about 1500, has a body shaped in the form of a half-pear (the curved surface being pieced together out of flat strips of wood), a flat wooden top with a rosette as sound hole (or "sound-rose"), and a broad, flat attached neck, around which gut strings are tied as frets. The guitar, on the other hand, has a flat top and bottom, connected by a frame, with the strings stretched across the sound-box and attached to it, open sound hole, screw pegs at the rear, and usually wire strings. In the lute today there are usually six gut strings, but earlier there were often eleven (five pairs and a melody string), which run from the crossbar parallel to the top and neck in the usually slanted-off pegboard with pegs set into the side. The strings are tuned in the so-called lute tuning: the two middle strings at the interval of a third, the outside strings in fourths—for example, A-d-g-b-e'-a' (as for the guitar). The modern European lute is played without plectrum.

The lute is known to have existed as early as Sumerian times in the ancient East, and may have originated there. Quite various species are to be found in Africa, Asia, the Near East, the Balkans, and Eastern Europe. Forerunners of the modern European lute are encountered as early as the Middle Ages. Perhaps the Arabs, by way of Spain, introduced the instrument into Central Europe. In the flowering time of lute music, between about 1450 and 1650, there were also special forms known as the theorbo and chitarrone. In addition to the playing strings these had several parallel bass strings running alongside the fingerboard and thus not to be fingered but to be set in motion by sympathetic vibration. These were attached to a pegboard of their own that was set on the main pegboard. The chittarone had a smaller body and a longer connecting-piece between the two pegboards, the theorbo a normally large body and shorter connecting-piece.

The flowering time of lute-making occurred in the 16th and 17th centuries, there being a 16th-century center in South Germany, at Füssen, where the best-known lute-makers were the members of the Tieffenbrucker family. In the late 16th century they emigrated from Füssen to Italy and France. During the 17th century Joachim Tielke in Hamburg was particularly well known.

To the end of the 17th century lute music was not written in the mensural notation then normal, but in lute tablature, a fingering script that gave the positions of the fingers on the fretboard of the instrument instead of the pitches. The music for keyboard instruments was sometimes also notated in tablature, but keyboard tablature differs from lute tablature in that the former often uses mensural notation for the upper voice. Italian, French, and German lute tablatures differ from each other: the Italian and French sketch for each string of the instrument a horizontal line, on which the French indicate the fret to be fingered by a letter, the Italian by a number. The German lute tablature has no lines.

The placement of each finger on the string is marked with a letter, the succession of letters does not go upwards on the individual string chromatically but goes along the fret across all the strings. In all tablatures the note values are indicated separately over the fingering-signs.

There are more examples of late-15th-century and 16th-century lute tablature extant than there are of keyboard tablature. This does not mean, however, that the lute was played almost to the exclusion of other instruments. It simply means that one needed a transcription to play a motet on the lute, while one could play the motet directly on a harpsichord or organ from the voice parts. Thus more transcriptions for the lute got into print in the early period than did those for the keyboard. The tablatures for keyboard instruments, accordingly, reproduce the pieces mostly in but slightly altered versions, while the lute tablatures always represent a reworking and usually a reduction to a three-voiced composition.

In the 16th and earlier half of the 17th century the lute was the most widespread and favored instrument in the home. Not until the latter half of the 17th century was it supplanted by the clavichord and harpsichord, after having left behind it an important influence on the music for those instruments. Lute music was cultivated in all European countries, though in Spain after 1580 the guitar predominated. National peculiarities left a sharp imprint on the music and the forms. In terms of its extent and character, lute music has left a striking imprint on European musical culture. From the character and playing technique of the lute, composers developed a distinctive style and compositional technique for suggesting the polyphony and sketching out the harmony.

The unusually extensive and various repertoire for the lute consists of transcriptions, free forms, and dances. Vocal compositions were "set down" in lute tablature, for use either by a singer with lute accompaniment or by a lutenist playing solo. Freer forms were represented among pieces especially distinctive of the music for the instrument, including variation forms such as the ricercar or tiento and free instrumental forms such as the toccata or fantasia. Dance movements included the passamezzo, galliard, and pavane, which also served as the basis for variations and could be assembled into suites.

The lute was also significant in the late 16th and the 17th centuries as a thorough-bass instrument, not only for accompanying soloists but particularly also in the orchestra, where emphasis was always placed on the lower region of sound and the thorough-bass by a therobo or chitarrone or an ordinary lute—and usually a number of these instruments—alongside the harpsichord and a string bass.

Among the most important composers for the lute are some perhaps more widely known as organists, such as Sebastian Virdung, Arnold Schlick, and Martin Agricola. A notable lutenist in the German-speaking area was Hans Judenkunig (b. in Schwäbisch Gmünd *ca.* 1445–1450, d. 1526 in Vienna), with his *Utilis et compendiaria introductio* (about 1515) and *Aine schone kunstliche underweisung* (1523). Some of the lutenists were members of old lute-making families, e.g., Hans Gerle (d. in Nuremberg *ca.* 1570), with his *Musica teusch* (4th ed. 1546) and Hans Newsidler, or Neusiedler (b. *ca.* 1510 in Bratislava, d. in Nuremberg 1563), with his *Newgeordnet künstlich Lautenbuch* (1536) and *Ein newes Lautenbüchlein* (1540 and 1544). Still other German lutenists were Rudolf Wyssenbach, with his *Tabulaturbuch uff die Lutten* (1550) and Hans Jacob Wecker, with his *Lautenbuch* (1552).

In Spain the most significant 16th-century lutenist was Luis Milán, with his tablature book, *El Maestro* (1536).

In Italy, the most notable lutenist was Francesco da Milano (b. in Milan *ca.* 1490), court lutenist in Mantua, composer of *Intavolatura de Lauto die Ricercate, Madrigali e Canzoni francese* I (1536), II (1546), and III (1547). Another Italian lutenist was Peter Paul Borrono, with *Intabolatura de Liuto* (1546 and 1563). Also active in Italy was Johann Hieronymus Kapsberger (d. Rome, 1650), who published three books of *Intavolatura di Chitarrone* (1604, 1616, and 1626).

Of the English lutenists, one of the most significant is John Dowland (b. near Dublin 1562, d. in London 1625 or 1626), from 1598 to 1606 court lutenist in Denmark and after 1612 in London.

In France, Denis Gaultier (b. 1597 or 1603, d. in Paris 1672), member of a well-known family of lutenists and the most significant composer for the lute in the 17th century, exerted decided influence on the French clavecinists and remained a model for the lutenists until well into the 18th century. His principal work was entitled *La rhétorique des dieux* (about 1655).

Another notable lutenist was Esajas Reus(s)ner (b. 1636, d. in Berlin 1679), with *Deliciae testudinis* (1667) and *Neue Lautenfrüchte* (1676). Well known musicians of the Bach period were Sylvius Leopold Weiss (1686–1750), chamber lutenist in Dresden, and Ernst Gottlieb Baron (1696–1760), lutenist to Frederick the Great. Johann Sebastian Bach wrote four compositions for lute and transcribed two of his works for that instrument. It is not known whether he himself played the lute or not.

In rather recent years, the lute has experienced a revival, at first under the stimulus of the Youth Movement in music and the new editions of older lute music issued by Chilesotti and others. This renewed interest perhaps justifies our surveying the literature for the instrument from the various countries.

In the German-speaking area, manuscripts and prints during the 16th century were almost without exception written in German lute tablature. In the 16th century the literature included particularly dances (most frequently the passamezzo, pavane, saltarello, galliard, padovan, and court dance) and French, Italian, and German song-settings in lute transcription from vocal material, such as that in the song books of Oeglin, Ott, and Forster. Toward the turn of the century the new vilanella style of composition became evident even in the lute style, supplanting it after having previously been stimulated by the technique and manner of the keyboard instruments. In the 17th century French lute style predominated, with its use of broken chords and its distinctly French dances.

In France, at the beginning of the second third of the 16th century, the first printed lute tablatures came from Attaignant's press. They had their own fingering script, which soon appeared also in the English,

Dutch, and Polish tablatures. The art of the French lutenists reached a culmination in the 17th century, with their arpeggiated style that influenced also the clavecinists.

In England, the flowering period occurred about the beginning of the 17th century, at the end of the Elizabethan era. It paralleled the art of the virginalists, developing and cultivating variations, characteristic pieces, and English, French, and Italian dances.

In Italy, the oldest printed tablature, dated 1507, consists of compositions and transcriptions by Francesco Spinaccino, including the first known ricercari and utilizing a fingering script of his own. Between 1550 and 1650 the lute was in full flower in Italy.

In Poland the lute tradition goes back to the beginning of the 15th century, and a flowering period occurred in the 16th.

Walenty Greff-Bakwark (1507–1576), of Hungarian ancestry, court lutenist of the military leader Janos Zapolya, was at the royal court in Vilna from 1546 to 1566 and later was at the courts of Vienna and Transylvania, eventually becoming a lute teacher in Padua. He wrote *Intabulatura . . . liber primus* (Lyons 1552, Paris 1564) and *Harmoniarum musicarum* (Cracow 1564, Antwerp 1569).

Wojciech Dlugoraj (*ca.* 1550 to some time after 1619) was court lutenist to Samuel Zborowski and for a while was at the court of Stefan Batory.

Jakub Reys (Jakub Polak) (*ca.* 1545 to 1605, at the French court) displayed elements of high virtuosity and artistic taste. His *Volta Polonica* is one of the best examples of a Renaissance stylization of Polish folklore.

Diomedes Cato (*ca.* 1570 to after 1615), of Italian origin, was court musician to Stanislaw Kostka and in 1600 became lutenist to King Zygmunt III Wasa.

Three additional 16th- and 17th-century Polish lute tablatures also are extant: the first Cracow lute tablature (from the latter half of the 16th century), the Danzig tablature (from the middle of the 17th century), and a tablature from the end of the 17th century.

General Bibliography

W. Apel, *Gesch. der Orgel- u. Klaviermusik bis 1700* (Kassel 1967); D. H. Boalch, *Makers of the Harpsichord and Clavichord* (N. Y. 1957); A. Cortot, *La Musique française du piano* (3 vols., Paris 1944); N. Dufourq, *La musique d'orgue fr. de J. Titelouze à J. Alain* (Paris 2nd ed. 1949); O. Eberstaller, *Orgeln u. Orgelbauer in Österreich* (Wiener musikwiss. Beiträge, Bd. I, Graz and Cologne 1955); H. Engel, *Das Instrumentalkonzert*, in Kretzschmar, *Führer d. d. Konzertsaal*, Bd. 3 (Lpz. 1932), and *Die Entwicklung d. dt. Klavierkonzertes v. Mozart b. Liszt* (Lpz. 1927); K. G. Fellerer, *Orgel u. Orgelmusik* (Augsburg 1929); G. Frotscher, *Gesch. d. Orgelspiels u. d. Orgelkomp.* (2 vols., Bln. 2nd ed. 1959); H. Grabner, *Die Kunst des Orgelbaus* (Bln. 1958); P. Hardouin, *La Facture d'orgues français* (AMl 1958); F. J. Hirt, *Meisterwerke des Klavierbaus. Gesch. d. Saitenklaviere von 1440–1880* (Olten-Lausanne 1955); O. Kinkeldey, *Orgel u. Klavier in d. Musik d. 16. Jh.* (Lpz. 1910); H. Klotz, *Über d. Orgelkunst d. Gotik, d. Renaissance u. d. Barock. Die alten*

Registrierungs- u. Dispositionsgrundsätze (Kassel 1934); A. Prosniz, *Hdb. d. Klavierlit. 1450–1904* (2 vols., Lpz. 1907–8); A. G. Ritter, *Zur Gesch. d. Orgelspiels im 14.-18. Jh.* (Lpz. 1884); Y. Rokseth, *The Instrumental Music of the Middle Ages and Early 16th Century* (NOHM III); L. Schierning, *Die Überlieferung der dt. Orgel- u. Kl.musik aus der ersten Hälfte des 17. Jh.* (Kassel 1961); M. Seiffert, *Gesch. der Klaviermusik, vol. 1, Die ältere Gesch. bis um 1750* (Lpz. 1899); M. A. Vente, *Die brabanter Orgel. Zur Gesch. d. Orgelkunst in Belgien u. Holland im Zeitalter d. Gotik u. d. Renaissance* (Amsterdam 1958) and *Lit. zum niederl. Orgelbau* (AMl 1958); W. Young, *Keyboard Music to 1600* (MD 1962–3); arts. Klavier, K.musik, K.spiel, Orgel, O.musik, O.spiel (MGG). *New eds. in coll. vols.:* Straube, *Alte Meister d. Orgelspiels* (2 vols., Lpz.); Guilmant and Pirro, *Archives des maîtres de l'orgue des XVIe, XVIIe, XVIIIe siècles* (Mainz); Straube, *Choralvorspiel alter Meister* (Lpz. 1907); Moser and Heitmann, *Frühmeister d. dt. Orgelkunst* (Lpz. 1930); Köhler, *Klaviermusik aus alter Zeit* (Litolff, Lpz.); Torchi, *L'arte musicale in Italia III* (Milan); *Liber organi* (8 vols., Mainz, early composers of Ger., Fr., It., and Sp.); *Organum,* 4. Reihe, 19 Hefte (Kassel, early Ger. composers); Tagliapietra, *Anthologie antiker u. moderner Musik* (18 vols., Ricordi, Milan); *400 Jahre europaischer Klaviermusik,* ed. W. Georgii (MW).

Keyb. Mus. to 1600: B. M. Add. 28550: facs. H. E. Wooldridge, *Early Engl. Harmony* (1897). *Codex Faenza 117:* facs. new ed. in MD 1959–60; D. Plamenac, *Keyboard Music of the 14th Century in Codex Faenza 117* (JAMS 1951) and *New Light on Codex Faenza 117* (Kongressbericht Utrecht, Amsterdam 1953); J. Wolff, *Zur Gesch. d. Orgelmusik im 14. Jh.* (KmJb 1899). *Squarcialupi Codex: facs. new ed. Adam Ileborgh:* art. Ileborgh von Stendal (MGG). *K. Paumann* "Fundamentum" facs. Kassel, new ed. in Chrysander's *Jahrbücher für die musikalische Wissenschaft II* (Lpz. 1867); Sch 48; F. W. Arnold, *Das Locheimer Liederbuch nebst der Ars organisandi von C. P.* (Lpz. 1926); B. A. Wallner, *K. P.* (Münchner Charakterköpfe der Gotik, Munich 1938); C. Wolff, *C. P.s Fundamentum organisandi und seine verschiedenen Fassungen* (AfMw 1968); art. Fundamentbuch (MGG). *Buxheimer Orgelbuch:* MfM 1887–8, facs. Kassel; new ed. in ED Bd. 37–39; Sch 36; E. Southern, *The Buxheim Organ Book* (IMM); H. R. Zöbeley, *Die Musik des Buxheimer Orgelbuchs* (Tutzing 1965); art. Buxheimer Orgelbuch (MGG). *16th-Century Germany:* E. Flade, *Lit. Zeugnisse . . . bei Orgel . . . in Deutschland ca. 1500–1620* (AMl 1956); G. Pietzsch, *Orgelbauer . . . in Deutschland bis zum Ende des 16. Jh.* (Mf 1958 ff.) A. *Schlick* "Tabulaturen": new ed. Hamburg 1924, 2nd ed. 1937, "Spiegel": new ed. MfM 1869, Mainz 1931, Kassel 1951, Mainz 1959. L. *Kleber* tablature: MfM 19. E. N. *Ammerbach* Sch 82, 83. P. *Hofhaimer:* H. J. Moser, *P. H.* (Stuttgart 1928); art. Hofhaimer (MGG). S. *Virdung:* PGfM 11, Kassel 1930. *16th-Century Italy:* new eds. in Torchi III; *Die Tokkata* (MW); *Werke für Tasteninstrumente von G. Gabrieli* (Kassel); Sch 92, 103, 149; W. Apel, *The Early Development of the Organ Ricercar* (MD 1949); H. H. Eggebrecht, *Terminus "Ricercar"* (AfMw 1952); H. Hering, *Das Tokkatische* (Mf VII, 1954); K. Jeppesen, *Die ital. Orgelmusik am Anfang des Cinquecento* (Copenh. 1943, 2nd enl. ed. in 2 vols., Copenh. 1960); J. Müller-Blattau, *Gesch. der Fuge* (Kassel 1963); M. Reimann, *Zur Deutung des Begriffs Fantasia* (AfMw 1953); arts. Canzone, Fantasie, Ricercar (MGG). *16th-Century Spain:* J. Bermudo, *Declaración de Instrumentos musicales, 1555* (facs., Kassel); A. de Cabezón, *Ges. Ausg.* in 5 vols., currently being issued (IMM, Brooklyn); F. Correa de Arauxo (in *Monumentos de la Música Española,* ed. M. Kastner, vols. 6 and 7, Barcelona 1948 and 1952); F. Pedrell, *Antología de Organistas Clasicos Españoles* (1908), *El organista liturgico español* (1905), and *Hispaniae scholae musica sacra III, IV, VII, VIII. 16th-Century France: 7 bks. publ. by Attaignant:* facs. new ed. of the first four (Munich 1914). *16th-Century England: The Mulliner Book:* new ed. MB I. *J. Redford:* C. F. Pfatteicher, *J. R.* (Kassel 1934). *Virginal Music,* new eds.: *Fitzwilliam Virginal Book* (2 vols., Lpz.); *Parthenia* (2nd ed. 1908); *The Mulliner Book* (MB, I, London 1951); *The Dublin Virginal Ms* (c. 1570), new ed. by J. Ward (1964); *My Ladye Nevell's Book* (1591), new ed. 1926; W. Byrd, keyboard music (vols. 18–20 of the coll. ed.); Tomkins, keyb. mus. (MB, V); Gibbons, keyb. mus. (MB XX); Bull, keyb. mus. I (MB XIV, XIX); Sch 147, 174. Studies: C. v. d. Borren, *Les origines de la musique de clavier en Angleterre* (Brussels 1912); J. Caldwell, *Keyboard Plainsong Settings in England 1500–1660* (MD 1965); M. II. Glyn, *About Elizabethan Virginal Music* (London 1924); R. Gress, *Die Entwicklung d. Klaviervariationen v. A. Gabrieli bis zu J. S. Bach* (Augsburg 1929); E. Lowinsky, *English Organ Music of the Renaissance* (MQ 1953); R. U. Nelson, *The Technique of Variation* (Berkeley and Los Angeles 1948); L. Neudenberger, *Die Variationstechnik der Virginalisten im Fitzwilliam Virginal Book* (Diss. Bln. 1937). *Poland:* new eds.: MMiP Ser. I, vol. 1 (facs. of Jan of Lublin's tablature); WDMP 20; MPO; MPR; MDK; MSt; studies: Z. Jachimecki, *Eine polnische Orgeltabulatur aus dem Jahre* 1548 (ZfMw 1919–20); J. R. White, *The Tablature of J. of Lublin* (MD 1963). *J. Podbielski* "Fantasia" new ed. WDMP, no. 18; *P. Żelechowski* "Fantasia sopra Primo Tono" new ed. MSt.

17th and 18th Centuries: E. Valentin, *Die Entwicklung d. Tokkata im 17. und 18. Jh.* (Münster 1930); art. Capriccio (MGG). *G. Frescobaldi:* coll. ed. of keyb. works (5 vols. 1950–   , Kassel); sel. organ comps. (Lpz.); Torchi III new ed. of "Fiori musicali" (Guilmant and Bonnet); "Fiori musicali" and sel. works (ed. H. Keller, Lpz. 1943); "Arie musicali" (Mainz); Sch 196; studies: F. X. Haberl, *F.* (KmJb 1887); L. Ronga, *F.* (Turin 1930); art. Frescobaldi (MGG). *B. Pasquini:* B. Haynes, *P.* (Diss. Indiana Univ. 1958). *D. Scarlatti:* coll. ed. of keyb. mus. in 11 vols., ed. A. Longo (Milan 1906–   ); sel. ed., ed. R. Kirkpatrick (N. Y.); Sch 282; W. Gerstenberg, *Die Klavierkomp. D. S.s* (Regensburg 1933); H. Keller, *D. S.* (Lpz. 1957); R. Kirkpatrick, *D. S.* (Princeton 3rd ed. 1962); A. Longo, ed., *Indice tematico delle sonate per clavicembalo* (Milan 1952). *B. Marcello:* W. S. Newman, *The Keyboard Sonatas of B. Marcello* (AMl 1957). *D. Alberti:* W. Wörmann, *Die Kl. Sonate Albertis* (AMl 27). *J. P. Sweelinck:* coll. ed. in 12 vols. (Lpz. 1895–1903); 46 organ chorales of S. and his German pupils; studies: C. v. d. Borren, *Les origines de la musique de clavier dans les Pays-bas jusque vers 1630* (Brussels 1919); M. Seiffert, *J. P. S. u. s. direkten dt. Schüler* (VfMw VII); R. L. Tusler, *The Organ Music of S.* (2 vols., Bilthoven 1958). *France:* E. Epstein, *Der frz. Einfluss auf d. dt. Kl. suite im 17. Jh.* (Diss. Bln. 1940); L. de la Laurencie, *La musique pour instruments à clavier* (Lav. Enc.); A. Pirro, *Les clavecinistes* (Paris 1925); M. Reimann, *Untersuchungen z. Formgesch. d. frz. Klaviersuite* (Regensburg 1940). *J. C. de Chambonnières:* coll. ed. Brunold and Tessier (Paris 1925); Sch 218. *Couperin family:* Sch 264; C. Bouvet, *Une dynastie de musiciens fr.: Les Couperins* (Paris 1919); J. Tiersot, *Les Couperins* (Paris 1926);

M. Reimann, art. "Couperin" (MGG). *L. Couperin:* coll. ed. (Paris 1936–   ). *F. Couperin le Grand:* coll. ed. 12 vols. Paris; 4 books "Pièces de clavecin" in DTD (Chrysander, vol. 4); them. index by M. Cauchie (Monaco 1949); "L'art de toucher" new ed. in Ger. and Engl.; W. Mellers, *F. C. and the French Classical Tradition* (London 1950). *J.-P. Rameau:* coll. ed. of keyb. works (Paris); Sch 296; "Pièces de clavecin" and "Nouvelles suites" new eds. Kassel. *N. de Grigny:* Sch 263. *Germany:* F. Dietrich, *Gesch. d. dt. Orgelchorals im 17. Jh.* (Kassel 1932). *J. J. Froberger:* coll. ed. DTÖ 4, 6, 10; also indiv. eds.; Sch 205; K. Seidler, *Untersuchungen über Biog. u. Kl.stil F.s* (Diss. Königsberg 1930). *J. K. Kerll:* DTB 2. *G. T. Muffat:* DTÖ 3 and 29; Sch 292. *F. X. Murschhauser:* DTB 18. *J. C. F. Fischer:* coll. ed. of keyb. works (Lpz.); R. Oppel, *Über J. K. F.s Einfluss auf J. S. Bach* (Bach-Jb. 1910). *J. Pachelbel:* new ed. keyb. works DTB 2, 4; DTÖ 8; Hexachordum Apollinis (Kassel); Sch 243; E. Born, *Die Variationen als Grundlage handwerklicher Gestaltung im Schaffen J. P.s* (Bln. 1941); H. H. Eggebrecht, *P. als Vokalkomponist* (AfMw 1954); F. Krummacher, *Kantate u. Konzert im Werk J. P.s* (Mf 1967). *J. E. Kindermann:* DTB 13, 21–24. *S. Scheidt:* coll. ed. (Hamburg 1923–   ); many sep. eds.; "Tabulatura nova" DDT 1, "Görlitzer Tabulaturbuch" new ed. 1940; Sch 185; C. Mahrenholz, *S. S.* (Lpz. 1924). *J. Krieger:* DTB 18. *J. Kuhnau:* DDT 4; Sch 244. *F. W. Zachow:* DDT 21–22. *G. P. Telemann:* K. Schaefer-Schmuck, *G. P. T. als Klav.komp.* (Diss. Kiel 1934). *J. G. Walther:* DDT 26–27; RD 9 (Orgelchoräle um Bach); facs. of the "Musikalisches Lexikon" (Kassel); Sch 291; O. Brodde, *J. G. W.* (Kassel 1937). *North German Organ Style:* G. Rietschel, *Die Aufgabe d. Orgel im Gottesdienst bis in d. 18. Jh.* (Lpz. 1892). *H. Scheidemann:* new ed. in Seiffert's Organum; W. Breig, *Die Orgelwerke von H. S.* (Wiesbaden 1967). *P. Siefert:* M. Seiffert, *Sweelinck u. s. direkten dt. Schüler* (VfMw VII). *M. Weckmann:* new ed. LD Schleswig-Holstein 4; M. Seiffert, *M. W. u. d. Collegium musicum in Hamburg* (SIMG II). *J. A. Reinken:* Sch 207. *F. Tunder:* W. Stahl, *T. u. Buxtehude* (AfMw 1926). *D. Buxtehude:* coll. ed. of the organ works (Lpz. 1876–7); coll. ed. (Hamburg 1925–   ); keyb. works (Copenh. 1942); Sch 249; J. Hedar, *B.s Orgelwerke* (Stockholm and Frankfurt a. M. 1951); H. Lorenz, *Die Kl. Musik D. B.s* (AfMw 1954); H.-J. Pauly, *Die Fugen in den Orgelwerken B.s* (1964). *N. Bruhns:* coll. works in LD Schleswig-Holstein 1–2; M. Geck, *N. B.* (Cologne 1968); H. Kölsch, *N. B.* (Kassel 1958). *V. Lübeck:* coll. ed. 1921. *G. Böhm:* coll. ed. Lpz. 1927 and 1932 (keyb. works repr. Wiesbaden 1952); Sch 253; R. Buchmayer, *Nachrichten über das Leben G. B.s* (Bach-Jb. 1908); J. Wolgast, *G. B.* (Diss. Bln. 1924). *Bohemia:* B. M. Černohorský: P 115. *J. Zach:* P 116. *F. I. Tůma:* P 117. *J. F. Seger:* P 123, 124. *F. X. Brixi:* P 125. *Summary:* F. Rotschild, *The Lost Tradition in Music. Rhythm and Tempo in J. S. Bach's Time* (London 1953); H.-P. Schmitz, *Die Kunst d. Verzierung im 18. Jh.* (Kassel 1955).

J. S. Bach: eds. of organ works, esp. that of the Bachgesellschaft coll. ed., also Peters, Steingräber, Augener, Novello, Schirmer; Sch 283; H. Keller, *B.s Orgelwerke* (Lpz. 1948), *B.s Klavierwerke* (Lpz. 1950), and *Das Wohlt. Klavier von J. S. B.* (Kassel 1965); F. Florand, *J. S. B., Das Orgelwerk* (Ger. tr., Lindau 1949); L. Hoffmann-Erbrecht, *Dt. u. ital. Kl. Musik zur B.-Zeit* (Lpz. 1954). *G. F. Handel:* keyb. works in vol. 2 of coll. ed.; coll. ed. of keyb. works, ed. by M. Schneider (Halle a. d. S.); Sch 279; F. Kahle, *Händels Cembalosuiten* (Diss. Bln. 1928); N. K. Nielsen,

H.'s Organ Concertos Reconsidered (Dansk Aarbog for Musikforskning 1963); P. G. Pauly, *H.s Klavierfugen* (Diss. Saarbrücken 1961).

Organ Music after Bach: K. G. Fellerer, *Studien z. Orgelmusik d. ausgeh. 18. u. frühen 19. Jh.* (Kassel 1932); H. Kelletat, *Zur Gesch. d. dt. Orgelmusik in d. Frühklassik* (Kassel 1933). *J. L. Krebs:* Sch 302. *F. Mendelssohn-Bartholdy* "6 Sonatas": Ges. Ausg. Ser. XII. *R. Schumann* "6 Fugues on B-A-C-H": Ges. Ausg. Ser. VIII. *C. Franck:* H. Haag, *C. F. als Orgelkomponist* (Kassel 1936). *M. Reger:* coll. ed. in prep. (35 vols., Weisbaden); *Them. Verzeichnis der im Druck erschienenen Werke,* ed. F. Stein (Lpz. 1953); H. Rösner, *M. R. Bibliog. 1893–1966* (Bonn 1968); R. Huesgen, *Der junge M. R. u. s. Orgelwerke* (Freiburg Diss. 1935); H. Keller, *R. u. d. Orgel* (Munich 1923); H. Rahner, *R.s Choralfantasien* (Diss. Heidelberg 1933); F. Stein, *M. R.* (Potsdam 1939). *Trends since 1920:* T.-H. Langer, art. Orgelmusik (MGG). *O. Messiaen:* A. Goléa, *Entretiens avec M.* (Paris 1960); E. Seidel, *M.s Livre d'orgue* (Musik u. Altar, X, Heft 6, 1958).

Piano Music after Bach: North German Style: H. Riemann, *Die Söhne Bachs* (in "Präludien u. Studien," vol. 3, Lpz. 1897). *W. F. Bach:* M. Falck, *W. F. B.* (Lpz. 2nd ed. 1919). *C. P. E. Bach:* Urtext ed. of 6 collections "Für Kenner u. Liebhaber"; DDT 29–30; new ed. of "Versuch" Lpz. 1906, Engl. version N. Y. 1948, facs. Lpz. 1957; Sch 303, 304; P. Barford, *The Keyboard Music of C. P. E. B.* (London 1965); L. Hoffmann-Erbrecht, *Sturm u. Drang in der dt. Kl.-Musik 1753–63* (MF 1957); E. Stilz, *Die Berliner Klaviersonate z. Z. Friedrichs d. Gr.* (Diss. Bln. 1929). *J. C. Bach:* sel. keyb. sonatas (Lpz.) *J. Schobert:* H. T. David, *J. S. als Sonatenkomp.* (Kassel 1928). *J. G. Eckard:* coll. ed. of keyb. works, Amsterdam and Kassel 1956; art. Eckard (MGG). *L. Honauer:* art. MGG. *G. C. Wagenseil:* new ed. DTÖ XV, 2; also indiv. eds.; I. Pelikant, *Die Klavierwerke v. G. C. W.* (Diss. Vienna 1926). *J. Haydn:* coll. ed. of keyb. works (Ges. Ausg., Ser. XIV, 3 vols.); H. Abert, *H.s Klavierwerke* (ZfMw II and III); E. F. Schmidt, *J. H. u. C. P. E. Bach* (ZfMw XIV). *W. A. Mozart:* Urtext ed. of sonatas (Lpz.); H. Dennerlein, *Der unbekannte M., die Welt seiner Kl.werke* (Lpz. 1951, 2nd ed. 1955); C. M. Girdlestone, *M. et ses concertos pour piano* (2 vols., Paris 1939; Engl., London, 2nd ed. 1958). *M. Clementi:* R. Allorto, *Le Sonate per pianoforte di M. C.* (Florence 1959); A. Tyson, *Thematic Catalogue of the Works of M. C.* (1967). *J. N. Hummel:* K. Benyovszky, *J. N. H.* (Bratislava 1934). *J. Field:* new ed. of piano concerti (MB 18); C. Hopkinson, *A Biogr. Thematic Catalogue* (London 1961). *F. Kuhlau:* coll. ed. of piano works, ed. H. Riemann (Mainz). *Parisian Developments:* G. Favre, *La musique française de piano avant 1830* (Paris 1953).

The 19th Century: L. van Beethoven: coll. ed.; Urtext ed.; E. Fischer, *B.s Kl.sonaten* (Wiesbaden 1956); A. B. Marx, *Anleitung z. Spiel B.-scher Kl.werke* (1863, new ed. Regensburg 1912); W. Nagel, *B. u. s. Kl.-sonaten* (2 vols., Lpz. 2nd ed. 1923–4); J. G. Prod'homme, *Die Kl.-sonaten B.s* (Ger. tr., Wiesbaden 1948); C. Reinecke, *Die B.schen Kl.-sonaten* (Lpz. n. d.); H. Riemann, *Ästh. u. formaltechnische Analyse v. B.s sämtl. Kl.-sonaten* (3 vols., Bln. 4th ed. 1920); R. Rosenberg, *Die Kl. Sonaten B.s* (2 vols., Olten and Lausanne 1957). *Romantic Piano Music:* P. Egert, *Die Klaviersonate im Zeitalter d. Romantik* (Bln. 1934); H. Heussner, *Das Biedermeier in der Musik* (Mf 1959); W. Kahl, *Das Charakterstück* (MW). *C. M. v. Weber:* W. Georgii, *C. M. v. W. als Kl.-komponist* (Lpz. 1914). *F. Schubert:* coll. ed. (Lpz.); W. Kahl, *Das lyrische Klavierstück S.s und seiner Vorgänger seit 1810* (AfMw 1921); H. Költzsch, *S.s Klaviersonaten* (Lpz. 1927); E. Ratz, *Chronologie der S.-Sonaten* ("Stimmen," Jg. 1, 1948); F. Salzer, *Die Sonatenform bei S.* (StMw 15). *F. Mendelssohn-Bartholdy:* coll. ed. (Lpz.); W. Kahl, *Zu M.s "Lieder ohne Worte"* (ZfMw III). *R. Schumann:* coll. ed. (Lpz.); W. Boetticher, *Neue textkritische Forschungen zu S.s Kl.werk* (AfMw 1968); W. Gertler, *R. S. in seinen frühen Kl.werken* (Wolfenbüttel 1931).

F. *Chopin:* coll. ed. (Lpz. 1878–80); new ed. (Warsaw 1956–   ); *Them. Verzeichnis* (Lpz. 1888); M. J. B. Brown, *C., an Index of his works in chronol. order* (London 1960); monographs by A. E. Cherbuliez (Rüschlikon-Zurich 1948), A. Cortot (Zurich 1954), P. Egert (Potsdam 1936), A. Hedley (London 1947), F. Hoesick (Warsaw 1910–1), J. Huneker (Ger. 1917, Engl. orig. 1900), Z. Jachimecki (Cracow 1927), F. Liszt (orig. 1852, tr. H. Kühner, Basel 1948), F. Niecks (2 vols., Lpz. 1890); sp. studies by G. Abraham (*C.'s Musical Style*, London 1939), L. Binental (*C. Dokumente u. Erinnerungen aus seiner Heimatstadt*, Lpz. 1932), L. Bronarski (*C.s Harmonik*, Warsaw 1935, and *Etudes sur C.*, Lausanne 1944–6), J. M. Chomiński (*C.s Präludien*, Cracow 1950, and *C.s Sonaten*, Cracow 1960), K. R. Jüttner (*Um C.s Geburtsjahr*, Mf VII, 1954, and *C.s Vater*, Mf 1957), J. Kleczyński (*C.s grössere Werke einschl. C.s Notizen zu "Méthode des Méthodes,"* Lpz. 1898), K. Kobylańska (*C. in der Heimat*, Cracow 1955), H. Leichtentritt (*Analyse d. C.-schen Kl.werke*, 2 vols., Bln. 1921–2), E. Meister (*Stilelemente u. d. gesch. Grundlage d. Kl.werke C.s*, Diss. Hamburg 1935), J. Miketta (*C.s Mazurkas*, Cracow 1949), and M. Ottich (*Die Bedeutung des Ornaments im Schaffen C.s*, Berl. Diss. 1937); Letters (Lpz. 1911, Munich 1921, 1928, Paris 1952); The Book of the First Intl. Musicological Congress devoted to the work of F. C. (Warsaw 1963); *L'Oeuvre de F. C. Discographie générale* (Paris 1949); B. E. Sydow, *C.-Bibliographie* (Warsaw 1954); *Chopin-Jahrbuch* 1956; *Annales C.* (5 vols., Warsaw 1956–60); art. Chopin (MGG).

F. *Liszt:* coll. ed. 1907–   ; H. Dobiey, *Die Kl.technik d. jungen F. L.* (Diss. Bln. 1931); Z. Gárdonyi, *Die ung. Stileigentümlichkeiten in den mus. Werken F. L.s* (Diss. Bln. 1931); H. Hering, *Übertragung u. Umformung. Zur Klavieristik im 19. Jh.* (Mf 1959); R. Kokai, *F. L. in s. frühen Kl.werken* (Lpz. 1933); D. Presser, *Die Opernbearbeitung des 19. Jh.* (AfMw 1955); P. Raabe, *F. L.* (2 vols., Stuttgart 1931). *J. Brahms:* coll. ed. (Lpz.); V. Luithlen, *Studie zu J. B.' Werken in Variationsform* (Vienna 1927); W. Nagel, *Die Kl.sonaten von J. B.* (Stuttgart 1915).

Transition to the More Recent Period and the Present: W. Georgii, *Klaviermusik* (Zurich and Freiburg i. B. 1950); R. Teichmüller and K. Herrmann, *Internationale moderne Kl.musik* (Lpz. and Zurich 1927, vol. 2 as addendum 1934). *French Impressionism:* H. Kölsch, *Der Impressionismus bei Debussy* (Diss. Cologne 1937); E. R. Schmitz, *The Piano Works of Debussy* (N. Y. 1966); G. Schulz, *Mus. Impressionismus u. impr. Kl.-stil* (Würzburg 1938). *M. Reger:* coll. ed. in prep. (35 vols., Wiesbaden); H. Rösner, *M. R. Bibliog. 1893–1966* (Bonn 1968); F. Stein, *M. R.* (Potsdam 1939). *A. Scriabin:* P. Dickenmann, *Die Entwicklung der Harmonik bei A. S.* (Lpz. 1935). *C. Ives:* H. and S. Cowell, *Ives and his Music* (N. Y. 1955). *A. Schönberg:* G. Krieger, *S.s Werke für Klavier* (Göttingen 1968); J. Maegaard, *A Study in the Chronology of op. 23–26 by A. S.* (Dansk Aarbog for Musik Forskning 1962); J. Romano and J. Zulueta, *A. S. La obra completa para piano* (Madrid 1965); J. Rufer, *Das Werk A.*

S.*s* (Kassel 1959). *B. Bartók:* H. U. Engelmann, *B.s Mikrokosmos* (Würzburg 1953); E. v. d. Nüll, *B. B.* (Halle a. d. S. 1930); H. Stevens, *The Life and Music of B. B.* (N. Y. 1953); J. Uhde, B.*s Mikrokosmos* (Regensburg n. d.) *E. Satie:* R. H. Myers, *E. S.* (London 1949).

Lute Music: Gen. Bibl.: W. Boetticher, *Studien z. solist. Lautenpraxis* (Bln. 1943); O. Chilesotti (see bibl. of works in art. Chilesotti in MGG); I. Dieckmann, *Die in dt. Lautentaubulaturen überlieferten Tänze d. 16. Jh.* (Kassel 1931); K. Geiringer, *Vorgesch. u. Gesch. d. europäischen Laute bis zum Beginn d. Neuzeit* (ZfMw X); O. Gombosi, *Der Lautenist Valentin Bakfark* (Kassel 1967); J. Jacquot, *Le Luth et sa musique* (AMl 1958); O. Körte, *Laute u. Lautenmusik bis z. Mitte des 16. Jh.* (PGfM Beiheft III, Lpz. 1901); W. Merian, *Der Tanz in den dt. Tabulaturbüchern* (Lpz. 1927); W. W. Newcomb, *Studien zur engl. Lautenpraxis im elisabeth. Zeitalter* (Kassel 1968); E. Radecke, *Das dt. weltl. Lied in d. Lautenmusik des 16. Jh.* (VfMw VII); A. Simon, *Die Lautenmusikbestände der kgl. Bibl. in Berlin* (Kongressbericht Vienna 1909); H. Sommer, *Die Laute* (1920); E. Vogl, *Lautenisten der böhmischen Spätrenaissance* (Mf 1965); W. J. v. Wasielewski, *Gesch. d. Instr.musik im 16. Jh.* (Bln. 1878); H. Zuth, *Hdb. d. Laute u. Gitarre* (Vienna 1926–8); art. Laute (MGG); eds.: DTÖ XVIII, 2, and XXV, 2; W. Trappert, *Sang u. Klang aus alter Zeit* (Bln. 1906); Sch 63, 74, 90, 93–95, 115, 138, 150, 181, 215, 216. *H. Judenkunig:* DTÖ XVIII, 2. *H. Gerle:* R. Eitner, *Tänze des 15. u. 16 Jh. aus den Quellen gezogen* (MfM VII); W. Tappert, *Die Lautenbücher des H. G.* (MfM XVIII). *H. Newsidler:* DTÖ XVIII, 2; R. Eitner, *Zwei Lautenbücher von 1536 und 1566* (MfM III, 1871). *L. Milán:* PäM II (1927);˙*Monumentos de la Musica Española;* G. Morphy, *Les Luthistes espanoles du XVIe siècle* (2 vols., Lpz. 1902). *Francesco da Milano:* O. Chilesotti (SbIMG IV 1902–3 and X). *D. Gaultier:* O. Fleischer, *D. G.* (Lpz. 1886, from VfMw II, 1886); W. E. Häfner, *Die Lautenstücke des D. G.* (Diss. Freiburg i. B. 1939); A. Tessier (Publications de la société française de musicologie, 1e série VI and VIII, Paris 1932–3). *E. Reusner:* RD 12; G. Sparmann, *E. R. und die Lautensuite* (Diss. Bln. 1926).

Poland: W. *Greff-Bakwark:* DTÖ XVIII, 2; MDK. W. *Dlugoraj:* Opieński, *La mus. polonaise* (Paris 1918); MPO; WDMP 23; art. in MGG. J. *Reys:* MPO, WDMP 22. D. *Cato:* MPO, WDMP 24. *Cracow Lute Tablature:* ZHMP 2; MDK. *Danzig Lute Tablature:* WDMP 30, 3.

30.   Violin Music

The Instrument

The violin, according to Sachs, originated from the fiddle, which came from Asia Minor to Europe by way of Byzantium during the 10th century. Originally shaped somewhat like a ham, it had rear pegs and usually five strings. It was the principal stringed instrument during the Middle Ages. Only gradually did it take on the rounded and pointed edges characteristic of the modern violin.

Around 1500 the fiddle, called *lira da braccio* in Italy, had the appearance of a violin, but with seven strings and rear pegs. At this time three families of instruments took their point of departure from the fiddle: the *lira*, the *viola da gamba*, and the *viola da braccio*. The first family, the lira, was a perfected fiddle, with seven strings and rear pegs, and was built in various sizes of lira da braccio and lira da gamba. The second family, the viola da gamba, was at first the bass instrument of the lira family and was held between the legs—the word viola being simply the Italian designation for "fiddle" and the viola da gamba being, literally, the "leg fiddle." In the 16th century this instrument was built in various sizes, from the descant to the double-bass level; yet for all of them it retained the same name, even though the smaller instruments were held in the arm. The designation for the third family, viola da braccio, means "arm fiddle." Originally the name was applied to an instrument with an alto level, though it was also built similarly in all sizes. The viola da gamba and the viola da braccio differ, according to Sachs, in the following ways:

Viola da gamba	*Viola da braccio*
five to seven strings	four strings
back sloped off at the upper end	back not sloped off
deep ribs	shallow ribs
flat back	bulging back
edges of sound box and back not projecting	projecting edges
sloping shoulders	round shoulders
c-holes, or flame holes	f-holes
pale and flat sound	round and full sound

The violin, viola, and violoncello are members of the viola da braccio family. The violin was developed around 1480–1530 and is first referred to in the literature about 1580. The improvement in the construction of the instrument was principally due to the families of violin builders living in Cremona—the Amati, Guarneri, and Stradivari.

The viola d'amore, a form of descant gamba especially favored in Germany during the 18th century, had a number of fine wire strings that lay behind the bowed gut strings and vibrated sympathetically with them when they were sounded. The result was a fuller and at the same time a milder tone. The use of resonating strings was due to influence from India.

Transition from 16th to 17th Century

The development of a literature specifically for the violin was limited by the fact that Renaissance musicians characteristically instrumented their pieces *ad lib.* The predominant instrument of this period was the viol. In sonority and range it was quite close to the human voice and thus was easier to use in *ad lib.* instrumentation than was the violin, which offered a greater contrast to the singing voice. The specific technique of violin playing was slow in developing and gaining recognition. Its rise began after 1600, stimulated also by the polar tension between descant and bass in thorough-bass music.

Since there is no actual virtuoso literature extant, it is to be assumed that the cultivation of the instrument was a matter of improvisation and oral tradition.

Diego Ortiz published accompanied solo compositions for the viol as early as 1553. The development of violin playing, accordingly, was related to that of monody. It arose on the basis of solo melody and *cantabile* style. Cantilena became characteristic of instrumental music. The development was quite parallel to that in opera, with its expression-filled dramatic melody for the voice.

The first extant composition intended for the violin is a five-voiced sinfonia by Luca Marenzio, brought out by Cristofano Malvezzi in 1591 in a printed volume of intermezzi. The instrumentation of the piece includes a harp, two liras, a string bass, two lutes, a violin, a viola bastarda, and a chitarrone.

The violin as an orchestral instrument with sonority of independent significance is first traceable in such works as Giovanni Gabrieli's *Sonata pian e forte,* Monteverdi's *Orfeo* (1607), and Salomone Rossi's *Sinfonie e Gagliarde* (1607–8).

The instrument at this time was referred to by various forms of the word corresponding to "violin." In Italy it was called a "violino" or "violina" and included also the alto violin, or present-day viola. In France the word was spelled *violon* and meant "small fiddle," the designation referring not only to all the stringed instruments but also all the players in the string choir. In Germany the word used was "violin" or "figlin."

17th Century

Italy

The Violin as an Orchestral Instrument in Italy

In Italy, during the first third of the 17th century, the violin was increasingly used as an orchestral instrument, with recognition of the significance of its distinctive sound. Claudio Monteverdi (1567–1643) was highly regarded at the court of the Gonzagas in Mantua for his playing of the violin. He considerably increased the demands made on the instrument in his *Orfeo* (1607) and *Combattimento* (1624). In addition to introducing forte-piano and echo effects he invented the tremolo and pizzicato.

Orazio Benevoli called for the high E (e''') in his orchestral part for the violin, for example, in the festival Mass composed for the dedication of Salzburg Cathedral (1628).

In the middle of the 17th century the composers of church sonatas developed a rich literature for the orchestral violin, characterized less by violinistic effects than by the development of a distinguished *cantilena*. The culmination of this trend occurred in Arcangelo Corelli. His predecessors were Giovanni Legrenzi (1626–1690), choirmaster at St. Mark's Cathedral in Venice; Maurizio Cazzati (*ca.* 1620–1677); Giovanni Battista Vitali (*ca.* 1644–1692); Agostino Steffani (1654–1728); Giovanni

Battista Bononcini (1670–*ca.* 1750); and Giovanni Battista Bassani (*ca.* 1657–1716).

Arcangelo Corelli (1653–1713) was the central figure in the highly significant Roman school of violinists. He organized great string concerts that were highly acclaimed in his day. Among his works are the following groups of compositions, each group bearing an opus number and consisting of twelve pieces: op. 1 (1683) and op. 3 (1689), church sonatas; op. 2 (1685) and op. 4 (1694), chamber sonatas; op. 5 (1700), violin solo sonatas; and op. 6 (published in 1714), concerti grossi.

Corelli influenced violin practice throughout Europe. His style was adopted by the Italians Antonio Veracini, in Florence; Antonio Caldara (*ca.* 1670–1736), court choir director in Vienna; Giuseppe Torelli (1658–1709), of Ansbach and Bologna; Tommaso Albinoni (1674–1745); and Giuseppe Valentini (1681–*ca.* 1740), of Florence. Corelli, moreover, had quite a great number of private pupils.

The Violin as a Solo Instrument in Italy

Giovanni Gabrieli seems to have been the first to use the violin as a solo instrument in his *Sonata con tre violini* (published posthumously in 1615). Solo pieces are also represented by the six sonatas of Andrea and G. P. Cima, published in G. P. Cima's *Concerti ecclesiastici* (1610).

Claudio Monteverdi, a leader both as soloist and as discoverer of new playing methods, founded the Mantuan school of violinists. Presumably one of his pupils was Biagio Marini, of Mantua and Venice, who significantly fostered violin technique and composed the first solo violin sonata (1617). His symphonies *La Orlandina* and *La Gardana* are the first known independent solo pieces for the violin.

Dario Castello, Monteverdi's concertmaster in Venice, was a leading technician. He is famous principally for his *Sonate concertate in stile moderno* (1621). Double-stop technique was first used by Ottavio Maria Grandi in 1628. The first vocal piece with solo violin was the *Sfera armoniosa* by P. Quagliati (1623). In the middle of the 17th century the range of the violin was extended to the sixth position. Though written accounts do not tell us that Corelli went beyond this in virtuoso technique, he may have done so in actual performance.

As over against the trio sonata, the solo sonata for violin significantly declined. Its place was taken by the violin sonata, even in the church, where it was heard mostly as the consecrated Host was being exposed.

Germany

The first appearance of the violin in Germany cannot be precisely established. The solo fiddler who provided music for dancing is a typically German figure. With the assistance of the lower open strings he managed to play chords. Harmonic and chordal feeling essentially differentiated 17th-century German fiddling from Italian.

As early as the suite literature of the first third of the 17th century, the violin belonged to the regular make-up of the orchestra. Non-soloistic treatment was accorded the instrument in the collections of suites by such composers as Hans Leo Hassler (*Lustgarten,* 1601), Valentin Haussmann, Melchior Franck, Paul Peuerl, and Johann Hermann Schein.

One of the first groups formed among German violinists was the Hanseatic school. Under the influence of English violinists active in Germany, particularly William Brade (d. 1630), a school of violinists arose in Hamburg. Brade was a significant virtuoso and was prominent as a composer of suites. One of his pupils, the German Nikolaus Bleyer (1590–1658), gained a wide reputation as a virtuoso through his double-stop technique and composed variations and miniature program pieces.

Italian influences also played a part in German violin playing, particularly through the activity of Biagio Marini and Carlo Farina in Germany. Biagio Marini (1597–1665) became in 1623 a music director at the court of the Wittelsbachs in Neuburg on the Danube and in Düsseldorf. His *Sonate, Symphoniae, Canzoni a 1–6 voci* that appeared in 1629 were epoch-making for German violin playing in multiple stops. He employed *scordatura,* or the arbitrary alteration of the regular tuning of the strings. Carlo Farina (*ca.* 1600–*ca.* 1640), violin virtuoso from Mantua, who played under Schütz in Dresden and then was in Danzig, composed program pieces with naturalistic imitation of such sounds as caterwauling and the barking of dogs.

In the second flowering period of the German orchestral suite, from about 1635 to 1680, the demands upon the violin as an orchestral instrument were further increased, for example in the suite collections of such composers as Andreas Hammerschmidt, Johannes Vierdanck, and Erasmus Kindermann.

Solo violin playing was particularly fostered in the middle of the 17th century by Johann Schop (d. 1667), music director to the Hamburg council. Among other innovations in technique, he introduced trills between major and minor sixths. Other violinists who helped develop solo violin technique were Christian Herwig, Caspar Förster, Nikolaus Adam Strungk (1640–1700), Samuel Capricornus (*ca.* 1629–1665) of Stuttgart, his pupil Johann Michael Nicolai, and Johann Pachelbel (1653–1706).

During this period Lully strongly influenced Philipp Heinrich Erlebach (1657–1714), Johann Sigismund Kusser (1660–1727), Georg Muffat (1653–1704), and Lully's pupil Johann Fischer (1646–*ca.* 1716). Muffat's *Florilegium* gave bowing indications after Lully's model. The influence of the French master also appears in the ballet character of the suites, the adoption of many new dances from France, the decided decline in violin virtuosity, and the introduction of short bowing.

At the same period there was a full flowering of sonata literature, which either had no dance movements or only suggested them. This trend is represented in the work of Johann Kaspar Kerll (1627–1693) in Munich, Johann Philipp Krieger (1649–1725) in Nuremberg and Weissenfels, Johannes Georg Rauch in Strasbourg, Johann Theile (1646–1724), and Henricus Albicastro.

There was special interest in violin playing at the Viennese court, where Italian influences fused with German. The Viennese style was particularly represented by Johann Heinrich Schmeltzer (*ca.* 1623–1680), assistant music director to the court in Vienna.

The most important German violinist of the 17th century was Heinrich Ignaz Franz Biber (1644–1704), music director at the Archbishop of Salzburg's residence. Among the features of his compositions that especially relate to the technique of the violin are the complicated *scordatura*, playing in the high registers (up to the seventh position), multiple stopping, broken unisons (*ondeggiando*), and flying staccato. Sacred pieces for the *XV Sacra Mysteria* of the celebration of the rosary—thus not program sonatas—are sixteen solo sonatas "for the glorification of the fifteen mysteries from the life of Mary," also called Passion sonatas or Christus sonatas, composed about 1674.

The Dresden school of violinists was significantly represented by two members of the court chapel, Johann Jakob Walther (b. 1650) and Johann Paul von Westhoff (1656–1705). They increased the use of more than single stops and of various kinds of bowing. Walther's main work was the *Hortus Chelicus* or *Wohlgepflanzter Violinischer Lustgarten* (1688), with program pieces and imitations of instruments. Westhoff's main strength was his multiple stopping, which had a direct influence on Johann Sebastian Bach. An outstanding violin virtuoso of the Dresden school was Vivaldi's pupil Johann Georg Pisendel (1687–1755).

France

The beginnings of violin playing in France are not as yet perfectly clear. The first extensive literature is connected with the ballet de cour, in which dance forms predominated. In a ballet de cour, partly composed by Orlando di Lasso, an *Air de guerre fort plaisant* was presented by some thirty stringed instruments in 1573. Five-voiced composition for strings, which became characteristic of France in the 17th century, had been established as early as 1581. Playing in the higher positions declined.

The instrumental ensemble set up by the French king was reorganized by Louis XIII during his reign from 1610 to 1643 as the *Vingt quatre Violons ordinaires du Roy*, or Twenty-Four Violins in Ordinary to the King. The master of the group was called the *roi des violons*. Their significant influence on the German court orchestra in Osnabrück, Wolfenbüttel, Celle, Brunswick, Lüneburg, Kassel, and Dresden was based on their providing a model for orchestral playing and discipline and on their fostering specifically French dance movements.

The culmination was reached under Jean-Baptiste Lully (1632–1687). In 1652 Lully became a member of the *Vingt quatre Violons* and was empowered by Louis XIV to establish the *Bande des Petits Violons* of sixteen (later twenty-one) performers. Lully's most important pupil was Pascal Colasse. European fame was also accorded the French gamba virtuoso Marin Marais.

During the last third of the 17th century multiple-stopped German playing and the Italian sonata style spread to France. In 1682–3 the German violinist Paul von Westhoff had great success as a virtuoso at Versailles. Of the Italians, Michele Mascitti (*ca.* 1670–1738), Giovanni Antonio Piani, Giuseppe Fedeli, and Antonio Giovanni Guido were active in Paris.

The French school of violinists began with Jean Féry Rebel, Elisabeth Claude, Jacquet de Leguerre, S. de Brossard, François Duval, and others. They responded to the new influences that were being manifested in sonatas, suites, and program pieces. From about 1715, efforts were made in France to oppose the Italian influence. They were particularly represented by Jacques Aubert (*ca.* 1687–1735). The aim, according to A. Moser, was a "violinistic, more homophonically oriented art for laymen, the salon, and society."

England

It is not easy to establish just when violin playing began in the British Isles, as the terminology for the instrument varies and accordingly remains not entirely clear. Compositions for strings are extant by Orlando Gibbons (1583–1625) and John Dowland (1562–1626). The leading violinist in England was the German emigré Thomas Baltzar, who was born in Lübeck about 1630 and was living in England by 1655. Charles II named him leader of the "Twenty-Four Fiddlers," a group established after the French model. Towards the end of the 17th century, in England, Italian string music by Corelli and others was preferred to that of the French. Italian influence was also exerted on Henry Purcell (1658 or 1659–1695) in his sonatas, which were of the church-sonata type.

18th Century

Italy

Composition for the violin and playing of the instrument were widespread during the 18th century in the cities of Rome, Venice, Bologna, Florence, Naples, Turin, and Padua. Taking them up in order, we might note that the Roman school included Francesco Montanari (*ca.* 1700–*ca.* 1730), Pietro Antonio Locatelli (1695–1764), Giovanni Mossi, and Eligio Celestino (d. 1812). Both Locatelli and Mossi were pupils of Corelli, and the former was technically quite gifted in handling wide leaps, double stops, and the higher registers.

At Venice the leading master of the violin in the earlier half of the 18th century in Italy was Antonio Vivaldi (before 1680–1743). From his work at the Pietà orphanage he gained great fame, and then from 1707 to 1713 he was perhaps in Mantua as music master to the governor there, the Prince of Hesse-Darmstadt. Otherwise, he was active in the chapel of St. Mark's in Venice. His concerti and sonatas notably reveal the advance in fingering and bowing technique that was occurring in Italy at this time. The twelve concerti op. 8, *Il Cimento dell'Armonia e dell'Invenzione,* represent the seasons, a storm at sea, and other program suggestions. Among Vivaldi's numerous pupils were Johann Georg Pisendel, Daniele Teofilo Fedele, and Giovanni Battista Somis. Further Venetian composers for the violin were Alessandro Marcello (1684–1750), Carlo Tessarini (b. 1690), and Francesco Bonporti (*ca.* 1675–*ca.* 1740).

In Bologna, a local school is represented by Giuseppe Aldrovandini (*ca.* 1673–*ca.* 1710); Girolamo Niccolò Laurenti; Giuseppe Matteo Alberti; Francesco Manfredini (*ca.* 1688–*ca.* 1748); Giuseppe Antonio Brescianello (*ca.* 1690–1757), mainly active in Stuttgart; and Evaristo Felice dall'Abaco (1675–1742), mainly active in Munich.

In Florence, the most important representative was the world-famous virtuoso and significant composer Francesco Maria Veracini (1685–1750), who from 1717 to 1722 was active in Dresden.

Naples seems, comparatively, to have declined in significance, apparently not having supported a school of violinists of distinct quality or a group of great virtuosi. There were, however, composers for the instrument who came from there, such as Francesco Mancini (1672–1737); Niccolò Porpora (1686–1768); Francesco Durante (1684–1755); Leonardo Leo (*ca.* 1694–1744); Emmanuele Barbella (1704–1773); Ignazio Raimondi (*ca.* 1735–1813), active in London; Giovanni Pergolesi (1710–1736), significantly gifted in his writing for the violin; and Niccolò Jommelli (1714–1774).

Turin became a center through the teaching activity of Giovanni Battista Somis (1676–1763), pupil of Corelli and Vivaldi. The Frenchman J. M. Leclair and Gaëtano Pugnani were among his pupils. Giovanni Battista Viotti was a pupil of Pugnani.

Padua achieved fame through the activity of Giuseppe Tartini (1692–1770), who set the style of violin playing in the earlier half of the 18th century. From the compositional point of view his best works are his more than eighty violin solo sonatas, particularly the *Devil's Trill Sonata* with its technical feature of the performer's leading two voices independently under one bow. Tartini's favorite pupil was Pietro Nardini (1722–1793), whose solo sonatas are musically quite outstanding. His 110 caprices anticipate Paganini's in difficulty, with passages of thirds and sixths carried up to the highest positions. Nardini trained numerous pupils, among whom a particularly significant virtuoso was Antonio Lolli (*ca.* 1730–1802).

Germany

The solo violin compositions of J. S. Bach, though written in the 18th century, are quite closely connected stylistically with the 17th century. In Weimar he became violinist to Prince Johann Ernst II in 1703 and concertmaster to Duke Ernst Wilhelm from 1714 to 1717.

Bach's works for violin include six sonatas for the solo instrument, of which three·are in four movements and have the character of church sonatas and the other three are suites. These six sonatas were written in Cöthen. The famous Chaconne is the last movement of the D minor Suite, and there are fugues in the three sonatas. Bach also wrote two violin concerti (a, E); a concerto for two violins (d); a sinfonia (D) for concertante violin; the Fourth Brandenburg Concerto, which is designated as a "concerto a violino principale"; and six sonatas for violin and clavier, of church sonata type, apparently written in Cöthen. Some further works, the genuineness of which has to some extent been questioned, are of less importance.

From one direction Bach was strongly influenced by the German violinists Biber, Walther, and Westhoff; and, from the other, by the

Italians. The solo sonatas belong among the technically and intellectually most demanding and difficult works for the instrument. The concerti combine a fresh trait of virtuosity with their content.

Among Bach's contemporaries the following stand out in the field of violin music as performers or composers: Georg Philipp Telemann (1681–1767), Johann Adam Birckenstock (1687–1733) in Kassel and Eisenach, Wilhelm Friedemann Bach (1710–1784), Carl Philipp Emanuel Bach (1714–1788), and Johann Ernst Bach (1722–1777), a son of one of Bach's older cousins.

In Dresden, Jean Baptiste Volumier trained the court chapel orchestra of the Elector of Saxony in French orchestral discipline. Francesco Maria Veracini also introduced Italian influences during his extended sojourn there. The leading violinist was Johann Georg Pisendel (1687–1755), a pupil of Vivaldi and Torelli.

At Berlin, in the court chapel under Frederick the Great, the outstanding violinists were Franz Benda (1709–1786) and Johann Gottlieb Graun (1702?–1771), who were succeeded by many of their pupils. Franz Benda had three sons and three nephews, all of whom became musicians. Johann Friedrich Reichardt (1752–1814) was also connected with Berlin. Johann Joachim Quantz (1697–1773), who played the flute for Frederick the Great, wrote an essay on how to play that instrument, *Versuch einer Anweisung, die Flöte traversière zu spielen* (Berlin 1752), containing important references to violin playing. The pupil of Benda's who emerged as the most significant composer in this group was Friedrich Wilhelm Rust (1739–1796), director of court music in Dessau, famous for his skill in managing double stops at high registers on the instrument.

The Mannheim school of violinists, which was founded by Johann Stamitz (1717–1757), introduced a new style of orchestral playing. Among his pupils were his sons Karl and Anton Stamitz (the latter becoming in turn the teacher of Rudolf Kreutzer), Christian Cannabich, Ignaz Fränzl (1736–1811), his son Ferdinand Fränzl (1770–1833), and Ignaz Jakob Holzbauer (1711–1783).

Leopold Mozart (1719–1787), who was assistant conductor at the Archbishop's court in Salzburg and the father of Wolfgang Amadeus Mozart, was regarded as occupying a middle position between Italian and South German violin playing. His *Gründliche Violinschule* (published in 1756) was based on precise awareness of Italian violin technique and literature, particularly that of Geminiani and Tartini. It is also a valuable source of information about the conception of music that prevailed at that time.

Wolfgang Amadeus Mozart (1756–1791), violin pupil of his father, became concertmaster in Salzburg as early as 1770. During his first Italian journey that same year, he came in contact with Nardini in Florence. According to accounts of the time, Nardini was an outstanding violinist. His special skills have left their imprint on Mozart's work in the form of passages, fluent violinistic style, and very noble song-like melody. His violin compositions include violin concerti (particularly those in B♭, D, G, D, and A, composed in 1775 in Salzburg), a Concertone for two violins and orchestra (in C, 1773), a Sinfonia concertante for violin and viola (1779), two duets for violin and viola (1783), and forty-two sonatas for violin and piano.

Karl Ditters von Dittersdorf (1739–1799), a violin virtuoso and conductor, composed violin concerti and chamber music.

Joseph Haydn (1732–1809), who was encouraged by the Eisenstadt concertmaster Aloiso Lodovico Tomasini to write for the violin, composed nine violin concerti. In the string quartets Haydn assigns to the first violin a particularly virtuoso part and allows it to dominate the other three parts. Mozart, on the other hand, took pains in his string quartets to equalize the significance of the four voices.

France

The formation of a national tradition was assisted by the *Concerts Spirituels* in Paris, founded in 1725 by Anne Danican Philidor. Italian influence, however, was strong, both before and after this time. L'abbéle-fils' *Principes du violon* (1761) gives an idea of the violin playing then prevailing.

A whole succession of French pupils proceeded from the school of the Italian Giovanni Battista Somis. Jean Marie Leclair (1697–1764) was their leader, with his violin sonatas, trio sonatas, and violin concerti.

Jean Joseph Cassanéa de Mondonville (1711–1772), director of the *Concerts Spirituels,* was especially significant in the development of violin technique in France, utilizing for the first time single and double natural flageolet tones.

The first professor of violin in the re-established Conservatory in Paris was Pierre Gaviniès (1728–1800), the composer of the celebrated *Vingt Quatre Exercices pour le Violon.* In addition to helping train numerous French pupils, he himself was one in a succession of great virtuosi.

Important influence on French violin playing was also exerted by Giovanni Battista Viotti (1752–1824), who was early trained by Pugnani, toured Europe in concert, was in Paris during the 1780's, then in England, and from 1819 to 1821 was again in Paris. Viotti's violin compositions—including concerti, solo sonatas, and chamber music—were stylistically decisive for the latter half of the 18th century. His best known pupil was Pierre Rode (1774–1830), who wrote violin concerti and twenty-four caprices.

Born in Versailles—his father having come from Silesia—Rodolphe Kreutzer (1766–1831) was the composer of the significant series of studies *40 Études ou Caprices pour un Violon seul* and numerous violin concerti. To him Beethoven dedicated his violin sonata op. 47, the *Kreutzer Sonata.*

England

Up to about 1770, England was entirely under the influence of the Italian school of violin playing and was the gathering-place of Italian violinists. But during the last third of the 18th century German musicians won predominance.

Italian musicians who principally were active in England were Francesco Geminiani (1674-1762), Pietro Castrucci (toward 1690-1769), and Felice Giardini (1716-1796). Geminiani's *The Art of Playing on the Violin* was published in London in 1751.

George Frederick Handel (1685-1759) wrote nineteen solo sonatas with thorough-bass accompaniment—eleven for flute, six for violin, and two for oboe. They are chamber sonatas and as a rule have as their four movements an Adagio, an Allegro, a Largo, and a Finale in the nature of a Gigue.

Georg August Polgreen Bridgetower (toward 1780-1860), son of an African father and a Polish mother and hence often referred to by his contemporaries as "the Mulatto," was the celebrated violinist for whom Beethoven wrote his Sonata in A (op. 47), the *Kreutzer Sonata*. With Beethoven he played it at the first performance in Vienna in 1803.

The leading German musicians were Karl Friedrich Abel (1723-1787), Johann Christian Bach (1735-1782), Wilhelm Cramer (1745-1799), and Johann Peter Salomon (1745-1815).

19th Century

Italy

Italy produced the greatest violin virtuoso in history, Niccolò Paganini, who was born in 1782 in Genoa. A pupil of Rolla in Parma, he was a child prodigy, giving his first public concert at eleven but not making concert appearances outside Italy until after 1828. Sensationally successful in Europe, he was also notably a virtuoso on the guitar. He died in 1840 in Nice.

His success as a virtuoso was based on the atmosphere of the fantastic, mysterious, and demoniac with which his figure and his presence were surrounded. There were also many special features of his technique, such as the quite novel possibilities in his playing on the G-string, his use of flageolet tones, double stops, pizzicati, and retuning of the strings. Also he possessed unique natural ability and particular physical features such as the great extension of his left hand. Early in his youth he had practiced assiduously, reputedly ten or twelve hours a day.

Paganini's compositions included violin concerti, the *Moto perpetuo*, variations, and particularly the twenty-four caprices composed in 1810, representing the epitome of violinistic virtuosity.

As virtuoso Paganini inspired the youthful Franz Liszt to develop quite new possibilities in piano playing. After hearing Paganini in 1829 at Frankfurt am Main, young Robert Schumann finally resolved to become a musician.

Many composers have written works based on Paganini's compositions. His etudes were transcribed by Franz Liszt for piano as his *Six Grandes Études de Paganini*. Schumann transferred Paganini's caprices to the piano as his op. 3 and op. 10. Brahms wrote piano variations, *Studie für Pianoforte*, on the theme of Paganini's twenty-fourth caprice, and Boris Blacher wrote orchestral variations on the same theme.

Virtuoso violin playing was also represented in Italy by Ernesto Camillo Sivori, Pietro Rovelli, Teresa and Maria Milanollo, Antonio Bazzini, Teresina Tua, and Enrico Polo.

France

In addition to Rodolphe Kreutzer, Pierre Baillot (1771–1842) had much to do with the character of French violin playing during the 19th century. Baillot's *Art du Violon* (1834) is still a standard work. Among his pupils were Habeneck, Mazas, and Dancla. François Antoine Habeneck (1781–1849), son of a Mannheim musician active in France, was concertmaster and later director of the Grand Opera, leader of the *Concerts Spirituels*, violin professor at the Conservatory, and leader of the *Concerts du Conservatoire*. With his exemplary performances he particularly made France aware of Beethoven's symphonies. From Habeneck's school there came many notable violinists. Jacques Féréol Mazas (1782–1849) composed studies and violin duets that are still in use today. Jean Baptiste Charles Dancla (1817–1907) also maintained the traditions of this school and, as a teacher, passed them on to a number of pupils who were later to become notable violinists.

Through various individuals, the French school has continued active into the present century. The Belgian Charles-Auguste de Bériot (1802–1870), though not an actual pupil of Baillot's, is to be accounted as belonging to this school. Appearing as virtuoso and teacher, he is still today significant for his *Méthode de Violon* (Paris 1858) and his etudes. Henry Vieuxtemps (1820–1881) was one of his pupils, and Vieuxtemps was in turn the teacher of the Belgian Eugène Ysaye (1858–1931). Among Habeneck's pupils was Delphin Alard (1815–1888), the editor of the series *Les Maîtres Classiques du Violon*. One of Alard's pupils was Pablo de Sarasate (1844–1908), to whom Lalo dedicated his *Symphonie espagnole*. The school of Habeneck was carried on further by Hubert Léonard (1819–1900), who was the teacher of Henri Marteau (1874–1934), active in Geneva and Berlin. His violin playing particularly occasioned Max Reger's writing many compositions. The Léonard pupil Martin Pierre Joseph Marsick (1848–1924) was the teacher of Carl Flesch and Jacques Thibaut (d. 1953). The school of Kreutzer was particularly perpetuated by Lambert Joseph Masart (1811–1892), who in turn taught Henri Wieniawski (1835–1880), Franz Ondřiček (1857–1922), and Fritz Kreisler (1875–1963).

Germany

The personality who for the last time in the history of violin playing in Germany united significantly the roles of virtuoso, composer, teacher, and creator of a style of his own was Louis Spohr (1784–1859), violin pupil of Franz Eck, who derived from the Mannheim School. In 1802 Spohr began to make concert tours, was concertmaster in Gotha, then conductor in Vienna, Frankfurt am Main, and from 1822 court conductor in Kassel. His violin works include fifteen concerti, of which the eighth, composed in 1816, is the *Konzert in Form einer Gesangszene*, or Concerto in the Form of a Vocal Scene, with recitative, aria, and stretta. He also wrote violin duets, many pieces of chamber music, and a *Violin School* (1832). His violin style represented the close of the Mannheim School and was the culminating point of the German Romantic expressive style, with its reliance on vibrato, bel canto, overt expressiveness, and lyrical style. Spohr was one of the most influential teachers in Germany and Austria.

His most significant pupil was Ferdinand David (1810–1873), who became in 1836 concertmaster at the Leipzig Gewandhaus under Mendelssohn. David also taught in the conservatory that was opened in 1843 and gained a wide reputation as a chamber musician. He edited many works of Classical literature and taught a whole generation of German violinists. David's most famous pupil was August Wilhelmj (1845–1908), an internationally celebrated virtuoso.

A further 19th-century German school of violinists goes back to Friedrich Wilhelm Pixis (1785–1842), who was born in the Rhenish Palatinate and was active at the Prague Conservatory. The best known pupil of Pixis was Moritz Mildner (1812–1865), his successor at the Prague Conservatory. From Mildner's school came Ferdinand Laub (1832–1875) and Ottakar Ševčik (1852–1934). Ševčik was, in turn, the teacher of Jan Kubelik (1880–1940).

As the 18th century drew to a close and the 19th began, violin playing in Vienna broke completely away from Italian influence. The circumstances that led to this rupture were partly based on the character of the Viennese Classical Era and partly on the intensive cultivation of chamber music in various circles of the Viennese nobility. The brothers Anton Wranitzky (1761–1819) and Paul Wranitzky (1756–1808) took a decisive role in this development. One of Anton Wranitzky's pupils was Ignaz Schuppanzigh (1776–1830), who as first violinist in his string quartet was particularly active in performing Beethoven's works. The leading violinist in Viennese musical life between 1810 and 1830 was Joseph Mayseder (1789–1863), also a pupil of Anton Wranitzky. A pupil of Mayseder's was Heinrich de Ahna (1835–1892), concertmaster of the Berlin court chapel and second violinist of the Joachim Quartet. Beethoven's violin concerto was played in 1806 by the significant violinist Franz Clement (1780–1842).

Joseph Böhm (1795–1876) helped mold the style of violin playing in 19th-century Vienna, especially by his teaching activities and his string-quartet performances. From Böhm the tradition went to Georg Hellmesberger (1800–1880) and further to his son and pupil Joseph Hellmesberger, Sr. (1828–1893), and Joseph Hellmesberger, Jr. (1855–1907). Joseph Hellmesberger, Sr., was the concertmaster of the court opera, violin professor at the Conservatory, and leader of a famous string quartet. A pupil of Böhm's, also, was Joseph Joachim (1831–1907), the first director of the Hochschule für Musik in Berlin, founded in 1869, who gave the decisive cast to Berlin musical life in the latter half of the 19th century. During some sixty years of activity as a teacher Joachim trained hundreds of pupils, and his influence has extended on into the immediate present. Among his pupils are Henri Petri (1856–1914), Jenö Hubay (1858–1922), Bram Eldering, and Karl Klinger. Hubay trained the violinists Joseph Szigeti and Franz von Vecsey.

Scandinavia

Though French and Italian violinists early came to Northern courts, violin music was not composed by native Scandinavian musicians until rather late. The only significant exception was the Swede Johan Helmich Roman (1694–1758). Besides sonatas with continuo he wrote music for violin solo that displayed a highly developed technique. By the end of the century J. M. Kraus (1756–1792)' had composed violin works, including four sonatas, and the Finn Erik Tulindberg (1761–1814) had written a concerto in the Viennese Classical style.

About the turn of the century in Copenhagen J. E. Hartmann (1726–1793) and his pupil Claus Schall (1779–1817) both wrote sonatas. Schall also wrote concerti. Johannes Frederik Frøhlich (1806–1860), Schall's pupil, was a capable violinist and successful composer of instrumental music, including four violin concerti and several pieces for violin and orchestra. In Sweden the Concerto in c♯ (1820) by Franz Berwald is significant.

The greatest of the Scandinavian violin virtuosi was Ole Bornemann Bull, who was born in Bergen, Norway, in 1810 and died there in 1880. From the age of twenty he concertized in Europe and America and continued active throughout the rest of his life. He was famous both as an interpreter and improviser. Inspired by Paganini, he followed this master's method and, concurrently, developed from the model of the Norwegian folk-instrument, the *hardingfele,* a technique of his own with flat bridge, which permitted him to play in four voices. He collected and transcribed Norwegian folk-music and encouraged the younger composers Grieg, Nordraak, and Svendsen to develop a Norwegian style from the folk-melodic heritage. In 1850 he founded in Bergen a national theater, *Den Nationale Scene.* His works include a concerto in e and many miniatures.

J. P. E. Hartmann wrote three sonatas, the third in g (1886), a most expressive work in Northern Romantic tone.

Niels W. Gade composed three sonatas, one in A (1842), one in d (1849), and one in B♭ (1885), the last two being mature, highly Romantic works.

Emil Sjörgren was inspired by Schumann and Brahms in his five sonatas, of which No. 2 in e (1889) and No. 5 in a (1914) are particularly significant.

Christian Sinding's violin works include three concerti (A 1898, D 1901, and a 1917), as well as several pieces for violin and orchestra—very energetic music in an international, Late Romantic style. He composed also four sonatas and four suites for violin and piano, and two serenades for two violins and piano in G (1903) and A (1909), the latter regarded as one of his most eminent creative works.

Jean Sibelius wrote a Concerto in d (1903–5), a work characteristic of his first creative period, and two serenades for violin and orchestra (D 1912, g 1913).

Carl Nielsen's violin works include a concerto in two movements (1911), developed in a thoroughly symphonic manner throughout, each movement with a slow introduction of virtuoso or lyrical character; two sonatas in A (1895) and g (1912), the second a principal work in Nielsen's chamber music, laid out as a sonata in a way much the composer's own; and violin soli, *Præludium og Tema med Variationer* (1923) and *Preludio e presto* (1928).

W. Peterson-Berger wrote a Concerto in f♯ (1928), stylistically Late Romantic and laid out like a symphony, one of his most substantial instrumental works.

Fartein Valen's Concerto, written in 1940 and published in 1948, is a one-movement, atonal work. Like Berg's concerto, it was composed on the occasion of a death—in Valen's case, that of a young man, his nephew Arne Valen—and it ends with a chorale by Crüger, *Jesus meine Zuversicht*. Valen's concerto is one of the first Scandinavian pieces to be constructed on a twelve-tone series. It has very great inwardness of expression. He also wrote a sonata op. 3 in 1916 (published in 1920), a youthful work in considerably expanded tonality.

Poland

The first known composer of specifically violin music in Poland was Feliks Janiewicz (1762–1848), who in 1777 became a violinist in the Warsaw royal chapel and later was a pupil of Nardini and Pugnani. For a while he was court violinist to the Duchess of Orléans and from 1792 to 1848 soloist and director of the Musical Society in Edinburgh. He wrote five violin concerti and much chamber music, with national accent. His writing for violin is much like that of Rode. Affiliated with the same stylistic circle was Jan Kleczyński (1756–1828), who lived in Austria.

The outstanding figure in Polish violin music of the 19th century was Karol Lipiński (1790–1861). A significant virtuoso, he made concert tours through Europe, and in 1839 he was first violinist in the Dresden court orchestra. As composer he is still known for various of his works: his capriccios for solo violin (op. 3, 10, 27, and 29), four violin concerti (op. 14, 21, 23, and 32), polonaises, and rondi alla polacca. He displays the virtuoso technique of the old Italian school and of Viotti, Kreutzer, and Rode; at the same time, he has melodic elements that are Slavic and predominantly Ukrainian. To the same generation belongs Stanisław Serwaczyński (1781–1859), of Vienna, Budapest, and Lvov. Serwaczyński taught Joseph Joachim and Henryk Wieniawski.

The second famous violinist in 19th-century Poland was Apolinary Kątski (1825–1879), a pupil of Paganini and incomparable interpreter of his teacher's work in Europe. In 1861 he was the first director of the Warsaw Musical Institute. His compositions are typically salon and concert miniatures, particularly mazurkas.

The third great violinist in this group was Henryk Wieniawski (1835–1880), pupil of Serwaczyński and Massart in Paris. A virtuoso, he made European concert tours with his brother, the pianist Józef Wieniawski, and later with Anton Rubinstein. As teacher he was active in Petersburg and Brussels. He belonged to the Belgian-French school of Bériot and Vieuxtemps. His works include violin concerti in f♯ and d, stylized Polish dances, etudes-caprices, and an *Ecole moderne pour violon seul*.

Karol Szymanowski (1882–1937) wrote significant and technically novel violin compositions during all his creative periods. His Sonata op. 9 and Romanze op. 25 have a Neo-Romantic character, sharing some traits with works of Scriabin and Wagner. He also has some quite Impressionistic works in *Myths* (1915) and in his First Violin Concerto (1917), both of which display delicate colors, choice means of articulation, and bold harmonic aspects. His Second Violin Concerto (1933) contains elements of Tatra folk-music and is deliberately simplified in compositional character.

Mieczysław Karłowicz (1876–1909) composed a Violin Concerto op. 8, of Classical construction, showing the influence of Brahms and Tchaikovsky, with Slavic elements particularly in the Romanza.

In the 20th century Polish composers include Zygmunt Stojowski (1869–1946), Emil Młynarski (1870–1935), Ludomir Różycki (1884–1953), Jan Adam Maklakiewicz (1899–1954), Zbigniew Turski (b. 1908), and particularly Grażyna Bacewicz (1913–1968).

Selected Violin Compositions of the 19th and 20th Centuries

Among violin concerti written in the 19th century and belonging today to the repertory of soloists in the concert hall and historically of special importance, the following might be named and briefly annotated thus, in chronological order:

Ludwig van Beethoven, Concerto in D, op. 61, composed in 1806. This work has a Classical three-movement layout and a symphonic basis. It is a work of Apollonian spirit, unique in the maturity and sense of consecration in its cantabile aspects. Also the "brilliant" passages of the solo instrument are expressive, with many new traits in the way the violin is brought into relationship with the orchestra and in the way the symphonic structure has been handled to accommodate the demands of a solo concerto.

Felix Mendelssohn-Bartholdy, Concerto in e, op. 64, composed in 1845. In this ideal virtuoso concerto there is a felicitous union of the highest technical demands, technical brilliance, musical ardor and poetry, and thoroughly balanced form. The violin is contrasted and interwoven with the orchestra in a novel way.

Robert Schumann, Concerto in d, composed in 1853, first published in 1937. The total impression that this work makes is of something that is divided within itself, though it is highly significant in individual themes of the first and second movements. It was written in a way not very effective for the soloist.

Louis Spohr, fifteen violin concerti. Of these, the eighth (1816) is the *Concerto in the Form of a Vocal Scene*, with Recitative, Aria, and Stretta.

Max Bruch, three concerti, the most successful being the first one, in g, op. 26, composed in 1864. This is a work especially distinguished by expressive melody and sonorous beauty.

Edouard Lalo, *Symphonie espagnole* in d, op. 21 (1875), particularly charming in sonority and highly effective.

Johannes Brahms, Concerto in D, op. 77, composed in 1877. Related in layout and attitude to the Beethoven Concerto, it takes its place beside it in significance.

Peter Tchaikovsky, Concerto in D, op. 35, composed in 1878. Highly virtuoso in character, it is linked with passionately Slavic melodic aspects and is quite gripping in certain passages.

Antonin Dvořák, Concerto in a, op. 53, composed in 1879. Peculiarly Slavic melodic and rhythmic traits are here united with the Classical tripartite structure into an effective whole with compelling energy.

Among outstanding violin concerti written in the 20th century are:

Jean Sibelius, Concerto in d, op. 47, composed in 1903, revised in 1905, a work characteristic of Sibelius, particularly in the slow movement with its melodic melancholy features.

Alexander Glasunoff, Concerto in a, op. 82, composed in 1904, strongly Russian in melody and rhythm.

Max Reger, Concerto in A, op. 101, published in 1908, more a symphony than a solo concerto.

Carl Nielsen, Concerto (1911), a monumental composition, with symphonic layout in two movements.

Rudi Stephan, Music for Violin and Orchestra, a significant work of symphonic proportions by a composer who died in 1915.

Maurice Ravel, *Tzigane,* a rhapsody with orchestra, composed in 1924 and representing a refined stylization of the Hungarian rhapsody.

Hans Pfitzner, Concerto in b, op. 34, composed in 1925, a quite impressive work consisting of four movements with tightly knit, mature melodic aspects.

W. Peterson-Berger, Concerto in f♯ (1928), a late-Romantic work, with symphonic layout.

Igor Stravinsky, Concerto in D, composed in 1931, Neo-classicistic in character, consisting of four movements: Toccata, Aria I and II, and Capriccio.

Karol Szymanowski, First Concerto (1917), of quite subjective emotion; Second Concerto (1933), of simplified and clarified style, with folkloristic influences.

Serge Prokofieff, First Concerto, in D (1916–7), strongly lyrical, with the solo part closely interwoven with the orchestra; Second Concerto, in g (1935), Classicistic, more polyphonic, and in chamber-music style.

Alban Berg, Concerto, dedicated "To the memory of an angel" (Manon Gropius, who had died while still young), Berg's last work, composed in 1935, a composition in two movements, highly significant expressive music, twelve-tone, with an allusion in the second movement to a chorale on death used by Bach.

Arnold Schönberg, Concerto, op. 36, composed in 1936, a work with twelve-tone aspects, quite strongly expressive music, extreme in its difficulties.

Béla Bartók, Concerto, composed in 1937–8, in three movements, rich in melodic maturity and multiplicity of moods.

Paul Hindemith, Concerto, composed in 1939, in three movements, lyrical, a significant work of compositional construction.

Fartein Valen, Concerto (1940, published in 1948), atonal, very expressive, with concluding chorale.

Among sonatas and other similar works for violin, the ten sonatas of Ludwig van Beethoven are outstanding compositions: op. 12 D, A, and E♭ (1798–9); op. 23 in a (1800–1); op. 24 in F, the so-called *Spring Sonata* (1800–1); op. 30 A, c, and G (1802); op. 47 in A, the *Kreutzer Sonata* (1803); and op. 96 in G (1811–2). The ten sonatas, significant works without exception, belong to the concert hall, especially the Sonata op. 47 with the great concertante layout of the first movement. The two romances, in F and G (1802), are smaller performance-pieces with orchestral accompaniment.

Franz Schubert composed three sonatinas, in D, a, and g, in 1816, charming occasional works; a Sonata in A, op. 162, in 1817, with larger, more virtuoso character; *Rondeau brillant* in b, op. 70, and *Fantasie*, op. 159, two works of virtuoso character.

Felix Mendelssohn-Bartholdy wrote a Sonata op. 4 in 1823, a worthy early work.

Robert Schumann, in 1851 during his later creative period, wrote two sonatas, one in a (op. 105) and another in d (op. 121).

Johannes Brahms has three sonatas, in G (op. 78, 1878, the so-called *Rain Sonata*), in A (op. 100, 1886), and in d (op. 108, 1887). The first sonata represents a new type of chamber music, in intimate collaboration as a duet. The most overtly effective is the second sonata. The third is passionate in character.

Edvard Grieg has three sonatas, in F (op. 8, 1865), in G (op. 13, 1867), and in c (op. 45, 1890). Melodically and rhythmically, these works are of strong intrinsic national significance.

César Franck composed a Sonata in A, in 1886, consisting of four movements, improvisatory in form, yet with all movements connected by a germinal motif.

Richard Strauss wrote a Sonata in E♭, op. 18, in 1887, a very energetic work, influenced by Schumann and Brahms.

Max Reger wrote several works for violin: sonatas op. 41 (A), op. 72 (C), op. 84 (f♯), op. 122 (e), and op. 139 (c), as well as a group of *Suites in Ancient Style,* op. 93. The sonata op. 72 intentionally uses the themes *Affe* (ape) and *Schaf* (sheep) in the first movement. The last sonatas op. 122 and op. 139 are especially significant.

Ferruccio Busoni wrote a notable Second Sonata in e, op. 36a, in 1901—a very individual work, with the last movement a set of variations on a Bach chorale.

Maurice Ravel's Sonata in G, composed in 1923–7, consists of three movements, of concertante character.

Hans Pfitzner's Sonata in e, op. 27, composed in 1918, is a work very characteristic of Pfitzner, in three movements, with its most significant content in the first two movements.

Claude Debussy's Sonata, composed in 1916–7, is from his late period and consists of three short movements of significant content as absolute music.

Béla Bartók notably wrote two sonatas, in 1921 and 1922, during his middle, strongly experimental stylistic phase.

Igor Stravinsky wrote a *Duo concertante for Piano and Violin* in 1932, consisting of the following movements: Cantilena, Eclogue I and II, Gigue, and Dithyramb.

Paul Hindemith wrote two sonatas, one in E (1935) and one in C (1939), the latter being especially significant, in three movements, with a triple fugue as the finale.

In music written in the United States, violin compositions figure steadily among the works of serious composers. Sonatas for violin and piano were written by Arthur W. Foote (1853–1937), John Alden Carpenter (1876–1951), and Daniel Gregory Mason (1873–1953). Charles Ives (1874–1954) wrote six sonatas for violin and piano. The influential teacher and composer Ernest Bloch (1880–1959) wrote a violin concerto (1938); and a somewhat early American atonalist, Wallingford Riegger (1885–1961), wrote a set of variations for violin and orchestra (1959). The Neo-classicistic trend that began to set in during the third decade of the present century favored works of this type. Violin sonatas or sonatinas appear among the compositions of Virgil Thomson (b. 1891), Walter Piston (b. 1894), Roger Sessions (b. 1896), Quincy Porter (b. 1897), Aaron Copland (b. 1900), Hugo Norden (b. 1909), Norman dello Joio (b. 1913), Gardner Read (b. 1913), Vincent Persichetti (b. 1915), Ben Weber (b. 1916), Louis Mennini (b. 1920), Harold Shapero (b. 1920), Lochrem Johnson (b. 1924), Easley Blackwood (b. 1933), and very many others. More extensive compositions for violin and orchestra, usually designated by the composer as concerti, figure among the works of Harl McDonald (1899–1955), Paul Creston (b. 1906), Ross Lee Finney (b. 1906), Samuel Barber (b. 1910), Gian-Carlo Menotti (b. 1911), Alan Hovhaness (b. 1911), Gail Kubik (b. 1914), David Diamond (b. 1915), Lou Harrison (b. 1917), Leon Kirchner (b. 1919), and Peter Mennin (b. 1923). This cursory mention of but a few of the active American composers today who have written or are writing works for the violin suggests that—in addition to some of the more sensational trends in contemporary music— this basic type of composition, like that of works for piano, chamber music, opera, and so on, continues to be steadily and seriously cultivated today.

Bibliography

Violin-playing: A. Moser, *Gesch. d. Violinspiels* (Bln. 1923, 2nd ed. suppl. by H.-J. Nösselt, Bd. 1, Tutzing 1966); W. Altmann, *Kammermusik-Katalog. Ein Verzeichn. von seit 1841 veröffentl. Kammermusikwerken* (Lpz. 5th ed. 1942); W. Bachmann, *Die Anfänge des Streichinstr.spiels* (Lpz. 1964); D. D. Boyden, *The History of Violin Playing from its Origin to 1761* (London 1965); H. Engel, *Das Instrumentalkonzert,* in *Kretzschmars Führer durch d. Konzertsaal,* vol. III (Lpz. 1932); H. Mersmann, *Die Kammermusik,* in *Kretzschmars Führer durch d. Konzertsaal,* 4 vols. (Lpz.

1930 ff.); A. Schering, *Gesch. d. Instr.konzertes* (Lpz. 1905); L. Torchi, *La Musica instr. in Italia nei secoli XVI, XVII e XVIII* (RMI 1897–1900); A. Tottmann, *Führer d. dt. Violin-Literatur*, 4th ed. rev. with W. Altmann (Lpz. 1935); W. v. Wasielewski, *Die Violine u. ihre Meister* (1869, Lpz., 6th ed. 1920). E. Heron-Allen, *De Fidiculis Bibliographia, being an Attempt towards a Bibliography of the Violin* (London 1890–4); D. D. Boyden, *The Violin and its Technique in the 18th Century* (MQ 1950); R. Fissore, *Les Maîtres Luthiers* (5th ed., Paris n. d.); J. Gallay, *Les Luthiers italiens aux XVIIe et XVIIIe siècles* (Paris 1869); G. Hart, *The Violin: its Famous Makers and their Imitators* (London 1825); W. Henley, *Universal Dictionary of Violin and Bow Makers* (1959– , Brighton, Sussex); K. Jalover, *Italian Violin Makers* (Prague 1957); W. L. v. Lütgendorff, *Die Geigen- u. Lautenmacher v. Mittelalter b. z. Gegenwart* (Frankfurt a. M. 4th ed. 1922); F. Niederheitmann, *Cremona. Eine Charakteristik der ital. Geigenbauer u. ihrer Instr.* (Lpz. 4th ed. 1909, rev. with E. Vogel); R. Rühlmann, *Atlas z. Gesch. d. Bogeninstr.* (Braunschweig 1882) and *Die Gesch. d. Bogeninstr.* (Braunschweig 1882); C. Sachs, *Die Musikinstrumente* (Breslau 1923) and *The History of Musical Instruments* (N. Y. 1940); P. Stoering, *Von der Violine* (Bln. 3rd ed. 1921).

17th Century: Germany: G. Beckmann, *Das Violinspiel in Deutschland vor 1700* (Diss. Bln. 1916); A. Moser, *Die Violinskordatur* (AfMw I, 1919). *F. Biber:* new eds. 16 Solo Sonatas (on the Passion) DTÖ 12, 2; 8 Solo Sonatas DTÖ 5, 2; Sch 238. *J. J. Walther:* sonatas RD 16; Sch 239. *J. G. Pisendel:* DDT 29–30. *France:* M. Pincherle, *La technique du violon chez les premiers sonatistes français* (Bulletin fr. de la S. J. M. 1911). *England:* "24 Fiddlers": Sch 237. *H. Purcell:* coll. ed.

18th Century: Italy: B. Studeny, *Beitr. z. Gesch. d. Violinsonate im 18. Jh.* (Munich 1911). *A. Vivaldi:* Sch 276. *E. F. dall'Abaco:* DTB 1 and 9; Sch 277. *G. Tartini:* Sch 295; M. Dounias, *Die Violinkonzerte T.s* (Wolfenbüttel 1935). *Germany: J. S. Bach:* A. Moser, *Zu J. S. B.s Sonaten u. Partiten f. Viol. allein* (Bach-Jb. 1907). *J. C. Pisendel:* DDT 29–30. *J. J. Quantz* "Versuch": new ed. 1906, facs. of 3rd ed. (1789) Kassel. *Austria: L. Mozart* "Violinschule": facs. 1922. *J. Haydn:* H. Neurath, *Das Violinkonzert in d. Wiener klass. Schule* (StMw 14). *France: L'abbéle fils* "Principes du violon," new ed. Paris 1961. *J. M. Leclair:* coll. ed. 16 vols. in prep. (ed. M. Pincherle, Paris); Sch 294; M. Pincherle, *J. M. L.* (Paris 1952). *G. B. Viotti:* R. Giazotto, *V.* (Milan 1956). *F. Geminiani* "The Art of Playing on the Violin": new ed. facs. London and N. Y. 1952.

19th Century: N. Paganini: J. Kapp, *P.* (Bln. 1913, rev. 1928). *F. A. Habeneck:* cf. Richard Wagner "Über das Dirigieren." *L. Spohr:* sel. works, ed. F. O. Leinert (Kassel). *Scandinavia: O. Bull:* M. Smith, *The Life of O. B.* (Princeton 1943).

31. Chamber Music

The designation "chamber music"—though originally referring to the place where the music-making occurred—actually has to do with instrumentation. In a narrower sense, it includes works for solo stringed instruments without piano. Beginning with Haydn's string quartets about

1775, the Viennese Classical composers developed this type of instrumentation, which to the present day has been generally regarded as having attained its artistic culmination in the string quartet. In a wider sense, also, the term "chamber music" applies to instrumental groups of soloistic strings or winds, separate or mixed, with or without piano. Sometimes, too, the term is used for Baroque works for soloistic voices and basso continuo or with soloistic instruments—as in the "chamber cantatas" or "chamber duets" of Agostino Steffani (1654–1728).

The designation "chamber music," however, is not applied to works for instruments used in choirs, as in the suite, symphony, overture, or solo concerto with orchestra—even if, as in certain divertimenti, the parts may be played as if they were solos. Also it is not applied to song for one or more solo voices accompanied by a keyboard instrument or to piano compositions.

The history of instrumental ensemble music accounts for some of these distinctions in terminology. In the 16th century music for instrumental ensemble and for orchestra served three purposes: dance music, social music of the aristocracy and the upper bourgeoisie, and representative church music. Around 1600 any sung or played music except that for the church or the opera house came to be called chamber music.

In terms of the history of forms, distinction was made among the canzone, orchestral sonata, church sonata or *sonata da chiesa,* and chamber sonata or *sonata da camera.* The canzone (*canzon da sonar*) and the sonata originated in the instrumental transcription of songs. Fiorenzo Maschera's *Canzoni a sonare,* published in 1584, are among the oldest datable orchestral compositions. In Giovanni Gabrieli the orchestral canzone or orchestral sonata often consists of two short sections—strongly contrasting in tempo, measure, and manner of setting—which constantly alternate and thus can be varied and concluded by a coda. His contemporaries and successors enlarged the independent sections to ten and more.

The church sonata, or *sonata da chiesa,* in time replaced the orchestral canzone and orchestral sonata. The designation is first encountered in Tarquinio Merula as being applied to the canzone. Arcangelo Corelli gave the church sonata its Classic form: four movements in the succession Grave-Allegro-Andante-Allegro. Its character was brilliant and festive, and the instruments were at least doubled.

The word "chamber," however, appeared with the chamber sonata, or *sonata da camera,* often consisting of a succession of movements, Fast-Slow-Fast. The movements were predominantly of a dance character, and the instrumentation was soloistic. The type was also occasionally referred to as a *partita,* which meant the same as "suite." The usual designation *per chiesa e camera,* or "for church and chamber," also points to the fact that the two forms, church and chamber sonatas, produced hybrids and often were not strictly separated. But it is from this mating that chamber music grew.

The trio sonata is a special form of this instrumentation for two soprano instruments with basso continuo—that is, for organ or harpsichord, the bass part of which was strengthened by cello, gamba, bassoon, or double-bass. The first monodic instrumental piece was by Giovanni Gabrieli (about 1555–1612) with his *Sonata con tre violini e basso se piace*. In it, the bass is the harmonic groundwork; the three voices are largely set note-against-note or in alternation. The possibilities thus opened up were quickly developed by Italian musicians. Biagio Marini (1597–1665) wrote in 1617 the first solo sonata for violin with continuo. Salomone Rossi (*ca.* 1570–*ca.* 1630) published in 1607 his *Primo libro delle Sinfonie e Gagliarde* (2nd book 1608), the first independent trio collection for two violas or cornette and nonfigured bass. Ludovico Grossi Viadana (1556–1645) published in his *Cento concerti ecclesiastici* (1602) the first thorough-bass trio in the sense of a trio sonata.

Up to the time of Arcangelo Corelli (1653–1713), numerous composers took part in developing these forms. Corelli's "commanding personality," according to Mersmann, "became the center of the following development."

Of particular historical significance are the twelve sonatas of Johann Sebastian Bach for a melody instrument and a harpsichord, written at Cöthen about 1720. There are three sonatas for flute, three for gamba, and six for violin. In them he included the written-out keyboard part, designated as *cembalo certato* or *cembalo obligato*. The figured bass and its improvised performance were replaced by a completely composed keyboard part. The harpsichord, accordingly, became an independent partner, taking over the second soprano voice. Thus arose the sonata for a melody instrument and keyboard. The form of the trio sonata was retained in Bach: the first voice is in the violin, the other two are in the harpsichord. It is not clear whether a second harpsichord performed the continuo; the participation of a cello as support of the bass voice is *ad lib.*

Similarly important are the *Pièces de clavecin en concerts* of Jean-Philippe Rameau (1741). There are five of these concerts, each consisting of three, four, or five movements, each all in the same key, and almost all movements with imaginative or personal titles. The harpsichord is the solo instrument, and the violin (or flute) and gamba (or second violin) are accompanying melody instruments. Jean Joseph Cassanéa de Mondonville's sonatas op. 3 (1734) for harpsichord and accompanying violin exhibit the same treatment.

A unique phenomenon in the Late Baroque—as in the history of music generally—is Bach's *Musical Offering*. This work was composed in 1747 in connection with the composer's visit to Frederick the Great in May of 1747 at Potsdam. The composition as a whole is based on the *Thema Regium*, a fugue theme which the King gave Bach for improvisation. The work consists of two ricercari, nine canons, a canonic fugue, and a trio sonata. It is a cyclic chamber work, with quite clever and esoteric combinatory implications, and accordingly is typical of Bach's conception of music in his old age.

The great 18th-century change in style—quite apart from its intellectual and artistic aspects—was manifested in three developments in chamber music. In the first place, thorough-bass practice was abandoned. The keyboard instrument (harpsichord or organ) dropped out entirely and thus gave place to new ideas of instrumentation embodied in such forms as the string quartet and string trio and in such new conceptions of composition as the written-out accompaniment. In the second place, a literature for solo instruments with piano came into being—the piano trio, the piano quartet, and the piano quintet. Finally, there was a change in forms, giving rise to the new sonata type as a cyclic form and to the sonata-allegro form.

The development of a number of novel features found their focal point in the string quartet, instrumented for a first violin, a second violin, a viola, and a violoncello. Its creator was Joseph Haydn (1732–1809), who wrote in this form throughout his long career as a composer. He composed his first six string quartets apparently at the suggestion of the nobleman Karl Joseph von Fürnberg in Weinzirl about 1755. They make up Haydn's op. 1, called by the composer *Quadri* and listed in the Breitkopf thematic catalogue of 1765 as *Quadri und Cassationes*. The string quartet today designated as op. 1, no. 5, however, originally did not belong to the compositional series of op. 1.

Referring to the string quartet, Goethe wrote to Zelter: "I have long found this kind of musical presentation the most understandable; one hears here four sensible people conversing, thinks he can get something from their discussion and become acquainted with the particular features of the instruments." Zelter's answer expands the idea: "Also the hearer does not know how it happens but one thinks he is playing along, one understands the unintelligible; one is captivated and knows not by what." Goethe's point of view reveals the attitude then prevalent among the music-lovers of the 18th century, when the playing of string quartets was a social diversion.

Before Haydn, there had been—as it were—prehistoric forms of the string quartet. At the beginning of the 17th century, in the work of Peuerl, Schein, Haussmann, and Franck, there had been four-voiced and five-voiced instrumental compositions that were especially favored for strings, without continuo, in a transparent manner of writing with extensively independent leading of the individual voices. Well before Haydn, Franz Xaver Richter and C. P. E. Bach were already writing quartets with obligatory viola and continuo, which are related to the trio sonata in their compositional structure. Also the first string quartets of Haydn are to be considered, in this period, as still belonging to works with continuo. In old printed editions the cello voice is regularly provided with figures as a matter of tradition, without much thought of their actually being used.

In Haydn's op. 1 (*Quadri und Cassationes*), elements of the suite and of the new cyclic sonata form coincide. With the exception of the later Quartet No. 5, the other five quartets of op. 1 are Divertimenti, having a five-movement over-all layout with two minuets each. The opening movement is in sonata-allegro form, the concluding movement is a quick ending, and the slow movement has a serenade-like cantilena in the first violin. These are genuine Haydn, despite their linkage with tradition, and are written in major.

The eighty-three string quartets of Haydn fall into a number of groups:

Nos. 1–6 are op. 1, consisting of six quartets. The quartet that originally was fifth was indicated by Haydn in his own listing of his works as belonging under "Divertimenti for various instruments."

Nos. 7–12 are op. 2, also consisting of six quartets. In style they form a unit with op. 1.

Nos. 13–18 are op. 3, again consisting of six quartets, but assigned by Geiringer to Haydn's second creative period between 1761 and 1770. The composer had here arrived at four-movement layout, and from now on it was to be retained almost without exception. Chamber-music style was here more clearly marked. The first movement gained in significance, especially as compared with the last movement. Expression in the slow movement was deepened. The four instruments were conceived of as fulfilling more of a solo role than before. Technical difficulties grew, especially for the dominating first violin.

Nos. 19–24 are op. 9, again consisting of six quartets, and composed in 1769, toward the end of the second creative period. In them, Haydn had attained true string-quartet style, almost entirely leaving behind the earlier relationship with the music of the suites and serenades. The first movement was the main movement of the work. After it, the slow movement was the most important in content. Individual thematic groups stood out distinctly. The principle of thematic work had not yet come to be recognized. Passages calling for violin virtuosity helped determine to some extent the musical structure. The concertante element maintained its old privilege. The richness of feeling and of expression had quite significantly grown. The harmonic element was here intensified and refined. The minuet was stylized dance music with increasingly individual traits. The finale was usually a crowded presto with decidedly terminal character. The six individual quartets here have each its own features, in this respect reflecting the influence of C. P. E. Bach.

Nos. 25–30 are op. 17, six quartets, composed in 1772, during Haydn's middle creative period, and related to op. 9.

Nos. 31–36 are op. 20, the six so-called "Sun" Quartets, composed in 1772. These form the culminating point of the groups op. 9, 17, and 20. There are new contrapuntal traits, which in Nos. 2, 5, and 6 lead to concluding fugues. Thus the earlier self-contained and rounded nature of the style was disturbed.

Nos. 37–42 are op. 33, the six so-called Russian Quartets, also sometimes referred to as *Scherzi* or *Jungfernquartette* (Maiden Quartets), composed in 1781. Haydn wrote on December 3, 1781, to Prince von Oettingen-Wallerstein about his "entirely new *à quadro* for two violins, alto, and violoncello concertante. They are written in an entirely new special way, for I have not written any for ten years." The hiatus in composing has been explained by A. Sandberger as having arisen from Haydn's inability to bridge the inner cleft between the contrapuntal style of op. 20 and the old cassation spirit of the quartet. The principle of thematic work which had been meanwhile discovered in the symphony was taken up in op. 33 also in the string quartet. Thus the modern string quartet was created. The first movement is the center of gravity of the whole work. The slow movements (Adagio to Allegretto) are of many kinds and of changing moods. The designation *Scherzo* in op. 33 (and later) changes nothing in its minuet character. In the finale the rondo-form was more clearly worked out. The harmonic aspects are more differentiated.

Nos. 43–48 are op. 50, six quartets, composed perhaps between 1784 and 1787. The influence of Mozart is particularly evident in the formation of the melodies. There is also a refining of the thematic work. Stylistically these quartets have somewhat the same character as those of op. 33. According to Mersmann, opuses 50, 54, 55, and 56 form a stylistic unit.

Nos. 49–56 are op. 51, *The Seven Words*, composed in 1785 on commission from the Canon of Cadix as instrumental compositions for orchestra and revised by Haydn as a cantata. The work scarcely belongs among the string quartets. It consists of an introduction, seven sonatas, and the description of the earthquake as conclusion in monumental style, at the expense of the chamber-music traits.

Nos. 57–59 are op. 54, three quartets, composed in 1789.

Nos. 60–62 are op. 55, three quartets, composed in 1789.

Nos. 63–68 are op. 64, six quartets, composed in 1790. These are the so-called Tost Quartets, dedicated to a wholesale merchant whose name was Tost. They show complete mastery on Haydn's part of his compositional resources and throw some light on his statement in connection with his symphonies that he had intended his works to have "a moral character." The forms here are given rich, universal, and surprising treatment. Homophonic and polyphonic means have become organic components of their architectural aspects.

Nos. 69–71 are op. 71, three quartets, and Nos. 72–74 are op. 74, three quartets, making up the six so-called Apponyi Quartets (dedicated to Count Apponyi), which were composed in 1793 between the two London journeys. Here there is further individualization as, for example, a slow introduction is placed before the first movement. There are also here numerous traits of orchestral invention. The first violin part is much enriched technically.

Nos. 75–80 are op. 76, six quartets, composed in 1797, the so-called Erdödy Quartets, dedicated to Count Josef Erdödy.

Nos. 81–82 are op. 77, two quartets, composed in 1799. As in op. 76, Haydn here reveals his supreme mastery. In each work the slow movement is now the culminating point and center. The minuet points to Beethoven's scherzi. There appear new possibilities of tonal gradation and new harmonic effects of contrast. The concluding movements often unite elements of the sonata-allegro form with the rondo. Op. 76, no. 3 contains the famous variations on *Gott erhalte Franz, den Kaiser* (God preserve Franz, the Emperor).

No. 83 is op. 103, Haydn's last quartet, consisting of a second and third quartet movement, composed in 1803.

Haydn's string quartets far surpass his many other works of chamber music in artistic and historical significance.

Also with Wolfgang Amadeus Mozart (1756–1791) the string quartet is the form in which the very spirit and form of chamber music is most significantly captured. In 1787, string quintets (K. V. 515 and 516) also achieved in his creative activity the artistic significance of the string quartets.

Mozart wrote his first string quartet (K. V. 80) in 1770 in Lodi, under Italian influence.

His 2nd–7th string quartets (K. V. 155–160) were written in 1772 and 1773, likewise in Italy. Haydn's influence is noticeable, though Italian influences predominate.

But the 8th–13th string quartets (K. V. 168–173) were composed in 1773 in Vienna under the influence of Viennese chamber music, especially that of Haydn's string quartets op. 17 and 20. These have four movements and the same formal innovations that we find in Haydn—a concluding fugue, variations as first movement, and an adagio introduction. In comparison with the earlier works, there is intensification of the compositional structure and of the expression.

The 14th–19th string quartets (K. V. 387, 421, 428, 458, 464, and 465), written between 1782 and 1785, were not commissioned works but were composed by Mozart on his own impulse and were dedicated to Joseph Haydn. They represent Mozart's coming to terms with Haydn's style as displayed in the Russian Quartets. Mozart, according to his own statement, had "learned from Haydn how string quartets are made" and these six quartets were the "fruit of long and hard work." But there are evidences in them also of Mozart's own world. He had made them more differentiated, more multiform, and more problematical than Haydn's—richer, but far less naturally flowing, more nervous, more highly refined, more fascinating, less folk-like. Mozart extended the form and enriched the harmony. Thus, in a sense, he achieved a chamber-music art of the miniature expanded to a larger form. In these quartets the principle of thematic work had been completely mastered.

The 20th string quartet (K. V. 499) was composed in 1786, between *The Marriage of Figaro* and *Don Giovanni*.

The 21st–23rd string quartets (K. V. 575, 589, and 590), the "three Prussian Quartets" and also sometimes called the "Cello Quartets," were written on commission from the Prussian king Friedrich Wilhelm II. They stand at the beginning of Mozart's last creative period, with great sensuousness of sound, cantabile melodic invention, and what Abert has called a "sense of joy in existence and delight in beauty but suffused with a gentle touch of melancholy." The part for the cello, which the King played, is well thought out. The works were composed in 1789–90.

The divertimenti (K. V. 136, 137, and 138) are presented in the complete edition as the 24th–26th string quartets.

The two quartets for piano, violin, viola, and violoncello (K. V. 478, composed in 1785, and K. V. 493, composed in 1786) were written in the years during which Mozart appeared as a clavier virtuoso in Vienna. They are closer to the clavier concerti, though in the collaboration with the strings they constantly maintain chamber-music style.

The string quintets form an independent group among Mozart's works. He was the first of his contemporaries to add a second viola to the string quartet to make a fifth instrument. Boccherini, it may be noted in passing, added a second violoncello. Mozart, with the additional viola, enriched the sound more darkly and fully in the middle register and at the same time gave it a new shading in association with the two violins as upper voices, in contrast to which the two violas with the cello could form a trio in the deeper register. The string quintets Nos. 4, 5, 7, and 8 link up with the string quartets in compositional art, richness of musical ideas, moods, and closeness of workmanship.

The 1st string quintet (K. V. 174), composed in 1768, exists in two versions, the second being the final one (1773). This quintet is in the nature of a divertimento.

The 2nd string quintet (K. V. 406), composed in 1787, is a reworking of a serenade (K. V. 406).

The 3rd string quintet (K. V. 407) is for violin, two violas, horn, and violoncello—or, in place of the horn, a second violoncello can be used (1782).

The 4th string quintet (K. V. 515) was composed in April 1787, and the 5th string quintet (K. V. 516) in May 1787. These were written in the same year as *Don Giovanni*. Both works are of the highest mastery, but they are quite different in content and expression.

The 6th quintet—actually a clarinet quintet—is for clarinet, two violins, viola, and violoncello (K. V. 581). Composed in 1789, it was written for the virtuoso clarinettist Anton Stadler. It blossoms forth in its euphony, but in its compositional aspects it is not to be compared with the string quintets of the late period. There is practically no polyphonic elaboration.

The 7th and 8th string quintets (K. V. 593 and 614), composed in 1790 and 1791, are—particularly the former—late works in style and character, in thematic invention, and in artful interweaving of counterpoint.

Among the string quintets is also counted K. V. 525, *Eine kleine Nachtmusik* (A Little Night-Music), composed in 1787. The instrumentation—for two violins, viola, violoncello, and bass—points to orchestral performance. It is a typical serenade. The fifth movement of the work, a second minuet, has been lost. First published in 1827, it is today one of Mozart's most popular works.

Further chamber music by Mozart includes the string trio, piano trios, the two duets for violin and viola, and the wind music with piano.

Also with Ludwig van Beethoven (1770–1827) the string quartet stands at the center of the composer's work in chamber music.

The first six string quartets, op. 18, nos. 1–6 (in F, G, D, c, A, and B♭), were composed between 1798 and 1800, partly with the aid of older sketches. The order in which they were written is apparently Nos. 3, 1, 2, 5; No. 4 was brought out while he was still at Bonn; and there is a question about the composition date of No. 6.

The Quartet op. 18, no. 1, was reworked before being brought out. The form of the string quartet had been settled by Haydn and Mozart when Beethoven began to write works of this type. In 1800 Beethoven noted in a letter that he "knew now for the first time how to write correct string quartets." With his op. 18 Beethoven made the style of this string quartet his own.

The 7th–9th string quartets, op. 59, nos. 1–3 (in F, e, and C) are the so-called Russian Quartets, dedicated to Count Rasumovsky. They were composed in 1805–6. The finale of op. 59, no. 3, is a fugue.

Between op. 18 and op. 59 there occur—along with piano sonatas and violin sonatas—particularly the Second and Third Symphonies and *Fidelio*. Thus the later, individualistic aspects of Beethoven made their appearance. The demands on performers and listeners appreciably increased. The works were accessible only to those who had studied them carefully. No longer could brief indications outline the content and significance.

The 10th string quartet, op. 75, in E♭, called the "Harp Quartet," written in 1809, stood between the E♭ piano concerto and the E♭ piano sonata op. 81a. The nickname "Harp Quartet" is to be explained by the somewhat harp-like effect of certain pizzicato passages in it.

The 11th string quartet, op. 95, in f, originated in the summer of 1810, in connection with the *Egmont* music. The manuscript was written in October of 1810. Commentators like to relate the passionate character of the work to the events of Beethoven's life: the first movement was sketched out shortly after his proposal of marriage to Therese Malfatti was rejected. In the autograph manuscript he headed the work *Quartett serioso*.

The 12th–16th string quartets, the so-called last quartets, present a slight discrepancy between the order in which they were composed and the opus numbers that have been assigned to them. They were written in this order:

> op. 127, E♭, 1822–5.
> op. 132, a, 1825.
> op. 130 (first version with the fugue op. 133 as finale), B♭, 1825–6.
> op. 131, c♯, 1826.
> op. 135, F, 1826.
> the finale, composed later, to op. 130, in place of the fugue, November 1826, Beethoven's last completed composition.

Op. 133, Great Fugue, B♭, the original finale of op. 130, was published after Beethoven's death.

Still today these "last quartets" are regarded as the utter culmination of chamber music. Here in Beethoven's work occurred the boldest ascent into a realm of expression that was most highly subjective, most his own; yet at the same time he maintained to some extent novel connections with traditional forms and techniques of composition.

These "last quartets" exhibit significant contrapuntal work—in the fugues, in the fusion of variation and fugue, in linear voice-leading, through the division and disintegration of the course of the harmony into a contrapuntal weft of voices. Fugal sections are to be found in the original finale of op. 130, brought out as *Grande Fugue tantôt libre, tantôt recherchée,* op. 133, and in the first movement of op. 131.

Beethoven used the technique of variation on a theme in the slow movements of op. 127, 131, 132, and 135—without, however, particularly labeling and numbering them as variations. He took some liberties with the traditional succession of movements, giving op. 130 six movements and op. 131 seven movements that are indicated as being intended to follow each other without pauses being left between them.

A hitherto unknown richness in contrasts is to be found in the individual movements and with relationship to each other; however, individual movements and various works are again linked with each other thematically. Contrast and unification are, as opposites, two basic tendencies in the "last quartets." There is opposition between brief motives and melodies of long breath, between thematic concentration in the fugues and thematic contrast in the sonata-allegro form and rondo, and between abrupt change of tempo within individual movements. There are folk-like turns (such as the suggestion of a German dance in the Alla danza tedesca in the fourth movement of op. 130) set over against passages of the highest spiritual intensity; cheerful humor and boisterousness over against deeply earnest concentration; very strict formation of periods over against complete freedom of compositional layout; and purely instrumental expressive treatment against insertion of instrumental recitatives in op. 131, 132, and 135.

There are also historicizing traits, such as a preference for polyphony and polyphonic forms. A chorale arrangement occurs in op. 132, Molto Adagio, using the Lydian mode. But this stands only ostensibly in opposition to the sonata-allegro or rondo forms, the "modern" forms of Beethoven's day.

The fusion of all these contrasts into a higher unity is one of the greatest creative accomplishments in the whole history of music—certainly the greatest in that of the 19th century.

There are also some programmatic suggestions in this late work. The slow movement of op. 130 (fifth movement), Adagio molto espressivo, is called *Cavatina*. The slow movement (Molto Adagio, chorale arrangement) of op. 132, moreover, is called *Canzone di ringraziamento in modo lidico offerta alla divinità da un guarito* (Song of thanksgiving in the Lydian mode offered to the divinity by a convalescent), the ensuing Andante *Sentendo nuova forza* (feeling new strength). The Finale of op. 135 is *Der schwergefasste Entschluss: Muss es sein? Es muss sein! Es muss sein!* (The difficult decision: Must it be? It must be! It must be!).

In Beethoven's late music the old unity of chamber music and domestic music was broken. Originally chamber music was a form of artistic activity cultivated in court circles or in middle-class society as a characteristic kind of domestic music, practiced by amateurs. In 1783, for example, there appeared in Cramer's *Magasin für Musik* a notice from Königsberg in which public request was made of Haydn that he write new quartets "commissioned by the German violinists who honor him." Beethoven's quartets, beginning with the "Russian" op. 59, however, represent the beginning of a momentous cleft: the technical and intellectual difficulties were constantly outgrowing the performing abilities of the amateur. With the "last quartets" this cleavage finally was complete. Performance by a professional ensemble became indispensable. Count

Rasumovsky, the Russian ambassador, maintained a string quartet in Vienna from 1808 to 1816, with Ignaz Schuppanzigh as first violinist—an ensemble of professional musicians, employed with fixed pay. In 1835 the quartet of the Müller brothers went on tour, to perform Beethoven's quartets in public concerts. Accordingly, this time marks the beginning of the split between chamber music as concert music and chamber music as domestic music-making. In 1803 Beethoven himself gave his *Kreutzer Sonata* its first performance in a public concert.

These late "chamber works" of Beethoven have many traits that point to the future. On into the immediate present the "last quartets" have given impulses to develop further possibilities outlined by Beethoven: further differentiation in the equal participation of the four instruments in the composition, relaxation of the harmonic procedures into an uninterrupted play of movement as ostensible contrapuntalism (as in Wagner's *Tristan und Isolde,* Acts II and III), strictly contrapuntal work in stretti, contrary movement, and so on (as in Bartók's Fifth String Quartet), beginning relaxation of the parts of the sonata-allegro form through the principle of constant development in one movement, as the movement became more and more a "development" in the sense of a continuing transformation (as in Schönberg), invention of axiomatic four-tone motives, which are in themselves laid out symmetrically (as in serial composition of the 20th century), working-over of such motives through their being taken up again in several quartets, indication of an "open form" or "centrifugal form," as for example the c♯ Quartet does not seem finished at the end, perhaps suggesting that all the "last quartets" together represent a cyclic unity.

The "last quartets" have a culminating place in the Viennese Classical period. Historical traits that connect directly with Haydn and Mozart are the fusion of thematic material reminiscent of folk-music and the contrast between the most highly developed music of art and of the folk. Perhaps Beethoven introduced themes here that were native to common urban song of his surroundings in Vienna or on the Rhine. Many impulses in the compositional work, such as the technique of development, are continuations of the consequences of the principle of thematic work already to be foreseen in Haydn and Mozart.

At the same time these "last quartets" have a highly significant position in Beethoven's own personal career. They were his last works, in the sense that death made it impossible for him to carry out numerous further plans, such as that for a Tenth Symphony. They are, however, not exactly his testament in the sense of the last thing that he had to say. Instead, they stand more in a new powerful wave of creative activity that he did not have the opportunity to carry on or develop further. In this sense they are Beethoven's late style, but by no means the works of his "old age" as are Monteverdi's, Schütz's, or Verdi's last works written at the age of over seventy.

In addition to the works of chamber music strictly for strings that have been mentioned, Beethoven wrote only five string trios (op. 3; op. 9, Serenade; and op. 9, nos. 1–3), of which the first two are still in the realm of the Serenade.

A quite different emphasis appears in his chamber compositions that include the piano: the seven piano trios, the wind quintet with piano (op. 16), and the chamber music compositions for winds (the Sextet op. 71, the Septet op. 20, and the Octet op. 103). Beethoven created a new relationship between the strings or winds and the piano, most noticeably in the piano trios. To the first three of these he gave the opus number 1 (1793–4). He raised the three instruments to complete equality of status in their demand for soloistic and virtuoso skill, in their sonorous individuality, and in their participation in the musical development. The Fourth Piano Trio (op. 11, 1798) originally had a clarinet instead of the violin. Op. 70, no. 1, nicknamed the *Geister* or Spirits' Trio, was written together with op. 70, no. 2, in 1808. The most mature piano trio is op. 97 (1811), in four movements, strongly symphonic in workmanship.

With the Viennese Classical period and in the hands of Haydn, Mozart, and Beethoven, chamber music was settled as a form in its style and as a world of artistic expression. As the history of music right on to the present time has again and again had to come to terms with the Viennese Classical era, many composers after Beethoven have written chamber music. It is the artistic standard and at the same time a confirmation of the classical model. The following survey covers the great composers and their central works. An exhaustive history of chamber music is still needed, as are also special studies that might clear up certain areas within it.

In the chamber-music compositions of Franz Schubert (1797–1828) the string quartet stands in the foreground, with fifteen extant compositions. Individual early quartets have been lost.

Schubert found his first occasion for writing string quartets at home, in works that he played with his father. During the time he was still attending boarding school he wrote the first five of the extant quartets, in 1812 and 1813, designated as Series V in the Complete Edition. They are apprentice work and are documents in his gaining of maturity. The first, in "changing keys," is an attempt to set up various movements according to a uniform head-motive; the second, with its two movements, is a torso. Reminiscences of Beethoven appear in the third. In the fourth and in the fifth (which has only two movements) there are some interesting chromatic themes and harmonic enrichments.

String Quartet No. 6 was also written in 1813, and No. 7 a year later. In this latter quartet Schubert, then seventeen, had found himself. The themes of the first movement are quite Romantic, in their lyricism, their lack of stress on the tensions in the dualism of contrast, and the "magic" of Schubertian feeling. New features appear in the sonata-allegro form, the first theme concluding the exposition and the first movement.

String Quartet No. 8 (1814) made the new expression into a style, through which the whole work achieved its self-contained form. The chronological sequence in the themes is noteworthy, as there are close relationships between the first and second movements, the chromatically ascending three tones of the first movement reappearing in the trio of the minuet and in the finale.

The 9th String Quartet (1815) seems like a piece of apprentice work on a higher level. It is "classicistic" work, with sharp contrasts and with the distinct formation of periods. The head-motive of the movement is directly dependent on Beethoven.

The 10th String Quartet, composed in 1813 (not 1817), is one of the works of traditional character, with thematic union of all the movements.

In 1816 Schubert wrote the 11th String Quartet, applying the Classical principles on a higher and henceforth quite personal level. In this, there is a striking relationship with Mozart.

The 12th String Quartet (in one movement, Allegro assai, in c) was written in 1820, over a period of eight years. The hiatus is comparable to that in Haydn's writing of quartets, but for Schubert it was still more important. The C minor composition stands in chronological proximity to the B-minor Symphony (the *Unfinished*) and is related to it; only the reconciling second movement is lacking. It exhibits a magnificent vision and a quite new style on the part of the composer.

The quartet movement in C minor introduces Schubert's last three string quartets. Here mastery has been achieved, independence, complete individuality, and highest maturity in the treatment of the quartet. Each of the three last quartets is a work with a distinctive character of its own.

In the 13th String Quartet, in a, written in 1824, Schubert in the slow movement quotes his own work, the stage music for *Rosamunde*, later also used in the 3rd Impromptu for Piano from op. 124.

The 14th String Quartet, in d, written in 1824, introduces variations on the song *Death and the Maiden* in the second movement. Viewed as a whole, it is a work in minor that is without equal.

The 15th String Quartet, in G, written in 1826, has very sharp rhythmic, dynamic, and melodic contrasts.

Schubert's other works of chamber music are typical individual compositions. The most significant one after the string quartets is the String Quintet in C, op. 163, written in 1828, with two violoncelli—that is, with the instrumentation Boccherini had introduced. The sonority of the five instruments attains here a completely new significance and with the melody and harmony enters into a new unity. The work entirely transpires in inner repose and beauty.

The "Trout" Quintet, in A, op. 114, written in 1819, in five movements, has in its fourth movement variations on the well-known Schubert song *Die Forelle,* or The Trout. The instrumentation is for piano, violin, viola, violoncello, and double bass.

The Octet, for two violins, viola, violoncello, double bass, clarinet, horn, and bassoon (in F, op. 166, written in 1824) is in six movements and presents a particularly charming interplay between the strings and the wind instruments.

There are also two piano trios (op. 99 and op. 100), written in 1826 and 1827.

Also in the chamber works of Felix Mendelssohn-Bartholdy (1809–1847) the eight string quartets predominate. The 1st String Quartet, op. 12, in E♭, 1829, was inspired by Beethoven. The 2nd String Quartet, op. 13, in a, 1827, is preceded by a solo song with piano accompaniment, *Ist es wahr?* (Is it True) as its "theme." Form is here subordinated to a poetic idea. In both these quartets new forms already make their appearance, with a Canzonetta and an Intermezzo in place of the Scherzo.

The 3rd String Quartet, op. 44, no. 1, in D, was written in 1838; the 4th, op. 44, no. 2, in e♭, in 1837; and the 5th, op. 44, no. 3, in E♭, in 1837–8. Thematic invention, elaboration, and thoroughness of formulation reveal Mendelssohn at a high point in his creative work.

His 6th String Quartet, op. 80, in f, was written in 1847, the year of his death; and the composer was not able to see the work through the press. In the gloomy and passionate moods there is an echo of this year, so fateful for him. To complete the account of Mendelssohn's chamber works, mention should also be made of two string quintets (op. 18, 1826, and op. 87, 1845) and of the octet for double string quartet (op. 20, 1825).

The three string quartets that Robert Schumann (1810–1856) wrote came into being during the summer of 1842 in Leipzig, within five weeks of each other. They constitute the first works of chamber music in his career as a composer, being preceded almost exclusively by piano compositions and songs. He had made beginnings towards the writing of string quartets as early as 1838 and 1839, but these were not carried to completion and are to be evaluated simply as studies. In the dedication to Mendelssohn, whose personality and creative activity Schumann in so many respects unreservedly admired, he articulated the meaning which he attributed to his own op. 41. Five years later he regarded his string quartets as his "best work of the earlier period."

Schumann took over the four-movement form of the quartet as it has been fashioned by the composers of the Classical Era and subjected the first movements to the sonata-allegro form. In accordance with his personal nature, he filled the form predominantly with melodic content and harmonic richness. The numerous polyphonic entries reveal his concern with Bach and Beethoven. The "Romantic" Schumann expressed himself in the Third Quartet most beautifully. Here he best succeeded in his generally evidenced intention to let the four voices individually join in the whole. Schumann's quartets have shown their vitality to the present day as expression of his personality. They are, for us, primarily concert works, while the composer still thought rather of intimate performance in a small domestic circle. With satisfaction, however, he found that they had a "very lively effect" when performed in the concert hall. The individual works are as follows:

1st String Quartet, op. 41, no. 1, in a, June 1842.
2nd String Quartet, op. 41, no. 2, in F, beginning of July 1842.
3rd String Quartet, op. 41, no. 3, in A, middle of July 1842.

In a piano quartet op. 47 (in E♭, 1842) and a piano quintet op. 44 (in E♭, 1842) Schumann perpetuated the tradition formulated in Beethoven's piano trios: chamber-music style, balance among the individual instruments, and important thematic work. He also wrote three piano trios: op. 63, in d, 1847; op. 80, in F, 1847–9; and op. 110, in g, 1851. Of these, the first two are particularly remarkable.

What Johannes Brahms (1833–1897) encountered was a Classically perfected form that Schumann and Mendelssohn had endowed with expressive nuances of their own. Brahms knew that he was not called upon to break this tradition. So he filled it with his own individuality and contented himself with making three quite important contributions. The first two, brought together as op. 51, belong only superficially to the summer of 1873, which proved for him a fruitful time for composition. Kalbeck expressed the belief that the second quartet is older and that its beginnings go back at least ten years. In his extended analysis he showed that Brahms conceived this second quartet with Joseph Joachim most definitely in mind and that probably he thought originally of also dedicating it to him. This quartet, in a, is a lyrical, sonorous, and sunny work. The First Quartet, in c, on the other hand, is intellectually quite close to the First Symphony and—like that work—is boldly outlined, passionate and heroic in character. Finally, the B♭ quartet, completed two years later, is of a humorous and cheerful nature and at the same time rounds out the triad of Brahms' quartets with a brilliantly lively and happy finale. His quartets, accordingly, are

> 1st String Quartet, op. 51, no. 1, in c, 1873.
> 2nd String Quartet, op. 51, no. 2, in a, 1873.
> 3rd String Quartet, op. 67, in B♭, 1875.

Like Schumann, Brahms no longer considered the string quartet the absolute center of chamber music. Perhaps Brahms, being a pianist, felt called upon to combine the piano with string and wind instruments into the chamber-music ensemble. He showed this tendency as early as his composition of numerous piano duets: three sonatas for violin and piano (op. 78, 100, and 108), two sonatas for violoncello and piano (op. 38 and 99), and two sonatas for clarinet and piano (op. 120). He also wrote five piano trios in op. 8, 87, and 101; the horn trio for piano, violin, and French horn, op. 40; and the clarinet trio for piano, clarinet, and violoncello, op. 114; three piano quartets in op. 25, 26, and 60; and one piano quintet, op. 34a. His works without piano include two string quintets op. 88 and op. 111; one clarinet quintet op. 115 (for clarinet, two violins, viola, and violoncello), and two string sextets for two violins, two violas, and two violoncelli, op. 18 and op. 36.

The predominance of the Viennese Classical composers and of the German Romantic movement up to Brahms in the 19th-century history of music obliged the other nations to come to terms with this historical situation. Many composers saw the touchstone of their own and their country's powers in the form of chamber music, as measured against the German tradition.

Alexander Borodin (1833–1887) wrote two string quartets (A, D), the latter being quite distinctively his own.

Peter Tchaikovsky (1840–1893) wrote three string quartets (op. 11 in D, op. 22 in F, and op. 30 in e♭) and a piano trio (op. 50 in a). In these works he fused creatively German forms (particularly those peculiar to the Romantic movement) with strongly individual traits and sporadic elements from folk-song.

Bedřich Smetana (1824–1884) wrote a first string quartet in e (*From My Life*), of a programmatic character, yet conforming to the four-movement formal layout; a piano trio in g; and a second string quartet in d, in 1882–3.

Antonin Dvořák (1841–1904) wrote eight string quartets: op. 16 in a, op. 80 in E, op. 34 in d, op. 51 in E♭, op. 61 ni C, op. 77 in G, op. 96 in F, and op. 106 in G. He also wrote a string quintet op. 77 in G (for two violins, viola, violoncello, and double bass), and a string quintet op. 97, in E♭ (with two violas); a string sextet op. 48 in A; four piano trios: op. 21 in B♭, op. 26 in g, op. 65 in f, and op. 90 in e; two piano quartets, op. 23 in D and op. 87 in E♭; and a piano quintet, op. 81 in A. There is a relationship with Beethoven and Brahms, and the union of a strong will-to-form with uninterrupted vital powers of melody and rhythm influenced by folk elements.

Leoš Janáček (1854–1928) wrote two string quartets, one in 1923 "Inspired by Tolstoi's *Kreutzer Sonata*" and the other in 1928, *Intimate Letters*. (An early string quartet of 1880 is no longer extant.) These two quartets are important works in his career, highly subjective, confessional, but of general human communication in their intensity and maturity of experience. In them he uses a special form by which thematic elements are handled like bits in a mosaic.

Giuseppe Verdi (1813–1901) wrote a string quartet in e, in 1872, after having composed *Aïda* and revealing strong influence from the operatic melodic "gesture," yet predominantly instrumental—i.e., non-vocal—in character.

In Scandinavian countries the Finn Erik Tulindberg (1761–1814) was a pioneer in the Viennese Classical style, composing six string quartets. He was followed by the Finn Bernhard Crusell (1775–1838), an eminent virtuoso on the clarinet, with chamber music for this instrument, including three quartets. Crusell was active in Sweden, where J. M. Kraus (1756–1792) and Johan Wikmanson (1753–1800) were writing string quartets and other chamber music. The tradition in Sweden, strongly marked by the Classical movement, was carried on primarily by Franz Berwald (1796–1868), A. F. Lindblad (1801–1878), and Ludvig Norman (1831–1888). Berwald's main works were the Second and Third String Quartets, in E♭ and a, both written in 1849; Norman's principal composition was the Third String Quartet in a (1884), inspired by Schumann and Swedish folk-melody.

At the beginning of the 19th century in Denmark, Friedrich Kuhlau (1786–1832) was the most productive composer. Among numerous works with flute, the then fashionable instrument, he wrote three flute quintets and a quartet for four flutes. Although his last work was a string quintet, he cannot be said to have formed any sort of school of chamber music. Among Danish composers in the 19th century, outstanding composers of chamber music include Niels W. Gade (1817–1890) with his Octet for Strings (1848), *Novelettes* for piano trio (1863), two string quartets (e, 1877, and D, 1888); Peter Heise (1830–1879) with his 'cello sonata and seven string quartets; and C. F. E. Hornemann (1840–1909) with his two string quartets (g, 1859, and D, 1861).

In Norway, Edvard Grieg (1843–1907) wrote two string quartets and a 'cello sonata; Christian Sinding (1856–1941) composed a piano quintet in e (1884) that is sometimes played and a qualitatively more significant string quartet in a (1904).

At the end of the 19th and during the 20th century chamber-music composition increased in significance. Primarily in Sweden this was a matter of the work of Wilhelm Stenhammar (1871–1927), with six string quartets, particularly No. 4 in a (1909) and No. 5 in C (1910). Carl Nielsen's four string quartets and his very significant wind quintet (1922) actively stimulated the writing of chamber music in Denmark. Among his followers were Jørgen Bentzon (1897–1951) with six *Racconti* (1935–49) and Vagn Holmboe (b. 1909), with ten string quartets (1949–69), which also show the influence of Bartók. The chamber music of Jan Maegaard (b. 1926) is to some extent influenced by the twelve-tone technique of the Schönberg tradition. Jean Sibelius wrote a Second String Quartet, *Voces intimae* (1909); and Hilding Rosenberg (b. 1892) composed twelve string quartets, the last six written as a separate group, representing the peak of his instrumental writing. Chamber music in Iceland was first written by Sveinbjörn Sveinbjörnsson (1847–1927), but only in rather recent times has it become a type with independent significance. Composers include Helgi Pálsson (b. 1899), Jón Leifs (b. 1899), Karl O. Runólfsson (b. 1900), and Thórarinn Jónasson (b. 1900).

In Poland there has been instrumental ensemble music since the Baroque, but chamber music in the strict sense of the term began to be written only during the latter half of the 18th century. The first representatives were Feliks Janiewicz (1762–1848), Jan Kleczyński (1756–1828), Franciszek Lessel (*ca.* 1780–1835), Karol Lipiński (1790–1861), and Franciszek Mirecki (1791–1862). They show influences of the Early Classical and traits of the Early Romantic periods. Pupils of Elsner were Józef Nowakowski (1800–1865), Ignacy Feliks Dobrzyński (1807–1867), Józef Krogulski (1815–1842), and Antoni Orłowski (1811–1861). Also in the work of Stanisław Moniuczko (1819–1872), Józef Wieniawski (1837–1912), and Adam Minchejmer (1830–1904) there was peripheral chamber-music composition. Not until Władysław Żeleński (1837–1921) was there a more fundamental interest and the writing of trios and quartets in the tradition of Schumann and Brahms. Toward 1900 Antoni Stolpe (1851–1872) wrote a sextet and a piano trio, and Juliusz Zarębski (1854–1885), a trio and a piano quintet, which is a masterpiece of Polish chamber music. Stolpe and Zarębski had somewhat Neo-Romantic tendencies. Numerous Polish composers around 1900 included Roman Statkowski (1859–1925), Henryk Opieński (1870–1942), Zygmunt Stojowski (1869–1946), and Witold Maliszewski (1873–1939), academically in the tradition of Schumann and Brahms.

Karol Szymanowski (1882–1937) wrote two outstanding works, his First String Quartet in 1917, marked by linear technique, and his Second Quartet in 1927, with its strong connections with folklore, the last movement taking the form of a fugue, a classical example of polytonality, each voice having the theme in a different key.

Chamber music in the 20th century has also been written by Ludomir Różycki (1884–1953), Kazimierz Sikorski (b. 1896), Bolesław Woytowicz (b. 1899), Jerzy Fitelberg (1903–1951), Arthur Malawski (1904–1957),

Roman Palester (b. 1907), Antoni Szałowski (b. 1907), Grażyna Bacewicz (b. 1913), and Michal Spisak (b. 1914).

In France during the 19th century two tendencies ran parallel: the one, proceeding from Berlioz, was that of program music and the other, connected with the absolute symphonic form of German tradition, resulted in significant works of chamber music, notably that of Camille Saint-Saëns (1835–1922), César Franck (1822–1890), and Gabriel Fauré (1845–1924).

César Franck's principal works of chamber music are the piano quintet in f (1880), of large, rather symphonic construction, and the string quartet of the same year, his only work of that type, in D, more distinctly chamber music, concentrated, Classically schooled, reaching its culmination and summary in the final movement.

The chamber music of Gabriel Fauré consists of a string quartet, a piano trio, two piano quartets, and two piano quintets. These works, written at various times throughout his career, are central to his total creative work. They are compositions of strongly French character, with a preponderance of the lyrical, without dramatically sharpened oppositions, and with a concentration on the form, a music of shifting sonority, but scarcely influential on the Impressionistic direction taken by music after 1890.

Through Impressionism a new relationship was established also with chamber music. It was subordinated in the work of Claude Debussy (1862–1918)—at least according to the number of works—in comparison with the works for piano and for orchestra, but it was not subordinated in significance. In 1893, when Debussy was founding the style of musical Impressionism, he wrote a single string quartet, in g, a principal work of the epoch and of French music. It is laid out cyclically in four movements, with the Scherzo in second place, and approaches the Classical form. The Impressionistic style is made here completely subservient to chamber music and to the character of the string quartet. Typical of Debussy's late style is the trio for flute, viola, and harp that he wrote in 1916.

The tendency to adhere to Classical forms was far stronger in Maurice Ravel (1875–1937) than in Debussy. Ravel's principal chamber works are a string quartet in F (1902) and a piano trio in A (1914), the third or slow movement of which is a Passacaglia.

The transition from the 19th to the present century was made in Germany by Max Reger (1873–1916). The scope and continuity of what he wrote show how much he as a musician felt himself indebted to tradition and how far he submerged his own artistic individuality in the nature and individual sphere of expression of German chamber music. He wrote his opus 1 as a sonata for violin and piano, composed works of chamber music at the height of his career, and again concentrated on such compositions during his last phase. His prolific creative work includes eleven sonatas for violin solo (a type of music in which he was the first, after Johann Sebastian Bach, to create works for a solo instrument without accompaniment). He also wrote thirteen preludes and fugues for violin alone; a serenade and a trio for strings, two serenades for violin, flute, and viola; a piano trio; five string quartets; two piano quartets; two piano quintets; a clarinet quintet; a string sextet; and numerous sonatas for a solo instrument with piano.

His work is strongly linked with forms such as the fugue, chaconne, passacaglia, sonata-allegro, rondo, and variation—in other words, Baroque and Classical forms. It also displays significant polyphonic development. Also the forms are suffused throughout with purely musical and non-sensuous aspects: there is unremitting struggle for organic structure, strong harmonic tensions without abandonment of tonality, gradual subordination of subjective or emotional impulses in favor of "purely musical" or objective procedures, and growing refinement and intensification of detail work and intimate traits in expression.

The significance of chamber music in contemporary writing, from about 1910 on, is shown by the fact that the stylistic change about 1920 was first distinctly marked in works of chamber music and that among the great style-creating masters of "modern" music, with the exception of Stravinsky, works of chamber music—particularly the string quartet—have stood in a pivotal position among their compositions, often at particularly decisive turning points. Schönberg wrote four, Bartók six, and Hindemith six string quartets. Chamber music is also central in the whole body of work written by other composers such as Milhaud and Honegger.

The emigration of so many of the composers prominent in this tendency to the United States during the 1930's, where—particularly through the universities—they continued to influence younger composers and the public in general, could not help having its effect on the further development of chamber music there. This was, of course, added to the fact that chamber music in the narrower sense of the term had been written in America almost as long as in Europe. From mid-18th century the Moravians in Bethlehem, Pennsylvania, had their *collegium musicum* and are represented by string quintets written by composers of American as well as European birth. Again, after the Civil War, American composers made contact with their German colleagues under somewhat academic auspices. W. W. Gilchrist (1848–1916), George W. Chadwick (1845–1931), Arthur W. Foote (1853–1937), and Horatio Parker (1863–1919), and a good many others, wrote chamber music.

Composers active in the United States after World War I made substantial contributions to this literature. Ernest Bloch (1880–1959) wrote several works, notably on Hebrew themes. Wallingford Riegger (1885–1961) was much concerned with sonority and rhythm on an atonal basis, beginning in the 1920's; in 1938–9 he composed his First String Quartet, and in 1948 his Second. Walter Piston (b. 1894) wrote four string quartets; Roger Sessions (b. 1896), two. Aaron Copland (b. 1900) wrote a certain amount of chamber music early in his career; in 1950 he wrote a piano quintet, and in 1961 a nonet for solo strings. Ross Lee Finney (b. 1906) composed eight string quartets. Samuel Barber (b. 1910) from early in his career was concerned with chamber music: his *Dover Beach* (1931) is for voice and string quartet, and his well-known Adagio for Strings comes from his string quartet (1936).

Important figures active today in carrying on traditional chamber music forms in novel directions are Elliott Carter (b. 1908) and Leon Kirchner (b. 1919), the former a pupil of Walter Piston and Nadia Boulanger, the latter acknowledging his indebtedness to Roger Sessions and Arnold Schönberg, under whom he studied in California. Carter, in string quartets written in 1951 and 1960, has been particularly concerned with rhythm and with conveying "varying rates of flux and change of material and character"; and Kirchner, in his string quartets of 1949 and 1958, conveys a strong sense of emotional expression.

In the works written by Americans, as well as by other composers in the past few decades, there has been a great deal of interest in ensembles other than those with the classic instrumentation, yet within the basic idea of chamber music. In part, this has been due to the fact that as composers wished to make linear aspects of their work clear, more distinctly differentiated instruments have been more to the purpose. Voice has often been introduced, as has percussion. But, thinking for the moment of chamber music in its more strictly historical sense, one cannot say that it has been neglected in the present century. In fact, particularly during the periods after the two world wars, it took its place in the forefront of musical development.

Bibliography

General: W. Altmann, *Hdb. f. Streichquartettspieler* (3 vols., 1927–9) and *Kammermusik-Katalog* (Lpz. 5th ed. 1942); W. W. Cobbett, *Cyclopedic Survey of Chamber Music* (3 vols., London 1963); H. Mersmann, *Die Kammermusik.* vol. 1: *Die Kammermusik des 17. und 18. Jh. bis zu Haydn und Mozart;* vol. 2: *Beethoven;* vol. 3: *Deutsche Romantik;* vol. 4: *Europäische Kammermusik des 19. u. 20. Jh.* (Lpz. 1933, Breitkopf & Härtel); E. H. Meyer, *English Chamber Music* (London 1946); W. S. Newman, *The Sonata in the Baroque Era* (Chapel Hill 1959) and *The Sonata in the Classic Era* (Chapel Hill 1963); T. Müller-Reuter, *Lexikon d. dt. Konzertliteratur* (Lpz. 1909); J. F. Richter, *Kammermusik-Katalog, Verzeichnis der 1944–58 veröffentl. Kammermusik-Werke* (Lpz. 1960); MW (Die italienische Triosonate); MW (Die Solosonate); art. Kammermusik (MGG). *J. S. Bach:* H. Eppstein, *Studien über J. S. Bachs Sonaten für ein Melodieinstrument und obligates Cembalo* (Uppsala 1966). *J. Haydn:* F. Blume, *J. H.s künstl. Persönlichkeit in s. Streichquartetten* (JbP 1931); U. Lehmann, *Dt. u. ital. Wesen in d. Vorgesch. des kl. Streichquartetts* (Würzburg-Aumühle 1939); A. Sandberger, *Zur Gesch. d. Haydnschen Streichquartetts,* in *Ausgew. Aufsätze z. Musikgesch.* (Munich 1921); M. M. Scott, *H. 's "83"* (M&L 1930). *L. van Beethoven:* T. Helm, *B.s Streichquartette* (Lpz. 2nd ed. 1910); J. Kerman, *The B. Quartets* (N. Y. 1967); E. Kreft, *Die späten Quartette B.s* (Bonn 1969); D. G. Mason, *The Quartets of B.* (N. Y. 1947); H. Riemann, *B.s Streichquartette* (Bln. 1903).

32. Song

"Song"—or, in German, *lied*—has two fundamental aspects, one appearing in the text, the other in the music. Considered textually and rather narrowly, a "song" is a short lyrical poem, sacred or secular, consisting of one or more stanzas, each in the same verse pattern. The immanent musical qualities come from the text as it is read—the symmetry of the lines, usually strengthened by end-rhyme, the constancy in the meter, and the accentuation and tone-color of the vowels. These features make it singable and constitute its song-like qualities—together, of course, with its content. From the musical and rather specific point of view, accordingly, songs consist of such compositions based on the stanzaic texts as relate closely to the structure of the poem. As the text has stanzaic structure, so the self-contained song has its tune, which finds its purest expression in the folk-song or church hymn and in art-songs written after these models.

The art-song in Italy was early called the solo cantata or chamber cantata (*cantata da camera*), a verbal distinction being made between something sung (*cantata*) and something played instrumentally (*sonata*). In the course of the history of music many and various forms of vocal music have been called "cantatas," and the word has come to contrast vocal and instrumental composition in only a quite general way, in terms of the basic intention.

The Italian cantata originated around 1600, in connection with monody. The word "cantata" itself was first used around 1620. A number of developments in music had prepared the way for the cantata, as an instrumentally accompanied vocal solo: Florentine monody, instrumentally accompanied villanelles and madrigals, the madrigal accompanied by thorough bass, and the madrigal composed primarily for a solo voice.

A whole new era of chamber music for solo voices began with Caccini's *Nuove Musiche* (1601) and Peri's *Varie Musiche* (1609). Composers set stanzaic poems to music as recitatives and solo madrigals and issued them in collections.

The 17th-century Italian cantata was an aristocratic type of vocal chamber music. It was a form of musical entertainment based on poems by current as well as earlier writers such as Petrarch and Tasso. Especially it favored love poems. It consisted, musically, of rather self-contained sections, with quasi-recitatives, varied treatment of different stanzas (including some over ostinato bass and others displaying melodic variation from stanza to stanza), and more or less rondo-like structures.

The first high point in the early development of the cantata was reached about the middle of the 17th century in Rome. Composers included Luigi Rossi (1598–1653), Giacomo Carissimi (1605–1674), Alessandro Stradella (1645–1682), and Agostino Steffani (1645–1728), who visited Germany in the course of his career.

Next in importance after Rome as a center was Venice, where there was clear influence from opera. Composers included Francesco Cavalli (1602–1676), Marc'Antonio Cesti (1623–1669), Giovanni Legrenzi (1626–1690), and Carlo Pallavicini (1630–1688). Another center was Bologna, where influences from both Rome and Venice appeared in the work of Francesco Gasparini (1668–1727).

The second culminating point occurred in the first half of the 18th century, at the same time as the Neapolitan school. There are similarities between this type of cantata and Neapolitan opera: the ostinato bass distinct from the singing voice and often moving in counterpoint to it, the recitative quite distinct from the aria, and the aria consisting of three sections. In fact, the cantatas were mostly a bipartite or tripartite succession of recitatives and arias (or ariosi). The layout eventually developed stereotyped features: a solo cantata normally contained two arias; a double cantata, two soli and four arias or two arias and a duet.

The poetic content usually included an "action," which opened with the delineation of a situation—often an amorous plaint. Then a decision was announced, and the conflict was resolved. At its height the cantata in Italy was the most important vocal form outside the church—the true art form for connoisseurs. But after the death of Alessandro Scarlatti in 1725 interest shifted, and opera and the operatic aria came to the fore.

Alessandro Scarlatti (1660–1725) wrote over six hundred solo cantatas. Other composers were Emanuele Giocchino Cesare Rincon d'Astorga (1680–ca. 1755), Antonio Lotti (ca. 1667–1740), George Frederick Handel (1685–1759), and Giovanni Battista Pergolesi (1710–1736). All were quite prolific: d'Astorga wrote over a hundred fifty, Lotti about fifty, and Handel seventy-two solo cantatas with basso continuo and twenty-eight with instruments.

The French chamber cantata reached a significant culmination in the first half of the 18th century. In character it was an operatic scene, the action of which was sketched very precisely by the music. Composers included André Campra (1660–1744), Jean–Philippe Rameau (1683–1764), and Louis-Nicolas Clérambault (1676–1749).

Germany, however, early favored the song and aria over the chamber cantata, and the 17th-century composers who led in the development of song there were Heinrich Albert and Adam Krieger.

17th Century

In the German-speaking area during the early 17th century, song with thorough-bass accompaniment had replaced song derived from cantus-firmus polyphony or the Italian madrigal. This development had begun with Johann Hermann Schein (*Musica bocareccia,* 3 books, 1621–8), Johann Staden (*Geistliche Monodien,* 1625), and Thomas Selle (1634). It continued during the middle third of the century as writers supplied poetry for song settings.

Influential poets included Simon Dach in Königsberg, Johann Rist in Hamburg, Gabriel Voigtländer, George Grefflinger (otherwise known as Seladon), Martin Opitz, and Paul Fleming. Rist issued his *Himmlische Lieder* in 1642 and his two collections of secular songs, *Galathea* and *Florabella.* Voigtländer also brought out *Allerhand Oden und Lieder* in 1642. Grefflinger was best known for his *Weltliche Lieder* (1651). Individual centers of song production arose in various cities: the Königsberg or Prussian poetic circle around Dach, the Hamburg school around Rist, the Saxon school around Fleming and Dedekind, the Thuringian school around Georg Neumark, and the Frankfurt circle around Grefflinger und G. H. Schreiber. Their texts dealt with many aspects of bourgeois life and included songs of nature, of love, and of student life. The style, though deriving in part from the folk, is highly charged with mythological and rather cerebral figures of speech. German song is typical of the bourgeoisie, compelled by external circumstances to withdraw from the political arena and to compensate for this withdrawal by using artistic means to heighten its idealistic and inward private life.

As for the composers of the music in these High Baroque song collections, Heinrich Albert (1604–1651), organist at Königsberg, was responsible for establishing some of the characteristics of the genre. He provided the music for eight books of *Arien* (Königsberg 1638–50). Using features from the German dance-song, Protestant chorale, and Italian monody, he was the first to develop a German type of song, including songs both for solo and for several voices. The polyphonic form is more in evidence in the latter portions of the collection, suggesting that the material was increasingly used by social groups. Albert was quite versatile, writing dance, madrigalesque, folk-like, sacred, and motet-like funeral songs. Usually composed stanzaically, they may well have been freely ornamented by the singers in performance. These songs, accordingly, involved more than just the transfer of Caccini's monodic principle to Germany. They had grown from the soil of the motet and madrigal. Polyphonic compositions which stressed the upper voice and possessed a song-like character gave rise to the solo song accompanied by thorough bass. Only very gradually did solo song yield place before the advancing tide of polyphonic song.

German song in the 17th century often vacillated between the more artful or monodic types of song and the more folk-like types. The music director of the Hamburg city council Johann Schop (d. 1667) composed the music for *Himmlische Lieder* (1642), which carries out an aim of achieving folk quality and symmetry—characteristic of the text-writer Johann Rist and the Hamburg circle.

Musically, song was enriched with brief preludes and postludes, with imitative and symbolical touches of tone-painting and figures of various kinds. Stringed instruments were added in *Weltliche Oden,* of which the first book appeared in 1642 at Freiberg in Saxony, the music composed by Andreas Hammerschmidt, organist in Freiberg and Zittau.

There was also frequent use of parodistic procedures, such as the adding of new texts to older melodies of songs or instrumental pieces. *Allerhand Oden und Lieder,* the first book of which appeared in 1642 at Sorø in Zealand, consists of such parodies—that is, of formerly wordless instrumental and dance pieces now provided with texts. The music is by the Danish court trumpeter Gabriel Voigtländer (d. 1643).

The artistic culmination of 17th-century German song was reached by the poet and composer Adam Krieger (1634–1666), an unusually gifted melodist. Having studied under Scheidt, he became court organist in Dresden. He was born the poet and composer of his *Arien,* which began to appear in 1657. With sparing use of basic melodic motives, the intimate form of the popular stanzaic song was here imbued with very great expressive intensity, effecting—according to Gudewill—a unique synthesis of folk quality and high art, for example in *Nun sich der Tag geendet hat* and *Die lob ich, die zu dieser Zeit.* Krieger represents the high point in the history of student song and of Baroque solo song generally.

Three further collections that appeared about this time and suggest the widespread interest in this type of song are *Aelbianische Musenlust* (Dresden 1657), a collection of pieces by Saxon poets set to music by the Dresden concertmaster Christian Dedekind (d. 1715); *Odae Sveticae* (Stockholm 1674), with texts by Samuel Columbus and music by Gustav Düben (1624–1690); and *Die musikalische Ergötzlichkeit* (1684), composed by Johann Krieger of Zittau (d. 1735).

Also the Italian cantata influenced German song. The *lied* was built up into the *"arie"* by the addition of ritornelli, richly constructed formal layout, and recitative-like passages intended for declamation. Johann Nauwach (*ca.* 1595–*ca.* 1630) was the first known composer of German songs with basso continuo, *Teutsche Villanellen* (1627), written under the influence of Caccini and Monteverdi. The collection issued by Kaspar Kittel (1603–1639) in Dresden, *Arien und Cantaten* (1638), used for the first time the German form of the word "cantata" in a title.

During the last third of the 17th century the influence of Italian opera prevailed, emanating from Dresden. The *da capo* aria found its way into song composition. Toward 1700 interest in song was displaced by the operatic aria in German, which, particularly during the heyday of the Hamburg opera, was circulated in collections of arias.

The *Augsburger Tafelkonfekt* (published in "four guises" between 1733 and 1746), which contained quodlibets, folk-songs, and solo songs by the Benedictine priest Valentin Rathgeber (1682–1750), is—according to Moser—a culmination of the South German popular Baroque and rather specifically Augsburgian polyphonic song collections.

18th Century

The Early Classical period from about 1730 to 1780 was a time of preparation for the potentialities of solo song with keyboard accompaniment, to be carried on during the 19th century to a realization of its full possibilities. The predominating type was the simple stanzaic song. The period brought with it a revival of German song. There was a conscious effort to achieve simplicity, naturalness, and folk-like quality. The folk-song movement gained particular influence through Herder and Goethe. The thorough-bass accompaniment, still retained at first, was then replaced by the written-out keyboard accompaniment. It increasingly gained in importance, in terms of the interpretation of the text, the tone-painting, and the enrichment of the harmony. The continuo song became the keyboard song. Johann Ernst Bach in 1749 was the first to write out a song on three staves, thus separating the singing voice from the keyboard accompaniment.

Leipzig Song-School

Three cities—Leipzig, Berlin, and Vienna—were focal points of the 18th-century renewal of interest in the German thorough-bass solo song. In Leipzig, a lawyer, Johann Sigismund Scholze, writing under the pseudonym Sperontes, issued his *Singende Muse an der Pleisse* in four books between 1736 and 1745. This was a collection of keyboard pieces with underlaid lyrics, some of them of a certain poetic value, by various authors, including Johann Christian Günther. The musical originals of these parodistically constructed songs were mostly French dances. This publication served to introduce a Leipzig song-school, which particularly emphasized songs of sociability.

Another song-writer who in the style of his work belonged to the Leipzig song-school was Georg Philipp Telemann, with his *24 Oden* (1741) and his *Sing-, Spiel- und Generalbassübungen* (1733). One of the best of the early 18th-century song collections was the *Sammlung neuer Oden und Lieder* in three books, the first of which appeared in 1742. In this collection Friedrich von Hagedorn, the founder of Anacreontic song-poetry, collaborated with Valentin Görner in creating a new relationship between word and tone.

As reaction to parodistic song and rejection of it, there appeared in Halle the collection of the musical amateur Friedrich Gräfe, *Sammlung verschiedener und auserlesener Oden,* in four books, from 1737 to 1743. The composers were Carl Philipp Emanuel Bach, Karl Heinrich Graun, Giovannini, and Konrad Friedrich Hurlebusch. For the most part these original songs are also dance tunes.

Another direction in the development of 18th-century German song was taken in 1749 by a son of one of J. S. Bach's cousins, Johann Ernst Bach (1722–1777), with his composition *Gellertsche Fabeln,* and in 1759 by Valentin Herbing, who constructed little cantata-like dramatic scenes with recitatives, arioso parts, and keyboard imitations of the instrumental movements. Thus he came upon the principle of the "ballad." The individual keyboard participation, however, belongs to the isolated exceptions in the literature of song. J. E. Bach used melodics with stanzas that varied in form and thus prepared the way for the principle of through-composition.

As the Leipzig school had dominated the early 18th century, the Berlin song-school assumed leadership after 1750. The continued influence of Telemann, however, is noticeable in *24 oder av våra bästa poëters arbeten* (24 Odes from the Works of Our Best Poets, Stockholm 1754) by Henrik Philipp Johnsen (1717–1779).

First Berlin Song-School

The Berlin song-school, the rise of which is associated with the flourishing musical life under Frederick the Great, began in 1753 with the collection *Oden und Melodien* (2nd book, 1755), compiled by Christian Gottfried Krause, Berlin lawyer and composer. The composers in the collection include Quantz, C. P. E. Bach, and K. H. Graun. In the preface Krause established his aesthetics of song: he urged a revival of popular song composition in connection with the French stanzaic chanson or *ariette*. The composer, he maintained, should start from singing and only later add the keyboard accompaniment. In 1752 Krause had brought out his essay *Von der musicalischen Poesie*. For the first time in the history of music the laity here seems to have manifested some explicit aesthetic reservations with regard to the professional musician. The vocal music of the Berlin schools is quite amateur and popular in intention.

Following Krause though not holding rigidly to his theories, other compilers issued numerous collections both in and outside of Berlin. In Leipzig the Saxon song-school was carried on further under Hiller. C. P. E. Bach supplied the music, in arioso and declamatory song style, for a book of Gellert's sacred odes, or stanzaic songs, in *Geistliche Oden und Lieder* (1758). Gottfried Krause in 1767-8 edited four books of *Lieder der Teutschen*, consisting of 240 texts, some from the 17th century. Musically Krause's collection is quite varied, as he included some through-composed songs and some canons and enriched the harmony of the thorough-bass. Christian Gottlob Neefe provided music for a volume of Klopstock's stanzaic songs, *Klopstocksche Oden* (1776, 3rd ed. 1785), in which he showed concern for correct declamation and admitted varying stanzaic structure. Neefe also provided music for a volume of serenades to be sung with keyboard accompaniment, *Serenaten beim Klavier zu singen* (1777), and a book with texts by Herder entitled *Bilder und Träume* (1780).

Christoph Willibald von Gluck's settings of seven texts by Klopstock, *Klopstocksche Oden und Lieder* (1785-6), are not confined to either the Berlin or the Viennese school and far surpass the rest of the song production of the period in the extent to which they achieve a union of text and music in declamation.

While the composers in the first Berlin song-school tried to achieve a popular manner, those who wrote *singspiele* actually succeeded in doing so. Johann Adam Hiller (1728–1804) led the way in 1766 and was followed by Christian Gottlob Neefe (1748–1798) and Johann André (1741–1799). The popular keyboard song and the song-numbers of German *singspiele* and operas are quite close to each other and proved mutually stimulating, as can be seen in Mozart's *Entführung* and *Zauberflöte*, in the *Freischütz,* in Lortzing, and in the Romantic Movement generally. Hiller also wrote special collections of children's songs with didactic tendencies as introduction to the technique of song.

The scope of German song was significantly extended in the latter half of the 18th century on beyond the Anacreontic. There were special types of song collections, such as cradle songs, songs for or about apprentices, students, tradesmen, country people, shepherds, and Masons. Also there were collections with explicitly stated aim, such as *Lieder für fühlende Seelen* (Songs for Feeling Souls, 1787), *Lieder der Freundschaft und Liebe* (Songs of Friendship and Love, 1774), and *Lieder der Weisheit und Tugend* (Songs of Wisdom and Virtue, 1790).

Carl Philipp Emanuel Bach stands in rank far above his contemporaries of the first Berlin song-school, particularly with his setting of the sacred songs of Gellert (1757–8) as artistic solo songs, with declamation stressing the sense, masterful writing for keyboard, and fine differentiation between the preludes and postludes, the harmonic aspects, the dynamics, and the characteristics of the keys. In 1773 after C. P. E. Bach became connected with the poets of the *Hainbund,* or "Band of the Sacred Grove," he attained new heights: mastery in secular song both of simple, unpretentiously folk-like setting and also of exaggerated sentiment. From 1775 on, synthesis was achieved in larger through-composed forms. After 1780 there ensued a clarification of the style, leading to very strong simplicity and limitation of the means.

Second Berlin Song-School

The second Berlin song-school was distinct from the first. Its members tended to set more significant lyric poems of the time to music, such as those of Goethe and Schiller. Thus working with poetry of higher quality, they showed greater artistic liveliness and freedom in handling it. Often they returned to genuine old folk-song. Also they established a closer connection with the instrumental music of the day. In both the First and Second Berlin schools, music was strictly conceived of as helping to fill out the ideas of the verse, and folk-like character was demanded. Songs of nature represented a special variety that included also parts for wind instruments. Songs with varying stanzas were rare. Harmony was simple. Both before and after the flourishing of this school, song was distinctly social.

One of the principal composers of this school was Johann Abraham Peter Schulz (1747–1800), who brought out his *Lieder im Volkston* in three books in 1785, as well as two collections of religious songs in 1784 and 1786. His main resources lay in simple folk-like melodies. He favored the lyrics of the Göttingen *Hainbund.* In individual solo songs with chorus he paved the way for the revival of choral song by a singing-society known as the Berlin *Liedertafel,* with such choruses as *Des Jahres letzte Stunde* and *Warum sind der Tränen?* Many of Schulz's songs are still popular today, such as *Der Mond ist aufgegangen.* Special artistic means that he employed are exact rhythmic and metric periodical structure, sequence, and repetition. Clavier interludes and postludes are rare, as is also interpretative tone-painting in the accompaniment. In the preface to the second part of *Lieder im Volkston* Schulz wrote: "I have chosen throughout only such texts from our best song-poets as seem to me to have been made for popular folk-singing, and have aimed in the melodies themselves towards the utmost simplicity and comprehensibility—indeed, in every way have sought to bring to them the appearance of the familiar. . . . In this appearance of the familiar lies the whole secret of the folk manner."

Johann Friedrich Reichardt (1752–1814) composed some seven hundred songs in about thirty collections. His uneven, often hasty, and varied work was influenced by Gluck and Mozart. It was of historical significance as he pioneered in the fully composed keyboard part with characteristic accompaniment, in various harmonic features, and in a general expansion of the form. His many settings of Goethe lyrics, such as *Rastlose Liebe, Erlkönig, Über allen Wipfeln,* and *Der du von dem Himmel bist,* make him the first notable composer to set the work of this poet. The character of the Berlin song-school thus showed aspiration for something more than sheer popularity.

Johann André (1741–1799) enriched the Berlin song-school expressively with his compellingly melodic manner. His books of songs included *Musikalischer Blumenstrauss* (1776), *Lieder und Gesänge beim Klavier* (1779), and *Neue Sammlung von Lieder mit Melodien* (1783).

Karl Friedrich Zelter (1758–1832) was a master mason in Berlin, director of the Berlin *Singakademie* which had been established in 1791 by Fasch, and founder of the first *Liedertafel.* He was a close friend of Goethe and decisively influenced the poet's judgment on musical matters. Also he was a teacher of Mendelssohn, an upholder of the Bach tradition in Berlin, and the first to organize Prussian music education. He wrote many solo songs with piano, not only simple stanzaic songs in the folk-like manner of the Berlin song-school but also ballads that anticipate the 19th-century lied as well as numerous settings of Goethe lyrics. Also of lasting significance are his men's choruses.

Johann Rudolf Zumsteeg (1760–1806), the leader of the Swabian song-school, was influential on Schubert as his significant predecessor in the setting of ballads such as *Ritter Toggenburg* and *Leonore* by Bürger. He also prepared the way for the typical Romantic mood-song.

The Swabian song-school followed the Berlin song-school and maintained somewhat similar aims, yet had a closer relationship to folk-song. Its founder was the poet, composer, and writer on music, Christian Daniel Schubart (1739–1791), with his three books of *Musikalische Rhapsodien* (1786), containing songs closely connected with the folk. He wrote some of his songs as early as 1763.

Third Berlin Song-School

The third Berlin song-school arose in the 19th century but perpetuated the musical style and social affiliations that had characterized the previous stages in the development of this tradition. In its general approach and use of musical means it did not go very far beyond its predecessor. Its principal representatives were Ludwig Berger (1777–1839), Bernhard Joseph Klein (1793–1832), and Felix Mendelssohn-Bartholdy (1809–1847). Berger was important as a composer of keyboard music. For a while he was active in Petersburg and London and, on his return, participated in the founding of the new Berlin *Liedertafel* in 1819 and was a teacher of Mendelssohn. The latter, in the course of his career, wrote 83 songs, 13 duets with piano accompaniment, and 28 quartets for mixed and 21 for men's voices. Some of his mixed-voice quartets he called *Lieder, im Freien zu singen* (Songs to be Sung Outdoors). General characteristics of his songs are the folk-like but somewhat sentimental melodic content, the stanzaic setting, the subordination of the accompaniment, the exclusive predominance of the lyrical mood, and the preference for Heine's lyrics. These songs enjoyed enormous favor and wide dissemination in Europe, particularly during the Biedermeyer period.

Viennese Song-School

Vienna also provided the scene for the development of a song-school in the German-speaking area. It flourished in connection with the Viennese national *singspiel*, which opened in 1778. In the same year Joseph Anton Steffan brought out his *Sammlung deutscher Lieder für das Klavier*.

The Viennese style involved a union of the folk-song, the typical singspiel-song, Viennese instrumental music, and Italian melody. Outstanding composers were Joseph Anton Steffan (1726–1797), Josef Holzer (*c.* 1780), Johann Christian Hackel (1758–1814), Johann Fuss (1777–1819), Maria Theresia Paradis (1759–1824), and Nikolaus Freiherr von Krufft (1779–1818). These composers were musically more elemental and close to the folk than their contemporaries in Berlin but showed somewhat similar tastes in their choice of texts. They favored the arietta, developed the sentimental aria, and derived from it the earnest and content-filled mood-song.

Haydn, Mozart, and Beethoven also belong to the history of the Viennese school of song, and Schubert's achievement had its roots in this tradition:

Joseph Haydn (1732–1809) issued two books of songs, in 1782 and 1784, each containing twelve songs on somewhat nondescript texts, largely influenced by operatic arias and notable only in details. The keyboard preludes, interludes, and postludes were, in certain passages, quite characteristic, revealing the sure hand of the master instrumental composer. In 1794 and 1795 in London, Haydn set some English texts as fourteen *Canzonettas and Songs*, which he then brought out in Vienna in German. Through their expression, which is to some extent significant, they point toward the arias of the two later oratorios. In 1797 he wrote one of the best known of his songs, *Gott erhalte*.

W. A. Mozart (1756–1791) composed thirty-four songs as occasional works, in which he utilized all the styles that had been developed by the Berlin and Viennese schools. Only some five of his songs were printed during his lifetime. Among them, *Das Veilchen,* with text by Goethe, is especially notable, as is also the through-composed lyric mood-song *Abendempfindung* (1787).

Ludwig van Beethoven (1770–1827) wrote seventy-nine solo songs with piano accompaniment, beginning in 1783. Most of his early songs are stanzaic. Within his first creative period the most significant one was the mood-song *Adelaide* (1795). In 1803 he wrote the six Gellert songs (op. 48), the first sacred songs of the Viennese school. In 1810 he set four Goethe texts. Beethoven's main lyrical work, the cycle of six numbers *An die ferne Geliebte,* with text by Jeittelles, was written in 1816. In this work he achieved a heightening of subjective feeling, moving into the Romantic realm. Beethoven's songs are not secondary works but stand at the very heart of his creative activity. They include all the forms of that time and bring together the North German and the South German traditions.

19th Century

The history of the piano-accompanied solo song as an independent artistic genre, freed from its previous ties with social music-making, did not begin until the 19th century with Franz Schubert; thus it falls within the Romantic period. German song, beginning with Schubert, has won international recognition and significance. Its greatest representatives after Schubert are Schumann, Brahms, and Hugo Wolf. It increasingly outgrew the character of music merely for the home and became the *lied* of the concert hall. As a concert piece it has artistic status alongside the symphony, chamber music, and piano music.

The Romantic *lied* has, in the main, four particular characteristics, which at first glance might seem contradictory in nature but which were conceived by the Romantics as a living unity. In the first place, it usually involves a flight from the reality of everyday life into the unreal, fantastic, or mystical realm. In the second, it invites the listener to relive ancient times in legend, history, and folk-song. Third, it maintains a simple folk-like quality in the poem and the music. Finally, it reveals a certain feeling for nature. The composer's aim is to interpret the content of the poem—so far as expression and mood are concerned—by musical means and to fill it with new vitality. By uniting the words and the music he brings about an entirely new artistic unity as an organic fusion. The piano comes forward as a factor coordinate with the singing voice, bringing with it quite new possibilities of interpretative tone-poetry, independent and often extensive passages of prelude, interlude, and postlude, development of accompanimental tone-painting, characteristic rhythm, and harmonic differentiation for expressive purposes. Beginning with Schubert, the various types of song were established and the later 19th-century composers of songs merely continued to exploit these types. Artistically the *lied* was carried by Schubert to the full realization of its possibilities.

He opened up to it all areas of life, utilizing them freely, and achieved perfect unity of all elements under the predominance of the melodic and harmonic aspects.

Franz Schubert

Franz Schubert was born in Lichtenthal near Vienna on January 31, 1797, and died in Vienna on November 19, 1828. His parents were of North Moravian origin, and he was the son of a teacher. Trained as a boy soprano at the Viennese court chapel under Ruzicka and Salieri, he was temporarily an assistant teacher and then became a freelance composer in Vienna without any regular job. Schubert was at the center of a great circle of friends sometimes referred to as the *Schubertiaden,* including Joseph Spaun, the poet Franz von Schober, Johann Mayrhofer, Eduardson Bauernfeld, Franz Grillparzer, Joseph von Sonnleithner, the painter Moritz von Schwind, the composers Anselm Hüttenbrenner and Franz Lachner, and the singer Michael Vogl. Sociologically, most of Schubert's work was originally connected with this group of friends, or with similar groups, during the period of the Austrian imperial "Restoration." In 1825 and 1827 Schubert applied unsuccessfully for the position of assistant master in the court chapel and of conductor at the Kärtner Tor Theater. The only public concert of his works during his lifetime was arranged in 1827. At his death only about a tenth of his work had appeared in print, and that only in Austria, though in 1826 the *Allgemeine Musikalische Zeitung* in Leipzig had dealt thoroughly with the Piano Sonata in A minor. Schubert had sent some songs to Goethe, but the poet neglected to acknowledge them.

Schubert's creative output falls into a number of separate groups of compositions. During the early years between 1810 and 1813 he made his youthful attempts at composition in the form of his first quartets. In 1814 he wrote *Gretchen am Spinnrade;* in 1815, *Wanderers Nachtlied, Heidenröslein,* and *Erlkönig.* Then, during the following three years, he wrote numerous instrumental works on the model of Haydn, Mozart, and Beethoven, including six symphonies and the piano sonatas op. 122, 147, and 164. Around 1818–9 he seems to have notably turned away from instrumental works. But beginning in 1822 and culminating in 1825, he wrote his most important symphonies (in C major and B minor), the string quartets in A minor and D minor, and the piano sonatas op. 42, 63, and the "posthumous" sonatas in C minor, A major, and B-flat major. In the final years of his work, Schubert attempted to connect his individual melodic and harmonic idiom more closely with Classical form. At all times he had at his disposal a great number of separate song forms, which he handled in an individual way.

In all, he composed over 660 lieder, of which sixty-six were on poems by Goethe. Schubert wrote his first lied (*Hagars Klage*) in 1811, and as early as 1814 and 1815 *Gretchen am Spinnrade, Erlkönig, Heidenröslein,* and *Wanderers Nachtlied.* He scarcely developed or heightened the formal aesthetic content during his long involvement with the lied. During his late period, however, he turned more and more to a symphonically laid-out type of mood-painting. Inexhaustible richness of melodic invention was his primary and strongest characteristic resource. He wrote two song cycles, *Die schöne Müllerin* (The Fair Maid of the Mill, 1823) and *Die Winterreise* (The Winter Journey, 1827), both on poems by Wilhelm Müller. The *Schwanengesang* (Swan Song) is no Schubert cycle, but includes fourteen songs from his last period, assembled by his friends after his death and issued under that title.

His lieder fall into three general types: those in strictly similar stanzas, such as *Heidenröslein;* those with occasional variation of individual stanzas in accordance with the text, such as *Des Baches Wiegenlied, Du bist die Ruh,* and *Der Lindenbaum;* and through-composed lieder, in which each stanza has its own melody and in which many different combinations of the musical means appear, such as declamation in alternation with arioso, aria, or strophe and unification through motivic and symphonic over-all layout, as in *Prometheus, Der Doppelgänger,* and *Letzte Hoffnung.* Historically, the through-composed lied is related to the operatic scene and the cantata.

Schubert had at least four ways of combining the vocal and pianistic components of his songs. One was to follow the pattern provided by folk-song, with the melody exclusively in the voice part and the piano merely supplying the accompaniment, as in *Das Wandern* and *Heidenröslein.* Another was to place the formally linking element in the piano part and to approximate the symphonic aspect through some distinctive coloristic or harmonic feature, as in *Die junge Nonne* and *Der Wanderer.* A third way was to compose declamatory songs in which the poem alone determined the musical layout of the whole, as in *Der Doppelgänger,* which with its chaconne or variation-lied structure pointed ahead to the future, right on into the present in the work of Schönberg and Hindemith, thus providing an example of German Expressionism in the Romantic Era. The fourth way was to bind the vocal and the instrumental elements together in a symphonic texture—organically, of equal rank, and indissolubly.

In addition to lieder, Schubert composed operas and singspiele, choral works, church music, nine symphonies (of which eight are extant), and chamber music, including fourteen string quartets, one string quintet, two piano trios, one piano quintet, the *Trout Quintet,* an octet, and some two-hand and four-hand piano works.

Composers of lieder between Schubert and Schumann include Franz Lachner, Anselm Hüttenbrenner, Johann Vesque von Püttlingen (who wrote under the pseudonym J. Hoven), Konradin Kreuzer, Carl Friedrich Rungenhagen, Heinrich Marschner, Ludwig Spohr, and Norbert Burgmüller.

Robert Schumann

Robert Schumann (1810–1856) also contributed significantly to the development of the lied. The beginning of his actual composition of songs occurred in 1840, which he spoke of as his "song-year." He married Clara Wieck that year and in the course of it wrote 138 lieder for piano and one or more voices. A second period that was productive of songs began in 1849. In contrast to Schubert, he heightened the expressive contribution of the piano to his songs as he continued to write in the genre. Often the melody is in the piano part, and the voice merely declaims the text, as in *Das ist ein Flöten und Geigen*. Characteristic and coloristic aspects often outweigh the melodic and euphonious features of the song. Schumann possessed the greatest mastery in briefly sketching mood, situation, and character, as in *Auf einer Burg* and *Die Lotosblume*. He took over Schubert's types, but sharply differentiated them. He extensively developed the free lied-forms and gave very great importance to the piano part, especially in the postludes, as in *Dichterliebe*. An outstanding connoisseur of literature, he usually displayed discrimination in his choice of texts and favored the Romantic lyric by such poets as Eichendorff, Heine, Chamisso, and Kerner. He preferred to bring poems together into series and cycles of lieder, as in the *Dichterliebe* (op. 48, on texts by Heine), *Liederkreis* (op. 24, also on Heine texts), *Myrthen* (op. 25, on texts by various poets), *Liederreihe* (op. 35, Kerner), *Liederkreis* (op. 39, Eichendorff), and *Frauenliebe und Leben* (op. 42, Chamisso). He composed these cycles in 1840.

More or less followers of Schumann, some two dozen lieder-composers appropriated, each in his own way, Schumann's artistic aims to their own purposes. Among them are Eduard August Grell (1800–1886), Karl Friedrich Curschmann (1805–1841), Wilhelm Taubert (1811–1891), Karl Reinecke (1824–1910), and Franz Abt (1819–1885).

Also a member of this group, Robert Franz (1815–1892) wrote some 350 lieder, beginning in 1843, predominantly in Romantic moods and with a preference for Romantic poets such as Heine. The harmonic setting was expanded by imitation of Bach and Handel and by use of the church modes. Even before Brahms, Franz went back to German song-melodies of the 15th and 16th centuries and to the older models of style.

Johannes Brahms

Johannes Brahms (1833–1897) composed more than two hundred songs for from one to four voices with piano. Along with Mendelssohn and Schumann, he was a representative of a conservative, classicistic trend in song-composition. His first published lied was *Liebestreu* (op. 3) in 1853, and his writing of lieder culminated in 1882–8. He once remarked that he regarded strictly stanzaic song as the highest of all song forms: to Clara Schumann he wrote, "Song now sails so false a course that one cannot too strongly bear in mind one ideal, and that is folk-song." His songs fall into three types. The first consists of serious lieder, which favored stanzaic form and rather seldom were through-composed, the vocal part making a great cantabile arch of serious and melancholy melody, with the accompaniment subordinated and usually simple, as in *Liebestreu* and *Feldeinsamkeit*, and also in significant late work such as the *Vier ernste Gesänge* on Biblical texts. The second of the song-types adopted by Brahms shows his love for folk-song, as in a group of "children's folk-songs" for the Schumann children written in 1858 and in his *Liebesliederwalzer*, which are folk-song arrangements. The third type consists, on the whole, of serene lieder, mainly constructed stanzaically with light and joyful melodic aspects and with simple but meaningful accompaniment, as in *Vergebliches Ständchen* and *Der Schmied.* To some extent Brahms wrote song cycles, in the *Vier ernste Gesänge* (1896), the 15 *Romanzen aus Tiecks Magelone* op. 33, and the *Daumer-Liederkreis* op. 57.

Hugo Wolf

Hugo Wolf (1860–1903) was born in Windischgrätz (Southern Styria) and studied at the conservatory in Vienna. In 1881–2 he was a conductor in Salzburg. From 1884 to 1887 he was a critic on the *Wiener Salonblatt* and, as partisan of Wagner and Bruckner, was unrelenting in his severity, particularly toward Brahms. After 1887 he lived entirely from his composition of music, but from 1898 on he was no longer creative, and he died in a Viennese mental hospital.

In all, he wrote some 250 lieder. They came into being mostly in whole series, from individual poets, composed in brief but fruitful working periods: fifty-three lieder to Mörike's texts, fifty-one to Goethe's, twenty to Eichendorff's, forty-four to poems in Heyse and Geibel's *Spanisches Liederbuch,* and forty-six to poems in Heyse's *Italienisches Liederbuch.* In the course of Wolf's career there occurred an increase in the declamatory style of the lied under Wagner's influence. The emphasis lay on characterization by the piano and on great strokes of harmonic boldness and freshness, achieved particularly by the use of chromaticism. The piano largely supplied the color, the sketching, the tone-painting, and extensive passages of prelude, interlude, and postlude. It was essentially during the years from 1888 to 1890 that Hugo Wolf wrote his lieder, the individual cycles taking shape eruptively, each within but a few months of the other.

In Hugo Wolf the history of the lied took a new turn under the influence of Wagnerian declamatory resources. Thus Wolf became representative of the "Neo-German trend" in the lied. Some of the cycles he called *Gedichte für eine Singstimme und Klavier,* or Poems for a Singing Voice and Piano. The "poetic idea" was for him the highest law.

Many composers of his day strove for something similar. In view of their individual significance, Wagner, Liszt, and Cornelius deserve special notice.

Richard Wagner (1813–1883) wrote twenty songs. The five Wesendonck lieder (*Der Engel, Schmerzen, Träume, Stehe still,* and *Im Treibhaus,* 1857–8) are preliminary studies in harmony and mood for *Tristan* and are without historical parallels in the period.

Franz Liszt (1811–1886) composed some sixty German songs, of which twenty-six were subsequently instrumented, to some extent influenced by Wagner in their declamatory and dramatic style. On occasion there are also suggestions of folk-song in Liszt. His lieder have a notably coloristic piano accompaniment, pointing ahead to Impressionism.

Peter Cornelius (1824–1874), poet and composer, was responsible for over a hundred songs, some for single voice, some for duet. He was an individual composer of lieder that have their own lyric and melodic qualities, in cycles to some extent sacred (*Vater unser, Weihnachtslieder, Trauer und Trost,* and *Brautlieder*).

Among more recent song-composers, the following deserve special mention for the significance, range, and success of their work: Gustav Mahler (1860–1911), with his cycles *Lieder eines fahrenden Gesellen* (1883), *Wunderhorn-Lieder, Rückert-lieder,* and *Kindertotenlieder;* Richard Strauss (1864–1949); Hans Pfitzner (1869–1949), with over a hundred lieder; Max Reger (1873–1916); and Hermann Reutter (b. 1900). In Switzerland, also, Othmar Schoeck (1886–1957) was an active composer of lieder, with 120 to his credit.

The Ballad

Settings of ballad texts were familiar to the 18th century through the Berlin song-school in two forms, as stanzaic songs and with recitative-like portions, as in opera. Johann Friedrich Reichardt, for example, wrote in the first form; Johann André, in the second. André's composition in 1775 based on Bürger's balled *Leonore* was of considerable significance, representing the first application of the principle of through-composition to this type of song. In this respect, also, Johann Rudolf Zumsteeg was influential on Schubert.

Schubert raised the ballad to an independent type in the composition of the lied. In so doing he utilized both the traditional and the free, improvisatory forms.

Karl Loewe (1796–1869), choir director and secondary-school music teacher in Stettin, wrote in 1818 his first ballads, *Edward* and *Erlkönig,* which were published as his op. 1 in 1824. He had four main periods of creative activity: 1818–27 (including *Heinrich der Vogler* and *Tom der Reimer*), 1830–40 (Goethe ballads, legends, and Polish ballads), 1843–7 (*Prinz Eugen* and *Tod und Tödin*), and 1850–69 (*Archibald Douglas*). Freely varied stanzaic form prevailed, with interchange among several strophic melodies. Succession and variation followed from the text. Loewe's strength lay in his folk-like, compelling effect, in his excellent characterization, particularly of the sinister, his bold harmonic aspects, and the creative immediacy of his ballads.

Further important ballad compositions were the work of Schumann (*Die Löwenbraut, Die beiden Grenadiere,* and *Der Schatzgräber*), Brahms (*Edward* and *Walpurgisnacht*), and Martin Plüddemann (1854–1897). The latter, influenced particularly by Wagner, introduced into the ballad the leitmotiv, dramatic characterization, and Late Romantic harmony.

German Choral Song

The rise of solo song with thorough-bass accompaniment in the 17th century tended strongly to supplant polyphonic song. It won new significance in the latter half of the 18th century in the work, for example, of Valentin Görner with his *Sammlung neuer Oden und Lieder* (1742 ff) and of Johann Abraham Peter Schultz with his *Lieder im Volkston.* There are many choral songs, somewhat hidden, in Johann Adam Hiller's songs of special type, such as his Freemasons' songs, in which only the melody and the thorough bass are written out but the middle voices were improvised. Monodic choral songs were written by Johann Friedrich Reichardt in his *Frohe Lieder für deutsche Männer* (1781). Reichardt is, however, also one of the most remarkable representatives of the new choral song, as exemplified in his *Lieder geselliger Freunde* (1796) and his Goethe songs (1809).

The rise of choral song is explained sociologically by the awakening and constantly growing feeling of nationalism, by the folk-song cult introduced by Herder, and by the social pleasure that people derived from choral singing.

In this connection, the term "men's chorus" implies a secular four-voiced *a cappella* composition for men's voices, in stanzaic form. Perhaps the first composer to write such pieces was Michael Haydn (1737–1806), a younger brother of Joseph Haydn and concertmaster in Salzburg, with his *Männerquartette* (1788).

Systematic attention to men's singing was introduced by Karl Friedrich Zelter (1758–1832), with his choral society founded in Berlin in 1809, the *Zeltersche Liedertafel,* a singing circle of a statutory twenty-five members distinguished as poets, singers, or composers. In 1819 the later Berlin *Liedertafel* was founded by Ludwig Berger (1777–1839), together with Bernhard Klein, Gustav Reichardt, and Ludwig Rellstab. The model was soon imitated in many cities. It became a matter of definite organization of clubs to sing men's choruses. The first *Deutsche Sängerfest,* or German Singers' Festival, was held in 1827 in Plochingen (Württemberg). A festival, first of its kind, had been held the year before in Switzerland.

In Switzerland the men's choral singing movement was led particularly by the notable music-educator of the people, Hans Georg Nägeli (1773–1836). The publication of his *Der schweizerische Männergesang,* a collection of men's choruses that he had begun writing in 1833, made a decisive contribution to the popularization of choral song also in South Germany.

Nägeli's work was continued by the Swabian Friedrich Silcher (1789–1860), who was academic music director in Tübingen; and it spread quite widely, in the form of the four-voiced folk-song. In South Germany a men's choral society was often called a *Liederkranz* or song-circle (literally, a "wreath"), in North Germany a *Liedertafel* or song board.

Leading composers of men's choral song during the earlier half of the 19th century were, after Zelter, particularly Bernhard Klein (1793–1832); Carl Maria von Weber (1786–1826), who set Körner's *Leyer und Schwert* to music; Friedrich Schneider (1786–1853), court conductor in Dessau; Karl Loewe (1796–1869); Karl Gottlieb Reissiger (1798–1859); Karl Friedrich Zöllner (1800–1860); Heinrich Marschner (1795–1861); Felix Mendelssohn-Bartholdy (1809–1847), with his op. 50, 75, 76, and 120 in this form; Franz Schubert (1797–1828); Konradin Kreutzer (1780–1849); and Wenzeslaus Kalliwoda (1801–1866).

In contrast to men's choral song, the song for mixed chorus aroused a popular response only much later and to a far less degree. The first significant composer of this latter type, who began working in it in 1839, was Felix Mendelssohn-Bartholdy. In his op. 41, 48, and 59 he wrote songs for soprano, alto, tenor, and bass "to be sung out of doors," and later he added to these works op. 88 and 100. He created the typical well-rounded song, melodically impressive and quite harmonious, which enjoyed very wide dissemination and extensive imitation and through its warmth and freshness maintains some of its vitality still today.

From his collaboration with choral organizations in Dresden, Robert Schumann wrote various men's choruses (op. 33 and 65) and mixed choruses (op. 76, 55, 59, and 146), in which he wished to improve the genre through artful, partially polyphonic composition and through careful choice of texts—though at the expense of the immediately folk-like effect.

The aims of Mendelssohn and Schumann were pursued also by Robert Franz (1815–1892), Moritz Hauptmann (1792–1868), Niels W. Gade (1817–1890), and others. Spontaneous effect and artful craftsmanship were combined by Johannes Brahms in a unique way in the men's choruses of his op. 41, the women's choruses of his op. 37, 44, and 113, and the mixed choruses of his op. 22, 29, 42, 52, 63a, 74, 104, 109, and 110. The choral writing of Max Bruch (1839–1920) and Peter Cornelius (1824–1874) is also of noteworthy artistic rank. On occasion Hugo Wolf and Anton Bruckner wrote for chorus. These works, at all events, always maintained an artistic standard that presents quite a contrast to the extensive literature that has come to be designated as mere *Liedertafel* numbers or *Liedertafelei,* too often marred by striving for effect, empty technical display, and fatuous sentimentality.

In the latter half of the 19th century and during the transition to the 20th, a particular leader in the field of men's choral literature was Friedrich Hegar (1841–1927). To his school belonged Rudolf Buck (b. 1866) and Mathieu Neumann (1867–1928).

A general reorganization of choral music, particularly for mixed voices, has taken place since 1920. It is connected with the stylistic revolution of these years, was influenced by the new spirit brought to music-making by the Youth Movement, and was also stylistically stimulated by contact with older choral music.

The Youth Movement had its beginning in 1897. The first musical evidence of its presence was the *Zupfgeigenhansl* (1909), edited by Hans Breuer. Jode's *Musikantengilde* and Hensel's *Finkensteiner Bund* inaugurated a great reform movement, leading to the founding of singing circles, madrigal choruses, amateur orchestras, and thus to the widespread cultivation of music on an entirely new basis. The older folk-song and the choral literature of the German flowering-time between 1500 and 1650 were made available for the practice of contemporary choral singing. Further steps were taken in school music (especially by Leo Kestenberg in Prussia), in the founding of people's music schools, the establishment of festivals and workshops (sometimes called "singing weeks," or *Singwochen*), training for choir-leaders, and a general movement to reform both Protestant and Catholic church music.

Present-day choral composition has been to a great extent stimulated by the German and Italian choral literature of the Renaissance and of the period up to the High Baroque. This relationship is revealed in numerous stylistic traits, such as the adoption of church modes, the combination of mixed linear and chordal composition, the use of older folk-songs, to some extent in arrangements with the character of the German tenor songs of the 15th and 16th centuries, the cultivation of madrigalesque composition in the sense of the Italians and of Hans Leo Hassler, and a stress on what might be roughly termed objectivity in contrast to 19th-century subjectivism and harmonic differentiation of sonority.

The number of composers who have devoted their skill—some even exclusively—to the service of choral composition is very great. Perhaps the two most significant creative personalities are Hugo Distler (1908–1941) and Ernst Pepping (b. 1901).

Solo Song Outside Germany

Among countries outside Germany, Russian and Scandinavian composers were the first to give their national song the attention that brought it high regard beyond their national boundaries. National coloring appeared in increasing distinctness in the some hundred songs of Michael Glinka (1804–1857), in the songs of Alexander Dargomishski (1813–1869), in those of Alexander Borodin (1833–1887), and above all in those of Modest Musorgski (1839–1881). Musorgski's song cycles were *Children's Room* (1868–72), to his own texts, and *Sunless* (1874) and *Songs and Dances of Death* (1875–7), to texts by Count Golenischev Kutusov. Musorgski also wrote many separate songs. His gift of intuitive feeling, his realism, naiveté with supreme psychological refinement, specifically Russian accents, psychological observation, affirmation of life and sadness at the thought of death, and his individual form—all these raise his songs far above the limitations of his period in the 19th century.

Peter Tchaikovsky (1840–1893) also made a contribution to song literature in his 103 songs, the texts for which include some by Alexei Constantinovich Tolstoi and others by Goethe and Heine, as well as French texts in the original language. His lyrical gifts were strong and many-sided.

In France, an upsurge of interest in solo songs with piano accompaniment began in 1789. In them, texts expressive of Romantic feeling and related to matters of immediate concern were set to music. The type was known as the "new romance." Around 1830 it became fashionable, was produced in quantity, and elicited a reaction in the artistically more prepossessing *mélodie*. The name for this type of song had been taken from Thomas Moore's *Irish Melodies*, which had widely circulated in France. In form the *mélodie* is not particularly dependent on the stanzaic song, and it shows a strong Schubertian influence. Hector Berlioz, Giacomo Meyerbeer, Félicien David, Henri Reber, and Victor Massé notably composed works of this type.

Charles Gounod (1818–1893) gave the *mélodie* its final form and became the model for many younger composers, such as Georges Bizet, Jules Massenet, Léo Délibes, César Franck, Edouard Lalo, and Camille Saint-Saëns.

The French song reached full flower about 1870, beginning with

639

Henri Duparc (1848–1933) and Gabriel Fauré (1845–1924). Duparc, who composed seventeen songs between 1868 and 1884, took Franck as a point of departure, particularly in his chromatic and harmonic manner of writing, and also revealed unmistakable influence of Wagner. According to Noske, Duparc raised song "to one of the most significant types of French music." Fauré began with Gounod and reformulated the Gounod song in a way very much his own. The most significant French song-composer, beside Fauré, was Claude Debussy (1862–1918), who composed over sixty songs, giving the text a more recitative-like treatment, heightening the color of the piano accompaniment, and enriching the harmony. The few songs of Maurice Ravel (1875–1937) are quite remarkable and distinctive.

Contemporary French composers of songs include Darius Milhaud (b. 1892), Francis Poulenc (1899–1963), Olivier Messiaen (b. 1908), and André Jolivet (b. 1905).

In Czechoslovakia, Antonín Dvořák (1841–1904) had a Brahmsian beginning in his *Písně milostné*, which are love-songs, originally called *Cypresses* (1865). Soon he found his own personal expression in his *Gypsy Melodies*, with text by A. Heyduk (1880), and *Biblical Songs* (1894) and thus brought out Slavic elements more prominently in his songwriting. *Echoes of Moravia*, op. 29 and 32 (1876) contributed to his world fame. The master of Czech lyric song was Joseph Bohuslav Foerster (1859–1951). His many song cycles include *Láska*, or Love (1899–1900), *Noční violy* (1899–1900), and particularly *Milostné pisně R. Thákura*, or Love Lyrics of R. Tagore (1914), with orchestral accompaniment—highly individual and subjective works. Other composers are Vítežslav Novák (1870–1949), with his ballads and cycles *Udolí nového království*, or The Valley of the New Kingdom (1903), and *Melancholické pisne o lásce*, or Melancholy Love-Songs (1906), and Jaroslav Křička (b. 1882), with children's songs. Song composition has been enriched in a typically dramatic vein by Leoš Janáček (1854–1928), particularly with his *Řikadla* or Proverbs (1927) and the excellent cycle of dramatized songs, *Zápisník zmizelého*, or The Diary of One Departed (1919).

In Poland the solo song is one of the favorite forms. From the latter half of the 17th century there is a manuscript (MS 10002 of the Jagiellonian Library in Cracow) with 59 dance-songs written out in two voices, solo with unfigured bass. The first Polish songs appeared at the end of the 18th century and the beginning of the 19th, on the model of the French *romance* and the Italian *arietta*—in, for example, romances by Michał Kleofas Ogiński. Patriotic traits appear, as in the songs of the Polish legions, including the Polish national anthem *Jeszcze Polska nie zginęła*, or Poland Is Not Yet Lost. During the November Uprising of 1830–1, there was strong intensification of patriotic song, its most notable composer being Karol Kurpiński (1785–1857), who wrote *Warszawianka*, still today a favorite song. Further song composers of this period were Józef Elsner, Antoni Radziwiłł, Jan Nepomucen Kaszewski, and Kazimierz and Franciszek Ksawery Kratzer. There are some rather anomalous solo songs by Chopin, published posthumously in 1859. They were, however, never as popular as those of Stanisław Moniuszko (1819–1872), who wrote 270 songs, the majority appearing in twelve *Household Song-Books* (1844, 1845–6, 1851, 1855, 1858, 1859, and six posthumous books). These were typical Romantic Polish songs, of great formal richness and expressive power in melodic and harmonic invention, significant in European song-writing, being of specifically national character and having a manner of their own, the so-called Moniuszko style.

A publication that served as a compendium and source of the national style in Polish music, especially of Polish song with folk coloring, was a collection of ethnographical material published from 1865 to 1890 in Cracow, *The Folk* . . . by Oskar Kolberg (1815–1890), in several volumes. This work included songs and dances from many regions in Central, Western, and Southern Poland.

An outstanding composer of songs in the latter half of the 19th century was Władysław Żeleński (1837–1921). His some seventy songs are related in mood to the Moniuszko type of song but are more modern in idiom, showing Brahmsian influence in the way the accompaniment often assumes the role of an atmospheric background.

After Żeleński there has been work in a more modern idiom, with new forms of expression in addition to the tradition-bound, stanzaic song which maintained decidedly folk coloring and simple accompaniment. Among composers who displayed a newer trend are Zygmunt Noskowski (1846–1909), with twelve song cycles, including a *Book of Songs for Children*, to texts by M. Konopnicka, close in style to Schubert. The Romantic phase was summed up by Jan Gall (1856–1912) and Stanisław Niewiadomski (1859–1936) in cycles including *Breath of Spring, Jasiek's Fate, Asters, The Dear Sun, Chanson d'Avril*, and *Poppy Flowers*, which display refined stylization of folk-music, fine shadings of expression, and great simplicity of setting. Eugeniusz Pankiewicz (1857–1898) enriched solo song with Late Romantic harmony. Stanisław Lipski (1880–1937) displayed unusual lyrical gifts, with influences from Brahms and Strauss.

The turn to the newer kind of song, with its rich accompaniment, strong effect of dissonance, and declamatory principle, was completed in the lyric compositions of Henry Melcer (1869–1928) and among the composers of "Young Poland," Mieczysław Karłowicz (1876–1909), Apolinary Szeluto (b. 1884), and particularly Karol Szymanowski (1882–1937). In the three phases of Szymanowski's career as a composer, the first or Romantic phase includes the cycles op. 11 and 20, with Oriental features in the *Love Songs of Hafiz* (1911) and the *Songs of the Mad Muezzin* (1918); the Impressionistic phase includes the *Songs of the Fairy-Tale Princess* (1915) and four songs on texts by Rabindranath Tagore (1918); and the final phase of clarification of his style appears in *Słopiewnie* (1921), *Children's Rhymes* (1923), and *Carpathian Songs* (1932).

In Denmark, proceeding from the second Berlin song school, a kind of solo song known as the "romance" was established, to become a repository for some of the best and most original of the native musical ideas. The instigator was J. A. P. Schulz, whose songs in the folk spirit and whose Copenhagen *singspiel* songs enjoyed special favor. Through his pupil C. E. F. Weyse (1774–1842), the first romance-composer, the simple folk-like quality took a turn to the lyrical, in part as a result of his choosing to set texts by J. L. Heiberg and B. S. Ingemann. The lyrical romance was marked by discriminating expression and modest but richly nuanced harmony along with simple melody and stanzaic structure, and thus it was quite different from the German romance, which was more closely linked with the ballad. Many of Weyse's romances came from his dramatic works. His romance style also appears in three collections which he later composed, to some extent for children: *Morgensange for Børn* (1837), *Syv Aftensange* (1838), and *Trestemmige Sange . . .* (1841).

While Weyse's music was still predominantly determined by the Classical Era in general and Mozart in particular, the songs and romances of J. P. E. Hartmann (1805–1900) and Niels W. Gade (1817–1890) were largely influenced—as far as harmony is concerned—by the Romanticism of the Leipzig School. Like Weyse, Hartmann set both secular and sacred texts to music. Gade wrote romances and several through-composed ballads. Notable examples of his romances appear in the cycle *Holger Danskes Sange* (1863), to texts by B. S. Ingemann. A highly regarded composer of children's songs was Johan Christian Gebauer (1808–1884). Some romances of Heinrik Rung (1807–1872), which often utilize the Danish folk-cadence, are sung still today.

Romantic song in Denmark reached a high point with Peter Heise (1830–1879). He was trained under Weyse's pupil A. P. Berggreen and under Hauptmann in Leipzig. Proceeding from Weyse's simple, stanzaic romance ideal, Heise began in the 1860's to develop a style of song under German Romantic influence, yet very much his own, with a piano part that became more and more distinctive, more often through-composed, occasionally even improvisatory with anticipations of Impressionistic traits. His texts were quite artistically chosen, and his interpretations of them were attractive. The best known of his some two hundred songs and romances, with their dates and the writers of the texts, are: *Verner og Malin* (1866), Christian Winther; *Gudruns Sorg* (1871), from the Elder Edda; *Finske Sange* (1874), Rafael Hertzberg; *Fire Sange fra Mittelalderen* (1875), Thor Lange; *Erotiske Digte* (1878), Emil Aarestrup; *Farlige Drømme* (1878), Holger Drachmann; and the cycle *Dyvekes Sange* (1878), Holger Drachmann.

Peter Erasmus Lange-Müller (1850–1926) was Heise's heir and successor. His most significant songs are in full-sounding, finely nuanced Late Romantic harmony, often Impressionistic, almost always stanzaic. There are about 250 songs, including some ballads, which for the most part are taken from dramatic works or are composed in cycles or little collections. The best known are his settings of poems by Holger Drachmann and of Thor Lange's translations from Slavic folk-songs. Heise and Lange-Müller also wrote many men's quartets for student vocal groups.

The songs and romances of Carl Nielsen (1865–1931), Poul Schierbeck (1888–1949), and Rued Langgaard (1893–1952) were inspired by Gade, Heise, and Lange-Müller. More recently Herman D. Koppel (b. 1908), Vagn Holmboe (b. 1909), and Per Nørgaard (b. 1932) have composed songs that to some extent are indebted to the romance tradition.

Paralleling Thomas Laub's reform of church song, song of a character much like that of folk-song experienced a successful and fundamental renewal, primarily through the people's high schools inspired by N. F. S. Grundtvig and general use in schools. Going back to J. A. P. Schulz's demand that song must have "the appearance of the familiar" and therefore be of the utmost simplicity, Carl Nielsen, Thomas Laub, Oluf Ring (1884–1946), Thorvald Aagaard (1877–1937), and Otto Mortensen (b. 1907) wrote many simple songs, which have become folk-songs. Melodically, these songs are strictly diatonic, anti-Romantic, dominated by pure triads, with harmony often colored by church modes.

In Sweden during the earlier half of the 19th century there were principally simple songs. From the Classical social song there developed, at first at the University of Uppsala, a native, sociable or lyrical vocal style in solo songs and men's quartets. The stylistic models of the composers of the so-called Uppsala School—particularly B. H. Crusell (1775–1838), E. G. Geijer (1783–1847), A. F. Lindblad (1801–1878), and J. A. Josephson (1818–1880)—were the second and third Berlin song schools. Many of the Uppsala songs and the somewhat sophomoric duet *Gluntarna* by G. Wennerberg (1817–1901) are popular still today.

After 1850 the Schumann-inspired art-song made itself more respected through the meritorious compositions of Ludvig Norman (1831–1885) and August Söderman (1832–1876), for example Söderman's cycle *Heather Rose* (1856) and Norman's *Skogssånger*, or Forest Songs (1867). An outstanding figure in this development was Emil Sjögren (1853–1918), whose songs, together with those of Grieg, Heise, and Sibelius, are high points in Northern song composition. Sjögren has astonishing breadth of expression and a fine ear for language. In setting the texts of various poets he used different styles. He displayed an Impressionism developed independently of Debussy, particularly in the setting of poems by J. P. Jacobsen and Verner von Heidenstam. The best known are his *7 spanska sånger* (1881), *Dikter av J. P. Jacobsen* (1887), *5 Fröding-Sånger* (1902), and *4 Sånger* (1918).

Further work along lines pursued by Söderman in the writing of songs was successfully carried on by W. Peterson-Berger (1867–1942), Hugo Alfén (1872–1960), and Josef Erikson (b. 1872). With the songs of Wilhelm Stenhammar (1871–1927) and Ture Rangström (1884–1947), the Romantic manner became the norm for the composers most gifted in this kind of composition during the 20th century. In the more recent period Gösta Nystroem (b. 1890) and Gunnar de Frumerie (b. 1908) have written neo-Romantic songs, stimulated by Honegger.

In Norway, Halfdan Kjerulf (1815–1868) was the first notable song composer. Inspired by Schumann, he wrote mostly stanzaic songs, with folk-song elements. His expression was his own, and he was decisive in the establishment of a Norwegian national Romantic movement. His successor was Rikard Nordraak (1842–1866), composer of the Norwegian national hymn, *Ja, vi elsker dette landet.*

The particular nature of Edvard Grieg (1843–1907) in songwriting is the richest but the most difficult to appreciate, as the linguistic subtleties are scarcely translatable. He used choice harmonic characterization, achieved spontaneity of expression, and enjoyed worldwide success. The best known of his songs are *6 Digte af Henrik Ibsen* (1876), *5 Digte af*

Johan Poulsen (1876), *Melodier til Digte af A. O. Vinje* (1873–80), *Digte af Vilhelm Krag* (1894), and the cycle *Haugtussa* (1895).

Contemporary with and following Grieg, Christian Sinding (1856–1941), Agathe Backer Gröndahl (1847–1907), Eyvind Alnaes (1872–1932), and Alf Hurum (1887–1952) wrote songs that reflect Continental developments. Fartein Valen (1887–1952) composed eleven songs, all in German, of which six are on texts by Goethe.

In Finland, a decisive influence on the development of a national style was exerted by the tonal idiom of Fredrik Pacius in his songs, which include the Finnish national anthem, *Suomis sång*. Also born in Germany, Richard Faltin (1835–1918) composed solo songs and men's quartets and arranged folk-songs. The Finnish-born composers F. A. Ehrström (1801–1850), A. G. Ingelius (1822–1868), Karl Collan (1828–1871), and Filip von Schantz (1835–1865) were all also active in song-writing.

Jean Sibelius (1865–1957) was the outstanding composer, though the main emphasis in his work was on instrumental music. The majority of his best-known songs were early works, such as the collections op. 36 and 37 (1898–1902). The eight songs op. 61, composed in 1910, have extended lines and piano parts full of tone poetry and expression. Further song composers are Armas Järnefeldt (1869–1958), Oskar Merikanto (1868–1924), Selim Palmgren (1878–1951), Ilmari Hannikainen (1892–1955), and—composing in a way quite his own—Yrjö Kilpinen (1892–1959). More recently, Erik Bergman (b. 1911) and Joonas Kokkonen (b. 1921) have written notable songs.

Iceland, during the latter half of the 19th century, gradually developed creative activity on its own, at first in song. Sveinbjörn Sveinbjörnsson (1847–1927), Iceland's first technically trained composer, wrote the national anthem *Ó, guð vors lands,* or O God of Our Land, as well as various songs, ballads, and choruses. Folk-like songs were composed by Jónas (1839–1903) and Helgi Helgason (1848–1922). Songs and duets of Jón Laxdal (1865–1928) were inspired by motives from the world of legend, as in the cycles *Helga hin fagra,* or Helga the Fair, and *Gunnar á Hildarenda.* In the 20th century at first Árni Thorsteinsson (1870–1962) and then Sigfús Einarsson (1877–1939) and Karl O. Runólfsson (b. 1900) came to the fore with songs, and more recently Emil Thoroddsen (1898–1944), Skúli Halldórsson (b. 1914), and Jón Thórarinsson (b. 1917) have achieved some prominence in this field.

In the United States there is a certain historical neatness to the fact that a native American, Francis Hopkinson (1737–1791), signer of the Declaration of Independence and early Secretary of the Navy, wrote the words and music for a group of Seven Songs published in 1788 with a dedication to George Washington—modest, graceful secular lyric compositions giving only the melody and bass. Hopkinson was a man of parts, one of which happens to be thus documented for posterity.

The political events of the late 18th century occasioned the emigration of several accomplished songwriters to the then new United States, such as C. P. E. Bach's friend Alexander Reinagle (1756–1809), Raynor Taylor (1747–1825), and Benjamin Carr (1768–1831). Some of their songs represented fairly advanced tendencies of the day: Carr, for instance, published in 1810 as No. 3 in his *Six Ballads* from the *Lady of the Lake* a setting of Sir Walter Scott's *Ave Maria* that foreshadows the well-known *Ellens Gesang* that Schubert wrote using the same text fifteen years later. Both compositions suggest a harp by means of the piano, and the voice soars above this busy accompaniment. It is a giant step from the slight songs of Hopkinson to the consciously composed lieder of Carr. Other important song composers who came to the United States in the 1790's and cast their lot with the new nation were James Hewitt, from England, and Victor Pelissier, from France. Pelissier's songs sometimes have the melody in the accompaniment beneath a single sustained tone in the vocal part.

Gottlieb Graupner (1767–1836), orignally from Hanover but also emigrating in the 1790's directly from England, is credited with one of the first black-face songs, *The Gay Negro Boy*, which he sang as an entr'acte in 1799. The outstanding composer of quasi-Negro songs, many actually written for a group of entertainers known as Christy's Minstrels, was Stephen Collins Foster (1826–1864). Some of these songs—such as *Old Folks at Home* and *Oh! Susanna*—have become a part of the American folklore. Many other composers flourished at this time, actively composing songs that undertook to convey the "appearance of the familiar": George J. Webb (1803–1887), Charles Edward Horn (1786–1849), F. W. Crouch (1808–1896), and J. P. Knight (1812–1887) with, for example, his *Rocked in the Cradle of the Deep* (1840).

If some of the songs of the first half of the 19th century may have become quite well-worn with the passage of the years, it must be realized that they represented a reaction against the rationalism of the previous century and that as the Central European revolutions of 1848 sent a new wave of musicians to the New World a more sophisticated level of Romantic composition could be achieved. By mid-century the writing of songs by American composers had a somewhat more solid basis. J. C. D. Parker (1828–1916) wrote a great deal of choral music, and the American art-song—according to W. T. Upton in his careful survey of this type of composition—"begins with Parker's imaginative setting of Tennyson's 'Come into the garden, Maud.' " Alfred H. Pease (1835–1882) also set poems by his contemporaries, such as Tennyson and Longfellow, in what was for that time a very sensuously chromatic way. Otto Dresel (1826–1890), who emigrated from Germany in 1848, wrote some twenty songs, all of high quality.

By about 1875 there were many American-born composers who received their higher musical training in Germany and became prolific composers of lieder, most notably Dudley Buck (1839–1909). Arthur Foote (1853–1937), George W. Chadwick (1854–1931), Edward MacDowell (1861–1908), and Horatio Parker (1863–1919) made important contributions to the literature of song in the United States as well as to that of various instruments.

As the 20th century dawned, German influence in song composition had begun to wane. Charles E. Ives (1874–1954) went his own way, publishing a volume of *114 Songs* (1922) extremely varied in mood and style, with a minimum of conventional musical rhetoric. The main emphasis is on the mood and content of the poem, in the most direct way.

French emphasis on delicacy and musical logic appeared in John Alden Carpenter (1876–1951). Charles T. Griffes (1884–1920) started out in his career from a rather Straussian early stage, but his later work reflects French and Russian influences.

By the second quarter of the present century a distinct revolt against Romanticism had become quite evident. Some composers wrote wordless songs, unaccompanied songs, and songs with accompaniments other than the piano. Though the bulk of the songs written towards mid-century were conventional enough, the presence of somewhat experimental efforts indicated either that there were so many active song composers that some had to distinguish themselves somehow, or—more likely—that composers and audiences were seeking in music something other than the inward, thoughtful, meditative or imaginative, highly subjective and individualized experience that had brought the *lied* so to the fore in the previous century. Whatever the reason, song did not occupy the central position in serious composition by Americans that it had in the previous century—and somewhat the same thing can be said of the musical situation in almost all the other countries.

There are, nevertheless, a great many songs being written and sung in the United States—on many different levels. A split between popular and art-song composition, with customary disregard of the former in most comprehensive accounts of the musical situation today, perhaps gives a misleading picture. Actually, folk-singing enjoys vast popularity; and the writing of songs that achieve "the appearance of the familiar" engages the talents of very many people and has widespread influence throughout the world. Art-song composition also continues. Just to pick almost at random three American composers out of many who might well be named, one might cite Aaron Copland (b. 1900), with his settings of Emily Dickinson's poems, Samuel Barber (b. 1910), with his settings of poems by James Joyce and others, and Ned Rorem (b. 1923), with over fifty individual songs and twenty song cycles to his credit.

Bibliography

General: M. Friedländer, *Das dt. Lied im 18. Jh.* (2 vols., Stuttgart and Bln. 1902); W. Krabbe, *Das dt. Lied im 17. u. 18. Jh.* (Adler Hdb.); H. Kretzschmar, *Gesch. d. neuen dt. Liedes von Albert bis Zelter* (Lpz. 1911); H. J. Moser, *Corydon, d. i. Gesch. d. mehrstr. Generalbassliedes u. d. Quodlibets im dt. Barock* (2 vols., Braunschweig 1933), *Das dt. Lied seit Mozart* (2 vols., Bln. 1937), and *Gesch. d. dt. Musik II;* G. Mueller, *Gesch. d. dt. Liedes. Vom Zeitalter d. Barock b. z. Gegenwart* (Munich 1925); F. Noske, *Das ausserdeutsche Sololied 1500–1900* (MW); F. E. Pamer, *Das dt. Lied im 19. Jh.* (Adler Hdb.); H. H. Rosenwald, *Das dt. Lied zwischen Schubert u. Schumann* (Diss. Hdlbg. 1929); W. Vetter, *Das frühdeutsche Lied* (2 vols., Münster 1928); E. Valentin, *Hdb. d. Chormusik* (Regensburg 4th ed. 1958); G. Schünemann, *Führer d. d. deutsche Chorliteratur* (2 vols., Wolfenbüttel 1935–6); art. Lied (MGG). *Aria and Cantata:* A. Einstein, *Der "stile nuovo" auf dem Gebiet d. pro-*

fanen Kammermusik (Adler Hdb.); M. Lange, *Die Anfänge d. Kantate* (Lpz. 1938); J. Racek, *Stilprobleme der ital. Monodie. Ein Beitrag zur Geschichte des einstimmigen Barockliedes* (Prague 1965); E. Schmitz, *Gesch. der Kantate u. des Geistl. Konzerts 1* (1914) and *Zur Gesch. des ital. Continuomadrigals im 17. Jh.* (SbIMG XI 1910); *Die Kantate* (MW); arts. Arie, Kantate (MGG); exs. Sch 242, 260.

17th Century: J. H. Schein: coll. ed. J. Staden: DTB 8, 1. G. Grefflinger: Sch 206. J. Rist: W. Krabbe, *J. R. u. d. dt. Lied* (Bln. Diss. 1910). Social Songs: Sch 186. H. Albert: DDT 12–13; Sch 193. A. Hammerschmidt: Sch 194. G. Voigtländer: K. Fischer, *G. V.* (Bln. Diss. 1910). A. Krieger: DDT 19; Sch 209; H. Osthoff, *A. K.* (Lpz. 1929). J. Krieger: Sch 235. J. W. Franck: DDT 45; Sch 254. P. H. Erlebach: DDT 46–47; Sch 262. Influence from Ital. Opera: Sch 210. V. Rathgeber: RD. 19.

18th Century: Sperontes: DDT 35–36. Leipzig School: Sch 289. G. P. Telemann: DDT 57. "Sing-, Spiel- und Generalbassübungen": new ed. 1921 and 1935; Sch 299. V. Görner: DDT 57; Sch 300. J. E. Bach: DDT 42. V. Herbing: DDT 42. Singspiellied: Sch 309. C. P. E. Bach: Sch 301; G. Busch, *C. P. E. Bach u. s. Lieder* (2 vols., Regensburg 1957). J. A. P. Schulz: partial new ed., Steingräber, Lpz.; C. Klunger, *S.' Lieder im Volkston* (Diss. Lpz. 1909); O. Riess, *S.' Leben* (SIMG 15); *Briefwechsel zwischen S. u. J. H. Voss* (Kassel 1960). J. Reichardt: various sep. new eds.; ed. of letters in prep. (IMBA); autobiog. in Berl. Mus. Zeitung 1805 (new ed. 1865); F. Flössner, *Beiträge z. Reichardt-Forschung* (Diss. Frankfurt 1929); W. Pauli, *J. F. R., sein Leben u. s. Stellung in d. Gesch. d. dt. Liedes* (Bln. 1903); R. Pröpper, *Die Bühnenwerke J. F. R.s* (1964); W. Salmen, *J. F. R.* (Zurich 1963); R. Sieber, *R. als Musikästhetiker* (Diss. Basel 1929). J. André: O. Pretzsch, *J. A. u. s. Stellung i. d. Berliner Liederschule* (Diss. Lpz. 1924). K. F. Zelter: sel. ed. (Mainz, Hanover); Goethe-Z. correspondence, 3 vols.; Schiller-Z. corr. in prep. (IMBA); autobiog., ed. W. Reich (Zurich 1956); H. J. Moser, *Z. u. d. dt. Lied* (JbP 1932); C. Schröder, *Z. u. d. Akademie* (Bln. 1959); G. Schünemann, *Z., der Begründer d. preussischen Musikpflege* (Bln. 1932). J. R. Zumsteeg: partial new ed.; L. Landshoff, *J. R. Z.* (Bln. 1902); F. Szymichowski, *Z. als Komponist von Balladen und Monodien* (Diss. Frankfurt 1932). L. Berger: D. Siebenkäs, *L. B.* (Bln. 1963). F. Mendelssohn-Bartholdy: L. Leven, *M. als Lyriker* (Diss. Frankfurt 1930). Viennese Song School: new eds. DTÖ 27, 2 (Das Wiener Lied von 1778 bis Mozarts Tod); DTÖ 42, 2 (1792–1815); J. Pollak-Schlaffenberg, *Die Wiener Liedmusik von 1778–1789* (StMw 5); E. Alberti-Radanowicz, *Das Wiener Lied von 1789–1815* (StMw 10). L. van Beethoven: H. Boettcher, *B. als Liederkomp.* (Augsburg 1928).

19th Century: F. Schubert: coll. ed. Lpz.; *Them. Verzeichnis*, ed. Nottebohm (Vienna 1874); new them. cat. by O. E. Deutsch (London 1951); new coll. ed. 1965– Kassel; monographs by M. J. E. Brown (London, N. Y. 1958), W. Dahms (Bln. 1912), A. Einstein (N. Y. 1951), R. Heuberger (Bln. 3rd ed. 1920), W. Klatte (Lpz. 1907), B. Paumgartner (Zurich 3rd ed. 1960), and W. Vetter (Potsdam 1934); M. Chusid, *S.s Cyclic Composition of 1824* (Acta 1964); O. E. Deutsch, *Die Dokumente des S.schen Lebens u. Schaffens* (2 vols., Munich 1914, new ed. London and N. Y. 1947, 4th ed. Vienna 1954; 3rd vol. *Schubert. Die Erinnerungen seiner Freunde*, Lpz. 1957); W. Kahl, *Verz. d. Schrifttums über S. 1828–1928* (Regensburg 1938); A. Orel, *Der junge S.* (Vienna 1939); W. Vetter, *Die Klassiker S.* (2 vols., Lpz. 1953).

R. Schumann: coll. ed. Lpz.; Them. Verzeichnis (Lpz., N. Y.); F. Feldmann, *Zur Frage des "Liederjahres" bei R. S.* (AfMw 1952); V. E. Wolff, *S.s Lieder in ersten und späteren Fassungen* (Lpz. 1914). *J. Brahms:* coll. ed. 26 vols., Lpz.; Them. Verzeichnis (Bln. 1907, enl. ed. N. Y. 1956); M. Friedländer, *B.' Lieder* (Bln. 1922); R. Gerber, *Formprobleme im Brahmsschen Lied* (JbP 1932); W. Hammermann, *B. als Liedkomp.* (Diss. Lpz. 1912); P. Mies, *Stilmomente u. Ausdrucksformen im Brahmsschen Lied* (Lpz. 1923); E. Rieger, *Tonarten-Charakteristik im einstim. Kl. Lied von J. B.* (StMw 22). *H. Wolf:* coll. ed. in prep. (Vienna); monographs notably by E. Decsey (4 vols., Bln. 1903–6) and F. Walker (London 1951); R. Egger, *Die Deklamationsrhythmik H. W.s in hist. Sicht* (Tutzing 1963). *P. Cornelius:* coll. ed. Lpz. *K. Loewe:* coll. ed. of L.'s ballads in 17 vols. (Lpz.); autobiog., ed. C. H. Bitter (Bln. 1870); K. Anton, *Beitr. z. Biographie C. L.s* (Halle 1912); H. Bulthaupt, *C. L.* (Bln. 1898); H. Kleemann, *Beiträge z. Ästhetik u. Gesch. d. L.schen Ballade* (Halle 1913); P. Spitta, *Ballade* (Musikgesch. Aufsätze, Bln., 1894).

German Choral Song: H. Blommen, *Anfänge u. Entwicklung des Männerchorwesens am Niederrhein* (Cologne 1960); A. Friedrich, *Beiträge zur Gesch. des weltl. Frauenchores* (Regensburg 1961); W. Krabbe, *Chormusik* (Adler Hdb.); S. Kross, *Die Chorwerke von J. Brahms* (Bln. 1958); H. J. Moser, *Das deutsche Lied seit Mozart* (Bln. and Zurich 1937); H. Osthoff, *Das dt. Chorlied* (MW); H. Thierfelder, *Vorgesch. u. Entwicklung d. dt. Männergesangs* (Hildburghausen 1923); arts. Chorkomposition, Jugendmusik, Männerchor (MGG). *F. Silcher:* sel. works, Kassel.

Solo Song outside Germany: E. Hardeck, *Untersuchungen zu den Kl.Liedern Debussys* (Regensburg 1967); F. Noske, *Das ausserdeutsche Sololied* (MW) and *La Mélodie française de Berlioz à Duparc* (Amsterdam and Paris 1954). *Poland:* A. Simon, *The Polish Songwriters* (Warsaw 1936). *Scandinavia:* P. Heise: W. Behrend, *P. H.* (Riemann-Festschrift 1909). *E. Grieg:* A. Desmond, *G.'s Songs* (ML 1941); C. W. Orr, *G.'s Songs* (Monthly Musical Record 1932); W. Weismann, *G. als Liederkomponist* (ZfMw 1932).

VI The Twentieth Century

33. On the Situation in the 20th Century

What should an account of the very recent and present era attempt to do, in a history of music? It should try to indicate the historical order already present in the material. Relying on documentary evidence, it should characterize individual tendencies, group musical traits according to style, and analyze works in terms of form, harmony, rhythm, expression, and symbolic force. It should not try to rate them in terms of value, for in the flux of the present one can only dimly foresee the future. To evaluate anything properly, one has to know what will come of it.

Unifying and Diverging Trends

If one assumes that the 20th-century musical situation forms a potentially intelligible whole, one observes considerable distance among the elements that compose it. Although the lines of cleavage between styles were evident in the 16th century, they had widened with increasing distinctness and speed by the 20th. Often they have produced a sense of extreme dissociation, on several levels—as between different styles, within individual types of composition, and among separate countries. When serial music, for example, appeared after 1951 in the work of Pierre Boulez in France, Luigi Nono in Italy, and Karlheinz Stockhausen in West Germany, a composer like Paul Hindemith was writing in an extremely moderated, tonally restrained, mature style, and Luigi Dallapiccola was writing in the strict twelve-tone system. Here we see different generations active at the same time. There is great distance between "true" jazz, "commercialized" jazz, and popular music; between symphonic works and pieces for sheer entertainment; and between opera and church music. The individual traits of the separate countries have moved apart during and after World War II, with political and ideological tensions between East and West limiting the exchange of artistic works and constricting the field of critical vision.

651

Not only is it a matter of distance, but also it is one of difference. The sharpness of the contrasts is greater than it has been before. Twelve-tone or serial music has become more individualized in idiom, expression, and choice of means, while commercial music has become more stereotyped in its functions as background for films, plays, television, and other activities. Extreme antitheses prevail between serial composition and "practical music," or *Gebrauchsmusik*, between computer music and improvised ensemble music. These contrasts are not easily bridgeable; for the "modern music" of Western Europe has largely lost creative contact with folk-song and other aspects of folklore.

Modernity

One of the terms frequently encountered in discussions of 20th-century music is "modern." Perhaps it might be appropriate first to look objectively at this word, and at some related terms such as "new," in their application to music. Phrases such as *Ars nova* and *Ars nova musicae* appeared in the history of Western music for the first time around 1320 in Paris. The extant theoretical and musical documents show unambiguously that a new direction was thus indicated—one that by its special nature contrasted with the older. The contrasts between the new and the not-so-new were then felt to be impossible to bridge and represented two generations distinct in age and point of view. This special situation, arising around 1320, limited itself first to Paris.

A century and a half later another situation came into being, quite closely related to that of 1320. Johannes Tinctoris, writing in the latter half of the 15th century, spoke of an *Ars nova*, saying: "The possibilities of our music have been so eminently increased that it seems almost like a new art" (*Proportionale musices*, around 1476). Also here we find a situation analogous to that of *Ars nova:* a new direction is taken, the leaders are aware that they are doing so, and there is a break between the generations. The scene, however, is now Cambrai, the episcopal see in Burgundy.

Somewhat over a hundred years later, in 1581, Vincenzo Galilei published his treatise in dialogue form, *Della Musica antica e della moderna.* Caccini's *Nuove Musiche* appeared in 1601. Monteverdi in 1605 wrote of *moderna musica* in the preface to his fifth madrigal book, formulating an antithesis in the history of style between *Prima Prattica* and *Seconda Prattica.*

During the first part of the present century the concept of modern or new music was reformulated every so often in novel terms. One notices considerable shifts in emphasis among them:

In 1909, Rudolf Louis wrote in *Die deutsche Musik der Gegenwart* (Munich) that the present in music as in other fields seemed to him "enormously multiform and rich in contradictions." Yet he tried to "characterize" his period "in a word." He said it lived "under the almost unanimously recognized . . . sway of a dogma peculiar to it," that of "musical progress." One had to recognize, he pointed out, that every living being constantly changes and that one has to have faith that all change is subject to strict legality—i.e., the laws of evolution. But he said that the concept of evolution does not necessarily imply any value judgment. The later stage of development does not necessarily need to represent a higher level of perfection. And in closing he said that evolution is not always and everywhere progress, though a dogmatic belief in progress would equate the two concepts as a matter of course.

In 1913, Walter Niemann in *Die Musik der Gegenwart* (Berlin) drew a distinction between modernism and classicism. "German musical modernism" Niemann saw as "embodied most clearly in Richard Strauss and his followers." The "Dionysian and Bacchic, that which whips up our nervous systems," he wrote, was "the decisive mark of all truly modern music."

In 1924, Ernst Bücken in his *Führer und Probleme der Neuen Musik* (Cologne) now recognized more sharply the historical connection. Impressionism and Expressionism were rooted, according to Bücken, "in Romantic soil." Expressionism, "the last phase in the development of music as expressive art," was derived from Schönberg.

In 1928, Hans Mersmann in *Die Tonsprache der Neuen Musik* (Mainz) considered it justified "in our time to speak of a new music, to reveal the laws of the new tonal idiom. This new music is not to be reduced to one common denominator." In the structure of its development so far and now completed, he saw three aims: a complete dissolution and replacement of the earlier musical picture, an elemental breakthrough of forces, and their new connection in form and shape. The problem of the New Music was traced back to the beginning of the century. It was Schönberg who fought out the problem of a whole generation. "Schönberg's music became the symbol of the new music in those circles in which it was not from the very start dismissed with passion or irony." Then, however, the situation changed. "There arose, in many places at the same time, a music which again attached itself to sound and rhythm, to folk-song and dance. That is New Music, as Stravinsky, Krenek, Bartók, and Milhaud first created it. No longer is Schönberg's work the symbol of a New Music. Now the New Music is an elemental reaction against him."

In 1950, Herbert Eimert in *Lehrbuch der Zwölftontechnik* (Wiesbaden) recognized twelve-tone music as "the most consistent attempt to find a new tonal order in the latest musical development." After the war, Eimert said, it has "entered the province of history as a new movement in music of international importance."

In 1954, the present writer in *Neue Musik in der Entscheidung* (Mainz) wrote: "The twelve-tone principle in its significance both as syntax and as means of artistic assertion makes a new presentation of the concept and nature of New Music necessary today, at the middle of the century."

In 1958, Wolf-Eberhard von Lewinski in *Junge Komponisten* in *Die Reihe* (Heft 4, Vienna) maintained: "New Music has so far borne its name unjustly. It has turned out that the composers who have already come to be familiarly called the 'classics of the new music' wrote in a way neither more nor less 'new' than the musicians of the last two centuries also. Of course the way of doing it has changed in detail.

But not the style. The crucial year for the beginning of a new stylistic epoch is 1950, with the beginning of polydimensional music."

In 1964, Leo Schrade in an address on the North German Radio said: "A new epoch in music has begun with the middle of the century."

The designations such as "modern" and "new" are obviously words of not very stable meaning. At most, "new" is a very relative and constantly changing concept; and "modern," with its obvious relationship to "mode" in the sense of what is fashionable at the moment, can be expected to vary from season to season. Perhaps, through the accelerated change in the stylistic and compositional situation in the 20th century, the concept "modern" has become finally a catchword, a rubber stamp, used from a feeling of insecurity toward that which is different, strange, or unfamiliar. Perhaps it has lost any normative value and as a cliché has descended to conveying a mere innuendo. Sometimes it is used for purposes of disparagement or discrimination, sometimes—like a catch-phrase in advertising or public speaking—to trigger off easily accessible emotional responses.

20th-Century Classicism

Obviously, any fruitful consideration of 20th-century music must be phrased in terms of slightly more stable meaning. One such term is "Classicism," which for music and the arts generally has a fairly definite referential content. At the beginning of the 1920's there arose in Europe and America a movement that has been called "Neoclassicism." By this is meant the tendency to fuse stylistic traits of 18th-century music with contemporary music. Igor Stravinsky was considered the instigator and leader in this direction. Beginning with the ballet *Pulcinella* (Paris 1920) and continuing in his Concertino for String Quartet (1920), Octet for Winds (1923), Concerto for Piano and Wind Orchestra (1924), and Sonata for Piano (1924), he drew inspiration from the 18th century and influenced numerous composers to a greater or less degree.

The Neoclassical movement, which was at its height between 1925 and 1950, is a reaction or "rebound" away from the strongly revolutionary trend that had prevailed in music during the years between 1909 and 1924. Those who followed this Neoclassical trend believed that they had to abandon the immediate past. Seen from another point of view, the tendency to go back to the Classical, Pre-Classical, and Late Baroque was a typically "anti-Romantic" reaction.

Neoclassicism as an anti-Romantic reaction at the beginning of the twenties is only one phase in the pendulum-like succession, the wave-like motion, which is characteristic of European music history since the Middle Ages. Viewed subjectively, the Neoclassical movement had to appear as "reaction," and so it did to those who had dared to take up an extremely advanced position. In reality they had never broken their ties with the past—not even during the "modern" movement—unrecognizable as these ties may have been to those who thought they were breaking them.

Classicism has been defined as "the voluntary seeking-out of a style that has been viewed historically and the attempt to fuse it with the composer's own idiom, bound as it is to his own time and personality." In this sense, Classicism was the phase of a tendency quite evident in the second quarter of the 20th century and incorporated in the great historical wave of Classicism since Mozart, which necessarily figures prominently in any account of the history of Western music. Composers during the second quarter of the 20th century usually adopted rather extreme positions, as if they were members of opposing armies at the front—somewhat as composers during the latter half of the 19th century had done. The party of progress was ranged against the Classicistic reaction. Thus they repeated the general configuration of a previous historical situation and tended to see an illusory antithesis between Schönberg and Stravinsky. However, this antithesis, like that of the 19th century, is resolvable into a higher unity.

This antithesis poses a historical question. Is it possible to compose today without continually reestablishing contact with tradition? In trying to answer this question, one has to investigate the past and the present historically, to recognize and expose the connections between the particular present and the past in its own special forms of tradition.

One can perhaps understand the dualism between Schönberg and Stravinsky more clearly from the point of view of sheer human psychology. Antitheses are not only a matter of artistic theory; they are also and primarily a matter of the human personality, the artistic psyche. Liszt and Wagner were basically different from each other, as also Brahms and Schumann in his late period were fundamentally strange to each other. Yet with all the differences that marked their music, it was bound to tradition in distinctly different ways—though the differences may have become manifest with any intensity only gradually. Oppositions of this sort establish the unity underlying a period. They are constantly repeated, only on other levels. Fifty years ago this antithesis was spoken of as Richard Strauss against Max Reger, thirty years ago as Schönberg against Stravinsky. The historian, however, must rise above the antitheses of the day and recognize the particular individual contacts with tradition.

Igor Stravinsky had already followed the younger composers and adopted serial composition when, looking back from the point of view of his later years, he felt obliged in 1958 in his conversations with Robert Craft to formulate the matter thus:

> Every period is a historical unity. To the partisans of the time it may seem to be entirely an Either–Or matter; yet the illusion grows apace, and at the right time Either and Or become the components of One and the Same. For example, the designation "Neoclassic" is used now for all composers between the two World Wars (not the concept of the Neoclassicistic composer as someone who plagiarizes his predecessors and everyone else and then arranges the theft in a new "style"). Schönberg, Berg, and Webern of the twenties were then designated as the most extreme iconoclasts, but today it seems that they used musical form as I have done, "historically." If I used it openly, they were more secretive about it (one might take, for example, the Rondo of Webern's Trio; the music magnificently interesting, but no one can recognize it as a rondo).

Of course in the twenties we learned about all the new music and delved into it; but we connected it all with the same tradition as we had so diligently grown out of, a decade before.

The formula "Neoclassicism" comes entirely from the French sphere of thinking and speaking. From Paris in the twenties Neoclassicism took its way artistically and propagandistically into the international world of music, having been formulated by Stravinsky, "The Six," and Cocteau. It would be factually more correct to speak of a Neoclassicism only when it concerns a matter of reworking stylistic elements of the Viennese Classical Era and to speak of Neo-Baroque when it concerns reaching back into the period of Bach, Schütz, or Gabrieli. In the same years as Stravinsky and some Frenchmen had resolved to look back to the 18th century, in Germany there occurred the trend toward the Neo-Baroque, with Paul Hindemith in the lead and with distinctive developments in the new choral music. This retrospective orientation lay entirely in the German line of tradition, as it came down through Mozart, Beethoven, Mendelssohn, Schumann, Brahms, and Reger. It also reflected the typically German concern with the world of Bach and Handel.

As seen from today, there is something a little misleading about the term "Neoclassicism" and about its application to the epoch from roughly 1924 to 1950; for during the first two decades of the 20th century the past had already exerted a strong effect as living consciousness on the music of the present. Many prominent composers bear witness to this fact—Claude Debussy and Maurice Ravel in the Franco-Roman cultural area, Wolf-Ferrari and Ferrucio Busoni in the Italian-Roman, and Mahler in the Austro-German. Debussy's three sonatas of 1915 bear the inscription "Claude Debussy, *musicien français.*" He called himself this because he felt, with a deep sense of shock, that a common European culture would not survive the war that broke out in 1914, and because in all his creative work he was deeply and consciously aware of the history of French music. Fundamentally, the Six, as well as Stravinsky, began where Debussy left off. Only in Debussy is the process of fusion with the French past truly sublime and perfect. It often appears more factitious and external than integral in Stravinsky and the Six. Gustav Mahler in his connection with tradition is the last great Austro-German symphonist.

In the mature culture of Western Europe the composer can look backwards to all phases and epochs of past style and adopt elements from the music of Oriental peoples or of primitives. He has available to him a great deal of musicological research and the numerous new editions of the monuments of older music and of the complete works of earlier composers—as well as the music of non-European peoples. Thus the history of music is today completely present and permits an unlimited abundance of points of contact and previously unsuspected possibilities of fusion. There are today works of art that fuse stylistic features ranging all the way from Gregorian chant and early medieval music to the Romantic Era—not to mention elements of even more radically divergent origin.

The future will be rich in surprises. Restrictions have not been imposed nor limitations set on creative artistic power. There is here only one standard, that of synthesis. The greatest composers, from Mozart on, have struggled to fuse historical style with the styles of their own period and personality. Only those works have remained alive that have this power of synthesis. They alone represent something new. They are the strokes of good fortune vouchsafed to us in the history of music.

The Concept of "Tradition"

Another term or concept that is frequently encountered in discussions of 20th-century music is "tradition." Tradition is the vitality of the past in the consciousness of the present. It is also something earned.

There are three ways in which the past may be operatively active in the present. It may be conscious and continuous. For example, Palestrina's presence in music since his death in 1594 has never been interrupted and has continued to manifest itself anew, through Fux's *Gradus* in 1725, Thibaut's essay in 1825, the Caecilian Movement, and the research in Palestrina carried on by Jeppesen, Fellerer, Hermelink, and others. Another example is instrumentation, which—with few exceptions —has represented something continuously present since about 1650. Many of the rules of contrapuntal composition, moreover, such as that regarding contrary motion among the voices (from 1100), imitation and canon (from 1300), and inversion and crab movement (from *Ars Nova*), have been present continuously. The juxtaposition of contrasts in musical structure has always been there—the opposition between slow and fast, the original pairing of dances, the over-all crescendo and accelerando, and the various linkages and gradations in the joining of musical motives, themes, and groups.

A second way in which the past may be present is as something that has been conscious but discontinuous. For example, we might observe the sharply changing evaluation of Joseph Haydn as a composer, the constantly varying judgment with reference to Wagner between that a century ago and that today, the process of revival of Baroque music that has occurred since Winterfeld's *Gabrieli und seine Zeitalter* (1834), the discovery of medieval music in present-day musical practice since about 1930, and the status of J. S. Bach—the fusing of his music with that of the present, beginning notably with Mozart in 1782, its penetration into the musical life of the day particularly since 1829 with the revival of the St. Matthew Passion, its utilization for teaching purposes since the beginning of the 19th century, the recognition of his greatness by the Romantic composers (as when Schumann asserted that "Bach is incommensurable"), and the Protestant use of Bach's music as a model of sacred music in the 20th century.

In a third way the past may be virtually present without anyone's being particularly conscious of it. For example, epochs may be manifestly similar but without the existence of direct or overt connections with each other. This may often be a matter of unconscious predispositions to certain common features, without objective influences. Specific musical gestures recur, doubtless prompted by the same expressive urges operating in related psychological situations. For example, certain formal tendencies may recur as a medium of exaggerated individual psychological character —the "Storm and Stress," Romanticism, Expressionism, and some tendencies of the immediate Present—and these may operate in a centrifugal direction. Another example, more specific, is the recurrence of an athematic form of composition in the monodrama *Ariadne* by Georg Benda (1775) and in *Erwartung* by Arnold Schönberg (1909). Also, linear chromaticism reappears as a highly subjective means of expression in the Italian madrigal of 1600, in Late Baroque, in the "Storm and Stress," and around 1850. To take a final example of this third way the past may be present, we might note the confrontation of distant keys—involving chromaticism through opposition of triads, chromatic modulation, and enharmonic modulation—that recurs in Baroque music around 1600, in Johann Sebastian Bach, in the "Storm and Stress," and in the latter half of the 19th century.

Folklorism

Another concept or tendency that has figured prominently in the music of the 20th century is the concern with folklore. In fact, it has been present in both its positive and negative forms—as folklorism and as anti-folklorism.

The first traceable influence of folk-music on art-music in the West occurred in the Carolingian Period and was connected with the trope and the sequence, as secular elements from music north of the Alps made their way into Gregorian chant. Probably folk-music influenced early English polyphony, but the documents that might establish the relationship have been lost. It is certain, however, that the music of the troubadours and trouvères derives in part from folk-music, transmitted through the minstrel repertoire. Since the Renaissance, documentation is ampler, though often it leaves something to be desired. Secular songs were adopted as cantus firmi in the Mass during the 15th century. The tenor song of the 15th and 16th centuries in Germany represents a popularly inspired, secular type of art, which in turn influenced the keyboard and lute music of the period. In the villanella, beginning about 1537, Southern Italian folk-melody at first played the predominating role. The Hussite chorale and other Protestant chorales did not reject folk-impulses, which again were reflected in the art music of the chorale preludes.

Art music has time and again resorted to folk-song and folk-dance. One first perceives their influence in early art-song and in the stylized form of dance music, the suite. This applies to the 17th century, the Baroque, as well as to the Classical Era, in instrumental music or in song, which in the Berlin School revived quasi-folk-song composition. The points of contact were no less close in the Romantic Era.

The latter half of the 18th century brought with it scholarly research into folk-song. A new stage was reached when composers themselves, with scholarly interest, took a hand in the research and then were again influenced by this work in their composition. The first composers to play this double role of scholar and creative artist were Janáček, Bartók, and Vaughan Williams, all of whom blazed new trails.

Looking at individual European countries in alphabetical order, we note significant interest in folk-song research in Bohemia and Moravia. Leoš Janáček (1854–1928) was the first in recent times, beginning in 1888, to pursue folk-song research both as a creative artist and as a scholar. Separating scholarly research and methodical collection of melodies from careful transcription, he left the character and nature of the original intact. He regarded the possible use of this material in composition as a task in itself. From folklore he gained the style, not the material of his compositions.

In England, Ralph Vaughan Williams (1872–1958) was the first significant composer to ally himself with the work of the English Folk-Song Society, founded in 1898. He himself collected folk-songs in Norfolk, and they very soon left their mark on his own compositions. He wrote three "Norfolk Rhapsodies" (1907), the Folk-Song Suite, the Fantasy on Christmas Carols, and folk-song transcriptions, mostly for *a cappella* chorus. Of the younger British composers, Benjamin Britten (b. 1913) especially has borrowed suggestions from folklore. He has transcribed a series of English folk-songs for voice and piano, and the spirit of the folk-songs has particularly entered into his treatment of speech. In his preface to the opera *Peter Grimes* (London, 1945), he sees the revival of idiomatic English in music as one of his main tasks.

In Germany, three developments are especially noteworthy: Carl Orff's *Schulwerk*, the Youth Movement, and the instrumental song-paraphrase. The internationally known composer and teacher, Carl Orff, has based his instructional method, *Schulwerk*, to a great extent on folk-song. The musical point of departure is the child's own world, children's song, and in the wider sense folk-song. The form of the pupil's own music-making is improvisation as the most elemental and ancient musical practice of man. Orff methodically undertakes to awaken and stimulate the dormant improvisatory capacities of the child to free development. He starts with children's play, of which music in the form of song and dance is an indispensable part. He then introduces calls and earlier forms of children's song, in which a still undeveloped pentatonicism is present. Then from this he proceeds to stimulate in the child's creative play the possibility of self-development. It is easy to move from children's song and play to folk-song. Alongside direct adoption of German folk-songs, particularly those of the earlier period, there appear original creations in numerous song and instrumental melodies.

A second folk-song development in Germany is the influence of the Youth Movement, the spirit of which resulted in widespread group singing. The style of this new choral music shows a preference for the church modes, constantly interchanging linear and chordal setting, and madrigalesque composition in the manner of such composers as Monteverdi, Hans Leo Hassler, and Heinrich Schütz. Often the older folk-song melodies are used, in part transcribed in the style of the 16th-century German tenor song, the setting being marked by what might roughly be termed objectivity in contrast to 19th-century subjectivism and harmonic differentiation in sonority. The restrospective tendency is shown also in the title of songs favored within this singing movement: madrigals, canons, choral songs, folk-song settings, folk-song transcriptions, folk-song variations.

Finally, a third tendency that represents a special instance of the use of folklore is the song-paraphrase. Composers have undertaken to rework folk-melody in instrumental variations, for example the concerto for viola and small orchestra based on old folk-songs, *Der Schwanendreher*, by Hindemith (1895–1963) and his *spielmusik* for strings and winds, *Ein Jäger aus Kurpfalz*.

In Hungary, Béla Bartók (1881–1945), together wtih Zoltán Kodály, began in 1905 to investigate what he referred to as the "hitherto simply unknown Hungarian peasant music." He had recognized that the Hungarian tunes erroneously circulated as folk-songs were more or less trivial popular art-songs. The work began in the Magyar-speaking area, extended to the linguistic regions of the Slovaks and Romanians, and finally included Arab peasant music. Bartók was not able to complete the scholarly evaluation of his activity as a collector. Discovery of folklore, however, brought him—according to his own statement—"to the possibility of a complete emancipation from the exclusive domination of the previous major and minor system." He studied the modal and pentatonic character of the melodies and became acquainted wtih their "quite varied and free rhythmic character when performed both *rubato* and *tempo giusto*." The use of modal tonalities led him to seek "emancipation from the petrified major-minor scale" and, as a final consequence, brought him "to the completely free use of every single tone in our chromatic twelve-tone system." Bartók said further: "To use folk-song is one of the most difficult tasks there is—possibly even more difficult than writing quite a large original composition." For "only a strongly form-creating art can make something out of the thematic raw material. Folk-music can be a source of inspiration for the music of the country only if the transplantation of its motivic material is the work of a creative natural capacity."

Bartók saw three ways in which he might be able to "put life into art music with elements of a fresh peasant music, uninfluenced by the work of the last centuries." One was to take over the peasant tune unaltered or only slightly varied and to write an accompaniment, perhaps also an introductory and concluding section for it. A second possibility was not to use the actual peasant melody but "rather to invent one's own imitations of this melody." The third possibility, he felt, was if "neither peasant tunes nor imitations of them are available, perhaps to absorb the music with its individual atmosphere." The composer would then have "taken the nature of the peasant music entirely into himself, and made it his own musical native tongue." He then would have "mastered it completely and poetically."

In Russia, during the 19th century, a highly significant and creative approach to folklore had been found. Rimski-Korsakov transmitted this impulse to his pupil Igor Stravinsky, leading to the compositions of Stravinsky's "Russian Period" before World War I, with the high point in the three ballets *Fire Bird* (Paris 1910), *Petrushka* (Paris 1911), and *Rite of Spring* (Paris 1913). In *Rite of Spring* the folkloristic element necessarily stands out most prominently. The opening theme is said to have been simply borrowed from a Lithuanian folk-song. All the other motifs represent—if they are his own invention—what Bartók called the "most clever and faithful imitations of folk-tunes." In *Les Noces* (Paris 1923) Stravinsky concentrated almost the entire thematic material on a motivic cell, a third subdivided into a minor third and a major second.

Since Stravinsky was so prominent in the 20th century, his career should be considered in some detail. Son of a well-known bass-baritone opera singer, Igor Feodorovich Stravinsky was born on June 18, 1882, in Oranienbaum, near St. Petersburg. At first a student of law and from 1905 to 1908 a composition pupil of Rimski-Korsakov, he wrote—among other works—two orchestral pieces, the First Symphony in E-flat major and the orchestral fantasy *Feu d'artifice*. His world success began with the first performance of the *Firebird* ballet in 1910, in Paris under Diaghilev, for whom he wrote the ballets *Petrushka* (1911) and *Le Sacre du Printemps* (1913) during the prewar period in Paris. From 1910 to 1939 Stravinsky lived principally in Paris and Switzerland, and thereafter in California. In 1934 he became a French citizen and in 1945 an American. He left his native Russia as a result of the political revolution in 1917 and returned only for brief visits in 1922 and 1962, as his separation from his homeland was largely of his own choice. Otherwise, however, he scarcely had a permanent dwelling place. In presenting his own works and otherwise discharging personal obligations he journeyed almost all over the world. He early appeared as an interpreter of his own piano works; later he conducted operas, concerts, and recording sessions. He also undertook to formulate his ideas in writing, usually by way of memoirs, and thus to arrive at a generally valid aesthetic.

To conceive adequately of Stravinsky as a composer, one has to begin with the history of 19th-century Russian music. It starts from Russian folklore, legends, and myths. But it also adopts the stylistic and formal heritage of secular music. At least, this was characteristic of Stravinsky up to about 1925. Then, however, there was increasing evidence of ancient and religious aspects in a somewhat neoclassical stratum of his music. His work falls into three periods. The first, or "Russian," goes up to about 1923; the second, or "Neoclassicistic," to the beginning of 1950; and the last, up to his death in 1971, involves his coming to terms with twelve-tone music. He derived creative stimulation partly from the past and partly from the present. Also important was his ability to transform the meaning of the material he took in hand. Stravinsky was not one of those talents who open up new worlds in a revolutionary way from their own impulses, like Schönberg, but was much more a genius of a deeply conservative nature who brought things together—in this respect one of the most significant phenomena in the 20th century.

Even a selective indication of his works constitutes an impressive list. His ballets and pantomimes include the *Firebird* (Paris 1910), *Petrushka* (Paris 1911), *Le Sacre du Printemps* (Paris 1913), *L'histoire du Soldat* (Lausanne 1918), *Pulcinella* (Paris 1920), *Renard* (Paris 1922), *Les Noces* (Paris 1923), *Apollon Musagète* (Paris 1928), *Le Baiser du Fée* (Paris 1928), *Persephone* (Paris 1934), *Jeu de Cartes* (New York 1937), *Orpheus* (New York 1948), and *Agon* (Paris 1957). His operas include *The Nightingale* (Paris 1914), *Mavra* (Paris 1922), *Oedipus Rex* (Paris 1927), *The Rake's Progress* (Venice 1951), and *The Flood* (New York 1962). As for orchestral works, he wrote *Le Chant du Rossignol* (Paris 1920), *Symphony for Winds* (1920), *Dumbarton Oaks* (1938), *Symphony in C* (1940), *Symphony in Three Movements* (1945), and *Variations* (1963–4); concerti and chamber music, *Piano Concerto* (1922–4), *Capriccio for Piano and Orchestra* (1929), *Violin Concerto* (1931), *Wind Octet* (1923), *Septet* (1953), *Piano Sonata* (1924), *Concerto for Two Pianos* (1931–5), and *Sonata for Two Pianos* (1943–4); and chamber works, *Le Roi des Étoiles* (1911), *Symphony of Psalms* (1930), *Canticum Sacrum* (1956), *Threni* (1957–8), and *Introitus* and *Requiem Canticles*. His literary works include his *Chroniques de ma vie* (Paris 1935–6), *Musical Poetics* (Cambridge, Mass. 1942), and dialogues with Robert Craft (1961–3).

The music of the USSR finds precedent in a remark of Glinka's: "Music is made by the people; and we, the artists, only arrange it." The composers have been encouraged to make contact with folklore. The results of extensive folk-song research are available and have produced a varied creative result.

In Poland at the beginning of the 20th century there was the movement in music known as "Young Poland" (*Młoda Polska*). Szymanowski, the most significant composer associated with it till his death in 1937, occasionally adopted Late Romantic expression, the Chopin tradition, and traits deriving from the folk. During his career he achieved wide international recognition, particularly with his *Harnasie*. The most important contribution of the group was the rapid spread of 19th-century Polish music beyond its national boundaries. It will be recalled that many of the gifted Polish musicians, such as Chopin, Wieniawski, and Zarebski, had gone abroad.

Influences stemming from the Parisian school of Nadia Boulanger began to affect Polish music in the work of Piotr Perkowski, Kazimierz Sikorski, and Tadeusz Szeligowski. Also the influence of Schönberg appeared in the works of Jósef Koffler. After 1945 there was a revived interest in the Szymanowski tradition, Neoclassicism, and folklore. After 1956, however, there was a shift, influenced by the Webern school, extreme experimentalism, and aleatory composition, often linked with quite individual stylistic traits. International recognition was quickly accorded many composers, such as Witold Lutosławski (b. 1913), Tadeusz Baird (b. 1928), and Krzysztof Penderecki (b. 1933).

In Spain, the great inaugurator of the rise of newer Spanish music was Felipe Pedrell (1841–1922). He wished to see Spanish music develop from the great musical tradition of his land and the national sources of his people. His aims were carried out by his pupils Isaac Albeniz (1860–1909), Enrique Granados (1867–1916), and subsequently Manuel de Falla (1876–1946), whose works up to 1914 bore the imprint of Andalusian folk-music. Their particular nature was determined by three factors: elements of Byzantine chant, Moorish influences, and the immigration of numerous gypsy tribes in the 15th century. In a folk-song, Falla said, the spirit is more important than the letter. Rhythm, mode, and melodic intervals are the primary consideration. "The people confirm this by constantly altering the melodic line. The rhythmic or harmonic accompaniment is as important as the song itself; hence one must take the inspiration also directly from the people." He maintained that one must go to its very heart and incorporate in oneself its very rhythm and tone color. De Falla's two ballets *El amor brujo* (Love, the Magician) and *El sombrero de tres picos* (The Three-Cornered Hat) represent high points in his assimilation of folklore, as does also his *Nights in the Gardens of Spain,* subtitled "Symphonic Impressions for Piano and Orchestra."

Anti-Folklorism or Internationalism

Over against the folklore movement and its many varieties in contemporary music, there stands a countermovement that might be designated anti-folklorism. It follows with a certain inevitability from the principle of twelve-tone music and serial composition, if they are carried out strictly. Exceptions are provided in the citation of folk-songs, as in Schönberg's Suite op. 29, Variations on *Aennchen von Tharau* or in Alban Berg's Violin Concerto with its quotation of a folk-song and a Bach chorale. In general, however, twelve-tone music is not directly influenced by folk-song. In fact, it rather avoids the limitations implied by the folk-idea.

Exoticism or Orientalism

Another trend in Western music has been sometimes referred to as exoticism or Orientalism. Since the 17th century, compositions have strikingly imitated foreign coloring. Mozart, for example, wrote "Turkish music" in his *Entführung;* Puccini, "Japanese music" in *Madame Butterfly;* and other composers, "Scottish," music that was recognized as "Moorish," or "Chinese." The World Exposition of 1889 and 1900 in Paris brought French composers for the first time in direct contact with the sonorities of the music of China, Japan, Java, and Annam. Indian rhythmic influence plays a part in the work of Olivier Messiaen (b. 1908).

A somewhat new development within the 20th century, however, has been a strong tendency on the part of some composers—particularly in the United States—to go more deeply into some of these non-European musics and to endeavor actually to work creatively in terms of them or to adopt essential assumptions that they make and then to follow out the results in terms of writing for conventional Western European musical means. This is a somewhat different matter from merely donning an exotic style in a spirit of fancy-dress masquerade. One of the early composers to address himself seriously to the task of understanding non-European musics both in a scholarly and in a creatively artistic way was Henry Cowell (1897–1965), with his *Persian Suite* (1958), *Ongaku* (1958) based on Japanese court music, and *Madras Symphony* (1959). Lou Harrison (b. 1917), Alan Hovhaness (b. 1911), and Colin McPhee (b. 1901) have each—in terms of different branches of non-European music—undertaken to do this same sort of thing. Some American composers have come to the act of writing music with distinctive non-European musical backgrounds, such as American Indian in Carlos Chavez (b. 1899),

Egyptian in Halem El-Dabh (b. 1921), and Chinese in Chou Wen-Chung (b. 1923). John Cage (b. 1912) has applied many assumptions from Zen Buddhism to the composition of music. Obviously, though the results may superficially seem to be characterized by exoticism or Orientalism, the spirit in which they have been approached by their composers is very different from that which appeared in Western music during the centuries before the 20th.

Primitivism

Still another tendency that has become particularly noticeable in 20th-century music and the other arts is sometimes referred to as primitivism. Beginning about 1910, individual composers have elaborated on impulses that emanated from so-called primitive music. What is here meant is not necessarily the music of primitive peoples directly, but in general that music which maintains its original character because it has not undergone the process of Western rationalization and differentiation in terms of tonal functions and polyphony. Striking stylistic elements of Western primitivism that appeared as a consequence of this encounter with primitive music are the stringing-together and piling-up of similar motives, rhythmic frenzy and orgy, free meters, asymmetric measures, and harmonic simplification. Siegfried Borris has distinguished five phases in this development:

1. Stile barbaro (1910–9), at the same time as Stravinsky and Bartók were concerned with elemental folk-styles.
2. Influence of jazz (1919–25).
3. Clarification of stylistic elements (1925–34).
4. Development of a Western primitivism (1934–5).
5. New encounter with jazz (1945–   ).

Probably no one can be completely happy with the word "primitivism." Particularly the West African musical practice which exists in the background of the development in America that is known as jazz is really not "primitive" in the sense of "simple" or in the sense of the "first" steps taken in music. If it is primitive harmonically, it is not primitive rhythmically. It is a music which is complicated in some ways that Western European music is not, and vice versa. The fact simply is that it makes different assumptions from Western European music and proceeds to carry them out to a point of considerable refinement.

Although jazz perpetuates some basic aspects of these assumptions, it does not exist natively in Africa but has been developed in America, and thus it is the end-result of a long process of acculturation, involving African and European elements. Two approaches to music here have come face to face with each other: one group-oriented, the other individual-oriented; one essentially auditory, the other basically intellectual; one utilitarian, the other aesthetic. In many instances the effect of this confrontation, so far as Western European music is concerned, has been simply to revive certain aspects that were characteristic of Western European music in certain periods before the 19th century. The reinstating of improvisation as a norm, or at least as an important part of music-making; the integral relationship between word and tone, according to which even instrumental technique is thought of in "speaking" terms; the balancing of the claims of melody and harmony, of the horizontal and vertical aspects of the music as it is written out; the skilful manipulation of polyrhythms—all these were normal in certain periods of Western European music before the 19th century. What the encounter with jazz has done to Western European music—according to one way of viewing the encounter—is simply to recall Western music to itself and to re-emphasize some fundamental aspects of its own essential nature.

Particularly in the United States many composers have devoted their efforts to bringing jazz and classical music into integral relationship, for example Gunther Schuller (b. 1925) with his "Third Stream" symphonic compositions and Lukas Foss (b. 1922) with his Improvisation Chamber Ensemble.

Harmonic Aspects of 20th-Century Music

Jazz with its originally simpler approach to tonal functions is but one indication that the harmonic aspects of music have been subject to many concentrated attacks and capitulations, particularly during the 20th century. To a great extent the orderly relationships provided by the major-minor system have been extended, reorganized, or abandoned.

There has been use of pentatonicism, or the five-degree scale, in-volving a succession of whole steps and minor thirds—for example, F G A C D.

Also some composers have used the whole-tone scale, constructed from a succession of equal whole steps, thus yielding six notes to the octave. With this approach there are only two possibilities: C D E F♯ G♯ A♯ or D♭ E♭ F G A B. Claude Debussy used the whole-tone scale throughout the prelude *Voiles* in the first book of his *Préludes pour le piano* (1910).

Composers have also used parallel chords. If a chord is shifted dia-tonically or chromatically up or down, the result may produce an effect of sonority or charm. Or a melody may be harmonized by chords of similar structure, as at the beginning of the second scene in Puccini's *La Bohème*.

Another indication of the breakdown of the order provided by the major-minor harmonic system—at least in the thought and practice of some composers—is the theory of the tonal center developed by Paul Hindemith. If one follows the overtone series, one can derive from C a succession of tones ("Series 1") which contains a certain natural order of rank. C is the "ancestral tone"; the C an octave higher, G, F, A, E, E♭, and A♭ are its "sons"; D, B♭, D♭, and B are its "grandsons"; and D♭ and G♭ are its "great-grandsons." From this, Hindemith inferred an "unam-biguous rank order in the relationships that exist among the tones" and an "evaluative measure for these relationships that retains its validity under all circumstances."

Many composers have used polytonality, or multiple keys, and poly-rhythms, or the simultaneous appearance of various rhythms within the same meter—this being one of the most striking features of African primitive music and of jazz. These tendencies also show the shift away from the former role of the major-minor system as the organizing device in Western music.

There has been some work with microtonal music, particularly according to a quarter-tone approach to the octave in which it is divided into twenty-four equal parts. The first experiments in this direction in recent times were undertaken by John Herbert Foulds in 1898 and Richard Stein in 1906. Alois Hába (b. 1893) was especially outstanding as a composer of quarter-tone music. The Mexican Julian Carillo, the Russian Vyshnegradsky, and the Californian Harry Partch (b. 1901) have also composed microtonal music.

Finally, the breakdown of the major-minor system has appeared in the use of bitonality and atonality. The former involves the simultaneous use of two keys. Two triads at the interval of the tritone are quite often used. An early example occurs in Stravinsky's *Petrushka* (1911) with the simultaneous and sudden juxtaposition of C major and F♯ major. Atonality is a music that is not organized according to key. The individual tones are not referable to a central tone or tonic. Historically, what is sometimes called the "period of free atonality" followed the disintegration of tonality and prevailed until tonality was replaced by twelve-tone music. The disintegration of tonality in the work of many European composers occurred around 1910; the beginning of the systematic twelve-tone epoch dates from 1923. The freely atonal compositions were mainly written during the period of German Expressionism. The principal representatives of free atonality in Germany were Arnold Schönberg with his compositions op. 11–22, Albert Berg with *Wozzeck*, written during this period, and Anton Webern. During the free atonal period, athematic compositions were also written—that is, compositions in which themes were not repeated or developed, such as Schönberg's *Erwartung*.

Twelve-Tone System (Dodecaphony)

Arnold Schönberg spoke of "composition with twelve tones related only to each other." In accordance with ideas derived from his work, the twelve-tone system involves the reorganization of the twelve half-tones within the octave, in such a way that the tonal organization is given up and the twelve half-tones of the octave are completely independent of each other and are entirely equal in significance.

From the number of twelve equal-ranking half-tones the composer chooses a series, an individual succession for a composition. This, according to Schönberg, "has to be the first creative thought." In the treatment of the series a great number of different methods have been developed. The first twelve-tone compositions come from Josef Matthias Hauer (1883–1959), who around 1918 provided also a clear theoretical exposition of the system. The first methodical twelve-tone compositions of Arnold Schönberg (1874–1951) are contained in his compositions op. 23–25, written between 1921 and 1924.

The period of "classical twelve-tone composition" began with the first formulation of the principle around 1923 and ended with Schönberg's death in 1951. The rudiments of the principle are as follows:

1. The series is to include, if possible, all the twelve tones.
2. A variety of intervals should be provided in the series.
3. Inversion is derived from the basic form of the series according to traditional contrapuntal principles, as are also the crab or backward movement and the crab of the inversion.
4. Each of the four forms can be transposed to each of the twelve steps of the octave, thus producing forty-nine possibilities.
5. Each individual tone can appear at whatever octave level is desired.
6. Immediate repetitions of a tone are permitted.
7. There are no restrictions on the rhythmic order in the succession of tones in the series.

The music of Schönberg's opera *Moses and Aaron*, of which the first two acts and some sketches for the third act were composed between 1930 and 1932, is built up exclusively on the following twelve-tone series: A, B♭, E, D, E♭, D♭, G, F, F♯, G♯, B, C. The inversion of this series is: A, G♯, D, E♭, F, B, C♯, C, B♭, G, F♯; the crab: C, B, G♯, F♯, F, G, D♭, E♭, D, E, B♭, A; and the crab of the inversion: F♯, G, B♭, C, C♯, B, F, E♭, E, D, G♯, A. On the basis of Schönberg's sketches for this opera it is clear that the series was derived from themes. With him, thematic invention was always primary.

Schönberg never conceived of his method of composition in any way other than as an organic part of the general theory of composition. After tonality had disintegrated for him as a form-producing principle of order around 1910, the twelve-tone series began to appear in 1924 as the vehicle for a new tonality in place of the old. "This new tonality," he said, "is connected, as previously the major-minor tonality was, with all other means of composition developed in Classical and pre-Classical music for composition with twelve tones." The rise of twelve-tone technique in Schönberg ensued with historical necessity, especially prepared for by the gradual and finally conclusive disintegration of tonality and the principle of constant transformation of the thematic material. The incursion of chromatic tones, opened up since Johann Sebastian Bach, led to the destruction of major-minor tonality. As early as the Franco-Flemish composers in their use of the cantus firmus technique, the idea of constant transformation had already become current. Both Mozart and Beethoven in their later works sought to avoid verbal repetitions; from the Romantic Era to Mahler there was a stronger and stronger drive toward the fusion of whole works through thematic relationships. The twelve-tone technique finally realized what Schönberg called the "unity of musical space."

In view of the great importance of Schönberg as leader in this particular development in 20th-century music, however, perhaps it should be noted that after he emigrated to the United States in 1934 he not only continued on occasion to use twelve-tone procedures but also on occasion composed tonally. Among the significant works he wrote in America, his *Kol Nidre* op. 37, Three Folk-Songs on 15th- and 16th-Century German Texts op. 49, and Variations on a Recitative for Organ op. 40 are tonal. His Violin Concerto op. 36, 4th String Quartet op. 37, and String Trio op. 54 are twelve-tone but oriented toward definite pitch areas, in a procedure falling somewhere between tonality and atonality. What has happened here is suggested by the title of an essay he wrote in 1948, "One Always Returns" (*On revient toujours*). Compositions with text, his *Ode to Napoleon* op. 41, *A Survivor of Warsaw* op. 46, and *De Profundis* op. 50b, are also basically twelve-tone, but have significant tonal implications. In other words, twelve-tone composition simply took its place as one of the possible resources along with many others that he used in his writing of music during the last seventeen years of his life. In this respect his relationship to it paralleled that of other serious composers in the United States, who tended to follow or not follow twelve-tone procedures in accordance with the particular purposes they had in mind. Also he thus exemplified his conception of "composing with twelve tones" as a matter of practice rather than as a doctrinaire system. Schönberg was different from the Schönbergians.

One of the most influential of Schönberg's pupils—and one most destined to suffer from the circumstances prevailing in Central Europe during his later years—was Anton Webern. Born February 12, 1883, in Vienna, son of a mining engineer, he grew up in Graz and Klagenfurt and in addition to his regular schooling received private instruction in piano, 'cello, and theory. An important musical experience of his youth was a trip to Bayreuth, given as a graduation present on his completing secondary school in 1902. At the University of Vienna he studied musicology under Guido Adler and completed a dissertation on Heinrich Issac's *Choralis Constantinus* in 1906. In 1908 he began his composition lessons with Arnold Schönberg in Vienna and—except for interruption while in military service during 1915 and 1916—continued until 1920. He coached and conducted in theaters at Bad Ischl, Vienna, Teplitz, Danzig, Stettin, and Prague. By 1920 he was back in Vienna as director and teacher, conducting the Vienna Schubert Society till 1922, the Mölding Men's Chorus till 1926, and the Viennese Workers' orchestra and chorus. In 1927 he became regular conductor for the Austrian radio, directing his own and other composers' works locally and in Switzerland, England, Spain, and Germany. In Vienna he won municipal music prizes in 1924 and 1932. But as a result of Nazi pressures from 1935 on, he withdrew from public activity and experienced increasingly straitened circumstances, giving private lessons and turning more and more to composition, completing his last seven opuses. At Easter 1945, to avoid the advancing Soviet forces, he withdrew to Mittersill near Salzburg but was shot by an American soldier of the occupation army.

Between 1908 and 1945 he wrote a total of 41 works, occupying about three hours in actual performance and now recorded in a single album under the direction of Robert Craft. These compositions display the utmost concentration. It has been said that Webern never repeated himself and never restated anything in a way similar or related to what he had stated before. Like Schönberg, he began tonally in his Passacaglia for Orchestra op. 1, moved on to free atonality in his Five Stefan George Songs op. 3, and adopted the twelve-tone technique in his Three Folk-Texts op. 17. But in his String Trio op. 20 and his Symphony op. 21 he made a very significant departure from the road Schönberg had been taking. While Schönberg always worked in terms of themes, Webern began to focus his attention on intervals, being concerned with intervallic rather than thematic structures. Thus, instead of linking theme with theme, he began relating tone to tone.

Of the thirty-one compositions printed during his lifetime, seventeen are vocal. For him, musical utterance was a matter of deeply responsible awareness. He expressed the matter thus: "It is like Goethe's idea of the original plant, in which the root is really nothing but the stem, and the stem no different from the flower: all variations on the same thought. . . . Wherever we cut into the piece the course of the series (*der Ablauf der Reihe*) must always be determinable."

New awareness of Webern's work began in 1953 under the leadership of Herbert Eimert and spread to the younger generation, led by Stockhausen, Boulez, and Nono. Stravinsky followed in 1955 without reservations. Especially from Webern's op. 20 on, there are many links between his work and the immediate present.

Serial Composition

A conception of music that has had much influence in the 20th century is serial composition. Serial music presupposes serial thinking, which attempts to mediate between whatever extremes may exist. In so doing, serial composers set up at least two intermediate stages between the two extremes. They may establish the transition between the extremes as either continuous or discontinuous. If continuous, it will appear as a *glissando,* as a completely transitionless change. If discontinuous, it will appear as a scale with the same distance between the degrees, as in the chromatic scale on the piano. If in a scale of equidistant degrees the succession of the scale steps is interchanged and brought into a new order, the result is a series or row (*Serie* or *Reihe.*)

Thus there is a characteristic drive to mediate, to transcend the antithesis, the dualism from which Classical form arose. Serial composers have established as the organizing principle in their works the idea of mediation, of setting up a scale between extremes and then forming a series with definite proportions by which one moves from one extreme to the other. They then observe these proportions strictly throughout the work and derive from them its character, its structure.

Universal mediation is the first basic thought; the second is that of equal recognition. Everything that belongs in a composition and that gives it form is brought under the law of equally recognized participation in the form.

In "special serial form," each individual formal area that is to be organized in the composition has to have its own special regulations or laws of order. Formal areas in this sense are the parameters of pitch, volume, rhythm, tone-color, and tonal placement. In "general serial form," on the other hand, all parameters are organized by one and the same law, by one single proportional series.

The American mathematician and composer Milton Babbitt (b. 1916) has been credited with being the first composer to work specifically and intensively with the aim of establishing "general serial form" or of "serializing everything" in the composition. His "Three Compositions for Piano" (1947) and—more thoroughly—his "Composition for Twelve Instruments" (1948) carry out the idea systematically. Since 1938 he had been teaching mathematics at Princeton and studying music there with Roger Sessions (b. 1896), to whom some of the background of this development must also be credited. In addition, there is a close tie-up between it and the use of electronic means of music-making: Sessions, Babbitt, Otto Luening (b. 1900), and Vladimir Ussachevsky (b. 1913) have since the 1950's been co-directors of the Columbia-Princeton Universities Electronic Music Center in New York City. Another personality in the background of this development is Edgar Varèse (1885–1965), who emigrated from France to the United States in 1915 and who began working during the 1920's with agglomerates of sonorities and densities, opening up all possible aural sensations for use as raw material for composition, embodied in such works as *Offrandes* (1921), *Amériques* (1922), *Hyperprism* (1922), *Octandre* (1924), *Intégrales* (1924), *Arcana* (1927), and *Ionisation* (1933)—works that have also contributed to the flourishing of percussion music in America during recent decades. Steps taken by Varèse and Sessions in their compositions have helped make serial composition and *musique concrète*, in the period since World War II, not only possible but also necessary, in a way that Babbitt seems to have been the first actually to realize.

The word *punktuelle* or "pointillist" is often applied to certain serial compositions, beginning—as far as the European developments of the movement are concerned—with Olivier Messiaen's piano etude *Mode de valeurs et d'intensités,* composed in 1949. The impression that the composition was a matter of points was gained from a general reaction to hearing it, with its individual tones forming a mosaic of sound, the level of each individual tone being fixed in pitch, duration, volume, and attack at the piano. In practice, there are no larger formal variants in music of this kind, no differences in shape that have been worked out in composition. All traditional criteria of musical relationship seem to have been eliminated.

Another term often applied in serial composition refers to groups of notes as the basis, "group composition." The next step taken after the formulation of "pointillist" composition was that the next-higher formal unit, groups, were formed from the isolated individual tones. Several tones were comprehended through characteristic properties of a higher order, and the law of the series was used not only for the peculiarities of the individual tones but also for the mutual relations between the groups. These can again be defined by a generally applied proportional series. Groups can be quantitatively differentiated, for example by the number of their tones, by their measured length, and the like. The number and the duration remain typical for a group; other peculiarities can be varied. Thus all the properties that were previously used for differentiation among the individual tones are now also applied to the differentiation of the groups.

At the other extreme from the distinctness of points of sound characteristic of "pointillist" form, there exists what is known as "statistical" form. If a certain limit of perception is overstepped in one parameter, several individual elements recombine into a conglomerate. The ear grasps the complex as something unresolvable, and the eye discovers relationships in the score. In such a situation, analysis should proceed not from the separate tone, but from the higher order of impression. By using statistical analysis one undertakes to grasp the essential part of it. Statistical form is a structure that is condensed into the complex. Therein a certain permutability of the tones in the succession plays a role; a tone may be exchanged with the neighboring tone without anything essential having been changed.

There are six criteria of statistical form: density, pitch levels, speed, fields of volume, tone color, and preponderance of a certain interval or group of intervals. With regard to the first of these criteria, density, the degree of density and the change in density may be regulated, as well as the change in pitch levels. So far as pitch levels are concerned, there are three basic forms that direction of movement can take: rising, constant, and falling. Similarly, with speed there are three basic forms: increasing, constant, and diminishing.

In addition to form deriving from the perception of definite points and from a statistical approach, there is also what is called "variable form." Statistical form has shown that within the context of a given set of elements there can appear a certain variability. It can be expressed as permutability of elements in certain densities, and it can be expressed in distinct realizations—for example, in the directions given on the score to the effect that a group of notes is to be played "as rapidly as possible." Thus there arise distinct playing areas, areas of variability, which are designated by composers as such. This is in sharp contrast to the situation that prevailed in earlier music, which is constantly subject to unlimited "interpretation" by performers. In *Klavierstück XI* by Karlheinz Stockhausen individual groups are interpreted in different ways.

There are also, in serial composition, possibilities of what are often referred to as "ambiguous form." All considerations that present themselves in the course of a context are so set down that many different solutions, of equal validity, are possible. The player's decision on which "version" he is choosing for the performance is incorporated into the composition. In *Zyklus für einen Schlagzeuger* Stockhausen uses nine different degrees of ambiguity.

Finally, there is what is often called "moment" form. A *moment* (which, as the word arises from German usage, has a meaning that lies somewhere between that of English "moment" and "momentum") is any formal unit recognizable by its own characteristic, which is noninterchangeable. A *moment*-group consists of several successive moments which are related to each other in one or more features but yet are not so closely related as to make their own characteristic questionable.

Moment forms (also referred to as present forms or endless forms, in view of their duration) are—*qua* forms—works with "endless duration."

Karlheinz Stockhausen has taken the most consistent road so far, starting from "pointillist" composition. He not only has fixed the new formal concepts in artistically significant works for the first time but also has been aware of these concepts theoretically and has undergirded them systematically. Born August 22, 1928, in Mödrath near Cologne, Stockhausen studied music education, piano, and composition at the Cologne Conservatory and Germanic philology and philosophy at the University. In 1951 he passed his state examination with distinction. He had begun to study composition with Frank Martin in 1950. In 1952 Stockhausen went to Paris and lived at the Cité Universitaire. He was strongly impressed by Messiaen's aproach to music. Contacts with other French musicians put him in touch with the Studio for Musique Concerète, where he began to experiment with synthetic sound-production on an electronic basis. After returning to Cologne in 1953 he was a regular participant in the activities of the Studio for Electronic Music of the West German Radio. He also traveled widely in Europe and America on lecture and concert trips.

If Messiaen had broken up the traditional concept of the theme, Stockhausen and some of his young colleagues tried to put the parts back together in a new way. Thus their aim was one of synthesis. Musical pointillism, or *punktuelle Musik,* had resulted from a process of analysis. The higher unity that was thus brought to bear on it was the "group" concept, or composition in terms of groups (*Gruppen*). Between 1955 and 1957 Stockhausen wrote two very important instrumental compositions in which this new idea is carried out: *Zeitmasse für fünf Holzbläser* and *Gruppen für drei Orchester.*

A further epoch-making step into new musical territory was the reorganization of the concept of time in music. The traditional idea of meter and rhythm, related to the bar-line and ultimately the human pulse, was abandoned. One factor leading to this was the availability of electronic means. Another was contained in the playing of the instruments themselves. As early as 1954, in *Klavierstück VI,* the intrinsic times of the sounds themselves—in place of clock or counting time—were introduced into the composition. Further steps along the same line were taken in *Zeitmasse* (1955–6). The intrinsic time of a sound is like and unlike a chord written with a fermata. The length of time the performer holds the chord is not left up to his feelings, nor is it determined by some value derived from the meter; instead, he is to proceed to the next chord only when the given chord has finished sounding.

Parallel to this reorganization of material is a completely new relationship between music and language. Heretofore, language as united with music has been thought of as communication, propositional statement, and conveyance of semantic meaning. But Stockhausen's work has moved in another direction. He has undertaken to remove precisely this character from the human voice when he has utilized it. He has spoken of removing the dualism between instrumental and vocal music. After his first attempt in *Gesang der Jünglinge,* he pressed on further in the *Carré für vier Orchester und Chöre.* He united singing voices and instruments in a uniform mixed sonority. The text, set to music from a purely musical point of view, manifests a whole gamut of most various differentiations in sound, ranging from voiceless consonants to vowels. A further stage in this new order in the relationship between music and language appears in the *Momente für Sopran, vier Chorgruppen und dreizehn Instrumentalisten.* Here the principle of ambiguity occupies a foreground position. Fragments of sound, scraps of words, and phrases are bound together in a most skillful way; and in principle the formal order is oriented toward *Momentform,* as a way of synthesizing the whole. In *Momentform* there are a number of individual sections, which may be played in any order one wishes or also may partly be omitted. In the treatment of language something occurs here that has its precedent in "Dadaism" or the completely new organization of language effected by James Joyce in *Finnegan's Wake.* More recent works, like the *Mikrophonie II* and the *Hymnen* show that Stockhausen is still pursuing the same course.

The following are the titles of his works: *Kreuzspiel* (1951), *Spiel* (1952), Percussion Quartet (1952), *Punkte* (1952, 1962), *Kontrapunkte* (1952–3), *Klavierstücke I–IV* (1952–3), *V–XI* (1954–61), *Zeitmasse* (1955–6), *Gruppen* (1955–7), *Gesang der Jünglinge* (1955), *Zyklus* (1959), *Carré* (1959–60), *Refrain* (1959), *Kontakte* (1959–60), *Originale* (1961), *Momente* (1962–4, 1965), *Punkte* (1952–62), *Plus/Minus* (1963), *Mikrophonie I* (1964), *II* (1965), *Mixtur* (1964, 1967), *Stop* (1965), *Solo* (1965–6), *Telemusik* (1966), *Adieu for Wolfgang Sebastian Meyer* (1966), *Hymnen* (1967), *Prozession* (1967), *Stimmung* (1968), *Kurzwellen* (1968), *Aus der sieben Tagen* (1968).

Statements anticipatory of the serial principle are to be found here and there in the late works of Anton Webern. The first model example for polydimensional serial organization in European music was given by Olivier Messiaen in the second number, *Mode de valeurs et d'intensités,* of his *Quatre Études de Rhythme* for piano (1949). Here there are at times pronounced sequences of tones (pitch), of time values (duration), of intensities (volume), and of touch (attack) that have been modally established. *Structures I* for two pianos (first performed in Paris in 1952) by Pierre Boulez (b. 1925) epitomizes the serial principle. Luigi Nono (b. 1924) first successfully brought the sung word into serial organization and treated it in accordance with tone colors in his *Canto sospeso* (first performed in Cologne in 1956).

Composers who have especially concerned themselves with serial music have contributed many novel features to contemporary composition. They have extensively and sometimes completely abandoned the traditional concepts of motive and theme, of the metrically organized and thus previously calculable expiration of time. Also they have abandoned every traditional harmonic aspect, both functional harmony and— to a great extent and often entirely—any tensional harmony. Having annulled the oppositions between instrumental and vocal music, they have incorporated space into their compositions functionally and have exploited new electronic sources of sound. With awareness of the implications of what they were doing they have extended a centrifugal formal tendency both as formal idea and as formal power. They have abandoned any relationship involving dramatic tension in the music, particularly in the 19th-century sense of the term "dramatic." Space and time have thus been combined and unified, the dimensions of the result being in the nature of space-time. Time thus has been established irreversibly, and its expiration is not previously determinable. Also there are no repetitions, for these exist only in finite time. In vocal compositions, the word has no longer primarily an informational character. Either it is absorbed into the musical whole, which is more important than the meaning of the text, or there is complete renunciation of any informational value in the language whatsoever, though the word may still be used in a prelogical, intuitive way or as a sort of instrumental sound.

If the present writer may be permitted a somewhat subjective interpretation of this music in terms of its content, he would begin by pointing out that composers active in developing serial composition have consistently carried through the principle of unrepeatability, of absolute uniqueness, of eternal change. They have succeeded in pinning down and fixing definitely some phenomena that are instantaneous and that—rationalized in terms of art—thus reflect the principle of that which has been organized. There is perhaps a relationship between this and the "interior monologue" or "stream of consciousness" in literature, which was notably exploited by James Joyce. Serial composers renounce every feature that might be associated with folklore, every imitation of naturalistic sounds that come from the outside world. Their work involves a dimension that is not otherwise physically utterable—which some people regard as the true world of artistic experience. They give us no poetic pictures, no dramatic course of action, for the course of action taken by serial music is not determined. The result is a music without the character of finality, without dialectic and dramatic situations. Instead it is quite personal and individual experience of the human situation, an artistic reflection of man today and of a new picture of the world. The language is polydimensional, with complex musical constellations always reaching into and over one another, inviting the listener to an act of audition in nonperspectived space. Thus the new image of the world reaches out beyond what is immediately compassable by the senses.

Among those who have notably developed this approach to music are Pierre Boulez (b. 1925) and Karlheinz Stockhausen (b. 1928). Also John Cage (b. 1912) has been especially significant as an instigator. A California pupil of Schönberg and of other teachers, Cage has been an influential figure among *avant-garde* composers since the 1940's. Starting from compositions for what he called the "prepared piano"—that is, a piano to which objects have been added to emphasize its percussive possibilities, he has also written significant pieces for percussion ensemble. In his compositions and in his essays—notably contained in a volume entitled *Silence* (1961)—he has stressed the essential importance of the relationship between sound and silence in music. He has also given considerable place in his practice to what he calls "aleatory composition," which means the incorporation of chance factors into the conception of the piece. Some of his works also bring in tape-recorded material and offer the performers specified alternatives. A good deal of his thinking about music and other matters proceeds from assumptions formulated in Zen Buddhism. Three composers closely associated with Cage are Morton Feldman (b. 1926), Earle Brown (b. 1926), and Christian Wolff (b. 1934).

A considerable number of European composers have also been active in the development of serial composition: Witold Lutoslawski (b. 1913), Bruno Maderna (b. 1920), Yanis Xenakis (b. 1922), Jacques Wildberger (b. 1922), Kazimierz Serocki (b. 1922), Ton de Leeuw (b. 1924), Luigi Nono (b. 1924), Giselher Klebe (b. 1925), Luciano Berio (b. 1925), Bengt Hambraeus (b. 1928), Tadeusz Baird (b. 1928), Henri Pousseur (b. 1929), Sylvano Bussotti (b. 1931), Mauricio Kagel (b. 1931), Niccolo Castiglioni (b. 1932), Krzysztof Penderecki (b. 1933), Peter Schat (b. 1935), and Bo Nilsson (b. 1937). Each of these composers stands in some way or other within the field of force of dodecaphonic or serial music.

In the United States the part played by twelve-tone and serial developments is a little different from that on the Continent. The United States is more extended, with a number of places within it where significant composition and performance may occur; and the feeling of personal discipleship or partisanship seems not so strong there. Thus twelve-tone and serial techniques have tended to become simply one among several means that an American composer is likely to use. One can find twelve-tone or serial aspects or movements or whole compositions in the works of Wallingford Riegger (1885–1961), Roger Sessions (b. 1891), Aaron Copland (b. 1900), Ross Lee Finney (b. 1906), Samuel Barber (b. 1910), George Perle (b. 1915), Ben Weber (b. 1916), George Rochberg (b. 1918), Mel Powell (b. 1923), Salvatore Martirano (b. 1927), and many others. To take one example of an American composer who might be regarded as a Schönbergian, Adolf Weiss, born in Baltimore in 1891, was a member of Schönberg's master class in Berlin and after returning to America wrote several twelve-tone works, but he has also written an orchestral piece in quartal harmony and some violin pieces based on Japanese court music. Similar cases could be cited from among the American pupils of Schönberg in California after his emigration in the 1930's— such composers, for instance, as John Cage (b. 1912), Leon Kirchner (b. 1919), and George Tremblay (b. 1911). Of course, there have been European composers originally of more or less Schönbergian persuasion who have also emigrated—Ernst Krenek (b. 1900), Stefan Wolpe (b. 1902), Lukas Foss (b. 1922)—but they have tended to move on in their musical development, as Schönberg and Stravinsky themselves did.

Another distinctive feature of the American situation is that considerable innovation has been undertaken there right from the beginning of the present century. It seems almost as if the drive to conformity, which had been so strong among the composers in the United States during the latter third of the 19th century, now had elicited its antithesis. Charles Ives (1874–1954), for example, was composing atonally—though proceeding on his own way rather than with any sense of leading a group or movement. By the 1920's George Antheil (1900–1959) was getting his atonal and athematic "musical abstractions" performed in Europe, Henry Cowell (1894–1968) was using "tone clusters," and Charles Ruggles (b. 1886) was limiting himself to not repeating notes within the melodic line. A string quartet brought out in 1931 by Ruth Crawford Seeger (1901–1953) is essentially serial, and—as already noted—Milton Babbitt was developing theoretical and practical aspects of this approach by the 1940's. Thus, when American composers encountered the work of Schönberg, Messiaen, and others, they often found it fitting in with aspects of composition that they were rather familiar with before and tended to give it a place within a total picture of 20th-century composition. Some of the Continental innovations did not create quite the degree of upset in America that they did in Europe.

New Sources of Sound

A development often related to this move to innovate—and, certainly, in the case of Babbitt quite closely connected with it—is a move to open up to potential music-making new sources of sound, other than the conventional instruments. Since times so ancient as to defy precise dating, the human spirit has labored at the instrumental resources of music. These efforts have been prompted by the impulse of the human spirit to play, its power of invention and craftsmanship, the magical realms of its imagination, and its practical drive to put things to use with what is given by the material itself. Different components have joined in helping create a powerful host of instruments. They may be separated into basically two groups, one—the larger group—in which man is the player, the driving force, and the other—the smaller group—in which man withdraws after he has intellectually achieved the propelling force, to let the outcome take place mechanically.

There have been mechanical instruments of music since the Renaissance, such as the "flute-clock," a miniature organ consisting of mechanical tracker, bellows, and pipes, in which clockwork turns a cylinder and by means of driven pegs and clamps opens the valves of the pipes. Many composers in the 17th and 18th centuries wrote for mechanical musical instruments—among others, Hans Leo Hassler, Handel, Carl Philipp Emanuel and Wilhelm Friedemann Bach, Haydn, Mozart, and Beethoven. In the 19th century and at the beginning of the 20th, the orchestrion was constructed in imitation of orchestral instruments; and there were also substitute forms of the piano that operated on pneumatic principles.

At the beginning of the 20th century a pioneering step was taken with the Welte-Mignon player pianos and the automatic "Welte Philharmonie." The playing of great composers was taken down on rolls, so that from the period before 1914—for the first time in human history—documents of solo interpretation became available in actual sound. Not only is this a precious part of the record for the so-called standard repertoire, but player-piano rolls have also recorded for us an early era of jazz playing, so-called ragtime, which otherwise would have been known to us only through second-hand reports, like much of the music of antiquity.

What was achieved up to the beginning of the 20th century in the field of mechanical musical instruments was child's play on the periphery of music, as compared with what came after World War I. In the 1920's there occurred a vehement incursion of technics into music through the discovery and full use of sound-transcription systems. Thus man was able to overcome the spatial and temporal barriers that heretofore had seemed unalterable, for up to this time players and listeners had to come together to serve the cause of music. Telephone and radio conquered spatial distances. Phonograph record and tape made it possible to repeat performances at will. We have come to take for granted these technical resources, as adjuncts to our lives.

New possibilities have been opened up by mechanico-electric and electronic instruments. In the former, mechanical and electric means serve in the formation of the sound. For example, in string instruments the resonating bodies may be replaced by an electro-acoustical tone reflector. The principle has led to the construction of many instruments, from the electrically reinforced guitar to the Neo-Bechstein grand, Thienhaus's electromagnetically strengthened harpsichord, and Vierling's Elektrochord. In electronic instruments, on the other hand, the electron tube is the starting point and the raw material. As electricity goes through a vacuum, vibrations are set up and appear in the loudspeaker as sound.

Two ways have appeared for using completely new electronic means. They may be employed merely to extend the previous sonorities and the instrumental resources with the aim of giving the new instruments a place in the domain of our existing music—as, for example, in the Trautonium, Ondes Martenot, Polychord organ, and its related type the Bode organ, Melochord, and Klavoline with keyboard accompaniment. Or the new electronic possibilities may be used to open up a completely new world of sound.

In detail, electronic instruments have so far served in at least five different recognizable areas, which represent gradations between these two extremes:

1. They have imitated the sound of conventional instruments, as for example in electronic church organs and chimes as substitutes for the traditional instruments.
2. They have collaborated as unique and individual sounding bodies in connection with the traditional instruments, such as the Ondes Martenot solo in Olivier Messiaen's *Turanglalia* or the concerto for trautonium and orchestra by Harald Genzmer.
3. They have been used soloistically without the traditional instrumentation, particularly in concert or mood-music, as background aids in radio, theater, and films, and for various "sound-effects."
4. A number of electronic instruments have been brought together to form an ensemble, as in Edgar Varèse's *Equatorial for two Theremin Instruments* (1934) and Olivier Messiaen's *Fêtes des belles eaux* for six Ondes Martenot (1937).
5. There has been some autonomous use of electronic instruments in so-called electronic music, such as that from the studio of the West German radio at Cologne or the studios of various radio stations in Europe and America or sponsored by various universities, particularly in the United States.

In considering the history of electronic music, one must distinguish between the history of the idea and the history of the apparatus, the discovery, and the practical realization of it. The idea appeared for the first time when composers felt the traditional means of sound production no longer adequate for their artistic ideas and began to take an interest in possibilities that technics had made available. Perhaps Ferruccio Busoni (1866–1924) was the first to reveal his openness to this possibility when he encountered the dynamophone of Thaddeus Cahill, one of the first discoveries in the field of electrical tone production (1906). Arnold Schönberg spoke of a music of tone color in 1911. Not until the beginning of the 1920's did the technical experiments get into full swing: the German discoverer Jörg Mager (b. 1880) with his *sphärophon*, the Russian physicist and musician Leo Theremin (b. 1896) with his *ätherophon*, Maurice Martenot with his *ondes*, and Friedrich Trautwein with his *trautonium*. First results of the experiments in the Cologne studio were made the subject of public discussion in 1951 at the International Vacation Courses for New Music in Darmstadt-Kranichstein. The first electronic compositions developed there were by Robert Bayer and Herbert Eimert.

Musique concrète, as a specific development, came from Pierre Schaeffer in Paris about 1948. It was not electronic music, but the transformation of natural sounds and noises through a sound-montage by means of magnetic tape.

"Computer music" is a recent development, related to the use of electronic means—here used as an adjunct to the process of composition. Obviously, computers can be of service in analyzing music that has been made. But what is envisioned by some users of the computer is not simply *ex post facto* analysis or simulation of familiar music. Rather they are attempting to synthesize a basically new music, in which the assumptions are consciously chosen and carried out with perfect consistency and in complete detail. There are a number of university programs aimed in this direction, notably one in New York at the Columbia-Princeton Center and one at the University of Illinois; and compositions, recordings, and discussions on the subject have been issued.

Terms Often Used in Discussions of 20th-Century Music

A number of specifically 20th-century developments, primarily in Central Europe, have focused around certain familiar phrases that are often encountered in discussions of the music of this period. The term *Gebrauchsmusik* (music for use), in connection with the related term *Gebrauchsoper*, was first used in an article in the music journal *Die Signale* for December 1918. To *Gebrauchsmusik* belong all works of contemporary composers that have as their aim and value the service of practical purposes, for example instructional works, exercises, background film music, and school operas. A great part of the musical literature that in the 1920's was comprehended under the term *Gebrauchsmusik* is today called *Sing- und Spielmusik* (music for singing and playing), which for a while was also designated as *Gemeinschaftsmusik* (group music).

Another phrase, "Late Romantic," is a blanket term for the late music of Wagner, Bruckner, Richard Strauss, and Mahler; thus it covers approximately the period from 1860 to 1914. The epoch is often called also the "Post Romantic" era—that is, the period following upon the "historical Romantic" one. It is characterized by a predominance of "expression." Frequently the composer undertakes to convey extra-musical and often religious or philosophical ideas through his music. In general, the development of Late Romantic music has been marked by increasing refinement and exaggeration of psychological characterization and symbolic interpretation. As far as the harmony is concerned, "Late Romantic" work reveals a preference for chromaticism achieved by so-called altered chords, enharmonic change, relationship of thirds, and enlargement of the orchestra. The fondness for some of these features became especially evident after *Tristan* (Munich 1865).

Impressionism

Still another term is "Impressionism," a word which appeared first in 1847 in connection with painting in France. Its transfer to music is justi-fied by the influence of Impressionist painting on Claude Debussy. Through his works from about 1890 on, he was the founder and most significant representative of Impressionistic music. Usually associating a program in the form of a title with his work, he sketched tone-pictures, which—as highly refined depictions of mood—suggest an impression, a pictorial aspect. Favorite objects of this mood-painting are nature, man in relationship to nature, and man himself. Impressionist composers sometimes use the whole-tone scale, pentatonicism, and church modes. Harmonically, their work often includes chords of the ninth, of the eleventh, of the thirteenth (usually without root). Chords are often left unresolved, or they may be shifted up or down with the component notes moving in parallel motion from chord to chord. Melodically, there is often influence from Gregorian chant. Rhythm often veils the center of gravity, and the sonorities are highly refined. Impressionism is a remarkable manifestation of the Roman and French manner. It also involves influ-ences from Oriental music, particularly from Javanese music.

Sometimes the word "Impressionism" appears with the prefix "Pseudo-." The "Debussy style" became, particularly between 1905 and 1920, a world-style. As the typically Impressionistic traits, however, were coarsened, they were sometimes spoken of as Pseudo-Impressionism. It was, especially during the years before and shortly after World War I, represented in individual works by a number of composers in different countries: in Spain by Manuel de Falla (1876–1946), in Italy by Ottorino Respighi (1879–1936), in Germany by Franz Schreker (1878–1934), in Poland by Karol Szymanowski (1883–1937), in England by Frederick Delius (1862–1934), and in the United States by Charles Martin Loeffler (1861–1935) and Charles Griffes (1884–1920). It also appears in Max Reger's *Four Tone Poems after Arnold Böcklin* (op. 128).

Among the lesser, but definite, movements in the 20th century is Futurism, which had its beginnings in a proclamation made by the Italian poet F. T. Marinetti in 1909 in the Parisian periodical *Figaro*. It called for a complete break-up of all traditional forms in favor of a new music-to-be. In the "Futurist Manifesto" of 1913 the Italian Luigi Rossolo developed the idea of *Geräuschmusik* (noise music). Also a lesser movement that appeared early in the century is Dadaism. This is an artistic tendency that manifested itself in 1916 in Switzerland and goes back to Tristan Tzara. Though it was without much influence on musical style, it is often referred to in discussions of 20th-century trends.

Vitalism, a direct, unreflective assertion of life, youthful and optimistic realism, was a characteristic phase of contemporary music from 1934 to 1945.

Expressionism

The word "Expressionism" occurred first in French in the catalogue of the *Salon des Indépendants* (Paris 1901). The painter Julien August Hervé so denominated his "Studies in Expression after Nature." These were academic and realistic, and from the present-day point of view scarcely Expressionistic at all. The term "Expressionists" appeared for the first time in April 1911 in the Preface to the 22nd Exhibition of the Berliner Sezession as a collective name for the "young Frenchmen" (Braque, Derain, Picasso, Dufy, and so on). Proceeding on from here the concept found general favor in critical writing about literature in 1912 and at the same time also in writing about music.

In the narrower sense, Expressionism in music refers to a definite movement of the 20th century. Early Expressionism extended from the beginning of the century, with Schönberg's *Pelleas and Melisande*, op. 5, Scriabin's Fourth Sonata, and works by Charles Ives; High Expressionism, from 1907–8 with works by Schönberg, Webern, Berg, Scriabin, Ives, Busoni, and Bartók; and Late Expressionism, with Scriabin around 1914, Schönberg around 1923, Bartók around 1924, and Carl Ruggles and Roger Sessions in the 1920's. As aspects of this movement in music at this period, tonality was vastly expanded or completely abandoned; traditional forms were explosively demolished, and there seemed to be great emphasis on the isolated egocentricity of man. There was also an attempt to regain and mobilize new collective powers with the beginning of a new time-space experience in music. Fundamental to some of the thinking about time here involved is the distinction explored philosophically by Henri Bergson, who distinguished between *temps escapé* and *temps durée*—that is, the time of being and the time of experience; absolute time and relative time; the one available and manipulable, the other unavailable and therefore irreversible.

The concepts underlying Expressionism were extended in music, leading to some fundamental rethinking of what is involved in the musical process. There is no music without meaning, and there is no music without *Ausdruck* or expression of some kind. Expressionistic music is music of subjective significance raised to a high degree; it is an extremely subjective, ego-centered art. It is avowal of the ego even where it appears for a collective group, as in the singing of shamans among primitive peoples. Expressionistic music is thus a special case in the history of music—a special case not as result or offshoot in the history of late cultures but a particular case, an exceptional case, a special direction present since the very beginnings of music. By its character it always falls outside the framework, it always raises itself above all that is around and about it. The ego-experience can be subjective, thus I-related; or it can be objective, in that it represents something that stands outside the ego but is reflected in a completely subjective way. Precisely this ego-related particularity, as reflection, differentiates Expressionistic music from realistic or naturalistic music.

Thus, within the general framework of Expressionism, there can be music that is primarily a personal representation of the ego, with fundamentally subjective meaning. With the subjectifying of expression, music is the language of individual feeling. The composer in his work or his play, insofar as he improvises, expresses himself. He communicates himself; in the composition he sets down his subjective feeling; he makes known his emotions, his affects, the agitations of his inner life. As Goethe expressed it, a god gave it to him to say what he suffers. His music is entirely personal expression.

Also, within the Expressionistic framework the unemotional can make its appearance, and the content of the meaning can be objective. Music is thus more or less able to represent processes of movement, material objects, and intellectual ideas. Processes of movement are depicted in music, hence the familiar idea of painting with tones, or "tone-painting." Material objects taken from the real world are only indirectly translatable into the idiom of musical meaning. The world of the abstract is to be made musically audible only by way of intellectual interpretation and disclosure.

It is no doubt correct to characterize the predominant tendencies that have so far appeared since the middle of the 20th century as derived from Expressionistic assumptions. Distinctive features of serious new music in the United States since 1950, for example, represent a reaction against the trends of the 1930's and '40's towards social conformity, when many composers were primarily concerned with simplifying extremely what they had to say in order to reach as broad a public as possible with their message, whatever it happened to be. With some composers it was a neo-nationalistic message, with others it was a message of social reform, with still others it was simply a message of the desirability of belonging to the group of listeners to the particular piece. One thinks, for instance, of the ballet and film scores by Aaron Copland (b. 1900) during the '30's and '40's, in contrast to the somewhat less group-oriented appeal of his earlier work and in contrast to his tendencies to dodecaphonic and serial composition in his later work. In full contrast, today, such a composer as Lukas Foss (b. 1922) is carrying out Expressionistic aims, giving place in his compositions for the performers to make choices and express themselves also. John Cage (b. 1912) has given large scope to whim and chance—which is an extension of the Expressionistic idea. The conception of music in spatial terms, as we find it in the work of Henry Brandt (b. 1913), Ralph Shapey (b. 1921), and Roger Reynolds (b. 1934), is more in the Expressionist than the Impressionist line of descent—more in the Ives than the Griffes tradition.

In the beginnings of man's becoming man, music arose from the magic relationship of man to his surrounding world. Music as the raising of spirits, as a means of magic, is of an expressionistic nature. It is an ego-stressed original sound, born of anxiety and defence. Expressionistic music has therefore existed since the early history of mankind and presumably still does in all places, among all peoples, and in all cultures. Expressionistic music of today, of the 20th century, is therefore not to be viewed as an isolated phenomenon; it stands rather in relationship to the past. This historical relation is, however, not continuous; therein lies its peculiarity. Expressionistic music today is not a member, the present is not the latest part of an unbroken chain in which the means of speech have continued from generation to generation, from epoch to epoch. An uninterrupted historical connection does not exist. Seemingly without obeying a law of periodicity, its appearance comes as an explosive outburst in individual periods, with individual personalities, and even among these often only in individual works or sections of individual works. In a manner of speaking, we can say that expressionistic music is created anew from instance to instance. Direct historical connections are rare. A history of expressionism in music is primarily a presentation of outstanding points.

In the course of its history music has gone through the establishment of relationships of a double nature: as change of the means for expression and as change of expression itself.

Judgments passed on works of art are reactions to artistic impressions. Expressionism in the history of music cannot be really clarified or measured by reference to the other expressionistic music being written at the same time. Historical relativism is in danger of obscuring judgment. A history of music, generally represented as a history of its meaning, specifically as a history of expressionism, calls necessarily for its being treated from a double perspective—from the way things appeared to people of the time and the way they do now.

Though recognizing that some of the terms for movements and developments that have been discussed are often met with in accounts of Continental European composition during the 20th century, one must inevitably feel that they fall short of adequately giving an idea of what has happened or is happening among composers in the United States during the present century. Musical life in the United States does not focus around some one city that is at once the political, business, and cultural center of the country, nor around some one central conservatory or set of musical institutions that bring the situation into the same kind of intense focus and engender the same kind of discipleship and partisanship as in Europe. Nevertheless there is a great deal of musical activity. More people in the United States are said to go to concerts than to baseball games, and almost three-fourths of the some two thousand symphony orchestras in the world are said to be in the United States—not to mention myriads of other instrumental and choral groups.

Since mid-century there have been three active sectors of American music: jazz, experimental, and classical.

In jazz since World War II there has been a reduction in the size of the large orchestras with completely written-out arrangements that characterized the "swing" era of the '30's and '40's—much as in Europe after World War I groups performing "serious music" tended to become smaller and more agile. So-called progressive jazz has marked a return to smaller ensembles, renewed interest in improvisation, and a generally more "hot" type of music.

In experimental music—serial, electronic, and aleatory—there has been much activity in the United States, particularly within the framework of the universities. Much of it has perhaps not been intended to be listened to and belongs more in the region of pure research—serving its purpose if it reasserts the importance of an abstract and intellectually unexceptionable basis for music. The ultimate implications of much of this remains yet to be seen—though, to judge from the actuality of the atomic bomb and the moon landing, one is not justified in dismissing the possibility of its having *some* implications and consequences, even if they are not immediately apparent to the outsider.

Among the composers who have connected with the quite large American musical public, somewhat eclectic and conservative tendencies prevail. Aaron Copland, Roy Harris, William Schuman, Samuel Barber, David Diamond, Leonard Bernstein, Vincent Persichetti, Alan Hovhaness, Norman Dello Joio, Peter Mennin, and Ned Rorem stand out among the many American-born composers of the present century.

Perhaps the most distinctive work by American composers has been done in music for the theater or for quasi-theatrical presentation—ballet, opera, films, television, and the like. If one were pressed to name a single composer whose work is much performed and has a good chance of remaining in the repertoire, one might perhaps single out Gian-Carlo Menotti (b. 1911). Born in Milan, he came to the United States at the age of seventeen for further musical study—thus reversing the pattern previously usual. His *Amalia Goes to the Ball* was produced at the Metropolitan Opera House in 1938, and since then he has composed several operas for the theater and television, notably *Amahl and the Night Visitors* (1951). Normally he has written the libretti for his own operas, and in addition he has also written libretti for Samuel Barber's *Vanessa*, (1958) and *A Hand of Bridge* (1960). Menotti's *The Last Savage* was first performed at the Paris Opera in 1963 and his *Martin's Lie* in England in 1964. He has also written ballets and instrumental works and has been active in promoting an international music festival at Spoleto, Italy. The style of his writing has been linked by some commentators with that of Puccini and Italian *verismo*. Working within a tradition, he has perfected his own abilities in the United States and has availed himself of the technical means at hand for projecting his work to both a national and a supranational audience.

Highly significant in the American situation, also, are many attempts by composers to bridge the gap between jazz, experimental, and classical music. Lukas Foss, another prominent figure in American music today, was born in Berlin in 1922 but came to the United States when he was fifteen. He has been applying the improvisational aspects so vital to jazz to classical music-making and has also introduced tape-recorded and performers'-choice procedures into his works. Native American composers have also been much concerned with bringing jazz and classical music together, notably Aaron Copland and Gunther Schuller.

Concluding Remarks

From having concerned ourselves with questions of musical origins, we end now with a question about the future of music. But we find that the final depths of the past are as darkly veiled as is the womb of the future, whereas the purpose of the present discussion is—so far as possible —to shed light. The origin of music is not to be separated from the magical link between man and his surrounding world, and the question of the future of music will perhaps be scarcely answerable other than by the indication of the function of music in the life of man and of society.

Music arose from magic and fulfilled the first task man assigned to it by virtue of its power to effect enchantment. China, Babylon, and Egypt placed music, by virtue of number, at the center of a spaciously constructed cosmology. The Greeks moved music into the midst of life itself and gave it ethical tasks of establishing connection and order among the components of existence. The Middle Ages theologized it, and the Renaissance turned it into a matter of playfulness and enjoyment. Music now became not only secularized but also a sort of maid-of-all-work. No longer was it merely the mistress of life; now it provided addition, stimulation, and help toward enhancing life in a positive way. It provided a sort of medication, dissipation, indulgence, and play.

If one asks what music means to 20th-century Western man, one encounters diversity among the answers that may be given within the framework of our late culture. The idea of the unity of culture has been long since lost.

What, nevertheless, is music today? Igor Stravinsky has written on the title page of his Symphony of Psalms: "*Composée à la gloire de Dieu.*" Olivier Messiaen says that music is for him an "act of faith." For many composers the task of music consists of its being the bearer of moral values, as Bach in the phrase of his day spoke of the "recreation of the *Gemüt*"—by which latter word he meant the feelings or the soul. Present-day music for singing and playing as a part of choral and instrumental music-making cultivates music as *ludus,* play, or—to use another 18th-century expression—delight, or *Ergötzlichkeit.* But much contemporary creative activity is made accessible today only to the ear of the specialist and is received as if it were purely aesthetic. As soon as music takes the form of being linked with some rather mundane purpose, such as incitement to movement, dance, marching, or common labor, it has the effect of an incantation. In the background and in other incidental functions such as for film or radio, music creates unconscious effects of response. Unaware of doing so, people respond to it. At worst, they take it as an accessory to life. At best they listen for something in it.

One can scarcely dispute the fact that music today in the West fulfils a multiplicity of functions—all, in fact, that have ever been, with possibly the exception of the magical. Nor can one dispute the right of each individual to establish his own relationship with music. The deep problem—unsolved perhaps because for us it is no longer solvable—lies in the complete lack of connection among the types, circles, and interest groups and in the constant confusion of values and of orders of value.

Fundamentally, music-making is an activity. One "makes music." This is a manner of speaking that characterizes with special clarity music-making as a form of doing. One "plays" an instrument. Playing as activity is indissolubly linked with music-making as activity. Nevertheless there are fundamental differences between the nature of play and that of music-making.

Music-making takes place in two forms essentially different from each other. The one is that of improvisation and free fancy, the other that of playing from notes.

"Improvisation" is a kind of music-making in which the player relies on something that has been previously given. This may be a given theme or a traditional form, a rhythm, a melody as model, or a composition. "Free improvisation" or extemporization, on the other hand, is music of the moment, a creation out of the intuition, out of the momentary impulse, without reliance on a plan, without something preconceived.

Playing from notes holds itself to something that has already been fixed, which according to its own very nature is final. Thus we come to the concept of composition. "Composition" is something created, made definite, brought into being according to a process, something finished, handed over, and binding—binding at least for the player, for whom the notated text of the composition has to be the authority. Even the usual insertion of free, improvised ornaments that was usual until far on into the 18th century changed nothing in the character of composition. It is the last will and testament—decisive, not to be abrogated.

The performance of purely technical exercises, for example finger-exercises or vocalises, does not represent a real form of music making. Here no music is being made, although musical elements are being utilized. The practice of techniques is a purely purposive activity, it is auxiliary, it is preparatory to music-making.

Music-making—and, for that matter, play in general—is usually either improvised or undertaken in accordance with some rules. Rules of play are an agreement, a settled convention, the unalterability of which assures the order and value of the game. There are, however, some fundamental differences between music-making and pure play, which may be comprehended under the headings of meaning, sense, and value.

For one thing, music-making is an activity filled with meaning. It always has about it some idea of communication. This can, according to its character, be either direct or indirect. It is the latter if the music-making occurs from notes—that is, it is mediate or indirect. Here the music-maker is simply transmitting the communication, he is its interpreter. He is the connecting link between the composition, the thing that is fixed, and the listener, wherein the one who is making the music—even if he plays alone and for himself—is himself the hearer and with his own person replaces the listener. The communication is direct or immediate, however, only in improvisation or extemporizing. The one making music is now not the *inter*preter, but the *auto*preter: he transmits himself, in direct form. Also here, in principle, it makes no difference whether he has other listeners or simply plays for himself.

The meaning contained in the music-making—and thus its substance—lies in the communication. Communication may be message, knowledge and news, notification, explanation, information, outcry.

Whoever steps out of himself uses—in order to manifest himself—a code of mutual understanding. What in music-making adds up to meaning is locked up in a number of codes, to which new ones are constantly being added as other, older signs become unintelligible and then disappear. It is not a matter of their losing their meaning, but they simply become uninteresting and are replaced by other signs. In practice they are often completely forgotten.

"Signify" includes the word "sign." To see something as a sign presupposes description of it. Description of the code means undertaking an analytic stock-taking of what the composer has notated. Music is coded meaning. Moments of meaning are to a certain extent comprehensible in the codes which they use. They are figures in the sense of being somewhat constant, fixed, and endowed with a specific content of significance. In their musical character these figures, or tropes, are often simply like formulae. It is also for this reason that the theory of rhetorical figures from the 16th to the 18th century had so meaningful an influence on composition.

As an activity filled with meaning, moreover, music-making has some sense to it. There is some sense in something if detail is related to a whole. Sense means fitting-in and arrangement. The activity of music-making is arranged in connections in which that which is fixed, the figures, the codes of meaning, represent the members. They fit into a higher order. Their union determines in general the organism of the musical form. The whole as such is musically conveyed with the individual formal types, the separate genres, and in the special case of program music, furthermore, the titles.

The sense, finally, is subordinated to a higher context. This is qualitatively determined and is classified in the frame of reference of *worth,* in a hierarchy of values.

Above the formal types and the genres there stand more comprehensive, further-reaching relationships of order. Their character is one of a *hierarchy of values.* The oldest and earliest value-category is incorporated into the magic circle. It is followed by cosmogony, and later by the connection between music and ethos. In the Middle Ages, for the first time, aesthetic aims became explicit.

Value concepts arise from at least three factors: the individual view and knowledge as manifested through an individual personality, the historical context, and sociological connections. These value concepts always have an ideological character. They can be private avowals or creeds, they can register official opinions and explain them as obligatory, or they can represent theologically viewed abstractions.

Thus, although the future of music is unavailable to objective description, we can speculate on it in terms of concepts that lie at the basis of all the arts.

Bibliography

On the Situation in the 20th Century: T. W. Adorno, *Philosophie der Neuen Musik* (new ed. Frankfurt a. M. 1958); Adler Hdb., vol. 2, *Die Moderne* (individual essays, arranged according to countries); W. W. Austin, *Music in the 20th Century* (N. Y. 1966); S. Borris, *Einführung in die moderne Musik* (Halle a. d. Saale, n. d.) and *Über Wesen u. Werden der neuen Musik in Deutschland. Vom Expressionismus zum Vitalismus* (Bln. 1948); P. Collaer, *Gesch. der modernen Musik* (Stuttgart 1963); U. Dibelius, *Moderne Musik 1945–65* (Munich 1966); K. v. Fischer, *Moderne Musik,* in *Moderne Literatur, Malerei u. Musik* (Zurich and Stuttgart 1963); P. Gradenwitz, *Wege zur Musik der Gegenwart* (Stuttgart 1963); M. Graf, *Gesch. u. Geist der modernen Musik* (Vienna 1953); H. Mersmann, *Die moderne Musik seit der Romantik* (Bücken Hdb.); A. Salazar, *Music of Our Time* (N. Y. 1946); N. Slonimsky, *Music since 1900* (N. Y. 3rd ed. 1949); R. Stephan, *Neue Musik* (Göttingen 1958); H. H. Stuckenschmidt, *Neue Musik* (Bln. 1951) and *Schöpfer der Neuen Musik* (Frankfurt a. M. 1958); K. H. Wörner, *Musik d. Gegenwart. Gesch. d. neuen Musik* (Mainz 1949) and *Neue Musik in d. Entscheidung* (Mainz 2nd ed. 1956); W. Zillig, *Variationen über Neue Musik* (Munich 1959).

12-Tone System: H. Eimert, *Atonale Musiklehre* (Lpz. 1924), *Grundlagen der mus. Reihentechnik* (Vienna 1964), and *Lehrbuch der Zwölftontechnik* (Wiesbaden 3rd ed. 1954); J. M. Hauer, *Vom Wesen des Musikalischen. Ein Lehrbuch der atonalen Musik* (Berlin-Lichterfelde 1920); H. Heiss, *Elemente der mus. Komposition* (Heidelberg n. d.); P. Hindemith, *Unterweisung im Tonsatz I. Theoretischer Teil* (new enl. ed., Mainz 1940); H. Jelinek, *Anleitung zur Zwölftonkomp.* (2 vols., Vienna 1952 and 1958); E. Krenek, *Studies in Counterpoint* (N. Y. 1940); R. Leibowitz, *Introduction à la musique de douze sons* (Paris 1949); M. Lichtenfeld, *Untersuchungen zur Theorie der Zwölftontechnik bei J. M. Hauer* (Regensburg 1964); O. Messiaen, *Technique de mon langage musical* (2 vols., Paris 1944); H. Pfrogner, *Die Zwölfordnung der Töne* (Zurich, Lpz., Vienna 1953); J. Rufer, *Die Komposition mit zwölf Tönen* (Bln. and Wunsiedel 1952); A. Schoenberg, *Style and Idea* (N. Y. 1950); W. Szmolyan, *J. M. Hauer* (Vienna 1965); K. H. Wörner, *Gotteswort u. Magie. Die Oper "Moses und Aron" von Arnold Schönberg* (Heidelberg 1959, enl. London 1963). *Serial Composition:* K. Boehmer, *Zur Theorie der offenen Form in der Neuen Musik* (Darmstadt 1967); P. Boulez, *Musikdenken heute I* (Mainz 1963); R. Heinemann, *Untersuchungen zur Rezeption der seriellen Musik* (Regensburg 1966); K. Stockhausen, *Texte* (2 vols., Cologne 1963–4); K. H. Wörner, *Karlheinz Stockhausen* (Rodenkirchen/Rhein 1963); *Darmstädter Beiträge zur Neuen Musik* (Mainz 1958–   ); *Die Reihe. Information über serielle Musik* (8 vols., Vienna 1955–62). *K. Stockhausen:* D. Schnebel, S. in *"Die Reihe,"* bk. 4, *Junge Komp.* (Vienna 1958, Universal Edition); K. H. Wörner, *K. H. Stockhausen. Werk und Wollen 1950–62,* Bd. IV of the series "Kontrapunkte," ed. H. Lindlar (Rodenkirchen/Rhein 1962, Tonger).

New Sources of Sound: A. Buchner, *Vom Glockenspiel zum Pianola*

(Prague 1959); E. Simon, *Mech. Musikinstr. früherer Zeiten u. ihre Musik* (Wiesbaden 1960); *Musik u. Maschine. Sonderheft der Musikblätter des Anbruch* (8. Jahrgang, Oct.–Nov. 1926); art. Mechanische Musikinstr. (MGG). *Musique concrète:* L. M. Cross, *A Bibliography of Electronic Music* (Toronto 1967); H. Eimert, ed., with K. Stockhausen, *Elektronische Musik. Die Reihe. Informationen über serielle Musik* (Vienna 1955) and art. Elektronische Musik (MGG); W. Meyer-Eppler, *Elektrische Klangerzeugung. Elektrische Musik u. synthetische Sprache* (Bonn 1949); W. Kaegi, *Was ist elektronische Musik* (Zurich 1967); F. K. Prieberg, *Musik des technischen Zeitalters* (Zurich 1956); P. Schaeffer, *A la recherche d'une Musique concrète* (Paris 1952); F. Winkel, *Elektrische Musikinstr.* (MGG). *Impressionism:* W. Danckert, *C. Debussy* (Bln. 1950); art. Impressionismus (MGG). *Expressionism:* L. Rognoni, *Espressionismo e dodecafonia* (1954); R. Vlad, *Storia della dodecafonia* (Milan n. d.); K. H. Wörner, *Die Musik in der Geistesgeschichte* (Bonn 1970); art. Expressionismus (MGG).

Bibliographical Resources

General Guides to Music Bibliography

V. Duckles, *Music Reference and Research Materials* (2nd ed., N.Y., 1967).
A. H. Heyer, *Historical Sets, Collected Editions and Monuments of Music* (Chicago 1957).

Catalogues of Sources

R. Eitner, *Bibliographie der Musiksammelwerke des 16. und 17. Jahrhunderts* (Berlin 1877, repr. N. Y. 1950, Hildesheim 1963); *Biographisch-Bibliographische Quellen-Lexikon der Musiker und Musikgelehrten der christlichen Zeitrechnung bis zur Mitte des 19. Jahrhunderts,* 10 vols. (Leipzig 1900–4), enl. ed. 1959–60.
F. Ludwig, *Repertorium organorum recentioris et motetorum vetustissimi stili* Vol. 1, Part 1 (Halle 1910), table of contents of Part 2 in F. Ludwig, "Die Quellen der Motetten ältesten Stils," *Archiv für Musikwissenschaft* V (1923); repr. of Vol. I and Vol. II, ed. L. A. Dittmer, Institute of Medieval Music, Brooklyn, N. Y.
RISM, Répertoire International des Sources Musicales, 1960–.
C. Sartori, *Bibliografia della musica strumentale italiana stampata in Italia fino al 1700* (Florence 1952).
E. Vogel, *Bibliothek der gedruckten weltlichen Vocalmusik Italiens aus den Jahren 1500–1700,* 2 vols. (Leipzig 1892); enl. ed. in Music Library Association *Notes II* (1944/5)-V (1947/8); new ed. Hildesheim 1962.

Source Readings

O. Strunk, *Source Readings in Music History* (N. Y. 1950).

Bibliographies

A. Aber, *Handbuch der Musikliteratur in systematisch-chronologischer Anordnung* (Leipzig 1922), repr. Hildesheim 1967.
J. N. Forkel, *Allgemeine Literatur der Musik* (Leipzig 1792), repr. Hildesheim 1967.

W. Kahl and W. M. Luther, *Repertorium der Musikwissenschaft* (Kassel 1953).
W. Lott, ed., *Verzeichnis der Neudrucke alter Musik*, 7 vols. (1936–42).
K. Taut, G. Karstädt, and W. Schmieder, *Bibliographie des Musikschrifttums* (Berlin 1936–51).
RILM, Répertoire International des Littératures Musicales, 1966–   .
E. Vogel, R. Schwartz, and K. Taut, "Verzeichnis der . . . Schriften über Musik," *Jahrbuch der Musikbibliothek Peters* (Leipzig 1895–1938).

Anthologies

D. von Bartha, *A zenetörténet antologiaja* (Budapest 1948).
A. della Corte, *Scelta di musiche per Co studio della storia* (Milan n. d.).
A. T. Davison and W. Apel, *Historical Anthology of Music*, 2 vols. (Cambridge 1946, 1950).
A. Einstein, *Beispielsammlung zur älteren Musikgeschichte* (Leipzig and Berlin 1917, 4th ed. 1930).
H. Feicht, *Muzyka Staropolska* (Cracow 1966).
K. G. Fellerer, ed., *Das Musikwerk* (Cologne 1951–   ).
H. Gleason, *Examples of Music before 1400* (N.Y. 1946).
Z. Lissa and J. M. Chomiński, *Muzyka Polskiego Odrodzenia* (Cracow 1953), *Music of the Polish Renaissance* (Cracow 1955).
C. Parrish and J. F. Ohl, *Masterpieces of Music before 1750* (N.Y. 1951).
C. Parrish, *A Treasury of Early Music* (N.Y. 1958).
Jaroslav Pohanka, *Dějiny české hudby v příkladech* (Prague 1958).
E. Reeser, *Stijlproeven van Nederlandse Muziek. Anthology of Music from the Netherlands 1809–1960* I (Amsterdam 1963).
H. Riemann, *Musikgeschichte in Beispielen* (Leipzig 1912, 4th ed. 1929).
A. Schering, *Geschichte der Musik in Beispielen* (Leipzig 1931, repr. N.Y. 1957).
Z. M. Szweykowski, *Muzyka w dawnym Krakowic. Music in Old Cracow* (Cracow 1964).
A. Tscherepnin, *Russische Musik-Anthologie* (Bonn 1965).
J. Wolf, *Sing- und Spielmusik aus älterer Zeit* (Leipzig 1926), repr. in U.S. as *Music of Earlier Time*.

Recordings

Anthologie Schweizerischer Musik (Arbeitsgemeinschaft zur Förderung Schweizerischer Musik).
Archiv-Produktion (Deutsche Grammophon Gesellschaft, Decca).
Harpsichord Suites of the Baroque (Haydn Society Records).
The History of Italian Music (R.C.A. Italiana).
The History of Music in Sound, 10 albums (R.C.A. Victor, His Master's Voice).
L'Anthologie Sonore (Haydn Soc. 1954–   ).
Lebendige Musik des Mittelalters und der Renaissance (Electrola).
Musica Antiqua Polonica (Polskie Nagrania).
Music of the Bach Family (Boston Records 1957).
Musik des Mittelalters und der Renaissance (Harmonia mundi).
Musik des Orients. A Musical Anthology of the Orient (UNESCO Series).
New York Pro Musica (Decca).
C. Parrish and J. F. Ohl, eds., *Masterpieces of Music before 1750* (N.Y. 1951)

and C. Parrish, *A Treasury of Early Music* (N.Y. 1958), albums accompanying anthologies previously listed.

Musicological Atlas

P. Collaer and A. van der Linden, *Atlas historique de la musique* (Brussels and Paris 1960).

Chronological Table of Music History

Arnold Schering, *Tabellen zur Musikgeschichte* (5th ed. enl. by H. J. Moser 1962).

Autographs of Musicians

E. Winternitz, *Musical Autographs from Monteverdi to Hindemith* (Princeton 1955).

Pictures Illustrative of Music History

H. Besseler and M. Schneider, eds., *Musikgeschichte in Bildern* (Leipzig 1962–).
G. Kinsky, ed., *Geschichte der Musik in Bildern* (Leipzig 1929).
K. M. Komma, *Musikgeschichte in Bildern* (Stuttgart 1961).
P. H. Lang and O. L. Bettmann, *A Pictorial History of Music* (N.Y. 1960).

Performance Practice

T. Dart, *The Interpretation of Music.*
A. Dolmetsch, *The Interpretation of Music of the XVIIth and XVIIIth Centuries* (London 1916, 2nd ed. 1946).
R. Donington, *The Interpretation of Early Music* (London 1963, 2nd ed. 1965).
F. Dorian, *The History of Music in Performance* (N.Y. 1942, 1965).
G. Frotscher, *Aufführungspraxis alter Musik* (Locarno 1963).
A. Geoffroy-Dechaume, *Les "secrets" de la musique ancienne* (Paris 1964).
R. Haas, *Aufführungspraxis der Musik* (Potsdam 1931), in E. Bücken, ed., *Handbuch der Musikwissenschaft.*
F. Rotschild, *Vergessene Traditionen in der Musik* (Zurich 1964).
A. Schering, *Aufführungspraxis* (Leipzig 1932).

Dictionaries and Encyclopedias of Music

W. Apel, *Harvard Dictionary of Music* (Cambridge 1944).
T. Baker, *Biographical Dictionary of Musicians*, 5th ed. rev. N. Slonimsky (N.Y. 1958).
F. Blume, ed., *Die Musik in Geschichte und Gegenwart* (1949–).
G. Grove, *Dictionary of Music and Musicians*, 1st ed. 1879–89, 5th ed. N.Y. 1954.
A. Lavignac and L. de La Laurencie, *Encyclopedie de la Musique et Dictionnaire du Conservatoire* (Paris 1913–31).

Handbooks and Histories

G. Adler, ed., *Handbuch der Musikgeschichte* (Frankfurt am Main 1924, 3rd ed. Tutzing 1961).

K. Ameln, C. Mahrenholz, and W. Thomas, eds., *Handbuch der Deutschen Evangelischen Kirchenmusik* (1935–   ).

E. Bücken, ed., *Handbuch der Musikwissenschaft,* 10 vols. (Potsdam 1927–34).

H. Wiley Hitchcock, ed., *Prentice-Hall History of Music Series,* 9 vols. (N.Y. 1965–   ).

J. A. Westrup *et. al., New Oxford History of Music* (London 1957–   ), projected as 11 vols., succeeding H. E. Wooldridge, ed. *Oxford History of Music,* 7 vols. (1901–34).

Series published by W. W. Norton, New York, including

C. Sachs, *The Rise of Music in the Ancient World* (1943).

G. Reese, *Music in the Middle Ages* (1940), *Music in the Renaissance* (1954).

M. Bukofzer, *Music in the Baroque Era* (1947).

A. Einstein, *Music in the Romantic Era* (1947).

Music and Collateral Fields

A. P. Merriam, *The Anthropology of Music* (Evanston 1964).

C. Sachs, *The Commonwealth of Art* (N.Y. 1946), *A World History of the Dance* (N.Y. 1937).

P. H. Lang, *Music in Western Civilization* (N.Y. 1952).

A. Hauser, *Social History of the Arts* (N.Y. 1951).

Periodicals

Acta Musicologica, journal of the Internationale Gesellschaft für Musikwissenschaft, 1931–   ; 1928–30: *Mitteilungen der IGMW.*

Archiv für Musikforschung (1936–43): continuation of *Archiv für Musikwissenschaft* and of the *Zeitschrift für Musikwissenschaft.*

Dansk Musiktidsskrift (Copenhagen 1925–   ).

Deutsches Jahrbuch der Musikwissenschaft (Leipzig 1957–   ).

Deutsche Vierteljahrsschrift für Literaturwissenschaft und Geistesgeschichte (1923–   ).

Jahrbuch der Musikbibliothek Peters Leipzig (1894–1940).

Journal of the American Musicological Society (1948–   ).

Journal of Renaissance and Baroque Music (1946, continued as *Musica Disciplina*).

Kirchenmusikalisches Jahrbuch (1886–   , previously *Cäcilienkalender* 1876–85).

Monatshefte für Musikgeschichte, ed. R. Eitner.

Music and Letters (1920–   ).

Musica Disciplina, yearbook of the American Institute of Musicology, 1947–   ; previously *Journal of Renaissance and Baroque Music,* 1946.

The Musical Quarterly (1915–   ).

Die Musikforschung, journal of the Gesellschaft für Musikforschung, 1948–.

Proceedings of the Royal Musical Association (London 1874–   ).

La Revue Musicale (1920–   ).

Rivista musicale Italiana (1894–   ).

Sammelbände der Internationalen Musikgesellschaft (1899–1914).

Svensk Tidskrift för Musikforskning (Stockholm/Uppsala 1919–   ).

Studien zur Musikwissenschaft, Beihefte der Denkmäler der Tonkunst in Österreich (1913–   ).

Vierteljahrsschrift für Musikwissenschaft (1885–94).

Zeitschrift der Internationalen Musikgesellschaft (1899–1914).

Zeitschrift für Musikwissenschaft (1918–35), continued as *Archiv für Musik-forschung*.

Series

F. Blume, ed., *Das Chorwerk* (Kallmeyer 1929–38, new ed. Möseler 1953–   ).

Cantica Selecta Musices Sacrae in Polonia (Posen 1928).

F. Chrysander, ed., *Denkmäler der Tonkunst* (1869–71).

Denkmäler deutscher Tonkunst (1892–1931); *Denkmäler der Tonkunst in Bayern* (1900–31); *Denkmäler der Tonkunst in Österreich* (1894–   ).

R. Eitner, *Publikationen älterer praktischer und theoretischer Musikwerke vornehmlich des XV. und XVI. Jahrhunderts* (1873–1905).

Das Erbe deutscher Musik, Reihe I: *Reichsdenkmale* (1935–42, cont'd. 1954); Reihe II: *Landschaftsdenkmale* (1935–42).

Istituzioni e Monumenti dell'Arte Musicale Italiana (1931–41).

T. Kroyer, ed., *Publikationen älterer Musik* (1926–41).

Musica Britannica, A National Collection of Music, publ. for The Royal Musical Association (London 1951–   ).

J. Surzyński, ed., *Monumenta Musices Sacrae in Polonia* (Posen 1885–96).

Muzyka Polskiego Odrodzenia (Cracow 1953).

L. Torchi, ed., *L'Arte musicale in Italia* (1897–1907).

Wydawnictwo Dawnej Muzyki Polskiej, Heft 1–50 (Warsaw-Cracow 1928–63).

Zródła do historii muzyki polskiej, Heft 1–7 (Cracow 1962–3).

Name Index

Subject Index